Date label over page.

I. Problem definition

    A. Plans, objectives, and decisions

    B. Boundaries of system

II. Information search

    A. Define the system

    B. Define possible cause and effects

III. Hypothesis/Theory/Model formulation

    A. Refine causal model

    B. Graphical exploration

    C. Postulate direction of causality

    D. Consider appropriate methods

IV. Experiment design

    A. Select in-sample fitting data

    B. Select out-of-sample validation data

V. Experiment execution

    A. Fit several in-sample models

    B. Forecast out-of-sample models

VI. Results analysis

    A. Are assumptions valid?

    B. Do results support theory?

    C. Experts agree?

    D. Perform out-of-sample validity tests

VII. Ongoing use of model/system

    A. Incorporate real-time judgment

    B. Implement model/system

Flowchart:

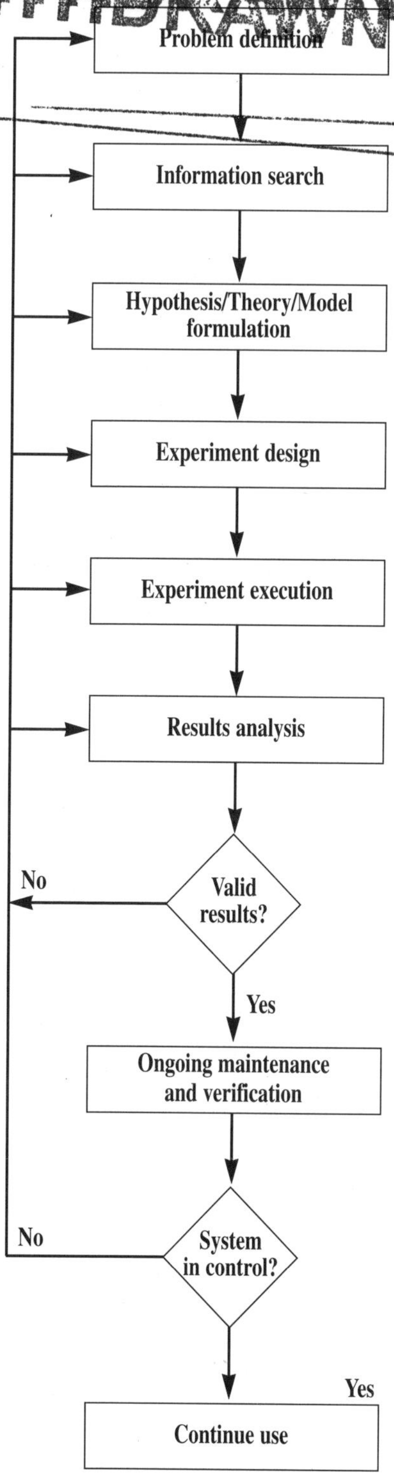

Problem definition → Information search → Hypothesis/Theory/Model formulation → Experiment design → Experiment execution → Results analysis → Valid results?

Valid results? — No → (loops back); Yes → Ongoing maintenance and verification → System in control?

System in control? — No → (loops back); Yes → Continue use

Figure 1-18

FORECASTING PRINCIPLES AND APPLICATIONS

THE IRWIN/McGRAW-HILL SERIES

FIRST EDITION

FORECASTING PRINCIPLES AND APPLICATIONS

Stephen A. DeLurgio
University of Missouri—Kansas City

**Irwin
McGraw-Hill**

Boston, Massachusetts   Burr Ridge, Illinois   Dubuque, Iowa
Madison, Wisconsin   New York, New York   San Francisco, California   St. Louis, Missouri

Irwin/McGraw-Hill

*A Division of The **McGraw·Hill** Companies*

FORECASTING PRINCIPLES AND APPLICATIONS

This book is printed on acid-free paper.

1 2 3 4 5 6 7 8 9 0 QPD 9 1 0 9 8 7

ISBN 0-256-13433-2

Publisher: *Tom Casson*
Executive editor: *Richard T. Hercher, Jr.*
Senior developmental editor: *Gail Korosa*
Project manager: *Lynne Basler*
Production supervisor: *Heather Burbridge*
Cover designer: *Michael Warrell*
Compositor: *New England Typographic Service*
Typeface: *10/12 Times Roman*
Printer: *Quebecor Printing Book Group/Dubuque*

Library of Congress Cataloging-in-Publication Data

DeLurgio, Stephen A., Sr.
    Forecasting principles and applications / Stephen A. DeLurgio, Sr.
      p. cm.
    Includes index.
    ISBN 0-256-13433-2
    1. Forecasting—Mathematical models. 2. Forecasting—Statistical methods. I. Title.
H61.4.D45   1998
658.15′224—dc21   —dc21
[003′.2′015195]   97-15142

http://www.mhhe.com

To my wife, Ina Kimmel, my parents, Louis and Amelia, and my sons, Steve and Pat

PREFACE

"I often say that when you can measure what you are speaking about, and express it in numbers, you know something about it; but when you cannot measure it, when you cannot express it in numbers, your knowledge is of a very meagre and unsatisfactory kind."

William Thomson, Lord Kelvin, 1824-1907

"If we could first know where we are, then whither we are tending, we could then decide what to do and how to do it."

Abraham Lincoln, 1809–1865

Today's computer-based analytical tools and systems provide users with effective forecasting technology. The challenges of the continuing revolutions in technology and information provide exciting opportunities for analysts and managers to make extraordinary contributions to their organizations. We can seize these opportunities by generating better plans based on better forecasts. This book is about better forecasting methods and processes. It is about modeling as much information as possible about the past, present, and future so that more effective plans can be made. This objective applies to all organizations whether public or private, profit or nonprofit, product or service oriented. It is especially relevant to emerging market economies and globally competitive firms. This forecasting challenge is not easily met, but nonetheless it is a necessary endeavor if we are to thrive—individually and collectively.

Purpose

The purpose of this book is to present forecasting principles and applications in an accessible way for students and researchers alike. The forecasting methods presented here are used by analysts and managers at successful retailers, wholesalers, manufacturers, and many service organizations such as health care, utilities, government offices, universities, financial institutions, research institutions, and others. As this book illustrates, the principles and applications of forecasting vary considerably whether short, intermediate, or long term forecasts are being made. Short-run methods are easier to understand and apply than other long-term methods such as multiple regression, econometric, and multivariate Box-Jenkins. However, our purpose is to make even these more sophisticated methods accessible to all while highlighting their strengths and limitations.

We have tried to make this book as comprehensive and theoretically valid as possible while still being accessible and understandable for all willing to study it. A clear, concise, and motivating writing style and layout are used to stimulate reader involvement and understanding. This style provides the substance of forecasting in a form that makes the topics interesting to the reader. To accomplish this task, this text has several important characteristics:

1. Comprehensiveness   More statistical forecasting methods are presented in this text than in other textbooks. Forecasting methods that are viewed by many as being difficult to understand are presented in this text including **Multivariate ARIMA, ARIMA Intervention, econometric methods, and neural networks.** It has been our experience that these methods are as easily learned as others when students have the correct study materials. This book includes pedagogically effective materials such as many more graphical illustrations, solved examples, exercises, and minicases.

2. Motivational Material   Special interest and motivating information is provided through short examples of successful and unsuccessful forecasts of the past as well as forecasting trivia, history, and applications. We hope these added bits of information and folklore will stimulate the readers' intellectual curiosity.

3. Evolving Statistical Sophistication   The level of mathematical and statistical rigor in this book progresses from the elementary to intermediate level. The mathematics of the earlier sections of the book (Parts I and II) is introductory, assuming that the reader needs to be eased into the material carefully. It is assumed that the students of the more advanced chapters either have studied the earlier chapters or had similar prerequisite courses.

4. Time Series Database   Approximately 250 actual time series are included on the enclosed diskette, and many are analyzed within the text. This database includes ASCII files of all series used in the text and problem sets. In addition, almost all of the homework problems use data from the diskette. For a large portion of the problems we recommend that the students have either a spreadsheet or statistical software package as a solution tool.

5. Continuing Minicases   Each chapter has 10 minicases which illustrate actual time series applications in an "integrative" format. These minicases continue throughout the book and by having a common thread of knowledge from chapter to chapter and method to method, we hope students will gain a better, more integrative understanding of alternative forecasting methods. In addition, these minicases and the other major exercises are tied together using a Master Forecasting Summary Table introduced at the end of Chapter 4.

6. Forecasting Process   Throughout the text, the process of forecasting is emphasized. This begins in Chapter 1 and continues throughout the book by way of reference to the **Master Forecasting Summary Table.** This table provides an overall perspective on the forecasting process by highlighting the effectiveness, advantages, and disadvantages of different methods. Completion of this table provides insights that are very much like those of past forecasting studies (e.g., the M-competition) of Makridakis et al. The table forces the forecaster to measure in and out-of-sample forecasting accuracy in a realistic setting and by doing so, he or she gains further insights to the principles and applications of forecasting.

7. Theoretical Underpinnings   Some chapters have appendices where the most technical derivations and theories are presented. These chapters can be used by students with varying statistical background and are intended to make the text useful for elementary through advanced forecasting courses. The serious student (i.e. manager or analyst) who earns a living using statistical forecasting methods will want to be familiar with the material in these appendices, while they may be skipped in some introductory classes.

8. Computer Software Support   We have not tied this book to specific computer software because to do so would diminish its value as a source of generic forecasting concepts and models. There are many "best" software packages available, more than can be integrated into a single textbook.

9. Spreadsheet Support Modern spreadsheets provide an extraordinary opportunity for students to learn and apply forecasting methods. To support such activities we have developed about 35 templates containing some of the techniques and tables of the text. Some of the more sophisticated methods do not lend themselves to easy spreadsheet implementation, consequently not all tables are included. Templates on the enclosed diskette use a generic wk1 format.

10. Classroom Tested The material in this book has been classroom tested by the author to achieve a teachable text, one that will free the instructor and student from many elementary questions. We hope the text will stimulate students to ask more thoughtful and advanced questions.

11. The Internet Connection In today's nearly instantaneous distribution of information, the Internet represents an important source of information. The publisher and author both maintain Internet websites in support of this book. The publisher's website (http://www.mhhe.com) is the primary locus of support materials for this textbook. A secondary source of information is the author's website; the address for this site is maintained on the publisher's website. These websites make the use of this book a dynamic process that motivates excitement and excellence in student learning.

Using this Book

This book is divided into six major sections.

I. Foundations of Forecasting (Chaps. 1 to 3) Introduction, Statistics, and Regression Analysis.

II. Univariate Methods (Chaps. 4 to 6) Simple Smoothing, Exponential Smoothing, Decomposition, Holt-Winters, and Fourier Series Analysis.

III. Univariate ARIMA Methods (Chaps. 7 to 9) ARIMA Basics, Applications, and ARIMA Forecasting/Estimation.

IV. Multivariate Forecasting Methods (Chaps. 10 to 13) Multiple Regression, Econometrics, MARIMA I (intervention analysis), and MARIMA II (transfer functions).

V. Cyclical, Qualitative, and Artificial Intelligence Methods (Chaps. 14 to 16) including Cyclical, Technological, and Neural Network forecasting methods.

VI. Validation, Qualitative, Managerial Issues (Chaps. 17 and 18) Combining, Validation and Control, Comparing and Selecting Methods.

Part I (Chapters 1 to 3) introduces the basic concepts and principles of forecasting including statistics and simple linear regression. This section is the foundation of the remainder of the book and is an essential part of bringing students "up to speed" in statistical modeling. It introduces the concepts of autocorrelations and cross correlations so that students can use them throughout the remainder of the text.

Part II (Chapters 4 to 6) introduces the simpler univariate forecasting methods including simple smoothing, exponential smoothing, decomposition, and Fourier Series analysis. Normally, at least some of these are covered before moving into Part III.

Part III (Chapters 7 to 9) develops an accessible presentation of ARIMA methods, including appendices of derivations for those desiring a more statistical presentation. These derivations should be accessible to all students completing Part I.

Part IV (Chapters 10 to 13) presents multivariate forecasting methods including advanced regression/econometric methods, intervention methods and multivariate ARIMA methods. As is true for all parts of this book, these methods are accessible to everyone completing part I and in the case of MARIMA methods, part III. If one wants a more statistically rigorous presentation of forecasting methods, then the appendices of these chapters should be included.

Part V (Chapters 14 to 16) presents a variety of important concepts and methods. Chapter 14 presents several methods of cyclical forecasting including leading indicators, cyclical indexes, and pressure cycles. Chapter 15 presents Qualitative and Technological forecasting methods. These methods continue to take on more importance as globally competitive markets require greater use of longer term forecast when little objective data exists. Chapter 16 presents important contemporary topics from the area of artificial intelligence, particularly neural networks.

Part VI (Chapters 17 and 18 and Appendices A and B) present important forecasting methods and managerial concepts. These can be introduced at any time, early within the course or as capstone summaries. Chapter 17 develops control, combining, and validation techniques that are applicable to all the forecasting methods and Chapter 18 presents a review of forecasting characteristic and accuracy studies. Appendix A presents an extensive listing of sources of forecasting data including sources on the Internet. Appendix B presents an elementary introduction to outlier detection and adjustment procedures. These Appendices are designed to be presentable at anytime in the term, or for independent study by the student.

The six sections of this book are intended to provide flexibility and some variety of levels for undergraduate to intermediate graduate level courses. If you are only interested in a good understanding of univariate forecasting methods without delving into the more technical multivariate methods, then parts I, II, III, and sections of parts V and VI yield a course of approximately 15 chapters. Those desiring a basic univariate/multivariate presentation might use parts I, II, and sections of parts IV, V and VI. If a more theoretical study is desired, then selected chapters and their appendices could be included. These basic combinations suggest the following:

Univariate Course (11 Chapters and Appendices A and B): Chapters 1 to 6, 14 to 18.

Univariate and Multivariate Course (13 Chapters and Appendices A and B): Chapters 1 to 6, 10, 11, 14, 15, 16, 17 and 18.

Intermediate Univariate Course (14 Chapters): Chapters 1 to 9, 14 to 18 with all appendices.

Intermediate Univariate/Multivariate Course (18 Chapters): Chapters 1 to 18 and their appendices, where some elementary chapters are skipped.

This book can also be used for self-study and reference by persons engaged in forecasting including those in marketing, finance, operations, management, engineering, and the social, health, and biological sciences.

Instructors Manual and Internet Support. An Instructor's Solutions Manual containing detailed solutions to all discussion questions, numerical problems, and minicases is available from the publisher for use by instructors. In addition, this manual has many programs and examples from the book written in RATS and SAS formats. This ancillary material will be updated on the Author's website. In addition, this website will be available to other instructors who want to electronically publish programs they have developed for use with this text. The author's website is available through the Irwin/McGraw-Hill website http://www.mhhe.com.

Acknowledgments

A book of this magnitude could not have been written without the substantial assistance of many individuals. A special thanks to my co-author of *Forecasting Systems for Operations Management,* Carl D. Bhame, Vice President of American Software Corporation for use of materials from that textbook. I am indebted to many contributors who have developed the theories, principles, and methods discussed in this book. First, I would like to express appreciation to the graduate students who took QA545, Forecasting Theory and Applications at UMKC. They helped in the development of this book in many ways and they had the very important and difficult job of using various drafts of the manuscript of this text for three years. Specific graduate students who assisted in notable ways include: Tony Sukadil and Chin-Kee Chiew who developed the Excel™ and Lotus™ Spreadsheets available from the website. Roseann Pakiz helped develop some of the SAS example programs included in the Instructor's Solution Manual. Zhihua Li assisted in several important ways including error checking the manuscript and some of the solutions of problems in the Instructor's Manual. Many other worked on the solutions of the Minicases, they are acknowledge in the instructors manual.

I am indebted to Professor J. Keith Ord, The Pennsylvania State University; J. Thomas Yokum, Angelo State University, Heejoon Kang, Indiana University, Gregory Hudak, Information Resources, Inc., Samuel Ramenofsky, Loyola University, Chicago, and Anne Koehler, Miami University; who all reviewed chapters in this text. In addition, Randy Dixon of Advanced Technology Transfer Group reviewed the chapter on Neural Networks and his product Neural Network Tutor™ is an extraordinarily good learning tool about Neural Networks. Professor Peter Eaton of the Economics Department of UMKC made insightful contributions when reviewing the multiple regression and econometrics chapters. Professor Haizhen Fu of The Pennsylvania State University provided important error checking of the manuscript. Also, I am indebted to Dr. Syed Hussain of Swift-Armour-Eckrich for his useful comments and review of the intervention chapter.

In addition, parts of Chapters 6, 11, and 14 were based on past jointly published articles with Professors Dean Booth, Art Williams, and Brian Belt, respectively, all of the Bloch School of Business at UMKC. In addition, S. Thomas Foster of Boise State University provided input to Chapter 3.

The insights and suggestions of all of these individuals were invaluable to the author.

Several individuals at Irwin/McGraw-Hill deserve our appreciation for excelling in their responsibilities. These include Richard Hercher, executive editor, Gail Korosa, development editor, and Lynne Basler, project manager. Without their suggestions, patience, and understanding this endeavor may have never been completed.

I am also greatly indebted to several individuals at UMKC who have assisted directly or indirectly in this book. These include Dean William B. Eddy and Business Division Directors Leon Robertson and George Pinches. Henry W. Bloch of the H&R

Bloch Foundation and the William T. Kemper Foundation continually provided significant financial and moral support to the scholarly activities of the business faculty at UMKC.

Special thanks to my brother, Louis J. DeLurgio, Jr. of IBM Inc., and to my sons Stephen and Patrick DeLurgio who provided important computer, engineering, and Internet expertise.

Finally, my family patiently bore the pressure and interruptions caused by my commitment to complete this book. I have benefited greatly from their understanding and many sacrifices.

Steve DeLurgio, Sr.

CONTENTS

PART II

UNIVARIATE METHODS

6   Trend-Seasonal and Holt-Winters Smoothing   204

PART V

CYCLICAL, QUALITATIVE, AND ARTIFICIAL INTELLIGENCE METHODS

FOUNDATIONS OF FORECASTING

1

PLANNING AND FORECASTING

The earth is degenerating these days. Bribery and corruption abound. Children no longer mind parents. Every man wants to write a book, and it is evident that the end of the world is approaching fast.

Assyrian tablet, 2800 B.C.

Chapter Outline

Introduction
The Importance of Forecasting
Financial and Strategic Importance of Forecasting
The Commonality of Forecasting
The Management Decision Hierarchy
Why Forecast?
What Is a Forecast?
What Should Be Forecast?
Common Time Series Patterns
Overview of Forecasting Methods
Parts of This Book
The Forecasting Process
Summary
Key Terms
Key Formulas
Problems
Minicases
References

Introduction

Predicting the future is one of the strongest cognitive desires of modern man. The actualization of this goal has resulted in scientifically based forecasting models of human health, behavior, learning, economics, weather, horse racing, and corporate sales, to name only a few. Historically, early man used forecasting methods that are now discredited; these included astrology, fortune-telling, and predictions based on the entrails of animal sacrifices—even today, astrology is considered by some to be a legitimate method of prediction.

Despite the inherent desires of individuals to forecast, studies have shown that most use highly subjective, nonquantitative methods. In contrast to this, it is shown in this book that the theory and practice of forecasting can be learned and applied with relative ease.

Purpose of This Book

The general purpose of this book is to present the art and science of forecasting in a manner that makes them accessible to manager and researcher alike. Those involved in planning and research should have a good understanding of forecasting. The methods presented here are used by successful retailers, wholesalers, large manufacturers, and many service organizations such as hospitals, utilities, government offices, financial institutions, and research institutes.

Because the benefits from improved forecasting are truly extraordinary, both the theory and application of effective forecasting are studied here. This book is designed to help you learn how to effectively forecast with simple and advanced techniques using simple and advanced software. It is important to share with you not only the science but also the art of forecasting because discussing one without the other would considerably diminish the value of this presentation. In most applied research, managers and analysts use both art and science.

Information Revolution

These are extraordinarily interesting and exciting times in forecasting and information systems. The information and electronics revolutions have now made it much more cost effective to collect and process data for use in integrated information systems. For example, electronic scanning devices of retailers, distributors, manufacturers, and hospitals make it possible for businesses and organizations to collect and process data in extraordinary volumes in real time and on-line; never before has more useful data been available for analysis. CD-ROMS, on-line data retrieval and information services such as America Online and Compuserve, as well as other, less commercial services such as the Internet and the Federal Reserve system provide vast sources of data and information. Book Appendix A lists many sources of forecasting data, quite a few of which were not available five years ago. However, this data is useless if we do not understand how to use it.

The Importance of Forecasting

For most organizations, no other investment has nearly as much immediate and long-term influence on profitability, customer service, and productivity as a good forecasting system. It can dramatically improve profits. It is not uncommon for the payback from these systems to be realized in less than a year. This is true because a good fore-

Computer Cost Justifications, the Early Days

The business computer has been in use since 1951 when the first commercial computer was installed in the U.S. Bureau of the Census. In the following three years, duplicates of this computer were being used by a few, very large companies at monthly rentals of about $25,000 (even more if we were to inflate to today's dollar). The Census Bureau finally retired its first computer to the Smithsonian Institution in 1964. In the early 1960s, the computer industry matured with a range of smaller and faster computers that rented for $700 to $300,000 per month. A 1964 book on computer applications provides this interesting perspective on the early days of computing.*

- Desktop computers—Monthly rentals of $700 to $3,000. Examples—Monorobot X1, Autonetics Recomp III, IBM 1620. Punched card input-output—Monthly rental of $1,500.
- Large-scale computers—Monthly rental of $15,000 to $300,000. Examples—IBM 704-7090, Univac

1105 and 1107, CDC 1604, Philco 2000. An IBM 7030 Stretch computer rented for $300,000 per month and could process tapes at 100,000 characters per second and execute instructions at 30,000 per second.

By today's standards, the above statistics are embarrassing. It is amazing that companies could cost-justify computer applications; the improved competitive position or labor productivity gains were enormous for large corporations. Today, the potential productivity gains from computer-based systems are not any less extraordinary. Because current performance/cost ratios are thousands to million of times greater than they were in 1964, the returns today are also extraordinary.

---

* Thomas H. Naylor and Eugene T. Byrne, *Linear Programming Methods and Cases,* (Belmont, CA: Wadsworth Publishing, 1964), pp. 116–18.

casting system is essential in eliminating waste such as inventory shortages and excesses, missed due dates, plant shutdowns, lost sales, lost customers, expensive expediting, and in the long run, missed strategic opportunities. The best manufacturers, distributors, retailers, and service organizations in the world are distinguished by the excellence of their forecasting systems.

Financial and Strategic Importance of Forecasting

The old marketing phrase that "nothing happens until somebody sells something" is really more appropriately stated as "nothing happens until somebody forecasts something." Forecasts are essential to all plans and decisions because nothing happens until someone makes a forecast.

At first thought, profitability, productivity, and forecasting seem to be only slightly related concepts; however, they are very strongly related. Consider the many benefits from improved forecasting:

Better strategic information.

Better marketing information.

Better financial information.

Better operations information.

Increased customer service.

Better allocation of scarce resources.

Increased manufacturing and operating efficiency.

Customer Service Is Often the Competitive Edge

Service, quality, and reliability are strategies aimed at loyalty and long-term revenue stream growth (and maintenance). The point of . . . a wonderful concomitant to a customer orientation is that the winners seem to focus especially on the revenue-generation side.*

* Thomas J. Peters and Robert H. Waterman, Jr., *In Search of Excellence—Lessons from America's Best-Run Companies,* (New York: Harper and Row, 1982), p. 157.

Higher productivity.

Stability in planning.

Reduced finished goods inventory.

Elimination of waste.

More flexibility to respond to customer preferences.

Increased profitability.

Increased return on investment.

Effective forecasts are essential in achieving the strategic and operational goals of all organizations. For corporations, forecasts drive the marketing, financial, and production information control systems. Forecasts are central to almost all decisions in organizations. In the public sector, forecasts are an integral part of policy and program designs, whether these concern national health care or education. The effects of a new law or regulation should be forecasted before becoming law.

The Pursuit of Knowledge

Although some of us are concerned about profitability, it is important to recognize the role of forecasting in expanding the knowledge base of organizations and whole societies. Theories are confirmed through forecasts and scientific inquiry; the tools of this book are an essential part of the attainment of better knowledge. Forecasting methods are generic, applying to a wide variety of phenomena that vary over time. The forecasting methods developed here are essential tools of researchers, whether they are studying issues of product demand, improved health care, better educational systems, or the biological, physical, and social sciences.

Public Policies and Forecasting
The budget should be balanced, the treasury should be refilled, public debt should be reduced, the arrogance of officialdom should be tempered and controlled, and the assistance to foreign lands should be curtailed lest Rome become bankrupt (Cicero, 106 B.C.–43 B.C.).

The Commonality of Forecasting

There is a commonality in the management of organizations, whether they are manufacturers or hospitals. This commonality is the need to make strategic decisions and resource allocations based on forecasts. In all organizations, the demands for products, labor, materials, and other resources must be estimated using either formal or informal forecasting methods. Figure 1–1 illustrates the commonality of forecasting in a variety

FIGURE 1–1

Commonality of forecasting systems in resource allocations

Type of Application	Data Collection	Information Processing	Forecasting Model	Operational Goals and Plans	Allocation Decisions
Supermarket chain	Cash register point of sale	Accumulation of store sales at distribution center	Forecasts of store demands by product	Keep probability of stockout to less than 1 percent	Shipments from distribution centers to stores
Hospital	Past and current patient admissions	Accumulation of demand by department and procedure type	Forecasts of the number of patients and the resources needed	Keep probability of stockout to approximately zero	Schedules of rooms, nurses, drugs, supplies, etc.
Manufacturer-distributor	Customer orders and EDI	Accumulation of demand for products by distribution center	Forecasts of demands by distribution center (DC)	Keep probability of DC stockout very low, less than 1–2 percent	Shipments from factory to DCs
School district	Student enrollment forms	Accumulation of demand for classes by school	Forecast of number of continuing and migrating students	Assure that class sizes are reasonable; faculty, staff, and budget sufficient	Assign faculty, staff, budget, and students as necessary
Utility repair service	Past and current work orders	Accumulation of demand by procedure type	Forecast of number of customers and resource type	Keep probability of stockout to less than 1 percent	Schedules of stock items and work force needed

of organizations. As shown there, this common sequence is data collection, information processing, forecasting, applying operational goals, and resource allocations.

The Management Decision Hierarchy

To better understand the many types and purposes of forecasts, look at the management decision hierarchy of organizations presented in Figure 1–2. This hierarchy is represented by the triangular sequence of decisions that progress from the highest decisions of strategic business planning, managerial planning, and operational control to the lowest-level decisions involved in transaction processing. This figure is a modification of a model popularized by Robert Anthony of the Harvard Business School. This hierarchical and sequential decision-making system assists in understanding the many functions and responsibilities in all organizations; it is used here to highlight the importance of forecasting.

The left-hand side of the figure presents the hierarchy of objectives in all organizations; the far-right column denotes the important decisions in a manufacturing organization. As shown in the second column, forecasts drive all decisions. You should

FIGURE 1–2

Hierarchy of goals, decisions, and functions

Objectives of Management	Forecast Horizon Length	Hierarchy of Decisions	Typical Decisions and Functions of Manufacturer
Planning goals of the organization	Long horizon: 3 to 20 years; planned by months, quarters, or years	Strategic business planning	Planning: Goals of profitabilty, quality, market share, customer service, automation, labor relations
Managing the acquisition of resources so as to achieve goals	Medium horizon: 3 months to 3 years; planned by weeks or months	Managerial planning	Managing: Finance, marketing, operations, sales, distribution; size, location, and number of facilities, aggregate production, master schedules
Effectively and efficiently managing the allocation of resources to achieve goals	Medium to short horizon: 1 month to 2 years; planned by weeks or months	Operational planning and control	Managing and controlling: Distribution of products, production of products, materials requirements, capacity requirements
Controlling day-to-day operations	Immediate horizon: 1 day to 1 month	Transaction processing	Controlling: Production, purchasing, order entry, accounts receivable, payables, transportation/traffic, quality

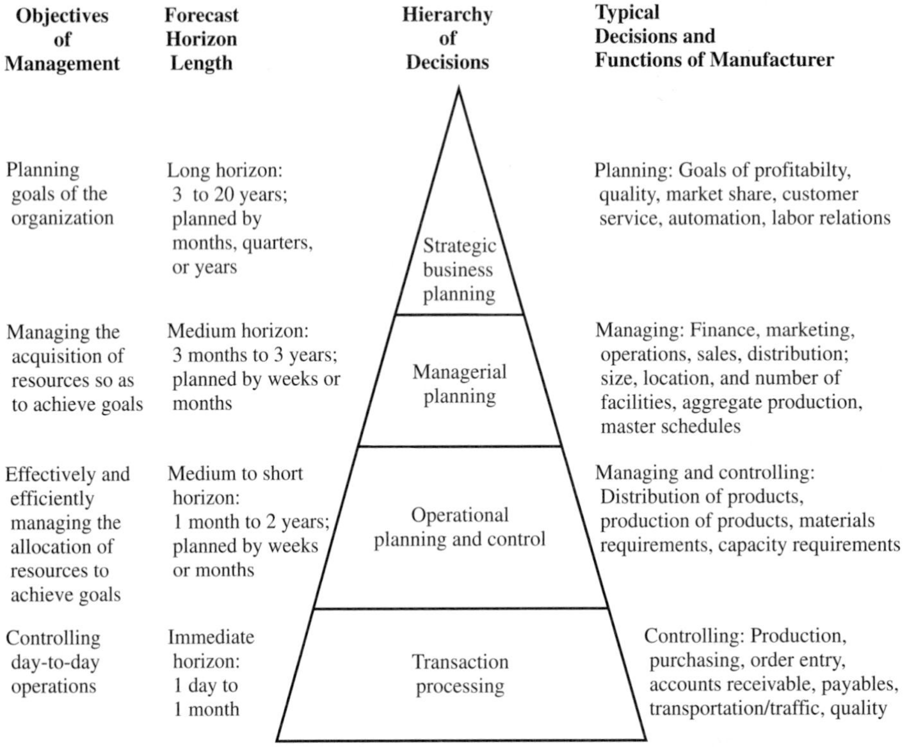

take a moment to study the objectives and decisions of each hierarchy and place these in the context of your own organization.

Consider this figure in greater detail. The first column, objectives of management, identifies the responsibilities of the different levels of management. Quite obviously, these objectives go from the very strategic, top management level to detailed day-to-day activities. The key concept of this figure is that managers are responsible for achieving these hierarchical objectives and need forecasting assistance. The next column, forecast horizon length, denotes the number of future periods planned at each level; for example, in business planning, the firm plans for 3 to 20 years into the future using either months, quarters, or years. Progressing down the hierarchy, the level of top management involvement decreases and that of lower management increases. Also, as shown in the figure, the horizon length (how far one plans in the future) decreases as the level of detail increases.

The forecast horizon lengths shown in this figure are prescriptive of the way firms should plan and descriptive of how the better-managed firms do plan. The decision or function column (the far-right column) denotes the major activity of each level of a typical manufacturing firm. Of particular interest here is that there is a hierarchy of forecasts that are the major inputs to respective management processes.

Moving down the decision pyramid, the level of information and system detail increases. Hence, a pyramid is used to represent the system. Also, the movement down the pyramid goes from ill-structured, nonprogrammable (i.e., nonroutine) decisions of top management to programmable decisions at lowest levels of the organization. For example, the management of inventory at lower levels of the hierarchy normally involves a more structured, programmable decision process. Once computer-based management systems are in place, many of the decisions of inventory management can be automated. Only when exceptions are detected does management need to be involved. To assist with these exception detections, reporting tools of tracking signals will be discussed in Chapter 17.

In summary, progressing down the hierarchy,

Decisions and forecasts become less strategic.

Top management involvement decreases.

Decision lead times decrease.

Forecast horizon lengths decrease from years to weeks.

Decisions and forecasts become more programmable.

Levels of detail increase greatly.

Levels of automation increase.

Computers are used to support more repetitive decisions.

As will be shown, a good forecasting system is hierarchical in nature, having most of the characteristics listed above.

Why Forecast?

Forecasts Are Necessary Because of Implementation Lead Times

Forecasting is most often part of a larger process of planning and managing. A forecast is necessary to provide accurate estimates of the future for this larger process. We have seen that in the hierarchy of decisions, some decisions take considerably longer to implement than others. If a decision requires a long time to implement, long-horizon forecasts are necessary to provide long-range information (e.g., for strategic business planning in Figure 1–2). In contrast, if a decision takes a short time to implement, it only requires a short-horizon forecast as an input (e.g., operational control).

One of the major benefits from reducing implementation lead times is the resulting reduction in the horizon length of the forecast. For example, when the just-in-time (JIT) philosophy is properly implemented, supplier and production lead times can be reduced significantly. Consider an example where order lead times are reduced from 16 to 2 weeks. In this situation, the forecast horizon decreases accordingly. That is, the forecast of demand for the next 2 weeks will be more accurate than the forecast for the next 16 weeks. This relationship between lead time and forecast accuracy yields the following principles:

Reducing forecast horizon lengths improves forecast accuracy.

Long lead times force future uncertainty on the present.

Long lead times require commitments of resources in the present despite the considerable uncertainty of the future.

What Is a Forecast?

A Forecast Should Be a Point, Range, and Probability Estimate

Because we all formally or informally make forecasts, we have an intuitive idea of what a forecast is—a forecast is a probabilistic estimate or description of a future value or condition. Although this is an adequate general definition, good planning and control require that a forecast includes a mean, range, and probability estimate of that

A 50-Year Planning Horizon—The Transamerica Transportation Corridor

Usually, planning horizons of 5 to 10 years are viewed as long; however, some endeavors are so large as to require extraordinary lead times. A preliminary study was recently completed on the construction of a high-technology multimodal transportation corridor across the United States from the coast of Virginia to California for the year 2040. The preliminary 15-month study was completed in 1993 at a cost of about $1,000,000. The study explored all transportation modes and technologies for a 3,000-mile high-speed "highway" named the Transamerica Transportation Corridor, including

- A rail system with 125 to 135 miles per hour (mph) passenger and 90 mph freight service, with access every 50 miles. Approximate cost, $33 billion.
- A 150 mph passenger highway system with intelligent electronic control of automobiles, with access every 20 miles. Approximate cost, $53 billion.
- A 300 mph high-speed rail system using magnetic levitation. Approximate cost, $51 to $78 billion.

The planning processes necessary for such an endeavor include technological forecasting and are studied in Chapter 15. There is the possibility that fusion will make electricity relatively inexpensive. Consequently, there is considerable uncertainty in the costs of alternative technologies and forms of transportation, particularly air travel. Air travel as it is known today did not exist 50 years ago. What are the implications of future vehicle developments, including electric cars, new trains, new trucks, new aircraft, and new hovercraft?

"The challenges of such a broad based and forward thinking study are mind-boggling. . . . success requires finding a large, highly polished crystal ball which will enable mere mortals to peer into the next half a century.*

———————

*Jim Haugen, "Designing the Next Interstate System," *Automotive Industries* 172, no. 1 (January 1992), p. 54.

range. The term *probability* emphasizes that a forecast should not be a single value, but a range of values. For example, a good forecast statement is "expected sales next month for product X is 400 units, with a 70 percent probability that sales will be 300 to 500 units" (i.e., a 35 percent chance of sales from 300 to 400 and a 35 percent chance from 400 to 500). The method used to arrive at this statement is developed in Chapter 2.

The probability estimates of forecasts are very important in contingency planning. Frequently, forecasts are wrong, so management should have plans for such contingencies. For example, if sales are 300 units instead of 400, management should have a plan that minimizes the negative effects of low sales. Likewise, if sales are 500 instead of 400, management should have an alternative contingency plan. Forecasting is designed to reduce the uncertainty or risk (i.e., the range of errors) in decision making; however, it cannot completely eliminate uncertainty and risk. This is highlighted by the following principle: forecast accuracy is important, but valid contingency plans when the inevitable errors occur may be more important.

All Managers Forecast.   Although most managers are not aware that they are making probability statements when they forecast, they are nonetheless implicitly doing so. For example, when someone forecasts next month's demand as 900 units, he or she is implicitly stating that there is about a 50 percent chance that demand will be greater than 900 and a 50 percent chance demand will be less than 900.

Basic Assumption of Forecasting.   Many different methods can be used to forecast; however, the basic assumption of most methods is the same: the past patterns or behavior will continue into the future. Some managers state that their firms do not forecast, they simply assume that last month's sales will equal this month's sales; however, this is a simple method of forecasting. In fact, almost all forecasts are based on the assumption that the past will repeat.

What Should Be Forecast?

Dependent versus Independent Demands

Forecast independent demands and then calculate the many dependent demands. There is an important yet simple relationship concerning demands for products, services, and resources. A demand is considered to be **independent** when estimates of it have to be forecasted. In contrast, **dependent demands** can be calculated directly from known physical or technical relationships. For example, a firm that manufactures microcomputers must forecast the demand for their final assembly, called a system unit; this therefore is an independent demand. However, the demands for system circuit boards, disk drives, and computer housings do not have to be forecasted; instead, they can be calculated from the forecast of system units. Each forecasted system unit must have a case, circuit board, at least one disk drive, and a housing. Fortunately, most demands for resources in an organization are dependent and do not have to be forecasted; rather, they are calculated from the forecasts of independent demands.

Consider another example. If a company manufactures children's wagons, bicycles, and tricycles, it must forecast the demand for these products. However, the demand for the wheels, axles, and other parts of the wagons, bicycles, and tricycles can be calculated from those forecasts, depending on how the product is manufactured. The demand for wagon wheels is completely dependent on the assembly schedule for wagons; there are four wheels per wagon; therefore, 100 wagons requires 400 wheels.

Although many organizations recognize the principle of independent and dependent demands, it is surprising how many do not recognize or use it effectively. This distinction may at times be subtle. For example, a retailer-wholesaler might not recognize that demand at its regional distribution center is completely dependent on the demands at its stores. This most often means that the demand at retail stores should be forecasted and the demand at the distribution center should be calculated as the sum of retail store demands. Dependent demands are often difficult to forecast accurately; thus, a firm may be forecasting the wrong thing and doing it very badly. Forecast accuracy is difficult to achieve with dependent demands.

Table 1–1 presents some other very simple relationships between independent and dependent demand items in a variety of organizations.

Forecasting Hierarchy—The Process of Aggregation/ Disaggregation

The typical forecasting situation involves several different dimensions. That is, there is not one forecast made in an organization, but a whole hierarchy of forecasts. Consider Table 1–2, which presents the **forecasting hierarchy** for a computer manufacturer. These forecasts are made of aggregate and disaggregate demands for the products of the firm. For example, the forecasts progress from estimates of the macroeconomy, to industry demands, company demands, product-line (i.e., group) demands, company-wide demands for specific products, and finally, specific product demands at particular locations. Chapter 17 discusses important principles related to aggregating and disaggregating forecasts.

TABLE 1–1 Independent versus Dependent Demands

Organizations	Independent Demands Forecasted	Dependent Demands Calculated
Manufacturer	Product demands at the factory	Parts in the product; manpower schedules; machine schedules
Manufacturer-distributor	Product demands at distribution centers	Products at the factory; production of parts; manpower/machine schedules
Wholesaler	Product demands at distribution centers	Demands at central warehouses or suppliers
Retailers	Product demands at each store	Demands for customer service personnel
Retailer-distributor	Product demands at each store	Demands at distribution centers and warehouses
Hospitals	Number of patients by DRG or MDC	Number of nurses; material/drug demands; demand for beds
Utilities	Kilowatt hours of power; new home hookups; equipment breakdowns	Number of power plants on-line; power purchased from other utilities; home watt-meters; size of service crew
School districts	Number of students by grade	Number of faculty, classes, and labs.
Universities	Number of students seeking a course	Number of faculty, classrooms, laboratories
Municipalities	Traffic counts; applicants for licenses and permits	Number of roads, lanes, bridges, and lights
		Number of employees

TABLE 1–2 Multiple Forecasts of Demands for Computers
The Forecasting Hierarchy

Type of Demand	Example of Forecasts
Macroeconomy	Forecasts of income, productivity, employment, interest rates, technology
Industry demand	General demand for products of an industry, e.g., the industry demand for microcomputers, minicomputers, and mainframes
Company demand	The company's market share
Product-line demand	Three product lines exist (micros, minis, and mainframes); demands need to be estimated at each level
Companywide demand	National demand for 32-bit microcomputers; for 64 bit minis; and for 64-bit mainframes
Demand at each location	Demand for microcomputers at St. Louis, Los Angeles, and New York distribution centers

Common Time Series Patterns

This chapter previews the remaining text by introducing models of time series using several different methods. The most common methods of forecasting make estimates of the future on the basis of past patterns, past relationships, or subjective predictions. These three ways to estimate the future are used to classify forecasting methods as univariate (using past patterns), multivariate (using past relationships between multiple variables), and qualitative (using subjective judgments and methods). Univariate methods are the most widely used; thus, we first discuss the common patterns that are modeled by univariate methods. These patterns include random, trend, seasonal, cyclical, autocorrelated, outlier, promotional, and combinations of these patterns. We then discuss the characteristics of each of the three different classes of forecasting methods. By studying the different patterns of time series, we can better understand the different methods of modeling these patterns.

Time Series versus Cross-Sectional Analysis

A **time series** is a continuous set of observations that are ordered in equally spaced intervals (e.g., one per month). An example is a database of the performance of a single bank from 1970 to date. In contrast, cross-sectional data is collected at one point in time. A cross-sectional database might be the recent performances of 100 banks. Although we do not study cross-sectional applications, cross-sectional data can be collected over time (e.g., information about 100 banks for 26 years) and can be analyzed using time series analysis.

When a time series is plotted, common patterns are frequently found. These patterns might be explained by many possible cause-and-effect relationships. Some common patterns are shown in Figures 1–3 through 1–17.

Random Patterns

Random time series are the result of many influences that act independently to yield nonsystematic and nonrepeating patterns about some average value. Purely **random series** have a constant mean and no systematic patterns.

Figure 1–3 illustrates random demand for a product. Knowing only past demand, one appropriate forecasting model is to estimate future demand as equal to the mean of this random series (i.e., 850). Alternatively, if demand were randomly increasing or decreasing very slowly over time, an average of the most recent observations could be used. For example, an average of the last 12 months of series A yields a mean of 882 (see SERIESA.DAT). There are other simple but effective methods that can be used to forecast this series; these are discussed in Chapters 3 through 9.

Unless other time series are available to help predict a random series (e.g., number of printers in use to predict paper sales), simple averaging models are often the most accurate way to forecast them. Figure 1–4 presents another example of a random series; it illustrates worldwide airline fatalities from 1970 to 1989. Is this series random or is it decreasing? Clearly, this is not as random as the printer paper series. You may be asked to explain this series as a homework problem.

Trend Patterns

A **trend** is a general increase or decrease in a time series that lasts for approximately seven or more periods (e.g., seven months, where seven is a crude rule of thumb). Trends are caused by long-term population changes, growth during product and technology introductions, changes in economic conditions, and so on. Figure 1–5 illustrates a series with a trend. In this case, the trend is a period-to-period increase that follows a straight line, a pattern called a linear trend. Trends are not necessarily linear because there are a large number of nonlinear causal influences that yield nonlinear series; nonlinear and linear trends are discussed in Chapters 5 to 7.

FIGURE 1–3

Demand for printer paper, a series with random sales (SERIESA.DAT)

FIGURE 1–4

Annual worldwide airline fatalities, 1970–1989 (WWFATAL.DAT)

FIGURE 1–5

Demand for a product with trend (SERIESC.DAT, demand for advanced microcomputers)

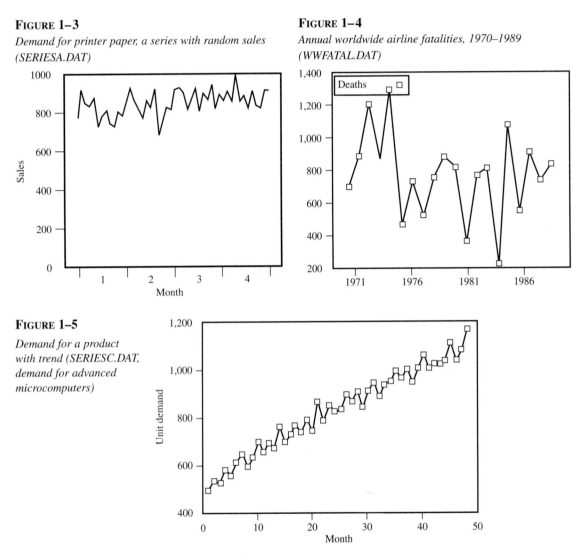

Figure 1–6 presents an example of two nonlinear trends; it shows the U.S. and German stock indexes. Clearly, whenever a series is trending and it is believed that the trend will continue into the future, it should be forecasted using a trend model.

Seasonal Patterns

Figure 1–7 illustrates a product demand with pronounced seasonality: soft drink sales. **Seasonal series** result from events that are periodic and recurrent (e.g., monthly changes recurring each year). Common seasonal influences are climate, human habits, holidays, repeating promotions, new-product announcements, and so on. Seasonality can occur many different ways, for example, by week of the year, month of the year, day of the month, day of the week (e.g., absenteeism on Friday or the greater demand on weekends), and hour of the day (e.g., telephone usage by hour). Figure 1–8 illustrates another seasonal time series, the quarterly number of births and marriages in the United States from 1970 to 1992.

A seasonal period may be for a year, month, day, and for some activities, even an hour. Consider the daily seasonality for trout tags at a Missouri state park in Figure 1–9. This series exhibits day-of-the-week and day-of-the-year seasonality. In some

FIGURE 1–6

U.S. versus German stock indexes (USGERM.DAT)

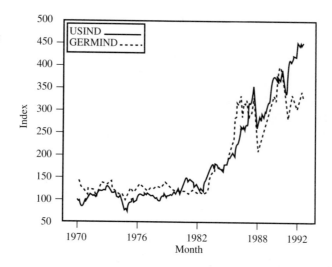

FIGURE 1–7

Demand for a product with strong seasonality (SERIESD.DAT, demand for a brand of diet soft drink)

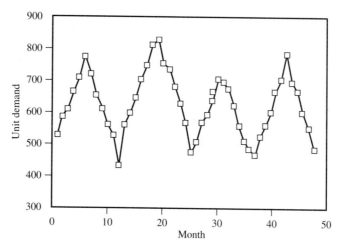

FIGURE 1–8

Quarterly marriages and births in the United States (BIRTHMAR.DAT)

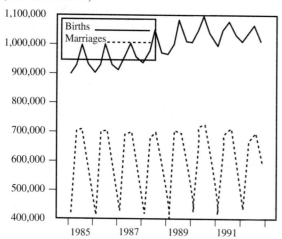

FIGURE 1–9

Daily demand for trout tags sold (TROUT.DAT)

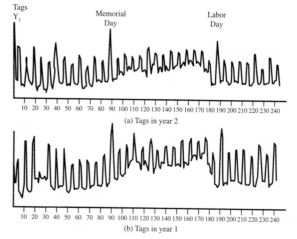

cases, the seasonal cycle may last for four years (e.g., the demand for Olympic athletic equipment). When seasonal influences are present, seasonal forecasting models should be used; these models are discussed in Chapters 5 through 13.

Cyclical Patterns

Economic and business expansions (increasing demand) and contractions (recessions and depressions) are the most frequent cause of **cyclical influences** on time series. These influences most often last for two to five years and recur, but with no known period. In the search for explanations of cyclical movements, many theories have been proposed, including sunspots, positions of the planets, stars, long-wave movements in weather conditions, population life cycles, growth and decay of new products and technology (e.g., phonograph records, tape cassettes, betamax VCRs), product life cycles, and the economy. Figure 1–10 illustrates the composite index of leading economic indicators published by the Department of Commerce. Note how this series expands and contracts over time.

Cyclical influences are difficult to forecast because, as shown in Figure 1–10, they are recurrent but not periodic (i.e., the times between peaks and troughs vary), unlike seasonal influences, which are periodic and recurrent. Because of their economic importance, considerable time and effort have been devoted to predicting cyclical variations. Analysts hope to find variables that predict the turning points of the series (turning points are changes from increasing to decreasing values or vice versa). As discussed in Chapter 14, these efforts have not been as fruitful as hoped; however, this is an area of continuing interest and development.

Autocorrelated Patterns

Another pattern that is often seen in time series is a concept called autocorrelation. **Correlation** measures the degree of dependence or association between two variables. The term **autocorrelation** means that the value of a series in one time period is related to the value of itself in previous periods. With autocorrelation, there is an *automatic* correlation between observations in a series. For example, if there is high positive autocorrelation, the value in June is positively related to the value in May. Frequently, this autocorrelation results from the momentum of the series. For example, customer preferences, brand loyalty, and so on may change slowly; thus, changes in demand may move slowly. Autocorrelated values are the result of high-volume influences and other systematic influences like trends and seasonality.

FIGURE 1–10

Composite index of 11 leading economic indicators (LEADIN.DAT)

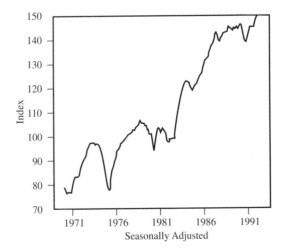

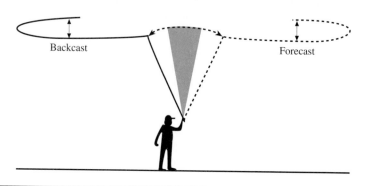

A Good Forecast Requires a Good Backcast

There is an insightful relationship between forecasting and one of the oldest known sports, fishing. In fishing as in forecasting, one casts a "line" forward. This cast is called a forward cast, or forecast. As shown below, a backcast in fly-fishing is the toss of a line backward overhead. This is analogous to the concept of modeling past demands in forecasting. In statistical forecasting, we model patterns of the past (the backcast) to throw those patterns forward to the future. Thus, as in fly-fishing, most often the determinant of a good forecast is a good backcast.

FIGURE 1–11

Price of common stock with a highly autocorrelated, random-walk pattern (SERIESB.DAT)

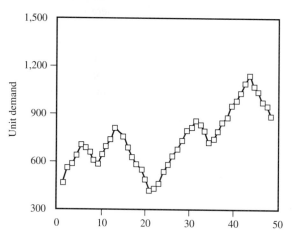

FIGURE 1–12

Price of IBM stock, March 1981–September 1993 (IBMMN.DAT)

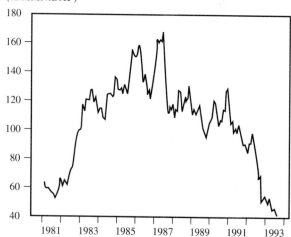

Figures 1–11 and 1–12 illustrate series that are highly autocorrelated; each observation is highly associated with (related to) the previous value. Positive autocorrelated series are characterized by the smooth pattern of the series. Autocorrelation is a general phenomenon that can occur with other patterns like those of Figures 1–3 through 1–10. As we will discuss, when high autocorrelation exists between adjacent values, very simple but accurate methods can be used to make forecasts one-period ahead. However, multiperiod-ahead forecasts are not usually as accurate. Highly positive autocorrelated series without trends or seasonality are often **random-walk series** like those of Figures 1–11 and 1–12.

Although negatively autocorrelated series exist, they are not as common as positively autocorrelated series. Such series consist of alternating high and low values. When they do occur, they might be the result of nonrandom processes (e.g., supply problems) that yield alternating highs and lows.

Finally, Chapter 2 discusses other measures of correlation between two variables, for example, demand and advertising. You may already be familiar with correlations in regression analysis. Figure 1–13 illustrates the relationship between demand and advertising for a bookstore, a relationship we study in greater detail in Chapters 2 and 3.

Some managers state that they do not forecast, but instead assume that the value in the following month will equal the value of the current month. However, the decision maker is really forecasting using a model that assumes values are highly autocorrelated. In fact, one very accurate short-term model for highly autocorrelated series is to predict the value for next month as that of this month. Figure 1–14 illustrates this situation using series B of Figure 1–11. As Figure 1–14 shows, the forecasted values track the actual values with a one-period lag; the actuals are just moved one period to the right to become forecasted values. As in all such plots, the vertical distance between the actual and predicted value is the error.

Although these forecasts may seem very accurate, multiperiod-ahead forecasts will be much less accurate (e.g., 10-period-ahead forecasts will be very inaccurate). Using the previous actual as a forecast of the demand of the next and many subsequent periods in Figure 1–14 yields inaccurate long-term forecasts. When using this or other simple models, the long-term forecasts are a constant, equal to some simple function of the most recent actuals. In the case of Figure 1–14, the forecasts for periods 25 through 30 all equal the actual demand in period 24, which is 558 (see SERIESB.DAT). Consequently, the forecast for periods 25 through 30 all equal 558; however, the actuals in periods 25 through 30 are 597, 654, 696, 746, 814, and finally, 826. The actual of period 24 is accurate in forecasting period 25; however, it is a poor forecast of periods 26 through 30.

Series B in Figure 1–14 is called a random-walk series because it moves randomly and smoothly about without a constant mean. When the mean of the series is al-

FIGURE 1–13

Demand versus advertising for Big City Bookstore (BIGCITY.DAT)

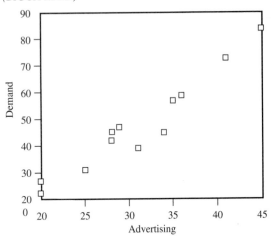

FIGURE 1–14

One-period forecasts of a autocorrelated, random-walk pattern (SERIESB.DAT, price of a common stock)

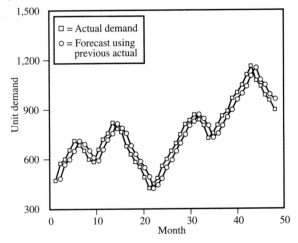

ways changing, the series is called a **nonstationary series**. Unfortunately, because series B is a random walk, there are no good univariate forecasting methods for long horizons. This is a problem that plagues all forecasters facing random-walk series, particularly those wanting to predict prices or demands more than one period ahead.

Not all highly autocorrelated series are random walks. Trending, seasonal, and those series with little variation might be highly autocorrelated. We discuss these in Chapters 4 and 5.

Outliers

The analysis of past data can be made very complex when the included values are not typical of the past or future. These nontypical values are called **outliers**, which are very large or small observations that are not indicative of repeating past or future patterns. Outliers include deviations that occur because of unusual events such as supply interruptions, strikes, earthquakes, floods, plant shutdowns, wars, and oil spills. However, in many cases, the cause of the outlier may be unknown. Figure 1–15 illustrates the data of Figure 1–3 before a low outlier was removed in period 31. As shown in Figure 1–15, demand in period 31 was originally 450 units. This value is so low as to be considered an outlier. As shown in Figure 1–3, it is adjusted to a more typical value, 811.

We must stress the importance of adjusting outliers prior to and during the analysis of a time series. The old adage "if you put garbage in, you will get garbage out" is very accurate in describing the effects of outliers in a model. Outliers are the worst type of forecasting garbage; consequently, it is very important to adjust these outliers. Book Appendix B and Chapters 12 and 17 discuss good methods of adjusting outliers; however, these methods often are not more accurate than eyeballing a new value, as was done with the observation for period 31 of Figure 1–15. When analyzing data in forecasting, a significant amount of computer programming or analyst time is devoted to detecting and removing outliers because outliers confound pattern-identification processes and should always be adjusted or modelled.

Interventions—
Unplanned and
Planned Events

Most often the patterns of past data reflect many **planned events,** such as product or price promotions or administrative or managerial interventions. When these events occur, their effects should be modeled so that their future impact can be anticipated. As discussed in Chapter 12, such interventions affect time series during and after the event. Some series are dominated by planned and unplanned interventions; conse-

FIGURE 1–15

Series with outlier
(SERIESA.DAT, boxes of
printer paper)

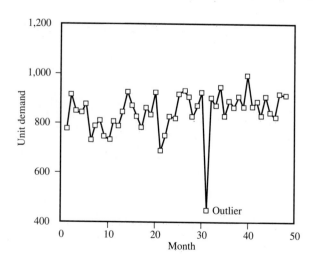

quently, it is important to be able to track the effects of the interventions. For example, promotional increases and decreases may be mistakenly identified as unexplainable outliers unless promotional timing and effects are measured. It is a simple task to measure the effect of a promotion as the difference between the expected demand (e.g., 1,000) and the actual demand (e.g., 1,600). This difference (600) should be captured by the forecaster or forecasting system. It will be useful in predicting the effect of future promotions on future values, and its identification eliminates the extreme value of that outlier. **Unplanned events** such as competitor actions (e.g., stockouts) should also be recorded. Book Appendix B further discusses this.

Modeling Combinations of Patterns

In general, a time series can possess a combination of patterns such as those shown in Figures 1–16 and 1–17. Figure 1–16 illustrates the demand for AM/FM personal radios having both pronounced trend and seasonality. The forecasting method chosen to model series F should include measures of the trend and seasonality. As discussed in Chapters 5 through 13, there are a number of methods that accurately represent series with trend and seasonality. The seasonal and trend patterns in Figure 1–17 are very pronounced; also surprising is how the seasonal variations have expanded over time, a condition called variance nonstationary, a topic discussed in Chapters 6 and 7. If a series has a combination of patterns, a model of it should include all those patterns.

FIGURE 1–16

A product with trend and seasonality (SERIESF.DAT, AM/FM personal radios)

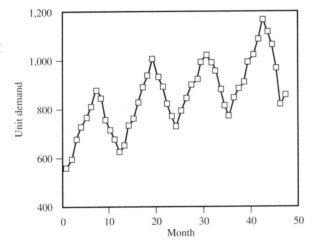

FIGURE 1–17

Monthly megawatts at an electric utility (MEGAWATT.DAT)

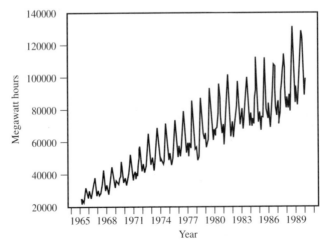

Overview of Forecasting Methods

Having defined a number of important time series patterns, let's consider the general methods of modeling these patterns. Three classifications of forecasting methods—univariate, multivariate, and qualitative—are discussed below.

Time Series (Univariate) Forecasting Methods

Univariate forecasting methods, also known as **time series methods,** use the past, internal patterns in data to forecast the future. Univariate methods include smoothing, exponential smoothing, decomposition, Fourier series analysis, ARIMA (i.e., Box-Jenkins), linear trends, and nonlinear growth models, among others. The purpose of these methods is to model the patterns of past values to project (cast) them into the future. Where cost and accuracy of short- to medium-horizon forecasts are important, univariate methods are almost always the most cost effective.

The basic concept of univariate forecasting is that future values of a series are a mathematical function (f) of past values. Mathematically, this is:

$$\text{Future values} = f(\text{Past values}) \qquad (1\text{--}1)$$

For example, consider a simple two-month average forecast model:

$$\text{Forecast of June sales } = \frac{\text{April sales } + \text{ May sales}}{2} = \frac{600 + 500}{2} = 550 \qquad (1\text{--}2)$$

Chapters 4 to 9 are devoted to univariate forecasting methods.

Causal (Multivariate) Forecasting Methods

Multivariate forecasting methods also known as **causal methods,** make projections of the future by modeling the relationship between a series and other series. For example, a forecast of furniture sales may be based on a relationship with economic indicators such as housing starts, personal income, number of new marriages, and number of new households. These external variables are called **predictor or independent variables,** and the furniture sales variable is referred to as the **predicted or dependent variable.**

Multivariate methods include simple- and multiple-regression, econometric, multi-equation econometric, multivariate time series, state space, and a few other more advanced techniques. In general, multivariate methods are more costly to develop than univariate methods; much of this additional cost results from necessary external data collection and analyst time. However, the wide availability of inexpensive microcomputer software has made this methodology much more cost effective.

A general mathematical statement of simple multivariate models is:

$$\text{Dependent variable} = f(\text{Independent predictor variable})$$

or

$$\text{Future values} = f(\text{Past values, Values of other variables}) \qquad (1\text{--}3)$$

Consider a simple three-variable model for furniture sales:

$$\text{Forecast of June demand} = 50 + .2 \times \text{LMS} + 1 \times \text{API} + .5 \times \text{NHS} \qquad (1\text{--}4)$$
$$= 50 + .2 \times 600 + 1 \times 250 + .5 \times 200 = 520$$

where the independent predictor variables are:

LMS = last month's furniture sales (i.e., sales in May).
API = average personal income.
NHS = new housing starts.

The synonym for multivariate methods, causal methods, indicates that the purpose in using multivariate methods is to model the causes of variations to better predict future values. However, modeling cause-and-effect relationships in many settings is costly and difficult. Also, when judged by the accuracy of short- to medium-term forecasts, causal models frequently are not as cost effective as univariate and simpler multivariate methods. However, the cost of using causal methods is declining. Finally, multivariate methods have the distinct disadvantage that in most cases the independent variables (e.g., LMS, API, and NHS) need to be forecasted in order to predict the future values of the dependent variable. However, if one wants to explain the cause-and-effect relationships (e.g., in the context of strategic planning), multivariate methods are the best approach.

The important differences between the purposes of causal (multivariate) and univariate models should be emphasized further. Univariate models are designed to model the past with mathematical relationships that mimic, but may not explicitly explain, past patterns. In contrast, multivariate methods are designed to model the cause-and-effect relationships of the past so as to forecast *and* explain behavior. Explanation of behavior (e.g., demand for furniture) as a function of other variables is the forte of causal methods. By explaining product sales as a function of external, independent variables, managers receive valuable information that can be used for short- to long-horizon decisions, including important strategic-management decisions.

Finally, all multivariate models are not necessarily causal models. In many situations, multivariate models are very accurate in prediction, but not necessarily a true representation of the underlying cause-and-effect relationships. When predictive accuracy is all that is desired from a multivariate model, the model may not be causal; nonetheless, it may be a best predictor of the future.

This book's presentation of multivariate models is more extensive than that of many other forecasting books because with readily available computer software, these methods are being used more extensively in forecasting by those not trained as economists. Therefore, Chapters 10 to 16 discuss multivariate methods in detail.

Qualitative Forecasting Methods

Qualitative forecasting methods are based on the judgment and opinions of others concerning future trends, tastes, and technological changes. Qualitative methods include Delphi, market research, panel consensus, scenario analysis, and historical analogy methods of predicting the future. Qualitative methods are most frequently used to make long-run predictions when there is little objective data concerning relevant past patterns or relationships. (As is common, the term **prediction** is used to denote a forecast based primarily on subjective (i.e., qualitative) methods.) These methods are as expensive as, and in many cases, more expensive than, causal methods. A very simple example of a qualitative prediction is illustrated by a group of executives agreeing upon the forecast for the following month. Consider a prediction forecast of a three-executive panel:

$$\text{June forecast} = \frac{\begin{array}{c}\text{Manager 1} \\ \text{forecast}\end{array} + \begin{array}{c}\text{Manager 2} \\ \text{forecast}\end{array} + \begin{array}{c}\text{Manager 3} \\ \text{forecast}\end{array}}{3} \qquad (1\text{--}5)$$

$$= \frac{400 + 600 + 600}{3} = 533$$

Qualitative methods are useful when there is little data to support quantitative methods. In business, they are used to predict the demand for new products, new technologies, new market shares, the cost or development time for new products or technologies, or the best competitive strategy. In the public sector, they are used to predict the effects of changes in public policy, constituents' views, demand for services, and so forth. They are sometimes called technological forecasting methods because of their frequent use in projecting long-run technological changes.

Formal qualitative methods are not used as much as univariate and multivariate methods because of their higher costs, lower accuracy, and the ready availability of data for other methods. However, because these subjective methods are used often in informal and intuitive ways, they should be studied by all forecasters.

The Art of Forecasting— Management Intuition and Involvement

The several qualitative methods discussed so far use subjective judgments of one or more individuals. It is important to highlight the very common practice of managerial "guesstimates" when data is unavailable or other methods are incapable of modeling a time series. Such procedures can be invaluable when necessary. Individuals have insights concerning appropriate assumptions and factors in a forecast. When sufficient data is not available, subjective management judgment is probably better than placing false hopes on sophisticated forecasting models that do not have an adequate database. Thus, the forecasting process should provide a method for input of subjective information from managers.

Although some forecasts are made by the computer in an automated environment, management review of all important forecasts is essential. Thus, management should have direct input to those forecasts. This management intervention may be prompted by an exception report highlighting a problem in the system. This may reflect a problem with outliers or the inability of the forecasting system to incorporate all relevant information about the time series. The intervention might be initiated by a manager because he or she knows of a future event that will be different than the past.

Some have a tendency to discount the validity of management forecasts because of the subjectivity of the input. However, experienced managers assimilate a large number of facts, both quantitative and qualitative, to arrive at their estimates. In fact, clearly some things repeat, but other phenomena, such as promotions and unusual events like floods, fires, earthquakes and war, have profound effects on the future; however, most are not forecastable. Consequently, these effects most often are incorporated into forecasts through management intervention. Although not obvious, the best forecasting approach is one that combines accurate objective and subjective forecasts to yield even more accurate forecasts. Such considerations are discussed further in Chapter 17.

Even when a model's forecast is accepted, in the end management is responsible for the consequences. Important future events like marketing promotions may not be included in the simple assumptions of univariate forecasts. Consequently, management involvement continues during all phases of the forecasting process. The forecast must be monitored, improved, and maintained. If the forecast is ineffective, the manager will be accountable for system failures. Conditions change too quickly and too often to depend solely on a single quantitative forecast.

Model Summary

Table 1–3 summarizes the preceding discussion and briefly defines many other methods of forecasting. Table 1–4 provides a listing of forecasting methods and the chapters in which they are developed.

TABLE 1–3   **Overview of Forecasting Methods**

Time Series Univariate Methods—Methods that model a time series as a function of itself, with no outside explanatory variables. For example a seasonal model might be, $Y_t = Y_{t-12} + (Y_{t-1} - Y_{t-13})$.

- *Moving averages*—Smoothing time series using moving averages reduces the period-to-period variation but tracks local movements above and below some long-run mean.
- *Exponential smoothing/Holts-Winters*—Time series are smoothed whereby most recent observations receive greater weight. Advanced methods include trend and seasonality through decomposition.
- *Classic decomposition Census II X-11*—A method that systematically decomposes a time series into trend, cyclical, seasonal, and error components. Developed by Julius Shiskin at the Department of Commerce and used heavily in deseasonalizing economic data.
- *Fourier series*—A method that models trend, seasonality, and cyclical movements using trigonometric sine and cosine functions. A method used in automated forecasting systems; however, it is not without its detractors.
- *ARIMA (Box-Jenkins)*—A method that models a series using trend, seasonal, and smoothing coefficients that are based on moving averages, autoregression, and difference equations. An accurate and very versatile approach.
- *Multimodel simulation methods*—A set of heuristic methods that have been found to be useful in forecasting. Intuitively appealing and reportedly relatively accurate in modeling many series, popularly known as focus forecasting.

Causal/Multivariate Methods—Explanatory models are used to define the cause and effect relationships in a system. For example, sales as a function of price, advertising, competition, and so forth. Some multivariate methods are used to model true cause and effect, but many multivariate models are focused solely on forecast accuracy.

- *Multiple regression*—Using the method of least squares, the relationship between one dependent and many independent variables is modeled. From a causal standpoint, multiple regression models may not be as valid as those of econometric, nonetheless they may forecast as accurately.
- *Econometric*—Using generalized least squares techniques, the relationships between one or more endogenous and exogenous variables are estimated. Small-scale, simple models are multiple regression models; however, the theoretical foundation of econometric models is much more rigorous and valid. Mutual causality using several simultaneous equations can be modeled with econometric methods.
- *Cyclical*—Methods that try to predict turning points in the economy using leading indicators, rate of change, and long-wave theories.
- *Mulivariate ARIMA (Box-Jenkins-MARIMA)*—A method that combines the strengths of econometric and ARIMA time series methods. Quite effective in applications when the effects of the independent variables lead one or more dependent variables.
- *State space*—An approach that is statistically equivalent to MARIMA models but more easily applied with automated software; however, its underlying mathematical foundations are complex.
- *Vector autoregression*—VAR models are a somewhat simpler approach than using MARIMA models when there are lagged effects of several independent variables on several dependent variables. However, while VAR estimation is simpler, the models often have many more coefficients than MARIMA models.
- *Input/output models*—Economic model that represents the relationships between the inputs and outputs of industries using matrices of influences.

Qualitative/Technological

- *Panel consensus*—This method is based on the assumption that the consensus of several experts will yield a better forecast than a single expert's opinion. The opinions of complementary experts yield improved predictions.
- *Sales force composite*—Methods for achieving an average or consensus forecast from the independent inputs of several salespersons who are closely involved with customers and understand customer's needs.
- *DELPHI*—An iterative process in which experts respond to questionnaires that are tabulated and modified in reaching conclusions.
- *Historical analogy*—Models a time series using a similar event from the past. Useful for new products and emerging technologies without past data.
- *Relevance trees*—Use of a tree representation of the relationships between goals and the means to achieve those goals; the importance of events and decisions are identified. By identifying the relationships between desired future events and the events necessary to achieve them, the organization attempts greater control of the future.

Other Quantitative

- *Artificial Neural Networks*—Mimic some of the parallel processing capabilities of the human brain as models of simple and complex forecasting applications. At times, these models identify nonlinear and interactive relationships which were anticipated by the analyst.

---

continued

TABLE 1–3 **Overview of Forecasting Methods**
concluded

• *Market research*—Characterized by formal hypothesis testing using a wide variety of statistical analyses of data collected by mail, telephone, and personal surveys.
• *Management science/operations research*—A wide variety of quantitative methods that are useful in modeling, including mathematical programming, simulation, network models, neural networks, and genetic algorithms.

TABLE 1–4 **Classification of Statistical Forecasting Methods**

Type	*Method*	*Chapter*
Time Series	Simple regression analysis	3
	Moving averages/exponential smoothing	4
	Classical decomposition/census X-11	5
	Holts-Winters	6
	Fourier series	Supplement to 6
	ARIMA (Box-Jenkins)	7, 8, & 9
Causal Methods	Multiple regression	3 & 10
	Econometric	11
	Cyclical	14
	Multivariate ARIMA (Box-Jenkins)	12 & 13
	State space	N/A
	Vector autoregression	N/A
Qualitative/ Technological	Expert opinion	15
	Sales force composite	15
	DELPHI	15
	Historical analogy	15
	S-growth curves	15
Other Quantitative	Market research	N/A
	Management science/operations research	N/A
	Expert systems	16
	Artificial Neural Networks	16
	Genetic Algorithms	16
	Combining methods	17

Parts of This Book

The layout of this book very much parallels the types of forecasting methods as shown in Tables 1–3 and 1–4 (where methods are referenced to specific chapters). This book is divided into six major sections, which are discussed in the preface.

    I. Foundations of Forecasting
    II. Univariate Methods
    III. Univariate ARIMA Methods
    IV. Multivariate Causal Methods
    V. Cyclical, Qualitative, and Artificial Intelligence Methods
    VI. Combining, Validation, and Managerial Issues

Forecasting Method Selection— A Preview

No Single Forecasting Method Always Works Best.   In the early literature of forecasting there was considerable time and effort spent in trying to find the best all-purpose statistical forecasting method, one that would forecast all situations accurately. Today, researchers realize that such a goal is unlikely to be achieved in the near future; instead, they recognize that some approaches to forecasting system design are better than others. The current state of the art is to use intelligent computer systems to forecast a time series using several methods; whichever method works best is then used to forecast that item. Forecasts are then reevaluated periodically to confirm that the best method is still being used for each item.

The Forecasting Process

Having previewed forecasting methods, let's preview the process of forecasting. The process can be relatively simple or complex, depending on the situation. This process, as most statistical/mathematical endeavors, is effectively approached using the scientific method. Figure 1–18 illustrates the following steps in applying the **scientific method** in forecasting:

I. *Problem definition*—There is a need to solve a problem or explain some phenomenon; that is, there is a need to plan or forecast some future event, for example, a product's demand.

II. *Information search*—This is the process of collecting information about the behavior of the system in which the problem or phenomenon resides (i.e., what influences the time series). For example, to understand the behavior of the series we need past data about sales of the product, out-of-stock conditions, prices, sales of competitors' products, advertising expenditures, out-of-stock conditions of competitors, and the number of customers.

III. *Hypothesis/theory/model formulation*—On the basis of the information and observations realized in step II, a hypothesis or hypothetical model is formulated to describe the important factors that influence the problem or phenomenon. For example, it may be hypothesized that demand is seasonal and trending or that demand is a function of price, advertising, number of competitors, and their prices.

IV. *Experimental design*—Using facts gathered in steps I, II, and III and statistical/mathematical tools, experiments are designed to test the hypotheses and theories (e.g., fit a model to all data except last year's, then see how well the model does in forecasting last year through this year). This might be as simple as selecting a model from several models or designing an experiment where data is collected and divided into two groups. The first group (called **in-sample data**) is used in constructing the model; the second group (called **out-of-sample data**) is used to validate the model in a simulated forecasting environment. Using out-of-sample data is an effective way to judge the effectiveness of a model or theory; most would argue that this is an essential step when sufficient data exists.

V. *Execute the experiment*—The experiment is designed and executed, then the results are measured and collected (e.g., fit the model to the data before last year and see how well it forecast last year through this year). Use the model fitted to in-sample data to forecast the out-of-sample data. We will learn how to do this for a variety of statistical forecasting methods as well as what statistics to analyze.

VI. *Results analysis*—The results of the experiment are analyzed in order to accept or reject the hypothesis or model (e.g., calculate appropriate error measures and perform statistical significance tests). Statistical diagnostic measures are used to

FIGURE 1–18

Scientific method of forecasting

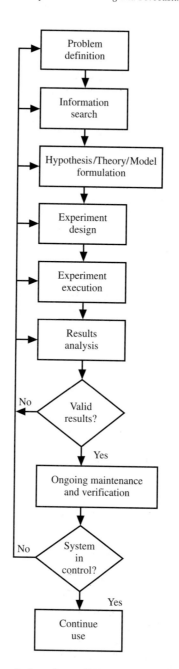

I.   Problem definition
   A. Plans, objectives, and decisions
   B. Boundaries of system

II. Information search
   A. Define the system
   B. Define possible cause and effects

III. Hypothesis/Theory/Model formulation
   A. Refine causal model
   B. Graphical exploration
   C. Postulate direction of causality
   D. Consider appropriate methods

IV. Experiment design
   A. Select in-sample fitting data
   B. Select out-of-sample validation data

V.   Experiment execution
   A. Fit several in-sample models
   B. Forecast out-of-sample models

VI. Results analysis
   A. Are assumptions valid?
   B. Do results support theory?
   C. Experts agree?
   D. Perform out-of-sample validity tests

VII. Ongoing use of model/system
   A. Incorporate real-time judgement
   B. Implement model/system
   C. Monitor model/system

judge the validity of the parts of the model and its forecasts. The model is either accepted, modified, or rejected. Depending on the results achieved, several iterations may be made before converging on a best model. Finally, because most forecasts support ongoing processes of planning, the seventh step addresses ongoing use of the theory or model.

   VII. *Ongoing maintenance and verification*—This is the process of ensuring that the model or theory is still valid and effective (e.g., diagnostic tools called tracking signals and other statistics can be monitored to ensure model validity).

   Table 1–5 illustrates a general presentation of the steps of developing an ongoing forecast. For some simple situations, this table may overstate the necessary activities; for others, it may understate them.

TABLE 1–5   Forecast Implementation—A General Outline

  I. Problem definition—Define the purpose of the forecast
     a. Plans and decisions—What plans and decisions require forecasts?
                           What information is needed to support the system?
     b. Initially define the variables to be forecasted.
     c. Define system boundaries—What factors affect the variables?
     d. Decisions/actions—What actions are taken based on the forecasts?
     e. Define the forecast horizon length/time periods used (e.g., 36 months, by month).
     f. Address the principles of forecasting developed in this text, for example, independent and dependent demands.
 II. Information search—Analyze the system to be modeled
     a. Define the general characteristics of the system, its parts, and the nature of their relationships.
     b. Identify important trends—socio, political, economic, ecological, global.
     c. Define seasonal and cyclical influences.
     d. Consider supply and demand factors.
     e. What casual relationships exists in the system?
     f. What unusual (outlier) events occurred and when?
III. Hypothesis/theory/model formulation
     a. Refine the Causal Model.
       1. Plot all variables (note behavior, usual/unusual).
       2. Perform statistical analyses of variables (e.g., correlation matrix).
       3. Define the cause-and-effect (CE) relationships between dependent and independent variables.
       4. Seek expert opinion as inputs to CE relationships.
       5. Flowchart the model showing CE relationships.
       6. Postulate the most important causes and relationships.
       7. Postulate the sign ($+$ or $-$)/strength of the influencing variables.
       8. Postulate the form of the relationship (linear versus nonlinear and the necessary data transformations).
       9. Plot all independent series versus the dependent series.
     10. Logarithms, power transformations, or outlier adjustments needed?
     b. Consider appropriate forecasting methods.
       1. Review alternative methods.
       2. Consider qualitative methods.
       3. Explore quantitative methods.
       4. Consider the need for subjective inputs.
       5. Consider the costs and benefits of alternative approaches.
     c. Identify resource requirements and availability.
       1. Define data requirements and sources.
       2. Assess personnel requirements.
       3. Consider computer requirements.
       4. Estimate costs versus benefits.
       5. What time and cost trade-offs exist?
       6. What cost and accuracy trade-offs exist?
IV. Experiment/model design—Consider alternative models
     a. Select experimental designs.
       1. Select fitting (i.e., in-sample) subset of data.
       2. Select out-of-sample validation subset of data.
       3. Consider jackknife/bootstrap
     b. Confirm data representativeness of past and future.
  V. Execute the experiment—fit and forecast with alternative models
     a. Fit univariate (time series) models.
       1. Postulate and confirm time series patterns.
       2. Define assumptions of patterns and underlying method.
       3. Apply data analysis/outlier adjustment procedures when necessary.
       4. Apply identification, estimation, diagnostic, and forecasting steps.

continued

TABLE 1–5 **Forecast Implementation—A General Outline**
concluded

    b. Fit multivariate models.
1. Confirm conceptual assumptions are valid.
2. Use graphs to define the relationships/transformations needed.
3. Are statistical assumptions valid? Signs of coefficients correct and significant?
4. Specification errors? Correct inclusion/exclusion of variables?
5. Autocorrelated errors? Heteroscedastic errors?
6. Multicollinearity problems?
7. Are residuals errors correlated with Y or X's?
8. Calculate and interpret S_x, S_y, S_{yx}, S_f, S_r, S_b, $\bar{R}^2$, AIC, BIC, F-test.
9. Generate fit and forecast confidence intervals.
10. Search for other casual independent variables.
11. Use residual analysis to identify nonlinearities.
12. Use residuals to determine new entering variables.
13. Interaction effects?
14. Interpret standardized coefficients for variable importance.
15. Should intervention effects be included?
16. Mutual causality?
17. Should simultaneous equations be used?

    c. Perform qualitative forecasting.
1. Determine as objective a method as possible.
2. Seek other sources and methods to confirm the forecast.

    d. Forecast out-of-sample data.
1. Apply diagnostic methods and statistics of previous sections Va and Vb to out-of-sample results.
2. Compare in-sample and out-of-sample results.

    e. Perform other experiments as designed.
1. Extreme value substitutions
2. Jackknife
3. Bootstrap

VI. Results analysis—Judge validity of models
    a. Are assumptions valid?
    b. Are equations plausible with respect to
1. Variables included
2. Relational form
3. Coefficients fitted
4. Actual forecasts

    c. Get expert opinions and management's acceptance.
    d. Ascertain the reasonableness of the forecasts.
    e. Is the model of practical significance?

VII. Ongoing use of model—Incorporate real-time judgment
    a. Build scenarios to ask and answer what-if questions.
    b. Experiment with subjective adjustments.
    c. Use Monte Carlo simulations to generate confidence intervals.
    d. Explore combining procedures with multiple models.

VIII. Implement the system
    a. Define the procedures of routinely collecting data.
    b. Assign responsibilities/maintain computer software.
    c. Design management's use of the model and interface.
    d. Assure management's acceptance.

IX. Monitor the effectiveness of the system
    a. Define model effectiveness.
    b. Measure actual versus forecasted.
    c. Track residual plots and calculate tracking signals.
    d. Refit, update, and revise the model.

The Scientific Method and Decision Making

Some think of the scientific method as some vague or un-necessarily methodical approach to problem solving. However, it only requires objectivity (truth) and attention to detail. In the 1970s, J.C. Penney, Inc. was identified as a very successful company; consider this particularly germane quote by its chairman during that period, William M. Batten, that characterizes the scientific method: "Get

the facts. Explore alternatives. Make the detailed study. Plan. After that, the decisions just leap out at you."*

---

* Joel E. Ross and Michael J. Kami, *Corporate Management in Crisis: Why the Mighty Fail,* (Englewood Cliffs, NJ: Prentice Hall, 1973).

This table assumes that an analyst needs to develop a forecasting model/process to support decisions in a relatively complex system where cause-and-effect relationships must be understood. In contrast, there are many situations in which only accurate predictions without explanations are desired. These situations frequently involve the use of univariate models and will therefore only relate to some of the considerations of Table 1–5. However, the prudent forecaster will consider all of the questions and methods presented in the table during the planning and execution of his or her forecasting process. Unfortunately, many of the details of Table 1–5 may be somewhat confusing until forthcoming chapters are studied. Nonetheless, if you are planning a forecasting project you should use this table as a preview, trying to understand the meanings of all considerations; no doubt some may be unclear now.

Summary

This chapter has presented important principles of forecasting. We have seen that

- Forecasts and forecasting systems are hierarchical.
- Forecasts should be point, range, and probability estimates.
- Forecasts are necessary because of the lead time in implementing decisions.
- The basic assumption of statistical forecasting is that the past repeats.
- Forecast independent demands, not dependent demands.
- The subjective input of management is an important part of the forecasting process.
- These forecasting principles should be incorporated in a good forecasting system.
- Univariate, multivariate, and subjective forecasting methods differ considerably in their purposes and processes.
- There is not one, single best method of forecasting.
- Forecasting is an ongoing process requiring the discipline and objectivity of the scientific method.

The importance of several of these principles is very clear now; however, some of these principles need to be more fully developed in later chapters.

In addition, this chapter has introduced a number of fundamental concepts in forecasting. Common time series patterns were introduced. These patterns include random, trend, seasonal, cyclical, autocorrelated, outliers, promotional, and combinations of these patterns. The selected forecasting method must be capable of modeling each of these time series patterns simultaneously. Finally, this chapter introduced the concepts and processes of univariate, multivariate, and qualitative forecasting.

Key Terms

autocorrelation	prediction
causal (multivariate) methods	predictor or independent variables
correlation	qualitative methods
cyclical influences	random series
forecasting hierarchy	random-walk series
independent and dependent demands	scientific method
in-sample data	seasonal series
nonstationary series	time series (univariate) methods
outliers	times series
out-of-sample data	trend
planned events	unplanned events
predicted or dependent variables	

Key Formulas

I. Univariate (time series) models:

$$\text{Future values} = f(\text{Past values}) \tag{1-1}$$

Simple two-month average forecast model:

$$\text{Forecast of June sales} = \frac{\text{April sales} + \text{May sales}}{2} = \frac{600 + 500}{2} = 550 \tag{1-2}$$

II. Multivariate (causal) models:

$$\text{Future values} = f(\text{Past values, Values of other variables}) \tag{1-3}$$

A three-variable model for furniture sales:

$$\begin{aligned}
\text{Forecast of June demand} &= 50 + .2 \times \text{LMS} + 1 \times \text{API} + .5 \times \text{NHS} \\
&= 50 + .2 \times 600 + 1 \times 250 + .5 \times 200 = 520
\end{aligned} \tag{1-4}$$

III. Qualitative model:

$$\text{June forecast} = \frac{\begin{matrix}\text{Manager 1} + \text{Manager 2} + \text{Manager 3} \\ \text{forecast} \qquad \text{forecast} \qquad \text{forecast}\end{matrix}}{3} \tag{1-5}$$

$$= \frac{400 + 600 + 600}{3} = 533$$

Problems

1-1 Choose an organization familiar to you and identify the common forecasting system characteristics of Figure 1-1.

1-2 Do you accept the near universality or commonality of the need for and uses of forecasting data suggested in Figure 1-1? Can you think of an actual organization that would not benefit from more accurate forecasts?

1-3 Do organizations or companies you are familiar with have formal forecasting systems? Speculate why or why not?

1–4 Explain the management decision hierarchy of Figure 1–2 and how it relates to forecasting.

1–5 What is a forecast? What characteristics should a good forecast have?

1–6 Explain the differences between dependent and independent demands and how these relate to forecasting.

1–7 List and define the common time series patterns described in the book. Also, define typical causes of these time series patterns.

1–8 What is an outlier and why are they so important? How do outliers relate to planned and unplanned events and interventions?

1–9 Give an example of forecasting hierarchy using an example different than that of Table 1–2.

1–10 Briefly explain the three general types of forecasting methods. Make up or relate to examples that are different from those of this chapter.

1–11 Describe the scientific method and how it relates to forecasting.

1–12 Describe the seven steps of the forecasting process discussed in this chapter.

1–13 Someone states that management intuition in forecasting is not legitimate. How do you respond to this?

1–14 Briefly describe any practical forecasting activities that you have personally been involved with or know about?

1–15 If you are to analyze an actual demand series in your use of this book or as a research project, identify that series and the source of the data. What types of patterns do you believe will dominate that series?

1–16 Choose a time series of interest to you on the enclosed data disk; plot this series and identify which common time series patterns are included in it. What is the dominant pattern? Explain the cause of this dominant pattern.

1–17 Go to your university or local library and choose a time series from a government publication such as the *Survey of Current Business, Federal Reserve Bulletin,* or the *Historical Statistics of the United States from Colonial Times to 1970.* Be sure to include at least 60 observations if it is a monthly time series. Plot this series and identify common patterns in it. What is the dominant pattern? Explain the cause of this dominant pattern.

1–18 Identify what has to be forecasted at a university for short-term planning and scheduling purposes and for long-term planning purposes.

1–19 Identify the short-term independent and dependent demands in your organization. (If you are a full-time student, your organization is your school.)

1–20 Using two selected series from the following list and their graphs from the text, identify the dominant pattern? Explain the cause of this dominant pattern.
   a. Figure 1–3, printer paper demand (SERIESA.DAT).
   b. Figure 1–4, worldwide airline fatalities (WWFATAL.DAT).
   c. Figure 1–5, advanced microcomputer sales (SERIESC.DAT).
   d. Figure 1–7, monthly soft drink sales (SERIESD.DAT).
   e. Figure 1–9, demand for daily trout tags (TROUT.DAT).
   f. Figure 1–10, composite index of leading indicators (LEADIN.DAT).
   g. Figure 1–11, monthly stock prices, stock unknown (SERIESB.DAT).
   h. Figure 1–12, monthly IBM stock prices (IBMMN.DAT).
   i. Figure 1–16, monthly AM/FM radio sales (SERIESF.DAT).
   j. Figure 1–17, monthly demand for electricity (MEGAWATT.DAT).

1–21 Plot selected time series from problem 1–20, using software chosen by you or your instructor. Confirm that the patterns identified in the text are evident in your plots.

1–22 Plot selected time series from the following, using your own software. Confirm that the patterns or relationships of the text are evident in your plots.
   a. Figure 1–6, German and U.S. stock indexes (USGERM.DAT).

b. Figure 1–8, quarterly births and marriages in the United States (BIRTHMAR.DAT).
c. Figure 1–13, Big City Bookstore (BIGCITY.DAT).

1–23 Plot selected time series from the following, and identify the common patterns in each. What is the dominant pattern? Explain the causes of the pattern.
a. JAPAN.DAT, the Japanese stock index.
b. BLOOD.DAT, the daily demand at a blood bank.
c. ELECT.DAT, the monthly demand for consumer electronics.
d. ERRORS.DAT, the hourly defects in the output of an in-control chemical process.
e. SALES.DAT, the quarterly manufacturer sales in the United States.

1–24 Define the purpose of each of the Roman numeral steps of the forecasting process shown in Table 1–5.

1–25 Review the general outline of the forecasting implementation of Table 1–5. List those sections that you do not understand and speculate on their meaning. Be prepared to discuss the meanings of those you do understand.

Minicases: Common Assignment for Minicases

Before plotting the data of the assigned minicase, speculate on the causes of the variation in that time series. What periods will have the greatest activity, which the least? What holidays occur during this time? What holidays do you believe significantly affect the activity? Now graph this data and confirm the accuracy of your estimates. Did you correctly identify the peaks and troughs? Did you correctly identify the effects of holidays? What surprised you the most about the pattern of demand? Speculate on how you would forecast this time series. In addition to the above, answer the following:

1. What dominant patterns are evident in this time series?
2. What are the peak and trough months?
3. What are the causes of these dominant patterns?
4. Does the series follow the patterns that you expected? Answer yes or no and explain why or why not.
5. What are the social and economic causes of activity? Are these changes evident in the time series. Hint: there are multiple causes of most dominant patterns; see if you can identify all of these.
6. Speculate on what other information would be useful for forecasting this time series. How would you forecast this series using time series analysis? How about causal analysis?

Minicase 1–1 Kansas Turnpike, Daily and Weekly Data If you have ever driven through Kansas, you have most likely driven its turnpike. The file TURNPIKD.DAT is a time series of the total number of vehicles that used the turnpike for each day for a 13-week period from June through August, and TURNPIKW.DAT is a time series of each week for five years, including the 13 weeks of TURNPIKD.DAT. The turnpike connects Kansas City, Missouri, to Lawrence, Kansas (where the University of Kansas is located), and further west to Topeka (where the State capital is), and from Topeka to Wichita.

Complete the Common Assignment for Minicases for both time series, the 13 weeks of daily values in TURN-PIKD.DAT and the 260 weeks of data in TURNPIKW.DAT.

Minicase 1–2 Air Passengers by Quarter The file PAS-SAIR.DAT contains a series of the quarterly passengers on flights in the United States from the first quarter 1982 through the second quarter of 1994; it includes 50 observations. This data is compiled by the Air Transport Association of Washington, DC, for use by its membership. Complete the Common Assignment listed previously. In addition, speculate on how you would forecast the number of passengers using a causal analysis?

Minicase 1–3 Hospital Census by Week The file CEN-SUSW.DAT is a time series of the weekly number of

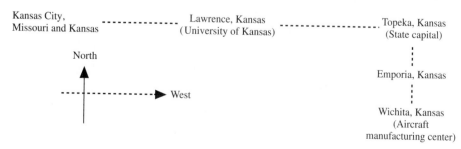

medical-surgical patients in a large midwestern hospital for three years. The number of patients in the hospital or ward is commonly called the patient census. Complete the Common Assignment listed previously. Note the several causal influences on the number of patients in a hospital. Which of these causes do you think are most important in this data?

Minicase 1–4 Henry Machler's Hideaway Orchids For many years the author's late uncle, Henry J. Machler, operated the Hideaway Orchid Nursery in Deerfield Beach, Florida, which is still in business under new ownership. This business sells orchid plants to amateur and professional orchid growers in southern Florida, including Dade, Broward, and Palm Beach counties. Orchids are found everywhere except at the polar regions; however, most beautiful species thrive in the tropics. Other than a few orchids like those of the genus *Vanilla,* which provides vanilla, orchids are sold for ornamental uses, to collectors, and to horticulturists. Most nurseries like Hideaway Orchids do not sell orchids for chemical or industrial uses.

Hideaway's business is very seasonal for a number of reasons that you should investigate. MACHLERM.DAT is a time series of eight years of monthly orchid sales in dollars. Graph this data and speculate on the causes of this seasonality as you answer the Common Assignment listed previously.

Minicase 1–5 Your Own Forecasting Project If you are required to do a forecasting project using this book and need to locate a good time series, review the data sources of book Appendix A. Identify and explain your choice of series. When you identify the time series, record the following information for review by your instructor. Source of data (e.g., *Survey of Current Business,* or STAT-USA on the Internet), the name of the series, the page or chart, the period of the data (e.g., from 1980 to 1996 by month), and the reason you chose this series. As a first step in your multichapter project, complete the Common Assignment listed previously.

Minicase 1–6 Midwestern Building Materials
LUMBER.DAT is a highly seasonal monthly series of lumber sales of a large Midwestern Building materials Company with 120 observations from January of year 1 through December of year 10. Complete the Common Minicase Assignment given above.

Minicase 1–7 International Airline Passengers
AIRLINE.DAT is a highly seasonal monthly series of international airline passengers with 12 years of 144 observations from 1949 through 1960, originally reported by R.G. Brown in 1962 and used by Box, Jenkins, and Reinsel (1995). As you plot the series note its increasing variance where the distance between peaks and troughs becomes wider. Explain this increasing variance. Because of this increasing variance, logarithms of the series should be analyzed. Complete the Common Minicase Assignment given above; however, you should plot both the original series and the transformed series. The transformed series should be natural logarithms of the original series.

Minicase 1–8 Automobile Sales AUTO.DAT is a highly seasonal monthly time series of automobile sales of a large automobile manufacture with 185 observations from January of year 1 to May of year 16. Complete the Common Minicase Assignment given above. Be sure to check this series for outliers caused by a faulty data entry.

Minicase 1–9 Consumption of Distilled Spirits
SPIRITS.DAT is a highly seasonal time series of 132 months (i.e., 11 years) of the shipments of alcoholic spirits in United States from January 1975 to December 1985. Complete the Common Minicase Assignment given above.

Minicase 1–10 Discount Consumer Electronics
ELECT.DAT is a highly seasonal time series of the sales of consumer electronics at a large retail discounter with 185 monthly observations from January year 1 to May of year 16. Complete the Common Minicase Assignment given above.

References

Capon, N., and J.M. Hulbert. "The Integration of Forecasting and Strategic Planning." *International Journal of Forecasting* 1 (1985), pp. 123–33.

Chatfield, C. "Simple Is Best?" *International Journal of Forecasting* 2 (1986), pp. 401–2.

Dalrymple, D.J. "Sales Forecasting Practices: Results from a United States Survey." *International Journal of Forecasting* 3 (1987), pp. 379–91.

DeLurgio, S.A., and Carl D. Bhame. *Forecasting Systems for Operations Management.* Burr Ridge, IL: Irwin Professional Publishing, 1991.

Dino, R.N., D.E. Riley, and P.G. Yatrakis.

"The Role of Forecasting in Corporate Strategy: The Xerox Experience." *Journal of Forecasting* 1 (1982), pp. 335–48.

Jenkins, G.M. "Some Practical Aspects of Forecasting in Organizations." *Journal of Forecasting* 1 (1982), pp. 3–21.

Klein, L.R. "The Importance of the Forecast." *Journal of Forecasting* 3 (1984), pp. 1–9.

Makridakis, S. "Forecasting in the 21st Century." *International Journal of Forecasting* 7 (1991), pp. 123–26.

Mentzer, J.T., and J.E. Cox. "Familiarity, Application and Performance of Sales Forecasting Techniques." *Journal of Forecasting* 3 (1984), pp. 27–39.

Miller, D.M. "The Anatomy of a successful forecasting implementation." *International Journal of Forecasting* 1 (1985), pp. 69–78.

Schultz, R.L. "Fundamental Aspects of Forecasting in Organizations." *International Journal of Forecasting* 7 (1992), pp. 409–11.

Sparkes, J.R. and A.K. McHugh. "Awareness and Use of Forecasting Techniques in British Industry." *Journal of Forecasting* 3 (1984), pp. 37–42.

STATISTICAL FUNDAMENTALS FOR FORECASTING

There is no inquiry which is not finally reducible to a question of numbers.

Auguste Comte, French positivist philosopher, founder of sociology, 1748–1857

Chapter Outline

The act of forecasting is pervasive in many human activities; consequently, many different analytical methods relate to forecasting, but none so much as statistics and probabilities. This chapter develops the fundamentals of statistical analyses for forecasting. It is designed to make these concepts as accessible and relevant as possible so that you can build on these in later chapters. As we will see, statistical measures of forecast errors and the normal distribution are central to forecasting. In this chapter you will learn the univariate measures of mean (μ, $\overline{X}$), standard deviation (σ, S), mean absolute deviation (MAD), mean square error (MSE), mean absolute percent error (MAPE), and residual standard error (RSE) as widely used statistics in forecasting. In addition, this chapter develops the important forecasting concepts of correlations (r_{xy}), and auto correlations (ACFs). These measures are powerful diagnostic tools in forecasting.

The Importance of Pattern

One of the fundamental assumptions of most univariate forecasting methods is that an actual value consists of a pattern plus error. That is,

$$\text{Actual value} = \text{Pattern} + \text{Error}$$

When the pattern of the actual value is a repeating pattern (e.g., seasonal pattern), this behavior can be used to predict the future value. We describe past patterns statistically. Thus, the importance of statistics.

Descriptive Statistics

Statistical analysis models the past to predict the future. Most methods of forecasting assume that the past behavior of a series or its relationship to other series (e.g., demand versus advertising) will continue into the future. Therefore, the first step in modeling a series is to plot it versus time. Figure 2–1 illustrates the demand for boxes of printer paper.

The plot of Figure 2–1 is very random, having no pattern; because of this, the series can be forecast relatively accurately by scaling an average from the graph (e.g., a straight line through the approximate center of points provides an estimate of the future). The mean of 850 is representative of the past and is, for this patternless data, a good forecast for month 49. However, many series have nonrandom patterns that must be modeled using more sophisticated methods; these methods are the focus of the rest of this book.

FIGURE 2–1

Demand for boxes of printer paper: A random monthly series (SERIESA.DAT)

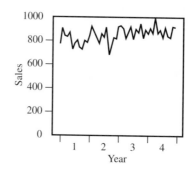

In forecasting, the most recent history of a series can frequently be used as a representative sample of past and future values. The past must be used in prediction because a random sample of the future is impossible; obviously, next month's value is unknown until the end of the month. However, to a surprising extent, the past repeats and is a good predictor of the future.

Descriptive and Graphical Tools

In the forecasting context, statistical analysis is used to extract information from the past. Based on more accurate forecasts, more effective decisions are possible, thus

Raw data → Information (i.e., pattern) → Forecasts → Decisions

Graphs and bar charts, such as Figure 2–1 and Table 2–1, are typical descriptive devices in forecasting. For example, frequency distributions such as Table 2–1 are used to summarize past data. It illustrates that demands for product A have varied between 675 to 1,024; 29.17 percent of past demands have been between 825 and 874; only 2.08 percent of demands were above 974, and 0 percent of the demands were above 1,024. Approximately 80 percent (25 + 29.17 + 25) of the time, demands have been between 775 and 924.

Combining Table 2–1 with the plot of Figure 2–1 provides a good graphical representation of the series. Such graphical devices are important because the ability of humans to detect patterns is extremely good. Consequently, graphical representations of the data are used throughout the modeling process. Also, as discussed below, graphics are very important in detecting unusual events, including outliers, planned and unplanned events, and seasonal influences. Therefore, good forecasting software provides good graphical support.

Probabilities

Because probabilities model uncertain future events, they are used extensively in forecasting. As shown next, there are three very simple ways to estimate probabilities.

Probability Estimates Using Past Percentage Frequencies. A percentage frequency is equal to the number of times a specific event has occurred (e.g., days it rained) divided by the total number of events that have occurred (total days). For example, if in the past there has been rain on 600 out of 1,000 days like tomorrow (i.e., days having the same climatic conditions as tomorrow), the probability of rain

---

TABLE 2–1   Frequency/Probability Distribution of Demands for Product A (SERIESA.DAT)

Demand Interval	Interval Midpoint	Frequency Distribution	Frequency Distribution	Percentage Frequency	Cumulative Percentage Frequency Below
≥ 1,025			0	.00%	
975 to 1,024	1,000	*	1	2.08	100.00%
925 to 974	950	****	4	8.33	97.94
875 to 924	900	************	12	25.00	89.61
825 to 874	850	**************	14	29.17	64.61
775 to 824	800	************	12	25.00	35.41
725 to 774	750	****	4	8.33	10.41
675 to 724	700	*	1	2.08	2.08
≤ 674			0	.00	.00
Total			48	100.00%	

Note: There may be some round-off error in totals.

The Pervasive Time Series Graph

Time series graphs are the most frequently used graphs in newspapers and journals. "A random sample of 4,000 graphics drawn from 15 of the world's newspapers and magazines published from 1974 to 1980 found that more than 75 percent of all the graphics published were time-series."*

* Edward R. Tufte, *The Visual Display of Quantitative Information,* (Cheshire, CT: Graphics Press, 1983), p. 28.

---

tomorrow is estimated as 600/1,000, .6, or 60 percent. Mathematically, this is expressed as:

$$P(rain) = 600/1,000 = .6 = 60\%$$

The .6 probability may be confusing because it will either rain or not rain; however, the essential concept of a probability lies in the percentage statements of the future. Because in the past, 6 out of every 10 days like tomorrow have had rain, it can be generalized that 6 out of every 10 days in the future with similar climatic conditions will experience rain. When we assume that a past frequency distribution represents the future, it becomes a **probability distribution.**

Probability Estimates Using Theoretical Percentage Frequencies.   In addition to using past actual frequencies to estimate probabilities, probabilities can be estimated theoretically using physical properties of the generating system. For example, if a true coin is tossed, the theoretical probabilities are .5 for each of heads or tails. Similarly, in tossing a true six-sided die, there is a 1/6 probability of each face appearing. Theoretically, if an outcome can yield x different results with equal probability, then there is $1/x$ probability of any one result occurring. Theoretical probabilities are used in much the same manner as past relative frequencies. The theoretical probabilities of random numbers are commonly used in different types of "what if" and simulation analyses. These are discussed in later chapters.

Probability Estimates Using Subjective Judgment.   Another way that probabilities can be estimated is through subjective judgment. Decision makers or experts subjectively estimate the probability of an event on the basis of their experience. For example, managers are often forced to subjectively estimate the probability of a new product being successful even though there is no past record of sales.

These subjective probability estimates are very important in forecasting because some events may have never occurred before and little objective information exists about the event. For example, in estimating the influence of a new sales promotion, a decision maker may state that he or she is 60 percent sure that sales will increase by 100 to 500 units and only 40 percent sure that sales will increase by more than 500 units.

Probability Distributions in Forecasting

A frequency distribution of the past becomes a probability distribution of the future when accepting the following assumptions:

Assumption 1: Past values are indicative of future values. That is, the past repeats.

Assumption 2: Past values are accurately represented by the sample of the past. For example, we assume that the 48 observations of Figure 2–1 accurately represent the past.

Is Forecasting a Game of Chance?

The oldest probabilistic game is that of casting bones or lots, as they were called. It is estimated that 40,000 years ago, cave dwellers were tossing cube-shaped bones in games of chance. Dice, as we know them, have been around for at least 3,400 years. In fact, the study of probability started with the analysis of dice games. Galileo, Pascal, and Cardano, in about 1600, studied the probabilities of dice games after being requested to do so by disillusioned participants. It is accurate to view forecasting as a game of chance in which the objective is to reduce the uncertainty of future events. Just as in dice games, we can never know with certainty what the next value will be; however, by looking at frequency distributions of past values or "tosses," we can state the probabilities of future values. For example, in tossing a six-sided die, there is a 1/6 or 16.67 percent probability of a 1 appearing because of the six sides of the die. We shall see that a good forecast is one yielding high probability statements about relatively tight ranges.

Consider the following. Given that the sales of product A in Table 2–1 are indicative of the sales next month, what is the probability that sales will be in the range of 825 to 874? In the past, 29.17 percent of the months have had sales in the range of 825 to 874; therefore, 29.17 percent of the time, future sales will be in this range. Alternatively, we can state that there is a 29.17 percent probability that sales may be in this range.

The use of probability statements is very important because a forecast should yield an average (850), a range (825 to 874), and a probability statement (29.17%). However, in forecasting there are no assurances that the future will behave as the past; thus, probability statements in forecasting are tenuous.

Another way that probability distributions are represented graphically is given in Figure 2–2. This figure is simply the frequency distribution of Table 2–1 turned on its

FIGURE 2–2

Probability Distribution of Demands for Product A (SERIESA.DAT)

Frequency	Percentage Frequency (probability)							
14	29.17%				*			
13	27.08				*			
12	25.00			*	*	*		
11	22.92			*	*	*		
10	20.83			*	*	*		
9	18.75			*	*	*		
8	16.67			*	*	*		
7	14.58			*	*	*		
6	12.50			*	*	*		
5	10.42			*	*	*		
4	8.33		*	*	*	*	*	
3	6.25		*	*	*	*	*	
2	4.17		*	*	*	*	*	
1	2.08	*	*	*	*	*	*	*
―	―――――	+	+	+	+	+	+	+
n = 48		7	7.5	8	8.5	9	9.5	10
					units in 100s			

side. Note the two left-hand columns represent the frequency and percentage frequency (probability) of sales shown on the horizontal axis.

Univariate Summary Statistics

***Predicting Values
Using Mean,
Median, or Mode***

Summary statistics are used to forecast future values. Frequently, it is effective to summarize a large amount of data through the use of summary statistics. For example, managers monitor monthly sales as useful summaries of performance.

The **mean,** also called the arithmetic average, measures that value about which 50 percent of the deviations are above and 50 percent of the deviations are below. That is, the sum of deviations about the mean equals zero. Given:

$$
\begin{array}{llllllll}
\text{Time } t & = & 1 & 2 & 3 & 4 & 5 & 6 & 7 \\
\text{Value } X_t & = & 11 & 4 & 5 & 12 & 9 & 2 & 6
\end{array}
$$

where X_t is the sales of a product in each of the last seven months, the mean sales is:

$$
\overline{X} = \frac{\Sigma X_t}{n} = \frac{11 + 4 + 5 + 12 + 9 + 2 + 6}{7} = \frac{49}{7} = 7 \qquad (2\text{--}1)
$$

where ΣX_t denotes the summation process from $t = 1$ to $t = 7$.

To illustrate the concept of the mean, deviations (x_t) are calculated below. A deviation is defined as an observed value (X_t) minus the mean. For this data, the deviations are the following:

$$
\begin{aligned}
X_t - \overline{X} &= x_t \\
(11 - 7) &= 4 \\
(4 - 7) &= -3 \\
(5 - 7) &= -2 \\
(12 - 7) &= 5 \\
(9 - 7) &= 2 \\
(2 - 7) &= -5 \\
(6 - 7) &= -1
\end{aligned}
$$

$$
\Sigma x_t = 4 - 3 - 2 + 5 + 2 - 5 - 1 = 0 \qquad (2\text{--}2)
$$

The **median** is an important summary statistic about which 50 percent of the values are above and 50 percent are below. As shown below, it is the middle value.

$$
2 \quad 4 \quad 5 \quad 6 \quad 9 \quad 11 \quad 12
$$

For these seven observations, three are above 6 and three are below 6; therefore, the median is 6. When sales were not equal to 6, 50 percent of the time in the past, sales have been greater than 6, and 50 percent of the time, sales have been less than 6. When an even number of observations exists, the median equals the mean of the middle two values.

The **mode** is that number or group of numbers that occurs most often. In the data below, the mode is 6 because it appears most frequently.

$$
1 \quad 2 \quad 5 \quad 6 \quad 6 \quad 7 \quad 10 \quad 11
$$

For the data in Table 2–1, the most frequent range of numbers (the modal range) is 825 to 874, which occurs 14 months out of 48 months. In general, a mode is expressed as a modal range such as 825 to 874.

*Comparisons
of Measures*

Each of the above measures of central values has slightly different advantages or uses in forecasting. However, note that for any distribution that is unimodal and symmetrical (i.e., the left and the right sides are mirror images), the mean, median, and mode are all equal. The series of Figure 2–2 is symmetrical, as is the following data set, which has mean, median, and mode equal to 6.

$$1 \quad 2 \quad 5 \quad 6 \quad 6 \quad 7 \quad 10 \quad 11$$

Finally, it is important to note that the most important distribution in forecasting, the normal distribution, is symmetrical. Consequently, its mean, median, and mode are equal.

*Properties of
Central Values*

Because it is the center of deviations, the mean is influenced greatly by extreme values. For example, a very large deviation (outlier) will greatly change the value of the mean. Thus, the mean is not the most appropriate statistic to use without first eliminating or adjusting the extreme values, a process called outlier adjustment.

In contrast to the mean, the median is not affected by extreme values and is therefore useful in describing the center of highly skewed data (*skewed* meaning a data set that has a few extremely high or low values, but not both). Finally, the mode, although not often used, does describe the most frequent number and is unaffected by extremes in the data.

Consider this sales time series for forecasting period 9.

Period t =	1	2	3	4	5	6	7	8
Value X_t =	100	70	90	110	1,200	110	130	80

In ascending order, the sales series is:

$$70 \quad 80 \quad 90 \quad 100 \quad 110 \quad 110 \quad 130 \quad 1,200$$

As shown by this data, sales have typically been in the range of 70 to 130; however, in period 5 something extraordinary happened: sales of 1,200 units. Which of the following statistics is the best for forecasting period 9?

$$\text{Mean} \quad = \frac{100 + 70 + 90 + 110 + 1200 + 110 + 130 + 80}{8}$$

$$= 236.25$$
$$\text{Median} = (100 + 110)/2 = 105$$
$$\text{Mode} \quad = 110$$

The effect of the 1,200 is rather dramatic on the mean; in contrast, the median and mode are much less affected. Assuming that the 1,200 is a typical value of the past and the future, the mean of 236.25 may be the best forecast. In contrast, if period 5 is abnormal and unlikely to recur, the median is the best forecast for period 9. However, the median is used infrequently because it is normally better to modify the mean by adjusting the extreme values. This is illustrated below.

If the 1,200 is a value that is not expected to occur in the future, it is referred to as an outlier. Formal methods of detecting and adjusting outliers are discussed in book Appendix B. For now, recognize that outliers should almost always be investigated to determine the cause and relevancy of the observation. Is the 1,200 a seasonal phenomenon (e.g., Christmas sales), a data entry error, or the result of some unusual promotional activity? After the cause is determined, appropriate action can be taken.

One should not eliminate the 1,200 but instead adjust it to a meaningful value. This way the data remains a complete time series with a continuous pattern. Assume that the best estimate of the fifth value is 130, therefore, the new statistics for this data are:

$$\text{Mean} = \frac{100 + 70 + 90 + 110 + 130 + 110 + 130 + 80}{8}$$

$$= 102.5$$

$$\text{Median} = 105$$

$$\text{Mode} = 110 \text{ and } 130$$

A good forecast of sales for this product is the modified mean of 102.5. As done in this example, outliers should almost always be replaced with typical values to retain the time series continuity.

Outlier Adjustments Are Essential

Conditions of normality are achieved through conscious and intelligent identification and elimination of the abnormal.

Mean Forecast Error   The mean is used in forecasting as a measure of the typical error. A good forecasting model should have a mean error of zero because it should overforecast and underforecast approximately the same. Because a good model is expected to have a mean error of zero, the **mean error (ME)** is a useful measure of systematic error, called **bias.** Bias is consistent over- or underforecasting that creates large cumulative errors. Thus, bias is very undesirable.

Measuring Errors—Standard Deviation and MAD

The central values (mean, median, and mode) give only one dimension of the distribution of data, the typical or center value. Other, equally important measures are the standard deviation and the mean absolute deviation (MAD). Four different distributions of demand are shown in Figure 2–3, each with considerably different scatter. As shown in this figure, a higher standard deviation denotes that there is more scatter of data about the mean; thus, it is a measure of the potential error distribution when using the mean to predict future values.

The **standard deviation** is the square root of the mean of the squared deviations, sometimes referred to as the root mean squared error (RMS). It is important to distinguish between two standard deviations: the sample standard deviation (S) and

FIGURE 2–3

Four distributions with the same mean but different scatter

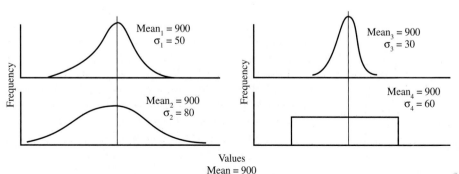

Values
Mean = 900
In order of most scatter to least scatter, distribution 2 > 4 > 1 > 3

The Longevity of U.S. Founding Fathers

A comparison between the longevity of U.S. presidents may be surprising. Has the life expectancy of the presidents increased or decreased over the history of the United States? Let's calculate a number of statistics using the first 10 presidents; you may be asked to do the same for the last 10 deceased presidents (exclusive of Kennedy, who was assassinated in office). The results may be a little surprising.

First 10 Presidents		*Last 10 Deceased Presidents*	
George Washington	67	William Howard Taft	72
John Adams	90	Woodrow Wilson	67
Thomas Jefferson	83	Warren G. Harding	57
James Madison	85	Calvin Coolidge	60
James Monroe	73	Herbert Hoover	90
John Quincy Adams	80	Franklin D. Roosevelt	63
Andrew Jackson	78	Harry S. Truman	88
Martin Van Buren	79	Dwight D. Eisenhower	78
William Henry Harrison	68	Lyndon B. Johnson	64
John Tyler	71	Richard M. Nixon	80

Approximate life expectancy of general population: about 1800, 35 years; 1994, 72.2 for men and 78.9 for women.

Source: *The Old Farmer's Almanac of 1994,* (Dublin, NH: Yankee Publishing Inc., 1994), pp. 92–93.

For the first 10 Presidents, the mean, median, mode, and standard deviation are:

Mean = 77.4

Ranking, low to high: 67   68   71   73   78   79   80   83   85   90

Median = (78 + 79)/2 = 78.5

Because no number appears more than once, a reasonably good mode is represented by the three center values, 78, 79, and 80; no other three-year range has as many observations, therefore,

Modal range = 78 − 80

The standard deviation (assuming that these represent a sample from a larger population) is:

$$S = \sqrt{\sum \frac{(X_t - \overline{X})^2}{n - 1}}$$

$$S = \sqrt{\frac{(67 - 77.4)^2 + (68 - 77.4)^2 + \cdots + (85 - 77.4)^2 + (90 - 77.4)^2}{(10 - 1)}}$$

$$= 7.56013$$

the population standard deviation (σ). The calculation of the standard deviation of the population (σ) requires a 100 percent sample or census. Consequently, the following population formula is used infrequently.

$$\sigma = \sqrt{\frac{\sum (X_t - \mu)^2}{N}} \qquad (2-3)$$

where μ is the population mean and N is the population size. And the summation sign, Σ, denotes addition over all N observations (i.e., a census).

In statistical analysis, most σs are estimated using the mean and standard deviation of large samples (i.e., sample sizes greater than 30) because these provide relatively accurate estimates of σ. Thus, the formula for the best estimate of σ when a census is not taken is the sample standard deviation (S):

$$S = \sqrt{\frac{\Sigma(X_t - \overline{X})^2}{n - 1}} \qquad (2-4)$$

where $\overline{X}$ is the sample mean that is used to estimate the population mean. The $n - 1$ denotes that the sample has n observations, and subtracting 1 makes S a better estimator of σ. The sample standard deviation for the seven observations below is:

$$t = 1 \quad 2 \quad 3 \quad 4 \quad 5 \quad 6 \quad 7$$

$$X_t = 11 \quad 4 \quad 5 \quad 12 \quad 9 \quad 2 \quad 6$$

$$\overline{X} = 7$$

$$S = \sqrt{\frac{(11 - 7)^2 + (4 - 7)^2 + (5 - 7)^2 + (12 - 7)^2 + (9 - 7)^2 + (2 - 7)^2 + (6 - 7)^2}{7 - 1}}$$

$$S = 3.742$$

Implicit in this calculation is the assumption that these seven observations are samples from a large population and that S is being used to estimate σ. Also, in calculating S, deviations are squared because the sum of all deviations about the mean is zero. In contrast, the sum of squared deviations is always greater than zero if one or more values differ from the mean.

Although the standard deviation has been introduced, its meaning may not be apparent without an understanding of the normal distribution.

Normal Distribution

As shown previously in Figure 2–3, the mean and standard deviation do not convey much information about the shape of the distribution; consequently, it is difficult to make probability statements based only on the mean and standard deviation. However, in many situations, means and standard deviations are presented as summary statistics of known distributions. One of the most important distributions is the normal distribution (ND). This distribution is useful in describing a wide variety of phenomena, including the error when using a good forecasting model. That is, the errors from good forecasts are typically normally distributed.

Characteristics of the Normal Distribution

1. As shown in Figure 2–4, the ND is a symmetrical, bell-shaped distribution with equal mean, median, and mode. Symmetry is important because an estimate of one central measure (e.g., mean) equals the other measures (e.g., median and mode).

2. ND phenomena are the result of a relatively large number of minor, independent, chance (random) influences. For example, if the diameters of turned shafts are influenced by a large number of minor independent events (e.g., temperatures of the shaft, cutting tool, machine, or room; minor variations in the material of the shaft, cutting tool, or machine setting) that act independently of each other, the variations of the shaft diameter will be a ND. *Independent* denotes that influences do not act together, they are not dependent on each other. Some influences will increase the diameter, while others will decrease the diameter. This is true because the tool

Modeling Is the Origin of the Normal Distribution

The ND has its origins in modeling and forecasting physical phenomena. Carl Friedrich Gauss (1777–1856) discovered the concept of the ND (also known as the Gaussian distribution) as a measure of error in predicting the orbits of planets. It was common then, as it is today, to repeat scientific measurements and then, using the law of large numbers, calculate the mean of the many repetitions as the typical value. Gauss went one step further and plot- ted the frequency of different values. When the error was random, denoting a good experimental measure, the frequency distribution normally was bell-shaped as shown in Figure 2–4. This was an extraordinary discovery, and we owe much of our understanding of the normal distribution to him. Gauss is also known for another important concept, the method of least squares regression, which is discussed in Chapter 3.

FIGURE 2–4

Normal distribution area

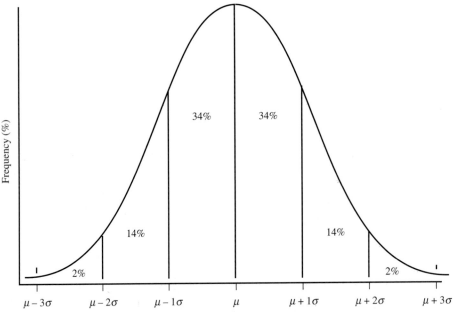

Approximate areas under the normal curve

Interval	Percent of Observations
$\mu \pm Z\sigma$	
$\mu \pm 1\sigma$	68.26%
$\mu \pm 1.96\sigma$	95.00
$\mu \pm 2\sigma$	95.44
$\mu \pm 2.33\sigma$	98.00
$\mu \pm 2.58\sigma$	99.00
$\mu \pm 3\sigma$	99.73

design engineers have eliminated all the large, major influences in the machine and tool design, and therefore, only small, minor influences remain; consequently, the output of the shaft turning process is a ND. Likewise, if the forecasting system has been well designed, all of the large, major patterns of the series have been modeled;

therefore, differences between the actual value and the forecasted value, the error, will be a ND.

3. The errors or deviations between the population mean and the means of large samples from that population, no matter how it is distributed, are NDs; large is defined as sample sizes greater than 30 to 120.

4. A ND is fully defined by its mean and standard deviation. For example, given a mean of 850 and a standard deviation of 40, one and only one ND is defined.

The table in Appendix D describes all possible NDs as a function of their mean and standard deviation. This table is referred to as a Z-table, where Z represents the number of standard deviations that an observation is above or below the mean of the ND. That is, the numbers in the table represent the area under the normal distribution between the mean and the mean plus (or minus) Z standard deviations; this is also illustrated in Table 2–2. The information in the Z-table in Appendix D and Table 2–2 can be proven accurate, but this is beyond our purpose.

Describing All Normal Distributions

A specific example is used to describe the ND; however, all results of this discussion can be generalized to any ND. Thus, "If you have seen one ND, you have seen them all." A firm uses a model that forecasts with a mean error of 0 and a standard deviation of 40, where the errors of the past are ND. By definition, forecast error is the difference between the actual value and forecasted value.

$$\text{Forecast error} = \text{Actual} - \text{Forecast}$$
$$\text{Actual} = \text{Forecast} + \text{Error}$$

Assume that the forecasted value for next month is 1,000 units and that the mean error is expected to be zero. Based on this information, the distribution of errors can be described using common ND intervals taken from the Z-table in Appendix D or Table 2–2. These intervals are universally true for all NDs and are commonly used to describe and make probability statements about forecasts.

The μ plus and minus σ contains 68 percent of the ND. For any ND, the interval defined by the mean plus and minus one standard deviation contains approximately 68

TABLE 2–2   Some Standard Intervals for the Normal Distribution

Interval $\overline{X} - ZS$ to $\overline{X} + ZS$	Percentage of Values in Interval from Z-Table	Example* $\overline{X} = 1{,}000$ $S = 40$ Forecast $-ZS$ to Forecast $+ ZS$
$\overline{X} - 1.00S$ to $\overline{X} + 1.00S$	68	1,000 − 40 to 1,000 + 40
$\overline{X} - 1.96S$ to $\overline{X} + 1.96S$	95	1,000 − 78.4 to 1,000 + 78.4
$\overline{X} - 2.33S$ to $\overline{X} + 2.33S$	98	1,000 − 93.2 to 1,000 + 93.2
$\overline{X} - 2.58S$ to $\overline{X} + 2.58S$	99	1,000 − 103.2 to 1,000 + 103.2
$\overline{X} - 3.00S$ to $\overline{X} + 3.00S$	99.73	1,000 − 120.0 to 1,000 + 120.0
$> \overline{X} + 2.06S$	2	> 1,082.4
$> \overline{X} + 2.33S$	1	> 1,093.2
$> \overline{X} + 3.00S$	$(100 - 99.73)/2 = .135$	> 1,120
$< \overline{X} - 3.00S$	$(100 - 99.73)/2 = .135$	< 880

* Given a forecasting model with mean forecast of 1,000 with a standard deviation of the forecast errors equal to 40.

percent of the population. In this case, 68 percent of the past errors produced by the forecast model have been in the interval 0.0 plus and minus 40 and, it is hoped, 68 percent of future errors. For example, approximately 7 (i.e., 6.8) of every 10 forecasts will have an error between −40 and +40 or alternatively, 7 out of 10 actual demands will be within 40 units of the forecasts. Therefore, approximately 7 out of 10 times the actual demand will be in the interval of the forecasted value of 1,000 plus and minus 40 units. When forecasting the future, this interval is called a prediction interval because when the model is valid, 68 percent of the time the forecast interval will contain the actual values.

$$\text{Actual values} = \text{Forecast} + \text{Mean error} \pm ZS$$
$$\text{Actual values} = 1,000 + 0 + \text{and} - 40 = 960 \text{ to } 1,040.$$

The μ plus and minus 1.96σ contains 95 percent of the ND. In this case, 95 percent of the forecasts will have an error in the interval of 0.0 plus and minus 1.96(40), that is, approximately −80 to +80 units. Another view is that approximately 9.5 out of 10 times the actual values will be in the range of 1,000 plus and minus 80 units; that is, 920 to 1,080. (Note: 1.96(40) equals 78.4, but 1.96 is commonly rounded to 2; therefore, 80 is used instead of 78.4.)

$$\text{Actual} = 1,000 + \text{and} - 80 = 920 \text{ to } 1,080, 95 \text{ out of } 100 \text{ times.}$$

The μ plus and minus 2.58σ contains 99 percent of the ND. These and other common intervals are summarized in Table 2–2.

Prediction Intervals   The intervals of Table 2–2 are called **prediction intervals** instead of confidence intervals, as commonly termed, because they are being used to predict future intervals. This distinction is made because of the added assumption about predictions of the future. That is, prediction intervals are based on the assumption that the past will repeat.

Prediction intervals are very useful in controlling the forecasting process. If, in the example, the actual values were greater than 1,000 plus 120 (greater than the mean + 3 standard deviations) there is cause for concern. If the forecasting process were in control, 99.73 percent of the time the actual value will be within 3 standard deviations and only .27 percent of the time (or 27 out of 10,000 times) will the actual value be outside 3 standard deviations, an extremely low number (see Table 2–2). Stated another way:

$$P(\text{Actual} > \text{Forecast} + 3S \mid \text{a good process}) = .0027/2 = .00135$$
$$P(\text{Actual} < \text{Forecast} - 3S \mid \text{a good process}) = .0027/2 = .00135$$

where P is the probability and | means given a good forecasting process.

Therefore, when an actual value falls outside the 3 standard deviation interval, then the logical conclusion is that the forecasting process (either the model or the actual value) is out of control. To infer that the process is in control is not logical, because only 27 out of 10,000 times will this occur when the process is in control; thus, we infer the model is no longer valid or an outlier has occurred.

MAD—An Easily Calculated Measure of Scatter   Before modern computers and handheld calculators were available, calculating the squares and square roots of the standard deviation was tedious. Another measure of dispersion popular at that time was the **mean absolute deviation (MAD).**

$$\text{MAD} = \frac{\Sigma |X_t - \overline{X}|}{n} \qquad (2\text{--}5)$$

Uncertainty Reduction Is Important in All Endeavors

The ND is an important tool in reducing uncertainty about the future. Our general, if not mystical, interest in reducing that uncertainty by studying the past may be more deeply rooted in our psyches than we realize. As

Sigmund Freud said, "The less a man knows about the past and present, the more insecure must be his judgment of the future."

Using data from the previous S calculation, 11   4   5   12   9   2   6   with $\overline{X} = 7$:

$$\text{MAD} = \frac{|11 - 7| + |4 - 7| + |5 - 7| + |12 - 7| + |9 - 7| + |2 - 7| + |6 - 7|}{7}$$

$$= 3.143$$

where | denotes the taking of absolute values (i.e., ignoring the sign of the deviations). The MAD of this data denotes that the average absolute deviation is 3.143. As in the case of the standard deviation, the MAD is not a particularly intuitive concept. It is more easily interpreted in the context of the ND. It can be shown that for the ND, the MAD is approximately 80 percent of the standard deviation.

$$\text{MAD} = .80S \qquad\qquad (2-6)$$
$$S = 1.25\text{MAD}$$

MAD intervals are used just like S intervals. In generating MAD intervals, we use K to designate intervals like Z values for the standard deviation. Let's calculate a 99.73 percent confidence interval given a ND with an S of 40, which is a MAD of 32 (i.e., .8S). In terms of S, the following interval results:

$$\text{Mean} + \text{and} - 3.00S = \text{Mean} + \text{and} - 3.00(40)$$
$$= \text{Mean} + \text{and} - 120$$

Because $K = 1.25Z$, the same interval in terms of MAD is:

$$\text{Mean} + \text{and} - 3.75 \text{ MAD} = \text{Mean} + \text{and} - 3.75(32)$$
$$= \text{Mean} + \text{and} - 120$$

In these examples, it appears that MAD and S are equivalent measures of dispersion, but this is only approximately true for normally distributed populations. Because the statistical properties of the standard deviation are well known and utilized in forecasting, it is the preferred measure despite the popularity of the MAD.

A Forecasting Example Using Sales of Product A

Consider the following forecasting example using series A of Figure 2–1 and Table 2–1. A firm desires to forecast sales so it is 98 percent confident of having enough inventory to preclude an out-of-stock condition next month. Given the facts below, what inventory level should be in stock?

Because the series varies randomly about a constant mean of 850 without any systematic pattern, an effective forecast is 850.

$$\text{Forecast} = 850$$
$$\text{Error} = \text{Actual} - \text{Forecast}$$
$$= \text{Actual} - 850$$

RMS—Root Mean Squared

The population standard deviation, σ, is known in the physical sciences as the **root mean squared (RMS)** value. It is exactly that, the squared root of the mean squared deviation. It is also interesting to get a physical sciences perspective on other descriptive statistics. Consider this quote.

Social scientists find that many of the frequency distributions they meet are skewed, with much of the data piled at one end. Examples are personal income or wealth and life expectancy in underdeveloped countries. With this type of distribution, where it makes a big difference which average you use, the

median is preferred. This type of problem seldom happens in physical sciences.*

When highly skewed data are collected over time, the median may be the best descriptive statistic for central values. However, the median might not be used if this skewness is the result of a few outlier values that should be adjusted.

_____

*William Lichten, *Data and Error Analysis in the Introductory Physics Laboratory,* (Boston: Allyn and Bacon, 1988), p. 10.

TABLE 2–3   **Frequency Distribution of Fitted Errors for Product A**
Forecasted Demand = 850; Error = Actual − 850

Error in Units	Midpoint	Frequency Distribution	Frequency Units	Percentage Frequency	Cumulative Percentage Frequency
125 to 174	150	*	1	2.08%	100.00%
75 to 124	100	****	4	8.33	97.92
25 to 74	50	************	12	25.00	89.59
− 25 to 24	0	**************	14	29.17	64.59
− 75 to − 26	−50	************	12	25.00	35.42
−125 to − 76	−100	****	4	8.33	10.42
−175 to −126	−150	*	1	2.08	2.08
Total			48	100.00%	

Note: There may be some round-off error in totals.

This calculation yields the error frequency distribution of Table 2–3. We use this distribution to solve the problem first, graphically, and then using ND intervals.

Frequency Distribution Solution

From Tables 2–1 and 2–3, it is clear that only during 2.08 percent of the time has actual demand exceeded 850 by more than 125 units. That is, if inventory equals 975, only 2.08 percent of the time will there be insufficient stock. Thus, from the frequency distribution of Table 2–3, we can assume that approximately 98 percent of the demands will be met when stocking 875 units. This graphical approach is an effective way of setting stock under conditions of non-normal distributions. Now consider the ND.

The mean error and the standard deviation of the errors were calculated using the actual data of series A. The standard deviation of the errors using the sample standard deviation formula of equation 2–4 is 64.53. The errors are nearly normally distributed, where the term *nearly* is used because it is rare that forecast errors are exactly normally distributed. On the basis of these error statistics, an interval can be calculated to achieve the desired product availability.

Table 2–2 illustrated important intervals of the normal distribution. As shown there, the mean plus 2.06 standard deviations has approximately 98 percent of the observations below that value and about 2 percent above. Thus, we can set inventory using the following relationships:

$$\text{Forecast} + 2.06S = 850 + 2.06(64.53) = 983$$

Thus, there should be sufficient stock about 98 percent of the time to meet customer demand. The inventory calculated using the normal distribution assumption is very nearly equal to the one calculated using the frequency distribution of Table 2–3 (983 versus 975). Herein lies the power of forecasting summary statistics under conditions of the normal distribution. The ability to model the past and predict the future using probability intervals is essential in forecasting. These statistical tools are refined further in the remainder of this book.

Fitting versus Forecasting

There is an important distinction between the process of fitting and forecasting. The process of **fitting** involves using past data to fit model coefficients. In contrast, the process of **forecasting** is the use of a model to forecast unknown future values. This simple sequence is (1) *fit* a model to past data and (2) use that model to *forecast* future data. Let's illustrate this process using the time series of worldwide airline deaths from 1970 to 1989, 20 years (WWFATAL.DAT). Without knowing the values of 1980 to 1989, a model is fitted to the actual values of 1970 to 1979. Then, the fitted model is used to forecast the actual values of 1980 to 1989. Table 2–4 and Figure 2–5 contain the 10 actual and fitted values for 1970 to 1979. A rather simple model is used for this data; it is assumed that the number of deaths is random about the mean and therefore:

$$\hat{Y}_t = \overline{Y}_t + e_t = 830.2 + e_t$$

where

$$\overline{Y}_t = \text{mean of 1970 to 1979} = 830.2.$$

FIGURE 2–5

Worldwide airline fatalities, 1970–1979 (WWFATAL.DAT)

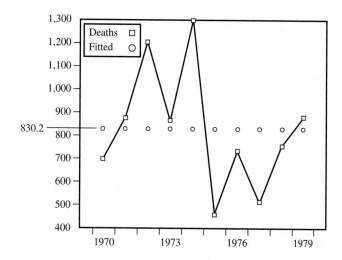

Absolute Error
Measures

If Y_t is the actual value and $\hat{Y}_t$ is the fitted or forecast value, the error is defined as

$$e_t = Y_t - \hat{Y}_t$$

Given $n = 10$ observations and errors in Table 2–4, the following statistics can be used to measure model accuracy:

$$\text{ME} = \sum_{t=1}^{n} \frac{e_t}{n} = 0/10 = 0 \tag{2-7}$$

$$\text{MAD} = \sum_{t=1}^{n} |e_t|/n = 1960/10 = 196 \tag{2-8}$$

$$\text{SSE} = \sum_{t=1}^{n} e_t^2 = 632{,}007 \tag{2-9}$$

$$\text{MSE} = \sum_{t=1}^{n} e_t^2/n = 63{,}200.7 \tag{2-10}$$

$$\text{RSE} = \sqrt{\sum e_t^2/(n-1)} = \sqrt{632{,}007/(10-1)} = \sqrt{70{,}223} = 265 \tag{2-11}$$

These measures of fit denote the following: the mean error (ME) of zero indicates that there is no bias in the fitted values. Thus, the errors are centered on zero. The mean absolute deviation (MAD) denotes that the absolute average error is 196, and if the distribution is symmetrical, 50 percent of the errors are above this value and 50 percent below. Note, however, that in general, absolute errors are not necessarily symmetrical even if the ME is zero. The **sum of squared errors (SSE)** and **mean squared errors (MSE)** are not easily interpreted by themselves, but are normally compared to other statistics as discussed below. Finally, note that the **residual standard error (RSE)** measures the dispersion of values about the mean error of zero, in this case 265. The RSE is a standard deviation (sometimes called the standard error of estimate) that is used to generate prediction intervals about the mean error of zero. Assuming that errors are approximately normally distributed and the past repeats, the Z-intervals of Table 2–2 apply.

As is true in most forecasting situations, the fitted and forecast accuracies differ; sometimes the forecast accuracy is the same or better than the fitted accuracy.

TABLE 2–4   Worldwide Airline Deaths—Actual and Fitted Values

Date	Deaths	Fitted	Error	$|Error|$	$Error^2$
1970	700	830.2	−130.2	130.2	16,952.04
1971	884	830.2	53.8	53.8	2,894.44
1972	1,209	830.2	378.8	378.8	143,489.44
1973	862	830.2	31.8	31.8	1,011.24
1974	1,299	830.2	468.8	468.8	219,773.44
1975	467	830.2	−363.2	363.2	131,914.24
1976	734	830.2	−96.2	96.2	9,254.44
1977	516	830.2	−314.2	314.2	98,721.64
1978	754	830.2	−76.2	76.2	5,806.44
1979	877	830.2	46.8	46.8	2,190.24
Total	8,302	8,302	.0	1,960	632,007
Mean	830.2	830.2	.0	196.0	63,200.7

Unfortunately, typically more than 50 percent of the time, forecast accuracy is inferior to that of fitted accuracy. Let's calculate the forecast error statistics in Table 2–5. This table assumes that the mean of the first 10 years (1970 to 1979) is the forecast of the actual values of 1980 to 1989. The forecast error measures are:

$$\text{ME} = \sum_{t=1}^{n} e_t/n = -1{,}260/10 = -126 \tag{2-7a}$$

$$\text{MAD} = \sum_{t=1}^{n} |e_t|/n = 1{,}873.2/10 = 187.32 \tag{2-8a}$$

$$\text{SSE} = \sum_{t=1}^{n} e_t^2 = 744{,}561.6 \tag{2-9a}$$

$$\text{MSE} = \sum_{t=1}^{n} e_t^2/n = 74{,}456.16 \tag{2-10a}$$

$$\text{RSE} = \sqrt{\sum e_t^2/(n-1)} = \sqrt{744{,}561/9} = \sqrt{82{,}729.1} = 287.6 \tag{2-11a}$$

These measures of forecast accuracy denote the following: the ME of -126 indicates that there is some bias in the forecasted values because, on average, the forecast is 126 units higher than the actual. This bias is also evident when comparing the mean of the actuals from 1980 to 1989 (704.2) with the mean of 830.2 for 1970 to 1979. Apparently, the number of deaths has declined during this period. The mean absolute deviation denotes that the absolute average error is 187.32, slightly lower than the MAD of the fitted value of 196. Although the forecasted MAD is lower than the fitted, it is not dramatically so, and all but two errors in Table 2–5 are negative, thus the bias of -126. The SSE and MSE of the forecasts are higher than the fitted values of Table 2–4, and thus the resulting RSE is higher. Because the forecasted RSE of 287.6 is higher than the fitted RSE of 265, the dispersion of errors is higher in forecasting. This RSE is used to generate prediction intervals; thus, the realized forecasted intervals are wider than the fitted intervals. In summary, we may be somewhat disappointed in the forecast accuracy of the model because of its bias (i.e., nonzero mean error) and its wider intervals (higher RSE), however, it performs nearly as well as the fit.

TABLE 2–5   Worldwide Airline Deaths—Actual and Forecasted Values

Date	Deaths	Forecast	Error	|Error|	Error²
1980	817	830.2	−13.2	13.2	174.24
1981	362	830.2	−468.2	468.2	219,211.24
1982	764	830.2	−66.2	66.2	4,382.44
1983	809	830.2	−21.2	21.2	449.44
1984	223	830.2	−607.2	607.2	368,691.84
1985	1,066	830.2	235.8	235.8	55,601.64
1986	546	830.2	−284.2	284.2	80,769.64
1987	901	830.2	70.8	70.8	5,012.64
1988	729	830.2	−101.2	101.2	10,241.44
1989	825	30.2	−5.2	5.2	27.04
Total	7,042	8,302.0	−1,260.0	1,873.2	744,561.60
Mean	704.2	830.2	−126.0	187.32	74,456.16

Occam's Razor and Parsimony

Occam's Razor is the principle of economy named for philosopher William of Occam (C. 1285–1350); it is also called the law of parsimony. Occam's Razor is a philosophical doctrine denoting that explanations or models should be as simple as possible. All other things equal, the simplest theory or model is the best. This is often called the principle of parsimony.

Parsimony is a synonym for frugality or thriftiness. This principle is used for choosing among explanations, theories, models, or equations. It denotes that the simpler, the better; or less is more. This makes sense when choosing from theories with approximately the same explanatory power, or conversely, the same error. It is most commonly applied in the context that the smaller the number of predictor variables or estimated parameters in a forecasting model, the more accurate the prediction, everything else being equal.

We frequently calculate all of these error measures because each provides some different information about fitted or forecasted errors. Nonetheless, the most frequent criteria used to choose one model over another is the minimization of the sum of squared errors, mean squared error, or residual standard error of *actual forecasts*. However, these statistics are unknown during the model fitting process. Unfortunately, as shown above, a model's goodness of fit (SSE, MSE, or RSE) does not necessarily assure a good forecast of future values. Also, the SSE of the fit can always be reduced by increasing model complexity (i.e., adding more terms to the model), but this complexity often does not increase forecast accuracy. Let's discuss this further.

Overfitting.   When adding model complexity only increases fit accuracy without improving forecast accuracy, this is called overfitting. In fact, experience and theory place more significance on simplicity than complexity. That is, a simple model that fits the past as well as a more complex model will almost always forecast the future better. This concept is commonly referred to as **parsimony** and is described in the Occam's Razor box.

The issue of model complexity and forecast accuracy at first may be confusing, but simplicity is a valuable attribute for a model to possess. Consider for example that in regression analysis it is possible to have a zero SSE for a model of 10 observations of a dependent variable by relating it to 10 observations of nine randomly chosen independent variables, even though there is no relationship between the individual independent variables and the dependent variable. That is, we can fit a model with zero MSE to the airline deaths of Table 2–4 by simply relating deaths to 10 observations of nine randomly chosen independent variables. For example, nine sets of random numbers will fit the 10 observations of 1970 to 1979 without error. This process of overfitting models the random variations, not the underlying pattern. We revisit the issues of fit, forecast, and overfitting throughout the remainder of the book.

Relative Measures of Error

We can enhance our understanding of a model's forecast accuracy by measuring both absolute and relative measures of error. This is so because the absolute measures are very much dependent on the scale of the dependent variable. Also, these absolute measures do not allow comparisons of results over time or between time series. Fortunately, there are several relative measures of forecast accuracy that facilitate model comparisons, including **percentage error (PE), mean percentage error (MPE),** and **mean absolute percentage error (MAPE):**

$$\text{PE}_t = \frac{(Y_t - \hat{Y}_t)}{Y_t} (100) \tag{2-12}$$

$$\text{MPE} = \sum_{t=1}^{n} \text{PE}_t / n \tag{2-13}$$

$$\text{MAPE} = \sum_{t=1}^{n} |\text{PE}_t| / n \tag{2-14}$$

The PE measures the ratio of the error to actual. Just as is true for the mean error for an unbiased model, the MPE should typically be near zero as positive errors are offset by negative errors. In contrast, absolute values are used in the MAPE; thus, positive and negative errors do not offset each other, a point made clearer in the results of Table 2–6.

Using the worldwide airline fatalities of Table 2–4 and 2–5, Table 2–6 illustrates that the MPE of fitted versus forecasted errors vary considerably. The fitted MPE is −9.8 percent and the forecasted MPE is −45.11 percent; the forecasted MPE confirms the bias found in the ME of Table 2–5. Although the MPE is useful in detecting bias, remember that with no bias (i.e., a MPE of zero), the MPE remains zero when

TABLE 2–6   Relative Measures of Fit and Forecast Errors

Date	Deaths	Fit	Error	PE	|PE|
1970	700	830.2	−130.2	−18.60	18.60
1971	884	830.2	53.8	6.09	6.09
1972	1,209	830.2	378.8	31.33	31.33
1973	862	830.2	31.8	3.69	3.69
1974	1,299	830.2	468.8	36.09	36.09
1975	467	830.2	−363.2	−77.77	77.77
1976	734	830.2	−96.2	−13.11	13.11
1977	516	830.2	−314.2	−60.89	60.89
1978	754	830.2	−76.2	−10.11	10.11
1979	877	830.2	46.8	5.34	5.34
Mean	830.2	830.2	.0	−9.80	26.30

Date	Deaths	Forecast	Error	PE	APE
1980	817	830.2	−13.2	−1.62	1.62
1981	362	830.2	−468.2	−129.34	29.34
1982	764	830.2	−66.2	−8.66	8.66
1983	809	830.2	−21.2	−2.63	2.62
1984	223	830.2	−607.2	−272.29	272.29
1985	1,066	830.2	235.8	22.12	22.12
1986	546	830.2	−284.2	−52.05	52.05
1987	901	830.2	70.8	7.86	7.86
1988	729	830.2	−101.2	−13.88	13.88
1989	825	830.2	−5.2	−.63	.63
Mean	704.2	830.2	−126.0	−45.11	51.11

extremely high positive errors are offset by extremely low negative errors; thus, it does not measure error scatter like the MAPE. As Table 2–6 illustrates, the forecast MAPE of 51.11 percent is greater than that of the fit, 26.3 percent. Thus, in comparison to fitted statistics, the model's forecasts are biased as shown by the MPE and less accurate as shown by the MAPE. The model's forecast performance is somewhat disappointing in comparison to the fitted statistics. However, our disappointment is somewhat dependent on how good other models perform with this data.

Cautions in Using Percentages

When using percentages or ratios, we must be cautious because extremely small denominators in equation 2–12 yield extremely high percentages or ratios, sometimes in the millions (i.e., the limit of division by zero is infinity). This problem is prevalent in forecasting whenever the actual values are very low. Thus, percentage measures have to be monitored for low denominators. Although such low actual values may be outliers, and therefore should be adjusted, frequently they are not.

Other Error Measures

There are many other measures of forecast error. Some measures are generated for making comparisons; some are calculated as part of the iterative process of identifying and diagnosing better models. These other error measures and brief explanations follow, with chapter numbers in parentheses:

- Autocorrelations (ACFs)—Used to detect patterns in a series of errors (2).
- Cross-correlations (CCFs)—Used to detect correlations between series over time (Supplement to 3).
- Durbin-Watson statistic (DW)—Used to detect patterns in a series of errors (3).
- Coefficient of determination R^2—Used to measure model accuracy (3).
- Schwarz Bayesian information criteria (BIC)—Used to determine the best from competing models (17).
- Akaike information criteria (AIC)—Same use as BIC (17).
- Demand filter—Used to detect outliers (Appendix B).
- Trigg and Leach tracking signal (TST), Cumsum tracking signal (TSC), and backward cumulative tracking signal—Tracking signals detect out of control cumulative errors (17).

Statistical Significance Test for Bias

Frequently, the question arises as to whether there is a systematic bias in a forecast (i.e., $\bar{e}_t \neq 0$). Fortunately, a simple classical hypothesis test can be used to confirm that the mean error is statistically significantly different than zero. This simple test is:

$$\text{Null hypothesis: } \bar{e}_t = 0.$$

That is, there is no bias.

If this hypothesis is proven wrong (i.e., nullified), then accept:

$$\text{Alternative hypothesis: } \bar{e}_t < 0 \text{ or } > 0.$$

That is, there is statistically significant negative or positive bias respectively.

These inferences are made by using a simple *t*-test. A calculated *t*-value is compared to a *t*-value from the *t* table. This *t*-test determines how many standard errors of the mean the error is away from the hypothetical mean of zero. The *t*-value is calculated by:

$$t\text{-calculated} = \frac{\bar{e}_t - 0}{\frac{Se}{\sqrt{n}}} \tag{2-15}$$

where S_e = standard deviation of errors about its mean, $\bar{e}_t$

If $|t\text{-calculated}| \leq t\text{-table}$, no statistically significant bias has been found.

If $|t\text{-calculated}| > t\text{-table}$, infer there is a statistically significant bias.

The denominator in equation 2–15 is the standard error of the mean (error), where *n* is the number of observed errors. For example, choosing a level of significance of .05 and given there are 10 observations, the *t*-value from Appendix C is

$$df = n - 1 = 10 - 1 = 9$$
$$t\text{-table} = 2.262$$
$$\text{significance} = .05$$

This test is based on the inference that, if there is no bias and errors are normally or nearly normally distributed, then 95 percent of the errors will lie within 2.262 standard errors of the mean value of zero. Only 5 times out of 100 will values be more than 2.262 standard errors away from their mean, and in this test the mean is selected to be the hypothesized mean of zero. That is, it is very unlikely that a value more than 2.262 standard errors away will occur when the true mean error is zero. Consequently, when rejecting the null hypothesis, we infer that the hypothesized value of zero is not the correct value and that the alternative hypothesis is true: the mean is significantly different than zero because there is a bias. Let's perform this test on the forecasts of the worldwide airline deaths of Table 2–5.

$$S_e = \sqrt{\frac{\Sigma(e_t - \bar{e})^2}{n - 1}} = 255.13$$
$$S_e/\sqrt{n} = 255.13/\sqrt{10} = 80.68 \text{ and}$$
$$\bar{e}_t = -126, \text{ thus}$$
$$t\text{-calculated} = \frac{\bar{e}_t - 0}{S_e/\sqrt{n} - 1} = \frac{-126}{80.68} = -1.562$$

From above, *t*-table = 2.262 and therefore

$$|t\text{-calculated}| < t\text{-table}$$
$$|-1.562| < 2.262$$

Therefore, accept the Null Hypothesis, no statistically significant bias has been found in the forecast.

Because there are so many negative errors in Table 2–5, these conclusions may not be consistent with our intuitive interpretations. However, note how many of these errors are relatively low, near zero values. More important, remember what the true conclusion of this test is: the statistical test results have not shown there to be a statistically significant bias in the 10 errors of Table 2–5. However, this is not a proof that there is no bias. As in all statistical significance tests, acceptance of the null hypothesis is rather inconclusive. Thus, these results are considerably less conclusive than rejection of the null hypothesis and acceptance of the alternative hypothesis.

Although in general, this statistical test is a very important one, there may be other information or facts that might confirm or deny the accepted hypothesis; thus, as in all statistical testing, we must cautiously accept or reject statistical conclusions.

Having developed a number of univariate statistical measures, let's study some essential multivariate statistics, concepts on which we can build more sophisticated knowledge of forecasting.

Correlation Measures

There are many situations in which measuring the relationship or association between two or more variables is important. For example, Figure 2–6 illustrates a graph of the demand for books at a bookstore versus advertising expenditures, both measured over time. Also, Table 2–7 illustrates the actual demand, advertising, and competition at that bookstore. Frequently, the question arises as to whether one variable can be used to predict another variable, or does one variable cause the other? As discussed later, useful predictions are much more easily obtained than proof of causality.

Predictive ability is achieved when it can be shown that the values of one variable move together with values of another variable (e.g., demand versus advertising), or alternatively, values of one variable move opposite to values of another (e.g., demand versus competition). The first case, demand and advertising, has positively related variables; the second case, demand and competition, illustrates a negative or inverse relationship between variables. Finally, we often find the situation in which two variables are not related at all, called statistical independence.

While the terms *positive* and *negative* are attributes of a relationship, they do not denote the strength or degree of association between each variable. Fortunately, there are several measures of the degree of association between two or more variables; four of these measures are developed below, the covariance, correlation, autocovariance, and autocorrelation coefficients. These concepts are developed using trivial data sets, then more realistic examples are illustrated. Through use of simple data sets you should gain further insight to the mathematics and theory of these measures.

As shown throughout the remainder of this book, measures of association are important tools for identifying and diagnosing forecasting relationships. We'll see that

Figure 2–6

Scatter plot, Big City Bookstore (BIGCITY.DAT)

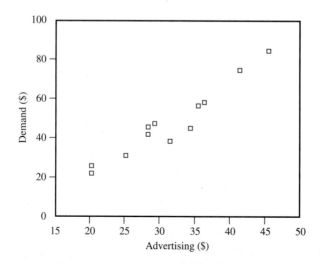

TABLE 2–7   **Big City Bookstore Demand, Advertising, and Competition (BIGCITY.DAT)**

Year	Demand (Y)	Advertising (X1)	Competition (X2)
1984	27	20	10
1985	23	20	15
1986	31	25	15
1987	45	28	15
1988	47	29	20
1989	42	28	25
1990	39	31	35
1991	45	34	35
1992	57	35	20
1993	59	36	30
1994	73	41	20
1995	84	45	20

Demand for books = Sales in $1,000.

Advertising = Expenditures in $1,000.

Competition = Square footage in competitor stores.

correlation measures can be used to detect association between *Y* and *X* or *Y* and lagged values of *Y* (e.g., Y_{t-1}) and lagged values of *X* (e.g., X_{t-1}).

Correlations and Covariances

A useful measure of association between two variables is the **covariance.** Often, this measure is not very insightful in itself, but it is important in understanding the second measure of association, correlation. So please follow the mathematics and logic of the covariance in preparation for the correlation coefficient.

The level of association between two variables can be measured by the degree that they covary (e.g., high values of *Y* with high values of *X* and low values of *Y* with low values of *X*). Equation 2–16 illustrates the formula for the covariance.

$$\text{COV}(X, Y) = \frac{\Sigma(X_t - \overline{X})(Y_t - \overline{Y})}{n - 1} \tag{2–16}$$

Thus, the covariance is the mean of the product of the deviations of two numbers from their respective means. As mentioned previously, a synonym for the mean is the expected value. Consider the data of example 1 in Figure 2–7, where there are three matched pairs of *X* and *Y*. (Please note that this was generated using $Y = .5X$; thus, there is a very strong relationship between *X* and *Y*, in fact, *X* predicts *Y* perfectly.)

Because they have a positive association, high deviations and low deviations of *Y* and *X* are paired together. Thus, the covariance between *X* and *Y* is 2. Unfortunately, because the covariance is an absolute number that can vary greatly by the scale of numbers used, there is no easy interpretation of the meaning of the covariance of 2. Before studying correlation measures, let's consider another covariance example (see Figure 2–8 of example 2).

Because in example 2, high and low deviations of *X* are associated with high deviations of *Y*, they are linearly independent and therefore, COV(*X*, *Y*) = .0.

FIGURE 2–7

Example 1 data
Perfect Linear
Covariance

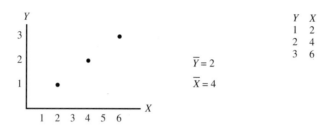

Covariance example 1:

X	Y	$X - \overline{X}$	$Y - \overline{Y}$	$(X - \overline{X})(Y - \overline{Y})$
6	3	2	1	2
4	2	0	0	0
2	1	−2	−1	2
				4

$$\text{COV} = \frac{4}{3 - 1} = 2$$

FIGURE 2–8

Example 2 data
Zero Linear
Covariance

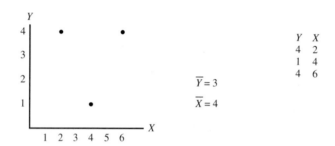

Covariance example 2:

X	Y	$X - \overline{X}$	$Y - \overline{Y}$	$(X - \overline{X})(Y - \overline{Y})$
6	4	2	1	2
4	1	0	−2	0
2	4	−2	1	−2
				0

$$\text{COV}(X, Y) = \frac{0}{3 - 1} = 0$$

Correlation—A
Relative Measure
of Association

A more useful measure of association is the correlation coefficient designated as r_{xy}. The **correlation coefficient** measures the proportion of the covariation of X and Y to the product of their standard deviations. (This measure is more properly called the **Pearson correlation coefficient.**) More conceptually, this correlation coefficient can be interpreted as the average standard deviation change in Y associated with a one standard deviation change in X. The values of the correlation coefficient will always range between 1 and −1; thus it provides information about the strength and direction of the association between Y and X. If the association is positive, r is positive; if the association is negative, r is negative.

If $r = -1$, there is a perfect negative relationship.
If $r = 0$, there is no relationship.
If $r = 1$, there is a perfect positive relationship.

Pearson correlation:

$$r_{xy} = \frac{\text{COV}(X, Y)}{S_x S_y} \tag{2–17}$$

where

$$S_x = \sqrt{\frac{\Sigma(X_t - \overline{X})^2}{n-1}} \qquad S_y = \sqrt{\frac{\Sigma(Y_t - \overline{Y})^2}{n-1}}$$

The correlation coefficient for example 1 of Figure 2–7 with perfectly related variables is:

$$S_x = \sqrt{\frac{2^2 + 0^2 + (-2)^2}{3-1}} = \sqrt{\frac{4+0+4}{2}} = \sqrt{4} = 2$$

$$S_y = \sqrt{\frac{1^2 + 0 + 1^2}{3-1}} = 1$$

$$r_{xy} = \frac{\text{COV}(X, Y)}{S_x S_y} = \frac{2}{2 \times 1} = 1$$

Thus, X and Y have a perfect correlation of $+1$.

Although it may not be obvious in this trivial example, a valid interpretation of the correlation coefficient is that an r_{xy} of 1 denotes that a one standard deviation change in X is associated with a one standard deviation change in Y. The reverse interpretation is true also: a one standard deviation change in Y is associated with a one standard deviation change in X. We expand on this later when looking at more realistic examples. For now, consider the correlation coefficient for example 2 of Figure 2–8, linearly, independent variables:

$$r_{xy} = \frac{\text{COV}(X, Y)}{S_x S_y} = \frac{0}{S_x S_y} = 0$$

The zero confirms information in Figure 2–8 that shows X and Y are linearly unrelated. The covariance is zero, therefore the correlation coefficient is also zero. Thus, the value of X does not indicate whether Y is high or low; therefore, X and Y are linearly independent (i.e., uncorrelated).

Correlation Coefficient— Big City Bookstore

Let's return to the Big City Bookstore example and calculate the covariance and correlation coefficients. Table 2–8 illustrates the calculation of several important sums of squares used in calculating the standard deviations and covariances.

From Table 2–8 we have:

$$(Y = \text{Demand}) \qquad S_y = \sqrt{\frac{\Sigma(Y_t - \overline{Y})^2}{n-1}} = \sqrt{\frac{3{,}612.67}{12-1}} = 18.1225$$

$$(X = \text{Advertising}) \qquad S_x = \sqrt{\frac{\Sigma(X_t - \overline{X})^2}{n-1}} = \sqrt{\frac{646.00}{12-1}} = 7.663$$

$$\text{COV}(X, Y) = \frac{\Sigma(Y_t - \overline{Y})(X_t - \overline{X})}{n-1} = \frac{1{,}473}{12-1} = 133.91$$

Given the standard deviations and covariance above, the correlation coefficient is easily obtained as the ratio of covariance and the product of the standard deviations:

$$r_{xy} = \frac{\text{COV}(X, Y)}{S_x S_y} = \frac{133.91}{18.12 \cdot 7.663} = .964$$

TABLE 2–8   Big City Bookstore Sums of Squares

Year	Demand Y	Advertising X	$(Y - \bar{Y})$	$(X - \bar{X})$	$(Y - \bar{Y})^2$	$(X - \bar{X})^2$	$(Y - \bar{Y})(X - \bar{X})$
1984	27	20	−20.67	−11.00	427.11	121.00	227.33
1985	23	20	−24.67	−11.00	608.44	121.00	271.33
1986	31	25	−16.67	−6.00	277.78	36.00	100.00
1987	45	28	−2.67	−3.00	7.11	9.00	8.00
1988	47	29	−.67	−2.00	.44	4.00	1.33
1989	42	28	−5.67	−3.00	32.11	9.00	17.00
1990	39	31	−8.67	.00	75.11	.00	.00
1991	45	34	−2.67	3.00	7.11	9.00	−8.00
1992	57	35	9.33	4.00	87.11	16.00	37.33
1993	59	36	11.33	5.00	128.44	25.00	56.67
1994	73	41	25.33	10.00	641.78	100.00	253.33
1995	84	45	36.33	14.00	1,320.11	196.00	508.67
Sum					3,612.67	646.00	1,473.00
Mean	47.67	31					

The correlation coefficient of .964 denotes that there is a very strong relationship between demand and advertising. It can be interpreted as each one standard deviation change in advertising is associated with, on average, a .964 standard deviation change in demand. An alternative interpretation is that a one standard deviation change in demand is associated with a .964 change in advertising. Thus, demand and advertising are highly correlated.

As cautioned below, correlation does not prove that causality exists between two variables. Causality can only be confirmed through statistical analysis; there must be considerable theory and control of data before we have proof of causality. We are content to infer that there is a high degree of association between demand and advertising. The concept of causality is studied in greater detail in Chapter 11. For now, study several other correlation coefficients in Figure 2–9.

Statistical Significance of the Correlation Coefficient

Although the correlation coefficient for the Big City Bookstore is high, there are many situations where the small sample size or low value of the coefficient makes one wonder about the significance of the association. Maybe the calculated r_{xy} occurs only because of chance and the true correlation coefficient is really zero? Even though r_{xy} is low, we may still want to know whether there is a significant relationship between the variables. That is, if r_{xy} equals a low value, does this denote no relationship between Y and X, or is there a statistically significant relationship? In such situations, it is helpful to be able to make a statement that this r_{xy} has only a .01 chance of being a sample from a population with a correlation coefficient of zero (i.e., with no association). To do this, we perform the significance tests developed below.

A **hypothesis test** can be used to determine whether a variable is statistically significantly different than another selected value. For example, we perform a test to determine whether the correlation coefficient is statistically significantly different than zero. If r is significantly different than zero, there is a significant association between Y and X. In the case of the Big City Bookstore, the hypothesis test will help to determine if advertising and demand are significantly correlated.

Figure 2–9

Several correlation coefficients

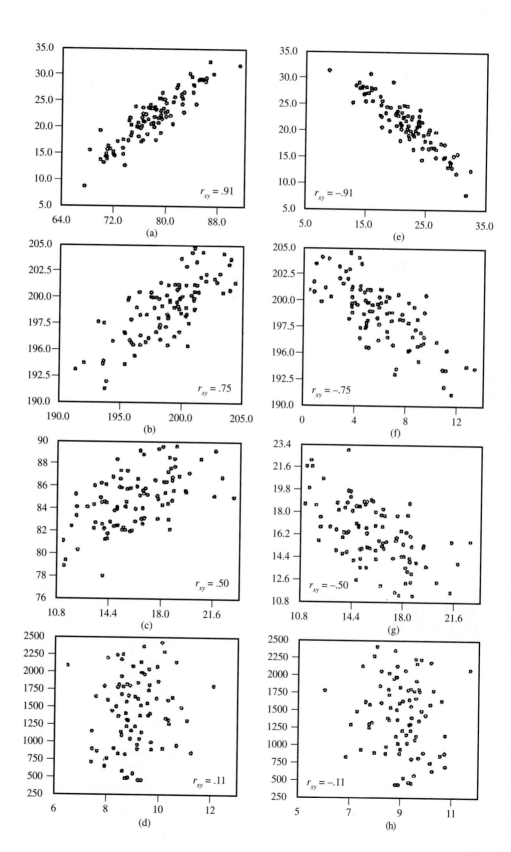

Below is a common procedure used in statistical hypothesis testing. A test statistic, t, is calculated and compared to a t-table value assuming the null hypothesis is true. Although the theory is not developed here, it can be shown that the sampling error in estimating the population correlation coefficient of two uncorrelated ND variables has a **standard error of the correlation coefficient** equal to:

$$Se_r = \sqrt{\frac{1 - r^2}{n - 2}}$$

where r equals r_{xy} and the adjustment of -2 in the denominator, called a degrees of freedom adjustment, makes Se_r a better estimate of the population standard error, σe_r. This standard error can be used to perform the **statistical significance test** of equation 2–18, which tests whether r is significantly different than zero.

$$t_r = \frac{r}{\sqrt{\frac{1 - r^2}{n - 2}}} \tag{2–18}$$

The statistical hypotheses are:

H_0: $r = 0$ The two variables are not associated. (population coefficient is zero)

H_1: $r \neq 0$ The two variables are associated. (population coefficient is not zero)

If $|t_r| \leq$ t-table with $n - 2$ degrees of freedom for $\propto = .05$ or less, infer there is no relationship between Y and X and accept H_0 and reject H_1.

If $|t_r| >$ t-table with $n - 2$ degrees of freedom for $\propto = .05$ or less, infer statistical significance and reject H_0 and accept H_1.

Consider this test in the context of the Big City Bookstore example. If the manager of the store is performing this test, she hopes to reject the null hypothesis and accept the alternative, therefore concluding that advertising and demand are positively correlated. If advertising and demand are unrelated, the calculated t-value will be low, for example, less than 2. In contrast, if they are related, the calculated t-value will be high, for example, greater than 2. Being greater than 2 is an event with a very low probability when H_0 is true. If the true r equals zero and the sample size n is 12 and the degrees of freedom are 10 ($n - 2$), then 95 percent of the time the calculated r will not deviate from zero by more than 2.228 (i.e., approximately 2) standard errors as shown in Table 2–9.

For the general case with other sample sizes, the t-table answers the question of how high t should be to conclude that there is a relationship between two variables.

The distribution of r when the true population correlation "is zero" is given in Figure 2–10. Assuming that $r = .9644$ and the population correlation coefficient is zero, t_r and Se are:

$$Se_r = \sqrt{\frac{1 - r^2}{n - 2}} = \sqrt{\frac{1 - .964^2}{12 - 2}} = \sqrt{\frac{.070}{10}} = \sqrt{.0070} = .084$$

$$t_r = \frac{r - 0}{\sqrt{\frac{1 - r^2}{n - 2}}} = \frac{.964 - 0}{.084} = 11.5$$

TABLE 2–9   Critical Values of *t* and *Z* for .05 and .01 Probabilities*

df	t-value		Z-value	
n − k	*.05*	*.01*	*.05*	*.01*
1	12.706	63.657	n.a.	n.a.
2	4.303	9.925	n.a.	n.a.
3	3.182	5.841	n.a.	n.a.
4	2.776	4.604	n.a.	n.a.
5	2.571	4.032	n.a.	n.a.
6	2.447	3.707	n.a.	n.a.
7	2.363	3.499	n.a.	n.a.
8	2.306	3.355	n.a.	n.a.
10	2.228	3.169	n.a.	n.a.
15	2.131	2.947	n.a.	n.a.
20	2.086	2.845	n.a.	n.a.
30	2.042	2.750	n.a.	n.a.
40	2.021	2.704	1.96	2.58
50	2.01	2.68	1.96	2.58
100	1.98	2.63	1.96	2.58
500	1.96	2.58	1.96	2.58

df = degrees of freedom (i.e., effective number of observations).

$k = 2$ for correlation coefficient significance tests.

n.a. = not applicable; use the *t*-value.

* Two-tail probability of *t* or *Z* being greater than these values is given by the column heading, either .05 or .01, respectively, when there is no relationship between the two variables. Finally, there are more extensive *t*- and *Z*-tables in Appendixes C and D.

Since 11.5 is greater than the critical value of 2.228 or 3.169 from Table 2–9 for *n − k* of 10, we conclude that advertising and demand are significantly correlated. The results of the statistical significance tests are shown in Figure 2–10. For the Big City Bookstore example, the calculated r_{xy} of .964 is so far off to the right that it is 11.5 standard errors away from zero. The probability of this if there were no relationship between demand and advertising is approximately zero; thus, we conclude that this is a statistically significant association.

FIGURE 2–10

Normally distributed r_{xy} *when population* $r_{xy} = .964, n − 2 = 10$

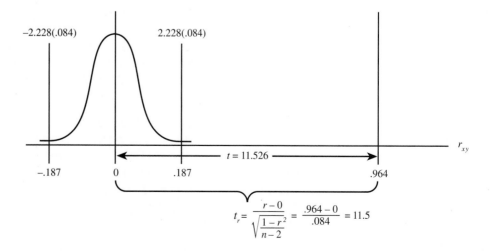

$$t_r = \frac{r - 0}{\sqrt{\dfrac{1 - r^2}{n - 2}}} = \frac{.964 - 0}{.084} = 11.5$$

A Note about Deviations from the Mean

Standard statistical notation is to use lowercase letters to denote deviations from the mean (for example, $x = X - \bar{X}$). This is called a simple linear transformation and does not affect the results of many statistical calculations such as the standard deviation, covariance, or correlation coefficients. Frequently, there are considerable mathematical advantages and simplicities in doing this transformation. For example, in calculating the covariance and correlations the formulas are considerably simplified.

Standard deviations using deviations from the mean:

$$S_x = \sqrt{\frac{\Sigma x^2}{}} \qquad S_y = \sqrt{\frac{\Sigma y_t^2}{n - 1}}$$

Correlation using deviations from the mean:

$$COV(XY) = \frac{\Sigma(x_t)(y_t)}{n - 1}$$

$$r_{xy} = \frac{COV(x, y)}{S_x S_y} = \frac{\Sigma(x_t)(y_t)}{\sqrt{\Sigma x_t^2 \Sigma y_t^2}}$$

Some of the formulas of this text will use X and Y in deviation form to save time and space. More important, this simplification makes formulas more easily understood. Note the simplicity of these equations in comparison to the nondeviational forms of 2–16 and 2–17.

If variables are unrelated, the absolute of the calculated t-value should be less than about 2. Remember that high absolute t-values come from related variables, low absolute t-values come from unrelated variables. The boundaries of high and low for different sample sizes are defined in the t-table, Table 2–9 and end-of-book appendix table C.

Cause and Effect

In the case of the Big City Bookstore, analysis showed that the two variables have a positive linear relationship. Consequently, we may be tempted to infer a **cause-and-effect relationship** between advertising and demand: an increase in advertising causes an increase in demand. While this seems logical, it is a mistake to assume that it is a true cause-and-effect relationship without spending more time analyzing it further. Other factors that influence demands may have occurred when advertising was measured.

In terms of cause and effect, past studies have shown a high correlation between women's skirt lengths and stock market performance, church attendance and beer consumption, and the price of scotch and clergy salaries. These nonsensical examples illustrate the need for care in concluding that a cause-and-effect relationship exists between two variables simply because they are highly correlated. *We can cautiously infer a cause-and-effect relationship only if we have measured and controlled for all other influencing factors on the dependent variable, and measured or manipulated the independent variables before the observed changes occur in the dependent variable.*

Correlation Coefficients Measure Linear Association

Correlation coefficients measure the linear association between two variables; consequently, there can be perfect *nonlinear* associations between variables, but the measured correlation coefficient is zero. Thus, it is important to understand whether linear or nonlinear association is expected between variables. To identify nonlinear relationships, it is important to have a theory and graphs for determining the appropriate form of association between two variables. Example 2 and Figure 2–8 illustrate Y and X having a correlation of zero. However, if instead X and Y are related nonlinearly, their correlation is perfect. That is, if a nonlinear transformation is made of X, there is perfect correlation between Y and X. If X is transformed to the new variable X', the correlation between X' and Y is 1.0. Proof of this is left to the reader to confirm in a homework problem. That is, you should show that there is perfect correlation between X' and Y when X' is calculated from X as:

$$X' = 13 - 6X + .75X^2$$

Autocorrelations and ACF(k)

One of the most frequently used statistical measures in forecasting is the autocorrelation coefficient. This measure is an important tool for discerning time series patterns. An autocorrelation measures the association between two sets of observations of a series separated by some lag. For example, with daily data, we might expect the demand for a product (e.g., beer) or service (electricity or telephone calls) to be related to the demand for the same day last week (this Saturday versus Saturday of last week); and frequently this occurs. One easy way to detect association in this example is to graph Y_t and Y_{t-7} on the same axis, and this can be very effective. In fact, early textbooks on statistics suggested plotting the same observations on transparent paper and overlaying the plots on a light table to discern lagged correlations. Fortunately, we can now do this very easily using the graphic capabilities of software. However, even with significant graphic capabilities, there is a need for objective measures of correlations over time; autocovariances and autocorrelations provide those objective measures.

As a simple example, Table 2–10 illustrates a time series with six observations, along with three lags. As shown, each lag reduces the usable observations by the length of that lag. Autocorrelations can be calculated several ways, one of which is using the Pearson coefficient (equation 2–19) and the other using an autocorrelation function, ACF(k) (equation 2–20).

Equation 2–19 provides a **Pearson autocorrelation** coefficient for Y_t and Y_{t-k}. As introduced previously in equation 2–17, correlation is the ratio of the covariance and the product of two standard deviations. Consider the example below.

$$r_{Y_tY_{t-k}} = \frac{\text{COV}(Y_t, Y_{t-k})}{S_{Y_t}S_{Y_{t-k}}} \tag{2–19}$$

Using the results of Table 2–11:

$$S_{Y_t} = \sqrt{\frac{16}{5-1}} = 2 \qquad S_{Y_{t-1}} = \sqrt{\frac{16}{5-1}} = 2 \qquad \text{COV}(Y_t, Y_{t-1}) = \frac{-4}{5-1} = -1$$

$$r_{Y_tY_{t-1}} = \frac{-1}{(2)(2)} = \frac{-1}{4} = -.2500$$

Thus, the correlation between Y_t and Y_{t-1} is $-.25$, denoting that a 1 standard deviation change in Y_{t-1} is associated with a $-.25$ standard deviation change in Y_t. Note that calculating correlations at many lags using equation 2–19 takes considerable computation time. Instead, there is a simplified form of equation 2–19, referred to as **autocorrelation function [ACF(k)]**.

$$\text{ACF}(k) = \frac{\sum\limits_{t=1+k}^{n}(Y_t - \overline{Y})(Y_{t-k} - \overline{Y})}{\sum\limits_{t=1}^{n}(Y_t - \overline{Y})^2} \tag{2–20}$$

TABLE 2–10   **Lagged Values of Y_t**

t	Y_t	Y_{t-1}	Y_{t-2}	Y_{t-3}
1	3			
2	6	3		
3	8	6	3	
4	4	8	6	3
5	4	4	8	6
6	8	4	4	8

Note: $\overline{Y}_t = 6$ and $\overline{Y}_{t-1} = 5$ for observations 2 to 6.

TABLE 2–11   **Calculation of Pearson Autocorrelation (r_{YtYt-1}) between Y_t and Y_{t-1}**

t	$Y_t - \overline{Y}_t$	$Y_{t-1} - \overline{Y}_{t-1}$	$(Y_t - \overline{Y}_t)(Y_{t-1} - \overline{Y}_{t-1})$	$(Y_t - \overline{Y}_t)^2$	$(Y_{t-1} - \overline{Y}_{t-1})^2$
1	n.a.				
2	0	−2	0	0	4
3	2	1	2	4	1
4	−2	3	−6	4	9
5	−2	−1	2	4	1
6	2	−1	−2	4	1
Sum	0	0	−4	16	16

The ACF of equation 2–20 uses an overall mean, $\overline{Y}$, without adjusting the denominator and numerator for equal numbers of observations as in equation 2–19. This results in the ACFs shown in Table 2–12. As shown in Table 2–12, ACFs deviate from the Pearson coefficient at extreme lags (in this case at $t - 2$ and $t + 2$ because there are fewer observations). Finally, note that Pearson autocorrelations and ACFs are symmetrical about the lag of zero (i.e., about $Y_t Y_t$). Thus, it is only necessary to calculate positive or negative lags of k, but not both.

In practice, accurate estimates of ACF(k) require a minimum of about $n = 50$ observations where k should not be larger than approximately $n/4$. Clearly, the example of Table 2–12 violates this rule, but it is meant to illustrate, if not exaggerate the effect of the loss of observations from relatively high lags (i.e., high k values).

We have developed the concept of statistical significance tests for the Pearson correlation coefficient in equation 2–18. That significance test can be applied to the autocorrelation function when these coefficients are calculated using that formula. However, when using the ACF there is a simpler approximation formula. This t-test is based on the standard error of the ACF. For series with no autocorrelations (i.e., the population autocorrelation is zero), the ACF can be expected to vary about zero with a standard error approximately equal to $(n)^{-1/2}$. That is,

$$Se_{\text{ACF}(k)} \simeq 1/\sqrt{n} \qquad (2\text{–}21)$$

where

Se_{ACF} = approximate standard error of ACF
n = number of observations in series

TABLE 2–12   Pearson Correlations versus ACFs

Variables	$Y_t Y_{t-2}$	$Y_t Y_{t-1}$	$Y_t Y_t$	$Y_t Y_{t+1}$	$Y_t Y_{t+2}$
Pearson	−.9113	−.2500	1.00	−.2500	−.9113
ACF	−.6170	−.2234	1.00	−.2234	−.6170

TABLE 2–13   ACFs of Series B

$B_t B_{t-1}$	$B_t B_{t-2}$	$B_t B_{t-3}$	$B_t B_{t-4}$	$B_t B_{t-5}$	$B_t B_{t-6}$
.9274	.8250	.6932	.5636	.4485	.3415
$B_t B_{t-7}$	$B_t B_{t-8}$	$B_t B_{t-9}$	$B_t B_{t-10}$	$B_t B_{t-11}$	$B_t B_{t-12}$
.2503	.1740	.1154	.0870	.0855	.0873

Equation 2–21 is an approximate formula that can be used as a guide in assessing statistically significant ACFs. Equation 2–21 is applied in the simple *t*-test of Equation 2–22.

ACF *t*-test:

$$t = \frac{\text{ACF}(k)}{Se_{\text{ACF}}} \qquad (2\text{–}22)$$

Consider a simple example $n = 100$, ACF(1) = .5

$$Se_{\text{ACF}} = \frac{1}{\sqrt{100}} = \frac{1}{10} = .10$$

$$t = \frac{.5}{.10} = 5 = t\text{-calculated}$$

Because this *t*-value is much greater than 2, we can infer that there is autocorrelation between Y_t and Y_{t-1}. Before applying equation 2–21 to some examples, note that there are other formulas for Se_{ACF} under different assumptions about the theoretical ACF(k)s. Several statistical software packages use different formulas, thus their Se_{ACF} values vary from equation 2–21. The assumptions of these alternative formulas are unclear unless you are familiar with ARIMA concepts of Chapter 7.

The $\pm 2 Se_{\text{ACF}}$ plots of your software may differ slightly from equation 2–21 because of the use of other formulas. For example, the Statistical Analysis System (SAS) uses equation 2–21a in its calculations and graphs.

$$Se_{\text{ACF}(k)} \approx (1 + 2\sum_{i=1}^{k-1}\text{ACF}_i^2)^{.5}/\sqrt{n} \qquad (2\text{–}21a)$$

Equation 2–21a and 2–21 yield identical results when $\Sigma \text{ACF}_i^2 = 0$.

Those desiring more information can refer to Chapter 7 and Box, Jenkins, and Reinsel, 1994, p. 188. For now, consider applications of equation 2–22.

Table 2–13 illustrates the ACFs for SERIESB.DAT, stock prices. These ACFs are very high, starting at .9274 at lag 1 to .0873 through lag 12. An approximate Se_{ACF} for the first $n/4$ (i.e. 12) of these 48 observations is:

$$Se_{\text{ACF}} = \frac{1}{\sqrt{48}} = \frac{1}{6.9282} = .1443$$

TABLE 2–14   *t*-Tests for ACFs of Table 2–13, $n = 48$ for Series B

Variables	$B_t B_{t-1}$	$B_t B_{t-2}$	$B_t B_{t-3}$	...	$B_t B_{t-6}$
Lag-*k*	1	2	3		6
ACF	.9274	.8250	.6932	...	.3415
Se_{ACF}	.1443	.1443	.1443		.1443
Calculated *t*-value	6.425	5.716	4.803		2.366

---

and the appropriate *t*-test is

$$t = \frac{\text{ACF}(1)}{Se_{ACF}} = \frac{.9274}{.1443} = 6.425$$

This calculated *t* is so high that we infer that this is statistically significant. Consider another lag, $k = 6$.

$$t = \frac{\text{ACF}(6)}{Se_{ACF}} = \frac{.3415}{1/\sqrt{48}} = \frac{.3415}{.1443} = 2.3666$$

Thus, we see that at least lags 1 to 6 have statistically significant correlations. Table 2–14 summarizes these calculations. In a moment we will use these facts to better identify the patterns in series B.

Pattern Recognition with ACFs. As mentioned, ACFs are so important in forecasting because they assist in identification, estimation, and diagnosis of forecasting models. We shall formally develop the concepts of modeling time series starting in Chapter 3; however, let's illustrate ACF pattern identification capabilities using four of the time series presented in Chapter 1.

ACFs of Random Series

Figure 2–1 of SERIESA.DAT illustrates the demand for printer paper. As shown, this series has considerable randomness and no discernible patterns. Logically, such series are not expected to have patterns in their ACFs because Y_t is not related to Y_{t-k} for all nonzero values of *k*. The ACFs for lags 1 to 12 for series A are presented in Table 2–15 and Figure 2–11. We can perform a simple *t*-test on these ACFs by dividing each by the approximate **standard error of ACF.** But as cautioned earlier, the minimum number of observations should be about 50 and *k* should be limited to about *n*/4. None of the 12 ACFs exceeds two times their standard errors; thus we infer that there is no pattern in the individual ACFs.

Upon closer inspection of Figure 2–11, we note that 11 out of 12 ACFs are positive, only one is negative. We are concerned that as a group these ACFs may have pattern. If a series is completely random, then 50 percent of the ACFs will be above and 50 percent below zero. Thus, there may be some pattern left in the ACFs. Fortunately, there is a statistical test to determine if a group of ACFs is patternless. This test is developed in Appendix 2B of this chapter. For now assume these ACFs are patternless.

Random Series and White Noise

When there is no pattern in a time series and its ACFs, a series is referred to as **white noise.** More correctly, a white noise series is completely random and has patternless ACFs and PACFs (a concept developed in Chapter 7), a constant variance, and a mean

FIGURE 2–11

ACF(k) of SERIESA.DAT—random demand for printer paper with lines at $\pm\ 2Se_{ACF} \approx \pm 2/(48)^{.5}$

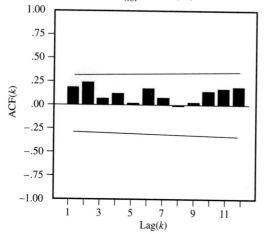

FIGURE 2–12

ACF(k) of SERIESB.DAT—random walk of stock prices, with lines at $\pm\ 2Se_{ACF} \approx \pm 2/(48)^{.5}$

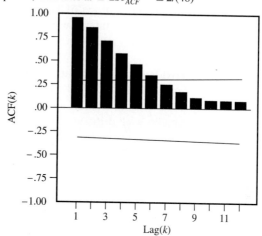

TABLE 2–15   ACFs of Series A

A_tA_{t-1}	A_tA_{t-2}	A_tA_{t-3}	A_tA_{t-4}	A_tA_{t-5}	A_tA_{t-6}
.17836	.22959	.07381	.12366	.01929	.17184
A_tA_{t-7}	A_tA_{t-8}	A_tA_{t-9}	A_tA_{t-10}	A_tA_{t-11}	A_tA_{t-12}
.08093	−.00548	.2409	.14669	.17109	.18924

of zero; (i.e., all observations are statistically independent). Series A becomes a white noise series if we subtract its mean from each observation. Also, a white noise series is best modeled using its mean, a procedure illustrated earlier in this chapter.

ACFs of Random-Walk Series

Reconsider the correlation patterns of series B in Figure 2–12; series B is illustrated in Figure 1–11. As you may recall, series B is the price of a common stock over the last 48 months. As is typical for common stocks, this series is a random walk because it randomly walks above and below its overall mean as shown in Figure 1–11. **Random walks** are characterized by extremely high autocorrelations. That is, adjacent observations are highly associated with each other. As shown in Table 2–13 and Figure 2–12, the ACFs of series B are very high and decline slowly, typical for random walks.

As shown before, a simple *t*-test on each of these ACFs is completed by dividing each ACF by the approximate standard error of the ACF. The *t*-values for Series B are calculated in Table 2–14, as shown, all of the first six ACFs exceed two times their Se's. Thus, we infer that there is a relationship between Y_t and Y_{t-k} for $k = 1$ to 6. The linearly declining ACFs of Figure 2–12 is the pattern for series that are either trends or random walks; the theory surrounding such declines is not developed until Chapter 7. Now consider a trending series.

ACFs of Trending Series

Consider the information in the ACF patterns of series C. Series C is illustrated in Figure 1–5 and SERIESC.DAT. Series C is the demand for advanced microcomputers over the last 48 months. This series has a very pronounced trend. As is true for random walks, trends are characterized by extremely high ACFs. That is, adjacent observations are highly associated with each other. As shown in Table 2–16 and Figure 2–13, the autocorrelations of series C are very high and decline slowly. As before, we can perform a simple *t*-test on each of these ACFs by dividing each by the approximate standard error of the ACFs. All of the first 10 autocorrelations exceed two times their Se's. Thus, we infer that there is relationship between Y_t and Y_{t-k} for $k = 1$ to 10, and therefore this is either a trending or random-walk series.

Trends versus Random Walks. The ACFs patterns of random walks and trends, Figures 2–12 and 2–13, behave similarly. Thus, the determination of whether a series is trending or walking involves statistical tests on the series itself. A series with a random walk drifts up and down over time. For series B and C, it is very clear how these series vary: they drift and trend, respectively. However, in some other situations, it may not be clear whether a trend or drift is occurring (i.e., the scatter plot and ACFs are ambiguous); in such situations, there is a simple *t*-test available. This *t*-test, which is similar to the significance test for bias, is discussed in Chapter 6.

ACFs of Seasonal Series

SERIESD.DAT is the demand for diet soft drinks and is illustrated in Figure 1–7. As we might expect, this series contains seasonality. In addition, as denoted by the high autocorrelations in low-order lags of the ACFs of Table 2–17 and Figure 2–14, the series either has a considerable amount of trend or drift in demand. In fact, the high autocorrelation at lags 1 and 2 denote that adjacent observations in series D are nearly equal to each other.

Thus, we see that there are two important patterns in the data of Figure 1–7 and the ACF patterns of Figure 2–14. The first is the strong association between adjacent observations, the second is the strong association between seasonally adjacent observations, that is, observations 12 periods apart. The ACF for $k = 12$ is .5107, a statistically significant value. Seasonal time series display high ACFs at seasonal lags as shown in Figure 2–14. Also, frequently there is a sinusoidal shape in the ACFs that reflect the relationships in the low order (i.e., 1 to 6 lags) and high order (12-period

TABLE 2–16   ACFs of Series C

C_tC_{t-1}	C_tC_{t-2}	C_tC_{t-3}	C_tC_{t-4}	C_tC_{t-5}	C_tC_{t-6}
.8558	.8199	.7611	.6948	.6417	.5705
C_tC_{t-7}	C_tC_{t-8}	C_tC_{t-9}	C_tC_{t-10}	C_tC_{t-11}	C_tC_{t-12}
.5481	.4691	.4197	.3614	.3156	.2704

TABLE 2–17   Autocorrelations of Series D

D_tD_{t-1}	D_tD_{t-2}	D_tD_{t-3}	D_tD_{t-4}	D_tD_{t-5}	D_tD_{t-6}
.7916	.4837	.0857	−.2920	−.5732	−.6690
D_tD_{t-7}	D_tD_{t-8}	D_tD_{t-9}	D_tD_{t-10}	D_tD_{t-11}	D_tD_{t-12}
−.5895	−.3541	−.0733	.2111	.4449	.5107
D_tD_{t-13}	D_tD_{t-14}	D_tD_{t-15}	D_tD_{t-16}	D_tD_{t-17}	D_tD_{t-18}
.4707	.2855	.0261	−.2200	−.4122	−.5802
D_tD_{t-19}	D_tD_{t-20}	D_tD_{t-21}	D_tD_{t-22}	D_tD_{t-23}	D_tD_{t-24}
−.4427	−.2942	−.0819	.1456	.3043	.3794

FIGURE 2–13

ACF(k) of SERIESC.DAT—trending demand for micro-computers, with lines at
$\pm 2Se_{ACF} \simeq \pm 2/(48)^{.5}$

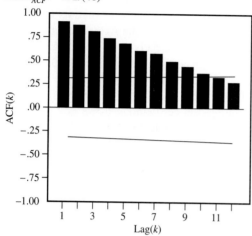

FIGURE 2–14

ACF(k) of SERIESD.DAT—seasonal demand for diet soft drinks, with lines at
$\pm 2Se_{ACF} \simeq \pm 2/(48)^{.5}$

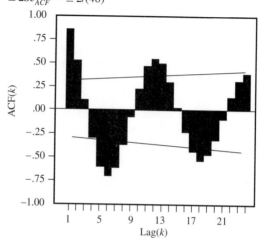

lag) ACFs. The sinusoidal pattern in ACFs of Figure 2–14 is typical of many but not all seasonal time series. If a graph of series D left any doubt about its seasonality, these ACFs eliminate that doubt. (Note, the seasonality of series D is confirmed more clearly by the Pearson autocorrelation at lag 12, it equals .821 versus the ACF(12) of .5107.)

In order to detect seasonality in ACF(k)s, it is good practice to calculate the ACFs using lags equal to two or three seasonal cycles. For example, for monthly data, it is recommended that $k = 36$. Also, it is necessary to have about eight to ten seasons of monthly data to get good estimates of ACF(24); this is necessary to have an adequate number of observations at the longest lag. Because series D is of insufficient length to calculate accurate ACFs at lag 36, we only consider the first two seasons of ACFs.

Back to Series B.   Some mistakenly believe that series B (Figure 1–11) is seasonal because its graph has a recurring up and down pattern; however, this pattern does not have a constant period between peaks and troughs as does the 12-period pattern of series D in Figure 1–7. Thus, we see that the ACFs of Figures 2–12 and 2–14 are very important in detecting or confirming seasonality. For example, we do not see seasonal patterns in the ACFs of series B, but those of series D have a very pronounced seasonality. The ACFs of series B provide evidence to the question of whether it is seasonal; clearly, series B is not.

Which Measure of Correlation?

As shown in Table 2–12 there can be considerable differences in the values of ACFs and Pearson correlation coefficients. Thus, the question arises: which measure of auto correlation should be used to identify patterns, particularly seasonal patterns? First, recognize that ACFs are calculated differently in some software packages, and some of these formulas are not as sensitive to the loss of data from lags. Thus, depending on your software, there may or may not be significant differences between the ACFs and Pearson correlations. Second, when dealing with a large data set and a small number of lags, there is little difference between the Pearson correlations and ACF(k)s. However, we can give some broad guidelines for when there might be significant differences between Pearson coefficients and ACFs.

When the number of observations is low (e.g., <60) and the number of lags is high (e.g., >10), there may be considerable differences in the coefficients. In such situations, it is important to calculate the Pearson coefficient at relevant long lags; for example, with monthly data and few observations (e.g., $n = 48$), the Pearson coefficient will be more accurate at a lag of 12 than the ACF. We have seen analysts misled by daily, monthly, weekly, and annual data; for example, when the ACFs for daily data at lags of 364 are being analyzed with only two years of daily data, the ACFs are very misleading. (Note: 364 days is often the lag of greatest interest because it separates the Monday of one year with the same Monday of an adjacent year; weeks are repeating patterns of 7 days, and there are 52 weeks per year, $7 \cdot 52 = 364$; more on this later.)

While the ACFs are less accurate than Pearson correlations, as we saw, ACFs are most often used as pattern recognition devices; consequently, at times the magnitude of the coefficients are not as important as the patterns they provide. Thus, ACFs can be used conveniently to discern significant lags through the patterns of plotted ACFs and not necessarily used in the interpretation of the exact magnitude of the correlation coefficient. Let's illustrate this pattern recognition process using another actual times series.

Autocorrelations of Births and Marriages.   Figure 2–15 and BIRTHMAR.DAT illustrate quarterly births and marriages in the United States from 1985 through 1992. As shown, both of these series have pronounced seasonality. Births peak in the third quarter (July, August, and September), and marriages are high in the second and third quarters of the year. Let's investigate the autocorrelation structure of marriages; then you might investigate births as homework.

Table 2–18 and Figure 2–16 illustrate the first eight ACFs for the number of marriages in the United States. As shown, there are statistically significant ACFs between Y_t and Y_{t-4}, and Y_t and Y_{t-8}, albeit the ACF(8) is less than ACF(4). Two standard errors of the ACFs are approximately .35 ($2/(32)^{.5}$). Thus, we can easily identify statistically significant ACFs by comparing them to two standard errors.

If an ACF is greater than .35, we infer that it is statistically significantly different than zero. In addition to lags 4 and 8, lags 2 and 6 are statistically significant; these high negative correlations denote that observations two and six periods apart vary in opposite directions. As we develop later, these two correlations are artifacts (i.e., harmonics) of the high positive correlations at 4 and 8. Consequently, all of these ACFs confirm the four-period seasonality of this series. The ACF(4) suggests that the number of marriages four quarters ago ($t - 4$) is useful in predicting marriages in this quarter (t). This can be determined easily by lagging marriages four periods and calculating errors.

$$\hat{Y}_t = Y_{t-4} \qquad\qquad \text{for } t = 5 \text{ to } 32 \qquad\qquad (2\text{–}23)$$
$$e_t = Y_t - Y_{t-4} \qquad\qquad \text{for } t = 5 \text{ to } 32 \qquad\qquad (2\text{–}24)$$

The predictions of equation 2–23 are shown in Figure 2–17, where Y_t and Y_{t-4} are plotted. As suspected, last year's quarterly values are good predictors of this quarter's values. To confirm whether there is still some pattern left in the data, consider Figure 2–18, which is a graph of the errors from equation 2–24; consider also Figure 2–19, a graph of their ACFs, and Table 2–19, the list of ACFs for the errors. As shown, the errors are very random: no discernible patterns exist either in the errors or their ACFs; also, no ACFs are statistically significant, denoting no remaining pattern in the errors. Because there are no patterns in the data, equation 2–23 appears to be a good forecasting model; marriages in $t - 4$ are a very good predictor of marriages in period t.

FIGURE 2–15

Quarterly marriages and births in the United States (BIRTHMAR.DAT)

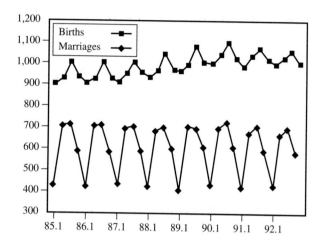

FIGURE 2–16

ACFs(k) for marriages—quarterly seasonal, lines at $\pm 2Se_{ACF} \approx \pm 2/(32)^{.5}$

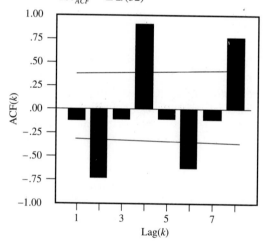

FIGURE 2–17

Marriages (t) versus marriage (t − 4)

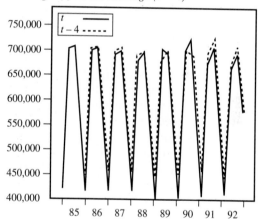

TABLE 2–18   ACFs of Marriages

Lag k	1	2	3	4	5	6	7	8
ACF	−.1250	−.7113	−.1088	.8753	−.1028	−.6130	−.1068	.7434

Quarterly data from 1985:01 to 1992:04, $n = 32$.

TABLE 2–19   ACFs of Errors = Marriages(t) − Marriages(t − 4)

Lag k	1	2	3	4	5	6	7	8
ACF	.0027	.2458	.1351	−.2034	−.0759	−.1055	−.2506	−.1890

Quarterly data from 1986:01 to 1992:04.

FIGURE 2–18

Errors in using marriage (t − 4) as predictor

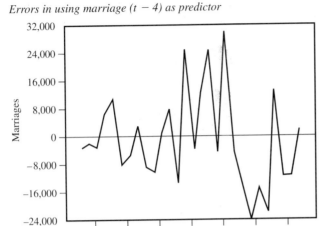

FIGURE 2–19

ACFs(k) for errors—*errors = marriage (t) − marriage (t − 4)*, $\pm 2Se_{ACF} \simeq \pm 2/(28)^{.5}$

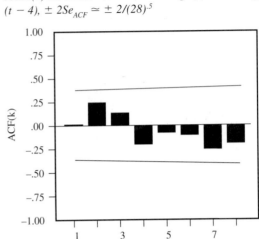

Summary

This chapter presents important statistical concepts that are essential in understanding forecasting methods. Even if you have had one or more statistics courses you may not have been exposed to the concepts of the autocorrelation and ACFs presented in this chapter. For those without adequate statistical prerequisites, this chapter is an important beginning in statistical forecasting. The concepts of $\overline{X}$, median, mode, standard deviation, outliers, probabilities, correlations, statistical significance, parsimony, ME, MSE, RSE, MAD, ACFs and MAPE are used in most forecasting applications.

We have introduced correlations and autocorrelations in this chapter because these are tools used throughout the book. These concepts are essential to proper forecasting and causal modeling of time series. As we develop more complex forecasting models it becomes important to understand how observations in one period are related to observations in other periods. There is a logical extension of the concept of the autocorrelation coefficient—cross-correlation coefficients. This important measure of association between, for example, Y_t and X_{t-3} is developed in the next chapter.

Key Terms

autocorrelation function (ACF(k))
cause-and-effect relationship
correlation coefficient
covariance
fitting
forecasting
hypothesis test
mean (X, μ), median, and mode
mean absolute deviation (MAD)
mean absolute percentage error (MAPE)

mean error (ME) = bias
mean percentage error (MPE)
mean squared errors (MSE)
normal distribution (ND)
overfitting
parsimony
Pearson autocorrelation
Pearson correlation coefficient
percentage error (PE)
prediction interval

probability distribution

random walks

residual standard error (RSE)

root mean squared (RMS)

standard deviation (S, σ)

standard error of ACF (Se_{ACF})

standard error of the correlation coefficient
   (Se_r)

statistical significance test

sum of squared errors (SSE)

white noise

Key Formulas

Basic time series formula: actual value = pattern + error

The mean:

$$\overline{X} = \Sigma X_t / n \tag{2-1}$$

The mean is center of deviations (x_t):

$$\Sigma x_t = 4 - 3 - 2 + 5 + 2 - 5 - 1 = 0 \tag{2-2}$$

The population standard deviation:

$$\sigma = \sqrt{\frac{\Sigma(X_t - \mu)^2}{N}} \tag{2-3}$$

The sample standard deviation as estimate of σ:

$$S = \sqrt{\frac{\Sigma(X_t - \overline{X})^2}{n - 1}} \tag{2-4}$$

The normal distribution: The μ plus and minus 1.96σ contains 95 percent of the *ND*.

Error Statistics:

$$MAD = \frac{\Sigma|X_t - \overline{X}|}{n} \tag{2-5}$$

$$MAD = .80S \quad \text{or} \quad S = 1.25MAD \quad \text{(for } ND\text{)} \tag{2-6}$$

$$ME = \sum_{t=1}^{n} e_t/n = 0/10 = 0 \tag{2-7}$$

$$MAD = \sum_{t=1}^{n} |e_t|/n = 1{,}960/10 = 196 \tag{2-8}$$

$$SSE = \sum_{t=1}^{n} e_t^2 = 632{,}007 \tag{2-9}$$

$$MSE = \sum_{t=1}^{n} e_t^2/n = 63{,}200.7 \tag{2-10}$$

$$RSE = \sqrt{\Sigma e_t^2/(n - 1)}$$
$$= \sqrt{7{,}022.3} = 265 \tag{2-11}$$

$$PE_t = \frac{(Y_t - \hat{Y}_t)}{Y_t}(100) \tag{2-12}$$

$$MPE = \sum_{t=1}^{n} PE_t/n \tag{2-13}$$

$$MAPE = \sum_{t=1}^{n} |PE_t|/n \tag{2-14}$$

Significance test for bias:

$$t\text{-calculated} = \frac{\bar{e}_t}{S_e/\sqrt{n}}$$

(2–15)

Covariance:

$$COV(X, Y) = \frac{\Sigma(X_t - \bar{X})(Y_t - \bar{Y})}{n - 1}$$

(2–16)

Pearson correlation coefficient:

$$r_{xy} = \frac{COV(X, Y)}{S_x S_y}$$

(2–17)

Standard error of the correlation coefficient:

$$Se_r = \sqrt{\frac{1 - r^2}{n - 2}}$$

Statistical significance test of r:

$$t_r = \frac{r - 0}{\sqrt{\dfrac{1 - r^2}{n - 2}}}$$

(2–18)

Pearson autocorrelation:

$$r_{YtYt - k} = \frac{COV(Y_t, Y_{t-k})}{S_{Yt} S_{Yt-k}}$$

(2–19)

Autocorrelation function (ACF):

$$ACF(k) = \frac{\displaystyle\sum_{t=1+k}^{n} (Y_t - \bar{Y})(Y_{t-k} - \bar{Y})}{\displaystyle\sum_{t=1}^{n}(Y_t - \bar{Y})^2}$$

(2–20)

Standard error of ACF(k):

$$Se_{ACF(k)} \simeq \frac{1}{\sqrt{(n)}} \simeq (1 + 2\sum_{i=1}^{k-1}ACF_i^2)^{.5}/\sqrt{n}$$

(2–21)

ACF(k) t-test:

$$t = \frac{ACF(k)}{Se_{ACF}}$$

(2–22)

Seasonally naive model:

$$\hat{Y}_t = Y_{t-4} \qquad \text{for } t = 5 \text{ to } 32$$

(2–23)

$$e_t = Y_t - Y_{t-4} \quad \text{for } t = 5 \text{ to } 32$$

(2–24)

Review Problems Using Your Software

R2–1 Repeat the analysis of the following tables, figures, or equations and include explanations.

   a. Table 2–4 and equations 2–7 to 2–11 for WWFATAL.DAT.

   b. Table 2–5 and equations 2–7a to 2–11a for WWFATAL.DAT.

   c. Table 2–6 and equations 2–12 to 2–14 for WWFATAL.DAT.

   d. Table 2–8 and correlation between demand and advertising for BIGCITY.DAT.

   e. Figure 2–8, Example 2 and explain the resulting inference.

   f. Table 2–11, and calculate the Pearson autocorrelation.

   g. Table 2–14, and explain the very high values, for SERIESB.DAT.

R2–2 Explain the use of the *t*-test of equation 2–15, and perform this test on the forecasts of worldwide airline deaths. What inferences do you make?

Problems

2–1 How are the patterns and forecasts of a time series related?

2–2 Why are graphs so important in forecasting analysis even when computers and expert systems are used to forecast?

2–3 What ways are probabilities estimated, and how are they used in forecasting?

2–4 How are probability distributions used in forecasting?

2–5 How are games of chance and forecasting related?

2–6 What is a mean, median, and mode? What are different about these? When is a median a better forecast than a mean?

2–7 Give a common English definition of the standard deviation. How is it used in forecasting? What is the RSE?

2–8 What are the characteristics of the normal distribution? How does the ND relate to forecasting?

2–9 What are prediction intervals? How are they different than confidence intervals?

2–10 What are the two common assumptions of statistical forecasting methods? Which of these is the most difficult to be sure of prior to realizing the future?

2–11 What is the difference between fitting and forecasting? Explain the difference between fitted errors and forecast errors.

2–12 Explain the meanings of the following forecasting accuracy measures: mean error (ME), mean absolute deviation (MAD), sum of squared errors (SSE), mean squared error (MSE), residual standard error (RSE).

2–13 What is the principle of parsimony? How does this relate to forecasting?

2–14 Explain the meanings of the following forecasting accuracy measures: percentage error (PE), mean percentage error (MPE), mean absolute percentage error (MAPE).

2–15 Explain the concept of correlation between *Y* and *X* using common English terms.

2–16 Explain the concept of correlation between *Y* and *X* using standard deviations. Now explain the meanings of correlation coefficients of -1 and $+1$.

2–17 Why is it necessary to test the significance of a measured correlation coefficient? What type of test is used for this significance test?

2–18 Explain the concept of statistical significance, particularly as it relates to the correlation coefficient.

2–19 Why is cause and effect so difficult to prove in business and economics?

2–20 What are the limitations of the correlation coefficient when nonlinear relationships exist between two variables? How can these problems be avoided?

2–21 What is a covariance? What is an autocovariance?

2–22 Distinguish between the concepts of autocorrelation and ACFs. Be sure to use an example.

2–23 What is the statistical significance test for an ACF at lag 10 when $n = 100$?

2–24 Is an ACF of .4 with a sample size of 100 at lag 12 statistically significant? What value of the ACF(12) for $n = 100$ is at the border of insignificant to significant when using a t-value of 2 to define significance?

2–25 What do the patterns of ACFs look like for the following common time series patterns?
   a. Random series
   b. Random-walk series
   c. Trending series
   d. Seasonal series
   e. A series with several outliers

2–26 Calculate the mean, median, and mode for the ages of the last 10 presidents that have died, use the data file PRESID.DAT. Compare these to statistics for the first 10 presidents calculated in this chapter. Are there any differences? What explains the differences, if any?

2–27 Calculate the standard deviation for the last 10 presidents that have died using the data file PRESID.DAT. Compare this standard deviation to the first 10 presidents. What might explain the differences if any?

2–28 Calculate the mean, standard deviation, and MAD for series A using any computer program you like, including a spreadsheet (SERIESA.DAT). Do your results agree with those of the textbook? Why or why not?

2–29 Calculate the ACF(k)s for the following series using k-values of 1 to 4. Compare your results with those in the book.
   a. SERIESA.DAT
   b. SERIESB.DAT
   c. SERIESC.DAT
   d. SERIESD.DAT
   e. Marriages using BIRTHMAR.DAT

2–30 Repeat problem 2–29 but for lags 1 to 12.

2–31 Using the data set BIRTHMAR.DAT, repeat the analysis done in Figures 2–16 to 2–19, but instead use births. Using graphs or other statistics, comment on how well the model of equation 2–23 fits this data. Why does it fit better or worse than the model for marriages?

2–32 Calculate the mean, standard deviation, and MAD for SERIESB.DAT.

Note: For problems 2–33 to 2–38: F_t = Forecast of period t; A_t = Actual of period t.

2–33 Use the naive forecasting model below to forecast SERIESB.DAT.

$$\text{Naive Model: } F_t = A_{t-1} \text{ and } e_t = A_t - F_t = A_t - A_{t-1}$$

   a. Calculate the ME, RSE, MPE, and MAPE.
   b. How well does the naive model forecast one period ahead?
   c. Generate prediction intervals for one-period-ahead forecasts using the results of *a.*
   d. Plot the errors.

2–34 For SERIESB.DAT, use the model below to the answer the following questions.

$$\text{Model: } F_t = A_{t-3} \text{ and } e_t = A_t - F_t = A_t - A_{t-3}$$

   a. Calculate the ME, RSE, MPE, and MAPE.
   b. Compare the performance of this model to that of problem 2–33. Comment on the results and explain the differences if any.
   c. Plot the errors.

2–35 For SERIESA.DAT, calculate the errors in using the two different models given below by forecasting periods 25 to 48.

$$\text{Model 1: } F1_t = \text{Mean for periods 1 to 24, and } e1_t = A_t - F_t$$
$$\text{Model 2: } F2_t = A_{t-1}, \qquad \text{and} \qquad e2_t = A_t - A_{t-1}$$

   a. Calculate the ME, RSE, MPE, and MAPE.

   b. Plot both errors.

   c. Which is better? Explain why or why not.

2–36 Use the naive forecasting model given below to forecast SERIESC.DAT.

$$\text{Naive Model: } F_t = A_{t-1}, \text{ and } e_t = A_t - F_t = A_t - A_{t-1}$$

   a. Calculate the ME, RSE, MPE, and MAPE.

   b. How well does the naive model forecast one period ahead?

   c. Generate prediction intervals for one period ahead forecasts using the results of *a.*

   d. Plot the errors of this model. Are there any patterns in the data? Explain the patterns.

2–37 Show that multiperiod-ahead forecasts are inaccurate with random-walk series by fore-casting SERIESB.DAT with two models for periods 13 to 48.

$$\text{Model 1: } F1_t = A_{t-1} \qquad e1_t = A_t - A_{t-1}$$
$$\text{Model 2: } F2_t = A_{t-12} \qquad e2_t = A_t - A_{t-12}$$

   a. Calculate the ME, RSE, MPE, and MAPE.

   b. Discuss the accuracy of the models. Which model provided the best forecast?

   c. Give an explanation why that model forecasted better.

2–38 Show that models should be based on patterns and that relatively accurate *n*-period-ahead forecasts are possible.

   a. Forecast SERIESD.DAT using the following model, $F1_t = A_{t-12}$.

   b. Now forecast using the following naive model, $F2_t = A_{t-3}$. Calculate the errors in using these two models to forecast periods 13 through 48.

   c. Calculate the errors, ME, and the RSE associated with these models for periods 13 through 48.

   d. Discuss the accuracy and appropriateness of each of these models using the ME, RSE, MPE, and MAPE.

   e. What do these results denote about the type of model and the patterns in the data?

2–39 Calculate the covariance COV(*X, Y*) and correlation coefficient (r_{xy}) for the Big City Bookstore variables sales and competition; interpret your results (use BIGCITY.DAT). Does a graph support your conclusions? Perform a statistical significance test on the correlation coefficient.

2–40 Repeat problem 2–39 using advertising and competition.

2–41 Using the data of example 2 in Figure 2–8, convert *X* to *X'* by making the nonlinear transformation identified in the chapter, then comment about the correlation between *Y* and *X'*. (Remember: $X' = 13 - 6X + .75X^2$)

2–42 Calculate the covariance COV(*X, Y*) and correlation coefficient r_{xy} for the following data and interpret your results. Does the graph support your interpretation? Perform a statistical significance test on the correlation coefficient.

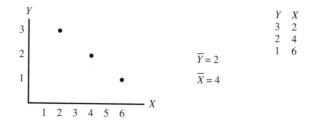

2–43 Calculate the ACFs for births in the U.S. from 1985 to 1992 (use BIRTHMAR.DAT, column 2). Illustrate the ACFs of the first eight lags and comment on their significance.

2–44 Calculate the Pearson correlation coefficient between births and marriages in the United States from 1985 to 1992 (use BIRTHMAR.DAT). Perform a statistical significance test on the coefficient. Comment on the results and the nature of causality between births and marriages.

2–45 Repeat the simple model of marriages (use BIRTHMAR.DAT) developed in the chapter: Marriages$_t$ = Marriages$_{t-4}$ + e_t. Calculate the ME, RSE, MPE, and MAPE. Comment on the accuracy of this model. Generate a 95 percent prediction intervals for one- to four-period-ahead forecasts.

2–46 Using the model and errors from the question above, calculate the ACFs of marriages and the ACFs of errors in predicting marriages for the first four lags. Is there any strong pattern in the errors? Are there any statistically significant ACFs?

2–47 Repeat the simple model of marriages developed in the chapter, but apply it to births (use BIRTHMAR.DAT): Births$_t$ = Births$_{t-4}$ + e_t. Calculate the ME, RSE, MPE, and MAPE. Comment on the accuracy of this model. Generate 95 percent prediction intervals for one- and-four-period-ahead forecasts.

2–48 Compare the ME, RSE, MPE and MAPE for the models of births and marriages in the three previous problems. Can you make any statements about which series is most accurately forecast?

2–49 Using the data below, calculate ACFs and Pearson correlation coefficients for lags 1, 2, and 3. Explain the differences.

$$t = 1 \quad 2 \quad 3 \quad 4 \quad 5 \quad 6$$
$$Y_t = 3 \quad 6 \quad 8 \quad 4 \quad 4 \quad 8$$

2–50 Using the monthly IBM closing stock prices (IBMMN.DAT) from 1985 to 1992, fit a naive model: $\hat{Y}_t = Y_{t-1} + e_t$. Calculate the ME, RSE, MPE, and MAPE. Comment on the accuracy of this model. Generate a 95 percent prediction interval for one-period-ahead forecasts. Calculate the ACFs of the original series and errors. Are there any patterns left in the ACFs? Are there any statistically significant ACFs in the errors?

2–51 Repeat problem 2–50 using the following model: $Y_t = Y_{t-3} + e_t$.

2–52 Compare the ME, RSE, MPE and MAPE for the models of IBM stock prices in the two previous problems. Can you make any statements about which model is best?

2–53 Repeat problem 2–50 using the S & P 500 index (SP500M.DAT) of monthly values from 1981 to 1992.

2–54 Repeat problem 2–51 using the S & P 500 index (SP500M.DAT) of monthly values from 1981 to 1992.

2–55 Compare the ME, RSE, MPE, and MAPE for the models of the S & P 500 stock index in the two previous problems. Can you make any statements about which model is best?

2–56 Repeat problem 2–50 using the Japanese stock index (JAPAN.DAT) of monthly values from 1970 to 1992.

2–57 Repeat problem 2–51 using the Japanese stock index (JAPAN.DAT) of monthly values from 1970 to 1992.

2–58 Repeat problem 2–52 using the Japanese stock index (JAPAN.DAT) of monthly values from 1970 to 1992.

Minicases: Common Assignment for Minicases

Minicases 6 to 10 were introduced in Chapter 1. For a selected minicase complete the following: Use the following two models to forecast the time series of the minicase.

$$Y_t = Y_t + e1_t \qquad e1_t = Y_t - Y_{t-1}$$
$$Y_t = Y_{t-12} + e2_t \qquad e2_t = Y_t - Y_{t-12}$$

Calculate the fitted errors in using these relationships to fit all but the last 12 months of data. Then calculate the forecast errors in using these relationships to forecast the last 12 months of data. Remember that none of the last 12 months of data are known at the time of forecasting. Discuss the accuracy of these two models using the ME, RSE, MPE, and MAPE for both their fit and forecast. What surprised you the most about these statistics? Discuss the practical significance of these two models for short-term (one-month ahead) and long-term forecasts (two to 12 months ahead). Which model do you recommend and why?

Minicase 2–1 Kansas Turnpike, Daily and Weekly Data
Case 1–1 introduced the daily and weekly demand figures of the Kansas Turnpike. The file TURNPIKD.DAT is a time series of the total number of vehicles that used the turnpike for each day during a 13-week period from June through August. For this time series, calculate the mean and standard deviation of the number of vehicles that travel the turnpike for each day of the seven days. That is, calculate the mean for the 13 Sundays, Mondays, . . . , and Saturdays; then divide each of the days by the mean volume per day for all days. This ratio, called a seasonal factor, is a measure of the seasonality of each day.

Which day of the week has the greatest traffic and which the least as measured by the mean and the seasonal factor? Are these numbers the result of holidays or purely the result of day-of-the-week seasonality? What holidays occur during this time? What holidays do you believe significantly affect the number of vehicles on the highway during this 13-week period? Did anything surprise you about the means, standard deviations, and seasonal factors? Speculate on how you would forecast the demand on this turnpike. If you wanted to test whether the means of the day of the weeks are statistically significantly different from each other, what general statistical significance test can you use?

Minicase 2–2 Air Passengers by Quarter Case 1–2 introduced the file PASSAIR.DAT, which is a time series of the quarterly passengers who have flown on domestic flights in the U.S. airlines from the first quarter of 1982 through the second quarter of 1994 (50 observations). For this time series, calculate the mean and standard deviation of the number of passengers who travel for each quarter of the year; that is, calculate the mean for the 12 quarters I, II, III, and IV (use only the first 48 observations). Then divide each of the quarterly mean volumes by the mean volume of all quarters. This ratio, called a seasonal factor, is a measure of the seasonality of each quarter. Which quarter of the year has the greatest volume and which the least as measured by the mean and the seasonal factor? Are these numbers the result of holidays or purely the result of quarter-of-the-year seasonality? Did anything surprise you about the means, standard deviations, and seasonal factors? How can these seasonal factors be used in short- and long-term forecasting.

Minicase 2–3 Hospital Census by Week Case 1–3 introduced the file CENSUSW.DAT, which is a time series of the weekly number of medical-surgical patients in a large midwestern hospital from January to December. Use the following two models to forecast the number of patients at the hospital:

$$\hat{Y}_t = Y_{t-1} + e_t \qquad e_t = Y_t - Y_{t-1}$$
$$\hat{Y}2_t = Y_{t-52} + e2_t \qquad e2_t = Y_t - Y_{t-52}$$

Calculate the errors in using these two models to forecast periods 53 to 104. Discuss the accuracy of these two models using the ME, RSE, MSE, MPE, and MAPE. In addition, calculate the correlations between Y_t and Y_{t-52} and Y_t and Y_{t-1} and test the significance of these two correlations. What surprised you the most about these statistics? Discuss the practical significance of these two models for short-term (one to two weeks) and long-term forecasts (more than two weeks into the future). Which model do you recommend?

Minicase 2–4 Henry Machler's Hideaway Orchids Case 1–4 introduced Henry J. Machler's Hideaway Orchid Nursery in Deerfield Beach, Florida. The file MACHLERD.DAT is a time series for daily sales over a 20-week period. As shown there, Hideaway Orchids is open seven days a week. Using this data, forecast using two models. Predict each day of one week as equal to the value of yesterday and the same day last week. That is,

$$\text{Model 1:} \quad Y_t = Y_{t-1} + e1_t \qquad e1_t = Y_t - Y_{t-1}$$
$$\text{Model 2:} \quad Y_t = Y_{t-7} + e2_t \qquad e2_t = Y_t - Y_{t-7}$$

Calculate the errors in using this relationship over the usable 12 weeks of data. Discuss the accuracy of these two models using the ME, RSE, MPE, and MAPE. In addition, calculate the correlations between Y_t and Y_{t-7} and Y_t and Y_{t-1} and test the significance of these two correlations. What surprised you the most about these statistics? Discuss the practical significance of these two models for short-term (one to two weeks) and long-term forecasts (more than two weeks into the future). Which model do you recommend?

Minicase 2–5 Your Forecasting Project Using the data you have selected for a forecasting project, fit two forecasting models, one a simple naive model. If your data is seasonal, fit a seasonal model as shown below; if the series is not seasonal, use the mean of the previous four observations:

Naive model 1: $Y_t = Y_{t-1} + e1_t \qquad e1_t = Y_t - Y_{t-1}$
Seasonal model 2: $Y_t = Y_{t-s} + e2_t \qquad e2_t = Y_t - Y_{t-s}$
Nonseasonal model 3:

$$Y_t = (Y_{t-1} + Y_{t-2} + Y_{t-3} + Y_{t-4})/4 + e3_t$$
$$e3_t = Y_t - (Y_{t-1} + Y_{t-2} + Y_{t-3} + Y_{t-4})/4$$

Calculate the error in using these relationships over the usable 13 weeks of data. Discuss the accuracy of these two models using the ME, RSE, MPE, and MAPE. What surprised you the most about these statistics? Discuss the practical significance of these two models for short-term (one to two weeks) and long-term forecasts (more than two weeks into the future). Which model do you recommend?

Minicase 2–6 Midwestern Building Materials
LUMBER.DAT is a highly seasonal monthly series of lumber sales of a large midwestern building materials company with 120 observations from January of year 1 through December of year 10. Complete the Common Minicase Assignment.

Minicase 2–7 International Airline Passengers
AIRLINE.DAT is a highly seasonal monthly series of international airline passengers with 12 years of 144 observations from 1949 through 1960. Complete the Common Minicase Assignment; however, first transform the original values using natural logarithms; use these in the models. Before calculating the error measures take the antilogs of the logarithmic fitted and forecasted values.

Minicase 2–8 Automobile Sales AUTO.DAT is a highly seasonal monthly time series of sales at a large automobile manufacturer with 185 observations from January of year 1 to May of year 16. Complete the Common Minicase

Assignment. Be sure to check this series for outliers from faulty data entry.

Minicase 2–9 Consumption of Distilled Spirits
SPIRITS.DAT is a highly seasonal time series of 132 months (i.e., 11 years) of the shipments of alcoholic spirits in the United States from January 1975 to December 1985. Complete the Common Minicase Assignment.

Minicase 2–10 Discount Consumer Electronics
ELECT.DAT is a highly seasonal time series of the sales of consumer electronics at a large retail discounter with 185 monthly observations from January year 1 to May of year 16. Complete the Common Minicase Assignment.

References

Aczel, Amir. *Complete Business Statistics.* Burr Ridge, IL: Irwin Publishing, 1993.

Box, G.E.P., G.M. Jenkins, and G.C. Reinsel, *Time Series Analysis.* Englewood Cliffs, NJ: Prentice Hall, 1994.

Cryer, J.D., and R.B. Miller. *Statistics for Business: Data Analysis and Modeling.* Boston: PWS-Kent, 1991.

DeLurgio, S.A., and C.D. Bhame. *Forecasting Systems for Operations Management.* Burr Ridge, IL: Irwin Professional Publishing, 1991.

Mansfield, E. *Statistics for Business and Economics: Methods and Applications.*

4th ed. New York: W.W. Norton and Company, 1991.

McClave, J.T., and P.G. Benson. *Statistics for Business and Economics.* 5th ed. San Francisco: Dellen Publishing Company, 1991.

Newbold, P. *Statistics for Business and Economics.* 3d ed. Englewood Cliffs, NJ: Prentice Hall, 1991.

Roberts, H. *Data Analysis for Managers.* 2d ed. Redwood City, CA: Scientific Press, 1991.

APPENDIX 2–A

EXPECTED VALUES, WHITE NOISE, AND CORRELATIONS

In Chapter 2, we discussed the mean and standard deviation of a time series. In this appendix, we discuss general methods for calculating the mean (expected value) and variance (squared standard deviation) using simple examples of discrete and continuous probability distributions. The forecast of a time series is a mean, and means are expected values; thus, for many forecasting formulas and derivations, it can be important to have some facility with the use of expected values.

Discrete Expected Values. The expected value of a distribution is its mean (i.e., 50 percent of the deviations above and 50 percent below). The *expected value* of a discrete random variable X_i is defined as

$$E(X) = \sum X_i P(X_i) \tag{2A–1}$$

where

$$X_i = \text{actual value}$$
$$P(X_i) = \text{probability of } X_i$$

By multiplying each X_i times its probability $P(X_i)$ and summing those products, the expected value is the equivalent of the mean, calculated by the formula

$$\bar{X} = \Sigma X_i \frac{f_i}{n} = \Sigma X_i P(X_i) \qquad (2A-2)$$

where

f_i = number of times X_i appears
n = total number of X's
$\dfrac{f_i}{n}$ = relative frequency (probability) of $X_i = P(X_i)$

Discrete Variance.   The variance is the principal measure of scatter for a probability distribution. The variance expressed in expected value form is equal to

$$\sigma^2 = \Sigma[(X_1 - E(X_i))^2 P(X_i)] \qquad (2A-3)$$

Again, this is equivalent to the variance calculation:

$$\sigma^2 = \Sigma\left[(X_i - \bar{X})^2 \frac{f_i}{n}\right] \qquad (2A-4)$$

Equations 2A–1 and 2A–3 are applied in the following example.

Example 2A–1.   Table 2A–1 illustrates the forecasts of demands for a product. From this information, calculate *(a)* the expected value (mean) of demand, *(b)* the variance of demand, and *(c)* the standard deviation.

(a) $E(X) = \Sigma\ X_i P(X_i)$
$\qquad = 1,200(.05) + 1,320(.15) + 1,440(.30) + 1,560(.35) + 1,680(.15)$
$\qquad = 1,488$

(b) $\sigma^2 = \Sigma\left[(X_i - E(X))^2 P(X_i)\right]$
$\qquad = (1,200 - 1,488)^2(.05) + (1,320) - 1,488)^2(.15) + (1,440 - 1,448)^2(.30) + (1,560 - 1,488)^2(.35) + (1,680 - 1,488)^2(.15)$
$\qquad = 16,416$

(c) $\sigma = \sqrt{\sigma^2} = 128.12$

Expected Value of Continuous Distribution.   In calculating the expected value of a continuous distribution, integral calculus is used to sum the continuous product of the random variable and its probability function $f(X)$. The expected value of the continuous random variable X is

$$E(X) = \int_{all\ X} X \cdot f(X)dX \qquad (2A-5)$$

TABLE 2A–1   Forecasts of Demand with Probabilities

Demand X_i	Probability $P(X_i)$
$X_1 = 1,200$	.05
$X_2 = 1,320$	.15
$X_3 = 1,440$	.30
$X_4 = 1,560$	.35
$X_5 = 1,680$	.15
	1.00

For example, given the probability function

$$f(X) = .05X - .0045X^2$$

valid over the $0 \le X \le 10$, the expected value is

$$
\begin{aligned}
E(X) &= \int_0^{10} X(.05X - .0045X^2)dX \\
&= \int_0^{10} (.05X^2 - .0045X^3)dX \\
&= \frac{.05X^3}{3} - \frac{.0045X^4}{4}\bigg|_0^{10} \\
&= 16.67 - 11.25 = 5.42
\end{aligned}
$$

Variance of Continuous Distribution.   The variance of a random variable (X) of a continuous distribution is

$$\sigma^2 = \int_{all\ X} (X - E(X))^2 f(X)dX$$

For the previous function,

$$
\begin{aligned}
\sigma^2 &= \int_0^{10} (X - 5.42)^2(.05X - .0045X^2)dX \\
&= \int_0^{10} (X^2 - 10.84X + 29.38)(.05X - .0045X^2)dX \\
&= \int_0^{10} (-.0045X^4 + .0988X^3 - .6742X^2 + 1.469X)dX \quad\quad\text{(2A–6)} \\
&= -\frac{.0045X^5}{5} + \frac{.0988X^4}{4} - \frac{.6742X^3}{3} + \frac{1.469X^2}{2}\bigg|_0^{10} \\
&= -90 + 247 - 224.73 + 73.45 \\
&= 5.7167
\end{aligned}
$$

Probabilities of Continuous Variables.   The integration of probability functions is used to calculate the areas and probabilities of continuous random variables. That is,

$$P(a \le X \le b) = \int_a^b f(X)dX \quad\quad\text{(2A–7)}$$

For the previous function,

$$
\begin{aligned}
P(0 \le X \le 10) &= \int_0^{10} (.05X - .0045X^2)dX \\
&= \frac{.05X^2}{2} - \frac{.0045X^3}{3}\bigg|_0^{10} \\
&= 2.5 - 1.5 \\
&= 1
\end{aligned}
$$

Verification of probability from 0 to mean:

$$
\begin{aligned}
P(0 \le X \le 5.42) &= \int_0^{5.42} (.05X - .0045X^2)dX \\
&= \frac{.05X^2}{2} - \frac{.0045X^3}{3}\bigg|_0^{5.42} \\
&= .7344 - .2388 \\
&= .4956 \approx .500
\end{aligned}
$$

The slight error between .4956 and the theoretical probability of .5000 is due to round off errors in computations.

Covariances, Correlations, and White Noise

The following identities are presented for clarification of the notations in this and other forecasting books. While we have tried to be consistent in the use of notation throughout this book, there are times when slightly different notations are necessary. Consequently, there are reasons why one notation is chosen over another. Remember that y_t is a deviation with a mean of zero.

Expected Values for Variables in Deviation Form.

$$\text{VAR}(y_t) = \frac{\Sigma(y_t y_t)}{n} = E(y_t^2), \text{ remembering that } y_t \text{ has a mean} = 0. \tag{2A-8}$$

$$\text{COV}(y_t y_{t-k}) = \frac{\Sigma y_t y_{t-k}}{n-k} = E(y_t y_{t-k}) \tag{2A-9}$$

$$\text{COR}(y_t y_{t-k}) = \frac{\text{COV}(y_t y_{t-k})}{\sqrt{\text{VAR}(y_t)\text{VAR}(y_{t-1})}} \simeq \text{ACF}(k) = \frac{E(y_t y_{t-k})}{E(y_t^2)} \tag{2A-10}$$

White Noise Residuals and Errors e_t.   The analyses of errors are much of the focus of model validation in forecasting. In statistical terms, white noise (WN) is normally and independently distributed (NID) with a mean of zero and a constant variance, zero autocovariances, and zero autocorrelations. A number of important properties result from these characteristics.

Given WN $\sim$ NID$(0, \sigma_{et}^2)$, which denotes a mean of zero and a constant variance, and remembering that $e_t \sim$ WN, the mean of e_t is zero, or in expectation form: $E(e_t) = 0$.

$$\bar{e}_t = \frac{\Sigma e_t}{n} = E(e_t) = 0$$

because WN errors should be unbiased.

The variance is constant and equals:

$$\text{VAR}(e_t) = \frac{\Sigma(e_t - E(e_t))^2}{n} = \frac{\Sigma(e_t - 0)^2}{n} = \frac{\Sigma e_t^2}{n} = E(e_t^2) \tag{2A-11}$$

Because WN errors have a constant variance:

$$\text{VAR}(e_t) = \text{VAR}(e_{t-k}) = E(e_{t-k}^2) = E(e_t^2)$$

Because they are statistically independent of each other, the autocovariances of e_t equal zero:

$$\text{COV}(e_t e_{t-k}) = E(e_t e_{t-k}) \tag{2A-12}$$

$$= \frac{\Sigma(e_t - E(e_t))(e_{t-k} - E(e_{t-k}))}{n-k} = \frac{\Sigma(e_t e_{t-k})}{n-k} = 0, \text{ for } k \neq 0$$

$\text{COV}(e_t e_{t-k})$ is notated as COV(k).

Because of independence, the autocovariances and all of the autocorrelations equal zero:

$$\text{ACF}(k) = \frac{\text{COV}(k)}{Se_t Se_{t-k}} = \frac{\text{COV}(e_t e_{t-k})}{\text{VAR}(e_t^2)} = \frac{\Sigma e_t e_{t-k}}{\Sigma e_t^2/n} = \frac{0}{\Sigma e_t^2/n} = 0 \text{ for } k \neq 0 \tag{2A-13}$$

This is why the ACF(k) = 0 for patternless data, for $k \neq 0$.

Given a series is white noise, the standard error of the autocorrelation function can be shown to be approximately:

$$Se_{\text{ACF}}(k) \simeq \frac{1}{\sqrt{n}} \tag{2A-14}$$

When plotted, the residuals are NID$(0, \sigma_{et}^2)$; that is, they are completely random, stationary, and independent with ACF(k) = 0, for all $k \neq 0$.

APPENDIX 2–B

Q-STATISTIC FOR WHITE NOISE ACF(*k*)S

The *Q*-Statistic and Diagnosing White Noise

When forecasting, we seek theoretically valid and intuitively appealing models with correct patterns. When the correct patterns of a time series have been included in the model, the resulting residuals will have no patterns and thus are white noise. White noise residuals will have ACFs without any remaining pattern, thus denoting that there is no opportunity for further model improvement. Consequently, one confirmation that a good model has been identified is patternless ACFs. Although we have studied how to perform t-tests of the significance of individual ACFs at specific lags, there are more complex patterns (e.g., seasonal ACF patterns) that might provide evidence for model improvement.

Fortunately, there is an objective diagnostic measure of white noise for a time series that assesses whether, as a group, there are patterns in the autocorrelations; this is commonly called the Q-statistic, Box-Pierce statistic, or Ljung-Box statistic. The Q-statistic measures whether as a group the autocorrelations are statistically significantly different than those expected from white noise. This is in contrast to the t-test on individual ACFs used in some previous examples. Equation 2B–1 illustrates this test statistic:

$$Q = n(n + 2) \Sigma[\text{ACF}(i)^2/(n - i)] \qquad \text{for } i = 1 \text{ to } k \qquad (2B-1)$$

This statistic is distributed as a chi-square distribution with $k - c$ degrees of freedom, where c is equal to the number of coefficients in the model. Thus, we see that Q is proportionate to the sum of the autocorrelations through lag k; where k is selected to be about the lesser of two seasonal cycles, about one-fourth of the observations, or 24 when two seasonal cycles is much greater than 24.

The *Q*-statistic is used to perform the following hypotheses tests.

Null Hypothesis:

H$_0$: ACFs are not significantly different than white noise ACFs.

$$\text{df} = k - c$$

If $Q \leq$ chi-square table,   then infer ACF patterns are not statistically significantly different than those of white noise.

alpha = .05

Alternative Hypothesis:

H$_1$: ACFs are statistically significantly different than white noise ACFs.

$$\text{df} = k - c$$

If $Q >$ chi-square table,   then infer ACF patterns are statistically significantly different than those of white noise.

alpha = .05

As mentioned, the *Q*-statistic has been refined several times by Box-Pierce and Ljung-Box; thus, your software may refer to the *Q*-statistic by those names. The *Q* of equation 2B–1 is the Ljung-Box statistic. Appendix E illustrates a chi-square table for use in the above hypothesis test. Consider an example of a white noise test.

Assume that a simple model with 2 coefficients is fit to a time series. The first 24 ACFs of the residuals of the model yield a Q of 10.2. This value is then compared to the chi-square value from the table:

$$\text{df} = k - c = 24 - 2 = 22$$

$$Q = 10.2 < \text{chi-square table} = 12.34$$

$$\text{alpha} = .05$$

Thus, because $Q <$ chi-square table, we infer that the ACFs are not statistically different than those of white noise. (As in all acceptances of null hypotheses, this does not prove that the residuals are white noise; it only denotes that they have not been shown to be statistically significantly different than white noise, an important difference.)

Many computer programs perform statistical significance tests directly by reporting the level of significance for the Q-statistic in their standard outputs. These programs report the alpha value or significance level denoting the probability that this Q-value came from a white noise series. For example, a significance value of .25 denotes that 25 percent of the time, Q-values this high or higher result from the sample ACFs of white noise processes. Thus, we commonly infer the series is not white noise when the level of significance is less than .05 and that it is consistent with white noise when the level of significance is greater than or equal to .05.

The Q-statistic is not a substitute for t-tests on individual ACFs; instead, it complements the individual ACF t-tests. At times, the t-test and Q-statistic may not agree because the model may not always yield unambiguous results. For example, it is possible to have models that are statistically and substantively defensible but lack white noise residuals as measured by the Q-statistic or individual t-tests, or both. Thus, judgment is necessary in the acceptance or rejection of models.

In most cases, lack of white noise is the result of a model deficiency and must be rectified; however, in some cases, a high t-value or high Q-statistic is an artifact of the particular sample. For example, Y_t might contain one or two near-outliers that are k periods apart. If these outliers are both high or both low, there may be a significant positive ACF at lag k. If these outliers are in opposite directions, there may be a significant negative ACF spike at lag k. A couple of sets of near-outliers may make the t-value or Q-statistic inconsistent with the white noise assumption. Thus, we are cautious when interpreting ACF patterns; do not overreact to marginally high t- or Q-values. Let's apply these concepts to the marriage series in the BIRTHMAR.DAT.

Q-Stat for Marriages.   The table below illustrates the first eight ACFs for the quarterly time series, marriages. As we saw before, the ACFs reveal the very seasonal nature of this time series, having very high peaks at 4 and 8. In addition, there are very high peaks at 2 and 6, which are harmonics of the underlying four-quarter seasonality. Immediately following the table is the calculated Q-statistic and significance level for the first eight ACFs. As shown, the level of significance denotes that the probability of a Q-statistic of 90.8147 is approximately zero if the time series marriages were a random sample from a white noise series. Thus, the Q-statistic confirms the highly seasonal behavior of the marriage series and its ACFs.

ACF(k) for Marriages—Quarterly Data from 1985:01 to 1992:04

k				
1:	$-.1250$	$-.7113$	$-.1088$	.8753
5:	$-.1028$	$-.6130$	$-.1068$	.7434

Ljung-Box Q-Statistics: $Q(8) = 90.8147$; significance level .00000000

Now, let consider the residuals of a seasonal fourth difference model of the marriage series.

$$Y_t = Y_{t-4} + e_t \tag{2B–2}$$

$$e_t = Y_t - Y_{t-4} \tag{2B–3}$$

The table below illustrates the first eight ACFs of the residuals of equation 2B–3. As shown, these ACFs do not have the very seasonal nature of the original time series (i.e., no significant peaks at 4 and 8). In fact, all of the ACFs are well within the approximate $2Se_{ACF}$ of .378 (i.e., $2/\sqrt{28}^{.5}$; thus, these ACFs are consistent with white noise. Immediately following the table is the calculated Q-statistic and its significance level for these first eight ACFs. As shown, the Q-statistic is only 8.66 and its level of significance denotes that these ACFs have about a 37 percent chance (i.e., .371) of having come from a white noise time series. Thus, we have not shown the ACFs as being inconsistent with white noise; the level of significance is well above the critical value of .05. This low Q-statistic and its level of significance confirm that the highly seasonal pattern of marriages has been modeled well by equation 2B–2.

ACF(k) for Residuals, Equation 2B–2, Quarterly Marriages

k				
1:	.0027	.2458	.1351	−.2034
5:	−.0759	−.1055	−.2506	−.1890

Ljung-Box Q-Statistics: $Q(8) = 8.661$, significance level $= .3717$.

Achieving White Noise

The pattern of the marriages time series was easily modeled using equation 2B–2. However, there was still some pattern left in the ACFs at lags of 2, 4, 6, and 8—albeit insignificant, as measured by the t- and Q-statistics in the previous table. Although we might be inclined to determine the cause of these slightly high ACFs, remember that they are individually and collectively insignificant. Thus, it appears that this model is valid.

Some analysts persist in extracting as much pattern out of a time series as possible. However, such analysis almost always violates the principle of parsimony. If all other aspects of a fitted model denote that it is a good representation of the underlying pattern, but nonetheless white noise is not achieved when using the t- or Q-statistics and it is not possible to improve the model, then, often, the best solution is to accept the model. The nonrandom behavior is most likely the result of minor sampling errors, not problems with the underlying model. However, extremely large deviations in the plots of the residuals, original series, and ACFs should be investigated. Those values of Y_t that adversely affect the model should be adjusted or controlled for. When only minor deviations from white noise occur, the best alternative is to accept the model that has less than white noise residuals.

Finally, some analysts continuously "torture" their time series to achieve white noise while not paying attention to the values of other more important measures such as the RSE or MAPE. In most cases, the modeling process should progress in directions that reduce the RSE while achieving statistically significant coefficients and subtantively defensible models. Thus, the RSE should be monitored during the modeling process and overly complex models avoided. A best statistic to monitor is the Schwarz Bayesian Information Criterion (BIC), which is developed in Chapter 17, you can review that section at any time.

Finally, note that several forecasting methods are commonly presented independent of any discussions of the Q-statistic or white noise. The methods of Chapters 4, 5, and 6, on simple smoothing methods, decomposition and Census II methods, and Winter's, often ignore consideration of the ACF patterns. When the RSE is reasonably low and only low values remain in the ACFs, then often, but not always, little harm is done by ignoring patterns. However, very high ACFs (e.g., .5) might be indicative of patterns that can significantly improve the model; these patterns should be identified and incorporated into the model. The use of ACF t-tests and Q-statistics are useful when analyzing the residuals of any forecasting model.

Problems

2B–1   Using the formula of equation 2B–1 or that of your software, calculate the Q-statistic for the following series. What inferences do you make from this value?
   a. SERIESA.DAT
   b. SERIESB.DAT
   c. SERIESC.DAT
   d. SERIESD.DAT
   e. Births using BIRTHMAR.DAT
   f. Marriage using BIRTHMAR.DAT

2B–2   Fit the model of equation 2B–2 to marriages using BIRTHMAR.DAT.

$$Y_t = Y_{t-4} \qquad\qquad (2B-2)$$

Confirm the previous results by calculating the residual ACFs; confirm the significance of any ACF(k)s and calculate the Q-statistic. What inferences do you make about this model? Compare the Q-statistic to the value from problem 2B–1f). Why are the values so different?

2B–3   Fit the model of equation 2B–2 to births using BIRTHMAR.DAT.

$$Y_t = Y_{t-4} \qquad\qquad (2B-2)$$

Now calculate the residual ACFs, confirm the significance of any ACF(k)s, and the Q-statistic. What inferences do you make about this model? Compare the Q-statistic to the value from problem 2B–1e). Why are the values so different?

2B–4   Fit the following model to SERIESD.DAT.

$$Y_t = Y_{t-12}$$

Now calculate the residual ACFs, confirm the significance of any ACF(k)s, and the Q-statistic. What inferences do you make about this model? Compare the Q-statistic to the value from problem 2B–1d). Why are the values so different?

2B–5   Fit the following model to SERIESB.DAT.

$$Y_t = Y_{t-1}$$

Now calculate the residual ACFs, confirm the significance of any ACF(k)s, and the Q-statistic. What inferences do you make about this model? Compare the Q-statistic to the value from problem 2B–1b). Why are the values so different?

CHAPTER 3

SIMPLE LINEAR REGRESSION ANALYSIS

Thinking is the hardest work there is, which is probably the reason why so few engage in it.

Henry Ford

Chapter Outline

Introduction
Purposes of Regression Analysis
Method of Least Squared Deviations
Regression Assumptions
Serial and Autocorrelation Problems
Sampling and Regression Analysis
Review of Regression Analysis Steps
Nonlinear Models Using Linear Regression
Regression Advantages and Disadvantages
Summary
Key Terms
Key Formulas
Review Problems Using Your Software
Problems
Minicases
References
Appendix 3–A Cross-Correlation Coefficients

Introduction

This chapter introduces regression analysis because it is one of the most frequently used forecasting methods. Also, regression analysis is an important general method in itself and a foundation of more sophisticated forecasting methods. It is a general approach to modeling the relationships between one variable, such as product sales, and one or more other variables, such as price, customer income, and competitor prices.

Dependent and Independent Variables

Regression analysis is often referred to as a causal method of statistical modeling. Causal methods include, but are not limited to, regression (Chapters 3 and 11), econometric (Chapter 12), and MARIMA methods (Chapters 13 and 14). Other synonyms for causal methods include multivariate and extrinsic methods. These methods differ from univariate methods in that causal models predict the future by modeling the past relationships between a **dependent variable** and one or more other variables called either **independent, predictor** or **exogenous variables.** The dependent variable is commonly denoted by Y and the independent variables by X or some other more descriptive notations such as A for advertising or C for competition.

Consider the following example of a regression application. The manager of the Big City Bookstore is reviewing sales of the past years. She notes that sales have fluctuated over time. She believes that there are several factors affecting sales such as the business cycle, advertising expenditures, the level of competition, the popularity of book reading, and population. To better understand these influences, she seeks a model relating book sales to these important market and demographic variables. The important variables she has chosen include:

Cyclical business influences (C).

Advertising expenditures (A).

Competition from other bookstores (O).

Population (P).

Thus, the manager believes that demand for books is dependent on the values of these independent variables:

$$Y = f(C,A,O,P) \qquad (3-1)$$

That is, Y is a function of, or dependent on, C, A, O, and P. Thus, we see that the first step in constructing a regression model is the theoretically based identification of the dependent and independent variables.

Table 3–1 illustrates a number of dependent and independent variables. At times it can be very difficult to understand and identify all of the relationships and interactions of the many independent variables influencing a dependent variable such as product sales. Thus, in most situations, it is difficult to model true cause-and-effect relationships. Typically, the most that can be done is to model how several independent variables are useful in predicting a single dependent variable and to hope that true cause and effect relationships are also being modeled. We study cause-and-effect modeling in greater detail in Chapters 10 through 13; for now, we consider predictive relationships.

Scatter Plots

Figure 3–1 shows graphs of matched pairs of hypothetical independent and dependent variables. As shown in Figure 3–1, there are a variety of relationships that can exist between two variables.

TABLE 3–1   **Example Dependent and Independent Variables**

Dependent Variable	*Independent Variables*
Product demand	Advertising, economic conditions, competition, prices, competitor prices
Crop yields	Rainfall, temperature, soil fertility, diseases, weeds, herbicides
Printer paper sales	Computer printer sales, number of computers, prices
Consumer product demands	Population, prices, competition
High-definition TV	Prices, economic conditions, popularity, competition

FIGURE 3–1

Some relationships between dependent and independent variables

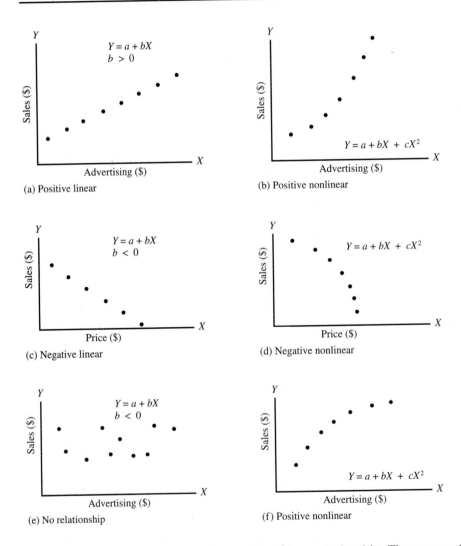

(a) Positive linear

(b) Positive nonlinear

(c) Negative linear

(d) Negative nonlinear

(e) No relationship

(f) Positive nonlinear

Figure 3–1(a) illustrates a perfect **positive linear relationship.** The term *perfect* refers to the fact that the correlation coefficient is 1 and all the actual values lie perfectly on a straight line; *positive* refers to the direction of the line as being up, or positive, to the right. In contrast, plot c shows a perfect **negative linear relationship.** Plots b, d, f are referred to as **nonlinear relationships** because the algebraic equations between the dependent and independent variables are nonlinear. In plots b, d, and f the squared independent variables are related to Y as:

$$\hat{Y} = a + bX + cX^2 \qquad (3-2)$$

The interpretation of plot b is that, as advertising expenditures increase, sales increase at an increasing rate; in contrast, plot f shows that as advertising increases, sales increase at a decreasing rate. Plot e shows a situation where sales and advertising are unrelated.

Returning to the Big City Bookstore example, suppose that the manager has gathered the data of Table 3–2 from previous years to predict sales using advertising expenditures [i.e., $Y = f(X)$, where X is advertising]. She plots these data in Figure 3–2, which shows clearly that there is positive linear relationship, where high sales are associated with high advertising and low sales are associated with low advertising expenditures. Having decided to model this relationship, she applies linear regression techniques. Before applying regression analysis to this specific example, consider the purposes of regression analysis.

TABLE 3–2   Big City Product Demands and Advertising Expenditures

Year	Sales (Y) ($000s)	Advertising Expenditures (X) ($000s)
1	27	20
2	23	20
3	31	25
4	45	28
5	47	29
6	42	28
7	39	31
8	45	34
9	57	35
10	59	36
11	73	41
12	84	45

FIGURE 3–2

Scatter plot, Big City Bookstore
BIGCITY.DAT

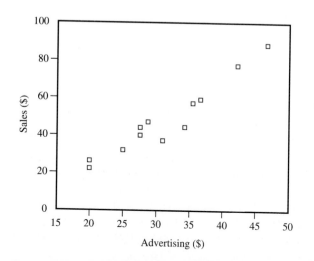

Purposes of Regression Analysis

Regression analysis has three general purposes:

1. To model the relationship between the dependent variable Y and one or more independent variables Xs.
2. To measure the error in using that relationship to predict the dependent variable.
3. To measure the degree of association (i.e., correlation) between the dependent and the independent variables.

Each of these purposes is illustrated in the context of the Big City Bookstore. The first purpose (relationship identification) is illustrated next. The second purpose (error estimation) is illustrated through the use of the **residual standard error (RSE)**, which in regression analysis is called the **standard error of estimate (SEE)**. The third objective (correlation measurement) is presented through discussion of the coefficients of correlation (r) and determination (R^2).

Method of Least Squared Deviations

The first objective in regression analysis is to accurately model the relationship between the dependent and independent variables. In our example, the most accurate model is that which yields a best fit (i.e., closest fit) line to the scatter plot in Figure 3–2. As we will see in a moment, the best model is the one having the minimum sum of squared deviations between actual and fitted values; hence, this method is called the **method of least squared deviations.** Remembering that an error or deviation is the vertical distance between the actuals (Y) and fitted values ($\hat{Y}$), the least squares method has the objective of minimizing the squared vertical deviations between actual and fitted values.

To define the best relationship between demand and advertising in Figure 3–2 requires finding the line that best fits the actual values. One might assume that the most representative line has the sum of the errors above and below equal to zero (i.e., $\Sigma e = \Sigma(Y - \hat{Y}) = 0.0$). However, there are an infinite number of lines that have this attribute; thus, this is an insufficient criterion. All lines that go through the intersection of $\bar{X}$ and $\bar{Y}$ have equal positive and negative errors; thus, the sum of errors (Σe) equals zero. This is shown in Figure 3–3, where there are two lines with the Σe equal to zero; the sum of high positive errors are negated by low negative errors. However, there is only one line passing through $\bar{X}$ and $\bar{Y}$ that yields the minimal value of Σe^2. That is, only one line has

$$\Sigma e_i = \Sigma(Y_i - \hat{Y}_i) = 0.0$$

and

$$\Sigma e_i^2 = \Sigma(Y_i - \hat{Y}_i)^2 = \text{minimum value}$$

This is called the least squares regression line and is illustrated in Figure 3–3. Remembering that a straight line is defined by two coefficients, a and b, the following formulas result:

$$Y = a + bX + e \qquad (3\text{–}3)$$
$$\hat{Y} = a + bX \qquad (3\text{–}4)$$
$$e = Y - \hat{Y} \qquad (3\text{–}5)$$

FIGURE 3–3

Two possible lines for Big City Bookstore

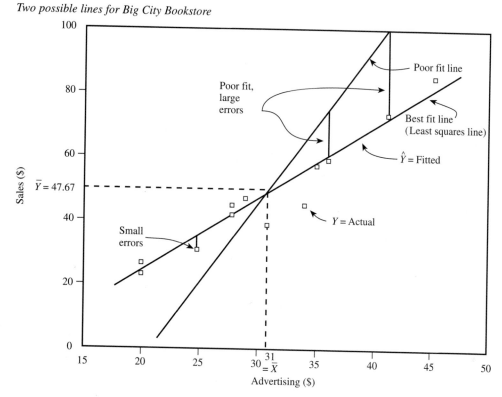

where

Y = actual value of sales,
$\hat{Y}$ = fitted value of Y,
a = value of Y when X equals zero, called the Y-intercept,
b = slope = change in Y resulting from a one-unit change in X,
e = residual error that remains after fitting the model.

The objective of minimizing the Σe^2 is shown in equation 3–6.

$$\text{MIN}[\Sigma(Y_i - \hat{Y}_i)^2] = \text{MIN}[\Sigma(Y_i - a - bX_i)^2] \tag{3–6}$$

The values of a and b that minimize these squared errors are called least squares coefficients and are calculated using equations 3–7 and 3–8. Remember that Y and X are known, only a and b are unknown in equation 3–6.

Partial differentiation and the maxima-minima theorems of calculus are used to estimate the values of a and b in equation 3–6 that yield the minimum Σe^2. Although not shown here, the results of differentiation yield two equations in two unknowns; these two unknowns are a and b as shown in equations 3–7 and 3–8. These equations are commonly called **normal equations.**

In summary, the least squares regression line is:

$$\hat{Y} = a + bX$$

where

$$a = \overline{Y} - b\overline{X} \tag{3-7}$$

$$b = \frac{\sum X_i Y_i - n\overline{X}\,\overline{Y}}{\sum(X_i^2) - n\overline{X}^2} = \frac{\sum(X_i - \overline{X})(Y_i - \overline{Y})}{\sum(X_i - \overline{X})^2} \tag{3-8}$$

where

$$\overline{Y} = \text{mean of the dependent variable} = 47.67$$
$$\overline{X} = \text{mean of the independent variable} = 31$$

Referring back to the Big City Bookstore example, the required summations are:

$$\sum Y = 572 \qquad\qquad \sum X = 372$$
$$\sum XY = 19{,}205 \qquad\qquad \sum(X^2) = 12{,}178$$

which yield:

$$b = \frac{19{,}205 - 17{,}732}{12{,}178 - 11{,}532} = 2.2802 \tag{3-9}$$

$$a = 47.667 - 2.2802(31) = -23.02 \tag{3-10}$$

$$\hat{Y} = -23.02 + 2.2802X \tag{3-11}$$

This final expression is the best-fit relationship for sales and advertising and is plotted in Figure 3–4. The *b* value of 2.2802 denotes that every $1 spent on advertising yields a $2.28 increase in sales for books. The *a* in equations 3–10 and 3–11 is the value of *Y* when *X* equals zero. To calculate past fitted or future predicted values, $\hat{Y}$, simply substitute the appropriate value of *X* into equation 3–11. The fitted values using past values of *X* are shown in Table 3–3. Although the relationship of equation 3–11 accurately fits past *Y* values, it may not predict future values of *Y* as accurately, a topic we address in a moment and later when discussing the standard error of forecast (S_f).

Interpretation of Y-Intercept (*a*).   There is a tendency to literally interpret the *a* value of equation 3–11 as the value of *Y* when *X* equals zero. However, this may be incorrect. Frequently, the *a* value does not represent the actual value of *Y* when *X* is zero. Stated another way, the *a* value is there to represent the influences of the many other independent variables that are not included in the relationship. Also, in many applications it is illogical to have independent variables with zero values. Even when

FIGURE 3–4

Least squares line,
Big City Bookstore

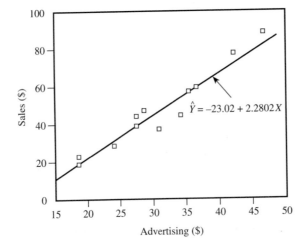

it is theoretically possible to have an X of zero, frequently X values of zero are not included in the data. Thus, it is difficult to estimate what Y equals when X equals zero. In our example, the interpretation of a is that sales will equal −\$23,020 when advertising is zero. Such a conclusion is illogical; there is no meaning to negative sales, nor is it likely that sales will even equal zero with no advertising, let alone be negative.

Table 3–3 and Figure 3–4 illustrate how closely the fitted and actual values are for the least squared regression line. Remember, in Figure 3–4 the **residual error** in fitting the relationship is equal to the vertical distance between the actual values and the regression line. Table 3–3 illustrates actual, fitted, residuals, and percent residuals. The model fits the data quite well because the residual errors are low relative to actual values. The term *residual* denotes the difference between the sample value of Y and the fitted value for each value of X.

$$\text{Residual error} = (Y - \hat{Y}) \tag{3–12}$$

Fitted Residual and Forecasted Error

There is an important distinction between the concepts of fitted and forecasted values. A **fitted value** results from the process of fitting a mathematical model to past data; thus, past values are used to arrive at fitted values (as in Table 3–3). In contrast, **forecasted values** are estimates of the future where actual values are unknown. Obviously, during the fitting process, the future values of Y do not influence the resulting model coefficients (i.e., a and b). Stated another way, the past actual values of Y were used to arrive at the fitted values of $\hat{Y}$ (a and b), while forecasted values are estimates of future Y values which are made after fitting model coefficients.

Because past actual values were used to generate model coefficients and the resulting fitted values, frequently there is less error between actual and fitted values than there is between actual and forecasted values. The greater errors in forecasting occur because of two assumptions we have already discussed: (1) the validity of the model

TABLE 3–3   Actual, Fitted, and Error Terms for Big City Bookstore

Year	Actual Sales (000s)	Fitted Sales (000s)	Residual Error (000s)	Percent Residual (%)
1	27	22.585	4.415	16.35
2	23	22.585	.415	1.81
3	31	33.985	−2.986	−9.63
4	45	40.826	4.174	9.28
5	47	43.106	3.894	8.28
6	42	40.826	1.174	2.79
7	39	47.667	−8.667	−22.22
8	45	54.507	−9.507	−21.13
9	57	56.787	.213	.37
10	59	59.068	−.068	− 0.11
11	73	70.469	2.531	3.47
12	84	79.589	4.411	5.25
Average	47.67		.00	−.46
Standard deviation	18.12	Residual standard error	5.039	11.69

in representing the past and (2) its continuing validity into the future. For example, in Table 3–3 there are 12 years of actual values used in regression analysis to determine the best fitted values. In contrast, the forecasted value for year 13 must be calculated using a budgeted advertising expenditure for that year. For example, assume that the budgeted advertising expenditure for year 13 is 46, therefore the predicted sales are

$$\hat{Y}_{13} = -23.02 + 2.2802 \cdot 46 = 81.87$$

However, the error in this estimate remains unknown until year 13 is over. Thus, the term **forecast error** is commonly used to denote the difference between a forecasted value and the actual value after the actual value becomes known. In contrast, the term residual error denotes the difference between the actual and fitted value.

$$\text{Residual error} = \text{Actual} - \text{Fitted}$$
$$\text{Forecast error} = \text{Actual} - \text{Forecasted}$$

Regression Output

Regression output can be reported several different ways; equation 3–13 and Table 3–4 show two possible presentations. Let's study these in greater detail.

$$\hat{Y} = -23.02 + 2.2802X \quad \text{[coefficients]} \qquad (3\text{–}13)$$
$$6.32 \quad .198 \quad \text{[standard errors]}$$
$$(-3.64) \quad (11.5) \quad \text{[t-values]}$$
$$S_{yx} = 5.039 \quad \bar{R}^2 = .923 \quad n = 12 \quad F = 132.2573 \quad DW = 1.13676$$

Before developing the theory of the statistics presented in Table 3–4 and equation 3–13, consider the following common English interpretation of Table 3–4. The equivalent statistics are in equation 3–13:

Row 1: Identifies the dependent variable as Big City Sales.

Row 2: Denotes that there are 12 observations; however, because there are two estimated regression coefficients (*a* and *b*), 2 degrees of freedom are lost and therefore 10 degrees remain.

Row 3: Gives the value of the adjusted R^2. We want this value to be as close to 1

TABLE 3–4   Big City Regression Output (BIGCITY.DAT)

Row					
1	Dependent variables sales				
2	Usable observations	12	Degrees of freedom	10	
3	$\bar{R}^2 = .923$				
4	Standard deviation of dependent variable 18.1225				
5	Standard error of estimate		5.0394		
6	Sum of squared errors		253.9530		
7	Regression $F(1, 10)$		132.2573		
8	Significance level of F		.00000044		
9	Durbin-Watson statistic		1.1368		
10	*Estimate*	*Coefficient*	*Standard Error*	*t-statistic*	*Significance*
11	Constant	−23.01909	6.3162	−3.644	.004504
12	Advertising	2.2802	.1983	11.500	.000000

as possible. It denotes that about 92 percent of the variance in sales have been explained by advertising; we define this in detail in a moment.

Row 4: Gives the standard deviation of the dependent variable; this statistic is compared to the SEE in row 5.

Row 5: Gives the standard error of estimate (SEE), which measures the dispersion of actual values of sales about fitted values. We would like this value to be low, near zero. More important, the SEE should be low relative to the standard deviation of Y (i.e., row 4). In this case, it is: $5.0394 < 18.1225$. A synonym for SEE is residual standard error (RSE).

Row 6: The sum of squared errors (SSE) is literally that; a and b were determined so as to minimize this sum.

Row 7: The F-value is used to measure the overall statistical significance of the relationship (see row 8 description below). In general, but not always, the higher the F-value, the more significant the relationship. The numbers in the parentheses represent the number of degrees of freedom in the numerator and denominator, a concept developed later.

Row 8: The significance level denotes the probability that the calculated F-value of row 7 would be this high, or higher, if in fact there were no relationship between Y and X. Thus, in this example, the probability of getting the calculated F-value of 132.26 if sales and advertising are not related is only 0.00000044, approximately zero. This is such a low probability that we infer that sales and advertising are related.

Row 9: Illustrates the calculated value of the Durbin-Watson statistic. This statistic is used to determine whether the fitted errors (i.e., residuals) have temporal pattern left in them. If there is a significant pattern left in the residuals, the standard error of estimate, F-value, and t-statistics (see row 10) may not be accurate measures. The Durbin-Watson statistic is supposed to be close to 2.0. We discuss this statistic later in the chapter. The DW statistic of Table 3–4 is low, and interpretation of the SEE, F, and t-values may not be valid, however any inferences are tenuous because of the small sample size. (More on this later.)

Rows 11 and 12: These rows identify the actual coefficients of the constant and independent variable. As shown in row 11, the coefficient for the constant is -23.01909, while the coefficient for advertising is 2.28019. To the right of these are three additional statistics. The standard error of these regression coefficients (S_b) is used to measure how much error there is in these estimates. Next is reported the number of standard errors the regression coefficients are away from zero (e.g., $(a - 0)/S_a = (-23.01909 - 0)/6.31623 = -3.64444$); this yields the t-value of -3.64444. If the absolute t-value is much greater than two or three, we conclude that this coefficient is not likely to be equal to zero, and thus the independent variable should be in the model.

Finally, consider the significance level, the last column of rows 11 and 12. This column shows, based on the t-distribution, the probability that these coefficients could be zero or of opposite sign. Thus, for example, the probability that the constant a could be zero or even positive is very small, .004504. Also, as shown in the last column of row 12, the probability that the coefficient for advertising could be zero or negative is approximately zero. Thus, there is a statistically significant relationship between advertising and sales of books.

Having provided a brief introduction to the statistics of regression analysis, let's study these in greater detail.

Standard Error of Estimate (S_{yx})

Having computed the relationship between sales and advertising, how closely do the actual values fit the regression line (i.e., fitted values)? The graph of Figure 3–5 shows a very good fit between actual and fitted values. However, it is useful to have an ojective measure of the goodness of fit. One measure of fit is the SEE (also known as the RSE). This standard error, which is developed in Chapter 2, measures the scatter of actual values (Y) about the regression line ($\hat{Y}$), its value is also shown at the bottom of Table 3–3. The formula for the SEE is:

$$S_{yx} = \sqrt{\frac{\Sigma(Y_i - \hat{Y})^2}{n - k}} = \sqrt{\frac{\Sigma e_i^2}{12 - 2}} = 5.039 \qquad (3-14)$$

where

$Y, \hat{Y},$ and e^2 were defined previously
n = Number of observations
k = Number of estimated parameters (a and b): here $k = 2$.

Note that the SEE is minimum when the sum of squared errors is minimum. A lower SEE denotes that the regression line is a better fit of Y values than a relationship with a higher SEE.

FIGURE 3–5

68 Percent intervals with and without regression model

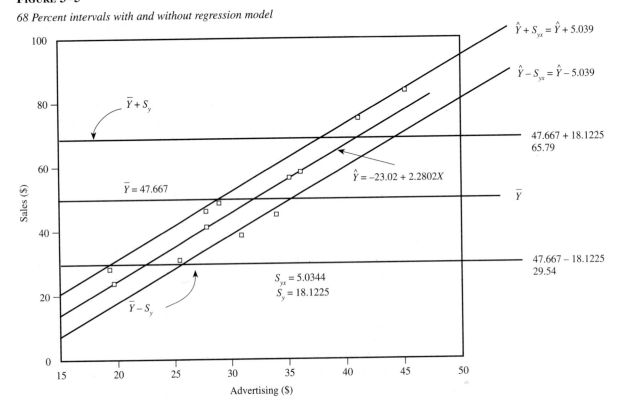

Which Is It? SEE, RSE, or S_{yx}?

Many of our problems in life are definitional, and no doubt the number of synonyms in statistics present great confusion. Historically, the standard error of estimate (SEE) has been noted as S_{yx}, the standard deviation of Y given X values, a useful way of expressing its meaning.

Thus, SEE, RSE, and S_{yx} are synonyms, used interchangeably. We would use only one term in this book were it not for the fact that different books and software use different notation for the same statistical calculation. Try to be comfortable with all three terms.

Let's consider the SEE for the Big City Bookstore example:

$$S_{yx} = 5.039$$

This standard error can be compared to that of the dependent variable sales (Y):

$$S_y = 18.12$$

By relating Y to X, the standard deviation has declined from 18.12 to only 5.039. Thus, X has reduced the scatter of Y from 18.12 to 5.039. That is,

$$S_{yx} = 5.039 < S_Y = 18.12$$

To better understand the significance of the standard error of estimate, consider the process of predicting Y with and without the relationship (i.e., equation 3–13).

Prior to relating Y to X, confidence intervals about future values of Y are based on the standard deviation of Y. However, by relating Y and X, the standard error of estimate gives tighter confidence intervals and greater accuracy. For example, not knowing Y's relationship with X, 68 and 95 percent confidence intervals for Y are

68%: $Y = \bar{Y} \pm S_y = 47.667 \pm 18.12$

95%: $Y = \bar{Y} \pm 2S_y = 47.667 \pm 36.24$

The 68 percent interval is plotted as the horizontal lines in Figure 3–5 as 29.54 to 65.79. Although not shown in Figure 3.5, the 95 percent confidence interval for the actual value of Y is expected to be in the range of 11.43 to 83.91, a very wide range (you might plot these yourself). In contrast, consider these two confidence intervals after relating Y and X. The confidence intervals for the fitted Y values given, for example, $X = 25$ are:

68%: $Y = \hat{Y} \pm S_{yx} = -23.02 + 2.28X \pm S_{yx}$
  $Y = -23.02 + 2.280(25) \pm (5.04) = 33.98 \pm 5.04$

95%: $Y = \hat{Y} \pm 2S_{yx} = -23.02 + 2.28X \pm 2 S_{yx}$
  $Y = -23.02 + 2.280(25) \pm 2(5.04) = 33.98 \pm 10.08$

As shown in Figure 3–5, the 68 percent interval with the forecasting model is considerably narrower than that without the model. In making confidence interval statements, it is not uncommon to use one and two standard error of estimates (5.04 and 10.08). Thus, the sales projection is expected to be within \$5,040 of the actual sales 68 percent of the time. As shown later, in this chapter, the intervals using S_{yx} are simplifications of the correct intervals. Also, note that this discussion has been general, using z values from the ND; instead, in the specific application t-values should be used with such small sample sizes.

Adjusted
Coefficient of
Determination ($\overline{R^2}$)

The S_{yx} is an *absolute* measure of the fit of a model because its value is dependent on the scale of Y. A very useful measure of *relative* fit is the **adjusted coefficient of determination,** which compares S_{yx}^2 to S_y^2. (Recall that the squares of standard deviations are called *variances*.) The adjusted coefficient of determination ($\overline{R^2}$) equals the proportion of the variance in the dependent variable Y that is explained or eliminated through the relationship with the independent variable X. In modeling a random dependent variable:

$$\text{Total variance} = \text{Explained variance} + \text{Unexplained variance}$$
$$S_y^2 = \text{Explained variance} + S_{yx}^2$$

Now we can estimate the total variance for actual values of Y, S_y^2, and, from regression analysis, the estimated unexplained variance, S_{yx}^2. Knowing these two values, the explained variance equals the total minus unexplained variance as shown below:

$$\text{Explained variance} = \text{Total variance} - \text{Unexplained variance}$$
$$= S_y^2 - S_{yx}^2$$

Thus, the proportion of explained variance is:

$$\text{Proportion explained} = \frac{\text{Explained}}{\text{Total variance}} = \frac{\text{Total} - \text{Unexplained}}{\text{Total variance}}$$

$$\overline{R^2} = \frac{\text{Total} - \text{Unexplained}}{\text{Total variance}} = 1 - \frac{\text{Unexplained variance}}{\text{Total variance}}$$

For Big City Bookstore:

$$\overline{R^2} = 1 - \frac{S_{yx}^2}{S_y^2} = 1 - \frac{5.039^2}{18.122^2} = 1 - \frac{25.392}{328.33} = .923 \tag{3-15}$$

In terms of sums of squares

$$\overline{R^2} = 1 - \frac{\dfrac{\Sigma(Y_i - \hat{Y})^2}{n - k}}{\dfrac{\Sigma(Y_i - \overline{Y})^2}{n - 1}} = 1 - \frac{\dfrac{253.92}{12 - 2}}{\dfrac{3611.63}{12 - 1}} = .923 \tag{3-16}$$

In this case, the total variance of Y equals 328.33, and the variance of the residual errors is only a fraction of this, 25.392. Thus, by relating Y to X, we have explained or eliminated 92.3 percent of Y's original variance. This was confirmed above when we considered confidence intervals.

In general, an $\overline{R^2}$ of 1 denotes that all the variance of Y has been eliminated because the standard error of estimate is zero; that is, all points are on the regression line. An $\overline{R^2}$ of zero indicates that the standard error of estimate equals the standard deviation of Y. When $\overline{R^2}$ equals zero, the regression model does not fit actual values better than the mean of Y; in fact, then the regression line is horizontal and fitted values are all equal to the mean of Y.

$$\overline{R^2} = 1 - \frac{S_{yx}^2}{S_y^2} = 1 - 1 = 0$$

only if $S_{yx}^2 = S_y^2$ and b = 0, therefore all $\hat{Y} = \overline{Y}$.

The $\overline{R^2}$ calculated in equations 3-15 and 3-16 is called the **adjusted R^2** because the denominator of S_{yx} is adjusted for the degree of model complexity as measured by

$\overline{R}^2$ Can Be Negative

Over the years we have been approached several times by students and colleagues believing that their computer programs had errors in them because the reported $\overline{R}^2$ was negative. However, negative values of $\overline{R}^2$'s are possible and have an important interpretation.

If the $\overline{R}^2$ is negative, it denotes that the b value in the regression relationship is nearly zero, and therefore all fitted values of Y nearly equal the mean of Y. That is, when $b = 0$, then

$$\hat{Y} = \overline{Y} \text{ for all values of } X$$

Consequently, when there are $n - 1$ and $n - k$ $(k > 1)$ degrees of freedom in the denominator and numerator of equation 3–16 respectively, the numerator is larger than the denominator as shown in the example below:

$$\overline{R}^2 = 1 - \frac{\dfrac{\Sigma(Y_i - \overline{Y})^2}{n - k}}{\dfrac{\Sigma(Y_i - \overline{Y})^2}{n - 1}} = 1 - \frac{\dfrac{3000}{25 - 2}}{\dfrac{3000}{25 - 1}} = 1 - \frac{130.44}{125} = -.04352$$

Note that the sums of squares are identical because all fitted values equal $\overline{Y}$. Because $b = 0$, there is no relationship between Y and X; a negative or zero-adjusted $\overline{R}^2$ confirms this situation.

the degrees of freedom, $n - k = n -$ number of coefficients in the equation (e.g., in equation 3–16, where $n - k = 12 - 2$). In general, when the number of independent variables increases, everything else being equal, S_{yx} increases because of the higher k in equation 3–16. However, when the sum of squares declines enough because of the added independent variables, the S_{yx} will then decline. Thus, we use the value of k to denote the complexity of the model: higher ks denote higher complexity and, everything else equal, will yield a higher S_{yx}.

Also, another term for $\overline{R}^2$ is R-bar squared.

In contrast to $\overline{R}^2$, some use and report another statistic called the **unadjusted R^2**. The unadjusted R^2 is unadjusted for model complexity, being calculated as

$$R^2 = 1 - \frac{\Sigma(Y_i - \hat{Y})^2}{\Sigma(Y_i - \overline{Y})^2} = 1 - \frac{253.953}{3612.667} = .9297$$

Thus, neither the denominator or numerator are adjusted for the loss of degrees of freedom, $n - k$ and $n - 1$. Consequently, the unadjusted R^2 will become larger and larger as more variables are added to a model, even though the adjusted $\overline{R}^2$ may be decreasing because of the term $n - k$. (Note: This is true because adding more independent variables will always decrease the sum of errors in the numerator.) Thus, the unadjusted R^2 may mislead one to believe that additional variables are useful in modeling Y when in fact they are not. The use of unadjusted R^2 may result in fitting models that are too complex. Thus, typically, the adjusted $\overline{R}^2$ is the better statistic. We will use $\overline{R}^2$ for the adjusted R^2; the unadjusted R^2 will be noted R^2.

Finally, note that R^2 is literally that: the square of the Pearson correlation coefficient, r, that is developed in Chapter 2. Thus, the square root of R^2, is r, where the sign of r equals that of the b value in the regression relationship.

If $R^2 = 1$, $|r| = 1$, there is a perfect linear relationship.

If $R^2 = 0$, $r = 0$, there is no relationship.

$\overline{R}^2$ **Is a General Statistic**

$\overline{R}^2$ is a general statistic that can be used to judge the relative accuracy of any model. For example, in using any model on a time series Y, assume that the RSE is 10 and the standard deviation of $Y(S_y)$ is 40. Then the $\overline{R}^2$ for this model is:

$$\overline{R}^2 = 1 - 10^2/40^2 = 1 - 100/1600 = .9375 \text{ or } 93.75\%$$

Thus, the model has explained 93.75 percent of the original variance of Y. $\overline{R}^2$ is a general statistic that is useful when making inter- and intramodel accuracy estimates.

The R^2 and r of other relationships are not always as high as those calculated here. In such situations, the question then arises as to whether there is a significant relationship between variables with a low R^2. That is, if R^2 or r does not equal a high value, does this denote no relationship between Y and X or is there a statistically significant relationship between Y and X? This question can be answered through the simple hypothesis test on r developed in Chapter 2. However, when more than one independent variable exists in the relationship, the simple t-test of Chapter 2 is not valid; instead the F-test is used. This statistical test is illustrated later in this chapter.

Testing the Significance of Regression Coefficients

Equation 3–13 shows two statistics under each regression coefficient b. The statistic immediately under b is the **standard error of the regression coefficient,** S_b, which measures how much the individual b_i's (i.e., the individual $\Delta Y_i/\Delta X_i$) vary about the mean b. That is, b is the mean of all the $\Delta Y_i/\Delta X_i$ and there is some scatter of these actual $\Delta Y_i/\Delta X_i$ about this mean; this scatter is measured by the S_b. Conceptually, if a regression coefficient (i.e., b value) is not statistically significantly different than zero, we infer that the independent variable has not been shown to be statistically related to the dependent variable. The question of statistical significance is answered by comparing the b-value to its standard error, S_b. This is most easily done by dividing b by its standard error. This quotient, b/S_b is the second number under each b in equation 3–13. The value b/S_b is referred to as the t-value; that is, for equation 3–13,

$$t = \frac{b - 0}{S_b} = \frac{2.2802}{.198} = 11.5 \qquad (3-17)$$

This t-value is used in the following hypothesis test:

Null hypothesis: The true regression coefficient (B) is not statistically significantly different than zero:

$$H_0: B = 0 \quad \text{Infer true if } |t| < t\text{-table.}$$

Alternative hypothesis: The true regression coefficient (B) is statistically significantly different than zero:

$$H_1: B \neq 0 \quad \text{Infer true if } |t| > t\text{-table.}$$

where t-table is a value chosen from the t-distribution, usually a value of about 2 depending on $n - 2$, the number of degrees of freedom.

Remembering that high t-values are statistically significantly different from zero, we reject H_0, accept H_1 and infer that the regression coefficient is not zero and that there is a significant relationship between advertising and sales.

The test of a regression coefficient is important in determining if a variable should be in the relationship. If there is no statistically significant relationship between the dependent and independent variable, then the slope B of the true regression line is zero. If the sample value b is significantly different than zero, we infer that there is a relationship between the variables. Although we do not derive equation 3–18, the standard error of the regression coefficient is:

$$S_b = \frac{S_{yx}}{\sqrt{\Sigma(X_i - \bar{X})^2}} \qquad (3\text{–}18)$$

Here, S_{yx} is the sample SEE and $\Sigma(X - \bar{X})^2$ describes the dispersion of X-values around their mean. As mentioned, the value S_b is a measure of the amount of sampling error in b, just as S_y is a measure of the sampling error in the mean of Y.

In the Big City example:

$$S_b = \frac{5.039}{\sqrt{646}} = .198$$

An inference about the population regression coefficient can be made either as a test of significance as in equation 3–17 or as a confidence interval. Consider these confidence intervals:

The 95 percent confidence interval for the regression coefficient in a large sample $(n - k > 30)$ is

$$b + tS_b$$
$$b \pm 1.96S_b$$

For the Big City example, however, with $n = 12$, use a t-value from Appendix C with $n - 2 = 10$ degrees of freedom and an alpha of .05 to find the confidence interval:

$$b \pm 2.23S_b$$

This is $2.2802 \pm 2.23(.198) = 2.2802 \pm .44154$. Therefore, we can make the statement that the true B is between 1.839 and 2.722, with a probability of about .95 that this statement is true.

We suggest calculating such confidence intervals when interpreting model results, particularly when the calculated t-value is low. That is, when the t-values of regression coefficients are only marginally significant, generation of these confidence intervals can be very insightful into the possible ranges of true coefficients.

Analysis of Variance in Regression Analysis

It is important to show that regression analysis is also an analysis of variance (here after, **ANOVA**). Regression relationships provide estimates of the total variance in the dependent variable that is associated with variance in the independent variable(s). ANOVA provides a powerful method of proving that there is a statistically significant relationship between a dependent variable and one or more independent variables. Let's work through an ANOVA using the Big City Bookstore and Figure 3–6.

Total, Explained, and Unexplained Variance

The components of total variation were introduced previously as
total variation = explained variation + unexplained variation:

$$\Sigma(Y_i - \bar{Y})^2 = \Sigma(\hat{Y}_i - \bar{Y})^2 \qquad + \Sigma(Y_i - \hat{Y})^2$$

FIGURE 3–6

Total, explained, and
unexplained variation

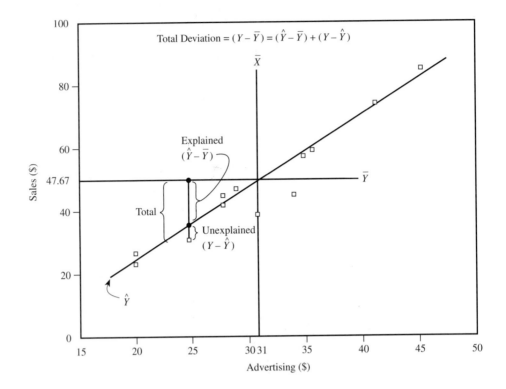

These two components of total variation are shown clearly in Figure 3–6. In the context of regression analysis, the following ANOVA notation is commonly used:

$$\text{Total sums of squares} = \text{TSS} = \Sigma(Y_i - \overline{Y})^2$$
$$\text{Explained variation} = \text{Regression sums of squares} = \text{RSS} = \Sigma(\hat{Y}_i - \overline{Y})^2$$
$$\text{Unexplained variation} = \text{Error sums of squares} = \text{ESS} = \Sigma(Y_i - \hat{Y}_i)^2$$

Thus, we see that:

$$\text{TSS} = \text{RSS} + \text{ESS}$$

Also, while it is not obvious, the degrees of freedom (*df*) in the total sums of squares are also related such that

$$df_{\text{TSS}} = df_{\text{RSS}} + df_{\text{ESS}}$$
$$n - 1 = (k - 1) + (n - k)$$

Dividing the sums of squares by their appropriate degrees of freedom yields the resulting variances:

$\text{TSS}/(n - 1) = \text{total variance}$
$\text{RSS}/(k - 1) = \text{explained variance} = \text{mean squared regression} = \text{MSR}$
$\text{ESS}/(n - k) = \text{unexplained variance} = \text{mean squared error} = \text{MSE}$

Two of these variances are used in the **F-test** of ANOVA developed next.

The F-Test
of ANOVA

The overall significance of a regression relationship can be tested with the ratio of the explained (RSS) to unexplained (ESS) variances. This variance ratio follows an

F-distribution with $k - 1$ and $n - k$ degrees of freedom in the numerator and denominator respectively.

Although we do not develop the general theory of the F-test here, it is an important statistical tool to verify whether the ratio of two variances is statistically significantly greater than one. If the variance ratio is significantly greater than 1, the variances are statistically different than each other. Thus, the test is designed to determine whether the numerator variance is greater than the denominator variance.

As with a t- or Z-test, a high F-value is indicative of a difference between two variances that is not due to chance. Or stated another way, the probability of high F-values is extremely low if there is no significant difference between the two variances. When high F-values occur, the most logical inference is that there is a significant difference between the two variances. The statistical test is

$$F_{k-1, n-k} = \frac{\text{RSS}/(k-1)}{\text{ESS}/(n-k)} = \frac{\Sigma(\hat{Y}_i - \bar{Y})^2/(k-1)}{\Sigma(Y_i - \hat{Y}_i)^2/(n-k)} \qquad (3\text{–}19)$$

For the Big City Bookstore, the appropriate sums of squares are

$$F_{k-1, n-k} = \frac{\text{RSS}/(k-1)}{\text{ESS}/(n-k)} = \frac{\Sigma(\hat{Y}_i - \bar{Y})^2/(k-1)}{\Sigma(Y_i - \hat{Y}_i)^2/(n-k)} = \frac{3358.714/(2-1)}{253.953/(12-2)} = 132.26$$

The calculated F-value of ANOVA is compared to values from book Appendix F with $k - 1$ degrees of freedom in the numerator and $n - k$ degrees of freedom in the denominator. This F-value is used to perform the following hypothesis test.

H_0 (*Null hypothesis*): There is no statistically significant relationship between Y and X.

If F (calculated) $\leq F_{k-1, n-k}$ (table)   Infer true H_0.

H_1 (*Alternative hypothesis*): There is a statistically significant relationship between Y and X.

If F (calculated) $> F_{k-1, n-k}$ (table)   Infer true H_1.

Hypothesis test results:

$$df_n = 1, df_d = 12 - 2 = 10$$

$$F\text{-calculated} = 132.26 > F\text{-table} = 10.0$$

$$\alpha = .01$$

Therefore, infer that there is a statistically significant relationship between Y and X.

The table below shows a commonly used format for reporting the ANOVA for a regression relationship.

Regression ANOVA Table

Source	SS	df	MS	F
Regression	3,358.714	$2 - 1 = 1$	$3,358.714 = \text{MSR}$	
Error	253.953	$12 - 2 = 10$	$25.395 = \text{MSE}$	
Total	3,612.667	11	328.424	132.26

Note: SS = sums of squares, df = degrees of freedom, MS = mean of squared sums, and F = value of F-statistic.

Some Software Reports Mean Squared Errors Only

Note that the mean squared values used in ANOVA are actually estimated variances. That is, the values of MSR (3358.714) and MSE (253.95) of regression analysis are actually the estimated explained variance of the regression line and the unexplained variance of the errors, respectively. When these variances (i.e., mean squared errors) are reported, the following F-test results:

$$F = \frac{MSR}{MSE} = \frac{\Sigma(\hat{Y}_i - \bar{Y})^2/(k - 1)}{\Sigma(Y_i - \hat{Y}_i)^2/(n - k)} = \frac{3358.714}{25.3953} = 132.26$$

Some regression routines do not provide an ANOVA and F-test; however, it is possible to perform an F-test using the unadjusted R^2. Applying this F-test to the Big City example:

$$F_{k-1, n-k} = \frac{R^2/(k - 1)}{(1 - R^2)/(n - k)} = \frac{.9297/(2 - 1)}{(1 - .9297)/(12 - 2)} = 132.26 \qquad (3-20)$$

F-Test and t^2

For simple linear regression, the calculated F-value equals t^2 for the regression coefficient of the independent variable (e.g., advertising). However, the equality of t^2 and F only holds true for simple bivariate regression relationships. Because most regressions involve more than one independent variable, the F-test becomes an important overall test of the significance of the relationship between Y and all independent variables taken as a group. This overall statistical significance test is necessary because the individual t-tests for coefficients do not provide such a test; additionally, the t-tests might be very misleading when the independent variables are highly correlated, a topic discussed further in Chapters 10 and 11.

Regression Assumptions

We have studied a number of statistical tests regarding the fit and significance of regression results. However, these tests are not necessarily accurate unless a number of regression assumptions are true. In order to make valid statistical inferences and generalizations about the true regression line based on a sample regression line, six specific assumptions must be true. These six assumptions are discussed below and shown in Figure 3–7. Note that Figure 3–7a to p illustrate relationships using graphs of Y versus X, e_t versus e_{t-1}, and e_t versus e_{t-1} X and Y; thus, be sure which variables are on the vertical and horizontal axes.

Assumption 1: The Fitted Relationship is of the Correct Form

When fitting a linear relationship to sample data, the true or population relationship should also be linear, otherwise the regression model will probably be misleading. The true underlying relationship may be expressed in the form:

$$Y_p = A + BX + v$$

$$\hat{Y}_p = A + BX$$

where A and B are the true (but unknown) population parameters, and v is the deviation of an actual value of Y from the true **population regression line** (Y_p); that is, $v =$

What Is the Level of Significance?

The output of most computer software includes the level of significance of test statistics. Consider Table 3–4, which shows three significance levels, .0000044, .004504, and .000000, for the F and two t-statistics respectively. In general, the level of significance is the probability that the reported statistic could be as high as this value *if the null hypothesis of the test statistic is true*. For example, the level of significance of F in Table 3–4 denotes that the calculated F-value of 132.3 has only a .00000044 probability) (i.e., a 44/100,000,000 chance) of occurring if the population F-value is 1.0. Stated another way:

$$P(F_{calculated} \geq 132.3 | F_{pop} = 1.0) =$$
$$.00000044 \text{ (approximately zero)}$$

An alternative statement is

$$P(F_{calculated} \geq 132.3 | H_0 \text{ is true}) =$$
$$.00000044 \text{ (approximately zero)}$$

where | is an abbreviation for *given that*. That is, the probability of $F_{calculated}$ being greater than or equal to 132.3 given that H_0 is true is approximately zero. Therefore, H_0 is inferred to be false. Now remember that the null and alternative hypotheses are:

H_0: There *is no* statistically significant relationship between Y and X.

H_1: There *is* a statistically significant relationship between Y and X.

Thus, a low numerical level of significance denotes that there is a very low probability that there *is no* relationship between Y and X; therefore, the logical conclusion is that there *is* a significant relationship between Y and X. A very low probability (i.e., $< .01$ or $.05$) is considered a very significant result.

The level of significance of the t-statistics in Table 3–4 is explained similarly using the hypotheses associated with equation 3–17.

$Y - Y_p$. Figures 3–7a to d illustrate linear and nonlinear relationships using graphs of Y versus X, e_t versus e_{t-1}, and e versus X and Y. If, as illustrated in Figure 3–7b, the true underlying relationship is nonlinear, then the regression coefficients, inferences, and statistics of the linear model discussed above are not valid. In multiple regression, this type of nonlinearity may not be so evident as it is in Figure 3–7b; however, a plot such as 3–7d is very useful in detecting nonlinearity. The interpretation of 3–7d is that some nonlinear form of X should be included in the relationship, for example X^2.

The consequences of using invalid mathematical forms for a relationship can vary from minor to extreme. For example, if the underlying relationship is nonlinear, but only slightly so, its linear approximation may be relatively accurate. Nevertheless, we must be very cautious not to always assume relationships are linear; many phenomena and relationships are nonlinear.

Assumption 2: Homoscedasticity of Errors

This assumption denotes that the standard deviation of the v's is the same for all values of X. This means that there is a uniform scatter or dispersion of points about the regression line (a concept known as **homoscedasticity**, equal scatter). Figures 3–7e, f, g, and h illustrate when this assumption is valid and invalid (a condition called **heteroscedasticity**, different scatter). Assuming that the other assumptions of regression are valid, then good estimates of the true residuals (i.e., the v's) are the observed residuals e's. Thus, these e's can be used to judge whether the homoscedasticity assumption is true.

When the residuals have different variances about the predicted values (i.e., are **heteroscedastic**), this denotes that the standard error of estimate (SEE) is not a constant and the F-test and other measures based on the sum of squared errors may be invalid. However, the regression coefficients still may be unbiased predictors of the true coefficients. Chapter 10 discusses tests for and ways of correcting heteroscedasticity.

Often when heteroscedasticity is a problem, this is a result of using the wrong functional form of one or more variables in the relationship. For example, maybe per capita data or logarithms should be in the relationship. Chapter 10 further develops these concepts.

Assumption 3: No Serial Correlation in the True Errors (v's)

For the t-values and F-test to be valid, the residuals in one time period should not be related to those in other periods; that is, residuals should be statistically independent of each other. This denotes that the deviation, e_t, of one point about the line is not related to the deviation of any other point, e_{t-m}. If e_t is autocorrelated with e_{t-m}, this is called **serial correlation.**

Unfortunately, this assumption of independence may not be valid for many time series models. Many series move in nonrandom patterns about the trend, so that adjacent values (e.g., in economic recessions and contractions) are closely related. Figures 3–7i, j, k, and l illustrate errors that are statistically independent (i and k) and serially dependent (j and l). Chapters 10, 11, and 13 develop techniques for least squares regression of time series when there is serial correlation in the errors. As developed later in this chapter, there are two important statistical tests for serial correlation of residuals: the Durbin-Watson test and the t-test for autocorrelations. Finally, note that serial correlation may exist in the residuals because some important variable has been left out of the relationship, a concept further explored in Chapter 10.

Assumption 4: The Distribution of Errors about the Regression Line Is Approximately Normally Distributed

This denotes that the errors are normally distributed (ND) about the regression line. Figures 3–7m and n illustrate errors that are and are not normally distributed about the regression line. When this assumption is not true, the regression coefficients and all the statistical inferences about the regression *may be* invalid.

When the errors are not ND about the regression line, then frequently some points might be more influential in determining the "best" least squares line. Consider the obvious problem with data in Figure 3–7n. The statistical significance of this relationship is completely dependent on the single high observation at the far right. This observation is extreme, and even if it is correct (i.e., not a data entry error), we still have to question how representative the relationship is, considering the large void of observations between this lone "outlier" and the cluster of lower values. Statistical analysis can help somewhat in answering the question of representativeness; however, it is theory and our understanding of the relationships that will help resolve the problem in Figure 3–7n.

The necessity of assumption 4 in determining the validity of regression measures is dependent upon the size of the sample. For small samples, normality of scatter is not necessary if one wishes only to estimate the values of the regression coefficients. However, the assumption is necessary for the valid use of the standard error of the regression coefficient S_b. Also, the normality assumption is necessary in order to make probability statements using S_{yx} and the standard error of forecast S_f as developed later.

For large samples, the normality assumption is not necessary to make valid inferences about the regression line (a, b, and S_b can be used to make inferences). The central limit theorem makes such inferences possible. However, normality is necessary to make probability statements using S_{yx}.

It is important to remember that graphs and regression results provide insights regarding the fit and consequences of inclusion and exclusion of observations. Therefore graphs should be used in all data analysis to provide insights and confirmation of the validity of a model and its assumptions.

113

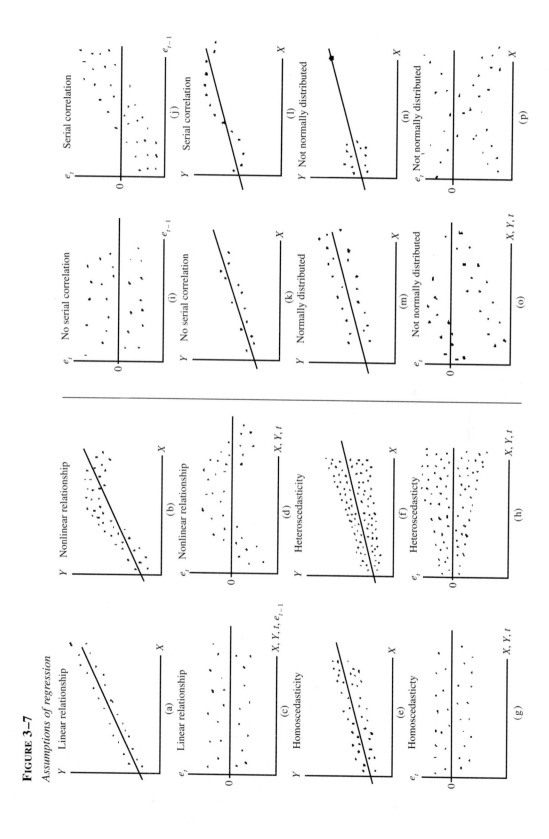

FIGURE 3–7

Assumptions of regression

Assumption 5: The Relationship Includes All Important Variables

The problem of including or excluding the wrong independent variables is a serious one. It denotes that the theory driving the analysis and the resulting relationship are wrong and misleading. When one wants to interpret the regression coefficients literally, that b is the change in Y that results from a unit change in X, it is important that all of the important independent variables are included in the relationship. If this is not true, the regression coefficients may be inaccurate.

Figures 3–7o and p illustrate two of many possible consequences of having important variables not included in the relationship. Figure 3–7o illustrates a situation where the variable X has been included in the relationship; however, a variable we'll call Z has been left out of the relationship. The variable Z appears to be one taking on two values—possibly high and low values, or 0 and 1—denoting when the event does or does not take place. The fact that this variable has been excluded results in the two patterns of errors.

Figure 3–7p illustrates a situation where the variable X interacts with another variable, again designated Z. This cross-pattern in the residuals denotes that Z and most likely the product of Z times X should be in the relationship. Such products of variables are called interactive variables that denote that combinations of low and high values of X behave differently with low and high values of Z.

Assumption 6: No Problems from Highly Correlated Xs

Sometimes when the independent variables are highly correlated, a condition called multicollinearity, more complex interpretations of the regression coefficients, may be necessary. Because of this high correlation, a change in one independent variable is associated with a change in another. When this occurs, the estimated relationship may or may not be accurate. We discuss the dependency of independent variables, that is, multicollinearity, further in Chapter 10.

Assumption Summary. When the above six assumptions are satisfied, the linear regression coefficients and the standard error of estimate computed from the sample are statistically efficient, consistent, and linearly unbiased estimators of true population values (this is commonly called BLUE, best linear unbiased efficient estimates). The term *efficient* denotes that no other methodology can provide more accurate estimates. The term *consistent* denotes that as the size of the sample increases, the standard error in estimating the coefficients decreases; that is, as the sample size increases so does the accuracy of the coefficient. Finally, the *unbiased* concept denotes that the coefficients of many samples have a mean equal to the true population mean. Thus, sample coefficients are not expected to over- or under-estimate the true population coefficient (i.e., they will not be biased). Finally, while not proven here, the BLUE property of estimated regression coefficients are proven in the Gauss-Markov Theorem of econometrics, Pindyck and Rubinfeld, 1991.

Serial and Autocorrelation Problems

Assumption 3 above denotes that residual errors should not be serially correlated. Serial correlation problems occur when the error terms in one period are correlated with those in previous periods (serial and autocorrelation are synonyms). When the serial correlation is one period apart, this is called first-order autocorrelation, as illustrated in Figures 3–7j and l. Problems of serial correlation (hereafter referred to as autocorrelation) can be very serious because high autocorrelations can result in very low (i.e., biased) estimates of the true S_{yx}, and consequently coefficient t-tests, overall F-test, and the S_{yx} can be wrong and misleading. When high autocorrelation exists, it is not uncommon to see what appears to be a very strong relationship disappear when the autocorrelation in errors is eliminated. We discuss the methods for eliminating the effects for autocorrelated errors in Chapter 10; for now, let's learn how to detect problems with autocorrelation.

Figure 3–8 clearly illustrates positive and negative autocorrelations, respectively, first as visible in a time series plot of errors and then as scatter plots.

Durbin-Watson Statistic

Autocorrelation can be detected through the use of several graphs and the t-test on the ACFs as developed in Chapter 2 or through the use of the **Durbin-Watson statistic (DW).** The DW is part of the standard output of most regression programs and is calculated as follows.

$$DW = \frac{\Sigma(e_t - e_{t-1})^2}{\Sigma e_t^2} \qquad (3-21)$$

Although not obvious from equation 3–21, the calculated value of the DW varies between 0 and 4, with a value of 2 denoting no autocorrelation and values of 0 and 4 denoting perfect positive and negative autocorrelations, respectively. The simple figure below illustrates the conclusions associated with different values of the DW statistic.

Positive	Inconclusive	No Autocorrelation	Inconclusive	Negative
0	dl	du	4 − du	4 − dl	4

FIGURE 3–8

Serial correlation problems

Time Series Plots

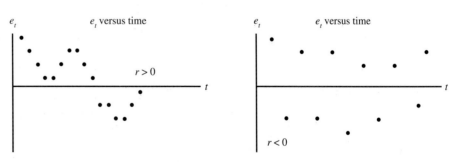

Scatter Plots

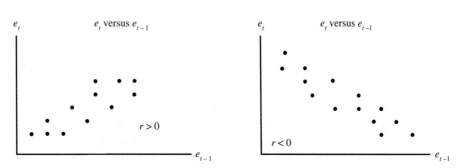

Appendix G provides a Durbin-Watson statistics table. As shown, there are two statistics associated with the DW, dl and du, which are lower and upper values used to make inferences. The DW-table statistic is determined by the number of observations, n, the number of independent variables (which equals $k - 1$). The following inferences result: When the

DW is between 0 and dl, infer there is positive autocorrelation.

DW is between dl and du, the test is inconclusive.

DW is between du and $4 - $ du, infer there is no autocorrelation.

DW is between $4 - $ du and $4 - $ dl, the test is inconclusive.

DW is between $4 - $ dl and 4, there is negative autocorrelation.

As reported previously in Table 3–4 and equation 3–13, the calculated DW for the Big City Bookstore example is:

$$n = 12, k - 1 = 1$$
$$/$$

Calculated DW $= 1.13676$

This calculated DW should be compared to that of Appendix Table G, where as mentioned, dl and du are based on n, the number of observations, and $k - 1$, the number of independent variables (remember that $k = $ number of coefficients in the relationship including the constant; thus, there are $k - 1$ independent variables). Unfortunately, Table G, as originally developed by Durbin-Watson has a minimum n of only 15. Thus, we cannot find the exact statistics with which to compare our results, and as discussed below, the results of samples as small as 12 or even 15 observations can be very unreliable. Nonetheless, we do have some basis of comparison (even if we didn't, we still want to illustrate the test). Consider the first three entries in this table as reproduced below; these provide some guidelines on the values to use. As shown, du and dl are both declining; thus, we will use the dl and du of $n = 15$ for this test.

n	dl	du
15	1.08	1.36
16	1.10	1.37
17	1.13	1.38

(One independent variable)

For discussion purposes, assuming that $n = 15$; then the following conclusion results: DW $= 1.13676$ is between dl $= 1.08$ and du $= 1.36$. Therefore, the result is inconclusive. We have not shown the residuals to have a statistically significant positive autocorrelation. In this analysis, plots of the residuals and the simple t-test on the first-order ACF from the appendix of Chapter 2 were also inconclusive.

The DW statistic, as many statistical tests, is accurate only with large samples. When small samples are used with statistical tests such as the DW, the results are very often unreliable because of the large variances of small samples. Finally, note that the DW test is only designed to detect first-order autocorrelations. The statistical tests of autocorrelation functions developed in Chapter 2 should be used to test for significant autocorrelations at other lags, and as mentioned, these are only reliable for reasonably large sample sizes.

The DW-statistic is not an accurate test when the relationship includes a lagged dependent variable Y_{t-1} as an independent variable. In that case, the recommended test is the Durbin *h*-test, which is presented in Pindyck and Rubinfeld (1991, p. 148).

Sampling and Regression Analysis

The matched pairs of *X*s and *Y*s used in regression are normally not a census but instead are samples from a larger population. That is, the estimated regression line is only one of many lines that might result from different samples drawn from the same population. Thus, the regression coefficients and therefore the regression line are subject to sampling error. This brings up the questions of how much error is there in the sample and the estimated regression line?

Fortunately, it is possible to generate probability intervals of the "true" population regression line based on the sample regression coefficients. An estimate of the error in a regression relationship is based on the sampling error associated with the estimates of *a* and *b*. Figure 3–9 illustrates four hypothetical different sample lines for the Big City Bookstore. As shown, the sample regression lines have slightly different constants and slopes. The net effect of errors in estimating the constant and slope is the hourglass shape about $\overline{X}$ and $\overline{Y}$. As you note, the potential error in the sample regression lines gets greater for *X* values further away from $\overline{X}$. Fortunately, we can estimate interval profiles of these errors using two new concepts, the standard error of regression (S_r) and the standard error of forecast (S_f).

FIGURE 3–9

Four sample regression lines with errors (Big City Bookstore)

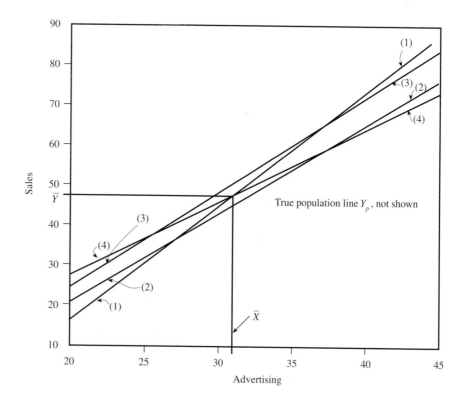

***Confidence and
Prediction Intervals***

Two intervals are useful for diagnosing and using regression models:

1. Confidence intervals for the true population regression line using the **standard error of the regression line (S_r).**
2. Prediction intervals for an individual forecast using the **standard error of forecast (S_f).**

These are illustrated in Figure 3–10 using 95 percent confidence intervals.

***Standard Error of
the Regression
Line (S_r)***

A regression line varies from the true regression line not only in its slope but also in its constant. The standard error of the regression line (S_r), for any value of X includes the standard errors of the constant and the slope b, S_b. This yields the following formula:

$$S_r = S_{yx} \sqrt{\frac{1}{n} + \frac{(X - \overline{X})^2}{\Sigma(X_i - \overline{X})^2}} \qquad (3\text{–}22)$$

Applying this to the Big City example, $S_{yx} = 5.039$, $n = 12$, $X = 20$, $\overline{X} = 31$, and $\Sigma(X_i - 31)^2 = 646$. Therefore,

$$S_r = 5.039 \sqrt{\frac{1}{12} + \frac{(20 - 31)^2}{646}} = 5.039 \sqrt{.2708} = 2.622$$

The S_r is not constant and is smallest at $\overline{X}$ and increases when moving away from $\overline{X}$. S_r values are shown in Table 3–5, column 4, for several values of advertising X.

The 95 percent confidence interval for the regression line when $n = 12$ is $\hat{Y} \pm 2.23 S_r$, as shown in Figure 3–10. The chances are 95 out of 100, therefore, that future values and the true regression line for the population fall within these limits.

FIGURE 3–10

*95% Confidence and
prediction intervals for
Big City Bookstore*

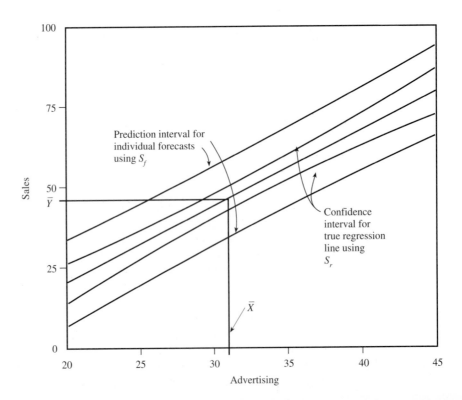

TABLE 3–5   Standard Error of Regression Line (S_r) and Individual Forecast (S_f)

				Line (S_r)			Individual (S_f)	
				Lower 95%	Upper 95%		Lower 95%	Upper 95%
X	Y	$\hat{Y}$	S_r	$\hat{Y} - 2.23S_r$	$Y + 2.23S_r$	S_f	$\hat{Y} - 2.23S_f$	$\hat{Y} + 2.23S_f$
20	27	22.58	2.622	16.7433	28.4260	5.680	9.9276	35.2416
20	23	22.58	2.622	16.7433	28.4260	5.680	9.9276	35.2416
25	31	33.99	1.879	29.7984	38.1727	5.378	22.0018	45.9693
28	45	40.83	1.572	37.3243	44.3280	5.279	29.0643	52.5879
28	42	40.83	1.572	37.3243	44.3280	5.279	29.0643	52.5879
29	47	43.11	1.508	39.7467	46.4659	5.260	31.3860	54.8266
31	39	47.67	1.455	44.4253	50.9080	5.245	35.9797	59.3536
34	45	54.51	1.572	51.0054	58.0091	5.279	42.7454	66.2691
35	57	56.79	1.657	53.0956	60.4792	5.304	44.9676	68.6072
36	59	59.07	1.760	55.1451	62.9900	5.338	47.1738	70.9614
41	73	70.47	2.459	64.9892	75.9479	5.607	57.9745	82.9626
45	84	79.59	3.134	72.6065	86.5720	5.934	66.3667	92.8119

Note: X values are in ascending order, not ordered in time.

Standard Error of Forecast (S_f)

It is important for a forecast to yield point and interval estimates. For example, assume we want to forecast the sales, Y, for an advertising expenditure, X, of 84. While the standard error of the regression line measures the error in the fitted regression line, it does not measure the scatter of *individual* observations, Y, about that true regression line (e.g., at X of 84). That is, to generate interval estimates we need to know how an individual Y-value might deviate from the true line. The standard error of forecast, S_f, measures the scatter of individual actuals about the sample regression line. That is, the standard error of forecast, S_f, is the estimated error when making a forecast of Y given the value of the independent variable, X:

$$S_f = \sqrt{S_{yx}^2 + S_y^2} \tag{3–23}$$

For the Big City Bookstore example when $X = 20$, the standard error of forecast is

$$S_f = \sqrt{5.039^2 + 2.622^2} = 5.680$$

Substituting the formula for the S_r, S_f becomes

$$S_f = S_{yx}\sqrt{1 + 1/n + (X - \overline{X})^2/\Sigma(X_i - \overline{X})^2} \tag{3–24}$$

This formula simply adds 1 under the radical of S_r.

The standard errors of forecast S_f for the 12 advertising expenditures (X) are given in Table 3–5, column 7.

If the calculations for the forecast errors are based on a large sample, and if the values are approximately normally distributed about the regression line, the chances are about 95 percent that a new observation (Y) equals $\hat{Y} \pm 1.96 S_f$.

In the present example, however, with a sample size of only 12, the 95 percent prediction interval for a new observation is based on the t-distribution and is $\hat{Y} \pm 2.23 S_f$. This interval is shown in Table 3–5. The chances are 95 out of 100 that an advertising expenditure will achieve sales within these limits.

Certain characteristics of Table 3–5 should be carefully observed. As is true for confidence intervals, the boundaries of the prediction intervals are curved. The further the X-value gets from its mean, the greater the interval width. This fact confirms the danger of extrapolating Y for values of X that are far from $\overline{X}$.

The standard error of forecast is useful not only for prediction but also for control. If an observation falls outside the S_f confidence limits, this may indicate that the model or observation is "out of control" and should be investigated. As a control chart, Table 3–5 and Figure 3–10 serve much the same purpose as a statistical quality control chart. In the present example, the manager can not only predict that an advertising expenditure of 84 achieves sales between 66.37 and 92.81 (with a 95 percent probability), but she can use these points as control limits; the chart warns the manager when to investigate high or low sales. For example, when advertising is 45, if sales fall below 66.37, it may be that the model is no longer valid or something unusual has happened to sales in that year.

Review of Regression Analysis Steps

In summary, these are the steps to follow in performing a simple linear regression, normally done by computer.

1. Determine the dependent and independent variables. Theory should indicate what independent variables should be included and the functional form of that relationship. We should consider all causal influences on the dependent variable.
2. Develop scatter plots of Xs and Y. Determine if the relationships appear to be linear or nonlinear. Transform the variables if nonlinearities are present (see section below concerning nonlinearities).
3. Compute the regression equation.
4. Compute standard errors of estimates S_{yx} and regression coefficients S_b. These provide measures of the fit of the data to the regression line.
5. Compute the adjusted coefficient of determination, $\overline{R}^2$. This measures the variance of Y that is eliminated by the relationship with X.
6. Perform a hypothesis test using the t-statistic of b/S_b to confirm that Y and X are significantly related.
7. Interpret the significance of the relationship, practically and theoretically, using F-test, $\overline{R}^2$, S_{yx}, S_b, and DW.
8. Using plots and appropriate statistics determine if the six assumptions of regression are valid. Check and correct for:
   - Appropriateness of linear or nonlinear relationship.
   - Homogeneity of errors (more on this in Chapter 10).
   - Serial or autocorrelations errors (more in Chapter 10).
   - Normality of errors (more in Chapter 10).
   - Multicollinearity and misspecification errors (more in Chapters 10 and 11).
9. Generate confidence and prediction intervals using S_f and S_r and interpret.
10. Interpret the practical, intuitive, and theoretical validity and significance of the relationship.

Cause and Effect   In the case of the Big City Bookstore, a scatter plot showed that the two variables had a positive linear relationship. This was confirmed by the standard error of the estimate, $\overline{R}^2$ and the F- and t-tests. We may be tempted to state that there is a definite cause-and-effect relationship between advertising and sales; in other words, an increase in advertising expenditures will lead to an increase in sales. Although this seems logical, it is a mistake to assume that it is a true cause-and-effect relationship without further analyzing the relationship. Other factors that influence sales may have occurred during this time. We expect a causal relationship between sales and advertising, but statistical significance is not sufficient to prove this. However, statistical significance is necessary to detect causality. We suggest a review of the cause-and-effect considerations in Chapter 2. In addition, we explore causality further in Chapters 10 and 11.

Nonlinear Models Using Linear Regression

Linear regression methods are versatile and can model many different types of **nonlinear relationships.** By using logarithms and other transformations of variables, many, but not all nonlinear functions can be modeled. When transformations cannot be used to make a nonlinear relationship linear, then nonlinear regression methods must be employed. Fortunately, many nonlinear relationships can be made linear, some of which are shown in Figure 3–11.

FIGURE 3–11
Nonlinear relationships

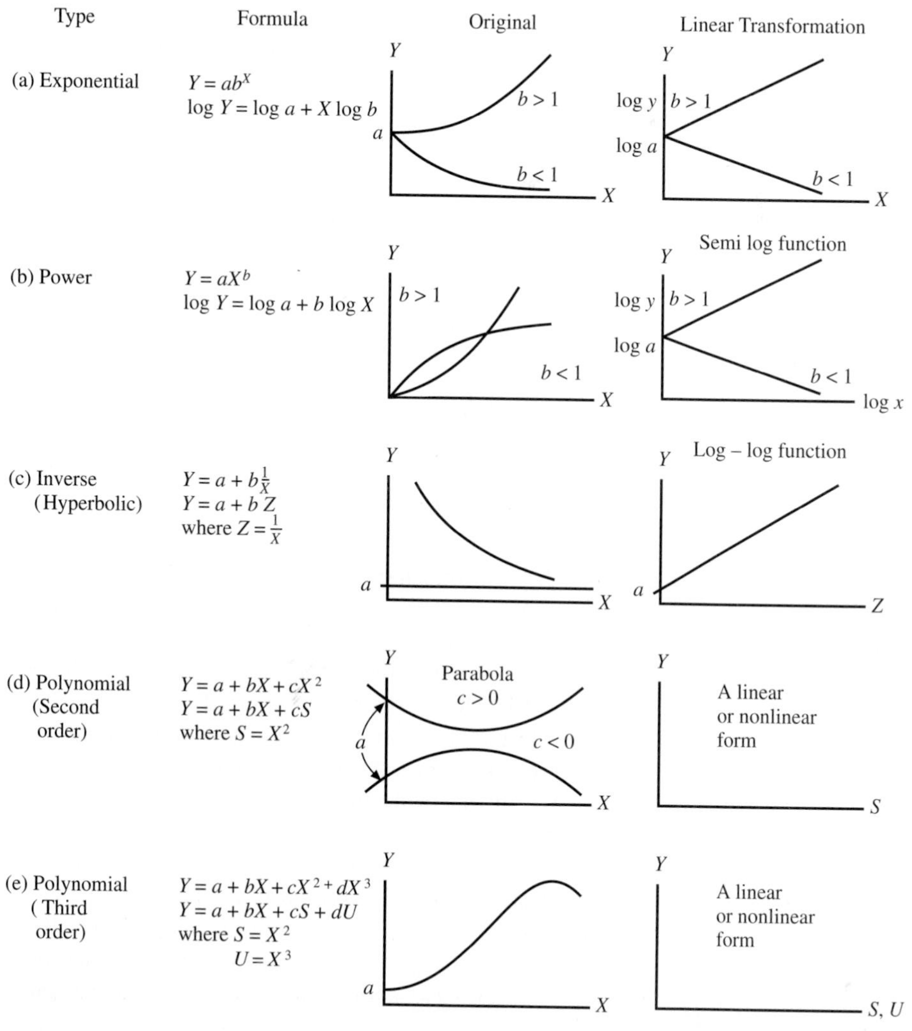
Type
Formula
Original
Linear Transformation
(a) Exponential
Y = ab^X
log Y = log a + X log b
b > 1
b < 1
log y
log a
(b) Power
Y = aX^b
log Y = log a + b log X
Semi log function
log x
(c) Inverse (Hyperbolic)
Y = a + b(1/X)
Y = a + bZ
where Z = 1/X
Log – log function
(d) Polynomial (Second order)
Y = a + bX + cX²
Y = a + bX + cS
where S = X²
Parabola
c > 0
c < 0
A linear or nonlinear form
(e) Polynomial (Third order)
Y = a + bX + cX² + dX³
Y = a + bX + cS + dU
where S = X²
U = X³
S, U

To apply linear regression to nonlinear relationships, the independent or dependent variables must first be transformed to yield a linear relationship. Consider equations 3–25 through 3–29 and Figure 3–11; also, remember that throughout this book, the term *log* denotes the process of taking a natural logarithm.

Exponential form:	$Y = ab^X$	(3–25)
Linear form:	$\log Y = \log a + X \log b$	(3–25a)

Power form:	$Y = aX^b$	(3–26)
Linear form log:	$Y = \log a + b \log X$	(3–26a)

Inverse form:	$Y = a + b(1/X)$	(3–27)
Linear form:	$Y = a + bZ$ where $Z = 1/X$	(3–27a)

Polynomial form:	$Y = a + bX + cX^2$	(3–28)
Linear form:	$Y = a + bX + cS$ where $S = X^2$	(3–28a)

Polynomial form:	$Y = a + bX + cX^2 + dX^3$	(3–29)
Linear form:	$Y = a + bX + cS + dU$ where $S = X^2, U = X^3$	(3–29a)

Remembering that the addition of logs is the equivalent of multiplication and the multiplication of logs is the equivalent of exponentiation, then equations 3–25 and 3–26 are much more easily interpreted. Also, remember that to convert logarithms back to original variables, the following transformations are performed:

$$e^{\log X} = X$$
$$e^{\log Y} = Y$$

Equation 3–25 is transformed to a linear relationship by taking logarithms of Y and regressing those versus X as shown in equation 3–25a. The estimated coefficients a and b can be used in either form of the equation where the appropriate transformations are made to the variables. The power function of equation 3–26 is fitted linearly by taking logs of both Y and X. Inverse relationships between variables are easily modeled by simply creating a new variable as shown in equation 3–27a. Also, the polynomial relationships of equations 3–28 and 3–29 and Figure 3–11d and e are only two of many possible polynomials. A polynomial can include as many powers of the independent variable as are necessary to model the nonlinear relationship. However, it is rare in business to have powers above 3 (e.g., X^3).

Cautions in Using Nonlinear Relationships

Although linear transformations of nonlinear relationships are a very effective use of linear regression analysis, we must be very cautious in using them. As always, there should be an underlying theory that supports the use of nonlinear functions. Second, we should be sure that the relationship is valid over all possible values of the independent variable. That is, the relationships of Figure 3–11 can behave strangely in the extremes. Most nonlinear relationships have turning points where positive slopes become negative or vice versa. Also, even more dramatic are the nonlinearities that result in explosive growths or declines from very slight increases or decreases in the independent variable. Such behavior is rarely expected in the real world; however, all the relationships in Figure 3–11 can yield indefensible results depending on the range of the independent variable. Such erroneous results erode the credibility of the model and the analyst, with the possibility that both the model and analyst may be discarded. Always explore the sensitivity of nonlinear relationships to the possible extremes of the independent variables. Let's apply these concepts to an example.

Nonlinear Example: Cell Phone Sales.   Consider the annual sales for cellular mobile telephones of a midwestern city in Table 3–6 and Figure 3–12a. As shown, the sales of this product have grown dramatically over the last 10 years. The patterns of Figures 3–12a and b are nonlinear; however, in c a linear relationship has been obtained by transforming both Y and X using natural logarithms. There are several possible ways to fit the relationships of Figure 3–12, including the following models:

$$Y_t = a + bX_t + cX_t^2 + e_t \qquad (3\text{–}12a)$$

$$\log(Y_t) = a + bX_t + cX_t^2 + e_t \qquad (3\text{–}12b)$$

$$\log(Y_t) = a + b\log(X_t) + e_t \qquad (3\text{–}12c)$$

TABLE 3–6   Sales of Cellular Mobile Telephones (Y) versus Time (X) CELLFONE.DAT

Year	Y	X	LOG(Y)	LOG(X)
1	148	1.0	5.000	.000
2	1,487	2.0	7.079	.693
3	3,807	3.0	8.296	1.099
4	10,498	4.0	9.159	1.386
5	17,551	5.0	9.828	1.609
6	34,057	6.0	10.375	1.792
7	48,905	7.0	10.838	1.946
8	76,987	8.0	11.238	2.079
9	109,193	9.0	11.592	2.197
10	147,413	10.0	11.908	2.303

FIGURE 3–12

Nonlinear cell phone sales

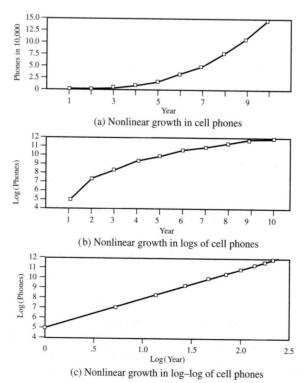

(a) Nonlinear growth in cell phones

(b) Nonlinear growth in logs of cell phones

(c) Nonlinear growth in log–log of cell phones

Clipping the Cost of MIPS

As users of computing power over four decades, we remain surprised at the continuing decline in the costs and increase in speed of computers. An overall statistic used to measure the speed of computers is the millions of instructions per second (MIPS), the speed at which computers perform additions and other functions. Consider the following speeds and costs of computer hardware.

An extrapolation of these performance and cost improvements yields extraordinary increases in computing and analytical capabilities. As shown below, each 10 years has resulted in about 100- to 1,000-fold decrease in computing costs; a computer of 10 years ago costs about 100 times that of a comparable computer today. This data is given in MIPS.DAT.

t		IPS	Price	$/IPS	
1	1964 IBM 7030	30,000	$3,600,000*	$120 =	$1.2 \times 10^{+2}$
12	1975 IBM Mainframe	10,000,000	10,000,000	1 =	$1 \times 10^{+0}$
13	1976 Cray I	160,000,000	20,000,000	.125 =	1.25×10^{-1}
15	1979 Digital VAX	1,000,000	200,000	.20 =	2.0×10^{-1}
18	1981 IBM PC	250,000	3,000	.012 =	1.2×10^{-2}
21	1984 SUN Microsystems-2	1,000,000	10,000	.01 =	1.0×10^{-2}
31	1994 Pentium-chip PC	66,000,000	3,000	.000045 =	4.5×10^{-5}
32	1995 Sony PCX-game	500,000,000	500	.00001 =	1.0×10^{-5}
32	1995 Microunity step-top box	1,000,000,000	500	.0000005 =	$5. \times 10^{-7}$

* Early computers were most often rented, not purchased; this is an annual rental price.

Table 3–7 shows the fit of the last equation, the log-log model of Figure 3–12c. As shown in Table 3–7, the log-log model fits the data very well, having a high $\overline{R}^2$ and extremely high t-statistics for each of the variables. Although the DW-statistic is high, denoting possible negative serial correlation, the sample size of this example is so low and the fit (i.e., $\overline{R}^2$ and t-values) are so high that we accept this model. However, we should be cautious in using this model because of its rapid growth. Considerations external to the fitted model should confirm the nonlinear growth of future years. Let's calculate those growths.

$$\log(\hat{Y}_t) = a + b\log(X_t)$$
$$\log(\hat{Y}_{11}) = 5.0778 + 2.9651\log(11)$$
$$= 5.0778 + 2.965 \cdot 2.39790 = 12.188$$
$$\hat{Y}_{11} = \exp(12.188) = 196,399.2$$
$$\log(\hat{Y}_{12}) = 5.0778 + 2.9651\log(12)$$
$$= 5.0778 + 2.9651 \cdot 2.48491 = 12.446$$
$$\hat{Y}_{12} = \exp(12.446) = 254,207.4$$

Table 3–8 illustrates the predicted growth of sales for cell phones for years 11 through 20. As the previous section admonished us, we should be cautious in naively extrapolating nonlinear relationships. Interestingly, the growth in cell phones continues throughout the United States, and these projections may or may not be very realistic for this midwestern city depending on its population; Chapter 15 explores this further.

TABLE 3–7   Log-Log Relationship for Cell Phone Sales

Dependent variable $\log(Y_t)$—estimation by least squares
Usable observations   10   Degrees of freedom   8
Adjusted R-square $\bar{R}^2$ .9984
Standard error of dependent variables   2.1750
Standard error of estimate   .0864
Sum of squared residuals   .0597
Regression $F(1, 8)$ 5693.532
Significance level of F .00000000
Durbin-Watson statistic   3.475

Coeff.	Estimate	Standard Error	T-Statistic	Significance
1. Constant	$a = 5.0778$	.06534	77.709	.00000000
2. $\log(X_t)$	$b = 2.9651$	.03930	75.455	.00000000

TABLE 3–8   Forecasted Cell Phone Sales

Year	$\log(\hat{Y}_t)$	$\exp(\log(\hat{Y}_t)) = \hat{Y}_t$
11	12.188	196,399.2
12	12.446	254,207.4
13	12.683	322,301.7
14	12.903	401,508.3
15	13.108	492,651.3
16	13.299	596,552.5
17	13.479	714,031.9
18	13.648	845,907.7
19	13.808	992,996.3
20	13.961	1,156,112.9

Regression Advantages and Disadvantages

The advantages of regression analysis include the ability to relate a single dependent variable to one or more independent variables. Its ability to find potentially causal relationships that not only predict but explain the dependent variable makes it a very powerful technique. Its many error and diagnostic statistics help in judging the validity of the relationships. Being widely and easily applied on computers, it is used heavily in sales forecasting.

The biggest disadvantage of regression methods in forecasting is that in order to forecast Y, future values of the independent variable must be known. Thus, multiple forecasts are needed to apply regression analysis. To the extent that the independent variables influence the dependent variables in later time periods (e.g., $Y_t = f(X_{t-2})$), this problem is lessened. Finally, although it is possible to fit causal models using regression analysis, it is very difficult to confirm that a true causal model has been identified. We discuss these matters further in Chapters 10, 11, and 13, where multiple linear regression, econometric, multi-equation econometric, and multivariate autoregressive integrated moving-average (MARIMA) methods are discussed.

Summary

This chapter has introduced statistical regression concepts that are the foundation of most forecasting methods in this book. These concepts include ordinary least squares regression analysis, coefficient statistical significance t-tests, analysis of variance statistical significance F-tests, and the Durbin-Watson statistic. In addition, we developed the several assumptions of ordinary least squares that apply to residual analysis. These statistics and concepts are important parts of sound statistical forecasting models. As developed here, it is normally much easier to fit good predictive models than to develop and validate good causal models. We develop the conceptual and methodological rigor needed for causal modeling in Chapters 10 and 11. However, after mastering the concepts of this chapter, you have statistical tools with which to start building powerful models of dependent variables.

The Appendix to this chapter introduces the concept of cross-correlations in time series data. Also discussed are problems in mutual causality. A study of this section is valuable before applying regression in time series analysis. Also, it is an essential topic before studying Chapters 10 through 16.

Key Terms

ANOVA	normal equations
adjusted $\overline{R}^2$	population regression line (Y_p)
adjusted coefficient of determination $(\overline{R}^2)$	positive linear relationship
dependent variable (Y_t)	predictor variable
Durbin-Watson statistic (DW)	regression analysis
exogenous variable	residual error
F-test	residual standard error (RSE)
fitted residual	serial correlation
fitted value	slope coefficient (b)
forecast error	standard error of estimate (SEE)
forecasted (predicted) value	standard error of forecast (S_f)
homoscedasticity and heteroscedasticity	standard error of regression (S_r)
independent variable (X_t)	standard error of regression coefficient (S_b)
method of least squared deviations	total, explained, and unexplained variance
negative linear relationship	unadjusted R^2
nonlinear relationships	Y-intercept (a)

Key Formulas

Functional relationship:

$$Y = f(C,A,O,P) \tag{3–1}$$

Nonlinear relationships:

$$\hat{Y} = a + bX + cX^2 \tag{3–2}$$

Method of least squared deviations:

$$\Sigma e = \Sigma(Y_i - \hat{Y}) = .0 \qquad \text{and}$$

$$\Sigma e^2 = \Sigma(Y_i - \hat{Y})^2 = \text{minimum value}$$

$\Big\}$ > Criteria of best fit

Actuals:

$$Y = a + bX + e \tag{3-3}$$

Fit and forecast:

$$\hat{Y} = a + bX \tag{3-4}$$

Errors:

$$e = Y - \hat{Y} \tag{3-5}$$

Minimum squared errors:

$$\text{MIN}[\Sigma(Y_i - \hat{Y}_i)^2] = \text{MIN}[\Sigma(Y_i - a - bX_i)^2] \tag{3-6}$$

Normal equations for least squares:

$$a = \overline{Y} + b\overline{X} \tag{3-7}$$

and

$$b = \frac{\Sigma X_i Y_i - n\overline{X}\,\overline{Y}}{\Sigma(X_i^2) - nX_i^2} = \frac{\Sigma(X_i - \overline{X})(Y_i - \overline{Y})}{\Sigma(X_i - \overline{X})2} \tag{3-8}$$

Typical regression output:

$$
\begin{aligned}
\hat{Y} = -23.02 &+ 2.280X \quad \text{(coefficients)}\\
6.32 &\qquad .198 \quad \text{(standard errors)}\\
(-3.64) &\quad (11.5) \qquad \text{(t-values)}
\end{aligned}
\tag{3-13}
$$

$$S_{yx} = 5.039 \qquad R^2 = .923 \qquad n = 12 \qquad F = 132.2573 \qquad DW = 1.13676$$

Standard error of estimate (S_{yx}):

$$S_{yx} = \sqrt{\frac{\Sigma(Y_i - \hat{Y})^2}{n - k}} = \sqrt{\frac{\Sigma e_i^2}{12 - 2}} = 5.039 \tag{3-14}$$

Adjusted coefficient of determination ($\overline{R}^2$):

$$
\begin{aligned}
\text{Total variance} &= \text{Explained variance} + \text{Unexplained variance}\\
S_y^2 &= \text{Explained variance} + S_{yx}^2\\
\overline{R}^2 &= \frac{\text{Total} - \text{Unexplained}}{\text{Total variance}} = 1 - \frac{\text{Unexplained variance}}{\text{Total variance}}
\end{aligned}
$$

For Big City Bookstore:

$$\overline{R}^2 = 1 - \frac{S_{yx}^2}{S_y^2} = 1 - \frac{5.039^2}{18.122^2} = 1 - \frac{25.392}{328.33} = .923 \tag{3-15}$$

In terms of sums of squares:

$$\overline{R}^2 = 1 - \frac{\dfrac{\Sigma(Y_i - \hat{Y})^2}{n - k}}{\dfrac{\Sigma(Y_i - \overline{Y})^2}{n - 1}} = 1 - \frac{\dfrac{253.92}{12 - 2}}{\dfrac{3611.63}{12 - 1}} = .923 \tag{3-16}$$

$$\text{Unadjusted } R^2 = 1 - \frac{\Sigma(Y_i - \hat{Y})^2}{\Sigma(Y_i - \overline{Y})^2} = 1 - \frac{253.92}{3612.667} = .9297$$

Testing the significance of regression coefficients:

$$t = \frac{b - 0}{S_b} = \frac{2.2802}{.198} = 11.5 \tag{3-17}$$

$$S_b = \frac{S_{yx}}{\sqrt{\Sigma(X_i - \overline{X})^2}} \tag{3-18}$$

Analysis of variance in regression analysis
Total Variation = Explained variation + Unexplained variation

$$\Sigma(Y_i - \overline{Y})^2 = \Sigma(\hat{Y}_i - \overline{Y})^2 + \Sigma(Y_i - \hat{Y}_i)^2$$

ANOVA notation commonly used:

$$\text{TSS}/(n - 1) = \text{Total variance}$$
$$\text{RSS}/(k - 1) = \text{Explained variance} = \text{Mean squared regression} = \text{MSR}$$
$$\text{ESS}/(n - k) = \text{Unexplained variance} = \text{Mean squared error} = \text{MSE}$$

Testing the overall relationship of the *F*-test of ANOVA:
     The statistical test is

$$F_{k-1,\,n-k} = \frac{\text{RSS}/(k - 1)}{\text{ESS}/(n - k)} = \frac{\Sigma(\hat{Y}_i - \overline{Y})^2/(k - 1)}{\Sigma(Y_i - \hat{Y}_i)^2/(n - k)} \tag{3-19}$$

Null hypothesis: There is no statistically significant relationship.

$$\text{If } F_{k-1,\,n-k}(\text{calc.}) \leq F_{k-1,\,n-k,\,\alpha=.05}(\text{table}) \quad \text{Infer true } H_0.$$

Alternative hypothesis: There is a statistically significant relationship.

$$\text{If } F_{k-1,\,n-k}(\text{calc.}) > F_{k-1,\,n-k,\,\alpha=.05}(\text{table}) \quad \text{Infer true } H_1.$$

F-test using R^2:

$$F_{k-1,\,n-k} = \frac{R^2/(k - 1)}{(1 - R^2)/(n - k)} = \frac{.9297/(2 - 1)}{(1 - .9297)/(12 - 2)} = 132.25 \tag{3-20}$$

The true underlying relationship may be expressed in the form:

$$Y_p = A + BX + v$$
$$\hat{Y}_p = A + BX$$

Durbin-Watson statistic for serial correlation:

$$\text{DW} = \frac{\Sigma(e_t - e_{t-1})^2}{\Sigma e_t^2} \tag{3-21}$$

Compare calculated DW to Table DW:

Positive	Inconclusive	No Autocorrelation	Inconclusive	Negative
0	dl	du	4 − du	4 − dl	4

Standard error of the regression line (S_r):

$$S_r = S_{yx} \sqrt{\frac{1}{n} + \frac{(X - \overline{X})^2}{\Sigma(X_i - \overline{X})^2}} \tag{3-22}$$

Standard error of forecasts (S_f):

$$S_f = \sqrt{S_{yx}^2 + S_r^2} \tag{3-23}$$

$$S_f = S_{yx} \sqrt{1 + 1/n + (X_i - \overline{X})^2/\Sigma(X_i - \overline{X})^2} \tag{3-24}$$

Nonlinear relationships:

Exponential form: $Y = ab^X$ (3–25)
  Linear form: $\log Y = \log a + X \log b$ (3–25a)

Power form: $Y = aX^b$ (3–26)
Linear form: $\log Y = \log a + b \log X$ (3–26a)

Inverse form: $Y = a + b(1/X)$ (3–27)
  Linear form: $Y = a + bZ$ where $Z = 1/X$ (3–27a)

Polynomial form: $Y = a + bX + cX^2$ (3–28)
  Linear form: $Y = a + bX + cS$ where $S = X^2$ (3–28a)

Polynomial form: $Y = a + bX + cX^2 + dX^3$ (3–29)
  Linear form: $Y = a + bX + cS + dU$ where $S = X^2$, $U = X^3$ (3–29a)

Review Problems Using Your Software

R3–1 Repeat the least squares regression of equation 3–13 and fully interpret.

R3–2 Repeat the analysis of Table 3–4, and interpret the results in detail as done following Table 3–4.

R3–3 Repeat the significance test on the regression coefficient of equation 3–17 and fully interpret.

R3–4 Repeat the F-test of equation 3–19 through 3–20 and interpret.

R3–5 Calculate the DW statistic for the Big City Bookstore example as in equation 3–21 and perform a statistical significance test and interpret the results.

R3–6 Confirm whether your software calculates the standard error of the regression line (S_r) and the standard error of forecasts (S_f); if so, then repeat the analysis of Table 3–5.

R3–7 Repeat the nonlinear analysis of Tables 3–6 and 3–7 and interpret.

Problems

3–1 What are the three general purposes of regression analysis?

3–2 In common English, describe the method of least squares.

3–3 Choose a product that you purchase and define it as the dependent variable; now define the independent variables that may be useful in explaining sales of this variable.

3–4 Explain the difference between:
  a. Correlation and causality.
  b. Linear and curvilinear relationships.
  c. S_{yx} and S_y.
  d. The regression coefficient and the coefficient of correlation.

3–5 Define the two criteria used to select best-fit linear relationships between Y and X.

3–6 Give a common English definition for the following regression concepts: $\overline{R}^2$, S_{yx}, Durbin-Watson statistic, the t-value of the regression coefficient, and its significance level.

3–7 Define the term $\overline{R}^2$ using explained, unexplained, and total variance.

3–8 Given $Y = 100$, $\hat{Y} = 98$, and $\overline{Y} = 90$, partition these values into explained, unexplained, and total variance.

3–9 If the variance about the regression line (S_{yx}^2) is 10 and the variance of Y (S_y^2) is 100, what is $\overline{R}^2$?

3–10 What is the relationship between the *F*-test and t^2 for bivariate relationship?

3–11 Explain the six assumptions of regression analysis.

3–12 Define serial correlation problems in regression analysis.

3–13 Define the concepts of the standard error of the regression line (S_r) and the standard error of forecast (S_f).

3–14 Explain the problems with proving cause and effect using regression analysis in business and economics.

3–15 Explain the difference between fit and forecast errors.

3–16 Repeat the Big City Bookstore example as illustrated in equation 3–13.
   a. Write out your model; does it agree with those in the text?
   b Explain any differences?
   c. Interpret your model as the book does.

3–17 Explain the following:
   a. How to test the significance of a linear relationship with several independent variables.
   b. How to estimate a 99 percent confidence interval for the regression coefficient for a large sample.
   c. S_f, S_r, and S_{yx}.

3–18 The following are average daily TV viewing and SAT (Scholastic Aptitude Test) scores for 36 years in the U.S. Investigate the relationship between these two (TVSAT.DAT).

Year	1960	1965	1970	1975	1980	1985	1990	1995
TV viewing (Hours)	5.10	5.48	5.93	6.11	6.60	7.11	6.92	7.04
SAT scores	975	969	948	910	890	906	900	899

(Sources: Nielson Media Research and the College Board.)

   a. Graph the relationship of SAT as a function of TV viewing.
   b. Fit a regression relationship between TV viewing and SAT scores.
   c. Fully interpret the results of your analysis.

3–19 The following are the percentage of children on welfare and teen suicide rates over the last 35 years (TEENSUI.DAT).

Year	1960	1965	1970	1975	1980	1985	1990
% of children on welfare	3.5	4.5	8.5	11.8	11.5	11.2	11.9
Suicide rate	3.6	4.0	5.9	7.6	8.5	10.0	11.3

(Sources: Bureau of the Census and National Center for Health Statistics.)

   a. Graph the relationship between these two variables.
   b. Fit a regression relationship.
   c. Fully interpret the results of your analysis.

3–20 The following two series are the violent crime rate in the United States per 100,000 people and median prison sentence for serious violent crimes (CRIMEPRI.DAT).

Year	1960	1965	1970	1975	1980	1985	1990
Crime rate	16.1	20.0	36.4	48.8	59.7	53.3	73.2

Year	1960	1965	1970	1975	1980	1985	1990
Median Prison Sentence	18.5	11.5	9.0	5.5	6.5	8.0	8.1

(Source: F.B.I. and National Center for Policy Analysis.)

   a. Graph this relationship.
   b. Fit a regression relationship.
   c. Fully interpret the results of your analysis.

3–21 A financial analyst wants to develop a model for predicting the relationship between the Japanese stock index and the U.S. stock index, hoping the U.S. index will be useful in predicting the Japanese index. Using the 48 months of matched pairs of indexes in USJAPAN.DAT, estimate this relationship. Comment on the degree of fit between these two variables.

3–22 Using the millions of instructions per second (MIPS.DAT) data from the special interest box of this chapter, estimate the relationship between the MIPS and time and the relationship between MIPS and cost. Interpret your results and forecast values for t equal to 35 to 40. Are these forecasts reasonable? If logarithms are used, be sure to express the MIPS in their original metrics.

3–23 A bank is interested in determining the amount that will be charged on its bankcard as a function of the cardholders' income. It has 50 observations of reported income on bankcard applications and the value of credit card charges for members for a one-year period. This data is given in CREDIT.DAT. Fit a relationship to this data and comment on its validity and usefulness.

3–24 Fifty months ago, a firm implemented a total quality management program and is interested in seeing if its market share has increased because of this program. The file TQM.DAT contains two variables; the first is the dependent variable market share, and the second is a variable denoting the percentage of individuals employed by the firm who have been through the TQM program. Estimate the relationship between these two variables and comment on whether the TQM program has had an effect on market share.

3–25 A hospital has surveyed its patients every month for the last 50 months regarding the quality of care they have received. During these 50 months the hospital has been training and educating its health care providers on how to better relate to patients and their families. The file CQI.DAT (continuous quality improvement) contains 50 monthly observations on the percentage of patients who are very pleased with their care and the dollars spent on training and quality awareness in the hospital. Estimate the relationship explaining satisfaction with the care provided and the amount spent on quality training and awareness. Comment on the DW statistic.

3–26 Historically, the level of long-term interest rates in the United States is correlated with the level of the stock market. The file INTMARK.DAT contains 139 monthly observations of yields of long-term AAA corporate bonds with the level of the S & P 500 during that time period. There is considerable evidence that the stock market anticipates the level of interest rates and therefore may be a better predictor of interest rates than vice versa. Analyze the usefulness of changes in the stock market in predicting changes in interest rates.

3–27 Record the daily stock price quotations in *The Wall Street Journal* for one stock and the level of the S & P 500. Fit a regression relationship using the S & P 500 to predict the value of the stock. Comment on the validity and the practical value of this relationship. Is there any lead-lag relationship between these two variables?

3–28 Model the lead-lag relationship of 270 observations of the U.S. leading and lagging economic indicators in LEADLAGG.DAT. Comment on the validity and the practical value of this relationship. Is there any lead-lag relationship between these two variables?

3–29 A direct marketing firm estimates the weight of its mail bags to forecast the number of orders that need to be processed for the day. Thirty days of mail were randomly sampled for the weight of mail bags and the number of orders. The file JUNKMAIL.DAT lists the weight of mail bags in hundreds of pounds and the number of orders in thousands of orders. Using this data, complete the following:
   a. Estimate the relationship between the number of orders and the weight of bags.
   b. What is the error is estimating the slope of this relationship?
   c. If a mail bag weighs 300 pounds, how many orders are expected to be in the mail.
   d. Assuming that values about the regression line are approximately normally distributed, estimate 95 percent prediction limits on the 300-pound prediction of *c*.

Minicases: Common Assignment for Minicases

For one of the continuing minicases—1–1 to 1–10—complete the following: Identify the possible causes of variations in the dependent variable. After some thought, write out an equation such as equation 3–1 that states the possible relationships between the dependent variable as a function of important variables and influences. Be sure to be comprehensive in the identification of important causal influences. Be sure to include an estimate of the importance of these variables by designating these variables as somewhat important (S), important (I), or very important (V). Next, identify the sign of the causality, that is, whether each variable positively (+) or negatively (−) influences the dependent variable and whether that influence is linear (L) or nonlinear (N). Now having defined a comprehensive causal model, identify potential sources of data that measure these causal variables.

References

Bowerman, B.L., and R.T. O'Connell. *Linear Statistical Models: An Applied Approach.* Boston: PWS-Kent, 1990.

Chatterjee, S., and B. Price. *Regression Analysis by Example.* 2d ed. New York: Wiley, 1991.

Draper, N.R., and H. Smith. *Applied Regression Analysis.* 2d ed. New York: Wiley, 1981.

Neter, J., M.H. Kuntner, C.J. Nachtsheim, and W. Wasserman. *Applied Linear Statistical Models.* 4th ed. Burr Ridge IL: Richard D. Irwin, 1996.

Newbold, P. *Statistics for Business and Economics.* 3rd ed. Englewood Cliffs, N.J.: Prentice Hall, 1991.

Pindyck, R.S., and D.L. Rubinfeld, 3rd Edition, New York: McGraw-Hill, 1991

Wiesberg, S. *Applied Linear Regression.* 2d ed. New York: Wiley, 1985.

APPENDIX 3–A

CROSS-CORRELATION COEFFICIENTS

I think and think for months and years. Ninety-nine times, the conclusion is false. The hundredth time I am right.

Albert Einstein

Cross-Correlations

We have studied the concepts of correlation coefficients and autocorrelations in Chapter 2; an extension of these two concepts is the cross-correlation coefficient. The **cross-correlation coefficient** measures the strength of the relationship between Y_t and X_{t-k}, where k is a positive or negative integer representing the lag or lead relationship between these variables. For example, we want to determine if Y_t is related to $X_{t-1}, X_{t-2}, X_{t-3}, \ldots$ and so forth. When there are lag relationships between X_{t-k} and Y_t, lagged values of X_{t-k} provide an effective way to estimate the future values of Y_t. For example, if Y_t is highly associated with X_{t-3}, the value of Y_t can be predicted three periods ahead more accurately than if there had been only a coincident relationship. The cross-correlation coefficient equals:

$$r_{Y_t X_{t-k}} = \frac{\text{COV}(Y_t, X_{t-k})}{S_{Y_t} S_{X_{t-k}}} \tag{3A–1}$$

Let's use a very simple example to demonstrate the meaning of this coefficient. This example is contrived and it is not statistically advisable to use data sets this small; in fact, about 50 matched pairs are recommended.

Table 3A–1 illustrates six weeks of Y and X over time. As shown, Y_t has varied from 16 to 35, and X_t has varied from 2.5 to 7. The coincident matched pairs of Y_t and X_t are in the second and fifth columns of the table. Columns 3, 4, 6, and 7 illustrate lags of $t + 2, t + 1, t - 1$, and $t - 2$, respectively, for X relative to Y. Each lag of a variable results in the loss of one observation as shown by the n.a. in several cells. The notation X_{t-1} denotes that the values of X have been moved *forward* one period relative to Y_t, the notation X_{t+1} denotes that X values have been moved *back* one period relative to t. Finally, a lag of one variable relative to another (e.g., X_{t-2} to Y_t) can be interpreted another way, that is, the other variable (Y_{t+2}) has been made to lead the first variable (X_t). You should confirm each of these concepts in Table 3A–1.

Hypothetical Example using Table 3A–1 Data

A consumer electronics firm believes there is an association between the weekly sales of a product and the level of TV advertising during that week. An analyst collects data concerning weekly product sales, Y_t, and expenditures for TV commercials during the same week, X_t, as shown in Table 3A–1. The analyst calculates the correlation between Y_t and X_t only to be disappointed by the result: $r_{xy} = .3367$. This result is disappointing because product management believes that advertising influences sales more.

In response to the low correlation, someone in product management suggests that TV advertisements appear on weekends and customers do not get to stores until the next week; also, the week in which the expenditure (X_t) is recorded precedes the advertisement by one week. Thus, there should be a two-week lag in the sales. Consequently, the analyst wants to determine the correlation between Y_t and X_{t-2}; to do so, she generates the data in Table 3A–2.

Table 3A–2 illustrates the matched pairs of Y_t and X_{t-2}, showing the loss of two observations. Columns 4 and 5 illustrate the deviation forms of Y and X, and columns 6 and 7 illustrate the squared deviations needed for the standard deviation calculations. Finally, column 8 illustrates the cross-products of deviations needed to calculate cross-covariances. The steps in calculating the cross-correlation coefficient are shown next.

TABLE 3A–1   Lagged Values of k for X_{t-k} on Y_t

$Week_t$	Y_t	X_{t+2}	X_{t+1}	X_t	X_{t-1}	X_{t-2}
1	26	3	6	4	n.a.	n.a.
2	16	7	3	6	4	n.a.
3	18	2.5	7	3	6	4
4	35	3	2.5	7	3	6
5	21	n.a.	3	2.5	7	3
6	29	n.a.	n.a.	3	2.5	7

TABLE 3A–2   Sums of Squares and Covariances for Y and X_{t-2}

Week	Y_t	X_{t-2}	y_t^*	x_{t-2}	y_t^2	x_{t-2}^2	$y_t \cdot x_{t-2}$
1	26	n.a.	.25				
2	16	n.a.	−9.75				
3	18	4	−7.75	−1.00	60.06	1	7.75
4	35	6	9.25	1.00	85.56	1	9.25
5	21	3	−4.75	−2.00	22.56	4	9.50
6	29	7	3.25	2.00	10.56	4	6.50
Mean	25.75	5.00					
Sums and Means for $t = 3$ to $t = 6$					178.75	10	33.00

* Remember, lowercase notation represents deviations from means.

Using the results of Table 3A–2:

$$S_Y = \sqrt{\frac{178.75}{4-1}} = 7.72$$

$$S_X = \sqrt{\frac{10.00}{4-1}} = 1.83$$

$$\text{COV}(Y_t\, X_{t-2}) = \frac{33.00}{4-1} = 11.00$$

$$r_{YtXt-2} = \frac{\text{COV}(Y, X_{t-2})}{S_Y \cdot S_{xt-2}} = \frac{11.00}{1.83 \cdot 7.72} = .7805 \tag{3A–2}$$

As shown by equation 3A–2, the correlation between Y_t and X_{t-2} is considerably greater than that between Y_t and X_t (.7805 > .3367); thus, there appears to be a significant association between the two variables. Consequently, within the limitations of this extremely small sample, there appears to be a two-week lag between advertising and sales.

Pearson Coefficient versus CCF

The coefficients calculated using equation 3A–2 are referred to as Pearson correlation coefficients. Table 3A–3 illustrates five **Pearson cross-correlation coefficients** for the consumer electronics example. As shown, these correlations vary from a high of .7805 for a two-period lag to a low of −.6308 for a one-period lag, that is, for X_{t-2} and X_{t-1} respectively. Statistical software will calculate the Pearson correlation coefficient when a correlation matrix or function is executed. However, when cross-correlations are calculated, another formula is used; in fact, this formula varies somewhat with different software products.

Equation 3A–3 illustrates one of the more popular methods of calculating cross-correlations using what is commonly called a cross-correlation function (CCF). The results of using equation 3A–3 are illustrated in the third row of Table 3A–3. It is common to use the term *CCF* to denote correlations calculated using this equation; and when the Pearson correlation coefficient is used, the term Pearson will be used. The differences between these two formulas are discussed next.

The calculation of cross-correlations is made easier through use of equation 3A–3:

$$\text{CCF}(k) = \frac{\sum_{t=1+k}^{n} (Y_t - \bar{Y})(X_{t-k} - \bar{X})}{\sqrt{\sum_{t=1}^{n}(Y_t - \bar{Y})^2 \sum_{t=1}^{n}(X_t - \bar{X})^2}} \quad k \geq 0 \tag{3A–3}$$

Note: for $k \leq 0$, sum $(Y_{t+k} - \bar{Y})(X_t - \bar{X})$ from $t = 1 - k$ to n in the numerator of Equation 3A–3.)

Table 3A–4 illustrates the calculation of the covariance sums of squares of Y_t and X_{t-2} for use in the numerator of equation 3A–3, and Table 3A–5 illustrates the calculations of the denominator sums of squares. As you might note in equation 3A–3, all observations are used in calculating the deviations of the denominator, not just $n - k$ values as used in the numerator, this is illustrated in Table 3A–4. Also, the means used in the numerator and denominator are means calculated over the full n observations. This is in contrast to the Pearson cross-correlation

TABLE 3A–3   Pearson Product Mommet versus Cross-Correlation Functions

Variables	$Y_t X_{t+2}$	$Y_t X_{t+1}$	$Y_t X_t$	$Y_t X_{t-1}$	$Y_t X_{t-2}$
Pearson	−.5166	−.2939	.3367	−.6308	.7805
CCF	−.4161	−.2806	.3367	−.5970	.5711

of equation 3A–2, where means are recalculated for each lag. Finally, note for equation 3A–3 that neither the numerator nor denominator is adjusted for (divided by) the number of degrees of freedom as was done in the Pearson coefficient. Although these simplifications reduce computation time, they make the CCF less accurate than the Pearson cross-correlation coefficient; the implications of this are discussed next.

Table 3A–5 illustrates the sums of squares used for Y_t and X_t. As mentioned, these sums of squares are not adjusted for degrees of freedom when used in equation 3A–3. Thus, in equation 3A–3, as the number of lags increases so does the difference in the number of observations between the numerator and denominator; this makes the CCF less and less accurate than the Pearson correlation. This effect can be seen in Table 3A–3 when comparing the two measures at extreme lags.

The value of the CCF(2), .5711, is shown in equation 3A–4 and reported in row 3 of Table 3A–3. As shown, it is important to recognize when CCFS are understatements of the Pearson coefficients.

$$\text{CCF}(2) = \frac{\Sigma((Y_t - \overline{Y})(X_{t-k} - \overline{X}))}{\sqrt{\Sigma(X_t - \overline{X})^2 \, \Sigma(Y_t - \overline{Y})^2}} = \frac{37.75}{\sqrt{258.83 \cdot 16.88}} = .5711 \qquad (3A-4)$$

Having studied the concepts of cross-correlation coefficients, consider an application.

Cross-Correlations between U.S. and German Stock Indexes (GERMUS.DAT)

The following is an analysis of the relationship between stock indexes in the United States (variable USIND) and Germany (GERMIND). This example uses autocorrelations and cross-correlations in determining whether there is a statistically significant relationship between these two

---

TABLE 3A–4   Autocovariance Function between Y and X_{t-2}

Week	Y_t	X_{t-2}	y_t	x_{t-2}	$y_t \cdot x_{t-2}$
1	26	n.a.	1.83		
2	16	n.a.	−8.17		
3	18	4	−6.17	−.25	1.54
4	35	6	10.83	1.75	18.96
5	21	3	−3.17	−1.25	3.96
6	29	7	4.83	2.75	13.29
Mean*	24.17	4.25			
Sum from $t = 3$ to $t = 6$			6.32	3.00	37.75

*Mean for $t = 1$ to 6 for both Y_t and X_t as in Table 3A-5

TABLE 3A–5   Sums of Squares for Y and X

Week	Y_t	X_t	y_t	x_t	y_t^2	x_t^2
1	26	4	1.83	−.25	3.36	.0625
2	16	6	−8.17	1.75	66.69	3.0625
3	18	3	−6.17	−1.25	38.03	1.5625
4	35	7	10.83	2.75	117.36	7.5625
5	21	2.5	−3.17	−1.75	10.03	3.0625
6	29	3	4.83	−1.25	23.36	1.5625
Mean	24.17	4.25				
Sum $t = 1$ to $t = 6$			.00	.00	258.83	16.88

indexes. Because a final determination of statistical significance requires concepts that we have not as yet learned, we can not reach a final conclusion until Chapter 11. Nonetheless, we will learn a number of important concepts that provide insights to valid time series modeling.

The profit motive has stimulated a large number of effective and ineffective investment strategies. One that has intrigued investors for some time has been the possibility of taking information about the behavior of one stock exchange as a predictor of the behavior of another located in a different time zone. Figure 3A–1 illustrates a time series plot of U.S. and German stock indexes. There are 271 monthly observations from January 1970 through July 1992. Let's analyze this data using the concepts of auto- and cross-correlations.

In Table 3A–6 and Figure 3A–1 there is an extremely high degree of association between the U.S. and German stock indexes. Figure 3A–2 illustrates a graph of 21 CCFs, 10 prior and 10 after CCF(0). Unfortunately, this high degree of cross-correlation is probably the result of a very high degree of autocorrelation in each variable. That is, because both series are increasing over

---

TABLE 3A–6   Cross-Correlations (CCF) of Series GERMIND(t) and USIND($t - k$) (GERMUS.DAT)

Monthly Data from 1970:01 to 1992:07 $n = $ 271

k

−24:	.7505	.7621	.7699	.7762	.7823	.7900
−18:	.7959	.8031	.8111	.8200	.8294	.8397
−12:	.8490	.8580	.8668	.8729	.8776	.8813
−6:	.8875	.8961	.9056	.9150	.9253	.9355
0:	.9437	.9312	.9159	.8991	.8834	.8672
6:	.8505	.8332	.8173	.8020	.7869	.7720
12:	.7568	.7424	.7288	.7149	.7010	.6878
18:	.6759	.6662	.6572	.6497	.6433	.6361
24:	.6286					

Approximate $2Se_{CCF} = 2/\sqrt{271} = .121$

TABLE 3A–7   ACF(k) of Series USIND for $k = 1$ to 30

1:	.9849	.9685	.9513	.9352	.9191	.9025
7:	.8853	.8708	.8569	.8428	.8285	.8136
13:	.7998	.7861	.7723	.7587	.7459	.7342
19:	.7257	.7169	.7097	.7034	.6961	.6877
25:	.6763	.6643	.6527	.6415	.6296	.6182

Approximate $2Se_{ACF} = 2/\sqrt{271} = .121$

TABLE 3A–8   ACF(k) of Series GERMIND for $k = 1$ to 30

1:	.9882	.9715	.9537	.9359	.9183	.9022
7:	.8886	.8768	.8648	.8522	.8369	.8207
13:	.8045	.7887	.7738	.7590	.7454	.7334
19:	.7212	.7090	.6987	.6890	.6792	.6666
25:	.6510	.6372	.6249	.6132	.6028	.5933

Approximate $2Se_{ACF} = 2/\sqrt{271} = .121$

FIGURE 3A–1

U.S. versus German stock indexes (GERMUS.DAT)

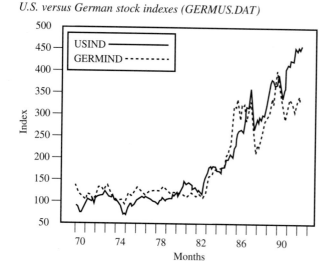

FIGURE 3A–2

CCF(k) of German and U.S. stock indexes—
$2Se(CCF(k)) = 2/\sqrt{271}$

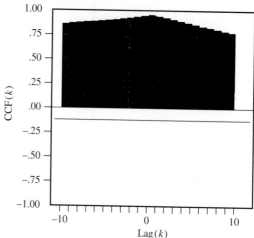

time, there is a built-in cross-correlation between the variables; the autocorrelations *within* each series make it appear that there is cross-correlation *between* the series. This is a very common situation that disappoints many analysts who anticipate extraordinary profits when having been misled by the spurious nature of the high cross-correlations.

It is very difficult to measure the degree of cross-correlation between two variables when there is extremely high autocorrelation within each variable. The most effective solution to this problem is to remove the autocorrelation of each series while not disturbing the cross-correlation between the pair, a procedure illustrated next.

Tables 3A–7 and 3A–8 illustrate the autocorrelations of the U.S. (USIND) and the German (GERMIND) indexes, respectively. As shown, each series has a very high degree of autocorrelation within it. Thus, we cannot interpret the cross-correlations of Table 3A–6 as reflecting only between-correlations, but also the high degrees of autocorrelation.

To measure the strength of the relationship between these stock indexes, first remove all of the autocorrelation in each and then cross-correlate that which remains. If the identical method of removing autocorrelations is applied to each variable, the between cross-correlations are preserved. A common first step in this process when the time series have trends or random walks is to take first differences of each series. First differences yield a series that represents changes from one period to the next:

$$dY_t = \text{GERMIND}_t - \text{GERMIND}_{t-1} \tag{3A–5}$$
$$dX_t = \text{USIND}_t - \text{USIND}_{t-1} \tag{3A–6}$$

If two variables are correlated over time, then logically so should be their incremental changes from period to period. By removing the autocorrelation with first differences of each variable, the cross-correlations still exist between the variables.

Figure 3A–3 illustrates a graph of first differences for dY_t and dX_t. As shown there, these series no longer have the trends or random walks seen in Figure 3A–1. Let's calculate the autocorrelations of these two new series.

Table 3A–9 and 3A–10 illustrate the ACFs for the differenced series of dY and dX respectively. As shown, almost all autocorrelations of the series have been removed. Let's now calculate the cross-correlations between dY_t and dX_{t-k}.

Tables 3A–11 and Figure 3A–4 illustrate the cross-correlations between the first differences of the German and U.S. stock indexes. As shown, the CCFs are very low. The coincident cross-correlation between the two series is .4944, and the lagged cross-correlation, CCF(1), is

Figure 3A–3

First differences of U.S. and German indexes— dY = German Index: dX = U.S. Index

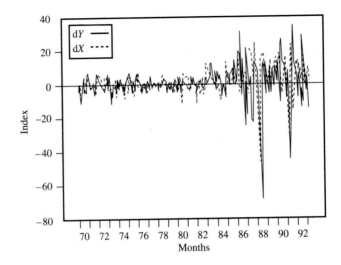

Figure 3A–4

CCF(k) of dY(t) = d(German), dX(t − k) = d(U.S.), 2Se(CCF(k)) ≈ 2/(270).⁵

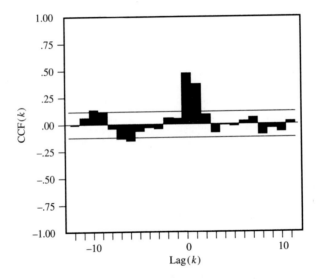

.3913. These correlations are between dY_t, the German stock index, and dX_{t-k}, the U.S. stock index. Thus, while there is some cross-correlation in the indexes that might be statistically significant, it is not nearly as high as before. The relationship between dY_t and dX_t may present some opportunity for predicting the German stock index as a function of the US.

Statistical Significance of Cross-Correlations

We have developed the concept of statistical significance tests for the Pearson correlation coefficient in equation 2–18. This significance test can be applied to the cross-correlation function when these coefficients are calculated using the Pearson formulas. However, when using CCF formulas, there is a simpler approximation formula. This *t*-test is based on the **standard error of the CCF.** For two series with no cross-correlations (i.e., the true cross-correlations are zero) the CCF can be expected to vary about zero with a standard error of approximately $(n)^{-.5}$. That is,

$$\text{Se}_{\text{CCF}} = \frac{1}{\sqrt{(n)}}$$

(3A–7)

TABLE 3A–9   ACF(k)s of dY for $k = 1$ to 24

Monthly Data from 1970:02 to 1992:07 $n = 270$

1:	.3047	.1095	.0246	−.0414	−.0980	−.1510
7:	−.0632	−.0699	.0310	.1195	.0850	−.0100
13:	−.0826	−.0078	−.0017	−.0498	−.0633	.1392
19:	−.1173	−.1296	−.0915	−.0671	.0102	−.0204

Approximate $2S_{ACF} = 2/\sqrt{270} = .122$

TABLE 3A–10   ACF(k)s of dX for $k = 1$ to 24

Monthly Data from 1970:02 to 1992:07 $n = 270$

1:	.3199	.0077	−.1144	−.0866	−.0266	.0081
7:	−.0249	−.0764	−.0129	.0163	.0973	−.0612
13:	−.0033	.0171	−.0651	−.0628	−.0565	.0026
19:	−.0490	−.0684	−.0603	.0007	−.0445	.0531

Approximate $2S_{ACF} = 2/\sqrt{270} = .122$

TABLE 3A–11   Cross-Correlations(CCF(k)) of Series dY_t and dX_{t-k}

Monthly Data from 1970:02 to 1992:07 $n = 270$
Lag = k

−24:	.0280	−.0495	.0395	−.0671	−.1049	−.0472
−18:	.0918	.0724	−.0055	−.0231	.0327	−.0091
−12:	−.0047	.0670	.1498	.1285	−.0406	−.1334
−6:	−.1514	−.0721	−.0163	−.0475	.0583	.0512
0:	.4944	.3913	.0939	−.0878	−.0052	−.0157
6:	.0249	.0551	−.1046	−.0422	−.0769	.0110
12:	−.0232	−.0491	.0391	−.0535	−.0427	−.1012
18:	−.0115	−.1103	−.1254	−.0963	−.0100	−.0420
24:	.0799					

Approximate $2S_{CCF} = 2/\sqrt{270} = .122$

---

where

Se_{CCF} = standard error of CCF

n = number of observations in series

k = the number of lags between Y_t and X_{t-k}

Equation 3A–7 is an approximate formula that can be used as a guide in assessing statistically significant correlations functions. Let's see how equation 3A–7 is applied in a simple *t*-test.

CCF *t*-test:

$$t = \frac{CCF(k)}{Se_{CCF}}$$

(3A–8)

Tree-Ring Time Series and Dating

Any outdoorsperson knows that the age of a tree can be determined by the number of concentric rings in its cross-section. In addition, the width of rings is related to its seasonal growth; and the growth is related to weather conditions, particularly rainfall. Thus, cross-sections of trees are really time series that document the passage of time and growing conditions. Interestingly, these cross-sections are also useful in determining the year in which a tree was cut or used in the construction of primitive dwellings. By dating the dwelling, the scientist can date the time period of construction. For example, scientists can determine when the dwellings of a particular primitive tribe was built by examining the pattern of the growth rings used in the construction of its beams and so forth. The sequence of patterns (i.e., sequences of relative ring widths) can be compared to the patterns in core samples from trees with known ages. Consider the two sequences of patterns at the right, one with dates known, the other taken from a dwelling of unknown age.

By matching patterns, we can determine that the unknown wood specimen was from the years 748 to 755, as shown by the near-perfect match of the unknown time series to the known series. The tools of time series studied in this text are useful in matching these time series. For example, regression analysis or cross-correlation coefficients can be used to find a match of sequences, a task you may do for homework using (TREERING.DAT).

Known Specimen		Unknown Specimen	
Date	*Estimated Rainfall*	*Date*	*Estimated Rainfall*
730	2.3	?	2.8
740	3.0	?	2.4
741	4.0	?	6.5
742	.5	?	9.0
743	3.5	?	5.9
744	6.0	?	1.0
745	7.8	?	2.1
746	2.0	?	3.9
747	3.0		
748	2.7		
749	2.3		
750	6.7		
751	8.9		
752	5.8		
753	.9		
754	2.0		
755	3.8		
756	2.6		
757	2.0		
758	1.0		
759	.9		
760	3.0		

For example, the Se_{CCF} for $k = 1$ in Table 3A–11 is:

$$Se_{CCF} = \frac{1}{\sqrt{270}} = \frac{1}{16.43} = .061$$

$$t = \frac{.3913}{.061} = 6.43 = t\text{-calculated}$$

Because this t-value is much greater than 2, we do not have to refer to the t-table of Appendix C to infer that there is a significant cross-correlation between Y_t and X_{t-1}; thus, there is a significant cross-correlation between the German and lagged U.S. stock indexes. When calculating the CCF, Se, and t-value remember that in practice a minimum of about 50 observations are necessary to have accurate estimates of these statistics. Also, k should not be larger than approximately one fourth of the observations; otherwise there will be large errors from the insufficient number of observations.

Using the above standard error of .061, we see that CCF(0) and CCF(1) are statistically significant. However, be cautious not to infer that the CCF(1) is only the result of cross-correlations; it might instead be a result of the significant ACF(1)s for each of the series dY and dX in Tables A3–9 and A3–10.

Unfortunately, some autocorrelation remains at lag 1 and possibly lag 2 for both series. As we have seen, the approximate standard error of the ACFs is $1/\sqrt{270}$, which is about .061.

Thus, a quick *t*-test of each of these yields significant ACFs at lag 1, but none of the other low-order or seasonal lags are statistically significant. We are cognizant of the autocorrelation at lag 1, particularly as it might relate to cross-correlation coefficients at lag 1. We will not be able to finish our analysis of these series until Chapter 11.

Our analysis of the relationship between the U.S. and German indexes has only begun. For example, as we will learn in Chapters 7 to 13, there are several modeling strategies that might be applied to this data. First, the relationship between stock indexes might better be modeled using percentage changes in the U.S. index versus those in the German index. Second, both the German and U.S. indexes display a considerable change in the variation (i.e., their standard deviations) as the level of the series increases. This variance change is called variance nonstationarity, and it must be eliminated before we can do valid analysis of these time series. Fortunately, logarithms are a relatively easy way to model percentage changes and the variance nonstationarity of most series, and this is developed in Chapters 5 to 7.

Key Terms

autocorrelation

cross-correlations

cross-correlation coefficient (CCF(*k*))

Pearson cross-correlation coefficient

standard error of CCF (Se_{CCF})

Key Formulas

Pearson cross-correlation coefficient:

$$r_{Y_t X_{t-k}} = \frac{\text{COV}(Y_t, X_{t-k})}{S_{Y_t} S_{X_{t-k}}} \tag{3A-1}$$

Cross-correlation function CCF(*k*):

$$\text{CCF}(k) = \frac{\sum_{t=1+k}^{n} (Y_t - \overline{Y})(X_{t-k} - \overline{X})}{\sqrt{\sum_{t=1}^{n}(Y_t - \overline{Y})^2 \sum_{t=1}^{n}(X_t - \overline{X})^2}} \tag{3A-3}$$

Removing autocorrelation to better measure CCF(*k*):

$$dY_t = \text{GERMIND}_t - \text{GERMIND}_{t-1} \tag{3A-5}$$
$$dX_t = \text{USIND}_t - \text{USIND}_{t-1} \tag{3A-6}$$

Statistical significance of cross-correlations:

$$Se_{CCF} = \frac{1}{\sqrt{n}} \tag{3A-7}$$

CCF *t*-test:

$$t = \frac{\text{CCF}(k)}{Se_{CCF}} \tag{3A-8}$$

The Se_{CCF} for Table 3A–11:

$$\frac{1}{\sqrt{270}} = \frac{1}{16.43} = .061$$

$$t = \frac{.3913}{.061} = 6.43$$

Problems

3A–1 Define the concept of cross-correlations using both the Pearson correlation coefficient and CCF(k). Explain the hypotheses that are tested using these significance tests. Which is most appropriate with a small number of observations?

3A–2 Calculate the two standard errors for CCF(k)s for 100 observations for k-values of 1 and 36. What happens to the standard error of the cross-correlation function as the lag, k, increases? Assume that the CCF(k)s are equal for the first 36 lags. What happens to the calculated t-values for $k = 1$ to 36?

3A–3 Using your computer software, verify the cross-correlations of Tables 3A–6 and 3A–11 for the German and U.S. stock indexes using time series GERMUS.DAT. Are your results the same? If not, discuss the possible reasons for these differences.

3A–4 Using TVSAT.DAT of problem 3–18
   a. Calculate ACF(k) for both series for $k = 0$ to 2.
   b. Calculate CCFs for TV and SAT scores for $k = 0$ to 2.
   c. Repeat *a* and *b* using first differences.
   d. Comment on your results by comparing the results of *a*, *b*, and *c*.
   e. Fit a regression model to the original or first differences.

3A–5 Calculate the cross-correlation coefficients (CCFs) between violent crime rates and median prison sentences using CRIMEPRI.DAT from problem 3–20. Only consider k-values (i.e., lags) of -2 to $+2$. Interpret your results.

3A–6 Calculate the Pearson cross-correlation coefficient between violent crime rates and median prison sentences for the data in problem 3–20. Only calculate these for k-values of -2 and $+2$. Compare your results to those of 3A–5. What do you feel is the direction of causality? Do your results confirm or deny the direction of causality?

3A–7 Determine whether there is a statistically significant lead-lag relationship between the U.S. leading and lagging economic indicators in the file LEADLAGG.DAT of problem 3–28. If there is high autocorrelation in these variables, use first differences of the variables to control for this autocorrelation. Perform the appropriate statistical significance tests.

3A–8 Use the data in TQM.DAT and described problem 3–24 to determine whether there is a statistically significant lead-lag relationship between market share and the percentage of individuals who have been through a TQM program at a midwestern hospital. If there is high autocorrelation in these variables, use first differences of the variables to control for this autocorrelation. Perform the appropriate statistical significance tests.

3A–9 Refer to problem 3–25. Determine whether there is a statistically significant lead-lag relationship between patient satisfaction and the percentage of individuals who have been through a TQM program at a midwestern hospital. If there is high autocorrelation in these variables, use first differences of the variables to control for this autocorrelation. Perform the appropriate statistical significance tests.

3A–10 Refer to problem 3–26 using INTMARK.DAT. Determine whether there is a statistically significant lead-lag relationship between the level of long-term interest rates in the United States and the level of the stock market.

3A–11 Refer to problem 3–27. Determine whether there is a statistically significant lead-lag relationship between the daily stock price quotations in *The Wall Street Journal* for one stock and the level of the S & P 500 during a 45-day period. Perform the appropriate statistical significance tests.

3A–12 Using the TREERING.DAT data of the special interest box, confirm the date of the unknown specimen. How did you verify this data?

3A–13 Repeat the analysis done on the German and U.S. stock indexes (GERMUS.DAT), but in this case use natural logarithms of the variables. Are your results the same as those of the text?

Common Assignment for Minicases

Using one of the continuing minicases, 1–1 to 1–10, discuss the possible lead-lag relationships and the sources of data available to identify those relationships.

UNIVARIATE METHODS

SIMPLE SMOOTHING METHODS

I know of no way of judging the future but by the past.

Patrick Henry, Virginia Convention, 1775

Chapter Outline

Because of the wide use of univariate methods in forecasting, eight chapters of this book are devoted to them. This chapter introduces elementary smoothing methods of moving averages, weighted moving averages, and single exponential smoothing. These are effective methods for short-term forecasts of very simple series that do not have cyclical, trend, or seasonal patterns. Chapter 6 presents more advanced smoothing methods, including Winters method and Fourier series analysis for modeling trends and seasonality. Chapter 5 presents seasonal and trend methods using several decomposition techniques. Several other chapters are devoted to the most sophisticated approach to univariate forecasting, ARIMA methods. Knowledge of the concepts and principles presented in this chapter is a prerequisite to understanding the other univariate methods of this book.

Simple smoothing methods are not sufficient as general forecasting approaches; instead they are the foundation on which to build more sophisticated general approaches to forecasting. Simple smoothing methods only forecast simple series accurately. They do not accurately forecast series with trends or seasonality. However, research has shown that single exponential smoothing is a particularly effective method when used with deseasonalized data.

Moving Averages

Simple Moving Averages (SMA)

One of the simplest methods of forecasting is to assume that a future value will equal an average of past values. This is the essential assumption of the moving average. The **simple moving average (SMA)** is useful in modeling a random series (i.e., one without trend or seasonality) because it averages or smooths the most recent actual values to remove the unwanted randomness.

The SMA is one of the easiest calculated forecasts. Table 4–1 illustrates the actual values of a series and shows the forecasts and errors for two-, four-, and eight-period moving averages. As the table shows, the simple four-period moving average forecast of May in year 1 is easily calculated as:

$$\text{SMA4(May)} = (\text{Jan} + \text{Feb} + \text{Mar} + \text{Apr})/4$$
$$= (120 + 124 + 122 + 123)/4 = 122.25$$
$$F_t = (A_{t-4} + A_{t-3} + A_{t-2} + A_{t-1})/4$$

In general, an *N*-period moving average denotes that each new forecast moves ahead one period by adding the newest actual and dropping the oldest actual. For example, the forecast for June, year 1, is

$$\text{SMA4(Jun)} = (\text{Feb} + \text{Mar} + \text{Apr} + \text{May})/4$$
$$= (124 + 122 + 123 + 125)/4 = 123.50$$
$$F_{t+1} = (A_{t-3} + A_{t-2} + A_{t-1} + A_t)/4$$

At the bottom of Table 4–1, several statistics are shown for each of the different SMAs. These error statistics while introduced in Chapters 2 and 3, are reviewed here. These are used to compare the accuracy of the different models and are defined as follows:

$$\text{ME} = \frac{\Sigma(A_t - F_t)}{n} = \bar{e}_t \tag{4-1}$$

$$\text{SSE} = \Sigma e_t^2 = \Sigma(A_t - F_t)^2 \tag{4-2}$$

$$\text{RSE} = \sqrt{\frac{\Sigma e_t^2}{n - k}} \tag{4-3}$$

TABLE 4–1   Two-, Four-, and Eight-Period Simple Moving Averages (TABLE 4–1.DAT)

Month	Period (t)	Actual	Two-Period SMA	Two-Period SMA2 Error	Four-Period SMA	Four-Period SMA4 Error	Eight-Period SMA	Eight-Period SMA8 Error
Year 1								
Jan	1	120						
Feb	2	124						
Mar	3	122	122.00	.00				
Apr	4	123	123.00	.00				
May	5	125	122.50	2.50	122.25	2.75		
Jun	6	128	124.00	4.00	123.50	4.50		
Jul	7	129	126.50	2.50	124.50	4.50		
Aug	8	127	128.50	−1.50	126.25	.75		
Sep	9	129	128.00	1.00	127.25	1.75	124.75	4.25
Oct	10	128	128.00	.00	128.25	−.25	125.88	2.13
Nov	11	130	128.50	1.50	128.25	1.75	126.38	3.63
Dec	12	132	129.00	3.00	128.50	3.50	127.38	4.63
Year 2								
Jan	13	131	131.00	.00	129.75	1.25	128.50	2.50
Feb	14	132	131.50	.50	130.25	1.75	129.25	2.75
Mar	15	133	131.50	1.50	131.25	1.75	129.75	3.25
Apr	16	130	132.50	−2.50	132.00	−2.00	130.25	−.25
May	17	132	131.50	.50	131.50	.50	130.63	1.38
Jun	18	134	131.00	3.00	131.75	2.25	131.00	3.00
Jul	19	134	133.00	1.00	132.25	1.75	131.75	2.25
Aug	20	133	134.00	−1.00	132.50	.50	132.25	.75
Sep	21	131	133.50	−2.50	133.25	−2.25	132.38	−1.38
Oct	22	135	132.00	3.00	133.00	2.00	132.38	2.63
Nov	23	137	133.00	4.00	133.25	3.75	132.75	4.25
Dec	24	138	136.00	2.00	134.00	4.00	133.25	4.75
Mean		129.88	129.57	1.02	129.68	1.73	129.91	2.53
SSE (for t = 9 to 24)				67.50		77.88		147.47
RSE (for t = 9 to 24)				2.12		2.28		3.14

where

A_t = Actual
F_t = Forecasted
n = Number of errors
k = 1 for estimating one coefficient, the moving average

As discussed in Chapter 2, a good forecasting model should not consistently over- or underforecast; consequently, the mean error should not vary greatly from zero. The sum of the squared errors is used to calculate the residual standard errors as in equation 4–3. Equation 4–3 is used throughout this book for calculating the standard deviation of the errors, commonly called the residual standard error or standard error of estimate; we shall use the term **residual standard error (RSE)** to denote this concept. The k value in equation 4–3 is the usual degrees of freedom adjustment that makes

RSE a better estimate of the true population RSE. As shown, the RSE is different than the usual standard deviation. The RSE is a standard deviation that assumes that the mean error is equal to zero, whether it is or not. You should note this because if you use a statistical program or spreadsheet to calculate the standard deviations of the errors, your solutions may not agree with those of equation 4–3.

Based on the RSE at the bottom of Table 4–1, the two-period moving average fits the past more accurately. However, the selection of the best forecasting model is considerably more complex than choosing the model with minimum RSE.

Choosing the Best Forecasting Model

There are a variety of criteria used to choose one forecasting model over another, and these are discussed in detail in Chapter 17. The most important general objective in forecasting is to decrease the width of the confidence intervals used to make probability statements about future values. A probability statement for the next actual value is:

$$\text{Actual} = \text{Forecast} \pm Z \cdot \text{RSE}$$

The probability that the actual value will be in this interval is determined by the *t*- or *Z*-value. If a *Z* of 1.96 is used and errors are normally distributed, approximately 95 percent of the actual values for one-period-ahead forecasts will be in this range, assuming the model of the past is accurate and the past repeats itself. For example, using a two-period average, the 95 percent prediction confidence interval for the actual value in period $t = 25$ (i.e., January of year 3) can be calculated using the last two actuals in Table 4–1:

$$\begin{aligned}
\text{Actual Jan } (t = 25) &= (\text{Nov} + \text{Dec})/2 \pm 1.96(\text{RSE}) \\
&= (137 + 138)/2 \pm 1.96(2.12) \\
&= 137.5 - 4.16 \text{ to } 137.5 + 4.16 \\
&= 133.34 \text{ to } 141.66
\end{aligned}$$

Thus, because 95 percent of the past actuals are within 1.96 RSE (i.e., standard deviations), there is a 95 percent chance that the one-period-ahead forecast interval will contain the actual demand.

As shown in Table 4–1, the two-period simple moving average has an RSE that is slightly lower than that of the four-period moving average, and significantly lower than that of the eight-period simple moving average. For this data, the RSE is 50 percent higher for the eight-period moving average than for the two-period moving average (3.14 vs. 2.12). Thus, we see that there are significant benefits from choosing the best moving average.

Optimal Number of Periods in a Moving Average

In general, the optimal number of periods to have in a SMA is that number minimizing the RSE. Figure 4–1 confirms that the two-period moving average most closely follows the actual series of Table 4–1. This figure illustrates that the number of periods in the moving average determines the length of the "memory" of the average. A two-period average only has a memory of two periods, and an eight-period average "remembers" eight observations.

As shown in Figure 4–1, longer moving-averages smooth the randomness of the series more. A long-period moving average yields the lowest RSE when a series is very random and erratic (an erratic series is one not possessing high levels of autocorrelation). However, if the series is random and moves smoothly up and down (is highly autocorrelated), a shorter-period moving average will yield a lower RSE. The series in Figure 4–1 does move rather smoothly over time; thus, a short-period moving average model works best for this series.

FIGURE 4–1

Two-, four-, and eight-period moving averages for data of Table 4–1

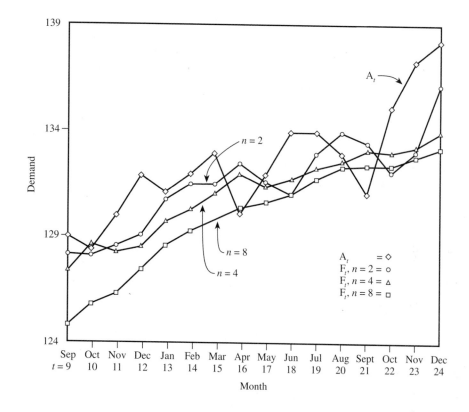

When to Use Simple Moving Averages

Moving average models work well with patternless demands. A patternless series is one that does not have a trend or seasonality in it. Such a series can have smooth or erratic variations (i.e., with or without high autocorrelation). When a series is patternless and erratic as shown in series A, Figure 1–3 of Chapter 1, a longer-period moving average is the more accurate forecasting model.

In contrast, as in series B, Figure 1–11, if the randomness is very smooth, with highly autocorrelated "walks" away from an overall mean, it should be modeled using a shorter-period average, for example, a one- or two-period moving average. Figure 1–11 is a very common pattern of prices for items sold in large competitive markets, such as stock, bond, and commodity markets. Also, it may describe the demand for very high-volume products that are not trending or seasonal. The pattern is referred to as a random walk because it randomly and smoothly walks up and down without any repeating pattern. As discussed in Chapter 1, random walks are characterized by high degrees of autocorrelation.

Weighted Moving Averages (WMA)

It is normally true that the immediate past is most relevant in forecasting the immediate future. For this reason, **weighted moving averages (WMA)** place more weight on the most recent observations. The simple moving average gives equal weight to each observation, but a weighted moving average uses different weights on each observation. The only restriction on the weights is that their sum equals one. Using a four-month moving average with weights .4, .3, .2, and .1 and the data of Figure 4–1 yields the following forecast for May, year 1.

$$WMA4(May) = .1 \text{ Jan} + .2 \text{ Feb} + .3 \text{ Mar} + .4 \text{ Apr}$$
$$= .1(120) + .2(124) + .3(122) + .4(123) = 122.6$$
$$F_t = .1A_{t-4} + .2A_{t-3} + .3A_{t-2} + .4A_{t-1}$$

An advantage of the weighted moving average is that the weights placed on past demands can be varied. However, the determination of the optimal weights can be costly. Table 4–2 and Figure 4–2 illustrates a comparison of a four-period weighted moving average (WMA4) versus a four-period simple moving average (SMA4) for the example of Figure 4–1. As shown in Table 4–2 and Figure 4–2, the WMA's RSE is slightly less than that of the SMA4. Consequently, it is the superior of the two. Although WMAs are not frequently used as stand-alone models, they are included in more advanced forecasting methods that use complex data smoothing such as the Department of Commerce's Census Method II as discussed in Chapter 5.

TABLE 4–2   Four-Period Simple versus Four-Period Weighted Moving Average Forecasts (TABLE 4–1.DAT)

Month	Period (t)	Actual Demand	Four-Period			
			SMA4	SMA4 Error	WMA4	WMA4 Error
Year 1						
Jan	1	120				
Feb	2	124				
Mar	3	122				
Apr	4	123				
May	5	125	122.25	2.75	122.6	2.4
Jun	6	128	123.50	4.5	123.7	4.3
Jul	7	129	124.50	4.5	125.5	3.5
Aug	8	127	126.25	.75	127.3	−.3
Sep	9	129	127.25	1.75	127.6	1.4
Oct	10	128	128.25	−.25	128.3	−.3
Nov	11	130	128.25	1.75	128.2	1.8
Dec	12	132	128.50	3.5	128.9	3.1
Year 2						
Jan	13	131	129.75	1.25	130.3	.7
Feb	14	132	130.25	1.75	130.8	1.2
Mar	15	133	131.25	1.75	131.5	1.5
Apr	16	130	132.00	−2	132.2	−2.2
May	17	132	131.5	.5	131.4	.6
Jun	18	134	131.75	2.25	131.6	2.4
Jul	19	134	132.25	1.75	132.5	1.5
Aug	20	133	132.5	.5	133.2	−.2
Sep	21	131	133.25	−2.25	133.4	−2.4
Oct	22	135	133.00	2	132.5	2.5
Nov	23	137	133.25	3.75	133.3	3.7
Dec	24	138	134.00	4	134.8	3.2
Mean		129.88	129.68	1.73	129.98	1.42
SSE (for *t* = 9 to 24)				77.88		68.27
RSE (for *t* = 9 to 24)				2.28		2.13

Limitations of the SMA and the WMA

The most distinct disadvantage of all moving average or smoothing methods is that they do not model seasonality or trend. A general forecasting method should be able to model seasonal and trend series. Also, historically the disadvantage of moving averages has been that all data needed to calculate the average must be stored and processed. For example, if a 12-period moving average is used, a database of 12 observations must be maintained. Although this created a serious data storage problem several decades ago when computer memory and calculations were expensive, it is no longer a matter of great concern. Today, it is recommended that at least 60 observations (i.e., five seasons) be stored for monthly series, regardless of the forecasting method.

When using a moving average, it is difficult to determine the optimal number of periods to include in the average; however this is not a problem for exponential smoothing, our next topic. Also, exponential smoothing is as accurate as moving averages while at the same time more computationally efficient.

Exponential Smoothing

As mentioned previously, when computer storage capacity was expensive, exponentially weighted moving averages (i.e., exponential smoothing) was advantageous. They are still very popular today, even though storage cost is not of much concern. **Exponential smoothing (EXPOS)** refers to a set of methods of forecasting, several of which are widely used. Brown's double, Holt's two-parameter, and Winters' three-parameter EXPOS methods are developed in Chapter 6. Below, we develop single exponential smoothing. An understanding of the more advanced methods of EXPOS and ARIMA is built on an understanding of simple EXPOS models.

FIGURE 4–2

Four-period simple versus four-period weighted moving average forecasts

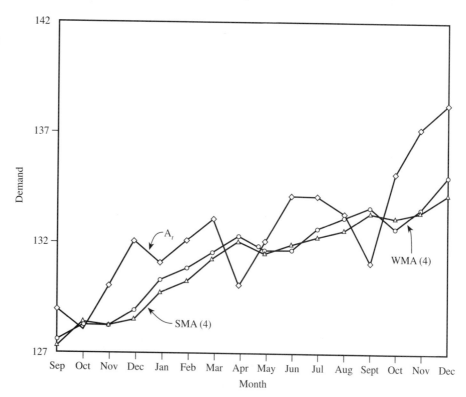

Additionally, EXPOS is important because it is one of the most widely used of all forecasting methods. Trend and seasonally adjusted exponential smoothing methods are used in many computerized forecasting systems for production, inventory, distribution, and retail planning. We owe the early development of exponential smoothing to Brown, Holt, and Winters.

Single Exponential
Smoothing (SES)

Single exponential smoothing (SES) is easy to apply because forecasts require only three pieces of data: the most recent forecast, the most recent actual, and a smoothing constant. The **smoothing constant** (α) determines the weight given to the most recent past observations and therefore controls the rate of smoothing or averaging. It is commonly constrained to be in the range of zero to one.

The equation for SES is the following:

$$F_t = \alpha A_{t-1} + (1 - \alpha) F_{t-1} \tag{4-4}$$

where

F_t = Exponentially smoothed forecast for period t
A_{t-1} = Actual in the prior period
F_{t-1} = Exponentially smoothed forecast of the prior period
α = Smoothing constant, alpha

Suppose a firm desires to forecast demand for a product using SES with an alpha .3. Last month's actual demand was 1,000 and the forecast was 900. Therefore, the forecast for this month is:

$$F_t = \alpha A_{t-1} + (1 - \alpha) F_{t-1}$$
$$= .3(1,000) + (1 - .3)900 = 300 + 630 = 930 \text{ units}$$

This formula states that the current forecast is equal to a weighted average of the most recent actual and forecasted values. Alpha (α) provides the relative weight given to each term in equation 4-4. With alpha equal to .3, the forecast is 30 percent of the most recent actual and 70 percent of the most recent forecasted value. As we will show, the alpha value can be chosen to achieve the desired level of averaging or smoothing. A high alpha smooths the previous actual very little by giving high weight to it.

Continuing the numerical example above, suppose that the demand for period t actually was 980. What is the forecast for period $t + 1$? Since

$$F_{t+1} = \alpha A_t + (1 - \alpha) F_t$$
$$= .3(980) + (1 - .3)930 = 294 + 651 = 945 \text{ units}$$

now given

$$A_{t+1} = 950$$

then

$$F_{t+2} = \alpha A_{t+1} + (1 - \alpha) F_{t+1}$$
$$= .3(950) + (1 - .3)945 = 285 + 661.5 = 946.5 \text{ units}$$

Another equally simple way to calculate the SES equation is:

$$F_t = F_{t-1} + \alpha (A_{t-1} - F_{t-1}) \tag{4-5}$$

According to this formula, the current forecast is equal to the old forecast plus a fraction (alpha) of the error in the previous forecast. However, note that equations 4-4 and 4-5 are the same equations written with terms combined in different ways.

Equation 4–4 is the preferred way of viewing SES in our discussions here. However, you will find that both equations are used in practice.

Getting EXPOS Started

To start using SES requires the choice of a smoothing constant, an initial forecast, and an actual value. The choice of a smoothing constant has been categorized by many as being arbitrary; however, this is not true. What is true is that the best choice of a smoothing constant might not be critical in some situations and often values between .1 to .5 are acceptable. However, there are many times when the choice of alpha can be very critical. With low-cost computers and the high costs of forecast errors, it is no longer advisable to choose a convenient or typical alpha value; instead, the best alphas should be chosen on the basis of minimal sum of squared errors. We provide other guidelines for choosing alpha later. For now, we use an alpha of .3.

After choosing a smoothing constant, the next step in application is to choose an initial forecast value. Very frequently, the first actual value is chosen as the forecast for the second period. Consider the situation below.

Period	Actual	Forecast
1	900	
2	1,000	900

Thus, to get SES started, we assume that the initial forecasted value for period 2 equals the actual value for period 1. It is now possible to forecast period 3.

$$F_2 = A_1 = 900$$
$$F_3 = \alpha A_2 + (1 - \alpha)F_2$$
$$= .3(1,000) + (1 - .3)900 = 300 + 630 = 930 \text{ units}$$

Although there are other methods of arriving at an initial forecast, this method is very popular and efficient for SES.

The Smoothing Constant

The function of the smoothing constant is to give relative weights to the most recent actual and forecasted values. Smoothing and averaging are synonyms in forecasting; consequently, exponential smoothing might also be called exponential averaging. Although it is not evident from our examples, an exponentially smoothed value is actually a weighted moving average of all past actual values. The exponential weights of the past actuals are completely determined by the smoothing constant, alpha. The first four weights, when alpha is .3, are given below. These weights are developed later in the chapter in equations 4–9 through 4–17.

Actuals	Weight
Most recent	$\alpha = .3000$
One period old	$\alpha(1 - \alpha) = .2100$
Two periods old	$\alpha(1 - \alpha)(1 - \alpha) = .1470$
Three periods old	$\alpha(1 - \alpha)(1 - \alpha)(1 - \alpha) = .1029$

Table 4–3 illustrates the values of the weights given to past actuals for smoothing constants of .1, .3, .6, and .9. As shown in the table, if an alpha value of .1 is chosen,

TABLE 4–3   **Exponential Weights with Different Smoothing Constants**

Past Period	Weight Smoothing	Weight When Alpha Equals			
		.1	.3	.6	.9
$t - 1$	α	.1	.3	.6	.9
$t - 2$	$\alpha(1 - \alpha)^1$	.09	.21	.24	.09
$t - 3$	$\alpha(1 - \alpha)^2$	.081	.147	.096	.009
$t - 4$	$\alpha(1 - \alpha)^3$	.0729	.1029	.0384	.0009
$t - 5$	$\alpha(1 - \alpha)^4$	.0656	.0720	.0154	.00009
$t - 6$	$\alpha(1 - \alpha)^5$	.0590	.0504	.0061	.000009
$t - 7$	$\alpha(1 - \alpha)^6$	.0531	.0353	.0025	.0000009
$t - 8$	$\alpha(1 - \alpha)^7$	.0478	.0247	.0010	.00000009
$t - 9$	$\alpha(1 - \alpha)^8$	.0430	.0173	.0004	.000000009
$t - 10$	$\alpha(1 - \alpha)^9$	.0387	.0121	.0002	.0000000009

the actual in the most recent period ($t - 1$) will be given a weight of .1 and, if an alpha of .9 is chosen, the recent actual will be given a weight of .9. Using an alpha of .1 results in weights of .1, .09, .081, .0729, and .0656 for periods $t - 1$ to $t - 5$, respectively. The second column of Table 4–3 defines the mathematical weighting term for each past value.

As shown in Table 4–3, if greater weight is to be given to the most recent actual values, a high smoothing constant is chosen. This is referred to as *low smoothing*. An alpha of 1.0 provides no smoothing because the forecast equals the most recent actual value. An alpha of 1.0 is called *zero smoothing;* that is

$$F_t = \alpha A_{t-1} + (1 - \alpha)F_{t-1} = 1 A_{t-1} + (1 - 1)F_{t-1} = A_{t-1} \qquad (4-6)$$

An alpha of 1.0 yields a one-period simple moving average. In contrast, a low-smoothing constant yields low weight to the recent actual and a great amount of smoothing or averaging; consider the values in third column of Table 4–3 showing the weights with an alpha of .1.

Estimating Alpha

Alpha Based on Autocorrelation

There are several ways to choose a smoothing constant for forecasting a particular data series. Using judgment and the following two principles, alpha can be selected subjectively. If a great amount of smoothing is desired, then a small alpha should be chosen. For example, a low alpha would be most appropriate for series A in Figure 1–3. In contrast, a very high alpha should be chosen for series B in Figure 1–11. This choice is based on the desire to greatly smooth the un-autocorrelated data of Figure 1–3 and not smooth the highly-autocorrelated data of Figure 1–11.

Alpha Based on Desired Simple Moving Average

There is an approximate relationship between alpha and the number of periods (i.e. N) included in a simple moving average. This relationship is expressed as follows:

$$\alpha = 2/(N + 1) \qquad (4-7)$$

$$N = 2/\alpha - 1 \qquad (4-8)$$

Managers Are Using Exponential Smoothing and Don't Know It

We have heard managers state that they do not forecast; they simply assume that this month's demand will equal last month's demand. However, this form of "not forecasting" is actually the use of exponential smoothing with a smoothing constant of 1. When alpha equals 1, the forecast equals the value of the most recent actual. This form of forecasting works well when the series is very smooth, without significant seasonality or trend. Even with a smooth series, these managers might be much better off by using an alpha that is chosen using one of the methods described here.

Consider the use of the following alphas:

For alpha of .1: $N = 2/.1 - 1 = 19.00$
For alpha of .3: $N = 2/.3 - 1 = 5.67$
For alpha of .6: $N = 2/.6 - 1 = 2.33$
For alpha of .9: $N = 2/.9 - 1 = 1.22$

This method of choosing alpha can be useful when converting to or from SMAs. However, because the RSE is a better way to set alpha, use of equation 4–8 is not recommended other than for insights or SMA conversions.

Alpha Based on Minimum RSE

The alpha that yields the most accurate forecasts is the one that achieves the lowest RSE. In other words, when choosing alpha, the object is to reduce the RSE of equation 4–3 to as low as possible. The RSE is minimized when the sum of the squared forecast errors is minimized. This is why in most forecasting systems alpha is chosen to minimize either the RSE or the sum of squared forecast errors. To achieve this, search methods are used to find the optimal alpha. That is, different alpha values are tried in fitting and the alpha that achieves the lowest RSE is chosen as the best. A crude search using three alpha values is illustrated in Table 4–4 using the data of Table 4–1. As Table 4–4 shows, the best alpha for this data is .9 with an RSE of 1.97; an alpha of .1 is much less accurate with an RSE of 5.72. There is little difference between the RSEs for alphas of .6 and .9. The best alpha may not be exactly .9; refining the estimate requires more precise searches between .6 and 1.0. Fortunately, most computer software will automatically provide the best alpha.

Figure 4–3 graphically illustrates the function of alpha and the inferiority of the forecasted values using alpha of .1. Obviously, the value of alpha can greatly affect the accuracy of the forecasts.

Derivation of Exponential Weights for Past Actuals

It is somewhat surprising that the single exponential smoothing model of equation 4–9 yields forecasts that are an exponentially weighted average of all past actual values. Consider this relationship in the derivations of equations 4–10 to 4–17.

The basic exponential smoothing model:

$$F_t = \alpha A_{t-1} + (1 - \alpha) F_{t-1} \qquad (4-9)$$

TABLE 4–4   Simple Exponential Smoothing Using Alpha of .1, .6, and .9 (TABLE 4–1.DATA)

Month	Period (t)	Actual	Alpha = .1 Forecast	Alpha = .1 Error	Alpha = .6 Forecast	Alpha = .6 Error	Alpha = .9 Forecast	Alpha = .9 Error
Year 1								
Jan	1	120						
Feb	2	124	120.00		120.00		120.00	
Mar	3	122	120.40		122.40		123.60	
Apr	4	123	120.56		122.16		122.16	
May	5	125	120.80	4.20	122.66	2.34	122.92	2.08
Jun	6	128	121.22	6.78	124.07	3.93	124.79	3.21
Jul	7	129	121.90	7.10	126.43	2.57	127.68	1.32
Aug	8	127	122.61	4.39	127.97	−.97	128.87	−1.87
Sep	9	129	123.05	5.95	127.39	1.61	127.19	1.81
Oct	10	128	123.65	4.35	128.36	−.36	128.82	−.82
Nov	11	130	124.08	5.92	128.14	1.86	128.08	1.92
Dec	12	132	124.67	7.33	129.26	2.74	129.81	2.19
Year 2								
Jan	13	131	125.41	5.59	130.90	.10	131.78	−.78
Feb	14	132	125.96	6.04	130.96	1.04	131.08	.92
Mar	15	133	126.57	6.43	131.58	1.42	131.91	1.09
Apr	16	130	127.21	2.79	132.43	−2.43	132.89	−2.89
May	17	132	127.49	4.51	130.97	1.03	130.29	1.71
Jun	18	134	127.94	6.06	131.59	2.41	131.83	2.17
Jul	19	134	128.55	5.45	133.04	.96	133.78	.22
Aug	20	133	129.09	3.91	133.61	−.61	133.98	−.98
Sep	21	131	129.48	1.52	133.25	−2.25	133.10	−2.10
Oct	22	135	129.63	5.37	131.90	3.10	131.21	3.79
Nov	23	137	130.17	6.83	133.76	3.24	134.62	2.38
Dec	24	138	130.85	7.15	135.70	2.30	136.76	1.24
Mean		129.88	125.27	5.38	129.07	1.20	129.44	.83
SSE (for t = 9 to 24)				490.80		61.33		58.05
RSE (for t = 9 to 24)				5.72		2.02		1.97

Thus, the following equations are also true:

$$F_{t-1} = \alpha A_{t-2} + (1 - \alpha) F_{t-2} \qquad (4\text{–}10)$$
$$F_{t-2} = \alpha A_{t-3} + (1 - \alpha) F_{t-3} \qquad (4\text{–}11)$$
$$F_{t-3} = \alpha A_{t-4} + (1 - \alpha) F_{t-4} \qquad (4\text{–}12)$$
$$F_{t-4} = \alpha A_{t-5} + (1 - \alpha) F_{t-5} \qquad (4\text{–}13)$$

Therefore, by substituting the right side of equation 4–10 for F_{t-1} in equation 4–9, we obtain equation 4–14.

$$F_t = \alpha A_{t-1} + (1 - \alpha)[\alpha A_{t-2} + (1 - \alpha) F_{t-2}] \qquad (4\text{–}14)$$

Equation 4–14 denotes that the forecast in t is equal to a weighted moving average of the actuals in periods $t - 1$ and $t - 2$ and the forecast of period $t - 2$. This moving average is expanded by substituting the right side of equation 4–11 for F_{t-2} in equation 4–14; this yields equation 4–16.

FIGURE 4–3

Single exponential smoothing with various alpha values

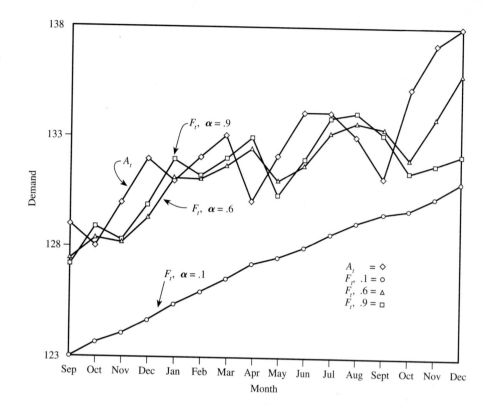

$$F_t = \alpha A_{t-1} + (1 - \alpha)[\alpha A_{t-2} + (1 - \alpha)(\alpha A_{t-3} + (1 - \alpha)F_{t-3})] \quad (4\text{–}15)$$

$$F_t = \alpha A_{t-1} + (1 - \alpha)^1 \alpha A_{t-2} + (1 - \alpha)^2 \alpha A_{t-3} + (1 - \alpha)^3 F_{t-3} \quad (4\text{–}16)$$

Now the forecast in t is equal to a weighted moving average of the past three actuals and a forecast of period $t - 3$. This process of substitution can continue indefinitely, in a theoretical sense. Mathematically, continuing this substitution process yields the following equation:

$$F_t = \alpha A_{t-1} + (1 - \alpha)^1 \alpha A_{t-2} + (1 - \alpha)^2 \alpha A_{t-3} + (1 - \alpha)^3 \alpha A_{t-4} + \quad (4\text{–}17)$$

$$(1 - \alpha)^4 \alpha A_{t-5} + (1 - \alpha)^5 \alpha A_{t-6} + (1 - \alpha)^6 \alpha A_{t-7} +$$

$$\cdots + (1 - \alpha)^n F_{t-n}$$

where n = total number of observations.

Although equation 4–17 seems complex, it simply states that the forecast in period t is equal to a weighted average of all past actual values and one initial forecast. Fortunately, this long equation is used only to demonstrate that the simple exponential smoothing formula of equation 4–9 yields an exponentially weighted moving average of all past actuals that is equal to the solution of equation 4–17. Also, the sum of the weights in equation 4–17 do equal 1.

Seasonal SES—Forecasting U.S. Marriages

The SES model of equation 4–9 can easily be applied to seasonal data that does not possess a trend. This simple model, Seasonal SES is expressed in equation 4–18

$$F_t = \alpha A_{t-s} + (1 - \alpha)F_{t-s} \quad (4\text{–}18)$$

where s is the length of the seasonal cycle, for example, 7 for daily data, 12 for monthly data, 4 for quarterly data, 24 for hourly data, and so forth. Consider the graph of marriages in the United States previously illustrated in Figure 2–16. As illustrated there, marriages are highly seasonal with a four-period, quarterly seasonality. This pattern suggests the following:

$$F_t = \alpha A_{t-4} + (1 - \alpha) F_{t-4}$$

Note that this equation yields forecasts of marriages using data of one year ago.

Table 4–5 illustrates the results of this analysis using an alpha value of .435. The statistics of the original series A_t and fitted errors are:

Mean	599,909.44	ME	−2,432.2
Standard deviation	116,739.84	RSE	12,823.98

As you may remember, Chapter 2 introduced the concept of autocorrelations and ACFs. The ACFs of marriages for quarterly data from 1985:01 to 1992:04 for lags 1 to 8 are:

ACF(k) for Marriages (BIRTHMAR.DAT)

1	2	3	4
−.12496	−.71134	−.10884	.87531
5	6	7	8
−.10276	−.61304	−.10676	.74338

Note the very high autocorrelations at lags 4 and 8; these are statistically significant as measured by the 2Se_{ACF} of .35. Because of the high ACFs at 4 and 8, we infer that equation 4–19 will be a useful model. The results of using a program to optimize alpha yields equation 4–19.

$$F_t = .435A_{t-4} + (1 - .435) F_{t-4} \tag{4–19}$$

The actuals, fitted, residuals, and percentage errors are given in Table 4–5. In addition, this model yields the following statistics:

$$\overline{R}^2 = .9879 \qquad \text{RSE} = 12823.98 \qquad \text{MAPE} = 1.79$$

Thus, this model explains almost 99 percent of the original variation in A_t; that is, $\overline{R}^2 = 1 - (12,823.98)^2/(116,739.84)^2 = .9879$. This is a surprisingly good fit for this model, and no doubt, we have considerable confidence in out-of-sample forecasts. Also, note that we do not include graphs of actuals versus fitted values because the differences are so low as to yield a graph with one point on top of the other. As a good measure of model fit, consider the percentage errors in the fifth column of Table 4–5. As shown, these have varied from −4.3 to 3.6, a very tight fit for one-year-ahead forecasts.

The ACFs of the residuals are given below. Note that none of these correlations are greater than the 2 standard errors of approximately .38 (i.e., $2/(28)^{.5}$). Thus, the residuals appear to have no pattern; they are white noise.

ACF(k) for Residuals of Equation 4–20

1	2	3	4
−.02162	.28913	.01340	.11240
5	6	7	8
−.08242	−.15865	−.18035	−.22533

TABLE 4–5 Fitted and Residuals of Marriages Using Equation 4–20

Date	Marriages A_t	Fitted F_t	Residual $A_t - F_t$	% Residual
1985:01	420240	n.a.	n.a.	n.a.
1985:02	703900	n.a.	n.a.	n.a.
1985:03	709010	n.a.	n.a.	n.a.
1985:04	579475	n.a.	n.a.	n.a.
1986:01	416040	420240.0	−4200.0	−1.0
1986:02	701072	703900.0	−2828.0	−.4
1986:03	705020	709010.0	−3990.0	−.6
1986:04	584967	579475.0	5492.0	.9
1987:01	425587	418413.1	7173.9	1.7
1987:02	692023	702669.9	−10646.9	1.5
1987:03	698699	707274.5	−8575.5	−1.2
1987:04	587069	581863.8	5205.2	.9
1988:01	416000	421533.5	−5533.5	−1.3
1988:02	681000	698038.9	−17038.9	−2.5
1988:03	698000	703544.4	−5544.4	−.8
1988:04	594000	584127.9	9872.1	1.7
1989:01	402000	419126.6	−17126.6	−4.3
1989:02	704000	690627.5	13372.5	1.9
1989:03	693000	701132.8	−8132.8	−1.2
1989:04	606000	588422.0	17578.0	2.9
1990:01	425000	411677.1	13322.9	3.1
1990:02	698000	696444.1	1555.9	2.2
1990:03	724000	697595.3	26404.7	3.6
1990:04	600000	596067.8	3932.2	.7
1991:01	411000	417472.1	−6472.1	−1.6
1991:02	674000	697120.9	−23120.9	−3.4
1991:03	709000	709080.5	−80.5	−.01
1991:04	578000	597778.2	−19778.2	−3.4
1992:01	423000	414657.0	8343.0	2.0
1992:02	662000	687064.0	−25064.0	−3.8
1992:03	697000	709045.5	−12045.5	−1.7
1992:04	579000	589175.3	−10175.3	−1.8
Mean	599,909	601,878	−2,432.2	−.39
Standard deviation	116,740	118,211	RSE 12,823.98	2.13

It should be highlighted that most exponential smoothing models do not yield white noise residuals. Thus, it is rare to see white noise discussed in the context of exponential smoothing because there is frequently some pattern left in the residuals. When this pattern is minor (i.e., has low ACFs) and the model yields a high $\bar{R}^2$ and low RSE, the potential additional explained variance left in the residuals is normally, but not always, small. Nonetheless, any good forecasting model should yield residuals that do not have significant patterns left in the residuals or ACFs.

As we have seen from this example, EXPOS is a versatile approach to forecasting. In addition to the methods of this chapter, Chapter 6 extends EXPOS methods to trending and seasonal time series.

Adaptive Response-Rate Exponential Smoothing (ARRES)

There are several methods of automatically choosing an alpha value based on the errors of previous time periods; these are called **adaptive response-rate exponential smoothing (ARRES)** methods because the smoothing constant adapts to the data. Trigg and Leach have suggested increasing alpha when errors are high and decreasing alpha when errors are low. As shown in equation 4–20, the adaptive response rate (TST_t) is the ratio of the absolute value of two means. These means are calculated using an exponentially weighted average, as shown in equations 4–21 and 4–22.

We call this ratio a **tracking signal** because, as we will see, it tracks errors over time. For example, when a series moves rapidly up or down, a high alpha value is automatically used. In contrast, if the series moves slowly and has low forecast errors, a low alpha value is used. Also, if the model is systematically under- or overforecasting, the alpha value is increased.

$$TST_t = \left| \frac{SAD_t}{MAD_t} \right| \tag{4-20}$$

$$SAD_t = \beta\,(A_t - F_t) + (1 - \beta)\,SAD_{t-1} \tag{4-21}$$

$$MAD_t = \beta\,\left| A_t - F_t \right| + (1 - \beta)\,MAD_{t-1} \tag{4-22}$$

where

TST_t = tracking signal in period t used for alpha in forecasting period $t + 1$

β = beta, a smoothing constant for SAD and MAD, typically chosen to be .2

SAD_t = an exponentially weighted average deviation (mean forecast error) in period t

MAD_t = an exponentially weighted mean absolute deviation (mean absolute forecast error) in period t

$|\ \ |$ = absolute values

Thus, alpha is replaced by the value of equation 4–20, and single exponential smoothing becomes

$$F_t = F_{t-1} + TST_{t-1}\,(A_{t-1} - F_{t-1}) \tag{4-23}$$

The value of TST can never be greater than 1 or less than 0; this is also the common constraint on alpha. Because it adapts to the magnitude of the errors, TST is referred to as an adaptive alpha. Note that SAD_t and MAD_t are simple exponentially weighted moving averages of past forecast errors and absolute values of errors respectively. If the model is forecasting accurately, SAD_t will be nearly equal to zero and the ratio TST will therefore be low. However, if the model consistently under- or overforecasts, SAD_t will approach the value of MAD_t.

Research has shown that if alpha is set equal to this tracking signal, under some conditions the forecast will more closely track the actual. Table 4–6 and Figure 4–4 illustrate the use of ARRES for the example of this chapter. As shown there, after the initialization phase of periods 1 to 3, the adaptive alpha has varied from .23 to as high as .76. The forecasts are quite accurate and follow the data well; however, as shown later, one has to be cautious when using ARRES when the series is very erratic.

The use of ARRES requires initial values of SAD, MAD, and TST. There are several procedures for doing so. When there is little information about these values, an arbitrary value of TST_1 can be used to initiate the process for several periods until representative values of SAD, MAD, and TST can be used in the calculations. Thus, in Tables 4–6 and 4–7, we set TST_t equal to .2 for the first two forecasting periods (periods 2 and 3). Thereafter, the calculated TST_t is used. Also, as is true for single

TABLE 4–6   Adaptive Response-Rate Exponential Smoothing (Random Series, TABLE 4–1.DAT)

Month	Period (t)	Actual (A_t)	Beta = .2		Adaptive Alpha (TST_t)	Forecast (F_t)	Error ($A_t - F_t$)
			SAD_t	MAD_t			
Year 1							
Jan	1	120	.000	4.000	.200		
Feb	2	124	.800	4.000	.200	120.000	4.000
Mar	3	122	.880	3.440	.256	120.800	1.200
Apr	4	123	1.083	3.131	.346	121.107	1.893
May	5	125	1.514	3.152	.480	121.762	3.238
Jun	6	128	2.148	3.458	.621	123.317	4.683
Jul	7	129	2.273	3.322	.684	126.225	2.775
Aug	8	127	1.594	2.882	.553	128.124	−1.124
Sep	9	129	1.574	2.605	.604	127.502	1.498
Oct	10	128	1.178	2.166	.544	128.408	−.408
Nov	11	130	1.305	2.095	.623	128.186	1.814
Dec	12	132	1.581	2.213	.714	129.316	2.684
Year 2							
Jan	13	131	1.218	1.817	.670	131.233	−.233
Feb	14	132	1.159	1.638	.708	131.077	.923
Mar	15	133	1.181	1.565	.755	131.730	1.270
Apr	16	130	.407	1.790	.228	132.689	−2.689
May	17	132	.310	1.447	.215	132.077	−.077
Jun	18	134	.636	1.546	.412	132.060	1.940
Jul	19	134	.737	1.465	.503	132.859	1.141
Aug	20	133	.503	1.258	.400	133.433	−.433
Sep	21	131	−.050	1.459	.034	133.260	−2.260
Oct	22	135	.324	1.530	.212	133.183	1.817
Nov	23	137	.945	1.911	.495	133.568	3.432
Dec	24	138	1.303	2.075	.628	135.266	2.734
Mean		129.88	1.025	2.332	.473	129.008	1.296
Standard deviation		4.64				RSE	2.316

FIGURE 4–4

Adaptive response-rate exponential smoothing

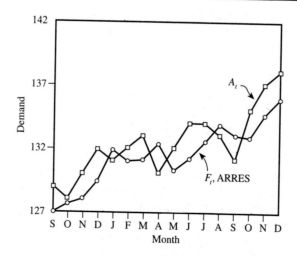

TABLE 4–7   **Adaptive Response-Rate Exponential Smoothing (Erratic Random Series, TABLE 4–7.DAT)**

Month	Period (t)	Actual (A_t)	Beta = .2 SAD$_t$	MAD$_t$	Adaptive Alpha (TST$_t$)	Forecast (F_t)	Error ($A_t - F_t$)	Single Forecast	EXPOS* Error
Year 1									
Jan	1	120	.000	4.000	.200				
Feb	2	124	.800	4.000	.200	120.000	4.000	120.00	4.00
Mar	3	168	10.080	12.640	.797	120.800	47.200	120.80	47.20
Apr	4	123	.976	17.200	.057	158.441	−35.441	130.24	−7.24
May	5	140	−2.505	17.046	.147	156.430	−16.430	128.79	11.21
Jun	6	101	−12.607	24.240	.520	154.015	−53.015	131.03	−30.03
Jul	7	167	−1.974	27.503	.072	126.442	40.558	125.03	41.97
Aug	8	180	8.550	32.132	.266	129.353	50.647	133.42	46.58
Sep	9	129	4.074	28.472	.143	142.830	−13.830	142.74	−13.74
Oct	10	180	11.089	30.607	.362	140.851	39.149	139.99	40.01
Nov	11	98	−2.536	35.893	.071	155.035	−57.035	147.99	−49.99
Dec	12	145	−3.230	29.915	.108	151.006	−6.006	137.99	7.01
Year 2									
Jan	13	131	−6.455	27.804	.232	150.357	−19.357	139.39	−8.39
Feb	14	145	−5.337	22.416	.238	145.863	−.863	137.72	7.28
Mar	15	110	−11.401	25.064	.455	145.658	−35.658	139.17	−29.17
Apr	16	130	−9.008	20.164	.447	129.438	.562	133.34	−3.34
May	17	180	2.856	26.193	.109	129.689	50.311	132.67	47.33
Jun	18	148	4.850	23.520	.206	135.174	12.826	142.14	5.86
Jul	19	100	−3.684	26.379	.140	137.819	−37.819	143.31	−43.31
Aug	20	142	−1.055	22.996	.046	132.537	9.463	134.65	7.35
Sep	21	158	4.162	23.403	.178	132.971	25.029	136.12	21.88
Oct	22	135	2.845	19.207	.148	137.422	−2.422	140.49	−5.49
Nov	23	169	8.663	21.753	.398	137.064	31.936	139.40	29.60
Dec	24	135	3.974	20.359	.195	149.783	−14.783	145.32	−10.32
Mean		139.92	.13	22.62	.24	139.96	.83	135.73	5.06
Standard deviation		25.26				RSE	32.71		28.82

* Alpha is fixed at .2 for the single exponential smoothing model.

exponential smoothing, the first actual value (120) is used to forecast demand for period 2. Finally, so that the initialization process will rapidly converge on a steady-state value, SAD$_1$ and MAD$_1$ are estimated. SAD$_1$ is estimated to be zero, because we expect the mean error to be zero. MAD$_1$ is estimated to be some typical value based either on the first several periods (e.g., periods 1 and 2) or, when past history is available, on the MAD of the past. We have chosen 4 as a typical MAD for period 1.

TST and Erratic Series

Adaptive response-rate exponential smoothing has a serious disadvantage: it does not work well for data that is very random and erratic (i.e., with low autocorrelation). Table 4–7 shows a series with more randomness than the previous series. As shown there, ARRES does not forecast as well as simple exponential smoothing. This is evident by the very large forecast errors in several periods. The last two columns of Table 4–7 illustrate the use of SES with a fixed alpha of .2. As seen by the RSE, the model with a fixed alpha has performed better than ARRES.

FIGURE 4–5

Adaptive response-rate EXPOS versus SES

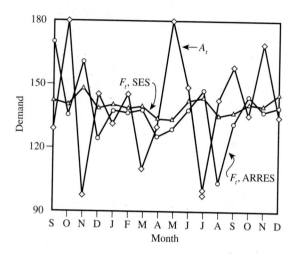

Although the series of Figure 4–5 is very random, it is not as erratic as many other series; it runs from a low of 98 to a high of 180. For the many series that are much more erratic than this one, the ARRES results in extraordinary errors. ARRES may be applicable in some situations; however, the forecaster that uses it must do so cautiously to avoid extremely inaccurate forecasts.

Accuracy of ARRES   Gardner and Dannenbring have researched the accuracy of adaptive smoothing models. In a simulation study using 9,000 time series, they showed that the adaptive response rate models more frequently generated unstable forecasts, even when average values were relatively stable. They recommended the use of trend-adjusted models to hedge against sudden changes in the series. Trend-adjusted models were shown to be more stable and more accurate than the adaptive models in a variety of situations. Trend models are the topic of Chapter 6. Gardner and Dannenbring's conclusions were confirmed in the Makridakis et al. 1982 study, which compared the accuracy of a variety of forecasting models using 1,001 actual time series. The Makridakis study found that adaptive smoothing models were significantly less accurate than models using constant alphas.

Forecasting Low-Value or Erratic Series

In many forecasting situations, some series have very low or erratic values. When this occurs, the selection of a good forecasting model can be very difficult. Low and erratic series are characterized as having very high standard deviations relative to the mean. The ratio of the standard deviation to the mean is called the **coefficient of variation.** Thus, when the coefficient of variation is high and no seasonal or trend patterns account for this high variation, it may be difficult to identify an accurate forecasting model. There are two solutions to this problem: (1) forecast the series as well as possible, probably using the mean, or a low alpha, or (2), when a meaningful group of similar, related series can be identified, group these data to improve the group forecast accuracy. However, no matter which solution is chosen, the RSE is likely to be high relative to the mean. Let's further discuss how to forecast low value and erratic series.

**Patterns in
Low-Value Series**

It is not too uncommon to find series that are relatively low and have repeating patterns; such series are more easily forecasted than those without patterns. These patterns result from the regularity in the generating process. For example, the low value might be the result of having many customers who regularly demand only a few units. In contrast, in many situations only a few customers may demand the product, but their demand is very erratic. In such situations, the resulting series will be very erratic, and difficult to forecast.

**Low-Values and
Erratic Series**

In these situations of no repeating patterns, simple smoothing methods are the best forecasting models. Single exponential smoothing with a low alpha value or simple moving averages with a large number of periods may be the best approaches. However, it is important to measure the errors and their RSE. The typically large RSEs are very important in setting forecast error confidence intervals and contingency plans. The tracking signals and control devices discussed in Chapter 17 become critical tools of monitoring and controlling the forecast of low-value and erratic series. The level of these series may shift, and we need to detect such shifts as soon as possible.

**Group Patterns in
Low-Value and
Erratic Series**

Although a series may have very erratic or low values, it may nonetheless be subject to some seasonal or trend patterns that are hidden by its high error variability (what is called low signal-to-noise ratio). In such situations, it can be helpful to combine series with similar items that are all members of a common group. Accumulating group totals makes it easier to model the seasonal patterns and to preclude large errors. As shown in the simple relationship below, the patterns in an individual series may not be pronounced enough to be identified; but when several series are added together, the resulting group pattern may be quite discernable. Individual series may, on average, be influenced 20 percent by patterns and 80 percent by random influences. Thus, the individual patterns may be difficult to identify. However, when this item is a member of a group, the patterns reinforce each other (i.e., are on average high or all low in any given time period), and the random values may cancel each other out. Thus, we may see that the group value is influenced 60 percent by patterns, such as trends and seasonality, and the random values account for only 40 percent of the group variation.

$$\text{Individual value} = f(20\% \text{ from pattern} + 80\% \text{ from random})$$
$$\text{Group value} = f(60\% \text{ from pattern} + 40\% \text{ from random})$$

The group pattern is then used to generate the individual series patterns with the pyramid method in Chapter 17. Thus, grouping low-value series with similar patterns may improve the pattern-recognition process and reduce forecast errors.

**Extremely Low
Values**

In some situations, mean values are extremely low, sometimes a fractional unit per period. In such situations, the errors in forecasting should be modeled with different methods. These methods include the use of distributions other than the normal distributions, such as the Poisson distribution, as discussed in Brown (1962).

Summary

This chapter has introduced several methods of averaging or smoothing data for short-term forecasting. All smoothing methods except ARRES work adequately well when forecasting patternless data. Because of its computational and storage efficiency, SES is the preferred method of those discussed here. However, the SES model of this chapter suffers from an inability to model series with seasonal and trend patterns. Because these patterns are not modeled, SES may be inadequate for even short-horizon forecasts of trend and seasonal data. We saw that a seasonal SES approach can be used in some situations such as the simple seasonal series of marriages; however, this is not a general purpose approach that will simultaneously model trend-seasonal models. Fortunately, there are several simple ways to incorporate trends and seasonality in models; these are discussed in the next 2 chapters.

Key Terms

adaptive response-rate exponential smoothing (ARRES)

coefficient of variation

exponential smoothing (EXPOS)

residual standard error (RSE)

seasonal SES

simple moving averages (SMA)

single exponential smoothing (SES)

smoothing constant (α)

smoothing constant (β)

tracking signal (TST$_t$)

weighted moving averages (WMA)

Key Formulas

Simple moving averages:

$$\text{SMA4(May)} = (\text{Jan} + \text{Feb} + \text{Mar} + \text{Apr})/4$$
$$\hat{Y}_t = (Y_{t-4} + Y_{t-3} + Y_{t-2} + Y_{t-1})/4$$

Mean forecast error

$$\text{ME} = \frac{\Sigma(A_t - F_t)}{n} = \bar{e}_t \tag{4-1}$$

Sum of squared errors:

$$\text{SSE} = \Sigma e_t^2 = \Sigma(A_t - F_t)^2 \tag{4-2}$$

Residual standard errors:

$$\text{RSE} = \sqrt{\frac{\Sigma e_t^2}{n-1}} \tag{4-3}$$

Weighted moving averages:

$$\text{WMA(May)} = .1\,\text{Jan} + .2\,\text{Feb} + .3\,\text{Mar} + .4\,\text{Apr}$$
$$\hat{Y}_t = .1Y_{t-4} + .2Y_{t-3} + .3Y_{t-2} + .4Y_{t-1}$$

Single exponential smoothing (SES[3])

$$F_t = \alpha A_{t-1} + (1 - \alpha) F_{t-1} \tag{4-4}$$
$$F_t = F_{t-1} + \alpha(A_{t-1} - F_{t-1}) \tag{4-5}$$

Alpha as a function of *n*:

$$\alpha = 2/(N + 1) \tag{4-7}$$

$$N = 2/\alpha - 1 \tag{4-8}$$

Exponentially weighted moving average of all past actuals:

$$F_t = \alpha A_{t-1} + (1 - \alpha)^1 \alpha A_{t-2} + (1 - \alpha)^2 \alpha A_{t-3} + (1 - \alpha)^3 \alpha A_{t-4} +$$
$$(1 - \alpha)^4 \alpha A_{t-5} + (1 - \alpha)^5 \alpha A_{t-6} + (1 - \alpha)^6 \alpha A_{t-7} + \ldots + (1 - \alpha)^n F_{t-n} \qquad (4\text{--}17)$$

Seasonal SES:

$$F_t = \alpha A_{t-s} + (1 - \alpha) F_{t-s} \qquad (4\text{--}18)$$

Tracking signal of Trigg and Leach:

$$TST_t = \left| \frac{SAD_t}{MAD_t} \right| \qquad (4\text{--}20)$$

Smoothed average deviation:

$$SAD_t = \beta (A_t - F_t) + (1 - \beta) SAD_{t-1} \qquad (4\text{--}21)$$

Mean absolute deviation:

$$MAD_t = \beta |A_t - F_t| + (1 - \beta) MAD_{t-1} \qquad (4\text{--}22)$$

Adaptive response-rate exponential smoothing (ARRES):

$$F_t = F_{t-1} + TST_{t-1} (A_{t-1} - F_{t-1}) \qquad (4\text{--}23)$$

Review Problems Using Your Software

R4–1 Repeat the analysis of the following tables and interpret your results as done in the book.
   a. Table 4–1
   b. Table 4–2
   c. Table 4–4
   d. Table 4–5
   e. Table 4–6
   f. Table 4–7

Problems

4–1 What criteria should be used in choosing the number of periods to include in a moving average? What criteria for the choosing the smoothing constant α?

4–2 What is the essential advantage or rationale for moving averages as opposed to an average over all observations?

4–3 In general, what is the biggest limitation of moving averages and simple exponential smoothing?

4–4 What is seasonal simple exponential smoothing?

4–5 Explain why a low α for SES or a large number of periods in moving averages should be used when the data is very erratic. Explain why a high α or low number of periods should be used in moving averages when the data is very smooth. Also, what value of alpha should be used for a random-walk series like SERIESB.DAT ?

4–6 What is a weighted moving average and why might it be preferred to a simple moving average?

4–7 What is the meaning of the term *exponential* in exponential smoothing or exponentially weighted moving average? Show by deriving the appropriate exponential terms.

4–8 How are the concepts smoothing and averaging related?

4–9 Explain the concept of adaptive response-rate EXPOS. How well has this method worked in practice?

4–10 The following data is the actual number of car miles driven in the United States in billions of miles (CARMILE.DAT).

1980	1981	1982	1983	1984	1985	1986	1987	1988
1,122	1,142	1,176	1,207	1,234	1,270	1,311	1,365	1,439

a. Forecast 1982 to 1988 using a simple two-period moving average.
b. Comment on your results from *a.* Is this a good model?
c. Forecast 1982 to 1988 using SES with an alpha you believe is best.
d. Comment on your results in *c.* Is this a good model?
e. Which method is better, the simple moving average or simple exponential smoothing? Why?
f. Forecast the out-of-sample 1989 to 1992 using the best model.

4–11 The following data is the ozone concentration in the United States in part per million of air (OZONE.DAT).

1980	1981	1982	1983	1984	1985	1986	1987	1988
.136	.127	.125	.137	.124	.123	.118	.125	.136

a. Forecast 1982 to 1988 using a simple two-period moving average.
b. Comment on your results from *a.* Is this a good model?
c. Forecast 1982 to 1988 using SES with an alpha you believe is best.
d. Comment on your results from *c.* Is this a good model?
e. Which method is better? Why?

4–12 The following data is the number of robberies in the United States per 100,000 people (ROBUS.DAT).

1980	1981	1982	1983	1984	1985	1986	1987	1988	1989
251	269	239	217	205	209	225	213	221	233

a. Forecast 1982 to 1990 using a simple two-period moving average.
b. Comment on your results from *a.* Is this a good model?
c. Forecast 1982 to 1990 using SES with an alpha you believe is best.
d. Comment on your results from *c.* Which method is better? Why?

4–13 For SERIESA.DAT determine the optimal number of periods to include in a SMA by forecasting using the following models: one-, four-, and six-period simple moving averages.

a. Calculate the mean errors and residual standard errors for each model and graph the forecasts.
b. Which model is the best model? Explain why.

4–14 For SERIESA.DAT use SES to forecast demand. Find the optimal smoothing constant using alpha values of .1, .3, .6, and .9.

a. Calculate the ME and RSE for each model, graphing each of them.
b. Which model is the best model? Explain why.
c. If your computer program has the capability, let it determine the optimal value of alpha. Comment and compare that smoothing constant to that of *b.*

4–15 For SERIESB.DAT use SES to forecast demand. Find the optimal smoothing constant using alpha values of .1, .3, .6, and .9.

a. Calculate the ME and RSE for each model, graphing each of them.
b. Which model is the best model? Explain why.
c. If your computer program has the capability, let it determine the optimal value of alpha. Comment and compare that smoothing constant to that of *b.*

Master Forecasting Summary Table

As you work homework in this text, your instructor may assign different forecasting problems using the same time series. By doing this, we gain insights into the similarities and differences of methods. The summary table below provides a good method for recording the performance of different methods. Depending on your series, the best type of forecasting method will vary. Note the summary statistics that are recorded for each time series; these provide important diagnostics on the validity and practical significance of the forecast.

Time Series: FILENAME.DAT = _____   Time Period Analyzed: _____
Mean = _____   Standard Deviation = _____   Transformations = _____

Method Prob.	Seasonal SES	Seasonal SES + ME	Seasonal SMA2	Seasonal SMA + ME	Other	Comments
FIT						
n						
ME						
RSE						
MPE						
MAPE						
$\bar{R}^2$						
DW						
Q-stat.						
FORECAST						
n						
ME						
RSE						
MPE						
MAPE						
$\bar{R}^2$						
DW						
Q-stat.						

4–16 For SERIESC.DAT use SES to forecast demand. Find the optimal smoothing constant using alpha values of .1, .3, 6, and .9.
   a. Calculate the ME and RSE for each model, graphing each of them.
   b. Which model is the best model? Explain why.
   c. If your computer program has the capability, let it determine the optimal value of alpha. Comment and compare that smoothing constant to that of *b.*

4–17 Using SERIESD.DAT as an example of a highly seasonal series, write out the seasonal single exponential smoothing (SSES) model that you would use to forecast this series.

4-18 Fit a SES model to the monthly price of IBMMN.DAT. What do you feel is the best smoothing constant to use in forecasting these prices? If your computer software has an optimization capability, use it and compare the results to your estimate. Which is better and why? Report the ME and RSE of fit. Why or why wouldn't your model be good in forecasting next year?

4-19 What type of model would you use to forecast births in the series BIRTHMAR.DAT? Apply that model and report the ME and RSE of the fit.

4-20 What type of model would you use to forecast the series of Table 4–1? Apply that model and report the ME and RSE of the fit.

Minicases: Common Assignment for Minicases—Seasonal Smoothing

Complete the following analysis using a time series from Minicases 4–1 to 4–10:

Forecast this series using seasonal exponential smoothing like Table 4–5 or a seasonal four-period moving average model or both. That is, fit and forecast with the following models:

a. Seasonal SMA2 (SSMA2)
$$F_t = (A_{t-S} + A_{t-2S}) / 2$$
b. Seasonal SES (SSES)
$$F_t = \alpha A_{t-S} + (1 - 2)F_{t-S}$$
where S is the length of the seasonal cycle (e.g., 4, 7, 12, 52, etc.)

Fit the models to all but the last season of data (i.e., withhold 12 months, 7 days, 52 weeks, or four quarters, depending on the type of data); then forecast the remaining withheld values. Be sure to estimate the ME, RSE, $\bar{R}^2$, MPE, and MAPE of both the fit and the forecast. Complete the first column of the Master Forecasting Summary Table. Plot the actual versus the fitted and forecasted values and their errors. Is there anything unusual in these plots? Comment about the accuracy and bias of the fit and forecast after completing the table. In what ways is this model deficient, if at all? In what ways can the forecast be improved? If there is bias in the fit (i.e., the ME is statistically significantly different than zero), this may represent a trend in the series (incidentally, Chapter 2 explained how to perform a simple statistical significance test of the ME). Estimate a new seasonal model by adding the fitted bias to the old model fit and forecast. That is,

$$F'_t = F_t + ME$$

where

F'_t = new trend enhanced fit and forecast
F_t = previous fit without ME
ME = mean error of the previous fitted values

Now, refit and reforecast with the trend enhanced model and repeat the analysis above.

Minicase 4–1 Kansas Turnpike, Monthly Data For the monthly time series TURNPIKM.DAT, complete the

common seasonal smoothing assignment; withhold and forecast the last 12 months of data.

Minicase 4–2 Air Passengers by Quarter For the quarterly time series PASSAIR.DAT, complete the common seasonal smoothing assignment; withhold and forecast the last 8 quarters of data.

Minicase 4–3 Hospital Census by Week For the weekly time series CENSUSW.DAT, complete the common seasonal smoothing assignment; withhold and forecast the last 52 weeks of data.

Minicase 4–4 Henry Machler's Hideaway Orchids For the monthly time series MACHLERM.DAT, complete the common seasonal smoothing assignment; withhold and forecast the last 12 months of data.

Minicase 4–5 Your Own Forecasting Project For your time series, complete the common seasonal smoothing assignment; withhold and forecast the appropriate number of observations.

Minicase 4–6 Midwestern Building Materials LUMBER.DAT is a highly seasonal monthly series of lumber sales of a large midwestern building materials company with 120 monthly observations starting in January. Complete the common seasonal smoothing assignment; withhold and forecast the last 12 months of data.

Minicase 4–7 International Airline Passengers AIRLINE.DAT is a highly seasonal monthly series of international airline passengers with 144 observations from 1949 through 1960, originally reported by Brown and used by Box, Jenkins, and Reinsel. Analyze the natural logarithms of the series. Complete the common seasonal smoothing assignment; withhold and forecast the last 36 months.

Minicase 4–8 Automobile Sales AUTO.DAT is a highly seasonal time series of automobile sales of an automobile manufacturer with 185 monthly observations starting in January of year 1. Complete the common seasonal smoothing assignment; withhold and forecast the last 12 months.

Minicase 4–9 Consumption of Distilled Spirits SPIRITS.DAT is a highly seasonal monthly time series of the consumption of alcoholic spirits in United States with

132 observations from January 1975 to December 1991. Complete the common seasonal smoothing assignment; withhold and forecast the last 12 months.

Minicase 4–10 Discount Consumer Electronics
ELECT.DAT is a highly seasonal monthly time series of the

sales of consumer electronics of a large wholesale distributor with 185 observations. Complete the common seasonal smoothing assignment; withhold and forecast the last 12 months.

References

Ameen, J.R.M., and P.J. Harrison. "Discounted Weight Estimation." *Journal of Forecasting* 3 (1984), pp. 285–96.

Bretschneider, S. "Estimating Forecast Variance with Exponential Smoothing: Some New Results." *International Journal of Forecasting* 2 (1986), pp. 349–55.

Brown, R.G. *Statistical Forecasting for Inventory Control.* New York: McGraw-Hill, 1959.

Brown, R.G. *Smoothing, Forecasting and Prediction of Discrete Time Series.* Englewood Cliffs, NJ: Prentice Hall, 1962.

Brown, R.G., and R.F. Meyer. "The Fundamental Theorem of Exponential Smoothing." *Operations Research* 9 (1961), pp. 673–85.

Chatfield, C. "Some Recent Developments in Time Series Analysis." *Journal of the Royal Statistical Society* A 140 (1977), pp. 492–510.

Chatfield, C. "The Holt-Winters Forecasting Procedure." *Applied Statistics* 27 (1978), pp. 264–79.

Chatfield, C., and M. Yar. "Holt-Winters Forecasting: Some Practical Issues." *The Statistician* 37 (1988), pp. 129–40.

Chatfield, C., and M. Yar. "Prediction Intervals for Multiplicative Holt-Winters." *International Journal of Forecasting* 7 (1991), pp. 31–37.

Chow, W.M. "Adaptive Control of the Exponential Smoothing Constant." *Journal of Industrial Engineering* 16 (1965), pp. 314–17.

Cox, D.R. "Prediction by Exponential Weighted Moving Averages and Related Methods." *Journal of the Royal Statistical Society* B 23 (1961), pp. 414–22.

Fildes, R. "Quantitative Forecasting—The State of the Art: Extrapolative Methods."

Journal of the Operational Research Society 30 (1979), pp. 691–710.

Gardner, E.S. "Automatic Monitoring of Forecast Errors." *Journal of Forecasting* 2 (1983), pp. 1–21.

Gardner, E.S. "The Strange Case of Lagging Forecasts." *Interfaces* 14 (1984), pp. 47–50.

Gardner, E.S. "Exponential Smoothing: The State of the Art." *Journal of Forecasting* 4 (1985), pp. 1–28.

Gardner, E.S., and D.G. Dannenbring. "Forecasting with Exponential Smoothing: Some Guidelines for Model Selection." *Decision Sciences* 11 (1980), pp. 370–83.

Gilchrist, W.G. "Methods of Estimation Using Discounting." *Journal of the Royal Statistical Society* B 29 (1967), pp. 355–69.

Gilchrist, W.G. *Statistical Forecasting.* London: Wiley, 1976.

Godolphin, E.G., and P.J. Harrison. "Equivalence Theorems for Polynomial-Projecting Predictors." *Journal of the Royal Statistical Society* B 37 (1975), pp. 205–15.

Golder, E.R., and J.G. Settle. "Monitoring Schemes in Short-Term Forecasting." *Operational Research Quarterly* 27 (1976), pp. 489–501.

Groff, G.K. "Empirical Comparison of Models for Short-Range Forecasting." *Management Science* 20 (1973), pp. 22–31.

Harrison, P.J. "Short-Term Sales Forecasting." *Applied Statistics* 14 (1965), pp. 102–39.

Harrison, P.J. "Exponential Smoothing and Short-Term Sales Forecasting." *Management Science* 13 (1967), pp. 821–42.

Harrison, P.J., and O.L. Davies. "The Use of Cumulative Sum (CUSUM) Techniques for the Control of Routine Forecasts of

Product Demand." *Operations Research* 12 (1964), pp. 325–33.

Holt, C.C. "Forecasting Seasonal and Trends by Exponentially Weighted Moving Averages." Office of Naval Research, Memorandum 52, 1957.

Ledolter, J., and B. Abraham. "Some Comments on the Initialization of Exponential Smoothing." *Journal of Forecasting* 3 (1984), pp. 79–84.

Makridakis, S., A. Anderson, R. Carbone, R. Fildes, M. Hibon, R. Lewandowski, J. Newton, E. Parzen, and R. Winkler. "The Accuracy of Extrapolation (Time Series) Methods." *Journal of Forecasting* 1 (1982), pp. 111–53.

Makridakis, S., and M. Hibon. "Accuracy of Forecasting: An Empirical Investigation." *Journal of the Royal Statistical Society* A 142 (1979), pp. 97–145.

Makridakis, S., and M. Hibon. "Exponential Smoothing: The Effect of Initial Values and Loss Functions on Post-Sample Forecasting Accuracy." *International Journal of Forecasting* 7 (1991), pp. 317–30.

McClain, J.O. "Dominant Tracking Signals." *International Journal of Forecasting* 4 (1988), pp. 563–72.

McKenzie, E. "The Monitoring of Exponentially Weighted Forecasts." *Journal of the Operational Research Society* 29 (1978), pp. 449–58.

McKenzie, E. "General Exponential Smoothing and the Equivalent ARMA Process." *Journal of Forecasting* 3 (1984), pp. 333–44.

Muth, J.F. "Optimal Properties of Exponentially Weighted Forecasts." *Journal of the American Statistical Association* 55 (1960) pp. 299–306.

Nerlove, M., and S. Wage. "On the Optimality of Adaptive Forecasting." *Management Science 10* (1964), pp. 204–224.

Newbold, P., and T. Bos. "On Exponential Smoothing and the Assumption of Deterministic Trend plus White Noise Data-Generating Models." *International Journal of Forecasting* 5 (1989), pp. 523–27.

Newbold, P., and C.W.J. Granger. "Experience with Forecasting Univariate Time Series and the Combination of Forecasts." *Journal of the Royal Statistical Society* A 137 (1974), pp. 131–165.

Reid, D.J. "A Review of Short-Term Projection Techniques." In *Practical Aspects of Forecasting,* ed. H. A. Gordon. London: Operational Research Society, 1975.

Sweet, A.L. "Adaptive Smoothing for Forecasting Seasonal Series." *AIIE Transactions* 13 (1981), pp. 243–48.

Theil, H., and S. Wage. "Some Observations on Adaptive Forecasting." *Management Science* 10 (1964), pp. 198–206.

Trigg, D.W. "Monitoring a Forecasting System." *Operational Research Quarterly* 15 (1964), pp. 271–74.

Trigg, D.W., and A.G. Leach. "Exponential Smoothing with an Adaptive Response Rate." *Operational Research Quarterly* 18 (1967), pp. 53–59.

Winters, P.R. "Forecasting Sales by Exponentially Weighted Moving Averages." *Management Science* 6 (1960), pp. 324–42.

Yar, M., and C. Chatfield. "Prediction Intervals for the Holt-Winters Forecasting Procedure." *International Journal of Forecasting* 6 (1990), pp. 127–37.

DECOMPOSITION METHODS AND SEASONAL INDEXES

If you don't know where you're going, you will wind up somewhere else.

Yogi Berra

Chapter Outline

This chapter presents one of the oldest commonly used forecasting methods, the classical time series decomposition method. An essential part of this method includes the concept of seasonal indexes. This concept is important because many business and economic times series are seasonal and seasonal indexes are an essential part of effective forecasting methods.

In addition, the strong seasonality of some series make it difficult to measure their trend and cyclical movements. Thus, measurement of the seasonal variation is an essential step in understanding a time series. In fact, most of the economic measures reported in the media by governments are seasonally adjusted. This is necessary because the high month-to-month seasonal variations confound identification of trends and cyclical movements. Were it not for seasonal indexes, the GDP and unemployment rates reported in the media would be difficult to interpret.

Many of us are familiar with simple ways of presenting seasonal data such as done in quarterly financial reports where the performances of quarters are presented simultaneously with the performance of the same quarter of the last year. For example, consider how clear such presentations are:

	Year 1	*Year 2*	*Year 2/Year 1*	*Year 2 − Year 1*
Quarter 1	12,000	13,200	1.100	1,200
Quarter 2	6,000	6,500	1.083	500
Quarter 3	4,000	4,300	1.075	300
Quarter 4	18,000	19,700	1.094	1,700

Although this method of presenting seasonal data is effective, we shall see that seasonal indexes present additional information about the time series.

This chapter is important as a prerequisite for understanding the other methods of forecasting in this book. These more sophisticated methods include the Department of Commerce's Census Method II X-11 used to generate seasonal indexes, the widely used Winters method (Chapter 6), Fourier series analysis (Appendix Chapter 6), and the versatile ARIMA model-building methods of Box and Jenkins (Chapters 7 to 9).

Seasonal indexes provide important insights regarding a time series when pronounced seasonality exists. For example, the detection and anticipation of peak seasonal demands often can mean the difference between effective and ineffective decisions.

Classical Decomposition Method

In decomposition, a time series is described using a multifactor model. The model is:

$$Y_t = f(T, C, S, e) \tag{5–1}$$

where

Y_t = actual value of time series at time t
f = mathematical function of
T = trend
C = cyclical influences
S = seasonal influences
e = error

As Chapter 1 developed, the trend component (T) in a time series is the long-run general movement caused by long-term economic, demographic, weather and technological movements. The cyclical component (C) is an influence of about three to nine years caused by economic, demographic, weather, and technological changes in an industry or economy. Frequently, the trend and cyclical components of equation 5–1 are modeled together as a single component, referred to as trend-cyclical components. This is done because it is very difficult to decompose a series into separate cyclical and trend components.

Typically, seasonal variations are the result of weather and man-made conventions such as holidays. Also, frequently they are thought of as being only quarterly or monthly movements; but there are seasonal variations that occur every four years (e.g., the Olympics), every 13 weeks, every seven days, every 24 hours, and so on. The key to identifying seasonal influences is whether the influence is recurrent and periodic. If an influence recurs every s-periods (e.g., every 12 months) it is called a seasonal influence regardless of the length of its cycle.

The error term in equation 5–1 is the residual component of a time series that is not explained by T, C, and S. Sometimes large errors can be caused by very unusual, irregular events; thus this term is often referred to as the irregular or random component. Irregular influences in a time series are unpredictable and can be caused by random events such as unusual weather, earthquakes, floods, hurricanes, wars, politics, or labor unrest. The error component of a time series is a catchall for all the unexplained variation in a time series. It is also referred to as residual error.

There are two general types of decomposition models, an additive and a multiplicative.

$$\text{Additive: } Y = T + C + S + e \qquad\qquad (5\text{–}2)$$

$$\text{Multiplicative: } Y = T \times C \times S \times e \qquad\qquad (5\text{–}3)$$

Since the **multiplicative decomposition method** is used most frequently, we will develop it first; however, there are many time series that can be and should be modeled using the additive model. Below we will provide guidelines for choosing between multiplicative and additive models. In the multiplicative model, Y is the product of the four components, T, C, S, and e. C and S are indexes that are proportions centered on 1. For example, a **seasonal index** of 1.10 or 110% in period t (e.g., July) denotes that the period is 10% higher than the trend-cyclical value. Similarly, a seasonal index of .90 or 90% (e.g., February) denotes that the period is 10% lower than the trend-cyclical value. In an identical manner, a cyclical index of .92 denotes a below-average cyclical influence in that period. Only the trend, T, is measured in the same units as the items being forecast. For example, the forecast of a product group for the month of April might be:

$$\hat{Y}_{\text{April}} = T \times C \times S = 240{,}000 \times 1.36 \times .98 = 319{,}872$$

where the cyclical effect of 1.36 is above the typical and seasonality below the typical period at .98. As you note in equation 5–3, e is shown as a proportion; however, in many applications of this method, e is an actual error ($Y_t - \hat{Y}_t$) that is simply added to equation 5–3. Because it is most commonly used, we use an additive error term in both equations 5–2 and 5–3.

Figure 5–1 illustrates the four components of a multiplicative time series. The procedure for identifying these is illustrated next.

FIGURE 5–1

Anatomy of a time series

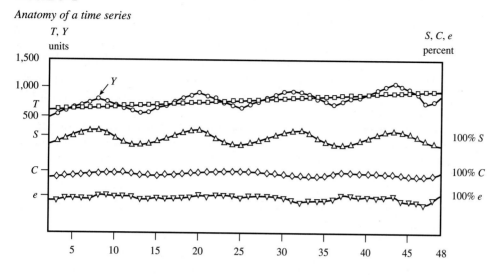

FIGURE 5–2

Additive and multiplicative seasonal influences

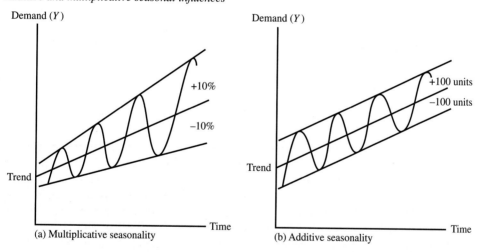

(a) Multiplicative seasonality   (b) Additive seasonality

Multiplicative versus Additive Models

The **additive decomposition method** is used when it is evident from plots of the data that seasonal and cyclical influences are unrelated to the general level of the series. That is, an additive seasonal model denotes that demand for soft drinks in July is always 100 units higher than the trend-cyclical of July, regardless of what the trend-cyclical value is. In contrast, a multiplicative model is used when the seasonal influence is a percentage of the trend-cyclical in July (for example, 10 percent higher than the trend-cyclical). Figure 5–2 illustrates each of these situations.

The determination of whether seasonal influences are additive or multiplicative is usually evident from a graph of the data. As shown in Figure 5–2a, if the differences of the peaks and troughs get greater as the trend increases, a multiplicative model is used. In contrast, as shown in Figure 5–2b, if the differences between the peaks and troughs stay the same—that is, are independent of the level of the series—an additive model is the correct choice.

Daylight Hours and Seasonality

Those of us not near the equator are very aware of the changes in the seasons, including temperature, humidity, and precipitation; and as farmers or outdoor persons, we see seasonal variations in the number of daylight hours. The enclosed figure illustrates the hour of the day at which sunrises and sunsets occur at 35° and 45° north in the United States. In the center of this figure are the differences between sunsets and sunrises, the number of daylight hours in the day for each latitude. The seasonality of daylight hours is rather obvious, peaking in weeks 12 (June 14) and 13 (June 29), which bracket the summer solstice, about June 21st. Note the differences in the profiles at the two different latitudes.

Viewing this graph, there is little wonder that many businesses are seasonal, even if they are not weather sensitive.

Daylight hours at 35 and 45 degrees north latitude

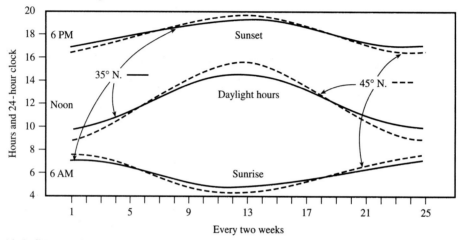

Note: January 1 is the first two weeks, December 26 is the last two weeks.

Seasonal Variation—The Ratio to Moving Average Method

The calculation of seasonal indexes is accomplished through the use of centered moving averages using a method called the **ratio to moving average method.** It is necessary to estimate seasonality first because it is very difficult to measure the trend of a highly seasonal series. Thus, by calculating seasonal indexes first, the trend can be estimated.

In principle, the decomposition of a time series is straightforward because the multiplicative time series model yields several simple identities for estimating the individual components. For example, given

$$Y_t = TCSe \qquad (5–4)$$

then

$$Se = \frac{Y_t}{TC} = \frac{\cancel{TC}Se}{\cancel{TC}} = Se \qquad (5–5)$$

This denotes that the actual value of period t divided by the trend and cyclical components equals the seasonal and error components. As shown next, the combined **trend and cyclical (TC)** components are estimated using moving averages.

Let us return to the Big City Bookstore example introduced in Chapter 3. Suppose the manager desires to identify the quarterly trend and seasonality of one of her stores.

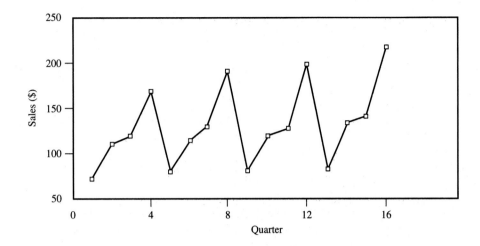

**TABLE 5–1   Seasonal Indexes Percent of Centered Moving Averages
(BIGQTR.DAT)**

Period (t)	Year	Quarter	Sales	Four-Period Average Simple	Four-Period Average Centered	Percent MA
1	1	1	72			
2		2	110	117.750		
3		3	117	118.750	118.250	.989
4		4	172	119.250	119.000	1.445
5	2	1	76	122.500	120.875	.629
6		2	112	128.000	125.250	.894
7		3	130	128.500	128.250	1.014
8		4	194	130.250	129.375	1.500
9	3	1	78	129.750	130.000	.600
10		2	119	131.500	130.625	.911
11		3	128	132.250	131.875	.971
12		4	201	136.00	134.125	1.499
13	4	1	81	139.250	137.625	.589
14		2	134	143.000	141.125	.950
15		3	141			
16		4	216			

Quarter	Average		Unadjusted Seasonal Indexes		Final Seasonal Indexes
1	(.629 + .600 + .589)/3	=	.606		.606
2	(.894 + .911 + .950)/3	=	.918	Times	.919
3	(.989 + 1.014 + .971)/3	=	.991	4.000	.992
4	(1.445 + 1.500 + 1.499)/3	=	1.481	3.997	1.482
			3.996		4.000

To do this, she plots the past four years' quarterly sales data (in Figure 5–3) and computes a centered moving average and seasonal indexes as show in Table 5–1.

To extract the trend-cyclical influence from this time series, a four-quarter centered moving average is used. Four quarter centered moving averages are used because the four-quarter total is a full year, and therefore, the average is neither seasonally high nor seasonally low because it contains all four seasons. In other words, the average of the sum of four quarters is neither seasonally high nor low.

To compute an annual centered moving average for quarterly data, first compute four-quarter moving averages. For example, the four-quarter moving averages centered on the ends of periods 2 and 3 are:

$$\text{Moving average for periods 1–4} = \frac{72 + 110 + 117 + 172}{4} = 117.75$$

$$\text{Moving average for periods 2–5} = \frac{110 + 117 + 172 + 76}{4} = 118.75$$

As shown in Table 5–1, the four-period moving average for periods 1 to 4 in column 5 is centered between periods 1 and 4, which is the end of period 2 and beginning of period 3. Also, the moving average for periods 2 to 5 is centered at the end of period 3 and beginning of period 4. To get the average centered on the middle of period 3 (i.e., $t = (3 + 4)/2 = 3.5$), the mean of these two averages is calculated in column 6 of Table 5–1.

$$\text{Centered moving average for period 3} = \frac{117.75 + 118.75}{2} = 118.250$$

Because it contains no seasonality, the centered moving average for period 3 equals the combined trend and cyclical components (TC) for that period. Using the identity of the seasonal-error terms, $Se = Y/(TC)$, we then find the combined seasonal and error component for period 3, which is:

$$Se = \frac{T\!\!\!/C\!\!\!/Se}{T\!\!\!/C\!\!\!/} = \frac{Y_3}{TC_3} = \frac{117}{118.250} = .989$$

where

Y_3 = actual value for period 3
TC_3 = centered four-quarter moving average for $t = 3$

After all of the combined seasonal error (Se) components are computed, they are averaged to eliminate the error and to isolate the seasonal indexes as shown at the bottom of the Table 5–1. That computation adjusts the seasonal indexes so that they equal 4.0, which is the number of periods per season. This is required because the average seasonal index should equal 1, and therefore the sum of all seasonal indexes total the number of periods per year. Otherwise, the final forecast will not be correct. In Table 5–1 the sum of the unadjusted seasonal indexes is 3.996. To adjust these to total 4, divide 4 by 3.996 and multiply this factor times each of the unadjusted indexes. This is shown at the bottom Table 5–1.

Interpreting Seasonal Indexes

The seasonal indexes for the Big City Bookstore are indicative of a repeating pattern. As shown at the bottom of Table 5–1, the first, second, and third quarters of the year are seasonally low, and the fourth quarter is seasonally high. The interpretation of the index for quarter 1 is that its sales are only 60.6 percent of the average quarterly sales of the year centered on quarter 1. In other words, the sales for quarter 1 are typically only 60.6 percent of the trend-cyclical values of that quarter. In contrast, the average sales for quarter 4 are 48.2 percent higher than the trend-cyclical values of that quarter (i.e., $S_{IV} = 1.482$).

In the brief time that it takes to calculate seasonal indexes, management can gain important knowledge about a time series. As we will see later, seasonal indexes are an important part of any good forecasting system. Also, seasonal indexes are used in the Winters and Fourier series methods discussed in Chapter 6.

Deseasonalizing Values to Identify Trend-Cycle

Having identified the seasonal component of demand, the trend-cycle of the series can be estimated. Decomposing the trend-cycle is done by **deseasonalizing** the actuals:

$$\frac{Y}{S} = \frac{TC\cancel{S}e}{\cancel{S}} = TCe \qquad (5\text{-}6)$$

where S = seasonal index for period t.

Using the identity of equation 5–6, column 6 of Table 5–2 shows the deseasonalized sales for the four-year period. These deseasonalized values are important in identifying movements in the trend over time. That is, just as we track deseasonalized inflation and unemployment rates in our economy, we should track deseasonalized activity in our organizations. The trend-cycle movement of sales in column 6 is clear in contrast to the not-seasonally-adjusted values of column 4 of Table 5–2.

Using Simple Linear Regression to Forecast Trend

Having calculated deseasonalized sales, simple linear regression can now be used to estimate the trend in sales. Figure 5–4 shows the deseasonalized sales of equation 5–6 versus time on the horizontal axis. In addition, we see a trend line, T, that is esti-

---

TABLE 5–2   Deseasonalized Sales for BIGQTR.DAT

(1)	*(2)*	*(3)*	*(4)*	*(5)*	*(6)*	*(7)*
					Deseasonalized	
Period					*Sales*	*Trend*
(t)	*Year*	*Quarter*	*Y_t*	*S_t*	*(TCe)*	*(T_t)*
1	1	1	72	.606	118.75	115.56
2		2	110	.919	119.69	117.41
3		3	117	.992	117.93	119.26
4		4	172	1.482	116.02	121.12
5	2	1	76	.606	125.35	122.97
6		2	112	.919	121.86	124.83
7		3	130	.992	131.03	126.68
8		4	194	1.482	130.86	128.54
9	3	1	78	.606	128.65	130.39
10		2	119	.919	129.48	132.25
11		3	128	.992	129.02	134.10
12		4	201	1.482	135.58	135.96
13	4	1	81	.606	133.59	137.81
14		2	134	.919	145.80	139.66
15		3	141	.992	142.12	141.52
16		4	216	1.482	145.70	143.37

$T_t = 113.700 + 1.1855t + 1.85t$ where $t = 1$ quarter 1 of year 1.

FIGURE 5–4

Deseasonalized values and trend, Big City Bookstore

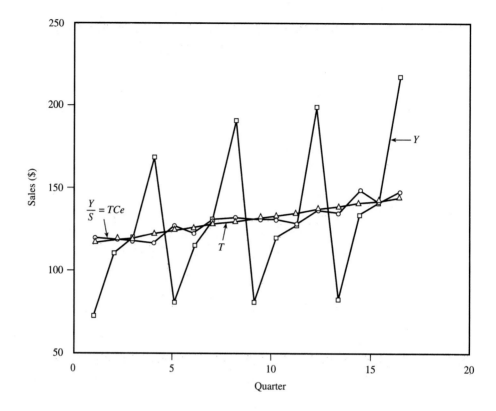

mated using the method of least squared deviations as developed in Chapter 3. The fitted trend line for column 6 is:

$$\text{Trend} = \hat{T}_t = a + bt$$
$$= 113.700 + 1.855t$$

where $t = 1$, quarter 1 of year 1. The resulting trend values, T_t, are shown in column 7 of Table 5–2. (We do not identify the cyclical index here, see Chapter 14.)

Having decomposed sales into trend and seasonal components, let us see how well the model fits the data. Table 5–3 shows the calculation of fitted values using T and S. Columns 5 and 6 show the seasonal indexes and trend values, respectively. The products of these two are shown in column 7 and are called the fitted values of sales. Finally, column 8 shows the resulting error from this fitting process. These errors are quite low, and as shown at the bottom of the table, the $\bar{R}^2$ is quite high. Of the original variance of Y (45.341^2), 99 percent has been removed by decomposing it into seasonal and trend components. The RSE shown in Table 5–3 is only 3.57, and its square (variance) is 12.75. This is a very good fit, a fact that we discuss later.

To this point, we have only fitted past history; how about forecasts? Table 5–4 illustrates two-year forecasts using the seasonal indexes and the trend equation. The pattern of the forecast very closely matches the pattern of the past data. Thus, if the past pattern persists, the resulting forecasts should be about as accurate as the past fit.

Now let's review the steps of classical decomposition.

Steps in Classical Multiplicative Decomposition

The steps in modeling and forecasting with the classical decomposition method are:

1. Calculate a moving average equal to the length of the season (e.g., four quarters, 12 months, etc.) to identify the trend cycle.

TABLE 5–3   Fitted Decomposition Time-Series Model

---

(1) Period (t)	(2) Year	(3) Quarter	(4) Sales	(5) Seasonal (S)	(6) Trend ($\hat{T}$)	(7) Fitted Values TS	(8) e Error
1	1	1	72	.606	115.56	70.062	1.938
2		2	110	.919	117.41	107.907	2.093
3		3	117	.992	119.26	118.324	−1.324
4		4	172	1.482	121.12	179.558	−7.558
5	2	1	76	.606	122.97	74.560	1.440
6		2	112	.919	124.83	114.725	−2.725
7		3	130	.992	126.68	125.684	4.316
8		4	194	1.482	128.54	190.556	3.444
9	3	1	78	.606	130.39	79.058	−1.058
10		2	119	.919	132.25	121.543	−2.543
11		3	128	.992	134.10	133.044	−5.044
12		4	201	1.482	135.96	201.554	−.554
13	4	1	81	.606	137.81	83.556	−2.556
14		2	134	.919	139.66	128.361	5.639
15		3	141	.992	141.52	140.404	.596
16		4	216	1.482	143.37	212.552	3.448
Mean			130.06				−.02803
Standard deviation			45.341			RSE	3.5674

$$\bar{R}^2 = 1 - \frac{3.570^2}{45.341^2} = .99 = 99\%$$

TABLE 5–4   Forecast of a Decomposed Time Series

---

(1) Period (t)	(2) Year	(3) Quarter	(4) Seasonal (S)	(5) Trend ($\hat{T}$)	(6) TS
17	5	1	.606	145.229	88.054
18		2	.919	147.083	135.180
19		3	.992	148.938	147.764
20		4	1.482	150.793	223.550
21	6	1	.606	152.647	92.552
22		2	.919	154.502	141.998
23		3	.992	156.356	155.125
24		4	1.482	158.211	234.548

---

2. Center the moving averages if the seasonal length is an even number.
3. Calculate the actual as a proportion of the centered moving average to obtain the seasonal index for each period.
4. Adjust the total of the seasonal indexes to equal the number of periods (e.g., 12-monthly seasonal indexes should sum to 12).
5. Deseasonalize the time series by dividing it by the seasonal index as in Table 5–2.
6. Estimate the trend-cyclical regression equation using deseasonalized data.

Seasonal Products and Contraseasonal Promotions

Many of the products we purchase at the supermarket are very seasonal. However, most providers of these products seek to reduce the seasonal troughs in demand while maintaining or increasing seasonal peaks. For example, Campbell Soup Co. promotes its products year round because approximately 50% of sales of canned soups occur in the winter. Campbell, ice cream producers, soft drink producers, and powered soft drink producers are all interested in lessening seasonal troughs using *contraseasonal marketing* techniques. Product and brand managers are well aware of the difficulty in bucking seasonal customs, often spending very large sums on promotions. Consider the following examples:

- Several pickle companies promote pickles year round, including giveaways for elementary and high school lunches. The price of pickles can vary from $.99 during seasonal promotions to $2.85 per 42-ounce jar in the off-season.

- Anheuser-Busch Co. increases beer consumption using Super Bowl promotions; these promotions increase January sales by 16% over industry averages.

- Several ice cream companies promote their products during off-season holidays.

- General Foods has pushed its diet drink, Crystal Light, in January.

- Kraft heavily advertises Kool-Aid in the winter to slowly change the custom of drinking Kool-Aid in just the summer.

However, many retailers are reluctant to devote shelf space to off-season products, believing such efforts may be unsuccessful and thereby displace bigger sellers from the shelves. To better understand the effectiveness of contraseasonal marketing, consider the following figure. As shown, the demand for soups and powdered drink mixes and ice cream are nearly mirror images of each other. The peak seasonal indexes are about 1.4 for drinks and soups, and the trough seasonal indexes are about .7, a 100 percent change. As shown, the demand for ice cream is not quite as seasonal. Such seasonal variations adversely affect the profits, revenues, costs, and internal operations of these firms. Reducing these seasonal fluctuations by increasing off-season sales increases profits and market share; however, these benefits are not without their cost; at times they can be ineffective efforts.

The seasonal modeling techniques studied in this book are invaluable tools in measuring and modeling the seasonality and impact of promotional programs.

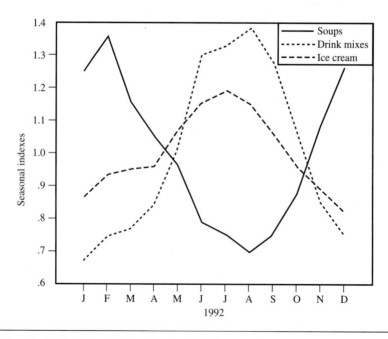

Source: "Ice Cream Seasonality's Gentle Hills," *Frozen Food Age* (September, 1994), 43, no. 2, p. 8 (1); "A Cure for Pickles," *Supermarket News* (April 24, 1995), 45, no. 17 p. 93 (4); and Eben Shapiro, "Food Firms Seek a Plan for All Seasons," *The Wall Street Journal,* July 29, 1993, p. B6.

7. Multiply the fitted trend values by their appropriate seasonal factors to compute the fitted values.

8. Calculate the errors and measure the accuracy of the fit using known actuals.

9. If cyclical factors are important, calculate cyclical indexes using one of the methods developed in Chapter 14.

10. Check for outliers, adjust the actuals and repeat steps 1 to 9 if necessary.

Remember, while completing each of these steps always check and adjust outliers. Having developed multiplicative decomposition, let's consider the additive decomposition method using the Big City Bookstore example.

Additive Decomposition Method

The steps in this method are very similar to those of the multiplicative except that instead of multiplications and divisions, additions and substractions are used in the following equation:

$$\text{Additive: } Y = T + C + S + e$$

Table 5–5 illustrates the following steps of the additive decomposition method.

1. Calculate a moving average equal to the length of the season (e.g., four quarters, 12 months, etc.), as in column 4 of Table 5–5.

2. Center the moving average as in column 5 to estimate the trend cycle.

3. Subtract the centered moving average to obtain the seasonal error factor for each period (column 6).

4. Adjust the total of the seasonal indexes to equal zero. The bottom of Table 5–5 illustrates these calculations where the mean unadjusted additive seasonal index is subtracted from each unadjusted index.

5. Deseasonalize the time series by subtracting the final additive seasonal indexes from the actual as in column 8 of Table 5–5. These deseasonalized values are estimates of trend-cyclical error.

6. Compute the trend-cyclical regression equation using deseasonalized data, column 9.

7. Add the fitted trend values and the seasonal indexes to estimate the fitted values, $\hat{Y}_t = T + S$ (column 10).

8. Calculate the errors and measure the fit using known actuals by subtracting the fitted from the actuals as in column 11.

9. If cyclical factors are important, calculate cyclical indexes using a method from Chapter 14.

10. Check for outliers, adjust the actuals, and repeat steps 1 to 9 if necessary.

The fit of the additive model in Table 5–5 is only somewhat less accurate than the multiplicative model of Table 5–3. This is evident in the calculated RSE of 5.456 and 3.570, respectively. If everything else is equal, we can use this slight difference as a basis of choosing one method over the other. Thus, the multiplicative model is somewhat better. Also, a multiplicative model is supported by the diverging shape of seasonal sales in Figure 5–4, where the differences in the peaks and troughs are greater as the series increases. Such percentage increases are indicative of a multiplicative time

TABLE 5–5   Additive Seasonal Indexes Using Centered Moving Averages (BIGQTR.DAT)

t	Qtr.	Sales	Four-Period Simple	Four-Period Centered	Average $S + e$	Seasonal Index	Deseas. Sales $= T + C$ $= 3 - 7$	Trend	$T + S$ Fitted $\hat{Y}_t$	Error
1	2	3	4	5	6	7	8	9	10	11
1	1	72				−50.802	122.802	115.208	64.406	7.594
2	2	110	117.75			−10.302	120.302	117.189	106.887	3.113
3	3	117	118.75	118.250	−1.250	−.760	117.760	119.170	118.410	−1.410
4	4	172	119.25	119.000	53.000	61.865	110.135	121.151	183.016	−11.016
5	1	76	122.50	120.875	−44.875	−50.802	126.802	123.132	72.330	3.670
6	2	112	128.00	125.250	−13.250	−10.302	122.302	125.113	114.811	−2.811
7	3	130	128.50	128.250	1.750	−.760	130.760	127.094	126.334	3.666
8	4	194	130.25	129.375	64.625	61.865	132.135	129.075	190.940	3.060
9	1	78	129.75	130.000	−52.000	−50.802	128.802	131.056	80.254	−2.254
10	2	119	131.50	130.625	−11.625	−10.302	129.302	133.037	122.735	−3.735
11	3	128	132.25	131.875	−3.875	−.760	128.760	135.018	134.258	−6.258
12	4	201	136.00	134.125	66.875	61.865	139.135	136.999	198.864	2.136
13	1	81	139.25	137.625	−56.625	−50.802	131.802	138.980	88.178	−7.178
14	2	134	143.00	141.125	−7.125	−10.302	144.302	140.961	130.659	3.341
15	3	141				−.760	141.760	142.942	142.182	−1.182
16	4	216				61.865	154.135	144.923	206.788	9.212
Mean		130.063							Mean	−.003
StdDev		45.341							RSE	5.456

Calculation of Seasonal Indexes

Quarters	Average Seasonal + Error		Unadjusted Seasonal Indexes	Final Seasonal Indexes
1	$(-44.875 - 52.000 - 56.625)/3 =$	−51.167	Each	−50.802
2	$(-13.250 - 11.625 - 7.125)/3 =$	−10.667	Plus	−10.302
3	$(-1.250 + 1.750 - 3.875)/3 =$	−1.125	.365	−.760
4	$(53.000 + 64.625 + 66.875)/3 =$	61.500		61.865
	Sum	−1.458		.000
	Mean	−.365		.000

$$\bar{R}^2 = 1 - \frac{5.4562^2}{45.3412^2} = .986$$

series. Thus, it is logical to choose the multiplicative model; the graph and the slightly inferior fit of the additive model support this conclusion.

Finally, note that if we have substantive or theoretical basis for choosing an additive model over a multiplicative model or vice versa, we should choose the model based on that substantive and theoretical knowledge.

Having developed two models using quarterly data, let's now consider a monthly time series.

Decomposition of Monthly Data

Table 5–6 illustrates the use of the decomposition method on SERIESF.DAT. As you may recall from Figure 1–16 of Chapter 1, this series is very seasonal with a pronounced trend. Let's review the steps of decomposition using the numbers given at the head of each column of Table 5–6.

TABLE 5-6 **Classical Decomposition Method Using Centered 12-Month Moving Averages, Seasonal Indexes, and Simple Linear Regression for Trend—(SERIESF.DAT)**

(1) Month	(2) Period	(3) Demand	(4) 12-Month Total	(5) 12-Month Total	(6) Centered 12-Month	(7) 12-Month Average	(8) Percent 12-Month Average
Jan	1	546					
Feb	2	578					
Mar	3	660					
Apr	4	707					
May	5	738					
Jun	6	781					
Jul	7	848	8,358	8,441	8,339.5	699.9583	1.2115
Aug	8	818	8,441	8,574	8,507.5	708.9583	1.1538
Sep	9	729	8,574	8,643	8,608.5	717.375	1.0162
Oct	10	691	8,643	8,734	8,688.5	724.0417	.9543
Nov	11	658	8,734	8,857	8,795.5	732.9583	.8977
Dec	12	604	8,857	8,979	8,918	743.1667	.8127
Jan	13	629	8,979	9,099	9,039	753.25	.8350
Feb	14	711	9,099	9,175	9,137	761.4167	.9337
Mar	15	729	9,175	9,306	9,240.5	770.0417	.9467
Apr	16	798	9,306	9,407	9,356.5	779.7083	1.0234
May	17	861	9,407	9,488	9,447.5	787.2917	1.0936
Jun	18	903	9,488	9,583	9,535.5	794.625	1.1363
Jul	19	968	9,583	9,727	9,655	804.5833	1.2031
Aug	20	894	9,727	9,834	9,780.5	815.0417	1.0968
Sep	21	860	9,834	9,976	9,905	825.4167	1.0418
Oct	22	792	9,976	10,060	10,018	834.8333	.9486
Nov	23	739	10,060	10,158	10,109	842.4167	.8772
Dec	24	699	10,158	10,234	10,196	849.6667	.8226
Jan	25	773	10,234	10,221	10,227.5	852.2917	.9069
Feb	26	818	10,221	10,252	10,236.5	853.0417	.9589
Mar	27	871	10,252	10,235	10,243.5	853.625	1.0203
Apr	28	882	10,235	10,233	10,234	852.8333	1.0342
May	29	959	10,233	10,240	10,236.5	853.0417	1.1242
Jun	30	979	10,240	10,363	10,301.5	?58.4583	1.1404
Jul	31	955	10,363	10,447	10,405	367.0833	1.1013
Aug	32	925	10,447	10,506	10,476	873	1.0696
Sep	33	843	10,506	10,593	10,549	879.0833	.9589
Oct	34	790	10,593	10,692	10,642.5	886.875	.8907
Nov	35	746	10,692	10,784	10,738	894.8333	.8336
Dec	36	822	10,784	10,929	10,856.5	904.7083	.9085
Jan	37	857	10,929	11,047	10,988	915.6667	.9359
Feb	38	876	11,047	11,142	11,094.5	924.5417	.9474
Mar	39	959	11,142	11,232	11,187	932.25	1.0286
Apr	40	981	11,232	11,229	11,230.5	935.875	1.0482
May	41	1,051	11,229	11,313	11,271	939.25	1.1189
Jun	42	1,124	11,313	11,413	11,363	946.9167	1.1870
Jul	43	1,073					
Aug	44	1,020					
Sep	45	933					
Oct	46	787					
Nov	47	830					
Dec	48	922					
Averages	24.5	827.44					

Seasonal Indexes

	Percent 12-Month MA						
(9) Season	(10) Year 1	(11) Year 2	(12) Year 3	(13) Unadjusted Index Mean	(14) Maximum	(15) Minimum	(16) Final Seasonal Index
S(1)	.83505	.9069665	.9359301	.8926482	.9359301	.8350481	.8874672
S(2)	.93379	.9589215	.9474965	.9467346	.9589215	.9337857	.9412396
S(3)	.94670	1.020354	1.028694	.9985835	1.028694	.9467020	.9927876
S(4)	1.0235	1.034200	1.048217	1.035292	1.048217	1.023460	1.02983
S(5)	1.0936	1.124212	1.118978	1.112271	1.124212	1.093623	1.105815
S(6)	1.1364	1.140416	1.187010	1.154604	1.187010	1.136385	1.147903
S(7)	1.2115	1.203107	1.101394	1.172000	1.21501	1.101394	1.165198
S(8)	1.1538	1.096876	1.059565	1.103416	1.153805	1.059565	1.097011
S(9)	1.0162	1.041898	.9589535	1.005685	1.041898	.9589535	.9998483
S(10)	.95436	.9486924	.8907681	.9312752	.9543650	.8907681	.92588699
S(11)	.89773	.8772381	.8336748	.8695482	.8977318	.8336748	.8645013
S(12)	.81274	.8226756	.9085801	.8479980	.9085801	.8127383	.8430761
Sum				12.07006			12.0

continued

TABLE 5–6   **Classical Decomposition Method Using Centered 12-Month Moving Averages, Seasonal Indexes, and Simple Linear Regression for Trend—(SERIESF.DAT)** concluded

				Trend Calculation			Forecast and Error				
(17) Period (t)	(18) Actual (Y_t)	(19) Seasonal Index (S)	(20) Deseasonalized (Y_t/S)	(21) (X-X)	(22) (X-Y)	(23) Trend	(24) Fitted ($S \times T$)	(25) Error (e)	(26) Percent Error (e/Y_t)	(27) Squared Errors (e^2)	(28) Z-Value of e^*
1	546	.88746	615.2340	1	615.234	663.8587	589.15	−43.15	−.0790	1,862.10	−1.120
2	578	.94123	614.0838	4	1,228.168	670.8607	631.44	−53.44	−.0924	2,855.90	−1.387
3	660	.99278	664.7948	9	1,994.384	677.8626	672.97	−12.97	−.0196	168.31	−.337
4	707	1.0292	686.8858	16	2,747.543	684.8646	704.91	2.08	.00294	4.33	.054
5	738	1.1058	667.3809	25	3,336.905	691.8666	765.07	−27.08	.0366	733.14	−.703
6	781	1.1479	680.3714	36	4,082.228	698.8685	802.23	−21.23	−.0271	450.83	−.551
7	848	1.1651	727.7733	49	5,094.413	705.8705	822.47	25.52	.03009	651.32	.663
8	818	1.0970	745.6624	64	5,965.299	712.8725	782.02	35.97	.04397	1,293.90	.934
9	729	.99984	729.1106	81	6,561.995	719.8744	719.76	9.23	.01266	85.28	.240
10	691	.92586	746.3252	100	7,463.252	726.8764	672.99	18.00	.02605	324.25	.468
11	658	.86450	761.1325	121	8,372.457	733.8783	634.43	23.56	.03580	555.13	.612
12	604	.84307	716.4241	144	8,597.089	740.8803	624.61	−20.62	−.0341	425.12	−.535
13	629	.88746	708.7586	169	9,213.862	747.8823	663.72	−34.72	−.0552	1,205.50	−.901
14	711	.94123	755.3868	196	10,575.42	754.8842	710.52	.47	.00066	.22	.012
15	729	.99278	734.2961	225	11,014.44	761.8862	756.39	−27.39	−.0375	750.27	−.711
16	798	1.0292	775.2969	256	12,404.75	768.8882	791.40	6.59	.00826	43.51	.171
17	861	1.1058	778.6111	289	13,236.39	775.8901	857.99	3.00	.00349	9.05	.078
18	903	1.1479	786.6522	324	14,159.74	782.8921	898.68	4.31	.00477	18.63	.112
19	968	1.1651	830.7601	361	15,784.44	789.8941	920.38	47.61	.04919	2,267.30	1.236
20	894	1.0970	814.9416	400	16,298.83	796.8960	874.20	19.79	.02214	391.88	.514
21	860	.99984	860.1305	441	18,062.74	803.8980	803.77	56.22	.06537	3,161.10	1.460
22	792	.92586	855.4118	484	18,819.06	810.9000	750.78	41.21	.05203	1,698.40	1.070
23	739	.86450	854.8281	529	19,661.05	817.9019	707.07	31.92	.04319	1,019.00	.829
24	699	.84307	829.1067	576	19,898.56	824.9039	695.45	3.54	.00506	12.55	.092
25	773	.88746	871.0181	625	21,775.45	831.9059	738.28	34.71	.04490	1,204.80	.901
26	818	.94123	869.0667	676	22,595.73	838.9078	789.61	28.38	.03470	805.80	.737
27	871	.99278	877.3277	729	23,687.85	845.9098	839.80	31.19	.03581	972.89	.810
28	882	1.0292	856.9071	784	23,993.40	852.9117	877.88	4.11	.00466	16.91	.107
29	959	1.1058	867.2335	841	25,149.77	859.9137	950.90	8.09	.00844	65.52	.210
30	979	1.1479	852.8599	900	25,585.80	866.9157	995.13	−16.13	−.0164	260.32	−.419
31	955	1.1651	819.6032	961	25,407.70	873.9176	1,018.2	−63.29	−.0662	4,005.20	−1.643
32	925	1.0970	843.2002	1,024	26,982.41	880.9196	966.37	−41.38	−.0447	1,712.10	−1.074
33	843	.99984	843.1279	1,089	27,823.22	887.9216	887.78	−44.79	−.0531	2,005.80	−1.162
34	790	.92586	853.2516	1,156	29,010.56	894.9235	828.58	−38.58	−.0488	1,488.60	−1.001
35	746	.86450	862.9253	1,225	30,202.39	901.9255	779.71	−33.72	−.0451	1,136.70	−.876
36	822	.84307	975.0010	1,296	35,100.03	908.9275	766.29	55.70	.06776	3,103.00	1.446
37	857	.88746	965.6695	1,369	35,729.77	915.9294	812.85	44.14	.05150	1,948.50	1.146
38	876	.94123	930.6876	1,444	35,366.13	922.9314	868.69	7.30	.00833	53.30	.190
39	959	.99278	965.9670	1,521	37,672.71	929.9334	923.22	35.77	.03730	1,279.70	.929
40	981	1.0292	953.0905	1,600	38,123.62	936.9353	964.37	16.62	.01695	276.50	.432
41	1,051	1.1058	950.4300	1,681	38,967.63	943.9373	1,043.8	7.17	.00683	51.55	.186
42	1,124	1.1479	979.1772	1,764	41,125.44	950.9393	1,091.5	32.41	.02883	1,050.60	.842
43	1,073	1.1651	920.8735	1,849	39,597.56	957.9412	1,116.1	−43.19	−.0402	1,865.40	−1.121
44	1,020	1.0970	929.7991	1,936	40,911.16	964.9432	1,058.5	−38.55	−.0377	1,486.30	−1.001
45	933	.99984	933.1415	2,025	41,991.37	971.9452	971.79	−38.80	−.0415	1,505.20	−1.007
46	787	.92586	850.0114	2,116	39,100.53	978.9471	906.37	−119.4	−.1516	14,251.00	−3.099
47	830	.86450	960.0911	2,209	45,124.28	985.9491	852.35	−22.35	−.0269	499.71	−.580
48	922	.84307	1,093.614	2,304	52,493.48	992.9510	837.13	84.86	.09204	7,202.30	2.203
1,176	SUM		39,763.43	38,024	1,038,706.					68,236.04	

Trend coefficients b = 7.0020 a = 656.86

Sum of squared errors   68,236.04

Standard deviation or series   130.97

RSE = 44.80 $\bar{R}^2$ = 88.30%

*Z value of error is error divided by RSE using $n - 2$ in denominator.

Columns 1 to 3 are self-explanatory. Columns 4 through 6 illustrate the calculation of the centered 12-month moving averages shown in column 7. Column 7 is the mean of column 6 and is centered on the middle month 7. Column 8, the percent of the centered 12-month moving average, results from the division of column 3, the actual time series, by the centered moving average of column 7. Thus, each month's actual value is expressed as a proportion of the moving average. Note that this procedure results in the loss of the first six and last six observations. The resulting percentages of column 8 can be viewed as seasonal-error factors.

Column 9 identifies each month of the season, January through December. Columns 10 to 12 illustrate the unadjusted seasonal factors for each of the three years. Column 13 illustrates the mean of columns 10 to 12, the unadjusted seasonal indexes. If more years of data were available, an adjusted mean might be calculated where the maximum (column 14) and minimum (column 15) would be eliminated before calculating this mean. Alternatively, with only three years of seasonal indexes, the median (i.e., middle value) might have been used for the unadjusted seasonal index.

As shown at the bottom of column 13, the sum of the 12 seasonal indexes is not 12; instead, it is 12.07. Logically, the sum of 12 seasonal indexes should be 12. To adjust these indexes, each unadjusted index of column 13 is multiplied by 12/12.07, which yields column 16, the final indexes with a sum of 12.000.

Having developed the seasonal indexes, we can calculate the deseasonalized values by dividing each actual value (column 18) by its appropriate seasonal index, (column 19). These deseasonalized values are shown in column 20. Having deseasonalized values makes estimating the trend more accurate. Columns 21 and 22 are used in the method of least squares to calculate the constant and trend coefficients shown at the bottoms of columns 19 and 20. These two parameters are used to generate the trends in columns 23.

The product of column 19, the seasonal indexes and column 23, the trend, yields the fitted values in column 24. Column 25, the fitted errors, is column 18 minus 24. From these errors we calculate the residual standard error from column 27, which equals the squared errors.

$$\text{RSE} = \sqrt{\frac{\Sigma(Y_i - \hat{Y})^2}{48 - 2 - 12}} = \sqrt{\frac{66236}{34}} = 44.80$$

where the 48-2-12 denotes that there are 48 observations, 2 degrees of freedom lost when the linear regression equation was estimated, and 12 degrees of freedom lost because of the 12 seasonal indexes.

This RSE can be used to calculate the $\overline{R}^2$ at the bottom of the table

$$\overline{R}^2 = 1 - \frac{\dfrac{\Sigma(Y_i - \hat{Y})^2}{48 - 2 - 12}}{\dfrac{\Sigma(Y_i - \overline{Y})^2}{48 - 1}} = .8830$$

This calculated $\overline{R}^2$ is very respectable and confirms the trend and seasonality of this series. The RSE can be used to identify residuals that are outliers as shown in column 28, where Z-values are calculated as

$$Z = \frac{e_t - 0}{\text{RSE}}$$

If a Z-value exceeds +2 or is less than −2, the residual is significantly greater than expected and denotes either a deficiency with the model or a very unusual actual

---

Two-Year-Ahead Forecasts Should Include Cyclical Influences

Sometimes we are surprised how well the decomposition method forecasts the next several months and, frequently, the next year or two. A good track record during one time period does not ensure a good one in future periods. Any organization that forecasts ahead two or more years without a business cycle correction is defying the laws of economics and documented history. Cyclical influences should be in forecasts, but sometimes are not because they are so difficult to predict. However, it is still very important to have forecasts that reflect cyclical influences. It is even more important to have contingency plans that are effective when significant changes occur in the business cycle. The value of future cyclical indexes can be estimated several ways, including econometric methods and other techniques developed in Chapters 6, 8, 11, and 14. These indexes can then be used to adjust the forecasts resulting from any of the other techniques developed in this book. Simply multiply the forecast by the cyclical index for multiplicative cyclical influences or simply add the cyclical index for additive influences.

---

value. As shown in column 2, observations 46 and 48 are outliers, but not extremely so. We choose to ignore these near outliers. In contrast, if we adjust one or more of these, the decomposition should be repeated.

Estimating Cyclical Indexes. As shown in column 25, there is considerable autocorrelation in the errors as evidenced by the series of continuous negative errors followed by a string of positive errors. Thus, there appears to be pattern in these errors. One explanation of these runs of positive and negative values is cyclical influences. Each of these errors can be divided by a centered four-month moving average to estimate the **cyclical index** for each period. As mentioned previously, this process is developed in Chapter 14, Table 14–4; if you are interested, you can review this material now.

Census Method II X-11

One of the most highly developed decomposition methods is the **Census Method II X-11,** procedure. This is the primary method that the federal government uses to deseasonalize the many macroeconomic times series data (e.g., GDP, unemployment, etc.) reported in the media. The predecessor of this method was developed by the National Bureau of Economic Research during the 1920s to forecast economic time series. It is often called the Shiskin decomposition method (for Julius Shiskin, the statistician responsible for its development) and was originally called the Census Method I, which was the computerization of the classical decomposition method. Because of its complexity, the Census Method II is infeasible without a computer.

This procedure is essentially the same as the centered moving average decomposition method developed here in Table 5–3, 5–5, and 5–6. The method decomposes a time series into three components:

$$Y = TC \times S \times I$$

where *TC* is the combined effect of trend and cycle components.

The components are estimated as follows:

1. Estimate the *TC* component via a centered moving average of *Y*.

2. Estimate *SI* as the ratio of *Y/TC*.

3. Adjust *SI* for extreme points (find extreme points and smooth by a moving average).
4. Estimate *S* by an averaging of *SI*.
5. Estimate *TCI* by the ratio of *Y/S*.
6. Estimate *I* by the ratio of *TCI* to *TC*.

This yields the following forecasting model using trend-cyclical and seasonal factors that can be the basis for a forecast. That is,

$$\hat{Y}_t = TC_t \times S_t$$

where $\hat{Y}_t$ is the forecasted value. The above six steps are repeated more than once for refinements during the following four major phases.

The first phase involves adjusting the data for trading days in a month or quarter. Trading day adjustments are made to a time series so that the number of days are consistent for the same periods (i.e., months) from year to year. That is, the number of working, sales, and trading days in the month of June will vary from year to year. For example, there may be 23, 24, or 25 trading or sales days in June for years 1, 2, and 3, respectively. To make these months more consistent, they are adjusted to have sales that reflect the same number of days. Thus, trading day adjustments can change the values of monthly data.

In the second phase of the X-II method, preliminary estimates of the seasonal indexes are made. These preliminary estimates are then used to calculate a trend-cycle component. Then, outlier adjustments are made to these trend-cycle components and this adjusted trend-cycle component is used to estimate better seasonal indexes in the next phase.

In the third phase, the preliminary seasonal indexes are refined. After the seasonal-index refinement, the trend-cycle and irregular components are refined further. These are output for use in reports and forecasts.

In the final phase, several summary statistics are generated as diagnostic tools. With these statistics, the user can confirm the appropriateness of the adjustments and final indexes.

Fortunately, software for executing this method is available in a number of commercial and public-domain software packages. To appreciate the complexity of this method, consider the SAS implementation of the Census Method II X-11. The user can specify a number of different options. The standard output involves 17 to 27 tables; the long output involves 27 to 39 tables; and the full output includes 44 to 59 tables.

Plots of the seasonal indexes, the trend-cycle curves, and other graphs are extremely useful in tracking trends and estimating turning points. In addition, this method is a very good way to identify and adjust the outliers in a time series. Because of its heavy computer requirements, the method is not used routinely in automated forecasting systems. However, this is a cost-effective method for important time series. Also, it is limited to time series with sufficient history (at least three years of monthly data). Its principal uses in business are in monthly and quarterly forecasting for seasonal time series for 1 to 10 years and in analyzing trend and seasonal factors for use in other forecasting methods.

Extensions and adaptations to the X-11 procedure have been developed. Levenbach and Cleary summarize the Seasonal Adjustment—Bell Laboratories (SABL) decomposition program, which has alternative methods of smoothing, summarizing, and displaying data. For details of the Census Method II, consult either the Bureau of the Census technical paper no. 15, "The X-11 Variant of the Census Method II Seasonal Adjustment Program" or Dagum or Makridakis, Wheelwright, and McGee.

In addition, the X-11 ARIMA is a popular method which Dagum (1988) develops. Fortunately, several X-11 computer codes are in the public domain.

Decomposition Using Regression Analysis

(This section may be omitted for those unfamiliar with multiple regression methods.)

As mentioned previously, multiple regression techniques are versatile in modeling a variety of relationships. This section illustrates their use in decomposing a time series using dummy (dichotomous) variables on the quarterly data of the Big City Bookstore in Table 5–1. This data is presented in Table 5–7. As previously mentioned, this firm desires to measure the trend and seasonal influences on the quarterly demand for its product. To do so, it must create **seasonal dummy variables**. These dummy variables will be used to model the seasonal increases or decreases in each quarter.

As Table 5–7 shows, four new variables have been created to perform the **regression decomposition** of this quarterly demand. Column 3 introduces a time variable, trend, which is used to measure the long-run change in demand over time. The last three columns (4, 5, and 6) have been created to represent the four quarterly influences on demands. These three variables are $Q2$, $Q3$, and $Q4$. Only three variables are necessary to measure the effect of four quarters because when all three are zero, the regression constant, q embodies the first quarter seasonality.

As shown in the table, for periods 1, 5, 9, and 13 each first quarter has columns 4,5, and 6 equal to zero. More important, for mathematical reasons multiple regression will not work if all four dummy variables are used to represent the four dependent events (i.e., quarters). That is, to represent p mutually exclusive, collectively exhaustive events (e.g., four quarters), we must use only p minus 1 dummy variable ($4 - 1 = 3$ dummies). To use p dummy variables for p events will result in indeterminate regression coefficients.

TABLE 5–7   Decomposition Using Multiple Regression (BIGDREG.DAT)

(1) Time	*(2)* Demand	*(3)* Trend	*(4)* Q2	*(5)* Q3	*(6)* Q4
1	72	1	0	0	0
2	110	2	1	0	0
3	117	3	0	1	0
4	172	4	0	0	1
5	76	5	0	0	0
6	112	6	1	0	0
7	130	7	0	1	0
8	194	8	0	0	1
9	78	9	0	0	0
10	119	10	1	0	0
11	128	11	0	1	0
12	201	12	0	0	1
13	81	13	0	0	0
14	134	14	1	0	0
15	141	15	0	1	0
16	216	16	0	0	1

The seasonal influences on demand in Table 5–7 can be modeled using either an additive model, equation 5–7, or a multiplicative model, equation 5–8. We briefly present both models.

$$D_t = a + b_1 t + b_2 Q2_t + b_3 Q3_t + b_4 Q4_t + e_t \tag{5-7}$$

$$Ln\,(D_t) = a' + b_1't + b_2'Q2_t + b_3'Q3_t + b_4'Q4_t + e_t' \tag{5-8}$$

where

$$D_t = \text{demand in period } t$$
$$t = \text{time value in period } t$$
$$Q2_t, Q3_t, Q4_t = \text{dummy variables for each quarter}$$
$$a, b_i, a', b_i' = \text{relevant regression coefficients; where } i \text{ equals 1 to 4}$$
$$Ln(D_t) = \text{logarithm of demand to the base of the natural}$$
$$\text{number } \mathbf{e}.$$

Additive Seasonal Regression Models

Using the data of Table 5–7 and multiple regression software, the following additive relationship results:

$$D_t = 62.88 + 1.98t + 40.02Q2_t + 48.29Q3_t + 113.06Q4_t \tag{5-9}$$
$$\quad\;\; (15.73)\;\;\; (5.62)\quad\;\;(8.96)\qquad (10.71)\qquad\;\; (24.71)$$

$$\overline{R}^2 = .981 \qquad F = 191.69 \qquad RSE = 6.296$$

The interpretation of this model is that demand increases 1.98 units each quarter, as measured by T_t. The additive seasonal influences of each quarter are interpreted relative to quarter 1. That is, each quarterly value is related to quarter 1. For example, the demand in quarter 2 is, on average, 40.02 units higher than demand in quarter 1. Similarly, quarters 3 and 4 are 48.29 and 113.06 units higher than quarter 1, respectively. Remember that at most only one of $Q2$, $Q3$, or $Q4$ is nonzero at time t. Finally, the parenthetical values below bs are t-values noting the statistical significance of each coefficient. Thus, insignificant coefficients can be eliminated from a model; in this case, all coefficients are statistically significant.

From a statistical standpoint, this is a very good model of demand. Its $\overline{R}^2$ is high, and all of the coefficients are statistically different than zero. Interestingly, the regression seasonal indexes are nearly the equivalent of the additive classical decomposition method. This near equivalency is shown in the following table.

Additive Classical Decomposition Indexes		Regression Indexes
Q1	−50.802	Embodied in constant
Q2	−10.302	40.02, Q2 > Q1 by 40.02 −10.302 − (−50.302) = 40.5 approx. 40.02
Q3	−.760	48.29, Q3 > Q1 by 48.29 −.760 − (−50.802) = 50.04 approx. 48.29
Q4	61.865	113.06, Q4 > Q1 by 113.06 61.865 − (−50.802) = 112.67 approx. 113.06

The multiplicative classical decomposition method of Table 5–2 had an RSE of 3.570 and the additive classical decomposition method had an RSE of 5.456; that of this method is 6.296. Thus, the multiplicative model appears better than either additive model. Also, Figure 5–2 confirms that this data is better modeled using a multiplicative model because the magnitudes of the seasonal peaks and troughs are a constant percentage of the level of the series. Thus, we choose the multiplicative model of Table 5–2 over the additive model of Table 5–7 and equation 5–9.

As shown in the next section, multiplicative regression models can be used to represent percentage-growth influences using logarithmic transformations.

Multiplicative Seasonal Regression Models

The modeling of percentage growth is most easily done using logarithms. To model the demand of Table 5–7 as a multiplicative model, first take natural logarithms of demand (i.e., logs to the base **e**), then use multiple regression to relate the logarithmic demands to the independent variables in equation 5–8.

Equation 5–10 illustrates the results of this multiple regression model. As shown, all regression coefficients are statistically significantly different than zero.

$$Ln\hat{D}_t = 4.239 + .01434t + .4200Q2_t + .489Q3_t + .891Q4_t \qquad (5\text{--}10)$$
$$\phantom{Ln\hat{D}_t =} (220.91) \quad (8.49) \quad\quad (19.59) \quad\quad (22.61) \quad\quad (40.56)$$

$$\overline{R}^2 = .992 \qquad F = 499.26 \qquad RSE = .030224$$

Unfortunately, the interpretation of equation of 5–10 is slightly more complicated because of the use of logarithms. To better interpret this model, we need to transform the log model using antilogs.

Equation 5–11 is the result of taking the antilogs of the right-hand and left-hand sides of equation 5–10. This was accomplished by taking the natural number **e** to the power of each side of the equation. Because the addition of logs is the equivalent of multiplication of antilogs, we see that equation 5–11 is a multiplicative model.

$$\hat{D}_t = (e^{a'})(e^{blt})(e^{b2Q2t})(e^{b3Q3t})(e^{b4Q4t}) \qquad (5\text{--}11)$$
$$\hat{D}_t = (e^{4.239})(e^{.01434t})(e^{.420Q2t})(e^{.489Q3t})(e^{.891Q4t})$$

Interpretation of this relationship is best accomplished by calculating a few examples. Let us consider the last four quarters of data in Table 5–7. (Remember as we fit demands using equation 5–11 that any number taken to the zero power equals one. Thus, when Q2 equals zero, **e** to the power of zero equals one.)

First quarter, $t = 13$, $Q2_{13} = Q3_{13} = Q4_{13} = 0$
$$\hat{D}_{13} = (e^{4.239})(e^{.01434(13)})(e^{.420(0)})(e^{.489(0)})(e^{.891(0)}),$$
$$= 69.338(1.2049) = 83.55$$

From Table 5–7: $D_{13} = 81$; $error_{13} = 81 - 83.55 = -2.55$.

Second quarter, $t = 14$, $Q2_{14} = 1$, $Q3_{14} = Q4_{14} = 0$
$$\hat{D}_{14} = (e^{4.239})(e^{.01434(14)})(e^{.420(1)})(e^{.489(0)})(e^{.891(0)}),$$
$$= 128.99$$

From Table 5–7: $D_{14} = 134$; $error_{14} = 134 - 128.99 = 5.01$.

Third quarter, $t = 15$, $Q2_{15} = 0$, $Q3_{15} = 1$, $Q4_{15} = 0$
$$\hat{D}_{15} = 69.338 \, (e^{.01434(15)})(e^{.489}) = 140.20$$

From Table 5–7: $D_{15} = 141$; $error_{15} = 141 - 140.20 = .8$.

Fourth quarter, $t = 16$, $Q2_{16} = Q3_{16} = 0$, $Q4_{16} = 1$
$$\hat{D}_{16} = 69.338 \, (e^{.01434(16)})(e^{.891(1)}) = 212.60$$

From Table 5–7: $D_{16} = 216$; $error_{16} = 216 - 212.60 = 3.40$.
These fitted values are quite accurate.

As shown below, the coefficients $b'_1, b'_2, b'_3,$ and b'_4 of equation 5–8 are meaningful measures of the relationship after transforming it back to original numbers.

The trend percentage-growth rate can be calculated from the coefficient of *t:*

$$e^{b'1} - 1 = e^{.01434} - 1 = .0144$$

This denotes that there is a 1.44 percent increase in demand each quarter.

Quarterly demands versus quarter 1 demand: Each of the coefficients of the dummy variables can be used to determine its seasonal index.

$$e^{b'2} - 1 = 1.522 \tag{5-12}$$

denotes that quarter 2 demand is 1.522 times quarter 1 demand.

$$e^{b'3} - 1 = 1.631 \tag{5-13}$$

denotes that quarter 3 demand is 1.632 times quarter 1 demand.

$$e^{b'4} - 1 = 2.438 \tag{5-14}$$

denotes that quarter 4 demand is 2.438 times quarter 1 demand.

As shown below, these quarterly demand ratios nearly equal those of the ratios of the classical decomposition multiplicative seasonal indexes of Table 5–2. That is, as shown next, the ratios of the classical multiplicative seasonal indexes of Table 5–2 are nearly equal to the transformed regression coefficients of equations 5–12, 5–13, and 5–14.

$$\frac{\text{Seasonal index quarter 2}}{\text{Seasonal index quarter 1}} = \frac{.918}{.606} = 1.515$$

$$\frac{\text{Seasonal index quarter 3}}{\text{Seasonal index quarter 1}} = \frac{.992}{.606} = 1.637$$

$$\frac{\text{Seasonal index quarter 4}}{\text{Seasonal index quarter 1}} = \frac{1.482}{.606} = 2.446$$

Thus, we see that the multiplicative regression model of equation 5–11 is nearly identical to the classical decomposition time series model of Table 5–3. This near-equivalency is not limited to classical decomposition and regression multiplicative models; it is common in the models we discuss in the next several chapters.

Testing the Significance of Seasonal Indexes

The following question should always be asked: Are the fitted seasonal indexes of the classical decomposition method statistically significant? Fortunately, there are several ways that seasonal indexes can be tested to confirm that they are statistically significantly different than 1.00 for multiplicative indexes or 0.00 for additive indexes. One of the easiest ways to test their significance is to create dummy variables as in the previous examples and to perform either an analysis of variance or regression analysis. In some cases where there is extremely high or nonlinear trends it is best to perform the regression on data that has been detrended using one of the methods developed in the next chapter.

Significance tests on seasonal indexes are important, because without them we may be misled to believe that there is seasonality when none exists. Unfortunately, many decomposition routines do not perform such tests; however, the Census Method

II X-11 does provide a statistical significance test. One of the advantages of using regression analysis is that the statistical significance of the seasonal indexes can be confirmed through the use of regression coefficient *t*-tests. Another way of testing the statistical significance of seasonality is through *t*-tests on the ACFs at seasonal lags as developed in Chapter 2; finally, the Kruskal-Wallis one-way analysis of variance can be performed.

Advantages

The classical decomposition of a time series is easily understood and applied. It provides management with an important perspective on the underlying cause-and-effect relationships in a time series. By decomposing a time series into its components, management can analyze and identify the causes of these variations. This method is easily implemented by simple spreadsheet programs, and the interpretation and use of seasonal indexes are intuitive yet insightful. The most sophisticated decomposition method is the Department of Commerce's Census II X-11-ARIMA method. This method is so computationally intense that is not routinely used in automated forecasting environments. However, it is one of the best techniques for decomposing an important time series, and its popularity is increasing as it becomes available from many microcomputer software vendors. Finally, decomposition methods provide a very easy way of generating deseasonalized values, which serves as an important early detection tool of management. These detection tools, called tracking signals, are discussed in Chapter 17.

Disadvantages

Because of the manner in which seasonal indexes and trends are calculated, overfitting models can be a problem with decomposition methods. This is true because the form of the model is decided before any analysis is done on the time series. There may be a tendency for decomposition methods to model large random variations as either seasonal or trend influences. That is, a large random error in only one period will influence the estimate of seasonal and trend values. Therefore, when calculating seasonal indexes, it is important to eliminate outliers and extraordinarily high or low indexes; then a modified mean or a median of the seasonal indexes should be used.

Another serious problem when deseasonalizing data and calculating trends is that the division by abnormally low seasonal indexes might generate extremely large forecasts. This creates large errors when forecasting. Consequently, it is important to check for outliers in each step of the method. We have seen badly designed commercial systems in which this is not done. The statistical tests for outliers discussed in book Appendix B should be applied to each of the deseasonalized trend values.

Because of these problems, the $\bar{R}^2$ of the fitted decomposition model may be quite high relative to actual $\bar{R}^2$ values realized when forecasting. Also, the multiperiod-ahead forecasts of a decomposition model may be greatly influenced by future changes in the cyclical influences. Consequently, we very cautiously forecast one to two seasonal cycles into the future using decomposition methods. We are even more cautious in forecasting several years into the future. Although this method has several disadvantages, it is useful in conjunction with other models of trend and cyclical variations. Thus, the more sophisticated the decomposition program, the better.

Finally, it is very difficult to simultaneously decompose trend and seasonality in a series when only a few seasonal cycles exist. The percentage of moving average method estimates the trend using deseasonalized values. However, the regression methods of equations 5–9 and 5–10 simultaneously estimate trend and seasonal values, not a good practice. Instead, we recommend estimating trends using the method of differences as developed in the next chapter. After estimating trends using differences, detrending the data is easily done; then apply regression analysis to estimate seasonal indexes as developed here. This is an easy modification of the method developed in this chapter, one you may be asked to do as homework in Chapter 6.

Summary

This chapter has introduced decomposition methods, including multiplicative, additive, regression, and Census Method II X-11. The classical decomposition method is important because it is effective for short-to-medium-term forecasts. The power and versatility of multiple regression applications in forecasting is clearly illustrated in the Big City Bookstore example. In addition, this chapter lays the groundwork for seasonal indexes in Winters' method and Fourier series analysis. The theoretical relationship between these methods are very strong. Each decomposes a time series into trend, seasonality, and randomness. Although the methods of estimating these components differ, the underlying models are similar. We develop these methods in the next chapter.

Finally, although we have highlighted some of the limitations of decomposition methods, they are nonetheless very important techniques. Widely available versions of the Census Method II X-11 are very sophisticated decomposition procedures that are valuable to those wanting to measure seasonality, track trends, and detect cyclical variations and outliers. A clear understanding of this chapter is an essential part of the effective use of these methods.

Key Terms

additive decomposition method
additive seasonal index
census method II X-11
cyclical index
deseasonalizing
multiplicative decomposition method

ratio to moving average method
regression decomposition
seasonal dummy variables
seasonal indexes
trend-cycle (TC)

Key Formulas

Classical decomposition method:

$$Y_t = f(T, C, S, e)$$

(5–1)

Additive:

$$Y_t = T + C + S + e$$

(5–2)

Multiplicative:

$$Y_t = T \times C \times S \times e$$

(5–3)

Multiplicative seasonal error:

$$Se = \frac{Y_t}{TC} = \frac{TCSe}{TC}$$

(5–5)

Multiplicative trend cyclical:

$$\frac{Y}{S} = \frac{TCSe}{S} = TCe$$

(5–6)

Least squares estimated trend:

$$\hat{T}_t = a + bt$$

Census method II-X11:

$$\hat{Y}_t = TC_t \times S_t$$

Decomposition using regression analysis:

Additive:

$$D_t = a + b_1t + b_2Q2_t + b_3Q3_t + b_4Q4_t + e_t$$

(5–7)

Multiplicative:

$$Ln(D_t) = a' + b_1't + b_2'Q2_t + b_3'Q3_t + b_4'Q4_t + e_t$$

(5–8)

Fitted additive:

$$D_t = 62.88 + 1.98t + 40.02Q2_t + 48.29Q3_t + 113.06Q4_t$$
$$(15.73)\ \ (5.62)\ \ \ \ \ (8.96)\ \ \ \ \ \ (10.71)\ \ \ \ \ \ (24.71)$$
$$\bar{R}^2 = .981\ \ \ \ \ F = 191.69\ \ \ \ RSE = 6.296$$

(5–9)

Fitted multiplicative using logs:

$$Ln(D_t) = 4.239 + .01434t + .4202Q2_t + .489Q3_t + .891Q4_t$$
$$(220.91)\ \ (8.49)\ \ \ \ \ \ (19.56)\ \ \ \ \ \ (22.61)\ \ \ (40.56)$$
$$\bar{R}^2 = .992\ \ \ F = 499.26\ \ \ RSE = 0.30224$$

(5–10)

Logarithmic reexpressed in original measure:

$$D_t = (e^{a'})(e^{b1t})(e^{b2Q2t})(e^{b3Q3t})(e^{b4Q4t})$$
$$D_t = (e^{4.239})(e^{.01434t})(e^{.420Q2t})(e^{.489Q3t})(e^{.891Q4t})$$

(5–11)

Trend percentage growth rate from coefficient of t:

$$e^{b'1} - 1 = e^{.01434} - 1 = .0144$$

Seasonal index from seasonal dummy variables:

$$e^{b'2} = 1.522$$

(5–12)

Review Problems Using Your Software

R5–1 Repeat the analysis of the following tables and interpret your results.

a. Table 5–1   *b.* Table 5–2
c. Table 5–3   *d.* Table 5–4
e. Table 5–5   *f.* Table 5–6

R5–2 Repeat multiple regression analysis yielding the following equations and interpret your results.
  a. Equation 5–9
  b. Equation 5–10
  c. Equations 5–12 to 5–14

Problems

5–1 Define the components of the multiplicative and additive classical decomposition methods. Explain the units of these components; first the multiplicative, then the additive components. Use some actual numeric examples.

5–2 Explain the forecasting significance of the special interest box, Daylight Hours and Seasonality. Why is this important in forecasting?

5–3 How do you interpret a seasonal index for an additive model? How about a multiplicative model?

5–4 Why is it important to deseasonalize a time series before fitting a trend of a time series.

5–5 What are typical causes of the following time series components? Use the soft drink industry as an example.
  a. Trend
  b. Cyclical
  c. Seasonal
  d. Irregular

5–6 Why is the simultaneous decomposition of trend and seasonality using regression not recommended?

5–7 Why are the sums of four quarterly seasonal indexes equal to 4?

5–8 How can cyclical indexes be incorporated in forecasts generated by a decomposition method that only has trend and seasonal components?

5–9 How can the statistical significance of seasonal indexes be tested? What are the null and alternative hypotheses?

5–10 Seasonal indexes of sales for the Werner Products Company are January .78, February .89, March 1.01, April 1.01, May 1.20, June 1.25, July 1.20, and so on. Company sales increased from 10,000,000 in January to 15,000,000 in April of the same year. Estimate the monthly trend between January and April? Using this information, forecast sales of May through July.

5–11 Repeat the multiplicative decomposition of Tables 5–3 and 5–4.
  a. Interpret your seasonal indexes.
  b. Interpret the trend.
  c. Forecast two years into the future.
  d. Do your results agree with those in the book?

5–12 Repeat the additive decomposition of Table 5–5.
  a. Interpret your seasonal indexes.
  b. Interpret the trend.
  c. Forecast two years into the future.
  d. Do your results agree with those in the book?

5–13 Repeat the decomposition of Table 5–7 using the regression method developed in this chapter. Choose the appropriate regression approach:
  a. Interpret your seasonal indexes.
  b. Interpret the trend.
  c. Forecast two years into the future.
  d. Do your results agree with those in the book?

5–14 The following data has been collected over the last 24 quarters (i.e., the last six years). This data in file COMPUTER.DAT represents the number of sophisticated personal computers sold through a large mail-order firm. The numbers are given in hundreds of units.

t	Units	t	Units
1	100	13	134
2	120	14	137
3	150	15	193
4	90	16	156
5	116	17	159
6	125	18	150
7	156	19	214
8	106	20	167
9	133	21	177
10	128	22	158
11	167	23	228
12	134	24	190

a. Plot this data. What type of model do you recommend?

b. Use the decomposition procedure you think appropriate, using only the first 16 observations, and interpret the results.

c. Plot the fitted values versus the actual values for these 16 observations. Comment on the validity of the model using appropriate error statistics and graphs.

d. Using the model fitted to the first 16 observations, forecast demands for periods 17 through 24. Calculate the forecast errors.

e. Calculate error statistics and comment on model validity and usefulness.

5–15 Midwestern University has reduced its undergraduate enrollments of night part-time students because of limited resources. In year 1, the school stopped offering night classes. Analyze the following fall (FA) and spring (SP) semester data using appropriate models. (UGDATA.DAT)

	Year 1		Year 2		Year 3		Year 4		Year 5	
t	1	2	3	4	5	6	7	8	9	10
Semester	FA	SP	FA	SP	FA	SP	FA	SP	FA	SP
Students	935	858	638	564	429	472	356	344	324	
Hours	7,902	7,275	6,212	6,047	5,242	6,047	4,578	4,025	3,828	

a. Is the trend linear or nonlinear? Is it seasonal?

b. Based on *a*, forecast the number of students for the spring semester of year 5 and years 6 and 7.

c. Does your model fit the data well? Use RSE, $\bar{R}^2$, and ME.

d. Comment on the validity of the forecast.

5–16 A northeastern university is facing declining enrollments because several new MBA programs entered the metropolitan area. The following is the number of students enrolled during the fall (FA), spring (SP), and summer (SU) semesters over the last 4.3 years. (MBADATA.DAT)

FA	SP	SU	FA	SP	SU	FA	SP	SU	FA	SP	SU	FA
632	612	355	585	542	292	464	429	233	392	369	210	356

Fit a classical decomposition model and answer the following:
a. What is the annual trend for enrollment?
b. What are the seasonal indexes?
c. Forecast the fall, spring, and summer of the fifth year and comment on the validity of the model.

5–17 A southeastern university is facing increasing enrollments in its MS in accounting program. Below find the number of students enrolled for fall (FA), spring (SP), and summer (SU) semesters over the last 4.3 years. (MSDATA.DAT)
Fit a classical decomposition model and answer the following:
a. What is the annual trend for enrollments?
b. What are the seasonal indexes?
c. Forecast the enrollments for the fifth year and comment on the validity of the model.

FA	SP	SU	FA	SP	SU	FA	SP	SU	FA	SP	SU	FA
90	91	77	118	109	84	129	137	100	160	148	128	182

5–18 A northwestern university is facing increasing enrollments in its master of public administration program. Below find the number of students enrolled for fall (FA), spring (SP), and summer (SU) semesters over the last 4.3 years. (MPADATA.DAT)
Fit a classical decomposition model and answer the following:
a. What is the annual trend for enrollments?
b. What are the seasonal indexes?
c. Forecast the fall, spring, and summer of the fifth year and comment on the validity of the model.

FA	SP	SU	FA	SP	SU	FA	SP	SU	FA	SP	SU	FA
122	117	60	127	131	80	157	132	76	139	146	91	152

5–19 Repeat problem 5–16 using regression decomposition analysis, where two dummy variables represent FA, SP, and SU as

FA	0	0
SP	1	0
SU	0	1

5–20 Repeat problem 5–17 using regression analysis as in problem 5–19.

5–21 Repeat problem 5–18 using regression analysis as in problem 5–19.

5–22 Repeat problem 5–15 using regression analysis.

5–23 The time series BIRTHMAR.DAT is the quarterly marriages in the United States. Fit an appropriate classical decomposition model to the first six years and judge the effectiveness of this model in forecasting the next two years by quarter. Be sure to calculate the ME, MPE, MAPE, RSE, and $\bar{R}^2$ for both the fit and forecast. Discuss the differences between the fit and forecast as measured by these statistics. Comment about anything you found unusual. Does this model fit the data well? Is the model useful from a practical standpoint? If you are analyzing this time series using several different methods, add these results to your master Forecasting Summary table and compare those results with the other methods as you complete this analysis.

5–24 The time series RETAIL.DAT is the monthly retail sales in the United States. Repeat the analyses of problem 5–23 using the first nine years and forecast the last two years.

5–25 The time series SUPEROIL.DAT is the sales of the Superoil Company in thousands of barrels during the last 108 months. Repeat the analysis of problem 5–23 using the first 8 years and forecast the last year.

Minicases: Common Assignment for Minicases

For each of the minicases complete the following analysis. Forecast with a decomposition method, being sure to calculate the ME, MPE, MAPE, RSE, AND $\overline{R}^2$ for both the fit and forecast. Discuss the differences between the fit and forecast performance as measured by these statistics. Comment about anything that you found unusual. Does this model fit the data well? Is the model useful from a practical standpoint? If you analyzed this series and filled out the Master Forecasting Summary Table in other chapters, combine these results with those already recorded.

Minicase 5–1 Kansas Turnpike, Daily Data Complete the common minicase forecasting assignment using TURN-PIKD.DAT of minicase 1–1. Use a decomposition model to forecast the number of vehicles that are using the turnpike each day. This method may not be in your statistical package, thus a spreadsheet may be the best method for fitting this model. Fit a decomposition model to the first 11 weeks, then compare the accuracy of that fit with the forecast of weeks 12 and 13.

Minicase 5–2 Domestic Air Passengers by Quarter Complete the common minicase forecasting assignment using the file PASSAIR.DAT, which is a time series of the quarterly passengers who have flown on domestic flights of U.S. airlines from the first quarter of 1982 through the second quarter of 1994, 50 observations. Fit to 42 observations and forecast 8.

Minicase 5–3 Hospital Census by Month Complete the common minicase forecasting assignment using the file CENSUSM.DAT. Fit this decomposition model to the first seven years, then compare the accuracy of the fit of the first seven years with the forecast of years 8 to 10.

Minicase 5–4 Henry Machler's Hideaway Orchids Complete the common minicase forecasting assignment using the file MACHLERD.DAT. Calculate the fitted error in using this relationship over the usable 19 weeks of daily data, then forecast the 20th week.

Minicase 5–5 Your Forecasting Project Complete the common minicase forecasting assignment using your time series.

Minicase 5–6 Midwestern Building Materials LUMBER.DAT is a highly seasonal series of lumber sales of a large midwestern building materials company with 120 observations starting in January. Complete the common seasonal smoothing assignment given above; withhold and forecast the last 12 months of data.

Minicase 5–7 International Airline Passengers AIRLINE.DAT is a highly seasonal monthly series of international airline passengers with 144 observations from 1949 through 1960. Because the variance of this series widens as the level increases, either logarithms should be used with an additive model or the original series should be analyzed with a multiplicative model. Complete the common seasonal smoothing assignment given previously; withhold and forecast the last 36 months. Fit a decomposition model to the first nine years, then forecast years 10 to 12.

Minicase 5–8 Automobile Sales AUTO.DAT is a highly seasonal monthly time series of auto sales of a large automobile manufacturer with 185 observations starting in January of year 1. Complete the common seasonal smoothing assignment given previously; withhold and forecast the last 12 months.

Minicase 5–9 Consumption of Distilled Spirits SPIRITS.DAT is a highly seasonal monthly time series of the consumption of alcoholic spirits in United States with 132 observations from January 1975 to December 1991. Complete the common seasonal smoothing assignment given previously; withhold and forecast the last 12 months.

Minicase 5–10 Discount Consumer Electronics ELECT.DAT is a highly seasonal monthly time series of the sales of consumer electronics from a large retail discounter with 185 observations starting in May. Complete the common seasonal smoothing assignment given previously; withhold and forecast the last 12 months.

References

Bell, W.R., and S.C. Hillmer. (1984). "Issues Involved with the Seasonal Adjustment of Economic Time Series." *Journal of Business and Economic Statistics,* 2 (1984), pp. 291–320.

Croxton, F.E., D.J. Cowdon, and B.W. Bolch. *Practical Business Statistics.* Englewood Cliffs, NJ: Prentice-Hall, 1969.

Dagum, E.B. *The X-11 ARIMA/88 Seasonal Adjustment Method.* Ottawa: Statistics Canada, 1988.

Dagum, E.B. *A Comparison and Assessment of Seasonal Adjustment Methods for Employment and Unemployment Statistics.* National Commission on Employment and Unemployment Statistics,

Background Paper No. 5. Washington, DC: Government Printing Office, 1978.

Frecka, T.J., P. Newbold, and P.A. Silhan. "Seasonal Adjustment at the Corporate Level Using X-11 Procedures." *Advances in Quantitative Analysis of Finance and Accounting* 1B (1991), pp. 39–53.

Makridakis, S, S.C. Wheelwright, and V.E. McGee. *Forecasting: Methods and Applications.* 2d ed. New York: John Wiley & Sons, 1983.

Makridakis, S., A. Anderson, R. Carbone, R. Fildes, M. Hibon, R. Lewandowski, J. Newton, E. Parzen, and R. Winkler. "The Accuracy of Extrapolation (Time Series) Methods." *Journal of Forecasting* 1 (1982), pp. 111–53.

Nerlove, M., D.M. Grether, and J.L. Carvalho. *Analysis of Economic Time Series: A Synthesis.* Orlando, FL: Academic Press, 1979.

Pierce, D.A. "A Survey of Recent Developments in Seasonal Adjustment." *The American Statistician* 34 (1980), pp. 125–34.

Shiskin, J., A.H. Young, and J.C. Musgrave. *The X-11 variant of the Census Method II seasonal adjustment program.* Technical Paper No. 15. U.S. Department of Commerce, Bureau of Economic Analysis, 1967.

Wallis, K.F. "Seasonal Adjustment and Relations between Variables." *Journal of the American Statistical Association* 69 (1974), pp. 18–31.

Wallis, K.F. "Seasonal Adjustment and Revision of Current Data: Linear Filters for the X-11 Method." *Journal of the Royal Statistical Society A* 145 (1982), pp. 76–85.

Wilson, J.H., and Barry Keating. *Business Forecasting.* Homewood, IL: Richard D. Irwin, 1990.

Young, A.H. "Linear Approximation to the Census and BLS Seasonal Adjustment Methods." *Journal of the American Statistical Association* 63 (1968), pp. 445–57.

Zellner A. (Ed.). *Seasonal Analysis of Economic Time Series.* Washington, DC: U.S. Department of Commerce, Bureau of the Census.

TREND-SEASONAL AND HOLT-WINTERS SMOOTHING

When we build, we first survey the plot, then draw the model.

William Shakespeare

Chapter Outline

The ability to model trend and seasonal patterns when forecasting is essential. Some have mistakenly been led to believe that the simple exponential smoothing methods of Chapter 4 are sufficient for many short-term forecasting situations. Most often, this is not true. Experience has shown that at least 50 percent of product demands possess either a trend or seasonal pattern, or both.

There are many methods for estimating trends and seasonality; some are rather simple and some complex. Somewhat surprisingly, the simple methods are very effective. In this chapter, we discuss the following methods of estimating trends: first differences, double moving averages, Brown's double exponential smoothing, Holt's two-parameter model, and Winters' three-parameter model. This chapter extends classical decomposition methods discussed in Chapter 5 into several smoothing methods. Here we discuss three methods of estimating seasonality, seasonal differences, Winters method and Fournier Series Analysis (FSA). Winters method and FSA are versatile methods because they model the level, trend, and seasonality of a time series. As will be shown, these decomposition methods are very similar to those studied in Chapters 5 and 7. The use of differences to model trends and seasonality is discussed first.

Estimating Trends with Differences

As discussed in Chapter 1, a trend is an increase or decrease in a series that persists for an extended time. For nonseasonal data, many use a rule of thumb that a trend exists when seven or more observations show a consistent trend. However, we must be cautious in using such rules because they are not always accurate. Trends can be difficult to detect when a series has significant randomness and seasonality. To better understand this, consider Figure 6–1, which shows two series with trends and one without.

The process of using differences to estimate trends is a simple one. However, the results are as meaningful as more complex models. **First differences** are:

$$Y_t - Y_{t-1} = \text{ change from period } t - 1 \text{ to } t$$

Remembering that a trend is a consistent change over time, we see that first differences estimate the trend. Consider the three series of Table 6–1 plotted in Figure 6–1. As shown in columns 3, 6, and 9 of Table 6–1, first differences yield actual period-to-period increases or decreases over time.

FIGURE 6–1

Series G, H, and I

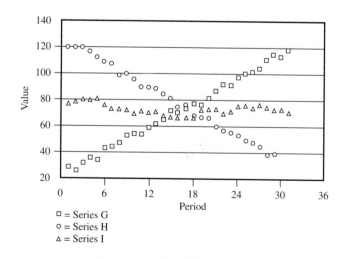

□ = Series G
○ = Series H
△ = Series I

TABLE 6–1   Three Series: Two with Trends and One Without (SERIESG, H, and I.DAT)

(1) Period (t)	(2) Series G Value	(3) First Difference	(4) Fitted Value	(5) Series H Value	(6) First Difference	(7) Fitted Value	(8) Series I Value	(9) First Difference	(10) Fitted Value
1	29.64			119.72			77.42		
2	27.14	−2.50	32.58	120.18	.46	116.80	78.79	1.37	77.42
3	32.70	5.56	30.08	120.72	.54	117.26	80.07	1.28	78.79
4	36.53	3.83	35.64	116.56	−4.16	117.80	79.53	−.54	80.07
5	34.96	−1.57	39.47	112.13	−4.43	113.64	81.17	1.64	79.53
6	44.00	9.04	37.90	108.78	−3.35	109.21	75.78	-5.39	81.17
7	45.17	1.17	46.94	107.49	−1.29	105.86	72.80	-2.98	75.78
8	48.02	2.85	48.11	98.99	−8.50	104.57	72.78	−.02	72.80
9	53.73	5.71	50.96	100.40	1.41	96.07	72.37	−.41	72.78
10	55.02	1.29	56.67	95.86	−4.54	97.48	69.24	−3.13	72.37
11	54.58	−.44	57.96	90.11	−5.75	92.94	71.48	2.24	69.24
12	59.49	4.91	57.52	89.90	−.21	87.19	69.77	−1.71	71.48
13	62.34	2.85	62.43	89.06	−.84	86.98	70.60	.83	69.77
14	65.41	3.07	65.28	85.12	−3.94	86.14	67.34	−3.26	70.60
15	72.23	6.82	68.35	81.34	−3.78	82.20	66.61	−.73	67.34
16	70.66	−1.57	75.17	75.50	−5.84	78.42	65.80	−.81	66.61
17	73.59	2.93	73.60	77.02	1.52	72.58	66.11	.31	65.80
18	77.50	3.91	76.53	68.63	−8.39	74.10	66.83	.72	66.11
19	76.78	−.72	80.44	67.10	−1.53	65.71	71.80	4.97	66.83
20	81.07	4.29	79.72	67.04	−.06	64.18	72.55	.75	71.80
21	87.15	6.08	84.01	60.30	−6.74	64.12	72.81	.26	72.55
22	91.78	4.63	90.09	57.52	−2.78	57.38	69.26	−3.55	72.81
23	91.29	−.49	94.72	55.95	−1.57	54.60	71.11	1.85	69.26
24	97.13	5.84	94.23	54.02	−1.93	53.03	74.57	3.46	71.11
25	99.96	2.83	100.07	49.75	−4.27	51.10	75.13	.56	74.57
26	100.91	.95	102.90	48.16	−1.59	46.83	73.81	−1.32	75.13
27	103.30	2.39	103.85	45.37	−2.79	45.24	75.82	2.01	73.81
28	109.99	6.69	106.24	38.84	−6.53	42.45	74.03	−1.79	75.82
29	113.93	3.94	112.93	39.69	.85	35.92	71.51	−2.52	74.03
30	112.28	−1.65	116.87	34.99	−4.70	36.77	72.12	.61	71.51
31	117.86	5.58	115.22	32.21	−2.78	32.07	69.83	−2.29	72.12
32			120.80			29.29			69.83
Mean	71.81	2.94		77.69	−2.92		72.54	−.25	
Standard deviation	27.43	2.97		27.91	2.78		4.11	2.26	

If a series exhibits a trend, on average the first differences should be equal to the increasing or decreasing trend by being greater or less than zero, respectively. That is, if first differences yield changes that are primarily above zero as measured by the mean, the series is increasing (series G of Table 6–1). In contrast, if differences yield a series with values primarily below zero, the series is decreasing (series H). Finally, if the values of first differences yield a series that is random about zero, sometimes positive and sometimes negative, we infer that there is no trend (series I).

As shown at the bottom of Table 6–1, the mean of first differences of series G is 2.94. This denotes that series G is increasing 2.94 units per period on average. The mean of first differences of series H is -2.92, and the mean of first differences of series I is -.25. On the basis of these numbers and an inspection of Figure 6–1, we infer there is no trend in series I, but G and H have trends. Columns 4, 7, and 10 of Table 6–1 illustrate fitted values (i.e., $\hat{Y}_t$ for $t = 1$ to $t = 31$) and a forecast of period 32 $\hat{Y}_t$ for each series. Let's use series G to illustrate the process of forecasting.

Forecasting with Differences

The fitting and forecasting equation for first differences is:

$$\hat{Y}_t = Y_{t-1} + \text{mean of the differences} \qquad (6-1)$$

Designating the mean of the differences as b:

$$\hat{Y} = Y_{t-1} + b \qquad (6-2)$$

$$\hat{Y}_{t+m} = Y_t + m \cdot b \qquad (6-3)$$

where m is the number of periods forecast into the future.

Assume that it is now the end of period 25; the forecasts of periods 26 through 28 are:

$$\hat{Y}_{26} = Y_{25} + b = 99.96 + 2.94 = 102.90$$
Actual $Y_{26} = 100.91$
Error $= 100.91 - 102.90 = -1.99$

$$\hat{Y}_{27} = Y_{25} + 2 \cdot 2.94 = 99.96 + 2 \cdot 2.94 = 105.84$$
Actual $Y_{27} = 103.30$
Error $= 103.30 - 105.84 = -2.54$

$$\hat{Y}_{28} = Y_{25} + 3 \cdot 2.94 = 99.96 + 3 \cdot 2.94 = 108.78$$
Actual $Y_{28} = 109.99$
Error $= 109.99 - 108.78 = 1.21$

As shown, this is a very simple method for forecasting trends.

While applying equation 6–3, we assumed that the mean of the first differences reflects a trend. However, the mean could have been the result of random influences. To have more confidence in the trend estimates, we must answer the question of whether a mean of first differences is or is not statistically different than zero. The value of zero is important because a mean nearly equal to zero is consistent with the assertion that there is no trend in the data. Table 6–2 illustrates frequency distributions of the three series of Figure 6–1. As shown, series G rarely has period-to-period changes less than zero; series H rarely has period-to-period changes greater than zero; and the values of positive and negative period-to-period changes of series I are nearly equal, hence the mean of near zero (i.e., $-.25$).

Statistical Significance Test for Trend

One of the advantages of using differences to estimate trends is that simple statistical tests can prove that a trend is significant. We can perform a **significance test for trend** on the mean of the first differences of each series shown in Table 6–1. It can be proven that series G and series H have trends and Series I does not. The statistical analysis and hypothesis test necessary to infer that trends exist are shown below.

Although the following illustrates the test on first differences, it can be generalized to any type of differences. We present the test using classical hypothesis-testing procedures.

TABLE 6–2   **Frequency Distributions of Differenced Series G, H, and I**

Difference Range	Series G	Series H	Series I
−10 to −8		2	
−8 to −6		2	
−6 to −4		7	1
−4 to −2	1	6	6
−2 to 0	6	8	8
0 to 2	3	5	11
2 to 4	9		3
4 to 6	7		1
6 to 8	3		
8 to 10	1		
Total	30	30	30

Null hypothesis: On average, $Y_t - Y_{t-1} = 0$; that is, there is no trend.

If this hypothesis is proven wrong (i.e., nullified), then accept:

Alternative hypothesis: On average, $Y_t - Y_{t-1} < 0$ or > 0; that is, there is a negative or positive trend, respectively.

These inferences are made by using a simple *t*-test. A calculated *t*-value is compared to a *t*-value from the table. This *t*-test determines how many standard deviations the mean of first differences is away from the hypothetical mean of zero. The *t*-value is calculated by:

$$t\text{-calculated} = \frac{b - 0}{S/\sqrt{n - d}} \tag{6–4}$$

where S = standard deviation of first differences

If $|t\text{-calculated}| \leq t\text{-table}$, infer there is no trend.

If $|t\text{-calculated}| > t\text{-table}$, infer there is a trend.

The denominator in equation 6–4 is the standard error of the mean, where n is the number of observations, d is the level of differencing, and therefore $n\text{-}d$ is the number of differenced values in the sample that yields b. The *t*-calculated value of equation 6–4 is compared to a *t*-value from the table. For example, assuming a level of significance of .05 and first differences of 30 observations, the *t*-value of Appendix C is

$$df = 30 - 1 - 1 = n - d - 1 = 28$$

t-table = 2.048, which we can round to 2 for our discussion

sign. = .05

For series G, the level of differences equals 1 for first differences. Note that in general $d = 2$ for second differences and $d = 12$ for monthly seasonal differences; thus, the number of differences taken, d, will always be less than the sample size because we lose one or more observations when differencing.

This test is based on the fact that if there is no trend, then the mean of the differences has a 95.5 percent probability of being within about two standard errors of zero (remember that zero indicates no trend). Alternatively, as discussed in Chapter 2, only 4.5 times out of 100 will sample means of trendless series be more than two standard deviations away from zero. Thus, in this test, the mean is selected to be the hypothesized mean of zero. It is very unlikely to get a value more than two standard errors away when the true mean difference is zero. Consequently, when accepting the alternative hypothesis, we infer that the hypothesized value of zero is not the correct value and that the null hypothesis is false. We logically infer that the mean is significantly different than zero because of the high t-calculated value.

Let's perform this test for the data of Table 6–1.

For series G, $S/\sqrt{n - d} = 2.97/\sqrt{31 - 1} = .542$ and b for series G is 2.94; thus

$$t\text{-calculated} = \frac{b - 0}{S/\sqrt{n - d}} = \frac{2.94}{.533} = 5.424$$

From above, t-table $= 2.048$ and therefore

$$|t\text{-calculated}| > t\text{-table}$$

$$5.424 > 2.048$$

Therefore, infer there is a positive trend.

For series H, $S/\sqrt{n - d} = 2.78/\sqrt{31 - 1} = .508$ and b for series H is -2.92 thus:

$$t\text{-calculated} = \frac{b - 0}{S/\sqrt{n - d}} = \frac{-2.92}{.508} = -5.748$$

From above, t-table $= 2.048$ and therefore

$$|t\text{-calculated}| > t\text{-table}$$

$$|-5.748| > 2.048$$

Therefore, infer there is a negative trend because t-calculated is negative and significantly different than zero.

For series I, $S/\sqrt{n - d} = 2.26/\sqrt{31 - 1} = .413$ and b is $-.25$; thus:

$$t\text{-calculated} = \frac{b - 0}{S/\sqrt{n - d}} = \frac{-.25}{.413} = -.605$$

From above, t-table $= 2.048$ and therefore

$$|t\text{-calculated}| > t\text{-table}$$

$$|-.605| < 2.048$$

Therefore, infer there is no trend.

These conclusions are consistent with our intuitive interpretations of Figure 6–1 and Table 6–1.

The statistical test for trend is a powerful one; however, this test may not identify significant trends when there are strong patterns left in the differences. In such situations, it is important to model the patterns using additional smoothing or other methods. Finally, when the results of statistical tests are inconclusive, your intuitive judgment or other empirical information should confirm or deny that a trend exists.

Advantages and Disadvantages of Forecasting with Differences

Using differences to model trends has advantages and disadvantages. The advantages are (1) the trend is easily calculated, (2) it is easily interpreted, and (3) its significance is easily tested using the previously illustrated hypothesis test.

The disadvantages of using differences arise from this method's weakness in dealing with outliers. Differences do not smooth out the effects of extreme outliers as much as smoothed averages, such as double moving averages and double exponential smoothing. Also, when there is strong pattern left in the differences, that pattern should be modeled using the methods described in Chapter 4, 5, 6 or 7. In addition, when applying equation 6–3, the value Y_{t-1} is critical in forecasting future values. Thus, Y_{t-1} should not be an unusual or outlier value. If it is, all future forecasts will be adversely affected. Instead, a good typical or smoothed value should be used as the point from which forecasts are made.

Because they do not smooth unusual values as much as smoothing methods, typically, differences are not used to estimate trends in automated forecasting systems. Instead, methods such as double moving averages or double exponential smoothing are used. We discuss these more fully below. Despite its disadvantages, differencing is a very powerful method for estimating trends when used intelligently.

Nonlinear Trends and Second Differences

The process of differences can be used to forecast **nonlinear trends** using either multiple differences or logarithms. Both of these methods are illustrated in Table 6–3. The actual data in Table 6–3 has a very slight nonlinearity as shown in Figure 6–2.

Logarithms are useful when the trend is a percentage growth function and second differences are useful when modeling quadratic functions. The formula for using **second differences** is:

$$Y_t - Y_{t-1} = \text{first differences} \qquad (6\text{--}5)$$

$$(Y_t - Y_{t-1}) - (Y_{t-1} - Y_{t-2}) = \text{first differences of first differences}$$
$$\text{(called second differences)};$$

thus, rearranging second differences yields:

$$Y_t - 2Y_{t-1} + Y_{t-2} \qquad (6\text{--}6)$$

First differences and second differences are shown in column 3 and 4 of Table 6–3.

In forecasting form, the process of second differences is:

$$\hat{Y}_t = 2Y_{t-1} - Y_{t-2} + b = Y_{t-1} + (Y_{t-1} - Y_{t-2}) + b \qquad (6\text{--}7)$$

FIGURE 6–2

Slight nonlinear trend

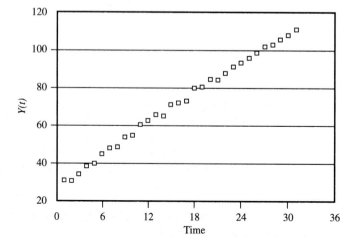

TABLE 6–3   Second Differences and Logarithms for Nonlinear Trends (NONLIN.DAT)

(1) Period (t)	(2) Actual Y(t)	(3) First Difference	(4) Second Difference	(5) Fitted Values	(6) Second-Difference Error	(7) Log (Y)	(8) Difference Log (Y)	(9) Fitted Values	(10) Error
1	31.16					3.439			
2	31.03	−.13				3.435	−.004	32.50	−1.47
3	34.57	3.54	3.67	31.00	3.57	3.543	.108	32.37	2.20
4	38.73	4.16	.62	38.21	.52	3.657	.114	36.06	2.67
5	40.15	1.42	−2.74	42.99	−2.84	3.693	.036	40.40	−.25
6	45.09	4.94	3.52	41.67	3.42	3.809	.116	41.88	3.21
7	48.01	2.92	−2.02	50.13	−2.12	3.871	.063	47.03	.98
8	48.67	.66	−2.26	51.03	−2.36	3.885	.014	50.08	−1.41
9	54.11	5.44	4.78	49.43	4.68	3.991	.106	50.77	3.34
10	55.21	1.10	−4.34	59.65	−4.44	4.011	.020	56.44	−1.23
11	60.50	5.29	4.19	56.41	4.09	4.103	.091	57.59	2.91
12	62.82	2.32	−2.97	65.89	−3.07	4.140	.038	63.11	−.29
13	65.83	3.01	.69	65.24	.59	4.187	.047	65.53	.30
14	65.32	−.51	−3.52	68.94	−3.62	4.179	−.008	68.67	−3.35
15	71.25	5.93	6.44	64.91	6.34	4.266	.087	68.13	3.12
16	72.27	1.02	−4.91	77.28	−5.01	4.280	.014	74.32	−2.05
17	73.37	1.10	.08	73.39	−.02	4.296	.015	75.38	−2.01
18	79.71	6.34	5.24	74.57	5.14	4.378	.083	76.53	3.18
19	80.18	.47	−5.87	86.15	−5.97	4.384	.006	83.14	−2.96
20	84.30	4.12	3.65	80.75	3.55	4.434	.050	83.63	.67
21	84.02	−.28	−4.40	88.52	−4.50	4.431	−.003	87.93	−3.91
22	87.55	3.53	3.81	83.84	3.71	4.472	.041	87.64	−.09
23	90.74	3.19	−.34	91.18	−.44	4.508	.036	91.32	−.58
24	92.76	2.02	−1.17	94.03	−1.27	4.530	.022	94.65	−1.89
25	95.40	2.64	.62	94.88	.52	4.558	.028	96.76	−1.36
26	98.18	2.78	.14	98.14	.04	4.587	.029	99.51	−1.33
27	101.41	3.23	.45	101.06	.35	4.619	.032	102.41	−1.00
28	102.55	1.14	−2.09	104.74	−2.19	4.630	.011	105.78	−3.23
29	105.30	2.75	1.61	103.79	1.51	4.657	.026	106.97	−1.67
30	107.55	2.25	−.50	108.15	−.60	4.678	.021	109.84	−2.29
31	110.42	2.87	.62	109.90	.52	4.704	.026	112.18	−1.76
Mean	71.55	2.64	.10	74.34	.00	4.205	.042	73.28	−.38
Standard deviation	24.45	1.84	3.32	23.03	3.32	.383	.037	24.79	2.18

where b is the mean of the second differences and represents a trend estimate when this mean is statistically significantly different than zero. This mean is shown at the bottom of column 4. Upon inspection, you should see that equation 6–7 has an intuitive explanation: Y_t equals Y_{t-1} plus the increase or decrease of $(Y_{t-1} - Y_{t-2})$ plus an additional constant of b (assuming b is statistically significantly different than zero).

Using the nonlinear trend data from Table 6–3, the forecast for period 32 is:

$$\hat{Y}_t = 110.42 + 2.87 + .10 = 113.39$$

In this case the b of .10 is not statistically significant and should be dropped, but for generality was left in Table 6–3.

Logarithms

Logarithms are used to model percentage trends or percentage seasonality (seasonal uses are discussed later). To use logs in modeling nonlinear trends, first take logarithms of the series (column 7 of Table 6–3), then take first differences of the logarithms (column 8), and finally perform a statistical significance test on the mean of the first differences. When the mean of first differences is significant, the following model results:

$$\widehat{Ln(Y)} = Ln(Y_{t-1}) + b \tag{6-8}$$

where Ln is the process of taking the natural logarithm of Y to the base **e,** and b is the resulting mean of the first differences. (Note: all logarithms in this book are taken in the base **e.**) After forecasting the Ln of Y, the actual value of Y is calculated by taking its antilog. The antilog is the natural number **e** to the power of the forecasted value of $Ln(Y_t)$:

$$\hat{Y}_t = \mathbf{e}^{\widehat{Ln(Y)}} \tag{6-9}$$

Finally, there is a simple yet powerful interpretation of the b value for logarithmic relationships. The anitlog of $b - 1$ is equal to the percentage change of the series.

Using the example of Table 6–3 yields the following forecasting form and interpretation of b:

$$\widehat{Ln(Y_{32})} = \widehat{Ln(Y_{31})} + b = 4.704 + .042 = 4.746$$
$$\hat{Y}_{32} = \mathbf{e}^{4.746} = 115.12$$

The **antilog of logarithmic b** yields:

$$\mathbf{e}^b - 1 = 1.0429 - 1 = .0429$$

The series of Table 6–3 has a period-to-period trend of approximately 4.29 percent.

Seasonal Differences to Model Seasonality and Trends

The method of estimating and testing for trends can be generalized to data that is highly seasonal. In such cases, we do not estimate trends using first differences, but instead use **seasonal differences**. Table 6–4 illustrates the use of 12th differences to model the trend and seasonality of a series. This is a very powerful method that is used in the general methods of ARIMA model building of Chapters 7 to 9. Note that the process of taking seasonal differences follows the theory and intuitive explanations of those used for first differences. Because of this, we do not develop seasonal differences further. However, please note that the process of taking seasonal differences includes performing a statistical test on the mean of the seasonal differences. If this mean difference is statistically significantly different than zero, trend exists in the series. Thus, we have a very simple model that includes trend and seasonal patterns. For monthly data:

$$\text{Forecast} = \text{Seasonal estimate} + \text{Trend}$$
$$\hat{Y}_t = Y_{t-12} + b$$

where b = mean of 12th differences $(Y_t - Y_{t-12})$ if statistically significant; otherwise, zero.

For quarterly data:

$$\hat{Y}_t = Y_{t-4} + b$$

where b = mean of 4th differences $(Y_t - Y_{t-4})$ if statistically significant; otherwise, zero.

TABLE 6–4   **Seasonal Differences for Modeling Seasonal Data (TABLE 6–4.DAT)**

Period (t)	Actual Value	12th Difference		Fitted Value	Error Actual − Fitted
1	15.29				
2	22.10				
3	28.25				
4	41.75				
5	52.19				
6	60.46				
7	68.87				
8	59.73				
9	56.73				
10	48.12				
11	58.33				
12	73.69				
13	31.12	15.83		50.76	−19.64
14	38.71	16.61		57.57	−18.86
15	57.28	29.03		63.72	−6.44
16	76.65	34.90		77.22	−.57
17	95.56	43.37		87.66	7.90
18	103.76	43.30		95.93	7.83
19	121.21	52.34		104.34	16.87
20	103.22	43.49		95.20	8.02
21	87.12	30.39		92.20	−5.08
22	78.44	30.32		83.59	−5.15
23	93.33	35.00		93.80	−.47
24	120.43	46.74		109.16	11.27
25	45.18	14.06		66.59	−21.41
26	62.92	24.21		74.18	−11.26
27	88.50	31.22		92.75	−4.25
28	110.08	33.43		112.12	−2.04
29	136.14	40.58		131.03	5.11
30	153.23	49.47		139.23	14.00
31	171.46	50.25		156.68	14.78
32	148.21	44.99		138.69	9.52
33	124.46	37.34		122.59	1.87
34	109.42	30.98		113.91	−4.49
35	126.11	32.78		128.80	−2.69
36	161.07	40.64		155.90	5.17
37			Forecast	80.65	
Mean	101.82	35.47			.00
Standard deviation	37.45	10.47			RSE 10.47

The process of using differences to estimate trends and seasonality is an intuitive, yet effective, statistical method. Through application of logarithms and second differences, it is possible to represent nonlinear trends and percentage growth in seasonality. Those desiring more information about differencing as a modeling method are encouraged to study Chapter 7.

Population Projections of Abraham Lincoln

As has been mentioned in this book, most methods of forecasting are based on projections of past patterns or relationships. We don't think of our presidents as forecasters, but certainly all decision makers, especially chief executives, are involved in the art of forecasting.

Consider the following data (LINCOLN.DAT) and projections from one of the best-known chief executives, Abraham Lincoln. In his annual state-of-the-union message to Congress, December 1, 1862, President Lincoln made the following statements and projections:

"Taking the nation in the aggregate, and we find its population and ratio of increase, for the several decennial periods to be as follows:

1790	3,929,827	
1800	5,305,937	35.02 percent ratio of increase
1810	7,239,814	36.45 percent ratio of increase
1820	9,638,131	33.13 percent ratio of increase
1830	12,866,020	33.49 percent ratio of increase
1840	17,069,020	32.67 percent ratio of increase
1850	23,191,875	35.87 percent ratio of increase
1860	31,442,790	35.58 percent ratio of increase

This shows an average decennial increase of 34.60 percent in population through the 70 years from our first to our last census yet taken. It is seen that the ratio of increase, at no one of these seven periods, is either 2 percent below, or 2 percent above, the average; thus showing how inflexible, and, consequently, how reliable, the law of increase, in our case, is. Assuming that it will continue, gives the following results:

	Projected Population
1870	42,323,341
1880	56,967,216
1890	76,677,872
1900	103,208,415
1910	138,918,526
1920	186,984,335
1930	251,680,914

These figures show that our country may be as populous as Europe now is, at some point between 1920 and 1930—say about 1925—our territory, at seventy-three and a third persons to the square mile, being of capacity to contain 217,186,000."

Obviously, the compound growth in U.S. population was extraordinary during Lincoln's time. It is easy to understand Lincoln's confidence in his projections; but as we know, these projections were much too large. Using hindsight, we see the following actual decennial populations and annual percentage growths.

	Lincoln's Projection	Actual	Actual % Annual Growth
1870	42,323,341	39,818,449	26.6
1880	56,967,216	50,155,783	26.0
1890	76,677,872	62,947,714	25.5
1900	103,208,415	75,994,575	20.7
1910	138,918,526	91,972,266	21.0
1920	186,984,335	105,710,620	14.9
1930	251,680,914	122,775,046	16.1

Double Moving Averages

As noted in Chapter 4, simple moving averages do not model trends. They lag trends; and when used to forecast, this lag is even greater. This section describes a modification of simple moving averages that includes an adjustment for the lag and trend.

Table 6–5 illustrates a simple series with 12 observations having a trend of three units from period to period. All random error has been removed so that the trend can be more easily identified. A three-period moving average [$MA(3)$] is used to forecast the series; thus, the first three periods are used to forecast the fourth period. As shown in column 6, the forecast of this three-period simple moving average has a systematic error of six units. Half of this error (i.e., lag), three units, occurs because the moving average for the first three periods cannot be computed until the end of period 3. That is, the average is centered on period 2. Thus, the moving average lags the series by the trend of one period; it is centered on period 2. Using the moving average of period 3 to forecast period 4 creates an additional one-period lag, thus the systematic lag is equal to the trend of two periods (i.e., 6 units). For $MA(3)$, the trend can be estimated using the differences between adjacent moving averages. Consider this method of estimating trend further.

To eliminate the systematic error just described, a method of **double moving averages, (DMAs)**, sometimes called **linear moving averages,** has been developed. This method calculates a second moving average from the original moving average. This is annotated as $MA(M \times N)$, an M-period moving average of N-period moving average; N is the length of the first average, M the second average. For example, a three-by-three double moving average is written as $MA(3 \times 3)$.

Table 6–6 illustrates double moving averages using the data of Table 6–5. The difference between the simple moving average and the double moving average is added to the simple moving average together with the trend estimate to get the forecast for the next period. For example:

$$F_{10} = (MA(3) \text{ at period 9}) + (MA(3) - MA(3 \times 3) \text{ at period 9}) + \text{Trend}$$

$$= 141 + 3 + 3 = 147$$

TABLE 6–5   Forecasting a Trending Series Using a Three-Period Simple Moving Average (TABLE 6–5.DAT)

(1) *Period* *(t)*	*(2)* *Observed* *Value*	*(3)* *Computed* *MA(3)*	*(4)* *Lag* *(2) − (3)*	*(5)* *Forecast* *MA(3)*	*(6)* *Error* *(2) − (5)*
1	120	—	—	—	—
2	123	—	—	—	—
3	126	123	3	—	—
4	129	126	3	123	6
5	132	129	3	126	6
6	135	132	3	129	6
7	138	135	3	132	6
8	141	138	3	135	6
9	144	141	3	138	6
10	147	144	3	141	6
11	150	147	3	144	6
12	153	150	3	147	6

TABLE 6-6 **Forecasting a Trending Series Using a Double Moving Average [*MA*(3 × 3)]** (TABLE 6–5.DAT)

(1) Period (t)	(2) Observed Value	(3) MA(3)	(4) Difference (2) − (3)	(5) MA(3 × 3)	(6) Difference (3) − (5)	(7) Forecast (3) + (6) + Trend	(8) Error (2) − (7)
1	120	—	—	—	—	—	—
2	123	—	—	—	—	—	—
3	126	123	3	—	—	—	—
4	129	126	3	—	—	—	—
5	132	129	3	126	3	—	—
6	135	132	3	129	3	135	0
7	138	135	3	132	3	138	0
8	141	138	3	135	3	141	0
9	144	141	3	138	3	144	0
10	147	144	3	141	3	147	0
11	150	147	3	144	3	150	0
12	153	150	3	147	3	153	0

where the trend is estimated from the following formula:

$$\text{Trend} = \frac{2}{N-1}(MA(3) - MA(3 \times 3))$$

and where N is the length of the simple moving average.

This trend formula is necessary because the lag between the simple and double moving averages is dependent on the number of periods in the averages. That is, the lag between these averages may be greater than one period, and so their difference may represent a multiperiod trend. The adjustment, $2/(N\text{-}1)$, ensures that the trend is adjusted to be only a one-period trend, not a multiperiod trend.

This example illustrates that with trending series, the systematic error produced by a simple moving average can be removed.

In summary, the double moving average is computed as follows:

1. Compute a simple moving average and a double moving average at time t (hereafter annotated as S'_t and S''_t).

2. Add to the simple moving average the difference between the simple and double moving averages. $S'_t + (S'_t - S''_t)$

3. Add the linear trend from period $t + 1$ (or to period $t + m$ for forecasting m periods ahead).

This procedure can be generalized through the following equations:

$$S'_t = \frac{Y_t + Y_{t-1} + \ldots + Y_{t-N+1}}{N} \tag{6-10}$$

$$S''_t = \frac{S'_t + S'_{t-1} + \ldots + S'_{t-M+1}}{M} \tag{6-11}$$

$$a_t = S'_t + (S'_t - S''_t) = 2S'_t - S''_t \tag{6-12}$$

$$b_t = \frac{2}{N-1}(S'_t - S''_t) \qquad\qquad (6\text{--}13)$$

$$F_{t+m} = a_t + b_t m \qquad\qquad (6\text{--}14)$$

where

a_t = smoothed level as of the end of period t
b_t = smoothed trend as of the end of period t
m = number of periods forecasted into the future (i.e., forecast horizon)

Table 6–7 is a more complete example of the application of double moving averages to a data set of 30 weekly values. With $N = 3$, the table shows the results of the intermediate steps as well as the final forecast value. Figure 6–3 shows these same results in graphics form. One can see in Figure 6–3 that the forecast from equation 6–14 fits the actual data fairly closely; the single and double moving averages fits, however, are low. The forecasts are above and below the actual values denoting that both positive and negative error occur (i.e., it is unbiased). This indicates that the systematic error of the simple moving average has been eliminated.

Advantages

When trend and randomness are the only significant demand patterns, this is a useful method. Because it smoothes large random variations, it is less influenced by outliers than the method of the first differences.

Disadvantages

In general, this method is too simplistic to be used by itself; it does not model the seasonality of the series. Also, as we see next, there are computationally simpler methods such as exponential smoothing that are as effective. Finally, when using this method, one faces the problem of determining the optimal number of periods to use in the simple and double moving averages.

FIGURE 6–3

Single and double moving averages

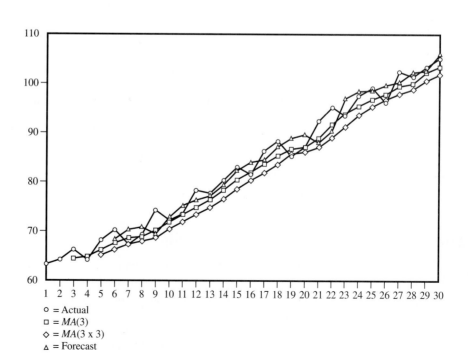

o = Actual
□ = MA(3)
◇ = MA(3 x 3)
△ = Forecast

TABLE 6–7   Double Moving Averages: Fitted and Forecasted (TABLE 6–7.DAT)

Period (t)	(1) Weekly Demand	(2) Three-Period Moving Average of (1)	(3) Three-Period Moving Average of (2)	(4) Value of a	(5) Value of b	(6) Fitted Value of a + b(m) (m = 1)	Error
1	63						
2	64						
3	66	64.33					
4	64	64.67					
5	68	66.00	65.00	67.00	1.00		
6	70	67.33	66.00	68.67	1.33	68.00	2.00
7	67	68.33	67.22	69.44	1.11	70.00	−3.00
8	69	68.67	68.11	69.22	.56	70.56	−1.56
9	74	70.00	69.00	71.00	1.00	69.78	4.22
10	72	71.67	70.11	73.22	1.56	72.00	.00
11	73	73.00	71.56	74.44	1.44	74.78	−1.78
12	78	74.33	73.00	75.67	1.33	75.89	2.11
13	77	76.00	74.44	77.56	1.56	77.00	.00
14	80	78.33	76.22	80.44	2.11	79.11	.89
15	83	80.00	78.11	81.89	1.89	82.56	.44
16	81	81.33	79.89	82.78	1.44	83.78	−2.78
17	86	83.33	81.56	85.11	1.78	84.22	1.78
18	88	85.00	83.22	86.78	1.78	86.89	1.11
19	85	86.33	84.89	87.78	1.44	88.56	−3.56
20	87	86.67	86.00	87.33	.67	89.22	−2.22
21	92	88.00	87.00	89.00	1.00	88.00	4.00
22	95	91.33	88.67	94.00	2.67	90.00	5.00
23	93	93.33	90.89	95.78	2.44	96.67	−3.67
24	97	95.00	93.22	96.78	1.78	98.22	−1.22
25	99	96.33	94.89	97.78	1.44	98.56	.44
26	96	97.33	96.22	98.44	1.11	99.22	−3.22
27	102	99.00	97.56	100.44	1.44	99.56	2.44
28	101	99.67	98.67	100.67	1.00	101.89	−.89
29	103	102.00	100.22	103.78	1.78	101.67	1.33
30	105	103.00	101.56	104.44	1.44	105.56	−.56
Mean	82.6					86.07	.05
Standard deviation	13.39					11.82	RSE 2.47

Brown's Double Exponential Smoothing

A method very similar to double moving averages is double exponential smoothing. This method accounts for trend and retains the advantage of requiring less data than moving averages, an attribute of all exponential smoothing methods.

Brown's doubling exponential smoothing uses a single coefficient, alpha, for both smoothing operations. As in double moving averages, this method computes the difference between single and double smoothed values as a measure of trend. It then adds this value to the single smoothed value together with adjustment for the current trend. Brown's model is implemented with the following equations (as before, S'_t denotes a single smoothed and S''_t denotes the double smoothed value):

$$S'_t = \alpha Y_t + (1 - \alpha)S'_{t-1} \tag{6-15}$$

$$S''_t = \alpha S'_t + (1 - \alpha)S''_{t-1} \tag{6-16}$$

$$a_t = S'_t + (S'_t - S''_t) = 2S'_t - S''_t \tag{6-17}$$

$$b_t = \frac{\alpha}{1 - \alpha}(S'_t - S''_t) \tag{6-18}$$

$$F_{t+m} = a_t + b_t m \tag{6-19}$$

where a_t = smoothed value as of the end of period t
   b_t = estimate of trend as of the end of period t
   m = forecast horizon

The application of these equations is illustrated in Table 6–8 and Figure 6–4.

Starting Values of S'_t and S''_t

As is true for simple exponential smoothing, double smoothing requires **starting values** to initialize the formulas. The equations below show common methods for estimating starting values for Brown's exponential smoothing.

$$S'_1 = S''_1 = Y_1$$
$$a_1 = Y_1$$
$$b_1 = \frac{(Y_2 - Y_1) + (Y_4 - Y_3)}{2}$$

Because there are 30 periods of historical data in this example, the starting values have little influence on period 31 forecasts. In instances where there is little historical data and the smoothing constant is small (close to zero), the choice of the initialization procedure can greatly influence the fits and forecasts of several periods.

FIGURE 6–4

Single (SES) and double (DES) exponential smoothing

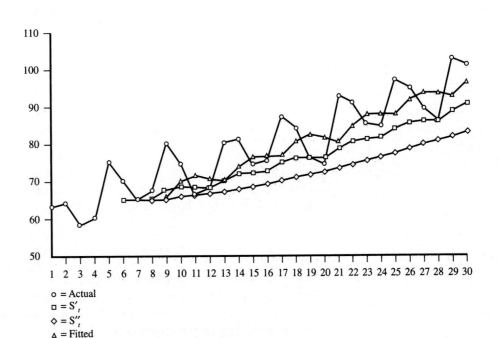

o = Actual
□ = S'_t
◇ = S''_t
△ = Fitted

TABLE 6–8   Brown's Double Exponential Smoothing Model (alpha = .15) (TABLE 6–8.DAT)

Period (t)	Weekly Demand	Single Exponential Smoothing	Double Exponential Smoothing	Value of a	Value of b	Fitted Value of a + b(m) (m = 1)	Error
1	63	63.000	63.000	63.000	1.500		
2	64	63.150	63.023	63.278	.023	64.500	−.500
3	58	62.378	62.926	61.829	−.097	63.300	−5.300
4	60	62.021	62.790	61.252	−.136	61.733	−1.733
5	75	63.968	62.967	64.969	.177	61.116	13.884
6	70	64.873	63.253	66.493	.286	65.145	4.855
7	64	64.742	63.476	66.007	.223	66.778	−2.778
8	67	65.080	63.717	66.444	.241	66.231	.769
9	80	67.318	64.257	70.380	.540	66.685	13.315
10	74	68.321	64.866	71.775	.610	70.920	3.080
11	66	67.973	65.332	70.613	.466	72.384	−6.384
12	68	67.977	65.729	70.224	.397	71.079	−3.079
13	80	69.780	66.337	73.224	.608	70.621	9.379
14	81	71.463	67.106	75.821	.769	73.831	7.169
15	74	71.844	67.816	75.871	.711	76.590	−2.590
16	75	72.317	68.491	76.143	.675	76.582	−1.582
17	87	74.520	69.396	79.643	.904	76.818	10.182
18	84	75.942	70.378	81.506	.982	80.548	3.452
19	76	75.950	71.213	80.687	.836	82.488	−6.488
20	74	75.658	71.880	79.435	.667	81.523	−7.523
21	93	78.259	72.837	83.681	.957	80.102	12.898
22	91	80.170	73.937	86.404	1.100	84.638	6.362
23	85	80.895	74.981	86.809	1.044	87.504	−2.504
24	84	81.361	75.938	86.783	.957	87.852	−3.852
25	97	83.706	77.103	90.310	1.165	87.740	9.260
26	95	85.400	78.348	92.453	1.245	91.475	3.525
27	89	85.940	79.486	92.394	1.139	93.698	−4.698
28	86	85.949	80.456	91.443	.969	93.533	−7.533
29	103	88.507	81.664	95.350	1.208	92.412	10.588
30	101	90.381	82.971	97.791	1.308	96.558	4.442
Mean	78.80						1.962
Standard deviation	12.350						RSE 7.0524

Optimal Smoothing Constant

Table 6–9 illustrates a simple trial and error search for the optimal value of alpha. As the table shows, the optimal value appears to lie between .1 and .2. The value of .15 appears to be optimal, on the basis of the residual standard error. We leave it to the reader to try an alpha of 0000.17.

Advantages

The advantages of Brown's double smoothing are:

- It models the trends and level of a time series.
- It is computationally more efficient than double moving averages.
- It requires less data than double moving averages. Because one parameter is used, parameter optimization is simple.

TABLE 6–9   A Search for a Good Alpha Value:
Brown's Double Exponential Smoothing

Alpha	RSE	Alpha	RSE
.05	10.02	.16	7.06
.02	14.76	.18	7.10
.10	7.43	.20	7.18
.12	7.16	.25	7.44
.14	7.06	.30	7.74
.15*	7.05	.70	10.47

* The best value of those calculated.

Disadvantages

Although parameter optimization is simple, there is some loss of flexibility because the best smoothing constants for the level and trend may not be equal. Brown's double smoothing model is not a full model; it does not model the seasonality of a series. Many times series have seasonality. Thus, it is not recommended unless the data is first deseasonalized, a procedure discussed in Chapter 5.

The next method we discuss is easier to understand than Brown's and has the flexibility of using two smoothing constants, one for trend and one for the level of the series.

Holt's Two-Parameter Trend Model

Holt's two-parameter double exponential smoothing model uses a second smoothing constant, β, to separately smooth the trend. Holt's model further adjusts each smoothed value for the trend of the previous period before calculating the new smoothed value. Holt's two-parameter trend model is implemented using the following equations:

$$S_t = \alpha Y_t + (1 - \alpha)(S_{t-1} + b_{t-1}) \qquad (6\text{–}20)$$
$$b_t = \beta(S_t - S_{t-1}) + (1 - \beta)b_{t-1} \qquad (6\text{–}21)$$
$$F_{t+m} = S_t + b_t m \qquad (6\text{–}22)$$

where

α = level smoothing constant
S_t = smoothed at end of period t
β = trend smoothing constant (called Beta)
b_t = smoothed trend in period t
m = forecast horizon

Notice that in equation 6–20, the smoothed level (S_{t-1}) of period t-1 is adjusted by the trend (b_{t-1}) from that period. This eliminates the natural lag of single smoothing. The first smoothing constant, α, is then used to smooth the new actual and trend-adjusted, previous smoothed level. The second smoothing constant, β, is used to smooth out or average the trend in equation 6–21. This removes some of the random error that would otherwise be reflected in the unsmoothed trend $(S_t - S_{t-1})$.

Holt's model is illustrated in Table 6–10 and Figure 6–5 using the data from the example. Table 6–10 shows that adjusting the previous smoothed level for trend as in equation 6–22 brings the new fitted values closer to the actual values. This is shown in columns 3, 4, and 5 of Table 6–10.

TABLE 6–10   Holt's Two-Parameter Trend Model (TABLE 6–7.DAT)

(1) Period (t)	(2) Weekly Demand	(3) Smoothed Level	(4) Smoothed Trend	(5) Fitted (m = 1)	(6) Error
1	63	63.000	−.500		
2	64	62.800	−.320	62.500	1.500
3	66	63.184	.102	62.480	3.520
4	64	63.429	.188	63.286	.714
5	68	64.494	.714	63.617	4.383
6	70	66.166	1.289	65.208	4.792
7	67	67.364	1.234	67.455	−.455
8	69	68.679	1.283	68.599	.401
9	74	70.769	1.767	69.961	4.039
10	72	72.429	1.703	72.536	−.536
11	73	73.906	1.567	74.132	−1.132
12	78	75.978	1.870	75.473	2.527
13	77	77.679	1.769	77.848	−.848
14	80	79.558	1.835	79.447	.553
15	83	81.714	2.028	81.393	1.607
16	81	83.193	1.699	83.742	−2.742
17	86	85.114	1.832	84.892	1.108
18	88	87.156	1.958	86.945	1.055
19	85	88.292	1.464	89.115	−4.115
20	87	89.205	1.134	89.756	−2.756
21	92	90.671	1.333	90.339	1.661
22	95	92.603	1.693	92.004	2.996
23	93	94.037	1.537	94.296	−1.296
24	97	95.859	1.708	95.574	1.426
25	99	97.854	1.880	97.567	1.433
26	96	98.987	1.432	99.734	−3.734
27	102	100.735	1.622	100.419	1.581
28	101	102.086	1.459	102.357	−1.357
29	103	103.436	1.394	103.545	−.545
30	105	104.863	1.414	104.829	.171
31				106.278	

Mean	82.6				.550
Standard deviation	13.39				RSE 2.361

Alpha = .20
Beta = .60
Starting trend, $b_1 = -.50 = (Y_2 - Y_1 + Y_4 - Y_3)/2$
Starting base, $S_1 = 63 = Y_1$

As with any exponential smoothing model, there are two basic questions to be answered: What smoothing constants should be used and how should the smoothing process be initialized? In our example, several values of α and β were tried until the good values of $\alpha = .2$ and $\beta = .6$ were found. The results with various smoothing values are shown in Table 6–11. To initialize the process, initial values for S_1 and b_1

FIGURE 6–5

*Holt's two-parameter
exponential smoothing*

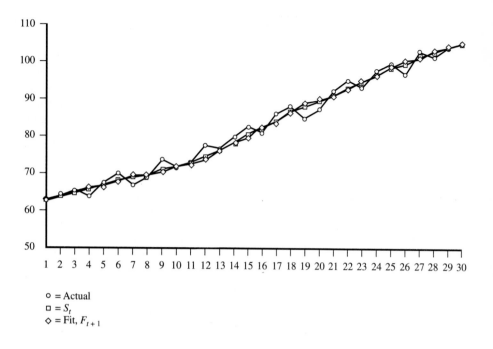

o = Actual
□ = S_t
◇ = Fit, F_{t+1}

TABLE 6–11 **Values of Alpha, Beta, and RSE for Holt's Two-Parameter Model**

Alpha	Beta	Residual Standard Errors
.3	.3	2.465
.3	.2	2.701
.3	.1	3.373
.25	.45	2.374
.25	.40	2.424
.25	.35	2.491
.25	.3	2.586
.2*	.6	2.361
.2	.55	2.395
.2	.5	2.442
.2	.45	2.505
.2	.4	2.590
.2	.35	2.704
.2	.3	2.859
.2	.25	3.068
.2	.2	3.360
.2	.1	4.565
.1	.3	4.798
.1	.2	5.889
.1	.1	8.544

* Best combination of alpha and beta of those tried.

are needed. For S_1, simply use Y_1, the observed value of period 1; however, the initial trend estimate, b_1, is not obvious. Some possible values are the differences between the first two observed values, some average of the observed slope for the first several periods, or an estimate of the series slope from a plot of the data. Any of these methods work if the data is well behaved. However, if it is not, inclusion of irregularities in the initial slope estimate can require a lengthy smoothing period. In such instances, it is better to estimate the trend from a data plot. In this example, we used the common starting conditions shown below.

$$S_1 = Y_1$$
$$b_1 = \frac{(Y_2 - Y_1) + (Y_4 - Y_3)}{2}$$

Advantages

Holt's method has the same advantages as Brown's double smoothing. In addition, Holt's is more flexible in that the level and trend can be smoothed with different weights.

Disadvantages

Holt's method requires that two parameters be optimized. Thus, the search for the best combination of parameters is more complex than for a single parameter. Holt's suffers the same limitation as other simple methods in that it does not model the seasonality of series.

Winters' Three-Parameter Exponential Smoothing

Winters' smoothing model extends Holt's two-parameter model to the seasonal case by including a third smoothing operation (and a third parameter) to adjust for seasonality. This method is often called the Holt-Winters method and is a very important approach to forecasting.

The underlying structure of one form of Winters model assumes that:

$$Y_{t+1} = (S_t + b_t)I_{t-L+1} + e_{t+1} \qquad (6\text{--}23)$$

where

$$S_t = \text{smoothed nonseasonal level of the series at end of } t$$
$$b_t = \text{smoothed trend in period } t$$
$$I_{t-L+1} = \text{smoothed seasonal index for period } t + 1$$
$$e_{t+1} = \text{error in period } t + 1$$

That is, Y_{t+1}, the actual value of a series, equals a smoothed level value S_t plus an estimate of trend b_t times a seasonal index I_{t-L+1}. These three components of demand are each exponentially smoothed values available at the end of period t. The equations used to estimate these smoothed values are:

$$S_t = \alpha \frac{Y_t}{I_{t-L}} + (1 - \alpha)(S_{t-1} + b_{t-1}) \qquad (6\text{--}24)$$

$$b_t = \beta(S_t - S_{t-1}) + (1 - \beta)b_{t-1} \qquad (6\text{--}25)$$

$$I_t = \gamma \frac{Y_t}{S_t} + (1 - \gamma)I_{t-L} \qquad (6\text{--}26)$$

$$\hat{Y}_{t+m} = (S_t + b_t m)I_{t-L+m} \qquad (6\text{--}27)$$

where

Y_t = value of actual demand at end of period t

α = smoothing constant used for S_t

S_t = smoothed value at end of t after adjusting for seasonality

β = smoothing constant used to calculate the trend (b_t)

b_t = smoothed value of trend through period t

I_{t-L} = smoothed seasonal index L periods ago

L = length of the seasonal cycle (e.g., 12 months or four quarters)

γ = smoothing constant, gamma for calculating the seasonal index in period t

I_t = smoothed seasonal index at end of period t

m = horizon length of the forecasts of y_{t+m}

Let's study each of these equations. Equation 6–24 calculates the overall level of the series as in other exponential smoothing models. It differs from single exponential smoothing models in two ways. First, the most recent actual value (Y_t) is deseasonalized by dividing it by I_{t-L}; second, the most recent trend b_t is added to the previous smoothed value prior to smoothing. Thus, S_t in equation 6–24 is the trend-adjusted, deseasonalized level at the end of period t. S_t is used in equation 6–27 to generate forecasts. As in Holt's and Brown's methods, equation 6–25 estimates the trend by smoothing the difference between the smoothed values S_t and S_{t-1}. This estimates the period-to-period change (trend) in the level of Y_t.

Equation 6–26 illustrates the calculation of the smoothed seasonal index, I_t. The denominator of the first term of this equation uses the most recent smoothed value of S_t. S_t reflects the trend-cycle and level patterns of Y_t, not the seasonal influence. By dividing Y_t by S_t, we have an estimate of an unsmoothed seasonal index for this period as shown below.

$$\frac{Y_t}{S_t} = \frac{\cancel{S_t} I_t}{\cancel{S_t}} = I_t \tag{6–28}$$

Then equation 6–26, which is repeated below, smoothes this estimate by averaging it with the index of the same period last year.

$$I_t = \gamma \frac{Y_t}{S_t} + (1 - \gamma)I_{t-L}$$

This seasonal factor is calculated for the next cycle of forecasting and used to forecast values one or more seasonal cycles ahead.

The forecast of equation 6–27 is made by adding the trend of equation 6–25 to the deseasonalized value (from equation 6–24) and then multiplying this result by the appropriate seasonal index. These forecasts can be readily extended beyond L periods in the future by repeating the L seasonal factors.

Table 6–12 is an example of the application of Winters' method to series F that reflects both trend and seasonality. A plot of actual values and forecasts is shown in Figure 6–6.

The bottom of Table 6–12 summarizes the errors realized during the coefficient-fitting process (periods 13 through 36) and the forecasting process (periods 37 through 48). As shown, these errors are somewhat comparable: the RSEs were not much different. Interestingly, the error statistics for forecasting (periods 37 to 48) are actually 1- to 12-period-ahead forecast errors. Each of the forecasts of periods 37 through 48 were made at the end of period 36. Thus, the forecast of period 48 is a full-year-ahead forecast.

The Dilemma of Random Walks, Trends, and Global Warming

The old adage "What goes up, must come down" is often true in short- to medium-term forecasting. Also, we can add the complement of that adage; "What goes down, may go up." This is true because for some time series, the short- to-medium-term behavior is a random walk. A random walk is characterized by its smooth movements up and down yielding very high first-order autocorrelations. If time series graphs of six months to a year are studied, random walks appear to have very strong upward or downward trends. That is, if we confine our analysis to only short periods of time, we may be misled into believing the time series has a sustainable trend. Herein lies a dilemma facing the forecaster and the forecasting system.

The dilemma is that detecting random walks may require more than a year of data. However, the last year of data is normally the most relevant. In general, this is a difficult dilemma. If enough data is included (i.e., several years) to identify the random walk for some time series, we may miss the recent trend if it is not a random-walk series. Or, if we do not include several years of data, then trends and random walks may both appear as trends, thus, we are correct for the trending series and grossly incorrect for the random-walk series.

How can a statistical model distinguish between a short-run period of a random walk and a trend? It can't.

The solution to this dilemma in most forecasting systems is to use smoothing methods that give more weight to recent data and to include multiple years of data to identify models. If a trend is strong enough or long enough to sustain a multi-year influence, it will be identified as a trend. This strategy may result in some trends being missed and some random walks being misidentified as trends, but it appears to be a reasonable trade-off. The problem has not been eliminated, but we hope it has been reduced to a cost-effective solution.

When random walks exist, we might have accurate one- or-two-period-ahead forecasts. But as horizons get longer than, for example, six-period-ahead forecasts, there will be extremely large errors.

Now, how does this relate to global warming? It relates directly.

Many scientists are debating the existence, causes, and effects of global warming. One group of scientists believes that the current increase in global temperatures is simply an aberration in temperatures caused by the many interacting global and solar influences on weather. They contend, but proof is not forthcoming, that the planet has undergone many similar, small temperature changes over time in a random-walk pattern. Thus, their position is one supporting a random walk of temperatures over tens of thousands of years; or possibly a cyclical variation in temperature where the period repeats so many hundred thousand or millions of years. In contrast, many scientists believe that recent global temperature increases are caused by man, including the burning of fuels in factories, homes, and cars and the depletion of the atmosphere's ozone layer and of rain forests. They contend that temperatures are rising and as long as the causes of these rises continue, the trend will continue; it is possible that even if the causes are removed, the system may continue with increasing temperatures. However, their theory is as equally difficult to prove as the random-walk theory.

Yet another groups contends that while the causes may be uncertain, the effects may not be. The net effect of small temperature rises includes the melting of polar ice caps and the flooding of many coastal cities, including some of the largest in the world. Thus, trends or random walks in the level of seas and the size of polar ice caps should be monitored to avoid massive loss of life or property.

No one predicts sudden catastrophic changes in sea levels over periods of days; instead predictions are over months or years. However, there may be profound changes in weather including more tropical storms. Also, as yet no one predicts that the Rockies will be on the West Coast or the Appalachians on the East Coast of the U.S. It will be many decades until the competing theories are confirmed or denied.

As Table 6–12 shows, the mean error during this 12-month period was 25.45; thus, the total cumulative error for the period is about +305 units (25.45 · 12) during a period when cumulative demand was actually 11,413. This yields an annual cumulative percent error of 305/11,413, or about 2.7 percent. We cannot generalize from this result; nonetheless, for this series Winters' method forecasted these 12 months quite accurately.

The procedure shown in Table 6–12 might be modified in actual practice because it uses unadjusted seasonal indexes in the forecasts. That is, the sum of the seasonal

TABLE 6–12   Winters' Three-Parameter Exponential Smoothing (additive trend, multiplicative seasonal, and smoothed model: $\alpha = .3$, $\beta = .05$, $\gamma = .75$) (SERIESF.DAT)

Period (t)	Y_t	Smoothed Trend S_t	b_t	$S_t + b_t$	Seasonal I_t	$\hat{Y}_t$	e_t
1	546			652.958	.836		
2	578			660.875	.875		
3	660			668.792	.987		
4	707	Initial $S_t + b_t =$		676.708	1.045		
5	738	for initial I_t		684.625	1.078		
6	781			692.542	1.128		
7	848			700.458	1.211		
8	818			708.375	1.155		
9	729			716.292	1.018		
10	691			724.208	.954		
11	658			732.125	.899		
12	604	740.196	7.917	748.113	.816		
13	629	749.344	7.978	757.322	.839	625.568	3.432
14	711	774.009	8.813	782.822	.908	662.353	48.647
15	729	769.588	8.151	777.739	.957	772.531	−43.531
16	798	773.560	7.942	781.502	1.035	812.554	−14.554
17	861	786.670	8.200	794.871	1.090	842.430	18.570
18	903	796.627	8.288	804.915	1.132	896.400	6.600
19	968	803.314	8.208	811.522	1.206	974.459	−6.459
20	894	800.323	7.648	807.971	1.126	937.110	−43.110
21	860	819.082	8.204	827.286	1.042	822.306	37.694
22	792	828.119	8.245	836.364	.956	789.351	2.649
23	739	832.130	8.034	840.163	.891	751.685	−12.685
24	699	845.100	8.280	853.380	.824	685.573	13.427
25	773	873.899	9.306	883.205	.873	715.644	57.356
26	818	888.629	9.578	898.206	.917	801.592	16.408
27	871	901.740	9.754	911.494	.964	859.725	11.275
28	882	893.726	8.866	902.592	.999	943.293	−61.293
29	959	895.673	8.520	904.193	1.076	984.146	−25.146
30	979	892.369	7.929	900.298	1.106	1023.619	−44.619
31	955	867.689	6.298	873.987	1.127	1086.133	−131.133
32	925	858.135	5.506	863.640	1.090	984.526	−59.526
33	843	847.277	4.687	851.965	1.007	899.829	−56.829
34	790	844.329	4.306	848.634	.941	814.329	−24.329
35	746	845.293	4.139	849.431	.885	755.921	−9.921
36	822	893.750	6.355	900.105	.896	700.221	121.779
37	857			906.459		785.842	71.158
38	876			912.814		831.484	44.516
39	959			919.168		879.699	79.301
40	981			925.523		918.140	62.860
41	1051			931.877		995.507	55.493
42	1124	Forecast		938.232		1030.497	93.503
43	1073			944.586		1057.455	15.545
44	1020			950.941		1029.654	−9.654
45	933			957.295		957.302	−24.302
46	787			963.650		900.525	−113.525
47	830			970.004		852.434	−22.434
48	922			976.359		869.003	52.997

Fitted Values Periods 13–36		Forecasted Values Period 37–48	
Mean error	= −8.1374	Mean error	= 25.4548
MAD	= 36.2905	MAD	= 53.774
RSE	= 50.2593	RSE	= 64.8303

FIGURE 6–6

*Winters' three-parameter
exponential smoothing
(SERIESF.DAT)*

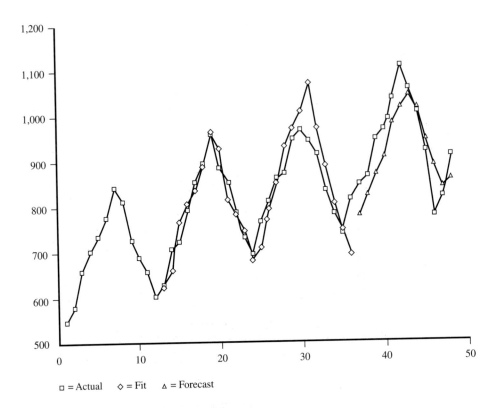

□ = Actual   ◇ = Fit   △ = Forecast

indexes for each year were not forced to equal 12, as is done in Chapter 5. The indexes were not adjusted because of the dynamic fitting computations. However, in actual practice, the final seasonal adjustment procedure used in Chapter 5 might be applied to the final set of seasonal indexes in Table 6–12.

Initialization of Starting Values

Table 6–12 reflects a combination of techniques in addition to the straightforward application of equations 6–24 through 6–27. Some method must be used to derive initial b_t, S_t, and I_t—the **initialization of parameters.** We initialize the model of Table 6–12 assuming only 15 observations were available to estimate b_t, S_t and I_t. In this case, the differences in the value of the series over three 12-month periods (period 13–period 1, period 14–period 2, and period 15–period 3) are summed and then divided by 36 to get an average monthly trend value of 7.9167. The average value of the first 12 periods (696.5) becomes a base upon which S_t and b_t are projected. This average value is centered on the period 6.5 [(12 + 1)/2]. Thus, to get the $S_t + b_t$ value for any particular month, we must use the appropriate multiplier on the trend value of 7.9167. Therefore, $S_t + b_t$ for period 1 is 696.5 − 5.5(7.9167) = 652.96. $S_t + b_t$ for period 2 is 696.5 − 4.5(7.9167) = 660.87, and so on. Each successive $S_t + b_t$ value is approximately 7.9167 greater than its preceding value. The actual values for periods 1 to 12 are then divided by their respective $S_t + b_t$ values to obtain the initial seasonal factors shown in periods 1 to 12. S_t for period 12 is the observed value for that period divided by the estimated seasonal index for that month (i.e., 604/.816 = 740.196), and b_t for period 12 is the average trend as estimated earlier. Fitted values for the next 24 time periods (periods 13 to 36) were used to determine the values of **alpha, beta,** and **gamma** that minimize the sum of the squared errors. The selected values of the parameters are then used to forecast the series for a full 12 periods ahead (periods 37 to

48), with period 36 as the origin of all 12 forecasts. In general, as the future rolls into the past, these forecasts are revised as each new observed value becomes known.

If the full 48 months of data exists at the time of initializing the model, then more accurate measures of initial values should be estimated. Consider the following alternatives:

Decomposition Method.   Initial values of b_1, S_1, and I_1 to I_{12} in Table 6–12 can be estimated using the seasonal indexes and trend line from the percent of moving average method of Chapter 5, Table 5–6. Alternatively, a regression decomposition method might be used to determine these initial values.

Backforecasting.   Backforecasting is a commonly used method to make it appear that there is a larger number of observations in a dataset. Backforecasting involves a simple process of reversing the order of the data, the most recent actual values are first and the oldest observations are the last in the dataset. For example:

$$
\begin{array}{llllllll}
t = & 1 & 2 & 3 & 4 & 5 & 6 & 7 & 8 \\
Y_t = & 12 & 14 & 16 & 17 & 19 & 21 & & & \text{Original data} \\
Y'_t = & 21 & 19 & 17 & 16 & 14 & 12 & & & \text{Backforecasting data}
\end{array}
$$

Now, a model is fitted to the reversed observations where the forecasted values (e.g., $\hat{Y}'_7$ and $\hat{Y}'_8$) of the model are actually backforecasts of Y_0 and Y_{-1}. These values can be used as starting values of the original series. (i.e., Y_0 and Y_{-1}, respectively). Such methods can be very effective when insufficient data exists, however, they are not substitutes for sufficient actual data.

In backforecasting the data of SERIESF.DAT in Table 6–12, a two-step procedure can be used. In step one the data can be used in reverse order in the computations of Table 6–12, this yields forecasted values, S_{49}, b_{49}, and seasonal indexes. Then, the forecasted values of periods 49 to 60 or the fitted seasonal indexes, S_{49} and b_{49} can be used as initial values of the original data in the second step. Thus, the second step uses the forecasts of the first step as starting conditions.

Backforecasting is an effective method that can be applied in many forecasting situations. It is easily implemented and effectively used.

Ongoing Use of the Model

After initializing the model, Winters method is used as follows.

1. At the end of period t, the actual demand, Y_t, is recorded.
2. Apply this value in equation 6–24 to calculate the smoothed value at time t. Note that all values in equation 6–24 are known at this time.
3. Calculate the new trend, b_t.
4. Next calculate the newest value of the seasonal index, I_t. Then adjust this and previous indexes so that they sum to the number of periods per year or season. These values will be used in the next forecast cycle.
5. Forecast future sales using equation 6–27.

Table 6–12 shows these steps using the Winters method with alpha equal to .3, beta equal to .05, and gamma equal to .75. Using a crude search method, these were found to be good values of the three smoothing constants.

Additive and Multiplicative Factors

Equation 6–27 of the previous example (shown below as equation 6–30) assumes that the trend is additive and that the seasonal influence is multiplicative. When a model results in the multiplication of two factors to yield a forecast, this is referred to as a mul-

Your Winter Blues May Be SAD

The underlying causes of seasonal demands for products can be complex. Demands for products such as pharmaceuticals are greatly influenced by changes in temperature, humidity, and precipitation. Although some of us thrive on seasonal changes, some do not. One of the stranger seasonal influences is seasonal affective disorder, or SAD. The American Psychiatric Association believes that approximately 10 million U.S. citizens (about 4 percent) are severely affected by this disorder. An additional 25 million people (about 14 percent) are mildly affected or hampered by the disorder. SAD affects people primar-

ily during winter months and is apparently caused by the hormonal and neurological changes that occur with decreases in the number of hours of daylight. Severely affected individuals may gain or lose weight, be lethargic, or have difficulty concentrating on their jobs. It is believed that having fewer daylight hours in the winter affects different parts of the brain, hormones, and biological rhythms. Fortunately, the disorder can be treated with therapies that typically involve exposure to special fluorescent lights.

tiplicative model. In equation 6–30, the seasonal index is multiplied by the current smoothed and trend values. In contrast, both the trend and seasonality in equation 6–29 is additive. The Holt-Winters method can be used to model four different combinations of trend and seasonal influences. Winters' method is commonly used to model additive trend and multiplicative or additive seasonality as in equations 6–29 and 6–30.

	Trend	Seasonality	
$F_{t+m} = S_t + b_t m + I_{t-L+m}$	Add.	Add.	(6–29)
$F_{t+m} = (S_t + b_t m) I_{t-L+m}$	Add.	Mul.	(6–30)
$F_{t+m} = S_t b_t^m + I_{t-L+m}$	Mul.	Add.	(6–31)
$F_{t+m} = S_t b_t^m I_{t-L+m}$	Mul.	Mul.	(6–32)

Additive trends are more popular than multiplicative trends because long-horizon forecasts that extrapolate a multiplicative trend have a tendency to significantly over- or underforecast demand. Because of this over- or underforecasting, multiplicative models are either avoided or the trend is dampened. Dampening is discussed in the next section of this chapter.

Data Requirements

Because Winters' method models seasonality, its data requirements are greater than other methods discussed in this chapter. To adequately measure seasonality, at least three seasons of monthly data (36 months), four or five seasons of quarterly data (16 to 20 quarters), and three seasons of weekly data (156 weeks) are suggested minimums. However, these are just that, minimums; in general, err on the high side, realizing you can always discard the oldest data.

Advantages

Winters' powerful method models trend, seasonality, and randomness using an efficient exponential smoothing process. Its seasonal indexes are easily interpreted; also, when these indexes are group indexes, they can be applied to new or low-volume products in the group. Because this is an exponential smoothing model, parameters can be updated using computationally efficient algorithms. The model's forecasting equations are easily interpreted and understood by management. The relationship between Winters method and other simple decomposition methods makes it more intuitive than other methods such as Fourier series analysis. Because of these advantages, Winters is popular in some commercial forecasting systems.

Disadvantages   Winters' method may be too complex for data that do not have identifiable trends and seasonality. The simultaneous determination of the optimal values of three smoothing parameters using Winters model may take more computational time than regression, classical decomposition, or Fourier series analysis. However, after fitting a model, these parameters can be updated very efficiently (see Brown, 1962). As in any multiplicative model, the division by very small numbers or multiplication by extremely large values is a problem with equations 6–30 to 6–32. Thus, outliers can have dramatic effects on forecasts, and should be eliminated.

Trend Dampening

Forecasters have noted the times that forecasts have been dramatically in error. One noted problem is the tendency of trend models to grossly overforecast the positive or negative trends of the past when long-term forecasts are made. Often, this occurs because it is difficult to distinguish between the trend and cyclical variations in a time series; consequently, most methods do not adequately decompose a series into separate trend and cyclical influences. Thus, trend and cyclical influences are modeled together in a single trend component (the trend may be higher or lower than it should be because of the cyclical up- or downward). **Trend dampening** is the process of reducing the trend value in proportion to the length of the forecast horizon. Thus, it offsets the over- or underforecasting caused by trend extrapolation.

One underlying assumption in justifying dampened trends is that the trend reflects the effects of the business cycle. These effects are not expected to extend indefinitely into the future. There is not much research on the use of trend dampening. However, the empirical evidence of some users suggests that dampening is more effective than not. Dampening is done by multiplying the trend estimate by a fractional constant to the power of m, the number of periods forecast into the future. The modified forecast equations are:

$$F_{t+m} = S_t + p^m b_t m + I_{t-L+m} \qquad (6\text{–}33)$$
$$F_{t+m} = (S_t + p^m b_t m) I_{t-L+m} \qquad (6\text{–}34)$$
$$F_{t+m} = S_t p^m b_t^m + I_{t-L+m} \qquad (6\text{–}35)$$
$$F_{t+m} = S_t p^m b_t^m I_{t-L+m} \qquad (6\text{–}36)$$

where

$p =$ fractional constant

Table 6–13 illustrates selected values of p^m for values of p and m.

We have seen little research on choosing the best dampening constant, p. It is suggested that very high values of p can be used to avoid unrealistically low projections for long-term values unless there is strong evidence to support rapid declines in the trend. Much subjective insight is needed in selecting p. The systematic bias caused by p-values can be very misleading when p is used across all items in an automated forecasting environment. We should be able to identify those groups of items that will have sustainable trends and those that will not. In all cases of dampening, we do not allow it to reverse the trend. Additive trends are not allowed to reverse their signs, nor

TABLE 6–13 p^m for Selected Values of p and m

				m		
p	1	2	3	6	12	24
.7	.7	.49	.343	.118	.014	.0002
.8	.8	.64	.512	.262	.069	.0047
.9	.9	.81	.729	.531	.282	.0800
.95	.95	.903	.857	.735	.540	.292
1.0	1.0	1.0	1.0	1.0	1.0	1.0

are multiplicative trends allowed to go below 1.00 or above 1.00 for increasing and decreasing trends, respectively. Thus, zero is an additive trend dampening bound, and 1.00 is a multiplicative trend dampening bound.

Summary

This chapter has illustrated a number of forecasting methods. The method of using first, second, and seasonal differences to model trend and seasonal patterns is simple and effective. However, because differences do not average or smooth the past, one must be cautious in using these methods since unusual values or outliers can adversely affect resulting forecasts. The trend-adjusted methods of linear moving averages, double exponential smoothing, and Holt's two-parameter exponential smoothing are effective methods of modeling trends. However, many series have seasonal patterns; thus, these methods are inappropriate for seasonal data. The most versatile method discussed here is Winters' method; it models randomness, trend, and seasonality. Another equally versatile method is Fourier Series Analysis which is developed in the appendix of this chapter.

Key Terms

α, β, γ
antilog of logarithmic b
Brown's double exponential smoothing
double moving averages (DMAs)
first differences
Holt's two-parameter trend method
initialization of starting values
linear moving averages

nonlinear trends
second differences
seasonal differences
significance test for trend
starting values
trend dampening
Winters' three-parameter trend-seasonal
  method

Key Formulas

First differences, naive model without trend:

$$\hat{Y}_t = Y_{t-1} + \text{ mean of first differences}$$

(6–1)

First differences model with trend:

$$\hat{Y}_t = Y_{t-1} + b \tag{6-2}$$

Significance test of trend:

$$\hat{Y}_{t+m} = Y_t + m \cdot b \tag{6-3}$$

$$t\text{-calculated} = \frac{b - 0}{S/\sqrt{n - d}} \tag{6-4}$$

$$t\text{-table} < \begin{cases} df = n - d - 1 = 28 \\ \text{sign.} = .05 \end{cases}$$

Second differences for nonlinear pattern:

$$(Y_t - Y_{t-1}) - (Y_{t-1} - Y_{t-2}) = Y_t - 2Y_{t-1} + Y_{t-2} \tag{6-6}$$

Second differences for nonlinear pattern with trend:

$$\hat{Y}_t = 2Y_{t-1} - Y_{t-2} + b = Y_{t-1} + (Y_{t-1} - Y_{t-2}) + b \tag{6-7}$$

Logarithmic nonlinear trend model:

$$\widehat{Ln(Y_t)} = Ln(Y_{t-1}) + b \tag{6-8}$$

$$\hat{Y}_t = e^{\widehat{Ln(Y)}} \tag{6-9}$$

The antilog of b yields percentage growth:

$$e^b - 1 = 1.0429 - 1 = .0429$$

Seasonal differences model with trend, monthly:

$$\hat{Y}_t = Y_{t-12} + b$$

For quarterly data:

$$\hat{Y}_t = Y_{t-4} + b$$

Double moving averages method:

$$S'_t = \frac{Y_t + Y_{t-1} + \ldots + Y_{t-N+1}}{N} \tag{6-10}$$

$$S''_t = \frac{S'_t + S'_{t-1} + \ldots + S'_{t-M+1}}{M} \tag{6-11}$$

$$a_t = S'_t + (S'_t - S''_t) = 2S'_t - S''_t \tag{6-12}$$

$$b_t = \frac{2}{N-1}(S'_t - S''_t) \tag{6-13}$$

$$F_{t+m} = a_t + b_t m \tag{6-14}$$

Brown's double exponential smoothing:

$$S'_t = \alpha Y_t + (1 - \alpha)S'_{t-1} \tag{6-15}$$

$$S''_t = \alpha S'_t + (1 - \alpha)S''_{t-1} \tag{6-16}$$

$$a_t = S'_t + (S'_t - S''_t) = 2S'_t - S''_t \tag{6-17}$$

$$b_t = \frac{\alpha}{1 - \alpha}(S'_t - S''_t) \tag{6-18}$$

$$F_{t+m} = a_t + b_t m \tag{6-19}$$

Holt's two-parameter trend model:

$$S_t = \alpha Y_t + (1 - \alpha)(S_{t-1} + b_{t-1}) \tag{6-20}$$

$$b_t = \beta(S_t - S_{t-1}) + (1 - \beta)b_{t-1} \tag{6-21}$$

$$F_{t+m} = S_t + b_t m \tag{6-22}$$

Winters' three-parameter exponential smoothing:

$$Y_{t+1} = (S_t + b_t)I_{t-L+1} + e_{t+1} \tag{6-23}$$

$$S_t = \alpha \frac{Y_t}{I_{t-1}} + (1 - \alpha)(S_{t-1} + b_{t-1}) \tag{6-24}$$

$$b_t = \beta(S_t - S_{t-1}) + (1 - \beta)b_{t-1} \tag{6-25}$$

$$I_t = \gamma \frac{Y_t}{S_t} + (1 - \gamma)I_{t-L} \tag{6-26}$$

$$\hat{Y}_{t+m} = (S_t + b_t m)I_{t-L+m} \tag{6-27}$$

$$\frac{Y_t}{S_t} = \frac{S_t I_t}{S_t} = I_t \tag{6-28}$$

Multiplicative (mul) and additive (add) Winters' models:

$$F_{t+m} = S_t + b_t m + I_{t-L+m} \qquad \text{trend = add, season = add} \tag{6-29}$$

$$F_{t+m} = (S_t + b_t m)I_{t-L+m} \qquad \text{trend = add, season = mul} \tag{6-30}$$

$$F_{t+m} = S_t b_t^{\ m} + I_{t-L+m} \qquad \text{trend = mul, season = add} \tag{6-31}$$

$$F_{t+m} = S_t b_t^{\ m} I_{t-L+m} \qquad \text{trend = mul, season = mul} \tag{6-32}$$

Trend dampening:

$$F_{t+m} = S_t + p^m b_t m + I_{t-L+m} \tag{6-33}$$

$$F_{t+m} = (S_t + p^m b_t m)I_{t-L+m} \tag{6-34}$$

$$F_{t+m} = S_t p^m b_t^{\ m} + I_{t-L+m} \tag{6-35}$$

$$F_{t+m} = S_t p^m b_t^{\ m} I_{t-L+m} \tag{6-36}$$

Review Problems Using Your Software

R6–1 Repeat the analysis of the following tables and interpret your results as done in the book.

- *a.* Table 6–1   *b.* Table 6–3
- *c.* Table 6–4   *d.* Table 6–7
- *e.* Table 6–10   *f.* Table 6–12

R6–2 Repeat the analysis of equations 6–1 to 6–4 and interpret.

Problems

6–1 What do the terms *first differenced model with* and *without trend* denote? Write out the forecasting and error equations of these two models.

6–2 What are the differences between first differences and DMA methods?

6–3 What is the main disadvantage of Brown's method in general and specifically relative to Holt's method?

6–4 Explain the meaning of the null hypothesis of the statistical significance test for trend.

6–5 What are the advantages and disadvantages of forecasting with differences?

6–6 How are differenced models used with seasonal and nonlinear time series? What are second differences?

6–7 Explain the meaning of taking first differences of logarithms. How are logarithmic fits and forecasts converted into original values? How do you interpret the logarithmic trend parameter, b, in terms of the original series?

6–8 What is a double moving average and how does it model trend?

6–9 Are double moving averages more like Brown's double smoothing or Holt's two-parameter smoothing?

6–10 For Brown's or Holt's methods, how are optimal smoothing constants found?

6–11 What is the relationship between Holt's two-parameter and Winters' three-parameter exponential smoothing?

6–12 In what ways are Winters' method and the classical decomposition method similar and different?

6–13 In general, what are starting values and what characteristics should they have when using exponential smoothing models?

6–14 What is trend dampening and why is it important?

6–15 Write out the forecasting forms of the four possible combinations of trend and seasonal Winters' models. Relate these to different forms of classical decomposition methods.

6–16 Repeat the test of significance for trend using SERIESG.DAT of Table 6–1.

6–17 Repeat the test of significance for trend using SERIESI.DAT of Table 6–1.

6–18 Midwestern University has reduced its undergraduate enrollments of night part-time students. In year 1 the school stopped offering night classes and stopped admitting part-time students. Analyze the following fall (FA) and spring (SP) semester data using appropriate trend models with or without seasonality as you deem appropriate.

UGDATA.DAT	Year 1		Year 2		Year 3		Year 4		Year 5	
t	1	2	3	4	5	6	7	8	9	10
Semester	FA	SP	FA	SP	FA	SP	FA	SP	FA	SP
Students	935	858	638	564	429	472	356	344	324	
Credit										
Hours	7,902	7,275	6,212	6,047	5,242	6,047	4,578	4,025	3,828	

a. Is the number of students undergoing a linear or nonlinear decline? Does there appear to be seasonality in the data or its plots?

b. Based on *a*, identify an appropriate trend model for predicting the number of students (i.e., head count) for the spring semester of year 5 and the fall and spring semesters of years 6 and 7.

c. How well does your model fit the known past values? Use the residual standard error, $\overline{R^2}$, and the mean error to answer this question.

d. What is the annual trend of students. How about the semester trend?

6–19 Repeat problem 6–18 using the credit hours.

6–20 Repeat problem 6–18 using credit hours per student.

6–21 Given the reported number of deaths from AIDS in the United States, find an appropriate model. (AIDSDIE.DAT)

Date	1982	1983	1984	1985	1986	1987	1988	1989
Deaths	444	1,436	3,266	6,404	10,965	14,612	18,248	21,675

a. Which should be used, a linear or nonlinear model?
b. Forecast the number of deaths in 1990 to 2000.
c. What is the percentage growth in AIDS deaths?

6–22 Given the actual per capita health expenditures for the United States, find an appropriate model. (HEALTHEX.DAT)

Date	1983	1984	1985	1986	1987	1988	1989
Dollars	1,407	1,518	1,638	1,749	1,887	2,061	2,274

a. Which should be used, a linear or nonlinear model?
b. Forecast the per capita health expenditures in 1990 to 2000.
c. What is the percentage growth in expenditures?

6–23 Given the number of AIDS cases reported in the United States beginning in 1982, forecast the number of cases in 1990 to 2000 and comment about the percentage growth in AIDS cases. (AIDSCASE.DAT)

Date	1982	1983	1984	1985	1986	1987	1988	1989
Cases	744	2,117	4,445	8,249	13,166	21,070	31,001	33,722

6–24 Given the following actual per capita red meat consumption for the United States in pounds, identify a best model for forecasting the annual pounds consumed from 1990 to 1995 and the percentage growth in red meat consumption. (REDMEAT.DAT)

Date	1983	1984	1985	1986	1987	1988	1989
Pounds	120.3	119.9	120.9	118.3	113.3	113.1	111.3

6–25 Given the standardized test scores of students in the United States from 1983 to 1989, forecast the scores for 1990 to 2000 using both the SAT and ACT. (SATACT.DAT)

Date	1983	1984	1985	1986	1987	1988	1989
SAT	963	965	977	1,001	1,080	1,134	1,088
ACT	18	18.50	18.60	18.80	18.70	18.80	18.60

6–26 Forecast the cost index for higher education in the United States for 1990 to 2000. Using the best model possible, predict future values and estimate the percentage growth in the index. Do you expect this growth to continue to the year 2000? (EDCOST.DAT)

Date	1977	1978	1979	1980	1981	1982	1983	1984	1985	1986	1987	1988	1989
Cost	61.1	65.2	70.2	77.2	85.5	94	100	105.4	111.6	116.3	120.9	126.3	134.1

6–27 Forecast the purchasing power (PP) of the U.S. dollar for years 1990 to 2000. Using the best model possible, forecast and estimate the percentage change in the index. Do you expect this percentage to continue to the year 2000? (USPP.DAT)

Date	1980	1981	1982	1983	1984	1985	1986	1987	1988	1989
PP	1.215	1.098	1.035	1.003	.961	.928	.913	.880	.846	.807

6–28 Given the composite index of leading economic cyclical indexes, develop a forecasting model of this series as you answer the following questions. Using the best model possible, forecast the growth in the index. Do you expect this growth to continue to the year 2000? (LEADIND.DAT)

Date	1980	1981	1982	1983	1984	1985	1986	1987	1988	1989
CPI	99.2	101.2	100	116.2	121.7	124.2	132.3	140.1	142.8	144.9

6–29 The following is the number of motor vehicle accidents in the U.S. from 1984 to 1989. Develop a forecasting model of this series as you answer the following questions. Using the best model possible, forecast and estimate the change in the index. Do you expect this change to continue to the year 2000? (MOTORACC.DAT)

Date	1984	1985	1986	1987	1988	1989
Accidents (000s)	18.8	19.3	17.7	20.8	20.6	12.8

6–30 The following is the number of U.S. aircraft shipments from 1983 to 1990. Develop a forecasting model of this series as you answer the following questions. Using the best model possible, forecast this series. Do you expect this relationship to continue to the year 2000? (AIRSHIPS.DAT)

Date	1983	1984	1985	1986	1987	1988	1989	1990
Aircraft	4,409	3,931	3,597	3,261	3,003	3,133	3,471	3,215

6–31 Calculate the error and percentage error in Lincoln's forecast of 1870 through 1930. Are there any general principles regarding forecasting illustrated by the errors in Lincoln's projections.

6–32 Using Lincoln's method of forecasting, forecast the population of the United States for 1940 to 1990; compare your results to the actual results given in problem 6–33. Calculate the errors in forecast using as many error statistics as you deem appropriate.

6–33 Let's see how well you can forecast the actual population of the United States for the years 1940 through 1990. Use whatever method you deem most appropriate to forecast 1940 through 1990 using LINCOLN.DAT. Justify your method, then compare your results to the actual results given below. Don't cheat; choose a method before you look at the following:

	Lincoln's Projection	Actual Population*	Actual % Increase
1940		131,669	7.2
1950		151,326	14.9
1960		179,323	18.5
1970		203,302	13.4
1980		226,546	11.4
1990		248,710	9.8

*in thousands.

6–34 Calculate the percentage change in the actual population figures for 1870 to 1990 given above and in LINCOLN.DAT. Are there any unusual percentage growths? How do you explain these percentage growths? How do you explain the long-run decline in percentage growths from 1870 to 1930? How do you explain the long-run decline in percentage growths from 1940 to 1990?

6–35 Using the data set TABLE6–7.DAT, choose an appropriate method to estimate the trend of the series. Calculate the mean error and standard deviation of the errors using this model, test the significance of the trend, calculate $\bar{R}^2$, plot first differences, and fully interpret your model.

6–36 For SERIESB.DAT, complete the following:
   a. Use appropriate differences to model this series for the first 36 observations.
   b. Using the model of *a*, forecast the remaining 12 observations.
   c. Calculate the ME, RSE, MPE, MAPE, and $\bar{R}^2$ for both the fit and the forecast.
   d. Discuss the validity of your model.

6–37 For SERIESC.DAT, complete the assignment given in problem 6–36.

6–38 For SERIESD.DAT, complete the assignment given in problem 6–36.

6–39 For SERIESF.DAT, complete the assignment given in problem 6–36. In addition, compare the ME and RSE for periods 13 to 36 and periods 37 to 48 as reported in Table 6–12. Which model performs better? Can you explain the difference?

6–40 For SERIESC.DAT, complete the following:
 a. Use the appropriate Holt's or Winters' model of this series on the first 36 observations.
 b. Using the model of *a*, forecast the remaining 12 observations.
 c. Calculate the ME, RSE, MPE, MAPE, and $\bar{R}^2$ for both the fit and forecast.
 d. Discuss the validity of your model.

6–41 For SERIESD.DAT, complete the assignment given in problem 6–40.

6–42 RETAIL.DAT is the monthly retail sales in the Unites States; fit models to all but the last 12 months and forecast those using the assignment given in problem 6–40.

6–43 SUPEROIL.DAT is the sales of the Superoil Company in thousands of barrels during the last 108 months. Complete the assignment given in problem 6–40 using the first eight years and forecast the last year.

Minicases: Common Assignment for Minicases

For each of the minicases complete the following analysis. Forecast with either Holt's or Winters' method and calculate the ME, MPE, MAPE, RSE, and $\bar{R}^2$ for both the fit and forecast. Discuss the differences between the fit and forecast performance as measured by these statistics. Comment about anything that you found unusual. Does this model fit the data well? Is the model useful from a practical standpoint? If you have filled out the Master Forecasting Summary Table in other chapters, combine these results with those already recorded in the table.

Minicase 6–1 Kansas Turnpike, Daily Data Complete the common assignment using TURNPIKD.DAT of Minicase 1–1. Use Winters method to forecast the number of vehicles that are using the turnpike each day. This method may not be in your statistical package; if not, apply a spreadsheet model or seasonally differenced models. Fit a model to the first 11 weeks, then compare the accuracy of that fit with the forecast of weeks 12 and 13.

Minicase 6–2 Domestic Air Passengers by Quarter Complete the common assignment using the file PASSAIR.DAT, which is a time series of the quarterly passengers who have flown on domestic flights in the U.S. airlines from the first quarter 1982 through the second quarter of 1994, 50 observations. Fit to 42 observations and forecast eight.

Minicase 6–3 Hospital Census by Month Complete the common assignment using the file CENSUSM.DAT. Fit a model to the first seven years, then compare the accuracy of the fit of the first seven years with the forecast of years 8 to 10.

Minicase 6–4 Henry Machler's Hideaway Orchids Complete the common assignment using the file MACHLERD.DAT Calculate the fitted error in using this relationship over 19 weeks of data and forecast the 20th week.

Minicase 6–5 Your Forecasting Project Complete the common assignment using your time series.

Minicase 6–6 Midwestern Building Materials LUMBER.DAT is a highly seasonal monthly series of lumber sales of a large midwestern building materials company with 120 monthly observations from January to December. Complete the common seasonal smoothing assignment given above; withhold and forecast the last 12 months of data.

Minicase 6–7 International Airline Passengers AIRLINE.DAT is a highly seasonal monthly series of international airline passengers with 144 observations from 1949 through 1960. Because the variance of this series widens as the level increases, either logarithms should be used with an additive model or the original series should be analyzed with a multiplicative model. Complete the common seasonal smoothing assignment given previously; withhold and forecast the last 12 months. Fit a model to the first seven years, then forecast years 8 to 10.

Minicase 6–8 Automobile Sales AUTO.DAT is a highly seasonal monthly time series of automobile sales of large automobile manufacture with 185 observations from January to May of year 16. Complete the common seasonal smoothing assignment given previously; withhold and forecast the last 12 months.

Minicase 6–9 Consumption of Distilled Spirits SPIRITS.DAT is a highly seasonal monthly time series of the consumption of alcoholic spirits in United States with 132 observations from January 1975 to December 1985. Complete the common seasonal smoothing assignment given previously; withhold and forecast the last 12 months.

Minicase 6–10 Discount Consumer Electronics
ELECT.DAT is a highly seasonal monthly time series of the sales of consumer electronics from large retail discounter with 185 observations from January to to May of year 16. Complete the common seasonal smoothing assignment given previously; withhold and forecast the last 12 months.

References

Ameen, J.R.M., and P.J. Harrison. "Discounted Weight Estimation." *Journal of Forecasting* 3 (1984), pp. 285–296.

Bretschneider, S. "Estimating Forecast Variance with Exponential Smoothing: Some New Results." *International Journal of Forecasting* 2 (1986), pp. 349–355.

Brown, R.G. *Statistical Forecasting for Inventory Control.* New York: McGraw-Hill, 1959.

Brown, R.G. *Smoothing, Forecasting and Prediction of Discrete Time Series.* Englewood Cliffs, NJ: Prentice Hall, 1962.

Brown, R.G., and R.F. Meyer. "The Fundamental Theorem of Exponential Smoothing." *Operations Research* 9 (1961), pp. 673–685.

Chatfield, C. "Some Recent Developments in Time Series Analysis." *Journal of the Royal Statistical Society A* 140 (1977), pp. 492–510.

Chatfield, C. "The Holt-Winters Forecasting Procedure." *Applied Statistics* 27 (1978), pp. 264–279.

Chatfield, C., and M. Yar. "Holt-Winters Forecasting: Some Practical Issues." *The Statistician* 37 (1988), pp. 129–140.

Holt-Winter. "*International Journal of Forecasting* 7 (1991), pp. 31–37.

Chow, W.M. "Adaptive Control of the Exponential Smoothing Constant." *Journal of Industrial Engineering* 16 (1965), pp. 314–317.

Cox, D.R. "Prediction by Exponential Weighted Moving Averages and Related Methods." *Journal of the Royal Statistical Society B* 23 (1961), pp. 414–422.

Fildes, R. "Quantitative Forecasting the State of the Art: Extrapolative Methods." *Journal of the Operational Research Society* 30 (1979), pp. 691–710.

Gardner, E.S. "Automatic Monitoring of Forecast Errors." *Journal of Forecasting* 2 (1983), pp. 1–21.

Gardner, E.S. "The Strange Case of Lagging Forecasts." *Interfaces* 14 (1984), pp. 47–50.

Gardner, E.S. "Exponential Smoothing: The State of the Art." *Journal of Forecasting* 4 (1985), pp. 1–28.

Gardner, E.S., and D.G. Dannenbring. "Forecasting with Exponential Smoothing: Some Guidelines for Model Selection," *Decision Sciences* 11 (1980), pp. 370–383.

Gilchrist, W.G. "Methods of Estimation Using Discounting." *Journal of the Royal Statistical Society B* 29 (1967), pp. 355–369.

Gilchrist, W.G. *Statistical Forecasting.* London: Wiley, 1976.

Godolphin, E.J., and P.J. Harrison. "Equivalence Theorems for Polynominal-Projecting Predictors." *Journal of the Royal Statistical Society B* 37(1975), pp. 205–215.

Golder, E.R. and J.G. Settle. "Monitoring Schemes in Short-Term Forecasting." *Operational Research Quarterly* 27 (1976), pp. 489-501.

Groff, G.K. "Empirical Comparison of Models for Short-Range Forecasting." *Management Science* 20 (1973, pp. 22–31.

Harrison, P.J. "Short-Term Sales Forecasting." *Applied Statistics* 14 (1965), pp. 102–139.

Harrison, P.J. "Exponential Smoothing and Short-Term Sales Forecasting." *Management Science* 13 (1967), pp. 821–842.

Harrison, P.J., and O.L. Davies. "The Use of Cumulative Sum (CUSUM) Techniques for the Control of Routine Forecasts of Product Demand."*Operations Research* 12 (1964), pp. 325–333.

Holt, C.C. "Forecasting Seasonal and Trends by Exponentially Weighted Moving Averages." Office of Naval Research, memorandum 52, 1957.

Ledolter, J., and B. Abraham. "Some Comments on the Initialization of Exponential Smoothing." *Journal of Forecasting* 3 (1984), pp. 79–84.

Makridakis, S., A. Anderson, R. Carbone, R. Fildes, M. Hibon, R. Lewandowski, J. Newton, E. Parzen, and R. Winkler. "The Accuracy of Extrapolation (Time Series) Methods." *Journal of Forecasting* 1 (1982), pp. 111–153.

Makridakis, S., and M. Hibon. "Accuracy of Forecasting: An Empirical Investigation." *Journal of the Royal Statistical Society A* 142 (1979), pp. 97–145.

Makridakis, S., and M. Hibon. "Exponential Smoothing: The Effect of Initial Values and Loss Functions on Post-Sample Forecasting Accuracy.' *International Journal of Forecasting* 7 (1991), pp. 317–330.

Makridakis, S., S.C. Wheelwright, and V.E. McGee. *Forecasting: Methods and Applications*, 2d ed. New York: John Wiley & Sons, 1983.

McClain, J.O. "Dominant Tracking Signals." *International Journal of Forecasting* 4 (1988), pp. 563–572.

McKenzie, E. "The Monitoring of Exponentially Weighted Forecasts." *Journal of the Operational Research Society* 29 (1978), pp. 449–458.

McKenzie, E. "General Exponential Smoothing and the Equivalent ARMA Process." *Journal of Forecasting* 3 (1984), pp. 333–344.

Muth, J.F. "Optimal Properties of Exponentially Weighted Forecasts." *Journal of the American Statistical Association* 55 (1960), pp. 299–306.

Nerlove, M., and S. Wage. "On the Optimality of Adaptive Forecasting." *Management Science* 10 (1964), pp. 207–224.

Newbold, P., and T. Bos. "On Exponential Smoothing and the Assumption of Deterministic Trend plus White Noise Data-Generating Models." *International Journal of Forecasting* 5 (1989), pp. 523–527.

Newbold, P., and C.W.J. Granger. "Experience with Forecasting Univariate Time Series and the Combination of Forecasts." *Journal of the Royal Statistical Society* A 137 (1974), pp. 131–165.

Reid, D.J. "A Review of Short-Term Projection Techniques." In *Practical Aspects of Forecasting*, London: ed. H.A. Gordon Operational Research Society, 1975.

Sweet, A.L. "Adaptive Smoothing for Forecasting Seasonal Series." *AIIE Transactions* 13 (1981), pp. 243–248.

Theil, H., and S. Wage. "Some Observations on Adaptive Forecasting." *Management Science* 10 (1964), pp. 198–206.

Trigg, D.W. "Monitoring A Forecasting System." *Operational Research Quarterly* 15 (1964), pp. 271–274.

Trigg, D.W. and A.G. Leach. "Exponential Smoothing with an Adaptive Response Rate." *Operational Research Quarterly* 18 (1967), pp. 53–59.

Wilson, J.H., and Barry Keating. *Business Forecasting.* Burr Ridge, II: Richard D. Irwin, 1990.

Winters, P.R. "Forecasting Sales by Exponentially Weighted Moving Averages." *Management Science* 6 (1960), pp. 324–342.

Yar, M., and C. Chatfield. "Prediction Intervals for the Holt-Winters Forecasting Procedure." *International Journal of Forecasting* 6 (1990), pp. 127–137.

APPENDIX 6–A

FOURIER SERIES ANALYSIS

If we do not change our direction, we are likely to end up where we are headed.
Chinese proverb

This appendix describes a method known by several different names, including **Fourier series analysis, spectral analysis,** and **harmonic smoothing.** Also this appendix develops the time series tools known as **line spectrum** and **periodogram.** We have chosen to use the most common name, Fourier series analysis (hereafter FSA), for the topics discussed here. Because FSA has advantages in automated forecasting, it is used in several commercial software packages. Also, FSA supplements other forecasting methods, including decomposition and ARIMA analysis. However, as with all methods, it does have some disadvantages.

FSA was developed in about 1822 by Joseph Fourier, a French mathematician and physicist. Fourier showed that any periodic observation can be represented by a series of trigonometric functions of sines and cosines. FSA is used extensively in science and engineering, where the patterns of alternating current, vibrating springs, and the oscillations of structures are similar to repeating patterns of seasonal and cyclical time series.

One of the most important advantages of FSA is its simple way of modeling a series with seasonality or cyclicalness. FSA can be used to model a seasonal variation using several seasonal peaks per year. Based on statistics generated during the modeling process, the unimportant seasonal patterns of the model can be dropped without reestimating the remaining model. Most other methods require a refitting of the model when one or more terms are dropped. The classical decomposition method and Winters' approach also allow several seasonal cycles per year. However, FSA is more methodical in identifying significant and insignificant peaks and eliminating those that are not significant. The ability to model a series as if it were a complex one and to eliminate the nonsignificant peaks is a distinctive advantage of FSA.

FIGURE 6A–1

$Y = Sin(X)$

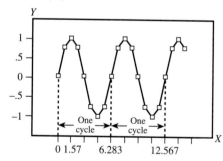

TABLE 6A–1 $Y = \sin(X)$

X Values	sin(X)	sin(X) Graph
		−1 0 +1
0	0	
.785398	.7071068	
1.570796	1	
2.356194	.7071068	
3.141593	0	
3.926991	−.707107	
4.712389	−1	
5.497787	−.707107	
6.283185	0	
7.068583	.7071068	
7.853982	1	
8.639380	.7071068	
9.424778	0	
10.21018	−.707107	
10.99557	−1	
11.78097	−.707107	
12.56637	0	
13.35177	.7071068	
14.13717	1	
14.92257	.7071068	

Trigonometric Functions

Understanding **sine and cosine functions** will increase your understanding of FSA. Figure 6A–1 and Table 6A–1 illustrate a simple sine function.

A **sine wave** is a repeating pattern that goes through one cycle every 6.283185 units of time (i.e., every 2π, where pi(π) equals approximately 3.141592). As shown in Table 6A–1, the value of sin(X) varies smoothly from 0 to +1 to 0 to −1 to 0 as X varies from 0 to 1.5708 to 3.14 to 4.71 to 6.283185. Also, the sin(6.283185 + X) varies the same way as X varies from 0 to 1.5708 to 3.14 to 4.71 to 6.283185. Thus, the repeating patterns of Figure 6A–1 and Table 6A–1 are identical for X values of 0 to 6.2832 versus 6.2832 to 12.5664. It is this repeating patterns of trigonometric functions that makes them useful in modeling the repeating patterns of seasonal and cyclical time series. To better understand the anatomy of sine waves, consider Figure 6A–2 and Table 6A–2.

Sine Wave Phase Shifts.   Different time series have peaks and troughs in different periods; these differences are called *phases*. Figure 6A–2 and Table 6A–2 show two sine waves with different phases.

$$Y = \sin(X) \tag{6A–1}$$

$$Z = \sin(X + 1.5708) \tag{6A–2}$$

Series Y is the sine function previously plotted in Figure 6A–1, while Z is the same sine wave shifted to the left by 1.5708 or $.5\pi$ units. This 1.5708 shift is called a **phase shift.** Different constants (i.e., phases) can be added to or subtracted from the X value of trig functions to change the location of the peaks and troughs. As shown, the shape of Z at $X = 0$ is the same

TABLE 6A–2 $Y = \sin(X)$ and $Z = \sin(X + 1.570796)$

X Values	y sin(X)	sin(X) Graph −1	0	+1	z sin(X + 1.5708)	sin(X + 1.5708) Graph −1	0	+1
0	0		•		1			•
.785398	.7071068			•	.7071068			•
1.570796	1			•	0		•	
2.356194	.7071068			•	−.707107	•		
3.141593	0		•		−1	•		
3.926991	−.707107	•			−.707107	•		
4.712389	−1	•			0		•	
5.497787	−.707107	•			.7071068			•
6.283185	0		•		1			•
7.068583	.7071068			•	.7071068			•
7.853982	1			•	.0		•	
8.639380	.7071068			•	−.707107	•		
9.424778	0		•		−1	•		
10.21018	−.707107	•			−.707107	•		
10.99557	−1	•			0		•	
11.78097	−.707107	•			.7071068			•
12.56637	0		•		1			•
13.35177	.7071068			•	.7071068			•
14.13717	1			•	0		•	
14.92257	.7071068			•	−.707107	•		

value of Y starting at $X = .5\pi$ (i.e., 1.5708). The ability to identify different phase shifts is an advantage of FSA.

Amplitude.   Figure 6A–3 and Table 6A–3 show a simple sine wave that has been multiplied by 25.

$$Y = 25*\sin(X) \tag{6A–3}$$

The 25 is called the amplitude (A) or intensity of the sine wave. The value of $25*\sin(X)$ varies from 0 to 25 to 0 to -25 back to 0 during one cycle. Thus, the amplitude can be changed to model the variations in different time series.

Various amplitudes and phases can be used to model simple sinusoidal functions. However, a

FIGURE 6A–2

$Y = \sin(X) \text{ and } Z = \sin(X + 1.5708)$

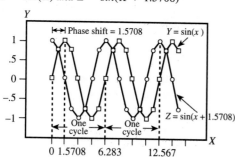

FIGURE 6A–3

$Y = 25 * \sin(X), \text{ amplitude} = 25$

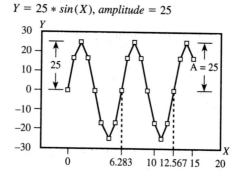

TABLE 6A–3   Selected Sine Wave Values for Figures 6A–1 and 6A–3

X Value	Figure 6A–2 sin(X)	Figure 6A–3 25*sin(X)	25*sin(X) Graph −25	0	+25
0	0	0		•	
.785398	.7071	17.68			•
1.570796	1	25			•
2.356194	.7071	17.68			•
3.141593	0	0		•	
3.926991	−.7071	−17.68	•		
4.712389	−1	−25	•		
5.497787	−.7071	−17.68	•		
6.283185	0	0		•	
7.068583	.7071	17.68			•
7.853982	1	25			•
8.639380	.7071	17.68			•
9.424778	0	0		•	
10.21018	−.7071	−17.68	•		
10.99557	−1	−25	•		
11.78097	−.7071	−17.68	•		
12.56637	0	0		•	
13.35177	.7071	17.68			•
14.13717	1	25			•
14.92257	.7071	17.68			•

Modeling Cyclical Variations Such as Earthquakes

Consider how we might model economic and other cyclical time series using FSA. Assume we have 700 years of data to analyze, where the intensities (number of quakes or Richter scale readings) of earthquakes are recorded for each of the 700 years. For example, in Japan, large earthquakes are approximately 70 years apart. Thus, we expect high intensities to occur with a frequency of 10 in 700 years and a wavelength of 70. That is:

$$f = n/L = 700/70 = 10$$

or 10 times in 700 years, or:

$$L = n/f = 700/10 = 70$$

That is, 70 years between peaks.

single-peak formula is not sufficient to model more complex seasonal behavior. Few seasonal cycles have a peak season that is a mirror image of the off-season (i.e., +25 to −25). Fortunately, as shown next, more complexity can be modeled by additional trigonometric terms.

Combining Amplitude, Phase, Frequency, and Wavelength.   Trigonometric functions such as sine waves have four characteristics for modeling seasonal patterns: frequency, phase, amplitude, and wavelength.

$$Y_t = \text{Amplitude} * \sin[2\pi ft/n + \text{Phase}]$$

$$Y_t = A * \sin(2\pi ft/n + P) \tag{6A–4}$$

where

t = Time ($t = 1, 2, 3, \ldots, n$)
Y_t = Value of the time series at time t
A = Amplitude or intensity of the series
f = Frequency, number of peaks or troughs in n observations
n = Number of periods in the time series
2π = 6.283185 . . . = One complete cycle
P = Phase shift that determines the horizontal position of the repeating pattern
$2\pi f/n$ = Often known as **ω, omega,** or Fourier frequency.

Consider each of these below.

A, the **amplitude** of the wave, determines the magnitude of the seasonal or cyclical effect on the series. It is the height of peaks and depths of troughs about the mean value of the series.

f, the **frequency,** is the number of peaks or troughs in the whole series. For example, with monthly data, a frequency of 4 is expected if there is one peak and trough per year and four years of observations (i.e., 48 months) in the series. Two peaks per year yield a frequency of eight in 48 months; that is, two peaks every 12 months. It is common to use frequency per series. Thus, the frequency normally relates to time series length, n.

P, the **phase,** refers to the horizontal position of the sine wave at its start. The phase determines where peaks or troughs occur relative to time.

L, the **wavelength,** is expressed in time units and is inversely related to the frequency. It represents the number of periods from one peak or trough to the next. This is the term often used to define seasonality (e.g., $L = 12$ month seasonality). L is the number of observations (n) in the series divided by the frequency (f).

$$L = \frac{n}{f} = \frac{48}{4} = 12 \tag{6A–5}$$

$$Lf = n \tag{6A–6}$$

Trend-Seasonal Patterns in Fourier Series.   Figures 6A–4 and 6A–5 illustrate several different functions with different wavelengths, phases, and amplitudes. The equations used to generate these graphs are included in each figure. Note that the X axis is the time (t) axis; the frequency (f), number of observations (n), and the phase (P) are given beside each graph.

Figure 6A–4 illustrates two series of seasonal monthly observations with two different amplitudes and phases. Figure 6A–5 illustrates two series with trend and seasonal influences. The trends are linear, equaling 8 and -10 units per month for Z and Y, respectively. Consider how these parameters are estimated.

Modeling Sinusoidal Behavior

Fitting sine functions to a time series requires estimation of several parameters. Consider Equation 6A–7:

$$Y = A*\sin(2\pi ft/n + P) = A*\sin(\omega t + P) \tag{6A–7}$$

where

$$\omega = 2\pi f/n = 6.283185 f/n$$

All of the parameters in Equation 6A–7 are known before a model is estimated except for A and P, the amplitude and the phase shift, respectively. However, as Equation 6A–7 is currently defined, it is difficult to simultaneously estimate A and P. Fortunately, there is a relationship in trigonometry that makes multiple regression estimates of A and P possible:

$$A*\sin(\omega t + P) = a_1\cos(\omega t) + b_1\sin(\omega t) \tag{6A–8}$$

FIGURE 6A–4

Two seasonal patterns with different phases and amplitudes

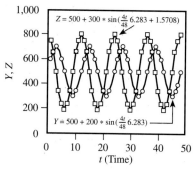

Series	Constant	Amplitude	f	P	n	L
Z	500	300	4	1.5708	48	12
Y	500	200	4	0	48	12

FIGURE 6A–5

Two-trend-seasonal patterns

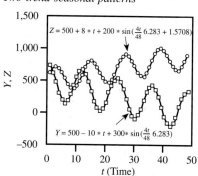

Series	Constant	Trend	Amplitude	f	P	n	L
Z	500	8	200	4	1.508	48	12
Y	500	-10	300	4	0	48	12

Equation 6A–8 shows that a sine function is equal to the sum of a sine and cosine function. (Note: A cosine function equals a sine function with a phase shift of π units (i.e., 3.1416 units).

After estimating a_1 and b_1 (a process shown in a moment), the value of the amplitude, A, is estimated from Equation 6A–9.

$$A_1 = \sqrt{a_1^2 + b_1^2} \qquad (6A-9)$$

Also, if we are interested in determining the phase shift, P, then the following relationships can be used:

$$\sin(P) = a_1/A_1 \qquad (6A-10)$$

$$\cos(P) = b_1/A_1 \qquad (6A-11)$$

Significant Frequencies.   There is a simple statistical test to determine if an amplitude (A) should be included in a FSA model. This statistical significance test compares the As to the residual standard error (RSE). If an A is less than .5RSE, then we infer that its frequency is not a statistically significant contributor to explaining the seasonal component of the series. Let's see how these facts are combined to yield a FSA model.

Combining Functions in Fourier Series Analysis

When modeling a time series, the amplitudes of the seasonal peaks and troughs are rarely equal. To model these various amplitudes and phases requires combining several trigonometric terms in a single model. Equation 6A–12 illustrates one general FSA model used in forecasting time series.

$$\hat{Y}_t = a_0 + b_0 t + a_1 \cos(\omega t) \ + b_1 \sin(\omega t) \qquad\quad + a_2\cos(2\omega t) + b_2\sin(2\omega t) \qquad (6A-12)$$
$$+ a_3\cos(3\omega t) + b_3\sin(3\omega t) + \ldots + a_k\cos(k\omega t) + b_k\sin(k\omega t)$$

where

$$\hat{Y}_t = \text{Fitted or forecasted value at time } t$$
$$a_0 = \text{Constant used to set the level of the series}$$
$$b_0 = \text{Trend estimate of the series}$$
$$a_1, b_1, a_2 \ldots = \text{Coefficients defining the amplitudes and phases}$$
$$\omega = 2\pi f/n, \text{ known as omega}$$
$$k = \text{Harmonic of } \omega$$

As shown in Equation 6A–12, it is easy to add a constant (a_0) and a trend (b_0) term to the relationship. Thus, three patterns are modeled—average, trend, and seasonal. These are the same as those modeled by Winters' exponential smoothing and the classical decomposition methods discussed previously. For many series, the models from these different methods are similar. While not obvious in Equation 6A–12, the trend and constant terms are estimated prior to estimating the terms a_1 to b_k.

Highest Harmonic, k.   It can be shown that the highest harmonic, k, in a FSA model is the number of observations per season divided by 2 for an even number of observations and $(n - 1)/2$ for an odd number of observations. When n is an even number, the last sine term is zero and should be omitted.

To better understand FSA models, consider a model for Series F shown in Equation 6A–13, Figure 6A–6, and Table 6A–4. The bottom of Table 6A–4 illustrates the coefficients for this model which were estimated using a method that is described later.

$$\hat{Y}_t = 654.18 + 7.07*t - 118.81*\cos(.5236t) - 1.294*\sin(.5236t) \qquad (6A-13)$$

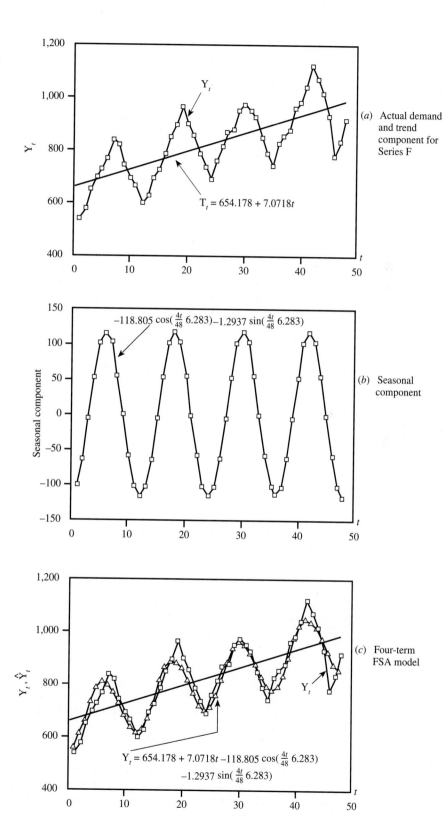

(a) Actual demand
and trend
component for
Series F

$T_t = 654.178 + 7.0718t$

$-118.805 \cos(\frac{4t}{48} 6.283) -1.2937 \sin(\frac{4t}{48} 6.283)$

(b) Seasonal
component

(c) Four-term
FSA model

$Y_t = 654.178 + 7.0718t -118.805 \cos(\frac{4t}{48} 6.283)$
$-1.2937 \sin(\frac{4t}{48} 6.283)$

TABLE 6A–4   **Four-Term FSA Model for Series F**

t	Y_t	$a_0 + b_0t$	$a_1cos(\omega t)$	$b_1sin(\omega t)$	Amplitude	$\hat{Y}_t$	Error	Squared Errors
1	546	661.25	−102.89	−.65	−103.53	557.71	−11.715	137.24
2	578	668.32	−59.40	−1.12	−60.52	607.80	−29.799	887.96
3	660	675.39	.00	−1.29	−1.29	674.10	−14.100	198.80
4	707	682.47	59.40	−1.12	58.28	740.75	−33.747	1,138.88
5	738	689.54	102.89	−.65	102.24	791.78	−53.778	2,892.11
6	781	696.61	118.81	.00	118.81	815.41	−34.414	1,184.31
7	848	703.68	102.89	.65	103.53	807.22	40.784	1,663.37
8	818	710.75	59.40	1.12	60.52	771.28	46.724	2,183.20
9	729	717.82	.00	1.29	1.29	719.12	9.882	97.66
10	691	724.90	−59.40	1.12	−58.28	666.61	24.386	594.68
11	658	731.97	−102.89	.65	−102.24	629.73	28.273	799.39
12	604	739.04	−118.81	.00	−118.81	620.23	−16.235	263.56
13	629	746.11	−102.89	−.65	−103.53	642.58	−13.576	184.32
14	711	753.18	−59.40	−1.12	−60.52	692.66	18.339	336.34
15	729	760.26	.00	−1.29	−1.29	758.96	−29.961	897.68
16	798	767.33	59.40	−1.12	58.28	825.61	−27.609	762.25
17	861	774.40	102.89	−.65	102.24	876.64	−15.640	244.61
18	903	781.47	118.81	.00	118.81	900.28	2.724	7.42
19	968	788.54	102.89	.65	103.53	892.08	75.922	5,764.27
20	894	795.61	59.40	1.12	60.52	856.14	37.863	1,433.62
21	860	802.69	.00	1.29	1.29	803.98	56.020	3,138.30
22	792	809.76	−59.40	1.12	−58.28	751.48	40.524	1,642.24
23	739	816.83	−102.89	.65	−102.24	714.59	24.411	595.94
24	699	823.90	−118.81	.00	−118.811	705.10	−6.096	37.16
25	773	830.97	−102.89	−.65	−103.53	727.44	45.562	2,075.90
26	818	838.04	−59.40	−1.12	−60.52	777.52	40.478	1,638.47
27	871	845.12	.00	−1.29	−1.29	843.82	27.177	738.59
28	882	852.19	59.40	−1.12	58.28	910.47	−28.471	810.57
29	959	859.26	102.89	−.65	102.24	961.50	−2.501	6.26
30	979	866.33	118.81	.00	118.81	985.14	−6.137	37.66
31	955	873.40	102.89	.65	103.53	976.94	−21.939	481.31
32	925	880.48	59.40	1.12	60.52	941.00	−15.998	255.95
33	843	887.55	.00	1.29	1.29	888.84	−45.841	2,101.41
34	790	894.62	−59.40	1.12	−58.28	836.34	−46.337	2,147.12
35	746	901.69	−102.89	.65	−102.24	799.45	−53.450	2,856.87
36	822	908.76	−118.81	.00	−118.81	789.96	32.042	1,026.70
37	857	915.83	−102.89	−.65	−103.53	812.30	44.700	1,998.13
38	876	922.91	−59.40	−1.12	−60.52	862.38	13.616	185.41
39	959	929.98	.00	−1.29	−1.29	928.68	30.315	919.03
40	981	937.05	59.40	−1.12	58.28	995.33	−14.332	205.41
41	1,051	944.12	102.89	−.65	102.24	1,046.36	4.636	21.50
42	1,124	951.19	118.81	.00	118.81	1,070.00	54.001	2,916.15
43	1,073	958.27	102.89	.65	103.53	1,061.80	11.199	125.43
44	1,020	965.34	59.40	1.12	60.52	1,025.86	−5.860	34.34
45	933	972.41	.00	1.29	1.29	973.70	−40.703	1,656.71
46	787	979.48	−59.40	1.12	−58.28	921.20	−134.20	18,009.28
47	830	986.55	−102.89	.65	−102.24	884.31	−54.311	2,949.72
48	922	993.02	−118.81	.00	−118.81	874.82	47.180	2,226.01
Mean	827						.0004	1,719.27
Standard deviation							39.70	

$a_0 = 654.178$ $b_0 = 7.0718$ $a_1 = -118.805$ $b_1 = -1.2937$

$f = 4$ $n = 48.00$ $\omega = .52360$

where

$$a_0 = 654.178 = \text{Constant}$$
$$b_0 = 7.0718 = \text{Trend}$$
$$a_1 = -118.81 \text{ for amplitude and phase}$$
$$b_1 = -1.294 \text{ for amplitude and phase}$$
$$n = 48$$
$$f = 4$$
$$\omega = (2\pi f/n) = (6.283185*4/48) = .52360$$

Figure 6A–6a through c illustrates the patterns of Equation 6A–13. Figure 6A–6a illustrates the constant and trend components of the relationship. As shown, the trend relationship fits the general movement of the series but does not follow its seasonal pattern. As shown in Figure 6A–6b, the trigonometric terms of Equation 6A–13 represent the seasonal movement of the series. The coefficients of this component, a_1 and b_1, have been determined using least squares regression. Finally, Figure 6A–6c shows the sum of the trend and seasonal models—that is, the fitted values, $\hat{Y}_t$, plotted with the actual series values, Y_t.

Model Fitting and Parameter Estimates

The steps of FSA are shown in Tables 6A–5 and 6A–6. The column numbers of these tables are explained in each step. The 11 steps of this method include estimating trends using seasonal differences, estimating Fourier seasonal parameters, eliminating those amplitudes that are insignificant, and, finally, forecasting future values.

Steps of Fourier Series Analysis

1. Take seasonal differences to estimate the mean annual trend. For the monthly data of Table 6A–5, the mean of the 12th differences shown in column 3 is 84.86.

$$\text{Mean}(Y_t - Y_{t-12}) = 84.86$$

2. Calculate the monthly trend by dividing the annual mean by the length of the season, 12.

$$\text{Mean}(Y_t - Y_{t-12})/12 = 84.86111/12 = 7.0718 \text{ units per month}$$

3. Center the trend on the mean of Y_t and the mean of time, t. This is done by finding the value of a_0 that forces the trend line through the intersection of the mean of the actual series Y_t and t. The mean of t is:

$$(\text{Ending value } t + \text{Beginning value } t)/2 = (48 + 1)/2 = 24.5$$

$$\text{Mean of } Y_t = 827.4375$$

The best fit trend line has the form:

$$T_t = a_0 + 7.0718t$$

We determine a_0 knowing the trend line goes through the intersection of the mean of T_t and Y_t.

$$T_{24.5} = 827.4375 = a_0 + 7.0718t = a_0 + 7.0718*24.5$$

Therefore:

$$a_0 = 827.4375 - 7.0718*24.5 = 654.178$$

Thus, the trend line is:

$$T_t = 654.178 + 7.0718t$$

4. Calculate the trend values from $t = 1$ to $t = 48$. See column 4 of Table 6A–5.
5. Calculate the deviations from the trend by subtracting the projected trends from each actual observation to yield a new series that is centered on zero. The resulting series is called a **detrended** series and is shown in column 5 of Table 6A–5. (Alternatively, when seasonality is

TABLE 6A–5   **Input Data for Six-Term FSA Model**

					Fourier Terms			
(1)	*(2)*	*(3)*	*(4)*	*(5)*	*(6)*	*(7)*	*(8)*	*(9)*
	Actual	Differences	Trend	Detrended				
t	Y_t	$Y_t - Y_{t-12}$	T_t	$Y_t - T_t$	$cos(\omega t)$	$sin(\omega t)$	$cos(2\omega t)$	$sin(2\omega t)$
1	546		661.250	−115.250	.8660	.5000	.5000	.8660
2	578		668.322	−90.3220	.5000	.8660	−.5000	.8660
3	660		675.394	−15.3938	0	1.000	−1.000	0
4	707		682.466	24.5344	−.5000	.8660	−.5000	−.8660
5	738		689.537	48.4626	−.8660	.5000	.5000	−.8660
6	781		696.609	84.3908	−.1000	0	1.000	0
7	848		703.681	144.319	−.8660	−.5000	.5000	.8660
8	818		710.753	107.247	−.5000	−.8660	−.5000	.8660
9	729		717.825	11.1754	0	−1.000	−1.000	0
10	691		724.896	−33.8964	.5000	−.8660	−.5000	−.8660
11	658		731.968	−73.9682	.8660	−.5000	.5000	−.8660
12	604		739.040	−135.040	1.000	0	1.000	0
13	629	83.00	746.112	−117.112	.8660	.5000	.5000	.8660
14	711	133.00	753.184	−42.1836	.5000	.8660	−.5000	.8660
15	729	69.00	760.255	−31.2554	0	1.000	−1.000	0
16	798	91.00	767.327	30.6728	−.5000	.8660	−.5000	−.8660
17	861	123.00	774.399	86.6010	−.8660	.5000	.5000	−.8660
18	903	122.00	781.471	121.529	−1.000	0	1.000	0
19	968	120.00	788.543	179.457	−.8660	−.5000	.5000	.8660
20	894	76.00	795.614	98.3856	−.5000	−.8660	−.5000	.8660
21	860	131.00	802.686	57.3138	0	−1.000	−1.000	0
22	792	101.00	809.758	−17.7580	.5000	−.8660	−.5000	−.8660
23	739	81.00	816.830	−77.8298	.8660	−.5000	.5000	−.8660
24	699	95.00	823.902	−124.902	1.000	0	1.000	0
25	773	144.00	830.973	−57.9734	.8660	.5000	.5000	.8660
26	818	107.00	838.045	−20.0452	.5000	.8660	−.5000	.8660
27	871	142.00	845.117	25.8830	0	1.000	−1.000	0
28	882	84.00	852.189	29.8112	−.5000	.8660	−.5000	−.8660
29	959	98.00	859.261	99.7394	−.8660	.5000	.5000	−.8660
30	979	76.00	866.332	112.668	−1.000	0	1.000	0
31	955	−13.00	873.404	81.5958	−.8660	−.5000	.5000	.8660
32	925	31.00	880.476	44.5240	−.5000	−.8660	−.5000	.8660
33	843	−17.00	887.548	−44.5478	0	−1.000	−1.000	0
34	790	−2.00	894.620	−104.620	.5000	−.8660	−.5000	−.8660
35	746	7.00	901.691	−155.691	.8660	−.5000	.5000	−.8660
36	822	123.00	908.763	−86.7632	1.000	0	1.000	0
37	857	84.00	915.835	−58.8350	.8660	.5000	.5000	.8660
38	876	58.00	922.907	−46.9068	.5000	.8660	−.5000	.8660
39	959	88.00	929.979	29.0214	0	1.000	−1.000	0
40	981	99.00	937.050	43.9496	−.5000	.8660	−.5000	−.8660
41	1,051	92.00	944.122	106.878	−.8660	.5000	.5000	−.8660
42	1.124	145.00	951.194	172.806	−1.000	0	1.000	0
43	1,073	118.00	958.266	114.734	−.8660	−.5000	.5000	.8660
44	1,020	95.00	965.338	54.6624	−.5000	−.8660	−.5000	.8660
45	933	90.00	972.409	−39.4094	0	−1.000	−1.000	0
46	787	−3.00	979.481	−192.481	.5000	−.8660	−.5000	−.8660
47	830	84.00	986.553	−156.553	.8660	−.5000	.5000	−.8660
48	922	100.00	993.625	−71.6248	1.000	0	1.000	0
Mean	827.4	84.86	827.4					

12-month trend = 84.86   Monthly trend = 7.07176

TABLE 6A–6   Regression Output and Amplitude Calculation for a Full Model

(1)	(2)	(3)	(4) Frequency (f) per Year (per Series)	(5) Residual Standard Error	(6) $\dfrac{A}{RSE}$	(7)
Coefficient	Value	A				Significant
a_1	118.80					
b_1	1.29	118.81	1 (4)	39.70	2.98	Yes
a_2	6.74					
b_2	22.32	23.31	2 (8)	36.76	.63	Yes
a_3	3.01					
b_3	3.64	4.72	3 (12)	37.46	.13	No
a_4	4.12					
b_4	1.15	4.27	4 (16)	38.24	.11	No
a_5	2.08					
b_5	.62	2.17	5 (20)	39.17	.06	No
a_6	1.72	1.72	6 (24)	39.67	.04	No

An amplitude is significant if A/RSE is greater than .50.

---

a percent of the trend, the actual observations can be divided by the trend series, or natural logarithms can be used as described in Chapter 5.)

6. Input the detrended series and trigonometric values to a multiple regression program; these are detrended actual values, $\cos(\omega t)$, $\sin(\omega t)$, $\cos(2\omega t)$, and $\sin(2\omega t)$ as shown in columns 5 to 9 of Table 6A–5, respectively. The values of the sine and cosine are easily generated using your software. Table 6A–5 only shows 4 trigonometric terms, but all 11 trigonometric terms were input in the analysis discussed below. These 11 are:

$$a_1\cos(\omega t) \;+\; b_1\sin(\omega t) \;+\; a_2\cos(2\omega t) + b_2\sin(2\omega t) \;+$$

$$a_3\cos(3\omega t) + b_3\sin(3\omega t) + a_4\cos(4\omega t) + b_4\sin(4\omega t) \;+$$

$$a_5\cos(5\omega t) \;+\; b_5\sin(5\omega t) + a_6\cos(6\omega t)$$

where

$$\omega = 6.283185(4/48) = .52360$$

7. Fit FSA model coefficients to the detrended series using a multiple regression program that determines the values of $a_1, b_1, a_2, \ldots, a_6$ that minimizes the sum of the squared errors. Column 2 of Table 6A–6 shows this model with its 11 estimated coefficients.

8. Calculate the amplitudes of each frequency. These values are calculated in column 3 of Table 6A–6. The values of $a_i'S$ and $b_i's$ are transformed to amplitudes A_i to test their significance:

$$A_i\sqrt{a_1^2 + b_1^2} = \sqrt{118.8^2 + 1.29^2} = 118.81$$

9. Discard all insignificant frequencies above the highest significant frequency. The test statistic in column 6 of Table 6A–6 is used to determine whether an amplitude of a frequency is sufficient to justify inclusion of that frequency. As the table shows, some of the amplitudes are not very high relative to the RSE. The amplitudes at frequencies 3, 4, 5, and 6 per year (i.e., 12, 16, 20, and 24 cycles per four years, respectively) are only 4.72, 4.27, 2.17, and 1.72, respectively. If the amplitude of a frequency is greater than one-half of the RSE, then infer that it is a statistically significant part of the seasonal pattern. If the amplitude is less than one-half of the RSE of a model that includes all coefficients up to that frequency, then infer that it should be eliminated. The amplitudes of frequencies 3, 4, 5, and 6 cycles per year are insig-

nificant and are dropped, as shown previously in Table 6A–5. It is standard practice in most systems to use all frequencies up to and including the highest frequency that has a statistically significant amplitude.

Table 6A–7 illustrates the RSEs for seven different FSA models. However, only one set of coefficients needed to be estimated using regression analysis, the most complex model with 11 trig terms. Then coefficients are eliminated frequency by frequency. As shown in Table 6A–7, the RSE does not change much except when moving from a two-term model to a four-term model and then from a four-term to a six-term model. As shown, the six-term model has the lowest RSE. This also confirms our decision to include only six terms in the model, a_0, b_0, a_1, b_1, a_2, and b_2.

Table 6A–8 and Figure 6A–7 illustrate the fitted values of the six-term model along with the resulting errors. As shown in Table 6A–8, the fitted values are calculated in column 9 by adding the trend of column 3 to the seasonal estimate in column 8. The seasonal estimate is the sum of four trigonometric functions in columns 4, 5, 6, and 7. Note the repeating pattern of seasonality in column 8. This is an additive seasonality for each month of the year. The magnitudes of the seasonality of column 8 are easily interpreted as the quantity by which a month is higher or lower than the trend. (Note: Multiplicative models can be modeled using ratios or logs.)

The error in column 10 is the difference between the actual in column 2 and the fitted in column 9. Because minimizing the sum of squared errors is the criterion used to select the best model, these squared errors are shown in column 11.

10. Forecast the withheld or out-of-sample values by projecting the trend-seasonal components. Having selected a six-term FSA model (a_0 through a_2), it is a relatively simple matter to project the trend and seasonal function of that relationship.

TABLE 6A–7   Residual Standard Errors of FSA Models of Series F

Terms in Model	Residual Standard Error	k	Amplitude of Last Term	Significant Frequency	Pattern Modeled
2	94.29	0	n.a.*	Yes	Trend only
4	39.70	1	118.81	Yes	Trend and seasonal
6	36.76	2	23.31	Yes	Trend and seasonal
8	37.46	3	4.72	No	Trend and seasonal
10	38.24	4	4.27	No	Trend and seasonal
12	39.17	5	2.17	No	Trend and seasonal
13	39.67	6	1.72	No	Trend and seasonal

* n.a. = Not applicable. A two-term FSA model has only a constant and trend in the equation.

FIGURE 6A–7

Six-term FSA model for series F

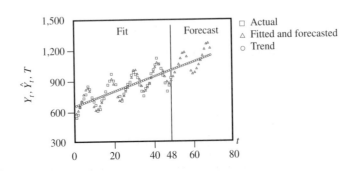

TABLE 6A–8   Fitted Values of Six-Term FSA for Series F

(1)	(2)	(3)	(4)	(5)	(6)	(7)	(8)	(9)	(10)	(11)
		$a_0 + b_0 * t$					Seasonal	Trend and Seasonal		Squared
t	Y_t	Trend	$a_1 cos(\omega t)$	$b_1 sin(\omega t)$	$a_2 cos(2\omega t)$	$b_2 sin(2\omega t)$	Amplitude	$\hat{Y}_t$	Error	Errors
1	546	661.25	−102.89	−.65	3.37	19.33	−80.84	580.41	−34.412	1,184.16
2	578	668.32	−59.40	−1.12	−3.37	19.33	−44.57	623.75	−45.755	2,093.50
3	660	675.39	.00	−1.29	−6.74	.00	−8.03	667.36	−7.359	54.15
4	707	682.47	59.40	−1.12	−3.37	−19.33	35.59	718.05	−11.051	122.11
5	738	689.54	102.89	−.65	3.37	−19.33	86.29	775.82	−37.822	1,430.52
6	781	696.61	118.81	.00	6.74	.00	125.55	822.15	−41.155	1,693.69
7	848	703.68	102.89	.65	3.37	19.33	126.23	829.91	18.087	327.16
8	818	710.75	59.40	1.12	−3.37	19.33	76.48	787.23	30.768	946.71
9	729	717.82	.00	1.29	−6.74	.00	−5.45	712.38	16.622	276.32
10	691	724.90	−59.40	1.12	−3.37	−19.33	−80.98	643.92	47.082	2,216.80
11	658	731.97	−102.89	.65	3.37	−19.33	−118.20	613.77	44.229	1,956.26
12	604	739.04	−118.81	.00	6.74	.00	−112.06	626.98	−22.975	527.86
13	629	746.11	−102.89	−.65	3.37	19.33	−80.84	665.27	−36.273	1,315.75
14	711	753.18	−59.40	−1.12	−3.37	19.33	−44.57	708.62	2.383	5.68
15	729	760.26	.00	−1.29	−6.74	.00	−8.03	752.22	−23.221	539.20
16	798	767.33	59.40	−1.12	−3.37	−19.33	35.59	802.91	−4.912	24.13
17	861	774.40	102.89	−.65	3.37	−19.33	86.29	860.68	.316	.10
18	903	781.47	118.81	.00	6.74	.00	125.55	907.02	−4.016	16.13
19	968	788.54	102.89	.65	3.37	19.33	126.23	914.77	53.226	2,833.01
20	894	795.61	59.40	1.12	−3.37	19.33	76.48	872.09	21.907	479.92
21	860	802.69	.00	1.29	−6.74	.00	−5.45	797.24	62.761	3,938.97
22	792	809.76	−59.40	1.12	−3.37	−19.33	−80.98	728.78	63.221	3,996.94
23	739	816.83	−102.89	.65	3.37	−19.33	−118.20	698.63	40.358	1,629.58
24	699	823.90	−118.81	.00	6.74	.00	−112.06	711.84	−12.837	164.79
25	773	830.97	−102.89	−.65	3.37	19.33	−80.84	750.13	22.865	522.82
26	818	838.04	−59.40	−1.12	−3.37	19.33	−44.57	793.48	24.522	601.33
27	871	845.12	.00	−1.29	−6.74	.00	−8.03	837.08	33.917	1,150.42
28	882	852.19	59.40	−1.12	−3.37	−19.33	35.59	887.77	−5.773	33.34
29	959	859.26	102.89	−.65	3.37	−19.33	86.29	945.55	13.454	181.03
30	979	866.33	118.81	.00	6.74	.00	125.55	991.88	−12.878	165.84
31	955	873.40	102.89	.65	3.37	19.33	126.23	999.64	−44.636	1,992.34
32	925	880.48	59.40	1.12	−3.37	19.33	76.48	956.95	−31.955	1,021.09
33	843	887.55	.00	1.29	−6.74	.00	−5.45	882.10	−39.100	1,528.84
34	790	894.62	−59.40	1.12	−3.37	−19.33	−80.98	813.64	−23.640	558.86
35	746	901.69	−102.89	.65	3.37	−19.33	−118.20	783.49	−37.494	1,405.77
36	822	908.76	−118.81	.00	6.74	.00	−112.06	796.70	25.301	640.17
37	857	915.83	−102.89	−.65	3.37	19.33	−80.84	835.00	22.003	484.16
38	876	922.91	−59.40	−1.12	−3.37	19.33	−44.57	878.34	−2.339	5.47
39	959	929.98	.00	−1.29	−6.74	.00	−8.03	921.94	37.056	1,373.16
40	981	937.05	59.40	−1.12	−3.37	−19.33	35.59	972.64	8.364	69.97
41	1,051	944.12	102.89	−.65	3.37	−19.33	86.29	1,030.41	20.593	424.07
42	1,124	951.19	118.81	.00	6.74	.00	125.55	1,076.74	47.260	2,233.57
43	1,073	958.27	102.89	.65	3.37	19.33	126.23	1,084.50	−11.497	132.19
44	1,020	965.34	59.40	1.12	−3.37	19.33	76.48	1,041.82	−21.816	475.95
45	933	972.41	.00	1.29	−6.74	.00	−5.45	966.96	−33.962	1,153.42
46	787	979.48	−59.40	1.12	−3.37	−19.33	−80.98	898.50	−111.50	12,432.67
47	830	986.55	−102.89	.65	3.37	−19.33	−118.20	868.36	−38.355	1,471.12
48	922	993.62	−118.81	.00	6.74	.00	−112.06	881.56	40.439	1,635.39

$a_0 = 654.2$ $b_0 = 7.07$ $a_1 = −118.81$ $b_1 = −1.2937$ $a_2 = 6.74$ $b_2 = 22.3163$
$f = 4$ $n = 48.00$ $\omega = .52360$

Table 6A–9 illustrates the process of forecasting. This process is identical to that of calculating the fitted values of Table 6A–8. Because we are forecasting, the actual values are unknown, as shown in column 2. The sum of the trend, column 3, and the seasonal, column 8, yields the forecasted values of column 9. As shown in Figure 6A–7, the fitted and forecasted values seem very reasonable for projecting this past behavior forward into the future. However, it is always important to perform a reasonableness check of any forecast.

11. Update model coefficients. To this point, we have illustrated the construction of a forecasting model. We have not discussed how this model is used in a forecasting system. In general, it is not efficient to refit model coefficients each week or month if a very large number of times series are being modeled. It is suggested that some form of smoothing or averaging be used to generate new model coefficients. As Brown (1982) points out, an efficient smoothing process might require only 5 percent of the computer resources needed to estimate and diagnose the original model. Thus, in some situations, it may be inefficient to reestimate models every month. However, computing power has increased so much recently that reestimation may be cost effective.

TABLE 6A–9   Forecasted Values Using Six-Term FSA for Series F

(1)	(2)	(3)	(4)	(5)	(6)	(7)	(8)	(9)
								Sum of Trend and Seasonal
		$a_0 + b_0 * t$					Seasonal	Seasonal
t	Y_t	Trend	$a_1 cos(\omega t)$	$b_1 sin(\omega t)$	$a_2 cos(2\omega t)$	$b_2 sin(2\omega t)$	Amplitude	$\hat{Y}_t$
49		1,000.70	−102.89	−.65	3.37	19.33	−80.84	919.86
50		1,007.77	−59.40	−1.12	−3.37	19.33	−44.57	963.20
51		1,014.84	.00	−1.29	−6.74	.00	−8.03	1,006.81
52		1,021.91	59.40	−1.12	−3.37	−19.33	35.59	1,057.50
53		1,028.98	102.89	−.65	3.37	−19.33	86.29	1,115.27
54		1,036.06	118.81	.00	6.74	.00	125.55	1,161.60
55		1,043.13	102.89	.65	3.37	19.33	126.23	1,169.36
56		1,050.20	59.40	1.12	−3.37	19.33	76.48	1,126.68
57		1,057.27	.00	1.29	−6.74	.00	−5.45	1,051.82
58		1,064.34	−59.40	1.12	−3.37	−19.33	−80.98	983.36
59		1,071.41	−102.89	.65	3.37	−19.33	−118.20	953.22
60		1,078.49	−118.81	.00	6.74	.00	−112.06	966.42
61		1,085.56	−102.89	−.65	3.37	19.33	−80.84	1,004.72
62		1,092.63	−59.40	−1.12	−3.37	19.33	−44.57	1,048.06
63		1,099.70	.00	−1.29	−6.74	.00	−8.03	1,091.67
64		1,106.77	59.40	−1.12	−3.37	−19.33	35.59	1,142.36
65		1,113.85	102.89	−.65	3.37	−19.33	86.29	1,200.13
66		1,120.92	118.81	.00	6.74	.00	125.55	1,246.46
67		1,127.99	102.89	.65	3.37	19.33	126.23	1,254.22
68		1,135.06	59.40	1.12	−3.37	19.33	76.48	1,211.54
69		1,142.13	.00	1.29	−6.74	.00	−5.45	1,136.69
70		1,149.20	−59.40	1.12	−3.37	−19.33	−80.98	1,068.23
71		1,156.28	−102.89	.65	3.37	−19.33	−118.20	1,038.08
72		1,163.35	−118.81	.00	6.74	.00	−112.06	1,051.28

$a_0 = 654.2$ $b_0 = 7.07$ $a_1 = −118.81$ $b_1 = −1.2937$ $a_2 = 6.74$ $b_2 = 22.3163$
$f = 4$ $n = 48.00$ $\omega = .52360$

Disadvantages of FSA

Overfitting and the Number of Parameters to Include.   As coefficients are added to a model, it becomes more complex, more time-consuming to estimate, more accurate in fitting the past, but eventually less accurate in forecasting the future. The additional terms that increase historical fit might not improve accuracy, a situation called *overfitting*. Added trig terms might only model events such as outliers that occurred in the past but are not going to occur in the future. Thus, the significance test on the choice of frequencies that should be included in the model is an important tool in model selection. However, it is not an infallible one. Overfitting is a general problem occurring no matter which forecasting approach is used.

Interpretability.   The primary disadvantages of the FSA method is that it may be difficult to relate the model parameters to commonly used or intuitive explanations of seasonal profiles. We have found the use of graphs very useful in describing the seasonal behavior of FSA. Also, these seasonal profiles can be used to express the amplitudes of each frequency as either an additive or percentage of the trend. See column 8 of Table 6A–8 for the additive interpretation.

Equal Weight to All Observations.   A FSA model uses least squares regression to determine seasonality or cyclical variations. One of the attributes of least squares is equal weight is given to all errors; that is, a recent error (e.g., $t = 46$) is squared just as a distant error (e.g., $t = 2$). Consequently, FSA models do not give more weight to the more recent actuals than to the distant actuals, as is done in exponential smoothing. Exponential smoothing methods such as Winters' method give more weight to the more recent actual values, and this is often advantageous because the recent past is normally a better predictor of the immediate future.

Advantages.   An advantage of FSA over other trend-seasonal methods is that it has coefficients that are statistically independent of each other (i.e., are orthogonal). For example, we used FSA to model a 13-term trend-seasonal model for Series F. Based on statistics in Table GA–6, the seasonal terms for a_3 through a_6 of the model were dropped without any necessity to reestimate the remaining model. In general, if all amplitudes are insignificant, then all will be dropped and the model will no longer include seasonal patterns. Finally, if the trend parameter, b_0 is found to be insignificant, it too can be dropped to yield a simple level model. Most other methods require a refitting of the model when one of more terms are dropped from the model. This makes FSA a versatile approach to modeling time series in operational forecasting systems.

The Line Spectrum and Periodogram

Using the Spectrum to Identify Patterns.   There is a useful method for identifying the seasonality and stationarity of time series using the amplitude and frequency of Fourier series components. The periodogram (also called the line spectrum) measures the amplitude of a time series for all possible frequencies and wavelengths. The line spectrum and periodogram can be interpreted as the amount of the total series sums of squares $\Sigma(Y - \mu)^2$ that is explained by specific frequencies. As we will see, the periodogram is useful in verifying:

1. White noise.
2. Seasonality.
3. Cyclicalness.
4. Significant positive or negative autocorrelations.

A FSA representation of a time series partitions the total variation (sum of squares):

$$\Sigma(Y_t - \mu)^2$$

Early Time Series Graphs

Early time series graphs

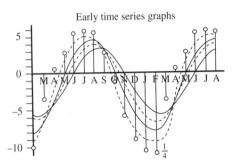

In the late 1700s, time series graphs first began to appear in scientific journals and books. The above drawing of Johann Heinrich Lambert, one of many, "shows the periodic variation in soil temperature in relation to the depth under the surface. The greater the depth, the greater the time-lag in temperature responsiveness."[a] The vertical axis is the observed temperature over a 20-month period. The four different sinusoidal curves represent different temperatures at different depths in the soil. Finally, the vertical lines with "balloons," the fifth variable, represent the ambient temperatures at the surface of the soil.

In terms of FSA, these five temperature series can be modeled very accurately with different amplitudes and phases. However, the frequency of each soil temperature–depth combination is the same. A frequency of one peak and trough every 12 months is expected for each series. The maximum variation (i.e., amplitude) in temperatures appears at the surface of the soil, with amplitudes declining as depth increases. The periods of the peaks and troughs (phase) is earliest at the surface of the soil, with phases delayed as depth increases. Thus, there is a delay to heat up and cool down the soil. The temperatures deeper in the soil have less peak-to-trough variations and the months in which these occur are later. Obviously, Fourier series analysis is an excellent model of this periodic and recurrent behavior.

---

a. Edward R. Tufte, *The Visual Display of Quantitative Information*, (Cheshire, CO: 1983), Graphics Press, p. 29.

Source: J. H. Lambert, *Pyrometrie*, Berlin, 1779.

into that which is explained by each frequency. It can be shown that the sum of squares of a frequency SS_f equals:

$$SS_f = n(a_f^2 + b_f^2)/2 \tag{A6–14}$$

where a_f and b_f are determined in Equation 6A–12 and in general the trend, t, component is excluded from the model. The SS_f is the portion of the $\Sigma(Y_t - \mu)^2$ accounted for by that frequency. Consequently:

$$\Sigma(Y_t - \mu)^2 = \Sigma SS_f = n\Sigma(a_f^2 + b_f^2)/2 \tag{6A–15}$$

The individual SS_f can be graphed as a histogram so that the area of each bar is proportionate to SS_f. The height of each bar of the histogram is proportionate to the amplitude, as measured by the Intensity of each frequency, $I(f)$:

$$I(f) = n(a_f^2 + b_f^2)/2 \tag{6A–16}$$

The plot of these $I(f)$ versus frequencies and wavelengths is called the periodogram. Consider the periodogram of the detrended series F shown in Table 6A–10. Column 1 shows the frequency, f, as in equations 6A–4 and 6A–12. Column 2 shows ω_f, commonly called the Fourier frequency, column 3 the wavelength or period between peaks and troughs, column 4 the calculated intensity, $I(f_k)$, and column 5, the spectral density, a concept defined in a movement. Let's interpret these results.

TABLE 6A–10   Line Spectrum and Periodogram for Detrended SERIESF.DAT

(1) Frequency *f*	*(2)* ω_f $2\pi f/n$	*(3)* Wavelength (L) Period	*(4)* I(f)	*(5)* SI(f)
	.00000	.	.00	579.01
1	.13090	48.0000	7,356.89	2,227.37
2	.26180	24.0000	2,139.35	3,918.97
3	.39270	16.0000	17,145.22	5,608.79
4	.52360	12.0000	338,780.39	7,182.56
5	.65450	9.6000	6,261.04	5,487.86
6	.78540	8.0000	1,781.18	3,780.13
7	.91630	6.8571	3,600.37	2,066.91
8	1.04720	6.0000	13,040.11	406.17
9	1.17810	5.3333	2,545.38	303.35
10	1.30900	4.8000	318.38	238.41
11	1.43990	4.3636	608.39	182.86
12	1.57080	4.0000	535.62	152.67
13	1.70170	3.6923	6,449.15	184.19
14	1.83260	3.4286	741.36	181.33
15	1.96350	3.2000	2,716.39	176.72
16	2.09440	3.0000	438.65	152.13
17	2.22529	2.8235	3,439.63	126.41
18	2.35619	2.6667	812.63	101.23
19	2.48709	2.5263	807.85	74.76
20	2.61799	2.4000	113.09	55.48
21	2.74889	2.2857	540.98	38.68
22	2.87979	2.1818	623.25	35.31
23	3.01069	2.0870	345.03	32.89
24	3.14159	2.0000	284.83	33.74
Total			411,425.16	

As shown in columns 1, 2, 3, and 4 of Table 6A–10, the frequency, ω_f, and wavelength having the highest intensity are 4, .52360, and 12, respectively. These correspond to:

$$f = 4, \text{ four peaks per 48 months}$$

$$\omega_f = .52360 = 2\pi f/n = 2\pi 4/48$$

$$L = n/f = 48/4 = 12$$

The intensity $I(f)$ can be plotted against either the Fourier frequency or wavelength, as shown in Figures 6A–8 and 6A–9, respectively. Thus, we see that the detrended series F is very seasonal, with a wavelength of 12 and a frequency of 4 per 48 observations. This confirms the previous analysis of Table 6A–8.

As shown at the bottom of the Table 6A–10, the total of the $I(f)$ should equal the total sums of squares $\Sigma(Y_t - \mu)^2$ of the detrended time series. Ignoring a slight round-off error:

$$\Sigma I(f) = \Sigma(Y_t - \mu)^2 = 411,425.16 \qquad (6A\text{–}17)$$

The larger the intensity of a frequency, the larger its contribution to the total sums of squares. Thus, the $I(f)$ at a frequency is proportionate to its contribution to the variance of the series. In

FIGURE 6A–8

Periodogram for detrended series F

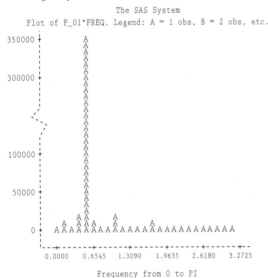

FIGURE 6A–9

Periodogram for detrended series F

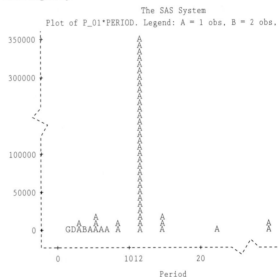

Table 6A–10, the intensity at the frequency of 4 and wavelength of 12 are the largest contributors to the total sums of squares.

If the time series is white noise, then the periodogram and intensities will have the same expected values for all fs. As we will see, high positive autocorrelations have low frequencies with high intensities and, while not shown, high negative autocorrelations have high frequency with high intensities. Consider the periodogram of the Series B given in Table 6A–11, which, as you might remember, is predominantly a random walk. As shown, this time series has very high intensities at the lowest frequency and highest wavelength, 1 and 48, respectively. These are the expected patterns from a random walk, and this behavior confirms its high autocorrelations.

Power Spectral Density

The sample periodogram used previously in our analysis has been shown to have poor statistical properties for many time series; that is, it may be volatile to sampling errors. Many times, the analysis of periodograms can be improved by smoothing them. The smoothed periodogram, $SI(f)$, is an estimate of the power **spectral density** of the time series. The power spectral density is estimated by an *m*-period moving average of the periodogram. The $SI(f)$ of detrended Series F and Series B shown in column 5 of Table 6A–10 and 6A–11 were smoothed by a weighted moving average with centered weights of 1, 2, 3, 4, 3, 2, 1. The value of these weights may be set manually or automatically. This large a period moving average may make the graph too smooth, while a lower value that is too small may result in spurious peaks.

There are a number of statistical significance tests that can confirm whether an intensity is inconsistent with a while noise assumption. Because we present Fourier series and periodograms as supplementary tools of other time series methods, we do not develop these here. However, the Fisher's Kappa statistic tests whether the largest amplitude can be considered different from the mean of the other amplitudes. Critical values of the Fisher's Kappa statistic and other tests can be found in Fuller (1996) and SAS (1993).

We have seen in these examples that periodograms are useful in discerning white noise, nonstationarity, and seasonality. However, FSA and periodograms are not commonly used in time series, despite the fact that they provide useful information.

TABLE 6A–11   Periodogram and Line Spectrum for SERIESB.DAT

(1) Frequency f	(2) ω_f $2\pi f/n$	(3) Wavelength (L) Period	(4) I(f)	(5) SI(f)
0	.00000	.	.00	48930.26
1	.13090	48.0000	833365.55	45021.89
2	.26180	24.0000	188677.64	34784.76
3	.39270	16.0000	374823.33	23768.15
4	.52360	12.0000	47541.55	13288.30
5	.65450	9.6000	19433.78	6530.32
6	.78540	8.0000	31954.64	3774.26
7	.91630	6.8571	24203.40	1682.64
8	1.04720	6.0000	10044.04	1221.22
9	1.17810	5.3333	10135.49	928.14
10	1.30900	4.8000	8825.76	657.92
11	1.43990	4.3636	1352.52	467.91
12	1.57080	4.0000	6396.00	393.10
13	1.70170	3.6923	5432.14	313.27
14	1.83260	3.4286	1823.98	249.58
15	1.96350	3.2000	1665.24	239.46
16	2.09440	3.0000	1737.88	239.34
17	2.22529	2.8235	3972.99	273.32
18	2.35619	2.6667	5593.70	303.36
19	2.48709	2.5263	3989.34	314.68
20	2.61799	2.4000	3933.70	301.61
21	2.74889	2.2857	1724.28	258.05
22	2.87979	2.1818	5597.78	224.12
23	3.01069	2.0870	1409.95	190.17
24	3.14159	2.0000	.67	170.60

Summary

Because the FSA method is somewhat different, using trigonometric functions, some find it difficult to learn and apply. However, after achieving some comfort with a few new concepts, it is not more difficult than the other methods in this book. As we have seen, decomposition methods (Winters' and classical decomposition) are all very similar to FSA. A few forecasting studies that have included tests of FSA accuracy have shown it to be inferior to Winters' method. However, we believe that in many applications, this method is comparable to or better than Winters'. Some believe that its orthogonal coefficients and the ability to run statistical significance tests on all model coefficients give FSA an accuracy advantage over other methods. We feel that this may be true. However, it may be a moot issue because there is no best single method of forecasting systems. The methods used in good systems are, in general, less important than their intelligent use.

FSA is a method used in automated forecasting systems sold by a number of large commercial software houses. These software packages automate the routine forecasting of tens of thousands of items. Those selling these systems state that the efficiencies of including and excluding orthogonal coefficients give this method a distinct advantage over others when used in automated environments. However, those buying automated software must ascertain whether a specific implementation of a methodology is well executed. We have seen several very good methodologies executed very poorly in automated systems—a good implementation of a less effective method can outperform a poorly implemented "best" method.

Key Terms

amplitude (A)
detrended
frequency (f)
Fourier series analysis
harmonic analysis
line spectrum
ω, omega

periodogram
phase shift (P)
spectral analysis
spectral density $SI(f)$
sine and cosine trig functions
sine wave
wavelength (L)

Key Formulas

$$Y = \sin(X) \tag{6A-1}$$

$$Z = \sin(X + 1.5708) \tag{6A-2}$$

$$Y = 25*\sin(X) \tag{6A-3}$$

Combining amplitude, phase, frequency, and wavelength:

$$Y_t = \text{Amplitude}*\sin[2\pi ft/n + \text{Phase}]$$

$$Y_t = A*\sin(2\pi ft/n + P) \tag{6A-4}$$

$$L = n/f = 48/4 = 12 \tag{6A-5}$$

$$Lf = n \tag{6A-6}$$

$$Y = A*\sin(2\pi ft/n + P) = A*\sin(\omega t + P) \tag{6A-7}$$

where

$$\omega = 2\pi f/n = 6.283185 f/n$$
$$A*\sin(\omega t + P) = a_1\cos(\omega t) + b_1\sin(\omega t) \tag{6A-8}$$
$$A_i = \sqrt{a_i^2 + b_i^2} \tag{6A-9}$$
$$\sin(P) = a_i/A_i \tag{6A-10}$$
$$\cos(P) = b_i/A_i \tag{6A-11}$$
$$\hat{Y}_t = a_0 + b_0 t + a_1\cos(\omega t) + b_1\sin(\omega t) + a_2\cos(2\omega t) +$$
$$b_2\sin(2\omega t) + a_3\cos(3\omega t) + b_3\sin(3\omega t) + \ldots + a_k\cos(k\omega t) +$$
$$b_k\sin(l\omega t) \tag{6A-12}$$

Series F—four term FSA model:

$$\hat{Y}_t = 654.18 + 7.07t - 118.81\cos(.52t) - 1.294\sin(.52t) \tag{6A-13}$$

Line spectrum and periodogram.

$$SS_f = n(a_f^2 + b_f^2)/2 \tag{6A-14}$$

$$\Sigma(Y_t - \mu)^2 = \Sigma SS_f = n\Sigma(a_f^2 + b_f^2)/2 \tag{6A-15}$$

$$I(f) = n(a_f^2 + b_f^2)/2 \qquad\qquad (6A-16)$$

$$\Sigma I(f) = \Sigma(Y_t - \mu)^2 = 411{,}425.16 \qquad\qquad (6A-17)$$

Review Problems Using Your Software

R6A–1 Generate the values of $Y = \sin(X)$ for X equal to 0 to 26. Compare your results to those of Table 6A–1 or Figure 6A–1.

R6A–2 Generate the values of $Y = \sin(X)$, $Z = \sin(X + 1.5708)$, and $W = \cos(X)$ for X equal to 0 to 26. Discuss the relationships between these results, as shown in Table 6A–2.

R6A–3 Generate Z and Y, as shown in Figure 6A–4. Explain the amplitudes and phases of each.

R6A–4 Generate Z and Y, as shown in Figure 6A–5. Explain the trend, amplitudes, and phases of each.

R6A–5 Fit a four-term FSA model to the data of SERIESF.DAT. Compare your results to those of Table 6A–4. Interpret the coefficients of your model. Perform a statistical significance test on the frequency. Which frequencies are significant?

R6A–6 Fit a full-term FSA model to the data of SERIESF.DAT. Interpret the coefficients of your model. Perform a statistical significance test on the frequency. Which frequencies are significant? Compare your results to those of Table 6A–8.

R6A–7 Using the model of problem R6A–6, forecast periods 49 to 72 and compare your results to those of Table 6A–9.

R6A–8 Generate the periodogram of SERIESF.DAT, as in Table 6A–10.

R6A–9 Generate the periodogram of SERIESB.DAT, as in Table 6A–11.

Problems

6A–1 Explain the following concepts:
  a. Sine function   *b.* Cosine function
  c. Frequency, f *d.* Phase, P
  e. Harmonic, k *f.* Wavelength, L

6A–2 If a time series is daily data with seven periods per week, how many frequencies should be used to model that series? What are those frequencies?

6A–3 What is a statistically significant frequency? How do we test for statistical significance?

6A–4 If a time series is hourly data with 24 periods per day, how many frequencies should be used to model that series? What are those frequencies?

6A–5 Explain the concept of the line spectrum. How are the intensities $I(f)$ related to the variance of the series?

6A–6 Formulate a Fourier series equation for predicting earthquakes in Japan based on the information given in the chapter.

6A–7 Fit a full FSA model to the 48 months of the highly seasonal data of SERIESD.DAT. Remember that this series does not have a trend, and deviations from its mean can be input directly to the regression model. Interpret the coefficients of your model. Perform a statistical significance test on each of the frequencies. Which frequencies are significant?

6A–8 Explain the concept of orthogonal coefficients as related to Fourier series analysis. What efficiency does this concept yield in Fourier series analysis?

6A–9 Fit a full FSA model to the quarterly U.S. marriage series BIRTHMAR.DAT. Interpret the coefficients of your model. What frequencies are statistically significant? Eliminate any insignificant coefficients and refit the model. Forecast two seasonal cycles into the future.

6A–10 Fit a full FSA model to the quarterly U.S. births series BIRTHMAR.DAT. Is there a statistically significant trend? What frequencies are statistically significant? Eliminate any insignificant coefficients and refit the model. Forecast two seasonal cycles into the future.

6A–11 If a time series is not seasonal but rather cyclical, then how can Fourier series analysis be used?

6A–12 When should logarithms be used in Fourier series analysis?

6A–13 Develop a full FSA model for the electric utility demand data in file ELECT.DAT. Be sure to graph the data and identify the relevant patterns before modeling those patterns. Is there a statistically significant trend? What frequencies are statistically significant? Eliminate any insignificant coefficients and refit the model. Interpret the coefficients of the model. (Be sure to consider a nonlinear model for any time series you analyze.) Forecast the next three years using the identified model. List the 36 monthly forecasted values of electric demand.

6A–14 The time series RETAIL.DAT is the monthly retail sales in the United States. Complete the minicase assignment, forecast and withhold the last 12 months.

6A–15 The time series SUPEROIL.DAT is the sales of the Superoil Company in thousands of barrels during the last 108 months. Complete the minicase assignment, withhold and forecast the last 12 months.

Minicases

For a selected minicase or problem, complete the following analysis. Develop a full FSA model for a selected time series. Interpret the coefficients of your model. What frequencies are statistically significant? Eliminate any insignificant coefficients and refit the model. Forecast two seasonal cycles into the future. In addition, if you have been filling out the Master Forecasting Summary Table, add the appropriate model to that table.

Minicase 6A–1 Kansas Turnpike, Daily Data
TURNPIKD.DAT. Withhold and forecast the last two weeks.

Minicase 6A–2 Domestic Air Passengers by Quarter
PASSAIR.DAT. Withhold and forecast the last 8 quarters.

Minicase 6A–3 Hospital Census by Month
CENSUSM.DAT. Withhold and forecast the last 36 months.

Minicase 6A–4 Henry Machler's Hideaway Orchids
MACHLERD.DAT. Withhold and forecast the last week.

Minicase 6A–5 Your Forecasting Project

Minicase 6A–6 Midwestern Building Materials
LUMBER.DAT. Withhold and forecast the last 12 months.

Minicase 6A–7 International Airline Passengers
AIRLINE.DAT. Withhold and forecast the last 36 months.

MINICASE 6A–8 Automobile Sales AUTO.DAT. Withhold and forecast the last 12 months.

Minicase 6A–9 Consumption of Distilled Spirits
SPIRITS.DAT. Withhold and forecast the last 12 months.

Minicase 6A–10 Discount Consumer Electronics
ELECT.DAT. Withhold and forecast the last 12 months.

References

Bloomfield, P. *Fourier Analysis of Time Series*. New York: John Wiley & Sons, 1976.

Box, G.E.P.; G.M. Jenkins; and G.C. Reinsel. *Time Series Analysis Forecasting and Control*. 3rd ed. Englewood Cliffs, NJ: Prentice Hall, 1994.

Brown R.G. *Advanced Service Parts Inventory Control*. 2nd ed. Thetford, VT: Materials Management Systems, 1982.

Chan, H. and J. Hayya. "Spectral Analysis in Business Forecasting." *Decision Sciences* 7, no. 1 (January 1976), pp. 137–51.

Chatfield, C. *The Analysis of Time Series.* New York: Chapman and Hall, 1984.

Fuller, W.A. *Introduction to Statistical Time Series.* 2nd ed. New York: John Wiley & Sons, 1996.

Jenkins, G.M., and D.G. Watts. *Spectral Analysis and Its Applications.* San Francisco: Holden Day, 1968.

Kay, S.M. *Modern Spectral Estimation.* Englewood Cliffs, NJ: Prentice Hall, 1988.

Marple, S.L. *Digital Spectral Analysis with Applications.* Englewood Cliffs, NJ: Prentice Hall, 1987.

Prandit, S.M., and S.M. Wu. *Time Series and System Analysis with Applications.* New York: John Wiley & Sons, 1983.

Priestly, M.B. *Spectral Analysis of Time Series.* New York: Academic Press, 1981.

Reinmuth, J.E., and M.D. Geunts. "Using Spectral Analysis for Forecast Model Selection." *Decision Sciences* 8, no. 1 (January 1977), pp. 134–50

SAS. *SAS/ETS User's Guide—Version 6.* 2nd ed. Cary, NC; SAS Institute Inc., 1993.

Thomopoulos, N.T. *Applied Forecasting Methods.* Englewood Cliffs, NJ: Prentice Hall, 1980.

PART

III

UNIVARIATE ARIMA METHODS

7

UNIVARIATE ARIMA MODELS

Introduction

Things should be made as simple as they are, but not simpler.
Albert Einstein

Chapter Outline

ARIMA Overview
ARIMA Notation (p,d,q)
ARIMA Processes
ARIMA Model Identification
Time Series Examples
Variance Stationarity
The Backshift Operator
The Integrated Stochastic Process (0,1,0)
Autoregressive Processes: ARIMA(p,0,0) Models
Moving Average Processes: ARIMA(0,0,q) Models
ARIMA(p,d,q) Models
Summary
Key Terms
Key Formulas
Review Problems Using Your Software
Problems
Minicases
References
Appendix 7–A Useful Statistical Definitions Used in Derivations
Appendix 7–B White Noise and Stationarity
Appendix 7–C Theoretical ACFs for an ARIMA(1,0,0) Process
Appendix 7–D Theoretical ACFs for an ARIMA(0,0,1) Process
Appendix 7–E Bounds of Invertibility and Stationarity
Appendix 7–F Example ARIMA Data Sets
Appendix 7–G PACFs and the Yule–Walker Equations

Perhaps no other univariate forecasting method has been more widely discussed than ARIMA model building, where an ARIMA model has three components: **Auto**Regressive, **I**ntegrated, and **M**oving **A**verage. This chapter develops general ARIMA model-building strategies for univariate time series and is a prerequisite to the other ARIMA Chapters 8, 9, 12, and 13, which develop more advanced methods of univariate and multivariate ARIMA (MARIMA) models. The chapter also presumes a knowledge of the fundamental concepts of Chapters 1, 2, and 3, including their appendixes. Appendixes at the end of the chapter provide more theoretical material.

Chapter 7 is divided into two parts. The first part is an overview of ARIMA models, focusing on a simple intuitive presentation of ARIMA model building. The second part describes ARIMA model building procedures using several actual time series. These series exemplify problems encountered in practice, illustrating nonstationarity, seasonality, and alternative, competing models.

ARIMA Overview

A time series is a set of ordered observations equally spaced over time or space.

$$Y_1, Y_2, Y_3, \ldots, Y_{t-1}, Y_t, Y_{t+1}, \ldots$$

ARIMA models and time series are used in many disciplines, from anthropology, business, criminology, dendrochronology, through zoology. Many processes that at first might not seem to be time series actually are. For example:

The variations in crime rates by day of the month (criminology).

The pulsations of light from distant stars (physics).

The gas concentrations in arctic ice cores (geology).

The size of rings in cross sections of trees (botany, dendrochronology).

The daily seasonal variations in telephone usage (engineering).

The occurrence of diseases by day of the year (epidemiology).

The daily fluctuations in the stock market (business).

These series are influenced by underlying causal processes. ARIMA model building is designed to identify those processes.

Process (Population) versus Realization (Sample)

In time series analysis, there is a fundamental distinction between the terms "process" and "realization." The actual values in an observed time series are the realization of some underlying process that generated those values. We refer to the underlying process as the **stochastic** or **probabilistic generating process** (probabilistic and stochastic are synonyms). In time series analysis, the relationship between the realization (i.e., the observed sample values) and the process (i.e., the underlying stochastic process) is analogous to the relationship between the sample and the population as studied in statistical hypothesis testing. A time series, then, is a sample from the underlying stochastic process that generated the series.

The purpose of time series analysis is to use the realization of a process (i.e., the sample) to identify a model of the ARIMA process (i.e., the population) that generated the series. The procedures used to build models are broadly referred to as **Box–Jenkins** or **ARIMA model building methods**. ARIMA model building is an empirically driven methodology of systematically identifying, estimating, diagnosing, and forecasting time series. Graphs of actual data, empirically derived statistics, and theory are all used to decompose a time series into its three ARIMA components.

ARIMA Model Building Steps

The purpose of ARIMA analysis is to find a model that accurately represents the past and future patterns of a time series.

$$Y_t = \text{Pattern} + e_t \qquad (7\text{--}1)$$

where the pattern can be random, seasonal, trend, cyclical, promotional, or a combination of patterns. One of the many contributions that Box and Jenkins made to time series modeling in 1970 is the methodology of ARIMA model building, using three iterative steps (Box, Jenkins, and Reinsel, 1994). We've listed a fourth step, forecasting; these steps are common to all empirical modeling and are as follows:

Four Steps of ARIMA Model Building

- Model Identification
  Using graphs, statistics, ACFs, PACFs, transformations, etc., achieve stationarity and tentatively identify patterns and model components.
- Parameter Estimation
  Determine model coefficients through software applications of least squares and maximum likelihood methods.
- Model Diagnostics
  Using graphs, statistics, ACFs, and PACFs of residuals, determine if the model is valid. If valid, then use the model, otherwise repeat identification, estimation, and diagnostic steps.
- Forecast Verification and Reasonableness
  Using graphs, simple statistics, and confidence intervals determine the validity of forecasts and track model performance to detect out of control situations.

ARIMA Model Assumptions

In ARIMA terms, a time series is a linear function of past actual values and **random shocks** (i.e., error terms):

$$Y_t = f[Y_{t-k}, e_{t-k}] + e_t \qquad \text{where } k > 0 \qquad (7\text{--}2)$$

In time series analysis, our purpose is to extract all possible information (i.e., patterns) from a time series so that e_t's are distributed as white noise.

A useful way of viewing univariate ARIMA models is to consider them to be machines which convert past actual values into accurate forecasts and white noise errors. Therefore, an in-control forecasting machine is one that yields accurate forecasts and white noise residuals. This simple time series machine is:

$Y_t \longrightarrow$ Machine $\longrightarrow$ $\hat{Y}_t$ and e_t
(Actual)   (Model of   (Accurate forecasts and
              pattern)   white noise residuals and errors)

Thus, the objective of ARIMA analysis is to design the right machine (i.e., identify the right pattern) empirically; we do not choose a forecasting model *a priori* before analysis begins. Confirmation that the correct pattern has been identified requires meeting several diagnostic characteristics, including model residuals (e_t's) distributed as white noise. By definition, white noise is normally and independently distributed (NID), having no patterns, a zero mean, and an error variance that is lower than the variance of Y_t. Consequently, our task is to find the pattern that, when subtracted from

Y_t, has white noise residuals and satisfies several other criteria, including intuitive and theoretical appeal and parsimony.

As we saw in Chapter 2, different time series have different autocorrelation patterns, and these ACFs serve as guides in identifying the correct forecasting model. In ARIMA model building, the data and theory direct the modeling process while many other methods of forecasting commit the analyst to the functional form of the model before data analysis begins.

In many respects, ARIMA models resemble other univariate forecasting methods because they include trend, seasonal, and random components. Yet, in contrast to other univariate methods, ARIMA models are built empirically, using the four steps previously defined. Consequently, there is no general ARIMA model, such as the Winters or decomposition methods; instead, a model is chosen based on a combination of empirical evidence and theory. In this respect, ARIMA model building requires a more scientific and methodical approach than other univariate methods. (While these other methods may be methodically applied, ARIMA model building requires it.)

ARIMA Notation (p, d, q)

ARIMA model building methods use a simple, versatile model notation; they are designated by the level of autoregression, integration, and moving averages. This standard notation identifies the orders of autoregression by p, integration or differencing by d, and moving averages by q.

$$
\begin{array}{ccc}
(\text{AR} & \text{I} & \text{MA}) \\
| & | & | \\
(p & d & q)
\end{array}
$$

p = order of autoregression
d = order of integration (differencing)
q = order of moving average

As we illustrate these models, note how versatile and accurate they are.

ARIMA Processes

Autoregressive Process — ARIMA(1,0,0)

Autoregression is an extension of simple linear regression, which was developed in Chapter 3. An ARIMA(1,0,0) model, commonly called an AR(1) model, is

$$Y_t = \theta_0 + \phi_1 Y_{t-1} + e_t \tag{7-3}$$

where θ_0 and ϕ_1 are coefficients chosen to minimize the sum of squared errors. While Equation 7–3 uses different notation for coefficients than Chapter 3, it is a simple linear relationship between Y_t and its previous value Y_{t-1}.

Consider an example of Equation 7–3. (The method used to derive this model is developed later; for now, simply consider the results shown in Equation 7–4.) Assume $\theta_0 = 30$ and $\phi_1 = .3$, then

$$Y_t = 30 + .3Y_{t-1} + e_t \tag{7-4}$$

If $Y_{19} = 35$, then

$$\hat{Y}_{20} = 30 + .3Y_{19} = 30 + .3(35) = 30 + 10.5 = 40.5$$

If $Y_{20} = 38$, then

$$\hat{Y}_{21} = 30 + .3Y_{t-1} = 30 + .3(38) = 30 + 11.4 = 41.4$$

Although this model is a linear relationship between Y_t and Y_{t-1}, the values of θ_0 and ϕ_1 are estimated using nonlinear least squares, instead of ordinary least squares (OLS). This is discussed at greater length later.

Example 7–1 An ARIMA(1,0,0) Model

The actual number of mainframe computers sold in the United States over a 6-year period was 3.5, 3.5, 3.4, 3.4, 3.7, and 3.9 million.[*] Assuming that $\theta_0 = .4$ and $\phi_1 = .9$ were fitted to past data, use the following ARIMA(1,0,0) model to forecast years 2 through 8:

$$Y_t = .4 + .9Y_{t-1} + e_t$$

Forecast	Actual	Error
$\hat{Y}_2 = .4 + .9(3.5) = 3.55$	3.50	−.05
$\hat{Y}_3 = .4 + .9(3.5) = 3.55$	3.40	−.15
$\hat{Y}_4 = .4 + .9(3.4) = 3.46$	3.40	−.06
$\hat{Y}_5 = .4 + .9(3.4) = 3.46$	3.70	.24
$\hat{Y}_6 = .4 + .9(3.7) = 3.73$	3.90	.17
$\hat{Y}_7 = .4 + .9(3.9) = 3.91$	unknown	

The actual of year 7 is unknown, so the forecast for year 8 uses the forecasted value of year 7 (i.e, 3.91):

$$\hat{Y}_8 = .4 + .9\hat{Y}_7 = .4 + .9(3.91) = 3.92$$

The value of the most recent actual is input until unknown; thereafter, the previous forecasted values are input in place of unknown actuals.

For an ARIMA(1,0,0) model, the absolute value of the coefficient ϕ_1 is normally constrained to be less than 1. This constraint is called a **bound of stationarity:**

$$\text{Bound of Stationarity } |\phi_1| < 1 \tag{7–5}$$

If this bound is exceeded (i.e., if the absolute value of ϕ_1 is greater than 1), then the series is not autoregressive; it is either drifting or trending, and differences should be used to model the series, as in Example 7–3.

Moving Average Process — ARIMA(0,0,1)

ARIMA moving averages are similar to exponential smoothing (Chapters 4 and 6). Consider Equation 7–6:

$$Y_t - \mu = -\theta_1 e_{t-1} + e_t \tag{7–6}$$

$$Y_t = \mu - \theta_1 e_{t-1} + e_t \tag{7–6a}$$

where θ_1 is an estimated coefficient and Y_t is only correlated with the previous forecast error, e_{t-1}. Estimation of this coefficient is discussed later.

---

[*] Source: *Statistical Abstract of the United States.*

Consider the following simple example. Assume that $\mu = 20$ and $-\theta_1 = .3$. Then

$$Y_t = 20 + .3e_{t-1} + e_t \tag{7-7}$$

given

$$Y_{19} = 20 \qquad \text{and} \qquad \hat{Y}_{19} = 25$$

then

$$e_{19} = 20 - 25 = -5$$

therefore

$$\hat{Y}_{20} = 20 + .3e_{19} = 20 + .3(-5) = 18.5$$

While not obvious from the final equation, an expansion of this relationship shows that Y_t is is an exponentially weighted moving average of all past actual values; thus, the term moving averages (we illustrate this later).

Example 7–2 An ARIMA(0,0,1) Model

The actual number of VCRs sold in the United States over six years was 11, 11.9, 12.7, 11.7, 11.0, and 9.8.[*] Assuming that $\mu = 11$, $-\theta_1 = .3$, and $e_1 = 1.5$, forecast VCR sales using an ARIMA(0,0,1) model for years 2 to 6. Then forecast out-of-sample years 7 and 8.

$$\hat{Y}_t = 11 + .3e_{t-1} + e_t$$

Forecast		Actual	Error
$\hat{Y}_2 = 11 + .3(1.5)$	$= 11.45$	11.90	.45
$\hat{Y}_3 = 11 + .3(.45)$	$= 11.135$	12.70	1.57
$\hat{Y}_4 = 11 + .3(1.57)$	$= 11.47$	11.70	.23
$\hat{Y}_5 = 11 + .3(.23)$	$= 11.07$	11.00	−.07
$\hat{Y}_6 = 11 + .3(.07)$	$= 11.02$	9.80	−1.22
$\hat{Y}_7 = 11 + .3(-1.22)$	$= 10.63$	unknown	unknown

Because the actual and error for year 7 are unknown, the expected value of the error e_7 is .0. This expected value is used in forecasting period 8 sales.

$$\hat{Y}_8 = 11 + .3e_7 = 11 + .3(0) = 11$$

Because all future errors are expected to be .0 on average, all forecasted values for periods 8 onward equal 11, the mean.

As in the case of an autoregressive model and ϕ_1, the absolute value of θ_1 for a moving average model is constrained to be less than 1. This constraint is called the **bound of invertibility,** a concept related to stationarity.

$$\text{Bound of invertibility} \qquad |\theta_1| < 1 \tag{7-8}$$

If this bound is exceeded, the model is not stationary. Invertibility is developed later in the discussion of the implications of nonstationarity.

---

[*] Source: *Statistical Abstract of the United States.*

Integrated Processes — ARIMA(0,1,0)

Deterministic Trend and Drift. The patterns in time series are the result of fundamental processes. A deterministic trend is a systematic period-to-period increase or decrease that persists for many time periods. Because trends represent important long-run general movements in a time series, they are important to model.

Integrated processes are level-nonstationary series. Trends and random walks are level-nonstationary because their means (i.e., levels) are not constant (i.e., are not stationary). The means either randomly change as the series randomly walks or consistently increases (decreases). A random walk behavior (drift) is called a *stochastic trend,* while a consistent period-to-period change is called a *deterministic trend.*

Random Walk Process — ARIMA(0,1,0). **Integrated series** (i.e., summed series) include **random walks** and trends. As explained previously, if a series is a random walk, then the previous actual value is a best predictor of all future values. This yields the following ARIMA(0,1,0) random walk model:

$$\hat{Y}_t = Y_{t-1} \tag{7-9}$$

$$Y_t = Y_{t-1} + e_t \tag{7-10}$$

Assume that $Y_{19} = 30$ and it is the end of period 19. Then

$$\hat{Y}_{20} = Y_{19} = 30$$

Using this model at the end of period 19, the forecast is

$$\hat{Y}_{20} = Y_{19} = 30$$
$$\hat{Y}_{21} = \hat{Y}_{20} = Y_{19} = 30$$
$$\hat{Y}_t = 30 \quad \text{for all } t > 19$$

All future values are expected to equal 30, the last known actual value.

Example 7–3 An ARIMA(0,1,0) Model, Stochastic Trend (Drift)

The number of microwave ovens sold in the United States during a 6-year period was 9.0, 10.6, 12.7, 12.7, 11.2, and 10.8 millions of units.[*] Forecast these using an ARIMA(0,1,0) model for years 1 to 7. Then, forecast the out-of-sample values for years 8 and 9.

$$\hat{Y}_t = Y_{t-1}$$

t	Actual	Forecast	Error
1	9.0		
2	10.6	$\hat{Y}_2 = \ \ 9.0$	1.6
3	12.7	$\hat{Y}_3 = 10.6$	2.1
4	12.7	$\hat{Y}_4 = 12.7$	.0
5	11.2	$\hat{Y}_5 = 12.7$	-1.5
6	10.8	$\hat{Y}_6 = 11.2$	$-.4$
7	unknown	$\hat{Y}_7 = 10.8$	unknown

[*] Source: *Statistical Abstract of the United States.*

Because the actual for year 7 is unknown, its forecasted value is used in predicting year 8 sales.

$$\hat{Y}_8 = \hat{Y}_7 = 10.8$$

In fact, all forecasts for year 8 onward equal 10.8, because all future errors are expected to be .0 and the last actual is 10.8 for period 6.

Deterministic Trend Process— ARIMA(0,1,0)1

A deterministic trend model is an example of an integrated component of an ARIMA model. The second "1" of the notation ARIMA(0,1,0)1 is used when $d > 0$ (i.e., differences are taken) to denote that the series has a deterministic trend. This yields

$$\hat{Y}_t = Y_{t-1} + \theta_0 \tag{7-11}$$

$$Y_t = Y_{t-1} + \theta_0 + e_t \tag{7-11a}$$

where θ_0 is an estimated parameter equal to the mean of the period-to-period changes (i.e., the trend). Assume, for example, that

$$\theta_0 = 20 \quad \text{and} \quad Y_{19} = 30.$$

Then

$$\hat{Y}_{20} = Y_{19} + 20 = 30 + 20 = 50$$

$$\hat{Y}_{21} = Y_{20} + 20 = \hat{Y}_{20} + 20 = 50 + 20 = 70$$

$$\hat{Y}_{22} = Y_{21} + 20 = \hat{Y}_{21} + 20 = 70 + 20 = 90$$

In general

$$\hat{Y}_{t+m} = Y_t + m\theta_0$$

where t is the period of the last actual and m is the forecast horizon. In the next example, we model a trend using first differences.

Example 7–4 An ARIMA(0,1,0)1 Model, Deterministic Trend

The index of health care prices in the United States for an 11-year period is given below.[*] Determine θ_0 from years 1 to 6 and forecast years 7 to 11 using an ARIMA(0,1,0)1 model based on the trend of years 1 to 6.

First, to estimate θ_0, calculate the mean of first differences using years 1 to 6.

t	Actual (Y_t)	Differences $(Y_t - Y_{t-1})$	Fitted $(Y_{t-1} + \theta_0)$	Fitted Error (e_t)
1	74.9	na	na	na
2	82.9	8	82.62	.28
3	92.5	9.6	90.62	1.88
4	100.6	8.1	100.22	.38
5	106.8	6.2	108.32	−1.52
6	113.5	6.7	114.52	−1.02
Mean		$\theta_0 = 7.72$		ME = .00
Std Dev.		$S_{\text{diff}} = 1.333$		RSE = 1.333

---
[*] Source: *Statistical Abstract of the United States.*

Thus, the trend of this time series is estimated to be 7.72. The standard deviation of first differences is 1.333; this yields a standard error of the mean for first differences of .5961 (i.e., $1.3333/\sqrt{5}$).

The simple t-test on the trend (see Chapter 6) yields:

$$t = \frac{\theta_0}{S_{\text{diff}}/\sqrt{n - d}} = \frac{7.72}{1.333/\sqrt{6 - 1}} = 12.95$$

where, d is the number of observations lost from taking differences, which in this case is 1. The calculated t-value is so high that a t-table need not be checked; there is a statistically significant trend in the time series (however the small sample size makes any inference tenuous).

Multiyear-Ahead Forecasts

Forecasts for the end of period t are made with the mean of first differences $\theta_0 = 7.72$:

$$\hat{Y}_{t+m} = Y_t + m\theta_0 = Y_t + m7.72 \qquad (7\text{--}12)$$

For example,

$$\hat{Y}_{6+1} = Y_6 + 1\theta_0 = 113.5 + 7.72 = 121.22$$
$$\hat{Y}_{6+5} = 113.5 + 5(7.72) = 152.10$$

this yields the following forecasts:

t	Actual (Y_t)	Base (Y_6)	Trend $(m\theta_0)$	Forecast $(Y_{t-1} + \theta_0)$	Forecast Error (e_t)
7	122.0	113.5	$1 \cdot 7.72$	121.22	.78
8	130.1	113.5	$2 \cdot 7.72$	128.94	1.16
9	138.6	113.5	$3 \cdot 7.72$	136.66	1.94
10	149.3	113.5	$4 \cdot 7.72$	144.38	4.92
11	162.8	113.5	$5 \cdot 7.72$	152.10	10.70
Mean					ME = 3.90

While this model forecasts relatively well, note the apparent bias in this model as the errors increase each period, we discuss this problem later.

ARIMA Model Identification

Having developed the basics of ARIMA components, consider how the three components are empirically identified.

Several of the tools used to identify ARIMA models should be familiar to you:

1. Autocorrelation functions ACF(k)s.
2. Partial autocorrelation functions PACF(k)s.
3. Series graphs and plots.
4. Descriptive statistics.

The major identification and diagnostic tools of ARIMA analysis include ACFs and PACFs. ACFs were introduced in Chapter 2. For now accept PACFs as pattern recognition devices, their meaning is developed later in this chapter and expanded in Appendix 7–G. Typical ACF and PACF patterns of ARIMA components are shown in

Figure 7–1. Note that the approximate $+2$ and -2 standard errors for these ACFs are shown in all of these figures assuming the series has 100 observations; therefore, 2Se equals .2. These ACF and PACF patterns are very useful as recognition devices for identifying ARIMA processes, even without a theoretical understanding of the causes of these patterns.

The notation of ρ_k and ϕ_{kk} used in Figure 7–1 denote the true theoretical autocorrelation and partial autocorrelation respectively. The terms ACF(k) and PACF(k) are used to designate the sample autos and partials calculated from actual data.

Random Walk and Trend: ACFs and PACFs

As shown in Figure 7–1a, level-nonstationary series, whether trends or random walks, are distinguished by very high, statistically significant ACFs that decline in a distinctive straight line. For these series, at least the first 3 ACFs are statistically significantly different than zero; that is, they are above the two-standard-error limits. In addition, nonseasonal level-nonstationary series have only one statistically significant PACF, at lag 1. The PACF(1) and ACF(1) values are equal and are typically very high: for example, .7 or above. The distinguishing pattern for nonstationary processes is the linear decline in ACFs, typically with several ACFs well above the two-standard-error limits.

Autoregressive (1,0,0) ACFs and PACFs

The ACFs and PACFs of autoregressive processes can be just as distinct as those of level-nonstationary processes. The ACFs of an ARIMA(1,0,0) process with high values of ϕ_1 appear very similar to those of trends and random walks. However, as shown in Figure 7–1b and 7–1c, the ACFs decline at an exponential rate, rather than in a straight line. For example, for ϕ_1 values of .8 and .4:

$$ACF(1) = \phi_1 = .8 \qquad\qquad ACF(1) = \phi_1 = .4$$
$$ACF(2) = \phi_1^2 = .8^2 = .64 \qquad ACF(2) = \phi_1^2 = .4^2 = .16$$
$$ACF(3) = \phi_1^3 = .8^3 = .512 \qquad ACF(3) = \phi_1^3 = .4^3 = .064$$
$$\vdots \qquad\qquad\qquad\qquad\qquad \vdots$$
$$ACF(k) = \phi_1^k = .8^k \qquad\qquad ACF(k) = \phi_1^k \qquad = .4^k$$

Theoretically, these patterns should persist; in actuality, they may only be discernible for two or three lags. As shown by ϕ_1 of .4, such low values decline very rapidly to insignificant values: in this case, after only one lag. Fortunately, when confusion occurs regarding the level, order, or significance of the autoregression in the ACFs, the PACFs can provide a guide.

As discussed more fully later, the PACFs are very important in identifying p and q in stationary series. If a process is an ARIMA(1,0,0), there will be a single, statistically significant peak in the PACFs at lag 1. For all ARIMA processes, the value of PACF(1) equals the ACF(1). The PACFs for an ARIMA(2,0,0) process have two statistically significant spikes, at 1 and 2. In general, then, an ARIMA(p,0,0) process has significant PACF spikes thru p-lags.

An ARIMA(1,0,0) process with $\phi_1 < 0$ behaves much differently than processes with $\phi_1 > 0$. Figure 7–1c illustrates the distinctive alternating negative and positive patterns in the ACFs for $\phi_1 < 0$. For example, if $\phi_1 = -.8$, then:

$$ACF(1) = \phi_1 = -.8$$
$$ACF(2) = \phi_1^2 = -.8^2 = .64$$
$$ACF(3) = \phi_1^3 = -.8^3 = -.512$$
$$\vdots$$
$$ACF(k) = \phi_1^k = -.8^k$$

where even ks have positive ACFs and odd ks have negative ACFs.

FIGURE 7–1

Some first-order theoretical ACF(k)s and PACF(k)s

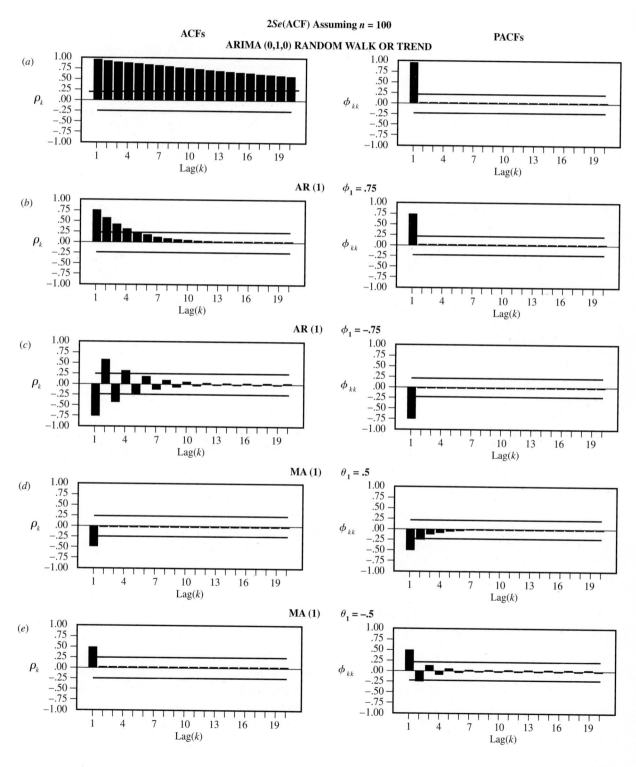

Moving Average (0,0,1) ACFs and PACFs

The ACFs and PACFs of ARIMA moving average models are also distinctive. As shown in Figures 7–1d and 7–1e, the ACFs for an ARIMA(0,0,1) are all zero except at lag 1, where there is a single significant peak or spike. If $\theta_1 > 0$, this spike is negative; if $\theta_1 < 0$, this spike is positive. The single significant ACFs can be extended to higher-order moving average models, an MA(2) having significant spikes at 1 and 2, an MA(3) having significant spikes at 1, 2, and 3, and so forth. Also, seasonal MA(1) models have significant ACF spikes at only one seasonal lag (e.g., at 12 for monthly data and 4 for quarterly data).

The PACFs can be used to confirm moving average models. As shown in Figures 7–1d and 7–1e, the PACFs of moving average models behave similarly to the ACFs of autoregressive models (Figures 7–1b and 7–1c). Also, the ACFs of moving average models behave similarly to the PACFs of autoregressive models. Thus for a moving average model, the PACFs have a negative exponential decline when $\theta_1 > 0$ and an alternating exponential decline when $\theta_1 < 0$. For example, for positive θ_1, if PACF(1) equals $-.8$, then PACF(2) equals $-.64$, PACF(3) equals $-.512$ and so on. This is the distinctive pattern of this MA(1) model: all negative PACFs that decline exponentially. When $\theta_1 < 0$, the exponential decline of the PACFs is alternating at $+.8$, $-.64$, $+.512$, and so on. Note that for either positive or negative θ_1 values, the ACF(1) can be used to derive the PACF values; however, the actual coefficient does not equal the value of ACF(1).

Table 7–1 illustrates the theoretical relationship between the true autocorrelation designated rho, ρ_1 and the true θ_1 value. This table is generated from Equation 7–13.

$$\rho_1 = \frac{-\theta_1}{1 + \theta_1^2} \qquad (7\text{–}13)$$

White Noise (0,0,0) ACFs and PACFs

While not shown in Figure 7–1, the ACFs and PACFs of patternless series are themselves patternless. Theoretically, no statistically significant ACFs and PACFs exist. However, in practice, with white noise series, there is a 5 percent chance that any single lag will be greater than 2 $Se(\text{ACF})$ away from zero. Thus, simply because of random chance, there may be one or two marginally significant spikes. When these spikes are not at low-order lags (i.e., 1, 2, or 3) or at seasonal lags, or no theory explains a spike, then we infer that these high correlations are indicative of the sample, not the underlying generating stochastic process. Do not model statistically significant spikes that represent random sampling error. However, sometimes ACF t-values are misleading, values as low as 1.25 may denote the need to add coefficients.

First Order ACFs and PACFs

In summary, there are many different ARIMA processes with many different ACF and PACF patterns. Some of the simple ARIMA processes are shown in the ACFs–PACFs Table.

Unfortunately, many time series do not behave as neatly as those in Figure 7–1 and the ACF–PACF Table. Herein lies the "art" of ARIMA model building. Through theory, intuition, graphs, ACFs, and PACFs, we iteratively build a model of a time series. Before illustrating this process, however, we must first review another important tool for identifying and diagnosing ARIMA models and white noise residuals: the Q-statistic.

TABLE 7–1   Theoretical Relationship of θ_1 and ρ_1 for Moving Average(1) Models

ρ_1	θ_1	ρ_1	θ_1
.500	−1.000	.000	.000
.499	−.950	−.050	.050
.497	−.900	−.099	.100
.493	−.850	−.147	.150
.488	−.800	−.192	.200
.480	−.750	−.235	.250
.468	−.700	−.275	.300
.457	−.650	−.345	.350
.441	−.600	−.349	.400
.422	−.550	−.374	.450
.400	−.500	−.400	.500
.374	−.450	−.422	.550
.349	−.400	−.441	.600
.315	−.350	−.457	.650
.275	−.300	−.468	.700
.235	−.250	−.480	.750
.192	−.200	−.488	.800
.147	−.150	−.493	.850
.099	−.100	−.497	.900
.050	−.050	−.499	.950
.000	.000	−.500	1.000

The value of ρ can be estimated by using ACF(1).

Note the maximum and minimum values of ρ for an MA(1) process; higher ρ typically denotes other processes.

ACFs–PACFs Table

Process	ACFs	PACFs
ARIMA(0,0,0)	No significant lags	No significant lags
ARIMA(0,1,0)	Linear decline at lag 1, with many lags significant	Single significant peak at lag 1
ARIMA(1,0,0) $\phi_1 > 0$	Exponential decline, with first two or more lags significant	Single significant peak at lag 1
ARIMA(1,0,0) $\phi_1 < 0$	Alternating exponential decline with a negative ACF(1)	Single significant negative peak at lag 1
ARIMA(0,0,1) $\theta_1 > 0$	Single significant negative peak at lag 1	Exponential decline of negative values, with first two or three lags significant
ARIMA(0,0,1) $\theta_1 < 0$ PACF(1)	Single significant positive peak at lag 1 No significant lags	Alternating exponential decline starting with a positive

The Q-Statistic and
White Noise
Diagnosis

In extracting information from a time series, we use the patterns in the ACFs to guide the identification of the ARIMA models. If a model has a high $\bar{R}^2$ (i.e., low sum of squares), statistically significant coefficients, nonredundant coefficients (a concept introduced later), and no patterns left in the ACFs, PACFs and residuals plots, we conclude that a good ARIMA model has been identified. That is, because no patterns are left in the ACFs, PACFs, and residuals plots, there is little opportunity for model improvement. However, while individual t-tests can be performed on specific lags of ACFs using the standard error of the ACFs, Se(ACFs), the definition of "no pattern" is subjective until it can be quantified. Even after quantification, there may still be some subjectivity in the "no pattern" conclusion.

Appendix 2–B discusses the use of the Q-statistic as an objective diagnostic measure of white noise for a time series, assessing whether there are patterns in a group of autocorrelations. The Q-statistic is

$$Q = n(n + 2)\sum_{}^{k}[ACF(i)^2/(n - i)] \qquad i = 1 \text{ to } k \qquad (7–14)$$

When the ACFs are from a white noise series this statistic is chi-square distributed with k–p–q degrees of freedom, where p and q are the number of AR and MA coefficients of the model. Thus, we see that Q is proportional to the sum of the ACFs through lag k, where typically k is selected to be two seasonal cycles or in general, about 20 when two seasonal cycles is much different than 20.

The Q-statistic is used in the following hypothesis test: The null hypothesis is that residual ACFs are consistent with white noise ACFs.

If $Q \leq$ chi-square-table, where $df = k$–p–q and alpha $= .05$, then infer that the ACF patterns are not statistically significantly different than those of white noise.

If $Q >$ chi-square table, then accept the alternative hypothesis: The residual ACFs are statistically significantly different than white noise ACFs.

The Q of Equation 7–14 is the **Box–Ljung statistic,** which is an enhancement of the Box–Pierce statistic. (Your software may refer to the Q-statistic by either name.) As we will show, the Q-statistic is an important diagnostic tool. However, we have noticed analysts who continuously "torture" their time series to achieve white noise (i.e., a low Q-statistic), while not paying attention to the values of other, more important measures, such as the RSE, or the sums of the squared errors. This raises the important question, what are the characteristics of a good ARIMA model?

Characteristics
of a Good
Model

Table 7–2 lists the characteristics of good ARIMA models. These characteristics are generic to all forecasting models and are therefore relevant to any modeling process. Note that almost always, the modeling process should progress in directions that reduce the RSE while achieving statistically significant coefficients and substantively defensible models. Thus, the $\bar{R}^2$ should be monitored during the modeling process, and overly complex models should be avoided. One of the best statistics for monitoring is the Schwarz Bayesian information criterion (BIC) which is developed in Chapter 17; that chapter can be reviewed at any time.

Time Series Examples

Having presented some of the basics of ARIMA model building, we will now study ARIMA components in greater detail.

TABLE 7–2   Characteristics of a good forecasting model

- It fits the past data well.
  - Plots of actual versus fitted are good.
  - $\bar{R}^2$ is high.
  - RSE is low relative to other models.
  - The MAPE is good.
- The model has intuitive appeal.
- It forecasts the future and withheld (i.e., out-of-sample) data well.
- It is parsimonious, simple but effective, not having too many coefficients.
- The estimated coefficients ϕ_p and θ_q are statistically significant and not redundant or unnecessary.
- The model is stationary and invertible. (See Appendix 7–A).
- No patterns left in the ACFs and PACFs.
- The residuals are white noise, or they have no patterns denoting model deficiencies.
- The Schwarz Bayesian or Akaike information criteria are lower than those of other models. (See Chapter 17).

White Noise Time Series

A completely random (i.e., patternless) series is:

$$Y_t = \mu + e_t \qquad (7\text{–}15)$$

where μ is the mean of the series. This is identified as an ARIMA(0,0,0) model.

Equation 7–15 denotes that Y_t varies randomly, without any patterns about its mean. As we know, a white noise process: (a) is **normally and independently distributed (NID)** about a mean of zero; (b) has a constant variance (σ^2); and (c) has autocorrelations [ACF(k)s] that are not statistically significantly different than zero. These properties apply to e_t and are all denoted in Equation 7–16:

$$e_t \sim \text{NID}\,(0, \sigma^2) \qquad (7\text{–}16)$$

where $\sim$ is notation meaning "is distributed as."

Because the mean of a white noise series is zero, the expected value of a completely random series is its mean, or

$$EY_t = \mu + Ee_t = \mu \qquad (7\text{–}17)$$

The expected value operator E denotes that the mean value of e_t is expected to be zero. While the ARIMA(0,0,0) model in Equation 7–15 seems somewhat simplistic, it is nonetheless the most accurate measure of random, patternless time series. Surprisingly, identification of this simple model can be difficult, because we are always looking for more complex models with patterns. In addition, outliers can make a patterned series appear to be graphically and statistically white noise; thus, it may be difficult to determine whether the series is random, or whether outliers have confounded its patterns.

A Random Walk Daily Stock Prices (STOCKA.DAT)

Figure 7–2 illustrates the daily price, Y_t, ACFs, and PACFs for a stock traded on a major exchange. As shown, this series drifts and therefore has a nonstationary (i.e.,

Demand at a Community Blood Bank

When starting the analysis of a time series, we should anticipate patterns in data but at the same time, remain objective. However, we are often surprised or disappointed at the lack of patterns in some time series. Consider the case of demand at a large community blood bank. It was anticipated that the demand for blood would be seasonal, by the day of the week or by the day of the year. However, in this stable community, the demand was uniformly distributed across all days of the week and year. No matter how we tortured the data, it would not confess!

No matter how many outliers were adjusted, there was no pattern. The best model was an ARIMA(0,0,0) model:

$$Y_t = \mu + e_t$$

Using the two years of daily data, the mean μ was the best predictor. In this case, the variation (i.e., standard deviation) in demand was quite low relative to the mean; thus, the forecasts were quite useful, and the confidence intervals using the standard deviation were very narrow and useful in avoiding inventory overstocks and shortages.

FIGURE 7–2

Daily stock prices (STOCKA.DAT)

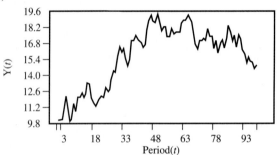

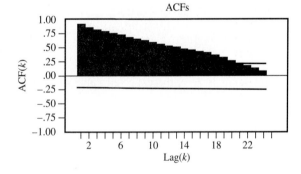

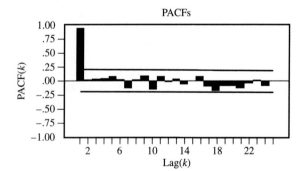

nonconstant) mean. This is verified by the plot, ACFs, and PACFs. The following stochastic trend, ARIMA(0,1,0) model of this series seems appropriate:

$$Y_t = Y_{t-1} + z_t$$

where

$$z_t = Y_t - Y_{t-1}$$

The plot, ACFs, and PACFs of first differences z_t are shown in Figure 7–3. As shown, the first differences have a mean of zero and are distributed as white noise, having no statistically significant ACFs and PACFs. Therefore, we designate z_t as e_t.

FIGURE 7–3

$z_t = e_t = (Y_t - Y_{t-1})$ *for daily stock prices (STOCKA.DAT)*

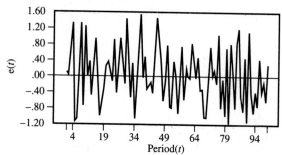

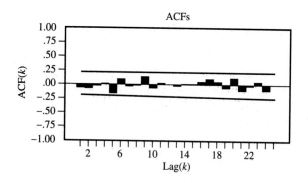

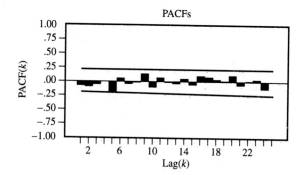

TABLE 7–3   ARIMA(0,1,0) for daily stock prices (STOCKA.DAT)

Usable observations	99
Degrees of Freedom	99
$\bar{R}^2$/BIC	.929/383.3
Mean of dependent variable	15.573
Std error of dependent variable	2.615
Standard error of estimate	.697
Sum of squared residuals	48.045
Durbin–Watson statistic	2.129
$Q(24-0)$	15.593
Significance level of Q	.902

Diagnostic statistics of this model are shown in Table 7–3. The model has an $\bar{R}^2$ of .929, the DW and Q statistics of the residuals are both consistent with a white noise assumption. The residuals of Table 7–3 shown in Figure 7–3 appear very random, with no outliers. The BIC should be compared to the BIC of other models, if they are fitted to this series. Thus, the modeling process yields the **random walk model:**

$$Y_t = Y_{t-1} + e_t \qquad (7\text{–}18)$$

In addition, Table 7–4 illustrates the ACFs, PACFs, and Q-statistics for Y_t and first differences. As shown, Equation 7–18 yields white noise.

TABLE 7–4   ACFs, PACFs, and *Q*-statistic for *Y_t* and *Z_t* (STOCKA.DAT)

For *Y_t*

ACF(*k*)	1:	.9437	.8925	.8475	.8095	.7816	.7555
	7:	.7154	.6784	.6528	.6122	.5852	.5568
PACF(*k*)	1:	.9437	.0178	.0309	.0450	.0805	.0171
	7:	−.1271	.0088	.0886	−.1563	.0857	−.0207

Ljung–Box *Q*-statistic: *Q*(24) = 922.21   Significance level .00000000

For $Z_t = Y_t − Y_{t-1}$

ACF(*k*)	1:	−.0705	−.0837	−.0300	.0096	−.1692	.0879
	7:	−.0249	−.0094	.1344	−.0721	.0293	−.0047
PACF(*k*)	1:	−.0705	−.0891	−.0433	−.0037	−.1778	.0621
	7:	−.0478	−.0157	.1394	−.0957	.0774	−.0206

Ljung–Box *Q*-statistic: *Q*(24) = 15.59   Significance level .90219

TABLE 7–5   ACFs, PACFs, and *Q*-statistic of *Y_t* for DAIRY.DAT

ACF(*k*)	1:	.7484	.4961	.3706	.2427	.1505	.0914
	7:	.0850	.1220	.1913	.2251	.1599	.0730
	13:	−.0574	−.1574	−.1513	−.1715	−.1831	−.1526
	19:	−.1304	−.1847	−.1886	−.1953	−.2424	−.2039
PACF(*k*)	1:	.7484	−.1458	.1263	−.1190	.0343	−.0309
	7:	.0933	.0765	.1385	−.0037	−.1353	−.0707
	13:	−.2069	−.0104	.1017	−.0852	.0015	−.0440
	19:	−.0725	−.2148	.1222	−.0725	.0276	.1287

Ljung–Box *Q*-statistic: *Q*(24) = 169.30   Significance level .00000000

An Autoregressive Time Series (DAIRY.DAT)

Figure 7–4 illustrates the daily sales of a dairy product during a 100-day period. This product is known to be nonseasonal by day of the week and week of the year. The plot of *Y_t* seems somewhat random; however, there is some wandering of *Y_t* about its mean of 199.02. The ACFs of Figure 7–4 and Table 7–5 show an exponential decline from about .75 at lag 1; in addition, the PACFs have a single significant spike at 1. Both the ACFs and PACFs suggest an autoregressive model, ARIMA(1,0,0).

$$Y_t = \theta_0 + \phi_1 Y_{t-1} + e_t \qquad (7–19)$$

Figure 7–5 illustrates the residuals from fitting Equation 7–19. As shown, the series appears quite random, as confirmed by the white noise of the ACFs and PACFs. Table 7–6 illustrates the diagnostic statistics, which are all indicative of a good model: ϕ_1 is very significant, and the DW and *Q* statistics are consistent with white noise residuals. Table 7–7 illustrates the ACFs and PACFs of model residuals. As shown, no low-order or seasonal ACFs or PACFs are statistically significant; thus, this seems to be a statistically defensible model.

While not shown here, several other models were fitted to this data; none were as good as this model. Finally, note that the same data fitted in different software will have slightly different values, because of the iterative nature of nonlinear optimization programs; therefore, the coefficients of your software may deviate very slightly from the results reported here. Also, the BIC can be calculated several different ways.

FIGURE 7–4

Dairy product sales (DAIRY.DAT)

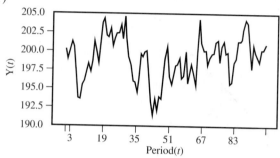

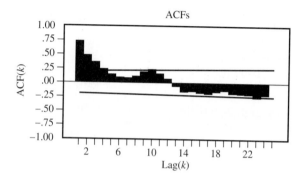

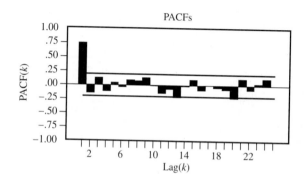

FIGURE 7–5

Residuals of AR(1) for DAIRY.DAT

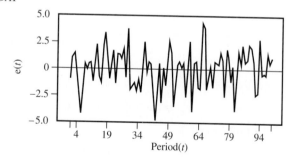

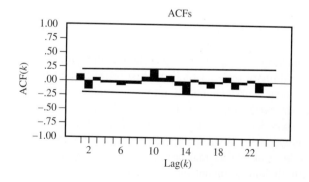

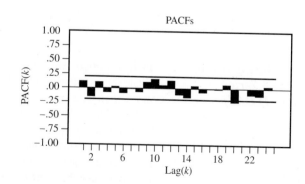

TABLE 7–6   ARIMA(1,0,0) for Y_t for DAIRY.DAT

Iterations taken	3
Usable observations	99
Degrees of freedom	97
$\bar{R}^2$/BIC	.560/592.4
Mean of dependent variable	199.011
Std error of dependent variable	2.9098
Standard error of estimate	1.9309
Sum of squared residuals	361.6545
Durbin–Watson statistic	1.7628
Q(24-1)	26.3432
Significance level of Q	.2849

Coeff.	Estimate	Std Error	t-Stat	Signif
θ_0	199.034	.783	254.052	.00000000
ϕ_1	.752	.067	11.205	.00000000

TABLE 7–7   Residual ACFs, PACFs, and Q-statistic for Equation 7–20

ACF(k)						
1:	.1154	−.1518	.0578	−.0296	−.0285	−.0655
7:	−.0455	−.0503	.0784	.2046	.0668	.0999
13:	−.0613	−.2120	.0370	−.0320	−.0990	−.0220
19:	.0907	−.1080	−.0287	.0403	−.1684	−.0442

PACF(k)						
1:	.1154	−.1673	.1017	−.0818	.0151	−.0934
7:	−.0167	−.0741	.1046	.1641	.0555	.1362
13:	−.1165	−.1665	.0521	−.0663	−.0095	−.0119
19:	.0758	−.2316	.0005	−.1078	−.1204	.0494

Ljung–Box Q-statistic: $Q(24) = 26.34$ Significance level .3360

Note that for AR models with constant terms, the constant θ_0 is calculated as

$$\theta_0 = (1 - \phi_1)\mu = (1 - .752)199.034 = 49.36$$

Thus, the final model is

$$Y_t = 49.36 + .752Y_{t-1} + e_t \tag{7–20}$$

In forecasting form this is

$$\hat{Y}_t = 49.36 + .752Y_{t-1} \tag{7–21}$$

A Moving Average Time Series (FAD.DAT)

In this section, we analyze a moving average series after taking first differences. Thus, this is initially a level-nonstationary series. This is the first series that embodies more than one component: an integrated I(1), and a moving average component MA(1). These are combined into an ARIMA(0,1,1) model.

Figure 7–6 illustrates the weekly demand for a fad product (FAD.DAT), which is known to be nonseasonal. As shown in the figure and in Table 7–8, this series has a nonstationary mean, and has ACFs and PACFs that are also indicative of a nonstationary series; they remain very high and significant for many lags.

FIGURE 7–6

Sales of a fad product (FAD.DAT)

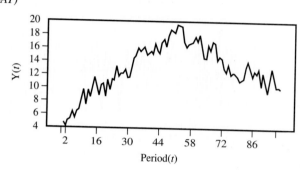

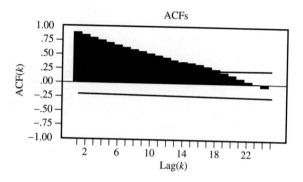

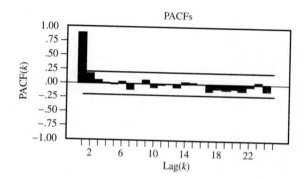

TABLE 7–8   ACFs, PACFs, and Q-statistic for FAD.DAT

ACF(k)	1:	.9049	.8517	.8063	.7634	.7201	.6875
	7:	.6354	.5941	.5694	.5281	.4911	.4591
	13:	.4178	.3886	.3670	.3421	.2978	.2551
PACF(k)	1:	.9049	.1811	.0645	.0197	−.0094	.0424
	7:	−.1014	−.0025	.0784	−.0679	−.0154	−.0007
	13:	−.0543	.0292	.0245	.0091	−.1197	−.0838

Ljung–Box Q-statistic: $Q(24) = 698.173$ Significance level .00000000

Because of the level nonstationarity, first differences of Y_t are taken:

$$z_t = Y_t - Y_{t-1}$$

As shown in Figure 7–7, the first differences z_t have a stationary mean; however, the ACFs and PACFs show a pattern at the low-order lags in the figure and Table 7–9. The single peak in the ACFs and the negative exponential decline in the PACFs starting at lag 1 are indicative of an MA(1) model. While not shown here, the mean of z_t is not statistically significantly different from zero, as expected since the series is not trending. Table 7–10 illustrates the results of fitting a first differences ARIMA(0,1,0) model to the FAD.DAT. As shown, the first differences yield an $\bar{R}^2$ of .8611. However, neither the Durbin–Watson nor the Q statistic is indicative of white noise residuals.

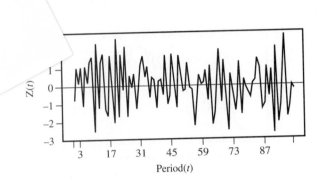

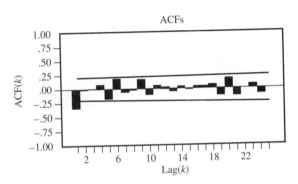

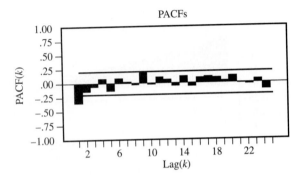

TABLE 7–9   ACFs and PACFs of First Differences of FAD.DAT

ACF(k)	1:	−.3493	−.0085	.0046	.0864	−.1834	.1842
	7:	−.0559	−.0233	.1668	−.1082	.0629	.0197
	13:	−.0469	.0478	−.0167	.0483	.0456	.0752
	19:	−.1188	.1864	−.1241	−.0018	.0830	−.0930
PACF(k)	1:	−.3493	−.1487	−.0591	.0774	−.1421	.0921
	7:	.0232	−.0206	.2010	−.0280	.1009	.0563
	13:	−.0493	.1069	−.0704	.0903	.1026	.0899
	19:	.0242	.1220	−.0063	−.0274	.0633	−.1191

Ljung–Box Q-statistic: $Q(24) = 37.7636$.   Significance level .03665365

TABLE 7–10   First Differences of FAD.DAT

Usable observations	99
Degrees of freedom	99
$\bar{R}^2$/BIC	.8611/509.1
Mean of dependent variable	12.9517
Std error of dependent variable	3.5276
Standard error of estimate	1.3149
Sum of squared residuals	171.1649
Durbin–Watson statistic	2.6898
$Q(24-0)$	37.7636
Significance level of Q	.0367

The ACFs and PACFs of Table 7–9 and Figure 7–7 suggest an MA(1) model for z_t:

$$z_t = e_t - \theta_1 e_{t-1} \tag{7–22}$$

Remembering that $z_t = (Y_t - Y_{t-1})$, Equation 7–23 is an ARIMA(0,1,1) model:

$$Y_t - Y_{t-1} = e_t - \theta_1 e_{t-1} \tag{7–23}$$

Table 7–11 illustrates the results of fitting an ARIMA(0,1,1) model to the series FAD.DAT. As shown, the $\bar{R}^2$ has increased and the BIC improves (decreases). θ_1 is statistically very significant, with a t-value of about -4.26. The DW and Q statistics are both indicative of white noise. Also, the ACFs and PACFs of Figure 7–8 and Table 7–12 are both indicative of white noise. Finally, the graph of the residuals in Figure 7–8 appears quite random. Our analysis of this series is therefore complete. Equation 7–23a illustrates the forecasting form of this model.

$$\hat{Y}_t = Y_{t-1} - .3958e_{t-1} \tag{7–23a}$$

This states that the forecast in period t equals the previous actual value minus some fraction of the previous error. This model seems to be very much like an exponential smoothing model, as developed in Chapter 4. In fact, an ARIMA(0,1,1) model is the

TABLE 7–11   ARIMA(0,1,1) of FAD.DAT

Iterations taken	6
Usable observations	99
Degrees of freedom	98
$\bar{R}^2$/BIC	.8792/498.8
Mean of dependent variable	12.9517
Std error of dependent variable	3.5276
Standard error of estimate	1.2262
Sum of squared residuals	147.3486
Durbin–Watson statistic	2.0077
$Q(24-1)$	17.9604
Significance level of Q	.7596

Coeff.	Estimate	Std Error	t-Stat	Signif
$-\theta_1$	$-.3958$	.0930	-4.2565	.00004760

TABLE 7–12   ACFs, PACFs of Residuals of ARIMA(0,1,1) for FAD.DAT

ACF(k)	1:	$-.0128$	$-.0066$	.0189	.0532	.1120	.1503
	7:	.0051	.0342	.1724	$-.0313$	.0664	.0361
	13:	$-.0156$	.0539	.0353	.1023	.1192	.1061
	19:	$-.0327$	.1496	$-.0777$	$-.0082$	.0593	$-.0629$
PACF(k)	1:	$-.0128$	$-.0067$	.0188	.0537	$-.1107$	.1506
	7:	.0019	.0395	.1857	$-.0649$	.1136	.0038
	13:	$-.0298$	.1048	$-.0546$	.1561	.0940	.0620
	19:	.0267	.0878	$-.0602$	$-.0167$	.0232	$-.1260$

Ljung–Box Q-statistic: $Q(24) = 17.9604$ Significance level .80492617

FIGURE 7–8

Residuals of ARIMA(0,1,1) for FAD.DAT

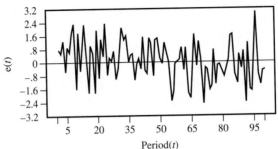

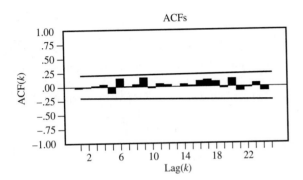

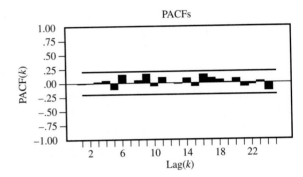

equivalent of an exponential smoothing model, a fact you may be asked to verify for homework.

This completes a basic introduction to ARIMA model building.

Variance Stationarity

Level stationarity is achieved when the mean of the series is the same over time; thus, no differencing is necessary. While level stationarity might be achieved in the ARIMA model-building process, another form of nonstationarity, that is, variance nonstationarity, must also be modeled. Some time series may have either level nonstationarity or variance nonstationarity, or both.

As discussed in Chapter 2, the variance is the expected value of the squared deviations. A process that has a stationary variance has a constant variance over all observations. For an initially stationary series, the variance is

$$E(Y_t - \mu)^2 = \sigma_y^2 = \text{constant variance for all subsets of } t$$

For an initially nonstationary series that has been appropriately transformed to yield a stationary z_t, the variance is

$$E(z_t - \theta_o)^2 = \sigma_z^2 = \text{constant variance for all subsets of } t$$

Thus, Y_t and z_t have level and variance stationarity.

However, many series have a nonstationarity variance. Consider a nonstationary-variance series and the method used to achieve stationarity. Figure 7–9 shows a time

White Noise versus Stationarity

We have noted that there can be some confusion regarding stationarity and white noise. White noise residuals are the residuals from a final model, confirmed in one of the last steps in the model-building process. In contrast, stationarity should be achieved in one of the first steps in the modeling process. Nonstationarity is an important component in its own right, and the ARMA structure of a nonstationary series is normally impossible to discern. Finally, white noise series are stationary; however, stationary series are not typically white noise.

FIGURE 7–9

Electric utility in California (MEGAWATT.DAT)

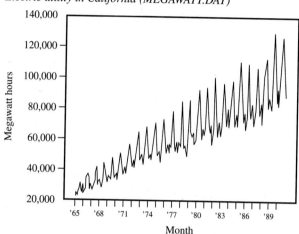

FIGURE 7–10

Logs of electric utility in California (MEGAWATT.DAT)

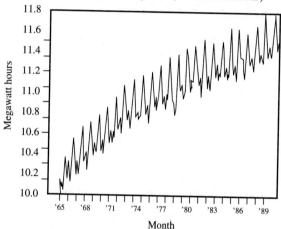

series of monthly demand for power at a utility in California. As shown, the series increases from January 1965 through 1990. Because the seasonal highs and lows diverge, this series is nonstationary in variance and should be transformed appropriately during the modeling process. As shown, the demand variance is greater when the level is higher; thus, the variance is not constant. Nonstationary variances cause ARIMA identification problems. Also, variance nonstationarity is a very important characteristic of a series and this condition should be explained and modeled. Figure 7–10 shows the natural logarithms of Y_t, which has a near constant variance. This illustrates that when the variance of a series is proportional to its level, or

$$\sigma_Y^2 = \propto(Y_t)$$

a logarithmic or power transformation of the series may be variance stationary. Frequently, the use of logs is appropriate for time series because they undergo percentage changes in trend or seasonality. Figure 7–9 shows that for this series, the seasonal increases or decreases are proportional to the level of the series in that month.

Because percentage growths in the demand for products, prices, and the economy are common, variance nonstationarity is also common in many time series. In many situations, we have

$$e_t^2 = Ke_{t-1}^2 \tag{7–24}$$

$$Y_t = KY_{t-1} \tag{7–24a}$$

where K is a constant of proportionality. Remembering that the addition (subtraction) of logarithms is the equivalent of the multiplication (division) of the original values, the use of logarithmic values yields appropriate nonlinear growth relationships for the original series. Consider the meaning of the first differences of logged transforms of a time series Y_t:

In logarithms	*In ratios*
$\ln(Y_t) = \ln(Y_{t-1}) + \ln(K)$	$Y_t = KY_{t-1}$
$\ln(Y_t) - \ln(Y_{t-1}) = \ln(K)$	$Y_t/Y_{t-1} = K$

Taking the logarithms of Y_t achieves variance stationarity and proper model structure. The use of logarithmic transformations to achieve variance stationarity and proper model structure is common in other statistical procedures, such as regression analysis and analysis of variance.

U.S. Stock Index (1,1,0)1,1 Model

Figure 7–11, illustrates 271 monthly values of a United States stock price index, from the *Survey of Current Business through 1992.* This series is clearly non-stationary in level, and its variance may also be nonstationary. Figure 7–12 is a graph of the first differences of this series. In general, the series is variance nonstationary about a mean slightly greater than zero; that is, the variance of first differences (i.e., period-to-period increases) in Figure 7–12 increases with the level of the series in Figure 7–11. This series therefore requires a transformation to achieve variance stationarity. Figure 7–13 illustrates the logarithms of the stock index, and Figure 7–14 shows that the first differences of Equation 7–25 have variance stationarity, the period-to-period changes are constant as $\ln Y_t$ increases. Thus, the percentage variation in Y_t is modeled well by taking natural logarithms, $\ln Y_t$

$$z_t' = \ln(Y_t) - \ln(Y_{t-1}) \tag{7–25}$$

where Y_t is the United States stock price index.

To assure that the steps taken have achieved stationarity and reduced the variance of the series, review the statistics of each transformation in Table 7–13.

As Table 7–13 denotes, both Y_t and z_t are nonstationary in variance; thus the need to take natural logarithms to achieve variance stationarity. The graph of $\ln(Y_t)$ appears nonstationary in level, but stationary in variance; thus, z_t' appears to be the variable for analysis. With that in mind, consider the ACFs and PACFs of z_t' delineated in Table 7–14 and illustrated in Figure 7–14.

As shown in Table 7–14, all ACFs except lag 1 are insignificant, and all PACFs except lag 1 are insignificant. The single positive spike in the ACFs of Figure 7–13 is

TABLE 7–13   Evolution of Descriptive Statistics of U.S. Stock Index (USIND.DAT)

	n	*Mean*	*Std Dev.*	*Minimum*	*Maximum*	*Level*	*Variance*	*White Noise*
						Stationarity		
Y_t	271	188.02	107.26	73.00	452.60	NO	NO	NO
$z_t = Y_t - Y_{t-1}$	270	1.31	7.72	−41.80	40.00	YES	NO	NO
$\ln(Y_t)$	271	5.10	.5151	4.29	6.12	NO	YES	NO
$z_t' = \ln(Y_t) - \ln(Y_{t-1})$	270	.0057	.0375	−.1343	.1102	YES	YES	NO
$(0,1,1)1,1$	270	.00006	.0357	−.1162	.1092	YES	YES	YES

FIGURE 7–11

Stock index, ACFs, and PACFs (USIND.DAT)

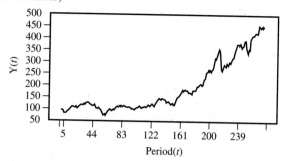

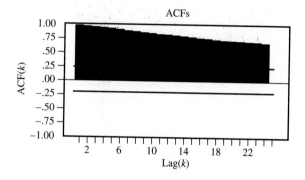

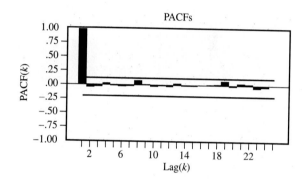

FIGURE 7–12

First differences of USIND.DAT

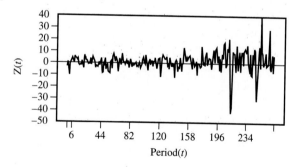

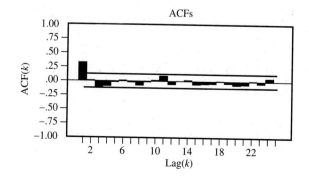

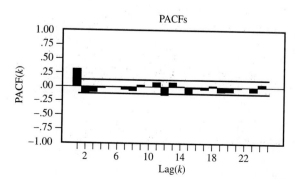

FIGURE 7–13

Ln(USIND.DAT)

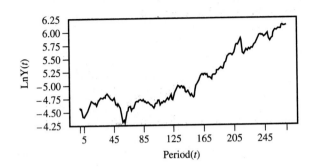

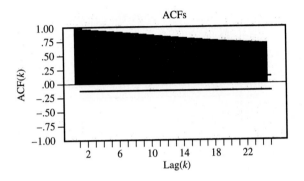

ACFs

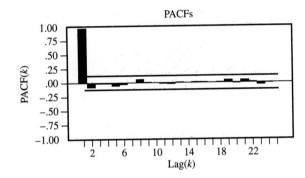

PACFs

FIGURE 7–14

First differences of ln(USIND.DAT)

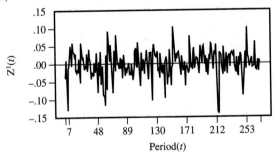

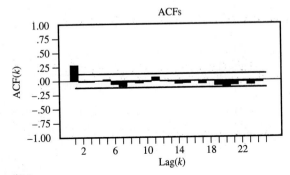

ACFs

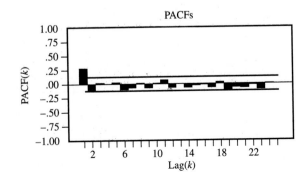

PACFs

TABLE 7–14   ACFs, PACFs of z'_t, First Differences of ln(U.S. Stock Index)

ACF(k)	1:	.2870	−.0119	−.0102	.0046	.0304	−.0618
	7:	−.1062	−.0230	−.0399	−.0178	.0635	−.0120
	13:	−.0178	−.0542	−.0498	−.0081	−.0555	−.0108
	19:	−.0896	−.1149	−.0794	−.0223	−.0749	−.0249
PACF(k)	1:	.2870	−.1028	.0254	−.0009	.0313	−.0880
	7:	−.0637	.0235	−.0559	.0097	.0740	−.0581
	13:	−.0013	−.0609	−.0215	−.0083	−.0525	.0348
	19:	−.1232	−.0572	−.0588	−.0047	−.0960	.0172

Ljung–Box Q-Statistic: $Q(24) = 41.5768$ Significance level .0144

FIGURE 7–15

Residuals of ARIMA(0,1,1)1 of ln(USIND.DAT)

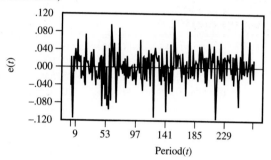

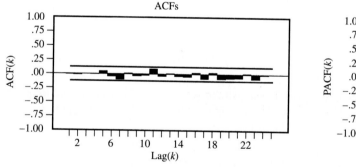

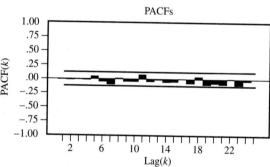

indicative of a moving average model MA(1). In addition, the first four alternating spikes of the PACFs confirm an MA(1) model. The anticipated MA(1) model will have a negative θ_1 (or positive $-\theta_1$) value.

The results of fitting an ARIMA(0,1,1)1 model to $\ln(Y_t)$, which is the equivalent of fitting an ARIMA(0,0,1)1 model to z'_t, are shown in Table 7–15 and Figure 7–15. From the results of Table 7–15, we make the following inferences:

1. The value of the constant θ_0 is marginally insignificant; thus, there is a trend in the series because its level of significance is .053. Because it is marginally insignificant, it would typically be dropped, however, we retain it here for discussion purposes.

TABLE 7–15   ARIMA(0,1,1)1 of ln(USIND.DAT)

Iterations taken	5
Usable observations	270
Degrees of freedom	268
$\bar{R}^2$/BIC	.9952/−227.3
Mean of dependent variable	5.0969
Std error of dependent variable	.5151
Standard error of estimate	.0358
Sum of squared residuals	.3435
Durbin–Watson statistic	2.0010
Q(36-1)	25.4012
Significance level of Q	.8832

Coeff	Estimate	Std Error	t-Stat	Signif
θ_0	.0056	.0029	1.942	.05313237
$-\theta_1$	.3236	.0579	5.592	.00000006

Residual ACFs and PACFs

ACF(k)						
1:	−.0035	−.0098	−.0049	−.0076	.0461	−.0474
7:	−.0956	.0153	−.0350	−.0321	.0837	−.0379
13:	.0059	−.0426	−.0453	.0269	−.0733	.0355
19:	−.0788	−.0725	−.0633	.0192	−.0800	−.0042

PACF(k)						
1:	−.0035	−.0098	−.0049	−.0077	.0460	−.0474
7:	−.0954	.0143	−.0366	−.0366	.0873	−.0325
13:	−.0048	−.0471	−.0440	.0079	−.0705	.0485
19:	−.0904	−.0704	−.0790	.0057	−.0923	−.0192

Ljung–Box Q-Statistic: $Q(24) = 16.73$ Significance level .8599

---

2. The first-order MA coefficient θ_1 is statistically significantly different than zero, with a very high t-value.

3. The $\bar{R}^2 = .995$ is quite high. The BIC of −277.3 should be compared to other BICs. In fact, the BIC improves (decreases) to −279.2 when dropping θ_0, thus confirming that it should be dropped.

4. The Q-statistic and D–W statistic are both indicative of white noise residuals. As shown, 88 percent of white noise residuals have a Q-statistic as high or higher than that found in this model. Thus, there appears to be no patterns left in the residuals, a fact confirmed in item 5.

5. The graph of the residuals in Figure 7–15 appears to be that of a white noise series, albeit there are some very large and small values, most likely from large market corrections..

6. The patternless ACFs and PACFs of Figure 7–15 appear to be those of a white noise series, because of the Q-statistic in item 4, and because none of the ACFs or PACFs is greater than two Se_{ACF} of about $2/(269)^{.5}$. Thus, this appears to be a good model.

7. The resulting model is:

$$\ln(Y_t) - \ln(Y_{t-1}) = \theta_0 + e_t - \theta_1 e_{t-1}$$

$$\ln(Y_t) = \ln(Y_{t-1}) + \theta_0 - \theta_1 e_{t-1} + e_t$$

In forecasting form this is:

$$\widehat{\ln(Y_t)} = \ln(Y_{t-1}) + \theta_0 - \theta_1 e_{t-1}$$

$$\widehat{\ln(Y_t)} = \ln(Y_{t-1}) + .0056 + .3236 e_{t-1}$$

Finally, in terms of the original time series we have

$$\hat{Y}_t = \mathbf{e}^{\widehat{\ln(Y_t)}}$$

Also we can interpret the constant $\theta_0 = .0056$ as a measure of the percentage growth in Y_t over time as:

$$\text{Growth} = \mathbf{e}^{\theta_0} - 1 = 1.00562 - 1 = .00562$$

This denotes that, on average, the stock index is growing at the rate of .562 percent per month, or about 7 percent per year (i.e., $1.00562^{12} - 1$).

Table 7–16 illustrates actual, fitted, residual, and percent error for this model. As shown, the model fits quite well. Finally, note that the residuals in Table 7–16 increase as Y_t increases, which is the logical consequence of the original variance nonstationarity and the reason the data was log transformed. However, note that the percent errors of the last column remain relatively constant.

We included the insignificant θ_0 to illustrate a deterministic trend; also, this choice illustrates that the purpose of the model can influence its structure. For example, in October 1987 there was a large drop in the index. This resulted from the large market

TABLE 7–16   **Actual Y_t, Fitted Values of $\mathbf{e}^{\widehat{\ln Y_t}}$, and Residuals: ARIMA (0,1,1)1,1 for U.S. Stock Index**

Date	Y_t	$\mathbf{e}^{\widehat{\ln Y_t}}$ Fitted	$Y_t - \mathbf{e}^{\widehat{\ln Y_t}}$ Residual	$(Y_t - \mathbf{e}^{\widehat{\ln Y_t}})/Y_t$ Error ratio
1970:01	98.2	NA	NA	NA
1970:02	94.8	98.75	−3.951	−.0416
1970:03	96.4	94.08	2.319	.0240
1970:04	93.5	97.70	−4.207	−.0450
1970:05	82.7	92.69	−9.994	−.1208
1970:06	82.2	80.14	2.050	.0249
1970:07	82.4	83.33	−.939	−.0114
1970:08	84.8	82.55	2.241	.0264
1970:09	89.8	86.01	3.781	.0421
1970:10	91.8	91.56	.230	.0025
1970:11	91.7	92.39	−.690	−.0075
1970:12	98.0	91.99	6.008	.0613
	• • •			
1991:01	354.1	362.74	−8.646	−.0244
1991:02	394.1	353.31	40.782	.1034
1991:03	405.0	410.57	−5.570	−.0137
1991:04	413.0	405.47	7.523	.0182
	• • •			
1992:05	451.2	445.25	5.943	.0131
1992:06	444.1	455.68	−11.582	−.0260
1992:07	451.5	442.88	8.613	.0190
Means	188.02	188.18	.167	−.00058
Std. dev.	107.26	107.04	7.39	.0360

correction known as "Black Monday." If our purpose was to model the effect of that crash, then our analysis is incomplete at this time. We investigate ways of modeling such interventions in greater detail in Chapter 12.

The Backshift Operator

An efficient notation used for ARIMA modeling, including differences, is the **backshift operator** B. By definition,

$$BY_t = Y_{t-1}$$

$$BY_{t-k} = Y_{t-k-1}$$

where B transforms Y_t backward one time period to Y_{t-1}. All algebraic laws of exponents and polynomial expansions are valid with the backshift operator. For example, the following are identities:

$$B^s Y_t = Y_{t-s}$$

$$B^{12} Y_t = Y_{t-12}$$

$$B^s B^d(Y_t) = B^{s+d} Y_t = Y_{t-s-d}$$

$$B^1 B^{12}(Y_t) = B^{1+12} Y_t = Y_{t-13}$$

First differences:

$$(1 - B)Y_t = Y_t - BY_t = Y_t - Y_{t-1}$$

Second differences:

$$(1 - B)^2 Y_t = (1 - 2B + B^2)Y_t = Y_t - 2Y_{t-1} + Y_{t-2}$$

Seasonal differences for quarterly data:

$$(1 - B^4)Y_t = Y_t - Y_{t-4}$$

Seasonal differences for monthly data:

$$(1 - B^{12})Y_t = Y_t - Y_{t-12}$$

Be cautious in specifying differences, because of the distinction between nonseasonal and seasonal differences. Consider the following:
Quarterly seasonal differences:

$$(1 - B^4)Y_t = Y_t - Y_{t-4}$$

Nonseasonal fourth-order differences:

$$(1 - B)^4 Y_t = (1 - B)(1 - B)(1 - B)(1 - B)Y_t$$

After expansion and combining terms we have

$$(1 - B)^4 Y_t = (1 - 4B + 6B^2 - 4B^3 + {}^{B4})Y_t$$

$$= Y_t - 4Y_{t-1} + 6Y_{t-2} - 4Y_{t-3} + Y_{t-4}$$

This is a difficult relationship to interpret, and is highly unlikely. Therefore, care must be taken to avoid misspecifications and excessive computational times when taking differences and using software. In the remaining time series chapters, we will use the backshift operator to identify and manipulate complex ARIMA models.

Integrated Stochastic Process (0,1,0)

A random walk process is one in which successive random shocks accumulate over time. In mathematics, accumulation or summation is referred to as integration; thus, a random walk is called an integrated process. To illustrate the generality of integrated processes, consider a gambler who bets one dollar on the flip of a fair coin. When the flip yields heads, a dollar is won; with tails, a dollar is lost. Using e_t for the random shocks (i.e., a loss or win) yields

$$e_t = \$1 \text{ for a head}$$

$$e_t = -\$1 \text{ for a tail}$$

Because flips of a fair coin are expected to result in equal numbers of heads and tails, the sum of coin flips is an integrated process with an expected value of zero.

$$P(\text{heads}) = P(\text{tails}) = .5$$

$$Ee_t = .5(\$1) + .5(-\$1) = 0$$

Therefore, over time, the gambler expects to break even.

Random shocks like coin flips have a mean of zero, a constant standard deviation, and no significant autocorrelations; they are white noise. However, the summation of random shocks is not distributed as white noise; instead, the distribution is nonstationary. That summation is the total won or lost after t coin flips:

$$Y_t = Y_0 + \Sigma e_t$$

where Y_0 is the initial sum held by the gambler. For example, after three flips, the total equals

$$Y_3 = Y_0 + e_1 + e_2 + e_3$$

In general, at the end of t coin flips we have

$$Y_t = Y_0 + e_1 + e_2 + \ldots + e_{t-1} + e_t \tag{7-26}$$

While not shown here, the summation of coin flips appears to be a random walk behaving very much like Figure 7–2, the daily stock prices. Over the long run, the average winnings will fluctuate about zero; however, there will be long excursions away from zero that appear as random walks. Also, if we only look at local behavior, there may appear to be trends, but these are actually local runs of either heads or tails.

As in Figure 7–2, it is surprising how high and low Y_t wanders from its mean, and at times, these drifts appear as strong trends. These random walks drift up and down slowly over time, instead of fluctuating about the mean because of runs of heads or tails. When a run of several heads or tails occurs, which is likely with many flips, the summation process drifts above or below the mean. The level of the process varies about the summed value until driven by another run, either up or down. However, it may take some time before an opposite run occurs.

Random walks are frequently encountered in forecasting when prices (e.g., stock prices or commodity prices) or product life cycles vary in efficient markets. Also, there are many processes in the physical and social sciences that are inherently summation or integration processes.

The first differences of a random walk time series yield random shocks, $e_1, e_2, e_3, \ldots, e_t$. Differencing transforms a random walk into a white noise process.

Just as in Figure 7–3, the first differences of the coin flip are white noise. The differenced series of Figure 7–3 does not drift; instead, it randomly and independently fluctuates about the mean.

Autoregressive Processes: ARIMA(p,0,0) Models

The most common autoregressive process is the first-order ARIMA(1,0,0) model:

$$y_t = \phi_1 y_{t-1} + e_t$$

Using backshift notation this is

$$(1 - \phi_1 B)y_t = e_t \qquad (7\text{–}27)$$

The general ARIMA(p,0,0) autoregressive model is

$$y_t = \phi_1 y_{t-1} + \phi_2 y_{t-2} + \cdots + \phi_p y_{t-p} + e_t \qquad (7\text{–}28)$$

where p denotes the pth (last) lag and y_ts are deviations from the mean or appropriate transformed values of Y_t.

Fortunately, p is very rarely above 2, except for seasonal series. Using the backshift operator notation, an ARIMA(p,0,0) is

$$(1 - \phi_1 B - \phi_2 B^2 - \cdots - \phi_p B^p)y_t = e_t$$

The p and q of ARIMA(p,d,q) processes are meaningful only if they represent the behavior of a stationary series. Thus, an AR(p) series is an initially stationary series, or one that has been transformed to stationarity by the appropriate transformation, such as first differences or logarithms, for example:

$$w_t = (1 - B)\ln Y_t$$

After stationarity is achieved, the appropriate value of p is found using w_t.

Let's assume that an initially nonstationary series Y_t is transformed to a stationary series z_t by taking first differences:

$$z_t = Y_t - Y_{t-1}$$

Analyses of ACFs and PACFs show that z_t is an autoregressive process

$$z_t = \phi_1 z_{t-1} + e_t$$

Through substitution, the model can be restated in terms of Y_t,

$$Y_t - Y_{t-1} = \phi_1(Y_{t-1} - Y_{t-2}) + e_t$$

which in forecasting form is

$$\hat{Y}_t = Y_{t-1} + \phi_1(Y_{t-1} - Y_{t-2})$$

As is true for most ARIMA models, this relationship has considerable appeal. It states that the value in period t (e.g., June) equals the value of period $(t - 1)$ (i.e., May) plus a fraction (i.e., ϕ_1) of how much that period $(t - 1)$ (i.e., May) is greater or less than the next previous period $(t - 2)$ (i.e., April). This illustrates that when fitting ARIMA models, you should consider their intuitive meaning. Do not simply accept a model without some verification of its meaning and appropriateness.

Fortunately, complex AR(p) series are not common, and a high value of p may be indicative of a moving average model, ARIMA(0,0,1), not an autoregressive model.

Let us reconsider the stationary series DAIRY.DAT in Figure 7–4. This series may have appeared completely random (i.e., white noise); however, as shown in Figure 7–4 there is a slight pattern in the series as it varies over time. This pattern is not as smooth as the random walk of Figure 7–2 (the daily STOCKA.DAT series). Even if the autoregressive pattern was undetectable in the Y_t plot of Figure 7–4, there are strong patterns in the ACFs and PACFs, shown in Figure 7–4 and Table 7–5. The strong exponential decline in ACFs and the single significant peak in the PACFs at lag 1 are the patterns of an autoregressive process with a p of 1, a consideration we discuss in more detail later.

Now let's consider the meaning of partial autocorrelations: PACFs measure the correlation between Y_t and Y_{t-k}, where all of the influences of other lags have been removed (i.e., partialed out). Thus, PACF(2) measures only the direct correlation between Y_t and Y_{t-2}, since the joint correlation between these two and the other lags, such as Y_{t-1} have been removed. (Again, see Appendix 7–F for further discussions.) Thus, for an AR process, a single significant PACF at lag one denotes that Y_t is only a function of Y_{t-1} as shown by the ARIMA(1,0,0) fitted to the dairy series in Table 7–6:

$$y_t = \phi_1 y_{t-1} + e_t$$

$$\phi_1 = .75$$

Model Relationships: AR(p), I(d), and MA(q)

Autoregression refers to stochastic processes in which the influences of random shocks decline exponentially over time. This autoregressive behavior requires that bounds be placed on the parameter ϕ_1:

$$-1 < \phi_1 < +1$$

As mentioned earlier, these are called the bounds of stationarity. If an ARIMA(1,0,0) model is written as

$$(1 - \phi_1 B)y_t = e_t \qquad \text{or} \qquad y_t = \phi_1 y_{t-1} + e_t,$$

the implication of these bounds becomes apparent: If $\phi_1 = +1$, then an ARIMA (010) model results:

$$(1 - B)y_t = e_t \text{ or } y_t = y_{t-1} + e_t$$

Thus, if ϕ_1 is greater than or equal to 1, then the ARIMA(1,0,0) model is a nonstationary ARIMA(p,1,q) model. As was shown previously, the nonstationary ARIMA(0,1,0) process gives equal weight to all past random shocks or

$$Y_t = Y_0 + e_1 + e_2 + \cdots + e_{t-1} + e_t$$

The influence of past random shocks does not decrease over time; there is no autoregression. The bounds of stationarity therefore relate to an important property of ARIMA(1,0,0) models: an ARIMA(1,0,0) model is equal to an infinite sum of exponentially weighted past random shocks. That is, the ARIMA(1,0,0) model is

$$y_t = \phi_1 y_{t-1} + e_t \qquad (7\text{–}29)$$

Therefore,

$$y_{t-1} = \phi_1 y_{t-2} + e_{t-1}$$

Substituting this equation for Y_{t-1} in Equation 7–29 yields

$$y_t = \phi_1(\phi_1 y_{t-2} + e_{t-1}) + e_t$$

$$= \phi_1^2 y_{t-2} + \phi_1 e_{t-1} + e_t$$

Continuing the substitution of

$$y_{t-2} = \phi_1 y_{t-3} + e_{t-2}$$

results in

$$y_t = \phi_1^2(\phi_1 y_{t-3} + e_{t-2}) + \phi_1 e_{t-1} + e_t$$
$$= \phi_1^3 y_{t-3} + \phi_1^2 e_{t-2} + \phi_1 e_{t-1} + e_t$$

Continuing the substitution process back to the first observation yields

$$y_t = \Sigma \phi_1^i e_{t-1} \qquad \text{for } i = 1 \text{ to } n \qquad (7\text{--}30)$$

which confirms that an ARIMA(1,0,0) process equals an infinite sum of exponentially weighted past random shocks, an ARIMA(0,0,q) where q is very large. An important property of simple ARIMA(1,0,0) models is their equivalency to a very complex ARIMA(0,0,q) model as shown in Equation 7–30.

Nonstationary ϕ_1 Values. We see now that if ϕ_1 exceeds 1, the series is nonstationary with an ever-increasing mean, where past random shocks (e.g., $\phi_1^{10} e_{t-10}$) have greater influence on y_t than recent random shocks ($\phi_1 e_{t-1}$). Therefore, transformations should be made to achieve stationarity before p or q can be found.

Consider a nonstationary relationship with $\phi_1 = 1.2$:

$$y_t = 1.2 y_{t-1} + e_t$$

Through substitution, we have

$$y_t = 1.2(1.2 y_{t-2} + e_{t-1}) + e_t = 1.44 y_{t-2} + 1.2 e_{t-1} + e_t \qquad (7\text{--}31)$$
$$= 1.44(1.2 y_{t-3} + e_{t-2}) + 1.2 e_{t-1} + e_t$$
$$= 1.728 y_{t-3} + 1.44 e_{t-2} + 1.2 e_{t-1} + e_t$$

and so forth. Thus, past values of y_{t-k} and e_{t-k} have greater and greater influence on y_t when the absolute value of ϕ_1 is greater than 1. Because y_t in Equation 7–31 is a level-nonstationary series, it should first be made stationary through appropriate transformations (i.e., differences).

As we have shown, an ARIMA(1,0,0) model is an exponentially weighted average of all past shocks. Because ϕ_1 is a fraction, powers of ϕ_1 converge to zero for high values of i. If $\phi_1 = .5$ and .75, for example, then:

$\phi_1 = .5$	$\phi_1 = .75$
$\phi_1^2 = .25$	$\phi_1^2 = .5625$
$\phi_1^3 = .125$	$\phi_1^3 = .4219$
$\phi_1^4 = .0625$	$\phi_1^4 = .3164$
. . .	. . .

$$\phi_1^i \longrightarrow 0 \qquad \phi_1^i \longrightarrow 0 \quad \text{as } i \longrightarrow \text{infinity}$$

where " $\longrightarrow$ " is read as "approaches." This means that an initial random shock stays in the process, but its influence diminishes exponentially.

***ARIMA(1,0,0)
Software Output***

There may be some confusion regarding Y_t versus y_t for ARIMA(1,0,0) processes. This confusion results from the manner in which ARIMA coefficients may be reported in some software. Most software programs define

$$Y_t = \theta_0 + \phi_1 Y_{t-1} + e_t$$

where

$$\theta_0 = (1 - \phi_1)\mu$$

However, some software programs only use

$$y_t = \phi_1 y_{t-1} + e_t$$

which must be converted using the simple transformation

$$y_t = Y_t - \mu \quad \text{and} \quad y_{t-1} = Y_{t-1} - \mu$$

where μ = mean of series. To convert results to the form used in regression analysis we first use

$$y_t = \phi_1 y_{t-1} + e_t$$

Substitute $Y_t - \mu$ for y_t to obtain

$$Y_t - \mu = \phi_1(Y_{t-1} - \mu) + e_t$$
$$Y_t = (1 - \phi_1)\mu + \phi_1 Y_{t-1} + e_t$$

Using the previous example, with $\phi_1 = .7523$, the value of Y_t is determined to be

$$Y_t = (1 - .7523)\mu + .7523 Y_{t-1} + e_t$$

In forecasting form, this is

$$\hat{Y}_t = (1 - .7523)\mu + .7523 Y_{t-1}$$

Since $\mu = 199.039$, then

$$\hat{Y}_t = (1 - .7523)199.039 + .7523 Y_{t-1} = 49.30 + .7523 Y_{t-1}$$

Moving Average Processes: ARIMA(0,0,*q*) Models

The moving average concept was introduced in the FAD.DAT series example. The general moving average process is designated ARIMA(0,0,*q*). For example, an ARIMA(0,0,2) model equals

$$y_t = e_t - \theta_1 e_{t-1} - \theta_2 e_{t-2}$$

or, in backshift notation,

$$y_t = (1 - \theta_1 B - \theta_2 B^2)e_t = e_t - \theta_1 e_{t-1} - \theta_2 e_{t-2}$$

where, by convention, a minus sign is shown for $\theta_1, \theta_2, \ldots, \theta_q$.

Similar to autoregressive processes, moving average processes are stationary; consequently, y_t is either deviations of an initially stationary series or it has been appropriately transformed to achieve stationarity.

In contrast to an AR process, the influence of the random shock in the moving average process lasts for only q periods. As in autoregressive ARIMA (p,0,0) processes, higher-order ARIMA(0,0,*q*) processes exist but q is rarely greater than 2, except for seasonal models.

Consider an ARIMA(0,0,2) process.

$$y_t = e_t - \theta_1 e_{t-1} - \theta_2 e_{t-2} + e_t$$

The value of y_t equals the sum of e_t, the current shock, and a fraction of the two previous shocks, e_{t-1} and e_{t-2}. Random shocks persist for two observations and then leave the process.

Consider the following expansion, which illustrates that an ARIMA(0,0,1) model is the equivalent of an infinite-order ARIMA(∞,0,0) model.

Given

$$y_t = e_t - \theta_1 e_{t-1} \tag{7-32}$$

then

$$e_t = y_t + \theta_1 e_{t-1}$$

Consequently

$$e_{t-1} = y_{t-1} + \theta_1 e_{t-2} \tag{7-33}$$

Substituting Equation 7–33 into 7–32,

$$y_t = e_t - \theta_1(y_{t-1} + \theta_1 e_{t-2})$$

Continuing this same substitution for e_{t-2} and e_{t-3} yields

$$y_t = e_t - \theta_1[y_{t-1} + \theta_1(y_{t-2} + \theta_1 e_{t-3})]$$
$$= e_t - \theta_1\{y_{t-1} + \theta_1[y_{t-2} + \theta_1(y_{t-3} + \theta_1 e_{t-4})]\}$$
$$= e_t - \theta_1 y_{t-1} - \theta_1^2 y_{t-2} - \theta_1^3 y_{t-3} - \theta_1^3 e_{t-4} \tag{7-34}$$

This expansion yields

$$y_t = e_t + \Sigma - \theta_1^i y_{t-i} \qquad \text{for } i = 1 \text{ to } n \tag{7-35}$$

This shows that an ARIMA(0,0,1) process is an exponentially weighted moving average of all past actual y_ts, where powers of θ_1 provide the weights.

Given that θ_1^i weights only past y_{t-i}, its magnitude is important. If the absolute θ_1 is greater than 1, then for high i values, y_{t-i} has greater weight in determining y_t than more recent values of y_{t-i} with low i values. Because it is important to model stationarity explicitly, θ_1 should be constrained. This constraint is called a **bound of invertibility,** which performs the same function as the bound of stationarity for autoregressive models; that is, the bound assures that the model is stationary. For an ARIMA(0,0,1) model, the bound of invertibility is

$$-1 < \theta_1 < +1$$

When absolute θ_1 is less than 1, the ARIMA(0,0,1) model is a parsimonious representation of a stationary ARIMA(p,0,0) process, where p is a very large number. If absolute θ_1 is greater than 1, then the resulting ARIMA(0,0,1) model denotes that the underlying process is nonstationary and should be transformed to stationarity before q is determined. (Alternatively, a nonstationary coefficient may result from an incorrectly transformed series due either to overdifferencing or some other inappropriate transformation.)

To understand invertibility better, let us use Equation 7–34 with a $-\theta_1$ of 1.2. This yields a nonstationary process:

$$y_t = e_t + 1.2y_{t-1} + 1.44y_{t-2} + 1.728y_{t-3} + \cdots + 1.2^i y_{t-i}$$

Thus, the weights for y_{t-i} become greater as i increases (i.e., goes back in time).

General Moving Average Process: ARIMA(0,0,q)

The general ARIMA(0,0,q) process is written as

$$y_t = (1 - \theta_1 B - \theta_2 B^2 - \cdots - \theta_{q-1} B^{q-1} - \theta_q B^q)e_t$$

As mentioned, most moving average processes have q values of less than 3. If higher values of q are found, these frequently represent misspecifications of the proper model; thus it's possible that an ARIMA(1,0,0) process exists, not an ARIMA(0,0,q). This relationship is illustrated in Equation 7–30; in other words, an ARIMA(0,0,q) model with high q values can sometimes be well-represented by an ARIMA(p,0,0) model, with p values of 1 or 2.

AR(2), MA(2), ARMA(1,1), and Seasonal Processes

While they are not as common as first-order models, AR(2), MA(2), and mixed ARMA (1,1) processes, and their ACFs and PACFs should be studied.

AR(2) Processes.   AR(2) processes can be identified by exponential or sinusoidal exponential declines in the ACF(k) and two significant PACFs at lags 1 and 2. Figure 7–16 illustrates four of the many possible theoretical ACFs and PACFs of AR(2) processes. The patterns of Figure 7–16 are quite distinct; unfortunately, the ACFs and PACFs for some time series may not be so clear. Because of their similarities, the patterns of AR(2) , MA(2), and ARMA(1,1) models may be difficult to discern when there are unclear ACF and PACF patterns. Fortunately, the correct models can be confirmed or denied during the estimation and diagnosis processes, during which model improvement and statistically significant coefficients can be confirmed.

MA(2) Processes.   In an MA(2) process, there are two significant ACFs at lags 1 and 2 and an exponential or sinusoidal exponential decline in the PACFs. Figure 7–17 illustrates four of the many possible theoretical ACFs and PACFs of MA(2) processes. Note the mirror patterns of AR(2) and MA(2) processes shown in Figures 7–16 and 7–17, where the ACFs for an MA(2) look like PACFs for an AR(2) and vice versa. These are similar to the mirror images of first-order models seen in Figure 7–1. As before, the correct models can be confirmed or denied during the estimation and diagnostic steps process.

ARMA(1,1) Processes.   Often an ARMA(1,1) process contains an AR pattern in the ACFs and an MA pattern in the PACFs. Figure 7–18 illustrates four of the many possible theoretical ACFs and PACFs of ARMA(1,1) processes. In other words, the ACF patterns of an AR(1) model and the PACF patterns of MA(1) model, as shown in Figure 7–1, apply to ARMA(1,1) models, commonly called mixed models. However, when fitting these models, be careful to avoid redundant coefficients, a topic discussed after presenting seasonal ARIMA models. As before, the correct models can be confirmed or denied during the estimation and diagnostic steps.

Seasonal Processes.   In seasonal processes, the ACF and PACF patterns of low-order, non-seasonal models occur only at the seasonal lags. This is most easily seen by comparing the patterns of Figure 7–1 with those of Figure 7–19. Figure 7–19 illustrates five of the many possible theoretical ACFs and PACFs of seasonal processes for quarterly data.

The similarities between seasonal models and low-order models is a general phenomenon. For example, seasonal second-order models follow the patterns of Figures 7–16 and 7–17 except these patterns occur at seasonal lags. However, when both low-order and seasonal processes exist in the same time series, these patterns may be difficult to separate and are most easily identified by using methodical and iterative identification, estimation, and diagnostic processes. These processes are studied in detail in the next chapter.

Stationarity and Invertibility.   When building nonseasonal and seasonal ARIMA models, it is important to ensure that the bounds of stationarity and invertibility are

FIGURE 7–16

Some theoretical ACF(k) and PACF(k) for AR(2) processes

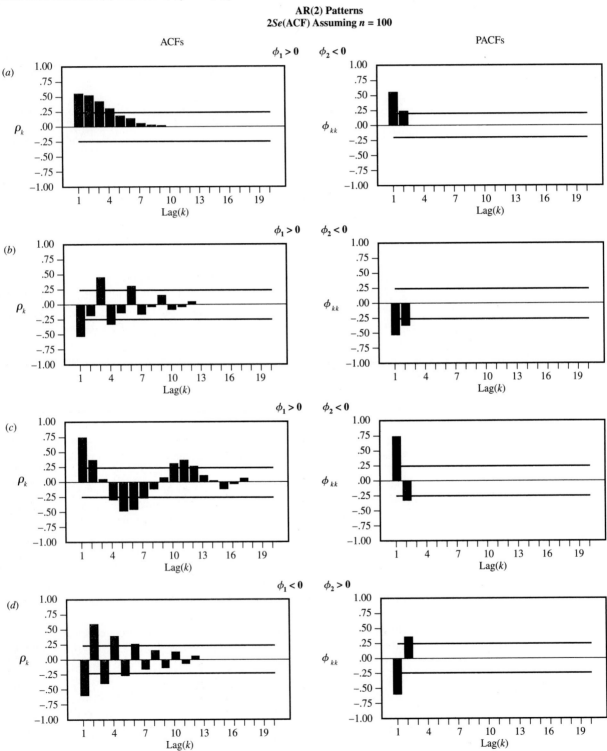

AR(2) Patterns
2Se(ACF) Assuming n = 100

FIGURE 7–17

Some theoretical ACF(k) and PACF(k) for MA(2) processes

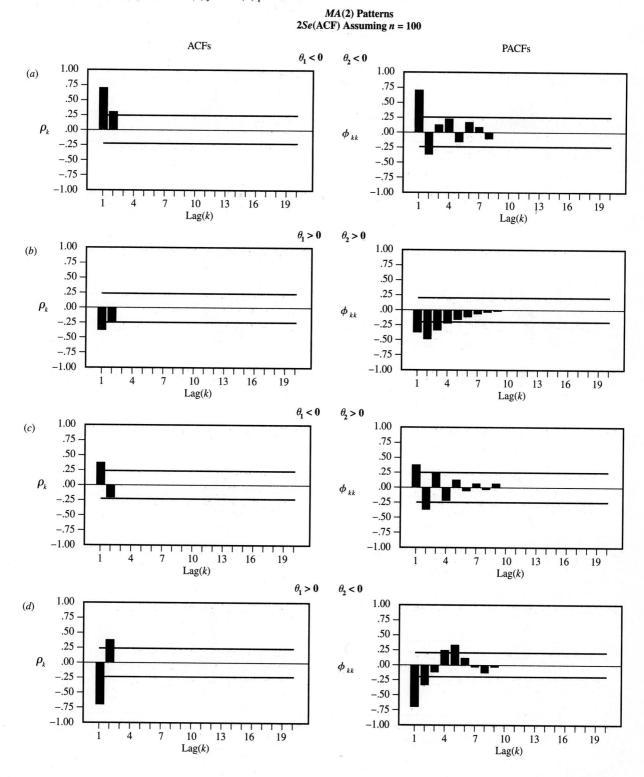

MA(2) Patterns
$2Se$(ACF) Assuming $n = 100$

307

FIGURE 7–18

Some theoretical ACF(k) and PACF(k) for ARMA(1,1) processes

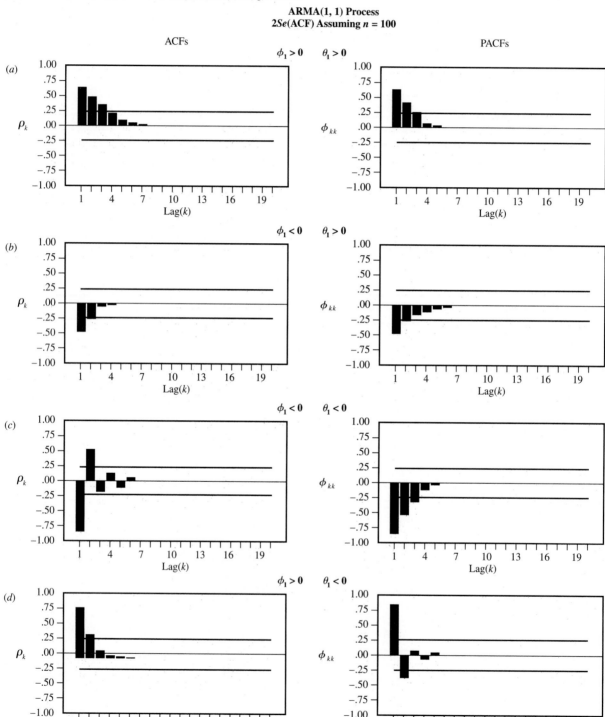

ARMA(1, 1) Process
2Se(ACF) Assuming n = 100

FIGURE 7–19

Some theoretical ACF(k) and PACF(k) for seasonal processes

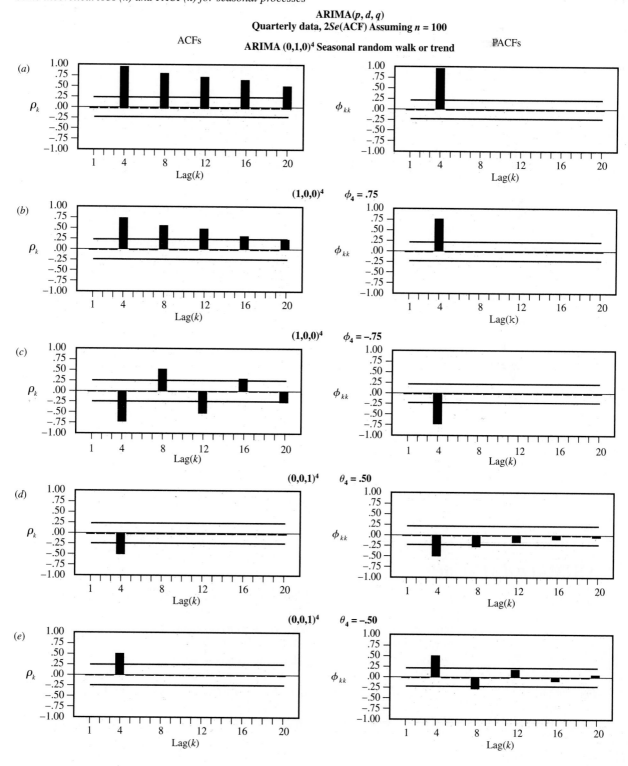

not exceeded. While not developed here, the bounds of stationarity and invertibility for ARIMA(2,0,0) and ARIMA(0,0,2) processes, respectively, are:

- Bounds of stationarity for an ARIMA(2,0,0) process:

$$-1 < \phi_2 < +1 \qquad (7\text{--}36)$$

$$\phi_1 + \phi_2 < +1$$

$$\phi_2 - \phi_1 < +1$$

- Bounds of invertibility for an ARIMA(0,0,2) process:

$$-1 < \theta_2 < +1 \qquad (7\text{--}37)$$

$$\theta_1 + \theta_2 < +1$$

$$\theta_2 - \theta_1 < +1$$

To confirm that a second-order model has achieved stationarity or invertibility, simply substitute the estimated coefficients into the appropriate formulas. All three conditions of these formulas must be true to achieve invertibility or stationarity.

For seasonal models, invertibility and stationarity are verified using the low-order model formulas, except the equivalent seasonal coefficient is substituted into either Equation 7–36 or 7–37. For example, a seasonal AR model achieves stationarity when

$$-1 < \phi_s < +1 \qquad (7\text{--}38)$$

where s is the length of the seasonal cycle, such as 4 for quarterly and 12 for monthly. Similarly, a seasonal MA(2) model achieves invertibility when all of the following relationships are true.

$$-1 < \theta_s < +1 \qquad (7\text{--}39)$$

$$\theta_s + \theta_{2s} < +1$$

$$\theta_{2s} - \theta_s < +1$$

Appendix 7–E provides summary formulas that are useful in checking the stationarity and invertibility of several ARIMA processes.

ARIMA(p,d,q) Models

The power of ARIMA model building is most evident when several components are combined as models. Frequently, after achieving stationarity, a time series contains both AR and MA components, which can be identified and used for forecasting. However, there can be complexities when both the AR and MA components are of the same order. Such models are referred to as mixed models.

Parameter Redundancy: Mixed Models

We need to be cautious when equal orders of p and q are in a model (e.g., ARIMA(1,d,1). This might be, but is not necessarily, an example of model misspecification because there are too many parameters in the model. Consider a situation in which y_t is a white noise series after μ is subtracted:

$$Y_t - \mu = y_t = e_t$$

If this is mistakenly modeled as an ARIMA(1,0,1) process, then

$$y_t - \phi_1 y_{t-1} = e_t - \theta_1 e_{t-1}$$

In backshift notation,

$$(1 - \phi_1 B)y_t = (1 - \theta_1 B)e_t \qquad (7-36)$$

If ϕ_1 and θ_1 are fit to this series, they may be mistakenly reported as statistically different than zero, even when they are redundant. When the coefficients in relationships such as Equation 7–36 are nearly equal to each other, and when dropping both of them does not adversely affect the RSE [or sum of squared errors (SSE)], then they are redundant coefficients, and it is likely that neither is necessary. This is illustrated in Figure 7–20, where the minimum SSE values of ϕ_1 and θ_1 are highly correlated, as shown by the 45-degree line on the xy plane and the trough SSE surface, which yields many equal minimum SSEs. The SSE trough denotes that an infinite number of combinations of ϕ_1 and θ_1 yield a minimum SSE, instead of a single combination.

As an example, assume that the coefficients are $\phi_1 = .4$ and $\theta_1 = .4$ and are mistakenly fitted. Consequently, this redundancy is clear in the following equation:

$$(1 - \phi_1 B)y_t = (1 - \theta_1 B)e_t$$

Knowing that $y_t = e_t$, we have

$$(1 - .4B) = (1 - .4B)$$

where the equal values in parentheses cancel, leaving the correct model

$$y_t = e_t$$

Remembering that

$$y_t = Y_t - \mu$$

we therefore have an ARIMA(0,0,0) model

$$Y_t = \mu + e_t$$

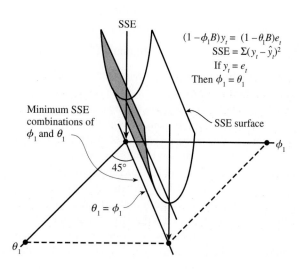

FIGURE 7–20

Redundant, highly correlated coefficients

A Needle in a Haystack

Patterns sometimes defy identification, even when theory dictates that a pattern should be there. When all methodical, legitimate attempts have been made to adjust the outliers, and yet no patterns have been found, we are forced to accept the patternless random model. What makes random ARIMA(0,0,0) models so hard to accept is the frequency with which they occur because of the outliers. Are outliers the problem, or is the series a patternless ARIMA(0,0,0) model? Sometimes the search for patterns progresses much like the proverbial search for a needle in a haystack. If there is no needle (i.e., pattern), we waste considerable time and effort in the search; however, we search until all alternatives have been eliminated and we are left with a patternless (0,0,0) model.

These redundant coefficients (ϕ_1 and θ_1) make the model, and our understanding of the process, incorrect, because they denote that the process is more complex than it actually is. Fortunately, redundant parameters can be identified relatively easily using a correlation matrix of model coefficients. This matrix is reported by almost all ARIMA estimation software. In the given case, for example, we have

Correlation matrix of coefficients	ϕ_1
θ_1	.95

Finally, note that when coefficient estimates are highly correlated, and when dropping one or both of these results in a significant increase in the RSE or a reduction in $\bar{R}^2$, it may not be advisable to drop either or both. In such situations, the coefficients may be highly correlated but not redundant. The partial F-test of Chapter 10 and the BIC of Chapter 17 can be used to accept or reject coefficients.

Parameter Estimates The coefficients estimated by ARIMA programs are selected using nonlinear search algorithms similar to, but more advanced than those illustrated in the exponential smoothing tables in Chapters 4 and 6. Nonlinear least squares methods are used to find the combination of coefficients that minimize the sum of squared residuals. For example, ϕ_i and θ_i are selected so as to produce

$$\text{Minimum } \Sigma(Y_t - \hat{Y}_t)^2$$

The most common nonlinear least squares methods require multiple iterations in search of the best coefficients (i.e., different ϕs and θs). At times, these search methods might not converge on least squares estimates. In such cases, the program will print a statement saying, "unable to converge," or "maximum iterations with no convergence." When this occurs, the model should be inspected, simplified, or altered in some way. Also, the maximum number of possible iterations can be increased and the model reestimated. Increasing the maximum number of iterations may solve the problem; on the other hand, it will not when the model is wrong.

When a large number of iterations are necessary, most commonly there is a problem with the selected model. Frequently, the model is being over-specified; that is, excessive or incorrect coefficients are being used in the model. If redundant coefficients are in the model, there may not be a single optimal combination of coefficient values.

Instead, there may be an infinite number of highly correlated combinations of, say, ϕ_1 and θ_1, that yield the same minimum sums of squares. As previously mentioned, the algorithm denotes this problem by highlighting the program's inability to converge on a unique solution for ϕ_1 and θ_1. In such cases, the model should be carefully evaluated to determine why different coefficients are included in the model, and an alternative modeling approach should be tried. Finally, remembering the principle of parsimony, simpler models almost always outperform more complex models in actual out-of-sample forecasts. Also remember that these models are built iteratively, which means you should avoid putting in more than one coefficient at a time, unless you are confident of the model.

Additional ARIMA Notation

Not all realistic time series are as simple as those used in our examples. Frequently, there are several different types of transformations and seasonal processes generating the time series. By convention, these processes are designated by the notation p, d, q, P, D, Q, C, T, s, and S as shown here:

$$(AR\ I\ MA)\ C,\ T\ (AR\ I\ MA)^s\ (AR\ I\ MA)^S \qquad (7\text{--}39)$$
$$\ \ \ (p\ \ d\ \ q)\ \ \ C\ T\ \ (P\ \ D\ \ Q)\ \ \ \ (P\ \ D\ \ Q)$$

where p, d, and q are as defined previously

P = seasonal level of autoregressions
D = seasonal level of differences
Q = seasonal level of moving averages
s = first period of seasonality
S = second period of seasonality
C = 1 for differenced models with nonzero θ_0, otherwise 0
T = power transformations of Y_t, 0 = none, 1 = logs, # = power, e.g., $T = .5$ for square roots

The designations of C and T are conventions of this book; the others are conventional ARIMA notations as originally proposed by Box and Jenkins.

We can see that the simple ARIMA components can be combined to yield a very large number of models. In fact, a very crude approximation of the combinations of $p, d, q, C, T, P, D, Q, s$, and S is $3 \cdot 3 \cdot 3 \cdot 2 \cdot 2 \cdot 3 \cdot 3 \cdot 3 \cdot 3 \cdot 3$ or 78,732 combinations, because each individual component commonly has three different values from 0 to 2. However, most models have only one to three components.

Consider the following examples of ARIMA notation:

A simple autoregressive series AR(1)	ARIMA(1,0,0)
A simple moving average series MA(1)	ARIMA(0,0,1)
A simple random walk series I(1)	ARIMA(0,1,0)
A simple trending series I(1)1	ARIMA(0,1,0)1
A seasonal monthly model with trend	ARIMA(0,1,0)^{12}1
A quarterly model with seasonal autoregression	ARIMA(1,0,0)^4
A monthly model with seasonal trend and nonseasonal autoregression	ARIMA(1,0,0)1(0,1,0)^{12}
A daily model with seasonality and nonseasonal autoregression	ARIMA(1,0,0)1(0,1,0)^7(0,1,1)^{364}

Summary

This chapter has presented the basics of ARIMA model building as developed by Box and Jenkins. This approach may appear strange until several successful applications are completed. Most forecasters are very familiar with the processes of regression (AR), moving averages (MA), and differences (I). However, initially some readers may have problems identifying which combinations of ARIMA components are the most effective in achieving low residual standard errors and white noise residuals. Unlike regression analysis or exponential smoothing, ARIMA modeling is not as easy as pulling a model "off the shelf". If done properly, ARIMA model building is a process of building a custom model for a time series. When building a model, we strive for a parsimonious one with a low RSE, low BIC, and white noise.

This is the first of five ARIMA model-building chapters in this book. The appendixes of this and the other ARIMA chapters, 8, 9, 12, and 13 extend this powerful methodology into several interesting applications.

Key Terms

ARIMA(0,0,1)

ARIMA(0,1,0)

ARIMA(1,0,0)

ARIMA(p,d,q)

ARMA(p,q) mixed models

autocorrelation (ACF)

AutoRegressive Integrated Moving Average

backshift operator

bounds of invertibility

bounds of stationarity

Box–Ljung, Q-statistic

correlated coefficients ρ_k

deterministic trend

level and variance nonstationarity

normally and independent distributed (NID)

$(1 - B^s)Y_t = Y_t - Y_{t-s}$

(p, d, q) C, T $(P, D, Q)^s$ $(P, D, Q)^S$

partial autocorrelation (PACF)

ϕ_1 and θ_1

process (population) vs. realization (sample)

redundant coefficients

ρ_k theoretical autocorrelation

stochastic process

stochastic trend

summation and integration

white noise residuals

Key Formulas

$$Y_t = \text{Pattern} + e_t \tag{7-1}$$

ARIMA(p, d, q)

$$Y_t = f[Y_{t-k}, e_{t-k}] + e_t \qquad \text{for } k > 0 \tag{7-2}$$

ARIMA(1,0,0)

$$Y_t = \theta_0 + \phi_1 Y_{t-1} + e_t \tag{7-3}$$

$$Y_t = 30 + .3Y_{t-1} + e_t \tag{7-4}$$

Bounds of stationarity

$$|\phi_1| < 1 \tag{7-5}$$

ARIMA(0,0,1)

$$Y_t - \mu = -\theta_1 e_{t-1} + e_t \tag{7-6}$$

$$Y_t = 20 + .3e_{t-1} + e_t \tag{7-7}$$

Bounds of invertibility

$$|\theta_1| < 1 \tag{7-8}$$

ARIMA(0,1,0)

$$\hat{Y}_t = Y_{t-1} \tag{7-9}$$

$$Y_t = Y_{t-1} + e_t \tag{7-10}$$

ARIMA(0,1,0)1

$$\hat{Y}_t = Y_{t-1} + \theta_0 \tag{7-11}$$

$$Y_t = Y_{t-1} + \theta_0 + e_t \tag{7-11a}$$

Trend *t*-test

$$t = \frac{\theta_0}{S_{\text{diff}}/\sqrt{n-d}} = \frac{7.72}{1.333/\sqrt{6-1}} = 12.95$$

m-period forecasts

$$\hat{Y}_{t+m} = Y_t + m\theta_0 = Y_t + m7.72 \tag{7-12}$$

ARIMA(0,0,1)

$$\rho_1 = \frac{-\theta_1}{1 + \theta_1^2} \tag{7-13}$$

White noise *Q*-test

$$Q = n(n+2)\Sigma[1/(n-i))\text{ACF}(i)^2] \qquad \text{from } i = 1 \text{ to } k \tag{7-14}$$

If $Q >$ Chi-square-table, the series is significantly different than white noise.

ARIMA(0,0,0)

$$Y_t = \mu + e_t \tag{7-15}$$

$$e_t \sim \text{NID}(0, \sigma_e^2) \tag{7-16}$$

ARIMA(1,0,0)

$$Y_t = \theta_0 + {}_{\phi 1}Y_{t-1} + e_t \tag{7-19}$$

$$\theta_0 = (1 - \phi_1)\mu$$

$$Y_t = 49.36 + .752Y_{t-1} + e_t \tag{7-20}$$

ARIMA(0,1,1)

$$z_t = e_t - \theta_1 e_{t-1} \tag{7-22}$$

$$z_t = Y_t - Y_{t-1} = e_t - \theta_1 e_{t-1} \tag{7-23}$$

Variance nonstationarity

$$\sigma_Y^2 = \propto(Y_t)$$

$$e_t^2 = Ke_{t-1}^2 \tag{7-24}$$

$$Y_t = KY_{t-1} \tag{7-24a}$$

$$\ln(Y_t) = \ln(Y_{t-1}) + \ln(K)$$

$$Y_t/Y_{t-1} = K$$

ARIMA(0,1,1)1,1

$$\ln(Y_t) - \ln(Y_{t-1}) = \theta_0 + e_t - \theta_1 e_{t-1}$$

USIND.DAT

$$\widehat{\ln(Y_t)} = \ln(Y_{t-1}) + 0.0056 + 0.3236e_{t-1}$$

Original series

$$\hat{Y}_t = \mathbf{e}^{\widehat{\ln(y_t)}}$$

$$\text{Growth} = \mathbf{e}^{\theta_0} - 1 = 1.00562 - 1 = 0.00562$$

Backshift operator

$$BY_t = Y_{t-1} \qquad\qquad BY_{t-1} = Y_{t-2}$$
$$BY_{t-k} = Y_{t-k-1} \qquad\qquad B^s Y_t = Y_{t-s}$$
$$B^{12}Y_t = Y_{t-12} \qquad\qquad B^s B^d Y_t = B^{s+d}Y_t = Y_{t-s-d}$$
$$(1 - B)Y_t = Y_t - Y_{t-1} \qquad (1 - B^4)Y_t = Y_t - Y_{t-4}$$
$$(1 - B)^4 Y_t = (1 - 4B + 6B^2 - 4B^3 + B^4)Y_t$$

ARIMA(0,1,0)

$$Y_t = Y_o + e_1 + e_2 + \cdots + e_{t-1} + e_t \tag{7-26}$$

ARIMA(1,0,0)

$$(1 - \phi_1 B)y_t = e_t \tag{7-27}$$

ARIMA(p,0,0)

$$y_t = \phi_1 y_{t-1} + \phi_2 y_{t-2} + \cdots + \phi_p y_{t-p} + e_t \tag{7-28}$$

ARIMA(1,0,0) equivalent to ARIMA(0,0,∞)

$$y_t = \Sigma \phi_1^i e_{t-i} \qquad\qquad \text{for } i = 1 \text{ to } i \tag{7-30}$$

ARIMA(0,0,1) equivalent to ARIMA(∞,0,0)

$$y_t = e_t + \Sigma - \theta_1^i y_{t-i} \qquad\qquad \text{for } i = 1 \text{ to } n \tag{7-35}$$

ARIMA(1,1) in backshift

$$(1 - \phi_1 B)y_t = (1 - \phi_1 B)e_t$$

Coefficient selection criteria

$$\text{Min(SSE)} = \text{Min}\Sigma (Y_t - \hat{Y}_t)^2$$

General ARIMA notation

$$(\text{AR I MA}) \; \text{C, T} \; (\text{AR I MA})^s \; (\text{AR I MA})^S \tag{7-39}$$
$$\begin{array}{ccccccccccc} | & | & | & | & | & | & | & | & | & | & | \\ (p & d & q) & C, & T & (P & D & Q) & (P & D & Q) \end{array}$$

Review Problems Using Your Software

R7–1 Repeat the analysis of Table 7–3 for the time series STOCKA.DAT. Interpret your results. Generate the equivalents of Tables 7–3, 7–4, and 7–5.

R7–2 Repeat the analysis of Tables 7–6 through 7–7 for the time series DAIRY.DAT. Interpret your results and generate the equivalents of Figures 7–4 and 7–5.

R7–3 Repeat the analysis of Tables 7–8 through 7–12 for the time series FAD.DAT. Interpret your results and generate the equivalents of Figures 7–6 through 7–8.

R7–4 Generate Figures 7–9 to 7–10 for MEGAWATT.DAT.

R7–5 Generate Figures 7–11 and 7–12 for the time series USIND.DAT and interpret the figures.

R7–6 Generate Figures 7–13 to 7–15 for the time series USIND.DAT and interpret the figures.

R7–7 Generate Table 7–13 for the time series USIND.DAT. Comment about each of the rows in the table.

R7–8 Generate Tables 7–14 and 7–15 for the time series USIND.DAT and interpret the results of the tables.

R7–9 Generate Table 7–16 for the time series USIND.DAT.

Problems

7–1 Define and explain the concepts of process and realization and their relationship to outlier adjustments and ARIMA model building.

7–2 Explain the meanings of level and variance nonstationarity and describe how they are achieved.

7–3 Sketch the patterns of the ACFs and PACFs for nonseasonal I(1), AR(1), AR(2), MA(1), and MA(2) models.

7–4 Give a common English definition of white noise.

7–5 Give a statistical definition of white noise.

7–6 Express the following in backshift notation:

    a. Y_{t-1} *b.* Y_{t-5}

    c. Y_{t-12} *d.* $Y_t - 2Y_{t-1} + Y_{t-2}$

    e. $Y_t - Y_{t-12}$ *f.* $Y_t - Y_{t-1} - Y_{t-12} + Y_{t-13}$

7–7 Sketch the patterns in the ACFs and PACFs for a monthly seasonal $I(1)^{12}$, $AR(1)^{12}$, $AR(2)^{12}$, and $MA(2)^{12}$.

7–8 Explain the meanings of fitted error, forecast error, and out-of-sample error.

7–9 Explain the attributes of a good forecasting model.

7–10 Give a common English definition of the concept of partial autocorrelation.

7–11 Give a statistical definition of the theoretical partial autocorrelation for an AR(2) process.

7–12 If an integrated ARIMA(0,1,0) model is used on the following data, what is the forecast for period $t = 6$?

t	1	2	3	4	5	6
Y_t	10	12	13	15	17	?

7–13 If an integrated ARIMA(0,1,0)1 model is used on the following data, what is the forecast for period $t = 6$?

t	1	2	3	4	5	6
Y_t	10	12	13	15	17	?

7–14 If an autoregressive ARIMA(1,0,0) model is used on the following data, what is the forecast for period $t = 6$, assuming $\theta_0 = 4$ and $\phi_1 = .8$?

t	1	2	3	4	5	6
Y_t	10	12	13	15	17	?

7–15 Fit an ARIMA(1,0,0) model to the following data, assuming $\theta_0 = 4$ and $\phi_1 = .8$. How well does this model fit? What is the forecast for period 6?

t	1	2	3	4	5	6
Y_t	17	15	13	12	10	?

7–16 Fit an ARIMA(0,1,0)1 model to the following data. How well does this model fit? What is the forecast for period 6?

t	1	2	3	4	5	6
Y_t	17	15	13	12	10	?

7–17 Fit an ARIMA(0,0,1) model to the following data, assuming $\mu = 10$ and $-\theta_1 = .8$. How well does this model fit?

t	1	2	3	4	5	6
Y_t	10	12	13	15	17	?

7–18 What is the notation for a forecast of period 100 made at the end of period 90?

7–19 Using Example 7–4, explain the differences between n-period ahead forecasts and one-period ahead forecasts.

7–20 Explain the cause of the bias in the model of Example 7–4.

7–21 Using your software, analyze IBM stock prices (IBMMN.DAT), as was done in this chapter for USIND.DAT.
   a. Is this series trending or drifting?
   b. Confirm your results with appropriate statistics.
   c. Write this model using backshift notation.

7–22 Fit an appropriate ARIMA(0,d,0) to the following data from PRB7–22.DAT.
   a Does this series trend or drift?
   b. Confirm your results with appropriate statistics.
   c. Write this model using backshift notation.
   d. Forecast Y_t from $t = 12$ through $t = 15$.

t	1	2	3	4	5	6	7	8	9	10	11
Y_t	10	12	13	15	17	19	21	22	24	27	28

7–23 Fit an appropriate ARIMA(0,d,0) to the following data from PRB7–23.DAT.
   a. Does this series trend or drift?
   b. Confirm your results with appropriate statistics.
   c. Write this model using backshift notation.
   d. Forecast Y_t from $t = 12$ through $t = 15$.

t	1	2	3	4	5	6	7	8	9	10	11
Y_t	10	12	11	10	9	11	13	14	15	13	12

7–24 Fit an appropriate ARIMA(0,d,0) to the following data from PRB7–24.DAT.
   a. Does this series trend or drift?
   b. Confirm your results with appropriate statistics.
   c. Write this model using backshift notation.
   d. Forecast Y_t from $t = 12$ through $t = 15$.
   e. If a transformation is used to forecast Y_t from $t = 12$ through $t = 15$, show the forecasts in the original metric scale.

t	1	2	3	4	5	6	7	8	9	10	11
Y_t	10	16	23	36	53	81	122	181	274	409	615

7–25 Analyze a Japanese index of stock prices using JAPAN.DAT.
   a. Is this series trending or drifting?
   b. Confirm your results with appropriate statistics.
   c. Write this model using backshift notation.
   d. If a transformation is used to forecast Y_t from $t = 12$ through $t = 15$, show the forecasts in the original metric scale.

7–26 Generate logarithmic transformations for JAPAN.DAT.
   a. Computer variances for the first and second half of this time series before and after logarithmic transformations.
   b. Are there differences between these variances?
   c. Explain these differences.

7–27 Confirm the manner in which your software presents the results of ARIMA(1,0,0) and ARIMA(0,0,1) models by fitting models to the following data sets of 100 observations:
  a. Fit a (1,0,0) model to AR1P.DAT.
  b. Fit a (0,0,1) model to MA1N.DAT.

7–28 If $\phi_1 = .5$ and $\theta_0 = 100$ in an ARIMA(1,0,0) model, write the model in terms of y_t and Y_t, showing the value of the constant.

7–29 The following series have been created to test your knowledge of ARIMA model-building methods. Each series consists of observations that have been coded to force you to identify the best ARIMA model. They are each in their own files, with an extension of .DAT (e.g., SERIESAA.DAT). Using your own computer software package, identify and estimate what you believe to be the best ARIMA model for each. (Refer to Appendix 7–F for the correct solution of each * example. Only your instructor will know the answer to those series without the asterisk.)

SERIESAA	SERIESAK
SERIESAB *	SERIESAL *
SERIESAC	SERIESAM
SERIESAD *	SERIESAN *
SERIESAE	SERIESAO
SERIESAF *	SERIESAP *
SERIESAG	SERIESAQ
SERIESAH *	SERIESAR *
SERIESAI	SERIESAS
SERIESAJ *	SERIESAT *

7–30 Heart surgeries, including bypass and angioplasty, have grown from 196,000 in 1980 to 839,000 in 1991[a]. Using the following data (HEART.DAT), fit an ARIMA model (surgeries are shown in 1000's). Comment on the goodness of fit, using whatever statistics you deem appropriate. Then, forecast 1992 and 1995 using your model.

Year	1980	1981	1982	1983	1984	1985	1986	1987	1988	1989	1990	1991
Surgeries	196	217	243	275	314	379	490	589	674	719	781	839

7–31 Show that an IMA(1,1) model is the equivalent of a single exponential smoothing model.

7–32 The time series BIRTHMAR.DAT includes the quarterly marriages in the United States. Complete the common minicase forecasting assignment.

7–33 The time series RETAIL.DAT is the monthly retail sales in the United States. Complete the common minicase forecasting assignment.

7–34 The time series SUPEROIL.DAT is the sales of the Superoil Company, in thousands of barrels, during the last 108 months. Complete the common minicase forecasting assignment.

Minicases: Common Assignment for Minicases

For a selected minicase, complete the following analysis. Generate ACFs and PACFs and tentatively identify an ARIMA model. Take appropriate differences and transformations to achieve a stationary series. Complete a table, such as Table 7–13, as you achieve stationarity.

Minicase 7–1 Kansas Turnpike, Daily Data
(TURNPIKD.DAT)

Minicase 7–2 Domestic Air Passengers by Quarter
(PASSAIR.DAT)

---

[a] Source: National Hospital Discharge Survey, 1991.

Minicase 7–3 Hospital Census by Month
(CENSUSM.DAT)

Minicase 7–4 Henry Machler's Hideaway Orchids
(MACHLERD.DAT)

Minicase 7–5 Your Forecasting Project

Minicase 7–6 Midwestern Building Materials
(LUMBER.DAT)

Minicase 7–7 International Airline Passengers
(AIRLINE.DAT)

Minicase 7–8 Automobile Sales (AUTO.DAT)

Minicase 7–9 Consumption of Distilled Spirits
(SPIRITS.DAT)

Minicase 7–10 Discount Consumer Electronics
(ELECT.DAT)

References

Abraham B.; and J. Ledolter. *Statistical Methods for Forecasting.* New York: Wiley, 1983.

Ansley, C.F.; and P. Newbold. "Finite sample properties of estimators for autoregressive-moving average models." *Journal of Econometrics* 13, (1980), pp. 159–183.

Bewley, R. "AUTOBOX: A review." *Journal of Applied Econometrics* 3, (1988), pp. 240–244.

Box, G.E.P.; G.M. Jenkins; G.C. Reinsel. *Time Series Analysis, Forecasting and Control.* 3rd ed. Englewood Cliffs, NJ: Prentice-Hall, 1994.

Box, G.E.P.; and D.A. Pierce. "Distribution of residual autocorrelations in autoregressive integrated moving average time series models." *Journal of the American Statistical Association* 65, (1970), pp. 1509–1526.

Davies, N.; and P. Newbold. "Forecasting with misspecified models." *Applied Statistics* 29, (1980), pp. 87–92.

Dickey, D.A.; W.R. Bell; and R.B. Miller. "Unit roots in time series models: tests and implications." *The American Statistician* 40, (1986), pp. 12–26.

Granger, C.W.J.; and M. Morris. "Time series modeling an interpretation." *Journal of the Royal Statistical Society* A, no. 139, (1976), pp. 246–257.

Granger, C.W.J.; and P. Newbold. *Forecasting Economic Time Series.* 2nd ed. Orlando, Fl.: Academic Press, 1986.

Hill, G.; and R. Fildes. "The accuracy of extrapolation methods: and automatic Box–Jenkins package sift." *Journal of Forecasting* 3, (1984), pp. 319–323.

Jenkins, G.M. *Practical Experiences with Modeling and Forecasting Time Series.* Lancaster, PA: GJP Publications, 1979.

Jenkins, G.M. "Some practical aspects of forecasting in organizations." *Journal of Forecasting* 1, (1982), pp. 3–21.

Jenkins, G.M.; and G. McLeod. *Case Studies in Time Series Analysis.* Lancaster, PA: GJP Publications, 1982.

Ledolter, J.; and B. Abraham. "Parsimony and its importance in time series forecasting." *Technometrics* 23, (1981), pp. 411–414.

Libert, G. "The M-competition with a fully automatic Box–Jenkins procedure." *Journal of Forecasting* 3, (1984), pp. 325–328.

Ljung, G.M.; and G.E.P. Box. "On a measure of lack of fit in time series models." *Biometrika* 65, (1978), pp. 297–303.

Nelson, C.R. *Applied Time Series Analysis for Managerial Forecasting.* San Francisco, CA: Holden Day, 1973.

Newbold, P. "ARIMA model building and the time series analysis approach to forecasting." *Journal of Forecasting* 2, (1983), pp. 23–35.

Pankratz, A. *Forecasting with Univariate Box–Jenkins Models: Concepts and Cases.* New York: Wiley, 1983.

Texter, P.A.; and J.K. Ord. "Forecasting using automatic identification procedures: A comparative analysis." *International Journal of Forecasting* 5, (1989), pp. 209–215.

Vandaele, W. *Applied Time Series and Box–Jenkins Models.* Orlando, Fl.: Academic Press, 1983.

APPENDIX 7–A

USEFUL STATISTICAL DEFINITIONS USED IN DERIVATIONS

$$y_t = Y_t - \bar{Y}_t \qquad (\text{Remember } \bar{y}_t = 0.0)$$

$$\bar{Y}_t = \frac{\Sigma Y_t}{n} = E(Y_t)$$

$$\text{VAR}(Y_t) = \frac{\Sigma y_t^2}{n-1} = E(Y_t^2) = \text{MSD}$$

(MSD = Mean of the Squared Deviations).

$$S(Y_t) = \sqrt{\frac{\Sigma y_t^2}{n-1}} = \sqrt{EY_t^2}$$

$$\text{COV}(Y_t Y_{t-k}) = \frac{\Sigma y_t y_{t-k}}{n-k-1}$$

$$\text{COR}(Y_t Y_{t-k}) = \frac{\text{COV}(Y_t Y_{t-k})}{S(Y_t)S(Y_{t-k})}$$

$$\text{ACF}(k) = \frac{E(Y_t Y_{t-k})}{E(Y_t^2)} = \frac{\Sigma y_t y_{t-K}}{\Sigma y_t^2}$$

Because of Stationarity:

$$EY_t = EY_{t-k} \qquad \text{(i.e., constant mean)}$$
$$EY_t^2 = EY_{t-k}^2 \qquad \text{(i.e., constant variance)}$$

White noise residual relationships

$$\bar{e}_t = \frac{\Sigma e_t}{n} = E(e_t) = .0$$

$$\text{VAR}(e_t) = \frac{\Sigma e_t^2}{n-1} = E(e_t^2)$$

Because of stationarity

$$E(e_t) = E(e_{t-k}) = .0 \qquad \text{(constant mean)}$$
$$E(e_t^2) = E(e_{t-k}^2) \qquad \text{(constant variance)}$$

Because of statistical independence with $k \neq 0$

$$\text{COV}(e_t e_{t-k}) = \frac{\Sigma e_t e_{t-k}}{n-k-1} = E(e_t e_{t-k}) = .0$$

$$\text{COR}(e_t e_{t-k}) = \frac{\text{COV}(e_t e_{t-k})}{S(e_t)S(e_{t-k})} = .0$$

$$\text{ACF}(k) = \frac{E(e_t e_{t-k})}{E(e_t^2)} = \frac{0}{E(e_t^2)} = 0$$

For AR(1) processes Y_t is not a function of e_{t-k} for $k \neq 0$, therefore:

$$\text{COV}(Y_t e_{t-k}) = \frac{\Sigma y_t e_{t-k}}{n-k-1} = E(Y_t e_{t-k}) = 0$$

$$\text{COR}(Y_t e_{t-k}) = \frac{\text{COV}(Y_t e_{t-k})}{S(Y_t)S(e_{t-k})} = \frac{0}{S(Y_t)S(e_{t-k})} = 0$$

$$\text{CCF}(k) = \frac{\Sigma(y_t e_{t-k})}{\sqrt{\Sigma y_t^2 \Sigma e_{t-2}^2}} = 0$$

For MA(1) processes Y_t is not a function of Y_{t-k} for $k > 1$ (see Appendix 7–D), therefore:

$$\text{COV}(Y_t Y_{t-k}) = \frac{\Sigma y_t y_{t-k}}{n-k-1} = E(Y_t Y_{t-k}) = 0 \qquad \text{for } k > 1$$

$$COR(Y_tY_{t-k}) = \frac{COV(Y_tY_{t-k})}{S(Y_t)S(Y_{t-k})} = \frac{0}{S(Y_t)S(Y_{t-k})} = 0 \qquad \text{for } k > 1$$

$$ACF(k) = \frac{\sum y_t y_{t-k}}{\sum y_t^2} = \frac{0}{\sum y_t^2} = 0 \qquad \qquad \text{for } k > 1$$

APPENDIX 7–B

WHITE NOISE AND STATIONARITY

Residuals analysis is the principal focus of the diagnostic stage of Box–Jenkins methodology (i.e., ARIMA model building). In statistical terms, white noise (WN) is normally and independently distributed (NID), with a mean of zero, a constant variance, zero autocovariances, zero autocorrelations, and zero partial autocorrelations.

A number of important properties result from these characteristics. Given $e_t \sim$ NID $(0, \sigma_{et}^2)$, the mean of e_t is zero or, in expectation form $E(e_t) = 0$.

The variance is constant and equals

$$E(e_t^2) = \frac{\sum(e_t - E(e_t))^2}{n - 1} = \frac{\sum(e_t - 0)^2}{n - 1} = \frac{\sum e_t^2}{n - 1}$$

Because they are statistically independent of each other, the autocovariances of e_t equal zero:

$$E(e_t e_{t-k}) = \frac{\sum(e_t - E(e_t))(e_{t-k} - E(e_{t-k}))}{n - k} = \frac{\sum(e_t e_{t-k})}{n - k}$$

$$= 0 \qquad \text{for } k \neq 0$$

Because of independence, the autocovariances, and therefore the autocorrelations, equal zero:

$$ACF(k) = \frac{E(e_t e_{t-k})}{E(e_t^2)} = \frac{COV(e_t e_{t-k})}{VAR(e_t^2)}$$

$$= \frac{\sum e_t e_{t-k}}{\sum e_t^2} = \frac{0}{\sum e_t^2} = 0$$

Given a series is white noise, the standard error of the autocorrelation function can be shown to be

$$Se[ACF(k)] = \ \simeq 1/\sqrt{n}$$

When plotted, the residuals will be NID$(0, \sigma_{et}^2)$; that is, they are completely random, stationary, and independent:

$$ACF(k) = PACF(k) = 0 \qquad \text{for } k \neq 0$$

APPENDIX 7–C

THEORETICAL ACFs FOR AN ARIMA(1,0,0) PROCESS

An ARIMA(1,0,0) process is

$$y_t = \phi_1 y_{t-1} + e_t \tag{7C–1}$$

where in these and other discussions e_t represents the true population random shock.

Multiplying both sides of this equation by y_{t-1} and taking expected values (i.e., calculating means) yields:

$$E(y_{t-1}y_t) = E[y_{t-1}(\phi_1 y_{t-1} + e_t)]$$

$$= E(\phi_1 y_{t-1}^2 + y_{t-1}e_t)$$

Remembering that y_{t-1} and e_t are independent, taking the expected values of individual terms and remembering that because of stationarity, $VAR(y_{t-1}) = VAR(y_t)$, we have

$$E(y_{t-1}y_t) = \phi_1 E(y_{t-1}^2) + E(y_{t-1}e_t) = \phi_1 VAR(y_{t-1}) + 0 = \phi_1 VAR(y_t)$$

$$COV(y_{t-1}y_t) = \phi_1 VAR(y_t)$$

Dividing both sides by $VAR(y_t)$, which is $E(y_t^2)$, yields ACF(1):

$$\frac{COV(y_{t-1}, y_t)}{VAR(y_t)} = ACF(1) = \frac{\phi_1 VAR(y_t)}{VAR(y_t)} = \phi_1$$

Thus,

$$ACF(1) = \phi_1$$

Continuing in a similar fashion for ACF(2), multiplying each side of Equation 7C–1 by y_{t-2}, we get

$$E(y_{t-2}y_t) = E[y_{t-2}(\phi_1 y_{t-1} + e_t)]$$

substituting $(\phi_1 y_{t-2} + e_{t-1})$ for y_{t-1}

$$E(y_{t-2}y_t) = E[y_{t-2}(\phi_1(\phi_1 Y_{t-2} + e_{t-1}) + e_t)]$$

$$= E(\phi_1^2 y_{t-2}^2 + y_{t-2}\phi_1 e_{t-1} + y_{t-2}e_t)$$

Taking expected values and remembering the independence of y_{t-2} and e_{t-1} and the independence of y_{t-2} and e_t yields

$$E(y_{t-2}y_t) = \phi_1^2 E(y_{t-2}^2) + 0 + 0$$

where each is the covariance and variances, respectively:

$$COV(y_{t-2}y_t) = \phi_1^2 VAR(y_{t-2})$$

Because of stationarity,

$$VAR(y_{t-2}) = VAR(y_t^2)$$

$$COV(y_{t-2}y_t) = \phi_1^2 VAR(y_t)$$

Dividing both sides by $VAR(y_t)$ yields

$$\frac{COV(y_{t-2}y_t)}{VAR(y_t)} = ACF(2) = \frac{\phi_1^2 VAR(y_t)}{VAR(y_t)} = \phi_1^2$$

Similarly derived, but not shown, for $k > 0$, the general formula for ACF(k) is:

$$ACF(k) = \frac{COV(k)}{VAR(y_t)} = \phi_1^k$$

APPENDIX 7–D

THEORETICAL ACFS FOR AN ARIMA(0,0,1) PROCESS

For an ARIMA(0,0,1) model, y_t is statistically independent of y_{t-k}. Also, because of white noise, e_t and e_{t-k} are statistically independent. An ARIMA(0,0,1) model is

$$y_t = (1 - \theta_1 B)e_t \tag{7D–1}$$

Multiplying each side of Equation 7D–1 by $y_{t-1} = (e_{t-1} - \theta_1 e_{t-2})$ and taking expected values, we have

$$E(y_t y_{t-1}) = E[(e_t - \theta_1 e_{t-1})(e_{t-1} - \theta_1 e_{t-2})]$$

$$= E(e_t e_{t-1} - \theta_1 e_t e_{t-2} - \theta_1 e_{t-1}^2 + \theta_1^2 e_{t-1}e_{t-2})$$

Recognizing the statistical independencies of e_t and e_{t-2} and calculating expected values yields

$$E(y_t y_{t-1}) = E(e_t e_{t-1}) - \theta_1 E(e_t e_{t-2}) - \theta_1 E(e_{t-1}^2) + \theta_1^2 E(e_{t-1} e_{t-2})$$

$$\text{COV}(y_t y_{t-1}) = \quad 0 \quad - \quad 0 \quad - \theta_1 E(e_t^2) \quad + \quad 0$$

Dividing each side by $\text{VAR}(y_t)$, which is the formula for the ACF(1), we get

$$\text{ACF}(1) = \frac{\text{COV}(y_t y_{t-1})}{\text{VAR}(y_t)} = \frac{-\theta_1 E(e_t^2)}{(1 + \theta_1^2)E(e_t^2)} = \frac{-\theta_1}{1 + \theta_1^2} \neq 0$$

where $\text{VAR}(y_t) = (1 + \theta_1^2)E(e_t^2)$ is shown at the end of this derivation.

Now consider the derivation of ACF(k) for $k > 1$. Multiplying each side of Equation 7D–1 by $y_{t-2} = (e_{t-2} - \theta_1 e_{t-3})$, taking expected values and expanding, we get

$$E(y_t y_{t-2}) = E[(e_t - \theta_1 e_{t-1})(e_{t-2} - \theta_1 e_{t-3})]$$

$$= E(e_t e_{t-2} - \theta_1 e_t e_{t-3} - \theta_1 e_{t-1} e_{t-2} + \theta_1^2 e_{t-1} e_{t-3})$$

Recognizing the statistical independence of all e_{t-k} and calculating expected values, we get

$$E(y_t y_{t-2}) = E(e_t e_{t-2}) - \theta_1 E(e_t e_{t-3}) - \theta_1 E(e_{t-1} e_{t-2}) + \theta_1^2 E(e_{t-1} e_{t-3})$$

$$= \quad 0 \quad - \quad 0 \quad - \quad 0 \quad + \quad 0$$

$$= \text{COV}(y_t y_{t-2}) = 0$$

$$\text{ACF}(2) = \frac{\text{COV}(y_t y_{t-2})}{\text{VAR}(y_t)} = \frac{0}{\text{VAR}(y_t)} = 0$$

Generalizing this result, we have

$$\text{ACF}(k) = 0 \text{ for } k > 1$$

Higher-order MA(q) ACFs can be derived in a similar manner.

To derive $\text{VAR}(y_t)$, we take the square of Equation 7D–1 and take expected values:

$$E(y_t^2) = E[(e_t - \theta_1 e_{t-1})^2] = E(e_t^2 - 2\theta_1 e_t e_{t-1} + \theta_1^2 e_{t-1}^2)$$

Remembering that $E(e_t e_{t-1}) = 0$ and $E(e_t^2) = E(e_{t-1}^2)$, we have

$$\text{VAR}(y_t) = E(e_t^2) + 0 + \theta_1^2 E(e_{t-1}^2) = (1 + \theta_1^2)E(e_t^2)$$

$$= (1 + \theta_1^2)E(e_t^2)$$

APPENDIX 7–E

BOUNDS OF INVERTIBILITY AND STATIONARITY

Students are often reluctant to check whether models exceed the bounds of invertibility and stationarity, even though these bounds are important guides in selecting models. When these bounds are not verified, the wrong model can be selected, or considerable time can be spent trying to refine invalid models. We urge you to check the bounds simply by substituting the fitted coefficient values into the following simple identities. If any of these bounds are exceeded, the model is either not invertible or not stationary and should be modified. When applying these bounds, note that they apply to both seasonal and nonseasonal models.

- Bounds of stationarity

ARIMA(1,0,0)

$$|\phi_1| < 1$$

$$ARIMA(2,0,0)$$

$$-1 < \phi_2 < +1$$

$$\phi_1 + \phi_2 < +1$$

$$\phi_2 - \phi_1 < +1$$

· Bounds of invertibility

$$ARIMA(0,0,1)$$

$$|\theta_1| < 1$$

$$ARIMA(0,0,2)$$

$$-1 < \theta_2 < +1$$

$$\theta_1 + \theta_2 < +1$$

$$\theta_2 - \theta_1 < +1$$

· Mixed model (1,0,1) bounds

$$|\phi_1| < 1$$

$$|\theta_1| < 1$$

APPENDIX 7–F

EXAMPLE ARIMA DATA SETS

The following data sets have been generated to illustrate ARIMA models for use in your software. These files contain 100 observations, with the ARIMA(p,d,q) structure identified in the file names. These are important learning data sets to familiarize you with ARIMA model building.

AR1N.DAT	I4.DAT
AR1P.DAT	I4T.DAT
AR2NN.DAT	I1T.DAT
AR2NP.DAT	MA1N.DAT
AR2PN.DAT	MA2NN.DAT
AR2PP.DAT	MA2NP.DAT
ARIMA110.DAT	MA2PN.DAT
ARMANP.DAT	MA2PP.DAT
I12.DAT	ARMAPN.DAT

Answers to Problem 7–23:

SERIESAB	ARIMA(1,0,0) series	AR1P.DAT
SERIESAD	ARIMA(2,0,0) series	AR2NP.DAT
SERIESAF	ARIMA(2,0,0) series	AR2PP.DAT
SERIESAH	ARIMA(0,1,0)^4 series	I4.DAT
SERIESAJ	ARIMA(1,0,1) series	ARMAPN.DAT
SERIESAL	ARIMA(0,0,1) series	MA1N.DAT
SERIESAN	ARIMA(0,0,2) series	MA2NN.DAT
SERIESAP	ARIMA(0,0,2) series	MA2PN.DAT
SERIESAR	ARIMA(1,0,0)1 series	I1T.DAT
SERIESAT	ARIMA(0,1,0)^{4}1 series	I4T.DAT

APPENDIX 7–G

PACFs and the Yule–Walker Equations

Partial autocorrelation measures are common to many types of modeling processes. In general, a partial correlation measures the degree of association between one variable (e.g., Y) and another (e.g., X) after partialing out (i.e., controlling for) the effects of other variables (e.g., Z or W). In time series analyses, a partial autocorrelation measures the degree of association between y_t and y_{t-k} (e.g., y_{t-2}) after partialing out the effects of the other lags of y (e.g., $y_{t-1}, y_{t-3}, \ldots$). For example, a partial autocorrelation measures the direct association between y_t and y_{t-2} that is independent of their mutual correlation with other lags of y_{t-k}.

The standard notation for partial autocorrelations is ϕ_p and estimated partial autocorrelation functions are notated as PACFs. As we have seen, PACFs are important aids for identifying higher-order ARIMA(p,d,q) processes, which are difficult to determine from the ACFs alone. These PACFs are estimated using the Yule–Walker equations (hereafter the Y–W equations).

Derivation of Yule–Walker Equations

Consider the meaning of the Y–W equations. If a series is an AR(2) process, as shown in Equation 7G-1,

$$y_t = \phi_1 y_{t-1} + \phi_2 y_{t-2} + e_t \tag{7G–1}$$

then the only variables that are directly correlated with y_t are y_{t-1} and y_{t-2}; all other autocorrelations results from the indirect autocorrelations of other lags of y_{t-k}.

Equation 7G–1 can be used to estimate initial values of ϕ_1 and ϕ_2 using two derived equations in two unknowns, where ϕ_1 and ϕ_2, the PACFs at lags 1 and 2, are the unknowns.

1. Multiply each side of Equation 7G–1 by y_{t-1}, to get

$$y_{t-1}(y_t) = y_{t-1}(\phi_1 y_{t-1} + \phi_2 y_{t-2} + e_t) = \phi_1 y_{t-1}^2 + \phi_2 y_{t-1} y_{t-2} + e_t y_{t-1}$$

2. Take the expected values (i.e., means) of each side.

$$E[y_t y_{t-1}] = E[(\phi_1 y_{t-1} + \phi_2 y_{t-2} + e_t)y_{t-1}]$$
$$= E[(\phi_1 y_{t-1}^2 + \phi_2 y_{t-2} y_{t-1} + e_t y_{t-1})] \tag{7G–2}$$

In taking expected values, remember that:

3. The expected values of the products of two deviations are covariances, unless the variables are the same, in which case variances result.

4. The covariances and correlations of independent events are zero.

5. Random shocks $e_t s$ are statistically independent of each other and, for an AR(2) process, $e_t s$ are not associated with y_{t-k} for $k > 0$.

Thus, Equation 7G–2 yields:

$$E(y_t y_{t-1}) = E[(\phi_1 y_{t-1}^2 + \phi_2 y_{t-2} y_{t-1} + e_t y_{t-1})]$$
$$\mathrm{COV}(y_t y_{t-1}) = \phi \mathrm{VAR}(y_{t-1}) + \phi_2 \mathrm{COV}(y_{t-2} y_{t-1}) + \mathrm{COV}(e_t y_{t-1})$$

By definition, $E(y_{t-1}^2) = \mathrm{VAR}(y_{t-1})$, and because of stationarity, $\mathrm{VAR}(y_t) = \mathrm{VAR}(y_{t-1})$. Also, because of stationarity, the covariances $E(y_{t-2} y_{t-1})$ and $E(y_t y_{t-1})$ are equal. Finally, $\mathrm{E}(e_t y_{t-1}) = 0$, because these are statistically independent events for an AR(2) process. (This assumption is not true for MA(q) processes.) Therefore, substituting the previous equations yields

$$\mathrm{COV}(y_t y_{t-1}) = \phi_1 \mathrm{VAR}(y_t) + \phi_2 \mathrm{COV}(y_t y_{t-1}) + 0$$

Dividing each side by VAR(y_t) yields

$$\frac{\text{COV}(y_t,y_{t-1})}{\text{VAR}(y_t)} = \phi_1 + \phi_2 \frac{\text{COV}(y_t,y_{t-1})}{\text{VAR}(y_t)}$$

Therefore, by definition,

$$\text{ACF}(1) = \phi_1 + \phi_2 \text{ACF}(1) \tag{7G–3}$$

Now ACF(1) is known, therefore this is the first of two equations in two unknowns.

Let us now develop the second equation. Multiply each side of Equation 7G–1 by y_{t-2} in a manner similar to the previous derivation:

$$y_{t-2}(y_t) = y_{t-2}(\phi_1 y_{t-1} + \phi_2 y_{t-2} + e_t)$$

Taking expected values, we get

$$\begin{aligned}
E(y_t y_{t-2}) &= E[(\phi_1 y_{t-1} + \phi_2 y_{t-2} + e_t)y_{t-2}] \\
&= E[(\phi_1 y_{t-1} y_{t-2} + \phi_2 y_{t-2}^2 + e_t y_{t-2})] \\
&= \phi_1 E(y_t y_{t-2}) + \phi_2 E(y_{t-2}^2) + 0
\end{aligned}$$

Dividing both sides by the variance, $E(y_t^2)$ and remembering some basic identities,

$$\frac{E(y_1 y_{t-2})}{E(y_t^2)} = \phi_1 \frac{E(y_t y_{t-1})}{E(y_t^2)} + \phi_2 \frac{E(y_{t-2}^2)}{E(y_t^2)}$$

Thus,

$$\text{ACF}(2) = \phi_1 \text{ACF}(1) + \phi_2 \tag{7G–4}$$

The two Equations 7G–3 and 7G–4 in two unknowns are easily solved, because estimates of ACF(1) and ACF(2) are calculated from the actual time series assuming a sufficient number of observations exist. Equations 7G–3 and 7G–4 are repeated as 7G–5 and 7G–6.

$$\text{ACF}(1) = \phi_1 + \phi_2 \text{ACF}(1) \tag{7G–5}$$

$$\text{ACF}(2) = \phi_1 \text{ACF}(1) + \phi_2 \tag{7G–6}$$

A useful interpretation of Equations 7G–5 and 7G–6 is

$$\frac{\text{Total}}{\text{autocorrelation}} = \frac{\text{Direct}}{\text{autocorrelation}} + \frac{\text{Indirect}}{\text{autocorrelation}} \tag{7G–5a}$$

$$\frac{\text{Total}}{\text{autocorrelation}} = \frac{\text{Indirect}}{\text{autocorrelation}} + \frac{\text{Direct}}{\text{autocorrelation}} \tag{7G-6a}$$

Consider these interpretations in more detail. Equation 7G–5 denotes that the total autocorrelation between y_t and y_{t-1} (i.e., ACF(1)) consists of two components. The first is the direct autocorrelation between y_t and y_{t-1}, as measured by the partial autocorrelation ϕ_1. The second is the indirect autocorrelation between y_t and y_{t-2}, as measured by the product of those portions of direct autocorrelation between y_t and y_{t-2} (i.e., ϕ_2) acting through ACF(1). That is, part of the total autocorrelation between y_t and y_{t-1} is attributable to the portion of the autocorrelation between y_t and y_{t-2} that acts through ϕ_2. Equation 7G–6 can be interpreted in a similar fashion, as shown in the following chart.

$$\text{ACF}(1) = \phi_1 + \phi_2 \text{ACF}(1) + e_t$$

$$\text{ACF}(2) = \phi_1 \text{ACF}(1) + \phi_2 + e_t$$

Direct ϕ_2

$$\xrightarrow{\hspace{3cm}} \phi_2 \xrightarrow{\hspace{2cm}} \text{Error}$$

$$y_{t-2} \xleftarrow{\hspace{0.8cm}} \text{ACF}(1) \xleftarrow{\hspace{0.8cm}} y_{t-1} \xleftarrow{\hspace{0.8cm}} \phi_1 \xleftarrow{\hspace{0.8cm}} y_t \xleftarrow{\hspace{0.8cm}} e_t$$

Indirect   ACF(2)

Consider some hypothetical coefficients for these equations. Given the autocorrelations ACF(1) = .6, and ACF(2) = .8 and the partials $\phi_1 = .1875$ and $\phi_2 = .6875$, we have

$$\text{ACF}(1) = \phi_1 + \phi_2 \text{ACF}(1) = .6 = .1875 + .6875 \cdot .6$$

$$\text{ACF}(2) = \phi_1 \text{ACF}(1) + \phi_2 = .8 = .6 \cdot .1875 + .6875$$

In this example, ACF(1) is .6, while ACF(2) is .8. However, because y_t, y_{t-1}, and y_{t-2} are interrelated, some of the autocorrelation between y_t and y_{t-1} is a result of the y_ts relationship with y_{t-2}. This interrelationship is given in Equation 7G–5. Thus, ACF(1) equals the sum of the partial autocorrelation between y_t and y_{t-1} and those portions of the indirect autocorrelation between y_t and y_{t-2} that act through y_{t-1}.

Solution of Y–W Equations for PACF(k)s

Consider how Equations 7G–5 and 7G–6 are used in practice to calculate partial autocorrelations. If the measured autocorrelations are ACF(1) = .6 and ACF(2) = .8, then the values of the partial autocorrelations ϕ_1 and ϕ_2 can be determined by solving Equations 7G–5 and 7G–6, which are

$$.6 = \phi_1 + .6\phi_2$$

$$.8 = .6\phi_1 + \phi_2$$

Solving these two equations in two unknowns yields

$$\phi_1 = .1875$$

$$\phi_2 = .6875$$

Also, the standard error of ϕ_1 and ϕ_2 is approximately

$$\text{Se(PACF)} = \frac{1}{\sqrt{n}}$$

Once Equations 7G–5 and 7G–6 are solved for the PACFs, statistical significance tests can be applied. If PACFs (1) and (2) are statistically significantly different than zero, if there are no other patterns in the PACFs, and if the ACFs are consistent, then it is inferred that an AR(2) process has generated the time series. This significance test is very easy to apply to a table of PACFs simply by dividing each PACF by the Se(PACF). An AR(2) process has two significant spikes, at lags 1 and 2 in the PACFs; an AR(1) process has one significant spike, at lag 1; and, while they are not as common, an AR(3) has three significant spikes, at lags 1, 2, and 3.

Let's consider how the PACFs of an AR(3) process are estimated. The applicable relationship is

$$y_t = \phi_1 y_{t-1} + \phi_2 y_{t-2} + \phi_3 y_{t-3} + e_t \tag{7G-7}$$

Three equations in three unknowns can be derived by multiplying Equation 7G–7 by y_{t-1}, y_{t-2} and y_{t-3}, and then taking the expected values, as follows:

$$E(y_t y_{t-1}) = E[y_{t-1}(\phi_1 y_{t-1} + \phi_2 y_{t-2} + \phi_3 y_{t-3} + e_t)] \tag{7G-8}$$

$$E(y_t y_{t-2}) = E[y_{t-2}(\phi_1 y_{t-1} + \phi_2 y_{t-2} + \phi_3 y_{t-3} + e_t)] \tag{7G-9}$$

$$E(y_t y_{t-3}) = E[y_{t-3}(\phi_1 y_{t-1} + \phi_2 y_{t-2} + \phi_3 y_{t-3} + e_t)] \tag{7G-10}$$

These equations are solved to provide initial estimates of ϕ_1, ϕ_2, and ϕ_3.

In actuality, the PACFs reported by computer software are:

PACF(1) = ACF(1)
PACF(2) = ϕ_2 from two equations, 7G–5 and 7G–6
PACF(3) = ϕ_3 from three equations, 7G–8, 7G–9, and 7G–10
PACF(4) = ϕ_4 from four equations in four unknowns
      . . .
PACF(k) = ϕ_k from k equations in k unknowns

In general, the value of a specific PACF(k) is estimated using k equations in k unknowns, where only the last PACF(k) is reported as the partial autocorrelation. That is, the PACF(4) (i.e., ϕ_4) is estimated from four equations in four unknowns, the value of PACF(5) (i.e., ϕ_5) is estimated from five equations in five unknowns, and so on. Only the last PACF of each solution is reported as a PACF. Consequently, the calculation of PACFs is computationally intense, and careful selection of k may be necessary. In general, it is unnecessary to calculate PACFs for more than three or four seasonal cycles.

Because the reported PACFs are calculated this way, they are designated using the double subscripted notation of ϕ_{kk}, where this is the k-th PACF from solving k equations in k unknowns.

PACF Patterns

The patterns that exist in PACFs assist in identifying both the ARIMA(p,0,0) and the general ARIMA(p,d,q) models. General PACF patterns were given previously some common patterns are as follows:

ARIMA	PACF Pattern
Low-order processes	
(1,0,0)	Single significant spike at lag 1.
(0,1,0)	Single significant spike at lag 1.
(0,0,1)	Significant spikes that decline exponentially.
(2,0,0)	Two significant spikes, one at lag 1 and one at lag 2.
(0,0,2)	Significant spikes with a sinusoidal exponential decline.
Seasonal order processes	
$(1,0,0)^S$	Single significant spike at lag S.
$(0,1,0)^S$	Single significant spike at lag S.
$(0,0,1)^S$	Significant spikes that decline exponentially at lags S, $2S$, $3S$, $4S$, … , nS.
$(2,0,0)^S$	Two significant spikes, one at lags S and one at lag $2S$.
$(0,0,2)^S$	Significant spikes with a sinusoidal exponential decline at lags S, $2S$, …, nS.

ARIMA
APPLICATIONS

Solving problems is a fundamental human activity . . . the greater part of our conscious thinking is concerned with problems . . . our thoughts are directed toward some end; we seek means, we seek to solve a problem.

G. Polya, *How to Solve It*

Chapter Outline

This chapter continues the development of ARIMA forecasting, using several hypothetical and real applications. In this chapter, we analyze four time series that display a variety of stochastic processes. Two nonseasonal time series are modeled: common stock prices, and a Japan stock index. Two seasonal models are analyzed: demand for an animal pharmaceutical, and demand for electricity at a California utility. These time series were chosen because they exemplify common time series patterns.

ARIMA models require the use of a methodical and intelligent forecasting process. These models are surprisingly versatile in their ability to represent a wide variety of trend, seasonal, random and other patterns. The statistical and intellectual challenges of ARIMA model building are significant; in return, the insights and intuitive models that result are even more significant. The successful process is gratifying, while the unsuccessful ones can leave the analyst with self doubt, particularly the less experienced analysts. As you might expect, the process of building such models takes time and practice.

The ARIMA Model-Building Process

The model-building strategy employed here consists of many iterative steps, as originally developed by Box and Jenkins in 1970. These steps are presented in Figure 8–1, which is a detailed flowchart of the ARIMA model-building process. This chart should be reviewed as necessary when completing these ARIMA model-building steps. The only caution is that this flowchart cannot possibly encompass all possible ARIMA problems, because the number and variety of models is staggering. However, the flowchart is useful for providing some structure, including the four general steps of model building: identification, estimation, diagnosis, and forecasting.

Four Iterative Steps of ARIMA Model Building

1. Model **Identification**
   - Achieve stationarity.
   - Are the variance and level stationary?
   - Tentatively identifying models.
        Are patterns discernible?
        With graphs, statistics, ACFs, PACFs, etc., identify the patterns in the time series.

2. Coefficient **Estimation**
   - Determine model coefficients through software applications of least squares and maximum likelihood methods. Did the estimation procedure converge on good coefficients?

3. Model and Residual **Diagnostics**
   - Does the model have a high $\bar{R}^2$ and low BIC and RSE?
   - Are the model coefficients statistically significant?
   - Are the coefficients stationary or invertible?
   - Are the residuals white noise?
   - Are the coefficients redundant or highly correlated?
   - Is the model too complex?
   - Is the model parsimonious?
   - Does a simpler model perform as well?
   - Is there theoretical and intuitive appeal in the model?

FIGURE 8–1

Flowchart of ARIMA model-building process

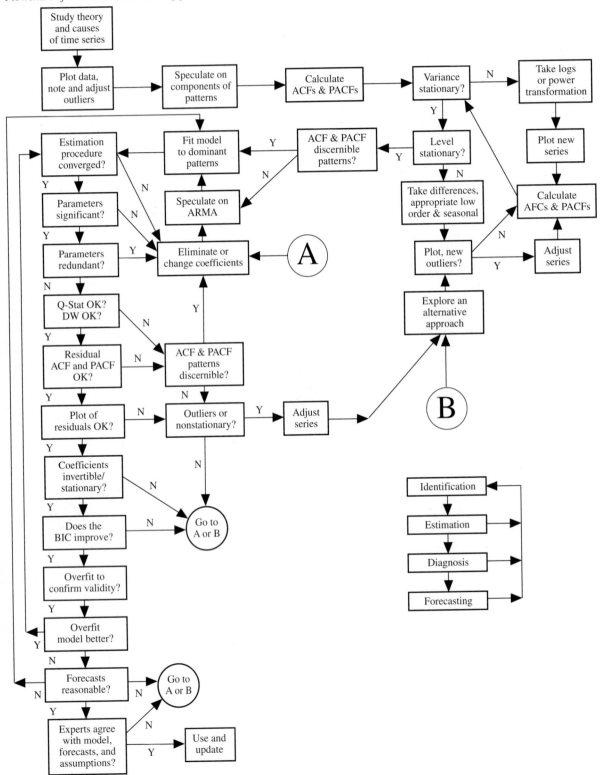

- Using graphs, statistics, ACFs, PACFs, etc of residuals, determine if the model is valid. If valid, then use the model; otherwise, repeat identification, estimation, and diagnosis steps.

4. **Forecasting** Verification and Reasonableness
   - Make forecasts using the verified model.
   - Are the forecasts reasonable, defensible?
   - Using graphs, simple statistics, and confidence intervals, determine the validity of forecasts and track model performance to detect out-of-control situations.

These four steps are highlighted in the ARIMA analyses presented in this chapter. It should be emphasized that a very short series is analyzed here: one series has only 48 periods. Do not be misled into believing that only 48 observations are sufficient to build ARIMA models. In general, it is difficult to identify models when time series are short (less than 60 observations) and not well behaved (i.e., ACF and PACF patterns are not clear). This is one of the disadvantages of ARIMA analysis; ARIMA models need sufficient observations with which to derive models empirically. However, as the successful analyses of these series illustrate, effective ARIMA models can be defined for some series, even if they do not have the suggested 60 or more observations.

SERIESB.DAT: Common Stock Prices

Identification

Figure 8–2 is a graph of SERIESB.DAT, a time series of the price of a common stock. As shown in the figure, the series appears to be a random walk, slowly increasing and decreasing over time. This highly-autocorrelated increasing and

FIGURE 8–2

SERIESB.DAT, ACF, PACF

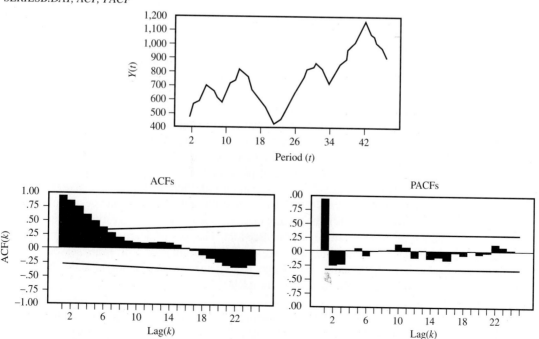

decreasing series has a nonstationary mean. We have already seen random walk series in Chapter 7. As discussed there, such series are easily modeled simply by taking first differences, which yield a white noise series. When the residuals possess no more pattern (i.e., are white noise) and other characteristics of the model are valid and defensible, the modeling process is complete.

Figure 8–2 and Table 8–1 illustrate the ACFs and PACFs for SERIESB.DAT. The patterns in these ACFs and PACFs are typical of a nonstationary series. Note the high autocorrelations that remain significant and slowly decline from lags 1 to 6. In fact, all of these ACFs are statistically significantly different than zero. (Remember that significant correlations are those with absolute values that are greater than about two standard errors.)

The first step in ARIMA analysis is achieving stationarity, because without stationarity, we cannot model the underlying ARMA process; that is, nonstationarity dominates the ACF and PACF patterns. More importantly, nonstationarity is an important attribute of the time series being modeled. Also, variance nonstationarity is often easily detected when differences or model residuals are analyzed. SERIESB.DAT does not seem to have variance nonstationarity, and as we will see, neither do its first differences, so we need not consider taking the logarithms or doing transformations of the data. A constant should be included in the model, to confirm that no trend exists. This is a good practice when there might be doubt about trend.

Estimation

Table 8–2 illustrates the fit of an ARIMA(0,1,0)1 model, where $d = 1$, thus first differences are taken, and a trend coefficient is estimated as

$$Y_t = Y_{t-1} + \theta_0 + e_t$$

After estimation, we have

$$Y_t = Y_{t-1} + 9.0851 + e_t$$

Table 8–2 is typical of several popular computer programs. The method used for fitting coefficients varies according to the software. However, most procedures use a nonlinear estimation method in a programmed, iterative search for the best coefficients. This search is similar to, but much more sophisticated than, the one shown in Chapter 4 used to find the optimal smoothing constant. Because the search algorithm tries a number of different coefficient values before converging on the optimum, these trials are called **iterations.** The estimation process of Table 8–2 took two iterations to converge on the optimal coefficient for the constant. When fitting more complex models, you should confirm that the estimation procedure converges on a solution, and that the number of iterations taken to find the coefficient is not excessive (e.g., greater than 20 to 50). Too many iterations may be indicative of a problem with the model, typically denoting the model is wrong or too complex.

As noted in Table 8–2, this estimation procedure had 47 usable observation, because one of the 48 was lost by taking first differences. Thus, one degree of freedom was lost because of differences and one was lost because of the estimated constant coefficient θ_0, leaving 46 degrees of freedom. The loss of degrees of freedom becomes great when seasonal differences are used. For example, if 12th-order seasonal differences are taken, then the sample size is no longer 48, but 36 observations. In general, this is an insufficient sample size for ARIMA analyses.

Diagnosis

Having fitted the model, our attention turns to the validity of the fit and the coefficients. As shown in Table 8–2, the mean of the original series is 756, with a standard deviation of 181.59. The standard error of estimate (i.e., residual standard

TABLE 8–1   ACFs and PACFs of SERIESB.DAT

ACF(k)	1:	.9274	.8250	.6932	.5636	.4485	.3415
	7:	.2503	.1740	.1154	.0870	.0855	.0873
	13:	.0955	.0847	.0580	.0068	−.0543	−.1223
	19:	−.1862	−.2494	−.3039	−.3308	−.3323	−.3041
PACF(k)	1:	.9274	−.2504	−.2384	.0059	.0523	−.0751
	7:	−.0109	.0132	.0208	.1213	.0920	−.1116
	13:	.0051	−.1144	−.0968	−.1410	−.0216	−.0596
	19:	.0030	−.0569	−.0273	.1244	.0629	.0226

Approximate $2Se_{ACF(k)} = 2S_{PACF(k)} = \dfrac{2}{(48)^{.5}} = .289$

TABLE 8–2   ARIMA(0,1,0)1 for SERIESB.DAT

Iterations taken			2	
Usable observations			47	
Degrees of freedom			46	
$\bar{R}^2$/BIC			.915/556.9	
Mean of dependent variable			756.085	
Std error of dependent variable			181.589	
Standard error of estimate			52.958	
Sum of squared residuals			129009.660	
Durbin–Watson statistic			.951	
$Q(11)$			36.342	
Significance level of Q			.000148	
Coeff.	*Estimate*	*Std Error*	*t-Stat*	*Signif*
θ_0	9.085	7.725	1.176	.2456

error) is 52.96; consequently, the $\bar{R}^2$ of the model is very good, at 91.5 percent. The sum of squared errors (residuals) is 129,009 and the DW statistic is not near 2. Also, the Q-statistic is inconsistent with an assumption that the residuals are white noise: that is, there is only a .000148 probability that a Q value of 36.3 or greater would result from the first 11 ACFs of a white noise series. Thus, we infer that (a) we have not achieved white noise residuals, and (b) some pattern is left in the series.

As suspected, from Table 8–2, the constant is not significant, having a t-statistic of 1.176, which is much less than 2, at a level of significance of only .2456. This level of significance denotes that there is a .2456 probability that this constant could be from a population with a parameter of zero or even a negative value.

Proper diagnosis should always include a plot of the residuals to insure that the process of taking differences has not created some very large and confounding outliers. For example, if there are large outliers in the residuals, it may appear that differences are not necessary, or that a constant is or is not necessary in the model. Consequently, the residuals of models should always be examined. Figure 8–3 illustrates a plot of the residuals of this model, and the plot does not seem very random.

Rediagnosis 1.   Because of the ACF and PACF patterns of Figure 8–3, we need to re-identify and estimate a new model.

FIGURE 8–3

Residuals, ACFs, and PACFs of ARIMA(0,1,0)1 for SERIESB.DAT

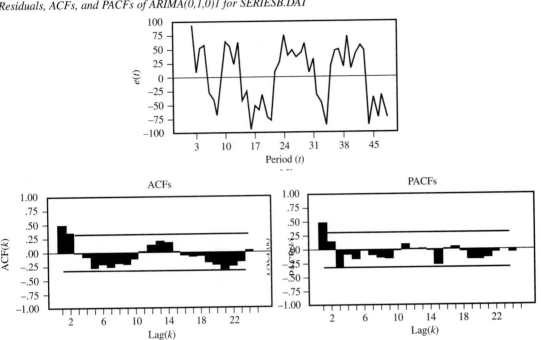

While the residuals are stationary in level and variance, there are discernible patterns in the ACFs and PACFs shown in Table 8–3 and Figure 8–3. Note the ACF spikes at lags 1 and 2, and the large PACF spike at lag 1; these resemble an AR(1) pattern. Also, the wide and sustained swings in the residuals of Figure 8–3 resemble the behavior of an autoregressive process. Table 8–4 shows the fit of an ARIMA(1,1,0)1 model. To confirm that no trend exists, a constant is included in this model; if this constant is insignificant, it will be eliminated.

The model of Table 8–4 has the highest $\bar{R}^2$ and lowest BIC of those fitted so far. In addition, the DW and Q statistics denote white noise. Note that the correlation matrix of the coefficients does not show any significant correlation between the estimates of the coefficients. As discussed in the previous chapter, if a model is well designed, the correlation between coefficients should not be high; for example, typically this correlation should not be higher than about .90. If these coefficients are highly correlated, then the model *may be* too complex, and one or more coefficients may be redundant, and should be dropped.

Rediagnosis 2.   Because the constant θ_0 is not statistically significantly different than zero, it is dropped. The resulting ARIMA(1,1,0) model is shown in Table 8–5.

The model of Table 8–5 appears to fit the data well. The $\bar{R}^2$ is higher, BIC lower, and the DW and Q statistics are consistent with white noise, and the coefficient ϕ_1 is statistically significant. As a final check on the adequacy of this model, let us analyze the ACFs and PACFs of the residuals, as shown in Table 8–6. Remember that statistically significant ACFs and PACFs are greater than approximately $2\mathrm{Se}_{\mathrm{ACF}} = \dfrac{2}{(47)^{.5}} = .292$.

TABLE 8–3 ACFs and PACFs of Residuals from ARIMA(0,1,0)1 for SERIESB.DAT

ACF(k)						
1:	.4745	.3439	−.0117	−.1027	−.2773	−.2347
7:	−.2687	−.2204	−.2258	−.1240	.0318	.1354
13:	.2166	.1840	.0059	−.0443	−.0806	−.0783
19:	−.1698	−.2094	−.2783	−.2214	−.1392	.0252
PACF(k)						
1:	.4745	.1532	−.2942	−.0741	−.1532	−.0311
7:	−.0940	−.1187	−.1210	−.0286	.1275	.0234
13:	.0243	−.0436	−.2345	.0056	.0569	−.0319
19:	−.1937	−.1842	−.1460	−.0444	−.0033	−.0606

Approximate $2S_{ACF(k)} = 2S_{PACF(k)} = \dfrac{2}{(47)^{.5}} = .292$

TABLE 8–4 ARIMA(1,1,0)1 for SERIESB.DAT

Iterations taken	3
Usable observations	46
Degrees of freedom	44
$\bar{R}^2$/BIC	.938/532.7
Mean of dependent variable	760.043
Std error of dependent variable	181.533
Standard error of estimate	45.361
Sum of squared residuals	90537.406
Durbin–Watson statistic	2.049
$Q(11)$	11.913
Significance level of Q	.2909

Coeff.	Estimate	Std Error	t-Stat	Signif
θ_0	3.737	13.3709	.280	.7812
ϕ_1	.495	.1289	3.843	.0004

Correlation matrix	θ_0
ϕ_1	−.22696

TABLE 8–5 ARIMA(1,1,0) model for SERIESB.DAT

Iterations taken	2
Usable observations	46
Degrees of freedom	45
$\bar{R}^2$/BIC	.939/528.9
Mean of dependent variable	760.043
Std error of dependent variable	181.533
Standard error of estimate	44.894
Sum of squared residuals	90694.414
Durbin–Watson statistic	2.061
$Q(11)$	11.843
Significance level of Q	.2957

Coeff.	Estimate	Std Error	t-Stat	Signif
ϕ_1	.5025	.12497	4.021	.0002

TABLE 8–6 ACFs and PACFs of residuals from ARIMA(1,1,0) for SERIESB.DAT, Table 8–5

ACF(k)						
1:	−.0558	.2281	−.1991	.0742	−.1795	.0162
7:	−.1764	−.1251	−.1675	−.1034	−.0026	.1257
13:	.1421	.2248	−.0590	.0210	−.0337	.0892
19:	−.0416	−.1106	−.2173	−.1611	−.1156	.0391
PACF(k)						
1:	−.0558	.2257	−.1867	.0152	−.1024	−.0439
7:	−.1140	−.1935	−.1331	−.1467	−.0262	.0935
13:	.0826	.1827	−.1307	−.1017	−.0037	.0286
19:	.0160	−.1450	−.1453	−.1023	−.0905	.0313

Approximate $2Se_{ACF(k)} = 2Se_{PACF(k)} = \dfrac{2}{(47)^{.5}} = .292$

The ACFs and PACFs of Table 8–6 have no statistically significant values in excess of $2Se_{ACF}$. Figure 8–4 illustrates the residuals of Table 8–5. As shown, the series is quite random and the ACFs and PACFs confirm that no strong patterns remain. We can therefore infer that the model of Table 8–6 is a good model for this time series. We can now confirm the model's forecasting form and function.

Forecasting

The model of Table 8–5 is an ARIMA(1,1,0) model that can be expressed in one of several ways:

$$(1 - \phi_1 B)(1 - B)Y_t = e_t$$

When expanded, this yields

$$(1 - B - \phi_1 B + \phi_1 B^2)Y_t = e_t$$

$$Y_t - Y_{t-1} - \phi_1 Y_{t-1} + \phi_1 Y_{t-2} = e_t$$

In forecasting form, this is

$$\hat{Y}_t = Y_{t-1} + \phi_1 Y_{t-1} - \phi_1 Y_{t-2} \tag{8–1}$$

$$= Y_{t-1} + \phi_1(Y_{t-1} - Y_{t-2})$$

$$= Y_{t-1} + .5025(Y_{t-1} - Y_{t-2})$$

While this equation may appear complicated, it is not, because it has a very intuitive explanation.

$$\text{Forecast}_t = \text{Actual}_{t-1} + .5025(\text{Actual}_{t-1} - \text{Actual}_{t-2})$$

FIGURE 8–4

Residuals of ARIMA(0,1,0)1 for SERIESB.DAT

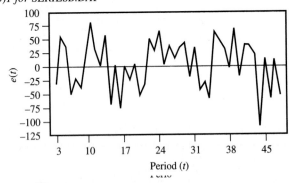

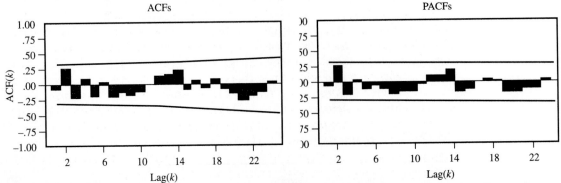

A Hint on Detecting Nonstationarity

As developed in Chapter 7, first differences and AR(1) models are identical when $\phi_1 = 1$, at which point first differences should be taken. This fact provides a very simple way to confirm when first differences are necessary. We can simply fit an AR(1) model and note whether the confidence intervals on ϕ_1 include 1.

Sometimes, however, this procedure is not conclusive; thus, when the modeling process yields AR coefficients that are close to 1 but not inclusive of 1, we should inves-

tigate two models, both the AR(1) and the first differences model I(1), and choose the one with the best attributes as presented in Chapter 7.

Consider the example of SERIESB.DAT. While not shown here, an ARIMA(1,0,0) model yielded $\phi_1 = 1.0082 \pm .0101$ (a 95 percent confidence interval); clearly, this series is best modeled with first differences.

The procedure of fitting AR(p) models can be used to detect nonseasonal and seasonal nonstationarity.

That is, the forecast equals the most recent actual plus about 50 percent of the difference between the most recent actual and the actual of two periods ago. As is true for many ARIMA models, the resulting relationship has an intuitive explanation that can frequently be confirmed by those familiar with the time series.

To forecast with this model, simply substitute known values of Y_t; when these are unknown, use previously forecasted values $\hat{Y}_t$. For example, assume that it is the end of $(t - 1)$ and therefore the forecasts through period $(t + 4)$ are:

$$\hat{Y}_t = Y_{t-1} + .5025(Y_{t-1} - Y_{t-2})$$

$$\hat{Y}_{t+1} = \hat{Y}_t + .5025(\hat{Y}_t - Y_{t-1})$$

$$\hat{Y}_{t+2} = \hat{Y}_{t+1} + .5025(\hat{Y}_{t+1} - \hat{Y}_t)$$

$$\hat{Y}_{t+3} = \hat{Y}_{t+2} + .5025(\hat{Y}_{t+2} - \hat{Y}_{t+1})$$

$$\hat{Y}_{t+4} = \hat{Y}_{t+3} + .5025(\hat{Y}_{t+3} - \hat{Y}_{t+2})$$

Note that the forecasts from $(t + 1)$ to $(t + 4)$ are based on previous forecasts.

Seasonal Time Series

The ability to model complex seasonal time series greatly increases the applicability and usefulness of ARIMA model building. Many time series have periodic and recurrent (i.e., seasonal) influences.

As discussed in Chapter 7, the ARIMA (p, d, q) components and patterns are generalized to seasonal ARIMA $(P, D, Q)^S$. Some other typical patterns are shown in Figure 7–19. However, there are many more possible seasonal models and combinations of seasonal models. For example, a single peak in the ACFs at a seasonal lag (e.g., 4 for quarterly or 12 for monthly) and an exponential decline in PACFs at the seasonal and harmonic lags (e.g., 4, 8, 12, 16, 20, 24, etc., for quarterly data) is indicative of a seasonal moving average model. Also, an exponential decline in the ACFs at seasonal lags and harmonics (e.g., 4, 8, 12, 16, 20, 24, etc.) and a single peak in the PACFs at only the seasonal lag (e.g., 4 for quarterly or 12 for monthly) is indicative of a seasonal autoregressive model. Nonstationary seasonal series have patterns that are similar to those of a seasonal autoregressive model, except the ACFs remain high for several seasonal lags. We will now analyze two seasonal time series.

Demand for an Animal Pharmaceutical (PHARMDEM.DAT)

Identification

Figure 8–5 illustrates the monthly demand for a drug used in the animal pharmaceutical business over the last 13 years. This drug is used to prevent a disease that is highly seasonal, and this seasonality is very pronounced. In addition, there appears to be some trend in the demand for the product.

Figure 8–5 and Table 8–7 illustrate the ACFs and PACFs for this series. As shown, the ACFs at 12, 24, and 36 dominate this very pronounced pattern. The linear decline in seasonal ACFs is indicative of **seasonal nonstationarity.** The PACFs show significant spikes at 1, 12, and 13, among others. The large PACF at 12 is further confirmation of the need for twelfth-order **seasonal differences** to attain stationarity.

Estimation

To confirm whether twelfth-order differences are necessary, let us estimate a seasonal autoregressive model to the data. This model, ARIMA(1,0,0)^{12}, is

$$y_t = \phi_{12} y_{t-12} + e_t$$

$$y_t = 1.000 y_{t-12} + e_t$$

The estimated coefficient confirms that the level of this time series is seasonally nonstationary. Let us now fit a seasonally differenced model with a trend (i.e., constant) coefficient.

FIGURE 8–5

Demand for an animal pharmaceutical (PHARMDEM.DAT)

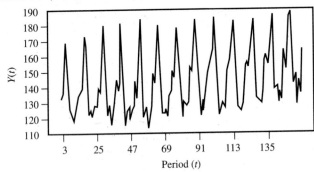

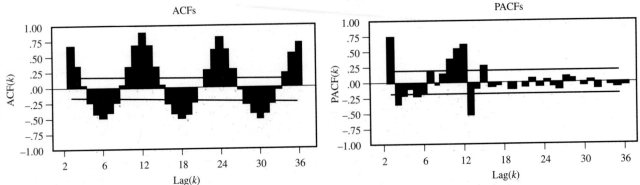

TABLE 8–7 **ACFs and PACFs for Animal Pharmaceutical, (PHARMDEM.DAT)** $n = 156$

ACF(k)							
	1:	.7216	.3617	.0298	−.2005	−.3660	−.4572
	7:	−.3608	−.1962	.0228	.3105	.6519	.8890
	13:	.6580	.3187	.0141	−.2054	−.3581	−.4451
	19:	−.3599	−.2004	−.0005	.2525	.5793	.7821
	25:	.5978	.2761	−.0124	−.2158	−.3519	−.4224
	31:	−.3486	−.1892	−.0218	.0215	.4976	.6715
PACF(k)	1:	.7216	−.3316	−.1839	−.0936	−.1969	−.1573
	7:	.1534	−.0376	.1132	.3543	.5121	.5755
	13:	−.4839	−.0791	.2396	−.0401	−.0189	−.0022
	19:	−.0929	.0023	−.0022	−.0519	.0624	−.0821
	25:	.0361	−.0388	−.0967	.0717	.0567	.0019
	31:	−.0341	.0302	−.0876	.0035	−.0179	−.0583

Approximate $2Se_{ACF(k)} = 2Se_{PACF(k)} = \dfrac{2}{(156)^{.5}} = .160$

TABLE 8–8 **ARIMA,1(0,1,0)^{12} model of PHARMDEM.DAT**

Iterations taken	2
Monthly data from 2:01 to 13:12	
Usable observations	144
Degrees of freedom	143
$\bar{R}^2$/BIC	.963/1118.3
Mean of dependent variable	145.155
Std error of dependent variable	20.778
Standard error of estimate	3.991
Sum of squared residuals	2278.224
Durbin–Watson statistic	2.143
$Q(36-0)$	25.407
Significance level of Q	.906

Coeff.	Estimate	Std Error	t-Stat	Signif
θ_0	2.0874	.3326	6.276	.00000000

The following model is reported in Table 8–8.

$$(1 - B^{12})Y_t = \theta_0 + e_t$$

In forecasting form this is

$$\hat{Y}_t = Y_{t-12} + \theta_0 \qquad (8-2)$$

Diagnosis   The model of Table 8–8 is a very good one; all diagnostic statistics are favorable. The $\bar{R}^2$ is high, the RSE is low, and the DW and Q statistics both denote that the residuals are white noise. Also, the constant coefficient is very significantly different than zero. Thus, there is an annual trend of 2.0874 units.

Table 8–9 and Figure 8–6 illustrate the ACFs and PACFs of the residuals of this model. As shown, there are no patterns or statistically significant coefficients in this

---

TABLE 8–9   ACFs and PACFs of e_t for ARIMA, 1(0,1,0)Y_t (PHARMDEM.DAT)

ACF(k)						
1:	−.0725	.1249	−.0682	−.0373	.0627	−.0616
7:	.1392	.0374	.0026	.0662	−.0949	−.0557
13:	−.0722	−.0041	.0997	−.0434	.0459	−.1055
19:	−.0252	−.0681	.0849	−.0638	−.0311	.0350
25:	.0132	.0637	−.0900	.0471	.0445	−.0254
31:	−.0288	−.0906	−.0706	.0396	.0167	.0311
PACF(k)						
1:	−.0725	.1203	−.0525	−.0610	.0734	−.0468
7:	.1136	.0741	−.0254	.0637	−.0647	−.1017
13:	−.0477	−.0107	.0807	−.0286	.0011	−.0739
19:	−.0202	−.0450	.1120	−.0779	−.0665	.0397
25:	.0248	.0680	−.0527	.0277	.0740	−.0373
31:	−.0924	−.0776	−.0867	.0514	.0404	−.0460

Approximate $2Se_{ACF(k)} = 2Se_{PACF(k)} = \dfrac{2}{(144)^{.5}} = .167$

FIGURE 8–6

Residuals of ARIMA1(0,1,0)^{12} PHARMDEM.DAT

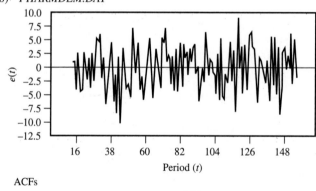

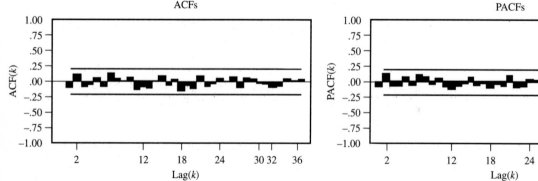

table; again, this is confirmation of white noise residuals. Finally, while not shown here, several other models of this series were tried (i.e., overfitted). AR(1), MA(1), and seasonal MA(12) and AR(12) coefficients were added individually to confirm that the simple model of Table 8–8 is the best. Its higher $\overline{R}^2$ and lower BIC confirmed that we had not overlooked anything in our modeling process.

Forecasting

A seasonal trend model is an effective forecasting tool. As shown here, 12 forecasts can be made based solely on past actual values, because this model reaches back 12 periods. Starting at the end of period $(t - 1)$, the forecasts are:

$$\hat{Y}_t = Y_{t-12} + \theta_0$$

$$\hat{Y}_t = Y_{t-12} + 2.087$$

$$\hat{Y}_{t+1} = Y_{t-11} + 2.087$$

$$\hat{Y}_{t+2} = Y_{t-10} + 2.087$$

$$\cdot \quad \cdot \quad \cdot$$

$$\hat{Y}_{t+11} = Y_{t-1} + 2.087$$

Forecasts for more than 12 periods into the future use previously forecasted values as follows:

$$\hat{Y}_{t+12} = \hat{Y}_t + 2.087 \qquad (8\text{–}3)$$

$$\cdot \quad \cdot \quad \cdot$$

$$\hat{Y}_{t+m} = \hat{Y}_{t+m-12} + 2.087 \qquad \text{for } m > 11$$

These forecasts seem very reasonable and defensible assuming past patterns continue; for further discussion of seasonal trend models see Appendix 8–A.

The next seasonal time series we will analyze is the demand for electricity at a California utility.

California Utility Electricity Demand (MWHRS.DAT)

Identification

Electric utilities face uncertain demands for power, particularly during seasonal peaks when wide temperature variations can occur. Figure 8–7 shows a plot of total monthly megawatt hours (MWHRS) of electricity demanded at a central California utility. During the summer, high temperatures require the use of air conditioners, which influence demand. In contrast, during the winter, low temperatures require the use of furnaces, which also influence demand, but at a different level. Consequently, the ten years (i.e., 120 observations) of peak demand shown in Figure 8–7 are clearly seasonal. In addition, the variance of this series appears slightly nonstationary when, Figure 8–7, without logarithmic transformations, is compared to those of Figure 8–8 with logarithmic transformations. Because of the divergence of lines in Figure 8–7, we will analyze the logs of MWHRS in Figure 8–8.

The consistent increase in the series indicates a trend. This trend can be modeled using the means of either the first-order or seasonal differences. Because the seasonality of the series dominates its pattern, seasonal differences will most likely be necessary to achieve stationarity. As we take differences, be aware that some model builders tend to take more differences than are necessary to achieve stationarity. However, because the seasonality of this particular series may be complex, seasonal, first–order, and a combination of the two differences are explored.

To identify seasonal models most easily, we should include at least three seasonal cycles of ACFs and PACFs; consequently, 36 ACFs and PACFs are included here. Figure 8–8 and Table 8–10 illustrate the ACFs and PACFs of LMWHRS.DAT. As shown, the seasonal peaks of the ACFs at lags 12, 24, and 36 are quite pronounced. Therefore, we take seasonal differences.

FIGURE 8–7

Electricity demand at a California utility (MWHRS.DAT)

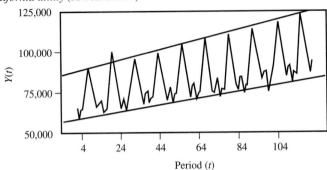

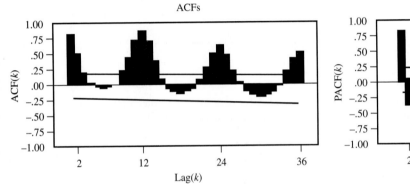

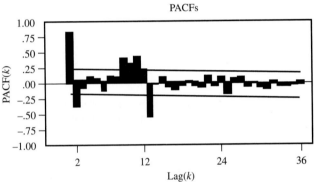

FIGURE 8–8

Logs of electricity demand (LMWHRS.DAT)

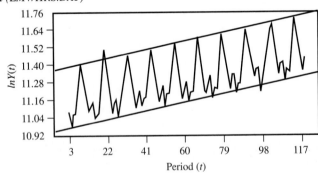

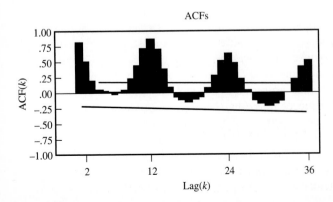

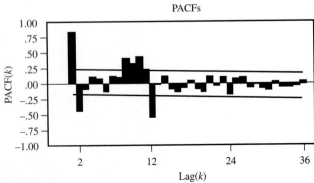

TABLE 8–10   ACFs and PACFs for LMWHRS.DAT

ACF(k)	1:	.7980	.4933	.2020	.02607	−.0237	−.0395
	7:	.0175	.0255	.1774	.4106	.6677	.8093
	13:	.6426	.3664	.1012	−.0582	−.1090	−.1198
	19:	−.0917	−.0465	.0836	.2918	.5116	.6352
	25:	.4870	.2424	.0112	−.1279	−.1644	−.1741
	31:	−.1551	−.1177	−.0042	.1761	.3714	.4830
PACF(k)	1:	.7980	−.3953	−.1036	.0995	.0776	−.1304
	7:	.0858	.0798	.3734	.3099	.4026	.2164
	13:	−.4995	−.0145	.0899	−.0884	−.1158	−.0526
	19:	.0264	−.0547	−.0684	.0975	−.0445	.0867
	25:	−.1555	.0664	.0839	−.0454	.0207	−.0509
	31:	−.0867	.0427	−.0312	−.0333	−.0205	.0524

$$\text{Approximate } 2Se_{ACF(k)} = 2Se_{PACF(k)} = \frac{2}{(120)^{.5}} = .183$$

FIGURE 8–9

$(1-B^{12})$ *Logs of electricity demand (LMWHRS)*

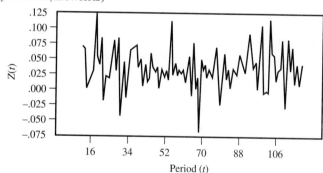

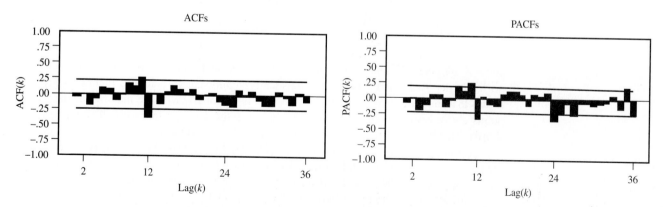

Figure 8–9 shows a graph of seasonal twelfth-differences of Z_t where

$$Z_t = LMWHRS_t - LMWHRS_{t-12}$$

   Table 8–11 presents the statistics of twelfth-order seasonal differences. As shown, the $\overline{R}^2$ is .92; however, this transformation does not achieve white noise residuals as measured by the DW and Q statistics. The ACFs and PACFs of twelfth-order differ-

---

TABLE 8–11   ACFs and PACFs for $(1-B^{12})$LMWHRS

ACF(k)							
	1:	−.0548	−.0066	−.1685	−.0729	.0775	.0726
	7:	−.0857	−.0127	.1504	.1153	.2400	−.3568
	13:	−.0109	−.1324	.0241	.1434	.0887	.0453
	19:	.0971	−.0416	.0125	.0243	−.0710	−.1243
	25:	−.1503	.0813	.0256	.0752	−.0479	−.1244
	31:	−.1202	.0783	−.0167	−.1082	.0295	−.0838
PACF(k)	1:	−.0548	−.0096	−.1700	−.0949	.0649	.0531
	7:	−.1092	−.0074	.1936	.1207	.2488	−.2951
	13:	.0344	−.0842	−.0972	.0818	.1158	.1210
	19:	.0786	−.0729	.0809	.0600	.1184	−.2913
	25:	−.1955	−.0327	−.2102	−.0220	−.0201	−.0498
	31:	−.0361	−.0219	.0655	−.1040	.2167	−.2012

Approximate $2Se_{ACF(k)} = 2Se_{PACF(k)} = \dfrac{2}{(108)^{.5}} = .192$

TABLE 8–12 $(1-B^{12})$LMWHRS

Iterations taken	11
Usable observations	108
Degrees of freedom	108
$\bar{R}^2$/BIC	.9125/−159.0
Mean of dependent variable	11.3396
Std error of dependent variable	.1558
Standard error of estimate	.0461
Sum of squared residuals	.2294
Durbin–Watson statistic	.9676
$Q(27-0)$	48.5163
Significance level of Q	.0067
No estimated coefficients	

ences Z_t are given in Table 8–11 and Figure 8–9. The ACFs and PACFs are stationary; no low-order ACFs and PACFs are statistically significant. In addition, Figure 8–9 shows that the plot of twelfth-order differences is stationary, with the majority of the points above zero, denoting that there is a trend in the series, a fact we will confirm shortly. Therefore, additional differences appear to be unnecessary.

To assure that first differences should not be used to achieve stationarity, consider the plot of $(1-B)LMWHRS_t$ in Figure 8–10. As shown there, the series appears to have a mean of zero, and the pattern is dominated by a repeating seasonal pattern. Also, the ACFs and PACFs of the first differences are nonstationary at the seasonal lags 12, 24, and 36 as shown in Table 8–13. In addition, the ACFs of lags 12, 24, and 36 show a linear decline; thus, twelfth-order seasonal differences of the first differences is necessary. Yet, as we noted previously, twelfth-order differences of the series are already stationary, without taking additional differences. Therefore, the use of first and twelfth differences is likely inappropriate because twelfth differences alone are stationary. To be sure, however, we will consider first *and* twelfth differences anyway.

FIGURE 8–10

Graph of first differences $(1-B)Y_t$

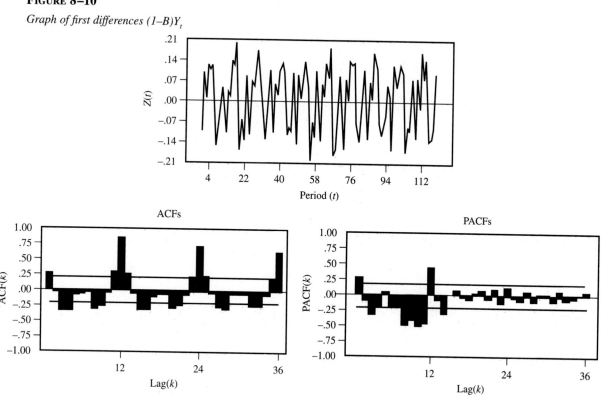

TABLE 8–13   ACFs and PACFs for $(1-B)$(LMWHRS.DAT)

ACF(k)						
1:	.2582	−.0278	−.3162	−.3253	−.0739	−.0631
7:	−.0486	−.2988	−.2389	−.0620	.2965	.8151
13:	.2731	−.0360	−.2858	−.2809	−.0796	−.0524
19:	−.0457	−.2509	−.2145	−.0446	.2486	.7191
25:	.2345	−.0316	−.2428	−.2687	−.0473	−.0500
31:	−.0417	−.2064	−.2013	−.0486	.2246	.6374
PACF(k)						
1:	.2582	−.1012	−.3055	−.1990	.0343	−.1818
7:	−.1975	−.4527	−.3940	−.4832	−.4635	.4214
13:	−.0787	−.2754	.0002	.0643	−.0461	−.0617
19:	.0172	.0681	−.0468	.0891	−.1081	.1173
25:	−.0345	−.0624	.0613	−.0787	.0263	.0334
31:	−.0776	.0680	−.0567	−.0323	−.0059	.0504

Approximate $2Se_{ACF(k)} = 2Se_{PACF(k)} = \dfrac{2}{(119)} = .183$

While not shown here, the first and twelfth differences appear stationary, with a mean of zero. This stationarity is confirmed in the ACFs and PACFs of Table 8–14, which are clearly stationary.

Consider the statistics in Table 8–15, which compares the results of three differences using a number of statistics, the most important being the standard deviation and

TABLE 8–14   ACFs and PACFs for $(1-B)$ $(1-B^{12})$LMWHRS

ACF(k)	1:	−.5237	.1099	−.1255	−.0258	.0689	.0629
	7:	−.1041	−.0343	.0845	−.0649	.3410	−.4489
	13:	.2244	−.1389	.0132	.0867	−.0062	−.0286
	19:	.0856	−.1045	.0309	.0465	−.0250	−.0129
	25:	−.1261	.1366	−.0420	.0802	−.0163	−.0445
	31:	−.0890	.1406	−.0069	−.1069	.1225	−.1567
PACF(k)	1:	−.5237	−.2265	−.2525	−.3154	−.2217	−.0556
	7:	−.1578	−.2938	−.1850	−.2640	.2852	−.0714
	13:	.0350	.0372	−.1465	−.1484	−.1182	−.0319
	25:	−.0472	.1080	−.1102	−.1084	−.0572	−.0469
	31:	−.0336	−.0965	.0649	−.2237	.2100	.0534

Approximate $2Se_{ACF(k)} = 2Se_{PACF(k)} = \dfrac{2}{(107)^{.5}} = .193$

$\bar{R}^2$. As shown, taking combined first and twelfth differences yields approximately the same $\bar{R}^2$ as the simpler twelfth differences. Therefore, there seems to be no advantage in taking both first and twelfth differences. More important, only twelfth differences are necessary to achieve stationarity. Finally, if first and twelfth differences were necessary and we mistakenly took only twelfth differences, then likely the inadequacy of the approach would be apparent in subsequent analyses of the ACFs and PACFs.

The process of taking differences is discussed at length here because over differencing is a very common mistake. Only take as many differences as are necessary to achieve a stationary series. Appendix 8–A discusses seasonal trend models further.

Estimation

Having chosen twelfth-order seasonal differences, we can now identify and estimate the ARMA components. The ACFs and PACFs of Table 8–11 and Figure 8–9 show a pattern of a single statistically significant, negative ACF at lag 12 and three statistically significant, negative, linearly declining PACFs at lags 12, 24, and 36. This pattern appears to be a twelfth-order moving average. We therefore fit an ARIMA,$1(0,1,1)^{12}$ model to LMWHRS.DAT, where the first "1" denotes that a constant is fitted with a seasonally differenced twelfth-order moving–average model. The model is:

$$(1-B^{12})\text{LMWHRS}_t = \theta_0 + (1 - \theta_{12}B^{12})e_t \tag{8–4}$$

$$\text{LMWHRS}_t = \text{LMWHRS}_{t-12} + \theta_0 - \theta_1 e_{t-12} + e_t$$

In forecasting form this is:

$$\widehat{\text{LMWHRS}}_t = \text{LMWHRS}_{t-12} + \theta_0 - \theta_{12}e_{t-12} \tag{8–5}$$

$$= \text{LMWHRS}_{t-12} + \theta_0 - \theta_{12}(\text{LMWHRS}_{t-12} - \widehat{\text{LMWHRS}}_{t-12})$$

which denotes that the forecast of LMWHRS_t equals the value of last year plus a trend and a fraction of the error from the same month last year.

Table 8–16 illustrates the results of fitting and ARIMA,$1(0,1,1)^{12}$ model to the series. As shown, the model converges on an optimal coefficient after 8 iterations.

Diagnosis

The model of Table 8–16 appears to be reasonably good. The $\bar{R}^2$ is high, the BIC low, and all coefficients, including the trend coefficient, are very significant. However, the Q statistic is only marginally consistent with the null hypothesis of white noise

TABLE 8–15   Comparison of Differences of LMWHRS

	Level-Stationary	Mean	Std. Dev.	R^2
LMWHRS	No	11.32	.1608	0
First differences (1–B)LMWHRS	No	.00303	.0997	.615
Twelfth differences $(1-B^{12})$LMWHRS	Yes	.0338	.0314	.912
First and twelfth differences $(1-B)$ $(1-B^{12})$LMWHRS	Yes	−.00016	.0458	.914

TABLE 8–16   Estimation of ARIMA,1(0,1,1)^{12} for LMWHRS.DAT

Iterations taken	8
Usable observations	108
Degrees of freedom	106
$\bar{R}^2$/BIC	.972/−275.7
Mean of dependent variable	11.33960
Std error of dependent variable	.15578
Standard error of estimate	.02595
Sum of squared residuals	.07138
Durbin–Watson statistic	1.857862
Q(27–1)	38.409
Significance level of Q	.0554

Coeff.	Estimate	Std Error	t-Stat	Signif
θ_0	.0328	.00072	45.508	.00000000
$-\theta_{12}$	−.8269	.05867	−14.094	.00000000

Correlation matrix of coefficients $-\theta_{12}$

θ_0	.10468

residuals. In addition, as shown in Table 8–17, none of the low-order ACF and PACF of the residuals for lags 1 to 5 are statistically significant. Also, the DW statistic denotes that ACF(1) is statistically insignificant (i.e., consistent with the white noise assumption). However, we are concerned that there are statistically significant ACFs and PACFs at lags 6 and 11, with 6 being a harmonic of 12, and 11 being very nearly equal to 12.

Figure 8–11 is a plot of the residuals and is fairly well behaved. The ACFs and PACFs in Table 8–17 and Figure 8–11 do not show a clear pattern. While not shown, several other models were tried. Each of these models failed by having one or more insignificant coefficients with no better residual, ACF, and PACF plots than those of the model presented here. Thus, we have converged on Table 8–16 as the best model. While the Q statistic is disturbing, we believe it is relatively unsolvable, unless several outliers of Figure 8–11 are adjusted or the series modeled using temperature or other independent variables in a MARIMA model as discussed in Chapter 13. Demand in a utility is driven by high and low average temperatures in summer and winter, respec-

TABLE 8–17 e_t **ACFs, and PACFs for ARIMA,1(0,1,1)^{12} for LMWHRS.DAT**

ACF(k)						
1:	.0618	−.0422	−.1083	−.0226	.1154	.2247
7:	−.0100	−.0622	.0889	.0700	.2875	.0984
13:	−.0578	−.1585	−.0212	.1192	.1015	.0990
19:	−.0112	−.0481	−.0001	−.0063	.0533	−.0931
25:	−.1874	−.0336	.0510	.0137	−.0364	−.0902
31:	−.1325	−.0037	−.0712	−.1198	−.0098	−.0769
PACF(k)						
1:	.0618	−.0462	−.1033	−.0116	.1106	.2048
7:	−.0291	−.0291	.1454	.0560	.2553	.0713
13:	−.0131	−.1154	−.0581	.0535	−.0451	.0699
19:	.0412	−.0524	−.0410	−.1385	.0299	−.1216
25:	−.1714	.0070	−.0494	−.0701	−.1244	−.0461
31:	−.0429	−.0144	−.0371	−.1377	.0648	.0046

Approximate $2Se_{ACF(k)} = 2Se_{PACF(k)} = \dfrac{2}{(108)^{.5}} = .192$

FIGURE 8–11

ARIMA,1(0,1,1)^{12} of LMWHRS.DAT

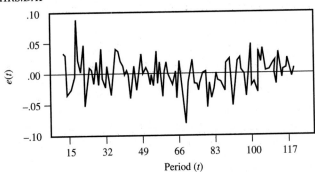

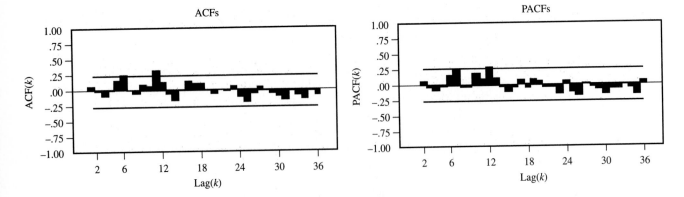

tively. During some seasons, very high (low) temperatures persist from month to month, as in an autoregressive process; in other seasons, there may be no temperature persistence; this creates the different patterns shown in Figure 8–11. Consequently, in some seasons, there will be runs of abnormally high or low temperatures, while in others, there will be short, independent periods of highs and lows.

Transforming Logs to Original Values

Having identified, estimated, and diagnosed this model, let's interpret its meaning. We have been modeling logarithms without discussion of the behavior of the original, non-logarithmic values; fortunately, it is very easy to convert or reverse the process of taking logs by taking the fitted or forecasted log values to the power of the natural number **e** as shown below:

$$\widehat{MWHRS}_t = \mathbf{e}^{\widehat{LMWHRSt}}$$

where $\widehat{LMWHRS}_t$ is calculated in Equation 8–5.

Finally, the nonlogarithmic errors are calculated as

$$e'_t = MWHRS_t - \widehat{MWHRS}_t = MWHRS_t - \mathbf{e}^{\widehat{LMWHRS}}{}_t$$

The essential behavior of a series of logarithms is that the series is undergoing percentage changes over time. In fact, if we were to transform the $MWHRS_t$ to a ratio $MWHRS_t/MWHRS_{t-12}$, it is nearly perfectly correlated with $\mathbf{e}^{(LMWHRSt - LMWHRSt-12)}$ because the subtraction of logs is a division process. That is,

$$\text{Correlation } [(\mathbf{e}^{(LMWHRSt - LMWHRSt-12)}, (MWHRS_t/MWHRS_{t-1})] \simeq 1.0$$

Trends using Logs

The trend coefficient $\theta_0 = .0328$ denotes that $MWHRS_t$ is $\mathbf{e}^{\theta}_0$ times that of period $t - 12$, $MWHRS_{t-12}$. That is:

$$\mathbf{e}^{\theta_0} = \mathbf{e}^{.0328} = 1.03334$$

Alternatively, there is a $1.00730 - 1 = 3.334$ percentage growth in demand per year. Thus, $MWHRS_t$ are on average 103.334% of those of $MWHRS_{t-12}$. These interpretations are reasonable and insightful.

Not only is the trend a percentage of the series, but also the errors are actually percentage processes. That is, the residual errors, e_t and some proportion of the error of 12 periods ago ($-\theta_{12} e_{t-12}$) are added to the logarithmic relationship, but the interpretation in terms of the original, nonlogarithmic time series is that these errors are multiplicative, increasing or decreasing the time series by some percentage error. It is this percentage variation that made the series variance nonstationary and thus required the use of logarithms to model this percentage variation.

This emphasizes that a series with variance nonstationarity is just that, a series without a constant standard deviation or variance. For such series, it is not meaningful to discuss $\bar{R}^2$ because there is no constant explained variance. The meaning of the $\bar{R}^2$ is accurate for the log data, but not so for the original, non-log data. Instead, it is better to interpret the standard error of estimate (i.e., RSE) as a percentage measure. That is, the RSE of Table 8–16 is .02595. In terms of variations of MWHRS, this means that the residuals of Equation 8–4 have a standard error that is .02629 of the level of the series. That is, the RSE of $\widehat{LMWHRS}_t$ is

$$\mathbf{e}^{RSE} = \mathbf{e}^{.02595} = 1.02629$$

This denotes that the error has a variance which is about .02629 of the actual value; that is, the error is 2.629 percent of the actual, where the actual value is nonstationary. Also, this denotes that a 68% prediction interval is a multiplicative interval calculated as:

$$\widehat{MWHRS}_t(1 - .02629) \leq MWHRS_t \leq \widehat{MWHRS}_t(1 + .02629)$$

A 95.45% prediction interval for MWHRS$_t$ is:

$$\widehat{\text{MWHRS}}_t(1 - 2*.02629) \le \text{MWHRS}_t \le \widehat{\text{MWHRS}}_t(1 + 2*.02629) \quad (8\text{–}6)$$

Thus, we see that the RSE is a constant percentage of the level of the series. When expressed this way, the accuracy of the model is reasonable. A 95.45 percent confidence interval of plus or minus 5.26 (i.e., 2*.02629) percent is quite good, but because of the extraordinarily high $\overline{R}^2$, we had hoped for a better fit. However, this disappointment is common with logarithmic processes. Obviously, the smaller the RSE, the lower percentage RSE.

Remembering that the process of adding logs is the equivalent of multiplication, the subtraction of logs is the equivalent of division, and the multiplication of logs is exponentiation, an alternative way of interpreting the ARIMA1(0,1,1) model of logarithms in equation 8–5 is:

$$\widehat{\text{MWHRS}}_t = \text{MWHRS}_{t-12}(e^{\theta_0})(e^{\theta_{12}e_{t-12}}) \quad (8\text{–}7)$$

$$= \text{MWHRS}_{t-12}(e^{.0328})(e^{-.8269e_{t-12}})$$

We leave it to the reader to verify that this calculation results in the equivalent fit of the model of Table 8–16.

The next time series we analyze is a nonseasonal logarithmic one which also illustrates these concepts.

Japan Stock Index (JAPAN.DAT)

*Identification
(JAPAN.DAT)*

Let's analyze a Japanese Stock Index series much as the U.S. Stock index was analyzed in Chapter 7. Because this times series is nonstationary in variance, logarithms are used to achieve variance stationarity. Figure 8–12 graphs the logs of this monthly index, showing that the level is still nonstationary. The ACFs and PACFs in Table 8–18 clearly show the nonstationarity; consequently, first differences of the logarithmic transformations are taken to achieve level stationarity.

Because this is a monthly stock index of a relatively efficient financial market, we do not anticipate statistically significant seasonality. On the other hand, the Japanese economy has been growing, and we do anticipate a trend parameter θ_0; thus, the trend should be estimated.

Estimation

Table 8–19 shows the statistics of a model with first differences and a trend coefficient for the log of the Japan Index. This is an ARIMA(0,1,0)1,1 model which is

$$\ln Y_t = \ln Y_{t-1} + \theta_0 + e_t$$

After estimation, this becomes

$$\ln Y_t = \ln Y_{t-1} + .00723 + e_t$$

Diagnosis 1

As shown in Table 8–19, taking first differences yields an $\overline{R}^2$ of 99.75 percent, which confirms the series is nonstationary. Next, we look at the statistical significance of the trend coefficient θ_0. As shown, this parameter is almost three standard errors away from zero, and the true population coefficient has only a .0042 chance of equaling zero or a negative trend.

FIGURE 8–12

Log (Japan Index)
n = 271

JAPAN.DAT
Source: Survey of Current Business, Table 15 of
Current Business Statistics.

TABLE 8–18   ACFs and PACFs of log(Japan Index)

ACF(k)	1:	.9930	.9847	.9761	.9675	.95730	.94667
	7:	.9359	.9248	.9131	.9007	.88825	.87528
	13:	.8623	.8494	.8368	.8244	.81201	.80008
PACF(k)	1:	.9930	−.0948	−.0129	−.0052	−.1256	−.0101
	7:	−.0116	−.0277	−.0301	−.0419	−.0140	−.0315
	13:	.0057	.0056	.0165	.0188	−.0123	.0282

Approximate $2Se_{ACF(k)} = 2Se_{PACF(k)} = \dfrac{2}{(271-1)^{.5}} = .121$

TABLE 8–19   First Differences of Log(Japan Index) = (1–B)Log(Japan Index)

Usable observations	270
Degrees of freedom	269
$\bar{R}^2$/BIC	.998/−206.8
Mean of dependent variable	6.3586
Std error of dependent variable	.8184
Standard error of estimate	.0411
Sum of squared residuals	.4553
Durbin–Watson statistic	1.2500
Q(36)	74.4910
Significance level of Q	.0002

Coeff	Estimate	Std Error	t-Stat	Signif
θ_0	.007228	.00250	2.887	.0042

Because this model has such a high $\bar{R}^2$ and a statistically significant trend coefficient, we examine whether the residuals e_t are white noise. If they are, then the model
may be valid. The DW is significantly different than 2, and the Q statistic has a level
of significance of .0002, which means it is very unlikely that the residuals of this
model are white noise. In other words, some pattern is left in the residuals. Consider
Table 8–20 and Figure 8–13 showing the ACFs and PACFs of e_t.

TABLE 8–20   ACFs and PACFs of (1–B)log(Japan Index)

ACF(k)	1:	.3720	.1067	.0527	.0365	.0262	−.0060
	7:	.0462	.0482	.1159	.1239	.0423	.0252
	13:	−.0167	−.0428	−.0006	.0071	.0215	.0742
	19:	−.0005	−.0080	−.0383	−.0144	.0283	.0358
PACF(k)	1:	.3720	−.0368	.0293	.0120	.0088	−.0232
	7:	.0642	.0108	.1061	.0497	−.0326	.0132
	13:	−.0391	−.0371	.0362	−.0068	.0132	.0657
	19:	−.0815	.0090	−.0401	.0139	.0520	.0233

$$\text{Approximate } 2S_{ACF(k)} = 2S_{PACF(k)} = \frac{2}{(269)^{.5}} = .122$$

FIGURE 8–13

e_t, ACFs and PACFs for ARIMA(0,1,0)1 of Log(Japan Index)

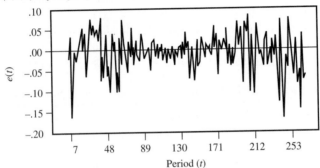

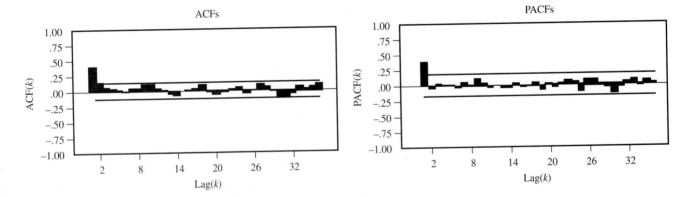

Both Table 8–20 and Figure 8–13 show that there are statistically significant ACFs and PACFs at lag 1 only. While these patterns are a little ambiguous, we assume that an AR(1) coefficient is necessary to achieve white noise. This interpretation is based on the near exponential decline in the first three ACFs and the single significant peak in the PACFs at lag 1. Also, there are no peaks in the ACFs and PACFs at lag 12 or 24; thus, seasonality is not apparent at this stage of the analysis. Subsequent model refinement may provide some minor seasonality. Table 8–21 illustrates the results of fitting an ARIMA(1,1,0)1 model to the logs of the Japan Index.

TABLE 8–21   ARIMA(1,1,0)1 for Log(Japan Index)

Iterations taken	3
Usable observations	269
Degrees of Freedom	267
$\bar{R}^2$/BIC	.9978/−241.1
Mean of dependent variable	6.3634
Std error of dependent variable	.8161
Standard error of estimate	.0383
Sum of squared residuals	.3914
Durbin–Watson statistic	1.961
$Q(36)$	25.718
Significance level of Q	.8738

Coeff	Estimate	Std Error	t-Stat	Signif
θ_0	.0072688	.003728	1.950	.0522
ϕ_1	.3737502	.056879	6.571	.00000000

Correlation Matrix of Coefficients θ_1

θ_0	−.00323

TABLE 8–22   ACFs and PACFs of residuals of ARIMA(1,1,0)1 of log(Japan Index)

ACF(k)							
	1:	.0159	−.0413	−.0060	.0222	.0241	−.0385
	7:	.0422	−.0049	.0815	.0910	−.0066	.0242
	13:	−.0104	−.0455	.0144	.0040	−.0064	.0801
	19:	−.0305	.0053	−.0398	−.0115	.0344	.0636
PACF(k)	1:	.0159	−.0416	−.0047	.0207	.0230	−.0376
	7:	.0458	−.0098	.0845	.0898	−.0024	.0303
	13:	−.0102	−.0543	.0186	−.0026	−.0145	.0828
	19:	−.0522	.0029	−.0403	−.0211	.0414	.0781

Approximate $2S_{ACF(k)} = 2S_{PACF(k)} = \dfrac{2}{(269)^{.5}} = .122$

Diagnosis 2

The residuals of the model in Table 8–21 are more consistent with a white noise assumption as shown by the DW and Q statistics. The $\bar{R}^2$ is higher and BIC lower, and all coefficients remain significant, while the constant is only marginally so. Table 8–22 and Figure 8–14 illustrate the ACFs and PACFs of the residuals. As shown, no patterns are discernible, and all values are essentially zero.

Figure 8–14 shows a graph of the model residuals. There is some hint of variance nonstationary, but there is no easy way of correcting this condition other than through an **autoregressive conditional heteroskedastic (ARCH)** model, which is discussed in Enders (1995). For now, we will ignore the variance nonstationarity shown in Figure 8–14.

An important issue is should the constant be included (i.e., is there a trend in the series)? Consider the results of fitting an ARIMA(1,1,0) model without the trend component. The resulting model varied little from that of Table 8–21: all statistics re-

FIGURE 8–14

e_t, ACFs and PACFs for ARIMA(1,1,0)1 of Log(Japan Index)

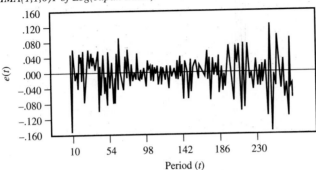

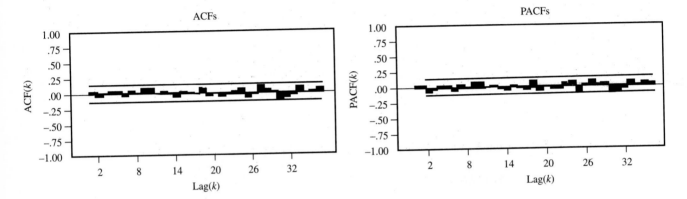

mained essentially the same, including $\overline{R}^2$, while the value of ϕ_1 changed only slightly, from .3738 to .3931. While not shown, the BIC with no trend (-243.1) is slightly better, nonetheless, the inclusion of the constant depends on the theory of the situation; that is, whether the trend of the series is expected to continue into the future.

From a statistical standpoint, the constant should be eliminated because of parsimony. As Box and Jenkins emphasize, deterministic trends are not as common in the social sciences as they are in the physical sciences. Unless there is strong evidence of a sustained trend, none should be included in the model. Thus, θ_0 should be dropped from the model. For explanatory reasons we will discuss both deterministic and stochastic trend models of this time series. The rapid and sustained economic growth in the Japanese economy since early 1950 suggests that a trend should be included in the model. However, the decline in the Japan Index from 1990 through 1992 is notable. These suggest hedging by forecasting both with and without the trend constant.

*Interpretation:
ARIMA(1,1,0)1,
Trend*

The simple model of Table 8–21 is

$$(1 - \phi_1 B)(1 - B)\ln Y_t = \theta_0 + e_t \tag{8–8}$$

Expanding this model yields

$$(1 - B - \phi_1 B + \phi_1 B^2)\ln Y_t = \theta_0 + e_t$$

$$\ln Y_t = \ln Y_{t-1} + \phi_1(\ln Y_{t-1} - \ln Y_{t-2}) + \theta_0 + e_t$$

In forecasting form, this is

$$\ln\hat{Y}_t = \ln Y_{t-1} + \phi_1(\ln Y_{t-1} - \ln Y_{t-2}) + \theta_0 \qquad (8-9)$$

where:

$\ln Y_{t-1}$ = log (Japan Index)
θ_0 = estimated trend coefficient
ϕ_1 = autoregressive coefficient

Substituting appropriate coefficients from Table 8–21 yields

$$\ln\hat{Y}_t = \ln Y_{t-1} + .37375(\ln Y_{t-1} - \ln Y_{t-2}) + .007269 \qquad (8-10)$$

For example,

$$\ln\hat{Y}_{\text{Jan}} = \ln Y_{\text{Dec}} + .37375(\ln Y_{\text{Dec}} - \ln Y_{\text{Nov}}) + .007269$$

This relationship has considerable intuitive appeal. The value of $\ln Y_t$ is equal to the previous value, $\ln Y_{t-1}$, plus a fraction of the difference between $\ln Y_{t-1}$, and $\ln Y_{t-2}$, plus a deterministic trend of .007269. Let us use this relationship to fit several in-sample values; we can then use it to forecast several out-of-sample values.

Table 8–23 shows the actual, fitted, and residual values of the model in Table 8–21. The third and fourth values of that table are calculated as follows:

$$\ln\hat{Y}_{262} = \ln Y_{261} + .37375\ln(Y_{261} - \ln Y_{260}) + .007269$$
$$= 7.3857 + .37375(7.3857 - 7.3734) + .007269 = 7.3949$$
$$e_{262} = \ln Y_{262} - \ln\hat{Y}_{262} = 7.4348 - 7.3949 = .0399$$
$$\ln\hat{Y}_{263} = \ln Y_{262} + .37375(\ln Y_{262} - \ln Y_{261}) + .007269$$
$$= 7.4348 + .37375(7.4348 - 7.3857) + .007269 = 7.4604$$
$$= -7.4578 \text{ (roundoff error; see note in Table 8–23)}$$
$$e_{263} = 7.3974 - 7.4578 = -.0604$$

TABLE 8–23   In-sample fit of ARIMA(1,1,0)1*

t	Date	$\ln Y_t$	$\ln\hat{Y}_t$	e_t
260	1991:08	7.3734	7.3908	−.0175
261	1991:09	7.3857	7.3671	.0186
262	1991:10	7.4348	7.3949	.0399
263	1991:11	7.3974	7.4578	−.0604
264	1991:12	7.3352	7.3880	−.0528
265	1992:01	7.2962	7.3165	−.0203
266	1992:02	7.2626	7.2862	−.0235
267	1992:03	7.1952	7.2546	−.0594
268	1992:04	7.0699	7.1745	−.1047
269	1992:05	7.1251	7.0276	.0975
270	1992:06	7.0699	7.1503	−.0804
271	1992:07	7.0306	7.0538	−.0232

* More exact coefficients used to fit the above values are:
$\ln Y_t = \ln Y_{t-1} + .0072687930 + .3737502423(\ln Y_{t-1} - \ln Y_{t-2})$

Transforming Logs to Original Values. As discussed previously, it is very easy to convert or reverse the process of taking logs by taking the fitted or forecasted log values to the power of the natural number **e** as follows:

$$Y_{262} = \mathbf{e}^{\ln Y_t} = \mathbf{e}^{7.4348} = 1693.92 \qquad (8\text{-}11)$$

$$\hat{Y}_{262} = \mathbf{e}^{\ln Y_t} = \mathbf{e}^{7.3949} = 1627.66$$

Finally, the error is calculated as

$$Y_{262} - \hat{Y}_{262} = \mathbf{e}^{\ln Y_t} - \mathbf{e}^{\ln Y_t} = 1693.92 - 1627.66 = 66.26$$

where **e** is the natural number 2.718282.

The essential behavior of a series of logarithms is that the series undergoes percentage changes over time. In fact, if we were to transform the Japan Index to a ratio $\dfrac{Y_t}{Y_{t-1}}$ it is nearly perfectly correlated with $\mathbf{e}^{(\ln Y_t - \ln Y_{t-1})}$ because the subtraction of logs is a division process. That is,

$$\text{Correlation}\left[\mathbf{e}^{(\mathrm{n}Y_t - \ln Y_{t-1})}, \left(\frac{Y_t}{Y_{t-1}}\right)\right] \simeq 1.0$$

Trends Using Logs. The trend coefficient $\theta_0 = .0072688$ denotes that the value in period t is $\mathbf{e}^{\theta_0}$ times that of period $(t - 1)$. That is,

$$\mathbf{e}^{\theta_0} = \mathbf{e}^{.0072688} = 1.00730$$

Alternatively, there is a $(1.00730 - 1) = .73$ percentage growth in the index per month. This equates to a $1.0073^{12} - 1 = .0912$ or 9.12 percent annual growth in the index during this time period. These interpretations are reasonable, and depending on our purpose in analyzing this series, we should not be too quick to discard this trend coefficient.

Remember that a series with variance nonstationarity is just that: a series without a constant standard deviation or variance. For such series, it is not meaningful to discuss $\overline{R}^2$, because there is no constant explained variance. The meaning of $\overline{R}^2$ is accurate for the log data, but not for the original data. Instead, it is better to interpret the RSE as a percentage measure. The standard error of Table 8–21 is .038287. In terms of variations of the Japan Index, this means that the random shocks have a standard error that is .03903 of the level of the series. That is, the RSE of the Japan Index is

$$\mathbf{e}^{\mathrm{RSE}} = \mathbf{e}^{.038287} = 1.03903$$

This denotes that the standard error is about .039 i.e., (3.9 percent) of the actual, where the actual value is nonstationary. This also means that a 68 percent confidence interval for Y_t is a multiplicative interval calculated as follows

$$\hat{Y}_t(1 - .03903) \leq Y_t \leq \hat{Y}_t(1 + .03903)$$

A 95.45 percent confidence interval for Y_t is

$$\hat{Y}_t(1 - 2 \cdot .03903) \leq Y_t \leq \hat{Y}_t(1 + 2 \cdot .03903) \qquad (8\text{-}12)$$

Thus, we see that the RSE is a constant percentage of the level of the series. When expressed this way, the accuracy of the model is a little disappointing. A 95.45 percent confidence interval, plus or minus 7.8 percent, is normally quite good. But because of the extraordinarily high $\overline{R}^2$, we had hoped for a better fit. However, this disappointment is common with logarithmic processes. Obviously, the smaller the RSE, the lower the percentage RSE.

Remember that the process of adding logs is the equivalent of multiplication, the subtraction of logs is the equivalent of division, and the multiplication of logs is exponentiation. Therefore, an alternative way of interpreting the ARIMA(1,1,0)1 model of logarithms is:

$$\hat{Y}_t = Y_{t-1}\left(\frac{Y_{t-1}}{Y_{t-2}}\right)^{\phi_1}(e^{\theta_0})$$

$$= Y_{t-1}\left(\frac{Y_{t-1}}{Y_{t-2}}\right)^{.37375}(e^{.0072688})$$

We leave it to the reader to verify that this calculation results in the equivalent fit and forecast of the model of Table 8–21.

Interpretation:
ARIMA(1,1,0),
No Trend

The interpretation of an ARIMA(1,1,0) model is identical to the previous equation, except there is no trend coefficient θ_0. Thus,

$$\ln Y_t = \ln Y_{t-1} + \phi_1(\ln Y_{t-1} - \ln Y_{t-2}) + e_t$$

In backshift notation, this is

$$(1 - \phi_1 B)(1 - B)\ln Y_t = e_t$$

Expanding this model yields

$$(1 - B - \phi_1 B + \phi_1 B^2)\ln Y_t = e_t$$

$$\ln Y_t = \ln Y_{t-1} + \phi_1(\ln Y_{t-1} - \ln Y_{t-2}) + e_t$$

In forecasting form, we have

$$\ln \hat{Y}_t = \ln Y_{t-1} + \phi_1(\ln Y_{t-1} - \ln Y_{t-2})$$

Substituting coefficients for the estimation process yields

$$\ln \hat{Y}_t = \ln Y_{t-1} + .393122443(\ln Y_{t-1} - \ln Y_{t-2})$$

Comparison

Figure 8–15 illustrates the fits of the two models, with and without trend. As shown, both models yield almost identical values. Despite similar fits, we will see that these models yield much different multiperiod forecasts; thus the significance of the choice of trend or no trend.

FIGURE 8–15

Fitted values with and without trend

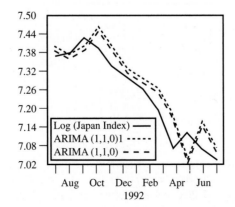

To better understand how each of these models performs in forecasting as opposed to fitting, consider Figures 8–16a and b and Figure 8–17. Figure 8–16a illustrates the accuracy of each model in the multiple-period forecasting of October 1991 through June 1992, made as of the end of September 1991, using fitted models for data from January 1970 through September 1991. Neither model performs very well; however, the trendless ARIMA(1,1,0) model is better.

Figure 8–17 illustrates 1-to 20-months-ahead forecasts made as of July 1, 1992. While the figure does not show which forecast is best, the significance of forecasts with or without trend is obvious. Table 8–24 illustrates the values of these forecasts, using both models.

FIGURE 8–16

Forecasts with and without trend

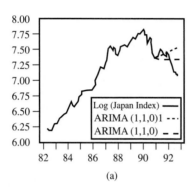

(a)

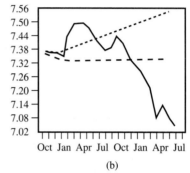

(b)

FIGURE 8–17

Forecasting out-of-sample data with and without trend

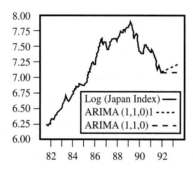

TABLE 8–24   **Forecasts as of July 1, 1992, for Log(Japan Index)**

t	*Date*	*Trend (1,1,0)1*	*No trend (1,1,0)*	*Actual*
271	1992:07	7.0538	7.0481	7.0306
272	1992:08	7.0523	7.0396	
273	1992:09	7.0563	7.0363	
274	1992:10	7.0624	7.0349	
275	1992:11	7.0692	7.0344	
276	1992:12	7.0763	7.0342	
	. . .			
288	1993:12	7.1634	7.0341	
289	1994:01	7.1707	7.0341	
290	1994:02	7.1780	7.0341	

Summary: Fit and Forecast, JAPAN.DAT

It appears that the analysis of this series is complete. (While not illustrated here, two models were overfitted to confirm that the modeling process was complete. These other models had coefficients that were insignificant.) As we have noted, the $\overline{R}^2$s of these two models are extremely high. However, a strict interpretation of $\overline{R}^2$ is inappropriate because the variances, total, explained, and unexplained values are not constant. Instead, we interpret the standard errors in terms of the percentage errors. In the ARIMA(1,1,0)1 model, the percentage errors have a standard error of approximately 3.9 percent of the level of the series. While we might not be completely satisfied with this percentage error, or confident regarding which model is the best, our understanding of the univariate behavior of the Japan Index is greatly enriched through this ARIMA model.

From this analysis we can build at least two scenarios: either the index randomly walks, or it has a slight trend. Historically, these indexes have globally trended upward with local random walks; we note that the Japan Index did not display a trend from 1990 to 1996, but instead was a random walk.

Summary and Conclusions

This chapter presented models for four time series that represent a variety of stochastic processes. In addition, we have illustrated a number of complex and subtle nuances of the modeling process. To better understand the process, Table 8–25 summarizes these models.

Two of the series required logarithmic transformations to achieve variance stationarity; two were seasonal, with various levels of complexity. The number of observations of the models analyzed varied from a low of 48 to a high of 270. Typically, ARIMA model building requires at least 60 observations. Thus, the number of observations in one of the series was low.

However, lack of data is a problem that plagues many forecasting situations. From our examples, we have seen the effectiveness of ARIMA models when the data quantity and quality support clearly defined ACFs and PACFs. Let's review the process used to choose these models.

The steps of ARIMA model building are iterative. Note, also, that the procedures described in this chapter apply to all forms of model building.

TABLE 8–25   **Summary of ARIMA applications**

Series	n	Logs	Final Model	$\overline{R}^2$/BIC	Coefficients	DW	Q
SERIESB.DAT Common stock prices	48	No RSE = 44.89	(1,1,0)	.92/528.9	$\phi_1 = .5025$ (.0002)	2.061	11.843 (.296)
PHARMDEM. DAT Pharmaceutical	156	No RSE = 3.991	$1(0,1,0)^{12}$	.96/1118.3	$\phi_0 = 2.087$ (.0000)	2.143	25.467 (.906)
MWHRS.DAT California utility	120	Yes RSE = .0260	$1,1(0,1,1)^{12}$	.97/−275.7	$\theta_0 = .0328$ (.0000) $\theta_{12} = −.8269$ (.0000)	2.12	38.41 (.0555)
JAPAN.DAT Stock index	270	Yes RSE = .0383	(1,1,0)1,1	.998/−241.1	$\theta_0 = .00727$ (.0522) $\phi_1 = .37375$ (.0000)	1.96	25.718 (.8738)

Identification

Before doing an analysis, study the series of interest. What is it? What are some of the cause and effect relationships of the series? What are some of the seasonal cause and effect relationships? How is the series measured? Is this one series, or two or more series? Analyze plots of the series. Is there a lot of noise in the series? If so, then this may be a very difficult series to analyze using ARIMA. Also, remember the principle of parsimony. Complex ARIMA models are not expected; normally, there are not more than two or three coefficients in the model, unless there is seasonality. Often, simpler models forecast out-of-sample values better than complex, overfitted models.

Plot the series, use a scatter diagram, use a histogram, and use standardized plots. Are summary statistics approximately normal distributed? If not, consider transformations, such as logarithms. Using plots, confirm that the expected patterns exist. Is there seasonality as expected? Why or why not? Is there variance stationarity? Why or why not? Is there level stationarity?

Look for outliers. Be careful to ensure that seasonality is not caused by outliers. Alternatively, do not mistakenly adjust seasonal values, thinking they are outliers. Investigate obvious outliers. Document the outliers with full explanation. Under all circumstances, keep a copy of your unadjusted original data.

Is the series stationary in level and variance, as evidenced by plots of the series, autocorrelations, and partial autocorrelations? If not stationary in variance, transform the series as needed, using logs or power transformations.

If not stationary in level, investigate the appropriate level of differencing. Consider both seasonal and nonseasonal differencing. Be careful not to overdifference. When in doubt, fit an autoregressive model with the appropriate ϕ lag: ϕ should be close to 1.0, but not necessarily exactly one. When in doubt about differencing, develop two models: one with AR(p), and the other with appropriate differences.

When taking differences assure that the standard deviation goes down. After taking differences, reevaluate the series. Particularly investigate the outliers created during the differencing process. Also, after taking differences, study auto- and partial correlations for significant patterns. These should provide a hint of the underlying stochastic process.

Be sure to use and confirm ACF and PACF patterns, using graphs of profiles. Remember basic patterns and their behavior with positive and negative ϕ and θ parameters.

Avoid a shotgun approach in which several coefficients are put in the relationship at the same time. Build all models iteratively.

Estimation

Estimate the model suggested from the ACFs and PACFs. Confirm that the nonlinear estimation procedure converges and terminates its search as expected. If the estimation has trouble converging on parameter estimates, increase the number of iterations, with 40 or 50 being the maximum. Also, investigate the cause of the convergence problem; typically, the model is too complex, has redundant coefficients or the wrong coefficients.

Request a correlation matrix between coefficients. If the correlation is very high, try dropping each and then both. If there is no significant change in the sum of the squared errors, they probably do not belong in the model. Remember the concept of parsimony.

Add coefficients one at a time; do not add several coefficients at once. If you do, go back and repeat the analysis step by step, coefficient by coefficient, to assure that you have not converged on the incorrect model.

Iteratively add and delete model components until no new improvements are possible.

Diagnosis

A good model should have the following statistical characteristics:

- Statistically significant coefficients.
- Stationary and invertible coefficients.
- Low RSE compared to the standard deviation of the original series.
- High $\bar{R}^2$.
- Low BIC in comparison to other models.
- White noise residuals.
- Q or Box–Ljung statistic indicates that there is no pattern in the ACFs for the first 20 to 30 lags.
- The ACFs and PACFs confirm that:
  - No significant correlations exist at low-order lags.
  - No significant correlations exist at or adjacent to seasonal lags.
- Plots of residuals show no outliers or nonstationarity. If significant outliers exist, then your model may not be as efficient as possible, and your analysis may be flawed. Compare the results of competing models.

Remember that achieving white noise is not the ultimate objective. Some models are defensible even if there are some high correlations. To better understand this, consider the fact that the results of using Winters, Fourier series analysis, or classical decomposition methods yield residuals (i.e., errors) that are extremely autocorrelated.

Forecasting

Forecasted (not fitted) values are reasonable, particularly when confirmed by expert opinion. Forecast error variance profiles are also reasonable (a topic of Chapter 9).

- Overfit the model to confirm that additional parameters are not necessary.
- When necessary, generate several alternative models of the series.
- Provide management with the results, forecasts, and assumptions, such as the continuation of a trend.
- When everything else is equal, parsimony is the principle in choosing one model over another.

Forecasts can differ significantly from one model to another. Forecast behavior is important in deciding which model to choose. Choose the model that best fits the data, confirms the expert opinion about the underlying behavior of the series, and provides relatively accurate forecasts for actual data withheld during the fitting process.

Also, everything else being equal, a model with narrower confidence intervals on the coefficients is a better than a model with wider confidence intervals.

A Fresh Perspective

When you need to ensure that an important alternative or more appropriate model has not been overlooked, consider alternative modeling strategies. For example, if outliers are not adjusted properly, an inappropriate model may be identified.

Try alternative types of differences to see if they might yield better models. Remember, however, that differences are only necessary to achieve stationarity. The second time you analyze a series goes much more quickly, possibly one fifth of the time needed for the first analysis.

Be sure to complete each of the required steps for the series analysis. Also, record summary statistics, such as those given in Table 8–25, for each model in your analysis. This is a very important step; otherwise, you may find yourself refitting the same models over again.

Pay particular attention to the concept of parsimony. Track the level of $\overline{R}^2$ as additional coefficients are added to the model. Are you modeling the underlying process, or its realization? Remember that a high-order AR series can often be modeled better as a first-order MA, and vice versa.

The Best Model

In summary, the best practical model will:

1. Make sense from an intuitive and theoretical standpoint. Some of the coefficients may not seem logical or intuitive, but differences and lags of the coefficients should make sense.
2. Yield out-of-sample forecasts that are accurate and theoretically sound.
3. Be parsimonious, simple and effective.
4. Have coefficients that are statistically significant and uncorrelated.
5. Yield the best intuitive forecasts and error variance profiles. (See Chap. 9)
6. Have high $\overline{R}^2$ and BIC.
7. Clearly represent the demand patterns expected.

Several different models may yield similar attributes. In such cases, discard all but one of the models, if the models are truly identical. If the models provide different insights into the series, use more than one model, especially if your goal is to achieve the highest accuracy of forecasts. Then, build scenarios with multiple models, when appropriate. The forecasts of several models can be combined effectively using the methods presented in Chapter 17.

In the next chapter, we present additional topics that we feel are essential for effective ARIMA model building. These topics include: more sophisticated methods for selecting from competing models and the generation of forecasting prediction intervals.

Key Terms

ARIMA flowchart
auto regressive conditional heteroscedastic
  (ARCH)
forecast reasonableness

iterations
overdifferencing
seasonal differences
seasonal nonstationarity

Key Formulas

SERIESB.DAT: Common stock prices

(0,1,0)1

$$Y_t = Y_{t-1} + \theta_0 + e_t$$

$$Y_t = Y_{t-1} + 9.0851 + e_t$$

(1,1,0)1

$$(1-\phi_1 B)(1 - B)Y_t = e_t$$

$$\hat{Y}_t = Y_{t-1} + \phi_1(Y_{t-1} - Y_{t-2})$$

$$\hat{Y}_t = Y_{t-1} + .5025(Y_{t-1} - Y_{t-2})$$

$$\text{Forecast}_t = \text{Actual}_{t-1} + .5025(\text{Actual}_{t-1} - \text{Actual}_{t-2})$$

(8–1)

PHARMDEM.DAT

$$(1-B^{12})Y_t = \theta_0 + e_t$$
$$\hat{Y}_t = Y_{t-12} + \theta_0$$
$$\hat{Y}_t = Y_{t-12} + 2.087 \tag{8-2}$$
$$\cdot \quad \cdot \quad \cdot$$
$$\hat{Y}_{t+11} = Y_{t-1} + 2.087$$
$$\hat{Y}_{t+12} = Y_t + 2.087$$
$$\cdot \quad \cdot \quad \cdot$$
$$\hat{Y}_{t+m} = \hat{Y}_{t+m-12} + 2.087 \qquad \text{for } m > 11 \tag{8-3}$$

MWHRS.DAT

$$(1 - B^{12})\text{LMWHRS}_t = \theta_0 + (1 - \theta_{12}B^{12})e_t \tag{8-4}$$
$$\widehat{\text{LMWHRS}}_t = \text{LMWHRS}_{t-12} + \theta_0 - \theta_1 e_{t-12} \tag{8-5}$$
$$= \text{LMWHRS}_{t-12} + \theta_0 - \theta_1(\text{LMWHRS}_{t-12} - \widehat{\text{LMWHRS}}_{t-12})$$

JAPAN.DAT

$$\mathbf{e}^{RSE} = \mathbf{e}^{.02595} = 1.02629 \tag{8-6}$$
$$\text{MWHRS}_t(1 - 2*.02629) \le \text{MWHRS}_t \le \text{MWHRS}_t(1 + 2*.02629) \tag{8-7}$$
$$\text{MWHRS}_t = \text{MWHRS}_{t-12}(\mathbf{e}^{.0328})(\mathbf{e}^{-.8269*e_{t-12}})$$

(1,1,0)1: Trend Model

$$(1 - \phi_1 B)(1 - B)\ln Y_t = \theta_0 + e_t \tag{8-8}$$
$$\ln\hat{Y}_t = \ln Y_{t-1} + \phi_1(\ln Y_{t-1} - \ln Y_{t-2}) + \theta_0 \tag{8-9}$$
$$\ln\hat{Y}_t = \ln Y_{t-1} + .37375(\ln Y_{t-1} - \ln Y_{t-2}) + .007269 \tag{8-10}$$
$$\hat{Y}_{262} = \mathbf{e}^{\ln Y_t} = \mathbf{e}^{7.3949} = 1627.66 \tag{8-11}$$
$$e_t = Y_{262} - \hat{Y}_{262} = 1693.92 - 1627.66 = 66.26$$
$$\text{Correlation}\left[\mathbf{e}^{(\ln Y_t - \ln Y_{t-1})}, \left(\frac{Y_t}{Y_{t-1}}\right)\right] \simeq 1.0$$

Trends using logs

$$\mathbf{e}^{\theta_0} = \mathbf{e}^{.0072688} = 1.00730$$

RSE using logs

$$\mathbf{e}^{RSE} = \mathbf{e}^{.038287} = 1.03903$$
$$\hat{Y}_t(1 - .03903) \le Y_t \le \hat{Y}_t(1 + .03903)$$

95.45 percent prediction interval

$$\hat{Y}_t(1 - 2 \cdot .03903) \le Y_t \le \hat{Y}_t(1 + 2 \cdot .03903) \tag{8-12}$$
$$\hat{Y}_t = Y_{t-1}\left(\frac{Y_{t-1}}{Y_{t-2}}\right)^{\phi_1}\mathbf{e}^{\theta_0}$$
$$= Y_{t-1}\left(\frac{Y_{t-1}}{Y_{t-2}}\right)^{.37375}(\mathbf{e}^{.0072688})$$

Review Problems Using Your Software

R8–1 Using SERIESB.DAT, fit an ARIMA(0,1,0)1 model and interpret your results. Also, interpret the ACF and PACF patterns of the residuals.

R8–2 Completely analyze one of the following, as was done in this chapter. Fully interpret the output of your software. What statistics are and are not reported by your software?
   a. SERIESB.DAT
   b. PHARMDEM.DAT
   c. MWHRS.DAT
   d. JAPAN.DAT

R8–3 Using your software, duplicate the final model reported in this chapter for selected time series. Interpret the output of your software, as was done in the textbook.
   a. SERIESB.DAT
   b. PHARMDEM.DAT
   c. MWHRS.DAT
   d. JAPAN.DAT

Problems

8–1 Define the four steps of ARIMA model building, using a brief paragraph to describe each step.

8–2 How do you detect seasonal, level nonstationarity in a time series? Be thorough in your answer.

8–3 How do you detect seasonal, variance nonstationarity in a time series? Be thorough in your answer.

8–4 How many observations are necessary to successfully identify an ARIMA model?

8–5 If a trend model and a random walk model fit a time series equally well, yet the trend coefficient is not clearly statistically significant, how should one model be selected over the other? How about choosing one over the other when the trend coefficient is clearly statistically significant?

8–6 Calculate the two standard error limits for ACF(k) and PACF(k) for $n = 100$ and $k = 1$, 10, and 24.

8–7 Why does variance nonstationarity make model identification difficult for a time series? Relate your answer to the formula for ACF(k) for the nonstationary series.

8–8 In terms of the original time series, describe the meaning of the constant and RSE for a time series fitted to a logarithmic relationship.

8–9 When is level stationarity achieved in ARIMA model building?

8–10 Graphically describe the ACF and PACF patterns for the following quarterly ARIMA processes:
   a. $(0,1,0)^4$ *b.* $(1,0,0)^4$
   c. $(0,0,1)^4$ *d.* $(1,0,1)^4$

8–11 What is the affect of outliers on ACFs and PACFs? Relate your answer to the formula of the ACF.

8–12 What are the formulas used to convert a logarithmic forecast into the original time series?

8–13 Show that an ARIMA $(0,1,1)^{12}$ is the equivalent of a seasonal single exponential smoothing model:

$$Y_t = \alpha Y_{t-12} + (1 - \alpha)\hat{Y}_{t-12}$$

8–14 Write out the best model fitted to SERIESB.DAT using standard, backshift, and forecasting ARIMA notation in the formulations.

8–15 The series BIRTHMAR.DAT includes quarterly marriages in the United States. Complete the common minicase forecasting assignment.

8–16 The time series RETAIL.DAT is the monthly retail sales in the United States. Complete the common minicase forecasting assignment.

8–17 The time series SUPEROIL.DAT is the sales of Superoil Company, in the thousands of barrels, during the last 108 months. Complete the common minicase forecasting assignment.

Minicases: Common Assignment for Minicases

For a selected minicase or problem, complete the following analysis. Develop an ARIMA model for the selected time series. As you achieve stationarity and white noise, fill out two tables: one the equivalent of Table 8–15, and the other the equivalent of Table 8–25. Also, if you have been filling out the Master Forecasting Summary Table, forecast the withheld quantities listed with each minicase.

Minicase 8–1 Kansas Turnpike, Daily Data
(TURNPIKD.DAT), withhold 14 days.

Minicase 8–2 Domestic Air Passengers by Quarter
(PASSAIR.DAT), withhold 8 quarters.

Minicase 8–3 Hospital Census by Month
(CENSUSM.DAT), withhold 36 months.

Minicase 8–4 Henry Machler's Hideaway Orchids
(MACHLERD.DAT), withhold 7 days.

Minicase 8–5 Your Forecasting Project

Minicase 8–6 Midwestern Building Materials
(LUMBER.DAT), withhold 12 months.

Minicase 8–7 International Airline Passengers
(AIRLINE.DAT), withhold 36 months.

Minicase 8–8 Automobile Sales (AUTO.DAT), withhold 12 months.

Minicase 8–9 Consumption of Distilled Spirits
(SPIRITS.DAT), withhold 12 months.

Minicase 8–10 Discount Consumer Electronics
(ELECT.DAT), withhold 12 months.

References

Abraham, B.; and J. Ledolter. *Statistical Methods for Forecasting*. New York: Wiley, 1983.

Ansley, C.F.; and P. Newbold. "Finite sample properties of estimators for autoregressive-moving average models." *Journal of Econometrics* 13, (1980), pp. 159–183.

Bewley, R. "AUTOBOX: A review." *Journal of Applied Econometrics* 3, (1988), pp. 240–244.

Box, G.E.P.; G.M. Jenkins and G. C. Reinsel. *Time Series Analysis, Forecasting and Control*. 3rd ed. Englewood Cliffs, NJ: Prentice-Hall, 1994.

Box, G.E.P.; and D.A. Pierce. "Distribution of residual autocorrelations in autoregressive integrated moving average time series models." *Journal of the American Statistical Association* 65, (1970), pp. 1509–1526.

Davies, N.; and P. Newbold. "Forecasting with misspecified models." *Applied Statistics* 29, (1980), pp. 87–92.

Dickey, D.A.; W.R. Bell; and R.B. Miller. "Unit roots in time series models: tests and implications." *The American Statistician* 40, (1986), pp. 12–26.

Enders, W., *Applied Econometric Time Series*. New York: John Wiley & Sons, Inc., 1995.

Granger, C.W.J.; and P. Newbold. *Forecasting Economic Time Series*. 2nd ed. Orlando, Fl.: Academic Press, 1986.

Hill, G.; and R. Fildes. "The accuracy of extrapolation methods: and automatic Box–Jenkins package sift." *Journal of Forecasting* 3, (1984), pp. 319–323.

Jenkins, G.M. *Practical Experiences with Modeling and Forecasting Time Series*. Lancaster: GJP Publications, (1979).

Jenkins, G.M. "Some practical aspects of forecasting in organizations." *Journal of Forecasting* 1, (1982), pp. 3–21.

Jenkins, G.M.; and G. McLeod. *Case Studies in Time Series Analysis*. Lancaster: GJP Publications, 1982.

Ledolter, J.; and B. Abraham. "Parsimony and its importance in time series forecasting." *Technometrics 23*, (1981), pp. 411–414.

Libert, G. "The M-competition with a fully automatic Box–Jenkins procedure." *Journal of Forecasting* 3, (1984), pp. 325–328.

Ljung, G.M.; and G.E.P. Box. "On a measure of lack of fit in time series models." *Biometrika* 65, (1978), pp. 297–303.

Nelson, C.R. *Applied Time Series Analysis for Managerial Forecasting*. San Francisco: Holden Day, 1973.

Newbold, P. "ARIMA model building and the time series analysis approach to forecasting." *Journal of Forecasting* 2, (1983), pp. 23–35.

Pankratz, A. *Forecasting with Univariate Box–Jenkins Models: Concepts and Cases.* New York: Wiley, 1983.

Texter, P.A.; and J.K. Ord. "Forecasting using automatic identification procedures: A comparative analysis." *International Journal of Forecasting* 5, (1989), pp. 209–215.

Vandaele, W. *Applied Time Series and Box–Jenkins Models.* Orlando, Fl.: Academic Press, 1983.

APPENDIX 8–A

SEASONAL ARIMA MODELS AND TRENDS

Some further clarification of seasonal models is appropriate. Consider the following model:

$$(1 - B)(1 - B^{12})Y_t = e_t \qquad (8A\text{–}1)$$

This very common model is easily interpreted after expansion:

$$Y_t = Y_{t-12} + (Y_{t-1} - Y_{t-13}) + e_t \qquad (8A\text{–}2)$$

The term $(Y_{t-1} - Y_{t-13})$ represents a stochastic trend of how much Y_{t-1} is higher or lower than Y_{t-13}. Now there are times when $(Y_{t-1} - Y_{t-13})$ might better be modeled by a deterministic trend coefficient, θ_0 of equation 8A–3, as in the PHARMDEM example. However, we must be very cautious to remember that stochastic trend models of equation 8A–2 are much more common than those of 8A–3, particularly in the social sciences, thus, when in doubt, drop the deterministic trend coefficient.

$$Y_t = Y_{t-12} + \theta_0 + e_t \qquad (8A\text{–}3)$$

Additive versus Multiplicative Seasonal Models.   There are many types of seasonal ARIMA models including those of equations 8A–4 and 8A–5. In equation 8A–4 the seasonality has multiplicative coefficients while in equation 8A–5 they are additive. Both additive and multiplicative relationships should be explored when modeling the general seasonal time series, some study of your software may be necessary to be able to fit additive models. Box, Jenkins, and Reinsel (1994, pp. 367–69) further explore such considerations. However, methodical use of the ARIMA model building methods developed in Chapter 8 should be sufficient to guide you in successfully modeling seasonal time series when caution is exercised to add only one component at a time.

$$w_t = (1 - B)(1 - B^{12})Y_t$$

$$w_t = (1 - \theta_1 B)(1 - \theta_{12}B^{12})e_t$$

$$w_t = e_t - \theta_1 e_{t-1} - \theta_{12}e_{t-12} + \theta_1\theta_{12}e_{t-13}$$

ACF values of w_t:

ACF(11), ACF(12), ACF(13) $\neq 0$ (8A–4)

$$w_t = (1 - \theta_1 B - \theta_{12}B^{12})e_t$$

$$w_t = e_t - \theta_1 e_{t-1} - \theta_{12}e_{t-12}$$

ACF(11), ACF(12) $\neq 0$, ACF(13) $= 0$ (8A–5)

ARIMA
FORECAST INTERVALS

An idea is only as good as its execution

Anonymous

A forecast is only as good as its projections.

Chapter Outline

Conditional and Unconditional ARIMA Forecasts
Forecast Mean Squared Error (FMSE) and Standard Error (FSE)
General EFSE(*m*) Values
ARIMA Prediction Intervals
Summary
Key Terms
Key Formulas
Review Problems Using Your Software
Problems
Minicases
References

This chapter presents ARIMA forecasting concepts, including conditional and unconditional forecasts, ψ-weight representations, and prediction intervals.

As you may recall, a **prediction interval** is a probability statement about a range of forecasted values, assuming that the fitted relationship is correct and continues into the future. An important advantage of ARIMA forecasting is its ability to define the shapes of forecast prediction intervals. The general shapes of prediction intervals of different ARIMA processes are presented in Figure 9–1. Figures 9–1a to h illustrate the 95 percent prediction intervals of ARIMA processes using the time series analyzed in Chapters 7 and 8. As this figure illustrates, these 95 percent prediction intervals vary dramatically depending on the type of ARIMA model used.

Figures 9–1a, b, and c illustrate stationary series, as shown, stationary series have relatively constant-width prediction intervals. In contrast, the nonstationary series in Figures 9–1d to h have ever-widening prediction intervals, albeit some do not widen as rapidly as others. These intervals provide important insights into ARIMA processes and model building, the figures are also useful for measuring the relative utility and validity of competing ARIMA models.

This chapter can be used in several ways. You can develop many of the derivations, or you can skim the more technical derivations and simply pay close attention to the conclusions and their significance. However, you should be able to follow the derivations of this chapter easily, by remembering the simple underlying assumptions of white noise, stationary series, statistical independence, and ARIMA processes. These assumptions are repeated during the derivations for emphasis and clarity.

Conditional and Unconditional ARIMA Forecasts

ARIMA models can provide very good short-term forecasts. However, in most applications, we need to know how well *m*-period-ahead forecasts perform. ARIMA models are insightful when used to generate prediction intervals for *m*-period forecasts. As is always true in forecasting, the validity of these intervals is contingent upon the validity of the model and the continuation of the past into the future.

As we saw in Chapters 7 and 8, a univariate ARIMA forecast is generated by substituting past actuals and forecasts into the model. The basic assumption of this procedure is that the forecast $\hat{Y}_t$ is the expected or mean value of the time series in period *t*, that is, $E(Y_t)$. We forecast by "assuming" that the underlying stochastic process of the past is time invariant (i.e., remains constant), even though this may not always be true.

Given that the current actual observation is Y_t, we want to accurately predict the values of $Y_{t+1}, Y_{t+2}, \ldots, Y_{t+m}$. (Remember that a forecast of $\hat{Y}_{t+m}$ made in period *t* can be designated $Y_t(m)$; for example, $Y_t(5)$ is a forecast for period $(t + 5)$ made as of the end of the period *t*.)

In forecasting, it is important to note that there are actually two types of forecasts (i.e., expected values): the unconditional, and the conditional expected values. An **unconditional forecast** is one in which none of the past actual values of the time series influence the forecast. In contrast, a **conditional forecast** is one that uses the most recently known actual values, thus, the conditional forecast is the more accurate of the two. Nevertheless, the unconditional forecast is of interest because it is the equivalent of a very-long-horizon conditional forecast.

Unconditional Forecasts

To illustrate the differences between conditional and unconditional forecasts, consider an AR(1) process

$$(1 - \phi_1 B)y_t = e_t$$

FIGURE 9–1

Prediction intervals

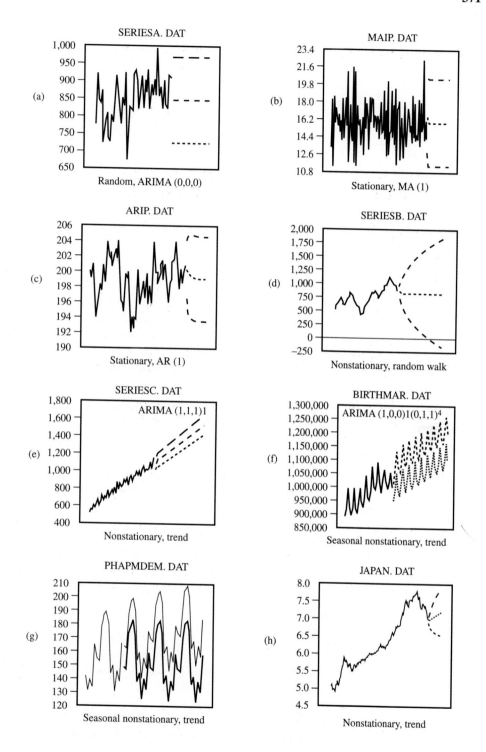

As shown in Chapter 7, this process can be inverted to an exponentially weighted sum of past random shocks:

$$y_t = (1 + \phi_1 B + \phi_1^2 B^2 + \cdots + \phi_1^n B^n + \cdots)e_t \tag{9-1}$$
$$= e_t + \phi_1 e_{t-1} + \phi_1^2 e_{t-2} + \cdots + \phi_1^n e_{t-n} + \cdots$$

Taking the expected value of this expression (i.e., calculating the mean) yields

$$E(y_t) = E(e_t) + \phi_1 E(e_{t-1}) + \phi_1^2 E(e_{t-2}) + \cdots + \phi_1^n E(e_{t-n}) + \cdots$$

Now assuming that all e_ts and y_t are unknown and because the expected value of random shocks is zero, the expected value of this series is zero; thus,

$$E(y_t) = 0 + \phi_1(0) + \phi_1^2(0) + \cdots + \phi_1^n(0) + \cdots = 0$$

Remembering that y_t represents deviations, that is, $y_t = Y_t - \mu$, we have

$$E(Y_t) = E(y_t) + \mu = \mu$$

Thus, the unconditional forecast, $E(\hat{Y}_t)$ for an AR(1) is the mean.

Extending this concept into the future yields

$$y_t(1) = E(y_{t+1}) = 0 \qquad Y_t(1) = \mu \qquad\qquad (9\text{--}2)$$

$$y_t(2) = E(y_{t+2}) = 0 \qquad Y_t(2) = \mu$$

$$\cdots \qquad\qquad\qquad \cdots$$

$$y_t(m) = E(y_{t+m}) = 0 \qquad Y_t(m) = \mu$$

Thus, the unconditional forecast of an ARIMA(1,0,0) process is the process mean, no matter how far into the future we forecast. This is so because the unconditional forecast is not "conditioned" by known actual values.

Conditional Forecast

When past values of y_t and e_t are known in period t, an unconditional forecast ignores the important information provided by recent values. This information can be used to generate more accurate conditional forecasts. The conditional forecast of y_{t+1} is the expected value, given the values of actual observations through y_t; that is:

$$E(y_{t+1}|y_t, y_{t-1}, \cdots, y_2, y_1) \qquad\qquad (9\text{--}3)$$

where $|$ is read as "given."

As shown in Equation 9–1, an AR(1) process is an exponentially weighted average of past random shocks; therefore, the conditional expectation of y_{t+1} is

$$E(y_{t+1}) = E(e_{t+1}) + \phi_1 e_t + \phi_1^2 e_{t-1} + \cdots + \phi_1^n e_{t-n-1} + \cdots \qquad (9\text{--}4)$$

because, for this conditional forecast, the values of all random shocks are known, except for e_{t+1}, the future shock in the next time period.

Substituting y_t of equation 9-1 into the equivalent part of Equation 9–4 yields

$$E(y_{t+1}) = E(e_{t+1}) + \phi_1 y_t \qquad\qquad (9\text{--}4a)$$

Because the expected value of the random shock, e_{t+1} is zero, we have

$$E(y_{t+1}) = \phi_1 y_t \qquad\qquad (9\text{--}4b)$$

Remembering that $E(y_{t+1})$ is, by definition, the same as $\hat{y}_{t+1}$ or $y_t(1)$, this confirms that we have been calculating conditional forecasts of ARIMA processes throughout Chapters 7 and 8.

Unconditional Forecast

If we expand the conditional forecast to the m horizon we note that a very-long-term conditional forecast evolves to an unconditional forecast. Consider the following starting with

$$y_t(1) = E(e_{t+1} + \phi_1 y_t)$$

Then, going another step into the future, we add another unknown future random shock:

$$y_t(2) = e_{t+2} + \phi_1 e_{t+1} + \phi_1^2 e_t + \phi_1^3 e_{t-1} + \phi_1^4 e_{t-2} + \cdots +$$

remembering that $y_t = e_t + \phi_1 e_{t-1} + \phi_1^2 e_{t-2} + \cdots +$
therefore

$$y_t(2) = e_{t+2} + \phi_1 e_{t+1} + \phi_1^2 y_t$$

Since $E(e_{t+2}) = E(e_{t+1}) = 0$, this becomes

$$y_t(2) = 0 + 0 + \phi_1^2 y_t = \phi_1^2 y_t$$

$$\cdots$$

In general,

$$y_t(m) = E(e_{t+m} + \phi_1 e_{t+m-1} + \cdots + \phi_1^{m-1} e_{t+1}) + \phi_1^m y_t \qquad (9\text{-}4c)$$

where the expected values of all $e_t = 0$. Thus,

$$y_t(m) = \phi_1^m y_t \qquad (9\text{-}4d)$$

However, remembering that $|\phi_1| < 1$, we have

$$\phi_1^m y_t \to 0 \qquad \text{as } m \to \infty \qquad (9\text{-}5)$$

Therefore,

$$Y_t(m) = y_t(m) + \mu = 0 + \mu = \mu \qquad \text{as } m \to \infty$$

Thus, the conditional forecast in Equation 9–3 eventually equals the unconditional forecast in Equation 9–2, because the known actual values become so "old."

Forecast Mean Squared Error (FMSE) and Standard Error (FSE)

An ARIMA model is normally chosen because it has the minimum mean squared error (MSE) or residual standard error (RSE) during the **fitting** process. However, we are really interested in minimizing **forecast** errors; thus, it is useful to measure the RSE of **m-period-ahead forecasts.**

Equation 9–6 defines the **forecast mean squared error, FMSE.** The equation is nearly identical to the MSE, except for a slight difference in the denominator, where j is used instead of $(n - k)$. The FMSE(m) is generated by subtracting the forecasts of, for example, $Y_{t+1}(3)$, $Y_{t+2}(3)$, . . . , $Y_{t+j}(3)$ from the actual values of these periods when they become known. That is, j three-period-ahead forecasts are made in order to calculate FMSE(3). Also note that, obviously, FMSE(3) cannot be calculated until the actuals are known for those periods.

$$\text{FMSE}(m) = \frac{\Sigma[Y_{t+i+m} - Y_{t+i}(m)]^2}{j} \qquad (9\text{-}6)$$

$$\text{FSE}(m) = \sqrt{\frac{\Sigma[Y_{t+i+m} - Y_{t+i}(m)]^2}{j}} \qquad (9\text{-}6a)$$

where

$$Y_{t+i+m} = \text{actual of that period}$$
$$Y_{t+i}(m) = \text{forecast made } m \text{ periods prior}$$
$$i = 1 \text{ to } j$$
$$j = \text{number of } m\text{-period forecasts}$$
$$m = \text{length of out-of-sample forecasts}$$

The value of FMSE(m) can be estimated through the use of forecasting experiments in which some data is withheld for that purpose. The FMSE(m) can then be used to select that model that most accurately forecasts the withheld time series.

Interestingly, it is possible to estimate FMSE(m) from the MSE of the fit before any future actual values are known. The estimated FMSE(m) can be used to generate prediction intervals about these m-period-ahead forecasts. This process is explained in the next section.

The estimated FMSE(m) is actually an expected value, so we can notate the expected FMSE(m) as EMSE(m); therefore,

$$\text{EMSE}(m) = \text{Expected }[\text{FMSE}(m)] \qquad (9\text{--}7)$$

Similarly, the estimated FSE is an expected value, which is notated EFSE(m)

$$\text{EFSE}(m) = \text{Expected }[\text{FSE}(m)] \qquad (9\text{--}7a)$$

Obviously,

$$\text{EFSE}(m) = \sqrt{\text{EMSE}(m)}$$

Table 9–1 illustrates the six different measures of residual and forecast errors. There are two measures of *fitted errors:* the MSE (i.e., variance), and the RSE (i.e., standard error). We have routinely used these measures to select models. There are also four measures of *forecast errors,* divided into two types: actual measures of realized forecast errors (FMSE and FSE), and estimated measures of expected forecast errors. The latter are of interest here.

General ARIMA Models: Psi Weights ψ

All ARIMA models can be expressed as a function of past errors i.e., past random shocks. By convention, the general model used to express any ARIMA process as a function of past random shocks is

$$y_t = e_t + \psi_1 e_{t-1} + \psi_2 e_{t-2} + \cdots + \psi_k e_{t-k} + \cdots \qquad (9\text{--}8)$$

where ψ's are determined by process coefficients and e_ts are the true population random shocks.

This representation of an ARIMA process is important for a number of reasons, one of which is the easy way it can be used to generate the EMSE(m) and its prediction intervals. This is most easily done by expressing a conditional forecast $\hat{Y}_t$ as a weighted sum of past random shocks e_t. These prediction intervals are often generated by computer software. However, manual derivations of these intervals is a worthwhile effort, because of the important information that the prediction intervals provide. This information includes the range and probability estimates of future actual values. It is therefore important to be able to calculate valid prediction intervals on m-period-ahead forecasts, as in Figures 9–1a through h.

The ψ weights are relatively easy to determine for most ARIMA processes. In fact, all moving-average models are expressed in ψ weight form, and the reexpression of nonstationary (i.e., integrated) models and autoregressive models is quite easy. Let us consider the generation of ψ weights for several different models.

The AR(1) model is

$$y_t = e_t + \phi_1 y_{t-1}$$

We have shown that an AR(1) process can easily be reexpressed in random shock form by successive substitutions of $(e_{t-k} + \phi_1 y_{t-k-1})$ for y_{t-k}, thus yielding Equation 9–1:

$$y_t = e_t + \phi_1 e_{t-1} + \phi_1^2 e_{t-2} + \cdots + \phi_1^k e_{t-k} + \cdots \qquad (9\text{--}9)$$

TABLE 9–1   Fit and Forecast Error Measures

Source of Deviation	Error Variances	Standard Errors	Typical Uses
Model residuals (Fit)	MSE = σ_e^2	RSE = σ_e	Model selection based on these fitted errors.
Actual forecast errors	FMSE(m)	FSE(m)	Measures of the goodness of fit of actual forecasts.
Expected forecast errors	EMSE(m)	EFSE(m)	Estimates of FMSE and FSE prior to forecasting. Provides model insights.

---

which in ψ weight form is

$$y_t = e_t + \psi_1 e_{t-1} + \psi_2 e_{t-2} + \cdots + \psi_k e_{t-k} + \cdots \tag{9-9a}$$

Now, equating equal time periods of e_t in Equations 9–9 and 9–9a yields

$$\psi_1 e_{t-1} = \phi_1 e_{t-1} \qquad \psi_1 = \phi_1$$
$$\psi_2 e_{t-2} = \phi_1^2 e_{t-2} \qquad \psi_2 = \phi_1^2$$
$$\psi_3 e_{t-3} = \phi_1^3 e_{t-3} \qquad \psi_3 = \phi_1^3$$
$$\cdots \qquad\qquad \cdots$$
$$\psi_k e_{t-k} = \phi_1^k e_{t-k} \qquad \psi_k = \phi_1^k$$

In a moment, these weights will be used to generate EMSE(m) and prediction intervals.

Let us now express another ARIMA model in ψ weight form. Consider a moving average ARIMA $(0,0,1)(0,0,1)^4$ model. In backshift notation, this is

$$y_t = (1 - \theta_1 B)(1 - \theta_4 B^4) e_t$$

Expanding this, we get

$$Y_t = (1 - \theta_1 B - \theta_4 B^4 + \theta_1 \theta_4 B^5) e_t \tag{9-10}$$
$$= e_t - \theta_1 e_{t-1} - \theta_4 e_{t-4} + \theta_1 \theta_4 e_{t-5}$$

where coefficients are easily equated to the ψ_i weights, as follows:

$$\psi_1 = -\theta_1$$
$$\psi_2 = 0$$
$$\psi_3 = 0$$
$$\psi_4 = -\theta_4$$
$$\psi_5 = +\theta_1 \theta_4$$
$$\psi_k = 0 \qquad \text{for all } k > 5$$

For our final example, consider the more complex model, ARIMA$(1,0,0)(1,0,0)^4$:

$$(1 - \phi_1 B)(1 - \phi_4 B^4) y_t = e_t$$
$$(1 - \phi_1 B - \phi_4 B^4 + \phi_1 \phi_4 B^5) y_t = e_t$$
$$y_t - \phi_1 y_{t-1} - \phi_4 y_{t-4} + \phi_1 \phi_4 y_{t-5} = e_t$$

Moving all terms except Y_t to the right-hand side, we get

$$y_t = \phi_1 y_{t-1} + \phi_4 y_{t-4} - \phi_1 \phi_4 y_{t-5} + e_t \qquad (9\text{–}11)$$

Now, substituting the following three relationships into Equation 9–11 yields Equation 9–12:

$$y_{t-1} = \phi_1 y_{t-2} + \phi_4 y_{t-5} - \phi_1 \phi_4 y_{t-6} + e_{t-1} \qquad (9\text{–}11a)$$

$$y_{t-4} = \phi_1 y_{t-5} + \phi_4 y_{t-8} - \phi_1 \phi_4 y_{t-9} + e_{t-4} \qquad (9\text{–}11b)$$

$$y_{t-5} = \phi_1 y_{t-6} + \phi_4 y_{t-9} - \phi_1 \phi_4 y_{t-10} + e_{t-5} \qquad (9\text{–}11c)$$

$$\begin{aligned} y_t = {}& \phi_1(\phi_1 y_{t-2} + \phi_4 y_{t-5} - \phi_1 \phi_4 y_{t-6} + e_{t-1}) \\ & + \phi_4(\phi_1 y_{t-5} + \phi_4 y_{t-8} - \phi_1 \phi_4 y_{t-9} + e_{t-4}) \\ & - \phi_1 \phi_4 (\phi_1 y_{t-6} + \phi_4 y_{t-9} - \phi_1 \phi_4 y_{t-10} + e_{t-5}) + e_t \end{aligned}$$

Multiplying these through, we get

$$\begin{aligned} y_t = {}& e_t + \phi_1^2 y_{t-2} + \phi_1 \phi_4 y_{t-5} - \phi_1^2 \phi_4 y_{t-6} + \phi_1 e_{t-1} + \phi_1 \phi_4 y_{t-5} \qquad (9\text{–}12) \\ & + \phi_4^2 y_{t-8} - \phi_1 \phi_4^2 y_{t-9} + \phi_4 e_{t-4} - \phi_1^2 \phi_4 y_{t-6} \\ & - \phi_1 \phi_4^2 y_{t-9} + \phi_1^2 \phi_4^2 y_{t-10} - \phi_1 \phi_4 e_{t-5} \end{aligned}$$

If we were to continue substituting similar expressions for y_{t-2}, y_{t-5}, y_{t-6}, and so on, and then combining the same time periods of e_{t-k}, the following would result:

$$\begin{aligned} y_t = {}& e_t + \phi_1 e_{t-1} + \phi_1^2 e_{t-2} + \phi_1^3 e_{t-3} + (\phi_1^4 + \phi_4)e_{t-4} \\ & + (\phi_1^5 - \phi_1 \phi_4)e_{t-5} + \cdots \end{aligned}$$

Therefore, the ψ weights of an ARIMA(1,0,0) (1,0,0)^4 model are:

$$\psi_1 = \phi_1$$

$$\psi_2 = \phi_1^2$$

$$\psi_3 = \phi_1^3$$

$$\psi_4 = \phi_1^4 + \phi_4$$

$$\psi_5 = \phi_1^5 - \phi_1 \phi_4$$

$$\cdots$$

As we see in Equations 9–9, 9–10, and 9–12, any ARIMA(p,d,q)(P,D,Q)^s model can be expressed in ψ weight form. Fortunately, as mentioned, some forecasting software automatically estimate these ψ weights.

As long as the ϕ and θ coefficients of an ARIMA process are within the bounds of stationarity and invertibility, the ψ weights eventually converge to zero. The value of the kth weight ψ_k is thus approximately zero; therefore, we need not compute the weights indefinitely. This is fortunate, because only n actual observations are available to estimate the ψ weights. Also, only the first m and $m - 1$ psi weights are needed to generate m-step-ahead forecasts and prediction intervals as shown in equations 9–4 and 9–22 respectively.

EMSE(m) and EFSE(m) Calculation

Now that we have expressed conditional forecasts as functions of all past random shocks, we can calculate interval estimates of these forecasts using EMSE(m). Prediction intervals for $y_t(m)$ of any ARIMA process can be generated by expressing the actual y_{t+1} as the series

$$y_{t+1} = e_{t+1} + \psi_1 e_t + \psi_2 e_{t-1} + \cdots + \psi_k e_{t-k+1} + \cdots \qquad (9\text{–}13)$$

Because e_{t+1} is unknown, its expected value of zero is substituted into this expression. Then, because past values of e_{t-k} are known, the conditional forecast of y_{t+1} is

$$E(y_{t+1}) = E(e_{t+1}) + \psi_1 e_t + \cdots + \psi_k e_{t-k+1} + \cdots \tag{9-14}$$

$$= \quad 0 + \psi_1 e_t + \cdots + \psi_k e_{t-k+1} + \cdots$$

When forecasting y_{t+1} [i.e., $y_t(1)$], the one-period-ahead forecast error is the difference between the actual y_{t+1} of Equation 9–13 and the predicted $E(y_{t+1})$ of Equation 9–14 or

$$e_t(1) = y_{t+1} - E(y_{t+1}) = e_{t+1}$$

where $e_t(1)$ designates the expected error for one-period-ahead forecasts. In general, $e_t(m)$ is the expected error for m-period-ahead forecasts.

The forecast error therefore equals the random shock e_{t+1}, and because random shocks are expected to have a mean of zero, the prediction variance or EMSE(1) is

$$\text{EMSE}(1) = E(e_{t+1}^2) \tag{9-15}$$

Because errors are stationary, we have

$$E(e_{t+1}^2) = E(e_t^2) = \sigma_e^2$$

which is the variance of the model's white noise residuals. Consequently, assuming a normal distribution of errors, the 95 percent interval forecast of Y_{t+1} is

$$Y_t(1) - 1.96\text{EFSE}(1) \le Y_{t+1} \le Y_t(1) + 1.96\text{EFSE}(1) \tag{9-16}$$

which for all ARIMA models is

$$Y_t(1) - 1.96\sigma_e \le Y_{t+1} \le Y_t(1) + 1.96\sigma_e \tag{9-16a}$$

Thus, for all ARIMA models, EFSE(1) equals the fitted RSE.

Two-Period-Ahead Prediction Intervals

Now let's calculate the EMSE(2), the variance for two-period-ahead forecasts. The ψ weight expression for the actual values of y_{t+2} is

$$y_{t+2} = e_{t+2} + \psi_1 e_{t+1} + \psi_2 e_t + \cdots + \psi_k e_{t-k+2} + \cdots \tag{9-17}$$

Because we are dealing with period t, the first two shocks are unknown. Thus, we must substitute their expected values into Equation 9–17.

$$E(y_{t+2}) = 0 + \psi_1 0 + \psi_2 e_t + \cdots + \psi_k e_{t-k+2} + \cdots \tag{9-18}$$

To calculate the error in two-period-ahead forecasts, we simply subtract Equation 9–18 from 9–17, as follows:

$$e_t(2) = y_{t+2} - E(y_{t+2})$$

$$= e_{t+2} + \psi_1 e_{t+1}$$

The variance of this error is

$$\text{EMSE}(2) = E(e_t(2)^2) = E[(e_{t+2} + \psi_1 e_{t+1})^2]$$

$$= E(e_{t+2}^2 + 2e_{t+2}\psi_1 e_{t+1} + \psi_1^2 e_{t+1}^2)$$

$$= E(e_{t+2}^2) + 2\psi_1 E(e_{t+2}e_{t+1}) + \psi_1^2 E(e_{t+1}^2)$$

Remembering that for stationary series,

$$E(e_{t+2}^2) = E(e_{t+1}^2) = \sigma_e^2$$

and that because of the independence of errors, the covariance $E(e_{t+2}e_{t+1})$ equals 0, the following results:

$$\text{EMSE}(2) = \sigma_e^2 + \psi_1^2\sigma_e^2 = (1 + \psi_1^2)\sigma_e^2 \qquad (9\text{--}19)$$

Equation 9–19 can be used in 95 percent prediction intervals of Y_{t+2}

$$Y_t(2) - 1.96\text{EFSE}(2) \le Y_{t+2} \le Y_t(2) + 1.96\text{EFSE}(2) \qquad (9\text{--}20)$$

Note that EFSE(2) is always larger than EFSE(1), except when $\psi_1^2 = 0$, which is commonly true with purely seasonal models, in that case they are equal.

Three-Period-Ahead Prediction Intervals

To generate three-period-ahead variances, we begin with the expression for the actual of y_{t+3}:

$$y_{t+3} = e_{t+3} + \psi_1 e_{t+2} + \psi_2 e_{t+1} + \psi_3 e_t + \cdots$$

When forecasting in period t, the first three errors are unknown, and their expected values of zero are substituted into the forecast of y_{t+3}, as follows:

$$E(y_{t+3}) = 0 + 0 + 0 + \psi_3 e_t + \cdots + \psi_k e_{t-k+3} + \cdots$$

Subtracting these equations, the three-period-ahead error is:

$$e_t(3) = y_{t+3} - E(y_{t+3})$$
$$= e_{t+3} + \psi_1 e_{t+2} + \psi_2 e_{t+1}$$

In a manner similar to previous derivations, the prediction variance is

$$\text{EMSE}(3) = E(e_{t+3}^2) = E[(e_{t+3} + \psi_1 e_{t+2} + \psi_2 e_{t+1})^2]$$
$$= (1 + \psi_1^2 + \psi_2^2)\sigma_e^2 \qquad (9\text{--}21)$$

As before, this variance can be used to calculate prediction intervals.

General EFSE(*m*) Values

The three EMSE calculated thus far are:

$$\text{EMSE}(1) = \sigma_e^2$$
$$\text{EMSE}(2) = (1 + \psi_1^2)\sigma_e^2$$
$$\text{EMSE}(3) = (1 + \psi_1^2 + \psi_2^2)\sigma_e^2$$

Continuing and generalizing the procedure, we see that the prediction variance of any ARIMA model for $y_t(m)$ is

$$\text{EMSE}(m) = E[(e_{t+m} + \psi_1 e_{t+m-1} + \cdots + \psi_{m-1} e_{t+1})^2] \qquad (9\text{--}22)$$
$$= (1 + \psi_1^2 + \psi_2^2 + \cdots + \psi_{m-1}^2)\sigma_e^2$$

As shown by EMSE(m), as the forecast horizon increases with non-zero ψ_{m-1}, the prediction variance increases about the conditional forecast of $Y_t(m)$. This is a logical result: the longer the horizon length, the wider the prediction interval.

Equation 9–22 can be used to calculate the prediction intervals once the appropriate ψ weights are known for the model. This calculation uses the following general prediction interval:

$$Y_t(m) - t \cdot \text{EFSE}(m) \leq Y_{t+m} \leq Y_t(m) + t \cdot \text{EFSE}(m) \qquad (9\text{–}23)$$

Equation 9–23 is used to generate m-horizon prediction intervals.

ARIMA Prediction Intervals

The shapes of the prediction intervals of ARIMA processes are referred to as **prediction interval profiles.** We have shown that for any ARIMA model, a conditional forecast for an ARIMA$(p,d,q)(PDQ)^s$ process can be made. Also, Equation 9–22 can be used to calculate the ARIMA model prediction variances. Thus, the variances of the ARIMA forecast can be estimated by the ψ weights of the process and the white noise RSE.

As we show in the next several sections, ψ weights behave similarly for similar ARIMA processes. They thus provide a way of characterizing the profiles of each type of ARIMA model. To illustrate this concept, we will consider several ARIMA prediction intervals.

White Noise Prediction Intervals

Consider a completely random process. This is an ARIMA(0,0,0) process with only one random shock affecting y_t:

$$y_t = e_t$$

Therefore, all ψ weights are zero, or

$$\psi_1 = \psi_2 = \cdots \psi_k = 0$$

Consequently, all forecasts of a white noise process are equal to the mean of the series:

$$y_t(1) = E(e_{t+1}) = 0 \qquad Y_t(1) = y_t(1) + \mu = \mu$$
$$y_t(2) = E(e_{t+2}) = 0 \qquad Y_t(2) = y_t(2) + \mu = \mu$$
$$\cdots \qquad\qquad \cdots$$
$$y_t(m) = E(e_{t+m}) = 0 \qquad Y_t(m) = y_t(m) + \mu = \mu$$

Interestingly, because all ψ weights are zero, variances about these conditional forecasts are constant for all horizons, or:

$$\text{EMSE}(2) = (1 + \psi_1^2)\sigma_e^2 = \sigma_e^2$$
$$\text{EMSE}(3) = (1 + \psi_1^2 + \psi_2^2)\sigma_e^2 = \sigma_e^2$$
$$\cdots$$
$$\text{EMSE}(m) = \sigma_e^2$$

These variances equal the variance of the white noise residuals of the model. For this simple ARIMA(0,0,0) model, the variances also equal the standard deviation of the original series. In addition, for white noise processes, the conditional and unconditional forecasts are the same.

As we know, the best forecast for a completely random process is its mean. Therefore, it is not surprising that the least complex model has the least complex prediction interval. However, it is interesting that this profile does not increase over time;

rather, it remains constant. When this profile is narrow, the forecasts of a random series can be very accurate.

Figure 9–2 illustrates the forecast and 95 percent prediction intervals for an ARIMA(0,0,0) process for SERIESA.DAT. As shown, the upper and lower 95 percent prediction intervals are constant about μ.

$$\mu - 1.96\sigma_e \leq Y_{t+m} \leq \mu + 1.96\sigma_e \tag{9-24}$$

For SERIESA.DAT, these values are $\mu = 850.08$ and $\sigma_e = 64.53$; thus, the 95 percent prediction interval is

$$850.08 - 1.96 \cdot 64.53 \leq Y_{t+m} \leq 850.08 + 1.96 \cdot 64.53 \tag{9-24a}$$

Autoregressive Prediction Intervals

Equation 9–9 shows the ψ weight representation of an AR(1) model. Contrary to the white noise process with no ψ weights, theoretically there are an infinite number of non-zero weights for AR models.

Consider a simple AR(1) process. As shown in Equation 9–9, this model has exponentially decaying ψ weights:

$$\psi_k = \phi_1^k$$

Thus, the conditional forecasts are

$$y_t(1) = E(e_{t+1} + \phi_1 e_t + \phi_1^2 e_{t-1} + \cdots + \phi_1^k e_{t-k+1} + \cdots)$$

After substituting zero for the expected values of future random shocks and remembering equation 9–1, we get

$$y_t(1) = 0 + \phi_1 e_t + \phi_1^2 e_{t-1} + \cdots + \phi_1^k e_{t-k+1} + \cdots +$$
$$= \phi_1(e_t + \phi_1 e_{t-1} + \cdots + \phi_1^{k-1} e_{t-k+1} + \cdots)$$
$$= \phi_1 y_t$$

Two-period-ahead forecasts yield

$$y_t(2) = E(e_{t+2} + \phi_1 e_{t+1} + \phi_1^2 e_t + \cdots + \phi_1^k e_{t-k+2} + \cdots)$$
$$= \phi_1^2 y_t$$

Thus, m-period-ahead forecasts yield

$$\cdots$$

$$y_t(m) = E(e_{t+m} + \phi_1 e_{t+m-1} + \cdots + \phi_1^m e_t + \cdots)$$
$$= \phi_1^m y_t$$

Therefore, on the basis of Equation 9–22, the prediction variances about the conditional forecasts are a function of the exponentially decaying ψ weights, or

$$\text{EMSE}(1) = \sigma_e^2$$

$$\text{EMSE}(2) = (1 + \phi_1^2)\sigma_e^2$$

$$\text{EMSE}(3) = (1 + \phi_1^2 + \phi_1^4)\sigma_e^2$$

$$\cdots$$

$$\text{EMSE}(m) = (1 + \phi_1^2 + \cdots + \phi_1^{2m-2})\sigma_e^2$$

The increase in the variance of the prediction intervals about the forecasts is determined by the value of ϕ_1. If ϕ_1 is low (high), then the increase in EMSE(m) as m in-

Figure 9–2

95 percent prediction interval for ARIMA(0,0,0) for SERIESA.DAT

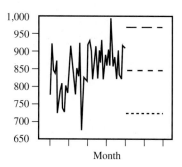

crease is small (large). Also, as m increases, the increase in the variance becomes smaller and smaller. The value of the variance EMSE(m) is a **Taylor series** asymptotically approaching the following value as m approaches infinity:

$$\underset{\lim\ m \to \infty}{\text{EMSE}(m)} = \frac{\sigma_e^2}{(1 - \phi_1^2)} \tag{9–25}$$

For example, assume $\phi_1 = .5$ and $\sigma_e^2 = 1$. Then

$$\underset{\lim\ m \to \infty}{\text{EMSE}(m)} = \frac{1}{(1 - .25)} = 1.33 \tag{9–25a}$$

If we have a high value of $\phi_1 = .95$ and $\sigma_e^2 = 1$, then

$$\underset{\lim\ m \to \infty}{\text{EMSE}(m)} = \frac{1}{(1 - .9025)} = 10.26 \tag{9–25b}$$

Finally as $\phi_1 \to 1$ and $\sigma_e^2 = 1$, we have

$$\underset{\lim\ m \to \infty}{\text{EMSE}(m)} = \frac{1}{(1 - \phi_1^2)} = \infty \tag{9–25c}$$

Therefore, the maximum variance EMSE(m) is dependent on the value of ϕ_1.

For low values of ϕ_1, the profile moves slowly; with high ϕ_1, the profile approaches that of a nonstationary process, as in Equation 9–25c. Obviously, $\phi_1 = 1$ represents a nonstationary process that should be differenced. Thus, Equation 9–25c shows that the limit of the prediction interval of a nonstationary ARIMA process is infinity. As we saw previously, for an ARIMA(0,0,0) white noise process, the limit of EMSE(m) is σ_e^2, while as just shown, for an ARIMA(0,1,0) process, the limit increases to infinity. Finally, depending on ϕ_1, an AR(1) model will be someplace between these two extremes.

Figure 9–3 and Table 9–2 show the forecasts and 95 percent prediction intervals for the AR(1) time series using the data of AR1P.DAT of Chapter 8. This prediction profile is typical of autoregressive profiles. Briefly, this model is

$$y_t = .75343y_{t-1} + e_t \tag{9–26}$$

As the horizon increases, the forecasts regress to the series mean, and the prediction intervals about the forecasts increase with increases in the horizon length; however, they increase asymptotically according to Equation 9–25.

FIGURE 9–3

*95 percent prediction
interval for AR1P.DAT*

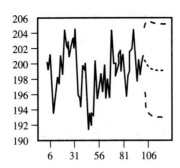

TABLE 9–2   **Prediction Intervals for AR1P.DAT ($\phi_1 = .75343$, $\sigma_e = 1.9248$)**

				Prediction Interval	
m	Time, $t + m$	Forecast	EFSE(m)	Lower 95%	Upper 95%
1	101	200.62	1.925	196.85	204.39
2	102	200.28	2.410	195.55	205.00
3	103	200.01	2.646	194.83	205.20
4	104	199.82	2.771	194.39	205.25
5	105	199.67	2.840	194.10	205.24
6	106	199.56	2.878	193.92	205.20
7	107	199.47	2.899	193.79	205.16
8	108	199.41	2.912	193.70	205.12
9	109	199.36	2.918	193.64	205.08
10	110	199.33	2.922	193.60	205.05
	. . .				
21	121	199.22	2.927	193.48	204.96
22	122	199.22	2.927	193.48	204.96
23	123	199.22	2.927	193.48	204.96
24	124	199.22	2.927	193.48	204.96

***Nonstationary
Prediction Intervals***

A random walk ARIMA(0,1,0) process is

$$Y_t = Y_{t-1} + e_t$$

Through successive substitutions, this yields

$$Y_t = (1 + B + B^2 + B^3 + \cdots + B^n)e_t$$

Thus, the ψ weights for integrated processes are all 1, or

$$\psi_1 = \psi_2 = \cdots = \psi_k = 1$$

Conditional forecasts of an ARIMA(0,1,0) process are

$$Y_t(1) = E(Y_t + e_{t+1}) = Y_t \qquad (9\text{–}27)$$

$$Y_t(2) = E(Y_t + e_{t+1} + e_{t+2}) = Y_t$$

. . .

$$Y_t(m) = E(Y_t + e_{t+1} + \cdots + e_{t+m}) = Y_t$$

As shown in Chapter 7, the best forecast of a random walk is the most recent actual. However, the resulting prediction variances increase as the horizon length increases, or:

$$\text{EMSE}(1) = E(e_{t+1}^2) = \sigma_e^2 \tag{9-28}$$

$$\text{EMSE}(2) = E[(e_{t+2} + e_{t+1})^2] = 2\sigma_e^2$$

$$\text{EMSE}(3) = E[(e_{t+3} + e_{t+2} + e_{t+1})^2] = 3\sigma_e^2$$

. . .

$$\text{EMSE}(m) = E[(e_{t+m} + e_{t+m-1} + \cdots + e_{t+1})^2] = m\sigma_e^2$$

For one-period increases in the horizon length, EMSE(m) increases by one unit of the residual variance σ_e^2.

Figure 9–4 and Table 9–3 show forecasts and prediction intervals for the stock prices SERIESB.DAT, introduced in Chapter 8. This is an ARIMA(1,1,0) series that is primarily a random walk process with an AR(1) coefficient. This prediction interval is

FIGURE 9–4

95 percent prediction interval for ARIMA(1,1,0) for SERIESB.DAT

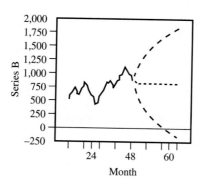

TABLE 9–3   SERIESB.DAT Prediction Intervals for ARIMA(1,1,0) ($\phi_1 = .5025$)

m	Time, $t + m$	Forecast	EFSE(m)	Lower 95%	Upper 95%
1	49	871.8422	46.6948	780.3221	963.3622
2	50	856.1839	84.2791	690.9999	1021.3679
3	51	848.3150	117.5560	617.9095	1078.7204
4	52	844.3604	146.7731	556.6904	1132.0305
5	53	842.3731	172.6199	504.0443	1180.7020
6	54	841.3744	195.7732	457.6659	1225.0829
7	55	840.8725	216.7860	415.9798	1265.7652
	. . .				
23	71	840.3655	433.3933	−9.0697	1689.8006
	. . .				
31	79	840.3655	508.2504	−155.7870	1836.5179
32	80	840.3655	516.8458	−172.6336	1853.3645
33	81	840.3655	525.3005	−189.2046	1869.9355
34	82	840.3655	533.6213	−205.5131	1886.2440
35	83	840.3655	541.8144	−221.5712	1902.3021
36	84	840.3655	549.8854	−237.3900	1918.1209

typical for nonstationary processes. After several steps into the future, the 95 percent prediction intervals become large, illustrating the great uncertainty associated with random walks. A nonstationary process has no constant mean; therefore, the variance and prediction interval become extremely large for large horizon lengths. In this case, the interval actually goes negative when m equals 23. As discussed previously, Equation 9–25c shows that for an integrated process, the limit of EMSE(m) as m increases to infinity is infinity.

Moving Average Prediction Intervals

An ARIMA(0,0,1) process has only one nonzero ψ weight:

$$y_t = e_t - \theta_1 e_{t-1} = (1 - \theta_1 B)e_t = (1 + \psi_1 B)e_t$$

where

$$\psi_1 = -\theta_1$$

Thus

$$\psi_2 = \psi_3 = \cdots = \psi_k = 0 \qquad \text{for all } k > 1$$

The conditional forecasts for an MA(1) process are

$$y_t(1) = E(e_{t+1} - \theta_1 e_t) = -\theta_1 e_t \qquad Y_t(1) = \mu - \theta_1 e_t$$

$$y_t(2) = E(e_{t+2} - \theta_1 e_{t+1}) = 0 \qquad Y_t(2) = \mu$$

$$\cdots$$

$$y_t(m) = E(e_{t+m} - \theta_1 e_{t+m-1}) = 0 \qquad Y_t(m) = \mu$$

Thus, the prediction variance is determined by only ψ_1:

$$\text{EMSE}(1) = E(e_{t+1}^2) = \sigma_e^2 \tag{9–29}$$

$$\text{EMSE}(2) = E[(e_{t+2} - \theta_1 e_{t+1})^2] = (1 + \theta_1^2)\sigma_e^2$$

$$\cdots$$

$$\text{EMSE}(m) = E[(e_{t+m} - \theta_1 e_{t+m-1})^2] = (1 + \theta_1^2)\sigma_e^2$$

After the first step into the future, the prediction interval and variance are constant. The limit of EMSE(m) is

$$\text{EMSE}(m) = (1 + \theta_1^2)\sigma_e^2$$
$$\lim m \to \infty$$

In Figure 9–5 and Table 9–4, the forecasts of an MA(1) time series MA1P.DAT are shown. With lead times greater than one observation, $Y_t(m)$ equals the series mean,

FIGURE 9–5

95 percent prediction interval for MA1P.DAT

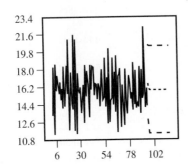

TABLE 9–4   **Prediction Intervals for MA(1) Process MA1P.DAT**
$(\theta_1 = .5428, \sigma_e = 2.0988, \mu = 15.97351)$

m	Time, $t + m$	Forecast	EFSE(m)	Lower 95%	Upper 95%
1	101	16.6305	2.0988	12.5169	20.7441
2	102	15.9735	2.3881	11.2930	20.6540
3	103	15.9735	2.3881	11.2930	20.6540
	$\cdots$				
22	122	15.9735	2.3881	11.2930	20.6540
23	123	15.9735	2.3881	11.2930	20.6540
24	124	15.9735	2.3881	11.2930	20.6540

while the EMSE(m) remains constant. Therefore, after one step into the future, an MA(1) behaves like an ARIMA(0,0,0) model.

Seasonal Nonstationary Prediction Intervals

Consider the impact of nonstationary seasonality on prediction intervals. An ARIMA(0,1,0)^{12} model is

$$Y_t = Y_{t-12} + e_t$$

Through successive substitutions of relationships such as

$$Y_{t-12} = Y_{t-24} + e_{t-12}$$

this yields the following:

$$Y_t = (1 + B^{12} + B^{24} + B^{36} + \cdots + B^{i \cdot 12})e_t \tag{9–30}$$

where i is an integer from 1 to INT $[\frac{n}{12}]$ where INT denotes the integer portion of $n/12$. Therefore, seasonal nonstationary processes only have nonzero ψ weights at seasonal lags, all of which equal 1.

$$Y_t = (1 + \psi_{12}B^{12} + \psi_{24}B^{24} + \psi_{36}B^{36} + \cdots + \psi_{i \cdot 12}B^{i \cdot 12})e_t \tag{9–31}$$

That is,

$$\psi_{12} = \psi_{24} = \cdots = \psi_{i \cdot 12} = 1 \qquad \text{All other } \psi_r = 0 \text{ for } r \neq i \cdot 12$$

Conditional forecasts of an ARIMA(0,1,0)^{12} process are

$$Y_t(1) = E(Y_{t-11} + e_{t+1}) = Y_{t-11}$$

$$Y_t(2) = E(Y_{t-10} + e_{t+2}) = Y_{t-10}$$

$$Y_t(3) = E(Y_{t-9} + e_{t+3}) = Y_{t-9}$$

$$\cdots$$

$$Y_t(11) = E(Y_{t-1} + e_{t+11}) = Y_{t-1}$$

$$Y_t(12) = E(Y_t + e_{t+12}) = Y_t$$

$$Y_t(13) = E(Y_{t+1} + e_{t+13}) = E(Y_{t+1}) = Y_t(1) = Y_{t-11}$$

This last relationship is true because the actual value of Y_{t+1} is unknown as of time period 13. Consequently, we substitute its expected value, Y_{t-11}. Thus the forecasts of a nonstationary seasonal monthly series equal the actual of 12 periods ago, which repeat as needed into the future. Therefore, the following repeating forecasts are obtained for such a series.

. . .

$$Y_t(24) = E(Y_{t+12} + e_{t+24}) = Y_t(12) = Y_t$$

$$Y_t(25) = E(Y_{t+13} + e_{t+25}) = Y_t(13) = Y_{t-11}$$

. . .

$$Y_t(36) = E(Y_{t+24} + e_{t+36}) = Y_t(24) = Y_t$$

$$Y_t(37) = E(Y_{t+25} + e_{t+37}) = Y_t(25) = Y_{t-11}$$

. . .

As we know, the best forecast of a random walk series is the last actual. However, for a seasonal nonstationary series, the forecast is a repeating pattern of the most recent S actual values. In this case, the last S actual values are the actuals of the last 12 periods.

Consider the prediction variances:

$$E(Y_{t+1}) = E(e_{t+1}) + \psi_1 e_t + \cdots + \psi_k e_{t-k+1} + \cdots$$

Referring back to Equation 9–22, which is

$$\text{EMSE}(m) = (1 + \psi_1^2 + \cdots + \psi_{m-1}^2)\sigma_e^2$$

substituting the known values of ψ, we can generate prediction variances.

The resulting prediction variances stay the same for 12 periods, but then increase to a higher value for the next 12 periods. That is, for a seasonal nonstationary process, as the horizon length continues to increase, the prediction variance only increases every 12 periods, as shown:

$$\text{EMSE}(1) = \sigma_e^2 \tag{9–32}$$

$$\text{EMSE}(2) = (1 + 0)\sigma_e^2 = \sigma_e^2$$

$$\text{EMSE}(3) = (1 + 0 + 0)\sigma_e^2 = \sigma_e^2$$

. . .

$$\text{EMSE}(12) = (1 + 0 + \cdots + 0)\sigma_e^2 = \sigma_e^2$$

$$\text{EMSE}(13) = (1 + 0 + \cdots + 0 + 1)\sigma_e^2 = 2\sigma_e^2$$

. . .

$$\text{EMSE}(24) = (1 + 0 + \cdots + 0 + 1 + 0 + \cdots + 0)\sigma_e^2 = 2\sigma_e^2$$

$$\text{EMSE}(25) = (1 + 0 + \cdots + 0 + 1 + 0 + \cdots + 0 + 1)\sigma_e^2 = 3\sigma_e^2$$

$$\text{EMSE}(m) = \; = \text{INT}\left[1 + \frac{(m-1)}{12}\right]\sigma_e^2$$

where INT denotes the integer portion of the term in brackets.

As the horizon length increases by 12 periods, the variance ESFE(m) increases by one unit of the random shock variance, as estimated by σ_e^2.

Figure 9–6 and Table 9–5 show the forecasts of the series PHARMDEM.DAT, which was introduced in Chapter 9. This is a seasonally nonstationary series with intervals typical of such nonstationary processes; the width of the 95 percent prediction intervals increase every 12 periods, as shown in Figure 9–7 and Table 9–5. This

FIGURE 9–6

Forecast of animal pharmaceutical PHARMDEM.DAT

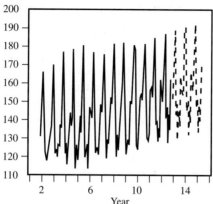

FIGURE 9–7

Prediction interval for PHARMDEM.DAT

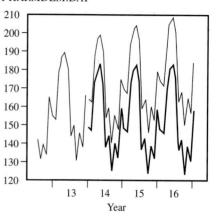

TABLE 9–5 **Prediction Interval for Seasonally Nonstationary Series PHARMDEM.DAT: ARIMA(0,1,0)^{12}1 ($\sigma_e = 3.9914$, $\theta_0 = 2.0873$)**

m	Time, $t + m$	Forecast	EFSE(m)	Lower 95%	Upper 95%
1	157	154.9974	3.9914	147.1743	162.8205
2	158	152.7774	3.9914	144.9543	160.6005
3	159	179.6174	3.9914	171.7943	187.4405
4	160	188.8874	3.9914	181.0643	196.7105
5	161	191.5574	3.9914	183.7343	199.3805
	...				
10	166	146.3274	3.9914	138.5043	154.1505
11	167	136.9974	3.9914	129.1743	144.8205
12	168	166.4174	3.9914	158.5943	174.2405
13	169	157.0847	5.6448	146.0212	168.1482
14	170	154.8647	5.6448	143.8012	165.9282
15	171	181.7047	5.6448	170.6412	192.7682
	...				
21	177	131.5347	5.6448	120.4712	142.5982
22	178	148.4147	5.6448	137.3512	159.4782
23	179	139.0847	5.6448	128.0212	150.1482
24	180	168.5047	5.6448	157.4412	179.5682
25	181	159.1721	6.9134	145.6221	172.7221
26	182	156.9521	6.9134	143.4021	170.5021
27	183	183.7921	6.9134	170.2421	197.3421
	...				
31	187	147.2221	6.9134	133.6721	160.7721
32	188	154.4921	6.9134	140.9421	168.0421
33	189	133.6221	6.9134	120.0721	147.1721
34	190	150.5021	6.9134	136.9521	164.0521
35	191	141.1721	6.9134	127.6221	154.7221
36	192	170.5921	6.9134	157.0421	184.1421

behavior is similar to that of the low-order nonstationary behavior of SERIESB.DAT; however, increases occur only at seasonal intervals. Also, it can be shown that the limit of EMSE(m) for the seasonal nonstationary process increases to infinity as m increases to infinity; however, because of seasonality, this increase does not occur as rapidly.

Table 9–5 shows the actual and prediction intervals for future periods of PHAR-DEM.DAT. As shown, the intervals continue to increase indefinitely. The prediction intervals of seasonal ARIMA models are interesting in that, often, they show little increase in error variances until after the end of the first seasonal cycle.

As you may recall, the animal pharmaceutical model is an ARIMA$(0,1,0)^{12}1$ process that includes a trend parameter. The forecasts track the pattern of seasonal variation quite well; however, because of the seasonal nonstationarity, prediction intervals become large. Thus,

$$\text{EFSE}(m) = 3.9914 \qquad \text{for } m = 1 \text{ to } 12$$
$$= \sqrt{2\sigma_e^2} = \sigma_e\sqrt{2} = 3.9914\sqrt{2} = 5.6448 \qquad \text{for } m = 13 \text{ to } 24$$
$$= \sqrt{3\sigma_e^2} = \sigma_e\sqrt{3} = 3.9914\sqrt{3} = 6.9134 \qquad \text{for } m = 25 \text{ to } 36$$

These EFSEs are confirmed in Table 9–5.

As you inspect these forecasts, remember that there is a trend coefficient, $\theta_0 = 2.0873$, in this model. Thus, the forecasts as of period t are:

$$Y_t(m) = Y_{t-12+m} + 1 \cdot 2.0873 \qquad \text{for } m = 1 \text{ to } 12$$
$$= Y_{t-24+m} + 2 \cdot 2.0873 \qquad \text{for } m = 13 \text{ to } 24$$
$$= Y_{t-36+m} + 3 \cdot 2.0873 \qquad \text{for } m = 25 \text{ to } 36$$

Other Prediction Intervals

Let us briefly review the prediction profiles of some other time series, as shown in Figures 9–8 through 9–13.

SERIESC.DAT ARIMA(1,1,1)1.   Figure 9–8 and Table 9–7 show the forecast and prediction intervals for SERIESC.DAT. As shown, SERIESC.DAT is a trending series and is thus nonstationary. The trend is very pronounced, and the prediction intervals, while not excessively wide, are increasing over time and will continue to do so indefinitely. Table 9–6 summarizes this model. This is a relatively complex model for the small sample size, nonetheless it exemplifies the profiles of trending series. Analysis using the BIC (i.e., Schwarz Bayesian Information Criterion) was used to select this model.

Quarterly Births in the United States.   Figures 9–9 and 9–10 and Table 9–9 show the forecasts and prediction intervals for the quarterly series BIRTHMAR.DAT. As shown, this series is trending. The trend is very pronounced, and the prediction

---

TABLE 9–6   SERIESC.DAT ARIMA(1,1,1)1 Model

Series	n	Logs	Model	$\overline{R}^2$	Coefficients	DW	Q
Series C microcomputer demand	48	no	(1,1,1)1 $\sigma_e^2 = 37.323$	.96	$\theta_0 = 12.518$ (.0000) $-\theta_1 = -.7816$ (.0000) $\phi_1 = -.5009$ (.0014)	2.187	10.698 (.297)

intervals, while not excessively wide, are increasing over time. Table 9–8 summarizes this model.

MWHRS at a California Utility.   Figures 9–11 and 9–12 and Table 9–11 show the prediction intervals for electricity demand in MWHRS. As shown, this series is a highly seasonal and trending series, and is thus nonstationary. The trend is very pronounced, and the prediction intervals, while not wide, are very slowly increasing

TABLE 9–7   Prediction Interval for SERIESC.DAT: ARIMA(1,1,1)1

m	Time, $t + m$	Forecast	EFSE(m)	Lower 95%	Upper 95%
1	49	1096.5158	37.3227	1023.3647	1169.6670
2	50	1151.9618	38.3167	1076.8625	1227.0611
3	51	1142.7736	41.1937	1062.0355	1223.5117
4	52	1167.0247	41.2896	1086.0985	1247.9510
5	53	1173.9756	42.2985	1091.0722	1256.8791
6	54	1189.8770	42.7063	1106.1742	1273.5797
7	55	1201.1477	43.3759	1116.1324	1286.1629
8	56	1214.8141	43.8919	1128.7875	1300.8407
	. . .				
32	80	1522.9258	55.7472	1413.6633	1632.1883
33	81	1535.7754	56.1864	1425.6522	1645.8987
34	82	1548.6250	56.6221	1437.6477	1659.6023
35	83	1561.4746	57.0546	1449.6497	1673.2995
36	84	1574.3242	57.4837	1461.6581	1686.9902

TABLE 9–8   Quarterly BIRTHMAR.DAT Model

Series	n	Model	R^2	Coefficients	DW	Q
Births	32	$(1,0,0)1(0,1,1)^4$	.89	$\theta_0 = 13{,}743\ (.0103)$	2.431	4.852
				$-\theta_4 = -.724\ (.0021)$		(.303)
		$\sigma_e^2 = 15{,}501.5$		$\phi_1 = .726\ (.0002)$		

FIGURE 9–8

95 percent prediction interval for SERIESC.DAT

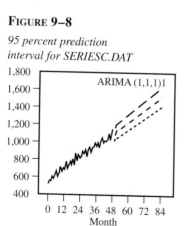

FIGURE 9–9

Forecasts of quarterly births (BIRTHMAR.DAT)

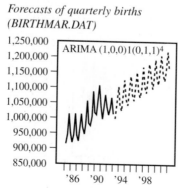

FIGURE 9–10

95 percent prediction interval for BIRTHMAR.DAT

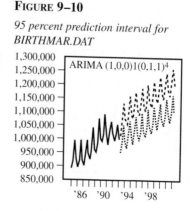

over time. The EFSE(*m*) remain constant until increases occur every 12 periods, at *m* = 13, 25, etc. Table 9–10 summarizes this model.

JAPAN.DAT Stock Index. Figure 9–13 and Table 9–13 show the prediction intervals for the Japanese Stock Index. As shown, this is a trending series and is thus nonstationary. The trend is evident and the prediction interval is increasing rapidly

TABLE 9–9   Prediction Interval for Quarterly BIRTHMAR.DAT: ARIMA(1,0,0)1(0,1,1)[4]

m	*Time, t + m*	*Forecast*	*EFSE(m)*	*Lower 95%*	*Upper 95%*
1	33	987036.84	15501.5	956654.41	1017419.26
2	34	1027606.86	19037.1	990294.81	1064918.91
3	35	1097548.49	20602.6	1057168.11	1137928.86
4	36	1035225.43	21354.2	993371.91	1077078.96
5	37	1014676.80	22056.4	971447.07	1057906.52
	...				
32	64	1138407.20	23927.9	1091509.33	1185305.07
33	65	1115914.09	24015.3	1068845.01	1162983.16
34	66	1151116.25	24059.5	1103960.41	1198272.08
35	67	1217231.30	24082.0	1170031.43	1264431.17
36	68	1152180.40	24093.4	1104958.17	1199402.63

TABLE 9–10   MWHRS.DAT Model

Series	*n*	*Logs*	*Model*	R^2	*Coefficients*	*DW*	*Q*
MWHRS	120	Yes	$1,1(0,1,1)^{12}$ $\sigma_e^2 = .0260$	.97	$\theta_0 = .0328 \ (.0000)$ $-\theta_{12} = -.8269 \ (.0000)$	2.12	22.73 (.019)

FIGURE 9–11

Forecasts of logs of MWHRS.DAT

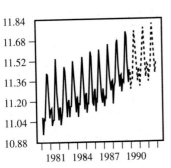

FIGURE 9–12

95 percent prediction interval of MWHRS.DAT

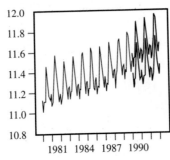

FIGURE 9–13

Forecasts and prediction intervals for logs of JAPAN.DAT

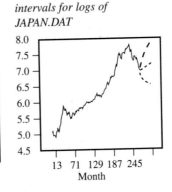

over time. The EFSE(m) increases greatly each period because of the nonstationarity of this series. Note how much more rapidly the EFSE(m) increases for this series compared to that of the previous MWHRS series. This is typical for a nonseasonal, nonstationary series. Table 9–12 summarizes this model. (As noted in Chapter 8, the trend coefficient θ_0 should be dropped from the model.)

TABLE 9–11   Prediction Interval for MWHRS.DAT: ARIMA,1,1(0,1,1)[12]

m	Time, $t + m$	Forecast	EFSE(m)	Lower 95%	Upper 95%
1	121	11.4482	.0260	11.3974	11.4991
2	122	11.3170	.0260	11.2661	11.3678
3	123	11.3952	.0260	11.3443	11.4461
11	131	11.3949	.0260	11.3441	11.4458
12	132	11.4704	.0260	11.4196	11.5213
13	133	11.4811	.0263	11.4295	11.5327
14	134	11.3498	.0263	11.2982	11.4014
	. . .				
23	143	11.4278	.0263	11.3761	11.4794
24	144	11.5033	.0263	11.4516	11.5549
25	145	11.5139	.0267	11.4616	11.5663
26	146	11.3826	.0267	11.3303	11.4350
	. . .				
36	156	11.5361	.0267	11.4837	11.5885

TABLE 9–12   JAPAN.DAT Model

Series	n	Logs	Model	R^2	Coefficients	DW	Q
Japan	270	yes	(1,1,0)1,1 $\sigma_e^2 = .0383$	.998	$\theta_0 = .00727\ (.0522)$ $\phi_1 = .37375\ (.0000)$	1.96	25.718 (.8738)

TABLE 9–13   Prediction Interval for Japan Stock Index: ARIMA(1,1,0)1,1

m	Time, $t + m$	Forecast	EFSE(m)	Lower 95%	Upper 95%
1	272	7.0203	.0382	6.9454	7.0953
2	273	7.0209	.0650	6.8935	7.1483
3	274	7.0255	.0870	6.8549	7.1961
4	275	7.0316	.1056	6.8246	7.2387
	. . .				
34	305	7.2423	.3507	6.5551	7.9296
35	306	7.2494	.3559	6.5518	7.9470
36	307	7.2564	.3611	6.5486	7.9642

Summary

The shapes and values of prediction intervals provide insights into ARIMA models and processes. As we have seen, prediction intervals vary dramatically from stationary to nonstationary series, as the stationary profiles are much narrower in forecasting. One of the more significant benefits of prediction intervals is their use in deciding whether a model has theoretical, intuitive, and practical validity. If the behavior of the forecasts or prediction intervals seems to be inconsistent with our understanding of the time series, we should reevaluate the model. Forecasts and prediction intervals are therefore important to understanding the differences between competing ARIMA models.

However, a model should not be selected because of its favorable prediction intervals. Instead, the correct model should be based on a number of measures, including the defensible behavior of its prediction interval. Remember: A model is chosen on the belief that it will accurately portray the future behavior of the series. Do not choose a model because you hope the future will behave as suggested by the model and its prediction interval. Also, narrow prediction intervals are not a basis for choosing one model over another. Instead, the relevant criteria should be the probability that this prediction interval reflects the future.

Key Terms

asymptotic values of EMSE(m)
conditional and unconditional forecasts
$e_t(m)$ m-period-ahead forecast error
expected mean squared error [EMSE(m)]
expected forecast standard error [EFSE(m)]
forecast mean squared error [FMSE(m)]

forecast standard error [FSE(m)]
m period forecasts
psi weight (ψ)
prediction intervals
Taylor series

Key Formulas

AR(1)

$$y_t = e_t + \phi_1 e_{t-1} + \phi_1^2 e_{t-2} + \cdots + \phi_1^n e_{t-n} + \cdots \qquad (9\text{--}1)$$

Unconditional forecast

$$E(Y_t) = E(y_t) + \mu = \mu$$

Conditional forecast

$$E(y_{t+1}|y_t, y_{t-1}, \ldots, y_2, y_1) \qquad (9\text{--}3)$$

$$y_t(m) = E(e_{t+m} + \phi_1 e_{t+m-1} + \cdots + \phi_1^{m-1} e_{t+1} + \phi_1^m y_t) = \phi_1^m y_t$$

Since $|\phi_1| < 1$,

$$\phi_1^m y_t, \to 0 \qquad \text{as } m \to \infty \qquad (9\text{--}5)$$

Then, $Y_t(m) = y_t(m) + \mu = 0 + \mu = \mu \qquad \text{as } m \to \infty$

Conditional forecast $\to$ Unconditional forecast as $m \to \infty$

Forecast Mean Squared Error (FMSE) and Standard Error (FSE)

$$\text{FMSE}(m) = \frac{\sum[Y_{t+i+m} - Y_{t+i}(m)]^2}{j} \qquad \text{FSE}(m) = \sqrt{\frac{\sum[Y_{t+i+m} - Y_{t+i}(m)]^2}{j}}$$

$$\text{EMSE}(m) = \text{Expected [FMSE}(m)] \qquad \text{EFSE}(m) = \sqrt{\text{EMSE}(m)}$$

General ARIMA Models: psi weights (ψ_1)

$$y_t = e_t + \psi_1 e_{t-1} + \psi_2 e_{t-2} + \cdots + \psi_k e_{t-k} + \cdots \qquad (9\text{–}8)$$

(e.g., AR(1))

$$y_t = e_t + \phi_1 e_{t-1} + \phi_1^2 e_{t-2} + \cdots + \phi_1^k e_{t-k} + \cdots \qquad (9\text{–}9)$$

General EMSE(m)

$$\text{EMSE}(1) = E(e_{t+1}^2) = \sigma_e^2 \qquad (9\text{–}15)$$

$$\text{EMSE}(2) = \sigma_e^2 + \psi_1^2 \sigma_e^2 = (1 + \psi_1^2)\sigma_e^2 \qquad (9\text{–}19)$$

$$\text{EMSE}(3) = (1 + \psi_1^2 + \psi_2^2)\sigma_e^2 \qquad (9\text{–}21)$$

$$\text{EMSE}(m) = (1 + \psi_1^2 + \psi_2^2 + \cdots + \psi_{m-1}^2)\sigma_e^2 \qquad (9\text{–}22)$$

P.I.

$$Y_t(m) - t \cdot \text{EFSE}(m) \le Y_{t+m} \le Y_t(m) + t \cdot \text{EFSE}(m) \qquad (9\text{–}23)$$

AR(1)

$$\text{EMSE}(1) = \sigma_e^2$$

$$\text{EMSE}(2) = (1 + \phi_1^2)\sigma_e^2$$

$$\cdots$$

$$\text{EMSE}(m) = (1 + \phi_1^2 + \cdots + \phi_1^{2m-2})\sigma_e^2$$

$$\lim_{m \to \infty} \text{EMSE}(m) = \frac{\sigma_e^2}{(1 - \phi_1^2)} \qquad (9\text{–}25)$$

ARIMA(0,1,0)

$$Y_t = Y_{t-1} + e_t$$

$$Y_t = (1 + B + B^2 + B^3 + \cdots + B^n)e_t$$

$$\psi_1 = \psi_2 = \cdots = \psi_k = 1$$

Conditional Forecasts

$$Y_t(m) = E(Y_t + e_{t+1} + \cdots + e_{t+m}) = Y_t \qquad (9\text{–}27)$$

$$\text{EMSE}(1) = E(e_{t+1}^2) = \sigma_e^2$$

$$\text{EMSE}(2) = E[(e_{t+2} + e_{t+1})^2] = 2\sigma_e^2$$

$$\cdots$$

$$\text{EMSE}(m) = E[(e_{t+m} + e_{t+m-1} + \cdots + e_{t+1})^2] = m\sigma_e^2 \qquad (9\text{–}28)$$

ARIMA(0,0,1), only one nonzero ψ weight, a one-period memory:

$$y_t = e_t - \theta_1 e_{t-1} = (1 - \theta_1 B)e_t = (1 + \psi_1 B)e_t$$

$$\text{where } \psi_1 = -\theta_1; \text{ thus, } \psi_2 = \psi_3 = \cdots = \psi_k = 0 \qquad \text{for all } k > 1$$

Conditional forecasts

$$y_t(1) = E(e_{t+1} - \theta_1 e_t) \quad = -\theta_1 e_t \quad y_t(1) = \mu - \theta_1 e_t$$

$$y_t(2) = E(e_{t+2} - \theta_1 e_{t+1}) = 0 \qquad y_t(2) = \mu$$

$$\cdots$$

$$y_t(m) = E(e_{t+m} - \theta_1 e_{t+m-1}) = 0 \quad y_t(m) = \mu$$

$$\text{EMSE}(1) = E(e_{t+1}^2) = \sigma_e^2$$

$$\text{EMSE}(2) = E[(e_{t+2} - \theta_1 e_{t+1})^2] = (1 + \theta_1^2)\sigma_e^2$$

$$\cdots$$

$$\text{EMSE}(m) = E[(e_{t+m} - \theta_1 e_{t+m-1})^2] = (1 + \theta_1^2)\sigma_e^2 \tag{9-29}$$

$$\text{EMSE}(m) = (1 + \theta_1^2)\sigma_e^2$$

$$m \to \infty$$

Seasonal nonstationary prediction interval

$$Y_t = Y_{t-12} + e_t$$

$$Y_t = (1 + B^{12} + B^{24} + B^{36} + \cdots + B^{i \cdot 12})e_t \qquad i = 1 \text{ to INT}\left(\frac{n}{12}\right) \tag{9-30}$$

$$Y_t = (1 + \psi_{12}B^{12} + \psi_{24}B^{24} + \psi_{36}B^{36} + \cdots + \psi_{i \cdot 12}B^{i \cdot 12})e_t \tag{9-31}$$

$$\psi_{12} = \psi_{24} = \cdots = \psi_{i \cdot 12} = 1, \qquad \text{all other } \psi_r = 0 \text{ for } r \neq i \cdot 12$$

Conditional forecasts ARIMA$(0,1,0)^{12}$

$$Y_t(1) = E(Y_{t-11} + e_{t+1}) = Y_{t-11}$$

$$Y_t(12) = E(Y_t + e_{t+12}) = Y_t$$

$$Y_t(13) = E(Y_{t+1} + e_{t+13}) = E(Y_{t+1}) = Y_t(1) = Y_{t-11}$$

$$\text{EMSE}(1) = \sigma_e^2$$

$$\text{EMSE}(2) = (1 + 0)\sigma_e^2 = \sigma_e^2$$

$$\cdots$$

$$\text{EMSE}(25) = (1 + 0 + \cdots + 0 + 1 + 0 + \cdots + 0 + 1)\sigma_e^2 = 3\sigma_e^2$$

$$\text{EMSE}(m) = \quad = \text{INT}\left[1 + \frac{m-1}{12}\right]\sigma_e^2 \tag{9-32}$$

Review Problems Using Your Software

If your software generates confidence intervals for ARIMA models, repeat the analysis of the following tables. Be sure to interpret your results.

a. Table 9–2, AR(1) model for AR1P.DAT.

b. Table 9–3, ARIMA(1,1,0) for SERIESB.DAT.

c. Table 9–4, MA(1) model for MA1P.DAT.

d. Table 9–5, ARIMA$(0,1,0)^{12}$1 for PHARMDEM.DAT.

e. Table 9–7, ARIMA(1,1,1)1 for SERIESC.DAT.

f. Table 9–9, ARIMA(1,0,0)1(0,1,1)^4 for BIRTHMAR.DAT.

g. Table 9–11, ARIMA,1,1(0,1,1)^{12} for MWHRS.DAT.

h. Table 9–13, ARIMA(1,1,0)1,1 for JAPAN.DAT.

Problems

9–1 Sketch the approximate prediction interval profiles for the following time series:
   a. ARIMA(0,0,0)
   b. AR(1), for low ϕ
   c. AR(1), for high ϕ
   d. ARIMA(1,1,0)
   e. MA(1)
   f. ARIMA(0,1,0)
   g. ARIMA(0,1,0)^{12}
   h. ARIMA(1,1,1)1
   i. ARIMA(1,0,0)1(0,1,1)^4
   j. ARIMA(1,0,0)1,1(0,1,1)^{12}
   k. ARIMA(1,1,0)1

9–2 If all else is equal during the fitting process, which type of ARIMA process has narrower prediction intervals?
   a. ARIMA(0,0,0) or ARIMA(0,1,0).
   b. ARIMA(0,0,0) or ARIMA(1,0,0).
   c. ARIMA(0,1,0) or ARIMA(0,1,0)1.
   d. ARIMA(0,1,0) or ARIMA(0,1,0)^{4}1 for two seasonal cycles.
   e. ARIMA(1,0,0)^4 or ARIMA(0,1,0)^4.
   f. ARIMA(1,0,0)^4 or ARIMA(1,0,0)^{4}1.

9–3 Define conditional and unconditional forecasts.

9–4 Define and distinguish between the following terms:
   MSE, RSE, FMSE, FSE, EMSE, and EFSE.

9–5 Explain how the following terms are used in forecasting:
   MSE, RSE, FMSE, FSE, EMSE, AND EFSE.

9–6 An analyst can choose between two alternative models: a (0,1,0), and a (0,1,0)1. Theory supports the (0,1,0) model; however, the (0,1,0)1 model fits the data somewhat better and has a marginally significant constant. Explain why the analyst might want to accept the (0,1,0)1 model, but should accept the alternative model instead. If the analyst and management are not confident of which model to select, what might be done to aid the decision?

9–7 For an AR(1) process, the following formula expresses the EMSE(*m*) at any horizon *m*:

$$\text{EMSE}(m) = \frac{\sigma_e^2(1 - \phi_1^{2 \cdot m})}{(1 - \phi_1^2)}$$

Using this formula, verify the prediction intervals of the AR(1) model of Table 9–2. Use of a spreadsheet is recommended for this problem. Now try $\phi_1 = .1$ and .9, and comment.

9–8 In what ways are the prediction interval profiles useful in accepting or rejecting a model? In what ways are the prediction interval profiles useful in explaining forecasts to management?

9–9 Manually derive the prediction intervals 1, 2 , 3, . . . , 6, and *s* for the following ARIMA processes.
   a. ARIMA(0,0,0)
   b. ARIMA(0,1,0)
   c. ARIMA(1,0,0)
   d. ARIMA(0,1,0)1
   e. ARIMA(0,1,0)^4
   f. ARIMA(1,0,0)^{4}1

9–10 Why might we expect the mean error in forecasting to have a greater bias as the horizon length *m* increases?

9–11 The time series BIRTHMAR.DAT is the quarterly marriages in the United States. Complete the common forecasting assignment I.

9–12 The time series RETAIL.DAT is the monthly retail sales in the United States. Complete the common forecasting assignment I.

9–13 The time series SUPEROIL.DAT is the sales of the Superoil Company, in thousands of barrels, during the last 79 months. Complete the common forecasting assignment I.

9–14 The time series MILK.DAT is the monthly milk production in the United States. Complete the common forecasting assignment I.

Minicases I

For a selected minicase or problem, complete the following analysis. If your software generates confidence intervals for ARIMA models, generate prediction intervals for two seasonal cycles, or 24 periods, whichever is less. Compare and comment on the EFSE(m) and the RSE of the fit. In general, comment on the meaning and usefulness of the resulting prediction intervals.

Minicases II

For a selected minicase, complete the following analysis. If you have withheld data and simulated out-of-sample forecasts, and your software generates confidence intervals for ARIMA models, compare the EFSE(m) generated by the software to the FSE(m) or the MAD(m) realized during the out-of-sample forecast period. Is there a relationship between these two measures? If not, speculate on why there is not. In completing this assignment, you need to make j m-period out-of-sample forecasts. For example, if 24 periods are withheld, it is possible to generate 24 one-period-ahead forecasts, 23 two-periods-ahead forecasts, 22 three-periods-ahead forecasts, . . . , 12 12-periods-ahead forecast. To generate these statistics, 24 out-of-sample forecasts must be generated, as shown in the following table. From each of these 24 out-of-sample forecasts, you can collect j samples for each m period.

m	j	Actual FSE (m) or MAD(m)	EFSE(m)
1	24		
2	23		
3	22		
. . .			
11	13		
12	12		

Complete this assignment by analyzing actual forecasting accuracy for at least two horizons: one of one-half and one full seasonal cycles. Comment on the accuracy of each measure.

References

Abraham, B.; and J. Ledolter. *Statistical Methods for Forecasting.* New York: Wiley, 1983.

Ansley, C.F.; and P. Newbold. "Finite sample properties of estimators for autoregressive-moving average models.: *Journal of Econometrics* 13, (1980), pp. 159–183.

Bewley, R. "AUTOBOX: A review." *Journal of Applied Econometrics* 3, (1988), pp. 240–244.

Box, G.E.P.; G.M. Jenkins; and G C. Reinsel. *Time Series Analysis, Forecasting and Control.* 3rd ed. Englewood Cliffs, N.J.: Prentice Hall, 1994.

Box, G.E.P.; and D.A. Pierce. "Distribution of residual autocorrelations in autoregressive integrated moving average time series models." *Journal of the American Statistical Association* 65, (1970), pp. 1509–1526.

Davies, N.; and P. Newbold. "Forecasting with misspecified models." *Applied Statistics* 29, (1980), pp. 87–92.

Dickey, D.A.; W.R. Bell; and R.B. Miller.

"Unit roots in time series models: tests and implications." *The American Statistician* 40, (1986), pp. 12–26.

Granger, C.W.J.; and M. Morris. "Time series modeling an interpretation." *Journal of the Royal Statistical Society A* 139, (1976), pp. 246–257.

Granger, C.W.J.; and P. Newbold. *Forecasting Economic time Series.* 2nd ed. Orlando, Fl.: Academic Press, 1986.

Hill, G.; and R. Fildes. "The accuracy of extrapolation methods: and automatic Box–Jenkins package sift." *Journal of Forecasting* 3, (1984), pp. 319–323.

Jenkins, G.M. *Practical Experiences with Modeling and Forecasting Time Series.* Lancaster, PA: GJP Publications, 1979.

Jenkins, G.M. "Some practical aspects of forecasting in organizations." *Journal of Forecasting* 1, (1982), pp. 3–21.

Jenkins, G.M.; and G. Mcleod. *Case Studies in Time Series Analysis.* Lancaster, PA: GJP Publications, 1982.

Ledolter, J.; and B. Abraham. "Parsimony and its importance in time series forecasting." *Technometrics* 23, (1981), pp. 411–414.

Libert, G. "The *M*-competition with a fully automatic Box-Jenkins procedure.

Journal of Forecasting 3, (1984), pp. 325–328.

Ljung, G.M.; and G.E.P. Box. "On a measure of lack of fit in time series models." *Biometrika* 65, (1978), pp. 297–303.

McCleary, R.; and R.A. Hay, Jr. *Applied Time Series Analysis for the Social Sciences.* Beverly Hills, CA: Sage Publications Inc., 1980.

Nelson, C.R. *Applied Time Series Analysis for Managerial Forecasting.* San Francisco, CA: Holden Day, 1973.

Newbold, P. "ARIMA model building and the time series analysis approach to forecasting." *Journal of Forecasting* 2, (1983), pp. 23–35.

Pankratz, A. *Forecasting with Univariate Box–Jenkins Models: Concepts and Cases.* New York: Wiley, 1983.

Texter, P.A.; and J.K. Ord. "Forecasting using automatic identification procedures: A comparative analysis." *International Journal of Forecasting* 5, (1989), pp. 209–215.

Vandaele, W. *Applied Time Series and Box–Jenkins Models.* Orlando, Fl.: Academic Press, 1983.

MULTIVARIATE/CAUSAL METHODS

MULTIPLE REGRESSION OF TIME SERIES

Theorize longer, analyze shorter. Don't be in a rush to run the program. Think about the model from every angle, hypothesize how different variables affect each other. When you have a theory, then try it. Impatience is the enemy of valid models. Contemplation is productive work.*

The Author

Measure twice, cut once.

The Carpenter's Rule

Chapter Outline

Linear Multiple Regression Models

In forecasting, building models that relate the dependent variable to multiple independent variables can be effective. Such models can be powerful analytical tools that provide predictions as well as insights into the cause and effect relationship between the dependent and independent variables. In the ultimate application of such **causal models**, policymakers use them to control the systems being modeled. Multiple regression is an important methodology in building such models because it measures the simultaneous influences of a number of independent variables upon one dependent variable.

We will develop several multiple regression estimation methods, including the least squares method (commonly called ordinary least squares), autoregressive methods (including the Cochrane–Orcutt iterative least squares), and weighted least squares methods. While these are presented primarily in the context of time series analyses, some discussion of cross-sectional analysis is also included.

In addition, this chapter covers methods of modeling nonlinear relationships using linear multiple regression. These and other methods of multiple regression are some of the most widely used in business and economic analysis. An understanding of multiple regression is a foundation upon which we can build an understanding of more advanced time series and multivariate data analysis techniques.

One important objective of this chapter is to explore the implications of several assumptions developed in Chapter 3: Linearity, uniform scatter, independence, and normality of errors. When these four assumptions are true, it is possible to measure the sampling error in regression results and to make inferences about the true population regression relationship.

In this book, we have constantly emphasized the importance of understanding and questioning the assumptions and theory upon which models are built, as well as the need to plot original variables and residuals as part of a methodical process of modeling multivariate relationships. Finally, we also emphasize the difficulties in constructing generalizable causal models.

General Multiple Regression Model

The general form of the multiple regression model is:

$$Y = a + b_1 X_1 + b_2 X_2 + \cdots + b_{k-1} X_{k-1} + e \qquad (10\text{--}1)$$

where this notation is similar to that already defined in Chapter 3. The number of independent variables included in a regression relationship $(k - 1)$ is typically low (e.g., < 6), because there are seldom more explanatory variables, except when dummy variables are used in the relationship. Fortunately, the bivariate concepts and statistics learned in Chapter 3 apply directly to multiple regression theory and models. A review of that chapter, particularly the discussion of Table 3–4, is very helpful in interpreting the results shown in this chapter.

Let us discuss multiple regression in the context of the Big City Bookstore example of Chapter 3. As you may recall, it was assumed that a relationship existed between sales and advertising at the bookstore. However, the store manager realized that sales were greatly influenced by the number and size of competing bookstores. Table 10–1 illustrates the data collected by the manager. She measured advertising in $1000 units, while competition was the total square footage of competitor stores in the area, measured in 1,000's.

Specific Multiple Regression Model

As shown in Table 10–1, during the given time period, competitor square footage varied from 10,000 to 35,000 square feet. It's reasonable to believe that the sales at a store are affected by the number and size of competing stores. As part of the normal

TABLE 10–1 Big City Bookstore Sales, Advertising, and Competition

Year	Sales (Y) ($1000)	Advertising (X1) ($1000)	Competition (X2) (sq. ft. in 1000s)
1	27	20	10
2	23	20	15
3	31	25	15
4	45	28	15
5	47	29	20
6	42	28	25
7	39	31	35
8	45	34	35
9	57	35	20
10	59	36	30
11	73	41	20
12	84	45	20

regression modeling process, Figures 10–1a, b, and c illustrate the graphical relationship between the three variables of this study. As shown in Figure 10–1a, sales and advertising seem highly related, while in Figure 10–1b the relationship between sales and competition is not nearly as strong. Finally, note that advertising and competition appear to have some relationship. To better understand the relationships between these variables, consider the following correlation matrix, which illustrates the correlation coefficients between the variables.

Correlation Matrix	Sales	Advertising	Competition
Sales	1	.964	.221
Advertising	.964	1	.426
Competition	.221	.426	1

These correlation coefficients confirm the speculations made using Figures 10–1a, b, and c. To better understand the relationships between sales, advertising, and competition, we will examine the relationships in Equations 10–2, 10–3, and 10–4, and will then peruse Table 10–2. Two simple linear relationships of sales with advertising and then with competition are shown in Equations 10–2 and 10–3; Equation 10–4 shows the fit of the multiple regression relationship of sales as a function of both advertising and competition.

Equation 10–2 was originally discussed in Chapter 3 and is consistent with the theory that increased advertising will increase sales. As shown in Equation 10–2, advertising has a very positive and significant relationship to the dependent variable, sales. The $\overline{R}^2$ and F values are quite high and significant. In addition, their t-values, given below the coefficients, in parentheses, are all very statistically significant. We did note in Chapter 3 that the Durbin–Watson statistic was low. The low DW statistic is indicative of a high autocorrelation in the residuals of this model. [Remember that the DW statistic is supposed to be approximately 2, with lower (higher) values denoting positive (negative) serial correlation.] Frequently, poor DW statistics are the result

FIGURE 10–1

Relationships for Big City Bookstore (BIGCITY.DAT)

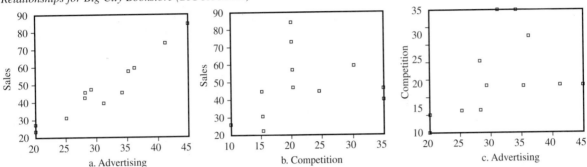

a. Advertising   b. Competition   c. Advertising

of omitting other important independent variables that have varied over time. Possibly, this autocorrelation in the residuals could result from the exclusion of the competition variable.

$$\hat{Y}_t = -23.02 + 2.280X1_t \qquad (X1_t = \text{advertising}) \qquad (10\text{–}2)$$
$$\phantom{\hat{Y}_t = } (-3.64) \quad (11.5)$$

where

$$S_{yx} = 5.039 \qquad \overline{R}^2 = .923 \qquad n = 12 \qquad F = 132.26 \qquad DW = 1.1368$$

The manager of the bookstore is interested in measuring the relationship between sales and competition. The results of this simple linear regression are shown in Equation 10–3:

$$\hat{Y}_t = 37.34 + .477X2_t \qquad (X2_t = \text{competition}) \qquad (10\text{–}3)$$
$$\phantom{\hat{Y}_t = } (2.339) \quad (.687)$$

where

$$S_{yx} = 18.574 \qquad \overline{R}^2 = -.050 \qquad n = 12 \qquad F = .472 \qquad DW = .3767$$

The results of Equation 10–3 are confounding. Based on theory, we expect increased competition to lower sales. However, the value of the coefficient for $X2$ is $+.477$. This denotes that every 1,000 square feet of competitor space yields a $477 increase in sales. This is inconsistent with the theory that competition will normally drive sales down. The t-value of the regression coefficient for Equation 10–3 is very low, .687. This denotes that the regression coefficient for competition is not significantly different than zero, or may even be negative. Thus, there appears to be no relationship between sales and competition. This is also confirmed by the $\overline{R}^2$ and F values. As we mentioned previously, this does not seem to be the right theoretical conclusion. (Don't be confused by the negative $\overline{R}^2$, this was discussed in Chapter 3.)

The problem with Equation 10–3 is that it is a flawed model (i.e., a misspecification). It does not measure the changes in sales that result from simultaneous changes in competition and advertising. Equation 10–3 does not control for the influence of advertising on sales while competition varies. Fortunately, multiple regression can be used to measure the simultaneous influence of several variables.

Finally, note the extremely low DW statistic, which is also indicative of problems with the model. Possibly, by leaving out the advertising variable, we have caused the residuals to be highly correlated. To better understand the problem of not accounting for or controlling for advertising when measuring the influence of competition, let us now fit a full model with both advertising and competition.

Equation 10–4 illustrates a more valid approach to measuring the effects of advertising and competition on sales.

$$\hat{Y}_t = -18.80 + 2.525X1_t - .545X2_t \tag{10-4}$$
$$(-4.879) \quad (19.50) \quad (-4.432)$$

where

$$S_{yx} = 2.978 \quad \overline{R}^2 = .973 \quad n = 12 \quad F = 199.21 \quad DW = 1.7705$$

As the results show, the $\overline{R}^2$ of this relationship is highest, the *t*-values of the regression coefficients are all very significantly different than zero (i.e., greater than 2 or 3), and the signs of the coefficients are all correct. Advertising has a positive effect on sales, and competition has a negative impact. Also, we see that the effect of advertising is greater after we have controlled for competition in the relationship: $2.525 here, versus $2.28 in Equation 10–3. Each dollar of advertising is associated with a $2.525 increase in sales; while each 1,000 square feet of competition is associated with a $.545 decline in sales. Finally, the DW statistic is now much closer to 2, denoting that likely there are no problems with serial correlation.

Only by simultaneously controlling for (i.e., including) each independent variable in the relationship were we able to better estimate the true relationship between sales, competition, and advertising. You may be asked to analyze these results further as a homework assignment.

As measured by the $\overline{R}^2$, *F*, and DW, this relationship is the most significant and accurate of those in Equations 10–2 to 10–4. While not shown here, good regression analysis includes plots of the residuals of Equation 10–4 versus *X*1, *X*2, and $\hat{Y}$. As we discuss later, any unusual patterns in these plots would suggest that the model has the wrong form (e.g., perhaps *X*1 should be squared, or maybe there is "heteroscedasticity" in the model results, a topic covered later in this chapter). From an analysis of Equation 10–4, the manager can gain insight into the complex relationship, and subject to the sampling errors in this small sample size, we seem to have a good relationship.

Table 10–2a, b, and c illustrate full regression outputs for Equations 10–2 to 10–4, respectively. You may want to study these tables now. The rows in these tables are defined well in Chapter 3, particularly the explanation given with Table 3–4.

There are some very minor differences in the way some statistics are interpreted when using multiple regression. These are briefly discussed in the next sections.

Adjusted Coefficient of Determination $\overline{R}^2$

As in simple regression analysis, the **adjusted coefficient of determination** is the ratio of explained variance to total variance, most easily calculated as 1 minus the unexplained variance over the total variance, or

$$\overline{R}^2 = \frac{\text{Explained variance}}{\text{Total variance}} = 1 - \frac{\text{Unexplained variance}}{\text{Total variance}} = = 1 - \frac{S_{yx}^2}{S_y^2}$$

The interpretation of this relationship is identical to that of the simple linear $\overline{R}^2$; that is, it represents the proportion of the total variance that is explained or removed by relating *Y* to one or more independent variables (i.e., *X*'s).

Partial (Net) Regression Coefficients

The regression coefficients in multiple regression measure the dependent variable response that results from a unit increase in an independent variable, after partialing out or holding constant the influences of the other independent variables. Because

TABLE 10–2   Simple and Multiple Regression for Big City Bookstore

a. Simple Linear Regression Sales = f(Advertising) — Equation 10–2

1 Dependent variable: Sales				
2 Usable observations	12	Degrees of freedom	10	
3 $\overline{R}^2$	.9227			
4 Std error of dependent variable	18.1225			
5 Standard error of estimate	5.0394			
6 Sum of squared residuals	253.9530			
7 Regression $F(1,10)$	132.26			
8 Significance level of F	.00000044			
9 Durbin–Watson statistic	1.137			

10 Variable	Coeff	Std Error	t-Stat	Signif
11 Constant	−23.0191	6.316	−3.644	.0045
12 ADVERT	2.2801	.198	11.500	.0000

b. Simple Linear Regression Sales = f(Competition) — Equation 10–3

1 Dependent variable: Sales				
2 Usable observations	12	Degrees of freedom	10	
3 $\overline{R}^2$	−.050			
4 Std deviation of dependent variable	18.123			
5 Standard error of estimate	118.574			
6 Sum of squared residuals	3449.780			
7 Regression $F(1,10)$	.472			
8 Significance level of F	.5076			
9 Durbin–Watson statistic	.377			

10 Variable	Coeff	Std Error	t-Stat	Signif
11 Constant	37.3372	15.960	2.339	.0414
12 COMP	.4767	.694	.687	.5076

c. Multiple Regression Sales = f(Adver. Comp.) — Equation 10–4

1 Dependent variable: Sales				
2 Usable observations	12	Degrees of freedom	9	
3 $\overline{R}^2$	.9730			
4 Std deviation of dependent variable	18.1225			
5 Standard error of estimate	2.978			
6 Sum of squared residuals	79.803			
7 Regression $F(2,9)$	199.2155			
8 Significance level of F	.00000004			
9 Durbin–Watson statistic	1.771			

10 Variable	Coeff	Std Error	t-Stat	Signif
11 Constant	−18.7958	3.8520	−4.880	.0009
12 ADVERT	2.5248	.1295	19.495	.0000
13 COMP	−.5449	.1230	−4.432	.0016

they partial the influences among several independent variables, the multiple regression coefficients are frequently called **partial** or **net regression coefficients.** They measure the effect of an independent variable while netting out the effects of the other independent variables.

Consider the meaning of holding the other variables constant. Given that the advertising of a store is $30,000, substitute this value into Equation 10–4:

$$Y_t = -18.80 + 2.525 \cdot 30 - .545X2_t + e_t \tag{10–5}$$

$$Y_t = -18.80 + 75.75 - .545X2_t + e_t = 56.86 - .545X2 + e_t$$

This equation relates sales to competitor store size, given a constant advertising of $30,000. In other words, the coefficient $-.545$ is the influence of competitor store size if advertising is held constant. The coefficient, b_2 shows the relationship between store sales and competitor store size, net of advertising effects.

The coefficient b_1 can be interpreted in the same way: It denotes that store sales are $2.525 higher for each dollar spent on advertising for a given level of competition. In other words, it is the relationship between sales and advertising, net of competition.

As in the case of simple regression, the intercept is a catchall for the mean influence of other variables not included in the relationship.

Regression Plane

In contrast to the bivariate regressions of Chapter 3, multiple regressions involve three or more dimensions. Consequently, we need to discuss errors that vary about a plane or **hyperplane,** in k-dimensional space rather than a line. Figure 10–2 illustrates the data of our example in three-dimensional space. As shown, the Y axis (the vertical axis) is sales, the $X1$ axis is advertising (with angle sloping \), and the $X2$ axis is competition (with angle sloping /).

Figure 10–3 illustrates the regression plane that results from the ordinary least squares model of Equation 10–4. This plane cuts through the three-dimensional space of the axis. As it goes through the top and bottom of the figure, the plane is truncated by horizontal planes. These horizontal planes limit the three-dimensional space.

As Figures 10–2 and 10–3 illustrate, the graphical representation of three-dimensional space is very easily accomplished; however, we may have considerable difficulty in understanding four-dimensional space, let alone presenting it graphically.

To better understand the relationship illustrated in Figure 10–3, consider the two added lines shown in Figure 10–4. When $X1 = 30$, Equation 10–3 is the nearly horizontal line that slopes slightly downward and to the right. This line goes through the intersection of $X1 = 30$, $X2 = 0$, and $Y = 56.86$ on the far lefthand side and $X1 = 30$, $X2 = 40$, and $Y = 35.06$ on the far righthand side, at point A. The value of $Y = 35.06$

FIGURE 10–2

Deviations about a plane or hyperspace

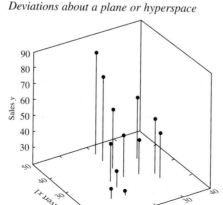

FIGURE 10–3

Regression plane for Equation 10–3

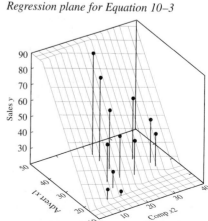

Misusing Graphical Presentations

Modern statistical software makes sophisticated graphical presentation possible, however, also, it can make data appear to be more than it is. When this software automatically interpolates and enhances data it can mislead the analyst. "Not so long ago, scientists had to be content with studying and presenting their data in simple charts, tables, graphs, and other rudimentary forms. But these techniques have faltered lately in the face of a rapidly swelling ocean of data."* Over-"glitzing" data is a phenomenon of recent advances in computer graphics. We have seen those most enthralled with computer capabilities make some serious mistakes. For example, with as few as 30 observations it is possible to present data in three dimensions where the software automatically provides the equivalent of missing values (i.e., interpolates) and through use of colors this three dimensional represen-

tation is further enhanced. In general, 30 observations is an insufficient amount of data with which to empirically derive multivariate relationships, however, the software makes it appear that there are many more than 30 observations. Thus, we should be very cautious in the use of advanced graphical methodologies. "It's easy to get caught up in the graphics candy store and to forget the scientific purpose of such representations. Sometimes the results really do look too good to be true."

---

*Ivars Peterson, "Going for Glitz . . . and other perils of scientific visualization," *Science News* 144, (October 9, 1993), pp. 232–33.

See also Wayne Lytle, "The Dangers of Glitziness and Other Visualization Faux Pas," 1993 SIGGRAPH Conference, Anaheim, CA, August, 1993.

FIGURE 10–4

Several regression lines on the regression plane

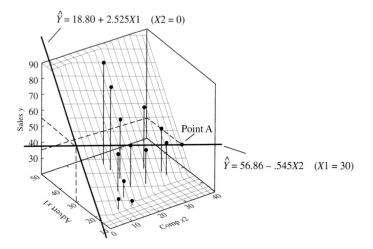

is projected around the back of the figure using a dotted line, to illustrate the change in Y from 56.86 to 35.06 as competition, $X2$, increases from 0 to 40.

The second added line of Figure 10–4 illustrates the relationship between Y and $X1$ when $X2$ is equal to 0. Assuming $X2$ equals 0, substitute different values of $X1$ into Equation 10–4 and project the resulting values of Y to the vertical axis of Figure 10–4.

While the interpretation of regression coefficients is straightforward, they can become more complex, particularly when the independent variables are not actually independent. We discuss such situations in greater detail later, in the multicollinearity section of this chapter.

No doubt these three-dimensional graphs are not as clear as simple two-dimensional graphs of linear relationships. Nonetheless, such graphs can provide some insight. Fortunately, many statistical software packages support such graphs, and you should include such plots in your analyses to confirm the reasonableness of your assumptions.

Multiple Regression Modeling Process

Figure 10–5 illustrates a flow chart of the general process of multiple regression analysis. At first, this chart may seem very complex; however, after completing this chapter, the terms, statistics, and decisions shown will be more meaningful.

The steps in the chart are iterative, repeated as many times as necessary to complete the modeling process. The chart also assumes that regression analysis is the best approach to modeling the relationship. (We will discuss choosing between different forecasting methods in Chapter 18.)

Note the importance of the earlier steps in laying the foundation for a valid model, which is based on a valid theory or understanding of the cause and effect relationships. Recognize the importance of using graphical methods throughout the modeling process to detect such problems as nonlinearities, outliers, and violations of regression assumptions.

One of the most common and serious mistakes is to accept a regression model without plotting the residuals against each independent variable, those variables not included in the model, Y, and residuals of the previous period. Figure 3–7 illustrates many of these examples. A quick review of the referenced figure can confirm the meaning of such plots. Consider several now:

- Residuals versus Included Independent Variable. This plot detects heteroscedasticity and model misspecification (e.g., nonlinear relationship between Y and X). Figures 3–7f, h, o, and p illustrate three examples.

- Residuals versus Excluded Independent Variable. This plot is useful in detecting the next variable to be included in the relationship, or the need to consider a nonlinear relationship between Y and the excluded X. Remember that correlation measures only the linear correlation between variables; therefore, if there is a perfect relationship between Y and X^2, we will not detect correlation unless either X^2 or plots of residuals versus X are included in the analysis. Figure 3–7d illustrates this situation.

- Residuals versus Y. This plot is useful in detecting serial correlation, heteroscedasticity, and other model misspecifications. The pattern in the residuals versus Y should be random; therefore, highly nonrandom patterns are indicative of one or more problems. Figures 3–7d and h illustrate this situation.

- Residuals$_t$ versus Residuals$_{t-1}$. This plot is useful in detecting serial correlation. With independent residuals, the pattern of e_t versus e_{t-1} should be random; there should not be any correlation between these two variables. Figure 3–7j illustrates this situation.

As you study the regression modeling process of Figure 10–5, note the terms of multicollinearity, serial correlation, and heteroscedasticity. These are developed throughout the remainder of this chapter. Finally, note that checking the validity of the model's predictions is one of the last steps in this chart. It is very possible to have a model that fits the data quite well, but when the reasonableness of the forecasts is checked, the model fails miserably and is therefore invalid.

Multicollinearity

When the independent variables in a multiple regression relationship are highly correlated with each other . . . a condition called **multicollinearity** . . . the regression coef-

FIGURE 10–5

Multiple-Regression modeling process

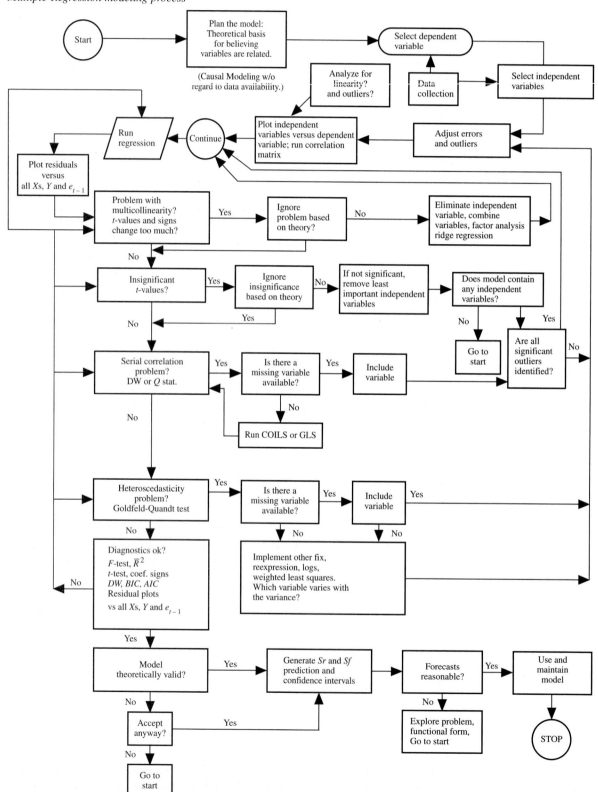

ficients may be unreliable, displaying incorrect signs and magnitudes. We emphasize the term "may be" because high multicollinearity between independent variables (i.e., correlation) does not always assure that there will be problems with the regression coefficients. Multicollinearity may or may not cause problems.

In Chapter 3, we introduced the formula for the standard error of the regression coefficient. The standard error of the partial regression coefficient for the three-variable case is shown in Equation 10–6.

$$S_{b1} = \frac{S_{yx}}{\sqrt{\sum x^2 (1 - r_{12}^2)}} \tag{10–6}$$

As shown, the standard error of the regression coefficient is related to the correlation between the independent variables, $X1$ and $X2$, r_{12}. Thus, when there is a problem with multicollinearity, both the coefficient and its standard error may be wrong. This standard error is smallest when r_{12}, the correlation between $X1$ and $X2$, is zero. However, as r_{12} approaches 1 and the denominator of the equation approaches zero, the standard error becomes very large; at the same time, the regression coefficient may become less reliable. Consequently, the standard error becomes sensitive to the degree of correlation between $X1$ and $X2$.

This sensitivity makes sense in that as $X1$ and $X2$ become more related, it can be difficult to distinguish between their separate effects on Y. The question that may be difficult to answer is, which of the variables affects Y when they move so closely together? In fact, when a relationship includes two independent variables that are perfectly correlated, $r_{12} = 1$, it is impossible to fit a unique regression model because of their redundancy. In this case, the computer program may abort and an error message regarding this problem may be generated. The message may read that the coefficients matrix has no inverse or is singular. With perfect multicollinearity, the problem is easily solved: one of the variables is removed from the relationship.

While perfect multicollinearity is evident immediately by an aborted solution, problems with high multicollinearity may not be evident unless a result that was not expected (e.g., the wrong coefficient sign or insignificant *t*-values) is reached. Also, an extremely high correlation between two independent variables does not necessarily mean there is a problem with multicollinearity.

We can best avoid multicollinearity by using good theory to direct the analysis, large sample sizes, or good procedures to detect problems when they occur. Based on theory, we should know which variables should be included in the relationship, as well as the direction of the influence (i.e., sign of the regression coefficient). If these variables have insignificant and incorrect regression coefficients, this may be a result of multicollinearity.

Sometimes, multicollinearity is simply the result of a small or unusual sample outcome. Finally, good analytical procedures help us anticipate, detect, and correct multicollinearity problems. This involves the use of graphs, correlation matrices, and theory verification, as illustrated in the previous Big City Bookstore example.

Multicollinearity can produce some strange regression results, but not always. For example, assume that we have two variables $X1$ and $X2$ that are highly correlated with Y and are positively correlated with each other. It is not uncommon to have one negative regression coefficient, even though positive signs are expected for both coefficients. Alternatively, it is not uncommon for one of these variables to be highly significant, with the correct sign and possibly (but not assuredly) the correct coefficient, while the other variable has an opposite sign and no statistical significance. Finally, one type of perfect multicollinearity that might not be anticipated by, and therefore might surprise the analyst, is multicollinearity among several variables.

Multicollinearity among More than Two Variables

It is possible to have perfect multicollinearity between more than two variables. It is not uncommon for the values of one independent variable to be perfectly correlated to two or more other independent variables. For example, in fitting Y as a function of $X1$, $X2$, and $X3$ the program aborts; however, there is no significant correlation between these variables. The problem is that some linear transformation of X_2 and X_3 perfectly defines $X1$. Functionally, this is

$$X1 = a + b_2 X2 + b_3 X2$$

with $S_{yx} = 0$, $\overline{R}^2 = 1$, and $r_{123} = 1$.

Thus, when an attempt is made to fit the following relationship,

$$Y = a + b_1 X1 + b_2 X2 + b_3 X3 + e$$

a solution is not possible. When this form of perfect colinearity occurs, the regression procedure aborts. We see this situation most often when analysts make mistakes in the use of **dichotomous variables**, also called **dummy variables**, which represent such events as promotions, seasons, and other interventions. Consider the following example.

An analyst wants to measure the seasonality of quarterly data, Y_t, using dichotomous variables, one for each quarter. These are designated $d1$, $d2$, $d3$, and $d4$. The proper use of these variables in regression analysis calls for including only three of them at one time in a regression relationship. The fourth variable is perfectly correlated with the other three dichotomous variables, as follows:

t	Y_t	$d1$	$d2$	$d3$	$d4$
1	10	1	0	0	0
2	20	0	1	0	0
3	30	0	0	1	0
4	5	0	0	0	1

Thus, $d1 = 1 - d2 - d3 - d4$, which is easily verified in the table.

Consequently, when OLS seeks a solution to the relationship between Y_t and the four dichotomous variables, a redundancy occurs in the data: any one of the three variables is a linear combination of the other three. This makes matrix inversion and a unique solution impossible. Avoid this problem by always defining one less dichotomous variable then is necessary to define the events; the excluded dichotomous variable is a part of the constant term.

Sometimes, several completely unrelated events result in perfectly correlated independent variables. Again, we have seen this in the analysis of sample survey data. Dichotomous variables are studied further in a later section of this chapter.

Multicollinearity Solutions

When multicollinearity exists, there are several potential solutions.

1. When the problem variables are redundant measures of the same underlying causal factor, simply delete the redundant variable. For example, if we were to include GDP and GNP in the same relationship, one of these variables would most likely be redundant. Often, such redundancies are not evident until they are investigated. Incidentally, good theory building should preclude most, but possibly not all, situations involving redundant variables.

2. Sometimes, multicollinearity problems are an artifact of a specific sample. When this occurs, additional observations may eliminate the problem.

3. Multicollinearity problems can result from a flawed understanding of the variables and their relationships to the dependent variable. For example, the two variables might actually be the same measure. Alternatively, when several measured variables each represent the same underlying causal factor but different dimensions of that factor, these separate variables might be combined into a single factor through the use of a statistical procedure called **factor analysis.** The resulting single factor can then be used in the regression analysis.

4. When the multicollinearity results from a unique sample and no additional observations can be gathered, an advanced regression technique called **ridge regression** can be used to partial out the individual effects of the highly correlated variables.

5. When all else fails and theory dictates that both variables should be included, then both variables should be included in the relationship. This is a viable solution; however, if our purpose is to model cause and effect, we should go one step further. In this case, we should investigate the relationships between variables, with attention to the possibility that several equations should be used. This topic is discussed in Chapter 11 on econometric methods.

While multicollinearity affects the reliability of the regression coefficients and their interpretability, it might not alter the predictive power of the regression model. That is, the overall relationship may still be useful for predictions. This can be confirmed by a low standard error of estimate and a high F-value. Consider the following example.

Example Multicollinearity Problem (MULT.DAT)

A researcher is interested in predicting the relationship between a dependent variable and four possible predictor variables. He expects all of these variables to be positively related to Y. As part of the analysis, he investigates the correlation between the five variables using the correlation matrix shown in Table 10–3. He is also interested in determining whether two or more independent variables are related. If they are very highly related, there may be a problem with multicollinearity.

As shown in Table 10–3, $X2$ is most highly correlated with Y, and the two independent variables most highly correlated with each other are $X1$ and $X4$. Because these two variables have a correlation coefficient of .9998, we can anticipate that there might be a multicollinearity problem in the regression model.

Table 10–4 illustrates the results of four regressions. We are interested in the manner in which the coefficients and t-values change as $X1$ and $X4$ are added to the relationship.

TABLE 10–3 Correlation Matrix (MULT.DAT)

	X1	*X2*	*X3*	*X4*	*Y*
$X1$	1.0000	−.1067	.1821	.9998	.4622
$X2$	−.1067	1.0000	.1031	−.1053	.7479
$X3$	.1821	.1031	1.0000	.1830	.5334
$X4$	.9998	−.1053	.1830	1.0000	.4638
Y	.4622	.7479	.5334	.4638	1.0000

TABLE 10–4   Models Illustrating Multicollinearity Problems

	X1	*X2*	*X3*	*X4*	$\bar{R}^2$	*F-value*	S_{yx}
	(t-Values Under Each Coefficient)					(Significance)	
Model 1		9.16	6.06		.7651	162.2	2166.5
		(14.3)	(9.4)			(.0000)	
Model 2	14.82	9.96	4.84		.9851	2188.9	544.9
	(37.9)	(61.26)	(29.33)			(.0000)	
Model 3		9.95	4.83	14.83	.9853	2217.0	541.4
		(61.61)	(29.47)	(38.17)		(.0000)	
Model 4	−7.07	9.94	4.83	21.89	.9852	1648.3	543.8
	(−.38)	(61.18)	(29.30)	(1.17)		(.0000)	

Consider each of the models in Table 10–4. Model 1 illustrates the inclusion of both $X2$ and $X3$, which were chosen because they are highly correlated with Y and not each other. This model has a low $\bar{R}^2$ and F-value. Model 2 includes $X1$, $X2$, and $X3$ together. These three variables result in a much better model than model 1. Model 3, with $X2$, $X3$, and $X4$, has the highest $\bar{R}^2$ and F-values and may represent the best model possible with these data.

Model 4 with multicollinearity problems includes all four variables. For this model, the coefficient of $X1$ has become negative and insignificant. Also, the sum of $X1$ and $X4$ coefficients equals 14.8, which is the value of their individual coefficients in models 2 and 3. In this situation, it appears that $X1$ and $X4$ are redundant measures of the same factor and one should be discarded. We should not hesitate to discard one of these variables if, from a theoretical standpoint, they are in fact redundant. If they are not theoretically redundant, we should investigate the cause of the multicollinearity and try either to remove it or model it using methods discussed later in Chapter 11. One of the most powerful tests to determine if a variable or group of variables is redundant is the partial F-test as described in the following section.

Partial F-test for Determining Inclusion of Variables

There are times when theory dictates that one or more variables should be included in a relationship; however, when these variables are included, their t-values are insignificant, even though $\bar{R}^2$ and F improve. The low t-values may result from multicollinearity. If the theory on whether to include the variables is ambiguous then should we include the variables or not? Fortunately, the partial F-test is useful in this situation.

In Chapter 3, we introduced the F-test as a measure of the overall significance of a relationship. With a slight modification, we can use that test to determine whether an individual variable or group of variables should be included in a relationship. That is, we can test the null hypothesis that some subset of the regression coefficients is zero. This is an important test because with multicollinearity problems, individual regression coefficient t-values are not reliable measures for determining whether or not to include a variable or group of variables.

Assume that we want to test whether a group of m variables should be included in the regression relationship, where m is some subset of the independent variables. The F-test statistic for this situation is calculated as follows:

$$F_{\text{calculated}} = \frac{(\text{SSE}_\text{R} - \text{SSE}_\text{U})/m}{\text{SSE}_\text{U}/(n - k)} \qquad (10\text{–}7)$$

where

SSE_U = Sum of squared errors with all variables in the relationship; called the unrestricted SSE.

SSE_R = Sum of squared errors with m variables excluded from the relationship; called the restricted SSE.

k = Total number of estimated coefficients.

m = Number of restricted (i.e., dropped) independent variables.

This test is used as follows:

1. Estimate a full, unrestricted model in which Y is related to all $k - 1$ independent variables and capture the SSE_U.

2. Estimate a partial, restricted model in which Y is related only to the $(k - m - 1)$ independent variables and capture the SSE_R.

3. Calculate F using Equation 10–7 and compare the result to the F from the end-of-book Appendix Table F with the correct degrees of freedom (i.e., m, $n - k$) and alpha value, that is $F_{m, n-k, \alpha}$, where α is typically .05 or .01.

4. If $F_{calculated}$ is greater than F_{table}, then SSE_R is statistically significantly greater than SSE_U. This denotes that the amount of variance unexplained by the restricted model is statistically greater than that of the unrestricted model; consequently, the model should not be restricted (i.e., the variables should be included). If the calculated F is less than or equal to the table F, then inclusion of the group of m variables has not significantly reduced the sum of squared errors. From a statistical standpoint, the variables do not improve the relationship (i.e., the variables should not be included). That is,

If $F_{calculated} \leq F_{table}$ then $SSE_R = SSE_U$ and there is no significant additional explained variance from the unrestricted model.

If $F_{calculated} > F_{table}$ then $SSE_R > SSE_U$ there is additional explained variance from the unrestricted model.

The null hypothesis says that inclusion of the m independent variables does not significantly increase the SSE_R relative to SSE_U; thus SSE_R has not been shown to be statistically greater than SSE_U after controlling for differences in degrees of freedom.

Let's use this test on the Big City Bookstore example, with $k = 3$ (i.e., coefficients, a, b_1, b_2) and $m = 1$ (i.e., advertising alone, with competition excluded). From Table 10–2c, SSE_U, with both advertising and competition in the relationship, is 79.8. While SSE_R, with only advertising in Table 10–2a, is 253.9. Thus,

$$F_{calculated} = \frac{(SSE_R - SSE_U)/m}{SSE_U/(n - k)} = \frac{(253.9 - 79.8)/1}{79.8/(12 - 3)} = 19.64 \qquad (10\text{–}7a)$$

$$F_{calculated} = 19.64 > F - table = F_{m, n-k, \alpha} = F_{1, 9, \alpha = .05} = 5.12$$

Let's also test at an α of 0.01

$$F_{calculated} = 19.64 > F - table = F_{1, 9, \alpha = .01} = 10.56$$

These F-table values were obtained from end-of-book Appendix Table F. As shown, the calculated value is statistically significant at .05 and .01 levels of significance. Thus, we find that SSE_R is significantly higher than SSE_U. Consequently, we infer that the competition variable makes a statistically significant contribution towards explaining the variation in the dependent variable. From a statistical standpoint, competition should be included in the relationship.

This is a powerful test when the regression coefficients do not have statistically significant *t*-values, but their inclusion increases $\overline{R}^2$ and reduces SSE.

Having developed the concepts and solutions to multicollinearity, we will now explore other problems in regression analyses. For additional discussion of multicollinearity see Neter et al. (1996).

Serial Correlation Problems

One of the assumptions of ordinary least squares regression analysis is that the residuals are independent. As shown in Chapters 3 and 7, statistical independence is characterized by a zero correlation between adjacent residuals. That is, ACF(*k*) = 0 for all $k > 0$, where *k* is the lag between residuals. (Don't confuse this *k* with *k* of the previous section.) Remember that **serial correlation** is a synonym for autocorrelation.

There are several methods of detecting when ACF(*k*) is not consistent with the independence assumption. The most commonly used statistic when $k = 1$ is the Durbin–Watson statistic. In addition, the *t*-test on individual ACF(*k*) and *Q*-statistics should be used, as in Chapters 3 and 7.

When the residuals of a model have significant first-order serial correlation (i.e., ACF(1) ≠ 0), there may be a deficiency in the estimated relationship. (We saw this with the Big City Bookstore example of Table 10–2a, b, and c.) This condition also denotes that the diagnostic statistics of the regression relationship may not be valid; that is, $\overline{R}^2$, S_{yx}, S_b, and the individual *t*-values of regression coefficients are invalid.

When first-order serial correlation exists, the following relationship exists:

$$Y_t = a + bX_t + \rho e_{t-1} + e_t \tag{10–8}$$

where ρ (rho) is the first-order regression coefficient.

Historically, the coefficient ρ is used to denote serial correlation of errors. This relationship implies that if ρe_{t-1} is included in the relationship, the resulting residuals are independent and the other related statistics are accurate. (Incidentally, the chronology of the development of related techniques has yielded different notations for the same concept. In ARIMA terms, ρ is $-\theta_1$ in Equation 10–8 and ϕ_1 in $e_t = \phi_1 e_{t-1} + v_t$; however, early writings in economics have resulted in the use of ρ. Because computer software and other references use this notation, it is used here.)

The question arises as how to estimate ρ. Estimating ρ requires an iterative process. There are several methods, including **Cochrane–Orcutt iterative least squares (COILS)** method, Hildreth–Lu method, and the Prais–Winston method. We will illustrate the COILS approach after demonstrating how Equation 10–8 can be estimated iteratively using OLS methods. While we use a bivariate relationship for our illustrations, the method is easily generalized to multiple regression relationships.

Given

$$Y_t = a + bX_t + \rho e_{t-1} + e_t \tag{10–9}$$

From the general definition of e_t

$$\rho e_{t-1} = \rho(Y_{t-1} - \hat{Y}_{t-1}) = \rho[Y_{t-1} - (a + bX_{t-1} + \rho e_{t-2})] \tag{10–10}$$

Substituting the right-hand-side of Equation 10–10 into 10–9 yields

$$Y_t = a + bX_t + \rho[Y_{t-1} - (a + bX_{t-1} + \rho e_{t-2})] + e_t$$

Expanding this equation and combining a's into new a^* and error terms into v_t.

$$Y_t = a + bX_t + \rho Y_{t-1} - \rho a - \rho bX_{t-1} + v_t \qquad (10\text{--}11)$$

$$Y_t - \rho Y_{t-1} = a^* + bX_t - \rho bX_{t-1} + v_t$$

Reintroducing the concept of the backshift operator from Chapter 7, by definition, we have

$$(1 - B)Y_t = (Y_t - Y_{t-1})$$

Therefore

$$(1 - \rho B)Y_t = (Y_t - \rho Y_{t-1})$$

Therefore, Equation 10–11 can be simplified to

$$(1 - \rho B)Y_t = a^* + b(1 - \rho B)X_t + v_t \qquad (10\text{--}12)$$

This relationship can be estimated iteratively by trial and error, using different values of ρ, a procedure similar to the Cochrane–Orcutt iterative least squares method (COILS). Fortunately, ρ can be determined using any ordinary least-squares software in the following manner:

1. Run OLS to determine an initial value of ρ by calculating ACF(1).
2. Using ρ, transform Y_t and X_t to Y_t^* and X_t^*:

$$Y_t^* = Y_t - \rho Y_{t-1} = (1 - \rho B)Y_t$$
$$X_t^* = X_t - \rho X_{t-1} = (1 - \rho B)X_t$$

3. Save these new variables for use in the following relationship:

$$Y_t^* = a^* + bX_t^* + v_t \qquad (10\text{--}13)$$

   (Note that with this method, we lose one observation in the process of back-shifting. Other methods, specifically the Prais–Winston and maximum likelihood (MAXL) methods, do not lose an observation and are preferred methods.)
4. For the relationship between X_t^* and Y_t^* in Equation 10–13, use systematically selected values of ρ and estimate a^* and b using ordinary least squares.
5. Through trial and error, search for that value of ρ that minimizes the sum of squared residuals.
6. After determining ρ, use the coefficients of Equation 10–13 in Equation 10–8 to fit and forecast Y_t in the usual manner, with the usual interpretations. However, a^* should be transformed back to a by the following relationship:

$$a = a^*/(1 - \rho)$$

Fortunately, this procedure has been automated in many statistical forecasting packages. These procedures are commonly known as **autoregressive regression procedures** (e.g., in SAS, it is known as the AUTOREG procedure; in MINITAB, SYSTAT, SORITEC, SPSS, and so on, it has similar names, including those mentioned previously). Let us illustrate this procedure on a simple bivariate relationship.

Figures 10–6 and 10–7 illustrate plots of X_t and Y_t. As shown, these two series are correlated.

FIGURE 10–6

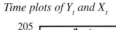

Time plots of Y_t and X_t

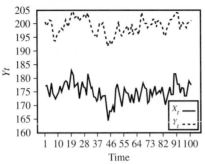

FIGURE 10–7

Y_t versus X_t

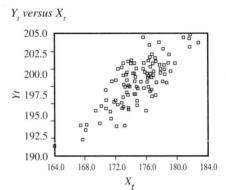

TABLE 10–5   OLS of the Relationship between Y and X: AR1DAT.DAT

Usable observations	100
Degrees of freedom	98
$\bar{R}^2$	.5924
Std error of dependent variable	2.898
Standard error of estimate	1.850
Sum of squared residuals	355.476
Regression F (1,98)	144.895
Significance level of F	.00000000
Durbin–Watson statistic	.905
$Q(25)$	61.009
Significance level of Q	.00008

Variable	Coeff	Std Error	t-Stat	Signif
Constant	79.894	9.899	8.071	.00000000
X	.681	.057	12.037	.00000000

TABLE 10–6   ACFs of e_t for OLS of Table 10–5

1:	.547	.239	.242	.147	.084	.049
7:	.005	−.003	−.025	−.141	−.103	.001

$$\text{Approx. } 2Se_{ACF} = \frac{2}{\sqrt{100}} = .20$$

Table 10–5 illustrates an OLS solution of Y_t as a function of X_t. As shown there, $\bar{R}^2$ is approximately 60 percent, the F-value is very significant, and the coefficients are very significant. However, the Durbin–Watson statistic and Q-statistic both denote problems with serial correlation. These problems may be sufficiently serious to invalidate any meaningful interpretation of the results.

As a first step in the procedure, we show the estimated ACFs of the residuals of this model in Table 10–6.

Using the ACF(1) of .547 as an initial estimate of ρ results in the following Y_t^* and X_t^* values:

$$Y_t^* = Y_t - .55Y_{t-1}$$
$$X_t^* = X_t - .55Y_{t-1}$$

(Note, if your software does not allow * in a variable name, substitute s for *.) Regressing these two variables yields Table 10–7.

The DW statistic is closer to 2.0 and, as measured by the Q-statistic, the residual ACFs, as a group, are consistent with the assumption of white noise. Continuing the procedure, we next try two other values of ρ, $\rho = .65$ and $\rho = .45$, to see if these yield lower sums of squares. (Remember: our purpose is to achieve the minimum sum of squares without significant first-order serial correlation.)

$$Y_t^* = Y_t - .45\,Y_{t-1}$$
$$X_t^* = X_t - .45\,X_{t-1}$$

Regressing these two variables yields Table 10–8. This model has a higher sum of squares, higher Q-statistic, and a less desirable DW statistic.

Consider a higher value of ρ, $\rho = .65$:

$$Y_t^* = Y_t - .65\,Y_{t-1}$$
$$X_t^* = X_t - .65\,X_{t-1}$$

Regressing these two variables yields Table 10–9.

This model yields a lower sum of squares and a DW statistic that is closer to 2.00 than that of Tables 10–7 and 10–8. This is the best result so far. (While not shown here, $\rho = .75$ yields a higher sum of squares.) Therefore, the experimental ρ yielding the lowest sum of squares is .65. Table 10–10 summarizes the manually derived values of ρ and the resulting sum of squares errors (SSE).

TABLE 10–7 $Y^* = f(X^*)$ for $\rho = .55$

Dependent variable Y^*—Estimation by least squares

Usable observations	99
Degrees of freedom	97
$\bar{R}^2$	.456
Std error of dependent variable	2.0089
Standard error of estimate	1.4823
Sum of squared residuals	213.145
Regression F (1,97)	82.99
Significance level of F	.00000000
Durbin–Watson statistic	1.637
$Q(24)$	22.958
Significance level of Q	.5223

Variable	Coeff	Std Error	t-Stat	Signif
a^*	49.731	4.3745	11.368	.00000000
X^*	.506	.0555	9.110	.00000000

TABLE 10–8 $Y^* = f(X^*)$ for $\rho = .45$

Dependent variable Y^*—Estimation by least squares

Usable observations	99
Degrees of freedom	97
$\bar{R}^2$	.483
Standard error of estimate	1.519
Sum of squared residuals	223.879
Regression F (1,97)	92.44
Significance level of F	.00000000
Durbin–Watson statistic	1.478
$Q(24)$	26.128
Significance level of Q	.34668

Variable	Coeff	Std Error	t-Stat	Signif
a^*	57.403	5.4164	10.598	.00000000
X^*	.541	.0563	9.615	.00000000

TABLE 10–9 $Y^* = f(X^*)$ for $\rho = .65$

Dependent variable Y^*—Estimation by least squares

Usable observations	99
Degrees of freedom	97
$\bar{R}^2$	.432
Standard error of estimate	1.465
Sum of squared residuals	208.201
Regression F (1,97)	75.52
Significance level of F	.00000000
Durbin–Watson statistic	1.795
$Q(24)$	23.328
Significance level of Q	.5005

Variable	Coeff	Std Error	t-Stat	Signif
a^*	40.549	3.353	12.09	.00000000
X^*	.476	.055	8.69	.00000000

TABLE 10–10 Iterations of ρ to Minimum SSE

ρ	SSE	DW Statistic
.00	535.5	.9053
.45	223.88	1.478
.55	213.15	1.637
.65*	208.20	1.795
.75	209.79	1.9331
.85	218.63	2.033
.95	235.22	2.082

* Denotes optimal value of ρ in manual search.

Forecasting

The results of the relationship with ρ of .65 are statistically defensible and denote that a very significant relationship exists between Y_t and X_t, as shown in Table 10–9 and as transformed here:

$$Y_t = a + bX_t + \rho e_{t-1} + e_t \tag{10–14}$$

$$= \frac{40.45}{(1 - .65)} + .476X_t + .65e_{t-1} + e_t$$

$$= 115.86 + .476X_t + .65e_{t-1} + e_t$$

for one-period-ahead forecasts made at the end of period $(t - 1)$.

$$\hat{Y}_t = 115.86 + .476X_t + .65e_{t-1}$$

For two-period-ahead forecasts made at the end of period $t - 1$, the value of e_t is unknown and its expected value of zero is substituted into the previous equation to yield

$$\hat{Y}_{t+1} = 115.86 + .476X_{t+1} + .65e_t \tag{10–15}$$

$$\hat{Y}_{t+1} = 115.86 + .476X_{t+1} + .65(0)$$

Note, because future values of e_{t-1} have an expected value of zero, the use of this relationship is identical to that of any other regression relationship for forecasted values of more than one period into the future.

Cochrane–Orcutt Iterative Least Squares (COILS)

All the previous time and effort of manually iterating towards the optimal ρ may be eliminated through the computer algorithm in your software. The results of the Cochrane–Orcutt method are shown in Table 10–11.

In Table 10–11, the optimal value of ρ is .677, very nearly equal to the manually selected ρ value of .65. All other statistics in the table are statistically appropriate. The DW and Q-statistics are consistent with independent residuals and, while not shown here, the ACFs and PACFs of the residuals have patterns consistent with this assumption. The estimated coefficients are statistically significant. Finally, note that the $\bar{R}^2$ of .7442 denotes that X_t and ρ together account for this percentage of explained variance. However, because ρ is so high, only a fraction of the explained variance is attributed to the relationship of Y_t to X_t. This $\overline{R}^2$ and RSE are indicative of one-period forecast errors; however, as shown above, after one period, the value of e_{t-1} equals zero, and the standard error of the residuals will increase for forecasts more than one period ahead.

What have we accomplished with COILS? The initial OLS of Table 10–5 yielded the following model:

$$Y_t = 79.894 + .681X_t + e_t \qquad \text{RSE} = 1.850 \qquad \text{DW} = .905$$

The correct coefficients from the COILS model are:

$$Y_t = 117.105 + .468X_t + .677_{t-1} + _t \qquad \text{RSE} = 1.472 \qquad \text{DW} = 1.835$$

This last model has more accurate coefficients and more accurate forecasts.

Cochrane–Orcutt Example #2

Consider another application of COILS to two series that appear to be statistically related. Figures 10–8 and 10–9 illustrate two series with an apparent negative relationship. The correlation coefficients between these two variables is $-.612036$. Thus, it seems appropriate to relate these two series using linear regression. Table 10–12 illustrates the output of this regression.

TABLE 10–11 $Y = f(X^*)$ Estimation by COILS

Usable observations		99		
Degrees of freedom		96		
$\overline{R}^2$		.744		
Std error of dependent variable		2.910		
Standard error of estimate		1.472		
Sum of squared residuals		207.954		
Durbin–Watson statistic		1.835		
$Q(24)$		24.037		
Significance level of Q		.4018		

Variable	Coeff	Std Error	t-Stat	Signif
Constant	117.105	9.592	12.208	.00000000
X_t	.468	.055	8.550	.00000000
e_{t-1}	.677	.077	8.815	.00000000

FIGURE 10–8

Time plots of Y_t and X_t

FIGURE 10–9

Y_t versus X_t

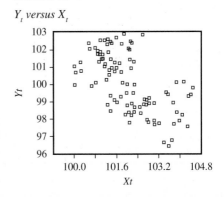

Because of the highly significant *t*-value of X_t, these two variables seem to be very strongly related. Also, the *F*-value is quite high (remember for the bivariate case, F equals t^2). However, the DW statistic and *Q*-statistic denote that there is an extremely high degree of residual autocorrelation. While not shown here, the ACFs and PACFs confirm this relationship.

Let us run a COILS procedure to model the relationship between Y_t and X_t more accurately. We do this because the high serial correlation makes the diagnostic statistics from the relationship unreliable. Possibly, *Y* and *X* are not related at all. The results of fitting COILS to these data are given in Table 10–13.

In contrast to the OLS, the COILS output in Table 10–13 denotes that Y_t and X_t may not be related, as indicated by the very low *t*-value on the regression coefficient of X_t. This shows that Y_t and X_t do not have a statistically significant relationship, even though the previous OLS estimation had extremely high *F* and *t*-values. The conflicting results of the OLS and COILS are very disturbing when one hopes to find a relationship between two variables. However, if all other methods of modeling Y_t and X_t are exhausted, the analyst can only infer that for this sample, there is no relationship between Y_t and X_t, even though Figures 10–8 and 10–9 seem to show one.

The results of the COILS procedure are consistent with the manner in which the data were actually generated. The data were generated using a random number generator in a popular spreadsheet program. Two numbers were generated as a summation process of six other random numbers, using the following relationship:

$$X_0 = 100 \qquad Y_0 = 100$$

$$X_t = X_{t-1} + [1.5 - (AN1_t + RAN2_t + RAN3_t)]$$

$$Y_t = Y_{t-1} + [1.5 - (RAN4_t + RAN5_t + RAN6_t)]$$

Stock Index Analyses Using COILS

Figures 10–10 and 10–11 show plots of the monthly U.S. and U.K. stock indexes from January 1970 to July 1992, in file UKUSIND.DAT, respectively. As shown, there appears to be a strong linear relationship between these two series. (The relationship in Figure 10–11 may be slightly nonlinear, but we ignore this to simplify the following discussions.) Is there really a relationship? Maybe they are both

TABLE 10–12	$Y = f(X)$ Estimation by OLS: ARDAT.DAT			
Usable observations		100		
Degrees of freedom		98		
$\bar{R}^2$		.368		
Std error of dependent variable		1.644		
Standard error of estimate		1.306		
Sum of squared residuals		167.243		
Regression F (1,98)		58.70		
Significance level of F			.00000000	
Durbin–Watson statistic		.211		
Q(25)		310.561		
Significance level of Q			.00000000	
Variable	*Coeff*	*Std Error*	*t-Stat*	*Signif*
Constant	192.602	12.077	15.948	.00000000
X_t	−.907	.118	−7.661	.00000000

TABLE 10–13	$Y = f(X)$ Estimation by COILS			
Usable observations		99		
Degrees of freedom		96		
$\bar{R}^2$		.910		
Std error of dependent variable		1.652		
Standard error of estimate		.497		
Sum of squared residuals		23.6708		
Durbin–Watson statistic		2.012		
Q(24)		25.823		
Significance level of Q		.30927		
Variable	*Coeff*	*Std Error*	*t-Stat*	*Signif*
Constant	114.298	12.331	9.269	.00000000
X_t	−.136	.120	−1.134	.2597
e_{t-1}	.952	.032	29.582	.00000000

increasing over time but are not correlated. The appearance of a relationship may be the result of independent autocorrelations.

Table 10–14 illustrates the results of an OLS of the U.K. index as a function of the U.S. index in times t and $(t - 1)$. Some analysis and discussion with those familiar with financial markets have suggested that the value of the U.K. index is related to the U.S. index in periods t and $(t - 1)$. Thus, periods t and $(t - 1)$ are included in the relationship.

The DW and Q-statistics in Table 10–14 are both indicative of high serial correlation. As shown in the residuals of this model, Figure 10–12, there is extremely high autocorrelation between adjacent values. This correlation violates one of the assumptions of regression analysis and makes OLS an inappropriate estimation technique. Therefore, we cannot interpret the t-values of the regression coefficients. We can correct for serial correlation by fitting an autoregressive model using COILS.

Table 10–15 illustrates the results of applying the COILS procedure to correct for serial correlation. As shown, the DW statistic is closer to 2 and the Q-statistic, while not indicative of white noise, is significantly lower than in the OLS model. The

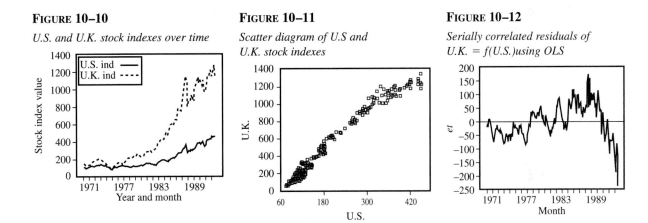

FIGURE 10–10

U.S. and U.K. stock indexes over time

FIGURE 10–11

Scatter diagram of U.S and U.K. stock indexes

FIGURE 10–12

Serially correlated residuals of U.K. = f(U.S.)using OLS

TABLE 10–14   U.K. Stock Index as a Function of U.S. Index, by OLS

Usable observations	270			
Degrees of freedom	267			
$\bar{R}^2$	.9729			
Std error of dependent variable	371.950			
Standard error of estimate	61.179			
Sum of squared residuals	999343.300			
Regression $F(2,267)$	4838.006			
Significance level of F	.00000000			
Durbin–Watson statistic	.1367			
$Q(36-0)$	2108.086			
Significance level of Q	.00000000			
Variable	*Coeff*	*Std Error*	*t-Stat*	*Signif*
Constant	−177.643	7.549	−23.532	.00000000
USIND(t)	2.839	.486	5.843	.00000001
USIND $(t - 1)$	.587	.491	1.195	.2330

COILS model has much less autocorrelation than the OLS. Interestingly, the *t*-values of both lags of the U.S. stock index increase significantly in the COILS estimation.

***First Order
Differences***

Sometimes, first-order serial correlation can be eliminated by taking first differences (i.e., by subtracting each variable from its previous value). However, first differences should only be used when theory suggests it or when ρ is very close to 1.

As shown in Table 10–15 the ρ value of the stock index is high enough to suggest the use of first differences. While not shown here, the results are nearly identical to those of Table 10–15. The use of first differences is a legitimate approach to modeling this data, a topic we return to in Chapter 13.

Normally, our analysis of the relationships of Table 10–15 would be complete at this time. That is, we would accept this model as a good one, were it not for the unusual scatter of residuals as shown in Figure 10–13. The residuals of Table 10–15 do not vary equally over time. This is a violation of one of the regression assumptions, **homoscedasticity** (i.e., variance stationarity). Therefore, our analysis of this time series is not complete.

The unusual scatter denotes that there is a problem in the model and possibly our understanding of the true relationship between these stock indexes. We will continue this analysis after discussing elasticities in preparation for further discussion of heteroscedasticity problems.

TABLE 10–15   U.K. Stock Index as a Function of U.S. Index, by COILS

Usable observations		269		
Degrees of freedom		265		
$\bar{R}^2$		.9966		
Std error of dependent variable		372.089		
Standard error of estimate		21.615		
Sum of squared residuals		123816.660		
Durbin–Watson statistic		1.747		
$Q(36-1)$		61.579		
Significance level of Q		.004		
Variable	*Coeff*	*Std Error*	*t-Stat*	*Signif*
Constant	−104.282	52.032	−2.004	.04607
USIND(t)	2.012	.171	11.752	.00000000
USIND (t − 1)	.993	.172	5.776	.00000002
$e(t − 1)$	.9634	.0195	49.407	.00000000

FIGURE 10–13

*Residuals of U.K. = f(U.S.)
using COILS*

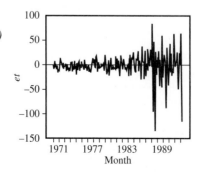

Elasticities and Logarithmic Relationships

It may be more theoretically sound to assume that a relationship between two variables is related to percentage changes; that is, a percentage change in X yields a b percentage change in Y, where b is the regression coefficient. When the variables in a regression are logs, the regression coefficients conform to this interpretation. That is, if variables are transformed to logarithms and are linearly related, the regression coefficients are a ratio of two percentage changes. This is the economic concept of **elasticity.**

Consider the following:

$$\ln Y_t = \log(Y_t) \qquad \ln X_t = \log(X_t)$$

where, as before, log is the natural logarithm to base **e**. Now the following least-squares relationship can be fitted.

$$\ln Y_t = a + b \ln X_t + e_t \tag{10–16}$$

This relationship yields a new interpretation of the regression coefficient b:

$$b = \Delta \ln Y_t / \Delta + X_t = \ln Y_t - \ln Y_{t-1} / \ln X_t - \ln X_{t-1}$$

This log–log form of b is interpreted as an elasticity. For example, in relating $\ln Y_t$ and $\ln X_t$, if $b = .8$, then a 1 percent change in X yields a .8 percent change in Y. Also, note that elasticities are unbounded and may be positive or negative.

Elasticities are useful in describing relationships that involve a percentage change (i.e., responsiveness) in one variable in response to percentage changes in another variable. Sometimes, the log form of an equation is preferred over the strictly linear form, because with the linear form, it is assumed that a unit change in an independent variable X produces the same change in Y, regardless of the level of Y, which is inappropriate in many situations. Frequently, we do not expect the change in Y to be the same from a unit change in X when X is, say, very high or very low. However, with the log form, since the changes are expressed as percentages, the percentage changes remain constant.

Equation 10–16 is actually a multiplicative one, equivalent to:

$$Y_t = \mathbf{e}^a X_t^b e_t$$

The general multiple regression, multiplicative model yields two equivalent forms:

$$Y_t = \mathbf{e}^a X 1_t^{b1} X_t^{-b2} e_t$$

$$\ln Y_t = a + b_1 \ln X 1_t + b2 \ln X 2_t + e_t$$

In general discussions of elasticities in economics and engineering, it is frequently pointed out that elasticities are not constant, that they vary about different values of X. Consequently, an elasticity is quoted either at the means of the variables or at some other relevant point. However, with logarithmic relationships, such as Equation 10–16, we see that the coefficient b is constant for all values of X. Thus, these relationships assume that the elasticity is constant over the range of included X values, an assumption that may or may not be true. We revisit this concept when we continue our analysis of the U.K. and U.S. stock index relationship.

Finally, it should be noted that the regression coefficient b of the simple linear regression $Y_t = a + b X_t$ can be used to calculate an elasticity at any point.

$$b = \Delta Y_t / \Delta X_t = Y_2 - Y_1 / X_2 - X_1$$

This yields the following formula for elasticity:

$$\text{Elasticity} = b\frac{X_1}{Y_1} = \frac{\Delta Y_t X_1}{\Delta X_t\, Y_1} = \frac{\Delta Y_t/Y_1}{\Delta X_t/X_1} \qquad (10\text{--}17)$$

The elasticity varies, depending on which matched pairs of X and Y are used in the calculation, typically $\overline{X}$ and $\overline{Y}$ are used as the base. This means that models with constant elasticities (e.g., log models like Equation 10–16) have variable slopes, and linear regression models without logs have constant slopes and variable elasticities.

As we will see in the next section, the concepts of logarithms and elasticities are very important in correcting heteroscedasticity.

Heteroscedasticity

Heteroscedasticity (variance nonstationarity) is a violation of one of the regression assumptions, homoscedasticity, presented in Chapter 3. Heteroscedasticity is the condition where the variation of errors about the regression line or plane S_{yx} is not constant. Graphically, heteroscedasticity can be detected in several ways, as shown in the Figures 10–14a and b. Because of heteroscedasticity, the estimated regression coefficients b may not be as accurate (i.e., efficient) as those obtained from a model with homoscedasticity.

Also, the standard errors of the regression coefficients S_b are biased, possibly overstated or understated. As shown previously in Equation 10–6, the standard errors of the regression coefficients S_b are a function of S_{yx}. Also, with heteroscedasticity, S_{yx} is not constant about the regression line; therefore, neither $\overline{R}^2$ nor S_b are known with any reliability. Thus, we cannot be sure of the statistical significance of individual regression coefficients. With serious heteroscedasticity, better estimates of the estimated regression coefficients are often, but not always, available using alternate estimation techniques, developed in the following sections.

Most often, heteroscedasticity results from the selection of an incorrect model; that is, from an incomplete understanding of the underlying theory of the relationship. These misspecifications include: choosing the wrong functional form (linear vs. nonlinear model); leaving important variables out of the relationship; or failing to transform variables prior to modeling. However, sometimes heteroscedasticity is simply an artifact of the sample.

Incorrect Functional Form

Improperly defined relationships can result in heteroscedasticity. This is illustrated well by further analysis of the U.S. and U.K. stock indexes. As you may recall, when these stock indexes were evaluated through OLS, there were serious problems with

FIGURE 10–14

Heteroscedasticity detection

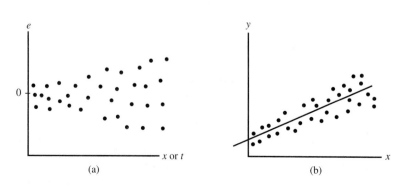

autocorrelation. We corrected the problem by changing the estimation procedure from OLS to COILS. The results in Table 10–15 showed the removal of most of the serial correlation. However, the residuals had considerable heteroscedasticity, (i.e., extreme variance nonstationarity) which is clearly illustrated in Figure 10–13.

It is possible that the model would be improved by relating percentage changes in the dependent variable to percentage changes in the independent variables, as discussed in the previous section. A reexpression of the variables using logarithms results in regression coefficients that are elasticities. The following transformation is made:

$$\ln UK = \log(\text{U.K. stock index})$$

$$\ln US = \log(\text{U.S. stock index})$$

Figure 10–15 illustrates a plot of logarithms for the U.K. and U.S. stock indexes. Table 10–16 illustrates the results of relating the logarithms lnUK and lnUS, respectively, using ordinary least squares at lags t and $(t - 1)$.

As shown by the results in Table 10–16, there is a serious problem with autocorrelated residuals: the DW statistic is extremely low and the Q-statistic is extremely high. As shown in the residuals in Figure 10–16, logarithms have not reduced the autocorrelations. While we did not expect logarithms to affect the autocorrelation problem, we felt obligated to fit OLS before fitting the COILS model to logarithmic values.

Table 10–17 shows the results of using the COILS procedure. The logarithmic relationship using COILS resulted in a much higher DW statistic that is more consistent with the assumption of no serial correlation. Note, however, that this DW statistic is still low enough to imply that there may be some slight serial correlation, but removing it must be delayed until our discussions in Chapter 13. Note also that while not shown, the ACF at lag 1 is only .233. This is so low as to be ignored at this time, a point we will return to later.

Having removed most of the autocorrelation, we can now confirm residual variance stationarity. Figure 10–17 illustrates a plot of the residuals for the model in Table 10–17. The residuals seem to be independent (i.e., no serial correlation) and, except for one very large outlier, they appear to have variance stationarity (i.e., are homoscedastic). Thus, logarithms have removed the heteroscedasticity dramatically, as shown by the plots of residuals in Figures 10–13 and 10–17, with and without the use of logarithms, respectively.

Up to this point, we have illustrated the detection of heteroscedasticity through the use of graphs. There are several more objective ways of detecting variance nonsta-

FIGURE 10–15

Logarithms of U.K. and U.S. stock indexes

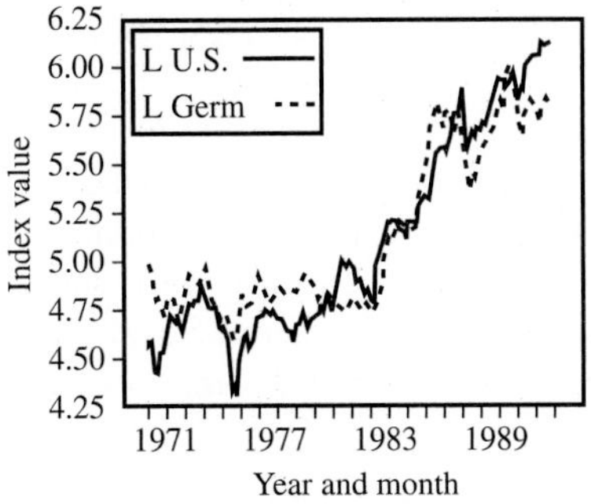

FIGURE 10–16

Residuals of lnUK = f(lnUS) using OLS

FIGURE 10–17

Homoscedastic residuals for log relationship

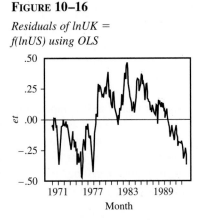

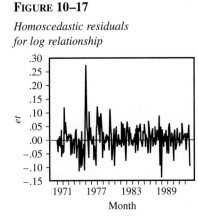

TABLE 10–16   Logs of U.K. and U.S. Stock Indexes

Dependent variable lnUK—Estimation by least squares

Usable observations	270
Degrees of freedom	267
$\bar{R}^2$	.940
Std error of dependent variable	.8313
Standard error of estimate	.2032
Sum of squared residuals	11.021
Regression $F(2,267)$	2118.352
Significance level of F	.00000000
Durbin–Watson statistic	.0678
$Q(36{-}0)$	3112.145
Significance level of Q	.00000000

Variable	Coeff	Std Error	t-Stat	Signif
Constant	−2.165	.124	−17.496	.00000000
lnUS(t)	1.561	.330	4.724	.00000374
lnUS($t{-}1$)	.004	.332	.013	.9896

TABLE 10–17   lnUK = f(lnUS) Using COILS

Usable observations	269
Degrees of freedom	265
$\bar{R}^2$	.9971
Std error of dependent variable	.8310
Standard error of estimate	.0447
Sum of squared residuals	.5293
Durbin–Watson statistic	1.514
$Q(36{-}1)$	49.278
Significance level of Q	.0553

Variable	Coeff	Std Error	t-Stat	Signif
Constant	.732	.5684	1.289	.1987
lnUS(t)	.780	.0756	10.320	.00000000
lnUS($t{-}1$)	.254	.0754	3.371	.00085943
$e(t-1)$	.9899	.0083	119.102	.00000000

---

tionarity: the Goldfeld–Quandt, Park, and Breusch–Pagan tests. We will only illustrate the Goldfeld–Quandt test, because it makes no significant assumptions about the form of the heteroscedasticity, is computationally simple, and it is effective. We apply this method to the stock index example: once to the relationship without logs, and once with the log relationship.

Goldfeld–Quandt Test

The **Goldfeld–Quandt test** (1965) compares the variances of the residuals for the low and high values of the variable that appears to be causing the variance nonstationarity. In Figure 10–13, which illustrates the residuals from the U.K. and U.S. index relationship using COILS, we see that because these stock indexes increase over time, the variances also increase over time. We will therefore measure the variances over time, a common practice in time series analysis.

The five steps of the Goldfeld–Quandt test are as follows:

1. Sort the data from low to high values of the independent variable that seems to be the cause of the heteroscedasticity. In time series analysis, this variable is often time. In cross-sectional analysis, this is the relevant independent variable.

2. Omit observations in the middle of the series; for example, the middle one-fifth or one-sixth. This procedure results in two groups with $\dfrac{(n-d)}{2}$ observations, where d is the number omitted.

3. Run two separate relationships, one for the first group of low values of the independent variable and one for the second half with high values of the independent variable. Each group should have the same number of observations.

4. Calculate or capture the error sums of squares for each relationship. Designate these as ESS_H and ESS_L for the high and the low variance groups, respectively.

5. Calculate the ratio of $\dfrac{ESS_H}{ESS_L}$. If there is no heteroscedasticity, this ratio will be distributed as an F-statistic with $\dfrac{n-d}{2}-k$ degrees of freedom in the numerator and denominator, where k is the number of coefficients.

6. If the ratio of $\dfrac{ESS_H}{ESS_L}$ exceeds F_{table}, the null hypothesis of homoscedasticity is rejected and we conclude that heteroscedasticity exists.

Let us run this test first on the original stock index data (i.e., without logs) and then on the logarithmic relationship using the COILS procedure. The data are divided into two groups: 1 to 107 for ESS_L and 165 to 271 for ESS_H. Each of these has 107 observations. Because COILS is being used with these data, one observation is lost through the use of $(t-1)$ in the transformation process; thus, there are effectively 106 observations in each group. The results of running the two regressions are:

$$ESS_L = 104685.85 \qquad ESS_H = 5164.41 \qquad (10\text{--}18)$$

$$F_{calculated} = \frac{ESS_H/[(n-d)/2-k]}{ESS_L/[(n-d)/2-k]}$$

$$= \frac{104685.85(106-2)}{5164.41(106-2)} = 20.27$$

$$F_{106-2,106-2,\,\alpha=.05} \approx 1.39 \qquad \text{(using } df = 100;\ 104 \text{ is not in F table)}$$

Because $F_{calculated} >> F_{table}$, we reject the homoscedasticity hypothesis and accept the conclusion of heteroscedasticity.

Now let us test the log model, where ESS_L is the variance of the first half and ESS_H is the variance of the second half.

$$ESS_L = .3094 \qquad ESS_H = .343$$

$$F_{calculated} = \frac{.1204(106-2)}{.3904(106-2)} = .3892$$

$$F_{106-2,106-2,\alpha=.05} = 1.39 \qquad \text{(using } df = 100)$$

We see that the use of logarithms dramatically reduces the *F*-value. Using this test, the variance of the second half is not statistically significantly higher than that of the second half. Thus the original heteroscedasticity has been removed.

Interestingly, now the variance of the first half is larger than that of the second half. What might explain this situation? If we reverse the definitions of ESS_L and ESS_H in the previous $F_{calculated}$, the following results:

$$F_{calculated} = \frac{.3094(106 - 2)}{.1204(106 - 2)} = 2.57$$

This test yields a statistically significant $F_{calculated}$ value. We might therefore infer that the residuals are heteroscedastic. However, we should not be too quick to reject this model based on this test. There is a dramatic difference between Figures 10–13 and 10–17. The variance nonstationarity of Figure 10–13 is systemic, continuously increasing as *t* increases. In contrast, the variance nonstationarity of Figure 10–17 is not nearly as continuous, being caused by outliers in the first half of the series. Therefore, we choose not to reject the log model. Instead we can further investigate or accept this model as is.

Alternatively, if we seek a more accurate model, or are uncomfortable with the heteroscedasticity of the logarithmic model, one of several things might be done. We might investigate the residual outliers and, where appropriate, make adjustments to the original data. This might also eliminate the marginally low DW statistic. Second, the series might be divided into two or more series. We consider this because 271 months may be too long a time period over which to have a constant relationship. Alternatively, we might try some other form of nonlinear transformation, such as the use of square roots, to see whether this eliminates the heteroscedasticity. The investigation of the correct form of transformation may be achieved through the use of Box–Cox transformations, which are discussed in Box, Jenkins, and Reinsel (1994).

Finally, we might consider another approach to modeling the data. The approach is called MARIMA and is developed in Chapter 13, where we continue this analysis. From a practical standpoint, however, we do not believe any of these strategies will significantly alter the final relationship defined in Table 10–17.

Weighted Least Squares

There are times when heteroscedasticity can and should be adjusted by weighting the observations. Consider the following example in which it is believed that there is a strong relationship between *Y* and *X*1 and *X*2. Figures 10–18a and b illustrate scatter diagrams of *Y* versus *X*1 and *X*2 using data in HETER.DAT. Clearly, *X*1 is related to *Y*; however, the relationship with *X*2 is not so clear. The OLS relationship is shown in Table 10–18.

FIGURE 10–18

Heteroscedasticity example

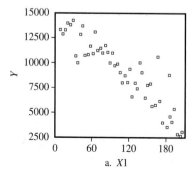
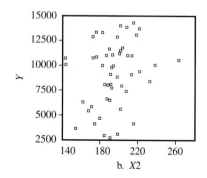

a. *X*1

b. *X*2

The OLS relationship appears acceptable: the $\bar{R}^2$, F, DW, and other statistics are very good. However, as shown in Figure 10–19, the residuals display significant heteroscedasticity when plotted against t and $X1$. Low values of $X1$ have low variances, while high values have high variances. These are such large differences that they may negate the results of Table 10–18. Normally, a Goldfeld–Quandt test would be run for heteroscedasticity, but the scatter of Figure 10–19 is so extreme that we are confident heteroscedasticity exists. How do we adjust for this problem?

The scatter of residuals in Figure 10–19 is indicative of the situation in which the residual variance S^2_{yx} is related to the level of $X1$, $X1^2$, $X1^{.5}$, or some other power of $X1$, such as $X1^P$. Frequently, heteroscedasticity denotes that the regression coefficients should be expressed in percentage terms. As mentioned, heteroscedasticity can often be eliminated through transformation of the variables. These transformations include logarithms, percentage changes, or a correction that involves dividing all variables (including the constant term) by some term related to the variance of errors. For example, each variable in the relationship can be divided by the square root of the variable that causes the heteroscedasticity.

Consider several simple hypothetical explanations of the heteroscedasticity of Table 10–18. In a study of bank profitability Y, the variability of Y might be highly correlated to the number of inner city loans, $X1$. That is, some banks may have had good returns from inner city loans, while others may have had much less luck with

TABLE 10–18 $Y = f(X1, X2)$ with Heteroscedastic Residuals

Dependent variable Y—Estimation by least squares

Usable observations	50
Degrees of freedom	47
$\bar{R}^2$	.9395
Standard error of estimate	797.215
Sum of squared residuals	29870960.896
Significance level of F	.00000000
Durbin–Watson statistic	2.220

Variable	Coeff	Std Error	t-Stat	Signif
Constant	5304.618	990.787	5.354	.00000252
X_1	−52.919	1.968	−26.884	.00000000
X_2	49.197	5.083	9.679	.00000000

FIGURE 10–19

Heteroscedasticity of residuals for X1 using OLS

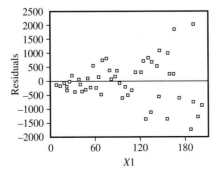

these loans. Thus, as the percentage of the inner city loans increases, the variance of Y increases, sometimes being very high and sometimes very low. The variance in bank performance is proportional to the level of the inner city loan value; consequently, so are the variances in the residuals of Y, the bank performance model.

Alternatively, assume we are measuring the purchases of luxury items as a function of several variables, including disposable income. Those individuals with higher disposable incomes are expected to have higher variances in the level of purchases, depending on family size and so on; therefore, the variances in the resulting residuals will be proportional to the level of disposable income. The classical setting for heteroscedasticity calls for per capita data (e.g., per capita income) to be used in a model.

The heteroscedasticity of Figure 10–19 hints at how to remove the unequal variances. As noted, the residual variances appear proportional to the level of $X1$; thus, we can divide all the variables in the relationship by $X1$. This suggests the following correction procedure:

Given

$$Y = a + b_1 X1 + b_2 X2 + e \tag{10-19}$$

divide each variable by $X1$ to yield

$$\frac{Y}{X1} = \frac{a'}{X1} + \frac{b_1' X1}{X1} + \frac{b_2' X2}{X1} + \frac{e}{X1} \tag{10-19a}$$

This transformation is easily completed using most computer software. With this reexpression, the coefficient a' is now the coefficient for $X1$, b_1' is the constant, and b_2' is the coefficient for $X2$, as it was before. These equivalencies are evident in the results of fitting this relationship as shown in Table 10–19.

As shown in Figure 10–20, there is no heteroscedasticity in residuals versus $X1$. The results of the weighted least squares are therefore statistically defensible. The t-

TABLE 10–19   Weighted Least Squares, $\dfrac{Y}{X1} = \dfrac{a'}{X1} + \dfrac{b_1' X1}{X1} + \dfrac{b_2' X2}{X1} + \dfrac{e}{X1}$

Dependent variable $\dfrac{Y}{X1}$—Estimation by least squares

Usable observations	50
Degrees of freedom	47
$\bar{R}^2$	.9995
Std error of dependent variable	254.1014
Standard error of estimate	5.9635
Sum of squared residuals	1671.482
Regression $F(2,47)$	44457.678
Significance level of F	.00000000
Durbin–Watson statistic	2.200

Variable		Coeff	Std Error	t-Stat	Signif
Constant (b_1)		−51.586	1.205	−42.798	.00000000
$\dfrac{1}{X1}$	(a)	5151.381	378.215	13.620	.00000000
$\dfrac{X2}{X1}$	(b_2)	49.359	2.117	23.320	.00000000

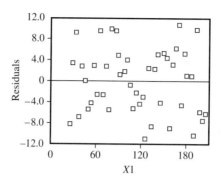

FIGURE 10–20

Residuals versus X1 with weighted least squares

values are all very significant, more significant in fact than those of Table 10–18. Equation 10–20 represents the results of Table 10–19 when expressed in terms of the original variables.

$$Y = 5151.381 - 51.586X1 + 49.359X2 + e \qquad (10-20)$$

Interestingly, these data were contrived using random number generators where the error is proportionate to $X1$. The relationship that was simulated is given in Equation 10–21.

$$Y = 5000 - 50X1 + 50X2 + e \qquad (10-21)$$

As shown here, the fitted relationship of Table 10–19 and Equation 10–20 are almost identical to the simulated values.

The effectiveness of using logs and weighted least squares has been quite good in the examples of this section. However, in practice, there may be problems with the use of weighted least squares. For one thing, it can be difficult to determine the best weighting scheme. Also, unless the heteroscedasticity is extreme, the resulting weighted least squares may not be as accurate as OLS. We should therefore be cautious using weighted least squares. The procedure illustrated here is a special case of a procedure called generalized least squares, which is discussed in the following section.

Generalized Least Squares

The general assumptions of the classical linear regression model include the assumptions that the errors are not autocorrelated or heteroscedastic. When these assumptions are not true, it is possible to compensate for their violation by using COILS and weighted least squares methods, as developed previously. There are times, however, when problems exist with serial correlation or heteroscedasticity and we are not sure how to correct for them. For example, we might not be able to determine the source of the heteroscedasticity and how to weight the relationship. Fortunately, there are methods that will achieve unbiased and efficient estimators of the regression coefficients under conditions of heteroscedastic or autocorrelated errors. These methods are referred to as **generalized least squares (GLS).** A full discussion of this procedure is beyond the scope of this text. It can be found in econometric and other advanced statistics test, such as Pindyck and Rubenfeld (1991), Greene (1993) or Neter et al. (1996).

Beta Coefficients

In general, the regression coefficients b_1 and b_2 measure the net effects of each independent variable on the dependent variable, while controlling for the influences of the other variables. When interpreting the influence of an independent variable on Y, it is important to keep the different scales of the variables in mind (e.g., 00's, 000's, etc.). However, there is a way to express all coefficients in a common unit, called **beta** (β) **coefficients.** A beta coefficient is the regression coefficient expressed in units of the standard deviation of the dependent and independent variables. For example, the beta coefficient β_1 is the change in Y expressed in standard deviations that result from a one-standard-deviation change in $X1$. These coefficients are therefore commonly called **standardized regression coefficients** to denote this standardization process.

The process of adjusting the coefficients puts them on a basis that clarifies the interpretation of their relative and absolute importance in explaining Y. Consider the following computation of β_1 and β_2:

$$\beta_1 = \frac{\Delta Y S_Y}{\Delta X1 S_{X1}} \qquad \beta_2 = \frac{\Delta Y S_Y}{\Delta X2 S_{X2}} \qquad (10\text{--}22)$$

Reexpressing b_1 and b_2 in Δ form, inverting, and multiplying yields

$$\beta_1 = b_1\left(\frac{S_{X1}}{S_Y}\right) \qquad \beta_2 = b_2\left(\frac{S_{X2}}{S_Y}\right) \qquad (10\text{--}23)$$

Thus, β_1 is the change in Y in standard deviation units (S_Y) resulting from a one S_{X1} change in $X1$. Likewise, β_2 is the change in Y expressed in S_y units resulting from a one S_{X2} change in $X2$. Consider an example, given the following relationship:

$$Y = a + .100X1 + 1000X2 + e$$

where $S_Y = 10$, $S_{X1} = 100$, and $S_{X2} = .005$. Because $b_1 = .100$ and $b_2 = 1000$, we might be led to believe that b_2 is more important in explaining Y than b_1; however the opposite is true. When the regression coefficients are standardized, the following beta coefficients result:

$$\beta_1 = .100\frac{100}{10} = 1 \quad \text{and} \quad B_2 = 1000\frac{.005}{10} = .5$$

The interpretation of these beta coefficients is straightforward. A one-standard-deviation change in Y results from a one-standard-deviation change in $X1$. In contrast, a .5-standard-deviation change in Y results from a one-standard-deviation change in $X2$. Thus, $X1$ has twice the influence on Y than $X2$; that is, variations in $X1$ have twice the influence as variations in $X2$. We also see that β's are pure numbers that are comparable across independent variables in a relationship.

Dichotomous (Dummy) Variables

Regression analysis is also effective in modeling the effects of qualitative attributes or events on the dependent variable. The procedure uses **dichotomous (dummy) independent variables** to model the occurrence of an event. Dummy variables have only two values, zero and one. These variables denote the occurrence of special events, such as outliers, promotions, price increases, new product introductions, seasonality, etc. The variables are treated much like any other variable in a regression analysis. We will consider two simple examples.

Event Influence

A product has the following 12-month sales (DUMMY.DAT). This nonseasonal product was promoted heavily in period 7, and management wants to measure the effect of this promotion.

Time (t)	1	2	3	4	5	6	7	8	9	10	11	12
Demand (Y_t)	13	16	18	22	24	28	42	34	39	41	44	46
Promotion (I_t)	0	0	0	0	0	0	1	0	0	0	0	0

These data are used in the following relationship:

$$Y_t = a + b_1 t + b_2 I_t + e_t$$

where

Y_t = sales
t = independent variable time
I_t = dichotomous variable for promotion, $I_t = 1$ for $t = 7$, otherwise 0

The following multiple regression relationship results:

$$Y_t = 9.36 + 3.13t + 10.75 I_t + e_t \qquad (10\text{--}24)$$
$$\quad\; (19.64)\;(48.48)\quad (13.34)$$

where

$$S_{yx} = .77 \qquad \bar{R}^2 = .996 \qquad n = 12 \qquad F = 1294.9 \qquad DW = 1.93$$

This relationship has a simple interpretation. The trend, measured by b_1 for the variable t, is 3.13 per month. In addition, in period 7, sales increased an additional 10.75 units, as measured by b_2 for I_t. This is the result of the promotional influence, I_7. Note that I_t is equal to zero for all t's except $t = 7$. Also note that this example can be generalized to any event that can be represented through zeros and ones.

Another important forecasting use of dummy variables involves measuring the seasonal effects on sales. This is fully developed in Chapter 5. Other uses of dummy variables to measure the effects of interventions are developed in the next section and in Chapters 12 and 13.

Changes in the Constant

Figure 10–21 illustrates the sales of a product during a 20-month period. The product is nonseasonal; thus, we expect only trend and randomness in the time series. In month 11, the product was improved so that it had appeal in another segment of the market. As clearly seen in Figure 10–21 and Table 10–20, sales increased to a new level in month 11. Consider the following regression model of this effect:

$$Y_t = a_1 + a_2 I_t + b_1 t + e_t$$

where

Y_t = sales of product
t = time
I_t = improvement in product at $t = 11$ $\begin{cases} I_t = 0 \text{ for } t = 1 \text{ to } 10 \\ I_t = 1 \text{ for } t - 11 \text{ to } 20 \end{cases}$

The results of fitting an OLS model to this data yields:

$$Y_t = 21.778 + 19.018I_t + 4.453t + e_t \qquad (10\text{--}25)$$
$$ (19.92) \quad (27.85) \quad (10.31)$$

where

$$S_{yx} = 2.054 \qquad \overline{R}^2 = .997 \qquad n = 20 \qquad F = 2781 \ (.00) \qquad DW = 2.26$$
$$Q = 2.35 \ (.799) \ (\text{sign. levels})$$

The interpretation of this relationship is very simple. The trend in this series is approximately 4.453 per month. As measured by the regression coefficient of I_t, the demand for this product shifts upward by 19.018 units in period 11; however, the trend remains constant. That is, the shift is permanent and the constant (i.e., Y intercept) of the relationship for periods 11 to 20 is 40.796 (i.e., 21.778 + 19.018).

Let us now consider a more complex situation, in which both the constant and the slope of the relationship change.

Changes in the Slopes

An event can influence both the constant in a relationship and the regression coefficient. Consider the sales of a company in Figure 10–22 and Table 10–21, before and after a price decrease in month 11. As shown, the price reduction increased demand, but not sufficiently to reverse the decline in sales. However, the slope of the decline is less after the price decrease. This suggest the following model:

$$Y_t = a_1 + b_1 t + a_2 I_t + b_2 X_t$$

TABLE 10–20   Product Improvement in $t = 11$, Shifting Sales Up (DUMMY2.DAT)

t	1	2	3	4	5	6	7	8	9	10
Y_t	25.91	31.81	33.86	38.07	42.90	49.56	51.12	60.93	63.86	64.67
$Y_t - Y_{t-1}$		5.9	2.05	4.21	4.83	6.64	1.56	9.81	2.93	.81
I_t	0	0	0	0	0	0	0	0	0	0
t	11	12	13	14	15	16	17	18	19	20
Y_t	87.21	97.13	98.27	106.25	107.31	113.10	116.16	117.08	125.25	130.40
$Y_t - Y_{t-1}$	22.54	9.92	1.14	7.98	1.06	5.79	3.06	0.92	8.17	5.15
I_t	1	1	1	1	1	1	1	1	1	1

FIGURE 10–21

Product sales before and after new market in month 11 (Dummy 2)

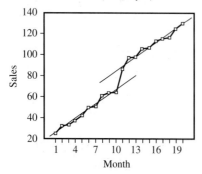

FIGURE 10–22

Change in intercept (constant) and slope (Dummy 5)

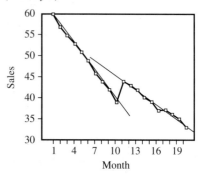

TABLE 10–21   *Product Improvement in t = 11, Shifting Sales Up*
                    (DUMMY5.DAT)

t	1	2	3	4	5	6	7	8	9	10	11	12	13	14	15	16	17	18	19	20
Y_t	60	57	55	53	51	49	46	44	42	39	44	43	42	40	39	37	37	36	35	33
$Y_t - Y_{t-1}$		−3	−2	−2	−2	−2	−3	−2	−2	−3	−5	−1	−1	−2	−1	−2	−0	−1	−1	−2
I_t	0	0	0	0	0	0	0	0	0	0	1	1	1	1	1	1	1	1	1	1
X_t	0	0	0	0	0	0	0	0	0	0	11	12	13	14	15	16	17	18	19	20

where

Y_t = sales of product
t = time
I_t = improvement in product at $t = 11$ $\begin{cases} I_t = 0 \text{ for } t = 1 \text{ to } 10 \\ I_t = 1 \text{ for } t = 11 \text{ to } 20 \end{cases}$
$X_t = I_t t \begin{cases} X_t = 0 \text{ for } t = 1 \text{ to } 10 \\ X_t \neq 0 \text{ for } t = 11 \text{ to } 20 \end{cases}$

The results of fitting an OLS model to the data of Table 10–21 is

$$Y_t = \underset{(208.13)}{62.0} - \underset{(-6.133)}{4.988 I_t} - \underset{(-46.96)}{2.2545 t} + \underset{(15.71)}{1.067 X_t} + e_t \qquad (10\text{–}26)$$

where

$$S_{yx} = .4361 \qquad \overline{R}^2 = .997 \qquad n = 20 \qquad F = 1999.73 \ (.00) \qquad DW = 1.933$$

$$Q = 6.013 \ (.305) \ (\text{sign. levels})$$

The fit of Equation 10–26 is shown in Figure 10–22.

Prediction and Confidence Intervals

One purpose of regression analysis is to estimate the error in using that relationship to predict future values. As discussed in Chapter 3, the values used as input to the modeling process are samples. Consequently, there is a sampling error in using the final relationship to describe the true population. A number of important statistics for ND errors were developed in Chapter 3 and are applicable to the multiple regression case, such as the standard errors of regression (S_r) and forecast (S_f).

Interval estimates can be determined for future values of the dependent variable, using specified values of the independent variables. The formulas used to set these intervals are considerably more complex than those shown for the simple regression model in Chapter 3. The results of these formulas are shown here for the three-variable example of the Big City Bookstore. In general, matrix methods are used in the formulas for more than two variables [see Neter et al. (1996)].

Assume we want to estimate the sales at a store, given an advertising expenditure of $30,000 and competitor display space of 20,000 square feet. From Equation 10–4, we find the point estimate for this case:

$$Y = -18.89 + 2.525(30) - .545(20) = 43.96$$

Consequently, the expected sales are $43,960 at this store, which seems to be a reasonable estimate. The probability that sales will exactly equal this value is virtually zero, but the probability of sales being in a range about this value is very high.

TABLE 10–22 Prediction and Confidence Intervals (BIGCITY.DAT)

Dep Obs	Var Y	Predict Value $\hat{Y}$	Std Err Regression S_r	Lower 95% Mean $\hat{Y} - 2.262S_r$	Upper 95% Mean $\hat{Y} + 2.262S_r$	Lower 95% Prediction $\hat{Y} - 2.262S_f$	Upper 95% Prediction $\hat{Y} + 2.262S_f$
1	27	26.251	1.756	22.2784	30.2240	18.4308	34.0716
2	23	23.527	1.564	19.9894	27.0637	15.9182	31.1349
3	31	36.151	1.213	33.4063	38.8949	28.8769	43.4243
4	45	43.725	1.136	41.1554	46.2947	36.5155	50.9347
5	47	43.525	.896	41.4984	45.5521	36.4908	50.5597
6	42	38.276	1.093	35.8044	40.7473	31.1006	45.4510
7	39	40.401	1.851	36.2135	44.5886	32.4694	48.3327
8	45	47.976	1.742	44.0347	51.9162	40.1713	55.7796
9	57	58.674	1.068	56.2590	61.0892	51.5181	65.8301
10	59	55.750	1.282	52.8505	58.6489	48.4161	63.0832
11	73	73.823	1.638	70.1166	77.5293	66.1345	81.5114
12	84	83.922	2.094	79.1851	88.6593	75.6872	92.1572

Note: *Y* values are not in ascending order, but ordered in time.

Alternatively, we could ask, what is the range of sales that describes the 95 percent prediction interval for sales given the previous values of *X*1 and *X*2? Fortunately, this interval is available from many statistical packages. As in the simple bivariate example of Chapter 3, we have two possible intervals that can be calculated. These are: a prediction interval for the variation describing sales at a specific store (S_f), and the confidence interval describing mean sales for many stores (or, alternatively, sales many times at the same store) (S_r).

These prediction and confidence intervals are shown in Table 10–22 using output from the statistical analysis system (SAS).

Parsimony and Data Requirements

The principle of **parsimony** applies to multivariate models (such as regression models) as much as, if not more than, to univariate models. Therefore, theory should drive the regression modeling process. The number of observations to include in a regression analysis is a common concern because parsimony is partially relative to the number of observations.

In order to derive models empirically, we should like to have as many relevant observations as possible. The term "relevant" has several dimensions: first, that the values are correctly recorded; second, that outliers and other irrelevant observations are controlled for; third, that the range of values for each independent variable varies over a wide range; and fourth, when the independent variables are not independent of each other, that a representative mix or combination of values of each variable is in the database.

Let's explore the meanings of the third and fourth data requirements. Simply stated, if the sample used in analysis is not representative, then most likely neither will be the model. Let's use the Big City Bookstore data to illustrate the need to have sufficient combinations of variables in a sample. Consider for example if the store manager unknowingly analyzed stores with approximately the same level of competitor square

"The real purpose of the scientific method is to make sure Nature hasn't misled you into thinking you know something you don't actually know."

Source: Robert Pirsig, *Zen and the Art of Motorcycle Maintenance* (1974).

footage. As we will see, this sample makes it appear that competition has no effect on demand.

Consider the representativeness of two different subsamples of 7 observations from the 12 years of BIGCITY.DAT. The first selected subsample is *not* representative of the underlying relationship because the competition variable does not vary over a sufficiently wide range of values. This subsample consists of data from years 2, 3, 4, 5, 9, 11, and 12, all observations with competitor square footage of 15,000 or 20,000. The second subsample is selected because it does contain a representative combination of demand, advertising, and competition. This second subsample consists of years 3, 4, 5, 6, 7, 9, and 12, having competitor square footage over the range of 10,000 to 35,000.

Nonrepresentative Sample

The results of fitting the nonrepresentative sample is given in Equation 10–27. As shown, because competition has not varied much, its coefficient is not statistically significant and is positive—a result inconsistent with the larger sample results and the accepted theory of this situation:

$$Y_t = -27.4935 + 2.390\text{ADVERT}_t + .1549\text{COMP}_t \qquad (10\text{–}27)$$
$$ (-3.167) \quad\;\; (10.988) \qquad\quad (.2135)$$

$$S_{yx} = 2.916 \qquad \overline{R}^2 = .9821 \qquad n = 7 \qquad F = 165.21(.0001431) \qquad DW = 2.566$$

Representative Sample

The results of fitting the more representative sample is given in Equation 10–28. This result is much more consistent with the underlying relationship of Equation 10–4, which is repeated in Equation 10–29.

$$Y_t = -20.1851 + 2.5314\text{ADVERT}_t - .4877\text{COMP}_t \qquad (10\text{–}28)$$
$$ (-2.354) \quad\;\; (10.846) \qquad\quad (-2.159)$$

$$S_{yx} = 3.809 \qquad \overline{R}^2 = .951 \qquad n = 7 \qquad F = 57.8875(.00105) \qquad DW = 1.391$$

When comparing Equation 10–27 and 10–28 to the results of Equation 10–29, the effects of the nonrepresentative sample (Equation 10–27) are quite clear. The competition coefficient has the wrong sign and is insignificant, thus the analyst is misled. If instead, a more representative sample is taken, then the model will be more representative, the condition shown in Equations 10–28 and 10–29, which vary only slightly.

$$Y_t = -18.80 + 2.525\text{ADVERT}_t - .545\text{COMP}_t \qquad (10\text{–}29)$$
$$ (-4.879) \;\; (19.50) \qquad\quad (-4.432)$$

$$S_{yx} = 2.978 \qquad \overline{R}^2 = .973 \qquad n = 12 \qquad F = 199.21(.0000000) \qquad DW = 1.7705$$

It is important to highlight the realism of the Big City Bookstore example as opposed to its expository value—normally 12 observations is an unrealistically small size. We must be emphatic to note that regression analysis and forecasting with only 12, let alone 7, observations is not recommended because of the problems illustrated in Equation 10–27 versus Equation 10–29; such a small sample may be unrepresentative.

Several references give guidelines on minimum sample sizes needed to fit valid statistical relationships. However, we have found these suggested rules of thumb to be less than effective. The minimum sample size is dependent on a number of factors, the most important being the strength and complexity of the relationship, the adequacy of the database, and the validity of the underlying theory. Figure 10–23 helps provide a better understanding of the number of observations that are needed to have a representative sample when there is little theory or knowledge on the part of the analyst (a situation arising frequently in student projects).

To better understand the problems with sample nonrepresentativeness, consider the situation in which theory suggests there are four independent variables useful in explaining the dependent variable. In addition, we are not sure whether these four variables are completely independent of each other. For example, it is possible that values of two variables are related or interact to greatly affect the dependent variable. Because of this possibility, the database should have combinations of high, medium, and low values of all variables that might interact.

Let's assume that all four variables are related. Thus, the specific question is, how many observations does it take to have all possible combinations of high, medium, and low values of each of the four variables? This is a simple combinatorial equal to 3^4 or 81 observations, as shown by the tree expansion in Figure 10–23.

Remember that the 81 observations are necessary only if we are concerned about the possible dependencies of variables. If no dependencies exist and sampling error is low, then theoretically only a very small number of observations are necessary to fit a meaningful relationship between the dependent and several independent variables.

As we can see from this discussion, the data requirements can be quite large when the relationship has great variation, or when there may be some relationship between the independent variables.

FIGURE 10–23

*Required sample size
with interactions between
four independent variables
(partial expansion shown)*

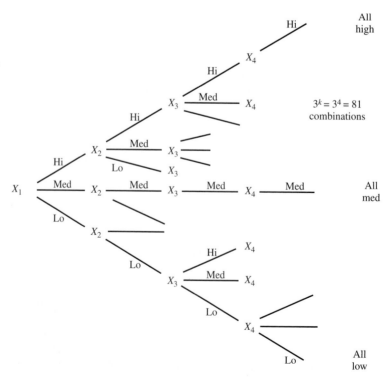

$3^k = 3^4 = 81$ combinations

In spite of our discussion here, one of the most common mistakes made by analysts is having too many potential independent variables in the database. In exploring a multiple regression relationship, if there are many possible independent variables (e.g., 20) in a database with, for example, only 30 observations of a dependent variable, then there is a very high probability that one or more variables might be selected by chance. This is a specification error, which should be avoided by wisely choosing the independent variables. Considerable theory exists to direct the choice of independent variables if the analyst seeks such theory. This problem is further discussed in the next chapter. The warning is very clear: Do not use automated software to choose independent variables if there are very few observations of the dependent variable or if a meaningful causal relationship is desired. Also, when it is important to know how high, medium, and low values of several variables are related, then the required sample size increases dramatically as shown in Figure 10–23.

Maximizing $\overline{R}^2$

We have noted analysts attempting to maximize $\overline{R}^2$ with considerable loss of parsimony. P.J. Dhrymes (1970) has shown that a maximum $\overline{R}^2$ can be achieved by including all variables in a relationship that have coefficient $|t\text{–values}|$ greater than 1. However such procedures are almost always misleading because they violate principles of parsimony and theory-directed-model building.

Automated Regression Modeling

This text stresses theory-based model construction. Unfortunately, this is almost always a difficult task; however, it is a best approach to identifying models with predictive and explanatory validity. Nonetheless, there are times when some form of automated regression method can be validly applied. Stepwise, forward, backward, and all possible subset regressions are typically available in software. While their use in exploratory analysis is valuable, they are not substitutes for intelligent, theory-directed-model building. It has been our experience that most students who have employed these approaches have been misled by automated model structures. Therefore, be cautious when using such methods. Remember the significance of the opening quote of this chapter.

Summary and Conclusions

This chapter has presented a number of important principles for modeling time series through the use of multiple regression methods. Important topics included autoregressive techniques, such as Cochrane–Orcutt iterative least square (COILS), and heteroscedasticity correction methods, including weighted least squares and power transformations. In addition, several important statistical tests for assuring valid regression models were presented, including the partial F-test for including variables, the Durbin–Watson and Q tests for serial correlation, and the Goldfeld–Quandt test. The concepts of elasticities, beta coefficients, and dichotomous variables were presented. Finally, cautions regarding parsimony, overfitting of models, and automated regression modeling were discussed.

This chapter is designed to be a best start in the study of regression methods in forecasting. Unfortunately, no single chapter can present the richness of all the methods and statistics of regression analysis. As you apply regression methods in a professional setting, we suggest you develop a library of books on these methods, including, at a minimum, the books written by Pindyck and Rubenfeld (1991) and by Neter, Kutner, Nachtsheim, and Wasserman (1996).

Key Terms

automated regression method

beta coefficients (β)

causal models

Cochrane–Orcutt iterative least squares (COILS)

coefficient of multiple determination (R^2)

collinearity

correlation matrix

dichotomous (dummy) variable

elasticities

$\dfrac{\text{ESS}_H}{\text{ESS}_L}$

factor analysis

generalized least squares

Goldfeld–Quandt test

heteroscedasticity

homoscedasticity

hyperplane

multicollinearity

ordinary least squares (OLS)

parsimony

Partial F-test

partial or net regression coefficients

perfect multicollinearity

regression plane

restricted and unrestricted SSEs and models

Rho (ρ)

ridge regression

serial correlation

standard error of the regression coefficient (S_{b1})

weighted least squares

Key Formulas

General multiple-regression model

$$Y = a + b_1 X_1 + b_2 X_2 + \cdots + b_n X_n + e \tag{10–1}$$

Big City Bookstore

$$\hat{Y} = -18.80 + 2.525 X1 - .545 X2 \tag{10–4}$$
$$\phantom{\hat{Y} = }(-4.879)\quad (19.50)\quad (-4.432)$$

$$S_{yx} = 2.978 \quad \overline{R}^2 = .973 \quad n = 12 \quad F = 199.21 \quad \text{DW} = 1.7705$$

Multiple adjusted coefficient of determination ($\overline{R}^2$)

$$\overline{R}^2 = \frac{\text{Explained variance}}{\text{Total variance}} = 1 - \frac{\text{Unexplained variance}}{\text{Total variance}} = 1 - \frac{S_{yx}^{\,2}}{S_y^{\,2}}$$

Partial regression coefficients, given $X1 = 30$

$$Y_t = -18.80 + 2.525(30) - .545 X2_t + e_t \tag{10–5}$$

$$Y_t = -18.80 + 75.75 - .545 X2_t + e_t = 56.86 - .545 X2 + e_t$$

Standard error of regression coefficient

$$S_{b1} = \frac{S_{yx}}{\sqrt{\Sigma x^2 (1 - r_{12}^2)}} \tag{10–6}$$

Partial F-test for restricted and unrestricted models

$$F_{\text{calculated}} = \frac{(\text{SSE}_R - \text{SSE}_U)\,/\,m}{\text{SSE}_U\,/\,(n - k)} \tag{10–7}$$

If $F_{\text{calc}} \leq F_{\text{table}}$, then $\text{SSE}_R = \text{SSE}_U$; no sign improvement.

First-Order serial correlation

$$Y_t = a + bX_t + \rho e_{t-1} + e_t \cdot .11 \tag{10-8}$$

Cochrane–Orcutt iterative least squares (COILS)

$$\rho e_{t-1} = \rho(Y_{t-1} - \hat{Y}_{t-1}) = \rho[Y_{t-1} - (a + bX_{t-1} + \rho e_{t-2})] \tag{10-10}$$

$$Y_t = a + bX_t + \rho Y_{t-1} - \rho a - \rho bX_{t-1} + v_t$$

$$Y_t - \rho Y_{t-1} = a^* + bX_t - \rho bX_{t-1} + v_t \tag{10-11}$$

$$(1 - \rho B)Y_t = a^* + b(1 - \rho B)X_t + v_t \tag{10-12}$$

Forecasting with serially correlated errors

$$\hat{Y}_t = 115.86 + .476X_t + .65e_{t-1} \qquad \text{(one period ahead)}$$

$$\hat{Y}_{t+1} = 115.86 + .476X_{t+1} + .65(0) \qquad (> \text{ one period ahead}) \tag{10-15}$$

Constant elasticity for logarithmic relationships

$$\ln Y_t = a + b\ln X_t + e_t \tag{10-16}$$

$$b = \frac{\Delta \ln Y_t}{\Delta \ln X_t} = \frac{\ln Y_t - \ln Y_{t-1}}{\ln X_t - \ln X_{t-1}}$$

Variable elasticity for linear relationships: like Equation 10–4

$$\text{Elasticity} = b\frac{X_1}{Y_1} = \frac{\Delta Y_t X_1}{\Delta X_t Y_1} = \frac{\Delta Y_t / Y_1}{\Delta X_t / \Delta X_1} \tag{10-17}$$

Heteroscedasticity: Goldfeld–Quandt test

$$\text{ESS}_L = 104685.85 \qquad \text{ESS}_H = 5164.41$$

$$F_{\text{calculated}} = \frac{\text{ESS}_H / [(n - d)/2 - k]}{\text{ESS}_L / [(n - d)/2 - k]} = \frac{104685.85 / (106 - 2)}{5164.41 / (106 - 2)} = 20.27 \tag{10-18}$$

$$F_{106-2, 106-2, \alpha=.05} \approx 1.39$$

$$F_{\text{calculated}} \gg F_{\text{table}}: \text{reject homoscedasticity hypothesis.}$$

Weighted least squares (e.g., variance proportional to $X1$)

$$\frac{Y}{X1} = \frac{a'}{X1} + \frac{b_1' X1}{X1} + \frac{b_2' X2}{X1} + \frac{e}{X1} \tag{10-19a}$$

Beta coefficients (standardized changes in variables)

$$\beta_1 = \frac{\Delta Y / S_Y}{\Delta X1 / S_{X1}} \qquad \beta_2 = \frac{\Delta Y / S_Y}{\Delta X2 / S_{X2}} \tag{10-22}$$

$$\beta_1 = b_1\left(\frac{S_{X1}}{S_Y}\right) \qquad \beta_2 = b_2\left(\frac{S_{X2}}{S_Y}\right) \tag{10-23}$$

Dichotomous (dummy) variables for modeling events: changes in the constant and slope, using dummy variables

$$Y_t = a_1 + b_1 t + a_2 I_t + b_2 X_t$$

$$t = \text{time}$$

$$I_t = \text{improvement in product at } t = 11 \begin{cases} I_t = 0 \text{ for } t = 1 \text{ to } 10 \\ I_t = 1 \text{ for } t = 11 \text{ to } 20 \end{cases}$$

$$X_t = I_t t \begin{cases} X_t = 0 \text{ for } t = 1 \text{ to } 10 \\ X_t \neq 0 \text{ for } t = 11 \text{ to } 20 \end{cases}$$

Review Problems Using Your Software

R10–1 Repeat the multiple regression analysis of the Big City Bookstore of Table 10–2c using your software. Are the same notation and terms used in your software? If not, highlight the differences in terms. Are there any additional terms or output from your software? Define those differences.

R10–2 Interpret the results of R10–1 as done in Chapter 3, Table 3–4.

R10–3 Generate Table 10–3, the correlation matrix for MULT.DAT. How do you interpret this correlation matrix?

R10–4 Using the time series MULT.DAT, duplicate the analysis of Table 10–4 and identify the best model.

R10–5 Repeat the analysis of Table 10–5 using AR1DAT.DAT and your software. Are there any differences in your results?

R10–6 If your software supports three-dimensional graphs, generate the regression plane of Figure 10–2.

R10–7 Repeat the analyses of Tables 10–5 to 10–7 using your software and AR1DAT.DAT. Confirm that your results are the same as those tables.

R10–8 If your software does COILS or a similar method for adjusting first-order serial correlation, repeat the analysis of Table 10–11. Do your results equal those of this table?

R10–9 Repeat the analyses of Tables 10–12 and 10–13 using ARDAT.DAT. Are there any differences in your results?

R10–10 Repeat the analyses of Tables 10–14 and 10–15 using your software. Are there any differences in your results?

R10–11 Confirm the SSE and DW statistics of three of the ρ values in Table 10–10.

R10–12 Repeat the Goldfeld–Quandt test of Equation 10–18.

R10–13 Repeat the analysis of weighted least squares of Table 10–19.

R10–14 Repeat the analysis of Equation 10–24 using DUMMY.DAT.

R10–15 Repeat the analysis of Equation 10–25 using DUMMY2.DAT.

R10–16 Repeat the analysis of Equation 10–26 using DUMMY5.DAT.

R10–17 If your software will generate prediction and confidence intervals of multiple regression relationships, generate Table 10–22 for the Big City Bookstore example.

R10–18 Repeat the analysis of Equations 10–27 to 10–29.

Problems

10–1 Does your software report the adjusted or unadjusted R^2?

10–2 Explain the meaning of the term "partial regression coefficient."

10–3 Review the flow chart of the multiple regression modeling process of Figure 10–5. Explain the regression process in four general steps.

10–4 Explain the importance of theory in regression analysis.

10–5 Identify the important diagnostic plots of residuals in regression analysis and describe how the plots should be distributed.

10–6 Define the concept of multicollinearity and answer the following:
  a. When is multicollinearity a problem?
  b. How is it detected?
  c. How is multicollinearity corrected?
  d. What is the effect of multicollinearity on the signs of the regression coefficients?

10–7 Explain the meaning of one independent variable being a perfect linear function of three other independent variables. What is the effect of this linear dependency on regression output?

10–8 What is the importance of a correlation matrix prior to and during the regression analysis?

10–9 Explain the purpose of the *F*-test. List the null and alternative hypotheses.

10–10 What are beta coefficients? Reexpress the Big City Bookstore relationship of Equation 10–4 in beta coefficients.

10–11 What are dichotomous variables and how are they used in modeling time series?

10–12 Explain the purpose of the partial *F*-test for including or excluding variables.

10–13 Explain the purpose of the Cochrane–Orcutt iterative least squares procedure.

10–14 Explain the steps of the COILS procedure.

10–15 Explain the concept of elasticity. How is it related to the use of logarithms in modeling?

10–16 What is the relationship between the COILS procedure and the use of the first differences of dependent and independent variables?

10–17 What is heteroscedasticity and what is its effect on OLS results?

10–18 Explain the purpose and steps of the weighted least squares procedure.

10–19 What is the purpose of the Goldfeld–Quandt test?

10–20 Describe the steps of the Goldfeld–Quandt test.

10–21 What are the causes of first-order serial correlation?

10–22 Explain the differences in one- and two-period-ahead forecasts using a COILS model.

10–23 Explain the concept of parsimony in regression analysis.

10–24 What are automated regression methods and what cautions apply to these methods?

10–25 If the independent variables in a relationship are not completely independent, what is the minimum number of observations that can represent all possible combinations of high, medium, and low values of four independent variables as predictors of the dependent variable? Assuming that the independent variables are completely independent, what is the minimum number of observations in a relationship that can represent all possible combinations of high, medium, and low values of four independent variables?

10–26 Express the Big City Bookstore regression coefficients in terms of beta coefficients. Interpret these results.

10–27 Perform a partial *F*-test on the Big City Bookstore assuming the full model includes advertising and competition and the restricted model includes only advertising. What inferences do you make from these results?

10–28 The chapter introduced the concept of elasticity. Apply that concept to the U.K.–U.S. stock index relationship of Table 10–16.

10–29 An analyst has estimated the following least-squares relationship with $\bar{R}^2$ of .98:

$$\hat{Y}_t = a + b_1 X_1 + b_2 X_2$$

Which of the following statements is true, which is false, and why?

a. b_2 measures the change in Y_t from a unit change in X_2 while holding X_1 constant.

b. If b_1 is 10 times larger than b_2, then X_1 is more important in explaining Y_t than X_2.

c. The coefficients a, b_1, and b_2 are all statistically significantly different than zero.

d. Variations in X_1 and X_2 account for a large proportion of the variation in Y_t.

e. There is a strong cause and effect relationship between Y_t and X_1 and X_2.

f. Because $\bar{R}^2$ is so high, the standard error of estimate will be quite low and forecasts will be quite accurate.

g. Because $\bar{R}^2$ is so high, the assumptions of multiple regression will not be violated.

h. The value of $\bar{R}^2$ will decline considerably if X_1 or X_2 are dropped.

10–30 A forecaster has estimated the following relationship explaining the sales of fishing boats:

$$Y_t = .09 - .24X_1 - .03X_2 + .015X_3$$
$$\quad (.10) \quad (.045) \quad (.0033) \quad (.0013)$$

where

$$S_{yx} = 15 \qquad \bar{R}^2 = .96 \qquad n = 60 \qquad F = 238.2 \qquad DW = 1.97$$

and

Y_t is sales in millions per year.
X_1 is the number of boats from all manufacturers on the market.
X_2 is the average price of competitor boats.
X_3 is the per capita disposable income each year.
(Values in parentheses are standard errors of the regression coefficients.)

Which of the following statements is true, which is false, and why?

a. The average price of competitor boats is a more important determinant of sales than per capita disposable income.
b. The constant is insignificant and should therefore be dropped.
c. The most statistically significant explanatory variable is X_3.
d. The standard deviation of Y_t is 75.
e. There appears to be some problem with serial correlation in the residuals.
f. The fact that the coefficient of X_1 is about eight times larger than X_2 means that X_1 explains much more variance in Y_t.
g. The overall relationship between Y_t and X_1, X_2, and X_3 is statistically significant.

10–31 A cost analyst for a manufacturing firm wants to model the determinants of manufacturing cost per unit for a major product. The analyst has measured the cost per unit over a 48-month period (COST), the percentage utilization of the capacity of the production line (CAP), and the cost of the raw materials used in the production of the product (RAWC). These data exist in the file PRODEXP.DAT.
a. Determine a best regression relationship for explaining COST.
b. Explain the meaning of the regression coefficients.
c. Discuss the goodness of fit of the relationship and its practical value.
d. Check to see if any of the assumptions of regression analysis are violated by your relationship. If so, explain how they might be corrected.

10–32 An express delivery service is interested in measuring the time it takes to load a package onto a truck. It has collected 25 observations of the time measured in .001 minutes, the weight, measured in .1 pounds, and the length, in .1 inches. These data exist in the file EXPRESS.DAT.
a. Determine the best regression relationship.
b. Fully interpret your model and perform appropriate significance tests.
c. Graph the residuals versus all relevant variables to assist in determining whether the model is valid.
d. Which one of the explanatory variables do you believe influences the time the greatest?
e. Check to see if any of the assumptions of regression analysis are violated by the relationship. If so, explain how they might be corrected.

10–33 A realtor is interested in determining the cost of lots in an area with various elevations and views of a western valley. The Realtor samples the selling price, elevation, and square footage of 20 lots. These data exist in the file REALTOR.DAT.
a. Determine the best regression relationship.
b. Fully interpret your model and perform appropriate significance tests.
c. Graph the residuals versus all relevant variables to assist in determining whether the model is valid.
d. Which one of the explanatory variables do you believe influences the price the greatest?
e. Check to see if any of the assumptions of regression analysis are violated by your relationship. If so, explain how they might be corrected.

10–34 The data MULT1.DAT is the sales for building materials supplies sold by a national chain in 40 different locations around the United States. The six variables are:

Y = Average monthly store sales in thousands of dollars (000s)
$X1$ = Households in 5-mile ring who are do-it-yourselfers (000s)
$X2$ = Average monthly advertising expenditure (0s)
$X3$ = Square footage of competitor stores in a 5-mile ring (000s)
$X4$ = Households in 5-mile ring who are below the poverty level (00s)
$X5$ = Weighted average daily traffic count at store intersection

Assist corporate management in forecasting store sales and good store locations by modeling sales as a function of the attributes of the economic environment of the store. To do so, you must complete the following tasks:

a. Based on your understanding of marketing and demographics, identify the direction in which sales will change as variables $X1$ to $X5$ increase.

b. Fit a regression relationship using all five variables as predictors of sales. Are the signs on the coefficients as you expected? Write out your equations and statistics as done in the text.

c. Interpret the results of your analysis in b. Be sure to interpret each coefficient, its statistical significance, and the significance of the total relationship. (Your computer output may include statistics that are unknown to you; ignore these for now.)

d. Comment on whether all five variables should be in the relationship.

e. If any variables are insignificant, remove them one by one and refit the model each time, until only significant variables remain in the relationship. Interpret the final results as you did in c.

10–35 The actual sales (demand) for the first store in Problem 10–34 were much lower than shown, because of management problems. The actual sales were estimated as if the problem did not exist, and this was the sales used in Problem 10–34; however, the actual sales for this store were 180, not 281. Correct the value of the data for store #1, as shown here; then complete the following tasks.

Y	X1	X2	X3	X4	X5	DUM
180	878	6575	175	7.94	2387	1
		. . .				0

a. Create an independent dummy variable with all zeros and only one 1, for store #1. Use this data to estimate the actual sales that would have been realized in store #1 were it not for the management problem. Write out your equations and statistics as done in the text.

b. Fully interpret the coefficient of the dummy variable. What does this denote? Did the values of the other coefficients remain approximately the same?

c. Remembering that Y represents average monthly sales, what is the annual effect of having poor store management?

10–36 The weekly demand at a community blood bank has recently increased because a nearby blood bank closed in week 135. Graph the data using BLOOD.DAT to determine the type of effect from the closing of the other blood bank. Using (a) dichotomous variable(s), fit a model to the data to explain the increase in demand that resulted from the closing of the other blood bank. Fully interpret the statistics of the relationship in statistical and practical terms. Are any of the assumptions of regression analysis violated?

10–37 The weekly demand for bottled water increased dramatically during the midwest floods of weeks 75 to 84. Graph the data using WATER.DAT to determine the type of effect from the flooding. Using (a) dichotomous variable(s), fit a model to the data to explain the increase in demand. Fully interpret the statistics of the relationship in statistical terms and practical terms. Are any of the assumptions of regression analysis violated?

10–38 Twelve years of monthly values of the closing value of the SP500 are given in the file SP500MN.DAT. In October and November 1987, the market declined permanently to new lows. Graph the data using SP500MN.DAT to determine the type of effect from the crash. When analyzing this series, it is most appropriate to use logarithms of closing prices, because of the percentage growth nature of this series. Using (a) dichotomous variable(s), fit a model to the data to explain the decrease from the market crash. Fully interpret the statistics of the relationship in statistical and practical terms. Are any of the assumptions of regression analysis violated?

10–39 AIRLINI.DAT is the monthly number of international airline passengers over a 12-year period. Beginning in year 11, a new advertising campaign was started with the introduction of a new fleet of jet aircraft. Graph the data to confirm that the introduction of the new fleet had an obvious effect on demand in period 121. When analyzing this series, it is most appropriate to use logarithms of passengers, because of the percentage growth nature of this series. Using dichotomous variables for different months of the year, fit a model to the data to explain the increase from the new advertising campaign. Fully interpret the statistics of the relationship in statistical and practical terms. Are any of the assumptions of regression analysis violated?

10–40 File IBMNYLN.DAT has 242 observations of the daily price of IBM stock on the New York and London stock exchanges. Use the methods of this chapter to model the relationship between prices on each exchange. In defining a relationship, first determine which price leads the other. Fully interpret the statistics of the relationship in statistical and practical terms. Are any of the assumptions of regression analysis violated?

Minicases: Common Assignment for Minicases

For a selected minicase or problem, complete the following analysis. Develop a multiple regression model for a selected time series as you achieve a valid model. Fill out a table the equivalent of Table 8–23, listing the important statistical validity measures of alternative models in tabular form. In addition, if you have been filling out the Master Forecasting Summary Table, add the appropriate model to that table, with holding the correct number of observations.

Note that these time series are previous time series with added input variables. These added independent variables are contrived for explanatory purposes.

Minicase 10–1 Kansas Turnpike, Daily Data
TURNPKMM.DAT includes two independent variables representing seasonal demand for daily travel.

Minicase 10–2 Domestic Air Passengers by Quarter
PASSAIRM.DAT includes three independent variables representing indexes of air travel. These are the first three variables of that dataset.

Minicase 10–3 Hospital Census by Month
CENSUSMM.DAT includes two independent variables representing seasonal monthly demand for health care.

Minicase 10–4 Henry Machler's Hideaway Orchids
MACHLRMM.DAT includes three independent variables representing the seasonal population of consumers (i.e., Northerners who stay for only five months or so in Florida, commonly called "snowbirds", who greatly affect demand). These are the first three variables of that dataset.

Minicase 10–5 Your Forecasting Project If there are independent variables in your project, fit a multiple regression model to your data. Use theory to guide your analysis.

Minicase 10–6 Midwestern Building Materials
LUMBERM.DAT includes two independent variables representing the seasonal demand for building material supplies.

Minicase 10–7 International Airline Passengers
AIRLINM.DAT includes two independent variables representing indexes of international travel. These are the first two variables of that dataset.

Minicase 10–8 Automobile Sales AUTOM.DAT includes two independent variables representing indexes of automobile affordability.

Minicase 10–9 Consumption of Distilled Spirits
SPIRITSM.DAT includes two independent variables representing the seasonal demand for alcoholic drinks, as estimated by liquor store managers.

Minicase 10–10 Discount Consumer Electronics
ELECTM.DAT includes two independent variables representing indexes of consumer demand, consisting of weighted averages of new product improvements and the number of outlets.

References

Bartels, R.; and J. Goodhew. "The Robustness of the Durbin–Watson Test." *Review of Economics and Statistics 63* (February 1981), pp. 136–39.

Bewley, R.; and D.G. Fiebig. "A flexible logistic growth model with applications in telecommunication." *International Journal of Forecasting 4* (1988), pp. 177–192.

Bowerman, B.L.; and R.T. O'Connell. *Linear Statistical Models: An Applied Approach.* Boston: PWS-Kent, 1990.

Box, G.E.P.; and P. Newbold. "Some comments on paper of Coen, Gomme and Kendall." *Journal of the Royal Statistical Society A, No. 134,* (1971), pp. 229–240.

Breusch, T.S.; and A.R. Pagan. "A Simple Test for Heteroskedasticity and Random Coefficient Variation." *Econometrical 47,* (1979), pp. 1287–94.

Chatterjee, S.; and B. Price. *Regression Analysis by Example.* 2nd ed. New York: Wiley, 1991.

Cochrane, D.; and G.H. Orcutt. "Application of Least-Squares Regressions to Relationships Containing Autocorrelated Error Terms." *Journal of the American Statistical Association* 44, (1949), pp. 32–61.

Dino, R.N. "Forecasting the price evolution of new electronic products." *Journal of Forecasting 4,* (1985), pp. 39–60.

Dhrymes, P.J. "On the Game of Maximizing $\bar{R}^2$." *Australian Economics Papers 9,* December 1970.

Draper, N.R.; and H. Smith. *Applied Regression Analysis.* 2nd ed. New York: Wiley, 1981.

Durbin, J.; and G.S. Watson. "Testing for Serial Correlation in Least-Squares Regression." *Biometrika* 38 (1951), pp. 159–77.

Durbin, J. "Testing for Serial Correlation in Least-Squares Regression When Some of the Regressors Are Lagged Dependent Variables." *Econometrica* 38 (1970), pp. 410–21.

Freedman, D.; T. Rothenberg; and R. Sutch. "On energy policy models." *Journal of Business and Economic Statistics 1,* (1983), pp. 24–32.

Granger, C.W.J. "Simple trend fitting for long range forecasting." *Management Decision,* (1967), pp. 29–34.

Granger, C.W.J.; and P. Newbold. "Spurious regressions in econometrics." *Journal of Econometrics 2,* (1974), pp. 111–120.

Granger, C.W.J.; and P. Newbold. *Forecasting Economic Time Series.* 2nd ed. Orlando, FL: Academic Press, 1968.

Greene, W.M. *Econometric Methods.* 2nd ed. Englewood Cliffs, NJ: Prentice-Hall, 1993.

Gujarati, D.N. *Basic Economics.* 2nd ed. New York: McGraw Hill, 1988.

Johnson, A.C.; M.B. Johnson; and R.C. Buse. *Econometrics: Basic and Applied.* New York: Macmillan, 1987.

Kmenta, J. *Elements of Econometrics.* New York: MacMillan, 1986; Judge, G.G. et al. *Introduction to The Theory and Practice of Econometrics.* 2nd ed. New York: Wiley, 1988; and Pagan, A.R.; and A.D. Hall. "Diagnostic Tests as Residual Analysis." *Econometric Reviews* 2 (1983), pp. 159–218.

Kunisawa, K.; and Y. Horibe. "Forecasting international telecommunications traffic by the data translation method." *International Journal of Forecasting 2,* (1986), pp. 427–434.

Maddala, G.S. *Introduction to Econometrics.* New York: Macmillan, 1988.

Meade, N. "The use of growth curves in forecasting market development — a review and appraisal." *Journal of Forecasting 3,* (1984), pp. 429–451.

Mendenhall, W.; and T. Sincich. *A Second Course in Business Statistics: Regression Analysis.* 2nd ed. San Francisco: Dellen, 1986.

Meyers, R.H. *Classical and Modern Regression with Applications.* Boston: Duxbury Press, 1986.

Neter, J.; M.H. Kutner; J. Nachtsheim; and W. Wasserman. *Applied Linear Regression Models.* 3rd ed. Burr Ridge, IL: Richard D. Irwin, 1996.

Newbold, P. *Forecasting Methods.* London: Her Majesty's Stationery Office, 1973.

Newbold, P. *Statistics for Business and Economics.* 3rd ed. Englewood Cliffs, NJ: Prentice-Hall, 1991.

Pindyck, R.S.; and D.L. Rubinfeld. *Econometric Models and Economic Forecasts.* 3rd ed. New York: McGraw Hill, 1991.

Weisberg, S. *Applied Linear Regression.* 2nd ed. New York: Wiley, 1981.

White, H. "A Heteroskedasticity-Consistent Covariance Matrix Estimator and a Direct Test for Heteroskedasticity." *Econometrica* 48 (1980), pp. 817–38.

Wonnacott, T.H.; and R.J. Wonnacott. *Regression: A Second Course in Statistics.* New York: Wiley, 1981.

Young, P.; and J.K. Ord. "Model selection and estimation for technological growth curves." *International Journal of Forecasting 5,* (1989), pp. 501–513.

APPENDIX 10–A

DERIVING NORMAL EQUATIONS AND REGRESSION COEFFICIENTS

Given: $Y_i = a + bX_i + e_i$ and $\hat{Y}_i = a + bX_i$

$$e_i = Y_i - \hat{Y}_i = Y_i - a - bX_i$$

$$e_i^2 = (Y_i - \hat{Y}_i)^2 = (Y_i - a - bX_i)^2$$

The sum of the squared errors equals

$$\Sigma e_i^2 = \Sigma(Y_i - a - bX_i)^2 \tag{10A–1}$$

Equation 10A–1 is to be minimized. Now, Y_i and X_i are knowns, a and b unknowns. Using Maxima–Minima Theorem of Partial Differentiation

$$\frac{\partial e_i^2}{\partial a} = -2\Sigma(Y_i - a - bX_i) \tag{10A–2}$$

$$\frac{\partial e_i}{\partial b} = -2\Sigma X_i(X_i - a - bX_i) \tag{10A–3}$$

Setting each of Equations 10A–2 and 10A–3 equal to zero and solving

$$-2\Sigma Y_i + 2na + 2bX_i = 0 \tag{10A–4}$$

$$-2\Sigma X_i Y_i + 2a\Sigma X_i + b\Sigma X_i^2 = 0 \tag{10A–5}$$

Dividing both sides of these equations by 2

$$-\Sigma Y_i + na + b\Sigma X_i = 0 \tag{10A–6}$$

$$-\Sigma X_i Y_i + a\Sigma X_i + b\Sigma X_i^2 = 0 \tag{10A–7}$$

Solving simultaneously Equation 10A–6 can be simplified to

$$na = \Sigma Y_i - b\Sigma X_i \tag{10A–8}$$

$$a = \frac{\Sigma Y_i}{n} - b\frac{\Sigma X_i}{n}$$

$$a = \overline{Y} - b\overline{X} \tag{10–8a}$$

Substituting Equation 10A–8 into Equation 10A–7 and simplifying

$$b = \frac{n\Sigma X_i Y_i - \Sigma X_i \Sigma Y_i}{n\Sigma X_i^2 - (\Sigma X_i)^2} \tag{10A–9}$$

Applying second-order conditions of the maxima–minima theorem confirms that

$$\frac{\partial^2 \Sigma e_i^2}{\partial a^2} > 0 \quad \frac{\partial^2 \Sigma e_i^2}{\partial b^2} > 0 \tag{10A–10}$$

Normal Equations with Deviations

Equation 10A–G can be simplified greatly when X_i and Y_i are deviations from their means x_i and y_i.

Remembering that for deviations of x_i and y_i:

$$\Sigma x_i = \Sigma y_i = 0$$

Therefore:

$$b = \frac{n\Sigma x_i y_i - 0(0)}{n\Sigma x_i^2 - (0)^2} = \frac{\Sigma x_i y_i}{\Sigma x_i^2}$$

From Equation 10A–8a, a can easily be derived as:

$$a = \bar{Y} - b\bar{X}$$

The reader interested in the general multiple regression case with more than one independent variable is referred to Neter et al. 1996, p. 279.

ECONOMETRIC METHODS

Mere qualitative knowledge for [Alfred Marshall] was not enough. He wanted to make it quantitative in the way physics is quantitative. Not just to be able to say that such and such an economic cause tends to produce this kind of effect; but that it tends to produce such and such an amount of this kind of effect.

A.G. Pigou about Alfred Marshall

Chapter Outline

Because we frequently want to model cause and effect, this chapter develops several analytical methods for modeling cause and effect in forecasting. To this point in this book, forecasting methods have been presented in the context of accurately predicting one dependent variable. This chapter extends multiple regression to structural equation modeling of **econometrics** in the context of the above quote about Alfred Marshall. Structural equations, causal order, causal closure, specification errors, simultaneous equations, Granger Causality, and two-stage least squares (2SLS) are presented in this chapter.

A single chapter on econometrics can only introduce the basics of econometrics and causal modeling. Thus, our purpose must be limited to introducing these concepts to those familiar with multiple regression. We view a basic understanding of causal models as a necessary knowledge set for forecasters. Most forecasting books avoid this topic because of its complexity; however, some introductory knowledge will greatly assist those wanting and needing to further study these topics.

Structural equations are used to *predict and explain* the values of two or more dependent variables as functions of several other variables. Because they model *systems* of interrelationships, they are some of the most powerful methods for measuring cause and effect. The most commonly used synonyms for structural equation models are econometric methods and, in the social sciences, path analysis or causal modeling.

Because of its popularity and versatility, there is a rich literature of structural equation modeling in a variety of disciplines. These methods have been used in political science, economics, business, and sociology to measure causal relationships. While used extensively in some large corporations, particularly in marketing research, structural equation methods are less widely developed in forecasting books where single-equation regression, smoothing, and ARIMA models dominate. Today, powerful microcomputer hardware and inexpensive software place econometric methods in the hands of most analysts. Thus, the chapter's purpose is to start you on the path of valid and insightful structural equation modeling; however, valid causal models are not easily obtained, requiring considerable science and art.

Biased Single-Equation Relationships

Structural equation methods are important because they statistically control or limit the effects of the biases that result from incorrect single-equation regression models. If the interrelationships among independent variables and error terms are not modeled, a single-equation regression model may have biased coefficients that make interpretations of the regression coefficients wrong, thus affecting explanatory validity. (Remember, in theoretical discussions, the error term is distinguished from the *residual* of the dependent variable. Errors are associated with the *true* regression model, while residuals arise from the *estimation* process.) While biased coefficients might not affect the accuracy of the forecast, they will mislead decision makers wanting to control the system based on the regression coefficients. For example, given:

$$Y = a + b_1 X_1 + b_2 X_2 + e$$

users may want to be sure that a one-unit change in X_1 yields a b_1 change in Y. Unfortunately, if the single-equation model is an oversimplification of causality, then b_1 is not an estimate of the true coefficient. This is important, for in a growing number of forecasting applications the accuracy of the forecast is secondary to valid and insightful models.

To be sure that regression coefficients are accurate, causal modeling processes place stringent requirements on the forecaster. These requirements include a significant theory justifying the included and excluded variables and a clear understanding of the direction and structure of causality. Given this theory, then, the structural equation method estimates the coefficients of the several independent variables on several dependent variables. Thus, we see that an understanding of the direction of causality is a prerequisite to valid causal modeling.

Recursive versus Nonrecursive Methods

This chapter presents both **recursive** and **nonrecursive structural equation methods.** Recursive models are those where the causality between two variables (e.g., Y and X) is in only one direction (i.e., X influences Y, but Y does not influence X). These are the types of relationships studied in Chapters 3, 10, 12, and 13. Fortunately, ordinary least squares (OLS) can be used to fit recursive models. However, recursive modeling is not just multiple regression analysis; it involves understanding the relationships between the variables on the right-hand side of the equation. Thus, when multicollinearity exists in a single-equation model, recursive methods provide models of these interrelationships. We will see an example of this in a moment.

In contrast to recursive methods, nonrecursive or reciprocal methods are those where X influences Y and Y also influences X, a situation that is referred to as **simultaneity.** Relationships that are simultaneous are modeled using simultaneous equation models. While recursive methods can be modeled validly using OLS procedures, nonrecursive methods require the use of other estimation methods, the most widely used being **two-stage least squares (2SLS)** and three-stage least squares (3SLS). We study 2SLS in the second half of this chapter.

Simultaneity biases (i.e., biased regression coefficients) result from relationships between jointly determined variables and the error terms in those relationships. In structural equations there are variables that are determined in the system of equations (called endogenous variables) and those that are predetermined outside of the relationship. The **predetermined variables** consist of externally determined variables and lagged endogenous variables.

Recursive System of Structural Equations

A Simple Recursive System

Let's use the Big City Bookstore data to introduce structural equations. Figure 11–1 presents the cause and effect between competition ($X1$), advertising ($X2$), and sales ($X3$) for Big City. Because the independent variable of one equation can be a dependent variable of another equation, we drop the use of Y as the dependent variable; thus, $X3$ is used for sales in Figure 11–1. In Chapter 10, the relationship between competition, advertising, and sales was measured. Assume that Big City has a corporate policy setting store advertising expenditures based on the competition in a two-mile ring around the store; thus, competition influences the advertising expenditures. We know theoretically why advertising and competition are related; we now estimate the magnitude of this relationship.

As shown in Figure 11–1, competition and advertising both influence sales. Also, we see that competition influences advertising. When we assume that these variables

FIGURE 11–1

Three-variable path analysis using Big City Bookstore example

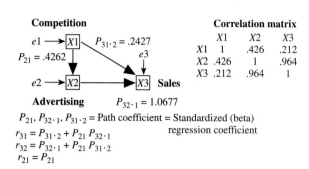

$P_{21}, P_{32\cdot1}, P_{31\cdot2}$ = Path coefficient = Standardized (beta) regression coefficient

$r_{31} = P_{31\cdot2} + P_{21}P_{32\cdot1}$
$r_{32} = P_{32\cdot1} + P_{21}P_{31\cdot2}$
$r_{21} = P_{21}$

are independent, then we oversimplify the causal structure. This results in misunderstanding of the actual relationship between sales, competition, and advertising. A single-equation representation of Figure 11–1 can mislead decision makers.

Endogenous, Exogenous, and Intervening Variables

In structural equation models, the variables sales ($X3$) and advertising ($X2$) are called **endogenous variables** and competition ($X1$) is an **exogenous variable.** The term *endogenous* denotes that at least part of the value of a variable is determined internally in the system of equations. The term *exogenous* denotes that the value is determined externally from the system of equations. Also, the variable advertising is referred to as an **intervening endogenous variable** because it is affected by competition and therefore intervenes between competition and sales. The $e1$, $e2$, and $e3$ terms of Figure 11–1 denote all other influences on each of the relationships.

The modeling of causality in this study requires analysis of the cause and effect structure between these three variables; thus, the term **structural equations.** After specification of the structure or path diagram, statistical analysis provides estimates of the coefficients that measure the influences of exogenous variables on the endogenous variables. The three equations that represent the system of Figure 11–1 are:

$$X1 = e1 \tag{11–1}$$

$$X2 = b_0 + b_1 X1 + e2 \tag{11–2}$$

$$X3 = b_2 + b_3 X1 + b_4 X2 + e3 \tag{11–3}$$

where

$X1$ = Competition
$X2$ = Advertising expenditures
$X3$ = Sales
$e1, e2, e3,$ = Error terms for each equation
b_i = Regression coefficients, including constants
$\overline{e1} = \overline{e2} = \overline{e3} = 0$

$$\text{COV}(e1,e2) = \text{COV}(e1,e3) = \text{COV}(e2,e3) = 0 \tag{11–4}$$

$$\text{COV}(em,Xn) = 0 \quad \text{within a relationship for all } m \neq n. \tag{11–5}$$

Equation 11–1 denotes that $X1$ is an exogenous variable influenced by variables not included in the system of equations. This relationship is shown for general purposes; it needs no estimation because it is an identity. Equation 11–2 expresses the relationship between $X2$, advertising, and $X1$, competition. Finally, Equation 11–3 represents the relationship between sales, $X3$, competition, $X1$, and advertising, $X2$ that is studied in Chapter 10. These three equations are a more accurate model of the relationships between these variables and therefore more useful in predicting and understanding sales. Because these equations are recursive (i.e., no mutual causality exists), each can be estimated independently using OLS methods.

Equation 11–4 is shown here even though it is implied in the underlying regression assumptions introduced in Chapter 3. Equation 11–4 denotes that the contemporaneous residual terms are unbiased estimates of the true error and that the error terms are not correlated with each other. If either of these assumptions is untrue, then the estimated coefficients in Equations 11–2 and 11–3 may be biased. Equation 11–5 denotes that the variables of a relationship are not correlated with the error term. If there is correlation between variable and the error term, then OLS will give biased estimates of the coefficients. This denotes that it may be necessary to estimate the model differently, possibly using simultaneous equations.

We avoid violations of the assumptions of Equations 11–4 and 11–5 by ensuring that we have good theory and sufficient sample sizes for the model-building process. Both of these topics are developed later in this chapter. However, before being able to fully understand these assumptions and structural relationships, we should be comfortable with a concept called **path coefficients.** Finally, remember that the sample size of this example is extremely low, with only 12 observations. The model of Figure 11–1 should have been estimated with many more observations, a reasonable minimum being 30 to 60, depending on the strength of the relationship.

Path Coefficients

Figure 11–1 includes a correlation matrix of the three variables of this system. The coefficients on the causal arrows of this figure, P_{21}, $P_{31.2}$, $P_{32.1}$ are called path coefficients and their arrows define the direction of causality. These coefficients are not ordinary regression coefficients but instead are standardized (i.e., beta) coefficients, as introduced in Chapter 10. As you may recall, beta coefficients, which are easily derived from the regression coefficients, measure the strength of the relationship between a predictor variable and the dependent variable. These coefficients were estimated from Equations 11–2 and 11–3, then standardized, as reported in Equations 11–6 and 11–7.

$$X2 = P_{21}X1 + e2$$
$$X2 = .4262X1 + e2 \tag{11–6}$$
$$X3 = P_{31.2}X1 + P_{32.1}X2 + e3$$
$$X3 = -.2427X1 + 1.0677X2 + e3 \tag{11–7}$$

Let's interpret these in the context of Figure 11–1. Remember, there is no constant in a standardized regression relationship. P_{21}, the beta coefficient between $X1$ and $X2$, denotes that a 1 standard deviation increase (decrease) in competition yields a .426 increase (decrease) in advertising; thus, competition and advertising are related. As you may recall from Chapter 10, a beta coefficient for a bivariate relationship equals the correlation coefficient for the two variables. Let's interpret the other path coefficients.

$P_{31.2}$ is the coefficient between $X3$ and $X1$ while holding $X2$ constant; thus, the dot between 31 and 2. However, as we mentioned, this is nothing more than the beta coefficient. $P_{31.2}$ denotes that a 1 standard deviation increase in competition yields a $-.2427$ standard deviation change in sales while holding advertising effects constant.

That is, independent of competition's effect on advertising and advertising's effect on sales, a 1 standard deviation increase in competition yields a .2427 standard deviation decrease in sales. However, we know from these structural equations that as competition varies, so does advertising. Thus, the effect of competition on sales is only correctly represented when competition's effect on advertising is also considered. Remember from Chapter 10 that when relating sales only to competition, there is a positive coefficient, .477, as shown in Equation 11–8. This occurred because the effects of advertising were not included. However, as shown in Figure 11–1, the path coefficient of competition, $P_{31.2}$, is a negative .2427.

$$X3 = 37.34 + .477X1 + e \qquad \text{(11–8 and 10–2)}$$

Equation 11–8 is a misspecification of the relationship between competition and sales because it does not include advertising as in Equation 11–3. Let's interpret the other beta coefficients. However, we will use the term path coefficient instead of beta coefficient.

The path coefficient $P_{32.1}$ denotes that a 1 standard deviation change in advertising yields a 1.0677 standard deviation change in sales, independent of the concurrent changes in competition that are denoted in Equation 11–6. However, we must remember that a 1 standard deviation change in advertising has been accompanied by a .426 standard deviation change in competition. This shows that because it is not possible to completely uncouple their influences, no single measure of influence is satisfactory when there is multicollinearity; we need to interpret the simultaneous influences.

Total, Direct, and Indirect Influences

One of the several advantages of structural equations is the ability to decompose the correlation between two variables into the sum of simple and compound paths. Frequently, but not always, the compound paths provide insights and substance regarding causal relationships. Thus, when interpreting path coefficients, it is insightful to partition the correlations shown in Figure 11–1 into **direct** and **indirect** effects using the following representation.

Total	Direct	Indirect
correlation =	causal influence +	causal or noncausal influence

Through a multistep derivation similar to the derivation of PACFs of Chapter 7, which is not shown here, Equation 11–7 (or 11–3) yields the following two relationships:

$$r_{31} = P_{31.2} + P_{21}P_{32.1} \qquad \text{(11–9)}$$
$$.212 = -.2427 + .426\,(1.0677)$$

Total correlation	= Direct causal	+ Indirect causal

$$r_{32} = P_{32.1} + P_{21}P_{31.2} \qquad \text{(11–10)}$$
$$.964 = 1.0677 + .426\,(-.2427)$$

Total correlation	= Direct causal	+ Indirect noncausal

where

r_{ij} = Correlation coefficient between variables i and j
P_{ij} = Path (beta) coefficient between i and j

Let's interpret the first of these relationships, noting that r_{31} is total correlation between competition, $X1$, and sales, $X3$. $P_{31.2}$ is the direct or partial influence net of advertising effects, and $P_{21}P_{32.1}$ is the indirect influence of competition's relationship with advertising. Thus, we see that Equation 11–9 expresses the following relationship between sales and competition:

$$
\begin{array}{ccc}
\text{Total} & \text{Direct} & \text{Indirect} \\
\text{correlation} = \text{causal influence} & + & \text{causal influence}
\end{array}
$$

$$.212 = -.2427 + .426\,(1.0677)$$

The measured total correlation between competition and sales is .212, where $-.2427$ is the direct (or partial) influence between competition and sales independent of the effect of advertising. In addition, because competition and advertising are related, there is an indirect causal influence of competition on sales that operates through advertising, as measured by $P_{21}P_{32.1} = .455$ (i.e., .426 (1.0677)). The sum of the direct and indirect causal influence for competition sums to the total correlation, .212.

Because we have theory (i.e., the corporate advertising policy) to support the direction of causality in Figure 11–1, the directions of the arrows are well established. Consequently, advertising influences sales, and while it does not influence competition, on average advertising is accompanied by increased competition. Thus, our interpretation of Equation 11–10 is different than that of 11–9. For advertising and sales:

$$
\begin{array}{ccc}
\text{Total} & \text{Direct} & \text{Indirect} \\
\text{correlation} = \text{causal influence} & + & \text{noncausal influence}
\end{array}
$$

$$.964 = 1.0677 + .426\,(-.2427)$$

The measured total correlation between advertising and sales is .964, where 1.0677 is the direct (or partial) influence between advertising and sales, independent of the effect of competition. In addition, because competition influences advertising, there is an **indirect noncausal influence** of advertising on sales, as measured by $P_{21}P_{31.2} = -.1034$. This noncausal correlation is sometimes referred to as **spurious correlation**. The sum of the direct causal and indirect noncausal influences for advertising is the total correlation.

The relationship between competition and advertising is more straightforward. Because this is a simple bivariate relationship, the path coefficient is a correlation coefficient, as shown in Figure 11–1. In general, there is a tendency to think of path coefficients as correlation coefficients. However, when there is multicollinearity in a multivariate relationship, then the beta coefficients are not equal to correlation coefficients. Only when there is no multicollinearity are correlation and beta coefficients equal. Consequently, the interpretation of beta coefficients can be confusing unless a diagram such as Figure 11–1 is used in the interpretation. Finally, to assist in the interpretation of beta coefficients, consider Table 11–1.

As shown in Table 11–1, the total correlation between two variables can be partitioned into several influences. As in Equations 11–9 and 11–10, these terms are best interpreted in the context of the two paths leading to the dependent variable, sales. Consider the following interpretations of the path coefficients.

For the data of this study, competition has two effects on sales. First, there is the direct effect, which yields a .2427 standard deviation decrease in sales from a 1 standard deviation increase in competition. Second, because of the corporate policy of increasing advertising when competition is higher, higher competition yields higher advertising, which yields higher sales. This second effect results in a .455 standard deviation change in sales from a 1 standard deviation increase in competition. The indi-

Stringent Causality Requirements and Smoking

There is no concept more difficult or controversial than proof of causality. Many (but not all) researchers would agree that to state X causes Y, three conditions must exist.

1. X must precede Y in time.
2. X and Y must covary (i.e., be correlated).
3. Nothing but X changed Y and explains (1) and (2).

Condition (3) is the most difficult to prove in business and economics. Confounding the determination of condition (3) is that many events are the result of multiple (i.e., combinations) of causes. Unfortunately, when multiple causes operate, then the number of possible causal theories increases exponentially. Even with controlled experi-

mentation (e.g., feeding rats a new drug), these three conditions may be difficult to obtain.

Few debates illustrate the controversies surrounding causality more than the relationship between smoking and several forms of cancer and heart problems. As nonsmoking laymen, we find the debate ridiculous. We feel that the associations between smoking and cancers (i.e., conditions 1 and 2) are sufficient proof of the need to better regulate or ban the sale of tobacco products. The debate continues as the tobacco industry continues to either negate cause and effect studies or to put other legal roadblocks in the way of improvements to the health of our society. Fortunately, the tide has reversed and the tobacco companies are being held more causally accountable.

TABLE 11-1   Decomposition of Big City Sales Relationships

	Comp, Advert. (X1, X2)	Comp, Sales (X1, X3)	Advert, Sales (X2, X3)
Total correlation (r)	.426	.212	.964
• Causal direct influence (P)	.426	−.2427	1.0677
• Causal indirect influence	.00	.455	.00
Total causal (c)	.426	.212	1.0677
Noncausal influence ($r - c$)	.00	.00	.1034

r = Simple correlation coefficient; P = path coefficients.

rect causal influence is dependent on continuing the corporate policy of increasing advertising. The net effect of these two actions is the resulting total correlation of .212. However, this correlation might seem illogical were it not for the fact that as competition increases, so does advertising.

Lest we forget, none of this discussion is meant to prove causality, only to support alternative causal explanations. Proof of causality is quite difficult to provide without controlled experimentation, much as is done in the biological sciences.

The interpretation of the effect of advertising may seem simpler than that of competition because there is no intervening variable. However, it also has two components. A 1 standard deviation change in advertising yields a 1.0677 standard deviation change in sales if the competition does not change. However, because of the intercorrelation of competition and advertising, the effects of advertising are less (i.e., $r = .964$) because higher competition is associated with higher advertising. So the interpretation of the path coefficient of 1.0677 is contingent on holding competition constant as advertising is increased. In this case, this is not a reasonable assumption—advertising and competition covary.

Remember that all of these coefficients are based on past data. There can be sampling and nonsampling error in these data. Also, there might be a third influence on sales; if so, it should be measured. This is particularly true when one considers the small sample size.

Also, note that our interpretation of the path coefficients is based on a known or hypothetical theory. The measured path coefficients confirmed this theory by being statistically significant and having the correct signs and magnitudes. However, these results alone do not prove the theory or direction of causality.

Alternative theories often are compatible with the same path coefficients, only the direction of causality changes with the alternative theories. For example, the results of Figure 11–1 may be completely compatible with a theory that states that advertising causes greater competition. Thus, an alternative theory might reverse the direction of the arrow between *X*1 and *X*2 in Figure 11–1. We address this situation in the next section on the general assumptions of recursive structural equations.

General Assumptions of Structural Equations

Structural equations should rarely be used to determine the direction of causality between two variables. Rather, the forecaster should assign or hypothesize the direction of causality before statistical modeling begins. Therefore, a good theory should identify the direction of causality among the several variables before statistical estimation. The results of analyzing these structural equations can then lend plausibility to "causal" patterns that meet the requirements of statistical tests. An important practical approach to confirming the direction of causality in structural equations is the use of the assumption of **weak causal ordering.**

Weak Causal Order Given two variables *X*1 and *X*2, a weak causal order exists if it can be assumed that *X*1 may or may not affect *X*2, but *X*2 cannot affect *X*1. That is:

$$X1 \rightarrow X2 \quad \text{but} \quad X2 \nrightarrow X1$$

where $\rightarrow$ is an operator denoting causal direction and $\nrightarrow$ denotes *X*2 does not cause *X*1.

For example, the effects of a drug might be different for male and female patients; thus, gender influences drug effects. However, it is impossible, in most instances, to hypothesize that the drug affects gender. Frequently, the causal order between variables is clear in forecasting because one variable precedes the other in time. As shown in Figure 11–1, it is assumed that the direction of causality is from competition (*X*1) to advertising (*X*2). This direction is expected because of the corporate policy of approving greater advertising budgets for larger competition areas and the assumption that advertising does not affect the competition of the area. Thus, it is logical in this situation that competition (*X*1) causes advertising (*X*2), and that advertising (*X*2) exerts little or no influence on (i.e., doesn't cause) competition (*X*1).

Causal Closure: No Specification Errors An important assumption of structural equations is **causal closure;** that is, all important variables have been measured and included in the system of equations, particularly intervening and confounding variables. Theoretically, it is very difficult to exactly meet causal closure, since this implies perfect knowledge of causes. If such knowledge existed, little analysis would be necessary. However, our knowledge is often lacking and alternative explanations of causality require a substantial research effort that builds on earlier findings.

Fortunately, causal closure is easier to attain with larger sample sizes because these larger sample sizes may randomize or cancel the effects of the excluded or unknown exogenous variables. Thus, **randomization** helps to control for or eliminate the influences of excluded variables. However, large sample sizes may not offset serious theoretical omissions of variables in the relationship when these omitted variables are associated with the included variables. In such situations, there will be considerable bias in the estimates of the coefficients of the included variables. Thus, the forecaster should study the current body of knowledge before determining causal closure. We have been surprised at the extraordinary time and effort that analysts devote to fitting alternative relationships without spending a fraction of that time prior to analysis studying theory to better guide their modeling process. Not only would their analysis go more efficiently but also the final results would be more valid.

To better understand the concept of causal order and closure, consider the concept of partial correlation coefficients.

Partial Correlation Coefficients

Partial correlation coefficients play an important role in good structural model building. For example, we have been discussing the partial standardized regression (i.e., beta) coefficient between $X2$ and $X3$. This is the influence that exists between these two variables after their mutual or shared influence with $X1$ has been "partialed out"(eliminated or controlled for). In addition to partial *regression* coefficients, there are partial *correlation* coefficients that provide great insight into the association between variables. For example, the partial correlation coefficient between $X3$ and $X2$ can be derived using the following steps.

1. Regress $X2$ as a function of $X1$ and save the residuals of this relationship, calling these residuals $X2.1$; that is, $X2$ having controlled for $X1$. That is, run the following regression analysis and save the residuals, notating these as $X2.1$.

$$X2 = a + bX1 + e = a + bX1 + X2.1$$

2. Regress $X3$ as a function of $X1$ and save the residuals of this relationship, notating these residuals as $X3.1$; that is, $X3$ having controlled for $X1$.

$$X3 = a + bX1 + e' = a + bX1 + X3.1$$

3. Calculate the correlation coefficient between $X2.1$ and $X3.1$. This coefficient measures the degree of association between $X2$ and $X3$ that is independent of their mutual association with $X1$.

Consider the example using the Big City Bookstore multiple regression example from Chapter 11. Let's calculate the partial correlation between sales and competition while holding the influence of advertising constant.

1. Regress sales, $X3$, as a function of advertising, $X2$, saving the residuals as $X3.2$, where 3.2 denotes the value of sales after having partialed out (i.e., controlled for) the influence of advertising.

$$X3 = -23.019 + 2.280X2 + X3.2 \qquad (11\text{--}11)$$

where

$X3 =$ Sales
$X2 =$ Advertising
$X3.2 =$ Residuals, sales controlled for advertising

2. Regress competition as a function of advertising, saving the residuals as $X1.2$, denoting competition after having partialed out the influence of advertising.

$$X1 = 7.750 + .4489X2 + X1.2 \qquad (11-12)$$

where

$X1 = $ Competition
$X2 = $ Advertising
$X1.2 = $ Residuals, competition having controlled for advertising

3. Calculate the correlation between $X3.2$ and $X1.2$.

Having controlled for the correlation between sales and competition each with advertising, the correlation coefficient is:

$$r_{31.2} = -.828$$

The negative sign of this correlation is expected. In contrast, when not controlling for advertising, the correlation between sales and competition is:

$$r_{31} = .212$$

Thus, the partial correlation coefficient $r_{31.2}$ measures the degree of association between sales and competition that is independent of their mutual association with advertising. Simply stated, the measured correlation coefficient between two variables consists of two components, the direct and indirect correlation. We introduced partial autocorrelation coefficients in Appendix 7–G and that discussion is germane to this one.

Now, let's study the concepts of causal order and causal closure in more detail, using the six examples shown in Figure 11–2a to f.

Causal Order and Closure

In Figure 11–2a, b, and c, the correlation between $X2$ and $X3$ is completely measured by relating $X2$ directly with $X3$. In other words, the correlation between $X2$ and $X3$ is unaffected by the influence $X1$. Thus, these two variables are causally closed. In contrast, the correlations between $X2$ and $X3$ in Figure 11–2d, e and f are influenced by a third variable, $X1$.

In 11–2e and f, the correlation between $X2$ and $X3$ is completely dependent on their common relationship with $X1$. The correlation coefficients, $r_{23.1}$, between $X2$ and $X3$ after partialing out the influence of $X1$, will be zero. Thus, there is no direct correlation between $X2$ and $X3$; they are indirectly dependent. In 11–2d, the total correla-

FIGURE 11–2

Some possible trivariate causal relationships

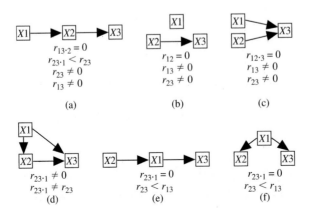

tion between $X2$ and $X3$ is due in part to a direct relationship between them and an indirect noncausal relationship with $X1$. In 11–2e and f, there is no direct correlation between $X2$ and $X3$, only indirect correlation operating through $X1$; thus, $r_{23.1} = 0$. In 11–2d through f, the correlations of $X2$ and $X3$ are not closed to outside influences; that is, they are not causally closed, the correlation is influenced by $X1$.

If one were to explore the relationship between $X2$ and $X3$ using a bivariate regression on a sample of sufficient size, the regression coefficients and their interpretations would be accurate under the causal structures identified in 11–2a, b, and c in Figure 11–2. However, estimates of the relationships between $X2$ and $X3$ under causal structures of Figure 11–2d, e and f will probably be incorrect if based solely on their bivariate relationship. Consequently, if you assume that the relationship between $X2$ and $X3$ are causally closed, then this is correct under structures 11–2a, b, and c and incorrect *under* 11–2d through f.

Thus, we see that in order to correctly model causal relationships, the researcher must correctly identify the direction of weak causal order and the variables that are necessary to have causal closure. While it is not possible to conclusively confirm a particular causal closure, it is possible, as Simon and Blalock illustrated, to test a specific causal model by comparing predicted to actual correlations (Blalock, 1964).

Consider the causal model of Figure 11–2a, $X1 \rightarrow X2 \rightarrow X3$. This model is confirmed if the correlation between $X1$ and $X3$ is much less than that between $X1$ and $X2$ and between $X2$ and $X3$, and the partial correlation between $X1$ and $X3$ with $X2$ held constant is zero; that is, $r_{13.2}$. If the actual results of analysis confirm these correlations, then the structure is also confirmed. If, in contrast, the measured correlations are inconsistent with the theory, then the theory may be incorrect in causal ordering, causal closure, or both. However, if the weak causal ordering is unsupported by theory, then the correlations mentioned are consistent with other directions of causality: $X3 \rightarrow X2 \rightarrow X1$ or $X2 \rightarrow X1$ and $X2 \rightarrow X3$. Herein lies the importance of theory-driven causal ordering and closure.

Finally note that for convenience, Figure 11–2 shows r, however, it is P (rho), the true population correlation coefficient that will equal the values shown there. Thus, the sample coefficient r will have sampling error, therefore it is unlikely that any r's will equal exactly zero. However, typically the r's should not be statistically significantly greater or less than zero given a ρ of zero if a sufficiently large sample size is used.

Therefore, if the direction of a causal order is unknown or unmeasured independent variables greatly influence the dependent variable, we may lack sufficient theory to construct structural equation models. However, these models may still be used to support exploratory work during the modeling process. Thus, alternative models may be specified when structures are uncertain. Then models may be confirmed on one data set and subsequently tested on other data. However, remember that causal closure does not preclude confounding influences.

Unfortunately, we have just touched the surface of causal modeling the relationship between correlations and the direction of causality. Those seeking additional information are directed to Ascher (1983) as a best starting point.

Specification Errors   Lack of causal closure is one form of model **specification error.** From a statistical standpoint, omitting relevant explanatory variables results in biased and inaccurate coefficients when these omitted variables are correlated with independent variables of the model. Substantively, these omissions denote a flawed understanding and representation of causal relationships. Other types of specification errors are inclusion of irrelevant variables, choosing incorrect functional forms (i.e., linear versus nonlinear

---

What Are Theories?

The theoretical physicist Stephen Hawking defines a theory as "a model of the universe, or a restricted part of it, and a set of rules that relates quantities in the model to observations we make" (1988, p. 9) While Hawking is interested in theories that explain the universe, his definition relates to causal modeling and forecasting. Hawking states that a good theory should:

1. Accurately represent (i.e., model) a large number of observations as simply as possible.
2. Accurately predicts future events.
3. Be stated in a way that can be disproved if it is incorrect.

Source: Stephen Hawking, A Brief History of Time, New York: Bantam.

---

functions), incorrect functional form of error terms or distribution of errors and disregard of interaction effects (Pindyck and Rubinfeld, 1991). Occasionally, specification errors may be detected on the basis of low explained variance (low $\overline{R}^2$) and incorrect signs of regression coefficients. However, detection of errors through such analysis may be unreliable (Theil, 1957) unless theory helps drive the error-detection process.

Finally, because OLS regression is used to estimate coefficients in recursive structural equations, the assumptions of regression analysis are operable. While ordinary least squares has been found to be robust, serious violations of its assumptions can invalidate inferences.

Specification Errors, Randomization, and Sample Size Effects

This section illustrates the consequences of specification errors by illustrating the effects of having a small sample size with imperfect theory (i.e., lack of causal closure). We see that:

- Erroneous coefficient estimates result when small sample sizes are used with specification errors.
- Less erroneous but nonetheless biased coefficient estimates are obtained with larger sample sizes and specification errors.
- Correct coefficient estimates are possible with small sample sizes and no specification errors.
- Most accurate coefficient estimates occur with large sample sizes and no specification errors.

These four conclusions are summarized in Table 11–2.

To illustrate these concepts, a simple three-variable relationship is used. The correct causal order of this relationship is illustrated in Figure 11–2c and below as $X1 \rightarrow Y$ and $X2 \rightarrow Y$, and $X1$ and $X2$ are uncorrelated; that is:

TABLE 11–2   Probability of Valid Model

	Small Sample	Large Sample
Correct specification	Medium	High
Incorrect specification	Very low	Low

The causal model that generated this data is:

$$Y = 1,200 + 300X1 + 300X2 + e \qquad \text{(Correct model)} \qquad (11\text{–}13)$$

where $\overline{X1} = 100, \overline{X2} = 100, \text{COV}(X1,X2) = .0$

In the next four sections, we fit two different samples with two different models having $X2$ included and excluded. However, the correct model is one with both $X1$ and $X2$, as shown in Equation 11–13.

Small Sample, Incorrect Specification

Assume that a researcher mistakenly assumes that Y is only related to $X1$ and not $X2$; then he or she fits the relationship

$$Y = a + bX1 + e$$

using a small sample size (e.g., $n = 30$). Figure 11–3 illustrates a scatter plot of the values of Y and $X1$ that result from a small sample. As shown, there does not appear to be a very strong relationship between these two variables. Table 11–3 illustrates the estimated regression relationship using this data. The negative $\overline{R}^2$ ($-.0094$) and the low t-value on the regression coefficient of $X1$ ($t = .85421$) denote that no statistically significant relationship has been found between Y and $X1$. These results mislead the researcher because in fact $X1$ does influence Y. Also, the researcher is unaware of the relationship between Y and $X2$.

In this sample, the influence of $X1$ on Y was confounded by the fact that by *chance*, the sampled values of Y were negatively correlated with the excluded variable $X2$. This is clear in Figure 11–4, where we see for this sample that $X1$ and $X2$ are negatively related. Thus, in the regression of Table 11–3, $X2$'s influence on Y masked the influence of $X1$ on Y.

After taking a larger sample, we find that the negative correlation between $X1$ and $X2$ is a result of the small sample. Also, it is not difficult to imagine such biased sampling when $X1$ and $X2$ are actually inversely related. Thus, the possibility of misspecifications will increase. Whatever the cause of the bias, the researcher using small sample sizes and incorrect specifications faces a difficult task in finding valid predictive and causal relationships.

Large Sample, Incorrect Specification, Hopes of Randomization

Let's assume that the researcher now takes a larger sample of the 100 observations shown in Figure 11–5. Consider the regression results in Table 11–4. While the sample is larger, the researcher still has incorrect specifications. The results exemplified in Table 11–4 are better than those of Table 11–3, but they are still flawed because the true regression coefficient for $X1$ is 300 while the fitted value is 256.9. Thus, the influence of $X2$ has not been completely randomized and it has influenced the estimated value of b_1.

FIGURE 11–3

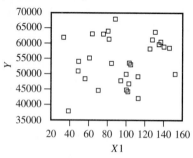

FIGURE 11–4

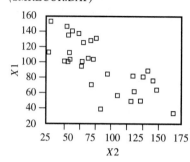

FIGURE 11–5

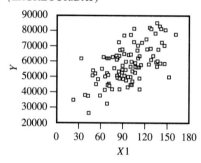

TABLE 11–3 Small Sample Regression, Not Controlling for $X2$ (SMRECUR.DAT)

Dependent variable Y—Estimation by least squares

Usable observations	30
Degrees of freedom	28
$\overline{R}^2$	−.0094
Standard error of dependent variable	7730.000
Standard error of estimate	7766.282
Sum of squared residuals	1688823727.7
Regression $F(1, 28)$	.7297
Significance level of F	.40024
Durbin–Watson statistic	2.426

Variable	Coeff	Std Error	t-Stat	Signif
Constant	50740.779	4399.217	11.534	.00000000
X1	37.170	45.513	.854	.40024

TABLE 11–4 Large Sample Regression, Randomization of $X2$ (LRGRECUR.DAT)

Dependent variable Y—Estimation by least squares

Usable observations	100
Degrees of freedom	98
$\overline{R}^2$	.3608
Standard error of dependent variable	12488.373
Standard error of estimate	9984.250
Sum of squared residuals	9769155147.0
Regression $F(1, 98)$	156.887
Significance level of F	.00000000
Durbin–Watson statistic	1.8498

Variable	Coeff	Std Error	t-Stat	Signif
Constant	33234.225	3450.863	9.631	.00000000
X1	256.939	34.066	7.542	.00000000

Because the effects of $X2$ are somewhat randomized, these results are quite good, not deviating greatly from the true values (e.g., 256.9 versus 300). While the researcher may be disappointed in $\overline{R}^2$, the relationship is nonetheless very significant; however, the low $\overline{R}^2$ denotes that a significant percentage of the variance of Y remains unexplained. This low $\overline{R}^2$ should suggest the need to find the cause of the remaining unexplained variance; that is, the missing variable $X2$.

Having seen the effects of incorrect specifications with two sample sizes, let's explore the effect of sample sizes when the correct causal closure exists.

Small Sample, Correct Specification

Table 11–5 illustrates the fitted regression relationship for the small sample size of Table 11–3 but with correctly specified variables. Because these results are obtained with $X1$ and $X2$ as predictor variables of Y, we see that the estimated model is more accurate than the one with the large sample size in Table 11–4. The estimated coefficients are very significant and nearly equal to those used to generate the data. Also, the $\overline{R}^2$ is quite high.

In general, a sample size of 30 is not sufficient to identify a valid model. However, as shown by this example, if the relationship is a strong one and good theory drives the analysis, the resulting model can be quite accurate. The model with the correct specifications and large sample sizes is even more valid.

Large Sample, Correct Specification

Table 11–6 illustrates the regression results using the same values of Y and $X1$ used in Table 11–4, the relationship without $X2$. However, Table 11–6 includes the variable $X2$. The fitted model of Table 11–6 is obviously the best of those estimated because it uses good theory and an adequate sample size. While there is some error in the fitted model, this error is certainly in the bounds of expected values. The model of Table 11–6 yields an $\overline{R}^2$ of .99 and regression coefficients that from a statistical standpoint equal those of the true underlying relationship. There is no need to interpret the slope constant a because as we have emphasized several times, it is a catchall for the influences of the other, minor variables not included in the relationship.

TABLE 11–5 **Small Sample Regression, Correct Specification (SMRECUR.DAT)**

Dependent variable Y—Estimation by least squares

Usable observations				30
Degrees of freedom				27
$\overline{R}^2$				.9649
Standard error of dependent variable				7730.000
Standard error of estimate				1448.538
Sum of squared residuals				56653107.687
Regression $F(2, 27)$				399.421
Significance level of F				.00000000
Durbin–Watson statistic				2.1535

Variable	Coeff	Std Error	t-Stat	Signif
Constant	795.063	1969.823	.4036	.68966982
$X1$	293.954	12.273	23.9504	.00000000
$X2$	296.636	10.636	27.8903	.00000000

There are many other possible misspecifications that might result in large sample bias when important variables are not included in the relationship. While not graphically illustrated here, the exclusion of $X2$ from the model might have had different effects depending on $X2$'s relationship with $X1$ and Y. For example, exclusion of $X2$ might have made the relationship with Y and $X1$ appear to be inverse if $X2$'s influence on $X3$ was strong and inverse. Also, note that if $X2$ had no influence on Y, then its exclusion would not have affected the relationship between Y and $X1$.

Table 11–7 summarizes the results of the four combinations of causal closure and sample sizes. It clearly illustrates the importance and effectiveness of having good theory and correct causal closure when fitting relationships.

TABLE 11–6   Large Sample Regression, Correct Specification (LRGRECUR.DAT)

Dependent variable Y—Estimation by least squares

Usable observations	100
Degrees of freedom	97
$\overline{R}^2$	.9933
Standard error of dependent variable	12488.373
Standard error of estimate	1025.285
Sum of squared residuals	101967402.83
Regression $F(2, 97)$	7295.4095
Significance level of F	.00000000
Durbin–Watson statistic	2.016

Variable	Coeff	Std Error	t-Stat	Signif
Constant	−118.6965	496.5304	−.2390	.8116
X1	299.8341	3.5267	85.0175	.00000000
X2	301.7198	3.1463	95.8971	.00000000

TABLE 11–7   Validity of Models with and without Causal Closure

	Small Sample (n = 30)	Large Sample (n = 100)
Correct specification	Medium validity $a = 795.67$ (.40) $b1 = 293.95$ (24) $b2 = 296.64$ (28)	High validity $a = -118.7$ (−.23) $b1 = 299.83$ (85) $b2 = 301.72$ (96)
Incorrect specification— X2 omitted	Very low validity $a = 50,740$ (12) $b1 = 37.17$ (.85)	Low validity $a = 33,234$ (9.63) $b1 = 256.9$ (7.54)
Population true values	$A = 1,200,$ $B1 = 300,$ $B2 = 300$	

Coefficients and (*t*-values) included in table.

Coincidences and Common Causes

"There is a familiar pattern of causal reasoning that we all use every day, usually without being consciously aware of it. Confronted with what appears to be an improbable coincidence, we seek a common cause. If the common cause can be found, it is invoked to explain the coincidence."[a]

In a posthumous book, the *Direction of Time*, Hans Reichenbach presented the principle of the common cause.

"When apparent coincidences occur that are too improbable to be attributed to chance, they can be explained by reference to a common causal antecedent."[b]

Consider a simple example. Assume that on average only 1 out of 1,000 individuals will randomly experience nausea after eating a properly prepared meal. However, after a dinner party with 10 diners, 8 experience severe intestinal distress. Immediately, we seek a common cause because the probability of 8 out of 10 individuals being ill if there is no common cause is calculated as a binomial probability of 8 out of 10 occurrences when the simple probability of 1 occurrence is 1/1,000. This is an extremely low probability of approximately zero.

In this illustration, on investigation, it was found that the 8 ill individuals all ate specially prepared mushrooms, while the 2 well individuals did not. We immediately infer that the mushrooms are the cause. A quick trip to the hospital and the analysis of the contents of 8 stomachs will confirm or deny the diagnosis.

While this example is so simple as to have an obvious explanation, other more complex situations commonly occur, and at times our diagnoses are incorrect. We must strive to objectively and methodically seek and confirm common causes.

———————

a. Wesley C. Salman, *Scientific Explanation and the Causal Structure of the World* (Princeton, NJ: Princeton University Press, 1984), pp. 158–59.

b. Hans Reichenbach, *The Direction of Time* (Berkeley and Los Angeles: University of California Press, 1956).

c. There is no medical basis for .001, in fact this may be too high a probability.

Source: Wesley C. Salman, *Scientific Explanation and the Causal Structure of the World* (Princeton, NJ: Princeton University Press, 1984).

Granger Causality

We have seen that it is difficult to prove that a causal relationship exists among phenomena. At a minimum, there appears to be agreement that causality requires at least three conditions:

1. Correlation among the variables.
2. Temporal asymmetry (i.e., time precedence) among phenomena.
3. Elimination of the possibility that other phenomena produced the observed covariation (Asher, 1983).

A useful test for causality in time series models related to conditions (1) and (2) is based on the research of C. W. J. Granger (1969). As Granger points out, it is difficult to determine the direction of causality when there are high degrees of autorecorrelation in variables. As we saw in Chapter 10, when high degrees of autocorrelation exist within X_t and Y_t, then OLS yields unreliable RSEs and therefore unreliable diagnostic statistics. Thus, the importance of the autoregressive procedures of Cochrane–Orcutt and Prais–Winsten. While these methods provide consistent RSEs and *t*-values, they do not provide a methodological confirmation of the direction of causality. Granger developed methods to determine whether variables are temporally related.

The **Granger causality test** is based on the fact that the future cannot affect the past. A test is made to show whether lagged values of X_t significantly explain Y_t. If Y_t is a mathematical function of X_{t-m} where m is positive, then causality may exist. As we will see, the Granger test uses the partial *F*-test described in Chapter 10. However, in this case, it is lagged variables that are included and excluded.

Granger-Causality Test

1. Run an **unrestricted** regression using arbitrarily long lags on the dependent and independent variables (i.e., use arbitrarily high m values on Y_{t-m} and X_{t-m} and note the unrestricted error sum of squares (ESS*u*). That is, fit the following relationships:

$$Y_t = f(Y_{t-1}, Y_{t-2}, \ldots, Y_{t-m}, X_{t-1}, X_{t-2}, \ldots, X_{t-m})$$

2. Omit all of the X_{t-m} terms from the relationship, run regression on the remaining variables, and retain the **restricted** error sum of squares (ESS*r*). That is, fit the following relationship:

$$Y_t = f(Y_{t-1}, Y_{t-2}, \ldots, Y_{t-m})$$

3. Perform an *F*-test on the following:

Null	$X \nrightarrow Y$	(*X* does not Granger-cause *Y*)
Alternative	$X \rightarrow Y$	(*X* does Granger-cause *Y*)

$$F_{r, n-m-k} = \frac{(\text{ESS}r - \text{ESS}u)/r}{\text{ESS}u/(n - m - k)} \tag{11–14}$$

where

n = Number of observations in total
m = Number of lags for dependent and independent variables, the number of degrees of freedom lost from lagging
r = Number of restricted terms when calculating ESS*r*
k = Number of coefficients in unrestricted model
$n - m - k$ = Degrees of freedom for unrestricted model

If the *F*-calculated value exceeds the *F*-table value at the selected level of significance (e.g., .05), then the null hypothesis is rejected and the alternative accepted; otherwise, the null hypothesis is accepted.

4. To confirm the direction of causality (i.e., weak causal ordering), then steps 1 through 3 are repeated to test whether Y_t Granger-causes X_t. That is, the roles of Y_t and X_t are reversed when performing the Granger causality test on whether movements in Y_t precede changes in X_t.

Example of Granger Causality Test

Let's run this test on the U.K. and U.S. stock index (UKUSIND.DAT) relationship developed in Chapter 10. Recall that two stock indexes were measured over time, using 271 monthly observations. Because these series are nonstationary, logarithmic values are used. The first unrestricted model is:

$$\ln\text{UK}_t = f(\ln\text{UK}_t, \ldots, \ln\text{UK}_{t-4}, \ln\text{US}_t, \ldots, \ln\text{UK}_{t-4} + e_t)$$

where

$\ln\text{UK}$ = Logarithm of U.K. stock price index
$\ln\text{US}$ = Logarithm of U.S. stock price index

In this model, it is assumed that the U.S. stock index influences or causes changes in the U.K. stock index. To test this, fit the unrestricted model and the following restricted model:

$$\ln\text{UK}_t = f(\ln\text{UK}_t, \ldots, \ln\text{UK}_{t-4} + e_t)$$

Here are the fits of these models:

- *Unrestricted model*

$$\text{SSE}u = .66195 \quad \overline{R}^2 = .9963 \quad Q\text{-statistic}(36) = 28.89 \quad (\alpha = .7940)$$

$$n = 271 \quad m = 4 \quad k = 9$$

- *Restricted model*

$$\text{SSF}r = .69634 \quad \overline{R}^2 = .9961 \quad Q\text{-statistic}(36) = 28.94 \quad (\alpha = .7922)$$

$$n = 271 \quad m = 4 \quad k = 5 \quad r = 4$$

$$F_{r, n-m-k} = \frac{(\text{ESS}r - \text{ESS}u)/r}{\text{ESS}u/(n - k - m)}$$

$$F_{4, 271-4-9} = \frac{(.69634 - .66195)/4}{.66195/258} = 3.351$$

$$F\text{-table } (4,400, \alpha = .01) = 3.37 \quad (4,258 \text{ not available})$$

Because $F_{4,271-4-9} > F$-table, reject the null hypothesis and accept the alternative, movements in X_{t-k} precede Y_t; that is, movements in the U.S. stock index in previous periods are associated with current movements in the U.K. index. Having shown a direction of influence from U.S. to U.K. indexes, let's ensure that there is no mutual association by testing the influence of lagged values of the U.K. index on the U.S. index.

The unrestricted model is:

$$\ln\text{US}_t = f(\ln\text{US}_t, \ldots, \ln\text{US}_{t-4}, \ln\text{UK}_t, \ldots, \ln\text{UK}_{t-4} + e_t)$$

In this model, it is assumed that the U.K. stock index influences or causes changes in the U.S. stock index. To test this, fit the unrestricted model and the following restricted model:

$$\ln\text{US}_t = f(\ln\text{US}_t, \ldots, \ln\text{US}_{t-4} + e_t)$$

Here are the fits of these two models:

- *Unrestricted model*

$$\text{SSE}u = .33167 \quad \overline{R}^2 = .9951 \quad Q\text{-statistic}(36) = 24.93 \quad (\alpha = .9174)$$

$$n = 271 \quad m = 4 \quad k = 9$$

- *Restricted model*

$$\text{SSE}r = .33926 \quad \overline{R}^2 = .9951 \quad Q\text{-statistic}(36) = 25.77 \quad (\alpha = .8967)$$

$$n = 271 \quad m = 4 \quad k = 5 \quad r = 4$$

$$F_{4, 271-4-9} = \frac{(.33926 - .33167)/4}{.33167/258} = 1.476$$

$$F\text{-table } (4,400, \alpha = .01) = 3.37$$

$$F\text{-table } (4,400, \alpha = .05) = 2.39$$

Because $F_{4,271-4-9} < F$-table, accept the null hypothesis and reject the alternative. Movements in $\ln\text{UK}_{t-k}$ do not precede those in $\ln\text{US}_t$. Thus, the value of the U.K. stock index in previous periods is not associated with current movements in the U.S. index. These are the same results as in Chapter 13 using the MARIMA methods.

Limitations of Granger Causality

The limitations of this method include:

1. The number of lags included in the unrestricted relationship can affect the level of significance of F. For example, with small samples, the choice of one lag of m versus longer lags (e.g., using m of 4 versus m of 8) affect the F-test.

2. In general, there is no good way to determine the lag length used for independent variables.

3. Econometricians have been able to show that the Granger test can yield conflicting results.

4. Granger causality is not proof of causality, it is confirmation of the direction of influence. It does not address the issues of causal closure. That is, there may be specification errors in the relationship.

However, Granger causality tests are still very useful in providing further confirmation of the direction of influence. Finally, when applicable, it is more appropriate to use the MARIMA methods of Chapter 13 to identify the direction of influence between the lags of several variables, particularly when there is considerable autocorrelated structure in the dependent and independent variables.

Simultaneous Equations—Nonrecursive Structural Equations

When variables are mutually related (e.g., $X \rightarrow Y$ and $Y \rightarrow X$), then their relationship should be modeled using a set of nonrecursive equations. In business and economics, nonrecursive equations are called **simultaneous equations.** This term is descriptive because X and Y are determined simultaneously; Y causes X while simultaneously X causes Y. This simultaneity presents problems when using OLS to estimate the structural equations. OLS yields biased and inconsistent coefficients, a condition referred to as **simultaneous equation bias.** Thus, nonrecursive relationships must be solved differently than recursive equations, the most common method being **two-stage least squares (2SLS)** which we illustrate in a moment. As we will see, to estimate consistent coefficients, the reduced-form equations of the model must be estimated. Reduced-form equations express each endogenous variable as a function of all predetermined variables in a system of equations.

Consider the following nonrecursive relationships between sales, advertising, population, and competition for the Building Materials Suppliers company (hereafter BMS). Based on past analysis, the management of BMS has arrived at the following causal structure:

$$S_t = a_0 + a_1 A_t + a_2 C_t + e1_t \tag{11-15}$$

$$A_t = b_0 + b_1 S_t + b_2 P_t + e2_t \tag{11-16}$$

where

S_t = Sales of 100 stores ($), an endogenous variable
A_t = Advertising ($), an endogenous variable
P_t = Do-It-Yourself population in five-mile ring, an exogenous variable
C_t = Weighted measure of market competition (000), an exogenous variable
ei_t = Errors in estimating each relationship

As shown in Equations 11–15 and 11–16, advertising affects sales, and sales affect advertising. Thus, sales and advertising are mutually dependent. Because

Equations 11–15 and 11–16 are mutually dependent, the values of sales and advertising are simultaneously determined. In order to get consistent estimates of population parameters, it is necessary to apply a procedure like two-stage least square (2SLS).

Simultaneity Problems

The problem with simultaneity is that with simultaneously determined endogenous variables OLS provides biased estimates of regression coefficients. Also, this bias does not decrease as the sample size increases.

The problem of bias is evident in Equations 11–15 and 11–16 because, for example, a change in $e1$ affects S in Equation 11–15. In turn, S affects A in Equation 11–16. As a result, A and $e1$ are correlated and estimates of the regression coefficients are biased and inconsistent.

There are a number of alternative methods for estimating parameters with nonrecursive structural equations, including indirect least squares (ILS), two-stage least squares (2SLS), and three-stage least squares (3SLS). In this chapter, we develop 2SLS and briefly discuss ILS and 3SLS.

Currently, there are no techniques that yield estimators with desirable properties when estimating simultaneous equations with small samples. However, for large samples, two-stage least squares (2SLS) provides efficient, consistent, and less biased estimates of regression parameters. In addition, the standard errors and t-values of individual coefficients are approximately correct for 2SLS.

Identification Requirements

In order to validly estimate a structural equation, it is necessary, but not sufficient, that the system be identifiable. Certain conditions must exist before it is possible to estimate coefficients (i.e., identify unique coefficients). In order for this to occur, the following conditions must be met: The number of **Excluded PRedetermined variables (EPR)** in an equation must be greater than or equal to the number of **Included ENdogenous variables (IEN)** minus 1. If EPR is less than IEN − 1, then the model cannot be estimated. This requirement yields the following simple rules:

Exactly identified	EPR = IEN − 1	Equation might be estimated using 2SLS.
Overidentified	EPR > IEN − 1	Equation might be estimated using 2SLS, but several solutions exist.
Underidentified	EPR < IEN − 1	Equation cannot be estimated.

These identification rules (called order conditions) are necessary, but may not be sufficient, rules. However, in most situations they are sufficient.[*]

If an equation of a system is **exactly identified,** then a unique value of the coefficients can be estimated from the reduced-form relationships. If an equation of a system is **overidentified,** then more than one numerical value can be calculated from some of the coefficients in the reduced-form relationships. If an equation of a system

_____

[*]A more technical definition of the identification rules as a sufficient condition for identification is given by the rank condition of the set of equations. A system of M equations is fully identifiable if, for all equations, it is possible to obtain one nonzero determinant of order $M − 1$ from the coefficients of the variables excluded from that particular equation but included in the other equations of the model. When this condition is satisfied, the order condition is also satisfied. Among other things, this rule precludes perfect multicollinearity in exogenous and endogenous variables (see Kmenta, 1986).

is **underidentified,** then no coefficients can be calculated from the reduced-form relationships. Let's apply 2SLS using these rules on the data of the Building Materials Supply company.

Two-Stage Least Squares (2SLS)

2SLS is a method for estimating consistent coefficients for both exactly and overidentified equations of a simultaneous set of relationships (a concept discussed in a moment). The term *two-stage* refers to fitting OLS models in two stages. Stage 1 yields fitted endogenous values to be used in stage 2 where these fitted values replace their original values on the right-hand sides of each original equation. Consider this two-stage procedure in greater detail.

1. In the first step of 2SLS, OLS is used to fit relationships of each endogenous variable versus all predetermined variables (i.e., exogenous and **lagged endogenous variables**). Thus, all endogenous variables are regressed as a function of all **predetermined variables.**

This first step is valid because it is possible to eliminate each right-hand-side endogenous variable (e.g., A and S of Equations 11–15 and 11–16, respectively) from all equations through a process of substitution. This process of substitution results in relationships where each endogenous variable is a function of all predetermined variables. This process yields what is referred to as a reduced form of the original equation (we illustrate this substitution in a moment.)

Using OLS, fit regression coefficients to the reduced-form equations. That is, estimate:

$$S_t = \Pi_0 + \Pi_1 C_t + \Pi_2 P_t + v1_t \tag{11–17}$$

$$A_t = \Pi_3 + \Pi_4 C_t + \Pi_5 P_t + v2_t \tag{11–18}$$

From the reduced-form OLS results, calculate fitted values of each of the endogenous variables.

$$\hat{S}_t = \Pi_0 + \Pi_1 C_t + \Pi_2 P_t \tag{11–19}$$

$$\hat{A}_t = \Pi_3 + \Pi_4 C_t + \Pi_5 P_t \tag{11–20}$$

2. Substitute the fitted values from the reduced-form equations into the right-hand sides of the original equations of step 1, (i.e., Equations 11–15 and 11–16):

$$S_t = a_0 + a_1 \hat{A}_t + a_2 C_t + e1_t \tag{11–21}$$

$$A_t = b_0 + b_1 \hat{S}_t + b_2 P_t + e2_t \tag{11–22}$$

Typically, the resulting coefficients of Equations 11–21 and 11–22 are more efficient and consistent estimators of the true model parameters than those of OLS. We'll apply this method in a moment. First, let's discuss reduced-form equations.

Reduced-Form Equations

As shown in step 2, 2SLS yields one reduced-form equation for each endogenous variable, and each reduced-form equation contains all of the predetermined variables of the system. Note that each of the reduced-form equations, 11–17 and 11–18, include only one endogenous variable and that each has the same set of independent variables. In general, for structural equation models, each exogenous variable is included as an independent variable in each reduced-form equation. In addition to exogenous variables, all lagged endogenous variables are included in the reduced-form equations. The exogenous and lagged endogenous variables are referred to as predetermined variables. Lagged endogenous variables are predetermined because it is not possible for values in time t to change or influence values in a previous time period—for example, $t - 1$. While not explanatory, these reduced-form equations are useful predictive relationships.

The reduced-form equations are easily derived as follows:

Given:
$$S_t = a_0 + a_1 A_t + a_2 C_t + e1_t \qquad \text{(First)}$$
$$A_t = b_0 + b_1 S_t + b_2 P_t + e2_t \qquad \text{(Second)}$$

Substituting the RHS of the second equation into the first:
$$S_t = a_0 + a_1(b_0 + b_1 S_t + b_2 P_t + e2_t) + a_2 C_t + e1_t$$

Then substituting the RHS of the first equation into the second:
$$A_t = b_0 + b_1(a_0 + a_1 A_t + a_2 C_t + e1_t) + b_2 P_t + e2_t$$

Now, simplifying each of the above as follows:
$$S_t = a_0 + a_1 b_0 + a_1 b_1 S_t + a_1 b_2 P_t + a_1 e2_t + a_2 C_t + e1_t$$
$$S_t - a_1 b_1 S_t = a_0 + a_1 b_0 + a_1 b_2 P_t + a_1 e2_t + a_2 C_t + e1_t$$
$$(1 - a_1 b_1)S_t = a_0 + a_1 b_0 + a_1 b_2 P_t + a_2 C_t + a_1 e2_t + e1_t$$
$$S_t = \frac{a_0 + a_1 b_0}{(1 - a_1 b_1)} + \frac{a_1 b_2 P_t}{(1 - a_1 b_1)} + \frac{a_2 C_t}{(1 - a_1 b_1)} + \frac{a_1 e2_t + e1_t}{(1 - a_1 b_1)}$$

Designating each term before each variable as a Π-coefficient:
$$S_t = \Pi_0 + \Pi_1 C_t + \Pi_2 P_t + v1_t \qquad (11\text{--}23)$$

This is called the reduced-form equation of (11–15). Now let's derive the reduced-form equation for A_t.

$$A_t = b_0 + b_1 a_0 + b_1 a_1 A_t + b_1 a_2 C_t + b_1 e1_t + b_2 P_t + e2_t$$
$$A_t - b_1 a_1 A_t = b_0 + b_1 a_0 + b_1 a_2 C_t + b_2 P_t + b_1 e1_t + e2_t$$
$$A_t = \frac{b_0 + b_1 a_0}{1 - b_1 a_1} + \frac{b_1 a_2 C_t}{1 - b_1 a_1} + \frac{b_2 P_t}{1 - b_1 a_1} + \frac{b_1 e1_t + e2_t}{1 - b_1 a_1}$$

Designating each term before each variable as a Π-coefficient:
$$A_t = \Pi_3 + \Pi_4 C_t + \Pi_5 P_t + v2_t \qquad (11\text{--}24)$$

Thus, we see that each endogenous variable in a system of equations is related to each exogenous variable of the system. These reduced-form equations are used in the 2SLS procedure developed below. However, before applying 2SLS, it is necessary to confirm that a system of equations is identifiable.

Building Materials Example of 2SLS (BMS.DAT)

1. Equations 11–15 and 11–16 are repeated next as Equations 11–25 and 11–26. Are these equations underidentified, exactly identified, or overidentified?

$$S_t = a_0 + a_1 A_t + a_2 C_t + e1_t \qquad (11\text{--}25)$$
$$A_t = b_0 + b_1 S_t + b_2 P_t + e2_t \qquad (11\text{--}26)$$

Noting that S and A are endogenous variables and P and C are exogenous, we see that Equations 11–25 and 11–26 are both exactly identified equations. In Equation 11–25, EPR is 1 (i.e., variable P is excluded) and this equals IEN minus 1 (i.e., S and A, 2–1). In Equation 11–26, EPR is 1 (i.e., variable C is excluded) and this equals IEN minus 1 (i.e., A and S, 2–1). Having established that each equation of this system of equations is exactly identified, let's perform 2SLS. (Note that in systems of equations, different equations have different order conditions, being over, under, or exactly identifiable. Thus, identification requirements are checked equation by equation.)

2. Stage 1. In this step, each endogenous variable is regressed versus all exogenous variables. Equations 11–27 and 11–28 illustrate the results of this fitting process. Note that the t-values of the regression coefficients are shown in parentheses below the estimated coefficients.

$$S = 10{,}511.55 - 1.341C + 7.337P + e \qquad (11\text{–}27)$$
$$(1{,}003.85)\ (-9.847)\quad (59.271)$$

$$\overline{R}^2 = .975 \quad \text{RSE} = 38.120 \quad F = 1{,}939.273(.000000) \quad \text{DW} = 2.007 \quad n = 100$$

$$A = 3{,}097.80 - .2065C + 2.565P + e' \qquad (11\text{–}28)$$
$$(306.88)\quad (-1.574)\qquad (21.497)$$

$$\overline{R}^2 = .8302 \quad \text{RSE} = 36.749 \quad F = 243.13(.0000000) \quad \text{DW} = 1.947 \quad n = 100$$

3. Given Equations 11–27 and 11–28, we can now calculate the fitted values of S and A, which are notated as usual as $\hat{S}$ and $\hat{A}$.

4. Stage 2. Replace right-hand side endogenous variables with fitted values, $\hat{S}$ and $\hat{A}$ from Equations 11–27 and 11–28, and fit an OLS of the original relationship. The 2SLS results are given in Equations 11–29 and 11–30.

$$S = 1{,}651.820 + 2.86\hat{A} - .750C + e \qquad (11\text{–}29)$$
$$(10.531)\quad (59.271)\quad (-5.434)$$

$$\overline{R}^2 = .975 \quad \text{RSE} = 38.120 \quad F = 1939.273(.0000000) \quad \text{DW} = 2.007 \quad n = 100$$

$$A = 1{,}478.376 + .154\hat{S} + 1.435P + e \qquad (11\text{–}30)$$
$$(1.447)\quad (1.574)\quad (1.924)$$

$$\overline{R}^2 = .8303 \quad \text{RSE} = 36.75 \quad F = 243.13\ (.0000000) \quad \text{DW} = 1.947 \quad n = 100$$

Both 2SLS relationships have good $\overline{R}^2$ and significant F-values; however, the t-values of Equation 11–30 are low. Because this relationship was chosen for its theoretical validity, it is accepted despite these low t-values. (Note also, that the t-values of Equations 11–29 and 11–30 may differ with different software procedures.)

To understand what is accomplished using 2SLS, consider inappropriate OLS estimations of Equations 11–15 and 11–16 shown in Equations 11–31 and 11–32.

$$S = 3{,}328.104 + 2.344A - 1.079C + e \qquad (11\text{–}31)$$
$$(8.360)\quad (19.141)\quad (-2.813)$$

$$\overline{R}^2 = .806 \quad \text{RSE} = 106.397 \quad F = 206.66(.000000) \quad \text{DW} = 1.807 \quad n = 100$$

$$A = 2{,}844.919 + .02312S + 2.420P + e \qquad (11\text{–}32)$$
$$(3.891)\qquad (.330)\quad (4.478)$$

$$\overline{R}^2 = .826 \quad \text{RSE} = 37.194 \quad F = 236.2(.00000) \quad \text{DW} = 1.949 \quad n = 100$$

Equations 11–31 and 11–32 should be compared to the 2SLS values and the theoretical values of Equations 11–33 and 11–34 used to generate this data. Table 11–8

TABLE 11–8   Comparison of OLS, 2SLS, and Theoretical Models (BMS.DAT)

Model	Dependent Variable	Constant (*t-values*)[a]	b_1	b_2	$\bar{R}^2$	F	DW
OLS	S	3,328.1 (8.30)	2.344A (19.14)	−1.079C (−2.813)	.806	206.7	1.807
2SLS	S	1,651.82 (10.53)	2.86$\hat{A}$ (59.27)	−.750C (−5.43)	.975	939.3	2.007
Theoretical coefficients		1,200.0	3.0A	−.55C			
OLS	A	2,844.92 (3.89)	.023S (.330)	2.42P (4.478)	.826	236.2	1.949
2SLS	A	1,478.38 (1.45)	.154$\hat{S}$ (1.574)	1.435P (1.924)	.830	243.1	1.947
Theoretical coefficients		1,000.00	.2S	1.0P			

a. *t*-values may vary depending on software used.

summarizes each of the two estimated models along with the actual simultaneous equations used to generate this data. Because this data was generated using known simultaneous equations, we know the underlying population equation:

$$S = 1,200 + 3A - .55C + e \tag{11–33}$$

$$A = 1,000 + .2S + 1.00P + e' \tag{11–34}$$

As shown in Table 11–8, the 2SLS results are considerably more accurate than those using OLS. This table clearly illustrates the advantage of 2SLS over OLS in estimating coefficients with simultaneity.

Quantity Demanded and Supplied— Equilibrium Simultaneity

A common identification problem in economics is that of estimating the relationship between the quantity demanded, Qd, the quantity supplied, Qs, and the market price, P. This problem is exemplified by a three-equation system:

Supply	$Qs_t = a_0 + a_1 P_t + e1_t$
Demand	$Qd_t = b_0 + b_1 P_t + b_2 Y_t + e2_t$
Equilibrium	$Qd_t = Qs_t$

Here, the lone exogenous variable is Y_t, consumer income, and the endogenous variables are the price and market-clearing quantity. The last of the three equations denotes that there is now a single quantity variable, Q_t. Thus, the equilibrium condition from a market-clearing quantity is:

$$Q_t = a_0 + a_1 P_t + e1_t \quad \text{(supply)}$$

$$Q_t = b_0 + b_1 P_t + b_2 Y_t + e2_t \quad \text{(demand)}$$

This system of equations is a simultaneous one because Q and P are mutually determined. Thus, if supply and demand equations are estimated independently, there will be simultaneous equation bias. Therefore, some estimation method other than OLS must be used to fit the system of equations. The first step in the process of fitting structural equations is to determine whether equations are identifiable.

Identification

The supply equation is exactly identified because the number of EPR variables, Y, is 1 less than the IEN variables, P and Q. However, the demand equation is underidentified because the number of EPR variables, which is zero, is smaller than the IEN variables minus 1: that is, 2 minus 1. In order to improve the model and to make identification possible, the theory of the supply equation needs to be improved. That is, in what ways can the supply equation be expanded to better reflect theory and be more validly estimated? For example, theory might denote that another determinant of Qs_t is the cost of components used in the production of the supply, designated as C_t. This yields

$$Qs_t = a_0 + a_1 P_t + a_2 C_t + e1_t$$

Now both the supply and demand equations are exactly identified, $EPR = IEN - 1$. The reduced form equations of market equilibrium are therefore:

$$Q_t = II_0 + II_1 C_t + II_2 Y_t + v1_t$$
$$P_t = II_3 + II_4 C_t + II_5 Y_t + v2_t$$

Note that the endogenous price, P_t, has been moved to the left-hand side which is indicative of the simultaneity of the equations. Finally, note how in this simple example, that theory and identification requirements have directed the analysis to a more comprehensive system of structural equations. These move the art of forecasting towards the science of econometrics.

Other Simultaneous Equation Methods

Indirect Least Squares (ILS)

ILS is a method for estimating structural equations for exactly identified equations. It uses OLS to estimate the reduced-form equations of the system and then uses the estimated coefficients to calculate the parameters. However, with ILS, it is not easy to calculate the standard errors of the structural coefficients, nor can ILS be used for overidentified equations as can 2SLS; thus, the 2SLS method dominates the ILS method. For these reasons, we do not develop ILS in this text.

Serially Correlated Errors and Lagged Dependent Variables

While 2SLS is a versatile method, it has limitations when the resulting errors are correlated and lagged independent variables exist in the estimated equations. That is, 2SLS does not provide good, consistent coefficient estimates when the equation contains a lagged dependent variable and the error terms are serially correlated. In such cases, it is suggested that the alternative method of Fair (1970) be used. Pindyck and Rubinfeld (1991) develop this methodology and we suggest review of this material when both lagged dependent variables and serially correlated errors exist in the relationship.

Seemingly Unrelated Regression (SUR) Model

If the error terms of two models are correlated, then the estimated coefficients may not be efficient. However, efficient coefficients can be estimated using a technique called seemingly unrelated regression (SUR). Consider an example where the demand equations for two related products are estimated:

$$D1_t = a_0 + a_1 P1_t + e1_t$$
$$D2_t = b_0 + b_1 P2_t + e2_t$$
$$COV(e1_t, e2_t) \neq .0$$

When their error terms covary, then more efficient estimates can be obtained using SUR, see Pindyck and Rubinfeld (1991) or Greene (1993).

Three-Stage Least Squares (3SLS)

The 2SLS method does not efficiently model simultaneous equations with correlated errors. A technique that does is called three-stage least squares (3SLS). The 3SLS method is completed in three stages. The first two stages are 2SLS to obtain estimates of the covariances and variances of the error terms in each equation. Then the method of Zellner (1962) is used to estimate all of the coefficients and their standard errors in all of the simultaneous equations at once. While this method is not as widely used as 2SLS, it is becoming more popular with more widely available software.

SUR and 3SLS methods are developed in several references, including Zellner (1962), Pindyck and Rubinfeld (1991), Kmenta (1986), and Judge et al. (1985).

Testing for Simultaneity

The BMS example has shown that when mutual causality exists, then one or more of the right-hand-side (RHS) variables will be endogenous. In such cases, the RHS variable is correlated with the error term. The question arises, how do we confirm that mutual causality exists between two variables? Fortunately, the **Hausman specification test** can be used to test for mutual causality.

Using the BMS system of equations, assume we want to test whether A and $e1$ are related in Equation 11–35.

$$S = a_0 + a_1 A + a_2 C + e1 \tag{11–35}$$

$$A = b_0 + b_1 S + b_2 P + e2 \tag{11–36}$$

To test for simultaneity of A, regress A versus the exogenous variables P and C, which is the reduced form of Equation 11–36.

$$A = c_0 + c_1 P + c_2 C + v1 \tag{11–37}$$

Then retain the residuals $v1$. In the second stage, $v1$ is added to the original relationship of Equation 11–35 to yield:

$$S = a_0 + a_1 A + a_2 C + a_3 v1 + e2 \tag{11–38}$$

The t-test of the coefficient $a3$ can be used to determine whether sales and advertising are simultaneous. The null hypothesis is that there is no simultaneity between A and S and the alternative is that there is simultaneity between A and S. Let's perform these steps.

1. Reduced-form equation for A:

   (BMS.DAT)

   $$A = 3{,}097.80 - .2065C + 2.565P + v1 \quad \text{(from Equation 11–28)}$$

2. Including $v1$ into an OLS of Equation 11–38 yields:

   $$S = 1{,}651.82 + 2.86A - .7499C - 2.976v1 + e \tag{11–39}$$
   $$(10.542) \quad (59.336) \quad (-5.439) \quad (-25.72)$$

$$\overline{R}^2 = .9751 \quad \text{RSE} = 38.077 \quad F = 1{,}296.12(.000000) \quad \text{DW} = 2.038 \quad n = 100$$

Because of the very high *t*-value of *v*1, a two-tailed *t*-test of the null hypothesis that there is no simultaneity, is rejected, and the alternative hypothesis of simultaneity accepted.

If there are lagged dependent variables or serial correlation in the residuals or a test for more than one pair of simultaneity is needed, this analysis becomes more complicated. We refer you to Pindyck and Rubenfeld (1991) for further information.

Summary

This chapter has studied causal modeling. We have seen that an understanding of causal ordering and causal closure are necessary before one can build valid causal models. Exactly meeting specifications is difficult theoretically since this implies perfect knowledge of cause. If such knowledge existed, the forecaster's job would be considerably easier—just collect data and estimate coefficients. However, forecasting analysts are being asked more often now to complete econometric studies. As we have seen, correct coefficient estimations are easier to attain with larger sample sizes because these larger sample sizes may randomize the effects of the excluded or unknown exogenous variables.

Structural equations are less widely used in forecasting because of concerns about identifying cause and effect as well as the concern that this approach is too advanced for some forecasters. Such concerns are necessary when catastrophic results may occur from forecasts. However, corporate planning processes and planners should study both OLS and simultaneous equations. While structural equations are more frequently used in marketing research, they can be used more in corporate planning and forecasting, at least as an exploratory tool to investigate causality. Successful econometric studies set the stage for more definitive and comprehensive planning models.

While this chapter has concentrated on simple three- and four-variable recursive and nonrecursive models, software is available for those who wish to do more complex analyses. Any statistical package that includes regression analysis can be used to fit recursive path models and simple nonrecursive models, such as two-stage least squares (2SLS). However, more complex nonrecursive models require programs such as LISREL, EZ-PATH, and EQS (Hayduk, 1987). These computer programs perform structural equation modeling for both causal and latent variable models, either separately or combined. While more difficult to use and describe than structural equations, these other methods have many advantages over other causal modeling methods, including measures of errors associated with latent variables and allowances for correlated error terms.

The SPSS/PC has LISREL, and structural equation models can be easily constructed using EGRET and PC versions of SAS. EZ-PATH and EQS offer structural equation modeling on mainframes and PCs, and mainframe versions of the above mentioned programs are widely available.

Finally, the greatest immediate contribution of causal modeling, such as structural equations, is in providing more accurate and valid multiple regression relationships for forecasting and policy decisions. We hope this chapter is useful in starting you on the path of improved causal forecasting. However, we must end this topic with the sobering reminder that an important limitation of multivariate methods is that good forecasts of predetermined variables are necessary to forecast the endogenous variables. Many studies have shown that univariate methods often yield more accurate short-to-intermediate term forecasts.

Key Terms

causal closure
controlling for influences
direct causal influence
econometrics
endogenous variables
exactly identified
excluded predetermined variables (EPR)
exogenous variables
Granger causality test
Hausman specification test
included endogenous variables (IEN)
indirect noncausal influence
instrumental variables
intervening variables
lagged endogenous variables
nonrecursive structural equations
overidentified
partial correlation coefficients

path analysis
path coefficients
predetermined variables
randomization
recursive structural equations
restricted model
simultaneity
simultaneous equation bias
simultaneous equations
specification errors
spurious correlation
structural equation modeling
total, direct, and indirect causal influences
two-stage least squares (2SLS)
underidentified
unrestricted model
weak causal ordering

Key Formulas

Recursive system of structural equations:

$$X1 = e1 \tag{11-1}$$

$$X2 = b_0 + b_1 X1 + e2 \tag{11-2}$$

$$X3 = b_2 + b_3 X1 + b_4 X2 + e3 \tag{11-3}$$

where $\overline{e1} = \overline{e2} = \overline{e3} = 0$, and

$$COV(e1,e2) = COV(e1,e3) = COV(e2,e3) = 0 \tag{11-4}$$

$$COV(em, Xn) = 0 \text{ within a relationship for all } m \neq n \tag{11-5}$$

Path (Beta) coefficients:

$$X2 = P_{21} X1 + e2 = .4262 X1 + e2 \tag{11-6}$$

$$X3 = P_{31.2} X1 + P_{32.1} X2 + e3 = -.2427 X1 + 1.0677 X2 + e3 \tag{11-7}$$

Total, direct, and indirect influences:

$$\begin{matrix} \text{Total} & \text{Direct} & \text{Indirect} \\ \text{correlation} = & \text{causal influence} + & \text{causal/noncausal influence} \end{matrix}$$

$$r_{31} = P_{31.2} + P_{21}P_{32.1} = .212 = .2427 + .426(1.0677) \tag{11-9}$$

$$r_{32} = P_{32.1} + P_{21}P_{31.2} = .964 = 1.0677 + .426(-.2427) \tag{11-10}$$

Generating partial correlation coefficients—Big City Bookstore:

$$X3 = -23.019 + 2.280 X2 + X3.2 \tag{11-11}$$

$$X1 = 7.750 + .4489 X2 + X1.2 \tag{11-12}$$

$$r_{31.2} = -.828 \text{ and } r_{31} = .212$$

Granger causality test:

Unrestricted	$Y_t = f(Y_{t-1}, Y_{t-2}, \ldots Y_{t-m}, X_{t-1}, X_{t-2}, \ldots, X_{t-m})$
Restricted	$Y_t = f(Y_{t-1}, \ldots, Y_{t-m})$
Null	$X \not> Y$ (X does not Granger-cause Y)
Alternative	$X > Y$ (X does Granger-cause Y)

Test statistics:

$$F_{r,\, n-m-k-1} = \frac{(\text{ESS}r - \text{ESS}u)/r}{\text{ESS}u/(n - m - k)} \tag{11–14}$$

Simultaneous equations—nonrecursive structural equations:

$$S_t = a_0 + a_1 A_t + a_2 C_t + e1_t \tag{11–15}$$

$$A_t = b_0 + b_1 S_t + b_2 P_t + e2_t \tag{11–16}$$

Two-stage least squares:
Reduced-form equation:

$$S_t = \Pi_0 + \Pi_1 C_t + \Pi_2 P_t + v1_t \tag{11–17}$$

$$A_t = \Pi_3 + \Pi_4 C_t + \Pi_5 P_t + v2_t \tag{11–18}$$

$$\hat{S}_t = \Pi_0 + \Pi_1 C_t + \Pi_2 P_t \tag{11–19}$$

$$\hat{A}_t = \Pi_3 + \Pi_4 C_t + \Pi_5 P_t \tag{11–20}$$

Second-stage estimated coefficients:

$$S_t = a_0 + a_1 \hat{A}_t + a_2 C_t + e1_t \tag{11–21}$$

$$A_t = b_0 + b_1 \hat{S}_t + b_2 P_t + e2_t \tag{11–22}$$

Reduced-form equation derivation:

$$S_t = \frac{a_0 + a_1 b_0}{(1 - a_1 b_1)} + \frac{a_1 b_2 P_t}{(1 - a_1 b_1)} + \frac{a_2 C_t}{(1 - a_1 b_1)} + \frac{a_1 e2_t + e1_t}{(1 - a_1 b_1)}$$

$$S_t = \Pi_0 + \Pi_1 P_t + \Pi_2 C_t + v1_t \tag{11–23}$$

$$A_t = \frac{b_0 + b_1 a_0}{1 - b_1 a_1} + \frac{b_1 a_2 C_t}{1 - b_1 a_1} + \frac{b_2 P_t}{1 - b_1 a_1} + \frac{b_1 e1_t + e2_t}{1 - b_1 a_1}$$

$$A_t = \Pi_3 + \Pi_4 C_t + \Pi_5 P_t + v2_t \tag{11–24}$$

Identification requirements:

Exactly identified	EPR = IEN − 1	Equation might be estimated using 2SLS.
Overidentified	EPR > IEN − 1	Equation might be estimated using 2SLS, but several solutions exist.
Underidentified	EPR < IEN − 1	Equation cannot be estimated.

Building materials example of 2SLS (BMS.DAT):
Reduced-form equations:

$$S = 10{,}511.55 - 1.341C + 7.337P + e \tag{11–27}$$
$$(1{,}003.85) \quad (-9.847) \quad (59.271)$$

$$\bar{R}^2 = .975 \quad \text{RSE} = 38.120 \quad F = 1{,}939.272(.000000) \quad \text{DW} = 2.007 \quad n = 100$$

$$A = 3,097.80 - .2065C + 2.565P + e' \tag{11-28}$$
$$(306.88) \quad (-1.574) \quad (21.497)$$

$$\overline{R}^2 = .8302 \quad \text{RSE} = 36.749 \quad F = 243.13(.000000) \quad \text{DW} = 1.947 \quad n = 100$$

Second-stage estimation:

$$S = 1,651.820 + 2.86\hat{A} - .750C + e \tag{11-29}$$
$$(10.531) \quad (59.271) \quad (-5.434)$$

$$\overline{R}^2 = .975 \quad \text{RSE} = 38.12 \quad F = 939.273 \, (.0000000) \quad \text{DW} = 2.007 \quad n = 100$$

$$A = 1,478.376 + .154\hat{S} + 1.435(P + e) \tag{11-30}$$
$$(1.447) \quad (1.574) \quad (1.924)$$

$$\overline{R}^2 = .8303 \quad \text{RSE} = 36.75 \quad F = 243.13 \, (.0000000) \quad \text{DW} = 1.947 \quad n = 100$$

Biased ordinary least squares:

$$S = 3,328.104 + 2.344A - 1.079C + e \tag{11-31}$$
$$(8.360) \quad (19.141) \quad (-2.813)$$

$$\overline{R}^2 = .806 \quad \text{RSE} = 106.397 \quad F = 206.66(.000000) \quad \text{DW} = 1.807 \quad n = 100$$

$$A = 2,844.919 + .02312S + 2.420P + e \tag{11-32}$$
$$(3.891) \quad (.330) \quad (4.478)$$

$$\overline{R}^2 = .826 \quad \text{RSE} = 37.194 \quad F = 236.2(.00000) \quad \text{DW} = 1.949 \quad n = 100$$

Theoretical:

$$S = 1,200 + 3A - .55C + e \tag{11-33}$$
$$A = 1,000 + .2S + 1.00P + e' \tag{11-34}$$

Quantity demanded and supplied—equilibrium simultaneity:

Supply	$Qs_t = a_0 + a_1 P_t + e1_t$
Demand	$Qd_t = b_0 + b_1 P_t + b_2 Y_t + e2_t$
Equilibrium	$Qd_t = Qs_t$

$$Q_t = II_0 + II_1 C_t + II_2 Y_t + v1_t$$
$$P_t = II_3 + II_4 C_t + II_5 Y_t + v2_t$$

Testing for simultaneity:

$$S = a_0 + a_1 A + a_2 C + e1 \tag{11-35}$$
$$A = b_0 + b_1 S + b_2 P + e2 \tag{11-36}$$

Reduced form of Equation 11–36:

$$A = c_0 + c_1 P + c_2 C + v1 \tag{11-37}$$

Include $v1$ in Equation 11–35:

$$S = a_0 + a_1 A + a_2 C + a_3 v1 + e2 \tag{11-38}$$

Perform *t*-test on a_3:

$$H_0(H_1)\text{: There is not (is) simultaneity between } A \text{ and } S.$$

Step 1: Reduced-form equation for A:

$$A = 3{,}097.80 - .2065C + 2.565P + 1 \qquad \text{(from Equation 11–28)}$$

Step 2: Including $v1$, t-test on a_3 of OLS of Equation 11–38 yields:

$$S = 1{,}651.82 + 2.86A - .7499C - 2.976v1 + e \qquad (11\text{–}39)$$
$$(10.542) \quad (59.336) \quad (-5.439) \quad (-25.72)$$

$$\overline{R}^2 = .9751 \quad RSE = 38.077 \quad F = 1296.12(.000000) \quad DW = 2.038 \quad n = 100$$

Review Problems Using Your Software

R11–1 Fit the beta coefficient relationships of Equations 11–6 and 11–7 using your software. Interpret the coefficients of those relationships to BIGCITY.DAT.

R11–2 Generate the path coefficients and correlations of Table 11–1 and relate these to Figure 11–1.

R11–3 Calculate the partial correlations coefficients $r_{31.2}$ for the Big City Bookstore example. Compare this value to r_{31} and explain the difference.

R11–4 Using SMRECUR.DAT repeat the analysis of Tables 11–3 and 11–5. Do your results agree? Explain why the results of Tables 11–3 and 11–5 differ so much. What principle is being illustrated?

R11–5 Using LRGRECUR.DAT repeat the analysis of Tables 11–4 and 11–6. Do your results agree? Explain why the results of Tables 11–4 and 11–6 differ so much. What principle is being illustrated?

R11–6 Using UKUSIND.DAT repeat the Granger causality test for the U.K. and U.S. stock indexes. First perform a test on the direction of causality from U.S. to U.K. and then from U.K. to U.S. Explain your results in terms of cause and effect.

R11–7 Repeat the 2SLS procedure on the example data of BMS.DAT as shown in Equations 11–25 to 11–30. Explain your results and compare them to the known population values.

R11–8 Perform the Hausman test for simultaneity, as illustrated for the BMS.DAT in Equation 11–39.

Problems

11–1 What is a system of structural equations?

11–2 What are the requirements necessary to prove causality? Why is it so difficult to prove causality?

11–3 Explain the difference between recursive and nonrecursive structural models. How is each type of model estimated?

11–4 Explain the concept of a path coefficient and give an example.

11–5 Explain the concept of the partial correlation coefficient and its importance in causal modeling.

11–6 What is denoted by the relationship between $X1$ and $X2$ when:
   a. $r_{12.3} = 0$.
   b. $r_{12.3} > 0$.
   c. $r_{12.3} < 0$.
   Can we make causal statements about their relationship based on these partial correlations?

11–7 Explain the differences between total, direct, and indirect influences as measured by path coefficients.

11–8 Explain the decomposition of influences for the Big City sales relationship, as shown in Table 11–1.

11–9 What is the meaning of a partial correlation coefficient of zero?

11–10 What is weak causal ordering, and why is it so important?

11–11 What is a specification error? List the several types of specification errors.

11–12 Explain the procedure of Granger causality.

11–13 What are the limitations of the Granger causality test?

11–14 Explain the two-stage least squares (2SLS) procedure.

11–15 Explain the meaning of instrumental variables and how they relate to reduced-form equations.

11–16 What are the identification requirements for simultaneous equations? In a system of equations, can some equations be identifiable while others are not?

11–17 Explain the Hausman simultaneity test.

11–18 When should 2SLS be used? Explain each step of the process.

11–19 What are the disadvantages of indirect least squares (ILS) as compared to 2SLS?

11–20 For the four trivariate relationships below, define the expected value of the specified correlation and partial correlation coefficients (i.e., $= 0, \neq 0, = ?$). What do the values of these correlations denote about the direction of causality?

a.

$$X2 \nearrow X3$$
$$\searrow X1$$

$$r_{12} = \underline{\quad}, r_{23} = \underline{\quad}, r_{13.2} = \underline{\quad}$$

b. $X3 \rightarrow X1 \rightarrow X2$ $r_{21} = \underline{\quad}, r_{23} = \underline{\quad}, r_{13} = \underline{\quad}, r_{13.2} = \underline{\quad}$

c.

$$X3$$
$$X2 \longrightarrow X1$$

$$r_{21} = \underline{\quad}, r_{23} = \underline{\quad}, r_{32} = \underline{\quad}, r_{21.3} = \underline{\quad}$$

d. $X3$

$$\searrow X2$$
$$\nearrow$$
$$X1$$

$$r_{12} = \underline{\quad}, r_{23} = \underline{\quad}, r_{13.2} = \underline{\quad}$$

11–21 For the four trivariate relationships below, define the expected values of the correlation and partial correlation coefficients you deem important in confirming the direction of causality. What do the values of these correlations denote about the direction of causality?

a.

$$X3 \nearrow X2$$
$$\searrow X1$$

b. $X2 \rightarrow X3 \rightarrow X1$

c.

$$X2$$
$$X3 \longrightarrow X1$$

d. $X3$

$$\searrow$$
$$\nearrow X2$$
$$X1$$

11–22 Determine the correlations and partial correlation coefficients for the Big City Bookstore example shown in Figure 11–1. What do these correlations denote about the direction of causality? Do they prove or confirm the suggested direction of causality? What other possible directions of causality might explain the values of the correlations?

11–23 When are the following methods applicable:

a. Fair's method.

b. SUR.

c. 3SLS.

11–24 The following two equations are a simple macroeconomic model:

$$Y_t = a_0 + a_1 R_t + e1_t$$

$$R_t = b_0 + b_1 M_t + b_2 Y_t + e2_t$$

where Y is income, R is the interest rate, and M is the money supply. From this relationship, answer the following questions.

a. Explain why this is a simultaneous equation model.
b. What are the effects of the simultaneity of this model?
c. Identify the exogenous and endogenous variables.
d. Derive the reduced forms of each equation.
e. Are the equations underidentified, overidentified, or exactly identified?

11–25 Given the following three-equation system, which of the equations are underidentified, overidentified, and exactly identified? Show how you determined this.

$$Y1_t = a_0 + a_1 Y2_t + a_2 X2_t + e1_t$$

$$Y2_t = b_0 + b_1 Y3_t + b_2 X1_t + e2_t$$

$$Y3_t = c_0 + c_1 Y2_t + e3_t$$

11–26 Two simultaneous relationships consist of two endogenous variables and two exogenous variables. These variables exist in the file TSLS.DAT. The following relationship is expected to exist:

$$EN1_t = a_0 + a_1 EN2_t + a_2 EX1_t + e1_t$$

$$EN2_t = b_0 + b_1 EN1_t + b_2 EX2_t + e2_t$$

a. Suggest a method for estimating these relationships and whether they are exactly, under, or overidentified.
b. Fit OLS models to each of these relationships.
c. Perform 2SLS.
d. Fully interpret the coefficients of the two simultaneous equations.
e. Verify that the error terms of the 2SLS are uncorrelated. If not, then recommend a better estimation procedure.
f. Compare the fits of the reduced-form equations and the 2SLS estimates. Which appears to better fit the endogenous variables?

11–27 Two simultaneous relationships consist of two endogenous variables and two exogenous variables. These variables exist in the file TSLS3.DAT. The following relationship is expected to exist:

$$EN1_t = a_0 + a_1 EN2_t + a_2 EX1_t + e1_t$$

$$EN2_t = b_0 + b_1 EN1_t + b_2 EX2_t + e2_t$$

a. Suggest a method for estimating these relationships and whether they are exactly, under, or overidentified.
b. Fit OLS models to each of these relationships.
c. Perform 2SLS.
d. Fully interpret the coefficients of the two simultaneous equations.
e. Verify that the error terms of the 2SLS are uncorrelated. If not, then recommend a better estimation procedure.
f. Compare the fits of the reduced-form equations and the 2SLS estimates. Which appears to better fit the endogenous variables?

11–28 Two simultaneous relationships consist of two endogenous variables and two exogenous variables. These variables exist in the file TSLS7.DAT. The following relationship is expected to exist:

$$EN1_t = a_0 + a_1 EN2_t + a_2 EX1_t + e1_t$$

$$EN2_t = b_0 + b_1 EN1_t + b_2 EX2_t + e2_t$$

a. Suggest a method for estimating these relationships and whether they are exactly, under, or overidentified.

b. Fit OLS models to each of these relationships.

c. Perform 2SLS.

d. Fully interpret the coefficients of the two simultaneous equations.

e. Verify that the error terms of the 2SLS are uncorrelated. If not, then recommend a better estimation procedure.

f. Compare the fits of the reduced-form equations and the 2SLS estimates. Which appears to better fit the endogenous variables?

Minicases: Common Forecasting Assignment

For a selected minicase or problem, complete the following analysis. Perform a Granger causality test for a selected time series as you achieve stationarity and white noise residuals. First identify how much the independent variable lags the dependent variable. In choosing *m*, the number of lags to include in your analysis, perform the test once with a full seasonal lag of dependent and independent variables and then with only one-half a seasonal cycle. Fully test and interpret your results, as done in the chapter. If the results vary with a full seasonal cycle and with one-half seasonal cycle, can you explain the cause? Note that these time series are previous time series where input variables have been added, these added independent variables are either real or contrived for explanatory purposes.

Minicase 11–1 Kansas Turnpike, Daily Data
TURNPIKG.DAT, where independent variables representing seasonal demand for daily travel are in that dataset.

Minicase 11–2 Domestic Air Passengers by Quarter
PASSAIRG.DAT, where independent variables representing indexes of air travel are in that dataset.

Minicase 11–3 Hospital Census by Month
CENSUSMG.DAT, where independent variables representing seasonal monthly demand for health care are in that dataset.

Minicase 11–4 Henry Machler's Hideaway Orchids
MACHLERG.DAT, where independent variables representing the seasonal population of consumers (i.e., Northerners who stay for only five months or so in Florida, commonly called "snowbirds") are variables in that dataset.

Minicase 11–5 Your Forecasting Project If there is an independent variable in your project, then complete the common forecasting assignment.

Minicase 11–6 Midwestern Building Materials
LUMBERG.DAT, where independent variables representing the seasonal demand for building material supplies are in that dataset.

Minicase 11–7 International Airline Passengers
AIRLING.DAT, where independent variables representing indexes for international travel are in that dataset.

Minicase 11–8 Automobile Sales AUTOG.DAT, where independent variables representing indexes of automobile demand are in that dataset.

Minicase 11–9 Consumption of Distilled Spirits
SPIRITSG.DAT, where independent variables representing the seasonal demand for alcoholic drinks as estimated by liquor store managers are in that dataset.

Minicase 11–10 Discount Consumer Electronics
ELECTG.DAT, where independent variables representing indexes of consumer demand consisting of a weighted average of new product improvements and the number of outlets are in that dataset.

References

Asher, H.B. *Causal Modeling*. 2nd ed. Newbury Park: Sage Publications, 1983.

Bassmann, R.L. "On Finite Sample Distributions of Generalized Classical Linear Identifiability Test Statistics." *Journal of American Statistical Association* 55 (1960), pp. 650–59.

Bentler, P.M. "Structural Modeling and Psychometrika: An Historical Perspective on Growth and Achievements." *Psychometrika*, 51 (1986), pp. 35–51.

Berry, W. *Nonrecursive Causal Models*. Newbury Park: Sage Publications, 1984.

Blalock, H.M., Jr. *Causal Inference in Nonexperimental Research*. Chapel Hill, NC: University of North Carolina, 1964.
_____. *Causal Models in the Social Sciences*. 2nd ed. Chicago: Aldine, 1985.

Christ, C. *Econometric Models and Methods*. New York: John Wiley & Sons, 1966.

Davis, J. *The Logic of Causal Order*. Newbury Park: Sage Publications, 1985.

Draper, N.R., and H. Smith. *Applied Regression Analysis*. 2nd ed. New York: John Wiley & Sons, 1981.

Duncan, O.D. *Introduction to Structural Equation Models*. New York: Academic Press, 1975.

Dwyer, J.H. *Statistical Models for the Social and Behavioral Sciences*. New York: Oxford University Press, 1983.

Dwyer, J.H.; M. Feinleib; P. Lippert; and H. Hoffmeister. *Statistical Models for Longitudinal Studies of Health*. New York: Oxford University Press, 1992.

Fair, R.C. "The Estimation of Simultaneous Equation Models with Lagged Variables and First Order Serially Correlated Errors." *Econometrica* 38 (May 1970), pp. 507–16.

Granger, C.W.J. "Simple Trend Fitting for Long Range Forecasting." *Mangement Decision*, 1967, pp. 29–34.
_____. "Investigating Causal Relations by Econometric Models and Cross-Spectral Methods." *Econometrica* 34 (1969), pp. 424–38.

Granger, C.W.J., and P. Newbold. "Spurious Regressions in Econometrics." *Journal of Econometrics* 2 (1974), pp. 111–20.
_____. *Forecasting Economic Time Series*. 2nd ed. Orlando, FL: Academic Press, 1968.

Greene, W.H. *Econometric Methods,* 2nd ed. Englewood Cliffs, NJ: Prentice Hall, 1993.

Hausman, J.A. "An Instrumental Variable Approach to Full Information Estimators for Linear and Certain Nonlinear Econometric Models." *Econometrica* 43 (1975), pp. 727–38.

Hayduk, L.A. *Structural Equation Modeling with LISREL*. Baltimore: Johns Hopkins University Press, 1987.

Heise, D.R. *Causal Analysis*. New York: John Wiley & Sons, 1975.

Helfenstein, U. "The Use of Transfer Function Models, Intervention Analysis, and Related Time Series Methods in Epidemiology." *International Journal of Epidemiology* (1991), 20 pp. 808–15.

Herting, J. "Multiple Indicator Models using LISREL." In Blalock (1985), pp. 263–319.

Herting, J. and H.L. Costner. "Respecification in Multiple Indicator Models." In Blalock (1985), 321–93.

Intrilligator, M.D.; R.G. Bodkin; and G. Hsiao. *Econometric Models, Techniques and Applications,* 2nd ed. Englewood Cliffs, NJ: Prentice Hall, 1996.

Johnson, A.C., M.B. Johnson, and R.C. Buse. *Econometrics: Basic and Applied*. New York: Macmillan, 1987.

Johnston, J. *Econometric Methods*. 3rd ed. New York: McGraw-Hill, 1984.

Joreskog, K.G. "A General Method for Analysis of Covariance Structures." *Biometrika* 57 (1970), pp. 239–51.

Joreskog, K.G., and D. Sorbom. *Advances in Factor Analysis and Structural Equation Models*. Cambridge, MA: Abt Bookstores, 1979.

Judge, G.G.; W.E. Griffiths; R.C. Hill; H. Lutkepohl; and T.-C. Lee. *The Theory and Practice of Econometrics*. 2nd ed. New York: John Wiley & Sons, 1985.

Kmenta, J. *Elements of Econometrics*. New York: Macmillan, 1986.

Kuhn, T. *The Structure of Scientific Revolutions*. 2nd ed. Chicago: University of Chicago Press, 1970.

Loehlin, J.C. *Latent Variable Models*. Hillsdale, NJ: Lawrence Erlbaum Associates, 1987.

Maddala, G.S. *Introduction to Econometrics*. New York: Macmillan, 1988.

Mandansky, A. "On the Efficiency of Three-Stage Least Squares Estimation," *Econometrica* 32 (1964), p. 55.

Muthen, B.O. *LISCOMP: Analysis of Linear Structural Relations Using a Comprehensive Measurement Model*. Mooresville, IN: Scientific Software, 1987.

Neter, J.; M.H. Kutner; C.J. Nachtsheim; and W. Wasserman. *Applied Linear Statistical Models*. 4th ed. Burr Ridge, IL: Richard D. Irwin, 1996.

Newbold, P. *Forecasting Methods*. London: Her Majesty's Stationery Office, 1973.

_____. *Statistics for Business and Economics*. 3rd ed. Englewood Cliffs, NJ: Prentice Hall, 1991.

Pedhazur, E.J. *Multiple Regression in Behavioral Research*. 2nd ed. New York: Holt, Rinehart & Winston, 1982.

Pindyck, R.S., and D.L. Rubinfeld. *Econometric Models and Economic Forecasts*. 3rd ed. New York: McGraw-Hill, 1991.

Rao, P. "Specification Bias in Seemingly Unrelated Regressions." In *Essays in Honor of Tinbergen*. Vol. 2. New York: International Arts and Sciences Press, 1974.

Savin, N.E., and K.J. White. "Testing for Autocorrelation with Missing Observations." *Econometrics* 46 (1978), pp. 59–66.

Snedecor, G.W., and W.G. Cochran. *Statistical Methods*. 6th ed. Ames, IA: Iowa State University Press, 1967.

Sokal, R., and F.J. Rohlf. *Biometry*. 2nd ed. New York: W. H. Freeman, 1981.

Stokey, N.L., and R.E. Lucas. *Recursive Methods in Economic Dynamics*. Cambridge, MA: Harvard University Press, 1989.

Theil, H. "Specification Errors and the Estimation of Economic Relationships." *Review of the International Statistical Institute* 25 (1957), pp. 41–51.

Wiesberg, S. *Applied Linear Regression*. 2nd ed. New York: John Wiley & Sons, 1985.

Williams, A. and S. DeLurgio "Path Analysis: Reflections on Causal Modeling," Manual for Clinical Practice Guidelines, Washington D.C., AHCPR, 1992.

Wright, S. "Path Coefficients and Path Regressions: Alternative or Complementary Concepts." *Biometrics* 16 (1960), pp. 89–202.

_____. "The Method of Path Coefficients." *Annals of Mathematical Statistics* 5 (1934), pp. 161-215.

Zellner, A. "An Efficient Method of Estimating Seemingly Unrelated Regressions and Tests for Aggregation Bias." *Journal of the American Statistical Association* 57 (1962), pp. 348–68.

_____. "Estimation of Functions of Population Means and Regression Coefficients: A Minimum Expected Loss (MELO) Approach." *Journal of Econometrics* 8 (1978), pp. 127–58.

Zellner, A., and H. Theil. "Three-Stage Least Squares: Simultaneous Estimation of Simultaneous Relations." *Econometrica* 30 (1962), pp. 54–57.

Zellner, A., and S. Park. "Minimum Expected Loss (MELO) Estimators for Functions of Parameters and Structural Coefficients of Econometric Models." *Journal of American Statistical Association* 74 (1979), pp. 185–93.

ARIMA
INTERVENTION
ANALYSIS

The whole of science is nothing more than a refinement of everyday thinking.
Albert Einstein (1936), *Physics and Reality*

Chapter Outline

This chapter presents methods for modeling influences that affect almost all time series. Consider such influences and some of the affected dependent variables:

Events	*Affected Variables*
October 1987 stock market crash	Wealth, income, investments
1991 Gulf War	Defense contracts, petroleum/civil engineering
Elimination of 55 MPH speed limit	Traffic deaths, gasoline, traffic tickets
European Economic Union creation	Global competition, European free trade
Demise of communism in USSR	Political/social stability, free enterprise
North American Free Trade Agreement	Hourly jobs, lifestyles, global competitiveness
Hurricane Andrew in 1992	Insurance claims, profits, building materials
1993 Midwestern flood	Building materials, bottled water, insurance costs

These events are just a few of the many interventions that can impact time series. In general, some of the most important influences on time series are events that may not recur but dramatically affect time series patterns. These significant events are called **interventions.** When modeling these influences, we may be interested in the event itself or in eliminating the confounding effects of the event on the nonintervention behavior of the time series. That is, intervention analysis can focus on the impact of an event as its purpose or on the elimination of the impact of that event on the time series. Both purposes require a model of the event. Our purpose here is to study those intervention models.

We have studied the use of dichotomous (i.e., dummy) variables in Chapters 3 and 10. This chapter presents more sophisticated uses of dichotomous variables with ARIMA models. The combination of an ARIMA model and dichotomous independent variables is called an **intervention model.** An *intervention* is an event that occurs. Common interventions include new laws, economic events, advertisements, earthquakes, wars, natural disasters such as those listed at the beginning of this chapter, and many other international, national, regional, company, and even product-specific events. Company-specific interventions include competitor and company stockouts, product promotions, new product introductions, and major advertising campaigns. In some cases, we may be faced with the alternative of modeling an intervention as an attribute or as a continuous variable. When the event has a magnitude that varies, then the methods of Chapter 13 can be used to model both the causal and ARIMA components of the model. However, we suggest studying this chapter before advancing to that chapter.

In general, an intervention model consists of two components: an intervention function and an ARIMA **noise model.**

$$\text{Intervention model} = \text{Intervention function} + \text{ARIMA noise model} \qquad (12\text{--}1)$$

$$Y_t = f(I_t) + N_t$$

where, the intervention function is designated $f(I_t)$ and:

$$N_t = \text{ARIMA}(p,d,q)(P,D,Q) \qquad (12\text{--}2)$$

$$I_t = \begin{cases} 1 \text{ when intervention occurs} \\ 0 \text{ otherwise} \end{cases}$$

In many cases, interventions dramatically impact the time series of interest. If we are unaware of the intervention or its effect, then our analysis of the time series is likely incorrect. Also, importantly, an intervention may represent an important event in its own right that we want to model.

Intervention time series methods were originally developed by Box and Tiao (1975), Campbell (1963), and Campbell and Stanley (1966). Prior to the popularization of the term *intervention* in the social sciences, much of the literature on the impact of events was called *longitudinal analysis* or *event studies*.

Sociological and legal applications of intervention models have been used to measure the impacts of new traffic laws, decriminalization, gun control laws, air pollution laws (Box and Tiao, 1975) and many other interventions. Thus, we see that intervention analysis as developed by Box and Tiao is a versatile tool for modeling time series. Recently, there has been great interest in using intervention analysis to model and control outliers that have known or unknown causes. The number of automated intervention software products has increased greatly and will continue to do so in the future.

Intervention functions are a subset of methods called *transfer functions*, a term commonly used in several disciplines. The next chapter extends intervention to MARIMA and transfer function modeling.

Common Intervention Types

I_t is commonly used to denote the occurrence of an intervention where I_t is 1 during the intervention, otherwise 0. There are several different types of intervention durations. The most common are pulse and step functions, as shown below.

t	$=$	1	2	3	4	5	6	7	8	9	10
Pulse function I_t	$=$	0	0	0	0	1	0	0	0	0	0
Sustained pulse I_t	$=$	0	0	0	0	1	1	0	0	0	0
Step function I_t	$=$	0	0	0	0	1	1	1	1	1	1

The **pulse intervention** represents an event that lasts for one time period (e.g., a single outlier). The **sustained pulse** affects more than one period, but only for a short time. The **step function** represents interventions that are permanent. How and when these are used will be clearer after several examples.

Zero-Order Intervention Functions

Figure 12–1 illustrates four common intervention functions where, for clarity, the errors and error terms are not shown. These four functions are called **zero-order intervention functions,** a term that will be more meaningful after studying first-order functions.

Pulse, Abrupt Temporary Impact

Figure 12–1a represents a very simple intervention model that is **abrupt** and **temporary.** For example, when the effect of the intervention is large and its cause unknown, these are outliers. While some outliers may be subjectively "eyeballed" to normal values, intervention models provide more exact estimates of outlier effects. Consider the model of Figure 12–1a in more detail:

$$Y_t = \theta_0 + \omega_0 I_t = 60 - 50 I_t \qquad (12–3)$$

where

$I_t = 1$ for $t = 9$ otherwise 0
$\theta_0 = $ Normal central value of the series
$\omega_0 = $ Effect of the intervention

This yields the following behavior:

t	Y_t	I_t	
1	60	0	$Y_1 = 60 - 50I_1 = 60$
2	60	0	
3	60	0	
⋮			⋮
8	60	0	
9	10	1	Intervention, $Y_9 = 60 - 50I_9 = 10$
10	60	0	$Y_{10} = 60 - 50I_{10} = 60$
⋮			
n	60	0	$Y_n = 60 - 50I_n = 60$

Thus, only one period is affected by this intervention—for example, a brief flood or a product stockout. The coefficients of θ_0 and ω_0 are estimated the same way as the coefficients in ARIMA analysis. However, the intervention of Equation 12–3 is so simple that it can be estimated using ordinary least squares of regression analysis (though the general model with an ARIMA noise model requires the use of nonlinear least squares). Let's consider a more complex intervention.

Abrupt, Temporary Impact

Figure 12–1b illustrates a slightly more complex intervention model that lasts for two periods. For example, a stockout occurs in period 9 and thus sales decline. However, when the item is back in stock, sales are higher than normal, as customers from last period (i.e., 9) had to wait until the item is back in stock in period 10. Consider the behavior of this model in more detail.

$$Y_t = \theta_0 + (\omega_0 - \omega_1 B)I_t \qquad (12\text{–}4)$$
$$= \theta_0 + \omega_0 I_t - \omega_1 I_{t-1} = 60 + (-50 + 10B)I_t$$

where

$$I_t = 1 \text{ for } t = 9; \text{ otherwise } 0$$
$$\theta_0 = \text{Normal central value}$$
$$\omega_0 = \text{Initial intervention effect}$$
$$-\omega_1 = \text{Delayed intervention effect}$$

FIGURE 12–1

Zero-order intervention functions

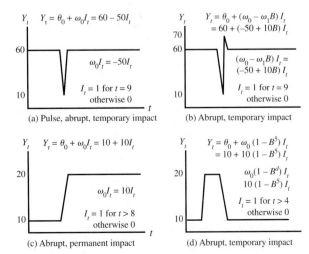

(a) Pulse, abrupt, temporary impact

(b) Abrupt, temporary impact

(c) Abrupt, permanent impact

(d) Abrupt, temporary impact

This yields the following behavior:

t	Y_t	I_t	
1	60	0	$Y_1 = 60 + (-50 + 10B)I_1$
2	60	0	
3	60	0	⋮
⋮			
8	60	0	$Y_8 = 60 - 50I_8 + 10I_7 = 60$
9	10	1	$Y_9 = 60 - 50I_9 + 10I_8 = 10$
10	70	0	$Y_{10} = 60 - 50I_{10} + 10I_9 = 70$
11	60	0	$Y_{11} = 60 - 50I_{11} + 10I_{10} = 60$
⋮			
n	60	0	$Y_n = 60 - 50I_n + 10I_{n-1} = 60$

Note that the series first decreases in period 9 and then increases slightly over the normal value in period 10. This model is one of many that can be constructed by combining several intervention terms. Later, this simple model is used with different fitted values of ω_0 and ω_1 to explain the October 1987 stock market crash. For now, consider the remaining models of Figure 12–1.

Abrupt, Permanent Impact

Figure 12–1c illustrates a very simple intervention model with an **abrupt permanent** shift in its value. Such a shift, for example, might result from fundamental changes in the demand or supply of a service or product. For example, this might occur with the introduction of a new product, an abrupt expansion of a sales area, or redefinition of those who are eligible to receive a service.

$$Y_t = \theta_0 + \omega_0 I_t = 10 + 10I_t \qquad (12\text{–}5)$$

where $I_t = 1$ for $t > 8$; otherwise 0. This yields the following behavior:

t	Y_t	I_t	
1	10	0	$Y_1 = 10 + 10I_1 = 10$
2	10	0	
3	10	0	⋮
⋮			
8	10	0	$Y_8 = 10 + 10I_8 = 10$
9	20	1	$Y_9 = 10 + 10I_9 = 10 + 10 = 20$
10	20	1	$Y_{10} = 10 + 10I_{10} = 10 + 10 = 20$
⋮			
n	20	1	$Y_n = 10 + 10I_n = 20$

Abrupt, Temporary Impact

Figure 12–1d illustrates a slightly different intervention model than the previous examples. In this case, an effect persists and then disappears. During the intervention period, the impact remains constant. Consider this behavior in the following relationship:

$$Y_t = \theta_0 + (1 - B^5)\omega_0 I_t = 10 + 10(1 - B^5)I_t \qquad (12\text{–}6)$$

where $I_t = 1$ for $t > 4$; otherwise 0.

As shown below by Y_t, the $1 - B^5$ term results in an impact for five periods:

t	Y_t	I_t	I_{t-5}	
1	10	0	0	$Y_1 = 10 + 10(1 - B^5)I_1 = 10$
2	10	0	0	
3	10	0	0	$\vdots$
4	10	0	0	
5	20	1	0	$Y_5 = 10 + 10(1 - B^5)I_5 = 20$
6	20	1	0	
7	20	1	0	
8	20	1	0	$\vdots$
9	20	1	0	
10	10	1	1	$Y_{10} = 10 + 10(1 - B^5)I_{10} = 10$
11	10	1	1	
$\vdots$				$\vdots$
n	10	1	1	$Y_n = 10 + 10(1 - B^5)I_n = 10$

Note here how the backshift operator, B^5, sets the time of the return to the preintervention value of Y_t in period 10. Depending on the capabilities of your software, I_t could be represented by a sustained pulse with the following values.

t =	1	2	3	4	5	6	7	8	9	10	11	12
Sustained pulse I_t =	0	0	0	0	1	1	1	1	1	0	0	0

First-Order Intervention Functions

Figure 12–2 illustrates four additional intervention models. As in Figure 12–1, the noise model is excluded for clarity. Figure 12–2 shows an additional term in the denominator of the intervention function. The term with delta, δ_1, $(1 - \delta_1 B)$, yields the gradual decreases and increases shown in the figure. The existence of the $\delta_1 B$ designates this as a **first-order function,** where the first order relates to the power of B (i.e., B to the first power). This term's function is easily seen in the following four examples.

Gradual, Permanent Impact

Figure 12–2a illustrates a **gradual, permanent impact** of a first-order transfer function.

$$Y_t = \theta_0 + \frac{\omega_0}{(1 - \delta_1 B)}I_t = 60 + \frac{-10}{(1 - 0.5B)}I_t \qquad (12\text{–}7)$$

To better understand this relationship, reexpress it by multiplying both sides by $(1 - \delta_1 B)$ as:

$$(1 - \delta_1 B)Y_t = (1 - \delta_1 B)\theta_0 + \omega_0 I_t$$

Because a backshift of the constant θ_0 equals the constant, we drop B from the right-hand side of the above equation, thus yielding:

$$Y_t - \delta_1 Y_{t-1} = (1 - \delta_1)\theta_0 + \omega_0 I_t$$
$$Y_t = \delta_1 Y_{t-1} + (1 - \delta_1)\theta_0 + \omega_0 I_t$$

Substituting the coefficients of Figure 12–2a into the above:

$$Y_t = .5Y_{t-1} + (1 - .5)60 - 10I_t = .5Y_{t-1} + (.5)60 - 10I_t$$

The following behavior results when I_t increases from 0 to 1.

t	Y_t	I_t	
0	60	0	
1	60	0	$Y_1 = .5Y_0 + (.5)60 - 10I_1 = 60$
2	60	0	
3	60	0	$\vdots$
4	60	0	
5	50	1	$Y_5 = .5Y_4 + 30 - 10I_5 = 50$
6	45	1	
7	42.5	1	
8	41.25	1	$\vdots$
9	40.63	1	
10	40.31	1	$Y_{10} = .5Y_9 + 30 - 10I_{10} = 40.31$
11	40.16	1	
$\vdots$			$\vdots$
$n \to \infty$	40.00	1	$Y_n = .5Y_{n-1} + 30 - 10I_n = 40.00$

This model illustrates the exponentially declining profile of Figure 12–2a, where the impact results in a decreasing decrease of Y_t. This decline is a Taylor series; as n approaches infinity, this intervention function yields an **asymptotic impact value** of:

$$\text{Asymptotic value} = \lim_{t \to \infty} \frac{\omega_0}{(1 - \delta_1)} = \frac{-10}{(1 - .5)} = -20$$

That is, the maximum decline of Y_t as a result of the intervention is -20 at infinity. However, practically, it is reached much sooner. As shown above and in Table 12–1, this decline progresses rather rapidly when $\delta_1 = .5$. You should confirm that different values of δ_1 yield different response rates.

FIGURE 12–2

First-order intervention functions

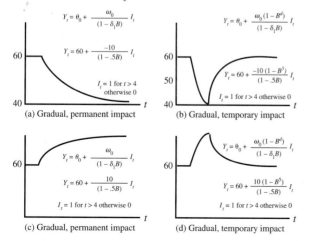

(a) Gradual, permanent impact

(b) Gradual, temporary impact

(c) Gradual, permanent impact

(d) Gradual, temporary impact

TABLE 12–1   Impact of Gradual, Permanent Intervention on Y_t

t	Periods after Intervention	$\dfrac{-10}{(1 - .5B)}I_t$	Summation of Impact on Y_t
5	1	−10	−10
6	2	−5	−15
7	3	−2.5	−17.5
8	4	−1.25	−18.75
9	5	−.625	−19.375
10	6	−.3125	−19.6875
11	7	−.15625	−19.84375
$\vdots$			$\vdots$
∞	∞	.0	−20.0

Past Relationships May Not Remain Constant

Causal models are based on the assumption that the past relationships between dependent and independent variables remain constant. Of course, some believe the only thing that remains constant in the long run is change. There are many times when changes affect our company, industry, country, or world. One notable event that made many econometric forecasts invalid throughout the world was the 1973 oil embargo. Middle Eastern suppliers restricted the flow of oil to the United States.

Gasoline, plastic, and many other products that are petroleum based, including pharmaceutical drugs, had very rapid price increases. Thus, the short-term forecasts of the price and demand for products throughout the world were very inaccurate.

However, there also were long-term effects from this crisis. The embargo and resulting price increases caused a near global effort to conserve oil and energy. Prior to the embargo, energy demand was increasing at the rate of about 3 percent a year. After the embargo and the nationwide effort to reduce energy demands, the rate of growth in the electric power industry went to approximately zero. Although the rate of growth has increased recently, it has not rebounded back to its previous preembargo rate.

The result was an oversupply of electricity capacity and last minute cancellations of nuclear power plants. Demands for electricity remain below their historical growth trends, and conservation and environmental concern will continue to keep these demands low. Neither of these events were predicted by the electric power industry prior to 1973.

Gradual, Temporary Impact

Figure 12–2b illustrates a gradual, temporary impact.

$$Y_t = \theta_0 + \frac{\omega_0(1 - B^5)}{(1 - \delta_1 B)}I_t = 60 + \frac{-10(1 - B^5)}{(1 - .5B)}I_t \qquad (12\text{–}8)$$

Reexpress this model by multiplying both sides by $(1 - \delta_1 B)$:

$$(1 - \delta_1 B)Y_t = (1 - \delta_1 B)\theta_0 + \omega_0(1 - B^5)I_t$$

$$Y_t - \delta_1 Y_{t-1} = (1 - \delta_1)\theta_0 + \omega_0(1 - B^5)I_t$$

$$Y_t = \delta_1 Y_{t-1} + (1 - \delta_1)\theta_0 + \omega_0(1 - B^5)I_t$$

$$= .5Y_{t-1} + (1 - .5)60 - 10(1 - B^5)I_t$$

$$= .5Y_{t-1} + (.5)60 - 10I_t + 10I_{t-5}$$

The following results from a permanent shift in I_t from 0 to 1:

t	Y_t	I_t	I_{t-5}	
0	60	0	0	
1	60	0	0	$Y_1 = .5Y_{t-1} + (.5)60 - 10I_t + 10I_{t-5} = 60$
2	60	0	0	
3	60	0	0	$\vdots$
4	60	0	0	
5	50	1	0	$Y_5 = .5Y_{t-1} + (.5)60 - 10I_t + 10I_{t-5} = 50$
6	45	1	0	$Y_6 = .5(50) + (.5)60 - 10 + 0 = 45$
7	42.5	1	0	
8	41.25	1	0	$\vdots$ *continued*

t	Y_t	I_t	I_{t-5}
9	40.63	1	0
10	50.32	1	1
11	55.16	1	1
12	57.58	1	1
13	58.79	1	1
14	59.39	1	1
$\vdots$			
∞	60.00	1	1

$$Y_{10} = .5Y_{t-1} + (.5)60 - 10I_t + 10I_{t-5} = 50.32$$

$$\vdots$$

$$Y_{\infty} = .5Y_{t-1} + (.5)60 - 10I_t + 10I_{t-5} = 60.00$$

As we see above, this model yields the profile that first decreases and then increases, as in Figure 12–2b and Table 12–2.

Other Examples

Figures 12–2c and d are the same intervention models as those of a and b, except the ω_0 terms are positive.

General Intervention Functions

As mentioned previously, the intervention functions of Figures 12–1 and 12–2 are special cases of transfer functions, as presented by Box, Jenkins, and Reinsel (1994). The general model is:

$$y_t = \frac{(\omega_0 - \omega_1 B - \omega_2 B^2 - \cdots - \omega_s B^s)}{(1 - \delta_1 B - \delta_2 B^2 - \cdots - \delta_r B^r)} x_{t-b} + N_t \tag{12-9}$$

where y_t and x_t represent either deviations from their means for stationary series or appropriately differenced or transformed series for initially nonstationary series Y_t and X_t.

The Noise Model

The notation used by Box and Jenkins (1976) is used in Equation 12–10 where the appropriate ARIMA noise model is of the form:

$$N_t = \frac{(1 - \theta_1 B - \theta_2 B^2 - \cdots - \theta_q B^q)}{(1 - \phi_1 B - \phi_2 B^2 - \cdots - \phi_p B^p)} e_t \tag{12-10}$$

For intervention modeling, the input series X_t is a dichotomous variable that is represented by the variable I_t.

As shown in Equation 12–9, intervention functions are identified by specifying the right-hand side values r, s, and b, where:

r = Level of autoregression or power of B in the denominator
$s + 1$ = Number of ω terms in the numerator
b = Delay in the intervention impact as shown by X_{t-b}

This is commonly used notation in intervention software.

Figure 12–3 illustrates various examples of intervention functions given r, s, and b. After using this figure as a reference in the following examples and your data analysis, you will be more comfortable with intervention functions.

TABLE 12–2   Impact of Gradual, Temporary Intervention on Y_t

t	Periods after Intervention	$\dfrac{\omega_0(1 - B^5)}{(1 - \delta_1 B)}I_t$	Summation of Impact on Y_t
5	1	-10	-10
6	2	-5	-15
7	3	-2.5	-17.5
8	4	-1.25	-18.75
9	5	.625	-19.375
10	6	9.69	-9.685
11	7	4.84	-4.845
12	8	2.42	-2.425
⋮	⋮	⋮	⋮
∞	∞	.0	.0

FIGURE 12–3

Intervention functions

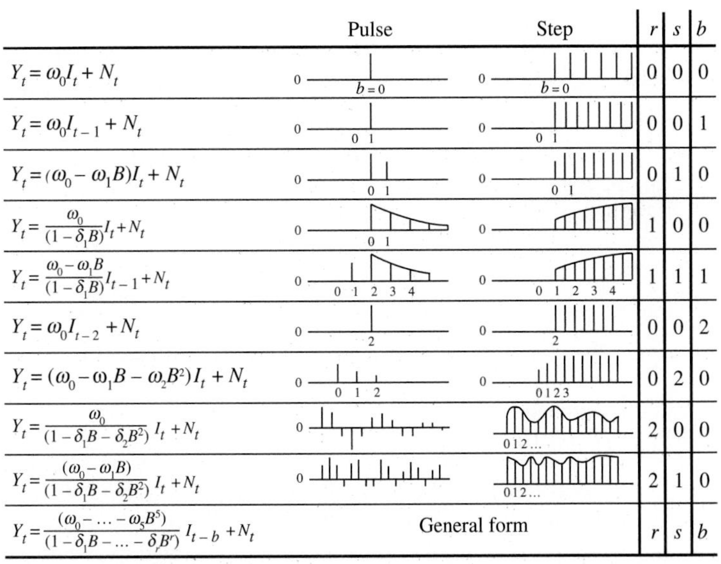

		Pulse	Step	r	s	b
$Y_t = \omega_0 I_t + N_t$				0	0	0
$Y_t = \omega_0 I_{t-1} + N_t$				0	0	1
$Y_t = (\omega_0 - \omega_1 B)I_t + N_t$				0	1	0
$Y_t = \dfrac{\omega_0}{(1 - \delta_1 B)}I_t + N_t$				1	0	0
$Y_t = \dfrac{\omega_0 - \omega_1 B}{(1 - \delta_1 B)}I_{t-1} + N_t$				1	1	1
$Y_t = \omega_0 I_{t-2} + N_t$				0	0	2
$Y_t = (\omega_0 - \omega_1 B - \omega_2 B^2)I_t + N_t$				0	2	0
$Y_t = \dfrac{\omega_0}{(1 - \delta_1 B - \delta_2 B^2)}I_t + N_t$				2	0	0
$Y_t = \dfrac{(\omega_0 - \omega_1 B)}{(1 - \delta_1 B - \delta_2 B^2)}I_t + N_t$				2	1	0
$Y_t = \dfrac{(\omega_0 - \ldots - \omega_s B^s)}{(1 - \delta_1 B - \ldots - \delta_r B^r)}I_{t-b} + N_t$		General form		r	s	b

Order of the intervention function and the power of B in the denominator, $\delta_r B^r$

$r + 1 = $ Number of denominator terms $\delta_r B^r$ and level of autoregression

$s + 1 = $ Power of B in numerator $= $ Number of ω terms

$b = $ Delay in start of effect, I_{t-b}

Nonstationary Series

As noted before, temporary and permanent impacts should be modeled using pulse and step functions, respectively. However, this can be confusing when modeling nonstationary series. Let's clarify the use of differences with nonstationary series using two examples, one with a permanent impact and the other with a temporary impact.

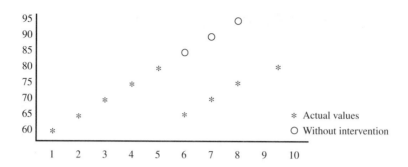

FIGURE 12–4

*Abrupt, permanent
intervention for a
nonstationary series*

Abrupt, Permanent Interventions for Nonstationary Series

Consider the time series in Figure 12–4, which has a trend and is interrupted in period 6 by an intervention.

t	1	2	3	4	5	6	7	8	9	10
Y_t	60	65	70	75	80	65	70	75	80	85
$(1 - B)Y_t$		5	5	5	5	-15	5	5	5	5
I_t		0	0	0	0	1	1	1	1	1

The event of period 6, I_t, significantly reduces Y_t from 80 in period 5 to 65 in period 6, even though in period 5, the expected value of Y_6 is 85 (i.e., $80 + 5$) as shown in Figure 12–4. That is, this event has a negative 20-unit impact on Y_t. Its first difference (i.e., trend) goes down from $+5$ to -15, for a net change or 20. To understand how to model this behavior, refer to the next table, where Y_t is given in row 2. As shown, the series permanently shifts down in period 6 by 20 units, albeit the trend continues upward from that point on.

t	1	2	3	4	5	6	7	8	9	10
Y_t	60	65	70	75	80	65	70	75	80	85
$(1 - B)Y_t$		5	5	5	5	-15	5	5	5	5
Trend $= \theta_0 = 5$ as estimated from the preintervention series										
$(1 - B)Y_t - \theta_0$			0	0	0	0	-20	0	0	0	0
$I_t =$ Step	0	0	0	0	0	1	1	1	1	1
$(1 - B)I_t$		0	0	0	0	1	0	0	0	0

Assume that our understanding of this series confirms the above behavior and denotes that the effect of the intervention should be permanent. Therefore, a step function should be used to model this series. However, when a time series is nonstationary and requires differencing, then to preserve the permanent step function between Y_t and I_t, differences should also be applied to the intervention, I_t.

If we had applied differences to Y_t but not to the I_t, the model is incorrect and identification difficult because of the strange behavior of $(1 - B)Y_t - \theta_0$. Remember that the decision to take first differences of I_t is based on the belief that the impact is permanent and the empirical evidence of the plot of the series. (Note: It has been our experience that improper specification of differences is the most common mistake in intervention modeling.)

The model fitted in the previous table is:

$$Y_t = \omega_0 I_t + \frac{\theta_0}{(1 - B)}$$

where cross multiplication of $(1 - B)$ yields the following model:

$$(1 - B)Y_t = \omega_0(1 - B)I_t + \theta_0$$

and in this specific case, ω_0, the intervention effect, is -20, and θ_0, the trend, is 5.

Therefore:

$$Y_t = Y_{t-1} + \omega_0(1 - B)I_t + \theta_0$$

$$Y_t = Y_{t-1} - 20I_t + 20I_{t-1} + 5$$

Finally, note that this model can more easily be expressed as:

$$Y_t = -_2 0I_t + \frac{5}{(1 - B)}$$

where

$$I_t = 1 \text{ for } t > 5; \text{ otherwise } 0.$$

Having acquired some insight into how permanent nonstationary interventions behave, now consider an abrupt temporary nonstationary intervention.

Abrupt, Temporary Interventions for Nonstationary Series

Figure 12–5 and the following table show a situation in which Y_t is impacted only in period 6 where it increases from 5 units to 25 units per period. In contrast to the previous table, the large increase in period 6 is followed by an equivalent decrease in period 7 that brings the time series back to the preintervention values as if the intervention had never taken place. Thus, we see that the value of period 7 is the same as was expected prior to the intervention (the value of period 5, 80, plus two periods of 5 each, 90). This behavior is considerably different than that of the previous example. By applying differences to the original times series, Y_t and the pulse of I_t, an effective model results.

t	1	2	3	4	5	6	7	8	9	10	11
Y_t	60	65	70	75	80	105	90	95	100	105	110
$(1 - B)Y_t$		5	5	5	5	25	−15	5	5	5	5
$\theta_0 = 5$ as estimated from the preintervention series.											
$(1 - B)Y_t - \theta_0$		0	0	0	0	20	−20	0	0	0	0
$I_t = $ Pulse	0	0	0	0	0	1	0	0	0	0	0
$(1 - B)I_t$		0	0	0	0	1	−1	0	0	0	0

Thus, even when I_t is a pulse, differences of I_t are necessary. And while the equation is identical to the permanent equation of the previous example, the effect is different because I_t is a pulse.

The notation for the above model is:

$$Y_t = \omega_0 I_t + \frac{\theta_0}{(1 - B)}$$

where the above shorthand notation yields the following model by multiplying both sides by $(1 - B)$:

$$(1 - B)Y_t = \omega_0(1 - B)I_t + \theta_0$$

and in this specific case, ω_0, the intervention effect, is −20, and θ_0, the trend, is 5.

FIGURE 12–5

Abrupt, temporary interventions for a nonstationary series

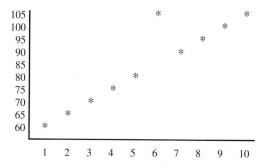

Therefore:

$$Y_t - Y_{t-1} = -20(1 - B)I_t + 5$$

$$Y_t = Y_{t-1} - 20I_t + 20I_{t-1} + 5$$

As before, this model can more easily be expressed as:

$$Y_t = -20I_t + \frac{5}{(1 - B)}$$

where

$$I_t = 1 \text{ for } t = 5; \text{ otherwise } 0.$$

Intervention Modeling

Figure 12–6 illustrates a flowchart of the intervention modeling process. We follow the discussion of this process with four intervention examples.

As shown in Figure 12–6, the first step in intervention modeling is to have a substantive basis for modeling the intervention effect. From a theoretical standpoint, intervention analysis should confirm the existence of an intervention; it should not be used in a blind search for possible events. That is, in order to correctly model an intervention, we should know of the existence and the date of the intervention. Thus, intervention analysis should normally flow from the research question or the purpose of the forecast, not from the data to the research question. Formally, a null hypothesis should be proposed that an event caused a change in the time series at point t, then the appropriate tests should be performed (e.g., a t-test on the intervention coefficient or an F-test on the relationship). This is an essential step when important decisions are made based on the intervention. However, there are many situations in which formal hypotheses should be formulated but are not. In these expedient or quick-and-dirty applications, intervention analysis is often used to measure or eliminate the effects of known or unknown events without formal hypotheses tests. However, such explorations must be done cautiously as discussed next.

When the date of an intervention is not known, then we might select the wrong period of intervention by choosing an unusually high or low value that occurred by chance. It is easy to find unusual values in any time series and then to hypothesize the causes of these unusual values. When independent verification of the date of an intervention can be made, then such activities may yield valid models. However, if one simply scans a time series looking for unusual values in order to fit intervention effects, then one is hardly involved with objective analysis. Such a search has a high probability of yielding a statistically significant result for no reason other than that an outlier of unknown origin occurred. Presenting unusual values as specific interventions without independent verification is misleading and violates the scientific method.

Steps of Intervention Analysis

In order to model the impact of an intervention, we need to model the time series without that impact. This almost always means modeling the **preintervention series** because most often the intervention effect is so large that it distorts the ACFs and the

FIGURE 12–6

Intervention modeling process

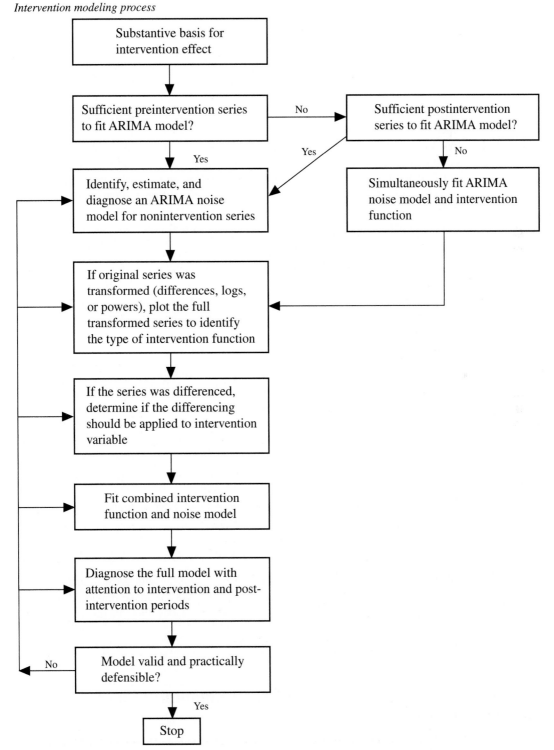

PACFs of the full series, just as any outlier distorts a time series. Because, prior to the intervention, only N_t exists in the series, the intervention function is best identified and estimated during this period.

While any univariate forecasting method can be used to model the preintervention period, the methods of ARIMA model building of Chapters 7 and 8 are used here.

Only after a good ARIMA model has been verified should the intervention function be identified and estimated. Hopefully, the intervention function will be based on theory. Then, the parameters of the noise model and intervention function are estimated simultaneously. If the coefficients are not statistically significant or are unacceptable because of violations of the bounds of stationarity or invertibility, then we seek an improved model. To confirm that a good intervention model has been found, we should diagnose both the noise model and intervention function. The same diagnostics that are used with univariate ARIMA models are used with intervention models. Thus, the residuals should not be significantly different than white noise. In addition, the overall validity measures applied to ARIMA models also apply to intervention models. The model should be parsimonious and estimated parameters significant and stable (a concept developed later). Also, the model should be theoretically and practically interpretable.

In summary, to empirically model an intervention we should have:

1. The date of intervention.
2. Theory suggesting the type of the impact on the time series.
3. Sufficient observations to identify the ARIMA noise model before the intervention.

   (When the preintervention observations do not support a preintervention model but the **postintervention** observations are sufficient and unaffected by the intervention function, then an ARIMA model can be fitted to the postintervention series. This model can then be applied to the full series. Finally, with some simple intervention models, the intervention function and the noise model can be identified and estimated simultaneously, however cautiously.)

4. Sufficient intervention and postintervention observations to identify the type of intervention effect. If there are not enough postintervention observations, then it may appear that the effect is permanent when it might instead be a temporary effect.

These four requirements suggest the sequence used to model an intervention, as shown in Figure 12–6.

We have seen that ARIMA models can be insightful with great intuitive appeal. This is even more the case for intervention models. We can make important statistical inferences using the results of intervention modeling. Let's illustrate this using several time series that have increasing complexity.

Zero-Order Intervention Model—Demand at a Community Blood Bank (BLOOD.DAT)

Figure 12–7 illustrates 187 weeks of demand for blood at a community blood bank located in the Midwest. In week 135, the market served by this blood bank expanded. Individuals at the blood bank confirm that because of the expansion, the demand

FIGURE 12–7

*Weekly demand at
blood bank
(BLOOD.DAT)*

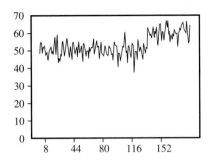

should shift permanently to a higher value. Thus, the following intervention function seems likely.

$$f(I)_t = \omega_0 I_t$$

where

$$I_t = 1 \text{ for } t > 134; \text{ otherwise } 0.$$

Thus, prior to the event, when $I_t = 0$, the value of $\omega_0 I_t$ is zero. However, when the event occurs, then $I_t = 1$ and the series increases by:

$$\omega_0 I_t = \omega_0 1 = \omega_0$$

Thus, the zero-order intervention function results in an abrupt, permanent shift in the level to ω_0, a step function. That is, at the time of the event, the series changes by ω_0.

Combining this behavior with the noise model yields:

$$Y_t = \omega_0 I_t + N_t \tag{12–11}$$

***Noise Model
Identification***

Thus, as shown in Figure 12–6 our task is to identify the noise model from the preintervention series; in this case Y_t for periods 1 to 134. Now let's fit the noise model to the preintervention periods. The ACFs and PACFs for periods 1 to 134 are:

Weekly data from 1 to 134

ACF(k)						
1:	.0357	−.1931	−.0595	.0132	−.1174	−.1450
7:	.0996	−.0028	−.1255	.0795	−.0434	−.0164
13:	−.0574	.0675	−.0288	.0546	.0865	−.0396
19:	.0202	.1386	−.0295	−.0381	.0135	−.0299

PACF(k)						
1:	.0357	−.1946	−.0462	−.0213	−.1435	−.1505
7:	.0582	−.0886	−.1289	.0655	−.1541	−.0146
13:	−.0830	−.0035	−.0948	.0859	.0058	−.0491
19:	.0719	.1280	−.0287	.0656	.0685	−.0781

Remembering that the 2 standard errors of the ACFs and PACFs are approximately $2/\sqrt{134} = .173$, there appears to be no clear patterns in the ACFs and PACFs, just as there are none in Figure 12–7. While there is a marginally significant peak at lag 2, we choose to ignore it, believing it represents sampling variation. Thus,

TABLE 12–3   An ARIMA(0,0,0) Model for Preintervention Blood (BLOOD.DAT)

Iterations taken	2
Usable observations	134
Degrees of freedom	133
$\bar{R}^2$	.000000
Mean of dependent variable	49.9191
Standard error of dependent variable	3.8502
Residual standard error	3.8502
Sum of squared residuals	1971.623
Durbin–Watson statistic	1.93
$Q(33-0)$	31.34
Significance level of Q	.5498

Coefficient	Estimate	Std Error	t-Stat	Significance
θ_0	49.919	.33261	150.084	.00000000

it appears that this is simply a random series (i.e., an ARIMA(0,0,0) model). Table 12–3 illustrates the fit of this model.

As Table 12–3 illustrates, simply taking the mean of the preintervention series yields white noise. That is, the following model of the preintervention series has white noise residuals:

$$Y_t - \mu = e_t$$

$$Y_t = \mu + e_t$$

Now using ARIMA notation, this is

$$Y_t = \theta_0 + e_t \qquad \text{(preintervention)}$$

where $\theta_0 = \mu$

While not shown here, plots of the residuals of the preintervention series and its ACFs and PACFs confirm that this is a good model. Having achieved a good noise model, let's estimate the intervention effect.

Because the effect of the intervention is quite pronounced in Figure 12–7, we expect the model of Equation 12–11 to be statistically valid. This is a model with $r = 0$, $s = 0$, and $b = 0$; that is, there is no right-hand side denominator δ_1 term. Thus $r = 0$, there is only one ω_0 term, $s = 0$, and finally, there is no lag in the effect, $b = 0$. The results of fitting this model are shown in Table 12–4.

The model of Table 12–4 appears to be a very good one. The t-statistics of the coefficients are both very significant and the DW and Q-statistics are compatible with a white noise assumption. The ACFs and PACFs of the residuals shown there have no discernible patterns and are indicative of white noise. Thus, we infer that this is a valid model of this time series.

Let's review this model. By simply taking deviations of Y_t from the mean during the preintervention period, white noise is achieved in the residuals. Also, during and after the intervention, there is an abrupt and permanent impact on Y_t. Thus, the following model results:

$$Y_t - \mu = \omega_0 I_t + e_t$$

$$Y_t = \mu + \omega_0 I_t + e_t$$

In forecasting form:

$$\hat{Y}_t = 49.91919 + 10.30920 I_t \qquad (12\text{--}12)$$

where $I_t = 1$ for $t > 134$; otherwise 0. Thus, the series has a mean of about 49.92 prior to the intervention, then increases to approximately 60.23 (i.e., 49.92 + 10.31) after the intervention. Figure 12–8 illustrates the fit of this step function, and this seems substantively defensible. Having fitted a correct model, let's consider the consequences of not modeling the intervention in the series.

TABLE 12–4   Zero-Order Intervention Model of Blood Demand, $r = 0$, $s = 0$, $b = 0$.

Dependent variable BLOOD—Estimation by Box–Jenkins

Iterations taken	2
Usable observations	187
Degrees of freedom	185
$\bar{R}^2$	.5933
Mean of dependent variable	52.8411
Standard error of dependent variable	6.0367
Standard error of estimate	3.8498
Sum of squared residuals	2741.88
Durbin–Watson statistic	1.84
$Q(24)$	27.99
Significance level of Q	.2606

Coefficient	Estimate	Std Error	t-Stat	Significance
θ_0	49.919	0.3326	150.1003	.00000000
ω_o	10.309	0.6247	16.5027	.00000000

ACFs and PACFs of the Residuals of Table 12–4

ACF(k)

1:	.0791	−.1526	−.0874	.0251	−.1170	−.1558
7:	.0603	.0196	−.0432	.0319	−.0593	−.0686
13:	−.0884	.0137	−.0278	.0787	.0508	.0029
19:	.0585	.1421	−.0310	−.0668	.0502	−.0145

PACF(k)

1:	.0791	−.1598	−.0628	.0142	−.1485	−.1417
7:	.0487	−.0620	−.0520	.0357	−.1337	−.0718
13:	−.0951	−.0478	−.0857	.0596	−.0374	−.0337
19:	.0631	.1210	−.0450	.0190	.0739	−.0656

FIGURE 12–8

Intervention model for blood demand

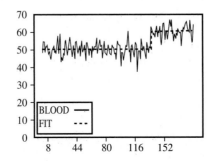

Univariate Analysis of Intervention Series

If, in univariate ARIMA analysis, we analyze a time series and mistakenly ignore a large intervention, then it may be impossible to fit a useful model. Table 12–5 illustrates the ACFs and PACFs for all 187 observations of the Blood Bank demand, inclusive of pre-, peri-, and postintervention periods. The ACFs and PACFs of Table 12–5 appear to come from a nonstationary time series having very high ACFs for the first 24 lags and a single large spike in the PACFs with other significant spikes through lag 4. This pattern is confounding in the context of univariate ARIMA modeling. Instead, it should be modeled as done in the previous section.

Zero-Order Intervention Model—Nonstationary Demand for Bottled Water (WATER.DAT)

Let's consider a zero-order intervention model for a nonstationary series. Just as in ARIMA modeling, it is necessary to achieve stationarity as the first step in intervention modeling. Figure 12–9 illustrates a nonstationary time series that undergoes an abrupt temporary impact. In this case, the series is trending with a sudden increase in periods 75 to 84.

This series is the weekly demand for bottled water before, during, and after the 1993 Midwestern floods. As shown in Figure 12–9, this series is nonstationary in level, and while not as evident, analysis has shown it to be nonseasonal. During weeks

TABLE 12–5   ACFs and PACFs of Full Blood Time Series, $n = 187$

Weekly Data from 1:01 to 187:01					
Autocorrelations					
1:	.6070	.5089	.5295	.5653	.4974	.4673
7:	.5347	.4970	.4604	.4693	.4173	.4020
⋮						
25:	.2926					
Partial autocorrelations					
1:	.6070	.2225	.2571	.2465	.0570	.0607
7:	.1892	.0301	.0333	.0672	−.0850	−.0047
⋮						
25:	−.1034					

FIGURE 12–9

Demand for bottled water (WATER.DAT)

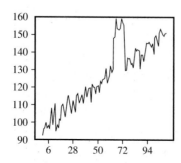

75 to 84, a flood struck a small community served by the bottled water company. The flood came quickly and disrupted the water supply from weeks 75 through 84. We see that the company experienced a considerable increase in demand. To better understand its behavior, consider the values of demand about the time of the flood.

Week	Y_t	I_t	
70	126.93	.0	
71	127.48	.0	
72	134.21	.0	
73	130.87	.0	
74	129.77	.0	
75	154.36	1.0	
76	155.00	1.0	
77	161.43	1.0	
78	160.36	1.0	
79	160.78	1.0	
80	157.60	1.0	Flood
81	158.49	1.0	
82	155.07	1.0	
83	162.92	1.0	
84	167.08	1.0	
85	140.00	1.0	
86	140.95	1.0	
87	140.25	1.0	

To analyze this series, we first must fit a preintervention model to periods 1 to 74. Consider the ACFs and PACFs for the preintervention period given in the following table.

			Preintervention Weeks 1 to 74			
ACF(k)						
1:	.8500	.7807	.7623	.7337	.7109	.6679
7:	.6631	.5862	.5537	.5586	.5118	.4793
13:	.4566	.4398	.3812	.3350	.2805	.2282
PACF(k)						
1:	.8500	.2098	.2245	.0822	.0796	−.0437
7:	.1152	−.2327	.0434	.0862	−.0811	−.0095
13:	.0387	−.0144	−.1138	−.0615	−.1967	−.0246

The ACFs and PACFs of this series confirm its preintervention nonstationarity, evident in Figure 12–9. A first differenced, trend model of the preintervention series, periods 1 to 74 is reported in Table 12–6.

The results of Table 12–6 confirm that first differences may be necessary but insufficient to achieve white noise residuals. We see that the Q-statistic is not indicative of white noise. In addition, the constant term is not statistically significant. Also, because there is a very significant ACF at lag 1 and several high negative PACFs at lags 1 to 4, the residuals appear to be an MA(1) process. Consequently, an ARIMA(0,1,1)1 model is fitted to the preintervention series. The results of this model are shown in Table 12–7. As shown, this model appears to be a very good one. All diagnostics are good. In addition, the residual ACFs and PACFs are consistent with white noise.

Figure 12–10 illustrates the fit of the following preintervention, univariate ARIMA model.

$$(1 - B)Y_t = \theta_0 + (1 - \theta_1 B)e_t$$

$$Y_t = \theta_0 + \frac{(1 - \theta_1 B)}{(1 - B)} e_t \qquad \text{(Preintervention model)}$$

This fit seems very good and, if the intervention of the flood in periods 75 to 84 had not taken place, the continuation of the trend of this model seems to be a very reasonable assumption.

Now that we have identified a good noise model, let's fit an intervention function. First consider how first differences have transformed Y_t and I_t about the time of the intervention. As the following shows, $(1 - B)Y_t$ has a large positive spike in period 75 and a large negative spike in period 85. Also, note that pulses in the first differences of the intervention, I_t and first differences of the 10-period lagged values of I_t match the spikes in Y_t for periods 75 and 85 respectively. Because of this behavior, terms $(1 - B)I_t$ and $(1 - B)I_{t-10}$ should both be included in a model.

Date	Y_t	I_t	$(1 - B)Y_t$	$(1 - B)I_t$	$(1 - B)I_{t-10}$
72	134.21	.0	6.73	.0	.0
73	130.88	.0	−3.34	.0	.0
74	129.78	.0	−1.10	.0	.0
75	154.36	1.0	24.59	1.0	.0
76	155.00	1.0	0.64	.0	.0
77	161.43	1.0	6.43	.0	.0
78	160.37	1.0	−1.07	.0	.0
79	160.79	1.0	.42	.0	.0
80	157.60	1.0	−3.19	.0	.0
81	158.50	1.0	.90	.0	.0
82	155.07	1.0	−3.43	.0	.0
83	162.92	1.0	7.85	.0	.0
84	167.08	1.0	4.16	.0	.0
85	140.00	1.0	−27.08	.0	1.0
86	140.95	1.0	.95	.0	.0
87	140.26	1.0	−.70	.0	.0

The following intervention function seems appropriate for this data:

$$Y_t = (\omega_0 - \omega_1 B^{10})I_t + \frac{\theta_0 + (1 - \theta_1 B)}{(1 - B)} e_t \qquad (12\text{–}13)$$

$$\text{where } I_t = \begin{cases} 0 \text{ for t} < 75 \\ 1 \text{ for t} > 74 \end{cases}$$

This intervention function is designated as $r = 0, s = 1, b = 0$ where there is a ten period lag between ω_0 and $-\omega_1$ corresponding to the start and stop of the flood. If your software supports this type of notation, then it is easy to estimate this model; if not, then refer to the end of this section for alternative methods for modeling this series.

TABLE 12–6 ARIMA(0,1,0)1 for Bottled Water Cases

Iterations taken	2
Usable observations	73
Degrees of freedom	72
$\bar{R}^2$	.7752
Mean of dependent variable	114.1143
Standard error of dependent variable	11.2585
Residual standard error	5.3373
Sum of squared residuals	2051.041
Durbin–Watson statistic	2.738
$Q(18-0)$	35.025
Significance level of Q	.00939

Coefficient	Estimate	Std Error	t-Stat	Signif
θ_0	.5511	.62468	.88222	.3806

ACFs and PACFs of $(1 - B)Y_t$

ACF(k)						
1:	−.3705	−.2288	.0959	.0082	.0394	−.1659
7:	.2550	−.0872	−.0807	.0504	.0101	.0001
13:	−.1878	.2504	−.0684	.0205	.0129	−.1050

PACF(k)						
1:	−.3705	−.4243	−.2574	−.2335	−.1089	−.3180
7:	.0438	−.0455	.0063	−.0093	.0411	−.0046
13:	−.2337	−.0406	−.1545	.0644	.0715	.0310

TABLE 12–7 ARIMA(0,1,1)1 for Bottled Water Demand (Weeks 1 to 74)

Iterations taken	11
Usable observations	73
Degrees of freedom	71
$\bar{R}^2$	.8612
Mean of dependent variable	114.114
Standard error of dependent variable	11.259
Residual standard error	4.195
Sum of squared residuals	1249.53
Durbin–Watson statistic	1.882
$Q(18-1)$	15.056
Significance level of Q	.5915

Coefficient	Estimate	Std Error	t-Stat	Signif
θ_0	.544002	.07538	7.217	.00000000
$-\theta_1$	−.860071	.06321	−13.607	.00000000

Correlation Matrix of Coefficients

	$-\theta_1$
θ_0	−.2136

continued

**TABLE 12–7   ARIMA(0,1,1)1 for Bottled Water Demand
Weeks 1 to 74
concluded**

Residual ACFs and PACFs: Periods 2 to 74

ACF (k)

1:	.0523	−.1808	.0275	.0412	.0390	−.0365
7:	.2061	−.0210	−.0994	−.0288	−.0388	−.0700
13:	−.0976	.2234	.0668	.0394	−.0077	−.0882

PACF(k)

1:	.0523	−.1841	.0502	.0029	.0521	−.0376
7:	.2358	−.0794	−.0062	−.0673	−.0518	−.1157
13:	−.0772	.1880	.0356	.1784	−.0048	−.0384

FIGURE 12–10

*Preintervention
fit for bottled water*

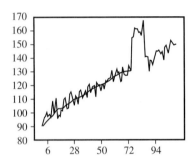

Table 12–8 illustrates the fitted model. The diagnostic statistics of this model are quite good. The $\overline{R}^2$ is quite high at about 95 percent. It appears that the residuals are white noise as measured by the DW and Q statistics. The coefficients are all statistically significant, having extremely high t-values. None of the estimated coefficients are highly correlated. The ACFs and PACFs of Table 12–8 are consistent with white noise. Let's interpret this model further.

This model has the following structure:

$$Y_t = (\omega_0 - \omega_1 B^{10})I_t + \frac{\theta_0 + (1 - \theta_1 B)}{(1 - B)}e_t$$

which when expanded yields:

$$(1 - B)Y_t = (1 - B)(\omega_0 - \omega_1 B^{10})I_t + \theta_0 + (1 - \theta_1 B)e_t$$

substituting the coefficients of Table 12–8,

$$(1 - B)Y_t = (1 - B)(23.658 - 25.851B^{10})I_t + .5431 + (1 - .9538B)e_t$$

In forecasting form:

$$(1 - B)Y_t = (1 - B)(23.658 - 25.851B^{10})I_t + .5431 - .9538e_{t-1} \tag{12-14}$$

$$\hat{Y}_t = Y_{t-1} + (1 - B)(23.658 - 25.851B^{10})I_t + .5431 - .9538e_{t-1}$$

Expanding the intervention function:

$$\hat{Y}_t = Y_{t-1} + 23.658I_t - 23.658I_{t-1} - 25.851I_{t-10} + 25.851I_{t-11} + .5431 - .9538e_{t-1} \tag{12-15}$$

Thus, this series has a trend of .5431 cases and a moving average component. In addition, when the flood struck in period 75, demand increased by 23.658 cases as I_t

TABLE 12–8   Full Intervention Model of Bottled Water Demand

Estimation by Box–Jenkins

Iterations taken	9	
Usable observations	99	
Degrees of freedom	95	
$\bar{R}^2$	.9517	
Mean of dependent variable	127.960	
Standard error of dependent variable	17.773	
Residual standard error	3.905	
Sum of squared residuals	1448.460	
Durbin–Watson statistic	1.741	
$Q(27-1)$	16.377	
Significance level of Q	.839	

Coefficient	Estimate	Std Error	t-Stat	Signif
θ_0	.5431	.0376	14.455	.00000000
$-\theta_1$	−.9538	.0413	−23.069	.00000000
ω_0	23.658	2.0245	11.686	.00000000
$-\omega_1$	−25.851	1.6485	−15.682	.00000000

Correlation Matrix of Coefficients

	θ_0	θ_1	ω_0	$-\omega_1$
θ_0	.00141	−.61166	−.63421	−.35144
$-\theta_1$	−.00095	.00171	.56237	.19011
ω_0				−.20406

Residual ACFs and PACFs

ACF (k)

1:	.1348	−.1134	.0136	.0173	.0365	.0204
7:	.2009	.0364	.0162	.0713	.0311	.0559
13:	−.0739	.0999	.0441	.0901	.0859	−.0349

PACF(k)

1:	.1348	−.1340	.0508	−.0081	.0444	.0089
7:	.2145	−.0292	.0754	.0463	.0266	.0458
13:	−.0944	.1043	−.0286	.1199	.0158	−.0225

went from 0 to 1 and when the flood subsided in period 85, the effect was reversed by the term $-25.851B^{10}I_t$. To better understand this model, consider its behavior during periods 74, 75, 76, 84, 85, 86, and 87 where previous actual values are known. (Remember, $I_t = 0$ prior to period 75 and 1 after period 74, and for our purposes, ignore the value of the lagged error term, $+ .9538e_{73}$.)

$$\hat{Y}_t = Y_{t-1} + 23.658I_t - 23.658I_{t-1} - 25.851I_{t-10} + 25.851I_{t-11} + .5431 - .9538e_{t-1}$$

$$\hat{Y}_{74} = Y_{73} + 23.658(0) - 23.658(0) - 25.851(0) + 25.851(0) + .5431 - .9538e_{73}$$

$$= 130.88 + 0 + 0 + 0 + 0 + .5431 + .9538e_{73} = 131.42 - .9538e_{73}$$

At $t = 75$, there is a 23.658 increase over the trend of .5431.

$$\hat{Y}_{75} = Y_{74} + 23.658(1) - 23.658(0) - 25.851(0) + 25.851(0) + .5431 - .9538e_{74}$$

$$= 129.78 + 23.658 + 0 + 0 + 0 + .5431 - 9538e_{74}$$

$$= 153.98 - .9538e_{74}$$

From $t = 76$ to 84, there is only the usual trend increase from period to period.

$$\hat{Y}_{76} = Y_{75} + 23.658(1) - 23.658(1) - 25.851(0) + 25.851(0) + .5431 - .9538e_{75}$$
$$= 154.36 + 23.658 - 23.658 + 0 + 0 + .5431 - .9538e_{75}$$
$$= 154.90 - .9538e_{75}$$

$$\cdots$$

$$\hat{Y}_{84} = Y_{83} + 23.658(1) - 23.658(1) - 25.851(0) + 25.851(0) + .5431 - .9538e_{83}$$
$$= 162.92 + 23.658 - 23.658 + 0 + 0 + .5431 - .9538e_{83}$$
$$= 163.46 - .9538e_{83}$$

At $t = 85$ there is a permanent decline of -25.851 cases which more than reverses the previous increase at period 75.

$$\hat{Y}_{85} = Y_{84} + 23.658(1) - 23.658(1) - 25.851(1) + 25.851(0) + .5431 - .9538e_{84}$$
$$= 167.08 + 23.658 - 23.658 - 25.851 + 0 + .5431 - .9538e_{84}$$
$$= 141.29 - .9538e_{84}$$

At $t > 85$ there are no further changes other than the trend of .5431.

$$\hat{Y}_{86} = Y_{85} + 23.658(1) - 23.658(1) - 25.851(1) + 25.851(1) + .5431 - .9538e_{85}$$
$$= 140.00 + 23.658 - 23.658 - 25.851 + 25.851 + .5431 - .9538e_{85}$$
$$= 140.54 - .9538e_{85}$$

$$\hat{Y}_{87} = Y_{86} + 23.658(1) - 23.658(1) - 25.851(1) + 25.851(1) + .535 - .9538e_{86}$$
$$= 140.95 + 23.658 - 23.658 - 25.851 + 25.851 + .5431 - 9538e_{86}$$
$$= 141.49 - .9538e_{86}$$

From $t > 85$, the series behaves as a simple ARIMA (0,1,1)1 model.

This behavior corresponds to other data collected by management. From sales records of new and pre-flood customers, the firm saw increased demand for water during the flood. However, this increased demand resulted in a slight increase in competition for bottled water. As the company struggled to meet customer demand during the flood, other firms entered the market and thus, a small share of the market ($23.658 - 25.8511 = -2.1931$) was lost by this company to others after the flood.

Figure 12–11 illustrates the fit of the full model. As shown, the fitted values track actual demands very closely. Because of this and its other attributes, we have considerable confidence in this model.

The model-building strategy outlined in this example is general. However, each time series presents unique problems that may require modifications of this strategy.

FIGURE 12–11

Pre-, peri-, and postintervention fit

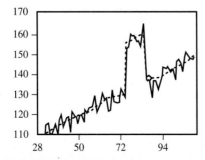

Finally, we note that in this example, a test of a null hypothesis was not at all in question. The impact was visually obvious. Intervention analysis nonetheless provided precise estimates of the form and magnitude of the effect.

We have shown the intervention function using backshift notation. However, some software products do not support this type of expression. When this is true, then either one of the following approaches may yield accurate intervention models using ordinary least squares regression.

Approach 1: Create one intervention variable that turns on and off at the appropriate time:

t	1	2 ...	74	75 ...	84	85 ...	110
I_t	0	0 ...	0	1 ...	1	0 ...	0

This intervention variable is used in the following simple, zero-order intervention function:

$$f(I_t) = \omega_0 I_t$$

With this model, the decrease in the series at time 85 is forced to equal the increase at time 75.

Approach 2: Create two intervention variables that turn on at different times:

t	1	2 ...	74	75 ...	84	85 ...	110
$I1_t$	0	0 ...	0	1 ...	1	1 ...	1
$I2_t$	0	0 ...	0	0 ...	0	1 ...	1

These two intervention variables are used in the following compound intervention function:

$$f(I_t) = \omega_0 I1_t + \omega_1 I2_t \tag{12–16}$$

In this case, the values of ω_0 and ω_1 are allowed to be different, and should not deviate from those of Table 12–8, if at all.

Modeling the Stock Market Crash of 1987 (SP500I.DAT)

Consider an intervention model of the stock market crash of October 1987. Figure 12–12 illustrates the S&P 500 before and after the crash. As shown, this stock index declined dramatically during the intervention period. Also shown is the level nonstationarity of the series, and, while not shown here, first differences yield a series with nonstationary variance. Fortunately, logarithms of this series achieve variance stationarity, thus, natural logs will be used in this analysis.

FIGURE 12–12

Monthly S&P 500

The Crash of '87: Black Monday

Over the last century and a quarter, there have been several severe stock market crashes, a recent one being the October 19, 1987, crash. On that date, the Dow Jones Industrial Average declined by more than 500 points, a 22.5 percent decrease. This decline was "blamed" on several factors, including weakness in the U.S. economy, computerized trading in the market that triggered automatic sell orders, and poor U.S. leadership in international trade. This large market decline resulted in large losses on international stock markets, including Tokyo and London. Also, in mid-October, before Black Monday, the New York Stock Exchange had three days of significant price declines before the "big one." However, by the end of 1987, the stock market had rebounded and the index had moved slightly above the average of the end of the previous year, 1986.

TABLE 12–9 $(1 - B)\mathrm{Ln}Y_t$ for Preintervention Closing Prices of S&P 500 (SP500I.DAT)

Iterations taken		2			
Usable observations		69			
Degrees of freedom		68			
$\bar{R}^2$		.9796			
Mean of dependent variable		5.2059			
Standard error of dependent variable		.2931			
Residual standard error		.0419			
Sum of squared residuals		.1192			
Durbin–Watson statistic		2.211			
$Q(17\text{–}0)$		14.659			
Significance level of Q		.6200			

Coeff	Estimate	Std Error	t-Stat	Signif
θ_0	.01399	.0050	2.777	.00709

ACF(k)						
1:	−.1159	.1126	−.0014	−.0850	.2365	−.1324
7:	−.0980	−.1337	−.0768	.0323	−.1242	.0399
13:	−.1488	.0624	.0171	−.0223	.0128	−.1058

PACF(k)						
1:	−.1159	.1005	.0225	−.0964	.2225	−.0755
7:	−.1814	−.1506	−.0403	−.0178	−.0981	.0591
13:	−.1013	.0046	−.0161	−.0200	−.0726	−.0878

Having previously analyzed this time series using univariate ARIMA methods, the preintervention series was found to be a trending ARIMA(0,1,0)1,1 series, as shown in Chapter 8. Table 12–9 shows the ARIMA(0,1,0)1,1 model of the logarithms of the closing prices of the S&P 500 for the preintervention series using SP500I.DAT. This simple model achieves white noise residuals and has intuitive appeal.

$$\widehat{\mathrm{Ln}Y_t} = \mathrm{Ln}Y_{t-1} + \theta_0 = \mathrm{Ln}Y_{t-1} + .013993 \qquad (12\text{–}17)$$

where

$$\mathrm{Ln}Y_t = \log(\text{S\&P500})$$

FIGURE 12–13

Alternative intervention effects of 1987 stock market crash

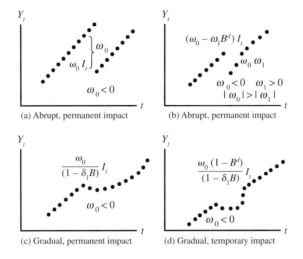

(a) Abrupt, permanent impact

(b) Abrupt, permanent impact

(c) Gradual, permanent impact

(d) Gradual, temporary impact

In modeling the impact of the 1987 crash, it is important to have theory denoting the shape and duration of the impact. There are many possible effects that this crash could have on the value of the S&P500. Figures 12–13a to d illustrate several possible impacts. As shown in Figure 12–13a, the influence could have resulted in an abrupt permanent impact on the index, where the price declines to a lower value and then continues the trend that existed prior to the intervention. Alternatively, in Figure 12–13c, the index might have gradually declined to a permanently lower point prior to continuing its trend upward. Other possible explanations are shown in Figures 12–13 b and d. As we will see, we choose the abrupt two-step permanent impact of b.

In deciding which intervention profile explains the effect, it is important to have a theory. If the event only influences the series for one period, then a pulse is used. If the event is expected to permanently influence the series, then it is represented by a step function. Because the change in the S&P 500 appears to be permanent, a step function is used. Therefore, we represent this intervention with the following:

$$I_t = \begin{cases} 0 \text{ prior to October 198, period} \\ 1 \text{ on and after October 1987, period} \end{cases}$$

To better understand this intervention, consider Figure 12–14, which illustrates the behavior of the S&P 500 immediately around and after October 1987. As shown, there was a dramatic decline in October 1987 followed by another smaller decline in November. These two declines were followed by an increasing trend that appears typical of the past trend. To further clarify the intervention effect, Figure 12–15 illustrates the first differences of the logs. As shown, the October and November first differences are large negative values, reflecting the crash. Because the November first difference is the third largest negative value, this suggests the intervention was still influencing the market. These scenarios suggest three alternative intervention models, the second one appearing to be the most likely.

- Abrupt, permanent single-month decline (Figure 12–13a)

$$\omega_0 I_t \qquad r = 0, s = 0, b = 0 \tag{12–18}$$

- Abrupt, permanent two-month decline (Figure 12–13b)

$$(\omega_0 - \omega_1 B)I_t \qquad r = 0, s = 1, b = 0 \tag{12–19}$$

FIGURE 12–14

Logs of monthly S&P 500

FIGURE 12–15

First differences of logs of S&P 500

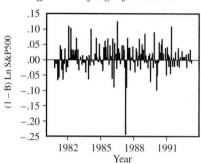

- Gradual, permanent decline (Figure 12–13d)

$$\frac{\omega_0}{(1 - \delta_1 B)} I_t \qquad r = 1, s = 0, b = 0 \qquad\qquad (12\text{--}20)$$

These models are reported in Tables 12–10, 12–12, and 12–13, respectively.

The model of Table 12–10 has acceptable goodness of fit measures. However, as shown in Table 12–11, the residual is large in November 1987, being about 2.46 times the standard error of estimate of Table 12–10 (i.e., $-.1020/.0415$).

The large residual in November 1987 and the previous graphs suggest Equation 12–19 as an alternative model; Table 12–12 illustrates the results of fitting this model. As shown, this model and its diagnostics are defensible. The ACFs and PACFs of the residuals shown in Table 12–12 are consistent with a white noise series. Also, while not shown, the large residual seen in November is no longer there. This model appears to be better than that of Table 12–10. To exclude the possibility that Equation 12–20 is the appropriate model, let's consider the results of fitting a first-order intervention model.

First-Order Model of Stock Market Crash

Table 12–13 illustrates the first-order intervention model of Equation 12–20. This model is a very good one except that the δ_1 parameter is not statistically significant. Unless there is some theoretical reason for selecting this model, the model of Table 12–12 dominates Table 12–13. Thus, we accept the model of Table 12–12 as the one that best explains the 1987 stock market crash, as measured by the monthly data.

Interpretation of Natural Log Intervention Models

The model of Table 12–12 is:

$$LnY_t = (\omega_0 - \omega_1 B)I_t + \frac{\theta_0}{(1 - B)} e_t \qquad\qquad (12\text{--}21)$$

$$LnY_t = (-.2597 - .1035B)I_t + \frac{.0143}{(1 - B)} e_t.$$

where

$LnY_t = $ Natural logs of monthly S&P 500

$$I_t = \begin{cases} 0 \text{ before October 1987} \\ 1 \text{ after September 1987} \end{cases}$$

TABLE 12–10 $(r = 0, s = 0, b = 0)$ **Model of $(1 - B)$ Logs of S&P 500 (SP500I.DAT)**

Iterations taken	2
Usable observations	97
Degrees of freedom	95
$\bar{R}^2$	.984
Mean of dependent variable	5.340
Standard error of dependent variable	.332
Residual standard error	.0415
Sum of squared residuals	.1639
Durbin–Watson statistic	2.233
$Q(24-0)$	13.958
Significance level of Q	.948

Coeff	Estimate	Std Error	t-Stat	Signif
θ_0	.0128	.00424	3.030	.00315
ω_0	−.2583	.04175	−6.186	.00000

Correlation of Coefficients

	ω_0
θ_0	−.1015

ACFs and PACFs of Residuals

ACF(k)						
1:	−.1410	.0477	−.0146	−.0041	.1057	−.0756
7:	−.0412	−.1488	−.0899	−.0435	.0158	−.0123
13:	−.1251	.0644	.0061	−.0111	.0068	−.0866
19:	.0175	.0075	−.0677	.0495	−.0150	.1254
PACF(k)						
1:	−.1410	.0284	−.0041	−.0082	.1069	−.0480
7:	−.0680	−.1624	−.1385	−.0848	.0149	.0067
13:	−.1096	.0294	.0031	−.0726	−.0510	−.1132
19:	−.0581	−.0123	−.1069	.0008	.0027	.1173

As you may recall, log transformations of time series are appropriate when the series variances are proportional to the level of the series. In estimating an intervention model of a logarithmic series, the ω_0 coefficient is interpreted as the pre- to postintervention percentage change in the time series. To better appreciate the meaning of this, consider the simple conversion of the logarithmic to original metric values.

- *Monthly trend in S&P 500.*

$$\mathbf{e}^{\theta_0} - 1 = \mathbf{e}^{.0143} - 1 = 1.014 - 1 = .014 = 1.4\%$$

Thus, during this period of time, the monthly increase in the S&P 500 is 1.4 percent. Historically, this is higher than normal; nonetheless, this agrees with the preintervention value of Table 12–9.

- *Permanent shift down in October 1987.* The theory of Table 12–12 is that the market shifted down permanently in October and then again in November, but then it continued its previous trend upward. The permanent shift down in October is:

$$\mathbf{e}^{\omega_0} - 1 = \mathbf{e}^{-.2597} - 1 = .7721 - 1 = -.2279 = -22.79\%$$

TABLE 12–11   Residuals in about October 1987

Observation	LnY_t	Residual	I_t
1987:JUL	5.7641	.0342	0
1987:AUG	5.7984	.0215	0
1987:SEP	5.7740	−.0373	0
1987:OCT	5.5285	.0000	1
1987:NOV	5.4393	−.1020	1
1987:DEC	5.5097	.0575	1
1988:JAN	5.5493	.0268	1

TABLE 12–12 $(r = 0, s = 1, b = 0)$ $(1 − B)$ Logs of S&P 500 (SP500I.DAT)

Iterations taken	2
Usable observations	96
Degrees of freedom	93
$\bar{R}^2$	0.9848
Mean of dependent variable	5.3485
Standard error of dependent variable	.3287
Residual standard error	.0405
Sum of squared residuals	.1524
Durbin–Watson statistic	2.1799
$Q(24–0)$	16.6270
Significance level of Q	.8641

Coeff	Estimate	Std Error	t-Stat	Signif
θ_0	.0143	.0042	3.415	.0009
ω_0	−.2597	.0407	−6.382	.0000
$−\omega_1$	−.1035	.0407	−2.542	.0127

Correlation of Coefficients

	ω_0	$−\omega_1$
θ_0	−.1026	−.1026
ω_0		.0105

ACFs and PACFs of Residuals

ACF(k)						
1:	−.1308	.0374	.0212	−.0264	.1233	−.1044
7:	−.0241	−.1671	−.0990	.0485	−.0031	−.0264
13:	−.1070	.0415	.0270	−.0627	.0370	−.0644
19:	−.0148	.0816	−.0396	.0325	−.0272	.1647

PACF(k)						
1:	−.1308	.0206	.0292	−.0212	.1178	−.0756
7:	−.0542	−.1842	−.1424	.0110	.0445	−.0145
13:	−.0934	.0046	−.0071	−.1077	−.0225	−.0469
19:	−.0416	.0646	−.0415	−.0122	−.0094	.1516

TABLE 12–13 $(r = 1, s = 0, b = 0)(1 - B)$ **Logs of S&P 500**

Iterations taken	23
Usable observations	97
Degrees of freedom	94
$\bar{R}^2$	.9848
Mean of dependent variable	5.3401
Standard error of dependent variable	.3318
Residual standard error	.0409
Sum of squared residuals	.1572
Durbin–Watson statistic	2.2017
$Q(24-0)$	14.8705
Significance level of Q	.9245

Coeff	Estimate	Std Error	t-Stat	Signif
θ_0	.0138	.0042	3.2583	.00156
ω_0	−.2642	.0410	−6.4409	.00000
$-\delta_1$	−.2386	.1430	1.6687	.09850

Correlation of Coefficients

	ω_0	$-\delta_1$
θ_0	−.0971	.1306
ω_0		.2163

ACFs and PACFs of Residuals

ACF(k)						
1:	−.1270	.0486	−.0029	−.0080	.1214	−.0827
7:	−.0454	−.1636	−.1001	.0081	.0140	−.0213
13:	−.1141	.0506	.0034	−.0325	.0192	−.0689
19:	.0105	.0506	−.0449	.0425	−.0179	.1529

PACF(k)						
1:	−.1270	.0330	.0074	−.0092	.1212	−.0542
7:	−.0744	−.1790	−.1473	−.0289	.0423	.0046
13:	−.0920	.0216	−.0216	−.1001	−.0393	−.0676
19:	−.0280	.0519	−.0564	.0007	−.0006	.1366

Thus, the market shifted down by 22.79 percent in October 1994. This shift was followed by another shift down in November 1987.

- *Permanent shift down in November 1987.*

$$e^{\omega_1} - 1 = e^{-.1035} - 1 = .902 - 1 = -.098 = -9.8\%$$

The market shifted down another 9.8 percent in November of 1987.

- *Combined permanent shift down as of November 1987.*

$$e^{\omega_0 + \omega_1} - 1 = e^{-.2597 - .1035} - 1 = .696 - 1 = -.304 = -30.4\%$$

The total of the October and November declines resulted in a 30.4 percent decrease in the market.

- *Ratio equivalences of logarithmic values.* Table 12–14 illustrates the ratio equivalences of the logarithmic values of Table 12–12. As shown there, the model of Table 12–12 is easily interpreted in terms of ratios. Now the percents calculated

TABLE 12–14   Ratios Related to Logarithmic Intervention Values

	Y_t	$\dfrac{Y_t}{Y_{t-1}}$	$1 - \dfrac{Y_t}{Y_{t-1}}$	$\left(1 - \dfrac{Y_t}{Y_{t-1}} - .014\right)$	Ratios Using ω_0 and ω_1
July	318.65				
August	329.77				
September	321.82				
October	251.77	.782	.218	.232	approx. .2284
November	230.28	.915	.085	.099	approx. .098

previously using the coefficients of Table 12–12 are least squares estimates while those of Table 12–14 are the ratios of the actual values of October and November to those of the previous values. As shown in Table 12–14, October is about .782 percent of September, a 21.8 percent drop. The ω_0 conversion denotes a 22.79 percent drop. However, this drop was assuming that the trend that existed on average through September would have persisted through October and November, so we must adjust for the trend that would have taken place if there were no crash. Thus, the trend-adjusted drop from September to November is even greater, as shown in the second last column, where the trend is subtracted from the simple ratios. As shown, the ratios are very nearly equal to the converted coefficients of Table 12–12. For example, November as a percent of October is, after adjusting for the expected trend .099, a 9.9 percent drop, while the ω_1 conversion denotes a 9.8 percent drop.

First-Order Intervention Function—Advertising Impact on Airline Passengers (AIRLINI.DAT)

Figure 12–16 illustrates the logarithms of the monthly number of international airline passengers (AIRLINI.DAT) over a 12-year period. This is the same series as AIR-LINE.DAT except that at the beginning of year 11, a new advertising campaign was started with the introduction of a new fleet of jet aircraft. The effect of the new fleet is rather obvious in period 121. While not shown here, univariate analysis of the preintervention series yields an ARIMA(0,1,1)0,1(0,1,1). Table 12–15 shows the resulting model of the preintervention series; while not shown, the residuals are distributed as white noise. (Note: This intervention was contrived for this discussion.)

Intervention Effect   While the type of intervention that describes the effect of the new advertising campaign may not be clear from Figure 12–16, what is clear is that the effect is permanent. To better help identify whether the effect is abrupt or gradual, consider Figure 12–17, which illustrates seasonal first (i.e., 12th) differences of this series. From this graph, it appears that the effect of advertising is gradual. Thus, the following intervention function appears likely:

$$\frac{\omega_0}{(1 - \delta_1 B)} I_t \qquad r = 1, s = 0, b = 0 \qquad (12\text{–}22)$$

However, in the spirit of building models iteratively, a zero-order model is fit, then a first-order model.

$$\omega_0 I_t \qquad r = 0, s = 0, b = 0 \qquad (12\text{–}23)$$

The Origins of Random Walks

On March 29, 1900, Louis Bachelier, a French student, defended his dissertation *Theorie de la Speculation*, in mathematics at the University of Paris. This was a mathematical treatment of how prices for stocks and bonds fluctuated on the Paris financial market, the Bourse. His dissertation was not well received, and while he did pass his defense, his grade was not as high as the significance of his theory. Explicitly, Louis Bachelier defined the random walk theory that is so well known on financial markets throughout the world. Here is a nonmathematical statement of that theory. Interestingly, as we have done in our analysis of stock prices and indexes, Bachelier recognized that stock prices were nonstationary in variance, therefore his analyses and the following properties relate to the logarithms of stock prices.

1. Changes (i.e. first differences of logs) in stock prices are white noise shocks.
2. Consequently, they are normally and independently distributed.
3. They are stationary in that price changes are invariant with respect to time; they are distributed identically in periods t to $t + k$ as they are in periods $t + 1$ to $t + 1 + k$.

This random walk theory is called the weak random walk theory in the financial community. It states that you cannot determine the movement of future stock prices based on univariate analysis of the past.

FIGURE 12–16

Logs of airline passengers with intervention in month 121.

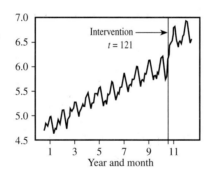

TABLE 12–15   ARIMA(0,1,1)0,1(0,1,1) of Preintervention Airline Passengers

Usable observations			120	
Degrees of freedom			118	
$\bar{R}^2$			.9879	
Mean of dependent variable			5.5034	
Standard error of dependent variable			.3482	
Residual standard error			.0384	
Sum of squared residuals			.1546	
Durbin–Watson statistic			1.9764	
$Q(26-2)$			17.7807	
Significance level of Q			.8135	
Coeff	*Estimate*	*Std Error*	*t-Stat*	*Signif*
$-\theta_1$	$-.3178$	.0935	-3.399	.00095
$-\theta_{12}$	$-.5671$	.0903	-6.279	.00000

Figure 12–17

*Seasonal differences
of airline passengers*

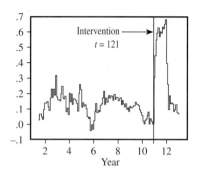

Table 12–16 $(r = 0, s = 0, b = 0)$ $X(0, 1, 1)$ $X(0, 1, 1)$ **Model of
Logs of Airline Passengers**

Usable observations	131
Degrees of freedom	128
$\bar{R}^2$	.9938
Mean of dependent variable	5.7007
Standard error of dependent variable	.5296
Residual standard error	.0417
Sum of squared residuals	.2229
Durbin–Watson statistic	1.9907
$Q(32$–$2)$	28.5009
Significance level of Q	.5439

Coefficient	Estimate	Std Error	t-Stat	Signif
$-\theta_1$	−.2142	.0871	−2.457	.01533
$-\theta_{12}$	−.6544	.0731	−8.949	.00000
ω_0	.3156	.0387	8.152	.00000

Correlation Matrix of Coefficients

	$-\theta_{12}$	ω_0
$-\theta_1$	−.0872	.09434
$-\theta_{12}$		.02079

The zero-order model of Table 12–16 appears to be a very good one; all diagnostics are consistent with a valid model having coefficients with high *t*-values and white noise residuals. Thus, the following model results:

$$LnY_t = \omega_0 I_t + \frac{(1 - \theta_1 B)(1 - \theta_{12}B^{12})}{(1 - B)(1 - B^{12})}e_t \tag{12–24}$$

$$LnY_t = .3156 I_t + \frac{(1 - .2142B)(1 - .6544B^{12})}{(1 - B)(1 - B^{12})}e_t \tag{12–24a}$$

Because differences are applied to the intervention term as well as Y_t, an expansion of this model to the fitting and forecasting form yields the following:

- Multiplying both sides by $(1 - B)(1 - B^{12})$:

$$(1 - B)(1 - B^{12})LnY_t = (1 - B)(1 - B^{12})\omega_0 I_t + (1 - \theta_1 B)(1 - \theta_{12}B^{12})e_t$$

- Moving all terms except Y_t to the right-hand side:

$$LnY_t = LnY_{t-12} + (LnY_{t-1} - LnY_{t-13}) + (1 - B)(1 - B^{12})\omega_0 I_t + (1 - \theta_1 B)(1 - \theta_{12}B^{12})e_t$$

Figure 12–18 illustrates the fit of this model for years 9 through 12. As shown there, the fit is quite good, except for a lag of the fitted from the actual during year 11, the first 12 months of the intervention. As shown, the fitted values (in solid line) are consistently lower than the actual values during year 11 (in dotted line). Now let's consider the fit of a first-order model.

Table 12–17 illustrates the fit of a first-order model. As shown, this model fits the data quite well, having high *t*-values, white noise residuals, and a slightly higher $\bar{R}^2$ than the zero-order model (.9950 versus .9938). While not shown here, the first-order model fits better during the intervention year of 11 than does the zero-order model of

FIGURE 12–18

Fitted and actual values of zero-order intervention Table 12–16

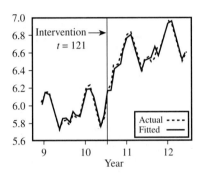

TABLE 12–17 $(r = 1, s = 0, b = 1)\ X(0, 1, 1)\ X(\theta, 1, 1)$ **Model of Logs of Airline Passengers**

Iterations taken	9
Usable observations	131
Degrees of freedom	127
$\bar{R}^2$	.9950
Mean of dependent variable	5.7007
Standard error of dependent variable	.5296
Residual standard error	.0376
Sum of squared residuals	.1793
Durbin–Watson statistic	1.9763
$Q(32-2)$	28.0954
Significance level of Q	.5654

Coeff	Estimate	Std Error	t-Stat	Signif
$-\theta_1$	−.3827	.08308	−4.6061	.00001
$-\theta_{12}$	−.5586	.07981	−6.9991	.00000
ω_0	.2758	.02937	9.3905	.00000
δ_1	.5172	.06179	8.3694	.00000

Correlation Matrix of Coefficients

	$-\theta_{12}$	ω_0	δ_1
$-\theta_1$	−.0855	.1163	−.0535
$-\theta_{12}$		.0810	−.0169
ω_0			−.6430

Figure 12–18. Because of its statistical defensibility and the fact that the intervention fit is better, we choose the first-order model for this series shown in equation 12–25.

$$\text{Ln}Y_t = \frac{\omega_0}{(1 - \delta_1 B)} I_t + \frac{(1 - \theta_1 B)(1 - \theta_{12} B^{12})}{(1 - B)(1 - B^{12})} e_t \qquad (12\text{–}25)$$

$$\text{Ln}Y_t = \frac{.2758}{(1 - .5172 B)} I_t + \frac{(1 - .3827 B)(1 - .5586 B^{12})}{(1 - B)(1 - B^{12})} e_t \qquad (12\text{–}25a)$$

Expanding this relationship by cross multiplying by the right-hand-side denominator terms:

$$(1 - \delta_1 B)(1 - B)(1 - B^{12})\text{Ln}Y_t = (1 - B)(1 - B^{12})\,\omega_0 I_t + (1 - \delta_1 B)(1 - \theta_1 B)(1 - \theta_{12} B^{12}) e_t \qquad (12\text{–}26)$$

To forecast with this model, move all terms except $\text{Ln}Y_t$ to the right-hand side after expanding the left-hand side. Let's interpret the intervention term of Equation 12–25a shown in Equation 12–27, where $\text{Ln}Y_t^*$ denotes only the intervention effect.

$$\text{Ln}Y_t^* = \frac{.2758}{(1 - .5172 B)} I_t \qquad (12\text{–}27)$$

Equation 12–27 denotes that the influence of the new fleet is a gradual, permanent increase in $\text{Ln}Y_t$, as shown in Table 12–18. As you may recall, the effect is permanent because I_t is a step function. As shown in Table 12–18, the asymptotic value of $\text{Ln}Y_t$ is:

$$\mathop{\text{Lim}}_{t \to \infty} \frac{\omega_0}{(1 - \delta_1 B)} = \frac{.2758}{(1 - .5172)} = \frac{.2758}{.4828} = .5719 \qquad (12\text{–}28)$$

TABLE 12–18   **Impact of Gradual, Permanent Intervention on Y_t**

(1) Period after Intervention	*(2)* $\dfrac{.2758}{(1 - .5172 B)}$	*(3)* Summation Of Impact on $\text{Ln}Y_t^*$	*(4)* Change in $e^{\text{Ln}Y_t^*} = \dfrac{Y_t}{Y_{t-1}}$ $e^{(2)}$	*(5)* Summation of Impact on $\dfrac{Y_t}{Y_{t-1}}$ $e^{(3)}$
1	.2758	.2758	1.3176	1.3176
2	.1428	.4186	1.1535	1.5198
3	.0739	.4926	1.0767	1.6365
4	.0383	.5308	1.0390	1.7004
5	.0198	.5507	1.0200	1.7344
6	.0103	.5609	1.0103	1.7523
7	.0053	.5663	1.0053	1.7617
8	.0028	.5690	1.0028	1.7665
9	.0014	.5704	1.0014	1.7690
10	.0007	.5712	1.0007	1.7703
11	.0004	.5716	1.0004	1.7710
12	.0002	.5717	1.0002	1.7714
13	.0001	.5719	1.0001	1.7715
14	.000053	.5719	1.0001	1.7716
15	.000028	.5719	1.0000	1.7717
16	.000014	.5719	1.0000	1.7717

Realizing that this is the limit of a logarithmic value, the asymptotic affect on Y_t is:

$$e^{.5719} = 1.77163 \tag{12-29}$$

This denotes that the asymptotic influence of the intervention will be to increase passengers by 77.163 percent over the preintervention trend.

Bounds of Stability for First-Order Intervention Functions

As we have seen, a gradual, permanent change in process level is implied by the first-order intervention function:

$$f(I_t) = \frac{\omega_0}{(1 - \delta_1 B)}$$

where the parameter δ_1 is constrained to the interval:

$$-1 < \delta_1 < +1$$

These constraints are called the bounds of system stability. If the value of δ_1 lies outside these bounds, the intervention model is unstable, a behavior identical to that of nonstationarity. When $\delta_1 > 1$, the postintervention time series is nonstationary, the event inducing a trend in the time series. Consider a simple first-order model.

$$Y_t = \theta_0 + \frac{\omega_0}{(1 - \delta_1 B)} I_t = 5 + \frac{20}{(1 - 1.3B)}$$

$$(1 - \delta_1 B)Y_t = (1 - \delta_1 B)\theta_0 + \omega_0 I_t = (1 - 1.3)5 + 20I_t$$

$$(1 - 1.3B)Y_t = (1 - 1.3)\theta_0 + \omega_0 I_t = (1 - 1.3)5 + 20I_t$$

Therefore:

$$Y_t = 1.3Y_{t-1} - .3\,(5) + 20I_t$$

Clearly, Y_t is nonstationary.

High values of δ_1 occur sometimes because the postintervention series is too short to reach a stable equilibrium. The postintervention series may appear to have a change in its slope and we may mistakenly infer that the postintervention series is nonstationary and trending. Instead, the intervention effect may be a gradual, permanent one that has not approached its asymptotic value. However, as more data become available, it is possible to determine if the value of δ_1 is 1 or greater and thus whether the postintervention process is trending or less than 1. If insufficient data exists, then additional judgment will be necessary to choose the correct intervention form. If a change in the slope seems reasonable, then when δ_1 is 1 (greater than 1), it is interpreted as a postintervention linear (nonlinear) trend.

Summary

This chapter has presented intervention modeling using several examples. Intervention modeling is a powerful methodology for measuring the impact of known and unknown events. These methods have become more important today with lower cost hardware and more sophisticated software. An understanding of the concepts of this chapter is important for those using modern statistical forecasting software introduced in the mid-1990s. Hopefully, the software you are using is capable of fitting intervention models. As we have suggested, you should experiment with simple intervention models using spreadsheets or simple programming languages such as C++ and BASIC; these provide useful insights to the form and function of intervention models. Software available from SCA (UTS and MTS), Automatic Forecasting Systems (AUTOBOX), Business Forecasting Systems (ForecastPro$_{tm}$), Estima (RATS), SAS (ETS), and others have intervention capabilities; however, many other software packages do not.

As you study the next chapter, you will realize the importance of this chapter as a prerequisite to the general transfer function modeling known as MARIMA–multivariate autoregressive integrated moving averages. Achieving comfort with this chapter will make the transition to the next much easier. We hope you find these methodologies as intriguing as we have.

Key Terms

abrupt permanent impact	noise model
abrupt temporary impact	preintervention series
asymptotic impact value	postintervention series
first-order intervention function	pulse intervention
gradual permanent impact	step intervention
gradual temporary impact	sustained pulse intervention
intervention model	zero-order intervention function
interventions	

Key Formulas

Intervention model:

$$Y_t = f(I_t) + N_t \tag{12-1}$$

$$N_t = \text{ARIMA}(p,d,q)\,(P,D,Q) \tag{12-2}$$

$$I_t = \begin{cases} 1 \text{ when intervention occurs} \\ 0 \text{ otherwise} \end{cases}$$

Zero-order $f(I_t)$:

$$Y_t = \theta_0 + \omega_0 I_t = 60 - 50I_t \qquad \text{(Figure 12–1a)} \tag{12-3}$$

$$Y_t = \theta_0 + (\omega_0 + \omega_1 B)I_t \qquad \text{(Figure 12–1b)} \tag{12-4}$$

$$= \theta_0 + \omega_0 I_t - \omega_1 I_{t-1} = 60 + (-50 + 10B)I_t$$

First-order $f(I_t)$:

$$Y_t = \theta_0 + \frac{\omega_0}{(1 - \delta_1 B)}I_t = 60 + \frac{-10}{(1 - .5B)}I_t \tag{12-7}$$

$$Y_t - \delta_1 Y_{t-1} = (1 - \delta_1)\theta_0 + \omega_0 I_t$$

$$Y_t = \delta_1 Y_{t-1} + (1 - \delta_1)\theta_0 + \omega_0 I_t$$

Asymptotic value:

$$\text{Asymptotic value} = \lim_{t \to \infty} \frac{\omega_0}{(1 - \delta_1)} = \frac{-10}{(1 - .5)} = -20$$

Gradual, temporary impact: If I_t is pulse:

$$Y_t = \theta_0 + \frac{\omega_0}{(1 - \delta_1 B)} I_t$$

Gradual, permanent impact: If I_t is step:

$$Y_t = \theta_0 + \frac{\omega_0}{(1 - \delta_1 B)} I_t$$

General intervention (r, s, and b):

$$y_t = \frac{(\omega_0 - \omega_1 B - \omega_2 B^2 - \ldots - \omega_s B^s)}{(1 - \delta_1 B - \delta_2 B^2 - \ldots - \delta_r B^r)} x_{t-b} + N_t \tag{12-9}$$

r = Level of autoregression or power of B in the denominator

$s + 1$ = Number of ω terms in the numerator

b = Delay in the intervention impact

S&P 500 example:

$$I_t = \begin{cases} 0 \text{ prior to October 1987} \\ 1 \text{ on and after October 1987} \end{cases}$$

Abrupt, permanent single-month decline (Figure 12–14a)

$$\omega_0 I_t \qquad r = 0, s = 0, b = 0 \tag{12-18}$$

Abrupt, permanent two-month decline (Figure 12–14b)

$$(\omega_0 - \omega_1 B) I_t \qquad r = 0, s = 1, b = 0 \tag{12-19}$$

Gradual, permanent decline (Figure 12–14d)

$$\frac{\omega_0}{(1 - \delta_1 B)} I_t \qquad r = 1, s = 0, b = 0 \tag{12-20}$$

Chosen model of Table 12–15

$$LnY_t = (\omega_0 - \omega_1 B) I_t + \frac{\theta_0}{(1 - B)} e_t$$

$$LnY_t = (-.2597 - .1035 B) I_t + \frac{.0143}{(1 - B)} e_t \tag{12-21}$$

LnY_t = Natural logs of monthly S&P 500

Monthly trend in S&P 500:

$$e^{\theta_0} - 1 = e^{.0143} - 1 = 1.014 - 1 = .014 = 1.4\%$$

Decrease in October 87:

$$e^{\omega_0} - 1 = e^{-.2597} - 1 = .7721 - 1 = -.2279 = -22.79\%$$

Decrease in November 87:

$$e^{\omega_1} - 1 = e^{-.1035} - 1 = .902 - 1$$
$$= -.098 = -9.8\%$$

Combined permanent decrease as of November 1987:

$$e^{\omega_1 + \omega_0} - 1 = e^{-.2597 - .1035} - 1 = .696 - 1 = -.304 = -30.4\%$$

Bounds of stability for first-order intervention functions:

$$\frac{\omega_0}{(1 - \delta_1 B)} \qquad -1 < \delta_1 < +1$$

Review Problems Using Your Software

R12-1 Study the documentation of your software and confirm whether it supports intervention modeling. If so, then explain how r, s, and b are specified in your software. In addition, how are differences applied to the intervention effect?

R12-2 Using a spreadsheet program of your choosing, calculate the gradual permanent intervention of Table 12–1 for 1 to 30. Do your results agree with Table 12–1?

R12-3 Using a spreadsheet program of your choosing, calculate the gradual permanent intervention of Table 12–2 for 1 to 30. Do your results agree with Table 12–2?

R12-4 Using BLOOD.DAT, repeat the analysis of Tables 12–3 and 12–4. Interpret your model. Plot actuals and fitted to judge the fit.

R12-5 Using WATER.DAT, repeat the analysis of Tables 12–6 to 12–8. Interpret your model. Plot actuals and fitted to judge the fit.

R12-6 Using SP500I.DAT, repeat the analysis of Table 12–12. Interpret your model. Plot actuals and fitted to judge the fit.

R12-7 Using AIRLINI.DAT, repeat the analysis of Table 12–17. Interpret your model. Plot actuals and fitted to judge the fit.

R12-8 Using ratios as in Table 12–18, confirm the meaning of the following logarithmic models.
  a. Table 12-12–SP500I.DAT
  b. Table 12-17–AIRLINI.DAT

Problems

12-1 Briefly define each step of intervention modeling.

12-2 How do you determine whether to apply differencing to the intervention term?

12-3 Explain the differences between a pulse and a step function. Give an example of each.

12-4 Explain the functions of r, s, and b for the general intervention model.

12-5 Using a spreadsheet or manual calculations, illustrate the bounds of stability for a first-order intervention function given values of $\omega_0 = 10$, $\delta_1 = .3, .6$, and 1.2 for $t = 1$ to 20 using:
  a. A step function originating in period 2.
  b. A pulse function originating in period 2.
  c. Compare the behavior of the two.

12-6 Draw the following intervention shapes for the given values of r, s, b:
  a. (0,1,0)
  b. (1,0,0)
  c. (0,0,1)
  d. (1,0,1)
  e. (1,1,1)

12-7 Express the following types of models in terms of r, pulse, and step functions:
  a. Abrupt, temporary impact.
  b. Abrupt, permanent impact.
  c. Gradual, temporary impact.
  d. Gradual, permanent impact.

12-8 What is the meaning of the asymptotic value of a first-order intervention function?

12-9 What should be known to be able to validly apply empirically driven intervention modeling?

12-10 What are the characteristics of a valid intervention model? Be complete in discussing the intervention and noise components.

12-11 What are the consequences of using univariate analysis on a series affected by an intervention?

12-12 How can intervention models be used if your software does not support models directly through the specifications of *r*, *s*, and *b*?

12-13 Explain the meaning of $\omega_0 = 10$, $\delta_1 = 0.3$ for a first-order intervention model in terms of the original time series when logarithms are used.

12-14 What is the effect of an intervention on ACFs and PACFs?

12-15 The time series BIRTHMAR.DAT is the quarterly marriages in the United States, where an intervention has occurred because of a favorable change in the tax laws. Complete the minicase.

12-16 The time series SALEI.DAT is the quarterly manufacturing sales in the U.S., where an intervention has occurred in period 82, Quarter 1, 1990. Complete the minicase.

Minicases

For a selected minicase or problem, complete the following analysis. Develop an intervention model for a selected time series. As you achieve stationarity and white noise, fill out two tables, one the equivalent of Table 8–15 and the other the equivalent of Table 8–25. In addition, if you have been filling out the Master Forecasting Summary Table, add the appropriate model to that table as you withhold the correct number of observations and forecast these.

Note that some of these time series are previous time series where interventions have been added in the appropriate period.

Minicase 12–1 Kansas Turnpike, Daily Data
TURNPIKT.DAT, Model holiday effects using either intervention or other methods suggested by your instructor. There are 1099 daily observations in this file.

Minicase 12–2 Domestic Air Passengers by Quarter
PASSAIRI.DAT, having an intervention in quarter 37, quarter 1 of 1991, *n* = 50.

Minicase 12–3 Hospital Census by Month
CENSUSD.DAT, Model holiday effects on the daily census during a 6 month period (i.e., 182 days). At least three intervention functions are needed.

Minicase 12–4 Henry Machler's Hideaway Orchids
MACHLERD.DAT, Using daily data, model the impact of Mother's Day using intervention methods.

Minicase 12–5 Your Forecasting Project If there is an intervention in your series?

Minicase 12–6 Midwestern Building Materials
LUMBERI.DAT, having an intervention in month 101 with a major promotional campaign (*n* = 120).

Minicase 12–7 International Airline Passengers
AIRLINI.DAT, having an intervention in month 121 when terrorists attack five major airlines (*n* = 144).

Minicase 12–8 Automobile Sales AUTOI.DAT, having an intervention in month 101, May 1988 when a major quality improvement effort is advertised heavily, *n* = 184.

Minicase 12–9 Consumption of Distilled Spirits
SPIRITSI.DAT, having an intervention in month 101 when a major health study was used to promote moderate alcohol consumption, *n* = 132.

Minicase 12-10 Discount Consumer Electronics
ELECTI.DAT, having an intervention in month 101 when new major market in the southwest was acquired, *n* = 185.

References

Aaker, J.; J. Carman; and R. Jacobson. "Modeling Advertising-Sales Relationships Involving Feedback: A Time Series Analysis of Six Cereal Brands." *Journal of Marketing Research,* February 1982, pp. 116–26.

BMDP Statistical Software. Berkeley: University of California Press, 1995.

Box, G.E.P.; G.M. Jenkins; and G. C. Reinsel. *Time-Series Analysis: Forecasting and*

Control. Englewood Cliffs, NJ: Prentice Hall, 1994.

Box, G.E.P. and G.C. Tiao. "Intervention Analysis with Applications to Economic and Environmental Problems." *Journal of the American Statistical Society* 70, (1975), pp. 70–79.

Cook, T.D., and D.T. Campbell. *Quasi-Experimentation Design and Analysis Issues for Field Settings.* Chicago: Rand

McNally College Publishing Company, 1979.

Draper, N.R., and H. Smith. *Applied Regression Analysis*. 2nd ed. New York: John Wiley & Sons.

Fuller, W.A. *Introduction to Statistical Time Series*. New York: John Wiley & Sons, 1976.

Glass, G.V. "Estimating the Effects of Intervention in Nonstationary Time Series." *American Educational Research Journal* 9, (1972), pp. 463–77.

Granger, C.W.J., and P. Newbold. *Forecasting Economic Time Series*, New York: Academic Press, 1977.

Haugh, L.D."The Identification of Times Series Interrelationships with Special Reference to Dynamic Regression Models." Unpublished doctoral dissertation, University of Wisconsin–Madison, 1972.

Helmer, R.M., and J.K. Johansson. "An Exposition of the Box-Jenkins Transfer Function Analysis with Application to the Advertising-Sales Relationship," *Journal of Marketing Research* 14, (1977), pp. 227–39.

Hussain, S.A. "The Effects of Persuasive Communication and Cognitive Dissonance in Influencing the Food Selection Behavior of University Cafeteria Patrons." Unpublished dissertation. School of Education, University of Missouri–Kansas City, 1983.

Jenkins, G.M. *Practical Experiences with Modeling and Forecasting Time Series*, Lancaster: GJP Publications, 1979.

Kotler, P., and G. Zaltman. "Social Marketing: An Approach to Planned Social Change." *Journal of Marketing Research*, 35, no. 3 (1977), pp. 3–12.

Leone, R. P. "Modeling Sales-Advertising Relationships: An Integrated Time Series-Econometric Approach." *Journal of Marketing Research*, August 1983, pp. 291–20.

McCleary, R., and R.A. Hay, Jr. *Applied Time Series Analysis for the Social Sciences*. Newbury Park: Sage Publications, 1982.

Marquardt, D.W. "An Algorithm for Least Squares Estimation of Nonlinear Parameters," *Journal of the Society of Industrial and Applied Mathematics*, 2 (1963), pp. 431–41.

Montgomery, D.C., and L. A. Johnson. *Forecasting and Time Series Analysis* New York: McGraw-Hill, 1976.

Nelson, C.R. *Applied Time Series Analysis for Managerial Forecasting*, San Francisco: Holden-Day, 1973.

Pack, D.J. *A Computer Program for the Analysis of Time Series Models Using the Box-Jenkins Philosophy*. Hatboro, PA: Automatic Forecasting Systems, 1977.

_____. "Revealing Time Series Interrelationships." *Decision Sciences* 8 (1977), pp. 377–402.

Phadke, M.S. *Multiple Time Series Modeling and System Identification with Applications*, Unpublished doctoral dissertation, University of Wisconsin-Madison, 1973.

Priestly, M.B. "Fitting Relationships between Time Series." Presented at 38th Session of the International Statistical Institute, Washington, D.C., 1971.

Tiao, G.C.; G.E.P. Box; and W. J. Hamming. "Analysis of Los Angeles Photochemical Smog Data: A Statistical Overview." *Journal of the Air Pollution Control Association* 25 (1975), pp. 260–68.

Tiao, G.C.; G. E. P. Box; M.R. Grupe; G.B. Hudak; W. R. Bell; and I. Chang. "The Wisconsin Multiple Time Series (WMSS-1) Program." Department of Statistic. University of Wisconsin–Madison, 1979.

Wichern, D.W., and R.H. Jones. "Assessing the Impact of Market Disturbances Using Intervention Analysis." *Management Science* 21 (1977), pp. 329–37.

MULTIVARIATE ARIMA TRANSFER FUNCTIONS

I would rather discover one cause than gain the kingdom of Persia.

Democritus, philosopher 460–370 B.C.

Chapter Outline

This chapter generalizes the concepts of Chapter 12 to systems where one or more independent variables (called input variables) are related to a dependent variable (called an output variable). In many applications in business, economics, and the sciences, there are causal relationships between a dependent variable and one or more lagged independent variables. This chapter introduces methods for modeling these lagged relationships using good **MARIMA** model-building practices and theories.

Consider Figure 13–1, which illustrates a plot of the jackpot in a lottery and the sales of tickets for that lottery. On some reflection, it is not hard to imagine that the sales of lottery tickets are related to the value of the jackpot for several previous periods—for example, the last three periods. That is:

$$\text{Ticket sales}_t = f(\text{Jackpot}_t, \text{Jackpot}_{t-1}, \text{Jackpot}_{t-2}) + \text{Noise}_t$$

Relationships such as this are best modeled using MARIMA models. Specifically, if a time series consists of one or more input series (i.e., independent variables) that influence a single output series (dependent variable), then MARIMA models may be the best form of the relationship.

In general, MARIMA models are combined univariate ARIMA and multivariate causal models having the attributes of both regression and ARIMA models—thus the term MARIMA, Multivariate ARIMA models. Alternatively, in the ARIMA context, MARIMA models are causal extensions of univariate ARIMA models. In the intervention sense, they are intervention models like those of Chapter 12, except that the input variables are not dichotomous. Finally, in the causal sense, MARIMAs are extensions of multiple regression and econometrics methods.

MARIMA models are very versatile and have found extensive practical applications in many disciplines, including:

Discipline	Example
Marketing	Sales = f(Advertising, Prices, Season of year)
Finance	Stock prices = f(Earnings, p–e ratio, Interest rates)
Production	Process output = f(Material thickness, Input voltage)
	Part dimensions = f(Process adjustments, Turning speed)
Engineering	Electricity usage = f(Temperature, Precipitation, Wind chill)
Economics	Product demand = f(Price, Competitor prices, Advertising)
Hydrology	Flood crests = f(Rain, Ground saturation, Tributary levels)
Meteorology	Rainfall = f(Temperature, Humidity, Barometer)

FIGURE 13–1

Lotto sales versus jackpot

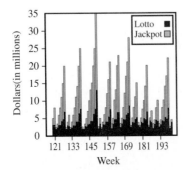

As we derive different models, remember that regression models are a subset of MARIMA models. Thus, you are already familiar with MARIMA models.

Transfer Functions

Assume you are interested in modeling a time series, Y_t, that is a function of a second time series, X_t. Complicating your analysis, is that Y_t and X_t have considerable autocorrelation and the relationship involves several lags of Y_{t-k} and X_{t-k}. Both of these complexities make it difficult to model the relationship using OLS regression or the simple autoregressive econometrics models of Chapter 10. Thus, in the general time series application, we expect Y_t to be related to past values of itself and X_t. In addition, the relationship between Y_t and X_t may involve several complexities, not necessarily being just a simple linear relationship but in many cases a dynamic, nonlinear relationship. MARIMA models are designed to model these general time series.

A MARIMA model consists of a transfer function (TF) and a noise model N_t.

MARIMA = Transfer function + Noise model

Because both the transfer function and noise model are difficult to identify from a nonstationary series, the first step in MARIMA model building is to achieve stationarity in the input and output variables. As is usual, we designate y_t and x_t as deviations from their mean values for stationary series or appropriately transformed values for initially nonstationary series.

To understand the notation of MARIMA models, consider the simplest case of a transfer function in Equation 13–1, a simple linear regression model. The ω_0 is the regression coefficient (b in regression terms), and because y_t and x_t are stationary deviations, there is no constant term. Note that in regression terms, N_t is simply the error term e_t. However, in the MARIMA case, N_t is an ARIMA model yielding normally and independently distributed (NID) errors with a mean of zero and constant variance (i.e., white noise).

$$y_t = \omega_0 x_t + N_t \qquad (13–1)$$

When the noise term, N_t, is an ARIMA model with seasonal or nonseasonal p, d, and q, ordinary least squares (OLS) regression should not be used to estimate Equation 13–1, because OLS will not estimate accurate coefficients. We discuss the noise model, N_t, in greater detail later. For now, study just the transfer function component.

Equation 13–1 is a much simplified version of the general transfer function, Equation 13–2:

$$y_t = \frac{(\omega_0 B^b - \omega_1 B^{b+1} + \ldots - \omega_s B^{b+s})x_t}{(1 - \delta_1 B - \delta_2 B^2 - \ldots - \delta_r B^r)} + N_t \qquad (13–2)$$

where y_t and x_t are called the output and input variables, respectively, $\omega_0, \omega_1, \ldots, \omega_s$ and $\delta_1, \ldots \delta_r$ are transfer function coefficients and as mentioned, N_t is a noise model. Note that the form of a transfer function is determined by three exponents, r, s, and b. Before studying the TF exponents, r, s, and b, consider some basics.

Zero-Order Transfer Functions (TFs)

Applications of transfer function models require identification of the lagged relationships between y_t and x_{t-k}. As you might recall, the greater the lag (i.e., k), the greater the forecasting utility. For example, if, in a relationship, X_{t-3} and X_{t-4} are related to Y_t, then $r = 0$, $b = 3$, and $s = 1$ and Equation 13–3 results:

$$y_t = \omega_0 x_{t-3} - \omega_1 x_{t-4} + N_t \qquad (13–3)$$

Clearly, such a relationship is very useful for 3- to 4-period-ahead forecasts. A more generalized relationship is one where the value of the output series is determined by a large number of the past values of the input series. This yields the general bivariate transfer function given $r = 0$:

$$y_t = \omega_0 x_{t-b} - \omega_1 x_{t-b-1} - \omega_2 x_{t-b-2} - \ldots - \omega_s x_{t-b-s} + N_t \qquad (13\text{--}4)$$
$$= (\omega_0 B^b - \omega_1 B^{b+1} + \ldots - \omega_s B^{b+s})x_t + N_t$$

Such relationships are extensions of regression models and are called **zero-order transfer functions** because in Equation 13–4, the value of r corresponding to the general Equation 13–2 is zero. We study the function of r after first considering zero-order functions.

Example 13–1 A Zero-Order Transfer Function

A national electronics retailer mails advertising inserts X_t (in millions of units) to customers each month. MARIMA analysis of the sales Y_t (in millions of dollars) in one of its major cities yields the following model:

$$y_t = (\omega_0 - \omega_1 B)x_t + N_t = (.5 + .3B)x_t + N_t$$

Given that the means of Y_t and X_t are 4.4 and .5, respectively, ignoring the noise model, and remembering that x_t and y_t are deviations, we substitute $Y_t - 4.4$ and $X_t - .5$ into the previous equation to yield:

$$Y_t - 4.4 = (.5 + .3B)(X_t - .5)$$
$$Y_t = 4 + (.5 + .3B)X_t = 4 + .5X_t + .3X_{t-1}$$

which in general notation is:

$$Y_t = \theta_0 + (\omega_0 - \omega_1 B)X_t \qquad (13\text{--}5)$$

Again, the methods used to arrive at the coefficients of this model will be discussed later. For now, review its behavior in Table 13–1.

For this zero-order transfer function, the output, sales in period t, (Y_t), is influenced by the last two values of the input series, X_t and X_{t-1}. The ability of transfer functions to model the length of the input's influence makes them an important dynamic modeling tool. Let's consider a more complex dynamic system.

TABLE 13–1   Zero-Order Model of Equation 13–5

t	X_t	Y_t	$= 4 + .5X_t$	$+ .3X_{t-1}$
0	.5	...		
1	.5	4.4	$= 4 + .5 * .5$	$+ .3 * .5$
2	1.0	4.65	$= 4 + .5 * 1$	$+ .3 * .5$
3	.5	4.55	$= 4 + .5 * .5$	$+ .3 * 1$
4	.5	4.4	$= 4 + .5 * .5$	$+ .3 * .5$
5	0	4.15	$= 4 + .5 * 0$	$+ .3 * .5$
6	0	4	$= 4 + .5 * 0$	$+ .3 * 0$

Note: $X_t = .5$ for $t < 0$

First-Order Transfer Functions

Equation 13–6 illustrates a **first-order transfer function** between y_t and x_t. As mentioned, the term *first-order* denotes a single delta term, δ_1, in the denominator of the right-hand side of the transfer function:

$$y_t = \frac{\omega_0}{(1 - \delta_1 B)} x_t + N_t \qquad (13-6)$$

To better understand the function of the denominator of Equation 13–6, consider a simple application.

Example 13–2 First-Order Transfer Function

To stimulate sales, an electronics discounter advertises weekly, where the number of minutes of TV exposure varies from week to week. After advertisements are aired, the effect of that week's advertising declines over time because of the decline in product recall by customers. Let X_t equal the number of TV advertisements aired throughout the market (in thousands) and Y_t equal the sales of the advertised products. Analysis of sales versus advertising yields the following relationship:

$$y_t = \frac{\omega_0}{(1 - \delta_1 B)} x_t + N_t = \frac{10}{(1 - .2B)} x_t + N_t \qquad (13-7)$$

where

ω_0 = Omega-zero = Influence of x_t on y_t in period t
δ_1 = Delta-one = Lagged influence of x_t on y_t through y_{t+k} for $k > 0$.

Consider the way this model explains sales. First, note that y_t and x_t are deviations from their respective means, $\mu_Y = 600$ and $\mu_X = 10$. Thus:

$$y_t = Y_t - \mu_Y = Y_t - 600$$
$$x_t = X_t - \mu_X = X_t - 10$$

Equation 13–7 is really a shorter form of Equation 13–8, where the denominator of the right-hand side of Equation 13–7 is multiplied times both sides to yield:

$$(1 - .2B)y_t = 10x_t + (1 - .2B)N_t$$

and therefore:

$$y_t = .2y_{t-1} + 10x_t + (1 - .2B)N_t \qquad (13-8)$$

In nondeviational form and ignoring N_t, Equation 13–8 becomes:

$$Y_t - \mu_Y = .2(Y_{t-1} - \mu_Y) + 10(X_t - \mu_X) \qquad (13-9)$$

Substituting the appropriate means and simplifying:

$$Y_t - 600 = .2(Y_{t-1} - 600) + 10(X_t - 10) \qquad (13-10)$$
$$Y_t = 600 - .2 * 600 - 10 * 10 + .2Y_{t-1} + 10X_t$$
$$= 380 + .2Y_{t-1} + 10X_t$$

Consider the behavior of the relationship in Table 13–2 and Figure 13–2. As shown there, the single increase in X_t in period 3 results in an immediate increase in Y_t that rapidly decreases, the speed of that decline determined by δ_1.

The first-order transfer function is the multivariate equivalent of a first-order univariate autoregressive model, an ARIMA(1,0,0). To better understand this, consider

TABLE 13–2   First-Order TF of Equation 13–10, $\delta = .2$

t	X_t	Y_t			
0	10	600			
1	10	600	$= 380 + .2Y_{t-1}$	$+ 10X_t$	
2	10	600	$= 380 + .2 * 600$	$+ 10 * 10$	
3	60	1100	$= 380 + .2 * 600$	$+ 10 * 60$	
4	10	700	$= 380 + .2 * 1100$	$+ 10 * 10$	
5	10	620	$= 380 + .2 * 700$	$+ 10 * 10$	
6	10	604	$= 380 + .2 * 620$	$+ 10 * 10$	
7	10	600.8	$= 380 + .2 * 604$	$+ 10 * 10$	

FIGURE 13–2

First-order TF with 13–11, $\delta_1 = .2$ and .8.

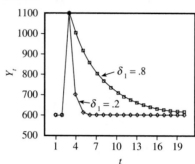

The influence of δ_1 with contrasting values of .2 and .8. For example, assume another relationship is fitted between sales Y_t' and advertising X_t' in Equation 13–11 this relationship results from improved advertising—thus, the notation of y' and x'. Remember that Equation 13–11 is Equation 13–7 with the $\delta_1 = .2$ replaced by .8.

$$y_t' = \frac{10}{(1 - .8B)}x_t' + N_t \qquad (13\text{–}11)$$

Again, ignoring N_t, remembering that y_t' and x_t' are deviations, and assuming previous input and output means:

$$Y_t' = 600 - .8 * 600 - 10 * 10 + .8Y_{t-1}' + 10X_t' = 20 + .8Y_t' + 10X_t'$$

The behavior of this TF is shown in Table 13–3 and Figure 13–2. Compare the influences of the two deltas in Figure 13–3. If δ_1 is high (e.g., .8), then X_ts influence remains high for several periods. If δ_1 is low (e.g., .2), then the influence declines very rapidly. The ability of transfer functions to capture such dynamic behavior is one reason they are so important in forecasting and time series analysis. Also note that it is not common to have negative values of δ_1 because these result in an alternating positive and negative exponential decline, as we saw with autoregressive models with negative ϕ_1 values.

Let's consider another example of transfer functions, in this case a second-order function.

Example 13–3 Second-Order Transfer Function

A precision machining process produces an outside diameter on a transmission roller bearing. This diameter is automatically controlled by a sensing device connected to a computerized controller. The computer automatically increases the voltage to a servo-mechanism that advances or retards a cutting tool in proportion to the voltage. However, because of uncontrollable mechanical tolerances in the mechanism, movements of the tool have been known to oscillate. Analysis of the diameter of the bearing, which is the **output series,** denotes that it is a function of the servo voltage, which is the **input series.** This analysis yields the following **second-order transfer function:**

$$y_t = \frac{\omega_0}{(1 - \delta_1 B - \delta_2 B^2)}x_t + N_t = \frac{20}{(1 - .8B + .6B^2)}x_t + N_t \qquad (13\text{–}12)$$

TABLE 13–3 First-Order TF of Equation 13–11, $\delta_1 = .8$

t	X'_t	Y'_t
0	10	600
1	10	600	$= 20 + .8Y'_{t-1} + 10X'_t$
2	10	600	$= 20 + .8 * 600 + 10 * 10$
3	60	1100	$= 20 + .8 * 600 + 10 * 60$
4	10	1000	$= 20 + .8 * 1100 + 10 * 10$
5	10	920	$= 20 + .8 * 1000 + 10 * 10$
6	10	856	$= 20 + .8 * 920 + 10 * 10$
7	10	804.8	$= 20 + .8 * 856 + 10 * 10$

FIGURE 13–3

Second-order TF of Table 13–4, a pulse

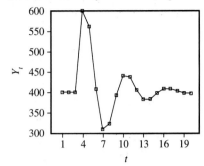

Again, for clarity, let's ignore the noise term and recognize that the means are 400 and 30, respectively:

$$y_t = Y_t - 400 \text{ and } x_t = X_t - 30$$

Rearranging the terms:

$$y_t = \delta_1 Y_{t-1} + \delta_2 Y_{t-2} + 20x_t = .8y_{t-1} - .6y_{t-2} + 20x_t \qquad (13\text{–}12a)$$

$$Y_t - 400 = .8(Y_{t-1} - 400) - .6(Y_{t-2} - 400) + 20(X_t - 30)$$

$$Y_t = 400 - .8(400) + .6(400) - 600 + .8Y_{t-1} - .6Y_{t-2} + 20X_t$$

$$Y_t = -280 + .8Y_{t-1} - .6Y_{t-2} + 20X_t$$

The behavior of this system with a constant input of 30 volts DC and a single voltage increase of 40 volts in period 4 is shown in Table 13–4 and in Figure 13–3.

As shown in Table 13–4 and Figure 13–3, this system reacts to a voltage increase or decrease by oscillating about a new value of the output series. This type of **oscillation** is typical of a second-order transfer function.

While we have illustrated this function using an industrial setting, many other systems might behave this way. Consider two other applications of Equation 13-12.

First Alternate Example 13–3

The output series Y_t is sales of a product and the input series X_t is advertising, where this advertising first increases demand in periods 4 to 6. However, some of this increase reduces demand in later periods 7, 8, and 9 as some customers bought products earlier than needed. Because these customers are satisfied through period 9, they again need to purchase more in periods 10, 11, and 12. This oscillation continues until the system reaches its old **steady-state** condition at 400 units.

Second Alternate Example 13–3

Consider a financial example where Y_t of Figure 13–3 is the price of a speculative stock. The input variable, earnings, is 30 until period 4, when it increases by 33 percent to 40. This increase results in a 50 percent increase in the stock price. However, because of the dynamics of the market, some stockholders sell off shares at the new highs in periods 4 and 5, thus driving the market to new lows, particularly when the

TABLE 13–4   **Second-Order Transfer Function of Equation 13–12**

t	X_t	Y_t			
0	30	400.00			
1	30	$400.00 = -280 + .8Y_{t-1}$	$- .6Y_{t-2}$	$+ 20X_t$	
2	30	$400.00 = -280 + .8 * 400$	$- .6 * 400$	$+ 20 * 30$	
3	30	$400.00 = -280 + .8 * 400$	$- .6 * 400$	$+ 20 * 30$	
4	40	$600.00 = -280 + .8 * 400$	$- .6 * 400$	$+ 20 * 40$	
5	30	$560.00 = -280 + .8 * 600$	$- .6 * 400$	$+ 20 * 30$	
6	30	$408.00 = -280 + .8 * 560$	$- .6 * 600$	$+ 20 * 30$	
7	30	$310.40 = -280 + .8 * 408$	$- .6 * 560$	$+ 20 * 30$	
8	30	$323.52 = -280 + .8 * 310.4$	$- .6 * 408$	$+ 20 * 30$	
9	30	$392.58 = -280 + .8 * 323.52$	$- .6 * 310.4$	$+ 20 * 30$	
10	30	439.95			
11	30	436.41	and so forth		
12	30	405.16			
13	30	382.28			
14	30	382.73			
15	30	396.81			
16	30	407.81			
17	30	408.16			
18	30	401.84			
19	30	396.58			
20	30	396.16			

earnings of period 4 are not continued. This yields a dampened oscillation as investors alternate between long (i.e., buying) and short (i.e., selling) positions.

Pulses and Shifts

An understanding of the **dynamics** of a system can be gained by studying its behavior using two different input changes, pulses and step functions. The previous examples illustrate transfer function behavior using abrupt, temporary changes in the input variable called **pulses**. Consider the behavior of the second-order transfer function of Example 13–3, Equation 13–12a, to a permanent **shift** (i.e., step) in the input. This step takes place in period 4, when the input value increases from 30 to 40 units and stays there. The results of this step are shown in Table 13–5 and Figure 13–4.

As shown in Table 13–5 and Figure 13–4, the second-order transfer function achieves a new level of approximately 650 after the input series shifts from 30 to 40 in period 4. However, the output series oscillates about 650 as it dampens to this new steady state value, a behavior considerably different than that of a pulse.

Simple simulations such as those of Examples 13–1 to 13–4 are essential to understanding TFs. An actual output series will not behave as regularly as these examples because there will be errors (i.e., noise) in the relationship and because the input series will not be as well behaved as these examples. Nonetheless, you should experiment with TFs using spreadsheets to ensure your understanding of these models.

For many, there is something intuitively appealing about the dynamics and explanatory power of TFs, particularly when the resulting models achieve good forecasts and insights. However, the empirical identification of valid TFs is not easily achieved without the methodical use of some old and new analytical tools. Now let's study these analytical tools.

TABLE 13–5   **Second-Order TF of Equation 13–12 with a Step in X_t**

t	X_t	Y_t			
0	30	400.00			
1	30	$400.00 = -280 + .8Y_{t-1}$	$- .6Y_{t-2}$	$+ 20X_t$	
2	30	$400.00 = -280 + .8 * 400$	$- .6 * 400$	$+ 20 * 30$	
3	30	$400.00 = -280 + .8 * 400$	$- .6 * 400$	$+ 20 * 30$	
4	40	$600.00 = -280 + .8 * 400$	$- .6 * 400$	$+ 20 * 40$	
5	40	$760.00 = -280 + .8 * 600$	$- .6 * 400$	$+ 20 * 40$	
6	40	$768.00 = -280 + .8 * 760$	$- .6 * 600$	$+ 20 * 40$	
7	40	$678.40 = -280 + .8 * 768$	$- .6 * 760$	$+ 20 * 40$	
8	40	$601.92 = -280 + .8 * 678.40$	$- .6 * 768$	$+ 20 * 40$	
9	40	$594.50 = -280 + .8 * 601.92$	$- .6 * 678.4$	$+ 20 * 40$	
10	40	634.44			
11	40	670.86	and so forth		
12	40	676.02			
13	40	658.30			
14	40	641.03			
15	40	637.84			
16	40	645.66			
17	40	653.82			
18	40	655.66			
19	40	652.24			
20	40	648.40			

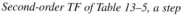

FIGURE 13–4

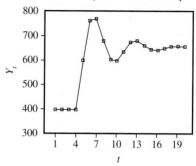

Second-order TF of Table 13–5, a step

Steps of MARIMA Modeling

As with ARIMA analysis, MARIMA modeling is best viewed in the three phases developed by Box and Jenkins—identification, estimation, and diagnostics forecasting—as shown in Figure 13–5. However, the identification and diagnostic phases require some additional steps using cross correlations. A preview of these steps follows:

I. Identification

- Study the theory, data, and plots.
- Achieve level and variance stationarity of Y_t and X_t.
- Fit a univariate model to x_t to estimate α_t.
- Fit a univariate model to y_t as a benchmark and possible N_t.
- Use prewhitened model of α_t and pretreat y_t to get β_t.
- Calculate CCF(k) of $\beta_t \alpha_{t-k}$ to identify r, s, and b.
- Examine CCFs for r, s and b.

II. Estimation of Model

- Estimate the Transfer Function using Y_t and X_t.
- Use the residual TF to identify N_t.
- Estimate the full model, r, s, b, p, d, q, P, D, Q.
- Confirm all estimation procedures converged.

III. Diagnostics

- Confirm significant, nonredundant parameters in model.
- Modify transfer function or noise model as needed.

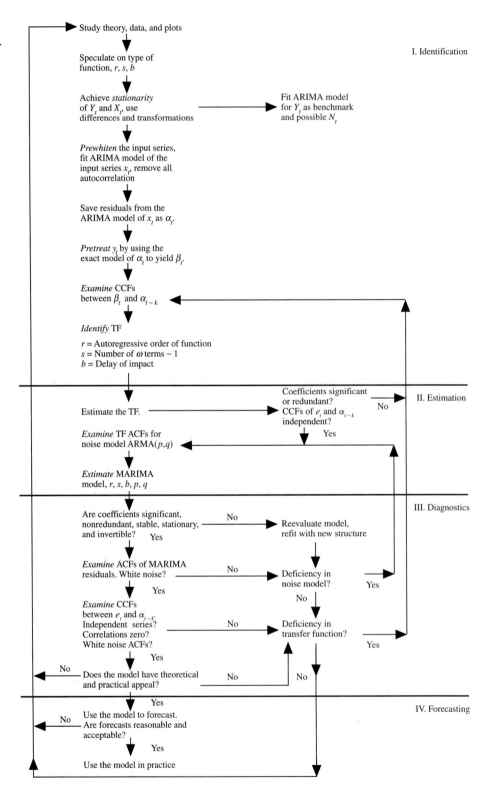

FIGURE 13–5

Steps of MARIMA transfer function modeling

- Confirm white noise residuals.
- Confirm residuals are not cross correlated with prewhitened α_{t-k}.
- Confirm that the fit and forecasts are reasonable.
- Confirm stationarity, invertibility, and stability.
- Confirm model parsimony.
- Overfit model.
- Interpret the model.
- Experiment with the transfer function.
- Confirm model intuitive appeal.

IV. Forecasting

- Confirm that forecasts are reasonable.

Let's discuss these steps very briefly before illustrating them with three actual examples. As you study Figure 13–6 and the following steps, recognize that both are general guidelines that describe most, but definitely not all MARIMA model building processes.

Identification Using Cross Correlation Functions (CCF(k))

Just as ARIMA model building focused on autocorrelation functions, so does MARIMA focus on the use of cross correlations. A review of Appendix 3–A is helpful in understanding CCFs. However, we provide a much abbreviated review here.

Most of the identification steps of MARIMA model building rely on cross correlations. Equations 13–13 and 13–14 illustrate the formulas for cross covariances and the resulting cross correlation coefficients for X and Y when X lags Y by k periods. That is $y_t = f(X_{t-k})$.

Cross covariance function

$$\text{COV}_{xy}(k) = \frac{1}{n} \sum_{t=1+k}^{n} (Y_t - \overline{Y})(X_{t-k} - \overline{X}) \quad k \geq 0 \qquad (13\text{–}13)$$

$$\text{COV}_{xy}(k) = \frac{1}{n} \sum_{t=1-k}^{n} (Y_{t+k} - \overline{Y})(X_t - \overline{X}) \quad k \geq 0$$

Cross correlation coefficient (i.e., standardized $\text{COV}_{xy}(k)$)

$$\text{CCF}_{xy}(k) = \frac{\text{COV}_{xy}(k)}{S_x S_y} \qquad (13\text{–}14)$$

As we will see, these CCFs are an important TF identification and diagnostic tool.

To detect significant correlation coefficients and patterns, Equation 13–15 provides an approximate standard error for the CCFs when two variables are statistically independent.

Approximate standard error of $\text{CCF}_{xy}(k)$:

$$Se\text{CCF}_{xy}(k) = 1/\sqrt{n} \qquad (13\text{–}15)$$

A simple *t*-test can be performed by dividing the Se[CCF] into the CCF. Quotients that are more than two are indicative of significant cross correlations. In addition, the Q-statistics can detect when patterns exist in a group of CCFs. Because these MARIMA statistics are used identically to those of ARIMA ACFs, we suggest review of the latter part of Chapter 2. Let's apply these concepts in a hypothetical example.

Two Hypothetical Applications

In this section, we analyze two very simple hypothetical bivariate MARIMA models using the steps of Figure 13–5. Assume we model a relationship between Y_t and X_t using a sample size of 100 observations.

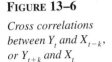

FIGURE 13–6

Cross correlations between Y_t and X_{t-k}, or Y_{t+k} and X_t

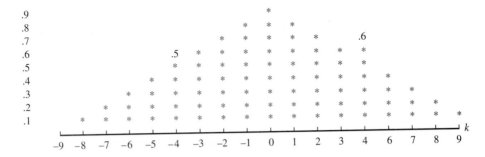

Achieving Stationarity of Input and Output

Because univariate ARIMA analysis of the input series is the first step in MARIMA model building, it is necessary to achieve stationarity in level and variance of the input series. If stationarity is not achieved in the input series, then the strong autocorrelations that exist in the two series make it difficult to measure the cross correlations between the series. This is illustrated in Figure 13–6, which is discussed next.

If we mistakenly calculate the CCF(k)s of Y_t and X_t before achieving stationarity as in Figure 13–6 these extremely high CCFs make it difficult if not impossible to identify the relationship between Y_t and X_t. Clearly, almost all of these cross correlations are significant because two standard errors of the CCF(k) for lags of zero to 25 are approximately:

$$2Se_{CCF(k)} = \frac{2}{\sqrt{n}} = \frac{2}{\sqrt{100}} = .200 \qquad (13\text{–}16)$$

for example:

$$t = \frac{CCF(4)}{Se_{CCF}} = \frac{.6}{.1} = 6$$

To clarify Figure 13–7, let's interpret the CCF(k) at 2 lags, 4 and −4.

$$CCF(4) = .6$$

This denotes that the correlation between X_{t-4} and Y_t is .6 or, if you prefer, between X_t and Y_{t+4} is .6. If we were expecting the direction of causality or influence to be from X to Y, then this is an expected result: X influences future values of Y. Consider the opposite lag of −4.

$$CCF(-4) = .5$$

This denotes that the correlation between X_{t+4} and Y_t is .5 or, if you prefer, X_t and Y_{t-4} is .5. If the direction of causality is supposed to be from X to Y, then this is an unexpected result. However, because of the high autocorrelations in Y and X, these CCFs are not meaningful and therefore their statistical significance cannot be used to measure the time precedence of association.

For simplicity, let's assume that X_t and Y_t are both initially stationary series, thus no differences or transformations are needed to achieve stationarity. The high CCFs of Figure 13–7 are likely related to the very high ACFs of both series. That is, while X_t is stationary, it nonetheless has extremely high autocorrelations as denoted by Figure 13–7.

To better measure true cross correlations, we must prewhiten and pretreat x_t and y_t, respectively. Remember that x_t and y_t denote appropriately transformed stationary Y_t and X_t.

FIGURE 13–7

ACFs and PACFs of X_t

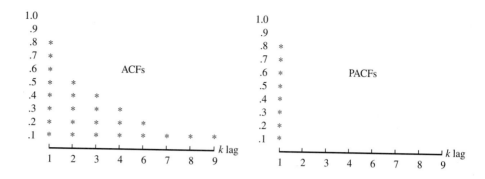

FIGURE 13–8

Cross correlations between β_t and α_{t-k}

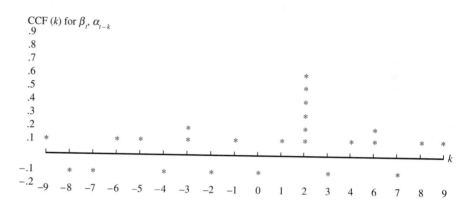

Prewhitening the Input Series

Prewhitening the input series consists of finding the ARIMA model for X_t that yields white noise residuals. By eliminating the auto-correlation in X_t, it is possible to better measure the between correlation of X_t and Y_t.

Figure 13–7 illustrates the ACFs and PACFs for X_t. These are both indicative of an ARIMA(1,0,0) model. Assume white noise residuals are achieved for this input series from the following model:

$$x_t = \phi_1 x_{t-1} + e_t = .8x_{t-1} + e_t$$

where x_t is the deviation of $X_t - \mu$ and $e_t s$ are white noise residuals. Reexpressing this relationship in terms of e_t yields:

$$e_t = x_t - \phi_1 x_{t-1} = x_t - .8x_{t-1}$$

To avoid confusion with the residuals of other models and to facilitate further analysis, designate e_t as α_t. Therefore:

$$\alpha_t = x_t - .8x_{t-1} \tag{13–17}$$

The series α_t is referred to as the **prewhitened input series** x_t because it is a white noise series.

Pretreating the Output Series

By treating y_t exactly as x_t was prewhitened, all of the direct cross correlation that existed before prewhitening is retained. That is, y_t is transformed to a new series using the exact model of Equation 13–17.

$$y_t = \phi_1 y_{t-1} + e_t' = .8y_{t-1} + e_t'$$

where y_t is the deviation of $Y_t - \mu$ and e'_t are the residuals. The pretreated output series is not expected to have white noise residuals because the model was chosen to whiten x_t.

Reexpressing this relationship in terms of e'_t yields:

$$e'_t = y_t - \phi_1 y_{t-1} = y_t - .8y_{t-1}$$

Again, to avoid confusion and to facilitate further analysis, define this e'_t as $\boldsymbol{\beta_t}$. Therefore:

$$\beta_t = y_t - .8y_{t-1} \qquad (13–18)$$

The series β_t is referred to as the **pretreated output series** y_t because it has been treated identically to the prewhitened model of x_t. Now, continuing the investigation of the relationship between y_t and x_t, Figure 13–8 illustrates the cross correlations between β_t and α_{t-k}.

Calculating CCFs to Identify r, s, and b

As Figure 13–8 shows, the high cross correlations seen previously in Figure 13–6 are gone. Now there is only one large correlation at lag 2. This correlation is indicative of a relationship between β_t and α_{t-2} and, therefore, y_t and x_{t-2}. Remembering that two standard errors of cross correlations is approximately $\dfrac{2}{\sqrt{n}} = 2\sqrt{100} = .2$, only the CCF(2) exceeds .2. These CCFs support the following model:

$$y_t = \omega_0 x_{t-2} + N_t \qquad (13–19)$$

In this hypothetical example, assume that the following TF results from estimation:

$$y_t = .6x_{t-2} + z_t \qquad (13–20)$$

where z_t residuals are probably not white noise.

Using Residuals of the TF to Identify TF Problems

Having identified a tentative TF, the next step is to determine whether the TF model is valid and then to identify a noise model. Assume that the model of Equation 13–20 has statistically significant coefficients and a high $\overline{R}^2$, however, the residuals are not white noise.

Diagnostics

Before an ARIMA noise model is fit to z_t, we should confirm that the TF model is complete. Confirmation that a MARIMA model is valid includes residuals that are not correlated with the prewhitened input series, α_t; this ensures that all pattern has been eliminated between Y_1 and X_t. Figure 13–9 shows the CCF(k) between z_t and α_{t-k}. If the MARIMA model has been correctly identified and estimated, then there should not be any pattern in the CCFs at any lags. Because there is no pattern in Figure 13–9, we infer that Equation 13–20 is a good MARIMA model. However, there may still be pattern left in the residuals that should be eliminated through a univariate ARIMA noise model.

FIGURE 13–9

Cross correlations between z_t and α_{t-k}

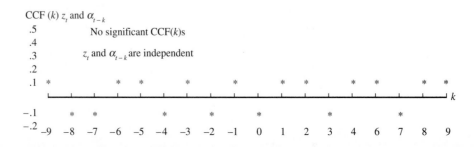

Using Residuals of the TF to Identify N_t

The next task is to determine the noise model of the MARIMA model. Sometimes an ARIMA model fitted to the output variable, Y_t, is valid as the noise model of the full transfer function. However, there are many exceptions to this rule. In general, the simplest method is to estimate N_t from the residuals of the transfer function model directly—that is, the residuals of the model of Equation 13–20. Figure 13–10 shows the residual ACFs and PACFs of Equation 13–20.

Moving Average Noise Model.   As seen in Figure 13–10, the residuals of Equation 13–20 are not white noise; the ACFs and PACFs have a clear MA(1) pattern. This suggests that the following is true:

$$z_t = (1 - \theta_1 B)e_t \qquad (13\text{–}21)$$

Thus, Figure 13–10 suggests that Equation 13–21 should be added to the MARIMA model. This yields the following model:

$$y_t = .6x_{t-2} + (1 - \theta_1 B)e_t \qquad (13\text{–}22)$$

Assume that the full MARIMA model estimation yields Equation 13–23:

$$y_t = .6x_{t-2} + (1 - .3B)e_t \qquad (13\text{–}23)$$

Model Diagnostics.   While not shown here, assume that the *t*-statistics of both coefficients are significant. Next to ensure that these residuals are white noise and uncorrelated with the prewhitened input variable, α_t, the analysis of Figures 13–9 and 13–10 was repeated using the residuals of Equation 13–23. Assume there is no pattern in the ACFs and CCFs and their *Q*-statistics confirmed model adequacy. Finally, if actual plots of residuals, fitted values, and forecasts are defensible, then this is a valid model. As always, the intuitive and theoretical appeal of the model is an important measure of validity that should not be overlooked. Given that all of the measures of model diagnostics are acceptable, our analysis of this relationship is complete. Now, let's consider another hypothetical MARIMA model.

Autoregressive Noise Model.   In this example, assume that analysis has been completed through Equation 13–20 of the previous example, which is repeated for convenience as Equation 13–24:

$$y_t = .6x_{t-2} + z_t \qquad (13\text{–}24)$$

As before the coefficients of Equation 13–24 are statistically significant and z_t is uncorrelated with α_{t-k}. Now analyze the autocorrelations of the residuals, z_t in Figure 13–11 in order to determine the ARIMA noise model.

The ACFs and PACFs of Figure 13–11 are indicative of an AR(1) in the noise series, z_t. This suggests the following possible ARIMA model:

$$(1 - \phi_1 B)z_t = e_t$$

FIGURE 13–10

ACFs and PACFs for z_t of Equation 13–20

FIGURE 13–11

ACFs and PACFs for residuals, z_t of Equation 13–24

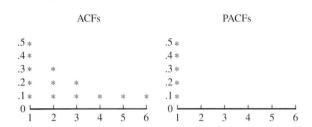

Given this model, a simple algebraic equivalent is:

$$z_t = \frac{e_t}{(1 - \phi_1 B)}$$

Substituting this into equation 13–24 yields:

$$y_t = \omega_0 x_{t-2} + \frac{e_t}{(1 - \phi_1 B)} \tag{13–25}$$

Assume that this model passes all diagnostics on the TF and N_t components, including no patterns in the ACFs of e_t and the CCFs of e_t and α_{t-k}. To clarify the meaning of Equation 13–25, consider its form:

$$(1 - \phi_1 B)y_t = (1 - \phi_1 B)\omega_0 x_{t-2} + e_t$$

Remembering that y_t and x_t are deviations from their means, the following results:

$$(1 - \phi_1 B)(Y_t - \mu_Y) = (1 - \phi_1 B)\omega_0(X_{t-2} - \mu_X) + e_t$$

Now combining all constants into a single constant, θ_0, yields:

$$Y_t = \theta_0 + \phi_1 Y_{t-1} + \omega_0(X_{t-2} - \phi_1 X_{t-3}) + e_t \tag{13–26}$$

The interpretation of this model, while not as straightforward as some, is Y_t varies about θ_0 where the variation equals an autoregressive fraction, ϕ_1 times Y_{t-1} plus a coefficient, ω_0, times the value of X_{t-2} minus a fraction, ϕ_1, of X_{t-3}. To have more confidence in this model, you should simulate it using spreadsheet software. Also, you might confirm the algebraic manipulations used to go from Equation 13–24 to 13–25.

Having analyzed several hypothetical examples, consider several actual applications.

New York and London IBM Stock Prices (IBMNYLN.DAT)

Identification of $NY_t = f(LN_{t-k})$

Because the London Stock Exchange closes earlier in the day than the New York Stock Exchange, a stock analyst believes that the closing price of IBM stock in London is useful in predicting the closing price in New York. (Note: As we will see, this analyst is wrong.) This analyst collects 242 days of daily stock prices on each exchange. These are shown in Figure 13–12, where the London prices are pounds sterling. The relationship between these two stocks is clear in this figure and has a coincident correlation coefficient of .97. As a first step in the analysis, the analyst calculates the cross correlations shown in Table 13–6. As shown there, all correlations are extremely high, as is expected with two random walk series.

The CCF(-1) of .9808 denotes that the correlation between New York price$_t$ and London price$_{t+1}$ is .9808; similarly CCF(1), the correlation between New York price$_t$

FIGURE 13–12

IBM stock price, New York and London

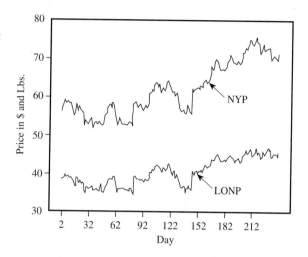

TABLE 13–6   Cross Correlations between New York$_t$ and London$_{t-k}$ Closing Prices

k					
−12:	.8026	.8185	.8323	.8474	.8654	.8820
−6:	.8975	.9103	.9256	.9412	.9592	.9808
0:	(.9701)	.9510	.9355	.9211	.9078	.8916
6:	.8745	.8551	.8389	.8268	.8113	.7972
12:	.7808	.7637	.7482	.7312	.7151	.7019

(Lag zero in parentheses)

and London price$_{t-1}$ is .9510. One might mistakenly believe that these time series have a strong mutual dependency at many lags because of their high mutual correlations. However, as we know, these correlations are not reliable measures of cross correlations. Clearly, it is necessary to take first differences to achieve stationarity and to prewhiten the input series (i.e., London prices) and pretreat the output series (i.e., New York prices) in order to estimate the true cross correlations. As a first step in the prewhitening process, Table 13–7 lists the ACFs and PACFs for the London prices. As expected, these are indicative of a random walk model, so first differences and a constant coefficient are fitted to this data.

Table 13–8 illustrates the fit of an ARIMA(0,1,0)1 model to the London stock price. As shown, the θ_0 is not statistically significant; thus, there appears to be no trend. However, the level of the Q-statistic denotes that the residuals of this model appear to be white noise. Because the constant is insignificant, the model is fitted without it. Table 13–9 shows the ACFs and PACFs for first differences of the input series. As shown, there is a marginally significant peak at lag 1 in the ACFs and PACFs. This is probably indicative of an MA(1) component.

Further analysis which is not shown, confirmed that an ARIMA(0,1,1) model has an identical fit to that of Table 13–8. This model with white noise residuals is:

$$X_t = X_{t-1} + (1 - \theta_t B)e_t$$
$$= X_{t-1} + (1 - .1477B)e_t$$
$$(-2.304)$$

TABLE 13–7   ACFs and PACFs for London IBM Stock Prices

ACFs					
k					
1:	.969	.947	.927	.908	.893	.873
7:	.853	.831	.813	.796	.778	.760
PACFs					
1:	.969	.127	.055	.016	.071	−.082
7:	−.017	−.051	.046	.005	−.008	−.002

TABLE 13–8   ARIMA(0,1,0)1 for London Price

Usable observations	241
Degrees of freedom	240
$\bar{R}^2$	.9486
Mean of dependent variable	40.500
Standard error of dependent variable	3.465
Residual standard error	.786
Sum of squared residuals	148.195
Durbin–Watson statistic	2.232
Q (36–0)	29.702
Significance level of Q	.76137

Coefficient	Estimate	Std Error	t-Stat	Signif
θ_0	.02956	.050617	.58407	.560

TABLE 13–9   ACFs and PACFs for Residuals of ARIMA(0,1,0) for London IBM Prices

ACFs					
k					
1:	−.1216	−.0750	−.0168	−.0722	.0943	.0062
7:	.0571	−.0761	−.0995	.0344	−.0420	.0370
PACFs					
1:	−.1216	−.0911	−.0387	−.0886	.0701	.0139
7:	.0728	−.0602	−.0970	−.0067	−.0555	.0024

$2Se(ACF) \approx 2/\sqrt{241} \approx .1288$

(Note: As part of the analysis, it was confirmed that first differences and residuals were variance stationary, therefore the series did not have to be transformed using natural logarithms.)

Thus, the prewhitened input series, α_t, is calculated as:

$$e_t = X_t - X_{t-1} - .1477e_{t-1} \tag{13–27}$$

By definition: $\alpha_t = e_t$.

Having defined the prewhitened series, we now pretreat Y_t. This series is made stationary by first differences and transformed by the following:

$$\beta_t = e'_t = Y_t - Y_{t-1} - .1477e'_{t-1} \qquad (13\text{–}28)$$

where e'_t are residuals given that e'_0, the first error, is 0.

By definition $\beta_t = e'_t$.

Cross Correlation Function

Having prewhitened and pretreated the input and output series, respectively, cross correlations are shown in Table 13–10. As shown for positive k values, the input variable, α_{t-k}, are uncorrelated with those of the output variable, β_t. Instead, values of the input variable, α_t, are correlated with lagged values of the output variable, β_{t-k}. That is, the direction of causality is from β_{t-k} to α_t, which is the opposite direction than hypothesized by the analyst.

$$\text{CCF}_{\beta_t, \alpha_{t-k}} = 0 \qquad \text{but} \qquad \text{CCF}_{\beta_{t-k}, \alpha_t} > 0 \qquad \text{for } k = 1$$

These CCFs are inconsistent with the belief that the London price changes precede New York prices. Instead, New York price changes precede London price changes. Those more familiar with this stock and its markets might have anticipated this result; however, our analyst did not.

Having arrived at the opposite conclusion than expected, let's now fit the correct transfer function. We do this by reversing the input and output variable. Now, the New York price is the input variable, X_t and α_t, and the London price is the output variable, Y_t and B_t.

Identification of London Price$_t$ = f(New York$_{t-k}$)

Prewhitening the Input Variable: New York Price. As shown previously, the ACFs and PACFs of the New York prices are nonstationary. Table 13–11 illustrates the fit of an ARIMA(0,1,0)1 model for New York stock prices of IBM. As shown, the constant is insignificant. The Q-statistic is consistent with the white noise assumption and, while not shown, there are no patterns in the ACFs and PACFs of the residuals, further confirming white noise. Let's refit the model as a pure random walk. While not shown, the process of taking first differences without a trend coefficient yields a model that has a high $\overline{R}^2$ and white noise residuals. Thus, the prewhitening and pretreating transformation for the input and output series is first differences, an ARIMA(0,1,0) model:

$$\alpha_t = X_t - X_{t-1} \qquad \text{New York price differences}$$
$$\beta_t = Y_t - Y_{t-1} \qquad \text{London price differences}$$

TABLE 13–10   Cross Correlations of Series β_t and α_{t-k}

k	B_t = Pretreated NY, α_{t-k} = Prewhitened London				
−12:	−.0230	.0189	−.1137	−.0596	.0523	.0420
−6:	.0513	−.0971	.0175	−.0823	.0936	.8554
0:	(−.1868)	−.0120	−.0471	−.0165	.0781	.0109
6:	.0728	−.0985	−.0949	.0085	−.0225	.0296
12:	.0226	−.0596	.0655	−.0238	−.0123	.0666

(Lag zero in parentheses)

**TABLE 13–11   ARIMA(0,1,0)1 Model for
New York Price**

Usable observations	241
Degrees of freedom	240
$\bar{R}^2$	.973784
Mean of dependent variable	62.1277
Standard error of dependent variable	6.8862
Residual standard error	1.1150
Sum of squared residuals	298.3560
Durbin–Watson statistic	2.1189
$Q(36-0)$	44.7267
Significance level of Q	.1509

Coefficient	Estimate	Std Error	t-Stat	Signif
θ_0	.06172	.07182	.85938	.3910

TABLE 13–12   Cross Correlation of Series β_t and α_{t-k}

k	B_t = Pretreated London, α_{t-k} = Prewhitened New York					
−12:	.0357	.02230	−.0253	−.0029	−.1096	−.0722
−6:	.0883	.01142	.0730	−.0350	−.0459	−.0324
0:	(−.0552)	.88641	−.0459	−.0937	.0151	−.0909
6:	.0712	.04191	.0367	−.0835	−.1032	.0318
12:	−.0196	.04295	−.0146	−.0933	.0409	−.0148

(Lag zero in parentheses)

***Identifying r, s,
and b***

Having prewhitened and pretreated the input and output series, respectively, we show cross correlations in Table 13–12. As shown, the lagged values of the input variable, α_{t-1}, are correlated with those of the output variable, β_t. The direction of causality is from α_{t-1} to β_t, which is the correct direction of time precedence.

$$\text{CCF}_{\beta_t, \alpha_{t-1}} = .8861$$

The time precedence of this relation shows that movements on the New York Stock Exchange precede those on the London Stock Exchange. The single peak in the cross correlations of Table 13–12 is indicative of the following transfer function:

$$y_t = \omega_0 x_{t-1} + N_t \tag{13–29}$$

***Estimation and
Diagnostics***

Table 13–13 shows the output of the transfer function of Equation 13–29. This model fits the data very well, having an $\bar{R}^2$ of .9889 and a very significant coefficient for the input series, the lagged price differences on the New York exchange. The constant in this relationship is not significantly different than zero. In addition, remember that the input variable and output variables are the differenced prices. While not shown, the residuals of Table 13–13 were not significantly cross correlated with the prewhitened input series, α_{t-k}; thus, the transfer function portion of this model appears adequate. Neither the Durbin–Watson nor Q-statistic are indicative of white noise residuals.

TABLE 13–13   Transfer Function of London Price
$r = 0, s = 0, b = 1$

Usable observations	240
Degrees of freedom	238
$\bar{R}^2$	.9889
Mean of dependent variable	40.5076
Standard error of dependent variable	3.4703
Residual standard error	.3650
Sum of squared residuals	31.7027
Durbin–Watson statistic	2.737
$Q(36-0)$	70.625
Significance level of Q	.00050

Coefficient	Estimate	Std Error	t-Stat	Signif
θ_0	−.01009	.02360	−.42767	.66928
ω_0	.62472	.02113	29.56621	.00000000

TABLE 13–14   ACFs and PACFs for Residuals of MARIMA(0,0,1)

ACFs					
k					
1:	−.3718	−.0690	.0262	−.0192	.1328	−.1428
7:	.0363	.0376	.0012	.0438	−.0845	.0327
13:	−.0188	.0850	−.0751	.0095	.0711	−.1143
19:	.0449	−.0394	−.0435	.0324	.0574	−.0482
PACFs					
1:	−.3718	−.2405	−.1170	−.0876	.1108	−.0527
7:	−.0095	.0240	.0380	.0735	−.0102	−.0059
13:	−.0423	.0803	−.0219	.0137	.0657	−.0718
19:	−.0392	−.0527	−.1132	−.0796	.0658	−.0232

Consequently, it is necessary to add an ARIMA noise model to the relationship. With that in mind, consider Table 13–14, which illustrates the ACFs and PACFs of the residuals of Table 13–13.

The patterns in the ACFs and PACFs of Table 13–14 are indicative of an MA(1) process; this noise model is added to the MARIMA model, which is now:

$$y_t = \omega_0 x_{t-1} + (1 - \theta_1 B)e_t \qquad (13-30)$$

The results of fitting this model are given in Table 13–15. As confirmed by the DW statistic, Q-statistic, and ACFs and PACFs of Table 13–16, this model has white noise residuals. The following estimated coefficients resulted:

$$y_t = .6205 x_{t-1} + (1 - .5067 B)e_t \qquad (13-31)$$

To verify that the MARIMA model of Table 13–15 is valid, cross correlations of the residuals and the input series should be consistent with the white noise assumption.

TABLE 13–15   MARIMA(0,0,1)ARIMA(0,1,1) Model for London Price

Usable observations	240
Degrees of freedom	238
$\bar{R}^2$	.9911
Mean of dependent variable	40.5076
Standard error of dependent variable	3.4703
Residual standard error	.3276
Sum of squared residuals	25.5395
Durbin–Watson statistic	1.9632
$Q(36-1)$	25.6936
Significance level of Q	.8745

Coefficient	Value	Std Error	t-Stat	Signif
$-\theta_1$	−.5067	.0559	−9.06	.00000000
ω_0	.6205	.0172	36.16	.00000000

TABLE 13–16   ACFs and PACFs of e_t for Model of Table 13–15

			ACFs			
k						
1:	.0101	−.0591	.0143	.0296	.1090	−.0879
7:	.0246	.0624	.0400	.0327	−.0638	.0123
13:	.0155	.0702	−.0479	−.0037	.0201	−.1220
			PACFs			
1:	.0101	−.0593	.0156	.0259	.1106	−.0885
7:	.0400	.0473	.0407	.0293	−.0457	−.0006
13:	−.0004	.0738	−.0532	.0181	−.0067	−.1287

Table 13–17 reports the cross correlations of these two variables. As shown, there are no statistically significant correlations. Thus, the transfer function and noise model are defensible.

Fit and Forecast   Having fitted and diagnosed this model, consider its meaning:

$$y_t = \omega_0 x_{t-1} + (1 - \theta_1 B)e_t \qquad (13\text{–}32)$$

Remembering that y_t and x_{t-1} are first differenced variables, this relationship is:

$$Y_t - Y_{t-1} = \omega_0(X_{t-1} - X_{t-2}) + (1 - \theta_1 B)e_t$$

$$\hat{Y}_t = Y_{t-1} + \omega_0(X_{t-1} - X_{t-2}) - \theta_1 e_{t-1}$$

Substituting the estimated parameters yields:

$$\hat{Y}_t = Y_{t-1} + .6205(X_{t-1} - X_{t-2}) - .5067e_{t-1} \qquad (13\text{–}33)$$

The meaning of Equation 13–33 is quite clear: Y_t is influenced by its past values and a fraction of the change in X_{t-1} minus another fraction of the most recent random shock. Now, let's see how well this relationship fits the actual data. Table 13–18 illus-

TABLE 13–17   CCFs of Residuals e_t and α_{t-k} for the Model of Table 13–15

k					
-12:	$-.0026$	$.0666$	$-.0000$	$-.0493$	$-.0727$	$.0648$
-6:	$.0040$	$-.0887$	$.0441$	$-.0786$	$.0242$	$.0049$
0:	$(-.0042)$	$.0549$	$-.0899$	$.0328$	$.0066$	$-.0016$
6:	$.0422$	$-.0242$	$-.0211$	$-.0063$	$-.0136$	$-.0184$
12:	$.1060$	$.0416$	$.0196$	$-.0413$	$.0311$	$-.0583$

$2Se[CCF(k)] = 2/(240) \approx .129$, (Lag zero in parentheses)

TABLE 13–18   Actual, Residuals, and Fitted Values for MARIMA Model

Day t	New York X_t	London Y_t	Fitted Y_t	Residual e_t
100	61.375	40.375	40.353	.0215
101	62.125	40.750	40.752	$-.0019$
102	61.750	41.375	41.216	.1586
$\vdots$				
146	61.375	40.875	40.073	.8025
147	62.250	40.000	39.848	.1521
148	62.375	40.625	40.466	.1591
149	62.500	40.875	40.622	.2531
150	62.250	40.688	40.824	$-.1363$

trates the fit of this relationship for several of the 242 observations. Consider a forecast of the London price on day 102:

$$\hat{Y}_{102} = Y_{101} + .6205(X_{101} - X_{100}) - .5067e_{101} \tag{13–34}$$

$$= 40.750 + .620519 * (62.125 - 61.375) - .506678 * (-.00192865)$$

$$= 41.216$$

The $\overline{R}^2$ of the model of Table 13–15 is rather impressive, but we should be cautious with series that are random walks because the $\overline{R}^2$ of first differences is normally quite high. A logical question is how much more accurate are the fitted values of the MARIMA model than those of an ARIMA(0,1,0) model. The ARIMA model for the London price is give in Table 13–8; it has an $\overline{R}^2$ of .94856 with a RSE of .7858. In contrast, the full MARIMA model has an $\overline{R}^2$ of .9911 and RSE of .32758, these being considerable improvements. To judge the relative advantage of the MARIMA model, we can calculate an $\overline{R}^2$ for the MARIMA versus the ARIMA model.

$$\overline{R}^2 = 1 - \frac{RSE^2(MARIMA)}{RSE^2(ARIMA)} = 1 - \frac{.32758^2}{.7858^2} = .8262 = 82.62\%$$

An 83 percent increase in the explained variance from the MARIMA model over the ARIMA model is quite high. This increase in accuracy would seem to make this modeling effort a worthwhile endeavor. Whether one can make money in the stock market using this particular relationship is speculative.

As with univariate analysis, overfitting models is sometimes useful as a model diagnostic tool. By fitting additionally coefficients, we can ensure that additional terms are unnecessary in the model, thus confirming the form of the parsimonious model. Unless there is strong theoretical justification for not doing so, statistically insignificant parameters should be dropped from the model and the remaining parameters reestimated. In this case all overfitted MARIMA models were inferior to the model of Table 13–15 and Equation 13–33; thus this model is accepted as a final one.

Cross Correlations and Identification

As we have seen from several examples, the cross correlation plots of prewhitened and pretreated series make it possible to identify:

    a. Significant CCFs.

    b. r, s, and b, and

    c. As Appendix 13–A shows, initial estimates of $\delta_1, \ldots, \delta_r, \omega_0, \ldots, \omega_s$

As regards to a, we saw that just as with autocorrelations, stationarity is achieved when cross correlations decrease quickly. However relative to b, the identification of transfer functions is often much more complex than the previous examples implied.

To better understand transfer function identification, let's explore the process of identifying r, s, and b with several examples. Refer to Figure 13–13, which provides several typical patterns. You should note in this figure that the values of r, s, and b are given with their corresponding CCFs and impulse response weights. These impulse response weights are the MARIMA equivalents of ARIMA psi weights. Some software provide estimated impulse response weights as the primary TF identification tool, just as CCFs are used here. Appendix 13–A further discusses impulse response weights.

As you study the CCFs of Figure 13–13, note that the principles of identifying r, s, and b are:

    a. r is identified just as with univariate ACF patterns for AR(p) models (e.g., an exponential decline is an AR(1) for ARIMA and $r = 1$ for the transfer function, an $r = 2$ has the same pattern as an AR(2) model).

    b. At b, the first significant CCF(k) is encountered; that is, for $b - 1$ lags CCF(k)s are insignificant.

    c. From b to $b + s$, CCF(k)s are significant, but no specific pattern may exist.

    d. After $b + s$ lags, the patterns of CCF(k) indicate r, but judgment is often needed to determine s and therefore r.

    e. Most transfer functions have very low values of r, s, and b; thus, parsimony should guide your selection.

Now consider several examples where only significant CCFs are shown.

Several Identification Examples

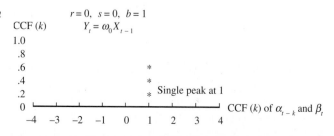

FIGURE 13–13

Example transfer functions, given r, s, and b.

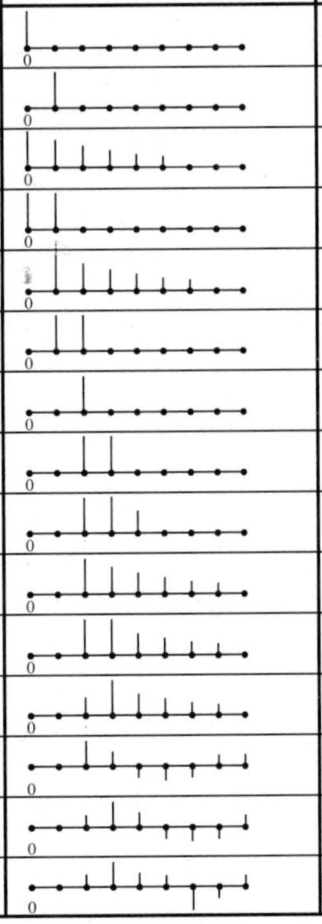

r s b	Transfer function	CCF and Impulse Response Weights	Significant CCFs at	Type of Decline
0 0 0	$Y_t = \omega_0 X_t$		0	
0 0 1	$Y_t = \omega_0 X_{t-1}$		1	
1 0 0	$Y_t = \dfrac{\omega_0 X_t}{(1 - \delta_1 B)}$		0, (+)	Expo at 1
0 1 0	$Y_t = \omega_0 X_t - \omega_1 X_{t-1}$		0, 1	
1 0 1	$Y_t = \dfrac{\omega_0 X_{t-1}}{(1 - \delta_1 B)}$		1, (+)	Expo at 2
0 1 1	$Y_t = \omega_0 X_{t-1} - \omega_1 X_{t-2}$		1	
0 0 2	$Y_t - \omega_0 X_{t-2}$		2	
0 1 2	$Y_t = (\omega_0 - \omega_1 B) X_{t-2}$		2, 3	
0 2 2	$Y_t = (\omega_0 - \omega_1 B - \omega_2 B^2) X_{t-2}$		2, 3, 4	
1 0 2	$Y_t = \dfrac{\omega_0}{(1 - \delta_1 B)} X_{t-2}$		2, (+)	Expo at 3
1 1 2	$Y_t = \dfrac{(\omega_0 - \omega_1 B)}{(1 - \delta_1 B)} X_{t-2}$		2, 3, (+)	Expo at 4
1 2 2	$Y_t = \dfrac{(\omega_0 - \omega_1 B - \omega_2 B^2)}{(1 - \delta_1 B)} X_{t-2}$		2, 3, 4, (+)	Expo at 5
2 0 2	$Y_t = \dfrac{\omega_0}{(1 - \delta_1 B - \delta_2 B^2)} X_{t-2}$		2, (+)	Sinu at 3
2 1 2	$Y_t = \dfrac{(\omega_0 - \omega_1 B)}{(1 - \delta_1 B - \delta_2 B^2)} X_{t-2}$		2, 3, (+)	Sinu at 4
2 2 2	$Y_t = \dfrac{(\omega_0 - \omega_1 B - \omega_2 B^2)}{(1 - \delta_1 B - \delta_2 B^2)} X_{t-2}$		2, 3, 4, (+)	Sinu at 5

Expo = Exponential, Sinu = Sinusoidal exponential, (+) = CCFs of decline may be significant

$$r = 0, \quad s = 0, \quad b = 3$$
$$\text{CCF}(k) \qquad Y_t = \omega_0 X_{t-3}$$

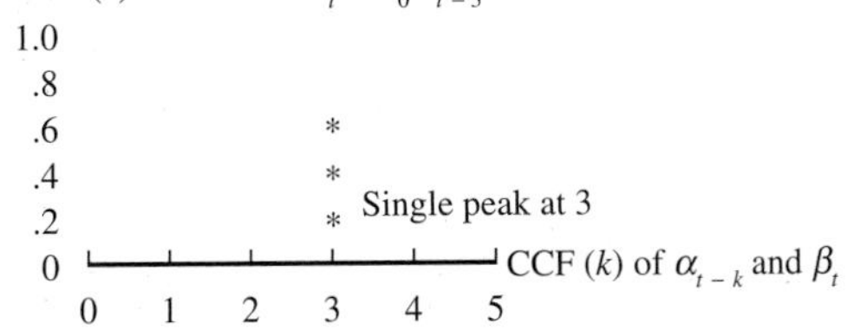

1.0
.8
.6   *
.4   *   Single peak at 3
.2   *
0 └────────────────────┘ CCF (k) of α_{t-k} and β_t
  0   1   2   3   4   5

$$r = 1, \quad s = 0, \quad b = 3$$
$$\text{CCF}(k) \qquad Y_t = \delta_1 Y_{t-1} + \omega_0 X_{t-3} = \dfrac{\omega_0 X_{t-3}}{(1 - \delta_1 B)}$$

1.0
.8   *
.6   *   *   Exponential decline after lag of 3
.4   *   *   *
.2   *   *   *   *   *
0 └──────────────────────────────┘ CCF (k) of α_{t-k} and β_t
  0   1   2   3   4   5   6   7

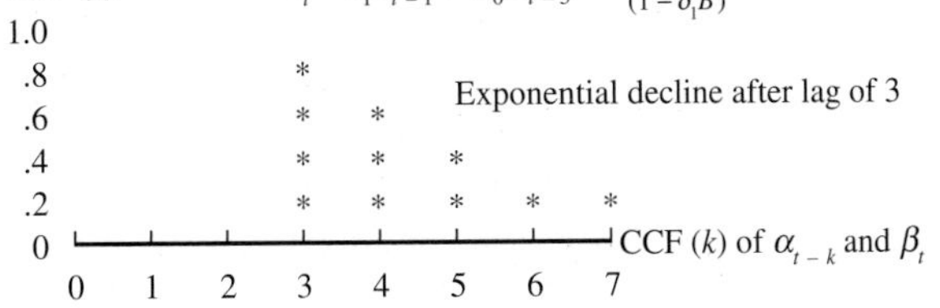

The autoregressive behavior of this series is evident from:

$$Y_t = \delta_1 Y_{t-1} + \omega_0 X_{t-3} + e_t$$
$$Y_t = \delta_1(\delta_1 Y_{t-2} + \omega_0 X_{t-4}) + \omega_0 X_{t-3} + e_t$$
$$Y_t = \delta_1(\delta_1(\delta_1 Y_{t-3} + \omega_0 X_{t-5}) + \omega_0 X_{t-4}) + \omega_0 X_{t-3} + e_t$$

and so forth.

$$r = 2, \quad s = 0, \quad b = 3$$

CCF (k) $Y_t = \delta_1 Y_{t-1} + \delta_2 Y_{t-2} + \omega_0 X_{t-3} = \dfrac{\omega_0 X_{t-3}}{(1 - \delta_1 Y_{t-1} - \delta_2 Y_{t-2})}$

```
1.0
 .8              *      Sinusoidal exponential decline after lag 3
 .6              *           *
 .4              *   *   *        *
 .2              *   *   *   *   *   *
  0  └──┴──┴──┴──┴──┴──┴──┴──┘  CCF (k) of α_{t-k} and β_t
     0  1  2  3  4  5  6  7  8
```

$$r = 0, \quad s = 1, \quad b = 3$$

CCF (k) $Y_t = \omega_0 X_{t-3} - \omega_1 X_{t-4}$

```
1.0
 .8                  *
 .6          *   *
 .4          *   *     Peaks at 3 and 4 only
 .2          *   *
  0  └──┴──┴──┴──┴──┘ CCF (k) of α_{t-k} and β_t
     0  1  2  3  4  5
```

Ambiguous Identifications

Consider an example of an ambiguous model identification in Figure 13–14. The estimated r, s, and b of this figure include several possibilities, including the following three models.

$$r = 0, s = 2, b = 3 \qquad Y_t = \omega_0 X_{t-3} - \omega_1 X_{t-4} - \omega_2 X_{t-5} + e_t$$
$$r = 1, s = 2, b = 3 \qquad Y_t = \delta_1 Y_{t-1} + \omega_0 X_{t-3} - \omega_1 X_{t-4} + \omega_2 X_{t-5} + e_t$$
$$r = 2, s = 0, b = 3 \qquad Y_t = \delta_1 Y_{t-1} + \delta_2 Y_{t-2} + \omega_0 X_{t-3} + e_t$$

The complexity of the patterns in the cross correlations in Figure 13–14 is not uncommon. As a general rule, rather simple transfer function models exist, usually of first or second order ($r, s \leq 2$). To avoid unnecessarily complicated models, we should use the principle of parsimony and select the simplest model that is consistent with the data and CCFs. This is fortuitous because the possible combinations of transfer functions and noise models are quite high. For now, let's consider two more actual MARIMA applications.

Lumber Sales = f(Advertising)(LUMBERAD.DAT)

A building materials firm is interested in measuring the influence of advertising, X_t, on the sales of a nonseasonal product, Y_t, over the last 100 months. Figure 13–15 illustrates a possible relationship between these two variables. However, an analyst in the advertising department correctly calculates the correlation between Y_t and X_t as only .0998. However, to correctly model the relationship between these variables, a MARIMA model should be fitted to this data.

Achieving Stationarity

As shown in Figure 13–15, both the output, Y_t, and input, X_t, appear to be stationary series, a fact confirmed by their ACFs and PACFs in Table 13–19. From Table 13–19, it appears that X_t is not only stationary but also white noise, while Y_t appears to be an autoregressive process. As mentioned previously, the univariate model for Y_t that achieves white noise residuals is sometimes a good predictor of the MARIMA noise model, N_t. Based on the ACFs and PACFs of Table 13–19, a tentative noise model for Y_t and a prewhitening transformation for X_t can be identified.

FIGURE 13–14

Ambiguous CCF(k)s, n = 64, 2S_{CCF} = .24

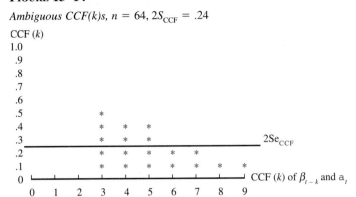

FIGURE 13–15

Lumber sales and advertising

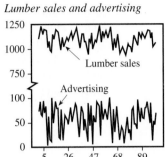

TABLE 13–19   ACFs and PACFs of X_t and Y_t ($n = 100$)

	Y_t autocorrelations					
1:	.4733	.2536	.1943	.1402	.1717	.0866
7:	.0625	−.0279	−.0732	.0206	−.0338	−.1484
13:	−.1273	−.1768	−.2107	−.2060	−.2057	−.2347
19:	−.1972	−.1759	−.1012	−.1477	−.0359	.0607
	Partial autocorrelations					
1:	.4733	.0382	.0785	.0189	.1057	−.0604
7:	.0189	−.1073	−.0452	.0884	−.0703	−.1489
13:	.0140	−.1049	−.1037	−.0491	−.0560	−.1066
19:	.0247	−.0718	.0404	−.0857	.1164	.0603
	X_t **autocorrelations**					
1:	.0559	.0649	.0816	−.0013	.1171	−.0560
7:	.0791	−.0159	−.0850	.1030	.0465	−.1487
13:	−.0309	−.0971	−.1016	−.0820	−.0657	−.1313
19:	−.1638	−.0794	.0059	−.1463	−.0478	.0767
	Partial autocorrelations					
1:	.0559	.0620	.0752	−.0133	.1095	−.0743
7:	.0770	−.0370	−.0795	.0934	.0651	−.1854
13:	−.0142	−.0773	−.1027	−.0493	−.0124	−.1559
19:	−.0845	−.0522	.0073	−.1151	.0066	.0801

Tentative N_t for Y_t   Based on its ACFs and PACFs, a tentative noise model for Y_t is fitted; while not shown, an AR(1) of Y_t yields white noise. Thus, the following may be a valid noise model for the full MARIMA model:

$$(1 - \phi_1 B)Y_t = \theta_0 + e_t = (1 - .474B)Y_t = 1{,}090.346 + e_t \qquad (13\text{–}35)$$
$$(5.300) \qquad\qquad (83.66)$$

$$n = 99 \qquad \overline{R}^2 = .2166 \qquad \text{RSE} = 68.1495$$

$$\text{DW} = 2.033 \qquad Q(24 - 1) = 19.014 \qquad (\text{SL} = .70)$$

Prewhitening X_t to Identify the TF

As shown in Table 13–19, X_t appears to be white noise simply by taking deviations from the mean. Further analysis confirms this. Thus, we should be able to identify r, s, and b directly from cross correlations between the original variables, X_{t-k} and Y_t. Table 13–20 and Figure 13–16 illustrate the cross correlations between X_{t-k} and Y_t.

As shown in Table 13–20 and Figure 13–16, there is a large spike in the CCF(k) at lag 1 and possibly exponential decline from lags 2 through 5. This suggests the following model:

$$r = 1, s = 0, b = 1$$

$$Y_t = \frac{\omega_0}{1 - \delta_1 B} X_{t-1} + N_t \tag{13–36}$$

Estimating and Diagnosing the TF

Table 13–21 illustrates the estimated MARIMA(1,0,1) transfer function of Equation 13–36 for Y_t. Note that all of the coefficients are quite significant. However, the residuals do not seem to be white noise. This is as expected because no noise model was estimated. While not shown, the CCFs for the prewhitened input and residuals of Table 13–21 do not indicate any deficiencies with this model. The ACFs and PACFs of Table 13–21 are shown in Table 13–22. There is a single spike at 1 in the ACFs and possibly an exponential decline at 2; the PACFs have a single spike at 1. These are indicative of an AR(1) process; thus, an AR(1) is added to the model. The results of this estimation are shown in Table 13–23.

TABLE 13–20   Cross Correlations between White Noise X_{t-k} and Y_t

−13:	−.1383	−.0751	−.1603	−.0305	.0923	−.0468
−7:	−.0332	.0352	.0026	.1194	.0702	.1142
−1:	.0963	(.0998)	.9098	.4078	.1993	.1469
5:	.0542	.1302	.0195	.0837	.0032	−.0863
11:	.0305	.0323	−.1071	−.0710	−.1090	−.1408
17:	−.1334	−.1105	−.1596	−.1596	−.1345	−.0279

2Se[CCF(k)] = $2/\sqrt{100}$. (Lag zero in parentheses.)

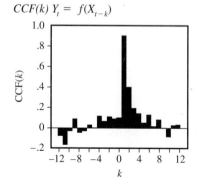

FIGURE 13–16

CCF(k) $Y_t = f(X_{t-k})$

TABLE 13–21   MARIMA(1,0,1) for Y_t

Iterations taken		8
Usable observations		99
Degrees of freedom		96
$\bar{R}^2$		.9731
Mean of dependent variable		1090.749
Standard error of dependent variable		76.995
Residual standard error		12.625
Sum of squared residuals		15300.821
Durbin–Watson statistic		1.372
$Q(24-0)$		36.647
Significance level of Q		.04744

Coefficient	Estimate	Std Error	t-Stat	Signif
θ_0	872.301	5.0604	172.379	.00000000
ω_0	25.101	.4750	52.845	.00000000
δ_1	.383	.0145	26.431	.00000000

The estimated model of Table 13–23 appears to be a good one. In addition, the ACFs and PACFs of Table 13–24 are consistent with white noise. The next check for model validity is to confirm that the residuals are not correlated with the prewhitened input variable; Table 13–25 illustrates these CCF(k). Remembering that two standard errors is approximately .2 (i.e., $2/\sqrt{100}$), there are no low-order statistically significant cross correlations in Table 13–25. Thus, there appears to be no relationship between the residuals and the prewhitened input series, X_t.

Note that the noise model of Table 13–23 is similar to the univariate ARIMA model estimated previously on Y_t in Equation 13–35. Next, to further confirm that there is no relationship between the residuals and prewhitened X_t, they were plotted against each other to confirm that there were no outliers confounding the relationship;

TABLE 13–22   Residual ACFs and PACFs of Table 13–21

			Autocorrelations			
1:	.3089	.0899	−.1031	−.0284	.0356	.1248
7:	.0609	−.0326	.0103	−.1314	−.0748	−.1466
13:	−.1103	−.2311	−.1046	−.0335	.0062	.1019
19:	−.0107	.0454	.0146	.0484	−.0555	.2133
			Partial autocorrelations			
1:	.3089	−.0061	−.1428	.0499	.0533	.0896
7:	−.0118	−.0605	.0721	−.1608	−.0187	−.1172
13:	−.0728	−.1948	−.0086	.0343	−.0182	.1279
19:	−.0342	.1009	.0343	−.0179	−.0798	.2055

TABLE 13–23   Final MARIMA(1,0,1) × ARIMA(1,0,0) Model

Iterations taken		9		
Usable observations		98		
Degrees of freedom		94		
$\overline{R}^2$		.975		
Mean of dependent variable		1090.196		
Standard error of dependent variable		77.193		
Residual standard error		12.114		
Sum of squared residuals		13794.302		
Durbin–Watson statistic		1.947		
$Q(24-1)$		24.139		
Significance level of Q		.396		

Coefficient	Estimate	Std Error	t-Stat	Signif
θ_0	872.6284	6.5658	132.905	.00000000
ϕ_1	.3166	.0987	3.208	.00000000
ω_0	24.9211	.4592	54.268	.00000000
δ_1	.3865	.0158	24.528	.00000000

	Correlation Matrix of Coefficients		
	θ_1	ω_0	δ_1
θ_0	.0693	−.4631	−.7516
ϕ_1		−.0790	−.0213
ω_0			−.1711

TABLE 13–24   **ACFs and PACFs of Residuals of Full MARIMA Model**

Autocorrelations

1:	.0010	.0270	−.1441	−.0093	.0066	.1345
7:	.0314	−.0699	.0667	−.1432	−.0066	−.1085
13:	−.0023	−.1990	−.0352	−.0066	−.0234	.1189
19:	−.0524	.0405	−.0114	.0760	−.1488	.1835

Partial autocorrelations

1:	.0010	.0270	−.1443	−.0094	.0148	.1167
7:	.0284	−.0771	.1034	−.1359	−.0316	−.1014
13:	−.0437	−.1977	−.0876	.0195	−.0600	.1168
19:	−.0199	.0696	.0595	.0264	−.1300	.1184

TABLE 13–25   **Cross Correlations of Residuals and White Noise X_t, α_t**

−24:	−.0411	.0697	.1108	−.0554	−.0789	−.1817
−18:	.1245	−.0879	−.1028	−.0682	−.0758	.0051
−12:	.0300	−.0145	−.0663	.1113	−.0368	−.0016
−6:	−.1273	.2278	.1084	.1628	.1158	−.0275
0:	(.0774)	−.0267	.0237	−.0973	−.0216	−.0130
6:	.0513	.1313	.0657	−.0848	−.1021	−.1856
12:	−.1364	.0620	−.0067	.0509	−.0118	−.0477
18:	−.0227	−.0439	.2744	−.0020	.1291	.0025

$Se[\text{CCF}(k)] = 2/\sqrt{(100)}$. (Lag zero in parentheses.)

None were found. Finally, to ensure that we have fitted the correct noise model, several MARIMA models were overfitted. While not shown here, the model of Table 13–23 was better; thus, this appears to be a best model.

We will leave it to the reader to fully interpret the results of this model. For now, consider the implications of coefficient redundancy. We may gain some insight into a model by examining the correlation matrix of parameter estimates. For our model, this matrix is given at the bottom of Table 13–23.

High correlations between parameter estimates are normally undesirable, denoting that the sum of squares surface occurs on a ridge, and thus there are many combinations of coefficients that minimize the sum of squares. This can mean that the model is too complicated, incorrectly specified, or that a particular data set yields such results. If two coefficients are redundant, then dropping either one or both of them will not significantly change the $\overline{R}^2$ and RSE. As shown in Table 13–23, the correlation between θ_0 and δ_1 is about .75, which indicates that either one of these may be redundant. However, even though these coefficients are highly correlated, dropping either significantly decreases the goodness of fit; thus, they are both retained in the model.

Multiple Input Transfer Functions—Automobile Market Share = f(Advertised quality, Price ratio)(AUTOMANU.DAT)

MARIMA can be extended to systems with multiple inputs. To illustrate this process, consider that a U.S. manufacturer of automobiles has seen its market share vary because of foreign competition. To better understand the relationship between market

FIGURE 13–17

*Market share, advertising
ratio, and price ratio of
auto manufacturer
(AUTOMANU.DAT)*

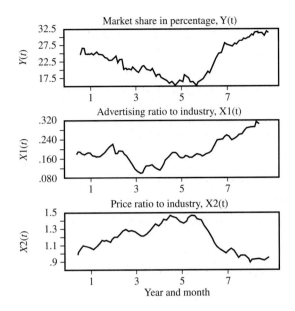

TABLE 13–26   Descriptive Statistics for Output and Input Variables

Series	Obs	Mean	Std Deviation	Minimum	Maximum
Y_t = MARKET (%)	100	22.817	4.886	15.034	31.692
$X1_t$ = ADVERT (%)	100	.18888	.05169	.09510	.31280
$X2_t$ = PRICE (%)	100	1.19711	.17552	.89554	1.48422

share, advertised quality, and price, the manufacturer studies the last 100 months (i.e., 8.333 years) of market share data. Figure 13–17 illustrates the following three variables:

Y_t = Market share of the manufacturer
$X1_t$ = Ratio of the amount spent on advertising its quality improvements to industry advertising expenditures
$X2_t$ = Ratio of the firm's prices to the average of industry prices

Thus, the independent variables are actually the ratio of the firm's variables (advertising expenditures and prices) to those of the whole industry. During this time, the firm improved its quality and oriented its advertisements to reflect quality improvements, as reported by consumer survey organizations such as J.D. Powers and Associates. To clarify these variables, their descriptive statistics are given in Table 13–26.

The firm seeks a model that explains Y_t as a function of $X1_t$ and $X2_t$:

$$Y_t = f(X1_{t-k}, X2_{t-k}, Y_{t-k}, e_{t-k})$$

This relationship is identified, estimated, and diagnosed in several steps by developing:

1. An ARIMA model of the output Y_t; this becomes a benchmark for judging the fit of the multiple input MARIMA model as well as a potential noise model.
2. An ARIMA model of the input variable, $X1_t$, in order to prewhiten it and to pretreat the output variable, Y_t.

3. A MARIMA model explaining Y_t as a function of $X1_{t-k}$ and $N1_t$.
4. An ARIMA model of the input variable, $X2_t$, in order to prewhiten it and to pretreat the output variable, Y_t.
5. A MARIMA model explaining Y_t as a function of $X2_{t-k}$ and $N2_t$.
6. A two-input MARIMA model explaining Y_t as a function of $X1_{t-k}, X2_{t-k}$, and N_t. The fitted one-input MARIMA models of steps (3) and (5) become a guide to the structure of the two-input MARIMA model of step (6).
7. The diagnostics of the MARIMA model, including cross correlations of the prewhitened input series, $\alpha1_t$ and $\alpha2_t$, and the residuals of the intervention model.

Consider each of these steps as we analyze this relationship.

1. Univariate model of the output variable Y_t
As shown in Figure 13–17, the output series appears to be very random; analysis of the series confirms that it is a random walk model, ARIMA(0,1,0).

$$Y_t = Y_{t-1} + e_t$$

$$n = 100 \qquad S_{Y_t} = 4.91 \qquad RSE = .9296 \qquad \bar{R}^2 = .964$$
$$DW = 2.149 \qquad Q = 25.407 \qquad \text{Significance of } Q(df = 24) = .3839$$

Thus, these residuals are white noise with a high $\bar{R}^2$ of .964. This $\bar{R}^2$ is compared to that of the one- and two-input MARIMA models developed next.

2. ARIMA model for advertised quality, $X1_t$
Univariate analysis of the advertising ratio yields the following model:

$$(1 - \phi_1 B)(1 - B)X1_t = \alpha1_t \qquad (13\text{–}37)$$

$$(1 - .3885B)(1 - B)X1_t = \alpha1_t$$
$$(-4.17)$$

$$n = 100 \qquad S_{X1t} = .0522 \qquad RSE = .00853 \qquad \bar{R}^2 = .973$$

$$DW = 1.95 \qquad Q = 24.48 \qquad \text{Significance of } Q(df = 24) = .3778$$

Remember that $\alpha1_t$ is simply the residuals, e_t.

3. MARIMA model for Y_t and $X1_t$
Having prewhitened $X1t$, the first step in MARIMA identification is to cross correlate the prewhitened variable, $\alpha1_t$, with the pretreated output variable, $\beta1_t$, calculated in Equation 13–38.

$$(1 - .3885B)(1 - B)Y_t = \beta1_t \qquad (13\text{–}38)$$

As shown in Table 13–27, the only marginally significant CCF is at lag 1; thus, $\beta1_t$ and $\alpha1_{t-1}$ are correlated. This pattern suggests that $r = 0$, $s = 0$, and $b = 1$. This MARIMA(0,0,1) model is fit with the following results:

$$Y_t = \omega_0 X1_{t-1} + \frac{e_t}{(1 - B)} \qquad (13\text{–}39)$$

$$= \underset{(2.117)}{20.72} X1_{t-1} + \frac{e_t}{(1 - B)}$$

$$n = 99 \qquad S_{Y_t} = 4.91 \qquad RSE = .896 \qquad \bar{R}^2 = .967$$

$$DW = 2.21 \qquad Q = 20.54 \qquad \text{Significance of } Q(df = 24) = .6656$$

The t–value of ω_0 has a .036 level of significance, and the residuals are white noise as measured by the DW and Q–statistics. While not shown, the ACFs and PACFs of the residuals have no patterns in them, implying that the appropriate noise model is an ARIMA(0,0,0). As a double check, several noise models were tried, including MA(1) and AR(1) models, none of which had statistically significant coefficients. Thus, the noise model is simply an ARIMA(0,0,0) model having no parameters.

The additional requirement of a MARIMA is that the residuals are not cross correlated with the prewhitened input variable, $\alpha1_t$; if there is a pattern left in these CCFs, then there is a deficiency in the model. Table 13–28 illustrates these CCFs, and as shown, none are statistically significant. Thus, this model appears to be the best for relating market share and the advertising ratio.

The proportion of explained variance from Equation 13–39, .967, is slightly higher than that of univariate analysis in Step 1, .964. While this model does explain the relationship between market share and advertising ratio, it is a rather weak relationship, with a t–value of about 2. This rather low t–value may be indicative of the need to include both price and advertising ratios in the relationship. We have several steps to complete before that full function is defined.

4. An ARIMA model for the price ratio, $X2_t$

Univariate analysis of the price ratio yields the following model:

$$(1 - \phi_1 B)(1 - B)X2_t = \alpha2_t \tag{13-40}$$

$$(1 - .46615B)(1 - B)X2_t = \alpha2_t$$
$$(-5.308)$$

$$n = 100 \qquad S_{X2_t} = .1757 \qquad RSE = .0221 \qquad \overline{R}^2 = .984$$

$$DW = 2.04 \qquad Q = 26.22 \qquad \text{Significance of } Q(df = 23) = .2904$$

where $\alpha2_t$ is simply the residuals, e_t.

TABLE 13–27   Cross Correlations of $\beta1_t$ and $\alpha1_{t-k}$

k					
-12:	$-.0696$	.1016	.0168	.0514	.0451	$-.0122$
-6:	.0586	.0698	.1385	$-.0492$	$-.0663$	.1530
0:	$(-.1773)$	.2003	.1126	$-.1084$	.0902	.0134
6:	$-.0220$	$-.0746$	.1156	$-.0697$	$-.0298$	.0822
12:	$-.0234$					

$2Se[CCF(k)] = 2/\sqrt{100}$. (Lag zero in parentheses.)

TABLE 13–28   Cross Correlations between e_t of Equation 13–39 and $\alpha1_t$

-12:	$-.0236$	.0627	$-.0104$	$-.0029$	.0977	$-.0906$
-6:	$-.0222$	.0487	.0844	$-.0726$	.1123	$-.0279$
0:	$(-.1509)$	.1512	$-.0591$	.0197	.1896	.1137
6:	.0826	.0529	.0914	.0353	.0255	.0602
12:	$-.0948$					

$Se[CCF(k)] = 2/\sqrt{99}$.

5. A MARIMA model for Y_t and $X2_t$

Having prewhitened $X2_t$, the first step in MARIMA identification is to cross correlate the prewhitened variable $\alpha2_t$ with the pretreated output variable $\beta2_t$ calculated in Equation 13–41.

$$(1 - .46615B)(1 - B)Y_t = \beta2_t \tag{13–41}$$

As shown in Table 13–29, the most significant CCF is at lag 1. Thus, $\beta2_t$ and $\alpha2_{t-1}$ are correlated. This pattern suggests that $r = 0$, $s = 0$, and $b = 1$. The fitted MARIMA(0,0,1) model results are:

$$Y_t = \omega_0 X2_{t-1} + \frac{e_t}{(1 - B)} \tag{13–42}$$

$$= -16.09X2_{t-1} + \frac{e_t}{(1 - B)}$$
$$(-4.942)$$

$$n = 100 \qquad S_{Y_t} = 4.91 \qquad RSE = .8195 \qquad \overline{R}^2 = .9722$$

$$DW = 2.76 \qquad Q = 43.50 \qquad \text{Significance of } Q(df = 24) = .0087$$

The model of Equation 13–42 has a very high $\overline{R}^2$, and the t–value of ω_0 is very significant. However, the residuals are not white noise, as measured by the DW and Q-statistics. As shown in Table 13–30, the ACFs and PACFs of the residuals have an MA(1) pattern in them, implying that such noise model should be added to Equation 13–42. Because the CCFs of e_t and $\alpha1_t$ in Table 13–31 do not show any patterns, the model is refitted with an MA(1) model.

TABLE 13–29   Cross Correlations of $\beta2_t$ and $\alpha2_{t-k}$ using Equation 13–41

−12:	.0309	.0459	−.0890	.0540	−.0691	−.0439
−6:	.1414	−.2129	.0669	.0198	−.0448	−.0073
0:	(−.0801)	−.2283	−.1353	.0324	−.0555	−.1674
6:	.1497	−.1821	.1127	.0232	−.1414	−.0081
12:	.0412					

$Se[CCF(k)] = 2/\sqrt{100}$.

TABLE 13–30   ACFs and PACFs of e_t of Equation 13–42

Autocorrelations					
1:	−.3851	−.1015	.1333	−.0278	.0557	−.1242
7:	.2597	−.0723	−.0910	.1350	−.0472	.0411
13:	−.1151	.1407	−.0213	−.0172	.1339	−.1274

Partial autocorrelations					
1:	−.3851	−.2934	−.0389	−.0084	.0977	−.0793
7:	.2447	.1326	.0371	.0801	.0284	.0458
13:	−.1064	.0076	−.0289	.0595	.1412	.0137

The estimation of Equation 13–42 with a MA(1) noise model yields the MARIMA(0,0,1) model of Equation 13–43:

$$Y_t = \omega_0 X2_{t-1} + (1 - \theta_1 B)\frac{e_t}{(1 - B)} \qquad (13-43)$$

$$= -22.22 X2_{t-1} + (1 - .6536B)\frac{e_t}{(1 - B)}$$

$$(-14.6) \qquad\qquad (-8.367)$$

$$n = 100 \qquad S_{Yt} = 4.91 \qquad \text{RSE} = .7069 \qquad \overline{R}^2 = .9793$$

$$\text{DW} = 1.95 \qquad Q = 16.60 \qquad \text{Significance of } Q(df = 23) = .828$$

The proportion of explained variance from the model of Equation 13–43, .9793, is higher than that of the univariate model of Step 1, .964.

While not shown, the ACFs and PACFs denote that the noise model of Equation 13–43 appears adequate. However, as shown in Table 13–32, there is a near significant CCF at lag 1. This .1906 may denote a deficiency in the transfer function. Consequently, we return to Table 13–29, the original CCF of $\beta 2_t$ and $\alpha 2_{t-k}$, to better identify the possible model deficiency. As shown there, the CCF(1) and CCF(2) are $-.2283$ and $-.1353$, respectively. These CCFs may be indicative of an exponential decline; therefore, let's try a first-order transfer function.

Equation 13–44 illustrates the fit of a first-order transfer function. As shown, $\overline{R}^2$ has improved, the t-values are approximately the same, and the other diagnostic statistics appear to be quite good. Because there is some theory to support a first–order model, the analyst accepts Equation 13–44 over the model of Equation 13–43.

$$Y_t = \frac{\omega_0 X2_{t-1}}{(1 - \delta_1 B)} + (1 - \theta_1 B)\frac{e_t}{(1 - B)} \qquad (13-44)$$

$$= \frac{-13.46 X2_{t-1}}{(1 - .4705B)} + (1 - .7515B)\frac{e_t}{(1 - B)}$$

$$(t_{\omega 0} = -8.32)\ (t_{\delta 1} = 7.25)\ (t_{\theta 1} = -10.7)$$

$$n = 100 \qquad S_{Yt} = 4.91 \qquad \text{RSE} = .6539 \qquad \overline{R}^2 = .9823$$

$$\text{DW} = 1.94 \qquad Q = 20.78 \qquad \text{Significance of } Q(df = 23) = .594$$

However, if we assume that there is no preference of Equation 13–43 over Equation 13–44 from a theoretical perspective, then the Bayesian information criterion (BIC) can be used to assist in the decision. Let's apply the BIC to these two alternative models. Recall that:

$$\text{BIC} = n\text{Ln (SSE)} + k\text{Ln}(n) \qquad (13-45)$$

TABLE 13–31   Cross Correlations of e_t and $\alpha 2_{t-k}$ for Equation 13–42

−12:	−.0782	.1225	−.0637	.0243	−.0053	−.0698
−6:	.1328	−.1423	−.0047	.0269	−.0198	−.0391
0:	(−.1094)	.0890	−.1458	−.0407	−.0402	−.2317
6:	.0557	−.1244	.0752	.0385	−.1214	−.0846
12:	−.0032					

2Se[CCF(k)] = 2/$\sqrt{100}$.

TABLE 13–32   Cross Correlations of e_t and $\alpha2_{t-k}$ for Equation 13–43

−12:	−.2069	.0395	−.0396	−.0006	.0164	−.0688
−6:	.1054	−.0651	−.0453	.0044	−.0013	−.0457
0:	(−.1588)	.1906	.0375	.0040	−.0046	−.2563
6:	−.1066	−.1783	−.0186	.0283	−.1184	−.1739
12:	−.1206	−.1110	−.0387	−.0776	.1489	−.0884

$2Se[\text{CCF}(k)] = 2/\sqrt{98}$.

TABLE 13–33   Cross Correlations of e_t and $\alpha2_{t-k}$ for Equation 13–44

−12:	−.1729	−.0017	−.0564	.0158	.0039	−.0545
−6:	.1500	−.0822	−.0319	.0299	.0003	−.0248
0:	(−.1447)	−.0812	−.0671	.0765	.1181	−.1141
6:	.0568	−.1044	.0652	.1403	−.0539	−.1267
12:	−.0840					

TABLE 13–34   ACFs and PACFs of e_t of Equation 13–44

	ACF(k)					
1:	.0052	−.1428	.0217	−.0151	.0221	−.0149
7:	.1714	−.0686	−.0900	.0997	.0237	.0463
13:	−.0118	.1343	−.0373	−.0434	.0110	−.2347
19:	−.1320	.0336	−.0321	.0615	.0525	.0076
	PACF(k)					
1:	.0052	−.1428	.0238	−.0366	.0298	−.0240
7:	.1850	−.0862	−.0323	.0711	.0191	.0589
13:	−.0039	.1358	−.0376	.0239	−.0542	−.2417
19:	−.1681	−.0297	−.1279	.0832	.0796	.0255

where

$$n = \text{Number of observations}$$
$$\text{SSE} = \text{Sum of squared errors}$$
$$k = \text{Number of coefficients estimated}$$

$$\text{BIC(Equation 13–43)} = 98\text{Ln}(47.97) + 2\text{Ln}(98) = 388.49$$

$$\text{BIC(Equation 13–44)} = 97\text{Ln}(40.61) + 3\text{Ln}(97) = 373.01$$

Thus, based on BIC, Equation 13–44 is the preferred model.

6. A MARIMA model of $Y_t = f(X1_t, X2_t)$

Having successfully fitted two bivariate MARIMA models, let's develop a trivariate model. The transfer functions to be included in the trivariate model of Equation 13–46 are those of Equations 13–44 and 13–39. Table 13–35 illustrates the fit of this model.

$$Y_t = \omega_0 X1_{t-1} + \frac{\omega'_0 X1_{t-1}}{(1 - \delta_1 B)} + \frac{N_t}{(1 - B)} \tag{13–46}$$

**TABLE 13–35   Trivariate TF Model,
Share = f(Advertising, Price),
Equation 13–46**

Iterations taken		6		
Usable observations		98		
Degrees of freedom		95		
$\bar{R}^2$		.975		
Mean of dependent variable		22.752		
Standard error of dependent variable		4.912		
Residual standard error		.775		
Sum of squared residuals		57.094		
Durbin–Watson statistic		2.881		
$Q(24-0)$		49.039		
Significance level of Q		.002		

Coefficient	Estimate	Std Error	t-Stat	Signif
ω_0	23.99	8.51	2.8201	.0059
ω'_0	-13.25	3.16	-4.1888	.0001
δ_1	43.01	.1546	2.7821	.0065

Correlation Matrix of Coefficients

	ω'_0	δ_1	ω_0
ω'_0	.0010	.7031	$-.1017$
δ_1			$-.0786$

TABLE 13–36   ACFs of Equation 13–45, the Model of Table 13–35

			ACF(k)			
1:	$-.4417$	$-.1564$	.1241	$-.0187$	.0239	$-.1161$
7:	.2072	$-.0744$	$-.1035$	.1146	$-.0580$	.0235
13:	$-.1429$	.1969	$-.0819$	$-.0028$	.0969	$-.1616$
19:	.0252	.1080	$-.0978$	.0076	.0410	.0553

			PACF(k)			
1:	$-.4417$	$-.4366$	$-.2578$	$-.2198$	$-.1094$	$-.2536$
7:	.0325	.0445	$-.0054$	.0635	.0041	.0228
13:	$-.2272$	$-.0739$	$-.1828$	$-.0465$	.0786	$-.0142$
19:	$-.0850$	.0872	$-.0807$	$-.1184$	$-.0842$	$-.0244$

All the coefficients of Table 13–35 are statistically significant. However, as expected, the residuals are not white noise. Table 13–36 illustrates the ACFs of the residuals. As shown, these behave as an MA(1). Thus, an MA(1) noise model is added to Equation 13–46 to yield Equation 13–47. (While not shown, there are no useful patterns in the CCFs of the residuals and the prewhitened input variables; thus, the TF is accepted for now.)

$$Y_t = \omega_0 X1_{t-1} + \frac{\omega'_0 X2_{t-1}}{(1 - \delta_1 B)} + (1 - \theta_1 B)\frac{e_t}{(1 - B)} \qquad (13\text{–}47)$$

7. Diagnostics of the MARIMA model

The model of Table 13–37 and Equation 13–47 appears to be a good one. All diagnostic statistics are good, and while not shown, there are no patterns left in the residuals. As shown in Tables 13–38 and 13–39, there are no patterns left between the prewhitened input variables and these residuals. And while not shown, the fit of this full model is quite good. Thus, both the transfer function and noise models appear very good and we accept this as the final model. To further confirm the effectiveness of this model, several other models were fitted to this data. However, each was found to be deficient.

The $\bar{R}^2$ of the model of Table 13–37 is quite high. A logical question is how much more accurate are the fitted values of the MARIMA model than those of an ARIMA(0,1,0) model? The ARIMA model for the market share is given in Step 1. It has an $\bar{R}^2$ of .964 with a RSE of .9269. In contrast, the full MARIMA model has an $\bar{R}^2$ of .9876 and a RSE of .5476, a considerable improvement. To judge the relative advantage of the MARIMA model, we can calculate $\bar{R}^2$ for the MARIMA versus the ARIMA model:

$$\bar{R}^2 = 1 - \frac{\text{RSE}^2(\text{MARIMA})}{\text{RSE}^2(\text{ARIMA})} = 1 - \frac{.5476^2}{.9269^2} = .6509 = 65.09\%$$

A 65.09 percent increase in the explained variance from the MARIMA model over the ARIMA model is quite high. This increase in accuracy would seem to make this modeling effort a worthwhile endeavor as summarized in Table 13–40.

TABLE 13–37   Trivariate MARIMA Model of Equation 13–47

Iterations taken	17
Usable observations	98
Degrees of freedom	94
$\bar{R}^2$	.9876
Mean of dependent variable	22.7523
Standard error of dependent variable	4.9124
Residual standard error	.5476
Sum of squared residuals	28.1832
Durbin–Watson statistic	2.1673
$Q(24-1)$	25.1043
Significance level of Q	.3449

Coefficient	Estimate	Std Error	t-Stat	Signif
$-\theta_1$	$-.9409$	.0375	-25.0671	.00000000
ω'_0	$-.1496$	.0132	-11.3128	.00000000
δ_1	.3770	.0555	6.7924	.00000000
ω_0	.1691	.0195	8.6514	.00000000

Correlation Matrix of Coefficients

	θ_1	ω'_0	δ_1	ω_0
θ_1	.0014	$-.0609$	.0297	$-.1845$
ω'_0			.9674	.0227
δ_1				$-.1375$

TABLE 13–38   CCFs of e_t and $\alpha2_{t-k}$ for Equation 13–46 and Table 13–37

−24:	−.0623	.0648	.0200	.1191	−.1151	.0005
−18:	.1191	−.1358	−.0936	.0473	.1808	−.0221
−12:	−.0701	.1301	.0605	.1847	.0613	−.0234
−6:	.2123	.0055	.0042	.0665	.0230	.0037
0:	(−.0909)	.0125	−.0369	.0559	.1167	−.1726
6:	.0112	−.1236	.0330	.1596	.0105	−.0730
12:	−.0051	−.0922	−.0466	−.0681	.1569	−.0577
18:	−.1034	.0356	.0699	−.0941	−.1040	.0767
24:	.0299					

TABLE 13–39   CCFs of e_t and $\alpha1_{t-k}$ of Equation 13–46 and Table 13–37

−24:	.0136	−.0917	−.1989	.0240	−.0595	−.0089
−18:	.1032	−.1568	−.0377	−.0523	.0312	−.1022
−12:	−.1777	.0321	.0500	.0344	.0408	−.0981
−6:	−.0558	.0055	.1607	.1163	−.1080	.0765
0:	(−.1429)	−.0305	.1283	−.1193	−.0256	−.0034
6:	.0222	−.1268	−.0002	−.0608	−.1364	.0311
12:	−.0649	−.1327	.0495	.0667	.0832	−.1635
18:	−.0331	.2603	−.1055	−.0760	.0523	.1119
24:	.0366					

TABLE 13–40   Summary of ARIMA and MARIMA Models for Market Share

Equation	ARIMA (p, d, q)	Transfer X1 (r, s, b)	Transfer X2 (r, s, b)	$\overline{R}^2$	RSE	DW	Q-stat	Q-stat sign
13–36	(0,1,0)	NA	NA	.964	.9296	2.15	25.41	(.3839)
13–39	(0,1,0)	(0,0,1)	NA	.967	.8960	2.21	20.59	(.6656)
13–44	(0,1,1)	NA	(1,0,1)	.982	.6539	1.94	20.78	(.5944)
13–47	(0,1,1)	(0,0,1)	(1,0,1)	.988	.5476	2.17	25.10	(.3449)

The MARIMA model of Equation 13–47 and Table 13–37 provides a good method for forecasting market share. As is true for most multivariate models, a forecast of the dependent variable requires past and forecasted values of the independent variables. Because there is a one-period lag in the relationship between Y and $X1$ and $X2$ in this relationship, one-period-ahead forecasts should have nearly the accuracy of the fit of Table 13–37. However, forecasts more than one period ahead require forecasts of the independent variables. In this case, we do have ARIMA models of $X1$ and $X2$ as fitted during the MARIMA modeling process. Thus, these can be used in MARIMA forecasting. While not developed here, forecasts of Y have increasing error, as do all models. There is an equivalent MARIMA forecast mean squared error identical to that of the FMSE, as developed in Chapter 9 for ARIMA models. This error measure can be generated in a similar manner, also, some software provide this output automatically.

Sex Makes Economy Go Round, Analyst Says[1]

"We have sex; we have kids; we buy new houses for the kids and stuff the houses with durable goods and appliances." Harry S. Dent, *Economic Demographer.*

In his book, *The Great Boom Ahead,* Mr. Dent suggests forgetting about politics, interest rates, econometrics, etc. One only needs to study one leading economic indicator, the U.S. birth rate. He suggests that all big economic expansions are preceded by a big birth surge 46 years prior. He predicts a continuous period of low inflation between now and 2006. The last big birth surge was the baby boom in the mid sixties which will result in economic growth peaking in about 2009, followed by a significant recession for about 10 years.

We are intrigued by Mr. Dent's assertions. Whether they are as accurate as he suggests, the MARIMA methods of this chapter and the topics of the next chapter on cyclical forecasting are essential for investigating the relationships of *The Great Boom Ahead.*[2]

---

[1]*Kansas City Star* headline, Fall 1996.
[2]Harry S. Dent, Jr. *The Great Boom Ahead: Your Comprehensive Guide to Personal and Business Profit in the New Era of Prosperity,* Hyperion, 1992.

Feedback Systems

Note that we have been fitting models with unidirectional causality or correlation. However, often, simultaneous causality occurs as discussed in Chapter 11. For example, assume that two time series are the number of hogs sold and their average price. If there is an increase in the number of hogs sold in year t, there is a tendency for the price to fall in that year due to increased supply. Also, the lower price in year t will usually generate a decrease in the number of hogs produced and sold in year $t + 1$ because farmers will reduce their breeding programs with lower prices. This year–to–year relationship is a form of **feedback**. With feedback between y_t and x_t, it is not appropriate to treat x_t as an input and y_t as output—they really alternate as input and output variables. Thus, the usual transfer function model may not be appropriate, particularly when this feedback is strong. In some cases, we can estimate simultaneous models, as developed in Chapter 11. However, this is not always possible. For more information on MARIMA models with feedback, see Jenkins (1979), Granger and Newbold (1977), and Box and MacGregor (1974).

Summary

This chapter has presented an introduction to modeling and forecasting time series using MARIMA. As we have seen in the examples of this chapter, MARIMA models can be very powerful. While these models have a general advantage over other multivariate and univariate models, their greatest advantage exists when lagged independent variables affect the dependent variable. Many applications of these methods in forecasting and control have been reported. However, many more potential applications exist. These applications will grow as more powerful and user friendly software become available to more users.

In general, the identification estimation and diagnostic steps used in MARIMA model building are nearly identical to those used in good univariate model building.

The transfer function models illustrated here are members of a general class of time series models. Jenkins (1979) identifies the class of models as follows:

1. Univariate ARIMA models for time series using only current and past values of the variable of interest (Chapters 7 to 9).
2. Transfer function models for relating a single output time series to several input time series (Chapter 13).
3. Intervention models that account for known events occurring in the time series, such as tornadoes, strikes, price changes, and so on (Chapter 12).
4. Multivariate stochastic models that are used to describe the interrelationships between several output time series having mutual interactions (Jenkins, 1979).
5. Multivariate transfer function models that are used to relate several mutually interacting output time series to one or more input time series (Jenkins, 1979).

There are a number of problems with MARIMA models that present considerable difficulty and require further research. With multiple inputs, it is hard to determine which subset of input variables results in the best model of the output variable. This problem is similar to the modeling problem in linear regression where we search iteratively using theory and empirical evidence to select the best model. Unfortunately, the methodology of selecting variables in MARIMA models is not as easy as that of regression analysis. One approach is to use a trial and error approach, much as developed in Chapter 10 on regression analysis. Another problem with fitting MARIMA models is the identification step. When theory does not dictate the form of transfer function, then we must use estimates of cross correlations or impulse response weights and match these against theoretical patterns to determine r, s, and b. Unfortunately, there is considerable art in this process because the possible patterns might have only slight differences. Thus, judgment is an important determinate of successful model building. Fortunately, automatic model identification software exists and is becoming more popular. However, it is difficult to incorporate enough intelligence in these systems. For further study of MARIMA and its extensions, see Box, Jenkins, and Reinsel (1994), Enders (1995), Jenkins (1979), Granger and Newbold (1977), Haugh (1972), Phadke (1973), and Priestly (1971).

Obviously, to efficiently fit MARIMA models, the steps of identification, estimation, and diagnostic checking should be done interactively and iteratively. Presently, there are several major software packages available for MARIMA analysis, including those from AFS, SCA, BMDP, SAS, SYSTAT, BFS, and ESTIMA. As these programs may differ slightly in their outputs, we have tried to use generic presentations in this chapter.

Key Terms

α_t and β_t
dynamics
feedback systems
first-order transfer functions
impulse response weights
input series
MARIMA
multiple input transfer functions
oscillation

output series
pretreated output series
prewhitened input series
pulses and shifts
rate coefficient, δ_1
second-order transfer functions
steady state
zero-order transfer functions (TF)

Key Formulas

$$\text{Ticket Sales}_t = f(\text{Jackpot}_t, \text{Jackpot}_{t-1}, \text{Jackpot}_{t-2}) + \text{Noise}_t$$

$$\text{MARIMA} = \text{Transfer function} + \text{model}$$

Zero-order model:

$$y_t = \omega_0 x_t + N_t \tag{13-1}$$

General transfer function (specified by r, s, and b):

$$y_t = \frac{(\omega_0 B^b - \omega_1 B^{b+1} + \ldots - \omega_s B^{b+s})x_t}{(1 - \delta_1 B - \delta_2 B^2 - \ldots - \delta_r B^r)} + N_t \tag{13-2}$$

Given $r = 0$, $s = 1$, $b = 3$:

$$y_t = \omega_0 x_{t-3} - \omega_1 x_{t-4} + N_t \tag{13-3}$$

General bivariate TF with $r = 0$:

$$y_t = \omega_0 x_{t-b} - \omega_1 x_{t-b-1} - \omega_2 x_{t-b-2} - \ldots - \omega_s x_{t-b-s} + N_t$$
$$= (\omega_0 B^b - \omega_1 B^{b+1} + \ldots - \omega_s B^{b+s})x_t + N_t \tag{13-4}$$

Example 13–1—A zero-order transfer function:

$$y_t = (\omega_0 - \omega_1 B)x_t + N_t = (.5 + .3B)x_t + N_t \quad \text{(in deviations)}$$

$$Y_t - 4.4 \text{ and } X_t - .5$$

$$Y_t - 4.4 = (.5 + .3B)(X_t - .5)$$

$$Y_t = 4 + .5X_t + .3X_{t-1}$$

Example 13–2—First-order transfer function:

$$y_t = \frac{\omega_0}{(1 - \delta_1 B)}x_t + N_t = \frac{10}{(1 - .2B)}x_t + N_t \tag{13-7}$$

Given $y_t = Y_t - 600$, $x_t = X_t - 10$:

$$y_t = .2y_{t-1} + 10x_t + (1 - .2B)N_t \tag{13-8}$$

$$Y_t = 380 + .2Y_{t-1} + 10X_t \tag{13-10}$$

Example 13–3—Second-order transfer function:

$$y_t = \frac{\omega_0}{(1 - \delta_1 B - \delta_2 B^2)}x_t + N_t = \frac{20}{(1 - .8B + .6B^2)}x_t + N_t \tag{13-12}$$

Given $y_t = Y_t - 400$ and $x_t = X_t - 30$, and rearranging terms:

$$Y_t = -{}_280 + .8Y_{t-1} - .6Y_{t-2} + 20X_t \tag{13-12a}$$

Cross covariances:

$$\text{COV}_{xy}(k) = \frac{1}{n}\sum_{t=1+k}^{n}(Y_t - \bar{Y})(X_{t-k} - \bar{X}) \quad k \geq 0 \tag{13-13}$$

Cross correlations CCF(k):

$$\text{CCF}_{xy}(k) = \frac{\text{COV}_{xy}(k)}{S_x S_y} \tag{13-14}$$

$$Se\text{CCF}_{xy}(k) = \frac{1}{\sqrt{n-k}} \tag{13-15}$$

Prewhitened input series:

$$x_t = \phi_1 x_{t-1} + e_t = .8x_{t-1} + e_t$$

$$\alpha_t = x_t - .8x_{t-1} \tag{13–17}$$

Pretreated output series:

$$y_t = \phi_1 y_{t-1} + e'_t = .8y_{t-1} + e'_t$$

$$\beta_t = y_t - .8y_{t-1} \tag{13–18}$$

Calculate CCFs to identify r, s, and b:

Given $r = 0 \; s = 0 \; b = 2$:

$$y_t = \omega_0 x_{t-2} + N_t \tag{13–19}$$

$$Y_t = .6X_{t-3} + z_t \tag{13–20}$$

IBM stock prices in New York and London:

$$\alpha_t = X_t - X_{t-1} \qquad \text{New York price differences}$$

$$\beta_t = Y_t - Y_{t-1} \qquad \text{London price differences}$$

Given $r = 0 \; s = 1 \; b = 1$:

$$Y_t - Y_{t-1} = \omega_0(X_{t-1} - X_{t-2}) + (1 - \theta_1 B)e_t$$

$$\hat{Y}_t = Y_{t-1} + .6205(X_{t-1} - X_{t-2}) - .5067e_{t-1} \tag{13–33}$$

Explained variance from MARIMA versus ARIMA model:

$$\bar{R}^2 = 1 - \frac{\text{RSE}^2(\text{MARIMA})}{\text{RSE}^2(\text{ARIMA})} = 1 - \frac{.32758^2}{.7858^2} = .8262 = 82.62\%$$

Lumber sales $= f(\text{Advertising})$ (LUMBERAD.DAT):

MARIMA(1,0,1) $$Y_t = \frac{\omega_0}{1 - \delta_1 B} X_{t-1} + N_t \tag{13–36}$$

Multiple input transfer functions—Automobile market share $= f(\text{Advertised quality, price ratio})$:

$$Y_t = \omega_0 X1_{t-1} + \frac{\omega'_0 \, X2_{t-1}}{(1 - \delta_1 B)} + (1 - \theta_1 B)\frac{e_t}{(1 - B)} \tag{13–47}$$

Review Problems Using Your Software

R13–1 Study the documentation of your software and confirm whether it supports MARIMA modeling and notation. If so, then explain how r, s, and b are specified in your software. In addition, how are differences applied in the model?

R13–2 Using a spreadsheet program of your choosing, repeat the zero-order transfer function of Table 13–1 for periods 1 to 6. Do your results agree with Table 13–1?

R13–3 Using a spreadsheet program of your choosing, calculate the first-order transfer function of Table 13–2 for periods 1 to 7. Do your results agree with Table 13–2? Use δ_1 of .2 and .8 (of Table 13–3)?

R13–4 Using a spreadsheet program of your choosing, calculate the second-order transfer function of Table 13–4 for periods 1 to 20. Do your results agree with Table 13–4?

R13–5 Using a spreadsheet program of your choosing, calculate the second-order transfer function of Table 13–5 for periods 1 to 20. Do your results agree with Table 13–5?

R13–6 Using IBMNYLN.DAT, repeat the analysis of New York and London IBM stock prices by completing the equivalent of the following tables. Interpret your results.

a. Table 13–10   *b.* Table 13–11
c. Table 13–12   *d.* Tables 13–13 and 13–14
e. Tables 13–15, 13–16, and 13–17   *f.* Table 13–18

R13–7 Using LUMBERAD.DAT, repeat the analysis of Lumber Sales and Advertising by completing the equivalent of the following tables. Interpret your results.
a. Table 13–19   *b.* Table 13–20
c. Tables 13–21 and 13–22   *d.* Tables 13–23, 13–24, and 13–25

R13–8 Using AUTOMANU.DAT, repeat the analysis of Automobile Market Share, advertised quality and price ratio, by completing the equivalent of the following steps. Interpret your results.
a. Step 1   *b.* Step 2
c. Step 3   *d.* Step 4
e. Step 5   *f.* Steps 6 and 7

Problems

13–1 Explain the relationship between MARIMA models and least squares regression.

13–2 Explain the relationship between MARIMA models and autoregressive methods like Cochrane-Orcutt Iterative Least Squares.

13–3 Briefly define each step of transfer function modeling.

13–4 Why are differences applied to the input and output variables?

13–5 Explain the differences between a pulse and a step function. Give an example of each.

13–6 Explain the functions of r, s, and b for the general transfer function model.

13–7 Using a spreadsheet or manual calculations, illustrate the bounds of stability for a first-order transfer function given values of $\omega_0 = 10$, $\delta_1 = .3, .6$, and 1.2 for $t = 1$ to 20 using:
a. A step function originating in period 2.
b. A pulse function originating in period 2.
c. Compare the behavior of (*a*) and (*b*).

13–8 Draw the following transfer function shapes for the given values of r, s, and b.
a. (0,1,0)
b. (1,0,0)
c. (0,0,1)
d. (1,0,1)
e. (1,1,1)

13–9 What is the meaning of asymptotic value of a first-order transfer function?

13–10 What should be known to be able to validly apply empirically driven transfer function modeling?

13–11 What are the characteristics of a valid transfer function model? Be complete in discussing the transfer function and noise components.

13–12 What are the consequences of using univariate analysis on a series affected by a transfer function?

13–13 How can transfer function models be used if your software does not support models directly through the specification of r, s, and b?

13–14 Explain the meaning of $\omega_0 = 1$, $\delta_1 = .3$ for a first-order transfer function model in terms of the original time series when logarithms are used.

13–15 Using one of the following combinations of stock index data sets fit a MARIMA model much as the IBMNYLN.DAT example
a. GERMUS.DAT
b. USJAPAN.DAT
c. UKUSIND.DAT

13–16 Using one of the following stock price time series on the London and New York stock markets, fit a MARIMA much as the IBMNYLN.DAT example
  a. British Airways stock price (BRITAIR.DAT)
  b. General Motors stock price (GM.DAT)

Minicases: Common Forecasting Assignment

For a selected minicase or problem, complete the following analysis. Develop a transfer function model for a selected time series as you achieve stationarity and white noise residuals. Fill out two tables, one the equivalent of Table 8–15 and the other the equivalent of Table 8–25. In addition, if you have been filling out the Master Forecasting Summary Table, add the appropriate model to that table.

Note that these time series are previous time series where input variables have been added, these added independent variables being contrived for explanatory purposes.

Minicase 13–1 Kansas Turnpike, Daily Data
TURNPIKG.DAT, where independent variables representing seasonal demand for daily travel are in that dataset.

Minicase 13–2 Domestic Air Passengers by Quarter
PASSAIRG.DAT, where independent variables representing indexes of air travel are in that dataset.

Minicase 13–3 Hospital Census by Month
CENSUSMG.DAT, where independent variables representing seasonal monthly demand for health care are in that dataset.

Minicase 13–4 Henry Machler's Hideaway Orchids
MACHLERG.DAT, where independent variables representing the seasonal population of consumers (i.e.,

northerners who stay for only five months or so in Florida, commonly called *snowbirds*) are variables of that dataset.

Minicase 13–5 Your Forecasting Project Is there a transfer function in your series? If so, fit a MARIMA to your data.

Minicase 13–6 Midwestern Building Materials
LUMBERG.DAT, where independent variables representing the seasonal demand for building material supplies are in that dataset.

Minicase 13–7 International Airline Passengers
AIRLING.DAT, where independent variables representing indexes for international travel are in that dataset.

Minicase 13–8 Automobile Sales AUTOG.DAT, where independent variables representing indexes of automobile demand are in that dataset.

Minicase 13–9 Consumption of Distilled Spirits
SPIRITSG.DAT, where independent variables representing the seasonal demand for alcoholic drinks as estimated by liquor store managers are in that dataset.

Minicase 13–10 Discount Consumer Electronics
ELECTG.DAT, where independent variables representing indexes of consumer demand consisting of a weighted average of new product improvements and number of outlets are in that dataset.

References

Bartlett, M.S. "On the Theoretical Specification of Sampling Properties of Autocorrelated Time Series." *Journal of the Royal Statistical Society*, 8 (1946), Series B, pp. 27–41.

Box, G.E.P., and J.F. MacGregor. "The Analysis of Closed Loop Dynamic Stochastic Systems," *Technometrics 16*, pp. 391–98. (1974).

Box, G.E.P., and P. Newbold. "Some Comments on a Paper of Coen, Gomme, and Kendall." *Journal of the Royal Statistical Society*, 134 (1971), Series A, Part II, pp. 229–40.

Box, G.E.P., and G.C. Tiao. "A Change in Level of a Non-Stationary Time Series." *Biometrika* 52 (1963), pp. 181–92.

————. "Intervention Analysis with Applications to Economic and Environmental Problems." *Journal of the American Statistical Association*, 70 (1975), pp. 70–79.

Box, G.E.P.; G.M. Jenkins; and G.C. Reinsel. *Time Series Analysis, Forecasting and Control*. 3rd ed. Englewood Cliffs, NJ: Prentice Hall, 1994.

Coen, P.J.; E.D. Gomme; and M.G. Kendall. "Lagged Relationships in Economic Forecasting." *Journal of the Royal Statistical Society*, 132 (1969) Series A, pp. 133–63.

Cook, T.D., and D.T. Campbell. *Quasi-Experimentation Design and Analysis Issues for Field Settings*, Chicago: Rand

McNally College Publishing Company, 1979.

Draper, N.R., and H. Smith. *Applied Regression Analysis*, 2nd ed. New York: John Wiley & Sons, 1981.

Enders, W. *Applied Econometric Time Series*. New York: John Wiley & Sons, 1995.

Fuller, W.A. *Introduction to Statistical Time Series*. New York: John Wiley & Sons, 1976.

Glass, G.V. "Estimating the Effects of Intervention into a Nonstationary Time Series." *American Educational Research Journal*, 9 (1972), pp. 463–77.

Granger, C.W.J., and P. Newbold. *Forecasting Economic Time Series*, New York: Academic Press, 1977.

Haugh, L.D. "The Identification of Time Series Interrelationships with Special Reference to Dynamic Regression Models." Unpublished doctoral dissertation, University of Wisconsin–Madison, 1972.

Helmer, R.M., and J.K. Johansson. "An Exposition of the Box-Jenkins Transfer Function Analysis with Application to the Advertising-Sales Relationship." *Journal of Marketing Research* 14 (1977), pp. 227–39.

Jenkins, G. M. *Practical Experiences with Modeling and Forecasting Time Series*, Lancaster: GJP Publications, 1979.

Marquardt, D.W. "An Algorithm for Least Squares Estimation of Nonlinear Parameters." *Journal of the Society of Industrial & Applied Mathematics* 2 (1963), pp. 431–44.

Montgomery, D.C., and L.A. Johnson. *Forecasting and Time Series Analysis*, New York: McGraw-Hill, 1976.

Nelson, C.R. *Applied Time Series Analysis for Managerial Forecasting*, San Francisco: Holden-Day, 1973.

Pack, D.J. "Revealing Time Series Interrelationships." *Decision Sciences* 8 (1977), pp. 377–402.

————. "A Computer Program for the Analysis of Time Series Models Using the Box-Jenkins Philosophy." Data Center, College of Administrative Science, The Ohio State University, 1977. [This computer program is now available from Automatic Forecasting Systems, Inc., Hatboro, PA 19040].

Phadke, M.S. "Multiple Time Series Modeling and system Identification with Applications." Unpublished doctoral dissertation, University of Wisconsin-Madison, 1973.

Priestly, M.B. "Fitting Relationships between Time Series." Presented at 38th Session of the International Statistical Institute, Washington, D.C., 1971.

Tiao, G.C.; G.E.P. Box; and W.J. Hamming. "Analysis of Los Angeles Photochemical Smog Data: A Statistical Overview." *Journal of the Air Pollution Control Association* 25 (1975), pp. 260–68.

Tiao, G.C.; G.E.P. Box; M. R. Grupe; G. B. Hudak; W.R. Bell; and I. Chang. "The Wisconsin Multiple Time Series (WMSS–1) Program." Department of Statistics, University of Wisconsin–Madison, 1979.

Wichern, D.W., and R.H. Jones. "Assessing the Impact of Market Disturbances Using Intervention Analysis." *Management Science* 21 (1977), pp. 329–37.

APPENDIX 13–A

ESTIMATING IMPULSE RESPONSE WEIGHTS AND INITIAL COEFFICIENTS

As was true for ARIMA models, where Y_t could be expressed as a function of e_t, it is possible to express Y_t as a function of past X_ts using **impulse response weights,** designated by vs.

Some software packages provide graphs of impulse response weights for model identification as illustrated in Figure 13–13. Also, these impulse response weight expressions are an efficient way to generate forecast confidence intervals. By definition:

$$Y_t = v_0 X_t + v_1 X_{t-1} + v_2 X_{t-2} + \ldots + e_t \qquad (13A-1)$$

Where vs are impulse response parameters. Because 13A–1 is true for Y_t and X_t, it is also true for the prewhitened α_t and the pretreated β_t.

$$\beta_t = v_0\alpha_t + v_1\alpha_{t-1} + \ldots - v_k\alpha_{t-k} + \ldots + e_t \qquad (13A\text{-}1a)$$

Remember that α_t is white noise having no autocorrelations, and therefore all α_t are statistically independent. To see how we estimate vs, consider the following derivation. Multiplying both sides of Equation 13A–1 by α_{t-k} yields:

$$\alpha_{t-k}\beta_t = v_0\alpha_t\alpha_{t-k} + v_1\alpha_{t-1}\alpha_{t-k} \ldots v_k\alpha_{t-k}\alpha_{t-k} \qquad (13A\text{-}2)$$

Remember that α_t is white noise, so the expected value (mean) is:

$$C_{\alpha\beta}(k) = v_k S_\alpha^2 \qquad (13A\text{-}3)$$

where $C_{\alpha\beta}(k)$ is the cross covariance, S_α^2 is the variance of prewhitened α, and all other terms have means of zero because of the independences of the lags of α—that is, $\alpha_{t-j} \neq f(\alpha_{t-k})$ for all $j \neq k$.

Now, calculate the cross correlation, $r_{\alpha\beta}$, by dividing Equation 13A–3 by $S_\alpha S_\beta$, to yield:

$$r_{\alpha\beta}(k) = \frac{C_{\alpha\beta}(k)}{S_\alpha S_\beta} = \frac{v_k S_\alpha^2}{S_\alpha S_\beta} = \frac{v_k S_\alpha}{S_\beta} \qquad (13A\text{-}4)$$

where $r_{\alpha\beta}(k)$ can be estimated from actual data. Rearrange Equation 13A–4 to yield Equation 13A–5. Also, the only unknown in Equation 13A–5 is v_k:

$$v_k = r_{\alpha\beta}(k)S_\beta/S_\alpha \qquad (13A\text{-}5)$$

Thus, v_ks can be *estimated* from cross correlations, and we have shown that v_ks are proportional to $r_{\alpha\beta}(k)$s:

$$v_k = r_{\alpha\beta}(k)S_\beta/S_\alpha$$

As shown below, the, v_ks are useful in solving for $\omega_0, \omega_1 \ldots \omega_s$ and $\delta_1, \delta_2 \ldots \delta_r$. Given the two relationships below:

$$\beta_t = (v_0 + v_1B + v_2B^2 + \ldots)\alpha_t$$
$$= \frac{(\omega_0B^b - \omega_1B^{b+1} - \ldots - \omega_sB^{b+s})\alpha_t}{(1 - \delta_1B - \delta_2B^2 - \ldots - \delta_rB^r)}$$

Now equating the right-hand sides of each of the above:

$$(v_0 + v_1B + v_2B^2 + \ldots) = \frac{(\omega_0B^b - \omega_1B^{b+1} + \ldots - \omega_sB^{b+s})}{(1 - \delta_1B - \delta_2B^2 - \ldots - \delta_rB^r)}$$

Cross multiplying by the denominator of the right-hand side:

$$(v_0 + v_1B + v_2B^2 + \ldots)(1 - \delta_1B - \delta_2B^2 - \ldots - \delta_rB^r) =$$
$$(\omega_0B^b - \omega_1B^{b+1} + \ldots - \omega_sB^{b+s})$$

By equating equal powers of B on both sides of these equations, we can solve for initial estimates of δs and ωs. This is illustrated next by substituting estimated values of v_ks into the left-hand side above and solving for δs and ωs.

Some Simple Examples.

1. $Y_t = \omega_0X_{t-2} = \omega_0B^2X_t$

$$(v_0 + v_1B + v_2B^2 + v_3B^3 + v_4B^4 + \ldots)1 = \omega_0B^2$$

Equating equal powers of B:

$$v_2B^2 = \omega_0B^2$$
$$v_2 = \omega_0$$

Remember that v_2 is known from the Equation 13A–4. Therefore, ω_0 is known:

$$v_2 = r_{\alpha\beta}(2)S_\beta/S_\alpha = \omega_0$$

2. $Y_t = \omega_0 X_{t-3} - \omega_1 X_{t-4}$

$$(v_0 + v_1 B + v_2 B^2 + v_3 B^3 + v_4 B^4)1 = \omega_0 B^3 - \omega_1 B^4$$

Equating equal powers of B:
B^3 terms:

$$v_3 B^3 = \omega_0 B^3$$

Therefore:

$$v_3 = \omega_0$$

B^4 terms:

$$v_4 B^4 = -\omega_1 B^4$$

Therefore:

$$v_4 = -\omega_1$$

3. $Y_t = \delta_1 Y_{t-1} + \omega_0 X_{t-3}$

$$(v_0 + v_1 B + v_2 B^2 + v_3 B^3 + v_4 B^4)1 = \frac{\omega_0 X_{t-3}}{1 - \delta_1 B}$$

$$(v_0 + v_1 B + v_2 B^2 + v_3 B^3 + v_4 B^4)(1 - \delta_1 B) = \omega_0 B^3$$

Now, equating equal powers of B yields two equations in two unknowns:

$$v_3 B^3 - v_2 \delta_1 B^3 = \omega_0 B^3$$
$$v_2 B^2 - v_1 \delta_1 B^2 = 0 B^2$$

Dividing each of the above by the appropriate power of B:

$$v_3 - v_2 \delta_1 = \omega_0$$
$$v_2 - v_1 \delta_1 = 0$$

From the last equation, we have:

$$\delta_1 = v_2/v_1$$

Therefore, δ_1 is known, and we can solve for ω_0 using the first of the two equations above:

$$\omega_0 = v_3 - v_2 \delta_1$$

Signal to Noise Ratio Problems Consider the following duplicate of Equation 13A–4. This will provide some insights into problems with identifying transfer functions. If S_β is significantly greater than S_α, then the $r_{\alpha\beta}(k)$ will be low and v_k may be difficult to identify as significant.

$$r_{\alpha\beta}(k) = \frac{C_{\alpha\beta}(k)}{S_\alpha S_\beta} = \frac{v_k S_\alpha}{S_\beta} \tag{13A–4}$$

This is so because the variance of $r_{\alpha\beta}$ is approximately $1/n$. Because the estimated v_k and $r_{\alpha\beta}(k)$ may be confounded by noise, S_α should be reasonably high compared to S_β unless the number of observations is quite large. Thus, successful identification requires that the population standard deviation of the pretreated input variable α_t be high compared to the variation in β_t.

CYCLICAL, QUALITATIVE, AND ARTIFICIAL INTELLIGENCE METHODS

CYCLICAL FORECASTING METHODS

Earnings momentum and visibility should continue to propel the [stock] market to new highs.

Report published by a well-known brokerage house, October 19, 1987.

Chapter Outline

In this chapter, we study business cycle forecasting with particular attention to the theory of cycles and practical methods for predicting them. The term **business cycle** is used to identify economic expansions and contractions. Except for irregular events, business cycles are the most difficult time series patterns to predict because they do not have a known period; they are recurrent but not periodic. Thus, the **turning points** (e.g., from expansions to contractions) are very difficult to predict. To better understand business cycles, this chapter discusses cycle theories, indicators of business activity, forecasting with decomposition methods, leading indicators, and pressure cycles.

Let's first explore some theories of business cycles and then methods for modeling those. If you want to go directly to discussions of cyclical forecasting methods, then you can skip to the Forecasting Recessions section. If you do so, remember how difficult it is to accurately predict recessions and recoveries. Some methods studied here reliably predict all recessions and recoveries, but unfortunately they predict more of each then actually occur. Thus, false signals in cyclical forecasting are not uncommon. These false signals can occur so frequently that some question the usefulness of these methods. However, we stress instead that the information these methods provide should be combined with information from other methods.

Theory Driven Analysis

This book has stressed that theory should drive the empirical processes of model identification, estimation, diagnosis, and forecasting. This chapter and its appendix review several cyclical and economic theories important in business forecasting, for without adequate theory, we have insufficient substantive knowledge. Many times, we have been surprised to find students spending weeks empirically fitting relationships without first researching the theory of the phenomena being modeled. However, in reviewing these cyclical theories, our discussion must be brief.

Why Model Business Cycles?

From a business planning perspective, there are several important reasons for measuring, modeling, and forecasting cyclical behavior.

1. A measure of past cyclical behavior is valuable in studying the causal influences on a business. These measures help answer questions such as:

- What economic variables seem to influence sales the most?
- How sensitive is our business to cyclical influences?
- For our industry, what are the typical cyclical amplitudes and timings of changes in production, inventory, sales, and material prices?
- Are there leads or lags in our sales relative to other economic series that will aid in forecasting?

2. Cyclical measures are important in strategic decision making by federal, state, and local governments and to businesses. The President's Council of Economic Advisors and other agencies evaluate cyclical indicators to reduce the chances of inflation, recessions, and depressions. Thus, accurate cyclical forecasts are necessary in modeling the effects of policies.

3. Several studies have shown that the accuracy of forecasts declines dramatically because of changes in cyclical variations. Thus, anticipating cyclical influences can greatly improve the accuracy of forecasts. As shown many times, forecasts made

for periods with continuing cyclical patterns (e.g., during economic growth) are relatively accurate; however, those made for periods with turning points (e.g., from expansion to contraction) have not been so (Eckstein, 1978).

Those in business and economics might view business cycles as opportunities to make profitable decisions. However, the macroeconomic impact of business downturns on many individuals and families can be devastating. Such individuals suffer economic hardships during recessions and depressions. Unfortunately, more and more employees are not covered by supplemental unemployment or health benefits and thus can be affected in catastrophic ways. Obviously, there is interest in business cycle theory because of the suffering and misery of humans, frequently by those least able to improve their lives.

Understanding Cyclical Influences

The Phases of Business Cycles

Typically, there are four phases in a business cycle: **prosperity**, **liquidation**, **recession** (or in the extreme, **depression**), and **recovery**. These four phases are the terms originally developed by Wesley Mitchell (1874–1948) and others. Some other researchers have identified six phases in business cycles: **growth**, prosperity, **warning**, recession, depression, and recovery. These six terms and the alternate four terms are shown in Figure 14–1. While the sequence of phases in business cycles is not difficult to predict, their timing and duration are.

Figure 14–2 shows three time series with highly cyclical variations. These are the **composite leading, coincident,** and **lagging economic indicators** developed by the U.S. Bureau of Economic Analysis of the Department of Commerce. While these are developed later in greater detail, they either lead, lag, or coincide with changes in macroeconomic output—specifically, gross domestic product, GDP. Please refer to these series as the phases of a business cycle are presented, starting with the prosperity phase.

During the prosperity phase, production, employment, wage and profit growth rates are higher than adjacent phases and, for example, culminate in the b coincident

FIGURE 14–1

Phases of the business cycle

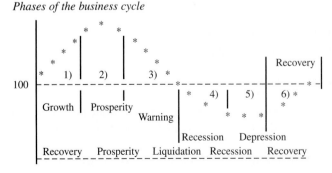

FIGURE 14–2

Leading, coincident, and lagging indicators

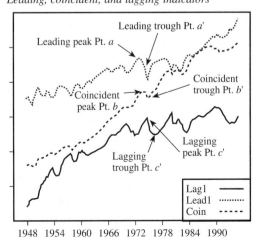

peak of Figure 14–2b. (Note that typically the peaks and troughs of Figure 14–2a and c lead and lag actual economic growth of 14–2b, respectively, as evident in the figure). However, as the business cycle continues, production costs and wages increase, material availability declines, prices rise, interest rates rise, and consumers become pessimistic because of increased prices. As customers buy less, demand declines below production (i.e., supply) and inventories rise. This causes businesses to reduce investment in new plant and equipment, reduce production, lay off workers, and reduce prices; thus, a period of liquidation begins. Management becomes more pessimistic about customer demands when prices and profits decline, and both businesses and consumers reduce expenditures in order to preserve financial security. This further reduces demand, and businesses react by reducing production and closing factories. As output (e.g., GDP) and employment decline, a recession or depression occurs, as shown respectively in the troughs of a′, b′, and c′ for leading, coincident, and lagging indicators of Figure 14–2.

The recovery from the recession may involve several actions on the part of consumers, businesses, and government. After significant price declines, consumers increase their purchases because of bargain prices. As is often the case, businesses may have reduced their production too much and now must expand output. In addition, the Federal Reserve Bank may stimulate credit by reducing interest rates and increasing the money supply. Finally, the government may cut taxes or provide incentives for consumption, thus further stimulating the economy. Then, as businesses become more confident of their economic futures, they invest in more materials, employees, equipment, and plants. This increased consumption and production lead to more prosperity; thus, the business cycle has gone full cycle. While this sequence of events is fairly accurate, the theoretical explanations of why consumers and businesses behave this way vary depending on whether one is monetarist, Keynesian, or neo-Keynesian. These theories are discussed in greater detail in Appendix 14–A.

Unfortunately, all business cycles do not have the same duration and severity. Table 14–1 provides a list of business cycles from the 1850s; as shown, the lengths of recession have declined since 1933. Some business cycles are mild, having a duration of only two to three years. Also note that the average length of full business cycles in the United States since 1919 has been about four to six years, with expansion periods typically twice as long as contraction periods. In summary, U.S. economic cycles from 1850 to 1995 have had the following characteristics:

- Expansions persisting from 10 to 106 months.
- Contractions persisting from 6 to 65 months.
- Full cycle durations from 17 to 121 months.

For 43 months in the 1930s, the most severe and widespread of all modern economic declines occurred: the Great Depression. While affecting the U.S. most, it quickly spread to western Europe. The U.S. recovery progressed from 1933 to 1937, but then it slipped back into a recession from 1937 to 1938 before full recovery at the onset of World War II in 1941.

Appendix 14–A provides a review of several economic theories that are important prerequisites for practical cyclical forecasting. If you are unfamiliar with this material, you should review it before starting a cyclical forecasting project. For now, consider some important measures of economic activity, many of which are reported in the media and through CD–ROMs and other electronic media such as the Internet and CompuServe.

TABLE 14–1   U.S. Business Cycle History

Dates of		Duration (in months)		
Trough	*Peak*	*Contraction*	*Expansion*	*Full Cycle*
December 1854	June 1857		30	
December 1858	October 1860	18	22	40
June 1861	April 1865	8	46	54
December 1867	June 1869	32	18	50
December 1870	October 1873	18	34	52
March 1879	March 1882	65	36	101
May 1885	March 1887	38	22	60
April 1888	June 1890	13	27	40
May 1891	June 1893	10	20	30
June 1894	December 1895	17	18	35
June 1897	June 1899	18	24	42
December 1900	September 1902	18	21	39
August 1904	May 1907	23	33	56
June 1908	January 1910	13	19	32
January 1912	January 1913	24	12	36
December 1914	August 1918	23	44	67
March 1919	January 1920	7	10	17
July 1921	May 1923	18	22	40
July 1924	October 1926	14	27	41
November 1927	August 1929	13	21	44
March 1933	May 1937	43	50	93
June 1938	February 1945	13	80	93
October 1945	November 1948	8	37	45
October 1949	July 1953	11	45	56
May 1954	August 1957	10	39	49
April 1958	April 1960	8	24	32
February 1961	December 1969	10	106	116
November 1970	November 1973	11	36	47
March 1975	January 1980	16	58	74
July 1980	July 1981	6	12	18
November 1982	August 1990	16	105	121
July 1990				
Average		17	34	51

Important Economic Indicators

There is interest in measures of economic performance because these provide information about the macroeconomy and possibly provide early warning signals of changes. Several of the more important measures of economic activity are defined next.

Leading, Coincident, and Lagging Indicators

Many businesses behave concurrently with the general business cycle; however, some are more sensitive to earlier or later stages. For example, the average workweek of manufacturing is more sensitive to economic changes than is other nonagricultural employment. New orders for durable goods and construction contracts occur before the acquisition of new plant and equipment. In addition, stock market movements anticipate changes in profits as much as six months ahead. Also, commodity sales and prices such as steel, aluminum, and corrugated box board (i.e., cardboard) are leading economic indicators of the macroeconomy. Before products can be fabricated, steel and aluminum must be ordered from the mills. Thus, these are among the first industries to be affected by economic upturns and downturns. Obviously, products must be packaged before being shipped; thus, the strong interest in box board shipments.

The construction industry has had cyclical variations of 16 to 20 years, including the two greatest depressions in 1872–73 and the 1930s. Also, some industries similar to the construction industry have downturns at the beginning of a general business decline and upturns at the beginning of the recovery. For example, often a recovery in the construction industry is a sign that a general economic recovery is underway.

Table 14–2 highlights just a few of the economic statistics that are monitored as gauges of economic activity. These are the components of the composite leading, coincident, and lagging economic indicators, as graphed previously in Figure 14–2. Review these with attention to why they might lead, coincide, and lag the general economy.

TABLE 14–2   Components of U.S. Composite Economic Indicators

Composite Index of Leading Indicators (Series 910)

Series 1:	Average weekly hours worked.
Series 5:	Average weekly initial claims for unemployment insurance.
Series 8:	Manufacturers' new orders—consumer and materials industries.
Series 19:	Stock prices.
Series 20:	Contracts and orders for plant and equipment.
Series 29:	New private housing units authorized.
Series 32:	Vendor performance.
Series 83:	Index of consumer expectations.
Series 92:	Changes in manufacturers' unfilled orders.
Series 99:	Changes in sensitive material prices.
Series 106:	Real M2 money supply.

Composite Index of Coincident Indicators (Series 920)

Series 41:	Employees on nonagricultural payrolls.
Series 47:	Industrial production.
Series 51:	Personal income less transfer payments.
Series 57:	Manufacturing and trade sales.

Composite Index of Lagging Indicators (Series 930)

Series 62:	Change in the index of labor costs of output in manufacturing.
Series 77:	Ratio of manufacturing and trade inventories to sales.
Series 91:	Average duration of unemployment.
Series 95:	Ratio of consumer installment credit outstanding to personal income.
Series 101:	Commercial and industrial loans outstanding.
Series 109:	Average prime rate charged by banks.
Series 120:	Smoothed change in CPI for services.

Series numbers are *Survey of Current Business* numbers.

Leading Economic Indicators

Government economists have assembled 11 leading indicators into an index of future economic activity (series 910 of Table 14–2). The government calculates and reports this index each month. It is expressed in percentages, with some year such as 1987 as the base year of 100 percent, as shown in Figure 14–2.

The index of leading economic indicators was created to predict economic patterns with a lead time of several months. The index has gone up, on average, three and a half months before an economic recovery, and down nearly nine months ahead of the start of a recession. For the investor, signs of economic strength often signal a time to consider stocks and stock mutual funds and a falling indicator denotes a time to consider bonds and bond mutual funds.

This index is no longer compiled by the Department of Commerce but instead by the Conference Board. Recently, there has been increased criticism about its usefulness as a leading indicator. However, as discussed later in this chapter, several research studies have confirmed its usefulness as a predictor of GDP and business cycle turning points. What most, if not all, research has confirmed is that several of the components of this index are at times not really leading indicators but instead are coincident and in one case more of a lagging indicator.

Cyclical Influences and Financial Markets

There is a tendency to view financial markets as having mechanisms that are different than those of product markets such as consumer electronics. However, the law of supply and demand determines prices in product and financial markets as well. While all aspects of financial markets cannot be described here, we will discuss cyclical influences and the use of financial markets as predictors of stock, bond, and commodity prices and business cycles.

The Fed's Influence

Federal Reserve Bank (Fed) actions and monetary policies have a direct effect on the general economy as well as on stock and bond markets. These financial markets in turn can greatly affect the whole economy. This is true because financial markets influence the cost and availability of the funds that are needed for investment in inventories, equipment, and plants.

Money Supply. Measures of the money supply or "money aggregates" are reported in a variety of general publications. *The Wall Street Journal*, for example, lists the money supply under Federal Reserve Data. The included money aggregates are M1, M2, and others. Because monetarists believe that the money supply causes inflation and deflation, they monitor these indicators closely. Obviously, without sufficient credit, it is more difficult to expand business activity. However, while low-cost credit (i.e., low interest rates) is a positive sign, it does not ensure economic growth.

Fluctuations in the growth rate of the nation's money supply can be significant. However, forecasters may not be concerned with the absolute level of the money supply but more with its trend and growth rate. For example, an increase in the money supply might signal an attempt by the Fed to reduce interest rates; this is often a positive sign for the general economy, especially for the stock and mutual fund markets.

Interest Rates. A change in prevailing interest rates may signal a change in the cost of borrowing money and the cost of maintaining or expanding businesses, particularly the cost of funds for expansion of plant and equipment. For example, from 1973 through 1974, the Fed tightened the money supply and caused a large rise in the interest rates. As inflation rose throughout 1974 (as reflected in the consumer price index, CPI), stock prices, as represented by the Dow Jones Industrial Average, sharply declined. Thus, it is important to monitor interest rates and the economic environment.

Long- and Short-Term Interest Rates.   The relationship between short-term and long-term interest rates has often been a useful stock market predictor, primarily because it reveals a traditionally favorable climate for stock prices. One measure of this short-term/long-term relationship is the ratio between three-month Treasury bills and long-term AAA-rated corporate bonds. Historically, when the ratio has risen over 1.20, this has been a buy signal for stock market investors. Other rules of thumb used to predict stock market price increases are when:

> The FED discount rate $>$ 3-month treasury (T-) bill rate
> The FED funds rate $<$ a year ago
> 3-month T-bill rate $<$ 7% and $<$ a year ago
> 7-year T-note rate and 30-year T-bonds $<$ 3 and 6-month T-bills

These rules of thumb are presented here, not as indicators with proven track records, but instead as indicators purported to be useful predictors of stock prices. Finally, the behavior of the term structure of interest rates (TSIR) (i.e., short-term vs long-term rates) discussed later is useful in predicting recessions.

Short-Term Instruments.   In anticipation of higher interest rates, investors will frequently lean toward more liquid investments such as Treasury bills (T bills), money market mutual funds, or short-term certificate of deposit (CDs). They do so because the yields on these relatively safe investments tend to increase with interest rates.

In contrast, an outflow of funds from short-term investments, as in 1991, indicates that investors anticipate lower short-term rates or a continuation of low interest rates. Outflows from these types of investments often precede big gains for stocks and stock mutual funds and decreased investment in bonds and bond mutual funds.

Long-Term Bonds.   Generally, a strengthening economy is poor news for the long-term bond investor. Bond investors generally fear economic growth because it can lead to higher inflation. This reduces the value of fixed-income securities as rates paid on newly issued securities go higher; thus, investors are wary of being locked-in to lower yielding long-term bonds.

Although high interest rates and a strengthening economy drive down prices on the bond market, at times bonds continue to enjoy high popularity. Sometimes, with a slow recovery (e.g., in 1993), many investors believe there will not be bond price-damaging inflation.

Other Economic Indicators

Consumer Confidence Indexes.   The Institute of Social Research at the University of Michigan compiles indexes of consumer sentiment. These indexes record the consumers' personal financial conditions and outlooks for the future. Another widely recognized and published consumer index is the Conference Board's index of consumer sentiment. These consumer indexes usually move in opposite directions to inflation because consumers can often see creeping inflation in their daily purchases. Personal experiences such as layoffs, current events, interest rate changes, and employment opportunities greatly affect how consumers perceive their personal and economic fortunes.

The Use of Regional Economic Performance

Recently, there has been increased interest in regional economics because regional statistics may provide more accurate measures of future economic growth statistics. The belief is that the macroeconomy is better forecasted using a bottom-up approach where local and regional trends are aggregated to yield national estimates. The national economy evolves regionally, and these business cycles move geographically. Thus, regional economists monitor states where manufacturing capacity is nearly fully utilized. By determining when manufacturing facilities are nearing their capacity, they can better predict contractions; when productive capacities are increasing from low levels, they can better predict expansions of the regions. Consider some recent statistics on regional unemployment. Clearly, some areas have been more adversely affected than others, typically because a dominant industry in that region has been adversely affected.

All economies walk the thin line of economic growth and overstimulation. If too much growth takes place too quickly, then the possibility of a downturn increases. Thus, as regions near peak economic activity, there are concerns about downturns in those economies. For example, if unemployment is very low during an economic upturn, then high wages yield higher costs and decrease a region's competitive advantage. These higher wages will slow down the growth in the expanding region and quite possibly increase the growth in bordering regions. If the regional economies grow too quickly, then the FED may put the brakes on by increasing interest rates, thus adversely affecting both the overheated and underutilized regions.

Adapted from Frederick Rose, "The Rise and Fall of Nation's Regions May Best Predict Growth, Analysts Say," *The Wall Street Journal*, October 31, 1994, p. A2.

Regional Unemployment

Region	Unemployment (%)
Pacific	8.1%
Rocky mountain	5.3
Midwest	4.9
Southwest	5.9
Northeast	6.5

Source: Salomon Brothers and Labor Department.

Consumer Price Index (CPI).   Inflation occurs when demand exceeds supply at current prices and therefore prices increase. The CPI attempts to chart the course of inflation. The Bureau of Labor Statistics releases CPI information about the fourth week of every month. Simply, the CPI is a market basket of goods and services purchased by the typical consumer. Included in this basket are food, clothing, public utilities, medical care, gasoline, and other purchased goods.

Because inflation usually coincides with rising interest rates, planners need to respond accordingly. For example, they should develop different strategies for inflation and deflation. During times of rising inflation, investors avoid interest-sensitive securities and long-term debt instruments. Common stocks of firms that own commodities such as oil or metals are good investment choices at such times because their asset values tend to increase during inflation.

In a period of declining prices (i.e., deflation), long-term debt obligations are typically sound investments. Investors should choose bonds or bond funds with excellent

"Once upon a Time There Was a Theory"

"Determining what drives economic growth or decline depends as much on storytelling as on data. For the past decade or so, a new crop of theorists, including Paul Romer of the University of California at Berkeley and Robert Lucas of the University of Chicago, have been pushing 'endogenous' growth. These economists argue that economic growth results entirely from endogenous factors; once upon a time the U.S. was poor; then its population grew and became urbanized, allowing business to exploit economics of scale. As a result the country became rich. . . .

"Economic historians such as Joel Mokyr of Northwestern University and Nathan Rosenberg of Stanford University meanwhile favor 'exogenous' explanations based on outside factors, in particular, technological changes and innovations. Once upon a time we were all poor; then a wave of gadgets swept over England. As a result, we are all rich, or well on our way to it, if we will let people alone. The story does a better job of explaining, for instance, why China's per capita income grows by 10 percent a year; the Chinese, like the Koreans and Japanese before them, adopt the best methods invented thus far and quickly catch up with more advanced nations, regardless of endogenous factors in their economy."

Source: Donald N. McCloskey, "The Analytical Economist," *Scientific American*, February 1995.

quality ratings, because deflation often begets bankruptcy, and therefore concerns about financial security and quality are well founded.

Producer Price Index (PPI).   The PPI shows the change in prices charged by producers of finished goods—changes that will eventually be reflected in consumer prices. The PPI can be found in *The Wall Street Journal* on the third Monday of the month.

Like the CPI, the PPI is also a measure of inflation. However, the CPI tends to follow the PPI. During a business expansion, with increases in output and capacity utilization, productivity drops and labor costs rise. These increase producer prices. Forecasters should consider inflationary or deflationary pressures as reflected by the CPI and PPI when forecasting demand and prices of plant and equipment.

Gross Domestic Products.   Gross domestic product (GDP), along with industrial production and capacity utilization, measure the economy's output. As one of the broadest available measures of economic activity, GDP provides the official scale with which fluctuations in the economy are measured. GDP figures are only available quarterly and are usually announced about three weeks after the end of each quarter. A rise in real GDP indicates a strengthening economy. For the investor, during a noninflationary economy, an increase in GDP signals a gain in stock market activity and a possible downward trend in bond markets.

"Buy stocks that go up. And if they don't go up, don't buy 'em."

Will Rogers
Famous American commentator

Stock Market Indicators.   Market indexes provide a barometer for the stock market as a whole. The Dow Jones Industrial Average (DOW) is a popular indicator of stock prices of 30 large industrial firms. In addition, the Standard & Poor's 500 index is a highly regarded, broader stock market gauge. These are excellent leading indicators because fluctuations in these indexes tend to lead those in the economy. This is true because investors buy stock in anticipation of future profit. Stock prices increase when earnings look good and decrease when they look bad.

Other Important Indicators. Previously, Table 14–2 listed other important economic indicators. In addition, the Bureau of Economic Analysis (BEA) of the Department of Commerce has classified over 100 data series as leading, lagging, and coincident indicators. These series and indexes have been published regularly since 1968. In the context of cyclical forecasting, after identifying a good theory, we should seek measures of the causal variables identified in that theory. There are many other causal variables, and book Appendix A discusses public and private sources for such variables.

The several economic indicators just defined provide a means of identifying and projecting future trends of the economy and financial markets. Let's use some of these concepts to predict recessions.

Forecasting Recessions

Roughly defined, a recession is two consecutive quarterly declines in GDP. However, this is not the only consideration of the National Bureau of Economic Research committee when they declare a recession is underway. A better definition is that a recession is an economy-wide decline measured by several indicators. The mix of indicators might change depending on the circumstances.

As a business cycle evolves toward a recession, changes appear in the behavior and constraints of financial and product markets. These changes include changes in levels as well as the relationship between interest rates at different maturities. The level of interest rates is heavily affected by current and anticipated inflation levels; thus, the **term structure of interest rates** (TSIR), or yield curve, can vary.

Figure 14–3 shows three different term structures of interest rates from equally risky issuers over differing maturities. The normal upward sloping TSIR of a* is referred to as normal because it has been most common during the post–World War II period. During good economic times, a lender expects to receive a higher interest rate for a longer term loan. Figure 14–3 also shows a downward sloping, or inverted, TSIR in c+. Generally, this structure occurs during periods of economic distress such as recessions. Since longer maturities are riskier (i.e., there is more uncertainty for borrowers and lenders), an inverted TSIR are expected to be short lived and infrequent. Even less frequent is the flat TSIR shown in Figure 14–3b, which usually happens in the transitions from normal to inverted structures.

FIGURE 14–3

Term structure of interest rates here

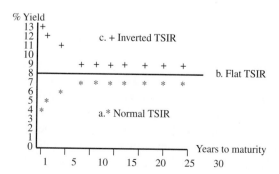

The Multivariate Nature of Cyclical Forecasting

Without a good model of a complex system, we tend to search for simple relationships—for example, if A is true, then B follows. Unfortunately, most relationships are more complex. Consider a simple model of the complexities of economic reactions to changes in the rate of inflation, interest rates, and economic growth. This model shows changes in stock, bond, and profits that most frequently occur with changes in inflation, interest rates, and economic growth. For example, if the economy declines with low inflation and low interest rates, then bond prices go up greatly. In contrast, if the economy declines under conditions of inflation, then interest rates go up and bond prices go down. This behavior is defined in the following model:[a]

Inflation up
Interest rates up
+

Transition of stagflation	+	**Overheated economy**
Stock prices up	+	Stock prices up
Bond prices down	+	Bond prices down
Dollar up	+	Dollar up
Gold prices up	+	Gold prices up
Profits improving	+	Profits up
	+	

Economic – – – – – – – φ+++++++++**Economic**
growth down   **growth up**

Recession/depression	**Healthy economy**
Stock prices down	Stock prices up
Bond prices up greatly	Bond prices up
Dollar down	Dollar up
Gold prices down	Gold prices down
Profits down	Profits up greatly

Inflation down
Interest rates down

While this model is enlightening, some might find it too simplistic. However, it is a good starting model for understanding the impact of business cycles on financial markets.

[a] This is a modification of a chart from Joseph E. Plocek, *Economic Indicators, How America Reads Its Financial Health*, (New York: New York Institute of Finance, 1991).

A simple rule for predicting recessions has been proposed by C.R. Harvey and is commonly called "Harvey's rule." **Harvey's rule** is that recessions follow two to five quarters after the term structure of interest rates (TSIR) shifts from a normal upward-sloping structure relative to maturity to an inverted, downward-sloping structure (Harvey, 1993). Using the spread between short- (three-month) and intermediate-term (five-year) rates, Harvey's rule correctly predicted the recent five recessions through 1997.

TABLE 14–3   Some Economic Data for Four Recent U.S. Recessions

Peak to Trough Recession	Real GDP Change	High to Low % Changes in Sales					
		All Mfg.	*Durable Mfg.*	*Nondurable Mfg.*	*Mining*	*Wholesaling*	*Retailing*
1973:4–75:1	−4.2%	−9.2%	−8.9%	−7.9%	n.a.	n.a.	n.a.
1980:1–80:3	−2.6	−1.5	−4.3	+1.2	−2.8%	−.5%	−9.5%
1981:3–82:4	−2.7	−9.7	−13.9	−6.5	−17.9	−12.4	−16.3
1990:3–91:2	−1.8	−7.9	−13.2	−7.3	−30.5	−7.9	−14.7
Average	−2.8	−7.1	−10.1	−5.1	−17.1	−6.9	−13.5

Source: B. Belt and S.A. DeLurgio, "How to Predict and Navigate A/R During Recessions," *The Credit and Financial Management Review*, Columbia, MD, January 1995, pp. 19–23; and various *Quarterly Financial Reports*, U.S. Dept. of Commerce.

Higher short term interest rates occur early in recessions during periods of economic constraints such as high manufacturing capacity utilization and during inflation. This assists in predicting recessions and, therefore, continuing peak economic times in specific industries when the TSIR is not inverted.

To better understand the effects of a recession on real GDP and sales, consider Table 14–3, which provides information on four recent U.S. recessions. As shown, real GDP and sales have both declined during recessions. All businesses in Table 14–3 experienced sales per day declines that averaged 5 to 17 percent. Not surprisingly, durable manufacturing is more volatile than nondurable, and mining is more volatile than wholesaling and retailing. Knowing when a recession may come is valuable business information. Using Harvey's rule, two guidelines emerge (Belt and DeLurgio, 1995):

1. Expect a recession two to five quarters after the inversion of the TSIR

Fortunately, the shape of the TSIR is easily monitored from many business newspapers. For example, *The Wall Street Journal* gives tables and charts each business day in its "Credit Market" column toward the back of Section C. If Harvey's Rule continues to work, the manager has 6 to 15 months of forewarning, so weekly or even monthly reviews are sufficiently timely.

2. Expect sales declines of 5 to 17 percent from peak to trough

As shown in Table 14–3, the cyclical declines are typically lower in wholesaling/retailing and highest in mining and durable manufacturing.

As long as Harvey's Rule remains a viable predictive tool, the timing of the next recession can be forecasted. The two rules discussed here cannot detail what will happen to any specific industry or firm. However, the macroeconomic effect of the recession on sales, accounts receivable, and cash flows can be anticipated. The test of time will prove or disprove Harvey's rule, so we remain cautious in its application.

Cyclical Forecasting Methods

As we have seen, there are several time series that lead the macroeconomic business cycle. Similarly, there are many time series that lead specific industry business cycles. These leading indicators provide an important historical database to explain past economic behavior and to project future business cycles. Before we develop methods for making these projections, however, be forewarned that from a practical perspective, at any one time, these leading indicators may not consistently generate accurate forecasts. Forecast accuracy suffers because of the great variation in the lead-lag lengths—recall the wide range given for Harvey's rule, two to five quarters (i.e., 6 to 15 months). In contrast to the general warning, however, there are applications where cyclical methods provide accurate forecasts of turning points in the time series.

A few of the methods that can be used to model cyclical influences and in some cases predict turning points include:

1. **Cyclical indexes** using the decomposition percent of moving average methods developed in Chapter 5. (Presented here)
2. Seasonal differences to isolate the trend-cycle. (Chapters 6 and 7)
3. Fourier series analysis of simultaneous seasonal, trend, and cyclical variations. (Supplement to Chapter 6)
4. Econometric and MARIMA models that relate a leading indicator to a firm's performance. (Chapters 11 and 13)
5. The use of paired indicators that combine leading indicators with percentage changes in firm performance. (Presented here)
6. The construction of company composite indexes from many other time series indicators (see McLaughlin, 1975).
7. The use of pressure cycles. (Presented here)

Method 1 is the first method discussed. Method 2 is discussed in several places in the ARIMA chapters. Also, note that seasonal differences can be used in Methods 4, 5, 6, and 7. Method 3 is a simple extension of Chapter 6, and therefore Fourier series analysis is not developed here.

Method 4, relationships with leading indicators, has a number of variations. One of these is simple regression analysis, where the firm's performance is the dependent variable and a leading indicator is the independent variable. However, be cautious using this because it is highly likely that there will be problems of serial correlation in such relationships. Therefore the econometric methods of Chapters 10 and 11 or the MARIMA methods of Chapter 13 should be applied to such relationships. Because these methods have already been studied in several chapters, we refer you to those chapters. You might recall how important the use of cross correlations and other diagnostics are in ensuring that a valid relationship exists between these variables. Several homework problems of these other chapters applied leading indicators and the methods of Chapters 10, 11, and 13 to cyclical forecasting.

Method 5, paired indicators, is developed as the second major method of this chapter. We refer you to McLaughlin (1975) and Zarnovitz (1992) for further discussion of Method 6. McLaughlin used approximately 50 indicators to determine when a specific firm's performance has peaked or bottomed out. Finally, Method 7, pressure cycles, is the last topic of this chapter.

Decomposition of Cyclical Indexes

The traditional method of estimating cyclical influences uses the classical decomposition method developed in Chapter 5. By eliminating the seasonal, trend, and irregular movements, the remaining residuals may show cyclical fluctuations. When annual data is used, there is normally no seasonality and therefore no need to seasonally adjust this data.

Table 14–4 illustrates the process of isolating the cyclical component of a time series after seasonal indexes have been determined using the decomposition method of Chapter 5. This table uses the example of Table 5–6 of Chapter 5 in the following procedure:

1. Adjust the data for calendar and trading days.
2. Determine whether the series has additive or multiplicative seasonality.

Assume multiplicative seasonality for the remainder of this discussion. Thus:

$$Y_t = T_t C_t S_t + e_t$$

3. Calculate seasonal indexes, S_t, using the percent of centered annual moving average method. The seasonal indexes derived in Table 5–6 are shown in column 3 of Table 14–4.
4. Using these seasonal indexes, deseasonalize the dependent variable:

$$Y_t/S_t \qquad \text{(Col. 4 of Table 14–4)}$$

5. Fit an appropriate trend equation to the deseasonalized values to generate fitted trend values, T_t.   (Cols. 5, 6, and 7)
6. Calculate the fitted trend–seasonal component by multiplying the trend times the seasonal component:

$$T_t S_t \qquad \text{(Col. 8)}$$

7. Isolate the cyclical-irregular ratio:

$$\frac{Y_t}{T_t S_t} = CI_t \qquad \text{(Col. 9)}$$

8. Compute centered three-month moving averages of the cyclical-irregular values to remove the irregular component, leaving initial cyclical indexes:

$$C_t = \frac{CI_{t-1} + CI_t + CI_{t+1}}{3} \qquad \text{(Col. 10)}$$

9. Confirm the theoretical and intuitive reasonableness of the cyclical indexes. For example, the cyclical indexes and cyclical-irregular values of Figure 14–4 can be compared to other series having a known cyclicalness such as the composite leading, coincident, and lagging economic indicators.
10. Calculate fitted values $\hat{Y}_t$ and e_t.

$$\hat{Y}_t = T_t C_t S_t \qquad \text{(Col. 11)}$$

$$e_t = Y_t - \hat{Y}_t \qquad \text{(Col. 12)}$$

11. Diagnose the residuals and the model

If the data are very erratic, then identification of the cyclical index may require averaging more than three months. In some applications, not all of the components of trend, seasonal, and irregular have to be eliminated before identifying the cyclical component. If these other movements are not large, then the cyclical behavior may be very apparent and easily extracted.

However, there are many times when it is difficult to extract valid cyclical indexes because the trend and cycle are so intermingled. This is why many decomposition methods, such as the Census II–X11, identify a trend-cycle component for the analyst.

TABLE 14-4 Cyclical Indexes Using Classical Decomposition Method

| Period (t) | Actual (Y_t) | Seasonal Index (S) | Deseasonalized (Y_t/S) | Trend Calculation | | | Trend-Seasonal (S*T) | Cyclical-Irregular Y/T*S | Smoothed Cyclical 3CMAV | Fitted Values T*C*S | Error Y-T*C*S e |
				(X*X)	(X*Y)	Trend					
1	546	.88747	615.2340	1	615.23	663.859	589.15	.93	.94	554.36	−8.36
2	578	.94124	614.0838	4	1,228.17	670.861	631.44	.92	.94	594.15	−16.15
3	660	.99279	664.7948	9	1,994.38	677.863	672.97	.98	.97	650.33	9.67
4	707	1.02928	686.8858	16	2,747.54	684.865	704.92	1.00	.98	692.77	14.23
5	738	1.10582	667.3809	25	3,336.90	691.867	765.08	.96	.98	750.05	−12.05
6	781	1.14790	680.3714	36	4,082.23	698.869	802.23	.97	.99	793.99	−12.99
7	848	1.16520	727.7733	49	5,094.41	705.870	822.48	1.03	1.02	836.34	11.66
8	818	1.09701	745.6624	64	5,965.30	712.872	782.03	1.05	1.03	805.45	12.55
9	729	.99985	729.1106	81	6,562.00	719.874	719.77	1.01	1.03	740.30	−11.30
10	691	.92587	746.3252	100	7,463.25	726.876	672.99	1.03	1.03	690.20	.80
11	658	.86450	761.1325	121	8,372.46	733.878	634.44	1.04	1.01	640.97	17.03
12	604	.84308	716.4241	144	8,597.09	740.880	624.62	.97	.98	614.59	−10.59
13	629	.88747	708.7586	169	9,213.86	747.882	663.72	.95	.97	644.99	−15.99
14	711	.94124	755.3868	196	10,575.42	754.884	710.53	1.00	.97	689.72	21.28
15	729	.99279	734.2961	225	11,014.44	761.886	756.39	.96	.99	749.53	−20.53
16	798	1.02928	775.2969	256	12,404.75	768.888	791.40	1.01	.99	784.97	13.03
17	861	1.10582	778.6111	289	13,236.39	775.890	857.99	1.00	1.01	862.75	−1.75
18	903	1.14790	786.6522	324	14,159.74	782.892	898.68	1.00	1.02	916.67	−13.67
19	968	1.16520	830.7601	361	15,784.44	789.894	920.38	1.05	1.03	944.68	23.32
20	894	1.09701	814.9416	400	16,298.83	796.896	874.20	1.02	1.05	916.26	−22.26
21	860	.99985	860.1305	441	18,062.74	803.898	803.78	1.07	1.05	843.29	16.71
22	792	.92587	855.4118	484	18,819.06	810.900	750.79	1.05	1.06	793.33	−1.33
23	739	.86450	854.8281	529	19,661.05	817.902	707.08	1.05	1.04	731.86	7.14
24	669	.84308	829.1067	576	19,898.56	824.904	695.46	1.01	1.03	718.00	−19.00

(continued)

25	773	.88747	871.0181	625	21,775.45	831.906	738.29	1.05	1.03	759.96	13.04
26	818	.94124	869.0667	676	22,595.73	838.908	789.61	1.04	1.04	821.23	−3.23
27	871	.99279	877.3277	729	23,687.85	845.910	839.81	1.04	1.03	861.58	9.42
28	882	1.02928	856.9071	784	23,993.40	852.912	877.89	1.00	1.02	892.62	−10.62
29	959	1.10582	867.2335	841	25,149.77	859.914	950.91	1.01	1.00	949.95	9.05
30	979	1.14790	852.8599	900	25,585.80	866.916	995.13	.98	.98	971.96	7.04
31	955	1.16520	819.6032	961	25,407.70	873.918	1,018.29	.94	.96	977.15	−22.15
32	925	1.09701	843.2002	1,024	26,982.41	880.920	966.38	.96	.95	916.31	8.69
33	843	.99985	843.1279	1,089	27,823.22	887.922	887.75	.95	.95	846.41	−3.41
34	790	.92587	853.2516	1,156	29,010.56	894.924	828.58	.95	.95	789.85	.15
35	746	.86450	862.9253	1,225	30,202.39	901.926	779.72	.96	.99	775.27	−29.27
36	822	.84308	975.0010	1,296	35,100.03	908.927	766.30	1.07	1.03	787.69	34.31
37	857	.88747	965.6695	1,369	35,729.77	915.929	812.86	1.05	1.05	849.55	7.45
38	876	.94124	930.6876	1,444	35,366.13	922.931	868.70	1.01	1.03	898.08	−22.08
39	959	.99279	965.9670	1,521	37,672.71	929.933	923.23	1.04	1.02	943.04	15.96
40	981	1.02928	953.0905	1,600	38,123.62	936.935	964.37	1.02	1.02	984.58	−3.58
41	1051	1.10582	950.4300	1,681	38,967.63	943.937	1,043.82	1.01	1.02	1,062.54	−11.54
42	1124	1.14790	979.1772	1,764	41,125.44	950.939	1,091.59	1.03	1.00	1,090.81	33.19
43	1073	1.16520	920.8735	1,849	39,597.56	957.941	1,116.19	.96	.98	1,099.29	−26.29
44	1020	1.09701	929.7991	1,936	40,911.16	964.943	1,058.55	.96	.96	1,017.96	2.04
45	933	.99985	933.1415	2,025	41,991.37	971.945	971.80	.96	.93	904.40	28.60
46	787	.92587	850.0114	2,116	39,100.53	978.947	906.38	.87	.93	846.60	−59.60
47	830	.86450	960.0911	2,209	45,124.28	985.949	852.35	.97	.98	836.29	−6.29
48	922	.84308	1093.6142	2,304	52,493.48	992.951	837.13	1.10	.98	821.35	100.65
Sum	48		39,763.4	38,024	1,038,706					39,664.04	52.96

Trend coefficients $a = 656.86$ $b = 7.0020$

Sum of squared errors   25,392.32

Residual Standard Error   23.495

$\bar{R}^2$ 96.78%

Standard deviation of series   130.97

FIGURE 14–4

Cyclical-irregular and cyclical indexes

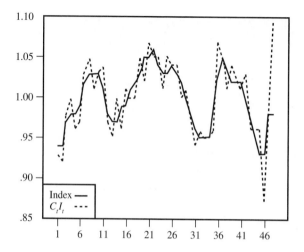

After identifying the trend-cycle variation, the two remaining components or changes in those components can be modeled using a variety of methods including methods 4 to 7.

Decomposition Forecasting

As discussed in Chapter 5, forecasts of next year can be made by combining the trend, seasonal, and cyclical components of the decomposition model. Projecting the trend and seasonal components is a simple process; however, projecting the cyclical index is difficult because it is not periodic.

To assist in projecting the cyclical index, the smoothed cyclical indexes of column 10 of Table 14–4 is a time series that can be used in subsequent analysis including methods 4, 5, 6, and 7. Also, there are a number of simple methods that can be used to forecast this cyclical index, including:

1. Assume the recent cyclical index will continue into the future (this is frequently a bad assumption).

2. Simulate the variations of the past several business cycles as optimistic and pessimistic forecasts and generate contingency plans.

3. Seek economic indicators that lead the cyclical index. If the lead is of sufficient length, then more accurate forecasts of the index are possible. The use of other economic indicators as predictors of cyclical indexes is a very effective method, particularly when good projections of the leading indicators are available from other sources such as the Department of Commerce. For example, the cyclical index can be related to other cyclical indicators, hopefully with long lead times, using econometric, MARIMA, or other methods.

4. Survey your customers about their specific business outlooks. Be sure to include a large enough sample size so that the weighted average outlook is accurate.

Cautions with Cyclical Indexes

Finally, note that the measures of fit such as $\overline{R}^2$ and RSE of the decomposition method are typically very optimistic estimates. As developed in Chapter 5, the users of the decomposition method must be cautious not to overfit a model. The likelihood of overfitting is high, because we have chosen the form of the model before data analysis and the fitting of seasonal and cyclical indexes and trends is so versatile as to model random variations or errors as repeating patterns. Unfortunately, there are no quantitative approaches that will guarantee success because of the variations in cycle intensity and length; there appears to be no way to avoid subjective judgment in the process of cyclical forecasting.

Paired Indicators and Change Analysis

In many situations, particularly in long-range and cyclical forecasting, an estimate of a growth rate may be more important than the actual value at any time. Also, the rate-of-change curve for one variable may be a leading indicator of another variable, a topic discussed in a moment. In general, the evaluation of differences and rates of changes can give early warnings of significant changes in a time series. For example, these may signal when to change production and inventory levels.

Change Measurements

Comparative change measurements involve a subtraction or ratio of a value and a base measurement; such comparisons can be made in a number of different ways:

Formula	*Example*
Absolute difference = Current − Base	$110 - 100 = 10$
Relative percent $= \dfrac{\text{Current}}{\text{Base}} \times 100$	$\dfrac{110}{100} \times 100 = 110\%$
Percentage change $= \left(\dfrac{\text{Current}}{\text{Base}} - 1\right) \times 100$	$\left(\dfrac{110}{100} - 1\right) \times 100 = 10\%$

Change analysis can be applied not only to raw historical data but also to deseasonalized or smoothed data such as those of Table 14–4. Because actual data tend to be erratic or seasonal, normally the data should be smoothed and deseasonalized.

Paired Indicators

The paired indicator method developed by McLaughlin and Boyle (1968) uses two concepts: leading indicators and percentage changes. Let's designate the leading indicator as X_t and an organizational performance measure, Y_t—for example, company sales, as in this example. This method is shown in Figure 14–5 and Table 14–5.

Figure 14–5a shows a graph of the leading indicator and sales. As shown, the leading indicator, X_t, does just that—it leads the time series, Y_t, by approximately three months. This is clearly seen in the typical underlined bold peak values of Table 14–5, columns (2) and (3) and points P_X and P_Y of Figure 14–5a. As shown, the peak of Y_t is preceded by a peak in X_t three months earlier (these are shown in bold). We might fit a relationship such as Equations 14–1a and b to these two series using the appropriate method from Chapters 10, 11, or 13.

$$Y_t = a + bX_{t-3} + e_t \qquad \text{Regression} \qquad (14\text{–}1a)$$

$$Y_t = \theta_0 + \omega_0 X_{t-3} + N_t \qquad \text{MARIMA} \qquad (14\text{–}1b)$$

This three-month lag is very clear in columns 2 and 3 of Table 14–5. Consider the implication of the lags. The values of X_{t-3} are known in periods 22, 23, and 24, while Y_t for those periods is unknown. The lead-lag relationship between Y_t and X_{t-3} can be used to estimate Y_t fairly accurately and thus predict a turning point. Assuming that the relationship between these two series remains stable, this is a useful relationship.

TABLE 14–5   Sales, Y_t, Leading Indicator, X_t, and Their Ratios (INDICATE.DAT)

	Figure 14–5a		Figure 14–5b		Figure 14–5c	
(1) Month	*(2)* X_t	*(3)* Y_t	*(4)* RX_t	*(5)* RY_t	*(6)* $RXRY_t$	*(7)* RXY_t
1	103.0	100.00	NA	NA	NA	103.000
2	101.0	101.50	98.058	101.500	96.609	99.507
3	98.7	102.50	97.723	100.985	96.769	96.293
4	98.0	102.91	99.291	100.400	98.895	95.229
5	97.0	100.97	98.980	98.115	100.881	96.068
6	97.5	98.80	100.515	97.851	**102.723**	98.684 Peak $RXRY_t$
7	99.0	98.06	101.538	99.251	102.305	100.959
8	100.0	97.09	101.010	99.011	102.019	102.997
9	101.0	98.06	101.000	100.999	100.001	102.998
10	103.5	99.40	**102.475**	101.367	101.094	**104.125** Peak RX_t and RXY_t
11	**104.0**	100.00	100.483	100.603	99.880	104.000 Peak X_t
12	103.4	101.20	99.423	101.200	98.244	102.174
13	101.0	102.91	97.679	**101.690**	96.056	98.144 Peak RY_t
14	100.0	**103.88**	99.010	100.943	98.085	96.265 Peak Y_t
15	97.5	103.70	97.500	99.827	97.669	94.021
16	97.0	100.97	99.487	97.367	102.177	96.068
17	96.0	100.00	98.969	99.039	99.929	96.000
18	96.5	97.70	100.521	97.700	102.887	98.772
19	98.0	97.09	101.554	99.376	102.192	100.937
20	99.0	96.12	101.020	99.001	102.040	102.996
21	101.0	97.09	102.020	101.009	101.001	104.027

Bold values are peak values.

However, McLaughlin and Boyle's method extends the relationship between the series of Figure 14–5a to those of Figure 14–5b.

Percentage Ratios

Figure 14–5b and Table 14–5, columns 4 and 5, illustrate the period-to-period ratios in the leading indicator and sales designated as RX_t and RY_t, respectively.

$$RX_t = \frac{X_t}{X_{t-1}} 100 \qquad (14\text{–}2)$$

$$RY_t = \frac{Y_t}{Y_{t-1}} 100 \qquad (14\text{–}3)$$

As shown by the peaks (designated as P_{RX} and P_{RY}) in Figure 14–5b and their bold values in Table 14–5, the proportionate change in the leading indicator, RX_t, is seen to lead the proportionate changes of the time series, RY_t, by the same amount as X_t and Y_t in Figure 14–5a, about three months. However, note now that the proportionate change in X_t, RX_t, leads the peak in Y_t by four months, thus providing an even longer lead time in which to detect a turning point.

$$RY_t = f(RX_{t-3}) \qquad \text{with a three-month lead} \qquad (14\text{–}4)$$

$$Y_t = f(RX_{t-4}) \qquad \text{with a four-month lead} \qquad (14\text{–}5)$$

FIGURE 14–5

Paired indicators (INDICATE.DAT)

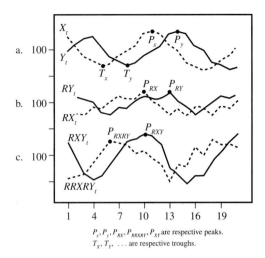

$P_x, P_y, P_{RX}, P_{RRXRY}, P_{XY}$ are respective peaks.
$T_X, T_Y, \ldots$ are respective troughs.

Thus, the percentage change information of Figure 14–5b and Table 14–5, columns 4 and 5, can be used to forecast four-period-ahead peaks and troughs in Y_t.

Also, note that in Figure 14–5c and Table 14–5, columns 6 and 7, that two additional ratios are calculated. These are:

$$RXRY = \frac{RX_t}{RY_t} 100 \tag{14–6}$$

$$RXY = \frac{X_t}{Y_t} 100 \tag{14–7}$$

These ratios have been found to be useful in anticipating turning points even earlier than the previous ratios. As shown in Table 14–5, column 6, the peak of $RXRY_t$ leads column 3, Y_t, by eight periods. This time precedence is quite strong and obvious. Also note that the peak in RXY_t, column 8, leads Y_t by four periods.

While in an actual application we would not expect as clear and strong a relationship as those in Figure 14–5 and Table 14–5, this method can be very effective in identifying turning points. When the lead-lag relationship is adequate, then the changes measured by these ratios provide an early warning of a turning point.

Obviously, it is the analyst's task to find the right paired indicators. Also, note that we have been implying that the leading indicator is a variable external to the firm. However, this variable can be one internal to the organization. In today's supply chain management era, the leading indicator might be sales at the retail level, which is used to forecast sales at the manufacturer level.

In summary, this method is applied to an indicator and time series as follows:

1. Deseasonalize the time series Y_t and X_t by dividing by their respective seasonal indexes, as developed in Chapter 5.

2. Calculate the trend-cycle values by smoothing the data as necessary to remove irregular components. This normally involves a centered moving average of the deseasonalized values, possibly using a three-period moving average, but in other cases different smoothing can be applied.

3. Standardize the estimated trend-cycle values by dividing each by the mean trend-cycle value and then multiply each by 100.

4. Calculate the period-to-period percentage ratios of trend cycles using:

$$RY_t = \frac{Y_t}{Y_{t-1}} 100 \quad \text{and} \quad RX_t = \frac{X_t}{X_{t-1}} 100$$

5. Calculate the percent index: Divide the standardized leading indicator index by the standardized time series.

$$RXY = 100 X_t / Y_t$$

6. Calculate the proportionate change:

$$RXRY = 100 RX_t / RY_t$$

7. Present these statistics as illustrated in Figure 14–5a, b and c and Table 14–5.

Ratio Behavior Explained

Why do ratios behave as shown in Figure 14–5? These ratios perform this way because cyclical indicators can, but certainly do not always, behave this way. Consider two artificially generated time series that are nearly identical but are offset by eight time periods, as shown in Figure 14–6. These were generated using sinusoidal functions because this is one type of cyclical behavior. These two time series have smooth transitions from growth to decline. First, let's consider the behavior of one indicator, X_t in Figure 14–6, and then compare the behavior of their ratios in Figure 14–7 and Table 14–6.

Figure 14–6 illustrates X_t and the ratio of X_t to X_{t-1}. This ratio, RX_t, is a measure of the proportionate increase or decrease in X_t over X_{t-1}. To better understand this behavior, consider points A, B, C, D, and E of Figure 14–6. The segments of these points behave as follows:

Segments	Cyclical Indicator	$RX_t = X_t / X_{t-1}$
A to B	Increasing at an increasing rate	Increasing
B to C	Increasing at a decreasing rate	Decreasing
C to D	Decreasing at an increasing rate	Decreasing
D to E	Decreasing at a decreasing rate	Increasing

These segments are underlined in Table 14–6 and the values of Figure 14–6 are shown in columns 1, 2, and 4. When there are smooth transitions in the behavior of a cyclical indicator, the lead-lag relationships of Figure 14–6 commonly occur. However, there is nothing to ensure that all transitions from growth to decline, or vice versa, will behave as well as the examples of Figures 14–5, 14–6, and 14–7. There are many cyclical influences that do not behave as shown in Figure 14–6, particularly those of volatile markets. Also, there is no assurance that the relationship between two cyclical indicators will remain constant into the future.

Having seen the behavior of a single cyclical indicator and its ratio, consider the behavior that might exist between two related indicators and their ratios. Table 14–6 and Figure 14–7 show the behavior of X_t, Y_t, and their ratios. As shown there, the

FIGURE 14–6

Theoretical behavior of a cyclical indicator

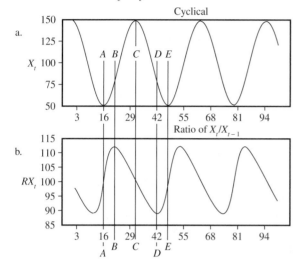

FIGURE 14–7

Ratio behavior of theoretical cyclical indicators

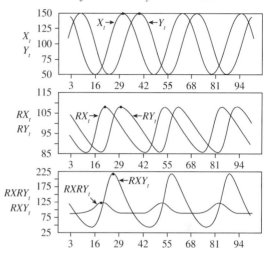

peak in Y_t occurs in period 39. This peak in Y_t is preceded by the peaks in X_t, RY_t, RXY_t, RX_t, and $RXRY_t$ in periods 31, 29, 26, 21, and 20, respectively. As the following summarizes, these ratios provide considerable lead time in predicting the peak of Y_t:

Peak Period	Variable	Lead
20	$RXRY_t$	19
21	RX_t	18
26	RXY_t	13
29	RY_t	10
31	X_t	8
39	Y_t	0

These lead-lag relationships are very clear. The fact that *RXRY* leads the changes the most is common for cyclical indicators that move smoothly about turning points. However, note its lower amplitude, it's not hard to imagine how these peaks might be confounded by noise in an actual application. Let's consider the results of some actual applications.

Ratio of U.S. Composite Coincident and Lagging Indexes

It can be shown that the ratio of the U.S. composite coincident index and composite lagging index (RCL_t) leads the economy for much the same reason that RXY_t of Figure 14–6 leads Y_t. Consider the meaning of such ratios. A coincident index tracks the actual economic behavior and thus the actual phase of a business cycle. As the economy grows, it grows most rapidly during the recovery, immediately after the end of a recession; then, as the recovery matures, it grows more slowly. In contrast, the lagging index lags the economy, and thus when the coincident indicator starts to increase rapidly, the lagging indicator is still declining. Thus, the ratio index increases because the numerator, the coincident indicator, increases, and the denominator, the lagging indicator, is still decreasing.

TABLE 14–6   Typical Cyclical Behavior of Two Indicators (with Peaks from Figure 14–6 Highlighted)(PAIREDIN.DAT)

	X_t	Y_t	RX_t	RY_t	RXY_t	$RXRY_t$	
1	149.00	109.93	NA	NA	135.54	NA	
2	146.05	119.47	98.02	108.68	122.25	90.19	
⋮							
15	50.50	107.06	95.48	91.70	47.17	104.13	
A16	50.09	97.08	99.18	90.68	51.59	109.37	
17	51.66	87.22	103.14	89.85	59.23	114.80	
18	55.16	77.87	106.78	89.28	70.84	119.60	
19	60.45	69.41	109.59	89.13	87.10	122.96	
20	67.32	62.16	111.36	89.56	108.30	**124.34** Peak in $RXRY_t$	
B21	75.49	56.42	**112.14**	90.77	133.79	123.54 Peak in RX_t	
22	84.63	52.42	112.12	92.91	161.45	120.67	
23	94.39	50.32	111.53	95.99	187.60	116.20	
24	104.37	50.19	110.58	99.75	207.95	110.85	
25	114.18	52.05	109.40	103.71	219.36	105.48	
26	123.43	55.83	108.09	107.25	**221.09**	100.79 Peak in RXY_t	
27	131.73	61.36	106.73	109.91	214.69	97.11	
28	138.78	68.44	105.35	111.53	202.78	94.46	
29	144.28	76.77	103.96	**112.18**	187.93	92.68 Peak in RY_t	
30	148.01	86.03	102.59	112.06	172.04	91.55	
C31	**149.83**	95.85	101.23	111.41	156.32	90.86 Peak in X_t	
32	149.66	105.83	99.89	110.41	141.42	90.47	
33	147.51	115.58	98.56	109.21	127.63	90.25	
34	143.47	124.71	97.26	107.90	115.05	90.14	
35	137.70	132.85	95.97	106.53	103.65	90.09	
36	130.42	139.68	94.71	105.14	93.37	90.08	
37	121.93	144.94	93.49	103.76	84.13	90.10	
38	112.56	148.40	92.32	102.39	75.85	90.17	
39	102.70	**149.93**	91.24	101.03	68.50	90.30 Peak in Y_t	
40	92.72	149.47	90.29	99.69	62.04	90.57	
41	83.04	147.04	89.56	98.37	56.48	91.04	
D42	74.04	142.73	89.15	97.07	51.87	91.84	
43	66.06	136.72	89.23	95.79	48.32	93.16	
44	59.45	129.25	89.98	94.53	45.99	95.18	
45	54.44	120.61	91.59	93.32	45.14	98.15	
46	51.26	111.14	94.15	92.16	46.12	102.16	
E47	50.02	101.24	97.58	91.09	49.40	107.12	
48	50.77	91.28	101.50	90.17	55.61	112.57	
49	53.48	81.68	105.34	89.47	65.48	117.74	
50	58.05	72.80	108.54	89.13	79.74	121.78	
51	64.29	65.01	110.75	89.30	98.89	124.03	
. . .							

A, B, C, D and E ranges for Figure 14–6
Peaks underlined and bold

A study by Oyen, along with several other studies, has shown that the RCL_t ratio leads the economy more than the composite index of leading economic indicators (CIL_t) (Oyen, 1991, p. 371). For the seven recessions from July 1953 to November 1987, the ratio of the coincident to lagging economic indicators (RCL_t) predicted the onset of recession by an average of 14.6 months with a range of 9 to 27 months, while the composite leading economic indicator predicted with a lead of only 9.7 months with a range of 2 to 20 months. This is a considerable advantage for the RCL_t. However, as is common with many such ratios, the RCL_t does not predict the trough and recovery as accurately. In this case, the composite leading indicator predicted a recovery sooner with an average of 4.6 months and a range of 1 to 10 months, as opposed to 2.6 months and a range of 0 to 10 months for RCL_t.

Unfortunately, RCL_t and the CIL_t give false signals at times. It is such false signals that negate the economic value of such ratios and indicators. However, by combining the early warning signals of several indicators, we may better filter false signals.

Cautions with Indicators and Ratios

The effectiveness of all these approaches depends on the smooth accelerations and decelerations in the original time series. Such accelerations and decelerations do not always occur. We have seen how well these methods work in these examples. However, be cautious not to overstate the inferences made from these statistical summaries. In addition, in an actual application, we should consider the identification of several possible leading indicators to ensure that an effective pair has been chosen. As in most forecasting applications, considerable experimentation should be performed to ensure an effective approach. Such experimentation should be done prior to acceptance and use of any single approach. Consider some of the controversies surrounding these indicators.

From a strategic planning and forecasting perspective, perhaps no other methods of forecasting are more controversial and difficult than cyclical forecasting. Indicative of the controversy surrounding cyclical indicators has been the recent shift of the compilation of the Index of Leading Indicators from the Commerce Department to the Conference Board. By privatizing the generation of the Index of Leading Economic Indicators, the Commerce Department saves about $450,000 per year.

Interestingly, the Commerce Department requested bids from several companies before awarding it to the Conference Board. However, some of the organizations not getting the bid may design their own leading economic indicators. In addition, several economists and planners have questioned the premise that modern economies have to have recessions or depressions as regularly as in the past. Several speculate that continuous growths of many economies may persist for several decades with only short interruptions of slower but nonetheless positive growth. Others believe, that through better fiscal and monetary management, the probability of recessions is quite low.

Some question whether the leading index accurately leads recessions. The reviews of the index are mixed, and like so many other measures and methods of forecasting, success depends on how it is used in a comprehensive forecasting system.

Michael Evans has stated that the index of leading economic indicators has not performed well over the long run. He examined the index's performance over the entire post–Korean War period, using the rule that the index has to decline two quarters in a row to confirm that a recession is imminent. As he reported, the leading indicators did indeed predict 15 of the last 7 recessions; that is, 8 false signals were generated. However, they never missed an actual downturn. Maybe the rule of two quarters of decline is too crude. He increased the rule to include more months while still accurately predicting each recession. However, while maintaining a perfect record for predicting recessions, it still yielded three false signals of recession in 1956, 1967, and 1984.

To reduce the number of false signals, many propose the inclusion of other economic series as part of the list of leading indicators. According to Evans, several of the economic indicators have become either coincident or even lagging.

Despite Evans' assertions, the CIL has been shown to be useful for forecasting turning points and GNP by several others (Hamilton and Perez-Quiros, 1996, and Niemira and Fredman, 1991).

Other Leading Indicators

Several other forms of leading indicators have been proposed. These include the Quarterly Leading Indicator (QLI) developed by Wallace Duncan (1977), an economist at the Federal Reserve Bank of Dallas, and the several experimental indexes sponsored by the NBER and NSF (Stock and Watson, 1989). James H. Stock and Mark W. Watson created three new indexes, an experimental coincident indicator (XCI), an experimental leading indicator (XLI), and an experimental recession indicator (XRI). While some initial research using these new indexes has been favorable, more recent literature should be explored to confirm their effectiveness.

For those desiring a more comprehensive discussion of business cycles and indicators, Zarnowitz (1992) provides a complete and carefully integrated study.

Pressure Cycles (PC)

A cyclical forecasting technique used by many firms since its development in the 1970s by the Institute for Trend Research in Contoocook, New Hampshire, is a method referred to as **pressure cycle (PC)** analysis. This section shows that the steps of pressure cycle (PC) analysis are very similar to the paired indicators but not identical.

Steps of Pressure Cycle (PC) Analysis

Figure 14–8 and Table 14–7 illustrate actual monthly orders for the U.S. capital equipment industry for the period of January 1985 to December 1994, a leading economic indicator (PLTEQP20.DAT). This seasonal monthly data is used to generate pressure cycles. The first step is to compute 12-month moving totals. As you may recall from decomposition methods, a 12-month total contains no seasonality in it; thus, seasonal variations have been eliminated. These 12-month totals are placed at the last month of the total. In step 2, calculate the ratio of each 12-month total to the 12-month total of the previous year and show it as a percentage (i.e., multiplied by 100, as shown in the 12/12 column). This percentage of the two 12-month totals is called a pressure cycle (PC) and is designated as a 12/12 PC (i.e., the ratio of 12-month totals 12 months apart).

FIGURE 14–8

Capital equipment orders

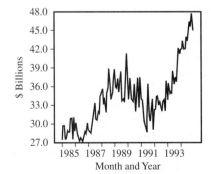

TABLE 14–7   **Pressure Cycles of Capital Equipment Contracts (PLTEQP20.DAT)**

Year:Month	Orders	12-Month Moving Totals	Ratio of 12-Month Moving Totals (12/12)
1985:01	27.41		
1985:02	29.78		
1985:03	29.73		
1985:04	27.53		
1985:05	27.77		
1985:06	29.08		
1985:07	28.77		
1985:08	28.82		
1985:09	30.99		
1985:10	30.94		
1985:11	27.51		
1985:12	31.20		
1986:01	28.76	350.880	
1986:02	30.39	351.490	
1986:03	28.55	350.310	
1986:04	27.82	350.600	
1986:05	27.27	350.100	
1986:06	27.98	349.000	
1986:07	27.50	347.730	
1986:08	27.09	346.000	
1986:09	28.31	343.320	
1986:10	29.02	341.400	
1986:11	28.51	342.400	
1986:12	30.28	341.480	
1987:01	29.06	341.780	97.407
1987:02	28.83	340.220	96.794
1987:03	28.52	340.190	97.111
1987:04	29.85	342.220	97.610
1987:05	30.92	345.870	98.792
1987:06	32.48	350.370	100.393
1987:07	33.63	356.500	102.522
1987:08	30.77	360.180	104.098
1987:09	30.68	362.550	105.601
1987:10	32.16	365.690	107.115
1987:11	31.72	368.900	107.739
1987:12	34.44	373.060	109.248
1988:01	35.36	379.360	110.995
1988:02	35.81	386.340	113.556
1988:03	32.96	390.780	114.871
1988:04	34.30	395.230	115.490
1988:05	31.72	396.030	114.503
⋮	⋮	⋮	⋮
1994:09	46.54	512.850	119.912
1994:10	45.54	519.470	120.078
1994:11	47.98	525.100	118.514
1994:12	44.90	528.800	118.252

Figure 14–9 shows the capital equipment expenditures and the 12/12 PC of Table 14–7. Note in the figure that the maximum value (point A) of the PC occurred in mid-1988 and late 1994 and the minimum value (point B) occurred in late 1991–early 1992. In contrast to the PC values, the maximum and minimum values for the original series occur later at points A′ and B′. It is the PC's ability to anticipate turning points that makes it a cyclical forecasting method.

There is some ambiguity of when the actual time series was at a trough in late 1991–early 1992. Thus, we might not be confident of the PC's ability to anticipate the trough and subsequent upturn or growth. Interestingly, while we might have some doubt about the trough in the series, there is no doubt about when the 12/12 PC denotes a growth or recovery phase at point B. Thus, after one or two periods starting at point B, the upturn in capital equipment contracts has started.

There are different PCs that can be calculated for different purposes. The most common PCs are 1/12, 3/12, and 12/12, where, respectively, these are one-month totals 12 periods apart, three-month totals 12 periods apart, and the previously illustrated 12-month totals 12 months apart. Obviously, PCs with lower numerators are more responsive to recent changes. However, they are more influenced by random variations that do not reflect fundamental changes or turning points.

Consider another example. Figure 14–10 illustrates a component of the coincident economic indicators, industrial production, along with a 12/12 PC (INDPRO47.DAT). As shown by the comparison of points A and A′, the 12/12 pressure denotes an impending downturn by giving an early warning in early 1988; however, the actual series did not decline until early 1989. Thus, the PC assisted in detecting the turning point. Somewhat surprising is the continual decline of the PC through 1991, a point where the time series once again starts a significant growth. If we had interpreted the segment after point A of the PC as signaling a downturn, we would have been correct, as the actual time series was level and then declined until about the first quarter of 1991.

Be cautious not to overestimate the ability of PCs based on historical fits and interpretations. PCs and their interpretations provide additional information that can add credence to other forecasts. To understand some of the difficulty in using PCs in real time, consider point B, where the PC of Figure 14–10 starts increasing very slightly. Does the slight increase denote a turning point or a slight inflection or hesitation in the downward movement of the time series? Not until following point C is there a strong signal of an increase in industrial production. Such interpretations are easily made in hindsight; however, the real-time interpretation are not so clear. Thus, we see that there is considerable art in the actual use of PCs. Always remember the implications and possibility of a false turning point.

FIGURE 14–9

Capital equipment and pressure cycle

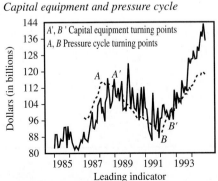

Leading indicator

FIGURE 14–10

Industrial production and pressure cycle

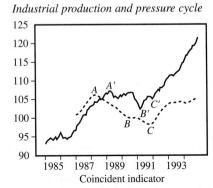

Coincident indicator

Multiple Pressure Cycles

The PCs of one or more variables can be compared to each other or to other variables using one of several time series methods. Let's compare the PC of capital equipment purchases, a leading indicator, to those of a coincident PC for industrial production. Figure 14–11 shows a 12/12 PC applied to each economic indicator. Interestingly, even though one series is typically a leading and the other a coincident indicator, the points at which peaks and troughs occur are nearly identical. In fact, the trough of the industrial production PC occurs earlier in 1991 than that of the leading series of capital equipment. Again, it is precisely for such reasons that PCs assist in detecting the turning points of economic time series.

At the corporate level, the PCs of a firm's sales, inventory, sales/inventory ratios, and other internal variables can be compared to industry and macroeconomic variables. For example, an early study by Sommer (1977) related a 1/12 PC of inventories to a 12/12 PC of orders. This relationship led to better inventory management.

Diffusion Indexes

Diffusion indexes measure how diffused or common a change is across the components of a composite index. Assume that a composite index of leading indicators for an industry consists of 10 individual series. Thus, the composite index is some average of these 10 series. A reported increase in the index will be the result of a net increase in one or more of the 10 series in the index. For example, an increase in the index can be explained by a large increase in a subset of its components or by a smaller increase in all of the components. In contrast, a diffusion index of .5 denotes that 50 percent (i.e., 5) of the components increased, while a .9 denotes that 9 of the 10 components increased. Thus, a diffusion index measures the percentage of the components of a composite index that have changed favorably.

A diffusion index is important because typically the more diffused the improvement, everything else being equal, the more significant the improvement. Thus, when a change is reported in an index such as a leading economic indicator, it is useful to know of the magnitude (i.e., the percentage change) and the diffusion of the change. For example, early in the growth of the index, its diffusion index is higher (i.e., more components of the series are moving favorably). As the growth in the index becomes less, its diffusion index is typically lower (i.e., fewer components of the series are moving favorably). Thus, a decline in the diffusion index denotes that there may be a subsequent decline in the composite index.

FIGURE 14–11

Capital equipment and industrial production pressure cycles

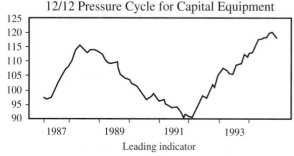

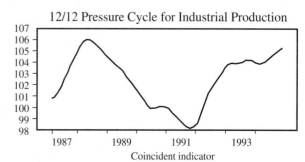

Seven Laws of Economic Forecasting

The following somewhat humorous laws of economic forecasting are presented for their relevance to short- and long-term forecasting.

1. History repeats itself; history does not repeat itself.
2. From time to time, major shocks throw the economy off course, and these are often not only unforecasted but unforecastable. (Economists fail to forecast large or unusual events such as wars, strikes, earthquakes, and technological breakthroughs.)
3. The consensus of economists' forecasts is more often right than wrong. (Over time, the average of several forecasts is more often better than any single forecast.)
4. Adherence to a single economic theory can be dangerous to your forecasting health. (The assumptions surrounding formal and informal theory may change without being anticipated in the forecast.)
5. Economic forces work relentlessly but on an uncertain timetable. One might predict that the demand will increase six months from now; however, demand increases one year later. This supports the old forecasting joke:

"Give them a number or a date, but not both."

6. Beware when something goes off the drawing board of historical experience. (When a ratio or trend departs dramatically from its historical bounds, we need to find out why and what risks it poses. Outlier detection is an essential part of this process.)
7. "The road is more important than the inn." (In general, the process of forecasting is more important than the final numbers. Improved decisions should result from a good process. The value in causal (i.e., multivariate) forecasting methods is in the assumptions made, the reasoning employed, the uncertainties described, and the factors identified as affecting the outcome.)

Source: Adapted from Gilbert Hebner, "Seven Laws of Economic Forecasting," National Association of Business Economists.

Summary

This chapter has presented a variety of theories and methods of forecasting the cyclical variations of time series. Because they can vary dramatically with equally dramatic impacts on organizational performance, cyclical variations should be studied and forecasted. We have noted over the years that students are very interested in cyclical forecasting but nonetheless have either forgotten or never learned some basic economic cyclical theories and principles. For that reason, this chapter provides a brief review of economic theory.

Many of the forecasting methods studied in this book are applicable to cyclical forecasting. In particular, the chapters on decomposition (5), ARIMA (7–9), multiple regression (10), econometrics (11), MARIMA (13), and the next chapter on technological forecasting (15) relate to cyclical forecasting.

Cyclical methods can be very useful in forecasting cyclical influences when a good economic indicator is available and forecastable. Thus, the cyclical indexes from classical decomposition can be related to some industry or macroeconomic variable in a lead–lag relationship. This is particularly effective when the independent variable is forecasted by some economic agency such as a regional, state, or federal agency.

The use of paired indexes can be very effective in cyclical forecasting, as illustrated by the examples of this chapter and the work of McLaughlin and Boyle (1968) and others. Very much related to this are pressure cycles. The examples using capital equipment expenditures and industrial production highlight the effectiveness of PCs.

No matter how effective these methods have been in the past, we must be cautious in applying them. As always, we should have significant substantive knowledge about what we are forecasting. Study the conventional and unconventional theories that might explain the variable of interest. Research the literature of the past to predict the movements of the future. In all cases, be cautious concerning cyclical projections and have contingency plans when what is supposed to go up instead goes down.

Key Terms

business cycle	multiplier effects of investment and
capital spending and inventory	consumption
change analysis	overinvestment
composite coincident economic indicators	paired indicators
composite lagging economic indicators	pressure cycles (PC)
composite leading economic indicators	prosperity
cyclical forecasting methods	psychological theory
cyclical indexes	recession
depression	recovery
diffusion indexes	RX, RY, RXY, RXRY
growth	Say's law
Harvey's rule	sunspots
innovation theory	term structure of interest rates
liquidation	turning points
long waves	underconsumption
monetarist	warning

Key Formulas

Decomposition of cyclical indexes:

$$Y_t = T_t C_t S_t + e_t$$

Estimate trend:

$$Y_t/S_t$$

Isolate the cyclical-irregular:

$$\frac{Y_t}{T_t * S_t} = CI_t$$

Smooth to remove irregular:

$$C_t = \frac{CI_{t-1} + CI_t + CI_{t+1}}{3}$$

Calculate fitted values and residuals:

$$\hat{Y}_t = T_t C_t S_t \qquad e_t = Y_t - \hat{Y}_t$$

Change measurements:

	Formula	*Example*
Absolute difference	$= \text{Current} - \text{Base}$	$110 - 100 = 10$
Relative percent	$= \dfrac{\text{Current}}{\text{Base}} \times 100$	$\dfrac{110}{100} \times 100 = 110\%$
Percentage change	$= \left(\dfrac{\text{Current}}{\text{Base}} - 1\right) \times 100$	$\left(\dfrac{110}{100} - 1\right) \times 100 = 10\%$

Paired indicators:

$$Y_t = a + bX_{t-3} + e_t \qquad \text{Regression} \qquad (14\text{--}1a)$$

$$Y_t = \theta_0 + \omega_0 X_{t-3} + N_t \qquad \text{MARIMA} \qquad (14\text{--}1b)$$

Percentage ratios:

$$RX_t = \frac{X_t}{X_{t-1}} \, 100 \qquad (14\text{--}2)$$

$$RY_t = \frac{Y_t}{Y_{t-1}} \, 100 \qquad (14\text{--}3)$$

$$RY_t = f(RX_{t-3}) \;\; \text{with a three-month lead} \qquad (14\text{--}4)$$

$$Y_t = f(RX_{t-4}) \;\; \text{with a four-month lead} \qquad (14\text{--}5)$$

$$RXRY_t = \frac{RX_t}{RY_t} \, 100 \qquad (14\text{--}6)$$

$$RXY_t = \frac{X_t}{Y_t} \, 100 \qquad (14\text{--}7)$$

Pressure cycles (PC):

12/12 = Ratio of two 12-month moving totals 12 months apart

3/12 = Ratio of two 3-month moving totals 12 months apart

1/12 = Ratio of two 1-month moving totals 12 months apart

Review Problems Using Your Software

R14–1 Repeat the percentage change analysis of Table 14–5 using your software and INDICATE.DAT. Comment on the resulting lead–lag relationships.

R14–2 By scaling the variables appropriately (adding or subtracting a constant so that they fit on the same graph), graph the results of problem R14–1, as done in Figure 14–5. Note the lead–lag relationships.

R14–3 Using the file PLTEQP20.DAT, generate a 12/12 pressure cycle for the capital equipment purchase series, as in Table 14–7.

R14–4 Graph the 12/12 PC of R14–3 with the original series, as in Figure 14–9. Note the lead–lag relationship on this graph using points A and B.

R14–5 Using the file INDPRO47.DAT, generate a 12/12 pressure cycle for the industrial production series, as in Figure 14–10.

R14–6 Graph the 12/12 PC of R14–5 with the original series, as in Figure 14–10. Note the lead–lag relationship on this graph using points A, B, and C.

R14–7 Graph the PCs for both the capital equipment and industrial production series, as in Figure 14–11. Comment on the original lead–lag relationship and the lead–lag relationships of the PCs.

Problems

14–1 Describe several reasons for modeling cyclical variations.

14–2 Why are cyclical variations so difficult to forecast?

14–3 Briefly describe the phases of the business cycle.

14–4 What does it mean to have a bottom-up approach in the use of regional economic performance?

14–5 Explain the mechanism of ratio analysis using the series X_t and RX_t of Table 14–6. How is it used to forecast X_t? How is it used to forecast Y_t?

14–6 What is a pressure cycle? Explain the mechanism whereby it leads the original variable.

14–7 Explain the meaning of the following concepts: *RX, RY, RXY,* and *RXRY.*

14–8 Explain the mechanism of the ratio analysis of two variables using the two series X_t, Y_t, and *RX/Y* of Table 14–6.

14–9 What is a diffusion index? Explain how it can be used to forecast.

14–10 What is a cyclical index and how can it be projected?

14–11 What is Harvey's rule? Explain how it can be used to forecast.

14–12 What is the term structure of interest rates (TSIR)? Explain how it can be used to forecast.

14–13 As discussed in Appendix 14–4 how are sunspots related to economic growth and decline?

14–14 Choose one each of the leading, coincident, and lagging economic indicators and explain theoretically why each leads, coincides and lags the economy.

14–15 Explain why the ratio of a cyclical indicator such as X_t shown in Figure 14–6 behaves the way it does in predicting turning points.

14–16 Perform a classical decomposition analysis on the series (SERIESD.DAT) using either regression, percent of moving averages, or another decomposition procedure. Calculate cyclical indexes and comment on their usefulness.

14–17 As an example of leading and lagging indicators, fit an appropriate model to Y_t and X_t of Table 14–6. Comment on the goodness of fit and whether the relationship is valid. Also, what is the measured lead–lag?

14–18 What are some of the controversies associated with ratios using the index of leading economic indicators? Do leading economic indicators forecast recessions and recoveries equally well? If not, what indicators have been shown to be better for recessions and recoveries?

The following time series of Table 14–2 exists on the data disk and each has about 600 observations.* These time series may be used in answering the following questions.

LEADI910.DAT: Composite Index of Leading Indicators (Series 910)
WORKHR1.DAT: Average weekly hours worked.
UCLAIM5.DAT: Average weekly initial claims for unemployment insurance.
MANNEW08.DAT: Manufacturers' new orders—consumers and materials industries.
STKPRI19.DAT: Stock prices.
PLTEQP20.DAT: Contracts and orders for plant and equipment.
PRIHOU29.DAT: New private housing units authorized.
VENDOR32.DAT: Vendor performance.
MANFIL92.DAT: Changes in manufacturers' unfilled orders.
MATPRI99.DAT: Changes in sensitive material prices.
M2106.DAT: Real M2 money supply.

COIND920.DAT: Composite Index of Coincident Indicators (Series 920)
EMPNAG41.DAT: Employees on nonagricultural payrolls.
INDPRO47.DAT Industrial production.
PERINC51.DAT Personal income less transfer payments.
MANSAL57.DAT: Manufacturing and trade sales.

LAGGI930.DAT: Composite Index of Lagging Indicators (Series 930)
ILABCS62.DAT: Change in index of labor costs of output, manufacturing.
INVSAL77.DAT: Ratio of manufacturing and trade inventories to sales.
DURUNE91.DAT: Average duration of unemployment.

---

*Source: Series numbers are *Survey of Current Business* numbers.

CRTPI95.DAT: Ratio of consumer installment credit outstanding to personal income.
LOANS101.DAT: Commercial and industrial loans outstanding.
PRIME109.DAT: Average prime rate charged by banks.
CPISM120.DAT: Change in consumer price index for services, smoothed.

14–19 Fit an appropriate relationship between the composite index of leading economic indicators (LEADI910.DAT) and the lagging economic indicator (LAGGI930.DAT). Comment on the goodness of fit and whether the relationship is useful. Also, what is the measured lead–lag?

14–20 Fit 12/12 pressure cycles to the composite index of leading indicators (LEADI910.DAT) and the lagging economic indicators (LAGGI930.DAT). Graph these two PCs versus each original series and then versus each other. Comment on the lead–lag relationship within and between the graphs. Are the PCs coincident? If not, how can this be used to an advantage?

14–21 Having completed Problem 14–20, fit an appropriate relationship between the following variable pairs:
a. The leading indicator and its PC.
b. The lagging indicator and its PC.
c. The PC of the leading indicator and original lagging indicator.
d. PCs of the leading and lagging indicators.
Note the lead–lag relationship. If more than one of (a) to (d) are completed, comment on which has the longest and most useful lead–lag relationship.

14–22 Choose any of the above 10 leading, 4 coincident, or 7 lagging indicators listed before problem 14–19 and complete the following:
a. Fit 12/12 PCs for one of each.
b. Fit a RXY_t between two of those from part a.
c. Compare the lead–lag relationships between the PC, RXY, X_t, and Y_t of parts a. and b.

14–23 Show that the ratio of coincident to lagging economic indicators, Series 920 and 930, is a leading economic indicator.

14–24 Compare the ratio of the coincident to lagging economic indicators to the index of leading economic indicators (Series 910). Which predicted the recession and recovery turning points of the coincident economic indicator better?

14–25 The time series RETAIL.DAT is the monthly retail sales in the United States. Complete the minicase assignment.

14–26 The time series SUPEROIL.DAT is the sales of the Superoil Company in thousands of barrels during the last 108 months. Complete the minicase assignment.

Minicases: Common Forecasting Assignment

For a selected minicase or problem, complete the following analysis. a) Speculate on what variables might be useful leading, coincident, or lagging indicators for each selected time series. b) If those variables exist in a usable form, then fit a cyclical forecasting model and judge its effectiveness. c) If you have been filling out the Master Forecasting Summary Table, then withhold the appropriate number of observations and complete that table and compare the cyclical model to other models in that table.

Minicase 14–1 Kansas Turnpike Monthly Data

Minicase 14–2 Domestic Air Passengers by Quarter

Minicase 14–3 Hospital Census by Month

Minicase 14–4 Your Forecasting Project

Minicase 14–5 Midwestern Building Materials

Minicase 14–6 International Airline Passengers

Minicase 14–7 Consumption of Distilled Spirits

Minicase 14–8 Automobile Sales

Minicase 14–9 Consumption of Distilled Spirits

Minicase 14–10 Discount Consumer Electronics

References

Adams, F. *The Business Forecasting Revolution.* New York: Oxford University Press, 1986.

Ashley, R. "On the Usefulness of Macroeconomics Forecasts as Inputs to Forecasting Models." *Journal of Forecasting* 2 (1983), pp. 211–23.

Auerbach, A.J. "The Index of Leading Indicators: Measurement without Theory Thirty-Five Years Later." *Review of Economics and Statistics* 64 (1982), pp. 585–95.

Belt, B., and S.A. DeLurgio. "How to Predict and Navigate A/R During Recessions." *The Credit and Financial Management Review,* Columbia, MD, January 1995, pp. 19–23.

Berlin, H.M. *The Handbook of Financial Market Indexes, Averages, and Indicators.* Burr Ridge, IL: Richard D. Irwin, 1991.

Bernstein, J. *The Handbook of Economic Cycles.* Burr Ridge, IL: Richard D. Irwin, 1991.

Boldin, M.D. "Dating Turning Points in the Business Cycle." *Journal of Business* 67 (January 1994), pp. 97–131.

Bowers, D.A. *An Introduction to Business Cycles and Forecasting.* Reading, MA: Addison–Wesley Publishing, 1985.

Colby, R.W. and T.A. Meyers, *Encyclopedia of Technical Market Indicators.* Burr Ridge, IL Business One Irwin, 1988

Cooley, T.F., ed. *Frontiers of Business Cycle Research.* Princeton: Princeton University Press, 1995.

Davis, G. "Managing Credit and Collections in Today's Economy." *Credit and Financial Management,* October 1982, pp. 15ff.

Dewey E.R. *Cycles—Selected Writings.* Pittsburgh: Foundation for the Study of Cycles, 1979, pp. 360–61.

Dhrymes, P.J., and S.C. Peristiani. "A Comparison of the Forecasting Performance of WEFA and ARIMA Time Series Methods." *International Journal of Forecasting* 4 (1988), pp. 81–101.

Diebold, F.X., and G. Rudebusch. Forecasting Output with the Composite Leading Index: A Real-Time Analysis." *Journal of the American Statistical Association* 86 (September 1991), pp. 603–10.

————. "Turning Point Prediction with the Composite Leading Index: An Ex Ante Analysis." In *Leading Economic Indicators: New Approaches and Forecasting Records,* ed. K. Lahiri and G. H. Moore. Cambridge: Cambridge University Press, 1991.

Diebold, F.X.; G. Rudebusch; and D. Sichel. "Further Evidence on Business-Cycle Duration Dependence." In ed. J.H. Stock and M.W. Watson. *Business Cycles, Indicators, and Forecasting.* Chicago: University of Chicago Press, 1993.

Doan, T. *Regression Analysis of Time Series.* Evanston, IL: Estima, 1994.

Dodosh, M.H. "Slump Leads Firms to Lag in Paying Bills." *The Wall Street Journal,* June 25, 1980, p. 34.

Duncan, W.H. "A New Leading Indicator." *Federal Research Bank of Dallas Economic Review,* March 1977, pp. 1–5.

Eckstein, O. *The Great Recession.* New York: North-Holland Publishing, 1978.

Eckstein, O., and A. Sinai. "The Mechanisms of the Business Cycle in the Postwar Era." In *The American Business Cycle: Continuity and Change,* ed. Chicago: University of Chicago Press, 1986, pp. 39–122.

Emery, G.W. "A Pure Financial Explanation for Trade Credit." *Journal of Financial and Quantitative Analysis,* September 1984, pp. 271–85.

Evans, M.K. "Farewell to the Leading Indicators: The Index Deserves a Decent Burial." *Industry Week* 244, no. 18, (October 2, 1995), p. 88(1).

Federal Reserve Bulletin. "Recent Developments in Industrial Capacity and Utilization." June 1990, p. 433; and subsequent issues.

Filardo, A.J. "Business Cycle Phases and Their Transitional Dynamics." *Research Working Paper 93–14.* Kansas City, MO: Federal Reserve Bank of Kansas City, 1993.

————. "Business Cycle Phases and their Transitional Dynamics." *Journal of Business and Economic Statistics* 12 (July, 1994), pp. 299–308.

Forrester, J.W. *World Dynamics*. New York: Wright-Allen, 1971.

Fuhrer, J.C. "Commodity Prices, the Term Structure of Interest Rates, and Exchange Rates: Useful Indicators for Monetary Policy?" *New England Economic Review*, November 1993, pp. 18–32.

Garner, C.A. "Market Indicators for Monetary Policy." *Research Working Paper 89–08*. Kansas City, MO: Federal Reserve Bank of Kansas City, 1989.

Gentry, J.A. "A State of the Art of Short-Run Financial Management." *Financial Management*, Summer 1988, pp. 41–57.

Gordon, R.A. *Economic Instability and Growth: The American Record*. New York: Harper & Row, 1974.

Granger, C.W.J., and P. Newbold. *Forecasting Economic Time Series*. 2nd ed. New York: Academic Press, 1986.

Green, G.R., and B.A. Beckman. "Business Cycle Indicators: Upcoming Revision of the Composite Indexes. *Survey of Current Business* 73 (October 1993), pp. 44–51.

Hamilton, J.D., and G. Perez-Quiros. "What Do the Leading Indicators Lead?" *The Journal of Business* 69, no. 1 (January 1996), p. 27(23).

Harvey, C.R. "Term Structure Forecasts Economic Growth." *Financial Analysts Journal*, May 1993, pp. 6–8.

————. "Forecasts of Economic Growth from the Bond and Stock Markets." *Financial Analysts Journal*, September–October 1989, pp. 38–45.

Klein, P.A., and G.H. Moore. "The Leading Indicator Approach to Economic Forecasting—Retrospect and Prospect." *Journal of Forecasting* 2 (1983), pp. 119–35.

Klein, P.A. "Leading Indicators of Inflation in Market Economies." *International Journal of Forecasting* 2 (1986), pp. 403–12.

Kling, J.L. "Predicting the Turning Points of Business and Economic Time Series." *Journal of Business* 60 (April 1987), pp. 201–38.

Koch, P.D., and R.H. Rasche. "An Examination of the Commerce Department Leading Indicator Approach." *Journal of Business and Economic Statistics* 6 (1988), pp. 176–87.

Long, M.S., et al. "Trade Credit, Quality Guarantees and Product Marketability." *Financial Management*, Winter 1993, pp. 117–27.

Larrain, M., and M. Pagano. "Forecasts from a Nonlinear T-Bill Rate Model." *Financial Analysts Journal*, November 1993, pp. 83–88.

Maddala, G.S. *Introduction to Econometrics*. 2nd ed. New York: Macmillan, 1992.

Makridakis, S. "Chronology of the Last Six Recessions." *Omega* 10, no. 1 (1982), pp. 43–50.

Makridakis, S., and S.C. Wheelwright, eds. *The Handbook of Forecasting: A Manager's Guide*. New York: John Wiley & Sons, 1982.

McLaughlin, R.L. "A Model of an Average Recession and Recovery." *Journal of Forecasting* 1, no. 1 (1982), pp. 55–63.

McLaughlin, R.L. and J.J. Boyle. *Short Term Forecasting*. New York: American Marketing Association, 1968.

————. "A New Five-Phase Economic Forecasting System." *Business Economics*, September 1975, pp. 49–60.

McNees, S.K. "The 1990–91 Recession in Historical Perspective." *New England Economic Review*, January 1992, pp. 3–22.

Moore, G.H. *Business Cycles, Inflation, and Forecasting*. 2nd ed. Cambridge, MA: Ballinger Publishing, for the National Bureau of Economic Research, 1983.

Neftci, S.N. "Lead-Lag Relations, Exogeneity, and Prediction of Economic Time Series." *Econometrica* 47 (1979), pp. 101–13.

Niemira, M.P., and G.T. Fredman. "An Evaluation of the Composite Index of Leading Indicators for Signaling Turning Points in Business and Growth Cycles." *Business Economics* 26, no. 4 (October 1991), p. 49.

Oyen, D.B. *Business Fluctuations and Forecasting*. Dearborn, MI: Financial Publishing, 1991.

Plocek, J.E. *Economic Indicators, How America Reads Its Financial Health*. New York: New York Institute of Finance, 1991.

Quarterly Financial Report, Washington, D.C.: U.S. Department of Commerce, various issues.

Reichenstein, W. "Touters Trophies: Ranking Economists' Forecasts." *Financial Analysts Journal*, July 1991, pp. 20ff.

Schumpeter, J.A. *Theory of Economic Development*. Cambridge, MA: Harvard University Press, 1934.

————. *Business Cycles*. Vol. 1. New York: McGraw–Hill, 1939.

Smith, J.K. "Trade Credit and Informational Asymmetry." *Journal of Finance*, September 1987, pp. 863–72.

Sommer, D.W. "Cycle Forecasting Spots Trends," *Industry Week,* New York, April 25, 1977, p. 71.

Stock, J.H., and M. Watson. "New Indexes of Leading and Coincidental Economic Indicators." In ed. O. Blanchard and S. Fischer. *NBER Macroeconomics Annual: 1989*. Cambridge, MA: MIT Press, 1989.

————. "Indexes of Coincident and Leading Economic Indicators." *NBER Reporter*, Spring 1989, p. 5.

U.S. Department of Commerce. *Handbook of Cyclical Indicators*. Washington, D.C.: Government Printing Office, 1984.

U.S. Government. *Business Conditions Digest*. Washington, D.C.: monthly publication.

Valentine, L.M. *Business Cycles and Forecasting*. 7th ed. Cincinnati, OH: South-Western Publishing, 1987.

Wecker, W.E. "Predicting the Turning Points of a Time Series." *Journal of Business* 52 (January 1979), pp. 35–50.

Wessel, D. "The Price Is Wrong, and Economists Are in an Uproar." *The Wall Street Journal*, January 2, 1991, p. B1.

Zarnowitz, V. *Business Cycles: Theory, History, Indicators, and Forecasting*. Washington, D.C.: NBER, 1992.

APPENDIX 14–A

SOME GENERAL THEORIES ABOUT CYCLES

"The opposite of a great truth is another great truth. You can recognize a small truth because its opposite is a falsehood."

Niels Bohr

There are many theories of business cycles for both the aggregate economy and specific industries. Many of these are long–wave cyclical theories. The underlying theories explaining long waves includes many phenomena, including **sunspots,** weather influences, and other natural or psychological phenomena. For example, it is believed that there are cycles in prices that last for 40 to 60 years shown by the cyclical wholesale prices of Table 14A–1. The causes of these and other recurrent patterns continues to be studied by many organizations. Consider a few explanations.

TABLE 14A–1   Major Long-Wave Cycles in Wholesale Prices

		Years for Full Cycle
1790 to 1815	Increases	
1815 to 1850	Decreases	1850–1790 = 60
1850 to 1865	Increases	1865–1815 = 50
1865 to 1890	Decreases	1890–1850 = 40
1890 to 1920	Increases	1920–1865 = 55
1920 to 1933	Decreases	1933–1890 = 43
1934 to 1978	Increases	1978–1920 = 58

A Mistaken Sense of Seasonal and Cyclical Stability

Despite what some consider to be incantations of others, many of us want to believe that the world is much more stable than it might be. However, maybe rain forests, fluorocarbons, and greenhouse effects should be taken more seriously by more individuals. Consider the following weather phenomena.

If there were a permanent drop in the energy reaching the Earth of only 1.6 to 2 percent, there would be snow cover to the equator and the oceans would eventually freeze. For example, in 1816, there was no summer in many parts of the globe because of volcanic dust; an eruption of a volcano in Tomboro, Indonesia, spewed dust that blocked the sun. In parts of New England, snow stayed on the ground all year long, and crops there and in Europe were ruined. This dust resulted in cold weather and red and brown snow that fell in Hungary, Italy, and the United States.

Source: Isaac Asimov, *Isaac Asimov's Book of Facts* (New York: Wing Books, 1979).

Long Waves, Sunspots, and Weather

Dewey (1979) identified a 33-month climatic cycle that affects other activities such as wheat and copper prices and residential construction. He also found a 30- to 41-month cycle in interest rates. Many others have concluded that there is a definite relationship between business, sunspot, and global temperature cycles. Consider the cyclical behavior of sunspots in Figure 14A–1, which are shown in actual and smoothed values. In fact, the British economist William Jevons (1835–1882) first proposed that sunspots affect weather and therefore agriculture. Sunspots are dark spots on the face of the sun that cause variations in the intensity of the solar energy reaching the earth. During periods of very low or high sunspot activity, variations in temperature, rainfall, and other weather conditions are more severe. Thus, sunspots affect the harvest of crops and therefore the prosperity of agricultural economies. As those involved in the telecommunications industry can confirm, sunspots have a 22-year cycle, with peaks followed 11 years later by troughs. These are the seasonal aspects of sunspots. However, as shown in Figure 14A–1, sunspots also vary cyclically. During extreme peak sunspot activity, some telecommunications are disrupted by high energy radiations.

In 1922, Lord William Beveridge found a 50- to 60-year cycle in European wheat prices. The famous Russian Nikolai D. Kondratieff (1892–1956) found that capitalistic economies have about a 50-year cycle in growth. Both Beveridge and Dewey studied 500 years of wheat prices and found strong evidence to support a 54-year cycle in wheat prices that correlates very strongly with the width of tree rings. Thus, a strong weather influence may exist. Other cycles include a 54-year cycle in the purchasing power of gold and a 25- to 27-year cycle in interest rates.

The important studies of economic cycles made by Nikolai Kondratieff showed patterns in a variety of economic variables, including consumption, exports, imports, materials, production,

FIGURE 14A–1

Wolfer sunspot measures

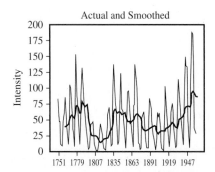

Actual and Smoothed

and wages in England and France. His research provided evidence that **long-wave** cycles exist in many economic variables. He identified three long waves of expansions and contractions that averaged about 50 years, from 1792 to 1850, 1850 to 1896, and 1896 to 1940. In recent years, there has been increased interest in Kondratieff's studies, in part because in 1990, many believed we were at the end of another 50-year cycle and poised for another growth phase.

While long-wave theories and empirical evidence are convincing, many economists feel that they are not conclusive. This discussion of cycles could go on for several chapters (Bernstein, 1991). However, let's focus on some of the causal theories of business and economic cycles.

There are many economic theories of business cycles, some of the most important being those of Arthur Pigou, Jean Baptiste Say, the Austrian-American economist Joseph Schumpeter (1883–1950), the British economist John Hobson (1858–1940), John Maynard Keynes (1883–1946), Milton Friedman (1912–   ), and others.

Psychological Theory of Business Cycles

"What concerns me is not the way things are, but rather the way people think things are."

Epictetus, Philospher (55–135)

The British economist Arthur Pigou (1877–1959) developed a **psychological theory** of business cycles. This theory proposes that the optimism or pessimism of business and political leaders often influence the economy. For example, if businesses expect the prices of their materials to increase, then they raise their prices and this becomes a self-fulfilling expectation. Many politicians subscribe to this psychological theory.

Recent U.S. presidents have espoused optimism about the economy to stimulate consumer and producer demand. Also, during the Great Depression, President Herbert Hoover used public optimism in hopes of stimulating consumer and business spending. Other examples of the importance of expectations in business cycles are the regular survey reports of the National Association of Purchasing Management, the many reports of the Survey Research Center of the University of Michigan, and the confidence index of the Conference Board.

Say's Law

The famous French economist Jean Baptiste Say (1767–1832), a contemporary of Adam Smith, is best known for his theory of markets and growth. One of the earliest theories of business cycles is **Say's law,** which states that supply creates its own demand and by implication is not demand driven. That is, as manufacturers hire workers and produce more product, this creates an equality of supply and demand. Deviations from this equilibrium, economic downturns and upturns, are only temporary phenomena. The theory is that goods and services are bought with other goods and services and that the production of goods creates a demand for other goods—in effect, goods are purchasing power and therefore production creates its own demand. Thus, as Say stated, "it is the aim of good government to stimulate production, of bad government to encourage consumption."

Innovation Theory

The famous Austrian economist Joseph Schumpeter (1883–1950) developed the **innovation theory** of business cycles, first presented in Austria and then at Harvard University. His theory is that business cycles result from new inventions that yield new technologies and innovations. These innovations stimulate the production of new products that stimulate consumer demand. However, because new inventions are discovered somewhat sporadically, economies expand and contract as the products of the new technologies expand and then contract. One of his more quoted ideas it the "creative gale of destruction," which says that real competition and growth come from the implementation of new technological innovations. Schumpeter (1939) believed that there are cyclical influences of 1 to 10 years within a longer cycle of about 30 years.

There has been increasing global interest in Schumpeter's theories as we have seen the development of many new technologies. Recent innovations in computers, information, telecommunications, microelectronics, microbiology, and genetic engineering have been and will continue to be determinants of the wealth of future economies. Very much related to cyclical forecasting is technological forecasting, discussed in Chapter 15.

Underconsumption

The British economist John Hobson (1858–1940) proposed that the causes of business cycles include low incomes, inequitable income distribution, and **underconsumption.** When product prices increase more than the incomes of consumers, then the profits from and demand for products decline. That is, demand declines because the workers cannot buy the products of their efforts, while the rich accumulate savings that are reinvested in nonproducing assets because of the low returns from manufacturing investments. The reduced investment in plant and equipment decreases the demand for labor and supply of products; thus, a cycle of decline in supply and demand begins.

Overinvestment

Two Austrian-born economists, Friedrich von Hayek (1899–1992) and Ludwig von Mises (1881–1973), developed an overinvestment theory of business cycles. Their theory says that cycles are the result of the law of diminishing marginal returns as production increases above efficient levels. That is, when production is increased to the point where less efficient allocations of resources are used, then costs increase. In addition, when the increased costs of production cannot be recovered through higher prices to consumers, then suppliers reduce production and employment levels. These actions start a cycle of supply and demand declines.

Monetarists

Milton Friedman (1912–   ) and Sir Ralph George Hawtrey (1879–1975) have developed **monetary theories** of business cycles. These theories stress the importance of the supply of money in economic systems. Because businesses must borrow money to operate, the cost of money (i.e., the interest rate) influences investment decisions. Thus, changes in interest rates determine whether businesses increase or decrease their investments in plant, equipment, and employees.

Capital Spending and Inventories

The importance of **capital spending and inventories** is seen directly or indirectly in all of the above theories. When demand decreases, inventories accumulate, thus sending a signal to slow down production and spending on new plant and equipment. Then, businesses reduce the number of employees and cut their capital expenditures because they fear that consumer spending will decline further and inventories will worsen. Not surprisingly, this simple relationship highlights why forecasters and planners focus on a number of key statistics, including shipments of capital equipment, sales-to-inventory ratios, and consumer expectation.

Multiplier Effects of Investment and Consumption

Common to all business cycle theories is the relationship between investment and consumption. Investments in plant, equipment, and housing have a **multiplier effect** on the economy. For example, when a company invests in new equipment and products, the money paid to workers and suppliers then becomes income to other workers; these workers then spend this income, thus providing more income to others. Therefore, when a company spends a dollar on wages, this dollar circulates throughout the economy. For example, if the Marginal Propensity to Consume (MPC) is .80, then 80 percent of wages are spent, 80 percent of which in turn is spent. The initial spending (i.e., wages, investment, welfare payments) starts a chain of spending that theoretically increases GDP by five times the amount spent.

Unfortunately, the multiplier effect also operates in the opposite direction. When a company reduces its wages by a dollar, this negative effect also multiplies through the economy. When employment and wages are reduced, the negative multiplying effect results in an even greater reduced demand for products and new factories and equipment.

Controlling Business Cycles

As is true in most forecasting applications, there is interest in making the forecast wrong if it is unfavorable, and true if it is favorable. That is, decision makers and policymakers forecast to make better decisions and thereby reduce the negative consequences predicted in the forecasts while accentuating the positive. In the U.S. economy, policies and programs are in place to reduce the severity of business cycles. These programs include unemployment benefits, social security, and pensions. In addition, the federal government provides price supports for agricultural and other strategic resources and direct interventions in attempts to counteract recessions. The three major types of interventions of government are monetary, fiscal and income policies. However, the popularity of these policies varies considerably. Complicating such policies are attempts by labor unions to maintain or increase wages, which can deepen recessions. The effects of these policies, while desirable, makes cyclical forecasting more difficult.

Milton Friedman of the University of Chicago is a vocal proponent of monetary policy, a policy favored by many conservatives. With monetary policy, the Federal Reserve Bank controls the money supply and interest rates and thus the availability and costs of consumer and business loans. By increasing the supply of money, consumers and businesses are encouraged to spend more on durable products, including housing, automobiles, plant, and equipment. By reducing the money supply, inflationary effects of increased demand can be decreased. However, when inflation and recession occur simultaneously (i.e., *stagflation*), then monetary policy is difficult to apply successfully.

In contrast to Milton Friedman, the famous British economist John Maynard Keynes (1883–1946) was a proponent of proactive fiscal policies. Keynes and the American economist John Kenneth Galbraith (1908–   ) propose the use of fiscal measures, increased deficit spending, decreased taxation of the poor, increased taxation of the wealthy, and wage/price controls. Keynes believed that there is no self-correcting mechanism that will bring an economy out of a recession or depression; thus, governments must intervene in recessions and depressions. However, many feel that such policies have not had much success since World War II.

Fortunately, because of a combination of anticyclical policies, the United States has not experienced a depression since the 1930s. However, the use of wage and price controls and deficit spending has not been without costs. In the 1970s, the economy fought problems of stagflation. In the 1980s, inflation and unemployment were brought under control during a sustained period of growth. However, during the 1980s, the federal debt almost quadrupled. Problems with the federal debt persist into the late 1990s, and there has been some reluctance to reduce some social programs and deficit spending.

With the breakup of the former Soviet Union, persistent problems in the Middle East, and the development of the unified European Economic Union, there is some concern in the United States about maintaining its competitiveness in world markets. Thus, policymakers are cautious to ensure that fiscal decisions do not cause a recession. The financial markets for stock and bonds continue to watch the actions of the Federal Reserve to ensure that interest rates do not increase and precipitate a recession.

15

TECHNOLOGICAL AND QUALITATIVE FORECASTING METHODS: LONG-TERM FORECASTING

Chance favors the prepared mind.

Louis Pasteur

Chapter Outline

Subjective Forecasting Methods
Exploratory Forecasting Methods
Normative Forecasting Methods
S-Curves of Growth
Summary
Key Terms
Key Formulas
Review Problems Using Your Software
Problems
References

This chapter discusses long-range forecasting methods including what methods exist, which are best for a specific application, and how to apply them. Until this chapter, forecasting methods have been based primarily on objective numeric data. The judgment of the forecaster was used only to select the type of model or to make subjective adjustments to the forecasts, but not as the primary numeric input to the forecast. However, this chapter covers a variety of qualitative and technological forecasting methods where judgment is the primary source of data used to generate forecasts. The methods discussed in this chapter are longer term methods that must use judgment as the primary input because there is little relevant numeric data—past data may not exist, or the forecasts are so far in the future that past data is irrelevant.

Because these methods use subjective judgment and qualitative estimates, they are either called **qualitative** or **judgmental forecasting** methods. In addition, because they are frequently used for **long-term forecasts** of new technologies, they are often called **technological forecasting** methods, even though they are used for a wider variety of other long-term applications. The terms *qualitative, judgmental,* and *technological* forecasting are often used interchangeably.

This chapter has four major sections. The first discusses forecasts using subjective estimates. The second section discusses structured procedures for exploring alternative futures using a variety of methods. The third section develops normative forecasting methods that define what needs to happen in the future to achieve some desired goal. Finally, the last section presents the technological forecasting methods called growth or S-curve models. These are called S-curves because of their shape. They have very small increasing slopes initially, but then the slopes increase rapidly and become nearly level as they approach a maximum. These curves have found considerable success in modeling the development, adoption, and decline of technologies. Consider this behavior in Figure 15–1, which shows the maturity (i.e., position of each technology on the S-curve) of the different technologies of automated manufacturing methods.

When studying technological forecasting, the term *technology* is used in a very general sense, including but not limited to the technology of products, services, processes, systems, economic markets, psychological behavior, scientific developments, and sociological phenomena. The importance of technological forecasting is clear when one considers the extraordinary events that have occurred recently that few people predicted. Consider these recent developments:

- The emergence of microprocessors.
- The development of microcomputers.
- Optical-digital (CD) electronics.
- Extremely low-cost CD-ROM readers and writers.

FIGURE 15–1

Maturity of various automated manufacturing technologies

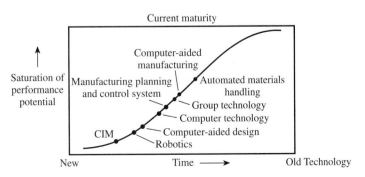

Source: Chase and Aquilano, *Production and Operations Management,* 7th *ed.*

- The fall of communism in the old Soviet Union and Eastern Europe. (How many people saw the role of advanced communications in this geopolitical change?)
- Stealth technology in the Gulf War.
- Advanced laser guidance system in the Gulf War.
- Genetic engineering of animals to produce pharmaceuticals.
- The impact of microcomputerization on all activities of life.
- Telecommuting.
- Nanotechnology yielding microscopic machines.
- The human genome project.
- The decline of nuclear power.
- The rise of electric solar cells to replace regulated power generation.
- Multimedia systems.
- Artificial intelligence, neural networks, and genetic algorithms.
- Organ transplants.
- Artificial organs.
- Superconductivity.
- The rise of AIDS, and the inability to cure AIDS and cancer.
- Cold fusion.
- Fuel cell uses as energy sources in homes and automobiles.

This list could be several pages long. As you review these developments, don't forget how difficult it would have been to anticipate them. Consider the blunders of the past, such as the early 20th-century debate over the effectiveness of airplanes in naval warfare. When General Billy Mitchell proposed using airplanes to bomb and sink battleships, Newton Baker, U.S. secretary of the War Department, stated, "That idea is so damned nonsensical and impossible that I'm willing to stand on the bridge of a battleship while that nitwit tries to hit it from the air." The secretary of the Navy, Josephus Daniels, stated, "Good God! This man (i.e., Billy Mitchell) should be writing dime novels." The popular and scientific literature was unbelieving and critical. The prestigious *Scientific American* stated in 1910 that "to affirm that the airplane is going to 'revolutionize' naval warfare of the Future is to be guilty of the wildest exaggeration." These types of statements were not restricted to the military and scientific communities. Consider the ridiculousness of the statements of experts in the "Technological Forecasting Is Difficult" box.

We are surprised at how many intelligent people make the wrong assumptions about the future. It is not easy to predict possible futures, but when we are prepared, we are better able to seize opportunities, as the Louis Pasteur quote at the beginning of this chapter pointed out.

This chapter presents a rich variety of long-term forecasting methods that can help prepare your mind for the future. Surprisingly, not enough companies use these methods. The U.S. economy would be much better today if, in the 1960s and 1970s, the steel industry, Ford, Chrysler, and General Motors had more fully explored the consequences of global competition, new technologies, oil cartels, globalization, environmentalism, and technological advances in materials and manufacturing.

In the 1980s, why did IBM and DEC not understand the importance of their microcomputer products?

Why did so many large corporations not understand the burdens of their bureaucracies?

Technological Forecasting Is Difficult!

The following humorous forecasting blunders exemplify the difficulty of accurate technological forecasting even when experts are making the projections.

"Everything that can be invented has been invented."

> Charles H. Duell, Director of the U.S. Patent Office, 1899

"Who the hell wants to hear actors talk?"

> Harry Warner, Warner Bros. Pictures, 1927

"Sensible and responsible women do not want to vote."

> Grover Cleveland, 1905

"There is no likelihood man can ever tap the power of the atom."

> Robert Millikan, Nobel Prize winner in Physics, 1923

"Heavier than air flying machines are impossible."

> Lord Kelvin, president of the Royal Society, 1895

"Home mortgage rates will never go below 10 percent in this century."

> Many financial experts, 1980

"With over 50 foreign cars already on sale here, the Japanese auto industry isn't likely to carve out a big slice of the U.S. market for itself."

> Business Week, August 2, 1968

"A severe depression like that of 1920–1921 is outside the range of probability."

> The Harvard Economic Society, November 16, 1929

"I think there is a world market for about five computers."

> Thomas J. Watson, chairman of IBM, 1943

"There is no reason for any individual to have a computer in their home."

> Ken Olson, president, Digital Equipment Corporation, 1977

"We don't like their sound. Groups of guitars are on the way out."

> Decca Recording Company executive, turning down the Beatles in 1962

"The phonograph . . . is not of any commercial value."

> Thomas Alva Edison, inventor of the phonograph, about 1880

"No matter what happens, the U.S. Navy is not going to be caught napping."

> Frank Knox, secretary of the Navy, December 4, 1941, just before the December 7th attack on Pearl Harbor

"They couldn't hit an elephant as this dist . . ."

> General John B. Sedgwick, last words, Battle of Spotsylvania, 1864

The source of several of these is C. Cerf and V. Navasky, *The Experts Speak* (New York: Pantheon Books, 1984).

Why have corporations that have invented new technologies not seen the value of those technologies?

We can try to avoid the failures of the past by anticipating the future.

In contrast to the mistakes made by so many in the past, consider the surprisingly accurate predictions of John Elfreth Watkins, Jr., in the "Forgotten Genius of Forecasting" box. Part of the reason his predictions were so accurate was his ability to assimilate the input from the "wisest and most careful men in our greatest institutions of science and learning" in a methodical application of technological forecasting. So that we might be better prepared and methodical, let's study long-term forecasting methods in greater detail.

Subjective Forecasting Methods

"Intelligence is quickness to apprehend as distinct from ability, which is capacity to act wisely on the thing apprehended."

> Alfred North Whitehead (1861–1947)
> British philosopher

Forgotten Genius of Forecasting:
Extraordinary Predictions of John Elfreth Watkins, Jr.[a]

In 1900, John Watkins did an extraordinary job of technological forecasting. He approached the "wisest and most careful men in our greatest institutions of science and learning . . . asking each in his turn to forecast . . . what, in his opinion, will have been wrought in his own field of investigation before the dawn of 2001—a century from now. These opinions (he) carefully transcribed." [b]

- Americans will be taller.
- Hot and cold air will be regulated in buildings.
- Mosquitoes, flies, and roaches "will have been practically exterminated."
- Ready-cooked meals will be bought.
- "Liquid-air-refrigerators will keep great quantities of food fresh for long intervals."
- "Coal will not be used for heating or cooking."
- Street cars will not be used in cities; instead subways and trains on "high trestles" will be used for mass transit.
- "Photographs will be telegraphed" around the world.
- Trains will run at 150 miles per hour.
- Automobiles will be cheaper than horses. [Few cars existed in 1900.]
- Everyone will try to keep fit by walking 10 miles a day.
- It will take two days to travel to England because ships will cross the ocean at more than a mile a minute using hydrofoils.
- "There will be air-ships."
- "There will be aerial war-ships and forts on wheels."
- "There will be no wild animals except in menageries."
- "Man will see around the world . . . brought within focus of cameras connected electrically with screens at opposite ends of circuits, thousands of miles at a span."
- "Wireless telephone and telegraph circuits will span the world."

- "Grand opera will be telephoned to private homes, and will sound as harmonious as though enjoyed from a theatre box."
- "Vegetables will be grown in cold weather by placing heat conducting wires in the soil and large electric lights at night."
- Black, blue, and green roses will be grown. "It will be possible to grow any flower in any color and to transfer perfume of a scented flower to another which is odorless."
- "Strawberries as large as apples."
- "Peas as large as beets."
- "Fast-flying refrigerators on land and sea will bring delicious fruits from the tropics and southern temperate zones within a few days."
- Few drugs will be taken orally. Instead, drugs "will be applied directly to those organs through the skin and flesh."
- "Store purchases by tube. Pneumatic tubes, instead of store wagons, will deliver packages and bundles."
- "A university education will be free to every man and woman."

Watkins' most inaccurate predictions were:

- "There will be no C, X, or Q" in our alphabet because they are not necessary sounds in our vocabularies.
- The population of the United States will be 350,000,000 to 500,000,000.

When you consider the accuracy of John Watkins' predictions, remember that most of the innovations he discussed did not exist at that time.

---

[a] Harold G. Shane and Gary A. Sojka, "John Elfreth Watkins, Jr., Forgotten Genius of Forecasting," *The Futurist,* October 1982.
[b] John Elfreth Watkins, Jr., "What May Happen in the Next Hundred Years," *The Ladies' Home Journal,* December 1900.

The art of forecasting requires subjective judgment and opinions of others concerning future trends, tastes, and technological changes. In this section, we present three methods for subjective forecasting: the jury of executive opinion, sales force composite, and formal survey methods. As we will see, these methods are often as expensive, and in some cases, more expensive than the causal modeling methods of econometrics and MARIMA. Nonetheless, for long-term forecasting, these often represent the most cost-effective methods of planning.

There are many informal applications of subjective methods in short-term forecasting. Subjective methods are used rather informally in routine forecasting when estimating the effects of new product introductions, promotions, price changes, competition, and so on. For example, a product manager might subjectively estimate that demand will be 50 percent higher in May because of special promotional effects. Because these subjective methods are used to adjust quantitative forecasts, they are presented in Chapter 17. For now, let's consider more formal methods of long-term, subjective forecasting.

Jury of Executive Opinion

A **jury of executive opinion** is a forecast generated during a meeting of executives. This method is sometimes called a *panel consensus method* and is based on the assumption that the consensus of several experts yields a better forecast than a single expert's opinion. In this method, open communication and interaction is encouraged. A very simple example of subjective forecasting is illustrated by a group of executives forecasting next year's sales as an average of their individual estimates:

$$\text{Next year's sales} = \frac{\begin{array}{c}\text{Executive 1}\\\text{forecast}\end{array} + \begin{array}{c}\text{Executive 2}\\\text{forecast}\end{array} + \ldots + \begin{array}{c}\text{Executive 8}\\\text{forecast}\end{array}}{8} \qquad (15\text{-}1)$$

$$= \frac{400 + 600 + \ldots + 600}{8} = 533$$

This is a very simplified example of what can be a much more involved process. The following characteristics are common to this approach:

1. Face-to-face discussion: This method uses open dialogue between jury members to arrive at a forecast. The final forecast may be a composite of the subjective values that are combined objectively, as in Equation 15–1, or some form of consensus.

2. Diversity of the jury: The jury should be composed of individuals from several different functional areas. This diversity makes complementary expertise possible. Thus, through jury interaction, the final forecast may be more insightful than the sum of the individual forecasts had there been no discussion.

One of the greatest advantages of this approach is its simplicity. Another significant advantage is the expertise and diversity that results from having a jury of experts or executives make predictions. Their complementary perspectives greatly enhance the effectiveness of the deliberations.

Offsetting the advantages of this approach are the disadvantages of bias induced by the influence of one or more members who might be managers of others in the group. That is, the open discussion might yield forecasts that are influenced (i.e., biased) by the social pressures of group dynamics and therefore may not reflect an objective consensus. Another disadvantage is that there are no generally accepted methods of combining or having competing forecasts converge on a final forecast. For example, after open discussion, the members of the jury might be asked to record their forecasts and have an average calculated, as in Equation 15–1. However, we have seen many situations in which an attempt is made to reach a consensus through less than free discussions: The estimate of the dominant person becomes the final opinion of the jury. Also, we have seen many meetings where through an attempt to build consensus the opinions

An Application of the Jury of Executive Opinion: Should Western College Offer an Executive MBA?

A west coast school of business is planning to offer an executive MBA (EMBA) program in its home city. As part of the planning process, eight human resource managers (HRM) from four large and four small corporations are assembled to discuss the EMBA market potential. While not representative of eight different functional areas, these managers represent the diverse firms in the geographic area. Because these individuals are active in the education and training of employees and because they are part of a local HRM network, their opinions are considered expert. These experts are asked to answer three questions:

1. How many qualified employees from their companies might be approved to take this EMBA program?

2. How large is the market for this EMBA program? That is, what are the anticipated enrollments for this degree?

3. What type of executive educational program has the greatest probability of success in this market?

These individuals are peers in the HR community, and an open and objective dialogue on this topic is expected. After some discussion, the group reaches the following conclusions:

1. Students from upper management represent a low demand for this MBA because of the success of several other EMBA programs in the market. Also, the low airfare to a well-known university to the south makes competition particularly strong.

2. The demand for an EMBA is high from low management, but financial support for these managers is low—few will get funding from their sponsoring corporations.

3. The demand for an EMBA may be skewed to less qualified candidates who do not have adequate prerequisite undergraduate degrees. Thus, the quality-oriented institution may not be able to attract enough qualified candidates.

4. Based on (1), (2), and (3), the group concludes that the market for an EMBA is saturated and thus competition will be high and the probability of financial and academic success low.

5. The group recommends enhancing the current night MBA program and offering short introductory, refresher, and contemporary courses for all executives in the community.

---

of key experts were diluted or the generation of averages was mistakenly avoided. These considerations emphasize the art needed for good collective decision making. If there is no vote or average calculated, then be careful when you assess the "consensus."

In addition to the problems of achieving good group averages or unbiased discussions, this method, like many qualitative methods, is costly because it uses the valuable time of executives. For more information about organizing groups for generating qualitative forecasts, see Sniezek (1989); for information about the use of product management in sales forecasting, see Edmundson, Lawrence, and O'Connor (1988); and finally, for information about the tendency of individuals to be biased by recent events, particularly dramatic events and outliers, see DeBondt and Thaler (1985).

Sales Force Composite Methods

Because they work closest with the customer and their geographic markets, salespersons are an important source of forecasting information. Part of their job is anticipating customer demands, and therefore they have insights into the trends occurring in their territories. Consequently, when possible, the insights and estimates of salespersons should be inputs to the forecasting process. The easiest way to include their input is to ask them for estimates of sales in their territory; then, these forecasts can be aggregated to a divisional or corporate-wide forecast. The aggregating principles of Chapter 17 can be applied to these regional forecasts. That is, bottom-up forecasts of the sales force can be rolled up and compared with other forecasts, including those of causal, time series analysis, or a jury of executive opinion.

Aggregating Sales Force Composites

Figure 15–2 illustrates the results of a sales force composite in the bottom row of the pyramid. These forecasts are summed in the second level (i.e., Regional Sales) of the pyramid using the principles of Chapter 17.

FIGURE 15–2

Aggregating sales force composite forecasts

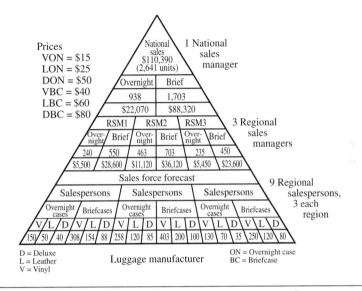

The advantages of **sales force composite methods** are the timeliness of opinions and their disaggregated regional forecasts. One of the disadvantages of this method is the tendency for salespersons to be very optimistic; thus, there is often a positive bias in the estimates from the sales force. In contrast to this bias, salespersons might be worried about meeting optimistic forecasts or quotas based on their forecast, in which case there will be a tendency for the sales force to inject a negative bias into forecasts. In many cases, carefully worded questionnaires can offset these biases. In addition, when there is trust between management and the sales force, more objective results are obtained. As a double check of individual forecasts, the sales manager can review the forecasts of those reporting to him or her and adjustments made where necessary.

An additional disadvantage of this method is that the sales force may not be aware of new developments or the condition of the macroeconomy. Also, the attributes of a good salesperson may not be those of a good forecaster. Salespersons have a tendency to generalize what may have occurred during a recent sales call. Judicious screening of forecasts can offset some of these problems.

Marketing Research and Survey Methods   We might view survey methods as extension of the sales force composite. However, in **marketing research,** actual and potential customers are surveyed statistically to estimate product demands, desirable attributes, and so on. These survey methods, which are studied in marketing research courses, use much larger sample sizes than the sales force and executive opinion methods. Marketing research is characterized by a systematic, formal, and objective application of the scientific method to estimate market data. Formal hypotheses are proposed and tested using a variety of statistical methods applied to data collected from e-mail, mail, telephone, or personal surveys.

A Simple Composite Forecast

The author surveyed an operations management class, asking students what percentage of workers in the United States were satisfied with their jobs. The average of the 26 students was 41.5 percent, varying from a low of 10 percent to a maximum of 80 percent. Because all students were currently working, it was assumed that they had insights into this question. Their estimate was surprisingly close to that of the Louis Harris poll reported below.

Harris Poll on Job Satisfaction

A worldwide poll asked workers if they were satisfied with their jobs. The following were the responses by country.

Country	Percent
United States	43
Canada	39
Japan	17

Source: Louis Harris and Associates, about 1993.

The types of surveys used depend on a number of considerations, including the number of customers, geographic dispersion, buyer behavior, and the probability of responses to different survey methods. If there are a large number of customers who buy small quantities of products, then statistical sampling methods can be used to survey them. In contrast, if there are a few very large customers, then significant time and effort can be expended in maintaining strong relationships, including the sharing of their forecasts with suppliers and customers. Recent sole-sourcing efforts of supply chain management, Just-In-Time, and quick response have made the sharing of forecast data more acceptable.

Frequently, a single marketing research survey may be conducted to fulfill several alternative purposes, thus providing great value to a variety of functions in an organization. An obvious disadvantage of marketing research is its cost. However, when the benefits are of strategic importance, then several functional areas can participate in the costs and benefits. Finally, marketing research is a natural fit for forecasting new product demand. We suggest several references for a more in-depth study of marketing research methods, Aaker et al. 1995 and Green and Tull 1978.

Exploratory Forecasting Methods

> "If we had a law that anybody who drilled a dry well would be shot, very few wells would be drilled. Our tolerance of dry wells does not seem to extend to research projects, which are always expected to gush."
>
> Kenneth Boulding (1910–1993)
> Economist

The purpose of exploratory forecasting methods is just that—to explore alternative futures. Exploratory forecasting methods can be used for a wide variety of forecasting applications. For example, a country may be interested in providing a higher standard of living for its citizens, a state in better economic development, a city in improving its viability, a firm in maintaining or improving profitability, an individual in ensuring that his or her life has been spent effectively.

This section briefly presents a variety of exploratory methods, including scenario analysis, Delphi method, cross impact analysis, and historical analogy methods.

Scenario Analysis

"Wisdom consists not so much in knowing what to do in the ultimate as in knowing what to do next."

Herbert Hoover (1874–1964)
37th president of the United States

The purpose of **scenario analysis** is to anticipate and influence future events so as to plan more effectively. In the scenario planning, we attempt to do the following:

1. Identify the interactions and integrative effects of several trends or events.
2. Avoid over- and under-estimating trends and the consequences of new or anticipated technological developments.
3. Provide several forecasts that are consistent with each other.

Through scenarios, we hope to predict how alternative futures will occur and to identify what actions might be taken to support or modify these alternatives. Obviously, our purposes is to attenuate negative outcomes and amplify positive ones.

The alternative scenarios of the future are based on assumptions such as population trends, changing product demands, technological improvements, and demographic changes. These scenarios present alternative courses of actions that can be taken by decision makers. Also, the results of these assessments are used to identify the scenario that will most likely occur.

By generating alternative scenarios, management has a better chance of choosing the right course of action under uncertainty as well as having a better chance of reacting to unlikely events that were identified in the scenario.

The generation of scenarios about possible futures is sometimes not thought of as a method of forecasting. However, it is an essential method for long-term forecasting, a method that should be (but may not be) used frequently in strategic planning. However, the writing of scenarios requires a breadth of knowledge and imagination greater than that needed for the typical quantitative and qualitative forecasting method. The box about John E. Watkins, Jr., presented earlier in this chapter, exemplifies the output of a simple scenario analysis, even though Watkins would not have used that term.

Often, scenario analysis is followed by discussions among experts who were not involved with the development of the scenario. This group can more objectively validate or modify the original scenario. For example, the generation of the scenarios might be done by staff planners and the subsequent discussion by top management. This procedure stimulates the interplay of theoretical possibilities, management insights, and intuitions. Through such forward-thinking exercises, the organization will be better prepared for the future.

While there is no standardized way to write a scenario, just as there is no standardized way of writing a book, the steps should include the following:

1. Identify the purpose of the scenario.

What organizational goals are being supported or achieved through this scenario?

2. Identify the system being modeled.

What are the bounds of the system? What are the parts of the system? What are the relationships between the parts? What trends are expected to continue influencing the parts? How will they change? Are there trends that can be modified? What decisions must be made and when, to influence the trends? What decision makers can influence the parts and relationships?

3. Determine alternative technologies of the future.

When and how will the technologies develop? How do the parts of the system change based on these technologies? How do the relationships between the parts change?

4. Explore alternative scenarios.

For alternative technologies and relationships, determine the timing of events and activities and what can be influenced by decisions. Determine if these alternative sequences of events are internally consistent.

5. Write the scenarios.

Develop the alternative series of events and decisions for steps (1) to (4) that seem plausible and relevant to the purpose of the study.

Consider the following examples:

- Royal Dutch/Shell has successfully used scenarios since the early 1970s as part of its strategic planning process, and Shell has better forecasts than other major companies.
- Early in the 1980s, the Anglo-American Corporation of South Africa assembled a group of international experts to investigate South Africa's future through scenarios.
- The Dutch Central Planning Bureau, a government agency that normally used econometrics and time series analyses, used scenarios to generate 25-year global futures.

In addition to these applications, Schoemaker has developed scenarios in a variety of settings with clients in environmental planning, health care cost containment and regulatory control, electric utilities, financial services, and R&D (Schoemaker, 1995). To better understand such applications, consider "A Simple Scenario" in the accompanying box.

An advantage of scenarios is that they provide a framework to simplify and reduce the large number of possible events and factors and their relationships. These are put into a smaller number of possible alternatives—that is, the many possible alternatives yield several scenarios that tell how the various events might interact under differing conditions. If the relationships between the events are well known, then these can be modeled formally (e.g., by quantitative models) or informally. Part of the scenario process is to evaluate each scenario for consistency and reasonableness. For example, in our Third World automobile trip, it is illogical to have mud roads, high-speed auto travel, and high precipitation all at the same time. While all possible events might not be defined initially, generating a detailed and realistic narrative of the possible scenarios will help identify events that you might otherwise overlook. The combination of adverse roads and weather conditions highlights the need for a suitable vehicle (e.g., one with four-wheel drive), communications abilities (e.g., radio communications), winches, and other devices for extricating your vehicle. These, in turn, highlight the need to start acquiring suitable equipment and licenses.

Advantages of Scenarios.   Scenarios are very beneficial in planning, particularly when the following conditions exist:

- There is great complexity in future uncertainties.
- Objective information is not available to reduce these uncertainties.
- The organization feels competitive pressure to innovate.

A Simple Scenario Example: An Automobile Trip through a Third World Country

Assume that you are planning an automobile trip through the backwoods of a Third World country where you cannot be confident of the availability of the usual infrastructure. On previous trips to other countries, you had maps, road condition reports, motel and hotel reservations, automobile repair, and hospital locations from your local travel club. In addition, for all of your North American trips, you were confident of the availability of high-quality roads.

Unfortunately, you are not confident of all of these factors for this trip. While your past experiences are very valuable in planning, this trip has much greater uncertainty. What kinds of roads will you encounter? How will these vary with the weather? What about safety and health? What are the laws about personal protection using firearms? Despite calls to officials in the provinces you are visiting, your information is incomplete. To better plan for the uncertainties in this trip, you assemble six expert travelers from the adventure travel club you belong to. These six travelers have all taken similar trips, though none exactly like yours. You ask these individuals to help develop the assumptions of the trip and scenarios. You are particularly interested in having a safe and successful trip, without any unexpected events ruining your pleasure. To ensure success, you complete the steps listed in this chapter.

- Previous long-range planning has been unsuccessful.
- The strategic plans of the past have lacked vision.
- Technological change is expected in the industry.
- A common and easily understood approach is needed to provide diverse input.
- The opportunities for conflict and strong differences of opinion are high.
- Competitors are successfully using scenario planning.

Additional advantages of scenarios are that they consider many uncertainties at the same time. They also provide a way to consider the effects of changing several variables at one time while not keeping others constant. They try to capture the results of major events or changes in key variables. Also, scenarios go beyond purely objective relationships and include subjective considerations. They attempt to model the full spectrum of possibilities and thereby prompt decision makers to consider alternative actions. The scenario accomplishes this while clearly presenting narratives that are easy to understand. Most importantly, scenarios accomplish all this while challenging conventional thinking.

After developing scenarios, it is common practice to circulate them throughout an organization to prompt further managerial input and thought. Such input can include opinions about the validity and consistency of the scenarios and alternative actions.

Several authors, including Schnaars and Topol (1987), have questioned the value of scenarios. These authors found that the study of multiple scenarios did not improve the accuracy of judgmental sales forecasts and that quantitative forecasts were more accurate. Also, despite expectations to the contrary, the use of scenarios did not provide forecasters with better contingency plans—they were just as surprised by unexpected outcomes despite the generation of multiple scenarios. Despite the conclusions of this study, many still feel that scenario analysis is a very valuable method for deterring alternative futures and facilitating contingency planning. Brauers and Weber (1988) discuss methods for analyzing scenarios, Huss (1988) and Schoemaker (1991) study methods of implementing scenarios, and Schoemaker (1995) provides a good guide on implementing scenarios and two examples. In addition, we refer you to Joseph Martino's 1993 edition of *Technological Forecasting and Decision Making*.

Delphi Method

"The mind is a strange machine which can combine the materials offered to it in the most astonishing ways."

Bertrand Russell (1872–1970)
British philosopher

The **Delphi method** is applicable in forecasting the probability and date of future events. To generate forecasts, a group of experts is assembled to identify emerging events, their likelihood, and their probable timing. The purposes of the Delphi method include building consensus and identifying competing opinions regarding alternative futures. Frequently, a consensus forecast is agreed on at the completion of this process.

The Delphi method was first used by the Rand Corporation when working on Air Force projects; it is one of the best-known qualitative methods. It is an effective method because the structured and independent surveys of experts yield relatively unbiased estimates of alternative futures. These experts iteratively fill out questionnaires concerning the future and thereby reveal facts that are important in influencing and predicting the future. By design, the experts are segregated from each other and the questionnaires are filled out independently. The results of the first questionnaires are used to generate the next set of questions. By generating questionnaires sequentially, expert opinions can be tabulated and shared with all participants. The independence of questionnaire responses eliminates much of the bias that might take place if the experts were to openly try to influence each other.

Thus, in the first round, questions are presented to experts, who must respond in writing. Their individual responses are summarized and then sent back to the experts. Then the experts can study the results and modify their comments for the next round. Three or more rounds are made in a similar fashion. When the administrators of the method believe that the participants have adequately developed their positions, they might work as a group to further refine their answers and projections. On completion of this process, the sponsors should have a better understanding of the probabilities of future events and can use these in organizational planning.

There are many variations of the Delphi method, including those with all experts in the same general locality (e.g., same hotel but different rooms), those with the experts geographically dispersed, and video conferencing of the concluding meetings of these experts. There have been several applications via the Internet, where a central site coordinates the process. Obviously, the rapid developments in the telecommunications industry have made this method much easier and less time-consuming to execute.

As mentioned, one of the greatest advantages of the Delphi method is the unbiased way in which experts from all over the globe can share ideas and conjectures. This rapid learning process yields a synergism where the whole is greater than the sum of the parts. Thus, a well-designed Delphi exercise should yield a general consensus and relevant scenarios.

In summary, the most important characteristics of the Delphi method are:

- A group of experts is selected.
- Questions or scenarios are presented to the experts.
- The first round of responses may vary greatly because of the different perspectives of the experts.
- Through iterative sharing of response summaries, the group opinion evolves.
- If significant differences exist between the consensus and minority opinions, these differences are studied.
- While the iterative rounds often yield a consensus, a consensus is not always necessary or desirable.

Example of the Delphi Method: Assessing General Aviation Developments

Phase 1. Eight expert aeronautical engineers were asked via electronic mail to identify the major developments in general aviation aircraft that may occur in the next 50 years. (General aviation aircraft are typically smaller one- or two-engine aircraft used by nonairlines such as corporations, small businesses, the wealthy, hobbyists, and others.) The experts were asked specifically what types of engines, materials, fuselages, control surfaces, avionics, and so on were expected in the future. In addition, they were asked about the regulatory environment of the FAA in accepting these new technologies for implementation on these aircraft. These participants sent their lists and dates back to the coordinator within two days. From these responses, a list of 36 items was generated, including the expected dates of the development.

Phase 2. Electronically, the list of 36 items was sent to the participants without the initial dates and the experts were asked to refine these and identify the mean date (i.e., year) of these developments. Again, these responses were sent back to the coordinator, who compiled the results.

Phase 3. The results of Phase 2 were sent back to the participants. However, now, the consensus dates were also forwarded. Those not agreeing with the consensus dates were asked to state the reasons why they did not agree. Some items had very different dates; in these cases, the respondents were asked to explain the differences and to justify their reasons. As is typical, some of the experts, after reevaluating their estimate and positions, converged on the consensus, while others maintained their original positions. At the end of this phase, there was considerable agreement on 28 of the items but still some significant differences on eight items.

Phase 4. In order to narrow the results of Phase 3, the same process was repeated as Phase 4, with particular attention focused on the developments and dates for which there was less consensus. At the end of this phase, there was considerable agreement on 32 of the original 36 items.

The general aviation company that initiated the study was successful in identifying 32 technological adoptions, implementations, or breakthroughs that might significantly impact the general aviation industry. For the remaining four items for which there was no consensus, the company had considerable information with which to refine and analyze its position.

As we see from this example, the purpose of the Delphi method is not to estimate a single number but to provide insights and estimates of the dates of adoption of new technologies and techniques. Also, we see that the participants did not even have to reach a consensus to benefit the sponsoring company. Gordon (1986), Martino (1993) and Levary and Han (1995) further describe the use of the Delphi method.

The Copy Was Better than the Original

In the late 1970s, Xerox was concerned about the influx of Japanese competitors in the copier market. In response, Xerox sponsored a conference to determine if the Japanese were a real threat. A conference of experts concluded that "the probability of a company manufacturing a copier—in Japan or in the Unites States—at a lower cost was very slight. Any new company entering the market, the conferees concluded, would lose money because the cost of entry would be prohibitive. Only a few weeks later, however, Canon launched a low-end copier (the Model NP210) that sold at a price lower than Xerox's manufacturing costs. The conclusion reached at Xerox's conference had proved to be dangerously incorrect."

We can only infer from the reports about this conference that there was considerable bias in its conclusion because participants were "sponsored" by the company and scientific objectivity might not have been formally requested or required. Most likely, many of the participants wanted to support Xerox and the status quo.

Source: Mohan Kharbanda, "Xerox Corporation: A Case Study in Revitalizing Product Development," in *Time Based Competition,* ed. Joseph D. Blackburn (Burr Ridge, IL: Richard D. Irwin, 1991).

- Differences in opinions often support the development of several scenarios.
- These different scenarios are important in identifying the spectrum of possible future developments.
- Delphi participants do not meet during the iterative rounds but may do so at the end of the analysis.

Cross Impact Analysis

There are many situations where developments in one field of knowledge or technology affect another. To model this, **cross impact analysis** estimates the effects of several related future events on the probability of another event such as the development of a new technology. Cross impact models formally define the dependence of one or more forecasts on one or more other forecasts. Using this method, we can assess the combined effects using the probabilities of their cross occurrence and therefore the probability and time of the new technology.

Cross impact analysis, which is often used with the Delphi method or scenario analysis, is discussed in detail by Helmer (1977) and Martino (1993). This method recognizes that the chance of one technology being developed is very much dependent on the development of other technologies or events. For example, if we were interested in the price of dairy products in the next decade, then the views of agricultural economists, Federal Reserve economists, farmers, and biologists are important in determining the quantity and price of milk. The essence of this method is to ask questions such as "If A happens, then what will happen to B?" This sounds very much like a formal conditional probability statement; it is this and a lot more.

Because cross impact analysis attempts to define the interrelationships between possible future events, it requires an understanding of a very broad system of interrelationships. Sometimes, we may have to look for these less obvious linkages and survey experts of diverse fields of knowledge. We hope to achieve accurate long-term forecasts as well as better decisions as the future unfolds and anticipated events occur. Some of the information needed to complete this analysis can be obtained from Delphi or scenario analysis. Consequently, the cost of application can be particularly high. Nonetheless, this method can be very cost effective for strategic decisions. Remember, our goal includes getting insights into alternative futures, including possible events and their probabilities. Experts should be able to shed some light on the future and the sensitivity of future events to other future events.

The advantages of cross impact analysis are that it forces experts to consider the interactions of two or more technologies. Because space does not permit a full development of this method we refer you to Martino (1993).

Analogy Methods

The use of historical **analogy** is a popular method of making short- to long-term forecasts of products or technologies that have characteristics similar to other products or technologies. For example, the demand during the introduction and growth of a new product might be expected to follow the demand patterns of similar products. Similar patterns are expected in the products because of similarities in their characteristics, uses, and customers. The use of historical analogies can be very effective in modeling the expected seasonal demand for a new product that is either replacing an old one or that will have the same seasonal demand pattern as an established product. However, our interest here is in longer term uses of analogies.

Examples of analogies include modeling the introduction of air travel by relating it to rail travel, automobile travel related to horse and buggy travel, personal computer (PC) adoptions related to color television adoptions, PC adoptions related to how early computer games were adopted, and so forth.

The modeling of analogies can be done using regression analysis and the concept of cross correlations when sufficient data exists regarding the new technology. However, when little quantitative data exists for the new technology, then subjective estimates are made about the adoption (i.e., timing and intensity) of the new technology. Let's consider the case where sufficient data exists.

In many cases, the univariate information available to forecast a variable is less than the information that can be discerned by relating one variable (e.g., the development of a new technology) to that of a past variable (e.g., the behavior of an old technology). Analogies using correlations and analysis fulfill this purpose; they can forecast the patterns of a new technology by relating them to those of existing technologies. Simply, if there is theoretical justification for believing an association (i.e., correlation) exists between two or more variables, then regression analysis or some other form of curve fitting can be used to model that association. These methods include identification of relationships using lead–lag correlations (i.e., cross correlations) as developed in the appendix to Chapter 3, learning curves of technological progress functions, as developed in most operations management textbooks, and the use of leading indicators, as developed in Chapter 14 of this book.

Once an association is established, it can be used to predict future values of the dependent variable (i.e., new technology) as a function of past values of the independent variable (i.e., old technology). The nature of the relationship between these variables is often assumed to be linear. Consider the simple correlation analysis illustrated in the "Analogy Using Correlation Analysis" box.

Trend Analysis

Trend analysis is a popular method of long-term forecasting. We have studied trend analysis several places in this book. This method works reasonably well when the linear or nonlinear trends of the past persist into the future. However, there are many situations where this is not true, and the many poor extrapolations of trends attest to the inappropriateness of the assumption of persistence. It is because trend projections are not effective that we need the many other methods of qualitative forecasting presented here.

We have used regression, ARIMA modeling, exponential smoothing, double smoothing, and decomposition methods to forecast trends. If the trends of the past persist, then this is an effective forecasting method. However, we expect many trends such as technological growth and product demands to undergo nonlinear growth, described by an S-curve analysis. In those situations, we should investigate the use of nonlinear S-curve functions as good predictors of future behavior, a topic we address in the last section of this chapter.

Nominal Group Process

The **nominal group process** (NGP) is another method similar to the Delphi method. This method uses a panel of experts who initially and independently write down their opinions on the probability of new technologies of developments. This information is then shared with all the experts. In contrast to the Delphi method, the NGP then involves open discussion of each member's opinion. Through open discussion, it is hoped that a consensus will be reached. To facilitate that process, a discussion leader is chosen. Obviously, the discussion leader's approach and opinion may affect the group's consensus. This is not as likely with the Delphi method, which involves little open discussion.

Case Study Method

In the **case study method,** studies are made of past and current technologies and the manner in which they evolved. After describing these actual cases, the similarities and differences between the potential new technology and the case studies are noted.

Analogy Using Correlation Analysis: European Market Penetration as a Function of American Penetration

A Japanese pharmaceutical company hopes to successfully create a new market for its products in the new European Economic Union. Fifteen years ago, it entered the U.S. market and has been very successful in gaining a significant share of that market. The firm believes that it will be as successful in the EU as it was in the United States. From the following information, forecast the market shares of the Japanese company in Europe.

	Market Share (percent)		
Year*	Actual United States	Forecast Europe	Actual Five Years Later[†]
1	1%	1%	.9%
2	2	2	1.8
3	3	3	3.1
4	5	5	4.9
5	8	8	9.0
6	10	10	
7	10.4	10.4	
8	10.8	10.8	
9	11.2	11.2	
10	12.6	12.6	
11	12.7	12.7	
12	12.8	12.8	
13	12.9	12.9	
14	13.0	13.0	
15	13.0	13.0	

* Year after entering the market.   [†] Five years after entering market.

High Definition TV Finally Arrives

"In the next six months, and maybe even sooner, you will be able to . . . have (TV) pictures that are made up of approximately 1,000 lines, instead of the prewar 525 lines."*

Interestingly, these comments after World War II from *Popular Science* were made in November 1945 by Dr. Peter C. Goldmark of CBS. Today, televisions still use the pre–World War II 525-line standard referred to by Dr. Goldmark. We hope that 50 years after his prediction, we will have high definition TVs with pictures of approximately 1,000 lines. We suspect that HDTV will be very popular near the turn of the century; however, we are uncertain of how rapidly the prices of these TVs will fall to current levels. We still remember our parents paying $600 for a very small color TV in 1959 with 1959 dollars.

* Wendi E. Black, "Looking Back," *Popular Science,* November 1995, p. 104.

Key Technologies for the 21st Century

Recently, *Scientific American* provided an insightful listing of "Key Technologies for the 21st Century" in its 150th anniversary issue. The table of contents of that publication provides an overview of future technological developments.

Information Technologies

    Microprocessors in 2020

    Wireless networks

    All-optical networks

    Artificial intelligence

    Virtual reality

    Satellites for a developing world

Transportation

    High-speed rail: Another golden age?

    The automobile: Clean and customized

    Evolution of the commercial airliner

    21st-century spacecraft

Medicine

    Gene therapy

    Artificial organs

    Future contraceptives

Machines, Materials, and Manufacturing

    Self-assembling materials

    Engineering microscopic machines

    Intelligent materials

    High-temperature superconductors

    Robotics in the 21st century

Energy and Environment

    Solar energy

    Fusion

    Industrial ecology of the 21st century

    Technology for sustainable agriculture

    Outline for an ecological economy

Source: John Rennie, Editor in Chief, "Key Technologies for the 21st Century," *Scientific American* 273, no. 3, (September 1995).

Based on what is generalizable from the case study, more enlightened predictions may be made about the development of the new technology.

Analytic Hierarchy Process

The **analytic hierarchy process** (AHP) is a general methodology for identifying the relationship between variables using pairwise comparisons. It models new technologies by making comparisons between the new and old technologies. Several experts are asked to make pairwise comparisons, and based on these estimates, a mathematical relationship can be identified. Applications of AHP can be found in textbooks on management science.

Normative Forecasting Methods

> "Our life is what our thoughts make it."
>
> Marcus Aurelius (121–180)
> Roman Emperor

Normative methods of forecasting are methods for determining how desired futures might be made to occur. These methods are based on the premise that the future can be influenced much more than many assume is possible. Organizations can achieve desirable futures by first defining these futures and then by taking the actions necessary to achieve those futures. In this section, we briefly present two normative methods, relevance trees and systems dynamics.

Relevance Trees (RT)   **Relevance trees** use methods and concepts similar to decision theory and decision trees to measure the effectiveness of future goals and to identify what is needed to achieve those desired goals. Their purpose is to identify the long-range developments that are most important to accomplishing desired goals. Relevance trees have been used in evaluating national objectives for military, space, and medical developments.

RTs are a good approach to technological forecasting based on a normative view of goals. The goals and purposes of a new technology are disaggregated into lower level goals and purposes in a decision tree or bill of material format. By doing so, the hierarchical structure of the technological development is identified for better planning and control. The probabilities of achieving the technology and higher level objectives can be better assessed and managed through this method. Thus, these probabilities can be used to forecast the probability of achieving the stated goals.

A Relevance Tree Example.   A midwestern school wants to be known as a preeminent executive business school. It has assembled a group of business executives and internationally known business educators. As a starting point, this group is presented with a scenario that describes the desired future. Also included in the scenario is a brief description of what the state of executive education may be like in the future. This scenario serves as an initial stimulus to help the experts identify the important developments and resources necessary to achieve international preeminence.

Using the scenario as a basis, the experts develop a relevance tree, part of which is shown in Figure 15–3. This tree shows the relationship between the objective and subobjectives, much as does a product structure tree (i.e., bill of materials). It is used to identify the subobjectives that are necessary to achieve the overall goal of the school. There can be considerable debate on the structure and precedence of the elements in this tree. Consequently, the coordinator must help resolve the conflicts in constructing the tree. For brevity, the RT of Figure 15–3 shows only six levels, and some of those levels are not fully developed.

By developing this tree, the experts become familiar with the many subobjectives that are necessary to achieve the main objective. After constructing this tree, the experts assign relevance numbers to each element, typically through a secret ballot. These relevance numbers are averaged, discussed, and modified by the participants.

FIGURE 15–3

Relevance tree for executive education

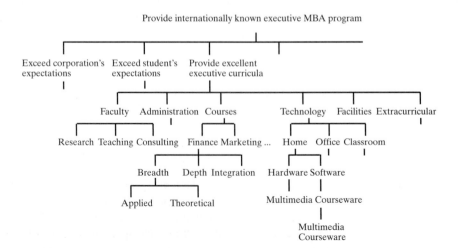

The relevance numbers for each element in the tree are added up the tree to compute a total relevance number. The relevance number of each element is multiplied by the relevance numbers of each element in the line above it to identify those parts of the tree that are most influential in achieving the goals of the organization. Those interested in more information about RTs should consult Martino (1993) or Makridakis, Wheelwright, and McGee (1983).

Systems Dynamics

Jay Forester of MIT developed **systems dynamics** in 1957 to study the dynamics of simple and complex systems using differential equations. Through this approach, the complex dynamic behavior of a process can be modeled. This and similar continuous simulation methodologies have been updated in recent years through the use of software systems such as I-Think™, SIMAN™, SIMSCRIPT™, and other continuous simulation programs. In fact, spreadsheet programs are capable of modeling many of the relationships of systems dynamics. If the assumptions and relationships modeled in these systems are correct, then the output provides insightful information.

The construction of these models may or may not be supported by significant empirical research. As Forester has stated, much of the knowledge of the world exists in the minds of people. Systems dynamics software makes it possible to quantify the intuition and knowledge of experts and to make this knowledge public and usable by others.

Senge (1990), and Martino (1993) provide further information about the use of systems dynamics in modeling long-term relationships.

S-Curves of Growth

"Businessmen go down with their businesses because they like the old ways so well they cannot bring themselves to change . . . Seldom does the cobbler take up with a new-fangled way of soling shoes and seldom does the artisan willingly take up with new methods in his trade."

Henry Ford
My Life and Work, 1922

In this section, we develop forecasting methods called *S-curves*—also called **growth, saturation,** or **substitution** curves—by studying Gompertz and logistics curves. An understanding of these curves is of strategic importance to all organizations. Thus, the potential benefits from S-curve analysis makes them an important tool of modern decision making. Possibly no other concept presents more persuasive reasons for encouraging innovations in organizations than S-curves.

Technological Life Cycles

The life cycles we associate with products are often related to **technology life cycles.** As do products, technologies usually have life cycles composed of four distinct phases:

1. Slow growth during an embryonic stage.
2. Rapid growth.
3. Slowing growth in the mature phase.
4. Decline during a final phase.

Growth curve identification, estimation, and diagnostics are very similar to the other quantitative methods of this book. While similar, this method is not as objective or as empirically driven as other methods because, as Martino (1993) points out, expert opinion is needed to identify the upper limit on growth curves in order to empirically derive their shape. However, in many applications, the upper limit of the growth curve is known to be 1. This is true because growth curves for predicting market share or the rate of technological substitution have upper limits of 100 percent. Whether the upper limit is 1 or not, growth curves provide important predictions of when new products or technologies will replace existing products or technologies.

In general, the modeling of growth curves is important because they can help identify the timing of each phase of the life cycle. Being able to predict the growth, maturity, and decline of a technology provides significant strategic advantage. Analyses of many time series have shown that as a new technology develops, its initial growth is at first slow. This results from the difficulties of solving technical problems (adaptations) as well as of market acceptance (adoptions). Fortunately, new technologies and innovations evolve in predictable patterns of the S-curves shown in Figures 15–4 to 15–6.

After an initial slow growth, the barriers to adaptations and adoptions decline and there is rapid growth. Frequently, this rapid growth cannot be sustained because there are physical laws and relationships that define the upper limit of that technology. The mature technology has slow growth because as scientists improve the process, diminishing marginal returns occur. Finally, sometimes as a result of these diminishing marginal returns, the search for other technologies intensifies. Consequently, new technologies are discovered and replace the old technology. Thus, a different growth curve soon describes the dominant technology, a situation illustrated in Figure 15–4.

FIGURE 15–4

Saturation of old and substitution of new technology

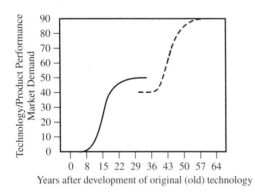

Years after development of original (old) technology

FIGURE 15–5

Capacity of worldwide nuclear power NUPOWER.DAT

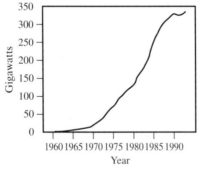

Source: World Watch Institute

FIGURE 15–6

Two S-curves
INFANSUR.DAT
MICROPRO.DAT

a. Newborn infant survivals per 1,000 births

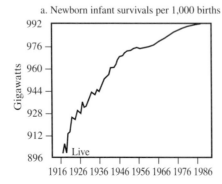

b. Density of Intel microprocessors

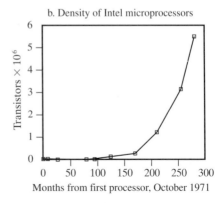

Months from first processor, October 1971

Figure 15–5 illustrates the worldwide capacity for nuclear power in gigawatts. As shown there, this curve starts with a small increasing slope, increases rapidly in the middle, then flattens out as it approaches a maximum value. This first stage represents a period of experimentation and slow growth; the second stage results from the rapid exploitation of the technology; and the third stage has slow growth because of the saturation of demands for this technology.

Consider Figures 15–6a and b, which illustrate the same behavior as the nuclear power example in Figure 15–5 but for two different technologies, Intel microprocessor densities and U.S. newborn infant survival rates. The similar behavior of these two phenomena are indicative of the change from technological growth and evolution.

Substitution Curves   When old and new technologies compete in the marketplace, this interaction may follow an S-curve. Thus, a common use of growth curves is to model the market share of existing products and the technologies they embody. The new technology or product has to overcome the older technology's momentum, and its adoption is slow early in its life cycle. Because the characteristics of the new technology are uncertain and users view the old technology as tried and true, the new technology must overcome problems of technical and market acceptance. However, as users become familiar with the new technology, the barriers to adoption and costs decline. These cost declines result from cumulative learning and experiences, commonly called learning curves (Chase and Aquilano 1995). Thus, users substitute the new technology for the old. This takes place at an accelerating pace until the upper limits of demand (customer uses) or supply (technological capabilities) are approached.

When forecasting market shares, the size of the total market can be forecasted using some general method and then the rate of substitution of one product or technology for the other can be forecasted using S-curves. Then, the substitution growth curve in percentages can be multiplied times the estimate of the total market to obtain a forecast of demand for the product.

Modeling Growth Curves   Modeling growth requires past data on the measure of interest, either market shares, product penetration, technology usage, or technology performance. The appropriate growth curve can then be fitted to this data. When the growth is expected to continue, the past behavior can be extrapolated into the future.

Growth curve models are based on the following assumptions:

1. The correct growth curve (i.e., nonlinear function) has been selected.
2. The past function is indicative of the future.
3. The estimated maximum level of the curve is correct.

This last assumption may need some explanation.

Because the nonlinearity of S-curves cannot be transformed to linear equivalents directly using, for example, logarithms, some manipulations of the relationships are necessary before estimating coefficients using linear regression. As Figures 15–7 and 15–8 illustrate, Gompertz and logistics S-curves are determined by three coefficients, a, b, and L, the asymptotic maximum value. To achieve a linear model solvable by least squares regression it is necessary to choose L prior to estimating the coefficients a and b. Consequently, the type of S-curve and its upper limit should be selected very carefully. Because the upper limit is so important, S-curves are often called *asymptotic* growth curves because each approaches an upper limit. See Martino (1993) and Girifalco (1991) for more information on this process, if necessary.

FIGURE 15–7

*Gompertz curves showing
functions of a and b*

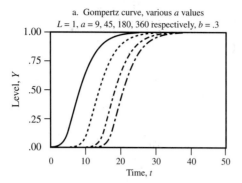

a. Gompertz curve, various *a* values
$L = 1$, $a = 9, 45, 180, 360$ respectively, $b = .3$

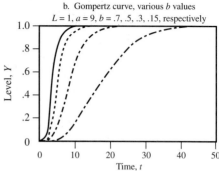

b. Gompertz curve, various *b* values
$L = 1$, $a = 9$, $b = .7, .5, .3, .15$, respectively

FIGURE 15–8

*Logistics curves showing
functions of a and b*

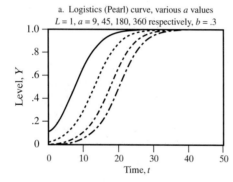

a. Logistics (Pearl) curve, various *a* values
$L = 1$, $a = 9, 45, 180, 360$ respectively, $b = .3$

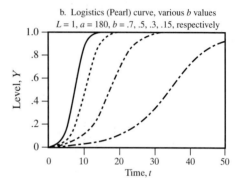

b. Logistics (Pearl) curve, various *b* values
$L = 1$, $a = 180$, $b = .7, .5, .3, .15$, respectively

The two most common types of S-curves are the Gompertz curve (see Figure 15–7) and Pearl–Reed, also known as the logistics curve shown in Figure 15–8. The Gompertz curve is discussed first, then the logistics curve.

Gompertz Curves

The **Gompertz curve** is named for the English actuary Benjamin Gompertz who developed it in his studies of growth. Equation 15–2 and Figure 15–7 illustrate this growth curve:

$$Y_t = Le^{-ae^{-bt}} \tag{15–2}$$

where

$$L = \text{Upper limit of } Y_t$$
$$e = \text{Natural number } 2.718282\ldots$$
$$a \text{ and } b = \text{Coefficients describing the curve}$$

The Gompertz curve ranges from zero to L as t varies from $-\infty$ to $+\infty$. As we will see, the inflection point of the Gompertz curve occurs where $t = \ln(a)/L$, which is where $Y_t = L/e$. As shown in Figure 15–7b, the Gompertz curve is not symmetrical. Also as shown in Figure 15–7a and b, the a value in Equation 15–2 determines the location of the curve, while the b value determines the shape of the curve. Consider the method for fitting these.

Because of its nonlinearity, the Gompertz is most easily estimated using the following procedure. First, after determining L, the maximum value of Y_t, Y_t is converted to y_t:

$$y_t = \ln(\ln(L/Y_t)) \tag{15–3}$$

TABLE 15–1   Microelectronic Density over Time (MICRO.DAT)

Year	1	2	3	4	5	6	7
Density	1	3	44	196	448	691	898
y_t	1.9587	1.7903	1.1957	.5944	−.0148	−.5943	−1.2382

Then the following relationship is fitted using OLS regression:

$$\hat{y}_t = a' + b't \tag{15–4}$$

where a' and b' are the usual regression coefficients and, while not proven here, a and b of Equation 15–2 can be determined by:

$$\ln(a) = a' \qquad \text{and} \qquad -b = b' \tag{15–5}$$

and therefore a' can be transformed to a using the following relationships:

$$a = e^{a'} \tag{15–6}$$

Thus, we have the estimated values of a and b for Equation 15–2 and forecasts can be generated. When modeling an actual time series, remember that the appropriateness of a Gompertz curve can be confirmed when a plot of y_t verus time is linear. Let's apply this method to the data of Table 15–1.

Microcircuitry Density.   A firm producing microelectronics wishes to determine the density of transistors that can be placed on integrated circuits (ICs). Table 15–1 shows the density of transistors that have been successfully etched on silicon ICs over the last seven years. Past studies by this firm have shown that the improvement in IC densities from the current photographic technology follows a Gompertz curve. Also, a plot of these observations is indicative of the embryonic and early growth stages of the Gompertz curve. The firm wants to forecast when the current technology will reach a density of 1,100 (the unit of density is not important for our purposes). Engineering physicists have determined that the maximum practical density for this technology is 1,200. Using this information, let's model the density of row 2 of Table 15–1 using a Gompertz curve, assess its fit, and then predict when this technology will reach a density of 1,100.

The transformation of the densities of Table 15–1 to y_t is completed using Equation 15–7.

$$y_t = \ln(\ln(1{,}200/Y_t)) \tag{15–7}$$

As shown in Table 15–1, y_t has a negative linear trend which is typical of y_t for Gompertz Y_t. Now let's fit the relationship between y_t and t. These results are shown in Table 15–2.

From Table 15–2, the fitted relationship is:

$$\hat{y}_t = a' + b't = 2.7518 - .5561t \tag{15–8}$$

Remembering that a' and b' can be transformed to a and b by the following:

$$\ln(a) = a' \qquad \text{and} \qquad -b = b'$$

and therefore:

$$a = e^{a'} = e^{2.7518} = 15.67020$$

TABLE 15–2   Estimated Gompertz Curve for y_t Table 5–1 (MICRO.DAT)

Dependent variable y_t—Estimation by least squares

Usable observations	7
Degrees of freedom	5
$\bar{R}^2$	.9855
Mean of dependent variable	.5274
Standard error of dependent variable	1.2086
Standard error of estimate	.1454
Sum of squared residuals	.1057
Regression $F(1, 5)$	409.4988
Significance level of F	.00000545

Coefficient	Estimate	Std Error	t-Stat	Signif
a'	2.7518	.12289	22.391	.00000330
b'	−.5561	.02748	−20.236	.00000545

TABLE 15–3   Gompertz Curve Fitted and Forecasted Densities

Year	Microelectronic Density Y_t	Fit/Forecast Y_t	Fitted Error e_t
1	1	.15	.85
2	3	6.94	−3.94
3	44	62.50	−18.50
4	196	220.44	−24.44
5	448	454.15	−6.15
6	691	687.38	3.62
7	898	871.80	26.20
8		999.10	
9		1,080.32	
10		1,129.83	
11		1,159.25	
12		1,176.46	
13		1,186.44	
14		1,192.21	
15		1,195.53	
16		1,197.43	
17		1,198.53	
18		1,199.15	
19		1,199.52	
20		1,199.72	

this yields the following Gompertz equation:

$$Y_t = \mathbf{L}e^{-ae^{-bt}} = 1{,}200e^{-15.67e^{.5561t}} \tag{15–9}$$

The results of applying Equation 15–9 are shown in columns 3 and 4 of Table 15–3. As shown, this model fits the data quite well and the density of transistors is expected to reach 1,100 sometime near the middle of year 10. Assuming that the technological improvements in this IC process follows a Gompertz curve, and the true maximum density is 1,200, then the predictions of Table 15–3 should be relatively accurate in forecasting future values of the IC densities.

Logistics (Pearl)
Curve

Having applied the Gompertz curve, consider the **logistics curve,** frequently called the Pearl or Pearl–Reed curve. This curve is illustrated in Equation 15–10 and previously in Figures 15–8a and b.

$$Y_t = \frac{L}{1 + a\mathbf{e}^{-bt}} \qquad (15\text{--}10)$$

As with the Gompertz curve, the upper limit of Y_t for the logistics curve is designated L and $\mathbf{e}$ is the base of natural logarithms. As is true for the Gompertz curve, the logistics curve ranges from 0 at $t = -\infty$ to L at $t = +\infty$. In a moment, you will see that the inflection point of this curve occurs at $t = (\ln(a))/b$, which is when $Y_t = L/2$, 50 percent of the maximum. Contrary to the Gompertz curve, the logistics curve is symmetrical about its inflection point.

The logistics curve is flexible in its ability to model different locations and shapes using a and b, respectively. As shown in Figures 15–8a and b, a positions the logistics curve on the x-axis, while b changes its shape.

The easiest way to fit a logistics curve is to first transform it to a linear function, a process requiring a known L. As is true for all growth curves, there should be some theoretical or practical basis for choosing L before the analysis starts. After L has been chosen, the logistics curve can be made linear by transforming it using natural logarithms in a procedure similar to that used with the Gompertz curve. This transformation is:

$$y_t = \ln\!\left(\frac{Y_t}{L - Y_t}\right) \qquad (15\text{--}11)$$

After transforming Y_t to y_t, run a linear regression of y_t as a function of time, t:

$$\hat{y}_t = a' + b't \qquad (15\text{--}12)$$

While not proven here, it can be shown that:

$$-\ln(a) = a' \qquad \text{and} \qquad b = b' \qquad (15\text{--}13)$$

and therefore these values can be substituted into Equation 15–10.

When applying these equations, remember that the appropriateness of a logistics curve is confirmed when a plot of y_t versus time is linear. Having developed the logistics curve, let's apply it.

Logistics Curve Application.   Table 15–4 and Figure 15–5 illustrate the available generating capacity of nuclear power in the world (NUPOWER.DAT). The shape of this curve in Figure 15–5 and a plot of y_t versus time appear to follow that of the logistics curve. Let's assume that the experts estimate that the maximum value, L, of global nuclear electricity capacity is 350 gigawatts. Using this information, let's fit a logistics curve and make projections regarding future capacities. Table 15–4 shows the transformed values of using Equation 15–14 with a maximum, L of 350.

$$y_t = \ln(Y_t/(350 - Y_t)) \qquad (15\text{--}14)$$

After calculating y_t, the linear regression of y_t as a function of time of Equation 15–14 is fitted in Table 15–5.

The relationship of Table 15–5 is quite strong.

TABLE 15–4 Y_t **and** y_t **Using**
Equation 15–14

Year	t	Y_t	y_t
1960	1	.8	−6.0788
1961	2	.9	−5.9607
1962	3	1.8	−5.2650
		⋮	
1969	10	13.0	−3.2551
1970	11	16.0	−3.0386
		⋮	
1979	20	121.0	−.6379
1980	21	135.0	−.4654
		⋮	
1989	30	321.0	2.4041
1990	31	329.0	2.7515
1991	32	326.0	2.6088
1992	33	328.0	2.7020
1993	34	337.0	3.2551

TABLE 15–5 y_t, **Transformed Gigawatts as a Function of** t

Dependent variable y_t—Estimation by least squares
Annual data from 1960 to 1993

Usable observations	34
Degrees of freedom	32
$\bar{R}^2$	.9934
Mean of dependent variable	−1.2514
Standard error of dependent variable	2.7415
Standard error of estimate	.2225
Sum of squared residuals	1.58446
Regression $F(1, 32)$	4977.210
Significance level of F	.00000000

Coeff	Estimate	Std Error	t-Stat	Signif
a'	−6.0537	.0780	−77.5739	.00000000
b'	.2744	.0039	70.5493	.00000000

The relationship of Table 15–5 is transformed to a and b using the relationship of Equation 15–13:

$$a = e^{-a'} = e^{6.05375} = 425.70644$$

$$b = b' = .2744$$

then these values can be substituted into Equation 15–10.

Table 15–6 and Figure 15–9 illustrates the fit and forecast of Y_t using the transformed coefficients of Equation 15–15.

$$\hat{Y}_t = \frac{L}{1 + ae^{-bt}} = \frac{350}{1 + 425.71e^{-.27442t}} \tag{15–15}$$

TABLE 15–6   Fitted and Forecasted Values

Year	t	Y_t	Fit/Forecast	e_t
1960	1	.8	1.078	−.278
1961	2	.9	1.418	−.518
1962	3	1.8	1.863	−.063
		⋮		
1969	10	13.0	12.336	.664
1970	11	16.0	16.053	−.052
		⋮		
1979	20	121.0	126.812	−5.811
		⋮		
1989	30	321.0	314.419	6.581
1990	31	329.0	322.281	6.718
1991	32	326.0	328.526	−2.526
1992	33	328.0	333.435	−5.435
1993	34	337.0	337.266	−.266
1994	35		340.237	
1995	36		342.530	
1996	37		344.293	
			⋮	
2001	42		348.535	
2002	43		348.885	
2003	44		349.152	
			⋮	
2019	60		349.990	

FIGURE 15–9

Capacity of worldwide nuclear power

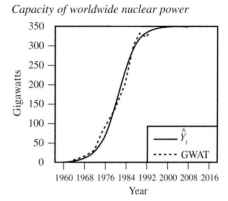

The fit and forecasts of Table 15–6 appear to be quite good. Note the importance of the maximum value, L, of 350. This value is the limit of the relationship at $t = \infty$; however, for practical purposes, that limit is reached at $t = 60$.

We have illustrated the logistics curve using natural logarithms. It is possible to use logarithms to the base 10. This yields the following equation:

$$Y_t = L/(1 + 10^{a - bt}) \tag{15–16}$$

where L is the upper limit of Y_t, as before. The coefficients a and b in Equation 15–16 are different than those of Equation 15–15 because of logarithmic base differences. The linear form of Equation 15–16 is:

$$y_t = \log_{10}\left[\frac{Y_t}{L - Y_t}\right] = -a + bt \tag{15–17}$$

When y_t is plotted versus time, it is a straight line. In Equation 15–17, the ratio of $Y_t/(L - Y_t)$ is 10 times higher for every increase in t by $1/b$. Let's refer to $1/b$ as the 10-fold time. From this fact, we can see that each $1/b$ (i.e., 10-fold) time period results in a 10-fold increases in Y_t. This yields two commonly referenced times, the 10 percent and the 90 percent of L times, Martino (1993).

Comparing Logistics (Pearl) and Gompertz Curves   Research has shown that models based on initial data for a growth curve are quite valid in later forecasts if the correct curve and upper limit have been identified. Thus, it is important to have insights into the correct form of the relationship and the maximum value of the relationship. One difference is the point of inflection, the Gompertz reaching the inflection earlier. In addition, consider the linear forms of each of these curves to better understand them.

Logistics	Gompertz
$\text{Ln}(Y/(L - Y))$	$\text{Ln}(\text{Ln}(L/Y))$
$\text{Ln}(\text{Current}/(\text{Max} - \text{Current}))$	$\text{Ln}(\text{Ln}(\text{Current}/\text{Max}))$

The logistics curve involves both Y and $(L - Y)$, the current value, and how far that current value is from the maximum. However, the Gompertz curve only involves how far the function has progressed relative to, or proportionate to, the maximum—it does not include a term denoting how close the current value is to the maximum. Figure 15–10 helps us better understand these characteristics. It illustrates fitted logistics and Gompertz curves for the global nuclear electricity capacity. As shown, the Gompertz curve grows more rapidly during the growth phase starting at point A, but then it does not grow as rapidly as the logistics curve during the maturing or saturation phase near the maximum, from B to the maximum. In contrast, during early growth, the logistics curve grows more rapidly than the Gompertz (i.e., logistics value > Gompertz value) until point A; however, the logistics value is less until point B. From point B onward, the logistics curve grows more rapidly toward the maximum than the Gompertz curve. The behavior of Figure 15–10 illustrates the difference between these two approaches.

Let's generalize these results. If, when considering the growth of a new technology, it is harder to achieve a constant improvement as we approach the maximum level, then the Gompertz curve is the best approach. However, if there are factors that assist in maintaining improvements (i.e., the slope at B), then the logistics curve is better to use. These assisting factors include momentum of the market, sustained assistance from technological improvements, and so forth.

Assuming that it is not easy to discern which of the two curves will best represent the time series, we can search for that combination of L, a, and b that fits the past data the best. However, with this practice there is always the high probability that the past will be fitted well, but because we do not understand the dynamics of the growth process, we have chosen an inferior forecasting model. Thus, care must be taken in the choices of L and type of S-curve fitted. If possible, data should include history of the item from its start. There should be theory that the growth rate varies with time and that the series is likely to reach a saturation point. For a fuller discussion of the use and fitting of these curves, see Cleary and Levenbach (1982), Girifalco (1991), Porter

FIGURE 15–10

Gompertz and logistics curves of worldwide nuclear power

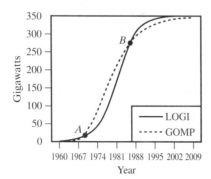

et al. (1991); and Martino (1993), who discuss general types of growth curves useful for long-term and technological forecasting.

Stability of Growth Curves

Marchetti (1983), when studying the adoption of automobiles in nine countries, found that accurate models could be identified when demand reached only 1 percent of final market demand. That is, if a model had been estimated after 1 percent of the market had been reached, then the coefficients of the model did not change much in the future as the growth continued to increase. Other studies (see Martino, 1993) have confirmed this further. Thus, even with very little data, it is possible to estimate growth curves that predict market or technological progress relatively accurately.

Summary

This chapter has presented a variety of qualitative and technological forecasting methods. We have seen that in many situations, the judgment of experts and forecasters is the only way to effectively generate alternative scenarios and forecasts, particularly when predicting long-term societal and technological changes. Even the more quantitative approaches of forecasting, S-curves, require significant subjective inputs.

The four types of long-term forecasting methods presented here are those using:

- Subjective judgment and estimates.
- Explorations of alternative futures.
- Normative models.
- S-growth curves.

Even though these methods are of strategic importance to the typical firm, they are often overlooked by those responsible for forecasting and planning. In contrast to other methods, which generate confidence intervals about forecasts, these methods are designed to represent a rich complement of information about the future.

While many firms use marketing research methods, many do not explore alternative futures, particularly as they relate to the decline and emergence of old and new products, technologies, industries, and economies. Fierce global competition from the Pacific rim, European Union, and China have made firms more aware of external threats. Consequently, there has been more interest in these methods in recent years. We need to speculate on the development of future economies, particularly those in our own hemisphere.

Related to the increased interest in competitiveness has been the greater interest in the research of Joseph Schumpeter and others. Inherent in longer term forecasting methods is the objective of identifying alternative decisions; thus, these are often more proactive than other forecasting methods.

When studying the past, three perspectives and two possible biases might occur. Familiarity with past trends may reduce the perceived uncertainty of the future when assuming persistence of these trends. Such hindsight may make the future seem more predictable than it is at the time of forecasts. In contrast, sometimes past failures negatively bias the perspective of long-range forecasters. However, the knowledge gained from the past should forearm one for a higher future success rate. Thus, one should offset such biases by objectively studying the past so that this objectivity will persist into future projections. Examining the successes and failures of the past, including past variability and unpredictability, are necessary to help us construct better scenarios.

Why Technology Forecasts Often Fail

Professor Nathan Rosenberg presents an interesting explanation of why technology forecasting is so difficult. He identifies six general causes of uncertainty in long-term forecasting.

Potential Uses.   All of the potential uses of new technologies are not known at the time of their development; thus, often the success of a new technology is dependent on the unknown, even though several other uses have been anticipated.

Complementary Innovations.   The success of a new technology is often dependent on the emergence of a complementary technology. For example, the inventors of the laser at Bell Laboratories did not recognize its telecommunications importance because fiber optics had not yet been developed.

Systems Integration.   Some new technologies do not yield spectacular breakthroughs quickly because the system use does not exist. Consider that cellular radio was developed in the 60s, but it did not become a market success until the microelectronics and telecommunications revolutions provided a cost-effective systems integration.

Problem-Solving Myopia.   Inventions are often solutions to more problems than those that stimulated the discovery. Thus, developers often overlook other applications of new inventions. For example, the steam engine was invented in the 18th century to pump water out of mines, not to power locomotives or ocean liners.

Passing the "Needs Test."   A new technology must not only be technologically better but also economically so. If the new technology is not economical, then it will not become widespread. Unfortunately, changes in social customs are very difficult to predict; thus, new technologies can fail for many socioeconomic reasons.

Competing with the Past.   The invention of a new way of doing something often stimulates improvements in the old technology, which may delay the adoption of the new technology.

Adapted from Nathan Rosenberg, "Why Technology Forecasts Often Fail," *The Futurist*, July–August 1995, pp. 15–21.

Recently, many companies did not plan for the discontinuities that have affected their viability because they did not try to innovate. As planners and long-term forecasters, we have to try to define alternative futures so that contemporary decisions build a viable future. While doing so, we must try to offset reasons why such forecasts fail. To this end, it is fitting to refer to the "Why Technology Forecasts Often Fail" box so that we will fail less.

Key Terms

aggregating sales force composites
analogy methods
analytic hierarchy process
case study method
cross–impact analysis
Delphi method
Gompertz curves
growth curves
judgmental forecasting
jury of executive opinion
logistics (Pearl) curve
long-term forecasting

marketing research and formal surveys
nominal group process
qualitative forecasting
relevance trees
sales force composite methods
saturation curves
scenario analysis
substitution curves
systems dynamics
technological forecasting
technological life cycles
trend analysis

Key Formulas

Jury of executive opinion:

$$\text{Next year's sales} = \frac{\begin{array}{c}\text{Executive 1} \\ \text{forecast}\end{array} + \begin{array}{c}\text{Executive 2} \\ \text{forecast}\end{array} + \cdots + \begin{array}{c}\text{Executive 8} \\ \text{forecast}\end{array}}{8}$$

$$= \frac{400 + 600 + \ldots + 600}{8} = 533 \tag{15-1}$$

Gompertz curve:

$$Y_t = Le^{-ae^{-bt}} \tag{15-2}$$

Linear transformation:

$$y_t = \ln(\ln(L/Y_t)) \tag{15-3}$$

$$\hat{y}_t = a' + b't \tag{15-4}$$

$$a' = \ln(a) \quad \text{and} \quad b' = -b \tag{15-5}$$

$$a = e^{a'} \tag{15-6}$$

Microelectronic density:

$$y_t = \ln(\ln(1{,}200/Y_t)) \tag{15-7}$$

$$\hat{Y}_t = a' + b't = 2.7518 - .5561t \tag{15-8}$$

$$\hat{Y}_t = Le^{-ae^{-bt}} = 1{,}200e^{-15.67e^{-.5561t}} \tag{15-9}$$

Logistics (Pearl) curve:

$$Y_t = \frac{L}{1 + ae^{-bt}} \tag{15-10}$$

$$y_t = \ln(Y_t/(L - Y_t)) \tag{15-11}$$

$$\hat{y}_t = a' + b't \tag{15-12}$$

$$-\ln(a) = a' \quad \text{and} \quad b = b' \tag{15-13}$$

Worldwide nuclear gigawatt generation:

$$y_t = \ln(Y_t/(350 - Y_t)) \tag{15-14}$$

$$\hat{Y}_t = \frac{L}{1 + ae^{-bt}} = \frac{35}{1 + 425.71e^{-.27442t}} \tag{15-15}$$

Logistic curve to the base 10:

$$Y_t = L(1 + 10^{a-bt}) \tag{15-16}$$

$$y_t = \log(Y_t/(L - Y_t)) = -a + bt \tag{15-17}$$

Review Problems Using Your Software

R15-1 Fit a Gompertz curve to the data of Table 15-1, microelectronic density data, MICRO.DAT. Show that your results agree with those of Tables 15-2 and 15-3.

R15-2 Fit a logistics curve to worldwide nuclear power capacity, NUPOWER.DAT. Show that your results agree with those of Tables 15-4, 15-5, and 15-6.

R15-3 Fit a Gompertz curve to NUPOWER.DAT. Generate Tables 15-4, 15-5, and 15-6, for the Gompertz curve. Which model fits the data better, the logistics curve or the Gompertz curve?

R15–4 Experiment with the values of *a* and *b* of the Gompertz curve, as in Figures 15–7a and b.

R15–5 Experiment with the values of *a* and *b* of the logistics curve, as in Figures 15–8a and b.

Problems

15–1 Define the four different approaches to the long-term forecasting methods surveyed in this chapter.

15–2 Give a one- or two-sentence description of each method developed in the following sections of this chapter.
  a. Subjective methods   *b.* Exploratory methods
  c. Normative methods   *d.* S-Curves

15–3 Why are subjective forecasting methods necessary?

15–4 In what sense is the term *technology* used in this chapter?

15–5 What are the characteristics of the jury of executive opinion approach to subjective forecasting methods?

15–6 What are the advantages and disadvantages of the sales force composite method?

15–7 What are the differences between marketing research and the other subjective forecasting methods?

15–8 What are the steps of scenario analysis?

15–9 What are the advantages of scenario analysis?

15–10 What are the most important characteristics of the Delphi method?

15–11 Explain Figure 15–1 in the context of multiple S-curves for each technology.

15–12 Contrast the characteristics of logistics and Gompertz curves.

15–13 What are the advantages and disadvantages of the jury of executive opinion versus the Delphi method?

15–14 You have been given the job of forecasting the demand for video telephones. How would you go about doing so? This product may be very important to your company, and success or failure of the product can have dramatic impact on the firm's survival. Thus, any reasonable forecasting costs will be acceptable to management.

15–15 It is 1985, and you have been given the job of forecasting the demand for cellular mobile telephones. Knowing what we know now about that market, how would you have gone about forecasting the demand for these products?

15–16 You are the campaign chairman for a national candidate for the presidency of the United States. How would you estimate the acceptance or rejection of the party's platform?

15–17 Select a new product that is not currently on the market but that you would like to buy. Discuss how the demand for this product can be estimated.

15–18 What is forecasting using analogies? Provide two examples of forecasting using analogies that have not already been mentioned in this book.

15–19 What is forecasting using relevance trees? Provide two examples of forecasting using this method that have not already been mentioned in this book.

15–20 Why would we expect inaccurate S-curve forecasts of NUPOWER.DAT?

15–21 Which of the following variables are more likely to require expert opinion, and which should more likely be estimated using quantitative methods? In addition, which one of the following should definitely be estimated both ways?
  a. The technological success of a new drug.
  b. The sales of a new drug.
  c. A federal judge's response to claims of a patent infringement.

d. Whether a new product line should be started by a firm.

e. Whether a firm should go into a new market.

15–22 If a committee is forecasting the demand for a new product, is it better to require that a consensus be reached or to have each committee member identify his or her forecasts and the rationale for those forecasts?

For the following time series, fit a logistics or Gompertz curve. Graph the time series and explain how you chose the upper limit and type of S-curve. Be sure to review each data set for missing values and a better definition.

15–23 Commercial AM radio stations, 1921 to 1970; AMSTAT.DAT.

15–24 Commercial FM radio stations, 1941 to 1970; FMSTAT.DAT.

15–25 Commercial TV stations, 1942 to 1970; TVSTAT.DAT.

15–26 Households with radios, 1921 to 1991; RADIOHH.DAT.

15–27 Households with TVs, 1946 to 1991; TVSETSH.DAT.

Graph the following time series, and explain the growth patterns that exist. Also, discuss how S-curves could or could not be fitted to these series. Be sure to review each data set for missing values and a better definition.

15–28 Annual world carbon emissions, 1950 to 1993; CARBON.DAT.[a]

15–29 Annual world paperboard production, 1950 to 1993; PAPER.DAT.[a]

15–30 Annual world crude oil production, 1950 to 1993; OIL.DAT.[a]

15–31 Annual world natural gas production, 1950 to 1993; NATGAS.DAT.[a]

15–32 Annual world grain production, 1950 to 1993; GRAIN.DAT.[a]

15–33 Annual fish harvest, 1950 to 1993; FISH.DAT.[a]

15–34 Intel microprocessor transistor densities, MICROPRO.DAT of Figure 15–6b.

Composite Forecast versus Individual Forecast Accuracy

Answer the following questions individually. Next, answer these questions in groups of four to eight students. Each group should discuss these questions as objectively as possible. For example, in question 15–35, you might estimate the composite percentage from the experiences of your group, then average these estimates to come up with a good projection. After your instructor provides the correct answer discuss why you got good or bad estimates.

15–35 What percentage of Americans are high school graduates?

15–36 What are the average monthly earnings of a person without a high school diploma in the United States?

15–37 What are the average monthly earnings of a person with a high school diploma in the United States?

15–38 What are the average monthly earnings of a person with a college degree in the United States?

15–39 What are the average monthly earnings of a person with a doctorate in the United States?

15–40 The number of homes constructed of steel frames is given below. Discuss the problems of fitting an S-curve to this data.

1992	500
1993	13,000
1994	40,000
1995	80,000

Source: An advertisement for steel-framed homes.

---

[a]Source: Lester R. Brown, Hal Kane, and David Malin Roodman, *Vital Signs,* World Watch Institute, W.W. Norton and Company, 1994.

15–41 As a group project, use scenario analysis to plan a trip from and to a location, duration, and date to be determined by your instructor. Define all of the details that are necessary to successfully complete the trip. Assume the trip is for a family of four—parents and two small children.

References

Aaker, D., V. Kumar, and G. Day. *Marketing Research.* New York: John Wiley & Sons, 1995.

Ang, S., and M. O'Connor. "The Effect of Group Interaction Processes on Performance in Time Series Extrapolation." *International Journal of Forecasting* 7 (1991), pp. 141–49.

Armstrong, J.S. "Relative Accuracy of Judgmental and Extrapolative Methods in Forecasting Annual Earnings." *Journal of Forecasting* 2 (1982), pp. 437–47.

————. *Long-Range Forecasting: From Crystal Ball to Computer.* 2nd ed. New York: John Wiley & Sons, 1985.

Ascher, W. "Political Forecasting: The Missing Link." *Journal of Forecasting* 1, pp. 227–39.

Austin, J.E., and D.B. Yoffie. "Political Forecasting as a Management Tool." *Journal of Forecasting* 3 (1984), pp. 395–408.

Ayres, R.U. *Technological Forecasting and Long Range Planning.* New York: McGraw-Hill, 1969.

Blattberg, R.C., and J. Deighton. "Interactive Marketing: Exploiting the Age of Addressability." *Sloan Management Review,* Fall 1991, pp. 5–14.

Bossert, R.W. "The Logistic Growth Curve: Reviewed, Programmed and Applied to Electric Utility Forecasting." *Technological Forecasting and Social Change* 10 (1977).

Brandt, J.A., and D.A. Bessler. "Price Forecasting and Evaluation: An Application in Agriculture." *Journal of Forecasting* 2 (1983), pp. 237–48.

Brauers, J., and M. Weber. "A New Method of Scenario Analysis for Strategic Planning." *Journal of Forecasting* 7, pp. 31–47.

Brockhoff, K. "Forecasting Quality and Information." *Journal of Forecasting* 3 (1984), pp. 417–28.

Brown, L.D. "Comparing Judgmental to Extrapolative Forecasts: It's Time to Ask Why and When." *International Journal of Forecasting* 4 (1988), pp. 171–73.

Bush, W.R. "The Case of Research Software Development." *Technological Forecasting and Social Change* 27 (1990).

Carbone, R., and W. Gorr. "Accuracy of Judgmental Forecasting of Time Series." *Decision Sciences* 16, pp. 153–60.

Cerf, C., and V. Navasky. *The Experts Speak.* New York: Pantheon Books, 1984.

Cetron, M.J., and C.A. Ralph. *Industrial Application of Technological Forecasting.* New York: John Wiley & Sons, 1971.

Cholette, P.A. "Prior Information and ARIMA Forecasting." *Journal of Forecasting* 1 (1982), pp. 375–83.

Clarke, A.C. *Profiles of the Future.* 2nd ed. New York: Harper & Row, 1973.

Cleary, J.P., and H. Levenbach. *The Professional Forecaster: The Forecasting Process through Data Analysis.* Belmont, CA: Lifetime Learning Publications, 1982, pp. 78–88.

Dalyrmple, D.J. "Sales Forecasting Practices: Results from a United States Survey." *International Journal of Forecasting* 3 (1987), pp. 379–91.

Dawes, R.M. *Rational Choice in an Uncertain World.* New York: Harcourt Brace Jovanovich, 1988.

De Bondt, W.F.M., and R. Thaler. "Does the Stock Market Overreact?" *Journal of Finance* 40 (1985), pp. 793–805.

de Geus, A. "Planning As Learning." *Harvard Business Review,* March–April 1988, pp. 70–74.

de Jong, A., and G. Zalm. *Scanning the Future.* The Hague, the Netherlands: Central Planning Bureau, Sdu Publishers, 1992.

Dietz, T. "Methods for Analyzing Data from Delphi Panels: Some Evidence from a

Forecasting Study." *Technological Forecasting and Social Change* 31 (1987).

Edmundson, B.; M. Lawrence; and M. O'Connor. "The Use of Nontime Series Information in Sales Forecasting: A Case Study." *Journal of Forecasting* 7 (1988), pp. 201–11.

Einhorn, H.J., and R.M. Hogarth. "Prediction, Diagnosis, and Causal Thinking in Forecasting." *Journal of Forecasting* 1 (1982), pp. 23–36.

Fischoff, B. "Judgmental Aspects of Forecasting: Needs and Possible Trends." *International Journal of Forecasting* 4 (1988), pp. 331–39.

————. "Hindsight [is not equal to] Foresight: The Effect of Outcome Knowledge on Judgment under Uncertainty." *Journal of Experimental Psychology: Human Perception and Performance* 1 (1975), pp. 288–99.

Fischoff, B., and D. McGregor. "Subjective Confidence in Forecasts." *Journal of Forecasting* 1 (1982), pp. 155–72.

Flores, B.E.; D.L. Olson; and C. Wolfe. "Judgmental Adjustment of Forecasts: A Comparison of Methods." *International Journal of Forecasting* 7 (1992), pp. 421–33.

Forrester, J.W. *Industrial Dynamics.* Cambridge, MA: MIT Press, 1961.

Gerstenfeld, A. "Technological Forecasting." *Journal of Business* 44 (1971), pp. 10–18.

Gilovich, J. "Seeing the Past in the Present: The Effect of Associations to Familiar Events on Judgments and Decisions." *Journal of Personality and Social Psychology* 40 (1981), pp. 797–808.

Girifalco, L.A. *Dynamics of Technological Change.* New York: Van Nostrand Reinhold, 1991.

Godet, M. "From Forecasting to "La Prospective": A New Way of Looking at Futures" *Journal of Forecasting* 1 (1982), pp. 293–301.

Godet, M. *Scenarios and Strategic Management.* London: Butterworths Scientific, Ltd., 1987.

Gordon, T.J. "The Delphi Method: An Illustration." In *Technological Forecasting for Industry and Government,* ed. J. Bright. Englewood Cliffs, NJ: Prentice Hall, 1986.

Green, P.E., and D.S. Tull. *Research for Marketing Decisions.* 4th ed. Englewood Cliffs, New Jersey: Prentice-Hall, Inc., 1978.

Hawken, P.; J. Ogilvy; and P. Schwartz. *Seven Tomorrows.* New York: Bantam Books, 1982.

Helmer, O. *Social Technology.* New York: Basic Books, 1966.

————. "Analysis of the Future: The Delphi Method." In *Technological Forecasting.* ed. J. Bright.

————. "Problems in Futures Research—Delphi and Causal Cross-Input Analysis." *Futures* 9 (1977).

Hogarth, R.M., and S. Makridakis. "Forecasting and Planning: An Evaluation." *Management Science* 27 (1981), pp. 115–38.

Homer, J.B. "A Diffusion Model with Application to Evolving Medical Technologies." *Technological Forecasting and Social Change* 31 (1987).

Huss, W.R. "A Move toward Scenarios." *International Journal of Forecasting* 4 (1988), pp. 377–88.

Jungerman, H. "Inferential Processes in the Construction of Scenarios." *Journal of Forecasting* 4 (1985), pp. 321–27.

Kahneman, D., and A. Tversky. "The Simulation Heuristic." in *Judgment under Uncertainty: Heuristics and Biases,* ed. D. Kahneman, P. Slovic, and A. Tversky. New York: Cambridge University Press, 1982, pp. 201–10.

Kirkwood, C.W., and S.M. Pollack. "Multiple Attribute Scenarios, Bounded Probabilities, and Threats of Nuclear Theft." *Futures,* February 1982, pp. 545–53.

Koriat, A.; S. Lichtenstein; and B. Fischhoff. "Reasons for Confidence." *Journal of Experimental Psychology: Human Learning and Memory* 6 (1980), pp. 107–18.

Lawrence, M. J. "An Exploration of Some Practical Issues in the Use of Quantitative Forecasting Models." *Journal of Forecasting* 2 (1983), pp. 169–79.

Lawrence, M.J.; R.J. Edmundson; and M.J. O'Connor. "An Examination of the Accuracy Judgmental Extrapolation of Time Series." *International*

Journal of Forecasting 1 (1985), pp. 25–35.

Levary, R., and D. Han. "Choosing a Technological Forecasting Method." *Industrial Management* 37 (January–February 1995), p. 14(5).

Linneman, R.E., and H.E. Klein. "The Use of Multiple Scenarios by U.S. Industrial Companries." *Long Range Planning* 12 (1979), pp. 83–90.

Linstone, H., and M. Turoff. *The Delphi Method: Techniques and Applications.* Reading, MA: Addison-Wesley Publishing, 1975.

Makridakis, S. "The Art and Science of Forecasting: An Assessment and Future Directions." *International Journal of Forecasting* 2 (1986), pp. 15–39.

Makridakis, S., S.C. Wheelwright, and V.E. McGee. *Forecasting Methods and Applications.* New York: John Wiley & Sons, 1983.

Mandel, T.F. "Scenarios and Corporate Strategy: Planning in Uncertain Times." Menlo Park, CA: SRI International, Research Report 669, 1982.

Marcetti, C. "The Automobile in a System Context: The Past 80 Years and the Next 20 Years." *Technological Forecasting and Social Change* 23 (1983).

Martino, J. "The Precision of Delphi Estimates." *Technological Forecasting and Social Change* 1 (1970), pp. 292–99.

————. *Technological Forecasting and Decision Making.* 3rd ed. Amsterdam: North Holland (1993).

Mentzer, J.T., and J.E. Cox. "Familiarty, Application, and Performance of Sales Forecasting Techniques." *Journal of Forecasting* 3 (1984), pp. 27–36.

Merino, D.N. "Development of a Technological S Curve for Tire Cord Textiles." *Technological Forecasting and Social Change* 37 (1990).

Mumpower, J.L.; S. Livingston; and T.J. Lee. "Expert Judgments of Political Riskiness." *Journal of Forecasting* 6 (1987), pp. 51–65.

Parenté, F.J.; J.K. Anderson; P. Myers; and T. O'Brien. "An Examination of Factors Contributing to Delphi Accuracy." *Journal of Forecasting* 3 (1984), pp. 173–82.

Porter, A.L.; A.T. Roper; T.W. Mason; F.A. Rossini; and J. Banks. *Forecasting and Management of Technology.* New York: John Wiley & Sons, 1991.

Russo, J.E., and P.J.H. Schoemaker. "Managing Overconfidence." *Sloan Management Review,* Winter 1992, pp. 7–18.

————. *Decision Traps.* New York: Doubleday, 1989.

Salancik, J.R.; W. Wenger; and E. Helfer. "The Construction of Delphi Statements." *Technological Forecasting and Social Change* 3 (1971), pp. 65–73.

Schnaars, S.P. *Megamistakes: Forecasting and the Myth of Rapid Technological Change.* New York: Free Press, 1989.

Schnaars. S.P., and M.T. Topol. "The Use of Multiple Scenarios in Sales Forecasting: An Empirical Test." *International Journal of Forecasting* 3 (1987), pp. 405–19.

Schoemaker, P.J.H. "When and How to Use Scenario Planning: A Heuristic Approach with Illustration." *Journal of Forecasting* 10 (1991), pp. 549–64.

————. "How to Link Strategic Vision to Core Capabilities." *Sloan Management Review,* Fall 1992, pp. 67–81.

————. "Multiple Scenario Development: Its Conceptual and Behavioral Basis." *Strategic Management Journal* 14 (1993), pp. 192–213.

————. "Scenario Planning: A Tool for Strategic Thinking." *Sloan Management Review* 36, no. 2 (Winter 1995), p. 25(16).

Schoemaker, P.J.H., and C.A.J.M. van de Heijden. "Integrating Scenarios into Strategic Planning at Royal Dutch/Shell." *Planning Review* 20 (1992), pp. 41–46.

Schwartz, P. *The Art of Long View.* New York: Doubleday, 1991.

Senge, P. *The Fifth Discipline.* New York: Doubleday, 1990.

Sharif, M.N., and V. Sundararajan. "A Quantitative Model for the Evaluation of Technological Alternatives." *Technological Forecasting and Social Change* 24 (1983).

Sniezek, J.A. "An Examination of Group Process in Judgmental Forecasting." *International Journal of Forecasting* 5 (1989), pp. 171–78.

Sparkes, J.R., and A.K. McHugh. "Awareness

and Use of Forecasting Technques in British Industry." *Journal of Forecasting* 3 (1984), pp. 37–42.

Sunter, C. *The World and South Africa in the 1990's.* Cape Town, South Africa: Human and Rousseau Tafelberg, 1987.

Toffler, A. *The Adaptive Corporation.* New York: McGraw-Hill, 1985.

Tversky, A., and D. Kahneman, "Extensional versus Intuitive Reasoning: The Conjunction Fallacy in Probability Judgments." *Psychological Review* 90 (1983), pp. 293–315.

Tyebjee, T.T. "Behavioral Biases in New Product Forecasting." *International Journal of Forecasting* 3 (1987), pp. 393–404.

Wack, P. "Scenarios: Uncharted Waters Ahead." *Harvard Business Review,* September–October 1985, pp. 72–89.

Welty, G. "Problems of Selecting Experts for Delphi Exercises." *Academy of Management Journal* 15 (1972), pp. 121–24.

Willemain, T.R. "Graphical Adjustment of Statistical Forecasts." *International Journal of Forecasting* 5 (1989), pp. 179–85.

————. "The Effect of Graphical Adjustment on Forecast Accuracy." *International Journal of Forecasting* 7 (1991), pp. 151–54.

Zentner, R.D. "Scenarios: Past, Present and Future." *Long Range Planning* 15 (1982), pp. 12–20.

ARTIFICIAL NEURAL NETWORKS, EXPERT SYSTEMS, AND GENETIC ALGORITHMS

Bees . . . by virtue of . . . forethought . . . know that the hexagon is greater than the square and the triangle and will hold more honey for the same expenditure of material.

Pappus of Alexandria, c. A.D. 340, Greek geometer

Chapter Outline

The forecasting methods discussed in this book are used in a variety of forecasting systems. Such systems have been some of the most successful applications of artificial intelligence (AI). Artificial intelligence programs provide an extraordinary opportunity to improve the effectiveness of all phases of forecast implementation. This chapter defines artificial intelligence (AI), expert systems (ESs), artificial neural networks (ANNs), and genetic algorithms (GAs) and their tremendous potential in forecasting. In addition, comments about forecasting accuracy are made using the well-publicized results of the Makridakis et al. competition of 1982.

Practical Implications of ESs, ANNs, and GAs

This chapter illustrates that in most settings, there are significant improvements in forecasting system performance from increased forecasting system intelligence. In fact, for most applications, greater benefits are achieved through the use of better systems, not through the use of more sophisticated methods. To better understand this assertion, consider the following discussion of forecasting accuracy and forecasting model complexity.

Forecast Accuracy and Model Complexity

Makridakis et al. (1982) using 1,001 actual time series performed one of the most extensive studies of forecast accuracy and is commonly called the M-competition. The M-competition involved the use of 24 different models in forecasting each of 1,001 series. The 1,001 series varied by type (e.g., industry data, national data) and the time period analyzed (e.g., monthly, quarterly, and annual). The results of that competition illustrated that for their seasonal data, there was very little difference between the performance of seasonal methods. That is, Makridakis, et al. (1982) reached the following conclusions based on the M-competition:

> If the forecasting user can discriminate in his choice of methods depending upon the type of data (yearly, quarterly, monthly), the type of series (macro, micro, etc.) and the time horizon of forecasting, then he or she could do considerably better than using a single method across all situations—assuming, of course, that the results of the present study can be generalized. . . . Furthermore, combining the forecasts of a few methods improves overall forecasting accuracy over and above that of the individual forecasting methods used in the combining. . . . Even though further research will be necessary to provide us with more specific reasons as to why this is happening, a hypothesis may be advanced at this point stating that statistically sophisticated methods do not do better than simple methods (such as deseasonalized exponential smoothing) when there is considerable randomness in the data. . . . Finally, it seems that seasonal patterns can be predicted equally well by both simple and statistically sophisticated methods.

Among the implications of these conclusions are the potential benefits and the necessity for improved expert system support. That is, forecasting systems with simple artificial intelligence (AI) and expert systems (ES) may be much more efficient and effective than systems with a single, more complex and sophisticated forecasting model. Simple AI/ES–based forecasting systems will typically outperform more sophisticated forecasting methods in many dimensions, including forecast accuracy, computational speed, user understanding, and cost effectiveness. This assertion is based on our experiences and the results of the M-competition. The concepts, applications, and advantages of AI/ES in forecasting systems are developed next.

Artificial Intelligence (AI)/Expert Systems (ES)

The field of **artificial intelligence (AI)** is an exciting one that has several dimensions of particular importance to forecasting. Artificial intelligence is the capability of a computer to perform functions usually completed with human intelligence such as reasoning, learning, and self-improvement. The general area of AI is broad, including the study of pattern recognition, robotics, process control methods, machine learning, expert systems, cognitive learning, artificial neural networks (ANNs), and genetic algorithms (GAs). To better understand AI in the context of forecasting systems, it is important to distinguish between two general areas and objectives of AI computer programs: the conventional program systems (CPS) approach and the expert systems (ES) approach (DeLurgio and Bhame, 1991).

Conventional Program Systems versus Expert Systems

In the **conventional program systems (CPS)** approach, "the researcher wants to create a system that is able to deal with interesting and difficult intellectual tasks, regardless of whether the methods and techniques used are similar or identical to those used by humans. There is a job to accomplish inexpensively, efficiently, and reliably—that is all that matters" (Ralston and Reilly, 1983). CPS are exemplified by the many good forecasting systems from IBM, American Software, Manugistics, SCA, Greystone, Business Forecasting Systems, AFS, Smart Forecast, and others.

In contrast, the **expert system (ES)** approach "has the basic objective of trying to gain an understanding of the inside mechanisms of a real life system and to explain and predict its behavior. We can put in this category, for example, those projects that simulate human problem solving, decision making, or learning behavior by building models of neural networks" (Ralston and Reilly, 1983). The ES approach to forecasting system development continues today; a number of general PC forecasting software packages are being marketed as forecasting expert systems. However, in some cases, these systems are not expert systems (ES) but instead are conventional program systems (CPS) that have considerable artificial intelligence built into them. In fact, most ES programs fall someplace between the two extremes of CPSs and ESs.

The difference between ESs and CPSs lies in the ES's emphasis on symbol manipulation, whereas non-ES programming relies primarily on number crunching and, to a lesser extent, logical relationships. ES programs solve problems by searching for patterns or logical relationships, not through simple algorithmic computations. ESs attempt to allow computers to act and react more like humans.

The major characteristics of an expert system are:

1. The ability to perform cognitive tasks at a level of an expert.
2. The representation of expert knowledge or recommendations in a domain-specific area.
3. The inclusion of explanations of why a decision or action is recommended.
4. Ways of handling uncertainty.
5. Systems directed to solving problems involving logical and symbolic representations, as opposed to number crunching.

Purpose of an Expert System

Another important way in which to distinguish an ES from a CPS is in the purpose of the system. An ES is designed to

1. Provide expert advice to nonexperts as problems are solved.
2. Assist experts as they solve problems.

3. Act as a teaching tool for the nonexpert.

Each of these purposes is relevant to forecasting systems.

Expert systems are best for problems that require large amounts of symbolic, unreliable, and uncertain input together with detailed knowledge of the subject in the domain. Unlike ES, conventional programs do not necessarily process qualitative data. Also, expert systems are particularly effective when the expert's knowledge is largely heuristic—that is, based on rules of thumb developed over time under conditions of uncertainty. Therefore, an expert system must have corrections for uncertainty, and explanations must be built into the system so the person using the system can understand how the conclusions have been derived.

Parts of an Expert System

As shown in Figure 16–1, the components of an expert system consist of:

1. A user interface, which supports conversation with the system. This is commonly called a **dialog structure**.
2. An **inference engine**, which controls the decision process using logical search and "thought" processes.
3. A **knowledge base**, which contains the knowledge of the expert.

The ES combines the body of information that is agreed on by experts in a field (i.e., the knowledge base) with heuristic solving techniques (i.e., the inference engine). The ES functions like a human expert: consulting others, asking questions, explaining reasoning when asked, and justifying conclusions. It should be able to function with incomplete data, without answers to some questions, just as a human consultant operates. To date, expert systems have only a limited, well-defined set of tasks through which they can reason. The expert system cannot as yet generate its own axioms or general theories: it cannot learn independently. Human users learn and adapt the program, adding new axioms and theories as that knowledge becomes available. Expert systems are designed to modify their queries as more information becomes known, allow the user to move on to new goals, keep traces of solution paths for review, record responses given by users, and record explanations and justifications for future reference.

Advantages of Expert Systems

An expert system has advantages over the human expert in terms of instant availability, consistency, and comprehensiveness. Unlike the human expert, the ES never for-

FIGURE 16–1

Expert system modules

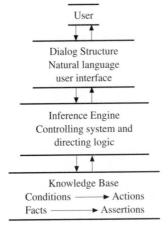

User

Dialog Structure
Natural language
user interface

Inference Engine
Controlling system and
directing logic

Knowledge Base
Conditions ⟶ Actions
Facts ⟶ Assertions

gets to check every possibility, never forgets an axiom. Additionally, there are four other significant advantages provided by ESs:

1. They are able to process qualitative information.
2. They process incomplete and/or uncertain information.
3. They provide permanent, documented, and duplicatable knowledge.
4. They are easy to maintain and modify.

In addition, ESs can be applied to problems that occur infrequently but that require a high level of expertise to solve, or that occur frequently at numerous sites. In the latter case, the ES expertise can be transferred to many other individuals dispersed throughout an organization.

Disadvantages of Expert Systems

There are several disadvantages to ESs, including:

1. The existing scarcity of skilled people. This includes those who are, or would be, knowledge engineers, as well as those who provide the system support from a data processing perspective.

2. The lack of standardization of development tools and operating system software, which makes it difficult to move applications of ESs from one system or computer platform to another.

3. The risk associated with defining any body of knowledge. Will the prospective users accept the authority of the knowledge base?

4. The unrealistic expectations of those who expect the knowledge base of the ES to be more comprehensive than it is.

5. The possibility of contradictions or inconsistencies in the knowledge base if it has been provided by more than one expert—that is, finding an expert is a task with some risk in itself.

Expert System Applications in Forecasting

What expert systems offer is the additional advice and problem-solving assistance of people who have built the expert system. In turn, by proper use of the expert advice, the forecast calculations and related techniques are used to greatest advantage to produce more efficient and effective forecasts. The expert system can be thought of as a manager of computational techniques. This is like having an assistant to the forecaster who is most familiar with the appropriate "knobs and levers" to use for a particular forecast problem. When we look at the types of problems or questions that arise during implementation of a forecasting system, some of them will lend themselves to expert system analysis.

Figure 16–2 is a simplified representation of a forecasting system. The three parts of the system denote potential areas in which ESs offer solutions to ill-defined problems. These three application areas are discussed separately as if they were separate expert systems; in fact, they are not. These systems include data entry and validation, model selection and forecasting, and system maintenance and control. Each of these is discussed below.

I. Data Entry and Validation Expert System

Forecasting systems can produce forecasts using any input data. However, it is independent demand data that is the most appropriate quantity to forecast, not distorted shipments data. Some data are more appropriate to particular business situa-

FIGURE 16–2

The parts of a simple forecasting system

I. Data Entry and Validation
  Logical filtering (e.g., demand versus supply or shipments).
  Special event filtering (promotions, price changes, product introductions).
  Initial outlier detection, adjustment, and classification.

II. Model Selection and Forecasting
  Model selection.
  Outlier detection, adjustment, and classification.
  Reasonableness test.
  Final forecast.

III. System Control and Maintenance
  Error measures.
  Tracking signal control.
  Data base updating and maintenance.
  Detection of system malfunctions and bugs.

tions or to the type of item that is being forecasted. Because the user of the forecasting system is (or should be) aware of the specifics of the input data, he or she should be able to guide and be guided by the ES in the selection of proper data.

Logical filtering of data used in the forecasting system can improve the quality of the forecast and resulting decisions. For example, shipments data may be distorted by supply restrictions. The ES can inquire and advise the user to modify the data to more closely reflect true demand.

As another example, the data may be distorted by an unusual mix of order transactions—perhaps an unusually high percentage of order cancellations or returns. A well-designed ES, having the intelligence of a well-informed manager, will discover these conditions and will suggest a course of action to modify the historical data.

Planned event filtering is managing the historical data adjustments associated with price changes, promotions, product introductions, product changes, and so on. These events are well identified ahead of time, should be organized in a database for analysis and recall, and thus can be treated more thoroughly than the unusual events of logical filtering. An ES offers a convenient method for programming the logical relationships identified through experience with planned or special events. Experienced product managers may pass on to others the likely effects of each kind of promotion or their distilled opinions regarding price increases. What percent demand increase occurred, for example, when a 3 percent price increase was announced one month ahead of the effective date? How did the effect vary among the product lines? Was there a difference in this market response when the inflation rate was twice as high? Thus, ESs provide an effective way of constructing and maintaining a data base of actual demand, adjusted demand, and measured effects of planned and unplanned events.

Data validation, then, is integral to data entry, to identify special events, unusual transactions, or poor data quality prior to model selection and forecasting.

An ES question–answer dialog that illustrates data validation might proceed as follows:

Q: Which of the following topics is selected? (Click the mouse on the appropriate item.)

> System Diagnostics
> Demand Data Characteristics
→ Forecast Model Selection

           Forecast Accuracy
           Graphics
           Input Preparation

Q: Is the item believed to be seasonal?
    → Yes   No

Q: How much demand history is being used?
    Less than one year
    → One to two years
    Two to three years
    More than three years

Q: Is the seasonality caused by
    → Natural market demand conditions
    Managed events, promotions etc.

Q: Is the market changing?
    Yes   → No

Q: What is the annual volume of this item?
    Less than 100
    → 100 to 1000
    Over 1000

Q: Are other items sold with the same seasonality?
    → Yes   No

Q: Do any of these other items have greater volume?
    → Yes   No

Q: Is there at least two years of history?
    → Yes   No

Q: Is that history distorted by either managed events or market changes?
    → Yes   No

Q: Are these distortions identified well enough to be replaced by better history?
    → Yes   No

Conclusion: Demand history should be adjusted on the selected larger volume items to form a basis for seasonality estimates. This should be done before using the group seasonality method to assign the seasonality to the initial item.

    Q: Do you want help with the procedure to adjust demand history?
        → Yes   No

At this point in the dialogue, the expert system has been asked to link to the input preparation portion of its knowledge base, a section that deals with screen inputs available to the user. The expert system will link to the procedure for adjusting demand history. Subsequently, the appropriate items will be selected to make the adjustment to history to compute the group seasonality factors and to assign those group seasonality factors to the initial item.

In this example, the first 11 questions took the user through many branches in a tree structure that could have had hundreds of different outcomes depending on the choices made during the dialogue. What has been done is to take advantage of a very efficient way to organize knowledge and to present it in a friendly and useful way to people who want to solve problems.

II. Model Selection and Forecasting Expert System

Because forecasting systems typically involve the processing of thousand of forecasts, routine forecasting will be done as in the past using background conventional program systems. However, when exceptions occur, the expert system can bring problems to the foreground so that they can be resolved effectively and efficiently by a forecaster.

Common problems requiring expert advice include initial selection of a forecasting model, resolution of outlier problems during the fitting/model selection process, and reasonableness checks of a final forecast. One of the most important advantages of ESs is that novice and pro alike can be guided to a resolution of the problem.

The initial selection of a forecasting model was illustrated in the Section I discussion when the ES guided the analyst to select the use of group seasonality factors. There are many other possible considerations in the model selection process that the ES can use to guide an analyst; these include several qualitative inputs such as cost (e.g., high, medium, or low), importance of or desire for accuracy (e.g., high, medium, or low), trends (e.g., likely or not likely), seasonality, relationship to other products, the manner in which promotions might be included in the model, and so on. This is a very effective, routine use of a forecasting ES when the cost trade-offs justify analyst–ES interactions.

When outliers or exceptions are detected, an ES can be used to guide the analyst in identifying the causes of outliers and means of correcting them. Not only are the causes important but also the numerical division of the outlier between normally expected demand and outlier effects. These divisions are critical for forecast accuracy.

When unusually large or small forecasts are detected, the ES can guide the analyst in resolving the problem. For example, it is very common for CPS to include a forecast **reasonableness test** in the software. This reasonableness test checks whether, based on past experiences and judgment, the forecast is in the bounds of reasonableness. For example, if the projected demand using a nonlinear model for a product yielded an effective annual rate of growth of 300 percent, this might trip an exception report and an ES session. Such "trip" points can be set based on objective and subjective input.

III. System Control and Maintenance Expert System

As the actual demand for a product is realized, important measures of forecast validity and accuracy will be calculated and updated; these include several error statistics and tracking signals, as discussed in Chapter 17. At this time, the system may detect out-of-control situations and opportunities to improve forecasting performance. Tasks such as explaining, adjusting, and classifying outliers are part of both this ES and the system described in Section II. In this case, the ES addresses an outlier not as a historical phenomenon but instead as a real-time occurrence. By having the ES generate a timely exception report, the analyst can devote the appropriate time and effort to resolution of the problem through the guidance of the ES. Statistics such as MAPE, RSE, and MAD can be calculated in real time and exceptions can trigger the ES to start an inquiry. Heuristic rules can be incorporated into the system and might even be tailored to the specific product or group of products.

At times, there may be questions as to whether the software is processing the data according to its design specifications. These are the questions related to diagnosis of bugs or suspected bugs in the software. Diagnostic expert systems are often chosen by first-time developers, perhaps because diagnostic services (problem solving) are a more traditional area in which special help is expected by customers.

Diagnostic questions and the expertise to answer them will usually be supplied most effectively by the designer of the forecasting system. For larger, well-established forecasting packages, there may be an experienced base of users who share information regarding software problems. Some of those problems will be diagnosed by using the documentation—that is, deciding that the system does not do what the documentation says it is supposed to do.

The evaluation of hardware and information systems is easier to perform with an expert system providing guidance in fault diagnosis. The expert system prompts the user for information concerning the symptoms of a particular malfunction. Using this information and the expert knowledge base, the expert system goes through the inference process to quickly provide the user with a diagnosis on which corrective action can be taken.

The diagnostic conclusions can fall into categories such as the following:

a. The system is performing as designed.

b. The system needs a fix in one or more particular modules.

c. No conclusion was reached; the inputs should be repeated for another item or forecast entity.

Good documentation, good training aids, and a diagnostic expert system can guide the user to a better understanding of the design and intended capabilities of the system. The user needs to be confident that the system is doing what it is supposed to do with the data it is given.

In summary, we see that there are ample opportunities for the use of expert systems in forecasting systems. There are few if any forecasting systems that incorporate all of the ES dimensions discussed here. Also, to date, many of the claims about dramatic improvements from ESs have yet to be realized. However, the use of ESs to support forecasting and decision support systems is increasing and offers great potential benefits.

Artificial Neural Networks (ANNs)

"When we do not understand the basics of our problems our solutions are too often too complex and wrong."

Oliver Wight
Production and inventory consultant

In this section, we introduce ANNs and apply some simple examples using one of the most versatile learning ANNs, the feedforward, backpropagation architecture. ANNs are approaches to forecasting using computer models with some of the architecture and processing capabilities of the human brain. The technology that attempts to achieve these results is called neural computing or **artificial neural networks (ANNs).** In some applications, this technology is extraordinarily successful, while in others it is disappointing. Computing based on emulation of the human brain originated more than 50 years ago. From the beginning, two basic approaches to ANN modeling have been attempted:

• Computers that more or less emulate human brain functions via their hardware designs.

• Programs of general purpose digital computers that contain data structures and logical connections enabling them to operate somewhat like a human brain.

Very successful emulation of **massively parallel** activity of the human brain within computer hardware architecture has yet to be obtained. However, program driven ANNs using digital computers have been used from the early days to develop an artificial, apparently intelligent representation of real-world systems using networks of connected **neurons.**

As we will see, the basic ANN is simple in principle, but large, complex ANNs provide very versatile and powerful ways to model complex systems. Many financial institutions have developed ANNs to perform tasks such as credit card validation, credit application acceptance, and stock and bond price predictions.

Interestingly, many of these models have remained secret because, we assume, they are so successful. Despite these successes, ANNs will be oversold as solutions to many problems that would better be solved using more traditional methods (thus, the opening quotation by Oliver Wight). However, valid ANN applications exist in forecasting, which is why this topic is presented here.

We assume in this chapter that you are to be users of ANNs; this is analogous to being users of ARIMA software without being software developers. Thus, our presentation provides you with insights to using ANNs but not all of the details of the designs of ANN software. However, this chapter is a good starting point for those wanting to develop ANN software. To assist you in the study of ANNs, we have included several spreadsheet ANNs on this book's data diskette. These several ANN spreadsheets are compatible with the wk1 format and thus should be easy to use in your spreadsheet package. Each spreadsheet has an explanation of its use. Finally, those desiring more information about ANNs after study of this chapter should refer to Blum (1992), Caudill and Butler (1992), Dixon and Bevan (1994), and Nelson and Illingworth (1991). We have found Dixon and Bevan to be a particularly good starting point, with excellent accompanying software.

ANNs mimic biological neurons by simulating some of the workings of the human brain. However, ANNs are only minuscule representations of the human brain. It is estimated that the number of neurons in a human brain is on the order of 100 billion. Also, there are hundreds of different types of neurons that are connected in networks to perform different functions. These networks are very complex when one considers that some neurons have as many as 10,000 interconnections with other neurons. In contrast, even the largest ANNs have only 10 million neurons, a number that is estimated to be somewhat less than the neurons of a cockroach.

An ANN is made up of processing elements called neurons or **neurodes** that are interconnected in a network (we use the term *neurodes* and *nodes* interchangeably here). These artificial neurodes receive inputs that are analogous to the electrochemical signals that natural neurons receive from other neurons. By changing the weights given to these signals, the network learns in a process that seems similar to that found in nature. For example, neurodes in an ANN receive signals or information from other neurodes or from external sources, perform transformations on the signals, and then pass those signals on to other neurodes. The way information is processed and intelligence stored in an ANN depends on the architecture and algorithms of the ANN.

One of the distinct advantages of ANNs is their ability to learn patterns in very complex systems. Through a learning or self-organizing process, they translate inputs into desired outputs by adjusting the weights given to signals between neurodes. As we will see, most learning processes require an extraordinary amount of computer time and software iterations.

While we will be modeling intelligence and learning using ANNs, it is important to remember that we do not really know how biological brains operate. The neurons in an ANN have nowhere near the richness of information found in natural neurons. However, by using massively parallel processes to imitate the brain, we achieve some of the advantages of such biological systems.

Before we get into the thick of ANNs, remember that from a macro standpoint, they function very much like other forecasting methods. Input data is provided a model, then coefficients are fitted to model the dominant patterns in the data. Just as in other forecasting applications, when deciding on the best model coefficients, some measure of goodness of fit is used, the most common being minimization of the residual standard error. (Actually, the RMS value is used in ANN software, and except for slight differences in the degrees of freedom in the denominator, it is essentially but not exactly equal to the RSE.) In contrast to methods such as ARIMA or MARIMA models, there is much greater complexity in an ANN. Just as we know there is not one MARIMA model, there is not one type of ANN. Theoretically, and practically, there are many more types of ANNs than there are types of ARIMA models. Thus, ANNs represent an approach to forecasting that includes many different types of networks, the variety of ANNs rivaling the variety of forecasting methods studied in this book.

ANNs are so powerful because of their ability to model complex mathematical and logical systems. However, this versatility of application and complexity is obtained at considerable cost. ANNs take extraordinary amounts of computer time to train, the best ANN design is not easily determined, and the weights (i.e., coefficients) of ANNs are not easily interpreted. Many ANN analysts suggest that ANNs are only partially insightful of the model and system. Thus, it is hard to make generalizations from the structure and weights of ANNs. Consequently, many users of ANNs are forced to consider these models as black boxes (*gray matter* may be a better term).

As always, it is important to be as knowledgeable as possible about your application so you will not be misled when constructing, using, and interpreting ANNs. For example, it is important to have as much understanding about your study as in an econometric application. Also, the principle of parsimony applies when using ANNs because of problems with overfitting, particularly when there is little theory to validate the output of the ANN.

Architecture of ANNs

New types of ANNs continue to be developed as research progresses. Fortunately, the number of well-established ANNs is limited. For example, in forecasting, most ANNs typically have at least three layers of neurodes: an **input layer,** a **hidden layer,** and an **output layer.** This **ANN architecture** is illustrated in Figure 16–3, where most of the elements of a general feedforward ANN are shown. While it is common to have only one hidden layer, very complex systems may require more hidden layers. However, there is always one input and one output layer in ANNs. Additionally, as

FIGURE 16–3

ANN for forecasting
Y_t and Y_{t+1}

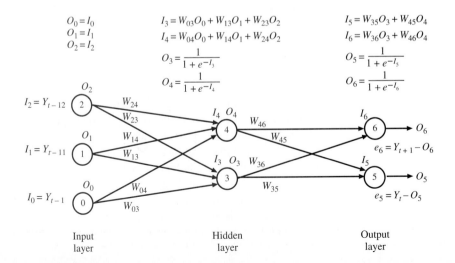

$$O_0 = I_0$$
$$O_1 = I_1$$
$$O_2 = I_2$$

$$I_3 = W_{03}O_0 + W_{13}O_1 + W_{23}O_2$$
$$I_4 = W_{04}O_0 + W_{14}O_1 + W_{24}O_2$$

$$O_3 = \frac{1}{1 + e^{-I_3}}$$
$$O_4 = \frac{1}{1 + e^{-I_4}}$$

$$I_5 = W_{35}O_3 + W_{45}O_4$$
$$I_6 = W_{36}O_3 + W_{46}O_4$$

$$O_5 = \frac{1}{1 + e^{-I_5}}$$
$$O_6 = \frac{1}{1 + e^{-I_6}}$$

Input layer   Hidden layer   Output layer

shown in Figure 16–3, ANNs can have more than one dependent variable, thus they can be used to forecast several variables (e.g., Y_t, Y_{t+1}, Y_{t+2}, . . .) using the same set of input variables.

Neurodes

The neurodes or **processing elements** (PEs) of an ANN receive inputs from other neurodes (e.g., nodes 0, 1, and 2 of Figure 16–3 feeding node 3). The neurodes process these inputs and then deliver output signals to other neurodes (e.g., node 3 feeding node 5). As we will see, these inputs will either activate or not activate the receiving neurodes depending on the signals, the weights given to the signals, and the form of the transfer function. The 0 to 1 output of nodes provides an important logical dimension to ANNs. Thus, some nodes will be active and others not active depending on the strength of the signal received from all feeding nodes. We see that an ANN is not a simple representation of a system such as an ARIMA model but instead consists of a network of logical and mathematical functions that model a system.

The two basic types of ANNs are those that have to be **trained** (e.g., **backpropagation**) and those that learn or organize on their own. Because training requires considerable time to complete, there is great interest in ANNs that learn on their own. These networks are called **self-organizing networks.** However, they often have unpredictable performance and the meaning of their outputs may be unknown. These self-organizing ANNs are at the cutting edge of ANN research. In contrast to self-organizing ANNs, the most popular and successful ANNs use training methods called backpropagation, developed by Werbos (1974) and Parker (1982). As Table 16–1 highlights, backpropagation is the most versatile method of the ANNs.

ANN Applications

As shown in Table 16–1, several different ANN applications and types of ANNs exist. The types of applications include the following:

- **Classification problems** consist of credit approval processes (i.e., acceptance or rejection) and defect identification (i.e., good or defective).
- **Mathematical modeling** occurs when the ANN is used to identify or emulate a mathematical function.
- **Forecasting and prediction** includes univariate and multivariate forecasting applications.
- **Reconstruction/Recognition** involves identifying a pattern in a noisy or unclear signal. For example, character recognition applications are indicative of

TABLE 16–1   Types of ANNs and Typical Applications

Application Problem Type	ANN Type					
	Backpropagation	*Adaptive Resonance*	*Feature Map Routing*	*Radical Basis*	*Recurrent*	*Temporal Difference*
Classification	X	X	X	X	X	
Math modeling	X			X	X	
Forecasting	X				X	X
Reconstruction	X					
Clustering		X	X			
Routing				X		

Source: Neural Network Utility: Installation and User's Guide, Ver. 3.1, p. 90, IBM Corporation, 1994.

FIGURE 16–4

A simple $2 \times 1 \times 1$ ANN before training for THREE.DAT

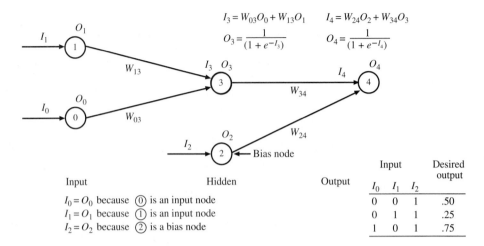

$I_3 = W_{03}O_0 + W_{13}O_1$ $I_4 = W_{24}O_2 + W_{34}O_3$

$O_3 = \dfrac{1}{(1 + e^{-I_3})}$ $O_4 = \dfrac{1}{(1 + e^{-I_4})}$

Input			Desired output
I_0	I_1	I_2	
0	0	1	.50
0	1	1	.25
1	0	1	.75

Input   Hidden   Output

$I_0 = O_0$ because ⓪ is an input node
$I_1 = O_1$ because ① is an input node
$I_2 = O_2$ because ② is a bias node

reconstruction. The character recognition methods in computer scanners and fax boards use ANNs.

- **Clustering** involves finding logical groupings of values in data—for example, in marketing, when trying to group the types of consumers and their responses to different types of promotions.

- **Routing** consists of determining the best route through a number of destinations, the traveling salesman problem being an example.

As mentioned, the ANN approach that is most relevant to forecasting is the backpropagation method, which we develop here. However, there are many other types of structures, including the ADALINE, MADALINE, Kohonen's, SOFM, BAM, Boltzmann, Hamming, Hopfield, and LVQ (see Dixon and Bevan, 1994, and Nelson and Illingworth, 1991, for further details). As the length of this list implies, the user of ANNs may have to search for the best ANN structure. Fortunately, there is a considerable literature associated with each type of application that provides guidance in selecting one structure over another.

Just as the typical user of forecasting software does not design the actual formulas used to calculate, for example, least squares coefficients, likewise the users of ANNs "simply" apply existing software based on the guidance of the software developers and the current body of knowledge. However, because of the complexity of ANNs, analysts may have to spend considerable time in experimenting with alternative ANN structures before an effective design is found.

To better understand the diversity of ANNs in forecasting, Table 16–2 illustrates some of the recent ANN applications that were found in the forecasting literature. This table represents a few of the ANN applications of a recent two-year period using an on-line search on the term "Neural Network" on ABI/Inform. This search yielded over 200 articles with neural network in their titles or abstracts.

To make these concepts and issues more concrete, let's study ANNs as we step through the calculations of the ANN of Figure 16–4.

Steps in Developing an ANN

In this section, we discuss the development of an ANN using Figure 16–4, a network with one input layer, one hidden layer, and one output layer; thus, the notation $2 \times 1 \times 1$ for the number of nodes in each layer. Let's assume we are forecasting using two ex-

TABLE 16–2   Typical Neural Network Applications

"Estimating Missing Values Using Neural Networks." Amit Gupta and Monica S. Lam. *Journal of the Operational Research Society* 47, no. 2 (February 1996), pp. 229–38.

"Residential Construction Demand Forecasting Using Economic Indicators: A Comparative Study of Artificial Neural Networks and Multiple Regression." Goh Bee Hua. *Construction Management and Economics* 14, no. 1 (January 1996), pp. 125–34.

"Forecast Combining with Neural Networks." R. Glen Donaldson and Mark Kamstra. *Journal of Forecasting* 15, no. 1 (January 1996), pp. 49–61.

"Neural Networks versus Conventional Methods of Forecasting." Chin Kuo and Arthur Reitsch. *Journal of Business Forecasting Methods and Systems* 14, no. 4 (Winter 1995/1996), pp. 17–22.

"Forecasting Electric Energy Consumption Using Neural Networks." S.S.A.K. Javeed Nizami and Ahmed Z. Al-Garni. *Energy Policy* 23, no. 12 (December 1995), pp. 1097–1104.

"A Neural Network Approach to Forecasting Model Selection." Jeffrey E. Sohl and A.R. Venkatachalam. *Information and Management* 29, no. 6 (December 1995), pp. 297–303.

"Neural Network Time Series Forecasting of Financial Markets." Nigel Meade. *International Journal of Forecasting* 11, no. 4 (December 1995), pp. 601–602.

"Forecasting Futures Trading Volume Using Neural Networks." Iebeling Kaastra and Milton S. Boyd. *Journal of Futures Markets* 15, no. 8 (December 1995), pp. 953–70.

"Forecasting Exchange Rates Using Feedforward and Recurrent Neural Networks." Chung-Ming Kuan and Tung Liu. *Journal of Applied Econometrics* 10, no. 4 (October–December 1995), pp. 347–64.

"Forecasting International Airline Passenger Traffic Using Neural Networks." Kyungdoo Nam and Thomas Schaefer. *Logistics and Transportation Review* 31, no. 3 (September 1995), pp. 239–51.

"A Neural Network for Classifying the Financial Health of a Firm." R.C. Lacher; Pamela K. Coats; C. Shanker Sharma; and L. Franklin Fant. *European Journal of Operational Research* 85, no. 1 (August 17, 1995), pp. 53–65.

"Ranking College Football Teams: A Neural Network Approach." Rick L. Wilson. *Interfaces* 25, no. 4 (July–August 1995), pp. 44–59.

"Backpropagation in Time-Series Forecasting." Gerson Lachtermacher and J. David Fuller. *Journal of Forecasting* 14, no. 4 (July 1995), pp. 381–93.

"Wily Weapons against Card Fraud." Mark Borowsky. *Credit Card Management* 8, no. 2 (May 1995), pp. 46–47.

"A Neural Network Approach for Smoothing and Categorizing Noisy Data." Young B. Moon and Rick Janowski. *Computers in Industry* 26, no. 1 (April 1995), pp. 23–39.

"The Application of Neural Networks and a Qualitative Response Model to the Auditor's Going Concern Uncertainty Decision." Mary Jane Lenard; Pervaiz Alam; and Gregory R. Madey. *Decision Sciences* 26, no. 2 (March–April 1995), pp. 209–27.

"Neural Networks versus Parameter-Based Applications in Cost Estimating." Jesus M. de la Garza and Khalil G. Rouhana. *Cost Engineering* 37, no. 2 (February 1995), pp. 14–18.

"Neural Networks in Finance and Investing." Olvi L. Mangasarian. *Interfaces* 25, no. 1 (January–February 1995), pp. 141–42.

"Neural Network System for Forecasting Method Selection." Chao-Hsien Chu and Djohan Widjaja. *Decision Support Systems* 12, no. 1 (August 1994), pp. 13–24.

"A Two-Stage Neural Network Approach for ARIMA Model Identification with ESACF." Jae Kyu Lee and Won Chul Jhee. *Decision Support Systems* 11, no. 5 (June 1994), pp. 461–79.

"A Decision Support System for In-Sample Simultaneous Equation Systems Forecasting Using Artificial Neural Systems." Louis E. Caporaletti; Robert E. Dorsey; John D. Johnson; and William A. Powell. *Decision Support Systems* 11, no. 5 (June 1994), pp. 481–95.

planatory variables (called *input variables*) and one dependent variable (called the *desired output variable*). We present 16 steps in the development of ANNs. As you study these, recognize that these 16 steps are part of the following four larger activities which are very similar to those of other forecasting methods:

Identification.   Design the ANN by selecting the input and output variables, its architecture, and validation (i.e., testing) experiment, while trying not to violate the principle of parsimony.

Estimation.   Train the ANN to minimize the RSE or RMS paying attention to whether the network is too simplistic or too complex.

Diagnosis.   Test the ANN on out-of-sample data and compare the out-of-sample RSE or RMS to that of the training data.

Forecasting.   Use the ANN to forecast, always monitoring its goodness of fit.

The following is a brief introduction to each step of training and validating an ANN. A full discussion of why these steps are taken will come later.

1. ***Determine the structure of the ANN*** based on some underlying theory about what influences the dependent variable. In this case, the structure is given in Figure 16–4. However, in general, this involves choosing input variables, the number of **input nodes,** the number of **hidden** layers and **nodes,** the **transfer function** type, and the number of **output nodes.**

2. ***Divide the input and output data into two groups,*** the first to be used to train (i.e., fit) the network, the second to be used to validate the network in an out-of-sample experiment or forecast.

3. ***Scale all input variables*** and the desired output variable to the range of 0 to 1. Because of its mathematical structure, it is necessary to rescale the values of the variables in an ANN to be between 0 and 1. This is a very simple process that does not affect the underlying patterns or values.

4. ***Set initial weights and start a training epoch*** using the training data set (only three observations in Figure 16–4) by repeating steps (5) to (13): An **epoch** is the calculation of errors and the adjustment of weights by processing (i.e., taking one pass through) all observations in the training set. Also, in this step, initial values are given to all of the **weights (w_{ij}s)** in the ANN. These initial values can influence the speed and RMS that result from the training process. Most programs allow weights to be initialized with all zeros or random numbers from, for example, -1 to 1.

5. ***Input scaled variables.*** The **scaled inputs** of an observation are received at the input nodes 0 and 1 of Figure 16–4.

6. ***Distribute the scaled inputs*** to each hidden node (in this case, there is only one hidden node). In general, each hidden node receives all scaled input variables, which results in a parallel processing of all inputs at multiple nodes. In some cases, these inputs are distributed to each output layer node as well as to the hidden layer nodes. Note that the **output O_j** of an input node equals its **input, I_j.** Thus:

$$O_0 = I_0 \tag{16–1}$$

$$O_1 = I_1$$

7. ***Weight and sum inputs to receiving nodes.*** At each hidden node (i.e., node 3), the outputs of the input nodes (i.e., nodes 0 and 1) are weighted and summed. Thus, the input to node 3 is:

$$I_3 = W_{03}O_0 + W_{13}O_1 \tag{16–2}$$

8. ***Transform hidden-node inputs to outputs.*** At each hidden node, the weighted inputs are transformed into an output in the range of 0 to 1.

$$O_3 = \frac{1}{(1 + e^{-I_3})} \qquad (16-3)$$

where, as always, **e** is the natural number of 2.718282. . . .

9. ***Weight and sum hidden node outputs as inputs to output nodes.*** The outputs of the hidden node O_3 and any bias nodes (node 2 in this case) are weighted and summed. As we will see, a bias node operates much like the constant term in regression analysis.

$$I_4 = W_{24}O_2 + W_{34}O_3 \qquad (16-4)$$

10. ***Transform inputs at the output nodes.*** At the output node 4, the weighted input I_4 is transformed into the output of O_4 in the range of 0 to 1. This is the final output of the ANN:

$$O_4 = \frac{1}{(1 + e^{-I_4})} \qquad (16-5)$$

11. ***Calculate output errors.*** The scaled output value O_4 is compared to the scaled desired output value D_4 and the error is calculated:

$$e_i = D_4 - O_4 \qquad (16-6)$$

where i is the observation number in the training set.

12. ***Backpropagate errors to adjust weights.*** Based on the errors of step (11), the weights throughout the network are modified so as to move toward minimization of the **RMS value.** (This is the backpropagation method, which is discussed in a later section of this chapter and Appendix A.)

13. ***Continue the epoch.*** Repeat steps (5) to (12) for all observations in the input data set (only three in the case of Figure 16–4). As mentioned, each pass through all observations is called an epoch. When all observations have been processed (i.e., one epoch completed), go to step (14).

14. ***Calculate the epoch RMS*** value of the errors. If this RMS is low enough, stop and go to step (15). If the RMS is not low enough, repeat steps (5) to (14) until the stopping condition is reached:

$$RMS = \sqrt{\frac{\Sigma(e_i)^2}{nt}} \qquad (16-7)$$

where

    RMS = Approximately the residual standard error
      e_i = Errors during each observation in latest epoch
      nt = Number of observations in the epoch/training set

15. ***Judge out-of-sample validity.*** Having trained the ANN using one set of input data, now it should be validated using out-of-sample data. That is, use the ANN trained in steps (1) to (14) to predict the withheld output variables. If the out-of-sample RMS is consistent with the training RMS, the model appears valid. If the model is not valid, repeat the experiment after you:

a. Try different initial values for the weights.
b. Redesign the ANN (i.e., use fewer/more layers/nodes).
c. Try a different ANN method.
d. Reject ANNs as a viable method.

FIGURE 16–5

A simple 2×1×1 ANN after 684 training epochs THREE.WK1

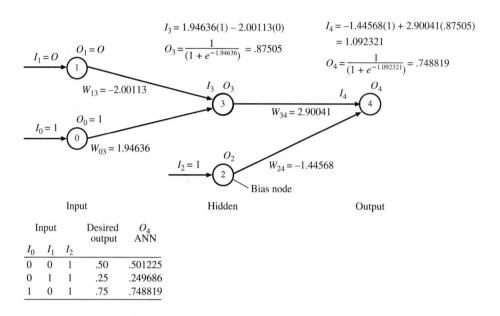

Input			Desired output	O_4 ANN
I_0	I_1	I_2		
0	0	1	.50	.501225
0	1	1	.25	.249686
1	0	1	.75	.748819

16. ***Use the model in forecasting.*** Use the model in an actual forecasting setting, being cautious to monitor it using tracking signals and other devices (see Chapter 17).

Having briefly presented each of the steps of developing an ANN, let's discuss some of these in greater detail using the trained version of the ANN of Figure 16–4 shown in Figure 16–5.

1. Determine the Structure of the ANN

The ANN of Figure 16–5 is rather simple. In contrast, most networks might have more input, hidden, and output nodes. In some cases, there is more than one hidden layer— sometimes as many as four.

Choosing the Architecture—Theory Driven Analysis. As mentioned, theory-based modeling applies equally well to traditional forecasting and ANN models. Because this is a contrived explanatory example, there is no need to discuss theory. However, consider the following general factors.

The number of input nodes in an ANN equals the number of input variables. For example, if the network is designed to approve or disapprove loans, one classical ANN problem, each attribute such as family income, credit card debt, age, home ownership, and so on requires an input neurode. Also, note that if we transformed any variables by taking logarithms or seasonal differences and these are input variables, each requires its own input node.

At the present, ANN modeling requires considerable art, and this is one of the more serious limitations of ANN. One of the "artistic" questions is exemplified by the lack of definite guidelines on the topology of ANN architecture. There are few well-established guidelines on choosing the best ANN architecture. Remember that the architecture includes all of the considerations we have discussed so far: the number of input variables and nodes, the number of hidden layers and nodes, the number of output nodes, also included are the choice of the transfer function used and values of other coefficients, considerations we discuss later. Fortunately, some ANN software include an expert system to guide the user in the design of the ANN.

Because the number of input nodes is established by the number of input variables, an understanding of the underlying theory of the output variable is important in determining which input variables should be included. Consequently, the usual questions exist concerning which variables to include and which to exclude. If too many variables are included, then the probability of overfitting a model increases. However, in ANN applications, there seem to be advantages to including more variables than not enough. For example, if the functional form of the relationship between the dependent and independent variables were known, most likely other forecasting methods discussed in this book would be more applicable than ANNs. In the limit, not knowing the functional form of a relationship means we are unsure of whether or not there is a relationship between the dependent and independent variables.

The Number of Hidden Layers.   In general, there is nothing that precludes having more than one hidden layer. However, the one hidden-layer network is very versatile. Sometimes though, it is necessary to have two or more hidden layers. But, just as we have seen with other forecasting methods, it is possible to have a model (i.e., network) that is too complex or too simple. If the ANN is too complex, the fitted weights will be designed to match the input data too closely instead of modeling the underlying patterns. Fortunately, this problem of overfitting can be detected during step (15). If the neural network is too simplistic, the training and validation RMS values will be too high.

2. Dividing the Data into Training and Validation Sets

For the reasons mentioned in the preceding paragraph, it is important to train and validate ANNs using two different data sets. The first data set is used to train the network and the second data set is used to validate the model. In this simple example, we use all of the data to train the ANN.

3. Scale All Input Variables

It has been our experience that the mathematics of ANNs are often the greatest barrier to understanding ANNs. Consequently, we illustrate these calculations in the simple example of Figure 16–5, which is the network of Figure 16–4 after 684 training epochs. Be aware that a full understanding of why these calculations are made requires more study, a task we undertake after this example.

Assume a firm wants to forecast demand Y using two inputs having the following values:

Inputs		Output
W	Z	Y
0	0	500
0	1	250
1	0	750

In modeling this relationship, we desire to minimize the error in predicting the output, Y. In fact, this is the same objective function of most ANNs, to minimize the RMS of Equation 16–7 when estimating the output.

Because the input variables in this simple example vary between 0 and 1, they do not need to be rescaled. However, the output variable Y must be rescaled. Let's assume that the **minimum value** of the output value could be 0 and the **maximum value**

1,000. Conveniently, the output can be made to vary between 0 and 1 by dividing it by 1,000.

Inputs		Output
SW	SZ	Y
0	0	.50
0	1	.25
1	0	.75

where *SW, SZ,* and *SY* are the scaled variables *W, Z,* and *Y,* respectively, and all have values in the range 0 to 1. This example is so trivial that an ANN is not needed to solve it:

$$SY = .50 + .25SW - .25SZ$$

Nonetheless, this is a useful introductory ANN example.

In general, when scaling the input data, it is important to anticipate actual maximums and minimums, even when these are not in the existing input data. This yields the simple scaling formula of Equation 16–8.

$$\text{Scaled value} = \frac{\text{Actual} - \text{Minimum}}{\text{Maximum} - \text{Minimum}} \tag{16–8}$$

where

Minimum = Expected minimum value in application
Maximum = Expected maximum value in application

When the training data set does not contain representative extreme values such as near maximum and minimum values of not only the output but also the input variables, the training process may not yield low out-of-sample errors. Of course, this is a problem with any model-building process—the data should be representative of future patterns and values.

In ANN terms, the inputs and actual output variables are notated as:

Inputs		Output
I_0	I_1	D_4
0	0	.50
0	1	.25
1	0	.75

As shown in Figure 16–5, there are two input nodes (0 and 1), one hidden node (3), one output node (4), and the additional **bias node** (2). As previously mentioned and discussed later, this node functions the same as the constant (i.e., *a*) in regression analysis.

4. Set Initial Weights and Start a Training Epoch

The initial values of the training weight can influence the required number of epochs and the final solution. Thus, when good starting values are unknown, the randomization of the initial training weights is often recommended, typically randomly distributed between −1 and 1.

5. Input Scaled Variables

The nodes 0 and 1 are simple nodes designating that I_0 and I_1 are inputs to the ANN. In general, the inputs to a node are designated as I_j and the outputs of nodes are designated O_j. Input nodes are the simplest types of nodes, as there is no transformation of the input variables; thus, the output of an input node equals its input value:

$$O_j = I_j \qquad (16\text{–}9)$$
$$O_0 = I_0$$
$$O_1 = I_1$$

6. Distribute the Scaled Inputs

In this step, each neurode in the input layer receives its value and distributes it to every node in the hidden layer. Thus, each neurode of the hidden layer receives all input values except that these signals are weighted to yield the input to the hidden neurodes in step (7). In this simple example, there is only one hidden layer neurode. However, in the general situation, there are several hidden neurodes and, as we noted, possibly more than one hidden layer.

It is the input of the same information to many nodes that is one of the distinctions of ANNs, resulting in the parallel processing power of ANNs. In general, but not always, each neurode in one layer receives all signals from its preceding layer. However, as mentioned, each signal to a neurode will have a different weight associated with it.

To make this discussion more concrete, assume that the actual inputs are:

$$I_0 = O_0 = 0$$
$$I_1 = O_1 = 1$$

7. Weight and Sum Outputs at Receiving Nodes

The weights and values in Figure 16–5 were determined by the many iterations of the training process. In a very real sense, the weights in an ANN contain its memory and intelligence. Just as with the coefficients in regression analysis, ANN weights express the relationship between the ANN layers and the final output. However, the weights in an ANN are more difficult to interpret than those in other modeling processes.

In this example, 684 training epochs were performed to yield the weights of Figure 16–5. Although this process probably remains somewhat of a mystery at this time, just remember that these weights were chosen so as to minimize the RMS. For now, let's feed these weights forward to see how they are used to generate the hidden node output and then the network output.

Along the arrows leading to node 3 are the weights given to each of the input values. At node 3, the inputs are summed using:

$$I_3 = W_{03}O_0 + W_{13}O_1 \qquad (16\text{–}10)$$
$$I_3 = 1.94636(1) - 2.00113(0) = 1.94636$$

In general, at each neurode, a weighted average of all inputs is calculated.

8. Transform Hidden Inputs to Outputs

The relationship between the input and output of a node is expressed by a **transfer function.** Because the **sigmoid transfer function** of Equation 16–11 (also called a **logistic function**) is used, the input value will result in a neurode output with a value of 0 through 1. This nonlinear transformation makes it possible to model nonlinear functions as well as to provide important logic in the network.

The input value to a neurode can be any value. However, the logistics transfer function transforms the input to an output level in the range of 0 to 1. Consider the output of node 3, given the input value of -1.94636:

$$O_3 = \frac{1}{(1 + e^{-I_3})} = \frac{1}{(1 + e^{-1.94636})} = .87505 \qquad (16\text{--}11)$$

Thus, we see that the input value to node 3 has been transformed to $O_3 = .87505$. This value is one input to node 4.

During the transformation of hidden node inputs to their outputs, some hidden neurodes will be activated (i.e., nonzero) and others will not (i.e., will equal zero). More importantly, as the network learns, the weights leading to the hidden layer neurodes are adjusted through backpropagation so as to minimize the ANN error. Thus, depending on the values of the input signals and the weights assigned to those signals, some combination of the hidden layer neurodes are activated. This sequence yields different outputs to next layer in the network.

When a hidden layer neurode is not activated, there is no signal from it to the output layer. When a hidden layer neurode is activated, and depending on the value of the summation at the output neurode, the output of the ANN is generated.

9. Weight and Sum Hidden Node Outputs at the Output Nodes

This next step is to sum inputs at the final node(s), the output node(s). We see that two nodes send signals to the output node, nodes 2 and 3.

$$I_4 = W_{24}O_2 + W_{34}O_3 \qquad (16\text{--}12)$$

$$I_4 = -1.44568(1) + 2.90041(.87505) = 1.092321$$

Node 3 is a hidden node and node 2 is a bias node. The bias node, 2, is used to change I_4 and therefore position the sigmoid function at a different location on the *x*-axis so that output O_4 has different values. It is a constant term where the added constant is determined by the weight from the bias node to the next node.

There is no transformation at a bias node, because the value of the bias output is always 1. However, the weight associated with a bias node is trained just as any other signal. Thus, W_{24} is trained like the other weights.

10. Transform Inputs at the ANN Output Nodes

The input value, I_4, is transformed to the output value, O_4:

$$O_4 = \frac{1}{(1 + e^{-I_4})} = \frac{1}{(1 + e^{-1.092321})} = .748819 \qquad (16\text{--}13)$$

11. Calculate Output Error

The output error is simply the difference between O_4 and the desired value, D_4. The ANN output is .748819 and the desired or true value is .75. Thus, there is very little error in this estimate:

$$e_i = D_4 - O_4 = .75 - .748819 = .001181$$

12. Backpropagate Errors to Adjust Weights

During this step, the weights are adjusted through a training process so as to yield the correct output variable. The **backpropagation of errors** in adjusting weights is discussed in the next section and Appendix 16–A.

13. Continue the Epoch

Process all inputs in the training data set once.

14. Calculate the Epoch RMS

Completing one epoch where all observations in the training data set are input to the ANN of Figure 16–5 yields Table 16–3. You should confirm the first and second

TABLE 16–3   Output and Errors of the ANN of Figure 16–5

Inputs		Desired Output	Actual Output		
I_0	I_1	D_4	O_4	e_4	e_4^2
0	0	.50	.501225	−.001225	.0000015
0	1	.25	.249686	.000314	.0000001
1	0	.75	.748819	.001181	.0000013
Summation				.000270	.0000029

Given the errors of Table 16–3, the RMS value of this epoch is:

$$\text{RMS} = \sqrt{\Sigma e_i^2 / nt} = \sqrt{.0000029/3} = .0017029 \qquad (16\text{--}14)$$

where nt is the number of observations in the training data set.

The epoch of Table 16–3 was the 684th training epoch.

15. Judge Out-of-Sample Validity

Because this is such a simple contrived example, there is no need to do this step here. However, this out-of-sample test is an essential step in an actual application.

16. Use the Model in Forecasting

To predict future outputs, simply input the scaled values of the input variables and calculate the output, O_4 using the previously fitted weights. This is about as easy as using other forecasting methods.

Having illustrated the computations of the feedforward steps of a simple ANN, let's discuss some of the more technical details of ANNs. First, consider the role of the sigmoid transfer function.

Understanding the Transfer Function

Because of the nonlinearity of the transfer function, there may be some confusion concerning its purpose. Consider the general summation process at a hidden or output node. (Remember, no transformations occur at input nodes.)

The general formula for the summation at a node is:

$$I_j = \sum_{j=f}^{s} W_{ij} O_i \qquad (16\text{--}15)$$

where

I_j = Net weighted input received by neurode j
W_{ij} = Weight of the connection from neurode i to neurode j
O_i = Signal from neurode i
j = Receiving node number
i = Sending node number
f, s = First and last number of sending nodes

After the summation of I_j is calculated, only the summation of the strength of the incoming signals is sent to the receiving node. The summation does not convey which neurode provided a strong signal and which did not. Consequently, it is the summation at the receiving node, not the source of each signal, that will activate a node. However, while the origins of specific input nodes are lost in the summation process, as the network is trained, the weights are adjusted so that only those input nodes that should influence the receiving node have high weights. Finally, it is possible to have a negative weight at a node. Such weights are referred to as inhibitors because they reduce the summation value, I_j, and thus may cause the output of the receiving node to be 0.

After summing the strengths of the incoming signals, these are transformed to an outgoing signal to the next layer of neurodes. As mentioned, the most commonly used function is the sigmoid:

$$O_j = \frac{1}{1 + e^{-I_j}} \qquad (16\text{–}16)$$

As shown in Table 16–4 and Figure 16–6, the sigmoid transfer function results in O_j varying between 0 and 1. Because the output of a sigmoid function is bounded by 0 and 1, it can operate as a binary output device. If the input, I_j, is very high, O_j is 1 as e^{-I_j} approaches zero; when I_j is very negative, O_j is 0 as e^{-I} approaches infinity. Thus, the signal from a neurode can easily be trained to either 0 or 1 depending on the value of I_j, which is determined by the values of the signal and weights of inputs from the layers feeding that neurode.

Just as in the human brain, a neuron either fires or does not fire. Thus, we see that a node is a mathematical device with logic generated by the sigmoid function. However, outputs between 0 and 1 yield signals of various strength to their receiving nodes.

To better understand the logical nature of the ANN, consider Table 16–4, which shows the value of the sigmoid transfer function from 1,000 to −1,000. We see that the values of 10 to 1,000 are essentially 1 and those of −10 to −1,000 are essentially 0. Thus, nodes activate (i.e., have an output greater than 0) or do not activate (i.e., have an output equal to 0) based on a fairly narrow range of inputs. Consequently, this activation range provides the logic and the memory of the ANN.

The Function of Bias

Typically, hidden and output layers should have a **bias** input. This input positions the transfer function on different locations on the horizontal axis, as in Figure 16–6. Without the bias weight, sigmoid transfer functions are centered on 0. Thus, the weight of the bias node positions the sigmoid function of the receiving node at the "best" value on the horizontal axis.

Consider a simple example. Assume that at a node the input of 1,000 should yield an output of .5; this is the underlying theoretical behavior of the hypothetical system. But, as we see in Table 16–4, the input of 1,000 yields a sigmoid output of 1, not .5. However, to achieve an output of .5, a constant can be subtracted from the 1,000 to yield an input of 0. This is precisely the function of the bias input. In this situation, the bias weight should be −1,000. In summary,

	Input I_j	Sigmoid Output O_j	Desired Output D_j
Without bias	1000	1	.5
With bias	1000 − 1000 = 0	.5	.5

Because the weights from a bias node are trained just as those from a regular node, the position of the sigmoid function is trained. Thus, we see that the bias node provides an additional flexibility to position the sigmoid transfer function on the horizontal axis and thereby have the correct output on the vertical axis.

TABLE 16–4   Sigmoid Transfer Function, Selected Values

I_j	$O_j = f(I_j)$	I_j	$O_j = f(I_j)$
1,000	1	−.25	.4378235
100	1	−.5	.37754067
10	.9999546	−1	.26894142
5	.99330715	−5	.00669285
1	.73105858	−10	.0000045398
.5	.62245933	−100	3.7201E-44
.25	.5621765	−1000	.00000000000
0	.5		

FIGURE 16–6

Sigmoid O_j of Table 16–4

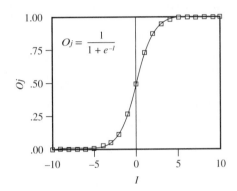

Other Transfer Functions

Typically, the transfer functions used in a ANN are the same for all neurodes in that network. While the sigmoid function of Equation 16–16 is the most common, some ANNs use other transfer functions more suited to that type of ANN. For example, some applications use a hyperbolic tangent function because it is symmetrical around zero (i.e., varies between −1 and +1). Another example is a threshold function, which operates by equating any input value—for example, .5 or less—to an output of 0 and any input value—for example, above .5 and—to an output of 1.

Most ANN software allows selection of the desired transfer function and will give guidelines on which transfer function to choose. Alternatively, additional study of ANNs may be necessary before you become comfortable enough to change the standard architecture for a particular application.

Describing Rates of Change in ANNs

Besides the nonlinear and logical behavior of sigmoid activation, the use of the sigmoid function is advantageous in an ANN because its derivative is easily computed as:

$$\frac{dO_j}{dI_j} = O_j(1 - O_j) \tag{16–17}$$

Thus, the rate of change in the value of the output of a neurode equals the product of O_j and $(1 - O_j)$. For example, several first derivatives of O_j with respect to I_j are:

Given $I_j = 0$	$dO_j/dI_j = .5(1 - .5) = .25$	This is the slope at $I_j = 0$.
Given $I_j = 10$	$dO_j/dI_j = 1(1 - 1) = .0$	This is the slope at $I_j = 10$.
Given $I_j = -10$	$dO_j/dI_j = 0(1 - 0) = .0$	This is the slope at $I_j = -10$.

These slopes can be confirmed by referring to Figure 16–6.

As shown in Appendix 16–A, the property of the first derivative of a sigmoid function is very useful when training an ANN (i.e., when adjusting its weights).

Forecasting Quarterly U.S. Marriages

Let's illustrate a more realistic ANN implementation process using the quarterly U.S. marriage series (BIRTHMAR.DAT) of Figure 16–7. Assume we want to predict this value using an ANN based solely on univariate information.

In this case, we have considerable understanding of the quarterly marriage series because most people are knowledgeable about the process of marriage. Because seasonality will dominate this series, we expect values of four quarters ago to be important inputs. Also, there may be some low-order or local memory, which might involve the level of marriages in the previous quarter. Thus, we anticipate at least two input variables, marriages one and four quarters ago.

Because the marriage data has only one strong pattern—seasonality—a **2 × 1 × 1 ANN** architecture seems appropriate. If, during the training process, only high RMS values result, then this might indicate that the ANN is too simplistic or the data set has too much noise in it. This ANN architecture is shown in Figure 16–8, which shows the trained ANN after 300 epochs.

Input Nodes.   Because the marriage time series is affected by seasonality and some drift, we have chosen two input nodes, one for Y_{t-1} and the other for Y_{t-4}. Note, however, that in the general application of ANNs, we might include more inputs, for example marriages for 1 to 8 quarters ago. Also, in general, it is good practice to choose several explanatory variables to include in the ANN. For example, the number

FIGURE 16–7

Quarterly U.S. marriages time series

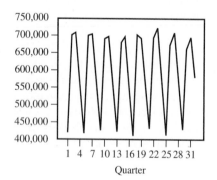

FIGURE 16–8

ANN for quarterly marriages MARRIAGE.WK1

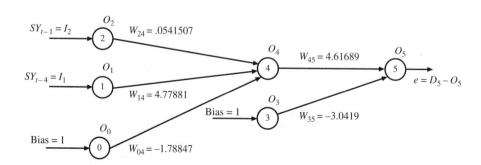

of men and women in the age bracket with the highest probability of marriage might have been included. It is doubtful that such causal variables will provide explanations of the seasonal nature of marriages that is so prevalent in this data, but they might explain the very slight up and down drift.

Hidden Nodes.   To simplify this presentation of ANNs, we have chosen a series that requires at most one hidden node. In fact, this ANN is so simple that the input nodes might have been connected directly to the output node without any hidden nodes. However, to illustrate another simple, general ANN, we include a single hidden node.

Output Nodes.   We have chosen to predict one output value. In general, ANNs have more than one output node. For example, in this situation, Y_t is being forecasted as a function Y_{t-1} and Y_{t-4}. A second output node for Y_{t+1} could easily be added to the ANN. In that case, the goal is to minimize one-and two-period-ahead errors. If we were to forecast two periods ahead, then surely we should include a third input variable, Y_{t-3}, which has a four-period lag with Y_{t+1}. However, we have limited the number of output nodes to simplify the discussions.

Table 16–5 illustrates the unscaled inputs and outputs for marriages.

Scaling Input Variables

As we have seen, scaling input variables is a necessary step because of the types of nonlinear transformations and logic built into an ANN. Let's assume that the maximum value of marriages in any quarter is likely to be about 850,000 and the minimum about 350,000. This yields:

$$SY_t = (Y_t - 350,000)/(850,000 - 350,000) \qquad (16–18)$$

Table 16–6 illustrates the scaled input data. As shown, these vary over a reasonable range of .104 to .748. When scaling variables ensure that the range of scaled actual variables is as wide as possible (i.e., minimum close to 0 and maximum close to 1)

TABLE 16–5   Unscaled Inputs and Desired Output Series

Period	Quarter	Input 1 Y_{t-4}	Input 2 Y_{t-1}	Output Y_t
1	1	NA	NA	420,240
2	2	NA	420,240	703,900
3	3	NA	703,900	709,010
4	4	NA	709,010	579,475
5	1	420,240	579,475	416,040
6	2	703,900	416,040	701,072
7	3	709,010	701,072	705,020
8	4	579,475	705,020	584,967
⋮				
25	1	425,000	600,000	411,000
26	2	698,000	411,000	674,000
27	3	724,000	674,000	709,000
28	4	600,000	709,000	578,000

Series	Obs	Mean	Std Error	Minimum	Maximum
Y_t	28	601,289.357	118,228.377	402,000	724,000

TABLE 16–6   Scaled Input and Output Variables

Period	SY_{t-4}	SY_{t-1}	SY_t
1	NA	NA	.140480
2	NA	.140480	.707800
3	NA	.707800	.718020
4	NA	.718020	.458950
5	.140480	.458950	.132080
6	.707800	.132080	.702144
7	.718020	.702144	.710040
8	.458950	.710040	.469934
⋮			
24	.512000	.748000	.500000
25	.150000	.500000	.122000
26	.696000	.122000	.648000
27	.748000	.648000	.718000
28	.500000	.718000	.456000

Series	Obs	Mean	Std Error	Minimum	Maximum
SY_t	28	.50258	.23646	.20400	.74800

while still encompassing the possible out-of-sample maximum and minimum. That is, scaled values should not vary little (e.g., from .4 to .6), but instead should vary over a wider range while assuring that future, scaled values are in the range of θ to 1.

Choosing the Target RMS

When **training** an ANN, some stopping value should be established. Commonly, the training is stopped when the ANN output value differs from the desired value by some sufficiently small amount. This stopping value is based on the RMS value of the output node during the most recent epoch. To assist in determining when training is to be terminated, some ANN software facilitates the choice of stopping value by clearly illustrating a graph of the RMS versus the epoch number. If too large an ANN is used or too many epochs are used to fit the ANN, there is the possibility that the data will be memorized (i.e., overfitted) by the ANN. Too many training cycles can occur when unrealistically low RMS values are chosen. Thus, some judgment is necessary in determining a stopping RMS.

To assist in determining a good stopping point, the plot of the RMS value can be monitored so that when learning no longer progresses at a "reasonable" rate, the ANN has been trained. That is, when the RMS graph becomes very flat, it is likely that the ANN has been trained sufficiently. Additional epochs are not necessary and might even result in overfitting weights. However, there are many times when so many epochs are needed to train the data that a graph of the RMS may be misleading. This is one reason we have to rely on the validation data to assess the ANN's validity after the training.

We have had some ANNs that require over 10,000 epochs before they were well trained. This can occur for a number of reasons, including poor starting values of the network weights. Such large numbers of required iterations make the determination of a good stopping value difficult. Thus, as mentioned earlier, judgment is necessary when stopping the training session.

TABLE 16–7   Output of Training 2×1×1 ANN for Marriages

Epochs = 300
RMS error = .025704
Eta = 1
Momentum = 0
Output delta = .01585

Input Layer
Node 0 is a bias node with value 1
Node 1 is an input node with output value .5
Node 2 is an input node with output value .718

Hidden Layer
Node 3 is a bias node with output value 1
Node 4 is a type hidden node with output value .659817

$$W_{04} = -1.78847$$

$$W_{14} = 4.77881$$

$$W_{24} = .0541507$$

Output Layer
Node 5 is an output node with value .505546 and target value of .456

$$W_{35} = -3.0419$$

$$W_{45} = 4.61689$$

A logical way in which to choose a stopping RMS value is the use of $\overline{R}^2$. To crudely estimate the target RMS, determine a reasonable $\overline{R}^2$ for the scaled output variable by, for example fitting an appropriate time series model to the variable. Because the marriage time series is very regular and previously fitted forecasting models yielded an $\overline{R}^2$ of about 99 percent, let's assume an $\overline{R}^2$ of .98 is desired. We know the value of s_D^2 from Table 16–6. Thus:

$$\overline{R}^2 = 1 - \frac{\text{Target RMS}^2}{S_D^2} = .98$$

$$= 1 - \frac{\text{Target RMS}^2}{.23646^2} = 1 - \frac{\text{Target RMS}^2}{.0559133} \tag{16–19}$$

$$\text{Target RMS}^2 = (1 - \overline{R}^2)S_d^2 = (1 - .98).0559133 = .00112 \tag{16–20}$$

$$\text{RMS} = \sqrt{.00112} = .03344$$

This RMS value seems fairly ambitious. Thus, we will cautiously watch the RMS value as the ANN is learning.

The Results of Training

During the training process, it was apparent that the RMS would be lower than expected, so the process was allowed to continue for 300 epochs. The results of this training process are shown in Table 16–7 and in Figure 16–8. Let's discuss these values.

As Table 16–7 illustrates, the weight, W_{24}, is quite low, .0541507. This weight is associated with the input variable Y_{t-1} and denotes that this variable has little influence on the value of the output variable. Thus, this variable might be dropped from the ANN and the new model refitted (you might try this yourself).

Using the weights of Table 16–7 yields the actual and desired outputs of Table 16–8. Column 3 shows that the errors have an RMS value of .0257. This RMS value corresponds to an approximate $\overline{R}^2$ of .988:

$$\overline{R}^2 = 1 - \frac{.0257^2}{.23646^2} = .988$$

Out-of-Sample Validation.   While not shown in this example, an essential step in ANN modeling is the forecasting of out-of-sample observations; commonly called validating the ANN using test data. Because of the simplicity of this very well behaved time series, we do not show this step here. However, you may be asked to test the ANN of Figure 16–8 on observations 29 to 32 for homework. For now, let's consider a more realistic ANN example.

TABLE 16–8   Output of 2×1×1 ANN for Quarterly Marriages

Period[a]	D_t	O_t	e_t
5	.13208	.13214	−.00006
6	.70214	.69001	.01213
7	.71004	.70061	.00943
8	.46993	.44273	.02720
9	.15117	.12829	.02289
10	.68404	.68638	−.00234
11	.69740	.69551	.00189
12	.47414	.45674	.01740
13	.13200	.13746	−.00546
14	.66200	.67353	−.01153
15	.69600	.68709	.00892
16	.48800	.46213	.02587
17	.10400	.12834	−.02434
18	.70800	.65645	.05155
19	.68600	.68650	−.00050
20	.51200	.47967	.03233
21	.15000	.11664	.03336
22	.69600	.69028	.00572
23	.74800	.67951	.06849
24	.50000	.51045	−.01045
25	.12200	.13702	−.01502
26	.64800	.68195	−.03395
27	.71800	.71746	.00054
28	.45600	.49521	−.03921
RMS			.0257

[a]First four observations are lost because Y_{t-4} is used.

Forecasting the S&P 500

Financial forecasting has been a widely used application of ANNs. For example, ANNs can be used to model fluctuations in one time series as a function of lagged daily values of other financial indexes. Assume that we want to predict the daily S&P 500 using an ANN and the following 14 financial market measures as input variables.

$$I_1 = \text{S\&P 500 close}_{t-1}$$
$$I_2 = \text{S\&P 500 high}_{t-1}/\text{low}_{t-1}$$
$$I_3 = \text{NYSE advancing}_{t-1}/\text{declining issues}_{t-1}$$
$$I_4 = \text{NASDAQ advancing}_{t-1}/\text{declining issues}_{t-1}$$
$$I_5 = \text{NYSE new highs}_{t-1}/\text{new lows}_{t-1}$$
$$I_6 = \text{NASDAQ new highs}_{t-1}/\text{new lows}_{t-1}$$
$$I_7 = \text{NYSE total volume}_{t-1}$$
$$I_8 = \text{NYSE advancing}_{t-1}/\text{declining issues volume}_{t-1}$$
$$I_9 = \text{NASDAQ total volume}_{t-1}$$
$$I_{10} = \text{NASDAQ advancing}_{t-1}/\text{declining issues volume}_{t-1}$$
$$I_{11} = \text{Three-month treasury bill yield}_{t-1}$$
$$I_{12} = \text{30-Year treasury bill yield}_{t-1}$$
$$I_{13} = \text{Price of gold}_{t-1}$$
$$I_{14} = \text{Dow Jones 30 industrial close}_{t-1}$$

These 14 variables require 14 input nodes. In addition, these variables can be used to generate other variables. For example, first differences, logarithms, or moving averages of these variables might be used. Obviously, each of these new variables must be scaled to values between 0 and 1. Then each of the scaled variables is input through an additional node.

When fully designed, the model should include all inputs that affect the S&P 500. Initially, the network might include about 7 hidden nodes. Depending on whether only one-period-ahead or, for example, five-period-ahead forecasts are desired, one to five output nodes are needed. Figure 16–9 illustrates an ANN having 14 input, 16 hidden, and 5 output nodes, a total of 1,120 weights and interconnections. However, the 16 hidden nodes of Figure 16–9 probably violate the parsimony principle. Experimentation with the network will likely reduce this number so that the ANN does not memorize the input data.

While we do not actually train and validate this model here, it is not difficult to do so because all of the input data is available publicly.

Sales with an Interaction Effect (INTERACT.DAT)

This example illustrates an ANN that has an unanticipated result. This result clearly illustrates the advantage of ANNs when there is uncertainty regarding the proper functional relationship between the input and output variables.

Consider a hypothetical situation where building materials sales (*SY*) is a function of the number of do-it-yourself (*DIY*) repair homeowners (*SX*1) and the value of housing (*SX*2) in a five-mile ring of 60 stores. (In this example, the variables have already been scaled in the range of 0 to 1). An analyst is exploring methods for explaining sales in such neighborhoods. In addition to the direct effects of *SX*1 and *SX*2 on *SY*,

FIGURE 16–9

ANN for S&P 500

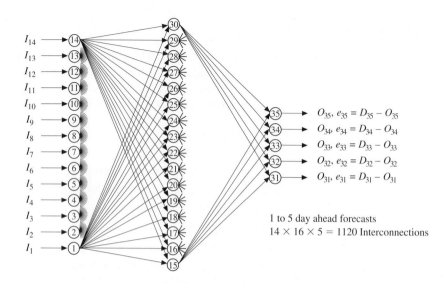

1 to 5 day ahead forecasts
14 × 16 × 5 = 1120 Interconnections

there is an interaction affect from the two independent variables (i.e., *SX1*∗*SX2*). This occurs when higher price houses exist in neighborhoods with large numbers of *DIY* homeowners. Let's consider the performance of regression analysis and ANNs.

Assume that an analyst is unaware of the interaction between the two variables *SX*1 and *SX*2 (the analyst did not study Chapter 3 and 10 well and did not plot the residuals against each of the independent variables). The analyst fits a regression model to this relationship as:

$$SY = -.2821 + .6606SX1 + .5218SX2 + e \qquad (16\text{–}21)$$
$$(-8.191) \qquad (16.388) \qquad (11.333)$$

$$\text{RSE} = .0985 \qquad \text{RMS} = .0979 \qquad \bar{R}^2\ 8738 \qquad n = 60 \qquad F = 205.2$$
$$(.00000000)$$

This model is a misspecification of the true relationship because the correct relationship is:

$$SY = .03828 + .02368SX1 - .02593SX2 + .9560SX1\ast SX2 + e \qquad (16\text{–}22)$$
$$(5.976) \qquad (2.117) \qquad (-2.525) \qquad (63.021)$$

$$\text{RSE} = .012 \qquad \text{RMS} = .0\text{-}115 \qquad \bar{R}^2 = .9982 \qquad n = 60 \qquad F = 10.989$$
$$(.00000000)$$

Incidentally, Equation 16–22 is a best model of any type to explain this data. But let's see how well an ANN will explain this data given the mistake of inputting just *SX*1 and *SX*2 into that ANN. Figure 16–10 and Table 16–9 illustrate the trained 2×2×1 ANN for this data. Now, this ANN is misspecified just as Equation 16–21 because an interaction input variable should have been included in the network—this requires a third input variable. However, our purpose is to see how well the misspecified ANN does relative to the misspecified and correctly specified regression Equations of 16–21 and 16–22.

Let's compare the performance of the four different fitted models of this series, the misspecified regression model (Equation 16–21), a correctly specified regression model (Equation 16–22), and the misspecified ANN of Figure 16–10 and a correctly

FIGURE 16–10

Trained 2×2×1 ANN for interaction data INTERACT.WK1

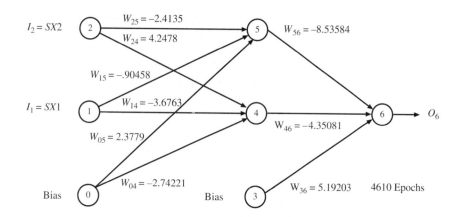

TABLE 16–9   Comparing Three Models of Building Material Sales

Model	Inputs	Estimation	RMS	Percent of Best
Equation 16–21	SX1, SX2	OLS	.0979	851
Equation 16–22	SX1, SX2, SX1*SX2	OLS	.0115	100
ANN (2×2×1)	SX1, SX2	4610 epochs	.0350	304
ANN (3×2×1)	SX1, SX2, SX1*SX2	4610 epochs	.0150	130

specified 3×2×1 ANN. As shown in Table 16–9, the misspecified ANN had a considerably better RMS and $\bar{R}^2$ than the misspecified regression model (.035 versus .0979). However, the ANN does not perform as well as the correctly specified regression of Equation 16–22—it is 204 percent higher. Finally, the correctly specified 3×2×1 ANN performs almost as well as the regression model, being only 30 percent higher.

This simple example illustrates how the ANN adapted to the relationship, even though the interaction was not known by the analyst. That is, the ANN performed much better than the misspecified regression model by including some, but not all of the effects of the interaction between the two variables. Also, as shown in Table 16–9, the correctly specified ANN with three inputs had an RMS that was better than all but the correctly specified regression model.

Backpropagation and Training ANNs

This section presents an overview of the backpropagation method of training an ANN. For some, it will be too technical; for others, not technical enough. Those wanting a more technical presentation should see Appendix 16–A and Dixon and Bevan (1994).

Just as in the estimation of regression coefficients using ordinary least squares, the weights in an ANN must be estimated. While there are several methods of training a network, the most successful and widely used is the feedforward, backpropagation method. The method of propagating information about errors at the output layers back to hidden layers was discovered in the mid 1970s, but this method was either unknown or ignored. It was rediscovered in the 1980s and the method termed *backpropagation* was refined and publicized by David Rumelhart and James McClelland (1986).

If the neurode output functions are differentiable, then the adjustment of the weights has a simple solution—adjust them in proportion to the negative of the change in the sum of squared errors with respect to the change in weights. It is logical that the changes in the weights in the ANN should be proportionate to the negative of the rate of change of the sum of squared errors (SSE) with respect to the weights because of the behavior of the slope of the SSE function. That is:

$$W_{ij}\,(\text{new}) = W_{ij}\,(\text{old}) + \Delta W_{ij}\,(\text{new}) \tag{16–23}$$

$$\Delta W_{ij} \propto - \frac{\partial \text{SSE}}{\partial W_{ij}} \tag{16–24}$$

where $\propto$ denotes "is proportionate to."

Figure 16–11 illustrates a hypothetical SSE versus the value of two network weights, W_{35} and W_{45}. Note that the slope prior to the minimum (i.e., point A) is negative. To increase the weight, some proportion of the negative of the rate of change should be added to the old weight. Also, the complement is true—the slope for weights after the minimum is positive (i.e., point B). When a weight "overshoots" the minimum, as in point B, it should be made lower. Thus, some proportion of the negative of the positive slope should be added to the old weight to yield the new weight.

In actuality, partial differentiation is used to change the weights in proportion to the derivative of the sum of squared error with respect to the weights. The training formula used in most software and the spreadsheets enclosed with this text use what is referred to as the **generalized delta rule.** As shown below, the generalized delta rule expands on Equation 16–23 by adding terms to accelerate or decelerate weight changes.

The Generalized Delta Rule

The training of an ANN using the generalized delta rule requires the adjustment of several parameters in the training algorithm. These include:

- Maximum number of epochs and stopping RMS value.
- Learning rate, η.
- Momentum rate, α.

Having already discussed the maximum number of epochs and the stopping RMS values, consider the concepts of the **learning rate (η), delta (δ),** and momentum rate (α) of the backpropagation method.

Using backpropagation, the errors in the hidden layers are backpropagated from the output layer and multiplied by the derivative of the hidden layers' output from the previous training step. Equation 16–25 defines the generalized delta rule:

$$\Delta W_{ij}\,(\text{new}) = \eta \delta_{ij} O_j + \alpha \Delta W_{ij}\,(\text{old}) \tag{16–25}$$

where

η = Learning coefficient, which users set between 0 and 1
δ_{ij} = Derivative of the sum of squared errors with respect to the weight at a node, sometimes referred to as that node's share of the error.
O_j = Output value at node j
α = Momentum coefficient varying between 0 and 1
$\Delta W_{ij}\,(\text{old})$ = Previous change in W_{ij}

Let's study the first part of the right-hand side of Equation 16–25, $\eta \delta_{ij} O_j$. This term states that the change in the weight from neurode i to the output neurode j equals

Figure 16–11

Sum of squared errors versus two weights

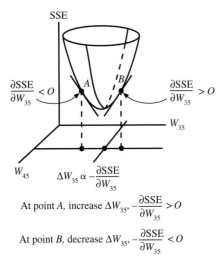

At point A, increase ΔW_{35}, $-\dfrac{\partial \text{SSE}}{\partial W_{35}} > O$

At point B, decrease ΔW_{35}, $-\dfrac{\partial \text{SSE}}{\partial W_{35}} < O$

some fraction, η, times the output neurode's share of the total squared errors, δ_{ij}, times the output of the jth neurode, O_j. The error at a neurode, δ_{ij}, should be viewed as that neurode's contribution to the total error of the network. The origin of this term may be somewhat mysterious. We do not show its mathematical derivation here but in Appendix 16–A, so to better understand the meaning of Equation 16–25, you should study Appendix 16–A if you are interested in these technical details. The typical user of ANNs need only understand the overall meaning of Equation 16–25. With that in mind, consider the functions of the learning and momentum coefficients.

The Learning Coefficient, η (eta). The learning coefficient is a fraction or smoothing constant set by the user so that the change in weights, $\Delta W_{ij}(\text{new})$, is not too rapid or slow. The learning coefficient is normally set above 0 and less than or equal to 1. Remembering that we adjust weights during the processing of each observation within an epoch and that the individuals within each epoch have various levels of error, it is often advantageous not to change the weights based on the error of a single observation but instead to change the weight by a fraction of the influence of several most recent observations.

Obviously, this adjustment process is wholly analogous to the concept of simple exponential smoothing, where the value of the weight is an exponentially weighted moving average of past weights. Thus, $W_{ij}(\text{new})$ is like an exponentially weighted moving average of past weights. If η is set too high, the weights may oscillate wildly about some optimal value and in some cases the training process may become unstable; if η is set too low, it may take many more epochs in which to train the ANN. Often, the best value of η can be found with simple experimentation during the training process.

Just as there are several types of exponential smoothing forecasting models, there are other ways of adjusting $\Delta W_{ij}(\text{new})$. For example, there are dynamic methods using adaptive response rate exponential smoothing (see Chapter 4). Such methods have many of the disadvantages in ANN training that they have in forecasting.

The Momentum Coefficient, α. One of the problems with searching for a minimum point on an SSE surface like Figure 16–11 is that local minima may interfere with the process of achieving a global minima. When nearing a minimum, whether local or global, the change in the weights decreases and may mistakenly stop at a local minimum. To offset the reduction in steepness that occurs at a local minimum, the momentum term is incorporated into the generalized delta rule. The basic concept with momentum is to continue with relatively large changes in the weights despite the tendency to reduce them because of a local optimal. By having large changes in the weights, local minimums may be stepped over. Also, the number of training epochs may decrease dramatically when the momentum term is included. However, if the momentum coefficient is too high, then the optimal point may be overstepped. Thus, some user manipulations or adjustments of α may be necessary as the training progresses.

The term $\alpha \Delta W_{ji}$ (old) is the momentum term that keeps the search moving and α is the weighting coefficient. Again, the function of this term in Equation 16–25 is very much like simple exponential smoothing, where a fraction of the old weight change is included in calculating the next weight. By including a fraction of the last weight change, the search has additional momentum in the direction of the previous change until sufficient force counteracts the momentum. Thus, during most iterations, we more rapidly approach the global optimal, hopefully overstepping local optimals.

Unfortunately, there are no universal rules regarding the best values of α; trial and error is the best way to determine good values. In all of the ANNs trained here, the momentum coefficient was set to 0. Also, note that there is no momentum coefficient in the enclosed spreadsheets.

ANN Summary

ANN models, like all forecasting methods, are not always the best approach to forecasting. In fact, the experiences to date give mixed reviews to the effectiveness of ANNs. A study by Lapedes and Farber (1987) showed that ANNs can outperform traditional forecasting models, sometimes being more than 10 times more accurate. However, this study was very limited in scope. Weigend, Huberman, and Rumelhart (1990) applied feedforward ANN to forecasting with realistic data, including sun spots. A trained ANN predicted out-of-sample values very accurately. Sharda and Patil (1990) used 75 times series from the M-competition and compared their results to those of an expert ARIMA (i.e., Box–Jenkins) forecasting system. Out of the 75 series, ANN performed better than 39 of the series and worse for 36 series. While the expert system they used in their comparison is very good, we believe that it is difficult to consistently outperform a good human ARIMA model builder.

Although backpropagation has been very successful, other very important ANN work continues. John Hopfield and David Tank have developed ANNs having fixed weights and adaptive output functions. These ANNs are very different than backpropagation methods but they have been successfully used to solve problems like the infamous traveling salesman problem. Although most ANNs use the backpropagation methods for learning, current research into nondeterministic ANNs shows great promise. These ANNs are capable of changing weights and outputs on the basis of probability distributions.

The power of ANNs includes their ability to perform pattern recognition, learning, classification, generalization, and interpretation of data. Because ANNs have some of the characteristics of human problem-solving approaches, they can analyze large quantities of data. ANNs can find patterns and relationships in systems where the rules are not known. ANNs have been found to be useful for financial applications such as forecasting stock prices and optimal portfolio mixes. Similarly, ANNs can find patterns in incomplete or noisy data.

Because of their parallelism and complexity, ANNs have several benefits:

- **Multiple output variables:** ANNs can be used to forecast multiple output variables such as $Y_t, Y_{t+1}, \ldots, Y_{t+s}$, where s is the length of the season.
- **Fault tolerance:** Because of the many processing nodes and layers, the loss of a few nodes or missing input data may not cause system failure.
- **Generalization:** When ANNs process noisy or out-of-sample data, they typically generate valid outputs.
- **Adaptability:** Once the architecture of an ANN is established, the ANN can rapidly learn in a new application.
- **Flexibility:** ANNs are effectively applied with multivariate data that are noisy, complex, or incomplete. In addition, as we saw in the building material sales interaction example, the complexity of the ANN makes it more flexible in modeling nonlinearities and interactions.
- **Hybrid systems:** ANNs can be incorporated into hybrid systems. For example, a hybrid system might use an ES or genetic algorithm to identify the correct ANN architecture, the correct transformations of the input variables, and so on.

Comparing ANNs and ESs

To place ANNs in perspective with expert systems, Table 16–10 compares these two methodologies.

The potential of ANNs is quite great. However, we must not be too optimistic or pessimistic. There are several vendors of ANNs, including the following:

Software Title	Vendor Name (in order by vendor)
ModelQuest	AbTech Corp.
Neural Net Tutor	Advanced Technology Transfer Group
BrainMaker Pro	California Scientific Software
Stock Prophet	Future Wave Software
ExploreNet 3	HNC
Neural Network Utility	IBM Corp. Mathworks Inc.
NeuralDesk 2.1	Neural Computer Sciences
MacBrain	Neurix
NeuralSolutions	NeuroDimension Inc.
DynaMind	NeuroDynamX
Neural Connection	SPSS Inc.
Neuroshell	Ward Systems Groups, Inc.

Most of these vendors can be found on the Internet through one or more of the search engines identified in book Appendix A.

In closing, we share some of the optimism expressed by ANN software vendors—the intelligence of ANNs can be extraordinary in the appropriate application. However this optimism must be tempered by the negative characteristics of ANN listed in Table 16–10.

TABLE 16–10   Comparing ANN and ES Characteristics

	Expert Systems	*ANNs*
Provides education of user	Yes	No
Coordination with other system	Yes	No
Good GUI interfaces	Yes	Maybe
Explains conclusions	Yes	No
Has mathematic capabilities	Yes	Some
Good development shells	Yes	Maybe
Technology well established	Yes	No
People skills required	Yes	Less
Extensive math skill required	No	Helpful
Experts needed to develop	Throughout	In setup
Useful in optimization	Yes	Some are
Useful in diagnosing problems	Yes	Much less so
Computer intensive	Sort of	Extraordinarily so
Easily embedded in other systems	Not easily	Easily
Expensive to develop	Yes	Yes, less so
Type of knowledge	Rules	Weights
Human input necessary to development	Great	Much less so

Adapted from Neural Network Tutor, Advanced Technology Transfer Group, www.attg.org.

Genetic Algorithms (GA)

As Darwin and others have so clearly shown, natural systems evolve following a number of different mechanisms. **Genetic algorithms** mimic these evolutionary processes as methods for solving complex problems. Specifically, genetic algorithms are search procedures that are based on natural selection and genetics. Consider the definitions of the terms, *genetic* and *algorithms*.

Algorithms are sets of instructions that are repeatedly executed to either solve a problem or provide system control. The term *genetic* refers to a process that evolves similarly to how a biological system might evolve. Genetic algorithms are self-organizing and adapt to changes in the environment much as do biological organisms. Because of their adaptive and self-organizing capabilities, genetic algorithms are used for categorization, pattern recognition, and association.

What Is a Genetic Code?

The following simple example illustrates the essence of a genetic code and GAs. Consider a situation where we seek a forecasting model which will minimize the sum of squared forecast errors. We have to choose from the following three combinations of forecasting model components to forecast a monthly time series, Y_t:

- *Seasonality (S)*
  - 0 = No, no seasonality in the model
  - 1 = Yes, seasonality in the model
- *Trend (T)*
  - 0 = No, no trend in the model
  - 1 = Yes, trend in the model

- *Exponential smoothing (E)*
  0 = Use no smoothing, simply use differences (e.g., $Y_t = Y_{t-12} + e_t$)
  1 = Use exponential smoothing

The number of possible combinations (i.e., genetic codes) from these three components is only 8 (i.e., $2^3 = 8$).

Enumeration of All Eight Possible Genetic Codes

Model Code			Forecast Model
S	*T*	*E*	*Sum of Squared Errors (SSE)*
0	0	0	100
1	0	0	95
0	1	0	80
0	0	1	90
1	1	0	65
0	1	1	75
1	0	1	80
1	1	1	60 *Optimum

This is an extremely simple situation where we can enumerate all possible combinations of genetic codes and resulting sums of squared errors as our measure effectiveness. However, in the general case, an exhaustive enumeration of codes and SSEs might not be possible. Now assume that we do not know the SSEs of each possible genetic code, but seek efficient and effective ways of determining the best code.

Evolutionary GA Processes

In general, GAs consist of three types of operations to converge on that genetic code with desirable properties. The desired property in this case is the lowest sum of squared errors. The three most common GA processes are selection, crossover, and mutation.

Selection.   **Selection** consists of algorithms that mimic survival of the fittest, where there are many combinations for achieving effective solutions. The methods of selection include rankings, tournaments, and proportionate methods that give preference to best performers.

Crossover.   **Crossover** is the process where parts of different genetic codes are exchanged. For example, given the following two genetic codes, several crossovers can occur.

Parent code 1	*011*
Parent code 2	*100*

Assume the first digit of each parent code is crossed over to (i.e., exchanged with) the other; this yields two offspring:

Offspring 1	*111*
Offspring 2	*000*

In a similar manner, assume that the last digit of each parent code is crossed over:

Offspring 3	*010*
Offspring 4	*101*

Selection and crossover are simple operations involving the use of random number generators, string copying, and partial string exchanges. Space does not allow a full discussion of the effective rules of crossover and selection; however, the previous four offspring illustrate the principle.

Mutation.   **Mutation** is the arbitrary change of genetic codes. Mutation can be used to keep an algorithm from converging on only one set of combinations. It injects change when the conditions seem to warrant such changes.

All three methods—selection, crossover, and mutation—are based on the principle of giving higher priority to the better individuals in the population.

A Simple Crossover Example

Let's assume that we randomly select four combinations from the population of eight forecasting methods (remember, assume we do not know the SSE values for each of these eight). We then apply those forecasting methods and calculate the SSE for a generation 0 of the population as:

Generation 0

S	T	E	Sum of Squared Errors	
1	0	0	95	
0	1	0	80	lowest
0	0	1	90	
1	0	1	80	lowest

We see that from generation 0, the lowest combinations are 0 1 0 and 1 0 1. We consider these combinations to be parents of the next generation. Using crossover, where the first and last code of the each parent are exchanged, yields the following two offspring:

Generation 1

S	T	E	Sum of Squared Errors	
0	1	0	80 parent	
1	0	1	80 parent	
0	0	0	100 offspring	
1	1	1	60 offspring	*Optimum

Thus, after one generation (i.e., two iterations) and evaluation of only six combinations, we have arrived at the lowest error combination of 1 1 1, a seasonal and trend exponentially smoothed forecasting model.

While we have illustrated the process of crossover using a simple example, the essential ideas of GAs are clear. Also note that a realistic application would have many more combinations of crossover than this simplistic example. Figure 16–12 illustrates a brief overview of the GAs process.

FIGURE 16–12

General flow diagram of GA process

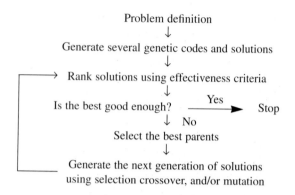

Benefits and
Applications of GAs

We have seen that GAs are iterative procedures solving a specific problem. During each iteration (sometimes called a generation), the current solutions are rated for their effectiveness. On the basis of these ratings, a new population of solutions is formed using genetic operations such as selection, crossover, and mutation.

GAs have several advantages, including the ability to quickly solve difficult problems, easily interface with other models or simulations, and easily integrate with other approaches such as ANNs. In fact, self-organizing ANNs have much in common with GAs, incorporating such evolutionary processes.

GA Applications

GAs have been used in applications such as:

- Time series prediction in currency trading.
- The selection of ANN structures (i.e., ANN topologies).
- Dynamic control of processes.
- Search for optimal decision rules in simulations.
- Coordination of engineering design systems such as finite element analysis, computational fluid dynamics, and discrete event simulations.

In summary, we see that based on Darwinian evolution theory, many possible codes are generated, evaluated, purged, and recombined to produce better offspring that will hopefully inherit the desirable traits of their parents. Occasionally, mutation is introduced to ensure that the algorithm is not trapped in a local minimum during the iterative process.

Goldberg (1994) and Austin (1990) provide interesting overviews and references for this exciting area, an area which will undergo its own considerable evolution.

Summary

Conventional programming solutions to forecasting system problems have existed for several decades and will continue to be very important in providing routine forecasts. The results of several forecasting studies have confirmed that increased forecast model sophistication may not result in improved accuracy with the typical data of forecasting systems. Consequently, a more fruitful way to improve forecasting system development is through AI. However, the potential benefits from the use of AI are just now being realized. This chapter has presented forecasting applications that can benefit from increased artificial intelligence in their implementations. These AI applications are currently under development at several firms and institutions. There are very significant potential improvements in forecasting efficiency and effectiveness from the use of ESs, ANNs, and GAs in the applications described here. This chapter has presented the basics of these methods so that you might start your journey toward improved forecasting systems.

Key Terms

actual ANN output, O_j

architecture of ANN

artificial intelligence (AI)

artificial neural networks (ANNs)

backpropagate errors

backpropagation

bias node

clustering

conventional program systems (CPS)

crossover

delta (δ_{ij})

desired output, D_j

dialog structure

epoch RMS

expert systems (ES)

generalized delta rule

genetic algorithms (GAs)

hidden layer

hidden nodes

inference engine

input layer

input nodes

input value, I_j

knowledge base

learning rate, η

logical filtering

massively parallel

maximum value

minimum value

momentum rate, α

mutation

neurodes

neurons

output layer

output nodes

processing elements (PEs)

reasonableness test

reconstruction/recognition

RMS value

routing

scaled inputs

scaled value

selection

self-organizing networks

sigmoid/logistic function

special event filtering

system control and maintenance

trained networks

training epochs

transfer function

weights, W_{ij}

$3 \times 2 \times 1$ ANN

Key Formulas

Artificial neural networks (ANNs)
Input Node:

$$O_0 = I_0$$
$$O_1 = I_1 \tag{16-1}$$

Weighted inputs at a node:

$$I_3 = W_{03}O_0 + W_{13}O_1 \tag{16-2}$$

Transform hidden node inputs to outputs:

$$O_3 = \frac{1}{(1 + e^{-I_3})} \tag{16-3}$$

Weight and sum hidden node outputs as inputs to output nodes:

$$I_4 = W_{24}O_2 + W_{34}O_3 \tag{16-4}$$

Transform inputs at the output nodes:

$$O_4 = \frac{1}{(1 + e^{-I_4})} \tag{16–5}$$

Calculate output errors:

$$e_i = D_4 - O_4 \tag{16–6}$$

Calculate the epoch RMS:

$$\text{RMS} = \sqrt{\frac{\Sigma(e_i)^2}{nt}} \tag{16–7}$$

where

$$\text{RMS} = \text{Residual standard error (approximately)}$$
$$e_i = \text{Errors during each observation in latest epoch}$$
$$nt = \text{Number of observations in the training set}$$

$$\text{Scaled value} = \frac{\text{Actual} - \text{Minimum}}{\text{Maximum} - \text{Minimum}} \tag{16–8}$$

	Input I_j	Sigmoid Output O_j	Desired Output D_j
Without bias	1000	1	.5
With bias	$1{,}000 - 1{,}000 = 0$	.5	.5

Describing rates of change in ANNs:

$$\frac{dO_j}{dI_j} = O_j(1 - O_j) \tag{16–17}$$

Forecasting quarterly U.S. marriages—scaling input variables:

$$SY_t = (Y_t - 350{,}000)/(850{,}000 - 350{,}000) \tag{16–18}$$

Choosing the target RMS:

$$\overline{R}^2 = 1 - \frac{\text{Target RMS}^2}{S_D^2}$$

$$= .98 = 1 - \frac{\text{Target RMS}^2}{.23646^2} = 1 - \frac{\text{Target RMS}^2}{.0559133} \tag{16–19}$$

$$\text{Target RMS}^2 = (1 - \overline{R}^2) * S_d^2 = (1 - .98) * .0559133 = .00112 \tag{16–20}$$

$$\text{RMS} = \sqrt{.00112} = .03344$$

Interaction Example:

$$SY = -.2821 + .6606SX1 + .5218SX2 + e \tag{16–21}$$
$$(-8.052) \quad\quad (16.388) \quad\quad (11.333)$$

Equation 16–21 is a misspecification of the true relationship:

$$SY = .03828 + .02368SX1 - .02593SX2 + .9560SX1 * SX2 + e \tag{16–22}$$
$$(5.864) \quad\quad (2.118) \quad\quad (-2.525) \quad\quad (63.023)$$

Backpropagation and training ANNs
Generalized delta rule:

$$W_{ij}(\text{new}) = W_{ij}(\text{old}) + \Delta W_{ij}(\text{new}) \tag{16–23}$$

$$\Delta W_{ij} \propto -\frac{\partial SSE}{\partial W_{ij}} \tag{16–24}$$

$$\Delta W_{ij}(\text{new}) = \eta \delta_{ij} O_j + \alpha \Delta W_{ij}(\text{old}) \tag{16–25}$$

Review Problems Using Your Software or Enclosed Spreadsheets

In completing this assignment note that several ANN spreadsheets are on this book's data disk, ANN211.WK1, ANN221.WK1, and ANN321.WK1 where the structure is clear from the file name. Instructions on how to use these programs are also on the spreadsheet. When using these, remember the trained weights in an ANN may be different depending on the starting conditions. In many cases, this is not indicative of a problem but a different combination of weights yielding the same outputs and RMS values. Consequently, your weights may differ from those in the book but the RMS value should not deviate greatly.

R16–1 Train the ANN of Figure 16–4 and confirm the weights. If your weights differ or the RMS value is considerably different, speculate why. (THREE.WK1)

R16–2 Train the ANN of Table 16–8 and confirm the weights. If your weights differ or the RMS value is considerably different, speculate why. (MARRIAGE.WK1)

R16–3 Train the Interaction ANN of Table 16–9 and confirm the weights. If your weights differ or the RMS value is considerably different, speculate why. (INTERACT.WK1)

Problems

16–1 Distinguish between conventional programming and expert systems.

16–2 Distinguish between expert systems and ANNs.

16–3 What are good applications of conventional programming, expert systems, and ANNs?

16–4 What is the function of a transfer function at a neurode? What is the most commonly used transfer function?

16–5 Describe the behavior of the sigmoid transfer function. What is the first derivative of a sigmoid transfer function? How is this first derivative used in a neural network?

16–6 Explain training and learning in an ANN?

16–7 Discuss the process of modifying the weights used in an ANN.

16–8 Explain the notation of $4 \times 4 \times 1$ ANN.

16–9 How is training an ANN different than programming a computer?

16–10 How are training and running an ANN different?

16–11 How do you determine the number of neurodes in the input layer of an ANN? How do you determine the number of neurodes in the hidden and output layers?

16–12 How do you determine the number of layers to include in the input, hidden, and output in an ANN?

16–13 In common, nonmathematical terms, explain the backpropagation training formulas.

16–14 How can we validate an ANN? Explain the process in as much detail as in the text.

16–15 What is the function of the bias weight at the hidden and output neurodes?

16–16 What variables are most logical inputs to an ANN model for forecasting the maximum temperature tomorrow?

16–17 What variables are most logical inputs to an ANN model for forecasting the closing Dow Jones Industrial Average tomorrow?

16–18 Explain the concepts of selection, crossover, and mutation in genetic algorithm terms.

16–19 Draw and label a $2 \times 2 \times 1$ ANN, being sure to show all of its components and formulas. Assume that each hidden and output node has a bias node as an input. Be sure to include the notation of all *I*s, *W*s, and *O*s.

16–20 Using the simple ANN of Figure 16–5 confirm that the ANN output of O_4 for the first two input patterns of the following table corresponds to those given in that table. Be sure to show all of the *I*s, *W*s, and *I*s.

Input I_0 I_1	Desired Output	ANN Output, O_4
0 0	.50	?
0 1	.25	?
1 0	.75	.748819

16–21 Validate the trained ANN for Quarterly Marriages in Figure 16–8 by forecasting periods 29 to 32 in the file MARRIAGE.DAT.
  a. What is the RMS value for these four periods?
  b. How does this RMS value compare to that reported in Table 16–7?
  c. What inferences do you make about this ANN?

16–22 Using ANN211.WK1, fit a $2 \times 1 \times 1$ ANN to the Big City Bookstore (BIGCITY.DAT) data of sales as a function of advertising and competiton. Interpret the weights at the input nodes and comment on their relationship to the regression weights shown in Chapter 10.

16–23 A firm faces the following quarterly demand. Using this data and the spreadsheet ANN, ANN211.WK1, answer the following questions. (PRB16–23.DAT)

Scaled Input Variables

Quarter	IO	I1	Actual Output (D)
I	0	0	.199
II	0	1	.401
III	1	0	.599
IV	1	1	.801
I	0	0	.201
II	0	1	.399
III	1	0	.601
IV	1	1	.799
			$S_D = .23905$

  a. Draw a $2 \times 1 \times 1$ ANN with bias on the output node only. Be sure to label all of the weights and nodes as done in this chapter.
  b. Fit a $2 \times 1 \times 1$ ANN using ANN211.WK1 with as many epochs as needed to achieve a reasonable $\bar{R}^2$, but not so many as to overfit the data.
  c. Interpret the output and place the weights in the figure drawn in (*a*).
  d. Discuss some measures of goodness of fit.

16–24 If you have an ANN software package that will accommodate four inputs, then train and forecast the multiple regression example (MULT.DAT) of Chapter 10. There is potential for *Y* to be a function of *X*1, *X*2, *X*3, and *X*4. Train a model to the first 75 observations, then confirm its validity by predicting the last 25 observations.

16–25 Using the ANN of Figure 16–10 for the INTERACT.DAT, confirm the following values of the network:
  $I_1 = .073442$ $I_2 = .388736$ $O_4 = .213656$ $O_5 = .799862$ $O_6 = .0715901$

16–26 Generate all possible combinations of the following genetic code:
  Trend 0,1   Seasonality 0,1   Nonlinearity 0,1   Smoothed 0,1

16–27 Given the following two genetic codes as parents from the genetic structure of the previous problem, generate the requested offspring using the crossovers requested.
  a. 1 1 1 1, 0 0 0 0   Parents, crossover the first and last codes.
  b. 0 1 1 0, 1 0 0 1   Parents, crossover the middle two.

       c. 1 1 1 1, 0 1 0 1   Parents, crossover the first two.

       d. 0 1 0 1, 1 1 1 0   Parents, crossover the last two.

16–28 The time series RETAIL.DAT is the monthly retail sales in the United States. Complete the minicase assignment.

16–29 The time series SUPEROIL.DAT is the sales of the Superoil Company in thousands of barrels during the last 108 months. Complete the minicase assignment.

Minicases I

For a selected minicase or problem, complete the following analysis. What variables are the most logical inputs to an ANN model for forecasting this time series? Identify these variables and any transformations that should be applied to them before use in the ANN. Assume that your purpose is to forecast one seasonal cycle into the future. Now how many hidden neurodes and output neurodes should be included in the ANN?

Minicases II

For a selected minicase or problem use the spreadsheet program ANN321.WK1 and three input series of your choice to forecast this time series. Train the series for as many epochs as necessary to achieve a reasonable $\bar{R}^2$, but not so many as to overfit the data. Withhold the appropriate periods for testing the network and add the results to the summary table from other chapter minicases.

Minicase 16–1 Kansas Turnpike, Daily Data Complete the minicase using TURNPIKD.DAT.

Minicase 16–2 Domestic Air Passengers by Quarter Complete the minicase using PASSAIR.DAT.

Minicase 16–3 Hospital Census by Month Complete the minicase using CENSUSM.DAT.

Minicase 16–4 Henry Machler's Hideaway Orchids

Complete the minicase using MACHLERD.DAT.

Minicase 16–5 Your Forecasting Project Complete the minicase using your project.

Minicase 16–6 Midwestern Building Materials Complete the minicase using LUMBER.DAT.

Minicase 16–7 International Airline Passengers Complete the minicase using AIRLINE.DAT.

Minicase 16–8 Automobile Sales Complete the minicase using AUTO.DAT.

Minicase 16–9 Consumption of Distilled Spirits Complete the minicase using SPIRITS.DAT.

Minicase 16–10 Discount Consumer Electronics Complete the minicase using ELECT.DAT.

References

Austin, S. "Genetic Solution to XOR Problems." *AI Expert,* December 1990.

Blum, Adam. *Neural Networks in C++.* New York: John Wiley & Sons, Inc., 1992.

Bochereau, L., and P. Bourgine. "Rule Extraction and Validity Domain on a Multilayer Neural Network." In *International Joint Conference on Neural Networks.* Vol. 1. San Diego, CA: 1990, pp. 97–100.

Brown, R.G. *Advanced Service Parts Inventory Control.* 2nd. ed. Norwich, VT: Materials Management Systems, Inc., 1982.

Caudill, M. and C. Butler. *Understanding Neural Networks: Computer Explorations.* Cambridge, MA: The MIT Press, 1994.

DeLurgio, Sr., S.A. and Carl D. Bhame. *Forecasting Systems for Operations Management.* Burr Ridge, IL: Irwin Professional Publications, 1991.

Dixon, R. and F. Bevan. *Neural Network Tutor.* Whitby, Ontario: Advanced Technology Transfer Group, 1994.

Dutta, S., and S. Shekhar. "Bond Rating: A Non-Conservative Application of Neural Networks." In *International Joint Conference on Neural Networks.* Vol. 2. (1988), pp. 443–50.

Fisher, D.H. and K.B. McKusick. "An Empirical Comparison of id3 and Back-Propagation." In *Proceedings of the*

Eleventh International Joint Conference on Artificial Intelligence, Detroit, MI, 1989.

Fishwick, P.A. "Neural Networks Models in Simulation: A Comparison with Traditional Modeling Approaches." In *Proceedings of Winter Simulation Conference,* Washington, D.C., 1989, pp. 702–10.

Frean, M. "The Upstart Algorithm: A Method for Constructing and Training Feedforward Neural Networks." *Neural Computation* 2, (1990) pp. 198–209.

Funahashi, K. "On the Approximate Realization of Continuous Mappings by Neural Networks." *Neural Networks 2,* (1989), pp. 183–92.

Goldberg, D.E. "Genetic and Evolutionary Algorithms Come of Age." *Communications of the ACM* 37, no. 3 (March 1994), pp. 113–99.

Hecht-Nielsen, R. "Theory of the Backpropagation Neural Network." In *International Joint Conference on Neural Networks.* Vol. 1. New York: pp. 593–605. (Washington, D.C.: IEEE, 1989.)

Hornik, K.; M. Stinchcombe, M. ; and H. White. "Using Multilayer Feedforward Networks for Universal Approximation." *Neural Networks* 3 (1990), pp. 551–60.

Jacobs, R. "Increased Rates of Convergence through Learning Rate Adaption." *Neural Networks* 1 (1988), pp. 295–307.

Kuo, C., and A. Reitsch. "Neural Networks versus Conventional Methods of Forecasting." *The Journal of Business Forecasting,* Winter 1995–96, pp. 17–22.

Kwong, K.K., and D. Cheng. "A Prototype Microcomputer Forecasting Expert System." *The Journal of Business Forecasting,* Spring 1988, pp. 21–26.

Lapedes, A., and R. Farber. *Nonlinear Signal Processing Using Neural Networks: Predictions and System Modelling.* Los Alamos, N.M.: Los Alamos National Laboratory, 1987.

Lee, C.J., and C. Chen. "Structural Changes and the Forecasting of Quarterly Accounting Earnings in the Utility Industry." *Journal of Accounting and Economics* 13 (1990), pp. 93–122.

Levine, R. I.; D. E. Drang; and B. Edelson. *A Comprehensive Guide to AI and Expert Systems.* New York: McGraw Hill, 1986.

Liebowitz, J. *Introduction to Expert Systems.* Santa Cruz, CA: Mitchell Publishing, 1988.

Lippmann, R. "An Introduction to Computing with Neural Nets." *IEEE ASSP Magazine,* 1987, pp. 4–22.

Makridakis, S.; S.C. Wheelwright; and V.E. McGee. *Forecasting Methods and Applications.* 2nd ed. New York: John Wiley & Sons, 1983.

Makridakis et al. "The Accuracy of Extrapolation (Time Series) Methods: Results of a Forecasting Competiton." *Journal of Forecasting* I (1982), pp. 111–53.

McCord, Nelson M., and W.T. Illingworth. *A Practical Guide to Neural Nets.* Reading, MA: Addison-Wesley Publishing, 1991.

Ralston, A., and E.D. Reilly, Jr., eds. *Encyclopedia of Computer Science and Engineering.* 2nd. ed. New York: Van Nostrand Reinhold, 1983.

Rumelhart, D.; G. Hinton; and R. Williams. "Learning Representations by Back-Propagating Errors." *Nature* 323 (1986), pp. 533–36. Reprinted in Anderson 1988.

Rumelhart, D.; J. McClelland; and the PDP Research Group 1986. *Parallel Distributed Processing: Explorations in the Microstructure of Cognition.* Vol. 1. Cambridge, MA: MIT Press, 1986.

Sales Forecasting. Atlanta, GA: American Software, Inc., 1983. (This book is indicative of forecasting system manuals available from companies such as IBM and Materials Management System, Inc., among others.)

Sharda, R., and T. Ireland. "An Empirical Test of Automatic Forecasting Systems." Technical Report ORSA/TIMS Meeting, New Orleans, 1987.

Sharda, R., and R. Patil. "Neural Networks as Forecasting Experts: An Empirical Test." In *International Joint Conference on Neural Networks.* Vol. 1. 1990, pp. 491–94. (Washington, D.C.: IEEE, 1990.)

Simpson, P. *Artificial Neural Systems: Foundations, Paradigms, Applications, and Implementations.* Elmsford, NY: Pergamon Press, 1990.

Singleton, J.C., and A.J. Surkan. "Modeling the Judgement of Bond Rating Agencies: Artificial Intelligence Applied to Finance." In *1990 Midwest Finance Association Meetings,* Chicago, IL, 1990.

Solla, S.; E. Levin; and M. Fleisher. "Accelerated Learning in Layered Neural Networks." *Complex Systems* 2 (1988), pp. 625–39.

Sontag, E. "On the Recognition Capabilities of Feedforward Nets." Technical Report Report SYCON-90-03, Rutgers Center for System and Control, 1990.

Tong, H., and K. Lim. "Threshold Autoregression, Limit Cycle and Cyclical Data". *Journal of Royal Statistical Society B* 42 (1980), p. 245.

Utans, J., and J. Moody. "Selecting Neural Network Architectures via the Prediction Risk: Application to Corporate Bond Rating Prediction." In *The First International Conference on Artificial Intelligence Applications on Wall Street*, Los Alamitos, CA: IEEE, 1991.

Weigend, A.; B. Huberman; and D. Rumelhart. "Predicting the Future: A Connectionist Approach." Technical Report, Stanford-PDP-90-01, Stanford University, Stanford, CA, 1990.

White, H. "Some Asymptotic Results for Learning in Single Hidden-Layer Feedforward Neural Models." *Journal of the American Statistical Association* 184 (1989), pp. 1003–13.

Widrow, B.; D.E. Rumelhart; and M.A. Lehr. "The Basic Ideas in Neural Networks." *Communications of the ACM* 37, no. 3 (March 1994), pp. 87–92.

―――――. "Neural Networks: Applications in Industry, Business and Science." *Communications of the ACM* 37, no. 3 (March 1994), pp. 93–105.

APPENDIX 16–A

MATHEMATICS OF A BACKPROPAGATION NEURAL NETWORK

As mentioned in this chapter, the backpropagation of an ANN assumes that there is supervision of the learning (i.e., training) of the network. The method of adjusting weights is designed to minimize the sum of the squared errors for a given training data set. In this simple discussion, remember that j identifies a receiving node and i, a node feeing that node (e.g., an input or hidden node).

Each noninput node has an output level O_j where:

$$O_j = \frac{1}{(1 + e^{-I_j})} \tag{16A–1}$$

$$I_j = \Sigma W_{ij} O_i \tag{16A–2}$$

where O_i is each of the signals to node j (i.e., the output of node of i).

The derivation of the backpropagation formula involves the use of the chain rule of partial derivatives and equals:

$$\delta_{ij} = \frac{\partial \text{SSE}}{\partial W_{ij}} = \left(\frac{\partial \text{SSE}}{\partial O_j}\right)\left(\frac{\partial O_j}{\partial I_j}\right)\left(\frac{\partial I_j}{\partial W_{ij}}\right) \tag{16A–3}$$

where by convention the left-hand side is denoted δ_{ij}, the change in the sum of squared errors attributed to W_{ij}. Now, remembering that:

$$e_i = (D_j - O_j) \tag{16A–4}$$

$$\text{SSE} = \Sigma(D_j - O_j)^2 \tag{16A–5}$$

therefore:

$$\left(\frac{\partial \text{SSE}}{\partial O_j}\right) = -2\Sigma(D_j - O_j) \tag{16A–6}$$

The output of an output node is:

$$O_j = \frac{1}{(1 + \mathbf{e}^{-I_j})} \tag{16A–7}$$

therefore:

$$\left(\frac{\partial O_j}{\partial I_j}\right) = O_j(1 - O_j) \tag{16A–8}$$

The input to an output node is:

$$I_j = \Sigma W_{ij} O_i \tag{16A–9}$$

Therefore, the change in the input to the output node resulting from the previous hidden node, i, is:

$$\left(\frac{\partial I_j}{\partial W_{ij}}\right) = O_i \tag{16A–10}$$

Therefore, from Equation 16A–3, the jth delta is:

$$\delta_{ij} = 2e_j O_j(1 - O_j)O_i \tag{16A–11}$$

Now the old weight is updated by the following equation:

$$\Delta W_{ij}(\text{new}) = \eta \delta_{ij} O_j + \alpha \Delta W_{ij}(\text{old}) \tag{16A–12}$$

For the hidden layers, the calculations are very similar. The only change is how the ANN output error is backpropagated to the hidden layer nodes. The output error at the ith hidden node depends on the output errors of all nodes in the output layer. This relationship is:

$$e_i = \Sigma W_{ij} e_j \tag{16A–13}$$

After calculating the output error for the hidden layer, the update rules for the weights in that layer are the same as the previous update, Equation 16A–11.

Inspection of the several spreadsheet ANNs will confirm the calculations of this appendix.

COMBINING, VALIDATION, AND MANAGERIAL ISSUES

CHAPTER 17

CONTROL, VALIDATION, AND COMBINING METHODS

To err is human, and to blame it on a computer is even more so.
A human

Chapter Outline

To a surprising extent, forecasting accuracy is dependent on how well unusual values are handled in the system. Relatively well-behaved patterns are accurately forecasted by many methods. However, unusual values present serious problems unless they are adjusted prior to forecasting.

The first section of this chapter develops several tools for detecting and controlling unusual values and forecast errors. It is an extension of outlier detection and adjustment methods of Appendix B of this book. The tools included here are tracking signals and forecast reasonableness tests. Each of these is an essential part of effective forecasting.

The second section of this chapter develops methods of combining the results of two or more forecasts to improve forecasting accuracy. This is an important topic because of the effectiveness of combining forecasts. Research has consistently shown that averaging the forecasts of two good models, on average, improves the accuracy of forecasts. We review this research and illustrate different ways of combining time series.

The third section of this chapter develops methods of validating forecasting models. This is an important topic because too often we have seen analysts choose forecasting models based on the accuracy of the fit. However, models should be chosen because they are expected to forecast accurately, and there are better ways to predict forecasting accuracy then to use simple historical fit measures such as RSE. We briefly explore several methods of selecting and validating alternative models. These validation methods include the use of the Schwarz Bayesian information criterion (BIC) and the effective use of withholding data to judge forecasting accuracy. Also, we discuss resampling methods such as the jackknife and bootstrap.

Finally, note that the three sections of this chapter are designed to be used anytime after Chapter 2. For example, the validation section on BIC might be introduced early in the use of this book.

Tracking Signal Control Methods

An ongoing forecasting process must detect outliers, otherwise, the old adage "garbage in, garbage out (GIGO)" will soon describe the model and the views of users. Large outliers must be removed from the data because these unusually large deviations will adversely affect the forecasting process. Unmanaged outliers and unusual observations are garbage into a forecast and probably will result in some garbage out—GIGO.

Even if large outliers are eliminated, the forecasting process can go out of control. In order to detect out-of-control situations as soon as possible, early warning devices called **tracking signals** (TS) are used. This section develops several tracking signals that detect out-of-control forecasts. These monitor accuracy and highlight when an automated or human intervention is necessary.

There are times when unreasonably high or low forecasts occur, even though everything appears correct prior to forecasting. These unusual forecasts should be detected and eliminated before any harm is done. Unless forecast reasonableness is checked prior to the decision process, unreasonably high and costly errors may occur.

Tracking Signals: Detecting Cumulative (Biased) Errors

One purpose in monitoring errors is to ensure that the forecast model is still valid. We infer that this is true when forecast errors are small individually and cumulatively. When a very large forecast error occurs, this can be detected using a z or t-test, as developed in Appendix B of this book. Cumulative errors can be detected statistically by

---

The Whole Distribution Is Important, So Be Cautious with Averages

The average error of a good forecasting model should not be significantly different than zero. However, a model with a mean error of zero is not necessarily a good forecasting model. Remember the example of the baker who states that on average he is comfortable because his head is in the refrigerator and his feet are in the oven. A good forecasting model has an average error of approximately zero and a low RSE.

---

use of a tracking signal. When a forecast goes out of control, bias occurs as the errors are primarily positive or primarily negative, but not both.

We infer that an out-of-control situation exists when the tracking signal exceeds some chosen trip point. When this occurs, it is assumed that the forecasts are biased and the mean error deviates significantly from the expected value of zero. Thus, it is inferred that the sum of errors is not random but is caused by some large or consistent over- or underforecasts. There are a number of theoretically and empirically derived rules of thumb for setting these trip points. However, the most common way is to choose the trip point directly from actual system performance.

Several tracking signals are studied here because there is not one best tracking signal for all applications. Thus, it is precisely because multiple forecasting methods are presented in this book, that we must present several different types of tracking signals.

CUSUM$_t$
Tracking Signal

One way to monitor forecasts is to use the sum of errors over time, sometimes called a **cumulative summation (CUSUM):**

$$\text{CUSUM}_t = \Sigma e_t = \text{CUSUM}_{t-1} + e_t \qquad (17\text{--}1)$$

When forecasts are unbiased, then the CUSUM fluctuates about zero. This CUSUM can be controlled using a simple *t*-test when errors are normally and independently distributed. Under these conditions, the standard error of the CUSUM is equal to the RSE times the square root of the number of errors. That is:

$$\text{Sc} = \text{RSE}\sqrt{k} \qquad (17\text{--}2)$$

where

$\quad \text{Sc} =$ Standard deviation of the CUSUM$_t$
$\text{RSE} =$ Residual standard errors in period t
$\quad\ k =$ Number of errors in the calculation of CUSUM$_t$

This results in the following *t*-test, which we call a tracking signal CUSUM (TSC):

$$\text{TSC}_t = \text{CUSUM}_t/\text{Sc}_t \qquad (17\text{--}3)$$

The TSC$_t$ value can be compared to a chosen *t*-value, typically 2 or 3.

While the TSC is a useful test statistic, it is not commonly used because Sc$_t$ gives equal weight to all past errors and frequently, past errors are not independent, particularly with exponential smoothing. Because the immediate past is a better indication of the immediate future, more recent errors should be given more weight than older errors. Also, an error once included in the CUSUM remains there indefinitely. For these reasons, the number of observations used in the calculations, k, should be small. But how many?

The question of how many periods to include in $CUSUM_t$ and Sc is very much like the question of how many periods to include in an exponential smoothing model. If too many are included, it may not be responsive enough to recent errors; if too few are included, the system may be too responsive. Not surprisingly, a popular method of detecting out-of-control situations is to use exponentially weighted values, where more weight is given to the most recent errors, as discussed next.

Tracking Signal: $CUSUM_t/MAD_t$

Brown (1963) defined a tracking signal that is a simple extension of TSC. We call this a tracking signal-cumulative using MAD (TSM). This is defined as:

$$TSM_t = CUSUM_t/MAD_t \qquad (17–4)$$

where

$$MAD_t = \alpha |e_t| + (1 - \alpha)MAD_{t-1} \qquad (17–5)$$

and $CUSUM_t$ is the cumulative sum of forecast errors that have occurred since the forecasting model was selected or reestimated. The value of $CUSUM_t$ is set to zero whenever the tracking signal is tripped or a major change is made in the forecasting environment. When tripped, the forecasting situation is investigated, corrected, and the $CUSUM_t$ reset to zero; however, the MAD_t is reset to a typical value.

The theoretical standard errors of TSC_t and TSM_t are not well defined when errors are not normally and independently distributed. Most often, when the exponential smoothing models of Chapters 4 and 6 are used, errors have significant autocorrelations. Because of this, the best trip values for TSM_t, TSC_t, or TST_t (which is discussed next) are unknown. Consequently, in most applications, the trip value is determined empirically, based on actual system performance. The choice of a trip value is limited by the necessity of attending to all of the exceptions. If too many models are tripped, making managerial or automated interventions an impossible task, the trip value should be increased. Common trip values are 4 to 7 for the TSM_t. When TSM_t exceeds the trip point, the forecasting situation is identified as out of control.

Note in Equation 17–4 that TSM_t uses MAD_t as opposed to the RSE. However, the denominator of Equation 17–4 can include an exponentially smoothed RSE_t instead of MAD_t. Brown (1982) makes a very strong case for the use of the RSE_t instead of MAD_t. He advocates the use of the square root of a smoothed MSE_t, which yields a smoothed RSE_t:

$$MSE_t = \alpha e_t^2 + (1 - \alpha)MSE_{t-1} \qquad (17–6)$$

$$RSE_t = \sqrt{MSE_t} \qquad (17–7)$$

$$TME_t = CUSUM_t/RSE_t \qquad (17–8)$$

MAD_t versus RSE_t. While this appears to be a best measure of error variation, there is some debate regarding the use of RSE_t. Some have suggested that an advantage of the MAD_t over the RSE_t is that MAD_t responds less to forecast errors that are almost, but not quite, outliers. This results from the fact that MAD_t involves no squared errors. Thus, as errors increase, MAD_t does not increase as rapidly as RSE_t. In contrast, some argue that the opposite problem exists; The MAD_t is not responsive enough and should be replaced by RSE_t. Also, MAD_t is more easily calculated than RSE_t. As shown next, this debate may not be important, because some use a different tracking signal, TST_t. Unfortunately, all tracking signals have limitations that must be offset using some very practical manual or automated overrides.

Trigg Tracking Signal: SAD_t/MAD_t

Trigg (1964) has provided another tracking signal based on the smoothed average of the deviations (i.e., forecast errors)—SAD_t—and the MAD_t. The SAD_t is calculated as:

$$SAD_t = \alpha e_t + (1 - \alpha)SAD_{t-1} \tag{17-9}$$

SAD_t is nothing more than a weighted moving average of past errors. The resulting Trigg tracking signal is:

$$TST_t = SAD_t/MAD_t \tag{17-10}$$

This tracking signal varies from -1 to $+1$. For unbiased errors, TST_t should fluctuate about zero. But when bias occurs, the TST_t will approach either $+1$ or -1 depending on the direction of bias. If error terms are approximately normally and independently distributed, the approximate standard error of SAD_t, $SSAD_t$ is:

$$SSAD_t = RSE_t\sqrt{\frac{\alpha}{2 - \alpha}} = 1.25MAD_t\sqrt{\frac{\alpha}{2 - \alpha}} \tag{17-11}$$

This standard error is used to set trip points for the TST_t, as shown below. When using MAD_t and an α of .1, a 95 percent trip point for TST_t is:

$$2*1.25\sqrt{\frac{\alpha}{2 - \alpha}} = 2*1.25\sqrt{\frac{.1}{2 - .1}} = .574 \tag{17-12}$$

Thus, when the TST_t exceeds .574, this indicates that the forecasting situation is out of control. However, as discussed previously, most errors are not independently distributed, particularly those from exponential smoothing. Thus, empirically derived trip values for TST_t should be used in an actual system. Brown (1963) suggests initial trip points based on an empirically derived standard deviation of TST_t, $STST_t$:

$$STST_t = .55\sqrt{\alpha}$$

With $\alpha = .10$:

$$STST_t = .55\sqrt{.1} = .174 \tag{17-13}$$

Using the usual two standard errors, when TST_t exceeds .35 (i.e., 2 times .174), the system is deemed to be out of control. However, the final trip points will be determined empirically from system performance. Gardner (1983) provides more refined guidelines on trip points. We will use Equation 17–13 in subsequent analysis.

An Example Application of TSM_t and TST_t

Table 17–1 simulates the use of the tracking signals of Brown and Trigg over a 24-month period. Brown's TSM_t is shown in column 5, while Trigg's TST_t is shown in column 7. Applying these tracking signals requires values for MAD_t, $CUSUM_t$, and SAD_t. The initial values of $CUSUM_0$ and SAD_0 are set to zero, as shown in Period 0, because these are expected to vary about zero. However, it is not logical for MAD_0 to be zero. An initial value of MAD_0 must be estimated. This initial value can be estimated from the model-fitting process or from some past mean absolute error. In this case, MAD_0 was chosen using the past 10 errors (these are not shown). The trip points for the two tracking signals are 4 and .35, respectively. The values of MAD_t and SAD_t are calculated using an alpha of .10.

TABLE 17–1   Use of Brown's TSM and Trigg's TST Tracking Signals (TRACK.DAT)

(1) Period (t)	(2) $Error_t$	(3) MAD_t	(4) $CUSUM_t$	(5) TSM_t	(6) SAD_t	(7) TST_t
0		59.22	.00	.00	.00	.00
1	−83.30	61.63	−83.30	−1.35	−8.33	−.14
2	78.60	63.33	−4.70	−.07	.36	.01
3	−9.50	57.94	−14.20	−.25	−.62	−.01
4	−42.60	56.41	−56.80	−1.01	−4.82	−.09
5	−82.10	58.98	−138.90	−2.36	−12.55	−.21
6	−96.00	62.68	−234.90	−3.75	−20.89	−.33
Tripped 7	−50.00	61.41	−284.90	−4.64	−23.80	−.39

Correct the System and Set CUSUM and SAD to Zero

(1)	(2)	(3)	(4)	(5)	(6)	(7)
7	−50.00	61.41	.00	.00	.00	.00
8	52.30	60.50	52.30	.86	5.23	.09
9	−21.50	56.60	30.80	.54	2.56	.05
10	−73.10	58.25	−42.30	−.73	−5.01	−.09
11	35.70	56.00	−6.60	−.12	−.94	−.02
12	−57.30	56.13	−63.90	−1.14	−6.57	−.12
13	−5.50	51.06	−69.40	−1.36	−6.47	−.13
14	−94.30	55.39	−163.70	−2.96	−15.25	−.28
15	68.80	56.71	−95.10	−1.68	−6.86	−.12
16	−87.80	59.82	−182.90	−3.06	−14.96	−.25
Tripped 17	−88.00	62.64	−270.90	−4.33	−22.26	−.36

Correct the System and Set CUSUM and SAD to Zero

(1)	(2)	(3)	(4)	(5)	(6)	(7)
17	−88.00	62.64	.00	.00	.00	.00
18	49.20	61.29	49.20	.80	4.92	.08
19	−80.20	63.18	−31.00	−.49	−3.59	−.06
20	94.30	66.29	63.30	.95	6.20	.09
21	−72.80	66.95	−9.50	−.14	−1.70	−.03
22	15.90	61.84	6.40	.10	.06	.00
23	−89.60	64.62	−83.20	−1.29	−8.91	−.14
24	72.70	65.42	−10.50	−.16	−.75	−.01

$\alpha = .10.$
Trip point $TSM_t = 4.$
Trip point $TST_t = .35.$
Underlined values are trip points.

As shown in Period 7 of Table 17–1, both tracking signals tripped because of the bias (i.e., all negative errors) of Periods 3 through 7. In Period 7 the situation was investigated, and the system was corrected and reset. As shown by the second Period 7 of the table, $CUSUM_7$ and SAD_7 were both reset to zero. The system continued to forecast without problems until Period 17. At that point, both TSM_{17} and TST_{17} tripped because of another run of negative errors. Again, the system was reset and the forecasting process continued without problems through Period 24.

These two tracking signals work well in this example, however, as we discuss in a moment, they are not always this effective. For now consider another good tracking signal.

Autocorrelation Tracking Signal, r_t

Quite logically, when there is bias in the errors, there is also autocorrelation in adjacent errors because biased errors have the same sign. Consequently, any significant positive autocorrelation in the errors denotes a problem with the forecasting process. Negative autocorrelations also denote a problem; however, not in terms of normal systematic bias.

As presented in Chapter 2, the first-order autocorrelation of errors can be calculated as:

$$r_t = \frac{\sum e_t e_{t-1}}{\sum e_t^2} \qquad (17\text{--}14)$$

However, with this form of autocorrelation coefficient, equal weights are given to all past error terms. In a manner similar to previous tracking signals, more distant errors should be given less weight. The following exponentially weighted forms result:

$$\text{SCOV}_t = e_t e_{t-1} + (1 - \alpha)\text{SCOV}_{t-1} \qquad (17\text{--}15)$$

$$\text{SMSE}_t = e_{t-1}^2 + (1 - \alpha)\text{SMSE}_{t-1} \qquad (17\text{--}16)$$

$$r_t = \frac{\text{SCOV}_t}{\text{SMSE}_t} \qquad (17\text{--}17)$$

where

SCOV = Exponentially smoothed covariance
SMSE = Exponentially smoothed mean squared error
r_t = Autocorrelation tracking signal

This tracking signal is discussed by Gardner (1983). While Equations 17–15 and 17–16 may appear to be incorrect in the first right-hand terms missing a smoothing parameter, they are nonetheless correct. The tracking signal, r_t, is a discounted least squares estimate of the true autoregressive parameter, ϕ_1. The discounting factor is $\beta = 1 - \alpha$.

Because this tracking signal is affected greatly by the high autocorrelation that remains in the errors of most exponential smoothing models, it is not recommended for use with errors from exponential smoothing models. For example, simple exponential smoothing models with smoothing constants above .1 have an increasing occurrence of negatively correlated errors, a phenomenon we will see in a moment. However, it is a very good tracking signal for controlling models that are expected to yield white noise residuals.

Table 17–2 illustrates the application of r_t on the example data of Table 17–1. Using a trip point of .35 (see Gardner, 1982), this tracking signal tripped at period 6 or 7 depending on your interpretation. Let's assume that it tripped at Period 6.

In Period 6, the covariance was reset to 0 and the tracking signal recalculated from there on. As shown in Period 16, the tracking signal was tripped again, but this time because of the negative autocorrelation of the errors. This is evident from the negative covariances that result from the nearly consistent alternating positive and negative signs on the errors. This is one of the characteristics of this signal: It is tripped by either negative or positive autocorrelations. As shown, the signal tripped again in Period 21 after having been reinitialized in Period 16. The behavior of this tracking signal is considerably different than that seen with TSC_t and TST_t in Table 17–1. In some applications of this tracking signal, such alternating positive and negative errors and the resulting negative covariances are ignored. However, the data of Table 17–2 should not have been controlled by r_t, because these are errors from an exponential smoothing model and thus have negative autocorrelations.

TABLE 17–2   Autocorrelation Tracking Signal, r_t (TRACK.DAT)
$$\beta = (1 - \alpha) = .90$$

(1) Period (t)	(2) $Error_t$	(3) $Error_{t-1}$	(4) $e_t e_{t-1}$	(5) $SCOV_t$	(6) $SMSE_t$	(7) r_t	
1	−83.30				11,400.00	.00	
2	78.60	6,938.89	−6,547.38	−6,547.38	10,260.00	−.64	
3	−9.50	6,177.96	−746.70	−6,639.34	16,172.89	−.41	
4	−42.60	90.25	404.70	−5,570.71	20,733.56	−.27	
5	−82.10	1,814.76	3,497.46	−1,516.18	18,750.45	−.08	
6	−96.00	6,740.41	7,881.60	6,517.04	18,690.17	.35	Tripped
7	−50.00	9,216.00	4,800.00	10,665.34	23,561.56	.45	

Correct System and Set $SCOV_6 = 0$, Retain $SMSE_6$

6	−96.00	6,740.41	7,881.60	.00	18,690.17	.00	
7	−50.00	9,216.00	4,800.00	4,800.00	23,561.56	.20	
8	52.30	2,500.00	−2,615.00	1,705.00	30,421.41	.06	
9	−21.50	2,735.29	−1,124.45	410.05	29,879.27	.01	
10	−73.10	462.25	1,571.65	1,940.70	29,626.63	.07	
11	35.70	5,343.61	−2,609.67	−863.04	27,126.22	−.03	
12	−57.30	1,274.49	−2,045.61	−2,822.35	29,757.20	−.09	
13	−5.50	3,283.29	315.15	−2,224.97	28,055.97	−.08	
14	−94.30	30.25	518.65	−1,483.82	28,533.67	−.05	
15	68.60	8,892.49	−6,468.98	−7,804.42	25,710.55	−.30	Tripped by
16	−84.80	4,705.96	−5,817.28	−12,841.26	32,031.98	−.40	$SCOV_{16} < 0$

Reset $SCOV_{16} = 0$, Retain $SMSE_{16}$ $r_t < 0$

16	−84.80	4,705.96	−5,817.28	.00	32,031.98	.00	
17	−88.00	7,191.04	7,462.40	7,462.40	33,534.75	.22	
18	49.20	7,744.00	−4,329.60	2,386.56	37,372.31	.06	
19	−80.20	2,420.64	−3,945.84	−1,797.94	41,379.08	−.04	
20	94.30	6,432.04	−7,562.86	−9,181.00	39,661.81	−.23	Tripped by
21	−72.80	8,892.49	−6,865.04	−15,127.94	42,127.67	−.36	$SCOV_{21} < 0$

Reset $SCOV_{21} = 0$, Retain $SMSE_{21}$ $r_t < 0$

21	−72.80	8,892.49	−6,865.04	.00	42,127.67	.00	
22	15.90	5,299.84	−1,157.52	−1,157.52	46,807.39	−.02	
23	−89.60	252.81	−1,424.64	−2,466.41	47,426.49	−.05	
24	72.70	8,028.16	−6,513.92	−8,733.69	42,936.66	−.20	

As illustrated by these examples, the behavior of different tracking signals is not simplistic. We discuss this behavior after briefly introducing the backward CUSUM V-mask tracking signal.

Backward CUSUM V-Mask Tracking Signal

A common problem with the above tracking signals is that in smoothing SAD_t, MAD_t, $SCOV_t$ and $SMSE_t$, there can be significant delays in the detection process. A system goes out of control in time t, but the problem is not detected until time $t + L$, where L is the length of delay. A more advanced tracking signal using cumulative summation

TABLE 17–3   Comparison of Different Tracking Signals

Method	Advantages	Disadvantages
CUSUM TSM$_t$	Performance is independent of smoothing constants used Independent of the variance of the time series and resulting errors	It never forgets large errors; they remain indefinitely. If system gives "exceptionally accurate forecasts, the signal may trip" Less effective than others with independent (i.e., white noise) errors
Smoothed-error TST$_t$	Works with independent errors Easy to use Independent of the variance of the time series and resulting errors Easy to update, only two parameters needed	Not recommended with high values of α For independent errors, not as good as autocorrelation tracking signal Trip points dependent on α
Autocorrelation signal r_t	Tracks positive and negative bias (i.e., autocorrelations) Best with white noise errors Independent of the variance of the time series and errors A better method except with dependent errors from exponential smoothing	Not recommended with exponential smoothing because of its autocorrelated errors Delayed trips occur when direction of bias changes—for example, from positive to negative, and vice versa
Backward CUSUM	A best or "most thorough tracking signal" Detects changes quicker than other methods	Difficult to apply Requires more data than other methods Detects changes only .5 periods sooner than r_t Trip points not easily determined Requires constant variance of time series Difficult to use with a short series

Adapted from E.S. Gardner, "Automatic Monitoring of Forecast Errors," *Journal of Forecasting* 2, no. 1 (1983), pp. 18–21.

techniques based on the use of V- or parabolic masks is designed to detect bias within a specific number of periods (Brown, 1971). These are derived from the sequential sampling techniques of Wald and are very effective methods. This TS method is implemented in a few forecasting systems. However, research by Gardner (1983) suggests that the **backward CUSUMs** do not appear to be worth the additional complexity and computer storage. The backward CUSUM tracking signal requires that the time series have a constant variance. Simpler methods that are as effective as those of the backward CUSUM do not require equal variances. The situations where other methods are better than the backward CUSUM are identified in Table 17–3, which summarizes the advantages and disadvantages of different tracking signals.

Graphical Support and Expert System Control

Automated controls are an essential part of a good forecasting process, but it is always important to have support for human review and modification. The highest degree of control in forecasting normally comes from periodic human intervention when the tracking signal trips or other exceptions occur. This is accomplished by having analysts and managers review the plots of actual values versus forecasted values as well as plots of errors. The pattern-recognition capabilities of the human mind are very good; thus, graphical presentations are an important part of a good forecasting system.

If the cost consequences of errors are low, it may not be effective to allocate analyst's time to all exceptions; this is one reason why trip points on tracking signals are set empirically. However, an out-of-control condition may be a serious matter. Therefore, controls should exist to ensure that bias is detected quickly.

With the advent of more powerful forecasting software, we have the opportunity to develop better automated methods of detecting and adjusting out-of-control situations (e.g., neural net control devices). While it is not easy to duplicate the pattern-recognition capabilities of humans, expert systems and neural networks are being developed to assist in this regard. These combine the best objective control techniques with the subjective assessment of humans. Artificial intelligence and expert systems (AI/ES) are already used in some systems to help identify, diagnose, and adjust out-of-control situations. Chapter 16 discusses AI/ES and neural network applications in forecasting.

Regression toward the Mean and Outliers

Around 1890, the term *regression* was coined during the study of natural phenomena such as child heights in relation to parent heights by the Reverend Francis Galton, a cousin of Charles Darwin. The Reverend Galton found that child heights regress toward the mean heights of all individuals. For example, if a child's parents are tall, it is likely that the child will also be tall, but not quite as tall as his or her parents. Likewise, if a child's parents are short, it is likely that the child will also be short, but not quite as short as his or her parents. As we all know, this is not a universal principle, but it is a common phenomenon that describes more situations than not. So, too, in forecasting we often see unusual behavior in a time series—unusually high or low values that yield unusually high or low forecasts errors. In many cases, this unusual behavior will regress (i.e., return) to normal values. Thus, many series may have outliers during one month or period followed by normal values in the next.

However, when several periods of outliers occur, the property of regression toward the mean is not operating—there is some systematic bias in the forecasting process. In this situation, we must detect and eliminate the cause of the bias.

Choosing a Simple Tracking Signal

Gardner (1983) provides an excellent review of tracking signals. He found that TST_t is more widely used than TSM_t. An advantage of TST_t is that it is less sensitive to certain types of false trips. It can be shown that if a very large error is followed by several small errors, TSM_t trips falsely. This occurs because the larger error has increased $CUSUM_t$ while the smoothed MAD_t becomes smaller as a result of the several very small errors. Thus, we see that the numerator of Equation 17–4 increases while the denominator decreases. To trip when forecast errors are low is unacceptable. However, the TST_t is not adversely affected by this behavior. As the MAD_t decreases because of smaller errors, so does the SAD_t. It is for this and other reasons that TST_t is used more frequently than TSM_t.

TABLE 17–4   One-Tail 95 Percent/99 Percent Trip
Points for Four Tracking Signals

	Independent Errors	*Exponential Smoothing (dependent errors)*		
		$\alpha = .1$	$\alpha = .2$	$\alpha = .3$
CUSUM	NR	5.6/7.5	4.1/5.6	3.5/4.9
Smoothed error	$\alpha = .1$ .54/.67	.42/.55	.57/.69	.69/.81
Autocorrelation	$\alpha = .1$ .35/.48	NR	NR	NR

NR = Not recommended.

Adapted from E.S. Gardner, "Automatic Monitoring of Forecast Errors," *Journal of Forecasting* 2, no. 1 (1983), pp. 18–21.

To assist in the better use of tracking signals, Gardner (1983) and others have defined the trip points of Table 17–4 for the three tracking signals discussed here.

Reasonableness Tests

Even though the forecasting process has been monitored through the use of outlier adjustments and tracking signals, there are times when the predicted values of otherwise good models yield unreasonable forecasts. These unreasonable forecasts can result from the interaction of several near outliers that greatly affect the next forecasted value. Simple reasonableness tests discussed here are important tools in precluding gross errors. As discussed below, these can be applied directly to actual values or to percentage change measures.

Reasonableness tests typically involve simple rules of thumb that result in exception reports. These exception reports prompt human intervention into the forecasting process. For example, it would be unusual for a series to grow at a 100 percent annual rate. While this does occur, it still may be decided that any series with a projection this high should be highlighted. The basic question of a reasonableness test is, "Does this projected value seem reasonable when compared to past values and future expectations?" Thus, one simple rule could be to highlight or identify as an exception any series with a deseasonalized monthly growth rate in excess of some number considered too large.

Reasonableness tests are determined empirically (i.e., based on experience). Even though such tests are easily determined and applied, they can dramatically improve the effectiveness of the forecasting process.

Combining Forecast Methods

There are many times when there are more than one forecast of the same series. We saw in ARIMA model building that frequently the analyst is confronted with a choice between two competing models. In addition, considerable research has shown that there is not one best method of forecasting. This leaves the analyst with a dilemma;

Which of the possible forecasting models should be chosen to forecast a time series? In such situations, it is not uncommon to apply several methods in a simulated contest to see which performs best.

When one model greatly dominates the other, the choice is clear. Alternatively, when models yield identical forecasts (i.e., highly correlated errors), the choice is to discard the least desirable model based on judgment, parsimony, or theory. However, there are times when two or more models seem to have some positive attributes and discarding one or more seems wasteful. Fortunately, it is possible to combine the results of several models to yield improved forecasts. In fact, research has shown that more often than not, forecasts that are averages of several other good forecasts are on average better than the individual forecasts. Thus, in most situations, it is better to combine the forecasts of several models into average forecasts. In this section, we discuss four ways of combining the forecasts of several models to yield better combined forecasts. These four **combining methods** are:

1. Simple averages.
2. Weighted averages.
3. Weights inversely proportionate to sum of squared errors.
4. Weights determined by regression analysis.

Simple Average Combinations

The simplest method for combining several forecasts is to average them. Consider a situation where two forecasts are combined:

$$\hat{Y}C_t = (\hat{Y}1_t + \hat{Y}2_t)/2 \tag{17–18}$$

where

$\hat{Y}C_t = $ Combined forecast
$\hat{Y}i_t = $ Individual forecasts of models 1 and 2.

It can be shown that when the individual forecasts are unbiased, the combined forecast will also be unbiased. Also, clearly, the combined error (ec) is simply the average of the errors:

$$\text{ec}_t = Y_t - \hat{Y}C_t = Y_t - (\hat{Y}1_t + \hat{Y}_{2t})/2 = (e1_t + e2_t)/2$$

Many times, this method of combining forecasts has been found to be as good as the other more sophisticated methods that are discussed next.

The combined variance associated with the variances of individual errors equals:

$$\sigma c^2 = (\sigma 1^2 + \sigma 2^2 + 2\rho\sigma 1\sigma 2)/4 \tag{17–19}$$

where ρ is the correlation coefficient between the two errors.

If the errors of the two models are independent—that is, $\rho = 0$—then this formula is:

$$\sigma c^2 = (\sigma 1^2 + \sigma 2^2)/4$$

Consequently, when the variances are nearly equal and independent, the combined error variance is considerably less than either of the other variances. For example, assume that $\sigma 1^2 = 100$ and $\sigma 2^2 = 100$:

$$\sigma c^2 = (\sigma 1^2 + \sigma 2^2)/4 = (100 + 100)/4 = 50$$

Even with correlations that are quite high between the individual forecast errors, the combined error variances will be smaller than either of the individual variances.

Consider another example where $\sigma 1^2 = 100$, $\sigma 2^2 = 100$, and $\rho = .8$:

$$\sigma c^2 = (\sigma 1^2 + \sigma 2^2 + 2\rho\sigma 1\sigma 2)/4$$

$$= (100 + 100 + 2*.8(10*10))/4 = 360/4 = 90$$

Even in this situation, there is a variance reduction from averaging the results of the two models. While these two examples yielded very favorable results, it is possible to have the combined variances that are greater than the lowest individual error variances. Consider the following example where $\sigma 1^2 = 100$, $\sigma 2^2 = 16$, and $\rho = .8$. Then:

$$\sigma c^2 = (\sigma 1^2 + \sigma 2^2 + 2\rho\sigma 1\sigma 2)/4$$

$$= (100 + 16 + 2*.8(10*4))/4 = 180/4 = 45$$

Thus, in this example, the combined variance is greater than the lower of the two variances. Consequently, it may not be advisable to use a simple average when there is such a large difference between the variances of the errors.

When the analyst has no preference for one method over another and the variances of the errors do not differ dramatically, the assumption of equal weights appears to be a reasonable one. However, there are situations where different weights might be assigned based on some objective or subjective criteria. Consider the following three forms of weighted averages.

Using Weighted Averages

If an analyst has no objective information concerning the performance of different models but can estimate subjective weights for each model, then a **weighted average** can be used to combine the forecasts. This is simply:

$$\hat{Y}C_t = w1\hat{Y}1_t + w2\hat{Y}2_t \tag{17-20}$$

where

$\hat{Y}C_t$ = Combined forecast
wi = Weights of individual forecasts, and $\Sigma wi = 1.0$
$\hat{Y}i_t$ = Individual forecasts of models 1 and 2

Obviously, higher weights should be assigned to those forecasts that have the lowest error variance. When historical fit or forecast accuracy data is available, it is more logical to use one of the following combining methods.

Weights Inverse to the Sum of Squared Errors

When the accuracy of past fits or forecasts are available, it may be best to use those accuracy measures to set the weights in Equation 17–20, higher weights given to the more accurate forecast models. Because models with lower squared errors are more accurate than other models, the sum of squared errors is a very good measure used to weight the different forecasts. However, accuracy and squared errors are inversely related; thus, the weights should be inversely related to the squared errors. A logical way to weight two models is:

$$w1 = \frac{1/SSE1}{1/SSE1 + 1/SSE2} \tag{17-21}$$

$$w2 = \frac{1/SSE2}{1/SSE1 + 1/SSE2} \tag{17-22}$$

where $SSE1 = (\Sigma e^2)$ for $i = 1$ to n for model 1; SSE2 is calculated in a similar manner.

For example, given SSE1 = 100 and SSE2 = 16:

$$w1 = \frac{1/100}{1/100 + 1/16} = \frac{.01}{.01 + .0625} = .1379$$

$$w2 = \frac{1/16}{1/100 + 1/16} = \frac{.0625}{.01 + .0625} = .8621$$

Thus, we see that much more weight is given to the more accurate model. Also, the sum of weights equals 1.

In using this relationship, we simply compile the errors from forecasting or fitting with each model. In addition, we need to determine how many observations to include in the sum of squared errors. Clearly, if too many observations are used, the accuracy measure may be tainted by very old forecast performance. Thus, as in exponential smoothing, we need to make a trade-off between having a reasonably large sample size of relevant (e.g., recent) performance measures but not data that is very old. For monthly data, the past two or three years appears to be adequate. For other series, somewhere between 12 to 40 observations is often appropriate.

In a moment, we will apply this method and review some of the research on the effectiveness of this combining method. For now, let's consider another logical way of combining forecasts.

Weights Determined by Regression Analysis

In Chapter 3, we developed the concept of regression analysis as weighting the influences of the independent variables on the dependent variable. This provides a logical way of determining weights. The following regression is fit to forecasted values:

$$\hat{Y}C_t = b1\hat{Y}1_t + b2\hat{Y}2_t \qquad (17\text{--}23)$$

where

$\hat{Y}C_t$ = Combined forecast
bi = Regression coefficients of individual forecasts
$\hat{Y}i_t$ = Individual forecasts of models 1 and 2

The predicted values of $\hat{Y}C_t$ are estimated using least squares where the actual value, Y_t, is the dependent variable and model 1 and 2 forecasts are independent variables. After estimation, the model can be used to forecast with the individual forecasts. This method has been used in practice with some success. However, there is nothing to ensure that the sum of the regression coefficients in Equation 17–23 will be 1; nor is there anything to ensure that the excluded constant, a (which is not shown), is zero. If the excluded constant is not zero, then there may be bias introduced into the resulting forecasts. Because of these problems, Granger and Ramanathan (1984) have suggested that a better approach is to leave the constant in:

$$\hat{Y}C_t = a + b1\hat{Y}1_t + b2\hat{Y}2_t \qquad (17\text{--}24)$$

However, with this approach, as in Equation 17–23, the regression coefficients may not sum to 1. Also, individual regression coefficients can be negative; thus, the weight given a forecast is negative. A common procedure when negative coefficients are found in Equation 17–24 is to delete that variable (i.e., that model) from the regression model and reestimate the model without those forecasts, however, some experimentation in the specific application can confirm whether to include or exclude a model.

From a theoretical standpoint, Equation 17–24 is a better approach to combining forecasts than Equation 17–23. However, it may have some drawbacks in that the error terms may be autocorrelated; thus, the regression coefficients may not be the most efficient. Also, when only a few observations are available for estimation, the results may not be accurate. Because of these and other problems, Equation 17–24 is not as popular as using simple averages or weights determined by the inverse SSE.

Past Research

The topic of optimal ways of combining forecasts has been researched considerably. This empirical evidence has yielded several important conclusions:

1. Most often, but not always, the process of combining forecasts of several models improves forecast accuracy even when compared to the best single model.
2. The use of simple, unweighted averages performs quite well—in several studies, better than other methods.
3. When one forecasting model is considerably better (i.e., has much lower SSEs) than the other models, the advantages of combining forecasts are not obtained. In such settings, it is better to drop the inferior models.
4. Because of the problems with weights determined by regression analysis, those of the inverse of the SSE are often better.
5. Some experimentation with and intelligent selection of combining methods is better than using one method exclusively. For example, it is better to compare the variances and correlation coefficients of several models and then choose a combining method consistent with the characteristics of the relationships. In some cases, there are no gains from combining forecasts.

Studies by Makridakis et al. (1982) and others have shown that simple averages do better than weighted averages when used indiscriminately across many time series. Bates and Granger (1969) introduced the concepts of weighting in inverse proportion to the sum of squared errors. Newbold and Granger (1974) studied the use of inverse sum of squared errors and regression-based weights using 80 time series and two best forecasting models, one being an ARIMA model. Their study showed that regression-based coefficients were somewhat inferior to inverse SSE weights.

Using 1,001 time series, Winkler and Makridakis (1983) confirmed the results of Newbold and Granger that regression-based coefficients are inferior to inverse SSE weights. In addition, Newbold and Granger (1974) illustrated that the addition of a third model somewhat improved the accuracy of the combined forecasts. Those desiring more information about combining methods are directed to an annotated bibliography by Clemen (1989). In addition, Mahmoud (1984) provides additional information about the performance of different combining methodologies.

Having illustrated several methods of combining time series, let's apply the simple average, inverse proportion, and regression methods in forecasting the U.K. stock index using models based on Chapters 8 and 10.

Using Combinations of Forecasts

In this example, we compare the performance of two models that are combined in the three different ways discussed previously. The first model used to fit the U.K. stock index is the Cochrane–Orcutt model of Chapter 10, Table 10–17. The second model is an ARIMA model. Hereafter, these will be called models 1 and 2, respectively.

Table 17–5 summarizes the results of applying three combination methods in the fitting process. Only the last 36 months of data were used out of the 270 observations to arrive at the weights and SSE. As shown in Table 17–5, the best method for this time series is regression-based weights. Let's consider the process used to generate Table 17–5 in more detail.

As shown by their sums of squared errors, the multivariate model had considerably less error than the univariate model (.52930 versus .70515). In addition, it was found that the errors of these two models have a correlation coefficient of .77170.

TABLE 17–5   Combining Forecasts for U.K. Stock Index (UKUSIND.DAT)

	Weights	SSE*
Multivariate Cochrane–Orcutt		.52930
$\quad$ LUK$_t$ = f(LUS$_t$, LUS$_{t-1}$ e_{t-1}) Cochrane–Orcutt		
Univariate ARIMA model		.70515
$\quad$ ARIMA(0,1,1)1,1		
Simple average of errors	.5/.5	.54372
Inverse proportion of SSE	.57132/.42877	.53278
Regression-based weights	.79957/.20043	.51760

*These are logarithmic models; thus, the low SSE.

Because there is high correlation between these two models and one model is much more accurate than the other, the likelikhood of a successful combination is low.

The results of using equal and inverse proportion weights on models 1 and 2 yielded an SSE that is much better than the univariate model but slightly inferior to the multivariate model. In contrast, the use of regression-based coefficients yielded a sum of squares that is lower than both models. An initial regression model including a constant yielded a low and insignificant constant value; thus, the model was reestimated without a constant. Both relationships, with and without a constant, had regression coefficients summing to 1. Thus, the regression-based weights were very reasonable and appear to be the best method. The regression-based model gave almost 80 percent of the weight to the better multivariate model.

The result of combining forecasts in this example was somewhat successful; however, these results were not unambiguous. The more complex method, the regression-based weights, is only slightly more effective than using the best single model, model 2. Considering the slight improvement in forecast accuracy and the fact that theory suggests a multivariate relationship between the dependent and independent variables, we have a preference for using model 2 without combining results. However, a more detailed analysis might change this conclusion.

This example and the cited research denote that there is considerable effectiveness in combining the forecasts of different methods. The next section illustrates another twist on combining forecasts, the concepts of cumulative and group forecasts.

Consistent Forecasts: The One-Number Principle

When different forecasts of the same series are made in an organization, there is the possibility that these different forecasts will not be equal. For example, operations might plan the production of 1,000 units, finance might budget the acquisition of 900 units, while marketing might forecast 1,400 units. Efficient forecasting and effective decisions are made by ensuring that the same forecast is used by all decision makers. This principle is sometimes called the **"one-number" principle.**

Table 17–6 illustrates an example of the one-number principle where the sum of forecasted regional distribution values equals national values and marketing revenue forecasts. Each of these six different forecasts are generated independently and initially were not equal to the others. However, management adjusted each so they would all be consistent. As discussed below, there are several different methods of "forcing" consistent forecasts.

TABLE 17–6   Consistent Forecasts at Different Levels of the Hierarchy

Item Being Forecasted	Forecasted Value	
	Units	(%)
Microcomputer demand		
Region I	1,309	21.2%
Region II	1,490	24.3
Region III	1,366	22.3
Region IV	1,977	32.2
Total regional demands	6,137	100.0%
National estimates of microcomputers	6,137	
Revenue forecasts 6,137 @ $3,500	$21,479,000	

Achieving Consistent Forecasts

The ways of generating consistent forecasts up and down the hierarchy are referred to as either top down or bottom up. The top-down approach is used when the company-wide value is estimated for a product (e.g., 6,137 microcomputers per year) and then historical ratios such as 21.2 percent (Region I), 24.3 percent (Region II), 22.3 percent (Region III), and 32.2 percent (Region IV) are used to generate specific regional values. In contrast, there is a bottom-up approach to forecasting where the individual forecasts of each region are generated and accumulated upward to arrive at a company value. There is a third way of forcing consistency, the pyramid principle, which will be discussed in a moment.

Item versus Cumulative Forecast Accuracy

The errors in specific item forecasts are normally higher than the errors that result from cumulative forecasts. For example, as shown in Table 17–7, the absolute forecast errors for each item of a four-item group were typically 10 to 16.7 percent; however, the **cumulative error** for the total four-item group was only 2.5 percent. Thus, while the individual forecast errors were sometimes high and sometimes low, the cumulative error was considerably less.

Similarly the errors for individual short time period forecasts are normally higher than the errors resulting from the accumulation of short time period forecasts. For example, if the first column of Table 17–7 referred to weeks rather than items, the absolute forecast errors for each week of the four-week period would be from 10 to 16.7 percent; while the cumulative error for the total four-week period would be only 2.5 percent. This illustrates that individual weekly forecast errors can sometimes be high and sometimes be low, yet the cumulative error for the four-week period is quite low, much less than the average weekly error. The principle of cumulative errors is the same whether accumulated over time or items.

Group Forecasts

In general, forecasts of groups are more accurate than forecasts of individual items. This principle states that the error in forecasting a specific series is normally greater than the error in forecasting the group from which this series was selected. Consider a group that consists of the four series (1, 2, 3, and 4) shown in Table 17–8. These series are each forecasted individually, as shown in row 2. In contrast, the past actual values

TABLE 17–7   **Cumulative Errors are Lower than Item Forecast Errors**

Item	Actual	Forecast	Error	*Percent Error**
1	1,000	900	100	10%
2	900	1,000	−100	−11
3	900	1,000	−100	−11
4	1,200	1,000	200	16.7
Cumulative	4,000	3,900	100	2.5%

*Percent error is error divided by actual.

TABLE 17–8   **Group Forecast Accuracy versus Individual Forecasts**

Item	1	2	3	4	Group	Cumulative*
Actual	460	676	283	284	1,703	1,703
Forecast	351	853	294	328	1,842	1,826
Error	109	−177	−11	−44	−139	−123
Percent error	24	−26	−4	−15	−8	−7

*Cumulative equals sum of Items 1, 2, 3, and 4.

of these items are also grouped and maintained as a separate series. This group is then forecasted as a single group.

In general, as confirmed in the table, the error in forecasting a group value will be less on a percentage basis than the typical percent error of the individual items. However, as shown by Item 3, the rule is not universally true. The group percentage error is much lower than the typical error, but it is not as low as that of Item 3.

In the last column, Table 17–8 also illustrates the cumulative principle of Table 17–7. This column shows the sums of the actuals, forecasts, and errors of the individual items to yield cumulative values. As shown, the cumulative error (−123) is the lowest of all, including the group error (−139). It is important to note that in general, both the cumulative and group errors are lower than the individual errors; however, the manner in which these two errors are calculated is considerably different.

The difference between cumulative and group errors is subtle but distinct. If you are confused, compare Tables 17–7 and 17–8. Both the cumulative and group principles are important in forecasting.

Finally, note that the group forecast and the cumulative forecasts can be combined into a single forecast using the methods discussed previously using the simple average, weighted average, inverse proportions, or regression-based weights.

Assumption of Independence

Each of the principles illustrated in Tables 17–7 and 17–8 are true when the forecasts are independent of each other. However, when forecast errors are dependent, all high or all low, then the cumulative forecast errors will equal the average of the individual errors. That is, cumulative errors will not be lower than the individual average errors but will equal the average of them; this is illustrated in Table 17–9. As shown in Table 17–9, the cumulative error is not lower than the typical item error because of the bias in all four item forecasts.

Forecasting Structures

"By dividing his problem into unsuitable parts, the unexperienced problem-solver may increase his difficulty."

Leibnitz
Philosophiesche Schriften

**TABLE 17–9   Cumulative Errors Are Equal to Item
Forecast Errors When Dependence Exists**

Item	Actual	Forecast	Error	Percent Error*
1	1,000	900	100	10%
2	1,000	900	100	10
3	900	800	100	11
4	1,200	1,000	200	16.7
Cumulative	4,100	3,600	500	12.2%

*Average individual error = (10 + 10 + 11 + 16.7)/4 = 11.9.

Using Groups in Forecasting Systems

Many corporate forecasting systems use the cumulative and group principles of Tables 17–7 and 17–8 in their design. This is effective because the planning process is hierarchical. For example, because the cumulative error for a group or a month is normally considerably less than the error for individual items or weeks, it is possible to plan higher level groups more accurately. Thus, forecasting and planning systems should be designed to take advantage of the increased accuracy of cumulative and **group errors** across items and time. For example, the group and cumulative forecast accuracy principles both denote that errors of group dollar sales will be less than the error in the dollar sales of the typical item in the group.

Pyramidal Forecasting Systems

There is another useful way in which to view the process of forecasting, sometimes called the pyramid principle. Figures 17–1 and 17–2 illustrate the pyramid for a brief-case manufacturer. As shown in these figures, the several forecasts used in a company can be viewed from the top down or the bottom up. The methods of integrating forecasts are part of this **pyramidal system** of forecasting.

As shown in Figure 17–1, the process of forecasting is hierarchical. At the peak of the pyramid is the original March group forecasts of 600 units at $50 per unit. In the middle of the pyramid we see the dollar sales for each item; these dollar projections were calculated from the lowest level, item forecasts. These two forecasts are uncoordinated at this time. This lack of coordination is apparent in the top section of the pyramid, which shows the group-forecasted dollars at $30,000 in comparison to the

FIGURE 17–1

Initial rollup forecasts of March as of January

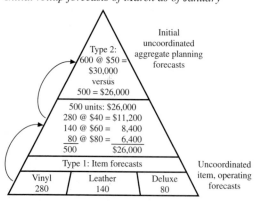

FIGURE 17–2

Force-down forecasts of March as of January

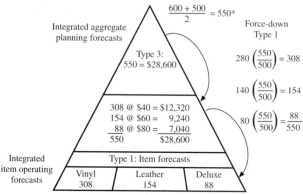

* This illustrates one of several ways to combine forecasts

item-forecasted dollars at $26,000. These forecasts need to be integrated, and the method of doing this is illustrated below using the pyramids of Figures 17–1 and 17–2.

The integration of forecasts requires two steps: the roll-up step and the force-down step.

Figure 17–1 illustrates the **rollup** of the item briefcase forecasts. This rollup yields the aggregate unit and dollar forecasts of the second level (500 units and $26,000). This forecast does not agree with the group forecast (600 units and $30,000). The next step is to combine each of these forecasts so that they are consistent.

Figure 17–2 illustrates the **force-down** step. As shown, the item and group forecasts are simply averaged to yield the combined forecasts. The mathematics of this example are also shown in Figure 17–2. However, there are several different methods of combining forecasts, including inverse weights and regression analysis. Note that all forecasts—aggregate and item—are consistent. Thus, different types of planning can proceed in harmony.

The pyramidal presentation is important because it is the basis of more realistic and complex corporate forecasting systems. Figure 17–3 illustrates the results of integrating forecasts in a more complex manufacturing–distribution network. In this case, two product lines are produced by the manufacturer, overnight cases and briefcases. These two products are produced in vinyl, leather, and deluxe models. These six products are distributed through three regional distribution centers, RDC1, RDC2, and RDC3.

As shown, there are 18 stockkeeping units (skus) in the three distribution centers. During the roll-up step, which is not shown here, the value for each of these skus or items is forecast, each product line is forecast at each distribution center, and national values for each product line are forecast. Thus, 18 item forecasts, 6 group forecasts at the distribution centers, and 2 national group forecasts (i.e., overnight and briefcase) are made during the roll-up step. Thus, the three levels of forecasts are not coordinated during the roll-up step. Thus, the sum of the item forecasts does not equal the product line forecast. The next step, the force-down step, is used to provide coordinated forecasts. This step yields the forecasts of Figure 17–3.

The benefits of coordinating forecasts and plans have already been stressed. However, we must emphasize that the process of combining forecasts shown in Figures 17–2 and 17–3 is essential to forecasting and planning effectiveness. Group,

FIGURE 17–3

*General hierarchical
structure in forecasting
systems: Forecasts of
March as of January*

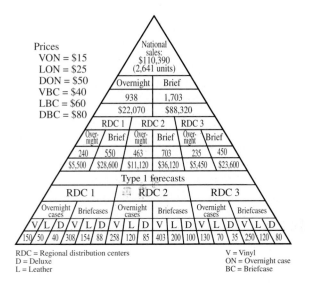

cumulative, and combined forecasts are inherently more accurate than item forecasts. However, item forecasts have important mix information that must be used in allocating items to locations. Plans should be coordinated and consistent. This is only achieved if there is a common database of forecasts.

Validation Methods: Occam's Razor and Parsimony

Some mistakenly choose models based almost exclusively on minimum sum of squared errors (SSE) in fitting. However, as we know, it is a fairly simple matter to reduce SSE by adding more complexity to the model, though forecast accuracy may not be enhanced by this increased complexity.

One of the more notable principles of model building is the principle of **parsimony.** Parsimony is a synonym for frugality or thriftiness. This principle is used for choosing among models or theories and denotes that, everything else being equal, simpler models are better. This principle has been found to be very effective when choosing between models with approximately the same explanatory power, or conversely, the same error. When applied in forecasting, it denotes that the smaller the number of predictor variables or estimated coefficients (i.e., the simpler the theory), the more accurate are the forecasts.

Occam's razor, the original statement of parsimony, is the principle of economy named for the philosopher William of Occam (AKA Ockham) (c. 1285–1349). It holds that explanatory principles should not be needlessly complex—the simplest proof or model is usually the best. All other things being equal, the simplest theory (e.g., the equation with the fewest predictors) is the best.

Parsimony should be the overriding principle in selecting one model over the other. We have been impressed with the near universality of this principle. The reason this principle is so important is because analysts have a tendency to select models with too many coefficients. These models fit the past data well but do not forecast future values well. Often, when overly complex models are chosen, the analyst may not have strong theory to select the best models. Fortunately, there are two statistical measures that embody the principle of parsimony and are very effective in selecting from competing models: the Schwarz and Akaike criteria.

Model Complexity versus Forecast Accuracy

In most statistical modeling, there exists a trade-off between model complexity (i.e., number of coefficients) and predictive accuracy (e.g., minimum sum of squared errors) in forecasting. Specifically, that model that fits the historical data most accurately is not necessarily the one that predicts future values most accurately. This phenomenon illustrates the principle of parsimony.

Figure 17–4 illustrates the typical trade-off between errors and complexity. The bottom curve shows the relationship between model complexity and errors during the model-fitting process, while the top curve illustrates the relationship between model complexity and errors during the actual forecasting process. As shown, if a model is selected based on the minimization of squared errors in fitting historical data, the model and its complexity are shown by point A (one with seven coefficients), the model with the lowest fitted squared errors. In contrast, the model that minimizes the error in actual forecasting is represented by the model and complexity of point B (the one with only four coefficients). That is, in actual forecasting, the model of point A has a higher sum of squared errors than the model of point B. This type of relationship is very common; thus, the importance of the principle of parsimony. Now, let's examine how to choose the model that forecasts most accurately.

Akaike and Schwarz Bayesian Criteria

Useful criteria for choosing a model from competing models include:

- Theory.
- Minimum sum of squared errors.
- Intuitive appeal.
- Parameter significance and lack of redundancy.
- Parsimony.
- Schwarz or Akaike criteria.

Unfortunately, there are times when these criteria give conflicting results. The last of the above criteria is one of the best when you do not have sufficient theory for choosing a model using the other criteria. While the other five criteria are important in selecting models, they might not provide a best guideline when there are confusing differences in the fits (i.e., RSEs) and complexities of the models.

Schwarz (1978) developed the **Bayesian information criterion (BIC)** and **Akaike** (1974) developed the **information criterion (AIC),** for selecting models that

FIGURE 17–4

Fit errors and forecast errors

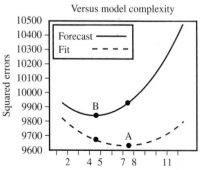

trade off model complexity and the error in fitting so as to achieve the most accurate out-of-sample forecasts. These two objective measures better balance model complexity and goodness of fit measures than does adjusted $\overline{R}^2$ or RSE. Akaike and Schwarz suggest selecting models that have the lowest AIC or BIC respectively.

Research has shown that use of these two measures improves out-of-sample forecast accuracy. Empirical research using 91 series from the M-competition shows that the BIC slightly outperforms the AIC (Koehler and Murphree, 1986). In addition, it appears that the BIC outperforms the AIC for the data that we usually encounter in forecasting.

Using theory beyond our scope, Akaike proposed Equation 17–25 as a useful way to select models:

$$AIC = n\text{Log}(SSE) + 2k \tag{17–25}$$

where

$\quad k =$ Number of parameters that are fitted in the model
$\text{Log} =$ Natural logarithm
$\quad n =$ Number of observations in the series
$SSE =$ Sum of the squared errors

Schwarz proposed the following criteria to choose from models:

$$BIC = n\text{Log}(SSE) + k\text{Log}(n) \tag{17–26}$$

Let's calculate these formulas using the data in Table 17–10, which illustrates the results of fitting six different variations of Winters' exponential smoothing model. The first model with no trend or seasonality is simple exponential smoothing; thus, it has only one coefficient, alpha. The last two models are models with three smoothing constants: alpha, beta, and gamma as discussed in Chapter 6. Table 17–10 illustrates only the BIC because it is generally recognized as the better of the two. Based on the Schwarz criterion, the best model of Table 17–10 is the one with linear trend and additive seasonality. Having analyzed this data in detail, we can confirm that this is the correct choice. However, these criteria are not infallible.

We illustrate the calculation of both the Schwarz and the Akaike for the first model in Table 17–10.

Schwarz Bayesian information criterion (BIC) for the first model:

$$BIC = 48*\text{LOG}(133026) + 1*\text{LOG}(48) = 570.190$$

Akaike information criterion (AIC) for the first model:

$$AIC = 48*\text{LOG}(133026) + 2*1 = 568.318$$

TABLE 17–10   Exponential Smoothing Model Selection for SERIESF.DAT

Trend	Seasonal	Sum of Squares	Schwarz	Coefficients (k)
None	None	133,026.683	570.190	1
None	Additive	81,314.714	550.434	2
None	Multiplicative	81,113.470	550.315	2
Linear	None	128,866.255	572.536	2
Linear	Additive	62,477.520	541.657	3
Linear	Multiplicative	75,404.444	550.683	3

As shown by these calculations, the Schwarz criterion penalizes model complexity more than the Akaike ($k\text{Log}(n)$ versus $2k$), a difference that some would say accounts for the improved out-of-sample performance of the Schwarz.

We cannot compare the AIC or BIC of one series with the AIC or BIC of another series; nor do we compare the AIC to BIC. In general, there is no easy interpretation of the magnitude of the AIC or BIC, nor is there any need for our purposes to understand the theoretical derivation of these statistics. Only the relative magnitudes of the statistics are important when comparing competing models of the same series.

Some suggest that the AIC or BIC should be the only criterion in choosing the best model from competing models. Studies have shown that the BIC is the best, single determinant of the best forecasting model. We have some difficulty using the AIC or BIC exclusively in choosing one model over another when other criteria provide clear reasons to choose other models.

Usually, there is no need to calculate both of these statistics; you should routinely calculate the BIC as part of your model selection process. When you do not have strong theoretical or empirical reasons for choosing one model over another, you should **choose the model with the lowest BIC**.

Fortunately, many computer programs routinely provide estimates of the AIC or BIC so that no additional calculations are necessary. SAS denotes BIC using the notation SBC; other programs use various notation. After some experience in using BIC, its effectiveness will be apparent.

The next three sections briefly describe other methods for selecting and validating forecasting models.

Split Sample and Out-of-Sample Validation

When there are sufficient observations in a time series, it is insightful to divide the data into two groups, where a model is fit to the first and validated with the second. This method can be applied in those situations that have sufficient observations, including time series, regression, econometric, and MARIMA methods.

When a data set is divided into two groups, models are built using the first data set using appropriate identification, estimation, diagnostic, and forecasting steps. For example, assume a multiple regression model relates a dependent variable to four independent variables. After fitting the model to the first set of data, the model is used to forecast the second set of data. The errors and standard errors from the second set of data can be compared to those of the first. Also, to judge the validity of the estimated coefficients, a second model can be fitted to the second data and the estimated coefficients compared to the first model. Then, statistical significance tests using t and F statistics can be applied to the RSE, the standard errors, and coefficient estimates. Because this procedure can provide additional confirmation of the validity of the underlying model, it is highly recommended when sufficient data exists.

Extreme Value Behavior

When fitting a model to data, the included database may or may not be representative of the variation of all possible combinations of variables. Assume we have fitted a regression model with four independent variables, $X1$, $X2$, $X3$, and $X4$. Assume that $X1$ and $X2$ are positively related to Y, and $X3$ and $X4$ negatively related. In addition, assume that these independent variables are uncorrelated with each. If the database is not representative of all valid combinations of these variables, then the model may not be valid. In such cases, it is insightful to enter realistic extreme values of the independent variables as follows:

$$\hat{Y}\text{max} = f(X1\text{max}, X2\text{max}, X3\text{min}, X4\text{min}) \qquad (17\text{–}27)$$

$$\hat{Y}\text{min} = f(X1\text{min}, X2\text{min}, X3\text{max}, X4\text{max}) \qquad (17\text{–}28)$$

If either $\hat{Y}$max or $\hat{Y}$min are unrealistic, then the model may be invalid. However, the complement is not true. That is, if $\hat{Y}$max and $\hat{Y}$min are very reasonable, this is not conclusive evidence of a valid model but only additional evidence.

The use of extreme values can be used for time series models. For nonlinear models, this may simply consist of advancing time to see if the forecasted value is realistic. For MARIMA models, the extreme value approach of Equations 17–27 and 17–28 can be used but still requires known realistic combinations of independent variables.

Clearly, the most stringent requirement of this validation method is to ensure that realistic combinations of variables can be determined. When independent variables are correlated, other methods are required such as the bootstrap (briefly defined in a moment) or Monte Carlo sampling, where correlations are used in the selection process. Nonetheless, such a simple method as Equations 17–27 and 17–28 can be very insightful and at times humbling. We have seen several models where realistic values of the independent variables are substituted, yet extreme negative values are forecast, even though such results were very unrealistic. Obviously, these methods are better completed by the analyst before submitting the model to management, rather than later, when bad decisions result.

Jackknife

The **jackknife,** named after the versatile knife carried by many outdoorsmen and women, is a method for better estimating the RSE of a model. The basic approach of this method is to take repeated subsamples of a time series and to leave one or more observations out of the model each time. For example, assume one observation is left out of n observations for n times; that is, n models of $n-1$ observations are fitted each with $n-1$ observations. Each time, the nth excluded variable is forecasted. The errors of each of these n out-of-sample forecasts are calculated, then the forecast RSE can be calculated. The resulting forecast RSE is a better estimate of forecast standard error than the fitted RSE.

An advantage of this approach is that it does not require any assumptions about the intercorrelations or autocorrelations of independent variables. However, it is not as easy to leave one observation out of a time series as it is for a cross-sectional study because of the importance of continuity. Nonetheless, sometimes time series are long enough to fit models using $n-k$ continuous observations. For example, if a time series consisted of 100 observations, the first 70 can be used to fit models, and the forecast accuracy for the last 30 can be determined by rolling the model forward 1 period 30 times. Depending on the appropriateness of doing so, the process can be reversed in backcasting. That is, fit models to the last 70 observations and then forecast the first 30 observations by rolling the model back 1 period 30 times. Such experiments are variations of the split-sample approach discussed previously. While we recommend study of Tukey (1977) and Mosteller and Tukey (1977) for those desiring further refinement of this approach, you should not hesitate to experiment with your data before doing so.

Bootstrap

Bootstrapping is a method for estimating the RSE and standard errors of the regression coefficients using repeated resampling from an original sample. The term **bootstrap** originates from the phrase "pull yourself up by your own bootstraps." Using the original database of n observations, we can better estimate the RSE and standard error of model coefficients.

Let's briefly consider the process of estimating a regression coefficient using a bootstrap. Assume we have fitted a regression coefficient b_1 and wish to better estimate the error in this estimate (i.e., better than simply using the usual standard error of the regression coefficient). To estimate the error, we randomly sample n independent observations from the original sample of n observations; however, our random sample is with replacement. That is, each observation (i.e., row of matched dependent and independent variables) can be chosen more than once. Thus, sampling with replacement denotes that the subsample of n observations may contain some duplicate observations from the original sample and consequently some original observations will be omitted from the subsample.

The next step is to perform least squares and then estimate the regression coefficient for that subsample. This provides the first bootstrap estimate of b_1, which we designate $b_{1,1}$. This estimate is retained, a new subsample of n is taken, and the process is repeated a large number of times. It is not uncommon that 1,000 subsamples of n observations are taken. Letting j equal the number of the subsample and m the total number of subsamples, we can calculate the mean and standard deviation of the $b_{1,j}$s.

The mean and the standard deviation of all m bootstrap estimates is an estimate of the variability of the true regression coeficient, B_1. These methods are extremely effective in providing better estimates of the true distributions of errors and standard errors. For a more comprehensive presentation of the bootstrap, we refer you to Neter et al. (1996), Tukey (1977), and Mosteller and Tukey (1977) for further study.

Summary

This chapter has presented important methods for controlling, combining, and validating forecasts. We have seen that there are many important principles for controlling, combining, and validating time series models.

Methods of detecting outliers and out-of-control forecasts are an essential part of a good forecasting process. While large, one-time errors can decrease forecast accuracy and system performance, we are equally concerned about bias—that is, consistent over- or underforecasting. Detecting bias is so important because it is usually the result of fundamental shifts in the pattern of the time series. The forecast system needs to be able to detect these fundamental shifts in order to provide accurate information. Also, the effects of bias are significant because of their cumulative detrimental impact. For example, in inventory control, over- and understock conditions may continue to worsen as a result of bias. High investment and low customer service are too costly a price to pay for poor forecasts. The control devices presented in this chapter are essential for achieving a good forecasting system.

The several methods of combining forecasts reviewed here are effective when no clear theory supports the selection of one model over the other. In ARIMA applications, we stressed the advisability of presenting experts with two or more models when each seems to have different, desirable attributes. This is an important service that the forecaster can provide. Interestingly, this service is enhanced when in addition the forecasts of each model are combined into an average forecast. Typically, these forecasts are more accurate than the individual forecasts.

Finally, we discussed methods of choosing from competing models and validation methods. The Schwarz and Akaike information criteria are important overall measures for selecting from competing models. As research has shown, the use of the Schwarz criteria is usually best. The split-sample, out-of-sample, jackknife, and bootstrap are important methods in validating models. Sometimes the data requirements of these methods preclude their use; however, when sufficient data exists, these are good methods for selecting best models.

The effectiveness of your forecasts will be enhanced greatly by studying and applying the methods of this chapter. Displeasure with forecasts is frequently directed toward the forecaster; consequently, the forecaster should learn how to better control, combine, and validate good forecasting models.

Key Terms

Akaike information criterion (AIC)	pyramidal system
backward CUSUM	r_t
biased errors	reasonableness test
bootstrap	rollup
combining methods	Schwarz Bayesian information criterion (BIC)
consistent forecasts—the one-number principle	simple averages
control methods	split sample and out-of-sample validation
cumulative errors	TME_t
$CUSUM_t$	tracking signals
extreme value behavior	TSC_t
force down	TSM_t
group errors	TST_t
jackknife	weighted averages
Occam's razor	weights determined by regression analysis
parsimony	weights inversely proportionate to SSE

Key Formulas

$$CUSUM_t = \Sigma e_t = CUSUM_{t-1} + e_t \tag{17-1}$$

$$\text{Standard deviation (CUSUM)} = Sc = RSE\sqrt{k} \tag{17-2}$$

$$TSC_t = CUSUM_t/Sc_t \tag{17-3}$$

Tracking signal—$CUSUM_t/MAD_t$:

$$TSM_t = CUSUM_t/MAD_t \tag{17-4}$$

where

$$MAD_t = \alpha|e_t| + (1 - \alpha)MAD_{t-1} \tag{17-5}$$
$$MSE_t = \alpha e_t^2 + (1 - \alpha)MSE_{t-1} \tag{17-6}$$
$$RSE_t = \sqrt{MSE_t} \tag{17-7}$$
$$TME_t = CUSUM_t/RSE_t \tag{17-8}$$

Trigg tracking signal—SAD_t/MAD_t:

$$SAD_t = \alpha e_t + (1 - \alpha)SAD_{t-1} \tag{17–9}$$

$$TST_t = SAD_t/MAD_t \tag{17–10}$$

$$SSAD_t = RSE\sqrt{\frac{\alpha}{2 - \alpha}} = 1.25MAD_t\sqrt{\frac{\alpha}{2 - \alpha}} \tag{17–11}$$

An α of 0.1, a 95 percent trip point for TST is:

$$2*1.25\sqrt{\frac{\alpha}{2 - \alpha}} = 2*1.25\sqrt{\frac{.1}{2 - .1}} = .574 \tag{17–12}$$

Empirically derived standard deviation of TST_t ($STST_t$):

$$STST_t = .55\sqrt{\alpha}$$

with $\alpha = .10$;

$$STST_t = .55\sqrt{.1} = .174 \tag{17–13}$$

Autocorrelation tracking signal, r_t:

$$r_t = \frac{\Sigma e_t e_{t-1}}{\Sigma e_t^2} \tag{17–14}$$

$$SCOV_t = e_t e_{t-1} + (1 - \alpha)SCOV_{t-1} \tag{17–15}$$

$$SMSE_t = e_{t-1}^2 + (1 - \alpha)SMSE_{t-1} \tag{17–16}$$

$$r_t = \frac{SCOV_t}{SMSE_t} \tag{17–17}$$

where

$SCOV_t$ = Exponentially smoothed covariance
$SMSE_t$ = Exponentially smoothed mean squared error
r_t = Autocorrelation tracking signal

Combining Forecasts
Simple average combinations:

$$\hat{Y}C_t = (\hat{Y}1_t + \hat{Y}2_t)/2 \tag{17–18}$$

Combined variance:

$$\sigma c^2 = (\sigma 1^2 + \sigma 2^2 + 2\rho\sigma 1\sigma 2)/4 \tag{17–19}$$

where ρ is the correlation coefficient of errors.
Using weighted averages:

$$\hat{Y}C_t = w1\hat{Y}1_t + w2\hat{Y}2_t \tag{17–20}$$

Weights inverse to the sum of squared errors:

$$w1 = \frac{1/SSE1}{1/SSE1 + 1/SSE2} \tag{17–21}$$

$$w2 = \frac{1/SSE2}{1/SSE1 + 1/SSE2} \tag{17–22}$$

Weights determined by regression analysis:

$$\hat{Y}C_t = b1\hat{Y}1_t + b2\hat{Y}2_t \tag{17–23}$$

$$\hat{Y}C_t = a + b1\hat{Y}1_t + b2\hat{Y}2_t \tag{17–24}$$

17–14 Do a roll-up and force-down forecast for the data of Figure 17–1, assuming that the firm believes that the group forecast is twice as accurate as the item forecasts. That is, roll up and force down the forecast assuming that 1/3 weight should be given to the item forecast and 2/3 to the group forecast.

17–15 Do a roll-up and force-down forecast for the data of Figure 17–1, assuming that the firm believes that the group forecast should be given all of the weight, but the item forecast should be used to develop the proper mix during the force-down step.

17–16 What would be a logical way to determine the best weights to give item and group forecasts when combining them? Explain the combining method of Figure 17–1.

17–17 Does your organization use group, item, and combined forecasts?

17–18 What is the "one-number" principle?

17–19 What are some of the political realities of integrating forecasting systems?

17–20 If you have a time series that is missing a few values, how is it possible to estimate values during those periods? List several ways of doing this.

17–21 What forecasting data is captured by your organization? Be explicit in terms of actual customer demand, shipments, sales, or production quantities. Is more than one of these captured by your company? If so, define these.

17–22 Distinguish between group and cumulative forecast errors. Distinguish between these concepts over time and space, as done in the text. Why are these distinctions so important?

17–23 Using the data in Table 17–11, calculate the average group and cumulative errors, as done in Table 17–7.

17–24 Using the data in Table 17–12, calculate the average group and cumulative errors over time, as done in Table 17–7.

TABLE 17–11   Cumulative Errors Are Lower than Item Forecast Errors

Item Percent	Actual Error	Forecast	Error	Percent Error	Cumulative Actual	Error
1	1,000	1,100			1,000	
2	900	1,000			1,900	
3	900	1,000			2,800	
4	1,200	1,000	___		4,000	___
Total	4,000			NA	4,000	

TABLE 17–12   Cumulative Time Period Errors Are Lower than Short-Time Period Errors

Week	Actual	Forecast	Error	Percent Error	Cumulative Actual	Error	Percent	Error
1	1,000	900			1,000			
2	900	2,000			1,900			
3	900	900			2,800			
4	1,200	1,000	___	___	4,000	___	___	___
Total	4,000				4,000			

Model Complexity versus Forecast Accuracy
Akaike (AIC) and Schwarz Bayesian (BIC) criteria:

$$\text{AIC} = n\text{Log(SSE)} + 2k$$

$$\text{BIC} = n\text{Log(SSE)} + k\text{Log}(n)$$

where

$k = $ Number of parameters that are fitted in the model
$\text{Log} = $ Natural logarithm
$n = $ Number of obervations in the series
$\text{SSE} = $ Sum of the squared errors

Extreme value behavior:

$$\hat{Y}\text{max} = f(X1\text{max}, X2\text{max}, X3\text{min}, X4\text{min})$$

$$\hat{Y}\text{min} = f(X1\text{min}, X2\text{min}, X3\text{max}, X4\text{max})$$

Review Problems Using Your Software

R17–1 Repeat the analysis of Table 17–1.

R17–2 Repeat the analysis of Table 17–2.

R17–3 Fit the two models referenced in Table 17–5 to the U.K. stock index UKUSIND.DAT. Now complete the combination forecasts of Table 1 results agree with those in Table 17–5? If not, speculate on why.

Problems

17–1 What is the purpose of a tracking signal?

17–2 What is the CUSUM_t? what is the disadvantage of the CUSUM_t track

17–3 What is the usual procedure for determining the trip points for TSM_t this necessary?

17–4 What aberrant behavior is there with the TSM_t that makes it less desi

17–5 What assumptions must be true for the autocorrelation tracking signa this assumption is not true, what are the consequences?

17–6 If a high smoothing constant is used in a simple exponential smooth why there will be a tendency to have negatively correlated residual underlying series is random.

17–7 What is the advantage of the backward CUSUM V-mask tracking si

17–8 What is a reasonableness test? Give three different possible reasona

17–9 What are four popular methods of combining forecasts? Briefly exp

17–10 What are the difficulties of using weights determined by regression without a constant?

17–11 Given that we want to combine the forecasts of two models, explai tions that combination will yield greatly improved forecasts over th and under what conditions the combination will yield forecasts wo single model.

17–12 In common English, explain the rationale for using weights invers the sum of squares errors to combine two forecasts.

17–13 What is the problem in using weighted averages to combine two f weights best determined?

17–25 Using the data in Table 17–13, calculate the individual and cumulative errors for the four items that belong to a common family. Comment on the relative magnitudes of the cumulative and individual errors.

17–26 Why are the principles of group and cumulative errors so important in forecasting?

17–27 Complete Table 17–14 and comment on the relative magnitudes of group, cumulative, and individual item forecast errors.

17–28 What trade-offs are made in the calculation of the Schwarz Bayesian information criterion?

17–29 What is the rationale of the extreme value validation method?

17–30 What is the problem in using the bootstrap and jackknife methods for model validation with time series data?

17–31 Explain the basic ideas of the following validation methods:
   a. Split sample   *b.* Extreme value
   c. Jackknife   *d.* Bootstrap

17–32 Choose a time series that you have successfully forecasted using several different methods. Now choose two different methods of forecasting, and fit these two models to all observations. Apply three methods of combining forecasts: the simple average, inverse proportionate weights, and the regression weights. Which combining method provided the lowest RSE of fit?

17–33 Do Problem 17–32 except withhold the last season of data. Fit to the first $n - s$ observations using two different forecasting models. Then measure the error of the fit from the three methods of combining forecasts. Now forecast one seasonal cycle into the future using each of the two methods, and combine these two forecasts using the three combining methods. Which methods worked best in fit and which worked best in forecasting? Can you explain any differences, if they occurred?

17–34 Table 17–15 illustrates the use of three combining methods on manufacturing sales, where 48 observations were used to fit models and 12 observations were used to judge

TABLE 17–13   With Bias, Cumulative Errors Equal Item Errrors

	Actual	Forecast	Percent Error	Item Error
1	1,000	900		
2	1,000	700		
3	900	800		
4	1,200	900	___	___
Cumulative	4,000			

TABLE 17–14   Group Forecast versus Individual Error Accuracy

Item	1	2	3	4	Group	Cumulative
Actual	460	676	283	284		
Forecast	360	700	300	322		
Error						
Percent Error						

the error in forecasting. Explain which forecasting method and which combining method had the lowest error during the fitting process and then during the forecasting process. Can you explain any differences, if they occurred?

17–35 Table 17–16 illustrates the use of three combining methods. Explain which forecasting method and which combining method had the lowest error during the fitting process and then during the forecasting process. Can you explain any differences, if they occurred?

TABLE 17–15   Errors and Weights for Quarterly U.S. Manufacturing Sales

Method Weight UBJ/WIN		FIT 77:02–88:01			Forecast 88:02–91:01 Errors				
		BIAS	SSE	SEE	BIAS	SSE	SEE	CUM	CUM%
UBJ*	1/0	.970	11,513	16.3	−5.5	6,023	23.4	−66	−.81
WIN	0/1	.760	28,031	26.1	7.5	6,585	24.5	90	1.10
AVG	.5/.5	.867	14,740	18.3	1.0	6,215	23.7	12	.15
IPW	.709/.291	.911	11,723	16.5	−1.7	6,114	23.6	−20	−.25%
REG	.854/.108	.439	11,352	16.1	−1.7	5,718	22.8	−20	−.25%

* = Best single model in fitting past data.
UBJ = Univariate Box–Jenkins model.
WIN = Winters' three-parameter exponential smoothing.
AVG = Simple average forecast.
IPW = Inverse proportion weight.
REG = Regression weights.
BIAS = Mean fitted or forecasted error.
SSE = Sum of squared errors fitted or forecasted.
SEE = Standard error of estimate (fitted or forecasted), same as the RSE.

TABLE 17–16   Errors and Weights for Monthly Product Sales

Method Weight UBJ/WIN		FIT n = 48			Forecast n = 12 Errors				
		BIAS	SSE	SEE	BIAS	SSE	SEE	CUM	CUM%
UBJ	1/0	−2.54	67,039	44.3	−12.8	2,242	13.7	−154	−2.18%
WIN*	0/1	2.32	21,135	24.0	−29.0	11,652	31.2	−348	−4.97%
AVG	.5/.5	−1.35	29,553	29.1	−20.9	5,856	22.1	−251	−3.58%
IPW	.24/.76	−.73	18,011	22.7	−25.1	8,604	26.8	−301	−4.30%
REG	−.096/1.131	−.21	11,403	18.1	−30.8	13,535	33.6	−370	−5.28%

* = Best single model in fitting past data.
UBJ = Univariate Box–Jenkins model.
WIN = Winters' three-parameter exponential smoothing.
AVG = Simple average forecast.
IPW = Inverse proportion weight.
REG = Regression weights.
BIAS = Mean fitted or forecasted error.
SSE = Sum of squared errors fitted or forecasted.
SEE = Standard error of estimate (fitted or forecasted), same as the RSE.

Minicases

For a selected minicase complete the following analysis. Fit two different models to the first $n - s$ observations of each time series, where s is the length of the seasonal cycle. These two different models can be those fitted in other chapters. Speculate on which of the two models is best in forecasting. Correlate the errors from these two models and speculate on whether a combining method will improve the fit. Then measure the error of the fit from three methods of combining forecasts (i.e., simple average, inverse proportionate, and regression weights). Now using the two forecasting models, forecast one seasonal cycle into the future using the s observations that were withheld during fitting. Measure the errors of the two models and the combined forecasts using the three combining methods. Which methods worked best in fit and which worked best in forecasting? Can you explain any differences, if they occurred? In what way is this experiment a validation procedure?

Minicase 17–1 Kanses Turnpike, Daily Data
TURNPIKD.DAT

Minicase 17–2 Domestic Air Passengers by Quarter
PASSAIR.DAT

Minicase 17–3 Hospital Census by Month
CENSUSM.DAT

Minicase 17–4 Henry Machler's Hideaway Orchids
MACHLERM.DAT

Minicase 17–5 Your Forecasting Project

Minicase 17–6 Midwestern Building Materials
LUMBER.DAT

Minicase 17–7 International Airline Passengers
AIRLINE.DAT

Minicase 17–8 Automobile Sales AUTO.DAT

Minicase 17–9 Consumption of Distilled Spirits
SPIRITS.DAT

Minicase 17–10 Discount Consumer Electronics
ELECT.DAT

References

Akaike, H. "A New Look at Statistical Model Identification." *IEEE Transactions on Automatic Control,* AC-19, 6, December 1974.

Bates, J.M., and C.W.J. Granger. "The Combination of Forecasts." *Operational Research Quarterly* 20 (1969), pp. 451–68.

Brown, R.G. *Advanced Service Parts Inventory Control.* 2nd ed. Thetford Center, VT: Materials Management Systems, 1982.

————. "Detection of Turning Points in a Time Series." Decision Sciences 2 (1971), pp. 383–403.

————. *Smoothing, Forecasting and Prediction.* Englewood Cliffs, NJ: Prentice Hall, 1963.

Bunn, D.W. "A Bayesian Approach to the Linear Combination of Forecasts." *Operations Research Quarterly* 26 (1975), pp. 325–29.

————. "Two Methodologies for the Linear Combination of Forecasts." *Journal of the Operational Research Society* 32 (1981), pp. 213–22.

————. "Statistical Efficiency in the Linear Combination of Forecasts." *International Journal of Forecasting* 1 (1985), pp. 151–63.

Clemen, R.T. "Combining Forecasts: A Review and Annotated Bibliography." *International Journal of Forecasting* 5 (1989), pp. 559–38.

Clemen, R.T., and J.B. Guerard. "Econometric GNP Forecasts: Incremental Information Relative to Naive Extrapolation." *International Journal of Forecasting* 5 (1989), pp. 419–26.

Clemen, R.T., and R.L. Winkler. "Combining Economic Forecasts." *Journal of Business and Economic Statistics* 4 (1986), pp. 39–46.

DeLurgio, S.A., and C.D. Bhame. *Forecasting Systems for Operations Management.* Burr Ridge, IL: Richard D. Irwin, 1991.

Diebold, F.X. "Serial Correlation and the Combination of Forecasts." *Journal of Business and Economic Statistics* 6 (1988) pp. 105–11.

Diebold, F.X, and P. Pauly. "Structural Change and the Combination of Forecasts." *Journal of Forecasting* 6 (1987), pp. 21–40.

Figlewski, S. "Optimal Price Forecasting Using Survey Data." *Review of Economics and Statistics* 65 (1983), pp. 13–21.

Figlewski, S., and T. Urich. "Optimal Aggregation of Money Supply Forecasts: Accuracy, Profitability and Market Efficiency." *Journal of Finance* 28 (1983), pp. 695–710.

Fullerton, R.M. "A Composite Approach to Forecasting State Government Revenues: Case Study of the Idaho Sales Tax." *International Journal of Forecasting* 5 (1989), pp. 373–80.

Gardner, E.S. "CUSUM versus Smoothed-Error Forecast Monitoring Schemes: Some Simulation Comparisons" *Journal of the Operational Research Society* 36 (1985).

————. "Automatic Monitoring of Forecast Errors." *Journal of Forecasting* 2 no. 1 (1983), pp. 18–22.

Granger, C.W.J. "Combining Forecasts—Twenty Years Later." *Journal of Forecasting* 8 (1989) pp. 167–73.

Granger, C.W.J., and P. Newbold *Forecasting Economic Time Series.* 2nd ed. New York: Academic Press, 1968.

Granger, C.W.J. and R.H. Ramanathan. "Improved Methods of Combining Forecasts." *Journal of Forecasting* 3 (1984) pp. 197–204.

Gupta, S., and P.C. Wilton. "Combination of Forecasts: An Extension." *Management Science* 33 (1987) pp. 356–72.

————. "Combination of Economic Forecasts: An Odds-Matrix Approach." *Journal of Business and Economic Statistics* 6 (1988), pp. 373–79.

Harrison, P.J. and O.L. Davies. "The Use of Cumulative Sum (CUSUM) Techniques for the Control of Routine Forecasts of Product Demand." *Operations Research* 12 (1963), pp. 325–33.

Koehler, A.B., and E.S. Murphree. "A Comparison of the AIC and BIC on Empirical Data." *Sixth International Symposium on Forecasting,* Paris, 1986.

Lawrence, M.J.; R.J. Edmundson: and M.J. O'Connor. "The Accuracy of Combining Judgmental and Statistical Forecasts." *Management Science* 32 (1986), pp. 1521–32.

Lobo, G.J. "Alternative Methods of Combining Security Analysts' and Statistical Forecasts of Annual Corporate Earnings." *International Journal of Forecasting* 7 (1991), pp. 57–63.

Mahmoud, E. "Accuracy in Forecasting: A Survey." *Journal of Forecasting* 3 (1984) pp. 139–59.

Makridakis, S. "Sliding Simulation: A New Approach to Time Series Forecasting." *Management Science* 36, no. 4 (April, 1990) pp. 505–11.

Makridakis, S., and R.L. Winkler. "Averages of Forecasts: Some Empirical Results." *Management Science,* 29 (1983) pp. 987–96.

Makridakis, S.; A. Anderson; R. Carbone; R. Fildes; M. Hibon; R. Lewandowski; J. Newton; E. Parzen, and R. Winkler "The Accuracy of Extrapolation (time series) Methods." *Journal of Forecasting* 1 (1982), pp. 111–53.

Makridakis, S., and M. Hibon. "Accuracy of Forecasting: An Empirical Investigation (with discussion)." *Journal of the Royal Statistical Society A,* no. 142, Part 2 (1979), pp. 97–145.

Miller, C.M.; R.T. Clemen; and R.L. Winkler. "The Effect of Nonstationarity on Combined Forecasts." *International Journal of Forecasting* 7 (1992), pp. 515–29.

Mosteller, F., and J.W. Tukey. *Data Analysis and Regression.* Reading, MA: Addison-Wesley, 1977.

Neter, J., M.H. Kutner; and C.J. Nachtsheim. *Applied Linear Statistical Models.* W. Wasserman, Richard D. Irwin. 4th ed. Burr Ridge, IL 1996

Newbold, P., and C.W.J. Granger. "Experience with Forecasting Univariate Time Series and the Combination of Forecasts." *Journal of the Royal Statistical Society A,* no. 137 (1974), pp. 131–65.

Newbold, P.; J.K. Zumwalt; and S. Kannan. "Combining Forecasts to Improve Earnings per Share Prediction: An Examination of Electric Utilities." *International Journal of Forecasting* 3 (1987) pp. 229–38.

Phillips, R.F. "Composite Forecasting: An Integrated Approach and Optimality Reconsidered." *Journal of Business and Economic Statistics* 5 (1987) pp. 389–95.

Reeves, G.R., and K.D. Lawrence. "Combining Multiple Forecasts Given Multiple Objectives" *International Journal of Forecasting* 1 (1982), pp. 271–79.

Schnaars, S.P. "A Comparison of Extrapolation Models on Yearly Sales Forecasts." *International Journal of Forecasting* 2 (1986) pp. 71–85.

Schwarz, G. "Estimating the Dimension of a Model." *Annals of Statistics* 6, no. 2 (1978), pp. 461–64.

Smith, B. *Focus Forecasting—Computer Techniques for Inventory Control.* Boston: CBI Publishing, 1984.

Trabelsi, A., and S.C. Hillmer. "A Benchmarking Approach to Forecast Combination." *Journal of Business and*

Economic Statistics 7 (1989), pp. 353–62.

Trigg, D.W. "Monitoring a Forecasting System." *Operational Research Quarterly* 15 (1964), pp. 2718–74.

Tukey, J.W. *Exploratory Data Analysis.* Reading, MA: Addison-Wesley, 1977.

Winkler. R.L. "Combining Forecasts: A Philosophical Basis and Some Current Issues." *International Journal of Forecasting* 5 (1989), pp. 605–09.

Winkler, R.L., and S. Makridakis. "The Combination of Forecasts." *Journal of the Royal Statistical Society A,* no. 146 (1983), pp. 150–57.

METHOD CHARACTERISTICS, ACCURACY, AND DATA SOURCES

Forecasters are far more artists than scientists, and their complex methods should not obscure the simplicity of their underlying assumptions.

Practical forecasters of the 20th century.

Chapter Outline

This chapter presents two major forecasting topics. First, we explore the general characteristics of different forecasting methods, second, several forecasting accuracy studies of Makridakis and others are discussed.

Because of the diversity of their uses, it is difficult to generalize the characteristics of forecasting methods. Nevertheless, some useful generalizations are possible (Murdick and Georgoff, 1986). However, note that we make such generalizations cautiously because they are just that — characterizations that are more often true than not.

The second section of this chapter presents research about the forecasting accuracy of different methods. This research provides guidance in the effective selection and use of many different forecasting approaches. Some surprising conclusions have been reached in these accuracy studies. As we will see, the forecasting performances of many methods are comparable. Also, there is not one best forecasting method.

Characteristics of Forecasting Methods

Table 18–1 presents the general characteristics of short-range through long-range forecasting methods. These are characteristics of the typical applications of different methods, thus, there are exceptions to these generalizations.

These forecasting model characteristics are listed in the columns of Table 18–1. As shown, the rows of this table present three general types of forecasting methods: univariate, multivariate, and qualitative. Each column presents a different characteristic of these methods and is discussed below under a separate heading. The letters after these section headings (e.g., (a) below) correspond to the column letters in Table 18–1.

Horizon Length (a)

Some forecasting methods have evolved to forecast different horizon lengths. Typically as shown in Table 18–1, the effective horizon length of different methods increases for those that are lower in the table. That is, the effective horizon lengths are longer as we move from univariate to multivariate to qualitative methods. In general, and for our purposes, forecasting methods are defined as either immediate, short-term, medium, or long-term methods. The horizons of these forecasts are, respectively, 1 second to 1 month, 1 to 3 months, 3 months to 3 years, and 3 to 20 years. However, your definitions might overlap these because there are no universally accepted ranges for these terms.

Accuracy at Each Horizon (b)

There are considerable differences in the relative accuracy of different methods at different horizons. As mentioned, longer-horizon accuracy increases for methods lower in the table. The term *accuracy* refers to the relative accuracy of methods; however, no percentage errors are given because percentage accuracy is dependent on the level and variance of the series. We can generalize that short-horizon forecasts are typically more accurate than longer-horizon forecasts. Long-horizon accuracy can vary dramatically depending on the validity of the model as well as the uncertainty of what is being forecast. For example, next month's demand can be forecasted much more accurately than the demand 48 months from now.

In general, smoothing methods such as Winters', Fourier series analysis, decomposition, and ARIMA can be more accurate for immediate to intermediate-term forecasting than are multivariate methods. However, there are many exceptions to this general principle, particularly when daily, weekly, or monthly multivariate data support methods such as multiple regression or multivariate ARIMA models. Thus, when

TABLE 18–1 Comparison of Forecasting Methods in Typical Applications

Methods	Book Chapters	(a) Horizon Length *Immediate (< 1 month) / Short (1–3 months) / Medium (3 months–3 years) / Long (> 3 years)*	(b) Accuracy at Each Horizon *Immediate / Short / Medium / Long*	(c) Development Cost *Very Low ($10s) / Low ($100s) / Medium ($1,000s) / High ($10,000s)*	(d) Data Period Used *Days / Weeks / Months / Quarters / Years*	(e) Frequency of Revision *Weekly / Monthly / Quarterly / Yearly*
Univariate						
Simple smoothing	4	I S M	H M L V	V	D ⟷ Y	W M
Complex smoothing	5, 6	I S M	H H M L	V L	D ⟷ Q	W M
ARIMA	7–9	I S M L	H H M L	L M	D ⟷ Y	W M
Cyclical—pressure cycles	14	I S M L	H H M L	L M	D ⟷ Y	M
Multivariate						
MARIMA—Intervention	12	I S M L	H H M L	L M	D ⟷ Y	W M Q
Multiple regression	3, 10	S M L	H M L	M H	W ⟷ Y	M Q
Single-equation econometric	10, 11	S M L	H H L	H	M ↔ Y	M Q
MARIMA	13	I S M L	H H H L	M H	D ⟷ Y	W M Q
Multiequation econometric	11	S M L	H H L	H	M ↔ Y	M Q Y
Cyclical—paired indexes	14	I S M L	H H M L	M H	D ⟷ Y	W M Q
Neural nets	16	I S M L	H H M S	M H	D ⟷ Y	M Q Y
Qualitative						
Delphi	15	M L	M M	H	Q Y	Y
Survey research	—	M L	M M	M H	Q Y	Q Y
Panel consensus	15	S M L	M M M	M H	M Q Y	M Q Y
Historical analogy	15	S M L	M M M	M H	M Q Y	M Q Y
Scenario analysis	15	M L	M	M H	Q Y	Q Y

H = High accuracy   M = Medium accuracy   L = Low accuracy   V = Very low accuracy

S = speculative because of newness   subj/obj = subjective and objective data.

continued

	(f) Type of Application	(g) Automation of Development	(h) Use of External and Subjective Data	(i) Pattern Recognition Ability	(j) Number of Observations Required
	Item-Level Plan / Production Plan / Aggregate Plan / New-Product Plan / Strategic Plan	*Very Low / Low / Medium / High*		*Trend / Seasonal / Cyclical / Explanatory*	*Low (<36) / Medium (24–48) / High (>48)*
Univariate					
Simple smoothing	I P	H	No		L
Complex smoothing	I P A N	H	No	+ + −	M H
ARIMA	I P A N S	M	No	+ + −	H
Cyclical—pressure cycles	P A N S	H	No	+ + +	M H
Multivariate					
MARIMA—Intervention	A N S	M	Yes (Dummies)	+ + − −	H
Multiple regression	A N S	M	Yes	+ + − −	H
Single-equation econometric	A N S	V L	Yes	+ + + +	M H
MARIMA	A N S	V L	Yes	+ + + +	H
Multiequation econometric	A N S	V	Yes	+ + + +	H
Cyclical—paired indexes	I P A N S	M	Yes	+ + + −	M H
Neural nets	P A N S	V L	Yes	+ + + −	H
Qualitative					
Delphi	N S	V	Yes subj/obj	← * →	L
Survey research	P A N S	V	Yes subj/obj	← * →	H
Panel consensus	P A N S	V	Yes subj/obj	← * →	L
Historical analogy	N S	V	Yes subj/obj	← * →	L M
Scenario analysis	N S	V	Yes subj/obj	← * →	L

+ = Good   − = Not so good   Blank = None   * = Depends on design

Origin of the Term *Forecasting*

One of the first written uses of the word *forecasting* was in 1400. The term is a combination of the Middle English words *fore* and *casten*. The term literally means to throw forward or to cast a set of dice forward as in a game of chance. Thus, a forecaster is one who will cast predictions forward in time. There are many different ways to cast forward. Most methods simply cast patterns or relationships forward into the future.

strong association exists between dependent and independent variables, multivariate methods can be much more effective than univariate methods. However, with multivariate methods, we are frequently required to predict both dependent and independent variables. Obviously, when forecasts of independent variables are in error, multivariate methods are much less accurate and lose their advantage.

For most situations, the accuracy of the forecast is dependent on the future accuracy and representativeness of past data. The forecaster must be aware of and adjust for any nonrecurring planned and unplanned events such as sales promotions, manufacturing interruptions, or lost sales caused by out-of-stock conditions. If such nonrecurring events are not adjusted for properly in the input data, accuracy suffers greatly. Consequently, to a very large extent, forecast accuracy is dependent on the ability of the model to represent the past patterns that recur in the future. Thus, both the input data and the model should reflect the repeating patterns of the data in the future.

Somewhat surprisingly, there are times when methods are not chosen for their lower errors but for the insights provided by the structure of the model. For example, univariate methods are sometimes more accurate than multivariate methods for immediate to short-horizon forecasts. However, a multivariate forecasting model might be chosen because it provides causal explanations of the relationship between the dependent and independent variables. That is, even though a multivariate model may be more costly to construct than a univariate model and might not be more accurate, it may nonetheless provide significantly higher benefits because of its ability to explain cause and effect relationships. This provides management with an improved framework for decisions.

Cost of Development (c)

The development costs of univariate methods are the lowest, while multivariate and qualitative methods can be very costly, depending on the method and application.

In selecting the best forecasting method, there are many trade-offs. It may be easy to make some choices, while other times it may take considerable analysis. For example, we may need to resolve the choice between a very simple and inexpensive method that provides a good forecast and a complex and expensive method that may provide a better forecast. The forecaster must determine if the incremental gain in accuracy is worth the increased cost of the more expensive method. The increased accuracy of a forecast will likely lead to better decisions; therefore, the costs of a more accurate forecast may be offset by the benefits from a better decision. Thus,

$$\text{Net benefit} = \text{Benefit from use} - \text{Cost of use}$$

Many times, these cost-and-benefit estimates and related decisions are made subjectively based on experience. Although much of forecasting is an art, the cost characteristics listed in Table 18–1 should help in forecasting method selection.

Ultimately, an organization should choose the technique that provides the greatest return on investment. For profit-oriented organizations, the DuPont model of financial management provides an important tool in this decision process. It models not only revenues and costs associated with forecasts but also the return that the firm receives from its investment in a forecasting system. An introductory textbook on financial management can be consulted in the development of a DuPont model.

Because forecasting benefits can vary widely by application, this chapter only discusses the relative costs and accuracies of different methods. However, these relative measures can be important in the initial forecasting method–selection process.

Additionally, the forecaster should consider developmental and operating costs separately. Developmental costs are associated with start-up costs of the forecasting method, which may include data analysis, data gathering, data entry, program acquisition, program modification, and development of ongoing data-gathering processes. Operating costs are those costs associated with producing the next forecast using the same technique. These costs will vary by company and technique and should be evaluated separately when determining the best choice. Obviously, operating costs are much lower than the development costs for univariate and multivariate methods. However, the operating costs of qualitative methods will not decline as much, likely following a slower learning curve.

Since data acquisition can sometimes be expensive, the forecaster should evaluate all internal data sources prior to purchasing external data. A cost–benefit analysis is helpful to determine the need for external data. Appendix A of this book provides an extensive list of potential external sources of data.

Data Period Used (d)   The data period analyzed (e.g., hours, weeks, months, quarters, or years) should increase as the forecast horizon increases. The multivariate and qualitative methods shown lower in Table 18–1 are more effective with longer horizons and are therefore used with longer data periods (e.g., quarters or years).

The size or length of the individual forecast period is an important determinant of the forecasting method and system design. Should weekly, monthly, quarterly, or yearly data be forecasted? If a general rule can be stated, it is to choose the longest data period that will give meaningful results. The trade-off in selecting the data period size involves, for example, the relationship between the number of periods per year versus the number of years being forecast. To illustrate, if five-year projections are needed, it is doubtful that daily data will be used; instead, weekly, monthly, quarterly, or annual data should be used. In other words, the farther into the future one needs to forecast, the longer the data period used in the model.

If a forecast is made for the next three years, monthly or quarterly data may be best. In contrast, to control inventory levels in a warehouse over the next month, most likely daily, weekly, or monthly data will be used. As we showed in Chapter 17, forecasts of groups of periods are more accurate than individual-period forecasts. Normally, the forecast of a single four-week period will be more accurate than the individual forecast of one of those weekly periods.

By far the most widely used period of analysis in forecasting has been the month. When necessary, these monthly forecasts can be disaggregated to weekly projections using simple rules based on the number of working days per month and week. Because dates fall on different days of the week, the number of working days varies from month to month (e.g., the number of working days in June versus July), and even year to year (e.g., the number of working days in May, year 1 versus May, year 2). This variation in the number of days per month frequently causes complexity in the forecasting process. Several different approaches are used to compensate for these differences, and fortunately some software packages facilitate this process by using *trading day adjustments.* Consider the following approaches.

Average Daily Demand with Trading Day Adjustments.   A common solution to the problem of months having different numbers of trading days is to average the monthly total based on the number of trading days in the month. For example, assume that a forecast is based on a simple model that predicts that the May, Year 2 daily sales rate will be equal to that of May, Year 1. However, these two months do not have the same number of trading days. Assume that May, Year 1 has 22 trading days, while May, Year 2 has 23 trading days. To forecast sales for May, Year 2, first divide sales of May, Year 1 by 22, then multiply that answer by 23. Assume that the sales of May, Year 1 were 2,500.

$$\text{Forecast May Year 2} = (\text{Daily sales May Year 1})*(\text{Days in May Year 2})$$

$$= (2,500/22)*23 = 2,613.6$$

The forecast based on daily average sales is considerably different than the total May Year 1 sales of 2,500. In general, this method is superior to simply ignoring monthly differences. This is a popular method, especially in retail businesses where the number of selling days is so important.

13-Period Years.   Another solution to the problem of forecasting nonstandard months is to divide the year into 13 periods or months of four weeks each. This method has been very popular with utilities and some larger corporations.

Quarterly, 4-4-5-Week Months.   An alternate method divides the year into 12 "months" that have a repeating pattern of **4-4-5-week months** starting with January. Also, other repeating patterns such as 5-4-4 or 4-5-4 are used. Thus, each month no longer follows the calendar but instead follows a repeating 13-week quarter in which the number of weeks in each month repeats in, for example, a 4-4-5 week pattern. One important disadvantage of this approach is that it introduces an artificial seasonality to the data. This can be offset by analyzing and forecasting average daily demand for each month, as developed previously.

Weekly Forecasts.   Finally, for some planning purposes, there has been movement from monthly to weekly data periods. This helps eliminate the differences in the number of days in each month. For many times series, weeks are much more homogeneous from year to year than are months. However, to forecast one year requires projecting 52 weeks. Herein lies the basic trade-off when choosing the forecast period: choosing shorter periods of analysis requires projections over larger numbers of periods. Consequently, when weeks or months are used for immediate to short-term forecasting, quarters or years may be used for longer-term forecasts.

Disaggregating Monthly Data to Weekly Data.   Our discussion here involves methods of disaggregating monthly data into weekly data. However, it can be generalized quite easily to other levels of aggregation. If decisions and allocations are made weekly, it would seem that weekly forecasts are most appropriate. However, frequently monthly forecasts are more accurate than weekly forecasts, and thus it can be more effective to forecast the demand for a month and then decompose that forecast into weekly forecasts using ratios of the actual number of trading days in the month and week, or historical ratios of a week's sales to a month's sales. These ratios are effective if they are not adversely influenced by large holidays that only affect one week of the month (e.g., the week of Labor Day and its effects on September). In general, the second ratio is better than the first because it measures the holiday influences that recur in the same week each year.

Frequency of Revision (e)

The expense of applying different methods affects the frequency of application. Logically, the most expensive methods may be applied only once or twice a year because of their cost. The frequency of revisions decreases for methods lower in Table 18–1 because they are more expensive to develop and apply. Univariate methods can be applied weekly or even daily. In contrast, qualitative methods may be applied only annually due to the high cost of data gathering and analyst/manager time. Revisions of forecasts are not normally made more frequently than the period of the data; a forecast of monthly data is not normally revised weekly simply because too little new data is available to warrant the weekly effort.

Type of Application (f)

Table 18–1 illustrates the types of business applications supported by forecasting using the hierarchy of decisions developed in Chapter 1—strategic planning, managerial control, operational planning and control, and transaction processing. The applicability of methods to short-horizon, lower-level decisions decreases while the use of methods for higher-level decisions increases as we move down the table. Higher-level decisions are normally decisions that take a long time to implement. Multivariate and qualitative methods are more useful for longer horizons and are therefore more useful for higher-level decisions. The required forecast horizon is important in choosing an appropriate forecasting method. Thus, as shown in Table 18–1, the most popular methods for short-term forecasting are simple smoothing, complex smoothing, ARIMA methods, and multiple regression techniques.

While we have been discussing planning applications in this section as if the forecasting needs of different applications were independent of each other, this is not true. As we discussed in Chapter 17, the forecasts of the same series (e.g., product A in January year 1) used in different planning applications should be equal; this is a requirement of the one-number principle. This equality is important across different departments in the organization (e.g., marketing versus operations) as well as over different time periods. Thus, the monthly forecasts for three years should be consistent with the quarterly forecasts for the same years. These various forecasts should be coordinated through aggregation methods discussed in Chapter 17.

Automation Potential (g)

The degree to which the estimation of forecasting methods can be automated decreases for those lower in the table. This is true because, as we move down the table, the complexity and subjectivity of the forecasting methods evolve from the highly programmable to the ill-structured qualitative methods. As the complexity of the method increases, the less likely will be its automation.

Causal methods such as regression and econometric techniques are complex to apply. It is not normally possible or cost effective to automate the causal modeling methods of multiple regression and econometric techniques; they require too much analyst time and expertise. However, there has been a continuing trend to develop sophisticated expert systems to support the construction of multivariate models. While we cannot have confidence that these are true cause and effect models, they are nonetheless good models for forecasting when verified by knowledgeable analysts.

Recent software products such as Forecast Pro™, and Autobox™ (i.e., Box–Jenkins), RATS™, SCA Multivariate™, and others have made automation of multivariate models much more feasible in recent years.

External and Subjective Data (h)

The use of external and subjective data increases for methods lower in the table. Because data sources are discussed in Appendix A of this book, see it for a detailed discussion of the sources of data.

Data Availability.   One of the important factors in choosing a forecasting method is the availability of data. As shown in Table 18–1, the data needs of methods differ. One of the distinct advantages of univariate forecasting methods is that the required data may be readily available from company records. However, this is not to say that there are no data-availability, cost, or quality problems. In contrast, multivariate data are frequently costly to obtain. Also, in order to make forecasts with multivariate models, it is necessary to make a forecast of the independent variables of the model. The necessity to obtain reliable forecasts of independent variables can make data more costly.

As discussed in Chapter 15, the data requirements for qualitative forecasting methods vary considerably by the method chosen. In general, external data for qualitative models are costly to obtain and maintain. Frequently, data are collected from many sources, including published government documents, sample surveys, and other database searches.

Pattern Recognition Capability (i)

It is important to match a method's **pattern recognition** capability to the patterns of the series being forecasted. Some forecasting systems use expert systems to detect different time series patterns and to subsequently choose the appropriate forecasting model. Whether automated or manual, a forecasting method should not be selected unless that method is capable of modeling the patterns of the time series.

Turning Points.   Another aspect of demand pattern capability is the ability to predict turning points. Turning points reflect changes in the trend or cyclical influences. These changes in direction are very difficult to predict. Examples of turning points are the cyclical expansions and contractions of the gross domestic product (GDP) and their effects on industrywide demands. Long-term forecasting of GDP turning points is difficult, and experts frequently disagree as to their timing, even after a turning point has occurred.

Short-term forecasts of the turning points of specific time series are even more difficult to predict. The responsible forecaster must be aware of the difficulty of predicting turning points and the potential for significant error. The models in Table 18–1 that are identified as having a cyclical pattern capability have a better chance of predicting turning points than other methods. Forecasting systems employ tracking signals to detect turning points after the fact, as discussed in Chapter 17. In addition, Chapter 14 discusses methods of detecting turning points in cyclical forecasting.

Number of Observations Required (j)

The number of observations required to use the methods of Table 18–1 varies considerably. In general, at least three to four seasons of observations should be used to model seasonal data using univariate methods. While trends might be estimated with fewer observations, the rule of thumb denoting that seven periods of increases or decreases imply a trend has to be applied intelligently (e.g., is it seven months showing a

---

Data Collection Is the First Step

"It is a mistake to theorize before one has data."

Sir Arthur Conan Doyle
"Scandal in Bohemia"
The Adventures of Sherlock Holmes, 1891

---

trend or seven years showing a trend?) As shown in Table 18–1, the number of required observations for multivariate methods is the highest of all methods.

The number of observations necessary to use univariate or multivariate ARIMA model building is in general quite large. Typically, six or seven seasonal cycles are recommended for use when the data is monthly. However, it is possible to successfully fit a model when only four or five monthly seasons exist when the data is well behaved (e.g., few outliers exist). We have seen this many times; however, this is not the usual situation. In contrast, we have often seen very long time series such as 15 seasonal cycles (e.g., 180 observations) that are difficult to analyze because either outliers were excessive or the long series really represented more than one time series. Because the series was so long, there were fundamental shifts in the process that generated it. For example, the relationship between dependent and independent variables might have changed significantly.

In general, all methods are more accurate when more observations are available. However, this increased accuracy will diminish when the oldest observations become irrelevant in representing future demand patterns.

Forecasts of New-Products and Erratic Time Series. With today's rapidly changing technologies, there are many time series for which three to four years or seasons of data are unavailable. Also, some time series may have such erratic values that patterns are hard to identify; nonetheless, patterns do exist. These problems need to be recognized and appropriate techniques used to ensure relatively accurate forecasts for trend and seasonal patterns. The methods that can be used in these situations include family trend and seasonal profiles and historical analogies (DeLurgio and Bhame, 1991).

In Summary   **Different Models with Different Horizons.** After studying Table 18–1 and the forecasting methods of this book, the information in Table 18–1 will be clearer. You may know instantly what method to use in a given situation. However, the trade-offs involved in forecasting are several and at times complex. For example, it is possible that a forecasting model is very accurate for immediate forecasts of one or two periods into the future while being grossly inaccurate for short-term forecasts 6 to 12 periods into the future. Thus, we have to be cautious in selecting a forecasting model by keeping in mind the forecasting horizon of greatest importance.

We have seen applications where two forecasting models of the same series were developed, one used for immediate-term forecasting and the other for longer-term projections. To assist you further in understanding such relationships, the next section of this chapter discusses the accuracy of different forecasting methods.

Forecast Accuracy

Accuracy of Time Series Methods

Several forecast accuracy studies have been completed over the years. Overall, the results of these studies have shown that more complex and more expensive methods are not necessarily significantly more accurate than simple time series methods. (The methods of Chapters 5 and 6, decomposition, Winters', and Fourier series, respectively, are not considered complex in this context.) An important assumption of this conclusion is that the models being compared each have the same pattern recognition capabilities.

M-Competition.   Three of the most comprehensive studies of forecasting method accuracy were completed by Makridakis and Hibon in 1979, Makridakis et al. in 1982, and Makridakis et al. in 1990. The first study in 1979 investigated the accuracy of 21 different methods in forecasting 111 different series. A second study conducted by Makridakis et al. (1982) involved seven experts who used 24 forecasting methods. They analyzed 1,001 different actual time series. This competition is now commonly called the **M-competition.** The 1,001 series varied by type (e.g., industry data, national data) and the time period analyzed (e.g., month, quarter, and year). The results of the M-competition are presented in Table 18–2. (The M-competition has been repeated, the most recent being the M3 competition involving 3,003 time series. The M3 results were not available when this book went to print.)

Because of the cost and time of applying some methods, not all 24 were used with all 1,001 series. To reduce application time, 111 series were selected from the 1,001 series. The procedures of the Box–Jenkins, Lewandowski, and Parzen methodologies were added to the 21 methods. Thus, Table 18–2 reports results of 21 methods with 1,001 series, while Table 18–4 reports the findings from 111 time series with 24 models; we discuss Table 18–4 later.

In the M-competition, the lengths of the forecast horizons ranged from 1 to 18 periods for monthly data, 1 to 8 periods for quarterly data, and 1 to 6 periods for annual data. The accuracy of these out-of-sample forecasts was measured on 21 methods using five different statistical measures. We report model performance using one of these measures—the forecast accuracy rank shown in Table 18–2. This rank runs from 1 to 21 for lowest to highest average errors. For example, a rank of 10 for one-period-ahead forecasts indicates that, on average, nine other methods had errors that were lower and 11 had higher errors. Each method receives a rank at each horizon length for each of 1,001 series. Then, the mean of the 1,001 rankings is recorded.

To increase the relevance of Table 18–2, Table 18–3 relates the methods used in the M-competition to those that are presented in this book. Table 18–3 shows that 20 out of the 24 methods are presented in this text. The remaining four methods are not developed because they are either simple extensions of the methods of this book or space doesn't permit their inclusion.

To better understand Table 18–2, consider the example of single exponential smoothing (Single EXP). The average ranking of 1,001 forecasts using Single EXP for one-period-ahead forecasts is 11.9 and for six-period-ahead forecasts, 11.6. When each of the 1,001 series is deseasonalized using the ratio-to-moving average method described in Chapter 5, the rankings of D Sing EXP (where D denotes deseasonalized values) are 10.3 and 10.5, respectively, for one- and six-period-ahead forecasts.

Table 18–4 provides summary results of Table 18–2. We report the rank of each method using the cumulative 18-month average of all forecast horizons. This is shown in column 2 of Table 18–4 and is the same as the last column of Table 18–2. This

TABLE 18–2 **Average Ranking of 21 Models Using 1,001 Series**

		Forecasting Horizons								Average of All Forecasts
Methods	Model Fitting	1	2	3	6	9	12	15	18	
Naive 1	15.8	11.9	12.4	12.3	12.0	11.6	10.0	11.1	11.2	11.62
Moving Average	13.3	11.8	12.3	11.9	11.5	10.8	10.9	10.4	10.6	11.28
Single EXP	12.9	11.9	12.2	11.9	11.6	10.4	10.6	10.5	10.6	11.18
ARR EXP	18.3	12.8	14.0	12.4	12.4	10.7	11.5	11.1	10.9	11.82
Holt EXP	10.5	10.9	10.9	11.0	11.0	11.7	11.3	12.0	11.8	11.41
Brown EXP	12.4	10.8	10.9	10.9	11.4	12.0	11.9	12.3	12.6	11.68
Quad. EXP	13.8	11.8	12.0	12.5	13.1	13.8	14.5	15.1	15.7	13.68
Regression	15.6	14.2	13.4	12.8	11.4	11.9	11.8	11.3	11.1	12.08
Naive 2	11.1	10.4	10.5	10.6	10.6	10.5	10.0	10.2	9.9	10.36
D Moving Average	8.1	11.4	11.9	12.3	11.6	11.2	10.9	10.8	10.8	11.34
D Sing Exp	7.6	10.3	10.4	10.6	10.5	9.6	9.8	9.7	9.4	10.00
D ARR EXP	13.6	11.4	12.4	11.6	11.5	10.4	10.5	10.3	10.0	10.87
D Holt EXP	4.8	9.4	8.9	9.3	9.9	10.7	10.7	10.7	10.7	10.09
D Brown EXP	6.6	9.4	9.0	9.5	10.0	10.6	10.9	11.0	11.3	10.29
D Quad. EXP	8.3	10.2	10.2	11.0	11.9	12.9	13.7	14.1	14.6	12.44
D Regress	12.3	13.3	12.0	12.1	10.9	11.4	11.2	10.7	10.0	11.21
Winters'	7.2	9.4	9.0	9.3	9.8	10.8	10.4	10.2	10.3	9.96
Autom. AEP	9.1	9.8	9.8	10.2	10.0	10.7	10.6	10.5	10.7	10.32
Bayesian F	15.6	11.0	10.0	10.1	10.4	10.3	10.7	10.4	10.2	10.38
Combining A	6.7	9.0	8.8	8.9	9.4	9.4	9.4	9.3	9.1	9.17
Combining B	7.5	9.8	10.0	10.0	10.1	9.7	9.8	9.6	9.6	9.80
Average	11.0	11.0	11.0	11.0	11.0	11.0	11.0	11.0	11.0	11.00

Source: Spyros Makridakis et al., "The Accuracy of Extrapolation (Time Series) Methods: Results of a Forecasting Competition," *Journal of Forecasting* 1 (1982), pp. 111–53.

average ranking is then ranked from the best to worst in column 3 of Table 18–4. Finally, for comparison purposes, we have reported the all-horizon, average rankings of the 111 series using all 24 methods in columns 1, 4, and 5 of Table 18–4. Let's study the results and conclusions of Tables 18–2 and 18–4.

Conclusions from M-competition. The conclusions of the M-competition were consistent with those of other studies. There was not one method that was best for all series or all forecast horizons. Some methods are better than others at short-horizon lengths, others at long-horizon lengths. There was a general conclusion that simple methods do as well or better than the more sophisticated methods, particularly over short-horizon lengths. While there is not one method that is best for all series and forecast horizons, we believe that there are better methods.

One of the more significant results of this study is the effectiveness of combining forecasting methods. As shown in Tables 18–2 and 18–4, Combining A and Combining B methods achieve much better performance than using only one method. Combining A method consists of deseasonalized ARR exponential smoothing, deseasonalized Holt, deseasonalized Brown, Winters', and automatic AEP. These are all easily implemented forecasting methods. This suggests that it may be better to combine a few methods than to rely on the chance that one can isolate a best method. As

---

TABLE 18–3   Relationship between M-Competition 24 Models and This Book

Name Used in Table 18–2*	Description of Method	Chapter(s) Where Method(s) Discussed
Naive 1	$Y_t = Y_{t-1}$	4
Moving Average	n-period moving average where n is chosen to minimize sum(e^2)	4
Single EXP	Single (simple) exponential smoothing with optimal alpha	4
ARR Exp	Adaptive response-rate exponential smoothing	4
Holt EXP	Holt's two-parameter exponential smoothing with optimal parameters	6
Brown EXP	Brown's single-parameter trend smoothing with optimal parameter	6
Quad. EXP	Brown's single-parameter quadratic, triple smoothing with optimal parameter	Not developed here
Regression	Simple linear regression with time as independent variable	3, 5
Naive 2[†]	Deseasonalized data used in Naive 1 model	5
D Moving Average[†]	Moving average using deseasonalized values	4, 5
D Single EXP[†]	Single EXP using deseasonalized values	4, 5
D ARR EXP[†]	ARR EXP using deseasonalized values	4, 5
D Holt EXP[†]	Holt EXP using deseasonalized values	5, 6
D Brown EXP[†]	Brown EXP using deseasonalized values	4, 5
D Quad. EXP[†]	Quad. EXP using deseasonalized values	Not developed here
D Regress[†]	Regression using deseasonalized values	3, 5
Winters'	Winters' three-parameter exponential smoothing with optimal parameters	6
Autom. AEP	An automatic adaptive estimation procedure developed by Carbone–Longini	Not developed here
Bayesian F	An adaptive Bayesian procedure developed by Harrison and Stevens	Not developed here
Combining A	A simple average of D Sing EXP, D ARR EXP, D Holt EXP, D Brown EXP, Winters', and Autom. AEP	4, 6, 17
Combining B	A weighted average of methods used in Combining A, weights determined by percentage error of each	4, 6, 17
Box–Jenkins[‡]	ARIMA model-building methods	7, 8, 9
Lewandowski[‡]	Lewandowski's FORSYS system	Not developed here
Parzen[‡]	Parzen's ARARMA methodology	Simple extension of 7, 8, 9

---

* The methods are presented in the order used in Table 18–2.

[†] The method of ratio to centered moving averages developed in Chapter 5 was used to determine seasonal indexes. Then the series were deseasonalized, forecasted using specified methods, and reseasonalized by multiplying the deseasonalized forecasts times the relevant seasonal indexes.

[‡] These methods are not included in Table 18–2 but are in Table 18–4.

---

we discussed in Chapter 17, there are several different methods of combining forecasts; however, simple averages seem to work as well as more sophisticated methods.

Combining A method uses a simple average of (i.e., gives equal weight to) the forecasts of several methods. Combining B method of forecasting is a weighted average of the methods used in Combining A, where the weights are inversely proportionate

TABLE 18–4   Ranking of Methods Based on Forecast Errors

(1) Method	(2) All-Horizon Average Rank 1,001 Series	(3) Rank of Rank 1,001 Series	(4) All-Horizon Average Rank (111 Series)	(5) Rank of Rank 111 Series
Combining A	9.17	1	10.40	1
Lewandowski	NA	NA	10.87	2
Combining B	9.80	2	11.30	6
Winters'	9.96	3	11.26	5
D Single EXP	10.00	4	11.57	9
Parzen	NA	NA	11.22	4
D Holt EXP	10.09	5	11.15	3
D Brown EXP	10.29	6	11.47	7
Box–Jenkins	NA	NA	11.53	8
Autom. EXP	10.32	7	11.77	10
Naive 2	10.36	8	12.32	12
Bayesian F	10.38	9	11.90	11
D ARR EXP	10.87	10	12.72	13
Single EXP	11.18	11	13.20	16
D Regress	11.21	12	12.94	14
Moving Average	11.28	13	13.09	15
D Moving Average	11.34	14	13.86	21
Holt EXP	11.41	15	13.25	18
Naive 1	11.62	16	13.83	20
Brown EXP	11.68	17	13.30	19
ARR EXP	11.82	18	13.95	22
Regression	12.08	19	14.61	23
D. Quad. EXP	12.44	20	12.23	17
Quad. EXP	13.68	21	15.27	24

NA = Not applicable.

Source: Spyros Makridakis et al., "The Accuracy of Extrapolation (Time Series) Methods: Results of a Forecasting Competition," *Journal of Forecasting* 1 (1982), pp. 111–53.

to the sum of squared errors of the methods. As shown in Table 18–1 and 18–4, the additional complexity of calculating inverse weights did not yield more accurate forecasts.

Another important conclusion of the study was that the sophisticated methods do not appear to be, on average, significantly better than simple methods. This is apparent when comparing the performance of the top eight methods of columns 4 and 5 of Table 18–4. Their performance rankings vary from 10.40 to 11.53. There is no practical difference between the most sophisticated methods of Lewandowski (10.87), Parzen (11.22), and Box–Jenkins (11.53) and the simpler methods of Combining A (10.40), Winters' (11.26), and D Holt EXP (11.15).

We remain cautious in accepting this last conclusion because average rankings can be misleading. Also, the wide variety of series included in the competition result in using methods that are appropriate for some of the series but clearly not for others. Further research by Makridakis in 1990 showed that by choosing different models for different horizons, one can dramatically improve accuracy. Thus, intelligent selection of different forecasting methods for different horizons and applications can dramatically improve forecasting performance in specific settings. Also, it is important to recognize that the little differences in performance between several methods likely occurs because these methods are capable of modeling the relevant patterns of each series. Consequently, we believe the following is in general true: When simple models have appropriate pattern capabilities, more sophisticated and more costly methods are not necessarily better.

While not presented here, Makridakis et al. (1982) presented the results of forecasting 60 seasonal series out of the 1,001 series. These results illustrated that, for the seasonal data of these 60 series, there is very little difference between the performance of the seasonally adjusted methods. As Makridakis et al., noted: "A hypothesis may be advanced at this point stating that statistically sophisticated methods do not do better than simple methods (such as deseasonalized exponential smoothing) when there is considerable randomness in the data. Finally, it seems that seasonal patterns can be predicted equally well by both simple and statistically sophisticated (seasonal) methods."

We can summarize the results of these and other studies as follows:

1. Choosing models based on out-of-sample (i.e., withheld) multiple-period-ahead forecasts is better than using historical fit.

2. Choosing different models for different horizon lengths appears better than using a single model for all horizon lengths.

3. Combining the forecasts of several different methods is an effective way of increasing forecast accuracy.

4. Frequently simple averages of several good forecasting methods work better than weighted average combinations.

5. More sophisticated and more costly methods are not necessarily better, as long as the pattern recognition capability of the model is good.

6. If one can ascertain the characteristics of the forecasting situation identified in Table 18–1 before selecting a method, forecasting accuracy can be greatly increased.

7. An implementation of a method should be tested to ensure that it can correctly handle unusual values (e.g., zero values and division by zero) without generating very inaccurate forecasts.

8. Forecasting method performance is dependent on how well that method is used in a system that adjusts for outliers and applies points (1) to (7).

Summary

The characteristics of the methods illustrated in Table 18–1 are very important in choosing one method over another; however, other factors enter into the choice. These include the availability of data, the expertise of the analyst, the availability of software and hardware, the benefits from increased forecast accuracy, and the costs of forecast errors. Fortunately, the choice of the forecasting method for many situations is quite easy, and most frequently, univariate methods have a cost-effectiveness advantage. This is true because they are relatively inexpensive to use, have high accuracy in immediate to medium-range forecasts, lend themselves to automated applications, and do not require forecasts of independent variables. In contrast, multivariate and qualitative methods are frequently unsuitable for the routine forecasting of hundreds or thousands of items because of their use of costly analyst time and effort. However, with the advent of lower-cost 64-bit microcomputers and relatively inexpensive expert forecasting systems, the advantages of multivariate techniques have increased greatly.

However, frequently, the most important determinant of successful multivariate applications is the expertise of the analyst.

Long-horizon forecasts are the basis of corporate long-horizon planning, including the functional areas of finance, marketing, operations, and logistics. These forecasts provide information for budgetary planning and cost control. Marketing depends on short- to long-horizon demand forecasts to plan new products and allocate sales and distribution resources. Production uses long-term forecasts to make long-term decisions involving process selection, capacity planning, and facility plans. Short-horizon forecasts are needed by production to support decisions about production planning, scheduling, and inventory control. Also, logistical plans depend on long-horizon forecasts for warehouse, transportation, and other supply chain planning.

Because forecasts always have errors, the search for the perfect method and forecast is futile; it is more important to have better methods and best systems. The best systems will have adequate control devices (e.g., tracking signals) and contingency plans or buffers for when the inevitable forecast errors occur. Such systems continuously review forecasts to achieve relatively accurate and unbiased predictions. By building low-cost but effective buffers for these inaccurate forecasts, overall system costs can be minimized despite the inaccuracy of the forecasts. This is not to say that we should not try to improve the forecasting model or system, but that we should try to find and use the most cost-effective forecasting method available for our application.

For long-horizon forecasts that lead to large financial commitments, greater care is justified in forecasting. Multivariate methods such as multiple regression analysis, econometrics, and MARIMA are important explanatory and policy planning tools. The effects of economic factors, product trends, growth factors, and competition should be modeled. Then, these effects can be used to adjust the forecast to reflect the influence of each. We have found that often, very simple percentage adjustments can be made to univariate forecasts to better reflect the possible impacts of such exogenous factors.

Short- to medium-horizon forecasts, such as required for inventory control, staffing, and scheduling, may use univariate methods such as exponential smoothing models that incorporate trend and seasonal adjustment procedures. In such applications, there are usually thousands of items to forecast. Such forecasting processes should therefore be simple and run efficiently on a computer. The system should also detect and respond rapidly to definite short-term changes in demand while at the same time ignoring the occasional outliers.

We have seen in this chapter that the accuracies of forecasting methods vary, but if several methods are capable of modeling the same times series patterns, typically their accuracy will not vary dramatically. Also, we have seen that there are different sources of data available to the forecasting system. When an external time series is needed to support forecasting and planning, its availability can be extremely valuable. On-line data retrieval systems, described in Book Appendix A, have increased dramatically in recent years. These are very cost-effective ways to routinely acquire the data needed for effective forecasts.

Key Terms

automation potential	M-competition
average daily demand	pattern recognition ability
4-4-5-week months	13-period years

Problems

18–1 List four major factors to be considered when determining whether to use a univariate, multivariate, or qualitative forecasting model.

18–2 List the many factors to be considered when selecting a forecasting method.

18–3 In modern applications what do you believe will be the trend in the proportion of univariate versus multivariate forecasting usage? What do you believe will be the trend in the absolute use of univariate versus multivariate forecasting applications? On a percentage basis, which will grow more rapidly?

18–4 What does it mean to use different models for forecasting different horizon lengths? Does this seem theoretically sound?

18–5 Using cost as a criteria, how should we determine the best forecasting method?

18–6 What is meant by forecasting ability versus explanatory power or ability?

18–7 What is the general principle concerning whether to forecast using small data periods such as daily activity versus larger periods such as quarterly activity?

18–8 Why would firms use 13-month years? Explain how monthly data from year to year can be made more homogeneous with respect to the underlying causes of variations.

18–9 Why would weekly data be more homogeneous with respect to the underlying causes of variations?

18–10 What is the general principle involved in determining when to revise a forecast?

18–11 What is meant by the term *automation potential*? How might the level of automation change over time as firms become more proficient at forecasting?

18–12 Which forecasting methods require the greatest number of observations? Are those methods requiring fewer observations less costly to apply?

18–13 What have been the conclusions of major forecasting competition studies relative to the accuracy of different seasonal forecasting models?

18–14 The conclusions from the M-competition are generalizations. In what circumstances are these results not valid?

18–15 What were the conclusions from the M-competition regarding the use of combining methods?

18–16 If you have forecasted the same series using several different methods, have your experiences confirmed or denied the conclusions of the M-competition?

18–17 If you were responsible for designing a forecasting system to forecast tens of thousands of items, in contrast to being responsible for forecasting a time series most accurately, which of the M-competition conclusions are most important to you? If you are responsible for forecasting a time series most accurately, as opposed to designing a forecasting system, which of the M-competition conclusions are most important to you?

Minicases: Common Assignment for Minicases

Answer the following questions using one of the continuing minicases which you have forecasted using several different methods. Have your results confirmed or denied the forecasting model accuracy conclusions of studies reviewed in this chapter? Compare and contrast the numerical results of your models in the context of the eight principles stated before the Summary of this chapter.

Minicase 18–1 Kansas Turnpike

Minicase 18–2 Domestic Air Passengers

Minicase 18–3 Hospital Census

Minicase 18–4 Henry Machler's Hideaway Orchids

Minicase 18–5 Your Forecasting Project

Minicase 18–6 Midwestern Building Materials

Minicase 18–7 International Airline Passengers

Minicase 18–8 Automobile Sales

Minicase 18–9 Consumption of Distilled Spirits

Minicase 18–10 Discount Consumer Electronics

References

Ahlburg, D.A. "Forecast Evaluation and Improvement Using Theil's Decomposition." *Journal of Forecasting* 3 (1984), pp. 345–51.

Boothe, P., and D. Glassman. "Comparing Exchange Rate Forecasting Models: Accuracy versus Profitability." *International Journal of Forecasting* 3 (1987), pp. 65–79.

Brodie, R.J., and C.D. De Kluyver. "A Comparison of the Short Term Forecasting Accuracy of Econometric and Naive Extrapolation Models of Market Share." *International Journal of Forecasting* 3 (1987), pp. 423–37.

Brown, L.R. et al. *State of the World.* New York: Worldwatch Institute and W.W. Norton, 1996.

———. *Vital Signs.* New York: Worldwatch Institute and W.W. Norton, 1996.

Carbone, R., and J.S. Armstrong. "Evaluation of Extrapolative Forecasting Methods." *Journal of Forecasting* 1 (1982), pp. 215–17.

Clemen, R.T., and J.B. Guerard. "Econometric GNP Forecasts: Incremental Information Relative to Naive Extrapolation." *International Journal of Forecasting* 5 (1989), pp. 419–26.

Cooper, J.P., and C.R. Nelson. "The Ex-Ante Prediction Performance of the St. Louis and FRB-MIT-Penn. Econometric Models and Some Results on Composite Predictors." *Journal of Money, Credit and Banking* 7 (1975), pp. 1–32.

DeLurgio, S.A., and C.D. Bhame. *Forecasting Systems for Operations Management.* Burr Ridge, IL: Irwin Professional Publishing, 1991.

Granger, C.W.J. "Prediction with a Generalized Cost of Error Function." *Operational Research Quarterly* 20 (1969), pp. 199–207.

Granger, C.W.J., and P. Newbold. *Forecasting Economic Time Series.* 2nd ed. New York: Academic Press, 1986.

———. "Some Comments on the Evaluation of Economic Forecasts." *Applied Economics* 5 (1973), pp. 35–47.

Kling, J.L. "Predicting the Turning Points of Business and Economic Time Series." *Journal of Business* 60 (1987), pp. 201–38.

Longbottom, J.A., and S. Holly. "The Role of Time Series Analysis in the Evaluation of Econometric Models." *Journal of Forecasting* 4 (1985), pp. 75–87.

Makridakis, S., and M. Hibon. "Accuracy of Forecasting: An Empirical Investigation (with discussion)." *Journal of the Royal Statistical Society* A, no. 14 (1979, Part 2), pp. 97–145.

Makridakis, S. et al. "The Accuracy of Major Extrapolation (Time Series) Methods." *Journal of Forecasting* 1, no. 2 (1982), pp. 111–53.

Makridakis, S. "Sliding Simulation: A New Approach to Time Series Forecasting." *Management Science* 36, no. 4 (April 1990), pp. 505–11.

Mincer, J., and V. Zarnowitz. "The Evaluation of Economic Forecasts." In *Economic Forecasts and Expectations,* ed. J. Mincer. New York: National Bureau of Economic Research, 1969.

Murdick, R.G., and D.M. Georgoff. "How to Choose the Best Technique—or Combination of Techniques—to Help Solve Your Particular Forecasting Dilemma." *Harvard Business Review,* January–February 1986, pp. 110–20.

Nelson, C.R. "The Prediction Performance of the FRB-MIT-Penn. Model of the U.S. Economy." *American Economic Review* 62 (1972), pp. 902–17.

Nelson, C.R., and S.C. Peck. "The NERC Fan: A Retrospective Analysis of the NERC Summary Forecasts." *Journal of Business and Economic Statistics* 3 (1985), pp. 179–87.

Stekler, H.O. "Who Forecasts Better?" *Journal of Business and Economic Statistics* 5 (1987), pp. 155–58.

———. "Macroeconimic Forecast Evaluation Techniques." *International Journal of Forecasting* 7 (1991), pp. 375–84.

Theil, H. *Economic Forecasts and Policy.* Amsterdam: North Holland, 1958.

———. *Applied Economic Forecasting.* Amsterdam: North Holland, 1966.

Zellner, A. "Biased Predictors, Rationality and the Evaluation of Forecasts." *Economic Letters* 21 (1986), pp. 45–48.

FORECASTING DATA
SOURCES

How dangerous it is to reason from insufficient data.
Sherlock Holmes

There has been an explosion in the number and availability of data for forecasting. Public bulletin boards, the Internet, and the emerging information superhighway have dramatically increased the potential sources of useful data. These data sources can be defined roughly on four dimensions that yield 24 ($3 \times 2 \times 2 \times 2$) combinations of data types:

> *Internal data*: Measures of activity internal to the organization.
> *External data*: Measures of activity external to the organization.
>   *Private sources*: Company, trade organization, industry, commercial, data services, and other data sources.
>   *Public sources*: Local, state, countrywide, regional or continentwide, data sources.
>
> *Domestic measures*: Regional and national data about an economy.
> *International measures*: International statistics.
>
> *Hardcopy media*: Data printed in books.
> *Computer/On-line media*: Either remote data access (e.g., Internet or dialin), diskette, or CD-ROM based services.
>
> *Primary data*: Data collected just for your forecasting process.
> *Secondary data*: Data collected for general use.

As you seek data to make forecasts, consider the combinations of types and sources of data using these attributes. We discuss several of the more popular combinations of these attributes after discussing the concepts of primary and secondary sources of data.

Primary versus Secondary Sources of Data

Secondary data refers to data that have already been collected and published for reasons other than for use in a specific application. These data include all data collected and published by private and public organizations for general use. In contrast, primary data are collected just to support the forecasting or research task at hand. Through research, sample surveys, and on-line computerized data collection devices, primary data is collected to support a specific forecasting system. Univariate and multivariate methods normally use secondary data in their databases.

That is, univariate methods will probably use data from an existing data processing system—for example—a perpetual inventory or order processing system.

U.S. Government Sources

The sources of external data include many governmental agencies, including those listed in Table A–1. (Note: In this section we discuss only hard copy publications, in a later section we discuss electronic media of many data sources including the U.S. government). Of particular interest is the Bureau of Economic Analysis (BEA) of the U.S. Department of Commerce. Each month, the BEA publishes the *Survey of Current Business (SCB)*. The *SCB* includes national income and product accounts (NIPA) data for the U.S. economy. The NIPA data included in the SCB can be grouped into eight subsets:

1. Gross national product and national income.
2. Personal income and outlays.
3. Government receipts and expenditures.
4. Foreign transactions.
5. Savings and investments.
6. Income and employment by industry.
7. Supplementary tables.
8. Implicit price deflators.

TABLE A–1   U.S. Government Data Sources

Arms Control and Disarmament Agency	Department of Labor
Board of Governors of the Federal Reserve System	Bureau of Labor Statistics
Council of Economic Advisers	Department of the Treasury
Council on Environmental Quality	Internal Revenue Service
Department of Agriculture	Department of Transportation
Economic Research Service	Coast Guard
Forest Service	Federal Aviation Administration
Statistical Reporting Service	Federal Highway Administration
National Agricultural Statistics Service	Research and Special Programs Administration
Department of Commerce	Environmental Protection Agency
Bureau of Economic Analysis	Federal Reserve Banks
Bureau of the Census	Federal Communications Commission
National Climatic Data Center	Federal Deposit Insurance Corporation
Department of Defense	House of Representatives
Army Corps of Engineers	Interstate Commerce Commission
Department of Energy	Library of Congress
Energy Information Administration	National Aeronautics and Space Administration
Department of Health and Human Services	National Science Foundation
Center for Disease Control	Office of Personnel Management
Health Care Financing Administration	Patent and Trademark Office
National Center for Health Statistics	U.S. Postal Service
Social Security Administration	
Department of the Interior	
Bureau of Mines	
Geological Survey	
Department of Justice	
Bureau of Justice Statistics	
Federal Bureau of Investigation	
Immigration and Naturalization Service	

Some of these national income series are available as annual and quarterly series. The annual data extends from about 1929 through the current year, and the quarterly series extends from 1946 through the current quarter. In addition, each issue contains about 32 pages of monthly and quarterly economic series. This data is in the section called Current Business Statistics. A list of the major headings defines the types of series included in the Current Business Statistics section:

- General Business Indicators.
- Commodity Prices.
- Construction and Real Estate.
- Domestic Trade.
- Labor Force, Employment, and Earnings.
- Finance.
- Foreign Trade of the United States.
- Transportation and Communication.
- Chemicals and Allied Products.
- Electric Power and Gas.
- Food and Kindred Products.
- Leather and Products.
- Lumber and Products.
- Metals and Manufacturers.
- Petroleum, Coal, and Products.
- Pulp, Paper, and Paper Products.
- Rubber and Rubber Products.
- Stone, Clay, and Glass Products.
- Textile Products.
- Transportation Equipment.

In addition, every month the *SCB* includes another section containing about 300 economic time series. This contains the Business Cycle Indicators section. These and other series are presented in detail in the *Handbook of Cyclical Indicators*. This publication contains historical data for these series, frequently as far back as the 1940s. You can obtain a booklet called *The Users Guide to BEA Information* from the BEA or from the January editions of the *SCB*. Finally, the BEA offers many electronic bulletin board and fax facilities from which you can obtain many of the aforementioned time series via telephone.

As we have seen, *The Survey of Current Business (SCB)* is a very valuable source of historical data for use in developing business forecasts. Comparable historical data can be found in *Business Statistics*, also published by the BEA.

The *Federal Reserve Bulletin*, published monthly by the Federal Reserve Board, is a useful source of economic and monetary data. In addition, at this time most Federal Reserve Banks offer computer bulletin boards that provide the capability of downloading many historical times series. This is a capability that only costs a telephone call. By using a high-speed modem and compressed files you can obtain valuable data for immediate use. Also of great interest is the data published by the U.S. Council of Economic Advisors in *Economic Indicators* and the *Economic Report of the President*. In addition, the Department of Commerce publishes the annual *U.S. Industrial Outlook*, which provides useful historical data as well as forecasts for all major industries. This is a particularly interesting source of industry-specific forecasts.

A publication we have used in several chapters for data sets is the *Statistical Abstract of the United States*, available at almost every library and from many bookstores, particularly the U.S. government bookstores. Also, a particularly interesting compilation of historical statistics is included in the *Historical Statistical Abstract of the United States*, with data going back to the 1790s or earlier. Also, the Census Bureau is an important source of data in the centennial censuses, these being available on electronic media from 1970, 1980, and 1990. Because these provide important economic and demographic characteristics, the census data can be an extremely valuable source of information. Many of the publications mentioned here are available at public libraries.

Finally, there are many additional references, two of which you may find very interesting: George Thomas Kurian, *Datapedia of the U.S. 1790 to 2000* (Lanham, MD: Bernan Press, 1994); and *Instant Investor*, a CD-ROM of thousands of economic and financial time series (Greenville, SC: Traders Press, 1995).

State Governments and Other Organizations

Table A–2 lists several important private sources of data, and while we have not listed any state governments, these are important sources of data. A few trade associations are listed in Table A–2, and these provide data to their members and nonmembers. Your local library can provide a list of addresses of the many hundreds of associations that exist in the United States. Also, there are many regional and metropolitan agencies that can assist you in forecasting regional and metropolitan behavior.

Included in Table A–2 are many other sources of information, including the Conference Board publications *Business Outlook* and *Guide to Consumer Markets*, and the Sales and Marketing Management's *Survey of Buying Power*. Interestingly, the first annual issue of *Business Week* includes an Industrial Outlook. There are several syndicated data services, including those from market research firms such as A.C. Nielsen. Also, there are economic series from sources such as *CITIBASE* from Citicorp Database Services. Another source of data for long-range planning is provided by the National Bureau of Economic Research. Some private organizations and research institutions provide additional data. For example, the J. Walter Thompson Company maintains a consumer panel of selected families to check the brands of food products being purchased. The A.C. Nielsen company collects detailed information on consumer purchase patterns at regular intervals. The F.W. Dodge Company collects data on various forms of construction activity. Often, these and other firms can supply needed data.

Table A–2 is not, nor could it be, comprehensive of the thousands of trade associations and commercial, state, and regional agencies providing time series data. A few minutes spent with a business reference librarian or on the Internet can be very fruitful in identifying other sources of data.

International Data Sources

The bottom of Table A–2 lists several international sources of data. The *International Financial Statistics*, published by the International Monetary Fund, contains a wealth of international data. Also, the United Nations provides many international times series by country. The national governments of other countries can be contacted; many gather statistics using classifications similar to those of the U.S. government. Finally, we subscribe to several publications of the WorldWatch Institute, which provide many interesting international and global time series.

Index and Abstract Services

Throughout this book, we've stressed the need to have models built on sound theory. To assist you in learning that sound theory, most university and public libraries subscribe to abstract services that review forecasting and econometric articles in business, engineering, and so on. Several abstract services of value to one needing assistance in identifying past research in forecasting are given below in alphabetical order.

Applied Science and Technology (H.W. Wilson, New York) indexes several hundred periodicals, including forecasting topics in industrial engineering, production engineering, scheduling, quality control, and computer technology.

Business Periodicals Index (H.W. Wilson, New York) is a cumulative subject index of several hundred periodicals published in the United States and abroad. This index is valuable

---
TABLE A–2   Associations, Research Institutes, and Other Publishers

---

American Academy of Political and Social Science
American Association of Fund-Raising Counsel, Inc.
American Association of Individual Investors
American Hospital Association
American Medical Association
Association of American Railroads
Citicorp Database Services
Conference Board, Inc.
Congressional Quarterly, Inc.
Dun & Bradstreet Corporation
Editor & Publisher Company
Elections Research Center
Eno Transportation Foundation, Inc.
Health Insurance Association of America
Macmillan Publishing Co., Inc.
McGraw-Hill, Inc.
Merrill Lynch Business Brokerage and Valuation
Motor Vehicle Manufacturers Association of the United States, Inc.
National Association of Purchasing Managers
National Association of Realtors
National Bureau of Economic Research, Inc.
New York Stock Exchange, Inc.
Northeastern University Press
PennWell Publishing Company
Population Reference Bureau, Inc.
Rutgers University Press
Standard & Poors Corporation
University of Michigan—Survey of Consumers, Survey Research Center

International Organizations

Food and Agricultural Organization of the United Nations
International Labour Office
International Monetary Fund
Traders Press Incorporated
United Nations Educational, Scientific and Cultural Organization
WorldWatch Institute, Washington, D.C.

---

for finding articles about state-of-the-art topics written in a style that will appeal to managers and generalists.

Dissertation Abstracts (University Microfilm Inc. (UMI), Ann Arbor, MI) provides abstracts of PhD dissertations available in the United States from UMI. These can be extremely valuable sources of methodology information and data.

Engineering Index (Engineering Information, Inc., New York) is a subject heading guide to engineering publications. There are hundreds of society publications cited in the index, including those of the ACM, AFIPS, IIE, SAE, SAM, and ORSA.

Government Reports Announcements and *Government Reports Index* (National Technical Information Service, Springfield, VA) are important sources of government sponsored research and development reports and other government analyses prepared by federal agencies, their contractors, or grantees. Sections are arranged in 22 subject fields, with all entries abstracted.

International Abstracts in Operations Research (Operations Research Society of America, Baltimore, MD) abstracts about 100 international journals. The abstracts are divided into subject sectors, allowing rapid access to specific titles.

Operations Research/Management Science Abstracts (ORMS) (Executive Sciences Institute, Inc., Whippany, NJ) abstracts over 100 international journals, including the transactions and meetings of many learned societies in the United States and abroad.

Predicast Publications (Predicasts, Inc., Cleveland) provides a wide variety of services, including abstracts, indexes, time series data, and forecasts. There are currently more than 1 million records on line in their *Predicasts* and *Worldcasts* database services. Most of these services are available on line using the Data-Star or DIALOG information services.

Readers' Guide to Periodical Literature (H.W. Wilson, New York) is an author-subject index to about 400 selected general interest periodicals. Included in the index are journals such as *Time, Life, Omni, Science, Forbes, Fortune*, and *Futurists*.

Science Citation Index (Institute for Scientific Information, Philadelphia, PA) is a useful resource for scientific applications and research in forecasting. Articles from 1,400 journals are indexed and cited.

Quality Control/Applied Statistics Abstracts (OC/AS) (Executive Sciences Institutes, Inc., Whippany, NJ) abstracts over 400 foreign and domestic periodicals and proceedings, including articles on forecasting.

On-Line Literature Retrieval Services

The most efficient way to research the forecasting literature is to use on-line literature retrieval services that provide access to the abstract services above. There are several on-line database services to assist in research. On-line literature searches can be done at your local library or through computer services such as Compuserve™ or America Online™. Electronic services include ABI/Inform, ERIC, Management Contents, Compendex, INFOTRACS, DIALOG, and SciSearch. Many of these services access multiple commercial databases. Unless you have studied several electronic services, it is recommended that you study search procedures or see a professional librarian to do the on-line literature search.

Internet Directory

By its nature, any directory of on-line and Internet information and data is out-of-date. However, it is important to highlight many of the possible sites of information on the Internet. No doubt you will be able to find other more specific sources of information on the Internet. We have found the following to be valuable sources of information:

Census Bureau (http://www.census.gov/) provides vast amounts of economic and demographical information about the U.S. economy.

Economic Report of the President (gopher://umslvma.umsl.edu:70/11/library/govdocs) at the University of Missouri at St. Louis provides the economic report of the president as well as much other government information.

Penn World Tables (http://cansim.epas.utoronto.ca:5680/pwt/pwt.html) from the University of Toronto provides an easy-to-use source of international economic data.

Regional Economic Information System (http://ptolemy.gis.virginia.edu:1080/reisl.html) of the University of Virginia provides a good source of regional, state, and local data.

The White House (http://www.whitehouse.gov/) provides daily press releases and the latest presidential budget.

Resources for Economists on the Internet (http://econwpa.wust1.edu/EconFAQ/Econ-FAQ.html) is a best starting point in the exploration of the Internet for business and economic forecasting and research. This site is managed by Prof. Bill Goffe of the Department of Economics and International Business at the University of Southern Mississippi, Hattiesburg, MS 39406. It lists vast sources of other sites and information.

STAT-USA (http://www.stat-usa.gov/inqsample.html) is an extraordinary source of government data and information. Unfortunately, it is not free; however, the annual subscription rate is only about $100. Also, site licenses to universities are very reasonable. The above Internet address will allow you to try this site for a limited free search. However, to get full utilization of this resource, you must subscribe. STAT-USA publishes the best business and economic information of the federal government. It gathers this data daily from over 50 federal agencies and distributes it centrally from this site. STAT-USA/Internet has over 300,000 reports and statistical series, the equivalent of 7 sets of encyclopedias, which are available to you at your computer. Publications of the Bureau of Economic Analysis (e.g., *Survey of Current Business*) and many other government agencies are available. The Internet interface to this site is extremely user friendly.

Table A–3 lists several additional Internet sites of interest to forecasters. No doubt some of these sites may no longer exist. However, popular search engines listed at the end of Table A–3 can be used to update this list for your purposes.

TABLE A–3   Additional Economic Internet Sites

Federal Reserve Board data	gopher://town.hall.org/1/other/fed
Federal Reserve Board	www.bog.frb.fed.us
Federal Reserve Bank of Chicago	www.frbchi.org
Federal Reserve Bank of Minnesota	woodrow.mpls.frb.fed.us
Federal Reserve Bank of Philadelphia	www.libertynet.org/~fedrserv/fedpage.html
Federal Reserve Bank of St. Louis	www.stls.frb.org
Federal Reserve Bank of Kansas City	www.kc.frb.org
FDIC	www.fdic.gov
World Bank	www.worldbank.org
American Bankers Association	www.aba.com/aba
Bureau of Labor Statistics (LABSTAT)	stats.bls.gov/blshome.html
Census Bureau	www.census.gov
USDA Agriculture Research	www.econ.ag.gov
Vienna Institute for Comparative Economic Studies	www.wsr.ac.at/wiiw-html/
World Wide Web Virtual Library	www.w3.org/hypertext/DataSources/bySubject/Overview.html
Internet public library	ipl.sils.umich.edu
Search Engines	
EXCITE	www.excite.com
InfoSeek	www2.infoseek.com
Lycos	www.lycos.com
Webcrawler	webcrawler.com
YAHOO	www.yahoo.com
Altavista	www.altavista.com
The Author's Website	http://forecast.umkc.edu
Banking Information	www.bankrate.com
American Stock Exchange	www.amex.com
New York Stock Exchange	www.nyse.com/public/home/html
NASDAQ	www.nasdaq.com
Investor Net	www.investor.com
Worldwide Banking	www.qualisteam.com/aconf.html

Final Comments

We urge you to explore the listed data sources in this Appendix. Several minutes spent at a library reference desk or the Internet will yield extraordinary returns. If you are required to analyze a time series of your choosing, then find a topic of interest to you by researching data sources of Table A–1 to A–3. It is disturbing to see students spending a semester studying a boring time series. Don't cheat yourself out of a very interesting intellectual pursuit by choosing a convenient time series without interesting patterns and relationships.

B

OUTLIER DETECTION AND ADJUSTMENT PROCEDURES

Better to ask twice than to lose your way once.
Danish proverb

Outliers

It is extremely important that the data used in fitting forecasting models be a good representation of the past and future so that we do not lose our way during the modeling process. To avoid misrepresentations in data, it is important to determine if there are problems in the data. Typically, time series have one or more observations that are not representative of the underlying time series pattern. Problems with the data used in forecasting can include large, one-time abnormal occurrences (i.e., outliers) or several minor events that cause the model to consistently over- or under-forecast (i.e., bias). Both of these cause large differences between the actual and expected values.

Because they are large deviations from the dominant patterns in a time series, outliers distort and confound the pattern recognition process of most forecasting methods. Even though outliers cause problems, they frequently provide important information that is worth retaining. Often, there is a causal explanation for the difference between the outlier and the dominant pattern, and therefore we don't want to simply discard the outlier but examine it in some detail.

While it may seem that outliers are easily detected, this is not necessarily true. When a series has great randomness in trend or seasonality, visual inspection of the data might not reveal the outlier. Also, outliers are difficult to detect because they can affect or arise in each step of the modeling process.

Causes of Outliers and Out-of-Control Forecasts

Outliers are caused by data entry errors, unusual events, unknown influences, planned events, incorrect forecasting models, and changes in patterns. Some of these are discussed below.

Unusual, Unknown, or Irregular Events.　Sometimes values change dramatically because of unusual events. For example, natural disasters, wars, strikes, competitors' out-of-stock situations, and competitors' promotional campaigns will likely cause values to vary from expected values. We should adjust outliers no matter what caused the unusual value; however, we need to record the date and magnitude of the outlier for use in forecasting and planning.

Planned Events.　Many time series are affected by events that are planned by decision makers. For example, marketing personnel can change prices, promotions, and so on. Unless these events are known, these influences may be viewed as unknown outliers. Consequently,

Coincidences and Outliers

"It is no great wonder if, in the long process of time, while fortune takes her course hither and thither, numerous coincidences should spontaneously occur."

Plutarch

It is no great wonder that outliers should occur spontaneously. The causes of these outliers are sometimes unknown and unknowable.

planned events that affect a time series should be managed and noted; otherwise, their effects will appear as outliers.

Incorrect Forecasting Models.   An outlier or out-of-control condition can occur when the wrong forecasting model is used. It might be wrong because past values were not representative of the future or because the model-selection process failed. For example, this could result in using single exponential smoothing on a series with significant trend or seasonality. The simpler model may appear to be good between seasonal peaks and troughs. Unfortunately, an incorrect model may forecast badly only during some periods, yet these might be the most important peak or trough values.

Changes in Time Series Patterns.   It is important to detect changes in patterns as soon as possible. For example, almost all products and services go through life cycles that result in differences in trends and seasonality, changes referred to as turning points. Products have slowly increasing demand during initial introduction followed by rapidly increasing demands that then decline after the product matures. Thus, a series that has had a positive trend might suddenly have a negative one. Or a random series might suddenly change from having a mean value of 1,000 to 2,000 per month. The sooner these can be detected, the sooner the proper decisions will be made. Thus, a good forecasting process should detect changes in life cycles or turning points; methods for detecting these shifts involve tracking signals, which are discussed in Chapter 17.

Outlier Detection

Formal statistical tests and informal judgment can be used to detect outliers. Both of these approaches use simple statistical tools such as time plots, frequency distributions, and simple *t*-tests. Our ultimate purpose is to understand how automated and judgmental outlier detection and adjustment procedures work. Both are important.

To better understand the practical problems of detecting outliers, consider the seasonal data of Table B–1. If we were to examine this data using simple frequency distributions like those illustrated in Chapter 2, we might not find any outliers because the order of data is lost in the distributions. However, by dividing the data into quarters, as in Table B–1, our ability to detect outliers improves. Thus, we see that detecting seasonal outliers requires detecting deviations from seasonal patterns.

By scanning the data of Table B–1 by quarters (i.e., by row), we can see that the value of 37 in Quarter 3 of Year 4 is very unusual. This is even more evident in Table B–2, which shows each observation with its seasonal difference in parentheses. For example, the parenthetical value for Quarter 1, Year 2 is Quarter 1, Year 2 minus Quarter 1, Year 1 (i.e., 32 − 31). The outlier of Quarter 3, Year 4 is evident now because of its extremely low value (−30). Interestingly, this single outlier creates two inconsistent seasonal values. Note that the seasonal differences of Quarter 3 in Years 4 and 5 are distorted by the single outlier. It is not hard to imagine how a forecaster might have problems in identifying the correct patterns when several outliers cause

TABLE B–1   **Detecting Outliers with Seasonal Presentations**

Year	1	2	3	4	5	6
Quarter 1	31	32	34	36	39	42
Quarter 2	40	41	45	53	58	60
Quarter 3	58	65	67	37	74	78
Quarter 4	42	44	49	51	52	53

TABLE B–2   **Detecting Outliers with Seasonal Differences (in parentheses)**

Year	1	2	3	4	5	6
Quarter 1	31	32 (1)	34 (2)	36 (2)	39 (3)	42 (3)
Quarter 2	40	41 (1)	45 (4)	53 (8)	58 (5)	60 (2)
Quarter 3	58	65 (7)	67 (2)	37 (−30)	74 (37)	78 (4)
Quarter 4	42	44 (2)	49 (5)	51 (2)	52 (1)	53 (1)

multiple problems like those in Table B–2 because each outlier distorts more than one observation when there are differences taken.

Plotting Values to Detect Outliers

To detect outliers, you should include plots of the original data, appropriate transformations, differences, or seasonal graphs (e.g., plot Quarters 1, 2, 3, and 4 data on separate graphs). Figure B–1 illustrates a plot of the data of Table B–2. The outlier in Period 15 is easily detected with this contrived data. In addition, we might plot seasonally differenced data for each season on the same graph, one under the other.

Statistical Tests for Outliers

One way to detect outliers is to measure each observation as a standardized deviation from its mean. Assuming that values are approximately normally distributed without pronounced seasonality or trend, actual observations should not deviate greatly from the mean. We can perform a simple z- or t-test to detect the outliers:

$$t = \frac{Y_t - \overline{Y}_t}{S_y} \tag{B–1}$$

where

$t = t$-value of each observation, Y_t
$\overline{Y}_t = $ Mean of Y_t
$S_y = $ Standard deviation of the observations

We can infer that an observation is an outlier when the calculated t value exceeds the t-table value. For the ND, approximately 95.45 percent of the values will be within 2 standard deviations. Approximately 99.73 percent will be within 3 standard deviations. It is common to use a t of 2 to 3 to detect outliers, however, we must be cautious in using such rules particularly with highly seasonal data.

Table B–3 illustrates the calculations of two t values for the data of Table B–1: one for the original data, the other for seasonal differences. The actual value is shown in column 2; the t

FIGURE B–1

*Quarterly demand of
Table B–2 data*

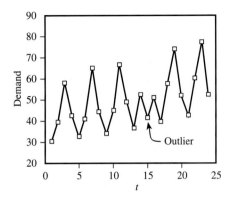

TABLE B–3   **Detection of Outliers Using Regular and Seasonal *t*-Values for Quarterly Data
(TABB–3.WK1)**

(1) Time (t)	(2) Demand	(3) t-Value	(4) Seasonal Differences	(5) Seasonal t-Values	(6) Adjusted Demand	(7) Outlier Effect (2) − (6)	(8) Type of Outlier*
1	31	−1.40			31		
2	40	−.71			40		
3	58	.67			58		
4	42	−.55			42		
5	32	−1.32	1	−.19	32		
6	41	−.63	1	−.19	41		
7	65	1.21	7	.35	65		
8	44	−.40	2	−.10	44		
9	34	−1.17	2	−.10	34		
10	45	−.32	4	.08	45		
11	67	1.36	2	−.10	67		
12	49	−.02	5	.17	49		
13	36	−1.01	2	−.10	36		
14	53	.29	8	.44	53		
15	37	−.94	−30	−3.00	71	−34	(a)
16	51	.14	2	−.10	51		
17	39	−.78	3	−.01	39		
18	58	.67	5	.17	58		
19	74	1.90	37	3.07	74		
20	52	.21	1	−.19	52		
21	42	−.55	3	−.01	42		
22	60	.83	2	−.10	60		
23	78	2.21	4	.08	78		
24	53	.29	1	−.19	53		
Mean	49.21	.00	3.10	.00	50.63		
Standard deviation	13.04	1.00	11.04	1.00	13.49		

*Explanation of outlier types:
a. Promotion
b. Price increase
c. Other influence
d. Unknown cause

values of each of these are in column 3. Assume we use a *t*-value of 3 to identify an outlier. As shown in column 3, no *t* value is greater than 3; thus, it appears that there are no outliers in the data. Using a simple *t*-test on the original data is not sufficient to detect a seasonal outlier.

When data are highly seasonal or trending, the check for outliers is more complex. In such cases, we can fit appropriate seasonal or trend models to the data and thereby search for unusual differences between the actual and fitted or forecast values. This is one of the most effective ways of detecting outliers. Another effective way of detecting seasonal outliers is to use seasonal differences as in Table B–2. Similarly, an effective way to detect outliers in trends is to use first differences. Thus, we should use appropriate difference values to help detect seasonal and trend outliers.

In Table B–3, the *t* values of the seasonal differences in column 5 denote two potential outliers. These *t* values are calculated using Equation B–1 on the seasonal fourth-order differences of column 4 (i.e., $Y_t - Y_{t-4}$). The first value is the actual outlier at Period 15, while the highest *t*-value is in Period 19; however, this second outlier is a result of the first outlier at Period 15. The Period 15 outlier should be adjusted to preserve the integrity of seasonal pattern. As this example illustrates, nonseaonal approaches to outlier detection and adjustment may be insufficient. Also, we should only adjust the observation(s) that causes the outlier.

A Word of Caution

We have noted novices adjusting too many observations in a time series without fully understanding the patterns of the series. More detrimental than outliers is the mistaken adjustment of seasonally high or low values because they appear to be nonseasonal outliers. To avoid wrongly deseasonalizing the data, only adjust true outliers which yield statistically significant differences in the fitted errors (i.e., residuals) of reasonably good models. Do not adjust seasonality out of the data by mistakenly believing they are outliers. When in doubt, do not adjust values, instead monitor the goodness of fit of outlier values. When outliers do not adversely affect the model, coefficients, or resulting forecasts, they can be ignored.

Comparing Actuals to Forecasts

The above methods of detecting outliers are particularly important in the initial phases of modeling. After a model has been selected, a more effective way to detect outliers is to compare actual values with the forecasts of a good model. If the difference between actual and forecast (i.e., the error) is large, then there may be a problem with either the model or outliers.

Errors are expected to be approximately normally distributed, with a mean of zero and a constant standard error. To detect an outlier, a simple *t*-test is performed. The *t* value is calculated as:

$$t = \frac{e_t - 0}{RSE} \tag{B–2}$$

where

$t = t$ value of an individual error, e_t
$RSE =$ Residual standard error as developed in Chapter 2

In detecting outliers, this calculated *t* value is compared to a *t*-table value, as discussed previously. In practice, it is common to use values of 3 or more, but only cautiously.

Filtering errors using Equation B–2 is an essential part of a good forecasting process; however, it does not control cumulative errors over time. Measuring cumulative errors is important in planning and control because the effects of the cumulative errors can be much more detrimental than single large errors. Also, the bias of cumulative errors can be indicative of fundamental changes in the time series pattern, changes that we want to detect as soon as possible. Methods for detecting large cumulative errors and pattern shifts are developed in Chapter 17.

Adjusting Outliers

When outliers adversely affect the patterns in the time series and the resulting model, they should be adjusted. Thus, after detection, the next step is to replace them with good values. When the outlier is due to measurement or human error, replacing the observation with the correct value solves the problem. When the outlier must be replaced with a hypothetical value, we need some guidance in the replacement. Rarely, if ever, are time series outliers simply deleted.

The correct adjustment of outliers is often apparent after some thought. Typically, the underlying pattern of values provides all of the information necessary to adjust the value. Consider the following methods.

1. If a reliable forecast exists for a series, an outlier can be replaced with the forecast.

2. If the series has no seasonality, replace outliers with several possible values. If the series is completely random, the outlier can be replaced with the mean of the series. In contrast, if the series is positively autocorrelated, either a random walk or trend, it can be replaced with the mean of the two adjacent values, as in Equation B–3, which uses the data of Table B–3.

$$(Y_{t-1} + Y_{t+1})/2 = (Y_{14} + Y_{16})/2 = (53 + 51)/2 = 52 \qquad \text{(B–3)}$$

However, this is not the correct adjustment for this data because of its strong seasonality.

3. If the series is seasonal, replace it with the mean of the two seasonally adjacent values when these are good representations of the underlying series. In Table B–3, this is:

$$(Y_{t-4} + Y_{t+4})/2 = (Y_{11} + Y_{19})/2 = (67 + 74)/2 = 70.5 \qquad \text{(B–4)}$$

4. If you want to preserve the unusually high or low value of the outlier, use the above rules but add or subtract some additional quantity. Normally, the adjusted value should not be an outlier but would still preserve some of its extreme value. This can be valuable when it is believed that future values will also be extreme but not quite as high or low as the outlier.

Retaining Actual, Adjusted, and Outlier Values

When adjusting outliers, it is important to retain both actual values (i.e., unadjusted values), adjusted values, and the outlier effect. These are shown in columns 2, 6, and 7 of Table B–3. The difference between the adjusted value and the actual values can provide important information about the outlier effect. For outliers that might recur in the future, it is important to retain the outlier effect with the notation of the cause of the outlier. This notation can be simply done, as shown in column 8 of Table B–3.

APPENDIX C Student t-Distribution

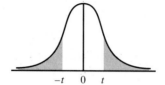

Two-tailed Area

df	.20	.10	.05	.02	.01	.001
1	3.078	6.314	12.706	31.821	63.657	636.619
2	1.886	2.920	4.303	6.965	9.925	31.598
3	1.638	2.353	3.182	4.541	5.841	12.941
4	1.533	2.132	2.776	3.747	4.604	8.610
5	1.476	2.015	2.571	3.365	4.032	6.859
6	1.440	1.943	2.447	3.143	3.707	5.959
7	1.415	1.895	2.365	2.998	3.499	5.405
8	1.397	1.860	2.306	2.896	3.355	5.041
9	1.383	1.833	2.262	2.821	3.250	4.781
10	1.372	1.812	2.228	2.764	3.169	4.587
11	1.363	1.796	2.201	2.718	3.106	4.437
12	1.356	1.782	2.179	2.681	3.055	4.318
13	1.350	1.771	2.160	2.650	3.012	4.221
14	1.345	1.761	2.145	2.624	2.977	4.140
15	1.341	1.753	2.131	2.602	2.947	4.073
16	1.337	1.746	2.120	2.583	2.921	4.015
17	1.333	1.740	2.110	2.567	2.898	3.965
18	1.330	1.734	2.101	2.552	2.878	3.922
19	1.328	1.729	2.093	2.539	2.681	3.883
20	1.325	1.725	2.086	2.528	2.845	3.850
21	1.323	1.721	2.080	2.518	2.831	3.819
22	1.321	1.717	2.074	2.508	2.819	3.792
23	1.319	1.714	2.069	2.500	2.807	3.767
24	1.318	1.711	2.064	2.492	2.797	3.745
25	1.316	1.708	2.060	2.485	2.787	3.725
26	1.315	1.706	2.056	2.479	2.779	3.707
27	1.314	1.703	2.052	2.473	2.771	3.690
28	1.313	1.701	2.048	2.467	2.763	3.674
29	1.311	1.699	2.045	2.462	2.756	3.659
30	1.310	1.697	2.042	2.457	2.750	3.646
40	1.303	1.684	2.021	2.423	2.704	3.551
60	1.296	1.671	2.000	2.390	2.660	3.460
120	1.289	1.658	1.980	2.358	2.617	3.373
∞	1.282	1.645	1.960	2.326	2.576	3.291

	.10	.05	.025	.01	.005	.0005

One-tailed Area

Source: Goldstein Software, Inc. for the program Goldspread Statistical, which was used to generate this table.

APPENDIX D Areas of the Standard Normal Distribution

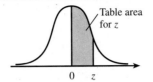

Table area for z

Second Decimal Place in z

z	.00	.01	.02	.03	.04	.05	.06	.07	.08	.09
.0	.0000	.0040	.0080	.0120	.0160	.0199	.0239	.0279	.0319	.0359
.1	.0398	.0438	.0478	.0517	.0557	.0596	.0636	.0675	.0714	.0753
.2	.0793	.0832	.0871	.0910	.0948	.0987	.1026	.1064	.1103	.1141
.3	.1179	.1217	.1255	.1293	.1331	.1368	.1406	.1443	.1480	.1517
.4	.1554	.1591	.1628	.1664	.1700	.1736	.1772	.1808	.1844	.1879
.5	.1915	.1950	.1985	.2019	.2054	.2088	.2123	.2157	.2190	.2224
.6	.2257	.2291	.2324	.2357	.2389	.2422	.2454	.2486	.2517	.2549
.7	.2580	.2611	.2642	.2673	.2704	.2734	.2764	.2794	.2823	.2852
.8	.2881	.2910	.2939	.2967	.2995	.3023	.3051	.3078	.3106	.3133
.9	.3159	.3186	.3212	.3238	.3264	.3289	.3315	.3340	.3365	.3389
1.0	.3413	.3438	.3461	.3485	.3508	.3531	.3554	.3577	.3599	.3621
1.1	.3643	.3665	.3686	.3708	.3729	.3749	.3770	.3790	.3810	.3830
1.2	.3849	.3869	.3888	.3907	.3925	.3944	.3962	.3980	.3997	.4015
1.3	.4032	.4049	.4066	.4082	.4099	.4115	.4131	.4147	.4162	.4177
1.4	.4192	.4207	.4222	.4236	.4251	.4265	.4279	.4292	.4306	.4319
1.5	.4332	.4345	.4357	.4370	.4382	.4394	.4406	.4418	.4429	.4441
1.6	.4452	.4463	.4474	.4484	.4495	.4505	.4515	.4525	.4535	.4545
1.7	.4554	.4564	.4573	.4582	.4591	.4599	.4608	.4616	.4625	.4633
1.8	.4641	.4649	.4656	.4664	.4671	.4678	.4686	.4693	.4699	.4706
1.9	.4713	.4719	.4726	.4732	.4738	.4744	.4750	.4756	.4761	.4767
2.0	.4772	.4778	.4783	.4788	.4793	.4798	.4803	.4808	.4812	.4817
2.1	.4821	.4826	.4830	.4834	.4838	.4842	.4846	.4850	.4854	.4857
2.2	.4861	.4864	.4868	.4871	.4875	.4878	.4881	.4884	.4887	.4890
2.3	.4893	.4896	.4898	.4901	.4904	.4906	.4909	.4911	.4913	.4916
2.4	.4918	.4920	.4922	.4925	.4927	.4929	.4931	.4932	.4934	.4936
2.5	.4938	.4940	.4941	.4943	.4945	.4946	.4948	.4949	.4951	.4952
2.6	.4953	.4955	.4956	.4957	.4959	.4960	.4961	.4962	.4963	.4964
2.7	.4965	.4966	.4967	.4968	.4969	.4970	.4971	.4972	.4973	.4974
2.8	.4974	.4975	.4976	.4977	.4977	.4978	.4979	.4979	.4980	.4981
2.9	.4981	.4982	.4982	.4983	.4984	.4984	.4985	.4985	.4986	.4986
3.0	.4987	.4987	.4987	.4988	.4988	.4989	.4989	.4989	.4990	.4990
3.1	.4990	.4991	.4991	.4991	.4992	.4992	.4992	.4992	.4993	.4993
3.2	.4993	.4993	.4994	.4994	.4994	.4994	.4994	.4995	.4995	.4995
3.3	.4995	.4995	.4995	.4996	.4996	.4996	.4996	.4996	.4996	.4997
3.4	.4997	.4997	.4997	.4997	.4997	.4997	.4997	.4997	.4997	.4998
3.5	.4998									
4.0	.49997									
4.5	.499997									
5.0	.4999997									
6.0	.499999999									

The table areas are probabilities that the standard normal random variable is between 0 and z.

Source: Amir D. Aczel, *Complete Business Statistics* (Burr Ridge, Ill.: Richard D. Irwin, 1996), p. 825.

APPENDIX E   Critical Values of Chi-Square

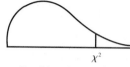

Possible values of χ^2

Degrees of Freedom df	Right-Tail Area			
	.10	.05	.02	.01
1	2.706	3.841	5.412	6.635
2	4.605	5.991	7.824	9.210
3	6.251	7.815	9.837	11.345
4	7.779	9.488	11.668	13.277
5	9.236	11.070	13.388	15.086
6	10.645	12.592	15.033	16.812
7	12.017	14.067	16.622	18.475
8	13.362	15.507	18.168	20.090
9	14.684	16.919	19.679	21.666
10	15.987	18.307	21.161	23.209
11	17.275	19.675	22.618	24.725
12	18.549	21.026	24.054	26.217
13	19.812	22.362	25.472	27.688
14	21.064	23.685	26.873	29.141
15	22.307	24.996	28.259	30.578
16	23.542	26.296	29.633	32.000
17	24.769	27.587	30.995	33.409
18	25.989	28.869	32.346	34.805
19	27.204	30.144	33.687	36.191
20	28.412	31.410	35.020	37.566
21	29.615	32.671	36.343	38.932
22	30.813	33.924	37.659	40.289
23	32.007	35.172	38.968	41.638
24	33.196	36.415	40.270	42.980
25	34.382	37.652	41.566	44.314
26	35.563	38.885	42.856	45.642
27	36.741	40.113	44.140	46.963
28	37.916	41.337	45.419	48.278
29	39.087	42.557	46.693	49.588
30	40.256	43.773	47.962	50.892

This table contains the values of χ^2 that correspond to a specific right-tail area and specific numbers of degrees of freedom df.

Source: Robert D. Mason and Douglas A. Lind, *Statistical Techniques in Business and Economics,* 9th ed. (Burr Ridge, Ill.: Richard D. Irwin, 1996), p. 806.

Denominator Degrees of Freedom (k2)	1	2	3	4	5	6	7	8	9	10	11	12	14	16	20	24	30	40	50	75	100	200	500	∞
1	161	200	216	225	230	234	237	239	241	242	243	244	245	246	248	249	250	251	252	253	253	254	254	254
	4,052	**5,000**	**5,403**	**5,625**	**5,764**	**5,859**	**5,928**	**5,981**	**6,022**	**6,056**	**6,083**	**6,106**	**6,143**	**6,170**	**6,209**	**6,235**	**6,261**	**6,287**	**6,303**	**6,324**	**6,334**	**6,350**	**6,360**	**6,366**
2	18.51	19.00	19.16	19.25	19.30	19.33	19.35	19.37	19.38	19.40	19.40	19.41	19.42	19.43	19.45	19.45	19.46	19.47	19.48	19.48	19.49	19.49	19.49	19.50
	98.50	**99.00**	**99.17**	**99.25**	**99.30**	**99.33**	**99.36**	**99.37**	**99.39**	**99.40**	**99.41**	**99.42**	**99.43**	**99.44**	**99.45**	**99.46**	**99.47**	**99.47**	**99.48**	**99.49**	**99.49**	**99.49**	**99.50**	**99.50**
3	10.13	9.55	9.28	9.12	9.01	8.94	8.89	8.85	8.81	8.79	8.76	8.74	8.71	8.69	8.66	8.64	8.62	8.59	8.58	8.56	8.55	8.54	8.53	8.53
	34.12	**30.82**	**29.46**	**28.71**	**28.24**	**27.91**	**27.67**	**27.49**	**27.35**	**27.23**	**27.13**	**27.05**	**26.92**	**26.83**	**26.69**	**26.60**	**26.50**	**26.41**	**26.35**	**26.28**	**26.24**	**26.18**	**26.15**	**26.13**
4	7.71	6.94	6.59	6.39	6.26	6.16	6.09	6.04	6.00	5.96	5.94	5.91	5.87	5.84	5.80	5.77	5.75	5.72	5.70	5.68	5.66	5.65	5.64	5.63
	21.20	**18.00**	**16.69**	**15.98**	**15.52**	**15.21**	**14.98**	**14.80**	**14.66**	**14.55**	**14.45**	**14.37**	**14.25**	**14.15**	**14.02**	**13.93**	**13.84**	**13.75**	**13.69**	**13.61**	**13.58**	**13.52**	**13.49**	**13.46**
5	6.61	5.79	5.41	5.19	5.05	4.95	4.88	4.82	4.77	4.74	4.70	4.68	4.64	4.60	4.56	4.53	4.50	4.46	4.44	4.42	4.41	4.39	4.37	4.37
	16.26	**13.27**	**12.06**	**11.39**	**10.97**	**10.67**	**10.46**	**10.29**	**10.16**	**10.05**	**9.96**	**9.89**	**9.77**	**9.68**	**9.55**	**9.47**	**9.38**	**9.29**	**9.24**	**9.17**	**9.13**	**9.08**	**9.04**	**9.02**
6	5.99	5.14	4.76	4.53	4.39	4.28	4.21	4.15	4.10	4.06	4.03	4.00	3.96	3.92	3.87	3.84	3.81	3.77	3.75	3.73	3.71	3.69	3.68	3.67
	13.75	**10.92**	**9.78**	**9.15**	**8.75**	**8.47**	**8.26**	**8.10**	**7.98**	**7.87**	**7.79**	**7.72**	**7.60**	**7.52**	**7.40**	**7.31**	**7.23**	**7.14**	**7.09**	**7.02**	**6.99**	**6.93**	**6.90**	**6.88**
7	5.59	4.74	4.35	4.12	3.97	3.87	3.79	3.73	3.68	3.64	3.60	3.57	3.53	3.49	3.44	3.41	3.38	3.34	3.32	3.29	3.27	3.25	3.24	3.23
	12.25	**9.55**	**8.45**	**7.85**	**7.46**	**7.19**	**6.99**	**6.84**	**6.72**	**6.62**	**6.54**	**6.47**	**6.36**	**6.28**	**6.16**	**6.07**	**5.99**	**5.91**	**5.86**	**5.79**	**5.75**	**5.70**	**5.67**	**5.65**
8	5.32	4.46	4.07	3.84	3.69	3.58	3.50	3.44	3.39	3.35	3.31	3.28	3.24	3.20	3.15	3.12	3.08	3.04	3.02	2.99	2.97	2.95	2.94	2.93
	11.26	**8.65**	**7.59**	**7.01**	**6.63**	**6.37**	**6.18**	**6.03**	**5.91**	**5.81**	**5.73**	**5.67**	**5.56**	**5.48**	**5.36**	**5.28**	**5.20**	**5.12**	**5.07**	**5.00**	**4.96**	**4.91**	**4.88**	**4.86**
9	5.12	4.26	3.86	3.63	3.48	3.37	3.29	3.23	3.18	3.14	3.10	3.07	3.03	2.99	2.94	2.90	2.86	2.83	2.80	2.77	2.76	2.73	2.72	2.71
	10.56	**8.02**	**6.99**	**6.42**	**6.06**	**5.80**	**5.61**	**5.47**	**5.35**	**5.26**	**5.18**	**5.11**	**5.01**	**4.92**	**4.81**	**4.73**	**4.65**	**4.57**	**4.52**	**4.45**	**4.41**	**4.36**	**4.33**	**4.31**
10	4.96	4.10	3.71	3.48	3.33	3.22	3.14	3.07	3.02	2.98	2.94	2.91	2.86	2.83	2.77	2.74	2.70	2.66	2.64	2.60	2.59	2.56	2.55	2.54
	10.04	**7.56**	**6.55**	**5.99**	**5.64**	**5.39**	**5.20**	**5.06**	**4.94**	**4.85**	**4.77**	**4.71**	**4.60**	**4.52**	**4.41**	**4.33**	**4.25**	**4.17**	**4.12**	**4.05**	**4.01**	**3.96**	**3.93**	**3.91**
11	4.84	3.98	3.59	3.36	3.20	3.09	3.01	2.95	2.90	2.85	2.82	2.79	2.74	2.70	2.65	2.61	2.57	2.53	2.51	2.47	2.46	2.43	2.42	2.40
	9.65	**7.21**	**6.22**	**5.67**	**5.32**	**5.07**	**4.89**	**4.74**	**4.63**	**4.54**	**4.46**	**4.40**	**4.29**	**4.21**	**4.10**	**4.02**	**3.94**	**3.86**	**3.81**	**3.74**	**3.71**	**3.66**	**3.62**	**3.60**
12	4.75	3.89	3.49	3.26	3.11	3.00	2.91	2.85	2.80	2.75	2.72	2.69	2.64	2.60	2.54	2.51	2.47	2.43	2.40	2.37	2.35	2.32	2.31	2.30
	9.33	**6.93**	**5.95**	**5.41**	**5.06**	**4.82**	**4.64**	**4.50**	**4.39**	**4.30**	**4.22**	**4.16**	**4.05**	**3.97**	**3.86**	**3.78**	**3.70**	**3.62**	**3.57**	**3.50**	**3.47**	**3.41**	**3.38**	**3.36**
13	4.67	3.81	3.41	3.18	3.03	2.92	2.83	2.77	2.71	2.67	2.63	2.60	2.55	2.51	2.46	2.42	2.38	2.34	2.31	2.28	2.26	2.23	2.22	2.21
	9.07	**6.70**	**5.74**	**5.21**	**4.86**	**4.62**	**4.44**	**4.30**	**4.19**	**4.10**	**4.02**	**3.96**	**3.86**	**3.78**	**3.66**	**3.59**	**3.51**	**3.43**	**3.38**	**3.31**	**3.27**	**3.22**	**3.19**	**3.17**
14	4.60	3.74	3.34	3.11	2.96	2.85	2.76	2.70	2.65	2.60	2.57	2.53	2.48	2.44	2.39	2.35	2.31	2.27	2.24	2.21	2.19	2.16	2.14	2.13
	8.86	**6.51**	**5.56**	**5.04**	**4.69**	**4.46**	**4.28**	**4.14**	**4.03**	**3.94**	**3.86**	**3.80**	**3.70**	**3.62**	**3.51**	**3.43**	**3.35**	**3.27**	**3.22**	**3.15**	**3.11**	**3.06**	**3.03**	**3.00**
15	4.54	3.68	3.29	3.06	2.90	2.79	2.71	2.64	2.59	2.54	2.51	2.48	2.42	2.38	2.33	2.29	2.25	2.20	2.18	2.14	2.12	2.10	2.08	2.07
	8.68	**6.36**	**5.42**	**4.89**	**4.56**	**4.32**	**4.14**	**4.00**	**3.89**	**3.80**	**3.73**	**3.67**	**3.56**	**3.49**	**3.37**	**3.29**	**3.21**	**3.13**	**3.08**	**3.01**	**2.98**	**2.92**	**2.89**	**2.87**
16	4.49	3.63	3.24	3.01	2.85	2.74	2.66	2.59	2.54	2.49	2.46	2.42	2.37	2.33	2.28	2.24	2.19	2.15	2.12	2.09	2.07	2.04	2.02	2.01
	8.53	**6.23**	**5.29**	**4.77**	**4.44**	**4.20**	**4.03**	**3.89**	**3.78**	**3.69**	**3.62**	**3.55**	**3.45**	**3.37**	**3.26**	**3.18**	**3.10**	**3.02**	**2.97**	**2.90**	**2.86**	**2.81**	**2.78**	**2.75**
17	4.45	3.59	3.20	2.96	2.81	2.70	2.61	2.55	2.49	2.45	2.41	2.38	2.33	2.29	2.23	2.19	2.15	2.10	2.08	2.04	2.02	1.99	1.97	1.96
	8.40	**6.11**	**5.18**	**4.67**	**4.34**	**4.10**	**3.93**	**3.79**	**3.68**	**3.59**	**3.52**	**3.46**	**3.35**	**3.27**	**3.16**	**3.08**	**3.00**	**2.92**	**2.87**	**2.80**	**2.76**	**2.71**	**2.68**	**2.65**
18	4.41	3.55	3.16	2.93	2.77	2.66	2.58	2.51	2.46	2.41	2.37	2.34	2.29	2.25	2.19	2.15	2.11	2.06	2.04	2.00	1.98	1.95	1.93	1.92
	8.29	**6.01**	**5.09**	**4.58**	**4.25**	**4.01**	**3.84**	**3.71**	**3.60**	**3.51**	**3.43**	**3.37**	**3.27**	**3.19**	**3.08**	**3.00**	**2.92**	**2.84**	**2.78**	**2.71**	**2.68**	**2.62**	**2.59**	**2.57**
19	4.38	3.52	3.13	2.90	2.74	2.63	2.54	2.48	2.42	2.38	2.34	2.31	2.26	2.21	2.16	2.11	2.07	2.03	2.00	1.96	1.94	1.91	1.89	1.88
	8.18	**5.93**	**5.01**	**4.50**	**4.17**	**3.94**	**3.77**	**3.63**	**3.52**	**3.43**	**3.36**	**3.30**	**3.19**	**3.12**	**3.00**	**2.92**	**2.84**	**2.76**	**2.71**	**2.64**	**2.60**	**2.55**	**2.51**	**2.49**
20	4.35	3.49	3.10	2.87	2.71	2.60	2.51	2.45	2.39	2.35	2.31	2.28	2.22	2.18	2.12	2.08	2.04	1.99	1.97	1.93	1.91	1.88	1.86	1.84
	8.10	**5.85**	**4.94**	**4.43**	**4.10**	**3.87**	**3.70**	**3.56**	**3.46**	**3.37**	**3.29**	**3.23**	**3.13**	**3.05**	**2.94**	**2.86**	**2.78**	**2.69**	**2.64**	**2.57**	**2.54**	**2.48**	**2.44**	**2.42**
21	4.32	3.47	3.07	2.84	2.68	2.57	2.49	2.42	2.37	2.32	2.28	2.25	2.20	2.16	2.10	2.05	2.01	1.96	1.94	1.90	1.88	1.84	1.83	1.81
	8.02	**5.78**	**4.87**	**4.37**	**4.04**	**3.81**	**3.64**	**3.51**	**3.40**	**3.31**	**3.24**	**3.17**	**3.07**	**2.99**	**2.88**	**2.80**	**2.72**	**2.64**	**2.58**	**2.51**	**2.48**	**2.42**	**2.38**	**2.36**
22	4.30	3.44	3.05	2.82	2.66	2.55	2.46	2.40	2.34	2.30	2.26	2.23	2.17	2.13	2.07	2.03	1.98	1.94	1.91	1.87	1.85	1.82	1.80	1.78
	7.95	**5.72**	**4.82**	**4.31**	**3.99**	**3.76**	**3.59**	**3.45**	**3.35**	**3.26**	**3.18**	**3.12**	**3.02**	**2.94**	**2.83**	**2.75**	**2.67**	**2.58**	253	**2.46**	**2.42**	**2.36**	**2.33**	**2.31**
23	4.28	3.42	3.03	2.80	2.64	2.53	2.44	2.37	2.32	2.27	2.24	2.20	2.15	2.11	2.05	2.01	1.96	1.91	1.88	1.84	1.82	1.79	1.77	1.76
	7.88	**5.66**	**4.76**	**4.26**	**3.94**	**3.71**	**3.54**	**3.41**	**3.30**	**3.21**	**3.14**	**3.07**	**2.97**	**2.89**	**2.78**	**2.70**	**2.62**	**2.54**	**2.48**	**2.41**	**2.37**	**2.32**	**2.28**	**2.26**
24	4.26	3.40	3.01	2.78	2.62	2.51	2.42	2.36	2.30	2.25	2.22	2.18	2.13	2.09	2.03	1.98	1.94	1.89	1.86	1.82	1.80	1.77	1.75	1.73
	7.82	**5.61**	**4.72**	**4.22**	**3.90**	**3.67**	**3.50**	**3.36**	**3.26**	**3.17**	**3.09**	**3.03**	**2.93**	**2.85**	**2.74**	**2.66**	**2.58**	**2.49**	**2.44**	**2.37**	**2.33**	**2.27**	**2.24**	**2.21**
25	4.24	3.39	2.99	2.76	2.60	2.49	2.40	2.34	2.28	2.24	2.20	2.16	2.11	2.07	2.01	1.96	1.92	1.87	1.84	1.80	1.78	1.75	1.73	1.71
	7.77	**5.57**	**4.68**	**4.18**	**3.85**	**3.63**	**3.46**	**3.32**	**3.22**	**3.13**	**3.06**	**2.99**	**2.89**	**2.81**	**2.70**	**2.62**	**2.54**	**2.45**	**2.40**	**2.33**	**2.29**	**2.23**	**2.19**	**2.17**
26	4.23	3.37	2.98	2.74	2.59	2.47	2.39	2.32	2.27	2.22	2.18	2.15	2.09	2.05	1.99	1.95	1.90	1.85	1.82	1.78	1.76	1.73	1.71	1.69
	7.72	**5.53**	**4.64**	**4.14**	**3.82**	**3.59**	**3.42**	**3.29**	**3.18**	**3.09**	**3.02**	**2.96**	**2.86**	**2.78**	**2.66**	**2.58**	**2.50**	**2.42**	**2.36**	**2.29**	**2.25**	**2.19**	**2.16**	**2.13**

continued

APPENDIX F The F Distribution for $\alpha = .05$ and $\alpha = .01$ (Bold) for Many Possible Degrees of Freedom

concluded

Denominator Degrees of Freedom (k2)	1	2	3	4	5	6	7	8	9	10	11	12	14	16	20	24	30	40	50	75	100	200	500	∞
27	4.21	3.35	2.96	2.73	2.57	2.46	2.37	2.31	2.25	2.20	2.17	2.13	2.08	2.04	1.97	1.93	1.88	1.84	1.81	1.76	1.74	1.71	1.69	1.67
	7.68	**5.49**	**4.60**	**4.11**	**3.78**	**3.56**	**3.39**	**3.26**	**3.15**	**3.06**	**2.99**	**2.93**	**2.82**	**2.75**	**2.63**	**2.55**	**2.47**	**2.38**	**2.33**	**2.26**	**2.22**	**2.16**	**2.12**	**2.10**
28	4.20	3.34	2.95	2.71	2.56	2.45	2.36	2.29	2.24	2.19	2.15	2.12	2.06	2.02	1.96	1.91	1.87	1.82	1.79	1.75	1.73	1.69	1.67	1.65
	7.64	**5.45**	**4.57**	**4.07**	**3.75**	**3.53**	**3.36**	**3.23**	**3.12**	**3.03**	**2.96**	**2.90**	**2.79**	**2.72**	**2.60**	**2.52**	**2.44**	**2.35**	**2.30**	**2.23**	**2.19**	**2.13**	**2.09**	**2.06**
29	4.18	3.33	2.93	2.70	2.55	2.43	2.35	2.28	2.22	2.18	2.14	2.10	2.05	2.01	1.94	1.90	1.85	1.81	1.77	1.73	1.71	1.67	1.65	1.64
	7.60	**5.42**	**4.54**	**4.04**	**3.73**	**3.50**	**3.33**	**3.20**	**3.09**	**3.00**	**2.93**	**2.87**	**2.77**	**2.69**	**2.57**	**2.49**	**2.41**	**2.33**	**2.27**	**2.20**	**2.16**	**2.10**	**2.06**	**2.03**
30	4.17	3.32	2.92	2.69	2.53	2.42	2.33	2.27	2.21	2.16	2.13	2.09	2.04	1.99	1.93	1.89	1.84	1.79	1.76	1.72	1.70	1.66	1.64	1.62
	7.56	**5.39**	**4.51**	**4.02**	**3.70**	**3.47**	**3.30**	**3.17**	**3.07**	**2.98**	**2.91**	**2.84**	**2.74**	**2.66**	**2.55**	**2.47**	**2.39**	**2.30**	**2.25**	**2.17**	**2.13**	**2.07**	**2.03**	**2.01**
32	4.15	3.29	2.90	2.67	2.51	2.40	2.31	2.24	2.19	2.14	2.10	2.07	2.01	1.97	1.91	1.86	1.82	1.77	1.74	1.69	1.67	1.63	1.61	1.59
	7.50	**5.34**	**4.46**	**3.97**	**3.65**	**3.43**	**3.26**	**3.13**	**3.02**	**2.93**	**2.86**	**2.80**	**2.70**	**2.62**	**2.50**	**2.42**	**2.34**	**2.25**	**2.20**	**2.12**	**2.08**	**2.02**	**1.98**	**1.96**
34	4.13	3.28	2.88	2.65	2.49	2.38	2.29	2.23	2.17	2.12	2.08	2.05	1.99	1.95	1.89	1.84	1.80	1.75	1.71	1.67	1.65	1.61	1.59	1.57
	7.44	**5.29**	**4.42**	**3.93**	**3.61**	**3.39**	**3.22**	**3.09**	**2.98**	**2.89**	**2.82**	**2.76**	**2.66**	**2.58**	**2.46**	**2.38**	**2.30**	**2.21**	**2.16**	**2.08**	**2.04**	**1.98**	**1.94**	**1.91**
36	4.11	3.26	2.87	2.63	2.48	2.36	2.28	2.21	2.15	2.11	2.07	2.03	1.98	1.93	1.87	1.82	1.78	1.73	1.69	1.65	1.62	1.59	1.56	1.55
	7.40	**5.25**	**4.38**	**3.89**	**3.57**	**3.35**	**3.18**	**3.05**	**2.95**	**2.86**	**2.79**	**2.72**	**2.62**	**2.54**	**2.43**	**2.35**	**2.26**	**2.18**	**2.12**	**2.04**	**2.00**	**1.94**	**1.90**	**1.87**
38	4.10	3.24	2.85	2.62	2.46	2.35	2.26	2.19	2.14	2.09	2.05	2.02	1.96	1.92	1.85	1.81	1.76	1.71	1.68	1.63	1.61	1.57	1.54	1.53
	7.35	**5.21**	**4.34**	**3.86**	**3.54**	**3.32**	**3.15**	**3.02**	**2.92**	**2.83**	**2.75**	**2.69**	**2.59**	**2.51**	**2.40**	**2.32**	**2.23**	**2.14**	**2.09**	**2.01**	**1.97**	**1.90**	**1.86**	**1.84**
40	4.08	3.23	2.84	2.61	2.45	2.34	2.25	2.18	2.12	2.08	2.04	2.00	1.95	1.90	1.84	1.79	1.74	1.69	1.66	1.61	1.59	1.55	1.53	1.51
	7.31	**5.18**	**4.31**	**3.83**	**3.51**	**3.29**	**3.12**	**2.99**	**2.89**	**2.80**	**2.73**	**2.66**	**2.56**	**2.48**	**2.37**	**2.29**	**2.20**	**2.11**	**2.06**	**1.98**	**1.94**	**1.87**	**1.83**	**1.81**
42	4.07	3.22	2.83	2.59	2.44	2.32	2.24	2.17	2.11	2.06	2.03	1.99	1.94	1.89	1.83	1.78	1.73	1.68	1.65	1.60	1.57	1.53	1.51	1.49
	7.28	**5.15**	**4.29**	**3.80**	**3.49**	**3.27**	**3.10**	**2.97**	**2.86**	**2.78**	**2.70**	**2.64**	**2.54**	**2.46**	**2.34**	**2.26**	**2.18**	**2.09**	**2.03**	**1.95**	**1.91**	**1.85**	**1.80**	**1.78**
44	4.06	3.21	2.82	2.58	2.43	2.31	2.23	2.16	2.10	2.05	2.01	1.98	1.92	1.88	1.81	1.77	1.72	1.67	1.63	1.59	1.56	1.52	1.49	1.48
	7.25	**5.12**	**4.26**	**3.78**	**3.47**	**3.24**	**3.08**	**2.95**	**2.84**	**2.75**	**2.68**	**2.62**	**2.52**	**2.44**	**2.32**	**2.24**	**2.15**	**2.07**	**2.01**	**1.93**	**1.89**	**1.82**	**1.78**	**1.75**
46	4.05	3.20	2.81	2.57	2.42	2.30	2.22	2.15	2.09	2.04	2.00	1.97	1.91	1.87	1.80	1.76	1.71	1.65	1.62	1.57	1.55	1.51	1.48	1.46
	7.22	**5.10**	**4.24**	**3.76**	**3.44**	**3.22**	**3.06**	**2.93**	**2.82**	**2.73**	**2.66**	**2.60**	**2.50**	**2.42**	**2.30**	**2.22**	**2.13**	**2.04**	**1.99**	**1.91**	**1.86**	**1.80**	**1.76**	**1.73**
48	4.04	3.19	2.80	2.57	2.41	2.29	2.21	2.14	2.08	2.03	1.99	1.96	1.90	1.86	1.79	1.75	1.70	1.64	1.61	1.56	1.54	1.49	1.47	1.45
	7.19	**5.08**	**4.22**	**3.74**	**3.43**	**3.20**	**3.04**	**2.91**	**2.80**	**2.71**	**2.64**	**2.58**	**2.48**	**2.40**	**2.28**	**2.20**	**2.12**	**2.02**	**1.97**	**1.89**	**1.84**	**1.78**	**1.73**	**1.70**
50	4.03	3.18	2.79	2.56	2.40	2.29	2.20	2.13	2.07	2.03	1.99	1.95	1.89	1.85	1.78	1.74	1.69	1.63	1.60	1.55	1.52	1.48	1.46	1.44
	7.17	**5.06**	**4.20**	**3.72**	**3.41**	**3.19**	**3.02**	**2.89**	**2.78**	**2.70**	**2.63**	**2.56**	**2.46**	**2.38**	**2.27**	**2.18**	**2.10**	**2.01**	**1.95**	**1.87**	**1.82**	**1.76**	**1.71**	**1.68**
55	4.02	3.16	2.77	2.54	2.38	2.27	2.18	2.11	2.06	2.01	1.97	1.93	1.88	1.83	1.76	1.72	1.67	1.61	1.58	1.53	1.50	1.46	1.43	1.41
	7.12	**5.01**	**4.16**	**3.68**	**3.37**	**3.15**	**2.98**	**2.85**	**2.75**	**2.66**	**2.59**	**2.53**	**2.42**	**2.34**	**2.23**	**2.15**	**2.06**	**1.97**	**1.91**	**1.83**	**1.78**	**1.71**	**1.67**	**1.64**
60	4.00	3.15	2.76	2.53	2.37	2.25	2.17	2.10	2.04	1.99	1.95	1.92	1.86	1.82	1.75	1.70	1.65	1.59	1.56	1.51	1.48	1.44	1.41	1.39
	7.08	**4.98**	**4.13**	**3.65**	**3.34**	**3.12**	**2.95**	**2.82**	**2.72**	**2.63**	**2.56**	**2.50**	**2.39**	**2.31**	**2.20**	**2.12**	**2.03**	**1.94**	**1.88**	**1.79**	**1.75**	**1.68**	**1.63**	**1.60**
65	3.99	3.14	2.75	2.51	2.36	2.24	2.15	2.08	2.03	1.98	1.94	1.90	1.85	1.80	1.73	1.69	1.63	1.58	1.54	1.49	1.46	1.42	1.39	1.37
	7.04	**4.95**	**4.10**	**3.62**	**3.31**	**3.09**	**2.93**	**2.80**	**2.69**	**2.61**	**2.53**	**2.47**	**2.37**	**2.29**	**2.17**	**2.09**	**2.00**	**1.91**	**1.85**	**1.77**	**1.72**	**1.65**	**1.60**	**1.57**
70	3.98	3.13	2.74	2.50	2.35	2.23	2.14	2.07	2.02	1.97	1.93	1.89	1.84	1.79	1.72	1.67	1.62	1.57	1.53	1.48	1.45	1.40	1.37	1.35
	7.01	**4.92**	**4.07**	**3.60**	**3.29**	**3.07**	**2.91**	**2.78**	**2.67**	**2.59**	**2.51**	**2.45**	**2.35**	**2.27**	**2.15**	**2.07**	**1.98**	**1.89**	**1.83**	**1.74**	**1.70**	**1.62**	**1.57**	**1.54**
80	3.96	3.11	2.72	2.49	2.33	2.21	2.13	2.06	2.00	1.95	1.91	1.88	1.82	1.77	1.70	1.65	1.60	1.54	1.51	1.45	1.43	1.38	1.35	1.33
	6.96	**4.88**	**4.04**	**3.56**	**3.26**	**3.04**	**2.87**	**2.74**	**2.64**	**2.55**	**2.48**	**2.42**	**2.31**	**2.23**	**2.12**	**2.03**	**1.94**	**1.85**	**1.79**	**1.70**	**1.65**	**1.58**	**1.53**	**1.50**
100	3.94	3.09	2.70	2.46	2.31	2.19	2.10	2.03	1.97	1.93	1.89	1.85	1.79	1.75	1.68	1.63	1.57	1.52	1.48	1.42	1.39	1.34	1.31	1.28
	6.90	**4.82**	**3.98**	**3.51**	**3.21**	**2.99**	**2.82**	**2.69**	**2.59**	**2.50**	**2.43**	**2.37**	**2.27**	**2.19**	**2.07**	**1.98**	**1.89**	**1.80**	**1.74**	**1.65**	**1.60**	**1.52**	**1.47**	**1.43**
125	3.923	3.07	2.68	2.44	2.29	2.17	2.08	2.01	1.96	1.91	1.87	1.83	1.77	1.73	1.66	1.60	1.55	1.49	1.45	1.40	1.36	1.31	1.27	1.25
	6.84	**4.78**	**3.94**	**3.47**	**3.17**	**2.95**	**2.79**	**2.66**	**2.55**	**2.47**	**2.39**	**2.33**	**2.23**	**2.15**	**2.03**	**1.94**	**1.85**	**1.76**	**1.69**	**1.60**	**1.55**	**1.47**	**1.41**	**1.37**
150	3.90	3.06	2.66	2.43	2.27	2.16	2.07	2.00	1.94	1.89	1.85	1.82	1.76	1.71	1.64	1.59	1.54	1.48	1.44	1.38	1.34	1.29	1.25	1.22
	6.81	**4.75**	**3.91**	**3.45**	**3.14**	**2.92**	**2.76**	**2.63**	**2.53**	**2.44**	**2.37**	**2.31**	**2.20**	**2.12**	**2.00**	**1.92**	**1.83**	**1.73**	**1.66**	**1.57**	**1.52**	**1.43**	**1.38**	**1.33**
200	3.89	3.04	2.65	2.42	2.26	2.14	2.06	1.98	1.93	1.88	1.84	1.80	1.74	1.69	1.62	1.57	1.52	1.46	1.41	1.35	1.32	1.26	1.22	1.19
	6.76	**4.71**	**3.88**	**3.41**	**3.11**	**2.89**	**2.73**	**2.60**	**2.50**	**2.41**	**2.34**	**2.27**	**2.17**	**2.09**	**1.97**	**1.89**	**1.79**	**1.69**	**1.63**	**1.53**	**1.48**	**1.39**	**1.33**	**1.28**
400	3.86	3.02	2.63	2.39	2.24	2.12	2.03	1.96	1.90	1.85	1.81	1.78	1.72	1.67	1.60	1.54	1.49	1.42	1.38	1.32	1.28	1.22	1.17	1.13
	6.70	**4.66**	**3.83**	**3.37**	**3.06**	**2.85**	**2.68**	**2.56**	**2.45**	**2.37**	**2.29**	**2.23**	**2.13**	**2.05**	**1.92**	**1.84**	**1.75**	**1.64**	**1.58**	**1.48**	**1.42**	**1.32**	**1.25**	**1.19**
1000	3.85	3.00	2.61	2.38	2.22	2.11	2.02	1.95	1.89	1.84	1.80	1.76	1.70	1.65	1.58	1.53	1.47	1.41	1.36	1.30	1.26	1.19	1.13	1.08
	6.66	**4.63**	**3.80**	**3.34**	**3.04**	**2.82**	**2.66**	**2.53**	**2.43**	**2.34**	**2.27**	**2.20**	**2.10**	**2.02**	**1.90**	**1.81**	**1.72**	**1.61**	**1.54**	**1.44**	**1.38**	**1.28**	**1.19**	**1.12**
∞	3.84	3.00	2.60	2.37	2.21	2.10	2.01	1.94	1.88	1.83	1.79	1.75	1.69	1.64	1.57	1.52	1.46	1.39	1.35	1.28	1.24	1.17	1.11	1.00
	6.63	**4.61**	**3.78**	**3.32**	**3.02**	**2.80**	**2.64**	**2.51**	**2.41**	**2.32**	**2.23**	**2.18**	**2.08**	**2.00**	**1.88**	**1.79**	**1.70**	**1.59**	**1.52**	**1.42**	**1.36**	**1.25**	**1.18**	**1.00**

Numerator Degrees of Freedom (k_1)

	$k = 1$		$k = 2$		$k = 3$		$k = 4$		$k = 5$	
n	d_L	d_U	d_L	d_U	d_L	d_U	d_L	d_U	d_L	d_U
15	.81	1.07	.70	1.25	.59	1.46	.49	1.70	.39	1.96
16	.84	1.09	.74	1.25	.63	1.44	.53	1.66	.44	1.90
17	.87	1.10	.77	1.25	.67	1.43	.57	1.63	.48	1.85
18	.90	1.12	.80	1.26	.71	1.42	.61	1.60	.52	1.80
19	.93	1.13	.83	1.26	.74	1.41	.65	1.58	.56	1.77
20	.95	1.15	.86	1.27	.77	1.41	.68	1.57	.60	1.74
21	.97	1.16	.89	1.27	.80	1.41	.72	1.55	.63	1.71
22	1.00	1.17	.91	1.28	.83	1.40	.75	1.54	.66	1.69
23	1.02	1.19	.94	1.29	.86	1.40	.77	1.53	.70	1.67
24	1.05	1.20	.96	1.30	.88	1.41	.80	1.53	.72	1.66
25	1.05	1.21	.98	1.30	.90	1.41	.83	1.52	.75	1.65
26	1.07	1.22	1.00	1.31	.93	1.41	.85	1.52	.78	1.64
27	1.09	1.23	1.02	1.32	.95	1.41	.88	1.51	.81	1.63
28	1.10	1.24	1.04	1.32	.97	1.41	.90	1.51	.83	1.62
29	1.12	1.25	1.05	1.33	.99	1.42	.92	1.51	.85	1.61
30	1.13	1.26	1.07	1.34	1.01	1.42	.94	1.51	.88	1.61
31	1.15	1.27	1.08	1.34	1.02	1.42	.96	1.51	.90	1.60
32	1.16	1.28	1.10	1.35	1.04	1.43	.98	1.51	.92	1.60
33	1.17	1.29	1.11	1.36	1.05	1.43	1.00	1.51	.94	1.59
34	1.18	1.30	1.13	1.36	1.07	1.43	1.01	1.51	.95	1.59
35	1.19	1.31	1.14	1.37	1.08	1.44	1.03	1.51	.97	1.59
36	1.21	1.32	1.15	1.38	1.10	1.44	1.04	1.51	.99	1.59
37	1.22	1.32	1.16	1.38	1.11	1.45	1.06	1.51	1.00	1.59
38	1.23	1.33	1.18	1.39	1.12	1.45	1.07	1.52	1.02	1.58
39	1.24	1.34	1.19	1.39	1.14	1.45	1.09	1.52	1.03	1.58
40	1.25	1.34	1.20	1.40	1.15	1.46	1.10	1.52	1.05	1.58
45	1.29	1.38	1.24	1.42	1.20	1.48	1.16	1.53	1.11	1.58
50	1.32	1.40	1.28	1.45	1.24	1.49	1.20	1.54	1.16	1.59
55	1.36	1.43	1.32	1.47	1.28	1.51	1.25	1.55	1.21	1.59
60	1.38	1.45	1.35	1.48	1.32	1.52	1.28	1.56	1.25	1.60
65	1.41	1.47	1.38	1.50	1.35	1.53	1.31	1.57	1.28	1.61
70	1.43	1.49	1.40	1.52	1.37	1.55	1.34	1.58	1.31	1.61
75	1.45	1.50	1.42	1.53	1.39	1.56	1.37	1.59	1.34	1.62
80	1.47	1.52	1.44	1.54	1.42	1.57	1.39	1.60	1.36	1.62
85	1.48	1.53	1.46	1.55	1.43	1.58	1.41	1.60	1.39	1.63
90	1.50	1.54	1.47	1.56	1.45	1.59	1.43	1.61	1.41	1.64
95	1.51	1.55	1.49	1.57	1.47	1.60	1.45	1.62	1.42	1.64
100	1.52	1.56	1.50	1.58	1.48	1.60	1.46	1.63	1.44	1.65

continued

Critical Values of the Durbin-Watson Test Statistic for $\alpha = .05$
concluded

n	$k = 1$		$k = 2$		$k = 3$		$k = 4$		$k = 5$	
	d_L	d_U	d_L	d_U	d_L	d_U	d_L	d_U	d_L	d_U
15	1.08	1.36	.95	1.54	.82	1.75	.69	1.97	.56	2.21
16	1.10	1.37	.98	1.54	.86	1.73	.74	1.93	.62	2.15
17	1.13	1.38	1.02	1.54	.90	1.71	.78	1.90	.67	2.10
18	1.16	1.39	1.05	1.53	.93	1.69	.82	1.87	.71	2.06
19	1.18	1.40	1.08	1.53	.97	1.68	.86	1.85	.75	2.02
20	1.20	1.41	1.10	1.54	1.00	1.68	.90	1.83	.79	1.99
21	1.22	1.42	1.13	1.54	1.03	1.67	.93	1.81	.83	1.96
22	1.24	1.43	1.15	1.54	1.05	1.66	.96	1.80	.86	1.94
23	1.26	1.44	1.17	1.54	1.08	1.66	.99	1.79	.90	1.92
24	1.27	1.45	1.19	1.55	1.10	1.66	1.01	1.78	.93	1.90
25	1.29	1.45	1.21	1.55	1.12	1.66	1.04	1.77	.95	1.89
26	1.30	1.46	1.22	1.55	1.14	1.65	1.06	1.76	.98	1.88
27	1.32	1.47	1.24	1.56	1.16	1.65	1.08	1.76	1.01	1.86
28	1.33	1.48	1.26	1.56	1.18	1.65	1.10	1.75	1.03	1.85
29	1.34	1.48	1.27	1.56	1.20	1.65	1.12	1.74	1.05	1.84
30	1.35	1.49	1.28	1.57	1.21	1.65	1.14	1.74	1.07	1.83
31	1.36	1.50	1.30	1.57	1.23	1.65	1.16	1.74	1.09	1.83
32	1.37	1.50	1.31	1.57	1.24	1.65	1.18	1.73	1.11	1.82
33	1.38	1.51	1.32	1.58	1.26	1.65	1.19	1.73	1.13	1.81
34	1.39	1.51	1.33	1.58	1.27	1.65	1.21	1.73	1.15	1.81
35	1.40	1.52	1.34	1.58	1.28	1.65	1.22	1.73	1.16	1.80
36	1.41	1.52	1.35	1.59	1.29	1.65	1.24	1.73	1.18	1.80
37	1.42	1.53	1.36	1.59	1.31	1.66	1.25	1.72	1.19	1.80
38	1.43	1.54	1.37	1.59	1.32	1.66	1.26	1.72	1.21	1.79
39	1.43	1.54	1.38	1.60	1.33	1.66	1.27	1.72	1.22	1.79
40	1.44	1.54	1.39	1.60	1.34	1.66	1.29	1.72	1.23	1.79
45	1.48	1.57	1.43	1.62	1.38	1.67	1.34	1.72	1.29	1.78
50	1.50	1.59	1.46	1.63	1.42	1.67	1.38	1.72	1.34	1.77
55	1.53	1.60	1.49	1.64	1.45	1.68	1.41	1.72	1.38	1.77
60	1.55	1.62	1.51	1.65	1.48	1.69	1.44	1.73	1.41	1.77
65	1.57	1.63	1.54	1.66	1.50	1.70	1.47	1.73	1.44	1.77
70	1.58	1.64	1.55	1.67	1.52	1.70	1.49	1.74	1.46	1.77
75	1.60	1.65	1.57	1.68	1.54	1.71	1.51	1.74	1.49	1.77
80	1.61	1.66	1.59	1.69	1.56	1.72	1.53	1.74	1.51	1.77
85	1.62	1.67	1.60	1.70	1.57	1.72	1.55	1.75	1.52	1.77
90	1.63	1.68	1.61	1.70	1.59	1.73	1.57	1.75	1.54	1.78
95	1.64	1.69	1.62	1.71	1.60	1.73	1.58	1.75	1.56	1.78
100	1.65	1.69	1.63	1.72	1.61	1.74	1.59	1.76	1.57	1.78

Source: Reproduced by permission from J. Durbin and G. S. Watson, "Testing for Serial Correlation in Least Squares Regression, II," *Biometrika* 38 (1951), pp. 159–78, as found in Amir D. Aczel, *Complete Business Statistics* (Burr Ridge, Ill.: Richard D. Irwin, 1996), pp. 843–844.

■ ■ ■ ■ Description of Data Files ■ ■ ■ ■

The enclosed diskette contains about 240 data files in the ASCII format and about 36 spreadsheets in the wk1 format. These files are found a:\data and a:\wk1, respectively. Subdirectory a:\data includes every dataset used in this text. These are identified by the name in the book. Many files contain only one variable; however, many contain variables in columns. The root directory of this disk contains a readme file with the extension of *.txt.

Write Protect and Save Your Diskette! Because you may be editing these files, you should write protect the original diskette and then copy it, being sure to get all the files from each directory. After copying the original, retain it in a safe but convenient place. Now study your copy of the files.

Diskette Format. The format used in all data files is illustrated below using BIRTHMAR.DAT.

DATE	BIRTHS	MARRIAGES
198501	896013	420240
198502	927850	703900
...		
199203	1059000	697000
199204	1002000	579000

N=32, Quarterly births and marriages in the United States.

As shown, each file has the data listed row-wise (i.e., by observation number). Under each column of data is the name of each variable in the dataset and a description of the dataset. Some software can use this format, while other applications may require some slight modification of the file to conform to their input formats. The best way to edit these files will vary, but typically, a DOS, WIN3.1, or WIN95 wordprocessor or spreadsheet can be used to modify the files. Remember that the files are in ASCII formats with spaces between columns. Your software will likely require you to save them in an ASCII format, but double check your software documentation.

Using Spreadsheets with Data Files. If you are using a spreadsheet to analyze this data, then it should be simple to import them as an ASCII file with space delimiters.

Neural Network Spreadsheets. Included in the subdirectory a:\wk1 are some spreadsheet tables from the text and several simple neural network spreadsheets with the file extensions of wk1. The wk1 format is a generic one that should be usable in your spreadsheet. Instructions for using neural network programs are given in each of the files.

Files in Subdirectories. The files of this book are in subdirectories because most operating systems limit the number of files in the root directory of a floppy diskette.